Marketing
Concepts and Strategies

William M. Pride
Texas A&M University

O.C. Ferrell
Colorado State University

Houghton Mifflin Company   Boston   New York

To Nancy, Michael, and Allen Pride

To Linda Ferrell

Executive Editor: George Hoffman
Associate Sponsoring Editor/Development Manager: Susan M. Kahn
Editorial Assistant: Kira Robinson-Kates
Senior Project Editor: Rachel D'Angelo Wimberly
Editorial Assistant: Sage Anderson
Art/Design Coordinator: Jill Haber
Photo Editor: Jennifer Meyer Dare
Composition Buyer: Sarah Ambrose
Senior Manufacturing Coordinator: Chuck Dutton
Executive Marketing Manager: Steven W. Mikels
Marketing Associate: Lisa E. Boden

Cover Image: © Michael Doret

Director of Custom Publishing: Dan Luciano
Custom Publishing Production Manager: Kathleen McCourt
Project Coordinator: Andrea Wagner

This book contains select works from existing Houghton Mifflin Company Resources and was produced by Houghton Mifflin Custom Publishing for collegiate use. As such, those adopting and/or contributing to this work are responsible for editorial content, accuracy, continuity and completeness.

Printed in the USA.

ISBN: 0-618-57831-5
N-04403

3 4 5 6 7 8 9 -CM- 08 07 06 05

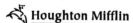 **Houghton Mifflin**
Custom Publishing

222 Berkeley St. • Boston, MA 02116

Address all correspondence and order information to the above address.

Brief Contents

Contents

Note: Each chapter concludes with a Summary, Important Terms, Discussion and Review Questions, Application Questions, and Internet Exercise & Resources.

4 Social Responsibility and Ethics in Marketing   87

5 Global Markets and International Marketing   117

Part Three   Using Technology and Information to Build Customer Relationships   145

6 E-Marketing and Customer Relationship Management   146

17 Retailing and Direct Marketing   443

Part Seven Promotion Decisions   471

18 Integrated Marketing Communications   472

19 Advertising and Public Relations   499

20 Personal Selling and Sales Promotion   527

Part Eight Pricing Decisions   557

21 Pricing Concepts   558

22 Setting Prices   585

Preface

The Challenges of Teaching and Learning Marketing

Teaching the introductory marketing course creates many challenges for most professors. Engaging and motivating students with diverse backgrounds and different interest levels in marketing requires stimulating and effective teaching and learning materials. This edition of *Marketing: Concepts and Strategies* has been revised to engage and motivate students to learn about marketing. We take cutting-edge marketing knowledge and make it interesting and relevant to students through the use of real-world examples, cases, and features. We connect marketing to the realities of the business world and relate marketing to students' personal lives. One of our goals is that students will view marketing as an important part of society that enhances our standard of living and can be used to achieve socially responsible individual and organizational objectives.

Our experience indicates that prior to taking their introductory marketing course, students believe marketing is mainly selling, advertising, and other elements of promotion. In addition, some students question whether marketing is an important and responsible business function. This limited view of marketing can be overcome by presenting a balanced, integrated, and comprehensive view of marketing in business and society. We accomplish this by focusing on a framework that provides complete coverage of marketing issues and best practices validated by the latest research. Our text is informative and interesting to enhance and create an effective learning environment.

Keeping Pace with the Challenges and the Changing World

In this new edition, as in previous editions, we continue to work hard, listening to adopters and students and keeping pace with changes. Many changes in the marketing environment have occurred since the last edition. Advancing technologies, including customer relationship management, help in understanding customers. The Internet and e-marketing strategies continue to create new opportunities for marketing success. Direct marketing, supply chain management, and growth of large retailers such as Wal-Mart, Best Buy, and The Home Depot are changing the competitive forces. Starbucks' success indicates that customers are trading up to services and experiences that provide enjoyment in a busy world. At the same time companies such as Starbucks are contributing more to society by providing environmentally responsible products and promoting fair trade activities to enhance the welfare of all marketing channel members. Ethics and social responsibility in marketing continue to be requirements—not options—in relating to customers and other stakeholders. All of these changes are emphasized in the content, examples, and boxes of this edition.

We examine the challenges that marketers face in developing global marketing strategies. Many of our products come from foreign markets, and foreign markets represent a sizable opportunity for U.S. products. For example, imported shrimp account for 90 percent of U.S. shrimp sales. Next year, General Motors expects to sell as many Buicks in China as in the U.S. With the help of a $124 billion U.S. trade deficit with China, this country has developed the second largest world economy in output behind the U.S. China is the largest broadband DSL market, and companies such as Motorola and Intel have invested billions of dollars in China. India's middle class of over 300 million consumers is buying consumer products from companies such as Procter & Gamble and Coca-Cola. These dramatic changes in international markets mean that students need to understand how global marketing strategies are developed and implemented in a changing world. We provide a revised chapter on this issue as well as global boxed features, cases, examples, and content throughout the text.

An introductory marketing text must be revised on a timely basis to stay current and reflect up-to-date changes in marketing and the marketing environment. In late 2004 the American Marketing Association finalized a new definition of marketing. This definition is included in Chapter 1 along with a more traditional definition so students can see how perceptions about marketing's role in business and society are changing. In Chapter 4, we provide the new American Marketing Association Code of Ethics that stresses appropriate values and norms for the practice of marketing. Throughout the text we have updated content with the most recent research that supports the frameworks and best practices for marketing.

Building on Established Strengths

Features of the Book

As with previous editions, this edition of the text provides a comprehensive and practical introduction to marketing that is both easy to teach and to learn. *Marketing: Concepts and Strategies* continues to be one of the most widely adopted introductory textbooks in the world. We appreciate the confidence that adopters have placed in our textbook and continue to work hard to make sure that, as in previous editions, this edition keeps pace with changes. The entire text is structured to excite students about the subject and to help them learn completely and efficiently.

- An *organizational model* at the beginning of each part provides a "roadmap" of the text and a visual tool for understanding the connection between concepts.

- *Learning objectives* at the start of each chapter present concrete expectations about what students are to learn as they read the chapter.

- An *opening vignette* about a particular organization or current market trend introduces the topic for each chapter. The issues in these vignettes surround a variety of products and services from diverse organizations such as Porsche Cayenne, McDonald's, Google, and Skechers. Through these vignettes, students are exposed to contemporary marketing realities and are better prepared to understand and apply the concepts they will explore in the text.

- *Key term definitions* appear in the margins to help students build their marketing vocabulary.

- Numerous *figures, tables, photographs, advertisements,* and *Snapshot* and *Net Sights* features increase comprehension and stimulate interest.

- Four types of *boxed features* reinforce students' awareness of the particular issues affecting marketing and the types of choices and decisions marketers must make.

 Tech Know boxes include discussions about the impact of technological advances on products and how they are marketed. Examples of topics include online auctions, cell phone competition, and using color preferences in packaging.

 Ethics and Social Responsibility boxes raise students' awareness of social responsibility and ethical issues and the types of ethical choices that marketers face every day. Some of the organizations on which we focus are Burger King, Qwest, and Wal-Mart.

 Global Marketing boxed features examine the challenges of marketing in widely diverse cultures for companies such as Conoco, Chupa Chups, and Gruma Tortillas.

Building Customer Relationships boxes look at how organizations try to build long-term relationships with their customers. Examples include Red Bull, Kodak, General Motors, and Dell.

- A complete *chapter summary* reviews the major topics discussed, and the list of *important terms* provides another end-of-chapter study aid to expand students' marketing vocabulary.

- *Discussion and review questions* at the end of each chapter encourage further study and exploration of chapter content, and *application questions* enhance students' comprehension of important topics.

- An *Internet exercise* at the end of each chapter asks students to examine a website and assess one or more strategic issues associated with the site. This section also points students to the various learning tools that are available on the text's website.

- Two in-depth *cases* at the end of each chapter help students understand the application of chapter concepts. One of the end-of-chapter cases is related to a video segment. Some examples of companies highlighted in the cases are BMW, Vail Resorts, New Balance, and Finagle A Bagel.

- A *strategic case* at the end of each part helps students integrate the diverse concepts that have been discussed within the related chapters. Some of the organizations highlighted in these cases include *USA Today*, Mattel, Bass Pro Shops, Napster, and XM Satellite Radio.

- *Appendixes* discuss marketing career opportunities, explore financial analysis in marketing, and present a sample marketing plan.

- A comprehensive *glossary* defines more than 625 important marketing terms.

Text Organization

We have organized the eight parts of *Marketing: Concepts and Strategies* to give students a theoretical and practical understanding of marketing decision making.

Part One   **Marketing Strategy and Customer Relationships**
Provides an overview of marketing, strategic marketing planning, and implementation.

Part Two   **The Global Environment and Social and Ethical Responsibilities**
Provides an overview of the marketing environment, social responsibility, global markets, and international marketing.

Part Three   **Using Technology and Information to Build Customer Relationships**
Focuses on e-marketing, customer relationship management, marketing research, and information systems.

Part Four   **Target Markets and Customer Behavior**
Covers target markets, segmentation, and consumer and business markets' buying behavior.

Part Five   **Product Decisions**
Discusses product concepts, developing and managing products, branding, packaging, and services marketing.

Part Six   **Distribution Decisions**
Provides coverage of marketing channels, supply chain managers, wholesaling, and physical distribution.

Part Seven   **Promotion Decisions**
Focuses on integrated communications, advertising, public relations, personal selling, and sales promotion.

Part Eight   Pricing Decisions
Covers pricing concepts and the setting of prices in a dynamic marketing environment.

What's New to this Edition?

This edition is revised and updated to address the dynamic issues emerging in the current technology-driven environment, and to still stress the importance of traditional marketing issues. These revisions assist students in gaining a full understanding of marketing practices pertinent today and helping them anticipate increasing future changes.

Organizational Changes

- *Consolidation of strategic planning and implementation.* The chapter on implementing and controlling marketing strategies has moved to the front of the text and been consolidated with Chapter 2 on planning marketing strategy. This should help students recognize that strategic planning is a comprehensive process that requires implementation and control in order to be successful.

- *Changes in the treatment of e-marketing and customer relationship management.* The chapter about marketing on the Internet has been moved forward in the text and combined with our discussion of customer relationship management. This chapter has also been updated to reflect new trends in the constantly changing environment of the Internet. This allows for greater integration of technology into the discussion of marketing mix elements throughout the remainder of the text.

Changes In Every Chapter

- *Opening vignettes.* All of the chapter opening vignettes are new. They are written to introduce the theme of each chapter by focusing on actual companies and how they deal with real-world situations.

- *Boxed features.* Each chapter includes two of the four types of boxed features that highlight important themes: "Building Customer Relationships," "Ethics and Social Responsibility," "Tech Know," and "Global Marketing." All of the boxed features are new in this edition.

- *New Snapshot features.* All twenty-three Snapshot features are new and engage students by highlighting interesting, up-to-date statistics that link marketing theory to the real world.

- *New illustrations and examples.* New advertisements from well-known firms are employed to illustrate chapter topics. Experiences of real-world companies are used to exemplify marketing concepts and strategies throughout the text. Most of these examples are new. Others have been updated or expanded.

- *End-of-chapter cases.* Each chapter contains two cases, including a video case, profiling firms to illustrate concrete application of marketing strategies and concepts. A number of the cases are new to this edition.

- *End-of-part Strategic Cases.* These cases incorporate issues found throughout all the chapters in each part and require students to integrate the content of these multiple chapters to answer the questions at the end of each case. Six of these cases are new and the other two have been updated.

A Comprehensive Instructional Resource Package

For instructors, this edition of *Marketing* includes an exceptionally comprehensive package of teaching materials.

- *Instructor's website.* This continually updated, password-protected site includes valuable tools to help design and teach the course. Contents include sample syllabi, downloadable text files from the *Instructor's Resource Manual*, role-play exercises, PowerPoint® slides, and suggested answers to questions posed on the student website. A downloadable game, *Who Wants to Be an "A" Student*, by John Drea, Western Illinois University, is useful for stimulating classroom participation. This easy-to-use game makes in-class review challenging and fun, and has been proven to increase students' test scores.

- *PowerPoint® slide presentations.* For each chapter, over twenty-five slides related to the learning objectives have been specially developed for this edition. The slides are original representations of the concepts in the book, providing a complete lecture for each chapter. These slides include key figures and tables from the textbook as well as additional data and graphics. The slides are available on the website.

- *HMClassPrep™ CD.* This software package provides all the tools instructors need to create customized multimedia lecture presentations for display on computer-based projection systems. The software makes available lecture outlines from the *Instructor's Resource Manual*, figures and tables from the text and transparencies, the PowerPoint® slides, and a link to the Web. Instructors can quickly and easily select from and integrate all of these components, and prepare a seamless customized classroom presentation.

- *Online/distance learning support.* Instructors can create and customize online course materials to use in distance learning, distributed learning, or as a supplement to traditional classes. The *Blackboard Course Cartridge*, *WebCT e-Pack*, and *Eduspace* course include a variety of study aids for students as well as course-management tools for instructors.

- *Test Bank.* The expanded *Test Bank* now provides more than 4,000 test items including true/false, multiple-choice, and essay questions. Each objective test item is accompanied by the correct answer, a main text page reference, and a key that shows whether the question tests knowledge, comprehension, or application. The *Test Bank* also provides difficulty and discrimination ratings derived from actual class testing for many of the multiple-choice questions. Lists of author-selected questions that facilitate quick construction of tests or quizzes appear in an appendix. These author-selected lists of multiple-choice questions are representative of chapter content. An outside consultant working with the authors was used to review, improve, and test this edition of the *Test Bank*.

- *HMTesting.* This computerized version of the *Test Bank* allows instructors to select, edit, and add questions, or generate randomly selected questions to produce a test master for easy duplication. An Online Testing System and Gradebook function allows instructors to administer tests via a network system, modem, or personal computer, and sets up a new class, records grades from tests or assignments, analyzes grades, and produces class and individual statistics. This program is available for use on IBM, IBM-compatible, and Macintosh computers, and is included on the *HMClassPrep* CD.

- *Marketing videos.* In this edition, about half of the videos for use with the end-of-chapter video cases are new. The *Instructor's Resource Manual* provides specific information about each video segment. The videos are now available on both VHS and DVD.

- *Color transparencies.* A set of over 250 color transparencies offers the instructor visual teaching assistance. About half of these are illustrations from the text. The rest are figures, tables, and diagrams that can be used as additional instructional aids.

- *Call-in test service.* This service lets instructors select items from the *Test Bank* and call our toll-free number to order printed tests.

- *Instructor's Resource Manual.* Written by the text's authors, the *Instructor's Resource Manual* includes a complete set of teaching tools. For each chapter of the text, there is (1) a teaching resources quick reference guide, (2) a purpose and perspective statement, (3) a guide for using the transparencies, (4) a comprehensive lecture outline, (5) special class exercises, (6) a debate issue, (7) a chapter quiz, (8) answers to discussion and review questions, (9) comments on the end-of-chapter cases, and (10) video information. In addition, the *Instructor's Resource Manual* includes comments on the end-of-part strategic cases and answers to the questions posed at the end of Appendix B, Financial Analysis in Marketing.

- *Role-play exercises.* Three role-play exercises that allow students to assume various roles within an organization are available in the *Instructor's Resource Manual* and on the instructor's website. The exercises are designed to help students understand the real-world challenges of decision making in marketing. Decisions require a strategic response from a class group or team. These exercises simulate a real-world experience, and give students an opportunity to apply the marketing concepts covered in the text. The *Instructor's Resource Manual* provides in-depth information concerning the implementation and evaluation of these exercises.

A Format and Supplements to Meet Student Needs

Text Format

We have heard students' complaints about price. In response, we continue to offer all the benefits of a comprehensive textbook, but in the convenient, low-cost loose-leaf format. Students have told us they like this format—they can carry only those chapters they need, and it is available for about two-thirds the cost of a hardcover textbook. For professors or students who want a bound book, we do offer the traditional hardcover, Library Edition version. We also offer a low-cost ebook version of the text. For more information about an ebook, contact your Houghton Mifflin sales representative.

Supporting Supplements

The complete package available with *Marketing: Concepts and Strategies* includes support materials that facilitate student learning.

- *Marketing Bonus Pack: Your Guide to an 'A.'* This guide to all the tools in the textbook and student supplements includes important study tips to help students achieve success in this class. Packaged with every new book, the *Marketing Bonus Pack* also includes a unique passkey for access to premium online study guide content on the student website. For students buying a used textbook, the *Marketing Bonus Pack* is available for less than the price of a traditional Study Guide.

- *Student Website.* With premium content accessible via the unique passkey provided in the *Marketing Bonus Pack*, this website contains a variety of study tools including

  - *ACE online self-tests.* By far the most popular online content with students, these questions allow students to practice taking tests and get immediate scoring results.

■ *Flashcards.* All the key terms in every chapter are presented as electronic flashcards (that can also be printed) to help students master marketing vocabulary.

■ *Marketing Plan worksheets.* These worksheets take students step-by-step through the process of creating their own marketing plan. Along with the text discussion and sample marketing plan, this is a project that will help students apply their knowledge of marketing theories.

■ *Career Center.* Downloadable "Personal Career Plan Worksheets" and links to various marketing careers websites will help students explore their options and plan their job search.

■ *Internet exercises.* Including the text exercises with links and updates as necessary, these reinforce chapter concepts by guiding students through specific websites and asking them to assess the information from a marketing perspective. Additional exercises are also offered for professors who want to assign them.

■ *Company links.* Hot links to companies featured in the text are provided so that students can further their research and understanding of the marketing practices of these companies.

■ *Online glossary* and *chapter summary.* These sections help students review key concepts and definitions.

■ *Study Guide.* Written by the text's authors, this printed supplement helps students to review and integrate key marketing concepts. The *Study Guide* contains questions different from those in the online study aids, and includes chapter outlines as well as matching, true/false, multiple-choice, and minicase sample test items with answers.

Your Comments and Suggestions are Valued

Bill Pride and O.C. Ferrell have been co-authors of *Marketing: Concepts and Strategies* for the past twenty-seven years. Their major focus has been on teaching and preparing learning material for introductory marketing students. They have both traveled extensively to work with students and understand the needs of professors of introductory marketing courses. Both authors teach this marketing course on a regular basis and test the materials included in the book, *Test Bank*, and other ancillary materials to make sure they are effective in the classroom.

Through the years, professors and students have sent us many helpful suggestions for improving the text and ancillary components. We invite your comments, questions, and criticisms. We want to do our best to provide materials that enhance the teaching and learning of marketing concepts and strategies. Your suggestions will be sincerely appreciated. Please write us, or e-mail us at w-pride@tamu.edu or oc.ferrell@colostate.edu, or call 909-845-5857 (Pride) or 970-491-4398 (Ferrell). You can also send a feedback message through the website at **http://www.pride ferrell.com.**

Acknowledgments

Like most textbooks, this one reflects the ideas of many academicians and practitioners who have contributed to the development of the marketing discipline. We appreciate the opportunity to present their ideas in this book.

A special faculty advisory board assisted us in making decisions during the development of the text and the instructional package. For being "on-call" and available to answer questions and make valuable suggestions, we are grateful to those who participated:

Sana Akili
Iowa State University

Katrece Albert
Southern University

Frank Barber
Cuyahoga Community College

Nancy Bloom
Nassau Community College

Sandra Coyne
Springfield College

Kent Drummond
University of Wyoming

Robert Garrity
University of Hawaii

John Hafer
University of Nebraska at Omaha

David Hansen
Texas Southern University

Kathleen Krentler
San Diego State University

Marilyn L. Liebrenz-Himes
George Washington University

Edna Ragins
North Carolina A&T State University

Janice Williams
University of Central Oklahoma

John Withey
Indiana University-South Bend

A number of individuals have made helpful comments and recommendations in their reviews of this and earlier editions. We appreciate the generous help of these reviewers:

Zafar U. Ahmed
Minot State University

Thomas Ainscough
University of Massachusetts—Dartmouth

Joe F. Alexander
University of Northern Colorado

Mark I. Alpert
University of Texas at Austin

David M. Ambrose
University of Nebraska

David Andrus
Kansas State University

Linda K. Anglin
Minnesota State University

George Avellano
Central State University

Emin Babakus
University of Memphis

Julie Baker
University of Texas—Arlington

Siva Balasubramanian
Southern Illinois University

Joseph Ballenger
Stephen F. Austin State University

Guy Banville
Creighton University

Joseph Barr
Framingham State College

Thomas E. Barry
Southern Methodist University

Charles A. Bearchell
California State University—Northridge

Richard C. Becherer
University of Tennessee—Chattanooga

Walter H. Beck, Sr.
Reinhardt College

Russell Belk
University of Utah

W.R. Berdine
California State Polytechnic Institute

Karen Berger
Pace University

Bob Berl
University of Memphis

Stewart W. Bither
Pennsylvania State University

Roger Blackwell
Ohio State University

Peter Bloch
University of Missouri—Columbia

Wanda Blockhus
San Jose State University

Paul N. Bloom
University of North Carolina

James P. Boespflug
Arapahoe Community College

Joseph G. Bonnice
Manhattan College

John Boos
Ohio Wesleyan University

Jenell Bramlage
University of Northwestern Ohio

James Brock
Susquehanna College

John R. Brooks, Jr.
Houston Baptist University

William G. Browne
Oregon State University

John Buckley
Orange County Community College

Gul T. Butaney
Bentley College

James Cagley
University of Tulsa

Pat J. Calabros
University of Texas—Arlington

Linda Calderone
State University of New York College of Technology at Farmingdale

Joseph Cangelosi
University of Central Arkansas

William J. Carner
University of Texas—Austin

James C. Carroll
University of Central Arkansas

Terry M. Chambers
Westminster College

Lawrence Chase
Tompkins Cortland Community College

Larry Chonko
Baylor University

Barbara Coe
University of North Texas

Ernest F. Cooke
Loyola College—Baltimore

Robert Copley
University of Louisville

John I. Coppett
University of Houston—Clear Lake

Robert Corey
West Virginia University

Deborah L. Cowles
Virginia Commonwealth University

Melvin R. Crask
University of Georgia

William L. Cron
Southern Methodist University

Gary Cutler
Dyersburg State Community College

Bernice N. Dandridge
Diablo Valley College

Lloyd M. DeBoer
George Mason University

Sally Dibb
University of Warwick

Ralph DiPietro
Montclair State University

Paul Dishman
Idaho State University

Suresh Divakar
State University of New York—Buffalo

Casey L. Donoho
Northern Arizona University

Peter T. Doukas
Westchester Community College

Lee R. Duffus
Florida Gulf Coast University

Robert F. Dwyer
University of Cincinnati

Roland Eyears
Central Ohio Technical College

Thomas Falcone
Indiana University of Pennsylvania

James Finch
University of Wisconsin—La Crosse

Letty C. Fisher
SUNY/Westchester Community College

Renée Florsheim
Loyola Marymount University

Charles W. Ford
Arkansas State University

John Fraedrich
Southern Illinois University, Carbondale

David J. Fritzsche
University of Washington

Donald A. Fuller
University of Central Florida

Terry Gable
California State University—Northridge

Ralph Gaedeke
California State University, Sacramento

Cathy Goodwin
University of Manitoba

Geoffrey L. Gordon
Northern Illinois University

Robert Grafton-Small
University of Strathclyde

Harrison Grathwohl
California State University—Chico

Alan A. Greco
North Carolina A&T State University

Blaine S. Greenfield
Bucks County Community College

Thomas V. Greer
University of Maryland

Sharon F. Gregg
Middle Tennessee University

Jim L. Grimm
Illinois State University

Charles Gross
University of New Hampshire

Joseph Guiltinan
University of Notre Dame

Richard C. Hansen
Ferris State University

Nancy Hanson-Rasmussen
University of Wisconsin—Eau Claire

Robert R. Harmon
Portland State University

Mary C. Harrison
Amber University

Lorraine Hartley
Franklin University

Michael Hartline
Samford University

Timothy Hartman
Ohio University

Salah S. Hassan
George Washington University

Manoj Hastak
American University

Del I. Hawkins
University of Oregon

Dean Headley
Wichita State University

Esther Headley
Wichita State University

Debbora Heflin-Bullock
California State Polytechnic University—Pomona

Merlin Henry
Rancho Santiago College

Lois Herr
Elizabethtown College

Charles L. Hilton
Eastern Kentucky University

Elizabeth C. Hirschman
Rutgers, State University of New Jersey

George C. Hozier
University of New Mexico

John R. Huser
Illinois Central College

Joan M. Inzinga
Bay Path College

Ron Johnson
Colorado Mountain College

Theodore F. Jula
Stonehill College

Peter F. Kaminski
Northern Illinois University

Yvonne Karsten
Minnesota State University

Jerome Katrichis
Temple University

James Kellaris
University of Cincinnati

Alvin Kelly
Florida A&M University

Philip Kemp
DePaul University

Sylvia Keyes
Bridgewater State College

William M. Kincaid, Jr.
Oklahoma State University

Roy Klages
State University of New York at Albany

Douglas Kornemann
Milwaukee Area Technical College

Patricia Laidler
Massasoit Community College

Bernard LaLond
Ohio State University

Richard A. Lancioni
Temple University

Irene Lange
California State University—Fullerton

Geoffrey P. Lantos
Stonehill College

Charles L. Lapp
University of Texas—Dallas

Virginia Larson
San Jose State University

John Lavin
Waukesha County Technical Institute

Marilyn Lavin
University of Wisconsin—Whitewater

Hugh E. Law
East Tennessee University

Monle Lee
Indiana University—South Bend

Ron Lennon
Barry University

Richard C. Leventhal
Metropolitan State College

Marilyn Liebrenz-Himes
George Washington University

Jay D. Lindquist
Western Michigan University

Terry Loe
Baylor University

Mary Logan
Southwestern Assemblies of God College

Paul Londrigan
Mott Community College

Anthony Lucas
Community College of Allegheny County

George Lucas
U.S. Learning, Inc.

William Lundstrom
Cleveland State University

Rhonda Mack
College of Charleston

Stan Madden
Baylor University

Patricia M. Manninen
North Shore Community College

Gerald L. Manning
Des Moines Area Community College

Lalita A. Manrai
University of Delaware

Franklyn Manu
Morgan State University

Allen S. Marber
University of Bridgeport

Gayle J. Marco
Robert Morris College

James McAlexander
Oregon State University

Debbie McAlister
Southwest Texas State University

Donald McCartney
University of Wisconsin—Green Bay

Anthony McGann
University of Wyoming

Jack McNiff
State University of New York College of Technology at Farmington

Lee Meadow
Eastern Illinois University

Carla Meeske
University of Oregon

Jeffrey A. Meier
Fox Valley Technical College

James Meszaros
County College of Morris

Brain Meyer
Minnesota State University

Martin Meyers
University of Wisconsin—Stevens Point

Stephen J. Miller
Oklahoma State University

William Moller
University of Michigan

Kent B. Monroe
University of Illinois

Carlos W. Moore
Baylor University

Carol Morris-Calder
Loyola Marymount University

David Murphy
Madisonville Community College

Keith Murray
Bryant College

Sue Ellen Neeley
University of Houston—Clear Lake

Carolyn Y. Nicholson
Stetson University

Francis L. Notturno, Sr.
Owens Community College

Terrence V. O'Brien
Northern Illinois University

James R. Ogden
Kutztown University of Pennsylvania

Mike O'Neill
California State University—Chico

Robert S. Owen
State University of New York—Oswego

Allan Palmer
University of North Carolina at Charlotte

David P. Paul, III
Monmouth University

Teresa Pavia
University of Utah

John Perrachione
Truman State University

Michael Peters
Boston College

Linda Pettijohn
Southwest Missouri State University

Lana Podolak
Community College of Beaver County

Raymond E. Polchow
Muskingum Area Technical College

Thomas Ponzurick
West Virginia University

William Presutti
Duquesne University

Kathy Pullins
Columbus State Community College

Edna J. Ragins
North Carolina A&T State University

Daniel Rajaratnam
Baylor University

Mohammed Rawwas
University of Northern Iowa

James D. Reed
Louisiana State University— Shreveport

William Rhey
University of Tampa

Glen Riecken
East Tennessee State University

Winston Ring
University of Wisconsin—Milwaukee

Ed Riordan
Wayne State University

Robert A. Robicheaux
University of Alabama

Robert H. Ross
Wichita State University

Vicki Rostedt
The University of Akron

Michael L. Rothschild
University of Wisconsin—Madison

Bert Rosenbloom
Drexel University

Kenneth L. Rowe
Arizona State University

Elise Sautter
New Mexico State University

Ronald Schill
Brigham Young University

Bodo Schlegelmilch
Vienna University of Economics and Business Administration

Edward Schmitt
Villanova University

Thomas Schori
Illinois State University

Donald Sciglimpaglia
San Diego State University

Stanley Scott
University of Alaska—Anchorage

Harold S. Sekiguchi
University of Nevada—Reno

Gilbert Seligman
Dutchess Community College

Richard J. Semenik
University of Utah

Beheruz N. Sethna
Lamar University

Morris A. Shapero
Schiller International University

Terence A. Shimp
University of South Carolina

Mark Siders
Southern Oregon University

Carolyn F. Siegel
Eastern Kentucky University

Dean C. Siewers
Rochester Institute of Technology

Lyndon Simkin
University of Warwick

Roberta Slater
Cedar Crest College

Paul J. Solomon
University of South Florida

Sheldon Somerstein
City University of New York

Eric R. Spangenberg
University of Mississippi

Rosann L. Spiro
Indiana University

William Staples
University of Houston—Clear Lake

Bruce Stern
Portland State University

Claire F. Sullivan
Metropolitan State University

Carmen Sunda
University of New Orleans

Robert Swerdlow
Lamar University

Steven A. Taylor
Illinois State University

Hal Teer
James Madison University

Ira Teich
Long Island University—C.W. Post

Dillard Tinsley
Stephen F. Austin State University

Sharynn Tomlin
Angelo State University

Hale Tongren
George Mason University

James Underwood
University of Southwest Louisiana

Barbara Unger
Western Washington University

Tinus Van Drunen
University Twente (Netherlands)

Dale Varble
Indiana State University

R. Vish Viswanathan
University of Northern Colorado

Charles Vitaska
Metropolitan State College

Kirk Wakefield
University of Mississippi

Harlan Wallingford
Pace University

Jacquelyn Warwick
Andrews University

James F. Wenthe
Georgia College

Sumner M. White
Massachusetts Bay Community College

Alan R. Wiman
Rider College

Ken Wright
West Australia College of Advanced Education—Churchland Campus

George Wynn
James Madison University

Poh-Lin Yeoh
Bentley College

Irvin A. Zaenglein
Northern Michigan University

We deeply appreciate the assistance of Gwyneth Walters and Marian Wood for providing editorial suggestions, technical assistance, and support. For assistance in completing numerous tasks associated with the text and supplements, we express appreciation to Dana Schubert, Robyn Smith, Adele Lewis, Sarah Scott, Clarissa Means, Alicia Delgado, Mark Stubbs, and Candice Suttie.

Nori Comello and Liza Hunn assisted in developing boxed materials. Michael Hartline, Samford University, helped in the development of the marketing plan outline and the sample marketing plan in Appendix C, as well as the career worksheets on the website.

We also wish to thank Kirk Wakefield, Baylor University, for developing the class exercises included in the *Instructor's Resource Manual,* and John Drea, Western Illinois University, for developing the *Who Wants to Be an 'A' Student* game. We especially thank Jim L. Grimm, Illinois State University, for drafting the financial analysis appendix.

We express appreciation for the support and encouragement given to us by our colleagues at Texas A&M University and Colorado State University. We are also grateful for the comments and suggestions we receive from our own students, student focus groups, and student correspondents who provide ongoing feedback through the website.

A number of talented professionals at Houghton Mifflin have contributed to the development of this book. We are especially grateful to Charlie Hartford, George Hoffman, Steve Mikels, Susan Kahn, Rachel D'Angelo Wimberly, Sage Anderson, Kira Robinson-Kates, Lisa Boden, Marcy Kagan, Penny Peters, and Katie Huha. Their inspiration, patience, support, and friendship are invaluable.

William M. Pride

O. C. Ferrell

Part One

Marketing Strategy and Customer Relationships

Part One introduces the field of marketing and offers a broad perspective from which to explore and analyze various components of the marketing discipline. **Chapter 1** defines *marketing* and explores several key concepts, including customers and target markets, the marketing mix, relationship marketing, the marketing concept, and value. **Chapter 2** provides an overview of strategic marketing issues, such as the role of the mission statement; corporate, business-unit, and marketing strategies; and the creation of the marketing plan.

1

1

An Overview of Strategic Marketing

OBJECTIVES

1. To be able to define *marketing* as focused on customers

2. To identify some important marketing terms, including *target market, marketing mix, marketing exchanges,* and *marketing environment*

3. To become aware of the marketing concept and marketing orientation

4. To understand the importance of building customer relationships

5. To learn about the process of marketing management

6. To recognize the role of marketing in our society

King's Saddlery and King Ropes

King's Saddlery and King Ropes in Sheridan, Wyoming, supplies cowboys around the world with high-quality ropes, saddles, and rodeo gear. Don King, the saddlery's founder, has been making ropes for more than 30 years and saddles for about 50 years. His Sheridan style of saddle making has become renowned worldwide and boasts a roster of prestigious customers. Many amateur and professional rodeo cowboys prefer King ropes, and the majority of the world's top calf ropers at the National Finals Rodeo in Las Vegas, Nevada, wield King ropes at the prestigious annual event. Many of the firm's customers have been buying King-branded products almost exclusively for many years. Such loyalty can come only from a company that is responsive to customer needs and makes every effort to satisfy demanding customers.

King's Saddlery prides itself on one-to-one customer service, an attribute that sets it apart from the competition. King's employees are highly knowledgeable about different kinds of rope, allowing them to find just the right product for each customer's problem or task. The materials that go into King's ropes are customized for each purchaser, with much of the work still done by hand. Although such work can be tedious and repetitive, King's employees take pride in doing the job right. All products made and sold by King's are guaranteed, and any product may be returned if the customer is not completely satisfied.

King's Saddlery and King Ropes does a large percentage of its business by mail order, and ships all over the world. Although customers cannot order merchandise online, they can request a catalog by phone. The firm's simple advertisements run semiannually in trade magazines and seasonally in local newspapers. The company also places brochures in local businesses, tourism boards, and gas stations to promote its products as well as the King's Western Museum, located inside the store. The picture-filled brochure offers consumers an interesting explanation of the businesses while providing a unique souvenir. The company has also received valuable publicity in the form of numerous articles appearing in a variety of publications on topics ranging from Don King himself to saddle making and rope making. Tourist publications, Internet sites, and brochures have highlighted King's as a must-see destination in Sheridan.

King's Saddlery has also received numerous awards and letters expressing thanks for its good business practices and exceptional customer service. The company received the Better Business Bureau Marketplace Ethics Torch Award in 2004. King's has also secured the business of a number of celebrities, including the Queen of England, who, while picking up a harness and some ropes for her daughter, was given a hand-tooled leather magazine holder and wastebasket. King's has also been patronized by presidents, including Ronald Reagan, who received a King's belt and halter, and Bill Clinton, who owns a King's belt. Even late-night talk show host David Letterman has sported King's products. Indeed, the walls of King's Saddlery are festooned with pictures, plaques, and letters from customers, organizations, and suppliers recognizing King's for the extra effort it takes with every single customer. Such effort and care have made King's Saddlery more than just a rope and saddle shop; it is also a piece of Western cowboy history.[1]

Like all organizations, King's Saddlery and King Ropes must develop products that customers want, communicate useful information about them to excite interest, price them appropriately, and make them available when and where customers want to buy them. Even if an organization does all these things well, however, competition from marketers of similar products, economic conditions, and other factors may affect the company's success. Such factors influence the decisions that all organizations must make in strategic marketing.

This chapter introduces the strategic marketing concepts and decisions covered throughout the text. First, we develop a definition of *marketing* and explore each element of the definition in detail. Next, we introduce the marketing concept and consider several issues associated with implementing it. We also take a brief look at the concept of value, which customers are demanding today more than ever before. We then explore the process of marketing management, which includes planning, organizing, implementing, and controlling marketing activities to encourage marketing exchanges. Finally, we examine the importance of marketing in our global society.

Defining *Marketing*

If you ask several people what *marketing* is, you are likely to hear a variety of descriptions. Although many people think marketing is advertising or selling, marketing actually encompasses many more activities than most people realize. In this book, we define **marketing** as the process of creating, distributing, promoting, and pricing goods, services, and ideas to facilitate satisfying exchange relationships with customers in a dynamic environment. Let's take a closer look at selected parts of this definition.

marketing The process of creating, distributing, promoting, and pricing goods, services, and ideas to facilitate satisfying exchange relationships with customers in a dynamic environment

◆ Marketing Focuses on Customers

As the purchasers of the products that organizations develop, promote, distribute, and price, **customers** are the focal point of all marketing activities (see Figure 1.1). Organizations must define their products not as what they produce but as what they do to satisfy customers. The Walt Disney Company, for example, is not in the business of establishing theme parks; it is in the business of making people happy. At

customers The purchasers of organizations' products; the focal point of all marketing activities

Figure 1.1 Components of Strategic Marketing

"Three car payments.
Three private colleges.
Three weddings.
I think I am having chest pains.
How are we going
to pay for all this?
Invest?
Invest in what?
The market is
more unpredictable
than our
daughters."

Emotional times require sound, unemotional financial advice.

Morgan Stanley
One client at a time.

Appealing to Target Markets
Morgan Stanley promotes its
financial services to parents.

target market A specific group of
customers on whom an organization focuses its marketing efforts

Disney World, customers are guests, the crowd is an audience, and employees are
cast members. Customer satisfaction and enjoyment can come from anything
received when buying and using a product.

In 2004, the American Marketing Association developed a new definition that
states "Marketing is an organizational function and a set of processes for creating,
communicating, and delivering value to customers and for managing customer relationships in ways that benefit the organization and its stakeholders." This definition
focuses on customers and customer relationships.

The essence of marketing is to develop satisfying exchanges from which both
customers and marketers benefit. The customer expects to gain a reward or benefit
in excess of the costs incurred in a marketing transaction. The marketer expects to
gain something of value in return, generally the price charged for the product.
Through buyer-seller interaction, a customer develops expectations about the seller's future behavior. To fulfill these expectations, the marketer must deliver on
promises made. Over time, this interaction results in interdependencies between the
two parties. Fast-food restaurants such as Wendy's and Burger King depend on
repeat purchases from satisfied customers—many often live or work a few miles
from these restaurants—while customer expectations revolve around quality food,
good value, and dependable service.

Organizations generally focus their marketing efforts on a specific group of customers, or **target market**. PepsiCo, for example, targets its regular and diet Mountain
Dew Code Red soft drink at teenagers and young adults looking for an extra jolt in
a high-caffeine soda.[2] Marketing managers may define a target market as a vast
number of people or a relatively small group. Rolls-Royce, for example, targets its
automobiles at a small, very exclusive market: wealthy people who want the ultimate in prestige in an automobile. Other companies target multiple markets, with
different products, promotion, prices, and distribution systems for each one. Nike
uses this strategy, marketing different types of shoes to meet specific needs of cross-
trainers, rock climbers, basketball players, aerobics enthusiasts, and other athletic-
shoe buyers. We explore the concept of target markets in more detail in Chapter 8.

◆ Marketing Deals with Products, Distribution, Promotion, and Price

Marketing is more than simply advertising or selling a product; it involves developing and managing a product that will satisfy customer needs. It focuses on making the product available in the right place and at a price acceptable to buyers. It also requires communicating information that helps customers determine if the product will satisfy their needs. These activities are planned, organized, implemented, and controlled to meet the needs of customers within the target market. Marketers refer to these activities—product, distribution, promotion, and pricing—as the **marketing mix** because they decide what type of each element to use and in what amounts. A primary goal of a marketing manager is to create and maintain the right mix of these elements to satisfy customers' needs for a general product type. Note in Figure 1.1 that the marketing mix is built around the customer.

marketing mix Four marketing activities—product, distribution, promotion, and pricing—that a firm can control to meet the needs of customers within its target market

Marketing managers strive to develop a marketing mix that matches the needs of customers in the target market. The marketing mix for Ralph Lauren's Polo brand of clothing, for example, combines a specific level of product design and quality with coordinated distribution, promotion, and price appropriate for the target market. The marketing mix for Ralph Lauren's Chaps clothing line differs from that for Polo, with lower prices and broader distribution.

Before marketers can develop a marketing mix, they must collect in-depth, up-to-date information about customer needs. Such information might include data about the age, income, ethnicity, gender, and educational level of people in the target market, their preferences for product features, their attitudes toward competitors' products, and the frequency with which they use the product. Such research helped convince Saturn to load its Ion sedan with stadium seating, a fold-down rear seat, and a multitude of options, including leopard-skin seats and brushed-steel interiors to appeal to Generation Y consumers (those born between 1977 and 1994).[3] In Chapter 7, we explore how organizations gather marketing research data. Armed with such data, marketing managers are better able to develop a marketing mix that satisfies a specific target market.

Let's look more closely at the decisions and activities related to each marketing mix variable.

The Product Variable. Successful marketing efforts result in products that become a part of everyday life. Consider the satisfaction customers have had over the years from Coca-Cola, Levi's jeans, Visa credit cards, Tylenol pain relievers, and 3M Post-it notepads. The product variable of the marketing mix deals with researching customers' needs and wants and designing a product that satisfies them. A **product** can be a good, a service, or an idea. A *good* is a physical entity you can touch. A Toyota Scion, a Nora Jones compact disc, a Duracell battery, and a puppy available for adoption at an animal shelter are examples of goods. A *service* is the application of human and mechanical efforts to people or objects to provide intangible benefits to customers. Air travel, dry cleaning, hair cutting, banking, insurance, medical care, and day care are examples of services. *Ideas* include concepts, philosophies, images, and issues. For instance, a marriage counselor, for a fee, gives spouses ideas to help improve their relationship. Other marketers of ideas include political parties, churches, and schools. Note, however, that the actual production of tangible goods is not a marketing activity.

product A good, a service, or an idea

The product variable also involves creating or modifying brand names and packaging, and may include decisions regarding warranty and repair services. Even the world's greatest golfer is a global brand. Tiger Woods, who has sparked a renewed interest in golf among teens and young adults, has endorsed products from American Express, Buick, and General Mills, as well as his own product line from Nike.

Product variable decisions and related activities are important because they are directly involved in creating products that address customers' needs and wants. To maintain an assortment of products that helps an organization achieve its goals, marketers must develop new products, modify existing ones, and eliminate those

A Product Can Be an Idea
The idea of fire prevention has been promoted heavily in drought-ridden western states.

that no longer satisfy enough buyers or that yield unacceptable profits. Microsoft, for example, introduced the Smartphone, which enables customers to access their e-mail, manage personal information, play music, and browse the Internet.[4] We consider such product issues and many more in Chapters 11 through 14.

The Distribution Variable. To satisfy customers, products must be available at the right time and in convenient locations. In dealing with the distribution variable, a marketing manager makes products available in the quantities desired to as many target market customers as possible, keeping total inventory, transportation, and storage costs as low as possible. With these objectives in mind, McDonald's expanded distribution by opening restaurants in Wal-Mart stores and in Amoco and Chevron service stations. This practice permits the fast-food giant to share costs with its partners and to reach more customers when and where hunger strikes. McDonald's now operates more than 31,000 restaurants in 119 countries, with annual sales of more than $41 billion.[5] A marketing manager may also select and motivate intermediaries (wholesalers and retailers), establish and maintain inventory control procedures, and develop and manage transportation and storage systems. The advent of the Internet and electronic commerce has also dramatically influenced the distribution variable. Companies can now make their products available throughout the world without maintaining facilities in each country. For example, Great Southern Sauce Company, a small firm in Little Rock, Arkansas, sells salsa, barbecue sauce, and other sauces through its website to buyers all over the United States and around the world.[6] We examine distribution issues in Chapters 15 through 17.

Snapshot

Wireless dialing in U.S.

The number of cellphone users is expected to rise about 13% by 2007. Annual user estimates (in millions):

2003	2004	2005	2006	2007
148	154	160	164	168

Source: Data from Yankee Group.

The Promotion Variable. The promotion variable relates to activities used to inform individuals or groups about the organization and its products. Promotion can aim to increase public awareness of the organization and of new or existing products. Ford Motor Company's Lincoln Mercury division, for example, is using basketball legend Earvin "Magic" Johnson in print and television advertisements to attract younger buyers to its vehicles.[7] However, as Building Customer Relationships reveals, using celebrities to promote products can be problematic if those celebrities fail to appeal to a product's target market. Promotional activities can also educate customers about product features or urge people to take a particular stance on a political or social issue, such as smoking or drug abuse. Promotion can help sustain interest in established products that have been available for decades, such as Arm & Hammer baking soda or Ivory soap. Many companies are using the Internet and the World Wide Web to communicate information about themselves and their products. Ragu's website, for example, offers Italian phrases, recipes, and a sweepstakes, while Southwest Airlines' website enables customers to make flight reservations. In Chapters 18 through 20, we take a detailed look at promotion activities.

The Price Variable. The price variable relates to decisions and actions associated with establishing pricing objectives and policies and determining product prices. Price is a critical component of the marketing mix because customers are concerned about the value obtained in an exchange. Price is often used as a competitive tool. For example, gardening products available at Lowe's home improvement stores cost 5 to

BUILDING CUSTOMER RELATIONSHIPS

The Perils of Using Celebrities in Advertising

When DaimlerChrysler signed a three-year, $14 million deal with recording artist Celine Dion to promote its automobiles, managers thought they were on to a good thing. The popular French-Canadian diva, who has issued a number of best-selling albums and smash hits, is adored by millions of fans around the world for her powerful vocals and unabashedly sentimental tunes. To Chrysler managers, she offered a sophisticated and polished image that seemed the perfect vehicle to steer the company on an unswerving "path to premium."

But just a year after signing the deal, Dion's image and voice were noticeably absent from the company's advertising. Although Dion's partnership with Chrysler helped increase record sales for Dion, it failed to move cars off the lot for Chrysler. Disgruntled dealers complained that the advertising campaign did more to sell the singer than sell Chrysler cars.

How did such a seemingly brilliant match fail to spark sales? Sources suggest that Chrysler's advertising agency had advised Chrysler *against* signing the deal with Dion on the grounds that her devoted audience was older than the buyers Chrysler sought to target. Despite this warning, however, Chrysler arranged for Dion to star in a

number of extravagant commercials and events as part of its "Drive & Love" campaign. The company even sponsored Dion's highly touted Las Vegas show called *A New Day.*

Dion's failure to appeal to car buyers as effortlessly as to listeners illustrates some of the pitfalls of using celebrities to endorse products. First, managers overawed by star power may be all too willing to sign deals, even when market research suggests that a celebrity is not a good match for a particular product or target market. Moreover, a celebrity with Dion's megastar power can easily overshadow the brand.

Another stumbling block is the possibility that a spokesperson will engage in scandalous behavior, as in the case of L.A. Lakers guard Kobe Bryant, who was accused of sexually assaulting a 19-year-old woman. Regardless of the outcome of an accusation, the scandal surrounding the charges threatened his endorsement deals with McDonald's, Nike, and Coca-Cola. The fallen-celebrity pitfall is illustrated by another of Chrysler's misfortunes when the automaker struck a deal with Martha Stewart, who shortly after was indicted on charges of securities fraud. Other problems may arise if celebrities become overexposed by being linked with too many products or become unable to perform and lose their status in their field.

50 percent less than comparable products available at nurseries and small garden centers.[8] Airlines develop complex systems for determining the right price for each seat on a specific flight. Zilliant, a pricing consulting firm, helps other companies model price alternatives and potential customer reactions to try to find the prices that will yield the highest profits.[9] Intense price competition sometimes leads to price wars, but high prices can also be used competitively to establish a product's image. Waterman and Mont Blanc pens, for example, have an image of high quality and high price that has given them significant status. We explore pricing decisions in Chapters 21 and 22.

The marketing mix variables are often viewed as controllable because they can be modified. However, there are limits to how much marketing managers can alter them. Economic conditions, competitive structure, or government regulations may prevent a manager from adjusting prices frequently or significantly. Making changes in the size, shape, and design of most tangible goods is expensive; therefore, such product features cannot be altered very often. In addition, promotional campaigns and methods used to distribute products ordinarily cannot be rewritten or revamped overnight.

◆ Marketing Builds Satisfying Exchange Relationships

exchange The provision or transfer of goods, services, or ideas in return for something of value

Individuals and organizations engage in marketing to facilitate **exchanges**, the provision or transfer of goods, services, or ideas in return for something of value. Any product (good, service, or even idea) may be involved in a marketing exchange. We assume only that individuals and organizations expect to gain a reward in excess of the costs incurred.

For an exchange to take place, four conditions must exist. First, two or more individuals, groups, or organizations must participate, and each must possess something of value that the other party desires. Second, the exchange should provide a benefit or satisfaction to both parties in the transaction. Third, each party must have confidence in the promise of the "something of value" held by the other. If you go to a Sting concert, for example, you go with the expectation of a great performance. Finally, to build trust, the parties to the exchange must meet expectations.

Figure 1.2 depicts the exchange process. The arrows indicate that the parties communicate that each has something of value available to exchange. An exchange will not necessarily take place just because these conditions exist; marketing activities can occur even without an actual transaction or sale. You may see an ad for a Viking refrigerator, for instance, but you may never buy the product. When an exchange occurs, products are traded for other products or for financial resources.

Marketing activities should attempt to create and maintain satisfying exchange relationships. To maintain an exchange relationship, buyers must be satisfied with the obtained good, service, or idea, and sellers must be satisfied with the financial reward or something else of value received. A dissatisfied customer who lacks trust in the relationship often searches for alternative organizations or products.

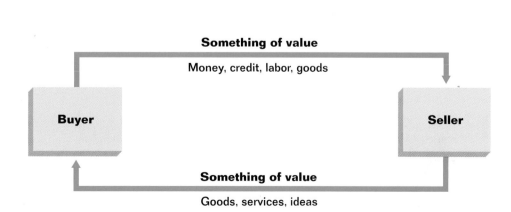

Figure 1.2 Exchange Between Buyer and Seller

◆ Marketing Occurs in a Dynamic Environment

Marketing activities do not take place in a vacuum. The **marketing environment**, which includes competitive, economic, political, legal and regulatory, technological, and sociocultural forces, surrounds the customer and affects the marketing mix (see Figure 1.1). The effects of these forces on buyers and sellers can be dramatic and difficult to predict. They can create threats to marketers, but they can also generate opportunities for new products and new methods of reaching customers.

The forces of the marketing environment affect a marketer's ability to facilitate exchanges in three general ways. First, they influence customers by affecting their lifestyles, standards of living, and preferences and needs for products. Because a marketing manager tries to develop and adjust the marketing mix to satisfy customers, effects of environmental forces on customers also have an indirect impact on marketing mix components. The merging of telecommunications and computer technologies, for example, allows FedEx Corporation to interact with customers via the World Wide Web. FedEx customers can track packages from their home or office computers and send e-mail feedback to FedEx about its services. This technology thus enables FedEx to gather marketing research information directly from customers. Second, marketing environment forces help determine whether and how a marketing manager can perform certain marketing activities. Third, environmental forces may affect a marketing manager's decisions and actions by influencing buyers' reactions to the firm's marketing mix.

Marketing environment forces can fluctuate quickly and dramatically, which is one reason marketing is so interesting and challenging. Because these forces are closely interrelated, changes in one may cause changes in others. For example, evidence linking children's consumption of soft drinks and fast foods to health issues such as obesity, diabetes, and osteoporosis has exposed marketers of such products to negative publicity and generated calls for legislation regulating the sale of soft drinks in public schools. Some companies have responded to these concerns by reformulating products to make them healthier. PepsiCo, for example, has begun removing trans fats, which have been linked to heart disease, from its Frito-Lay snack foods, while the Ruby Tuesday restaurant chain has switched to frying with canola oil, which does not contain trans fats, and begun offering low-carbohydrate menu items.[10]

Changes in the marketing environment produce uncertainty for marketers and at times hurt marketing efforts, but they also create opportunities. Marketers who are alert to changes in environmental forces can not only adjust to and influence these changes but also capitalize on the opportunities such changes provide. Sharper Image, for example, was once a high-tech gadget boutique, always looking for the next calculator, robot, or other hot product from Sony, Panasonic, and other manufacturers. Today the national retail chain stays on top of social and technological trends by stocking new inventions and designing and marketing its own ideas. With an average purchase of $128 per customer, 80 percent of Sharper Image's revenues now come from its own products, such as the Turbo-Groomer, the Automatic Eyeglass Cleaner, and the Saxxy, a software-powered kazoo.[11]

Marketing mix elements—product, distribution, promotion, and price—are factors over which an organization has control; the forces of the environment, however, are far less controllable. But even though marketers know they cannot predict changes in the marketing environment with certainty, they must nevertheless plan for them. Because these environmental forces have such a profound effect on marketing activities, we explore each of them in considerable depth in Chapter 3.

Understanding the Marketing Concept

Some firms have sought success by buying land, building a factory, equipping it with people and machines, and then making a product they believe buyers need. However, these firms frequently fail to attract customers with what they have to

The All-New BMW X3 Sports Activity Vehicle. Any weather. Any corner. Any pace. Any passion. Any weather. Any corner. Any pace. Any passion.

The Marketing Concept
BMW continually develops new automobiles to meet changing consumer needs and to stay ahead of the market.

marketing concept A philosophy that an organization should try to provide products that satisfy customers' needs through a coordinated set of activities that also allows the organization to achieve its goals

offer because they defined their business as "making a product" rather than as "helping potential customers satisfy their needs and wants." For example, when compact discs became more popular than vinyl records, turntable manufacturers had an opportunity to develop new products to satisfy customers' needs for home entertainment. Companies that did not pursue this opportunity, such as Dual and Empire, are no longer in business. Such organizations failed to implement the marketing concept. Likewise, the growing popularity of MP3 technology has enabled new firms, such as Apple Computer, to develop products like the iPod to satisfy consumers' desire to store customized music libraries. Instead of buying CDs, a consumer can buy songs for 99 cents per download at Apple's iTunes.com.

According to the **marketing concept,** an organization should try to provide products that satisfy customers' needs through a coordinated set of activities that also allows the organization to achieve its goals. Customer satisfaction is the major focus of the marketing concept. To implement the marketing concept, an organization strives to determine what buyers want and uses this information to develop satisfying products. It focuses on customer analysis, competitor analysis, and integration of the firm's resources to provide customer value and satisfaction as well as generate long-term profits.[12] The firm must also continue to alter, adapt, and develop products to keep pace with customers' changing desires and preferences. Ben & Jerry's, for example, constantly assesses customer demand for ice cream and sorbet. On its website, it maintains a "flavor graveyard" listing combinations that were tried and ultimately failed. It also notes its top ten flavors each month. Pharmaceutical companies such as Merck and Pfizer continually strive to develop new products to fight infectious diseases, viruses, cancer, and other medical problems. Drugs that lower cholesterol, control diabetes, alleviate depression, or improve the quality of life in other ways also provide huge profits for the drug companies. When a new product—like a new grape-flavored chewable form of the allergy medication Zyrtec for young allergy sufferers—is approved, the company must undertake marketing activities to reach customers and communicate the product's benefits and any potential side effects. Thus, the marketing concept emphasizes that marketing begins and ends with customers.

The marketing concept is not a second definition of *marketing*. It is a management philosophy guiding an organization's overall activities. This philosophy affects all organizational activities, not just marketing. Production, finance, accounting, human resources, and marketing departments must work together.

The marketing concept is also not a philanthropic philosophy aimed at helping customers at the expense of the organization. A firm that adopts the marketing concept must satisfy not only its customers' objectives but also its own, or it will not stay in business long. The overall objectives of a business might relate to increasing profits, market share, sales, or a combination of the three. The marketing concept stresses that an organization can best achieve these objectives by being customer oriented. Thus, implementing the marketing concept should benefit the organization as well as its customers.

It is important for marketers to consider not only their current buyers' needs but also the long-term needs of society. Striving to satisfy customers' desires by sacrificing society's long-term welfare is unacceptable. For example, while many parents want disposable diapers that are comfortable, absorbent, and safe for their babies, society in general does not want nonbiodegradable disposable diapers that create tremendous landfill problems now and for the future. Marketers are expected to act in a socially responsible manner, an idea we discuss in more detail in Chapter 4.

◆ Evolution of the Marketing Concept

The marketing concept may seem to be an obvious approach to running a business. However, businesspeople have not always believed that the best way to make sales and profits is to satisfy customers (see Figure 1.3).

The Production Orientation. During the second half of the nineteenth century, the Industrial Revolution was in full swing in the United States. Electricity, rail transportation, division of labor, assembly lines, and mass production made it possible to produce goods more efficiently. With new technology and new ways of using labor, products poured into the marketplace, where demand for manufactured goods was strong.

The Sales Orientation. In the 1920s, strong demand for products subsided, and businesses realized they would have to "sell" products to buyers. From the mid-1920s to the early 1950s, businesses viewed sales as the major means of increasing profits and came to adopt a sales orientation. Businesspeople believed the most important marketing activities were personal selling, advertising, and distribution. Today some people incorrectly equate marketing with a sales orientation.

The Marketing Orientation. By the early 1950s, some businesspeople began to recognize that efficient production and extensive promotion did not guarantee that customers would buy products. These businesses, and many others since, found they must first determine what customers want and then produce it rather than making the products first and then trying to persuade customers that they need them. As more organizations realized the importance of satisfying customers' needs, U.S. businesses entered the marketing era, one of marketing orientation.

marketing orientation
An organizationwide commitment to researching and responding to customer needs

A **marketing orientation** requires the "organizationwide generation of market intelligence pertaining to current and future customer needs, dissemination of the intelligence across departments, and organizationwide responsiveness to it."[13] Top management, marketing managers, nonmarketing managers (those in production, finance, human resources, and so on), and customers are all important in developing and carrying out a marketing orientation. Unless marketing managers provide continuous customer-focused leadership with minimal interdepartmental conflict, achieving a marketing orientation will be difficult. Nonmarketing managers must communicate with marketing managers to share information important to understanding the customer. Finally, a marketing orientation involves being responsive to ever-changing customer needs and wants. To accomplish this, Amazon.com, the online provider of books and compact discs, follows buyers' online purchases and

Figure 1.3 The Evolution of the Marketing Concept

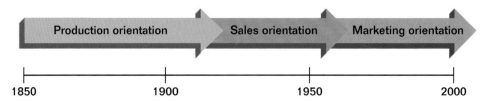

| Production orientation | Sales orientation | Marketing orientation |

1850   1900   1950   2000

recommends related purchases. Trying to assess what customers want, a difficult task to begin with, is further complicated by the speed with which fashions and tastes can change. Today businesses want to satisfy customers and build meaningful, long-term buyer-seller relationships.

◆ Implementing the Marketing Concept

A philosophy may sound reasonable and look good on paper, but that does not mean it can be put into practice easily. To implement the marketing concept, a marketing-oriented organization must accept some general conditions and recognize and deal with several problems. Consequently, the marketing concept has yet to be fully accepted by all American businesses.

Management must first establish an information system to discover customers' real needs and then use the information to create satisfying products. When M&M/Mars asked customers to choose a new M&M color to replace tan, 10.2 million people voted by mail, phone, fax, and e-mail. Blue received 54 percent of the vote, with purple, pink, and "no change" losing.[14] Within months, blue joined red, green, yellow, orange, and dark brown in the M&M lineup. Similarly, Parker Brothers encouraged customers to vote online for a new Monopoly piece (a biplane, bag of money, or piggy bank). These examples illustrate one technique marketers can use to obtain information about customers' desires and to respond in a way that forges a positive marketing relationship. An information system is usually expensive; management must commit money and time for its development and maintenance. But without an adequate information system, an organization cannot be marketing oriented.

To satisfy customers' objectives as well as its own, a company must also coordinate all its activities. This may require restructuring the internal operations and overall objectives of one or more departments. Nanotechnology, for example, represents opportunities for advances in pumps, gears, and switches to perform physical tasks. However, application and commercialization of this technology requires marketing knowledge related to customers' needs and product uses. If the head of the marketing unit is not a member of the organization's top-level management, a new technology may fail to sufficiently address actual customer needs and desires. Implementing the marketing concept demands the support not only of top management but of managers and staff across all functions and levels of the organization.

Managing Customer Relationships

Achieving the full profit potential of each customer relationship should be the fundamental goal of every marketing strategy. Marketing relationships with customers are the lifeblood of all businesses. At the most basic level, profits can be obtained through relationships by (1) acquiring new customers, (2) enhancing the profitability of existing customers, and (3) extending the duration of customer relationships. Implementing the marketing concept means optimizing the exchange relationship— the relationship between a company's investment in customer relationships and the return generated by customers' loyalty and retention.[15]

relationship marketing
Establishing long-term, mutually satisfying buyer-seller relationships

Maintaining positive relationships with customers is an important goal for marketers. The term **relationship marketing** refers to "long-term, mutually beneficial arrangements in which both the buyer and seller focus on value enhancement through the creation of more satisfying exchanges."[16] Relationship marketing continually deepens the buyer's trust in the company, which, as the customer's confidence grows, in turn increases the firm's understanding of the customer's needs. Successful marketers respond to customer needs and strive to increase value to buyers over time. Eventually this interaction becomes a solid relationship that allows for cooperation and mutual dependency. For example, customers depend on Coca-

Cola Company to provide a standardized, reliable, satisfying soft drink anyplace in the world. Due to its efforts to expand distribution to every possible location, Coca-Cola sells 30 percent of its volume in North America, 26 percent in Latin America, 21 percent in Europe, 16 percent in the Asian/Pacific region, and 7 percent in Africa and the Middle East.[17] The company continues to expand distribution and to maintain a high-quality product. Coca-Cola is also a good "corporate citizen," donating millions of dollars to education and health and human services each year.

To build long-term customer relationships, marketers are increasingly turning to marketing research and information technology. **Customer relationship management (CRM)** focuses on using information about customers to create marketing strategies that develop and sustain desirable customer relationships. By increasing customer value over time, organizations try to retain and increase long-term profitability through customer loyalty.[18] For example, AmSouth Bank, a financial institution with branches throughout the southeastern United States, promotes itself as "The Relationship Bank" and offers every financial service a business or consumer could conceivably need. Instead of focusing on acquiring new customers, AmSouth strives to serve all the financial needs of each individual customer, thereby acquiring a greater share of each customer's financial business.[19] Research has found that commitment and loyalty programs that provide economic incentives improve customer retention and increase share of business with each customer.[20]

Managing customer relationships requires identifying patterns of buying behavior and using that information to focus on the most promising and profitable customers.[21] Companies must be sensitive to customers' requirements and desires, and establish communication to build customers' trust and loyalty. Consider that the lifetime value of a Taco Bell customer is approximately $12,000, while a lifelong Lexus customer is worth about $600,000.[22] Identifying and analyzing the factors that influence the lifetime value of each customer has become an important activity for businesses.[23] Because the loss of a loyal potential lifetime customer can result in lower profits, managing customer relationships has become a major focus of strategic marketing today.

Through the use of Internet-based marketing strategies (e-marketing), companies can personalize customer relationships on a nearly one-on-one basis. A wide range of products, such as computers, jeans, golf clubs, cosmetics, and greeting cards, can be tailored for specific customers. At Priceline.com, for example, customers can specify the price they are willing to pay for a particular travel product and then find companies that are willing to sell at that price.[24] Customer relationship management provides a strategic bridge between information technology and marketing strategies aimed at long-term relationships with high-revenue customers.[25] This involves finding and retaining customers using information to improve customer value and satisfaction. For example, Amazon.com uses e-mail to inform customers about books, music, DVDs, or other products that may interest them. Amazon analyzes each e-mail campaign to determine which strategies yield the greatest response rates and additional purchases. When the company offered a $5 or $10 gift certificate to 1 million new customers, 150,000 customers purchased again.[26] Thus, information technology helps Amazon manage customer relationships to build value and increase sales and satisfaction. We take a closer look at some of these e-marketing strategies in Chapter 6.

customer relationship management (CRM) Using information about customers to create marketing strategies that develop and sustain desirable customer relationships

Value-Driven Marketing

value A customer's subjective assessment of benefits relative to costs in determining the worth of a product

Value is an important element of managing long-term customer relationships and implementing the marketing concept. We view **value** as a customer's subjective assessment of benefits relative to costs in determining the worth of a product (customer value = customer benefits − customer costs). From a company's perspective, there is a tradeoff between increasing the value offered to a customer and maximizing the profits from a transaction.[27]

Customer benefits include anything a buyer receives in an exchange. Hotels and motels, for example, basically provide a room with a bed and bathroom, but each firm provides a different level of service, amenities, and atmosphere to satisfy its guests. Hampton Inns offers the minimum services necessary to maintain a quality, efficient, low-price overnight accommodation. In contrast, the Ritz Carlton provides every imaginable service a guest might desire and strives to ensure that all service is of the highest quality. Customers judge which type of accommodation offers the best value according to the benefits they desire and their willingness and ability to pay for the costs associated with those benefits.

Customer costs include anything a buyer must give up to obtain the benefits the product provides. The most obvious cost is the monetary price of the product, but nonmonetary costs can be equally important in a customer's determination of value. Two nonmonetary costs are the time and effort customers expend to find and purchase desired products. To reduce time and effort, a company can increase product availability, thereby making it more convenient for buyers to purchase the firm's products. Another nonmonetary cost is risk, which can be reduced by offering good basic warranties or extended warranties for an additional charge.[28] Another risk reduction strategy is the offer of a 100 percent satisfaction guarantee. This strategy is increasingly popular in today's catalog/telephone/Internet shopping environment. L.L. Bean, for example, uses such a guarantee to reduce the risk involved in ordering merchandise from its catalogs and online store.

The process people use to determine the value of a product is not highly scientific. We all tend to get a feel for the worth of products based on our own expectations and previous experience. We can, for example, compare the value of tires, batteries, and computers directly with the value of competing products. We evaluate movies, sporting events, and performances by entertainers on the more subjective basis of personal preferences and emotions. For most purchases, we do not consciously try to calculate the associated benefits and costs. It becomes an instinctive feeling that Kellogg's Corn Flakes are a good value or that McDonald's is a good place to take children for a quick lunch. The purchase of an automobile or a mountain bike may have emotional components, but more conscious decision making may also figure in the process of determining value.

In developing marketing activities, it is important to recognize that customers receive benefits based on their experiences. For example, many computer buyers consider services such as fast delivery, ease of installation, technical advice, and training assistance to be important elements of the product. Customers also derive

Value-Driven Marketing
Macy's promotes its Hotel Collection™—a luxury line at great value.

Luxury at exceptional value. Hotel is the place to stay.

HOTEL COLLECTION™
BED | BATH | TABLEWARE

benefits from the act of shopping and selecting products. These benefits can be affected by the atmosphere or environment of a store, such as Red Lobster's nautical/seafood theme. Even the ease of navigating a website can have a tremendous impact on perceived value. For this reason, General Motors has developed a user-friendly way to navigate its website for researching and pricing vehicles. Using the Internet to compare a Saturn with a Mercedes could result in different customers viewing different automobiles as an excellent value. Owners have highly rated the Saturn as providing low-cost, reliable transportation and having dealers who provide outstanding service. A Mercedes may cost twice as much but has been rated as a better-engineered automobile that also has a higher social status than the Saturn. Different customers may view each car as being an exceptional value for their own personal satisfaction.

The marketing mix can be used to enhance perceptions of value. A product that demonstrates value usually has a feature or an enhancement that provides benefits. Promotional activities can also help create an image and prestige characteristics that customers consider in their assessment of a product's value. In some cases, value may simply be perceived as the lowest price. Many customers may not care about the quality of the paper towels they buy; they simply want the cheapest ones for use in cleaning up spills because they plan to throw them in the trash anyway. On the other hand, more people are looking for the fastest, most convenient way to achieve a certain goal and therefore become insensitive to pricing. For example, many busy customers are buying more prepared meals in supermarkets to take home and serve quickly even though these meals cost considerably more than meals prepared from scratch. In such cases, the products with the greatest convenience may be perceived as having the greatest value. The availability or distribution of products can also enhance their value. Taco Bell, for example, wants to have its Mexican fast-food products available at any time and any place people are thinking about consuming food. It has therefore introduced Taco Bell products into supermarkets, vending machines, college campuses, and other convenient locations. Thus, the development of an effective marketing strategy requires understanding the needs and desires of customers and designing a marketing mix to satisfy them and provide the value they want.

Marketing Management

marketing management The process of planning, organizing, implementing, and controlling marketing activities to facilitate exchanges effectively and efficiently

Marketing management is the process of planning, organizing, implementing, and controlling marketing activities to facilitate exchanges effectively and efficiently. Effectiveness and efficiency are important dimensions of this definition. *Effectiveness* is the degree to which an exchange helps achieve an organization's objectives. *Efficiency* refers to minimizing the resources an organization must spend to achieve a specific level of desired exchanges. Thus, the overall goal of marketing management is to facilitate highly desirable exchanges and to minimize the costs of doing so.

Planning is a systematic process of assessing opportunities and resources, determining marketing objectives, and developing a marketing strategy and plans for implementation and control. Planning determines when and how marketing activities are performed and who performs them. It forces marketing managers to think ahead, establish objectives, and consider future marketing activities and their impact on society. Effective planning also reduces or eliminates daily crises.

Organizing marketing activities involves developing the internal structure of the marketing unit. The structure is the key to directing marketing activities. The marketing unit can be organized by functions, products, regions, types of customers, or a combination of all four.

Proper implementation of marketing plans hinges on coordination of marketing activities, motivation of marketing personnel, and effective communication within the unit. Marketing managers must motivate marketing personnel, coordinate their activities, and integrate their activities both with those in other areas of the company and with the marketing efforts of personnel in external organizations, such as advertising agencies and research firms. If McDonald's runs a promotion advertising Big Macs for 99 cents, proper implementation of this plan requires that each of the company's restaurants has enough staff and product on hand to handle the increased demand. An organization's communication system must allow the marketing manager to stay in contact with high-level management, with managers of other functional areas within the firm, and with personnel involved in marketing activities both inside and outside the organization.

The marketing control process consists of establishing performance standards, comparing actual performance with established standards, and reducing the difference between desired and actual performance. An effective control process has four requirements. First, it should ensure a rate of information flow that allows the marketing manager to detect quickly any differences between actual and planned levels of performance. Second, it must accurately monitor various activities and be flexible enough to accommodate changes. Third, the costs of the control process must be low relative to costs that would arise without controls. Finally, the control process should be designed so that both managers and subordinates can understand it. We examine the development, organization, implementation, and controlling of marketing strategies in greater detail in the next chapter.

The Importance of Marketing in Our Global Economy

Our definition of *marketing* and discussion of marketing activities reveal some of the obvious reasons the study of marketing is relevant in today's world. In this section, we look at how marketing affects us as individuals and at its role in our increasingly global society.

◆ Marketing Costs Consume a Sizable Portion of Buyers' Dollars

Studying marketing will make you aware that many marketing activities are necessary to provide satisfying goods and services. Obviously these activities cost money. About one-half of a buyer's dollar goes for marketing costs. If you spend $12.00 on a new compact disc, about $6.00 goes toward activities related to distribution and the retailer's expenses and profit margins. The production (pressing) of the CD represents about $1, or 8.33 percent of its price. A family with a monthly income of $3,000 that allocates $600 to taxes and savings spends about $2,400 for goods and services. Of this amount, $1,200 goes for marketing activities. If marketing expenses consume that much of your dollar, you should know how this money is used.

◆ Marketing Is Used in Nonprofit Organizations

Although the term *marketing* may bring to mind advertising for McDonald's, Chevrolet, and IBM, marketing is also important in organizations working to achieve goals other than ordinary business objectives such as profit. Government agencies at the federal, state, and local levels engage in marketing activities to fulfill their mission and goals. The U.S. Army, for example, uses promotion, including television advertisements and event sponsorships, to communicate the benefits of enlisting to potential recruits. The U.S. Treasury Department plans to spend $53 million over a five-year period to promote the release of redesigned $20, $50, and $100 bills. As part of the effort, the new $20 bills were featured on episodes of *Wheel of Fortune, Jeopardy,* and *Who Wants to be a Millionaire?*[29] Universities and

colleges also engage in marketing activities to recruit new students as well as donations from alumni and businesses.

In the private sector, nonprofit organizations employ marketing activities to create, distribute, promote, and even price programs that benefit particular segments
of society. Habitat for Humanity, for example, must promote its philosophy of low-
income housing to the public to raise funds and donations of supplies to build or
renovate housing for low-income families who contribute "sweat equity" to the
construction of their own homes. In a recent year, such activities helped nonprofit
organizations raise nearly $241 billion in philanthropic contributions to assist them
in fulfilling their missions.[30]

◆ Marketing Is Important to Business and the Economy

Businesses must sell products to survive and grow, and marketing activities help sell
their products. Financial resources generated from sales can be used to develop
innovative products. New products allow a firm to better satisfy customers' changing needs, which in turn enables the firm to generate more profits. Even nonprofit
businesses need to "sell" to survive.

Marketing activities help produce the profits that are essential not only to the
survival of individual businesses but also to the health and ultimate survival of the
global economy. Profits drive economic growth because without them businesses
find it difficult, if not impossible, to buy more raw materials, hire more employees,
attract more capital, and create additional products that in turn make more profits.
Without profits, marketers cannot continue to provide jobs and contribute to social
causes.

◆ Marketing Fuels Our Global Economy

Profits from marketing products contribute to the development of new products
and technologies. Advances in technology, along with falling political and economic barriers and the universal desire for a higher standard of living, have made
marketing across national borders commonplace while stimulating global economic growth. As a result of worldwide communications and increased international
travel, many American brands have achieved widespread acceptance around the
world. At the same time, customers in the United States have greater choices
among the products they buy as foreign brands such as Toyota (Japan), Bayer
(Germany), and BP (Great Britain) now sell alongside American brands such as
Ford, Tylenol, and Chevron. People around the world watch CNN and MTV on
Toshiba and Sony televisions they purchased at Wal-Mart. Electronic commerce via
the Internet now enables businesses of all sizes to reach buyers worldwide. Global
Marketing highlights a Mexican firm that targets customers around the world. We
explore the international markets and opportunities for global marketing in
Chapter 5.

◆ Marketing Knowledge Enhances Consumer Awareness

Besides contributing to the well-being of our economy, marketing activities help
improve the quality of our lives. Studying marketing allows us to assess a product's
value and flaws more effectively. We can determine which marketing efforts need
improvement and how to attain that goal. For example, an unsatisfactory experience with a warranty may make you wish for stricter law enforcement so that sellers would fulfill their promises. You may also wish you had more accurate information about a product before you purchased it. Understanding marketing enables
us to evaluate corrective measures (such as laws, regulations, and industry guidelines) that could stop unfair, damaging, or unethical marketing practices. Thus,
understanding how marketing activities work can help you be a better consumer.

◆ Marketing Connects People Through Technology

New technology, especially technology related to computers and telecommunications, helps marketers understand and satisfy more customers than ever before. Through toll-free telephone numbers, customers can provide feedback about their experiences with a company's products. Even bottled-water products, such as Dannon Natural Spring Water, provide toll-free telephone numbers for questions or comments. This information can help marketers refine and improve their products to better satisfy consumer needs. The Internet, especially the World Wide Web, also allows companies to provide tremendous amounts of information about their products to consumers and to interact with them through e-mail. A consumer shopping for a personal digital assistant, for example, can visit the websites of Palm and Handspring to compare the features of the PalmPilot and Visor, respectively. Although consumers are often reluctant to purchase products directly via the Internet, many value the Internet as a significant source of information for making purchase decisions.

The Internet has also become a vital tool for marketing to other businesses. In fact, online sales are expected to account for 42 percent of all business-to-business

GLOBAL MARKETING

Gruma Tortillas Folds up U.S. Market

The next time you go to the grocery store, take a look at the tortillas. Chances are you'll find them in their own section, and you'll face a mind-boggling array of choices: flour, corn, garlic-herb, tomato-basil, fajita-size, super-size, fat-free, and other varieties. The humble tortilla—a staple in many Latin American diets—has come a long way.

The increasingly wide distribution of tortillas can be partially credited to Gruma Corporation, a Mexico-based company with U.S. and international subsidiaries. One of Gruma's U.S. brands, Mission Foods Corporation, claims to produce more than one-quarter of the tortillas consumed worldwide, with 68 million tortillas produced by just one of its plants. Mission and three other brands owned by Gruma accounted for almost half of U.S. supermarket sales in 2002.

Gruma's growing dominance of the U.S. market led 17 competitors to file a lawsuit claiming that Gruma had established a monopoly and was forcing other brands off the shelves by paying grocers for prime shelf space. They also argued that the variety of brands marketed by Gruma deceives consumers into thinking they have a choice in tortillas. Although the case against Gruma was

dismissed, the tortilla makers have filed an appeal for $70 million in damages.

How did Gruma come to dominate the U.S. market? Analysts say that Gruma, a tortilla-manufacturing giant in Mexico, entered the United States when no dominant national brand existed. Recognizing the tremendous potential for growth, Gruma began to buy small U.S. tortilla makers, including Mission. Today Gruma owns 13 manufacturing facilities and 5 corn-flour plants in the United States. In addition to its own brands sold at supermarkets, Gruma-owned companies manufacture many in-house products for stores and restaurants. Gruma has also expanded its tortilla empire to Europe, with a facility in Great Britain that distributes tortillas throughout the United Kingdom, continental Europe, Scandinavia, and even as far as the Middle East.

Regardless of whether allegations against Gruma hold up in court, U.S. tortilla makers have a product that seems poised for even greater growth. Not only is the tortilla firmly established in the mainstream American diet, but the number of traditional consumers of tortillas is growing as well. U.S. Census figures indicate that Latinos are now the largest ethnic minority group, with more than half of this group being Mexican Americans. Such market conditions should favor tortilla makers, provided they are willing to seize opportunities.

Marketing and the Growth of Technology
LG introduces a 60" wide-screen plasma HDTV, taking advantage of high-tech capabilities.

TOO MUCH IS NOT ENOUGH.

THE 60" WIDE-SCREEN LG PLASMA HDTV MONITOR: A NEXT GENERATION PANEL FOR INCREDIBLE PICTURE, FAROUDJA PROCESSOR, ADVANCED ZOOM AND FLEXIBLE PIP A BIT MUCH? YES. OVER THE TOP? DEFINITELY. WANT TO KNOW MORE? SEE THE FULL RANGE OF FLATPANELS AT WWW.LGUSA.COM OR CALL 1-800-243-0000.

LG
LIFE'S GOOD™

NET SIGHTS

*The World Wide Web has become a very useful information tool for consumers and marketers alike. Marketers can now turn to numerous websites for the latest information about consumer trends, industry news, economic data, competitors' products and prices, and much, much more. We highlight some of these sites in each chapter in a Net Sights box. One of the most useful sites is the Marketing Learning Center site for this textbook at **http://www.prideferrell.com**. There you will find chapter summaries, self-tests, and exercises, as well as career information and links to many more useful marketing-related websites.*

marketing by 2005, while currently 1 percent of all retail sales occurs completely online.[31] Successful companies are using technology in their marketing strategies to develop profitable relationships with these customers. We look more closely at marketing on the Internet in Chapter 6.

◆ Socially Responsible Marketing Can Promote the Welfare of Customers and Society

The success of our economic system depends on marketers whose values promote trust and cooperative relationships in which customers are treated with respect. The public is increasingly insisting that social responsibility and ethical concerns be considered in planning and implementing marketing activities. Although some marketers' irresponsible or unethical activities end up on the front pages of *USA Today* or *The Wall Street Journal*, more firms are working to develop a responsible approach to developing long-term relationships with customers *and* society. For example, Russell Simmons, who owns Phat Fashions, the Simmons-Lathan Media Group, and *OneWorld* magazine through his Rush Communications holding company, created the Rush Philanthropic Arts Foundation to donate funds to organizations that help underprivileged youth gain access to the arts.[32] By addressing concerns about the impact of marketing on society, a firm can protect the interests of the general public and the natural environment. We examine these issues and

The Importance of Marketing
The Nature Conservancy works to protect millions of acres of natural habitat around the world.

many others as we develop a framework for understanding more about marketing in the remainder of this book.

◆ Marketing Offers Many Exciting Career Prospects

From 25 to 33 percent of all civilian workers in the United States perform marketing activities. The marketing field offers a variety of interesting and challenging career opportunities throughout the world, such as personal selling, advertising, packaging, transportation, storage, marketing research, product development, wholesaling, and retailing. In addition, many individuals working for nonbusiness organizations engage in marketing activities to promote political, educational, cultural, church, civic, and charitable activities. Whether a person earns a living through marketing activities or performs them voluntarily for a nonprofit group, marketing knowledge and skills are valuable personal and professional assets.

SUMMARY

Marketing is the process of creating, distributing, promoting, and pricing goods, services, and ideas to facilitate satisfying exchange relationships with customers in a dynamic environment. As the purchasers of the products that organizations develop, promote, distribute, and price, customers are the focal point of all marketing activities. The essence of marketing is to develop satisfying exchanges from which both customers and marketers benefit. Organizations generally focus their marketing efforts on a specific group of customers, or target market.

Marketing involves developing and managing a product that will satisfy customer needs, making the product available in the right place and at a price acceptable to customers, and communicating information that helps customers determine if the product will satisfy their needs. These activities—product, distribution, promotion, and pricing—are known as the marketing mix because marketing managers decide what type of each element to use and in what amounts. Marketing managers strive to develop a marketing mix that matches the needs of customers in the target market. Before marketers can develop a marketing mix, they must collect in-depth, up-to-date information about customer needs. The product variable of the marketing mix deals with researching customers' needs and wants and designing a product that satisfies them. A product can be a good, a service, or an idea. In dealing with the distribution variable, a marketing manager tries to make products available in the quantities desired to as many customers as possible. The promotion variable relates to activities used to inform individuals or groups about the organization and its products. The price variable involves decisions and actions associated with establishing pricing policies and determining product prices. These marketing mix variables are often viewed as controllable because they can be changed, but there are limits to how much they can be altered.

Individuals and organizations engage in marketing to facilitate exchanges—the provision or transfer of goods, services, and ideas in return for something of value. Four conditions must exist for an exchange to occur. First, two or more individuals, groups, or organizations must participate, and each must possess something of value that the other party desires. Second, the exchange should provide a benefit or satisfaction to both parties involved in the transaction. Third, each party must have confidence in the promise of the "something of value" held by the other. Finally, to build trust, the parties to the exchange must meet expectations. Marketing activities should attempt to create and maintain satisfying exchange relationships.

The marketing environment, which includes competitive, economic, political, legal and regulatory, technological, and sociocultural forces, surrounds the customer and the marketing mix. These forces can create threats to marketers, but they also generate opportunities for new products and new methods of reaching customers. These forces can fluctuate quickly and dramatically.

According to the marketing concept, an organization should try to provide products that satisfy customers' needs through a coordinated set of activities that also allows the organization to achieve its goals. Customer satisfaction is the marketing concept's major objective. The philosophy of the marketing concept emerged in the United States during the 1950s after the production and sales eras. Organizations that develop activities consistent with the marketing concept become marketing-oriented organizations. To implement the marketing concept, a marketing-oriented organization must establish an information system to discover customers' needs and use the information to create satisfying products. It must also coordinate all its activities and develop marketing mixes that create value for customers in order to satisfy their needs.

Relationship marketing involves establishing long-term, mutually satisfying buyer-seller relationships.

Customer relationship management (CRM) focuses on using information about customers to create marketing strategies that develop and sustain desirable customer relationships. Managing customer relationships requires identifying patterns of buying behavior and using that information to focus on the most promising and profitable customers.

Value is a customer's subjective assessment of benefits relative to costs in determining the worth of a product. Benefits include anything a buyer receives in an exchange; costs include anything a buyer must give up to obtain the benefits the product provides. The marketing mix can be used to enhance perceptions of value.

Marketing management is the process of planning, organizing, implementing, and controlling marketing activities to facilitate effective and efficient exchanges. Planning is a systematic process of assessing opportunities and resources, determining marketing objectives, developing a marketing strategy, and preparing for implementation and control. Organizing marketing activities involves developing the marketing unit's internal structure. Proper implementation of marketing plans depends on coordinating marketing activities, motivating marketing personnel, and communicating effectively within the unit. The marketing control process consists of establishing performance standards, comparing actual performance with established standards, and reducing the difference between desired and actual performance.

Marketing is important in our society in many ways. Marketing costs absorb about half of each buyer's dollar. Marketing activities are performed in both business and nonprofit organizations. Marketing activities help business organizations generate profits and help fuel the increasingly global economy. Knowledge of marketing enhances consumer awareness. New technology improves marketers' ability to connect with customers. Socially responsible marketing can promote the welfare of customers and society. Finally, marketing offers many exciting career opportunities.

 Please visit the student website at **www.prideferrell.com** for ACE Self-Test questions that will help you prepare for exams.

IMPORTANT TERMS

Marketing
Customers
Target market
Marketing mix
Product
Exchange
Marketing environment

Marketing concept
Marketing orientation
Relationship marketing
Customer relationship management (CRM)
Value
Marketing management

DISCUSSION & REVIEW QUESTIONS

1. What is marketing? How did you define the term before you read this chapter?
2. What is the focus of all marketing activities? Why?
3. What are the four variables of the marketing mix? Why are these elements known as variables?

4. What conditions must exist before a marketing exchange can occur? Describe a recent exchange in which you participated.

5. What are the forces in the marketing environment? How much control does a marketing manager have over these forces?

6. Discuss the basic elements of the marketing concept. Which businesses in your area use this philosophy? Explain why.

7. How can an organization implement the marketing concept?

8. What is customer relationship management? Why is it so important to "manage" this relationship?

9. What is value? How can marketers use the marketing mix to enhance customers' perception of value?

10. What types of activities are involved in the marketing management process?

11. Why is marketing important in our society? Why should you study marketing?

APPLICATION QUESTIONS

1. Identify several businesses in your area that have not adopted the marketing concept. What characteristics of these organizations indicate nonacceptance of the marketing concept?

2. Identify possible target markets for the following products:
   a. Kellogg's Corn Flakes
   b. Wilson tennis rackets
   c. Disney World
   d. Diet Pepsi

3. Discuss the variables of the marketing mix (product, price, promotion, and distribution) as they might relate to each of the following:
   a. a trucking company
   b. a men's clothing store
   c. a skating rink
   d. a campus bookstore

Internet Exercise & Resources

Visit **www.prideferrell.com** for resources to help you master the material in this chapter, plus materials that will help you expand your marketing knowledge, including Internet exercise updates, ACE self-tests, hotlinks to companies featured in this chapter, and much more.

The American Marketing Association

The American Marketing Association (AMA) is the marketing discipline's primary professional organization. In addition to sponsoring academic research, publishing marketing literature, and organizing meetings of local businesspeople with student members, it helps individual members find employment in member firms. To see what the AMA has to offer you, visit the AMA website at **www.marketingpower.com.**

1. What type of information is available on the AMA website to assist students in planning their careers and finding jobs?
2. If you joined a student chapter of the AMA, what benefits would you receive?
3. What marketing mix variable does the AMA's Internet marketing efforts exemplify?

Video Case 1.1

Finagle A Bagel

Finagle A Bagel, a fast-growing New England small business co-owned by Alan Litchman and Laura Trust, is at the forefront of one of the freshest concepts in the food service business: fresh food. The stores bake a new batch of bagels every hour and receive new deliveries of cheeses, vegetables, and other ingredients every day. Rather than prepackaging menu items, store employees make everything to order to satisfy the specific needs of each *guest* (Finagle A Bagel's term for a customer). Customers like this arrangement because they get fresh food prepared to their exact preferences—whether it's extra cheese on a bagel pizza or no onions in a salad—along with prompt, friendly service.

"Every sandwich, every salad is built to order, so there's a lot of communication between the customers and the cashiers, the customers and the sandwich makers, the customers and the managers," explains Trust. As a result, Finagle A Bagel's store employees have ample opportunity to build customer relationships and encourage repeat business. Many, like Mirna Hernandez of the Tremont Street store in downtown Boston, are so familiar with what certain customers order that they spring into action when regulars enter the store. "We know what they want, and we just ring it in and take care of them," she says. Some employees even know their customers by name and make conversation as they create a sandwich or fill a coffee container.

Over time, the owners have introduced a wide range of bagels, sandwiches, and salads linked to the core bagel product. Some of the most popular offerings include a breakfast bagel pizza, salads with bagel-chip croutons, and BLT (bacon-lettuce-tomato) bagel sandwiches.

Round, flat, seeded, plain, crowned with cheese, or cut into croutons, bagels form the basis of every menu item at Finagle A Bagel. "So many other shops will just grab onto whatever is hot, whatever is trendy, in a 'me-too' strategy," observes Heather Robertson, director of marketing, human resources, and research and development. In contrast, she says, "We do bagels—that's what we do best. And any menu item in our stores really needs to reaffirm that as our core concept." That's the first of Finagle A Bagel's marketing rules.

To identify a new product idea, Robertson and her colleagues conduct informal research by talking with both customers and employees. They also browse food magazines and cookbooks for ideas about out-of-the-ordinary flavors, taste combinations, and preparation methods. When developing a new bagel variety, for example, Robertson looks for ideas that are innovative yet appealing: "If someone else has a sun-dried tomato bagel, that's all the more reason for me not to do it. People look at Finagle A Bagel as kind of the trendsetter."

Once the marketing staff comes up with a promising idea, the next step is to write up a formula or recipe, walk downstairs to the dough factory, and mix up a test batch. Through trial and error, they refine the idea until they like the way the bagel or sandwich looks and tastes. Occasionally Finagle A Bagel has to put an idea on hold until it can find just the right ingredients.

To further reinforce the brand and reward customer loyalty, Finagle A Bagel created the Frequent Finagler card. Cardholders receive one point for every dollar spent in a Finagle A Bagel store and can redeem accumulated points for coffee, juice, sandwiches, or a dozen bagels (actually a *baker's dozen,* meaning 13

instead of 12). To join, customers visit the company's website (**www.finagleabagel.com**) and complete a registration form asking for name, address, and other demographics. From then on, says Litchman, "It's a web-based program where customers can log on, check their points, and receive free gifts by mail. The Frequent Finagler is our big push right now to use technology as a means of generating store traffic."

Pricing is an important consideration in the competitive world of quick-serve food. This is where another of Finagle A Bagel's marketing rules comes in. Regardless of cost, the company will not compromise quality. Therefore, the first step in pricing a new product is to find the best possible ingredients and then examine the costs and calculate an approximate retail price. After thinking about what a customer might expect to pay for such a menu item, shopping the competition, and talking with some customers, the company settles on a price that represents "a great product for a fair value," says Robertson.

Although Finagle A Bagel's rental costs vary, the owners price menu items the same in both higher-rent and lower-rent stores. "We have considered adjusting prices based upon the location of the store, but we haven't done it because it can backfire in a very significant way," owner Laura Trust explains. "People expect to be treated fairly, regardless of where they live."

Although Finagle A Bagel competes with other bagel chains in and around Boston, its competition goes well beyond restaurants in that category. "You compete with a person selling a cup of coffee, you compete with a grocery store selling a salad," Litchman notes. "People only have so many 'dining dollars' and you need to convince them to spend those dining dollars in your store." Finagle A Bagel's competitive advantages are high-quality, fresh products; courteous and competent employees; and clean, attractive, and inviting restaurants.

Social responsibility is an integral part of Finagle A Bagel's operations. Rather than simply throwing away unsold bagels at the end of the day, the owners donate the bagels to schools, shelters, and other nonprofit organizations. When local nonprofit groups hold fund-raising events, the owners contribute bagels to feed the volunteers. Over the years, Finagle A Bagel has provided bagels to bicyclists raising money for St. Jude Children's Research Hospital, to swimmers raising money for breast cancer research, and to people building community playgrounds. Also, the owners are strongly committed to being fair to their customers by offering good value and a good experience. "Something that we need to remember and instill in our people all the time," Trust emphasizes, "is that customers are coming in and your responsibility is to give them the best that you can give them."

Even with 400-plus employees, the owners find that owning a business is a nonstop proposition. "Our typical day never ends," says Trust. They are constantly visiting stores, dealing with suppliers, reviewing financial results, and planning for the future. Despite all these responsibilities, this husband-and-wife entrepreneurial team enjoys applying their educational background and business experience to build a business that satisfies thousands of customers every day.[33]

QUESTIONS FOR DISCUSSION

1. Describe Finagle A Bagle's marketing mix.
2. What forces from the marketing environment provide opportunities for Finagle A Bagle? What forces might threaten the firm's marketing strategy?
3. Does Finagle A Bagle appear to be implementing the marketing concept? Explain your answer.

Case 1.2

Indy Racing League vs. Open Wheel Racing Series: Who Will Win the Race?

Championship Auto Racing Teams (CART) was created in 1978 when 18 out of 21 automobile racing team owners left the United States Auto Club (USAC) to form a new league for open-wheel racing in the United States. Originally sanctioned in the mid-1950s by the USAC, *open-wheel racing* refers to cars that have an open cockpit with the engine housed at the rear of the vehicle, typical of cars used in the Indianapolis 500 race each year. However, dissatisfaction with USAC's administration and promotion of open-wheel racing prompted Roger Penske, Dan Gurney, Pat Patrick, and 15 other highly respected figures in American motor sports to found CART.

During its first 17 years, CART dominated auto racing in the United States, and open-wheel racing enjoyed greater attention than other forms of racing, including stock-car racing associated with NASCAR. In the 1980s, CART attracted legendary driver Mario Andretti and gained further foreign media coverage when Formula 1 champion Nigel Mansell teamed up with Andretti and with Brazil's Emerson Fittipaldi for great finishes at CART races.

Although CART enjoyed increasing popularity in the early 1990s, Anton H. "Tony" George, president of the Indianapolis Motor Speedway, had concerns about CART's future direction. George, whose family founded the Indianapolis 500 and developed it into the world-renowned auto race, was concerned that CART was beginning to lose sight of the interests of American open-wheel racing. Despite CART's attempt to reorganize its board of directors to include Tony George, in 1994 he announced he was creating a new open-wheel

league to compete with CART beginning in 1996. His proposed Indy Racing League (IRL) was divisive to open-wheel racing in the United States as team owners were forced to choose whether to remain with CART or move to the new league. George further deepened the rift when he proposed a "25/8" rule for the 1996 Indianapolis 500: the first 25 positions in the 33-car field would go to IRL members.

Despite the apparent duplication of open-wheel racing by CART and IRL, there are significant differences between the two organizations. First, the leagues differ with respect to the types of racecourses employed. IRL races are held exclusively on oval tracks, whereas the majority of CART races are run on road courses—either permanent racetrack facilities or temporary courses that run through the streets of an urban area. Because it is more difficult for racers to pass on road courses, they place a premium on drivers' skills to successfully navigate a track. On the other hand, oval track racing is influenced more by the horsepower and aerodynamics of the race cars, placing an emphasis on engineering and technical expertise to gain an edge over competitors.

Second, CART and IRL differ in terms of the geographic scope of their leagues and drivers. The IRL is strictly an American circuit. In contrast, CART's drivers represent North America, South America, and Europe, and its 2004 schedule included races in the United States, Canada, Mexico, Australia, England, Germany, and Japan. CART also places greater emphasis on geographic allegiances with the

Nations Cup, an award that recognizes the country whose drivers scored the best overall finish during the CART Champ Car season. As a result of CART's international focus, it enjoys greater television exposure outside the United States as annually televised CART races reach more than 980 million fans in 195 countries.

CART has continued to be a dominant force in American open-wheel racing after the initial split with the IRL. In fact, in 1998, CART was incorporated and became a publicly traded company on the New York Stock Exchange. In 2000, two CART teams resumed racing in the Indianapolis 500, and one won. Then CART slowly began to lose ground against the IRL. CART races in Brazil and Texas were cancelled during the 2001 season, resulting in public relations embarrassments for the organization. Top management turmoil was evident, too, as CART went through four chief executive officers during 2000 and 2001.

When CART and IRL split before the 1996 season, the breakup did more than split the racing teams. Fans tended to follow the league in which their favorite drivers raced rather than following both leagues. More important, sponsorship support was split between the two open-wheel leagues. Television broadcasts of CART races could be instrumental in expanding the league's following, but CART has been mired in an unfavorable television rights deal. CART must pay to have its races broadcast, whereas IRL is paid by ABC for the rights to broadcast its races on ABC and ESPN. The limited reach of CART's television broadcasts may have contributed to additional problems with sponsor relationships. Three major partners left CART in recent seasons. Honda and Toyota, which provided engines and technical support to CART and its teams, left for deals with IRL. FedEx, which shipped a great deal of cargo to CART racing sites in foreign markets, discontinued its title-sponsor relationship with CART after the 2002 season. CART successfully enlisted two new major series sponsors for the 2003 season and renamed the Champ Car series "Bridgestone Presents Champ Car World Series Powered by Ford."

CART's viability as a major racing league was also harmed by the defection of key racing teams to IRL, including Roger Penske, Michael Andretti, and Chip Ganassi. Their absence meant that CART might not be able to field the 18 cars needed to hold races. CART responded by offering financial incentives to team owners to ensure enough cars would participate in its races. Also, CART was forced to become the promoter of its own races after losing promoters in some markets. The combined result of an unfavorable television deal, sponsor and team owner defections, and increased costs of holding races forced CART into a perilous financial position.

CART's financial position continued to deteriorate during 2003, with company reports of increased operating costs and sluggish advertising and sponsorship revenue. Soon after, CART's stock was delisted by the New York Stock Exchange. Shortly after that, a group of investors, including some CART team owners, purchased the embattled company for 56 cents per share. The group formed Open Wheel Racing Series LLC and planned to take CART private once again and continue operating under the same name, Champ Car World Series. A judge ruled that the Open Wheel Racing Series owns all assets of CART. In effect, the ruling guarantees that this organization will compete in 2004 and beyond. While the race schedule, television plans and team, driver, and sponsorship plans will be forthcoming, the series anticipates an eleventh consecutive season.

The new owners have many decisions to consider, including defining their product, how to promote races, where to race, and how to price their product for their race fans (customers). American auto racing fans prefer oval track racing, as evidenced by NASCAR's strong race attendance and television ratings. However, IRL races on many of the same oval tracks as NASCAR but draws a fraction of the fans, with the Indianapolis 500 being a notable exception. Moreover, proponents of street and road course racing point to the fact that such venues lend themselves to creating a festival atmosphere around a race, including concerts, volleyball games, and beer gardens. To survive, CART must carefully identify its target market and create a marketing mix to develop a successful marketing strategy.[34]

QUESTIONS FOR DISCUSSION

1. Identify the product that the Open Wheel Racing Series offers its race car fans (customers).
2. What can the Open Wheel Racing Series do to better promote its products? How should gaining sponsorships fit into its promotional plans?
3. How can the Open Wheel Racing Series use the strengths of its international driver and race events to its advantage? Relate its selection of racecourses and events to the concept of distribution presented in the chapter.

Planning, Implementing, and Controlling Marketing Strategies

2

OBJECTIVES

1. To describe the strategic planning process

2. To explain how organizational resources and opportunities affect the planning process

3. To understand the role of the mission statement in strategic planning

4. To examine corporate, business-unit, and marketing strategies

5. To understand the process of creating the marketing plan

6. To describe the marketing implementation process and the major approaches to marketing implementation

Fiji Water Profits from Bottled-Water Trends

Water is the most basic substance on earth. But once it has been bottled and put on store shelves, is all water created equal? Apparently some bottled-water brands sparkle more than others.

Fiji Natural Artisan Bottled Water reportedly contains high levels of natural silica, touted for its anti-oxidant and skin-beautifying properties. The company claims that no other bottled water shares Fiji's unusual and health-enhancing composition. One look at Fiji Water reveals the care with which the product has been positioned in the market. Filtered through volcanic rock on the island of Viti Levu in Fiji, the water comes in an alluring bottle decorated with orchid and hibiscus blossoms in the foreground and, shimmering through the water in the bottle, a tropical waterfall in the background. Upscale restaurants and hotels stock the water for their guests, and the brand has gained a loyal celebrity following, including Cameron Diaz, Whoopi Goldberg, and the entire cast of *Friends*. In short, Fiji is liquid gold, with more than 50 million bottles sold in 2002 and approximately 80 million in 2003.

Fiji Water's success reflects the growing market for bottled water in the United States. Long a popular option in Europe, where hundreds of brands are available, bottled water has only recently become a growth industry in the United States. In fact, bottled water is now the fastest-growing segment of the beverage industry, whereas carbonated beverages are declining. The bottled-water trend is driven in part by increasingly health-conscious consumers who want to avoid the sugar and caffeine of other beverages. Bottled-water companies such as Fiji are quick to remind consumers that health experts recommend at least eight glasses of water a day. But aside from the intrinsic health value of water, what else is there to promote?

Bottled water may be favored over public sources of water because of perceived consistency and purity, according to the International Bottled Water Association. Further, there is value in appealing presentation, as demonstrated by Fiji Water's lush packaging and by the practice by some restaurants of displaying bottles of water much as they do bottles of fine wine. Moreover, some companies claim added health benefits from the water, such as Fiji's natural silica or the vitamin and herbal extracts added by other brands. Finally, customers may succumb to the exotic appeal of the water's source, such as Fiji or, in the case of Perrier, the south of France. As companies such as Fiji demonstrate, playing up these factors can increase the flow of profits in a market that's far from saturated.[1] ■

With competition increasing, Fiji Water and many other companies are spending more time and resources on strategic planning, that is, on determining how to use their resources and abilities to achieve their objectives. Although most of this book deals with specific marketing decisions and strategies, this chapter focuses on "the big picture": all the functional areas and activities—finance, production, human resources, and research and development, as well as marketing—that must be coordinated to reach organizational goals. To effectively implement the marketing concept of satisfying customers and achieving organizational goals, all organizations must engage in strategic planning.

We begin this chapter with an overview of the strategic planning process. Next, we examine how organizational resources and opportunities affect strategic planning and the role played by the organization's mission statement. After discussing the development of both corporate and business-unit strategy, we explore the nature of marketing strategy and the creation of the marketing plan. These elements provide a framework for the development and implementation of marketing strategies, as we will see throughout the remainder of this book.

Understanding the Strategic Planning Process

strategic planning The process of establishing an organizational mission and formulating goals, corporate strategy, marketing objectives, marketing strategy, and a marketing plan

Through the process of **strategic planning**, a firm establishes an organizational mission and formulates goals, corporate strategy, marketing objectives, marketing strategy, and, finally, a marketing plan.[2] A marketing orientation should guide the process of strategic planning to ensure that a concern for customer satisfaction is an integral part of the process. Figure 2.1 shows the components of strategic planning.

The process begins with a detailed analysis of the organization's strengths and weaknesses and identification of opportunities and threats within the marketing environment. Based on this analysis, the firm can establish or revise its mission and

Figure 2.1 Components of Strategic Planning

Source: Figure adapted from *Marketing Strategy,* Second Edition, by O. C. Ferrell, Michael Hartline, and George Lucas, Jr. Copyright © 2002. Reprinted with permission of South-Western, a division of Thomson Learning: **www.thomsonrights.com.** Fax 800-730-2215.

goals, and then develop corporate strategies to achieve those goals. Next, each functional area of the organization (marketing, production, finance, human resources, etc.) establishes its own objectives and develops strategies to achieve them.[3] The objectives and strategies of each functional area must support the organization's overall goals and mission. The strategies of each functional area should also be coordinated with a focus on marketing orientation.

Because our focus is marketing, we are, of course, most interested in the development of marketing objectives and strategies. Marketing objectives should be designed so that their achievement will contribute to the corporate strategy and they can be accomplished through efficient use of the firm's resources. To achieve its marketing objectives, an organization must develop a **marketing strategy**, which includes identifying and analyzing a target market and developing a marketing mix to meet the needs of individuals in that market. Thus, a marketing strategy includes a plan of action for developing, distributing, promoting, and pricing products that meet the needs of the target market. Marketing strategy is best formulated when it reflects the overall direction of the organization and is coordinated with all the firm's functional areas. When properly implemented and controlled, a marketing strategy will contribute to the achievement not only of marketing objectives but also of the organization's overall goals. For example, the 2004 Chrysler Crossfire, which competes in the two-seat sports-car market, contains many Mercedes SLK parts. DaimlerChrysler executives hope this plan will improve the image of the Chrysler brand and help drive sales for DaimlerChrysler.

The strategic planning process ultimately yields a marketing strategy that is the framework for a **marketing plan**, a written document that specifies the activities to be performed to implement and control the organization's marketing activities. In the remainder of this chapter, we discuss the major components of the strategic planning process: organizational opportunities and resources, organizational mission and goals, corporate and business-unit strategy, marketing strategy, and the role of the marketing plan.

marketing strategy A plan of action for identifying and analyzing a target market and developing a marketing mix to meet the needs of that market

marketing plan A written document that specifies the activities to be performed to implement and control the organization's marketing activities

Assessing Organizational Resources and Opportunities

The strategic planning process begins with an analysis of the marketing environment. As we will see in Chapter 3, economic, competitive, political, legal and regulatory, sociocultural, and technological forces can threaten an organization and influence its overall goals; they also affect the amount and type of resources the firm can acquire. However, these environmental forces can create favorable opportunities as well—opportunities that can be translated into overall organizational goals and marketing objectives. Organizational culture and information use affect the extent to which managers perceive such opportunities as situations on which they can successfully capitalize.[4]

Any strategic planning effort must assess the organization's available financial and human resources and capabilities, as well as how the level of these factors is likely to change in the future. Additional resources may be needed to achieve the organization's goals and mission.[5] Resources can also include goodwill, reputation, and brand names. The reputation and well-known brand names of Rolex watches and IBM computers, for example, are resources that give these firms an advantage over their competitors. Such strengths also include **core competencies**, things a firm does extremely well—sometimes so well that they give the company an advantage over its competition. For example, the Chili's Grill & Bar restaurant chain has built an advantage over competitors such as Bennigan's and Houlihan's through superior menus and service, resulting in good food at moderate prices in a casual atmosphere.[6]

Analysis of the marketing environment involves not only an assessment of resources but also identification of opportunities in the marketplace. When the right combination of circumstances and timing permits an organization to take action to

core competencies Things a firm does extremely well, which sometimes give it an advantage over its competition

Both Have

Unsurpassed Engineering

And Red Hot Good Looks.

Both Blow Away The Competition.

But One Costs

Considerably Less Than $400,000.

MACH3 Turbo
CHAMPION
*The world's best shave.
Test drive one today.*

Gillette®
The Best a Man Can Get:

© 2004 The Gillette Company

Core Competency
Gillette's core competency is in developing superior blades and razors.

reach a particular target market, a **market opportunity** exists. For example, advances in computer technology and the growth of the Internet have enabled real estate firms to provide prospective home buyers with databases of homes for sale all over the country. At www.realtor.com, the website of the National Association of Realtors, buyers have access to a wealth of online information about homes for sale, including photos, floor plans, and details about neighborhoods, schools, and shopping. The World Wide Web represents a powerful market opportunity for real estate firms because its visual nature is perfectly suited to the task of shopping for a home. Such opportunities are often called **strategic windows**, temporary periods of optimal fit between the key requirements of a market and the particular capabilities of a firm competing in that market.[7]

When a company matches a core competency to opportunities it has discovered in the marketplace, it is said to have a **competitive advantage**. In some cases, a company may possess manufacturing, technical, or marketing skills that it can match to market opportunities to create a competitive advantage. For example, eBay pioneered the online auction and built the premier site where 75 million users around the world buy and sell products. By analyzing its customer base, eBay found an opportunity to improve growth by targeting the nearly 23 million small businesses in the United States, many of which already use the auction site to buy and sell construction, restaurant, and other business equipment. To appeal to this important market, eBay sought ways to improve customers' online shopping experience.[8]

market opportunity A combination of circumstances and timing that permits an organization to take action to reach a particular target market

strategic windows Temporary periods of optimal fit between the key requirements of a market and the particular capabilities of a firm competing in that market

competitive advantage The result of a company's matching a core competency to opportunities it has discovered in the marketplace

SWOT analysis Assessment of an organization's strengths, weaknesses, opportunities, and threats

◆ SWOT Analysis

One tool marketers use to assess an organization's strengths, weaknesses, opportunities, and threats is the **SWOT analysis**. Strengths and weaknesses are internal factors that can influence an organization's ability to satisfy its target markets. *Strengths* refer to competitive advantages or core competencies that give the firm an advantage in meeting the needs of its target markets. John Deere, for example, promotes its service, experience, and reputation in the farm equipment business to emphasize the craftsmanship used in its lawn tractors and mowers for city dwellers. *Weaknesses* refer to any limitations a company faces in developing or implementing a marketing strategy. For instance, PepsiCo, with fewer resources than Coca-Cola Company, has found it difficult to expand in the fountain market, which includes restaurants, theaters, and sports arenas, where Coca-Cola holds two-thirds of the market.[9] Both strengths and weaknesses should be examined from a customer perspective because they are meaningful only when they help or hinder the firm in meeting customer needs. Only those strengths that relate to satisfying customers should be considered true competitive advantages. Likewise, weaknesses that directly affect customer satisfaction should be considered competitive disadvantages.

Snapshot

Buying downloads instead of CDs

Spending on music downloads by Americans is expected to increase to $600 million by 2007.

Projected spending in millions:

2003 ♪ $10
2004 ♪ $30
2005 ♪ $125
2006 $300
2007 $600

Source: Data from PricewaterhouseCoopers.

Opportunities and threats exist independently of the firm and therefore represent issues to be considered by all organizations, even those that do not compete with the firm. *Opportunities* refer to favorable conditions in the environment that could produce rewards for the organization if acted on properly. That is, opportunities are situations that exist but must be exploited for the firm to benefit from them. *Threats,* on the other hand, refer to conditions or barriers that may prevent the firm from reaching its objectives. For example, consumers today are buying fewer music CDs, in part because many believe CD prices are too high. CD sales declined by 31 percent over a three-year period as consumers downloaded more music from online sharing networks such as Kazaa or shifted their entertainment dollars to video games and DVDs.[10] An organization must act on threats to prevent them from limiting its capabilities. For example, to counter the threat of declining music sales,

ETHICS AND SOCIAL RESPONSIBILITY

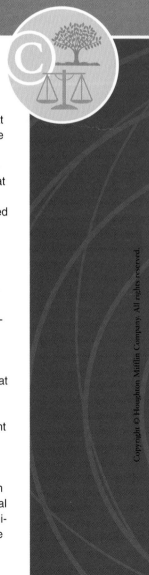

Recycling Disposable Cameras

Disposable cameras are increasingly popular because of their size and convenience. They account for 40 percent of worldwide film sales, which equates to about $2 billion annually. Fujifilm, the world's number two film maker, holds the key patent for disposable cameras, but Eastman Kodak obtained licensing rights from Fuji to produce and manufacture its own single-use cameras. Despite their convenience, disposable cameras add to the ever-growing amount of waste.

As landfills continue to bulge with waste and increasing demand for scarce natural resources threatens to harm wildlife habitats, companies have responded by looking for ways to protect and preserve the natural environment in a socially responsible manner. To accomplish this, Fuji initiated a recycling program for the QuickSnap camera in 1990 as part of the firm's commitment to worldwide environmental concerns. One challenge of Fuji's initiative was to get people to stop thinking "disposable" and start thinking "recyclable." Kodak also launched a recycling program as part of its design-for-the-environment initiative. Both companies are proud to be manufacturers of one of the most heavily recycled and most recyclable products in the world. Globally, the percentage of cameras returned is about 60 percent and growing. In the United States, rates of recycling of single-use cameras (74 percent) surpass those of corrugated containers (73 percent), aluminum cans

(63 percent), steel cans (58 percent), and bottles (33 percent). Since the programs began, hundreds of millions of cameras have been recycled, diverting 70 million pounds of waste from landfills. Another benefit of reusing instead of disposing is that the cameras can be recycled into new cameras more than three times on average.

However, Fuji's and Kodak's efforts were threatened by Jazz Photo Corporation and other firms that sought to profit from the phenomenal growth of disposable cameras. They had the idea to take the used Fuji and Kodak single-use camera cases discarded by film processors, put new film in them, color out the label, and market the "reloaded" cameras to retailers such as Wal-Mart Stores. The reloaded cameras sold for a dollar or two less than the name brand, and sales skyrocketed. By 1999, Jazz and other reloaders had captured 10 percent of the market, and Fuji decided to file suit against them for patent infringement and use of stolen technology. Kodak also warned retailers to exercise caution in selling the reloaded cameras because of the risk that buyers would be dissatisfied with their quality. A study of 500 reloaded cameras conducted for Fuji's lawsuit found that nearly 50 percent had a significant observable defect.

A jury ultimately ruled on behalf of Fuji and awarded the company $22.9 million in damages related to the reloading and relabeling of 41 million cameras between 1995 and 2001. The International Trade Commission eventually barred Jazz and similar firms from refurbishing single-use cameras. The ruling may help Fuji and Kodak eliminate at least one competitor from the growing market.

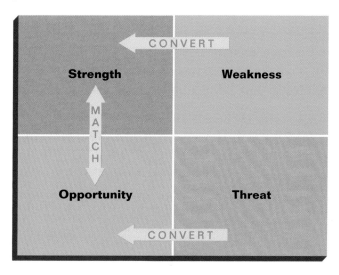

Figure 2.2 The Four-Cell SWOT Matrix
Source: Reprinted from Nigel F. Piercy, *Market-Led Strategic Change.*
Copyright © 1992 Butterworth-Heinemann Ltd., p. 371. Reprinted with
permission.

Universal Music Group slashed the wholesale price of CDs by artists such as Jay-Z and Shania Twain by as much as 31 percent.[11] Opportunities and threats can stem from many sources within the environment. When a competitor's introduction of a new product threatens a firm, a defensive strategy may be required. If the firm can develop and launch a new product that meets or exceeds the competition's offering, it can transform the threat into an opportunity.[12] Ethics and Social Responsibility (on p. 32) examines a product that represented an opportunity for one firm and a threat for another.

Figure 2.2 depicts a four-cell SWOT matrix that can help managers in the planning process. When an organization matches internal strengths to external opportunities, it creates competitive advantages in meeting the needs of its customers. In addition, an organization should act to convert internal weaknesses into strengths and external threats into opportunities. Ford Motor Company, for instance, converted the threats posed by rising gasoline prices and the growing acceptance of hybrid gas-electric cars from Japanese automakers into opportunities when it introduced a hybrid version of its Escape sport-utility vehicle, making the 40-mile-per-gallon Escape the first hybrid SUV available.[13] A firm that lacks adequate marketing skills can hire outside consultants to help convert a weakness into a strength.

Establishing an Organizational Mission and Goals

mission statement A long-term view, or vision, of what the organization wants to become

Once an organization has assessed its resources and opportunities, it can begin to establish goals and strategies to take advantage of those opportunities. The goals of any organization should derive from its **mission statement**, a long-term view, or vision, of what the organization wants to become. Herbal tea marketer Celestial Seasonings, for example, says that its mission is "To create and sell healthful, naturally oriented products that nurture people's bodies and uplift their souls."[14]

When an organization decides on its mission, it really answers two questions: Who are our customers? and What is our core competency? Although these questions seem very simple, they are two of the most important questions any firm must answer. Defining customers' needs and wants gives direction to what the company must do to satisfy them.

Our mission:
Deliver superior quality products and services for our customers and communities through leadership, innovation and partnerships.

Every day in Wendy's restaurants worldwide, we are focused on serving the very best. It's the foundation of our business – serve quality food, provide excellent service, superior value and a sparkling clean atmosphere.

Wendy's has a strong commitment to giving back. From corporate-sponsored initiatives, to the neighborhoods where the hard work and community service efforts of Wendy's employees make their corner of the world a little brighter, it's our responsibility to serve... and give back.

Wendy's International, Inc.

Tim Hortons.   WENDY'S   BAJA FRESH MEXICAN·GRILL

Diversity & Ethics Department
P.O. Box 256
Dublin, OH 43017

marketing objective A statement of what is to be accomplished through marketing activities

An organization's goals and objectives, derived from its mission statement, guide the remainder of its planning efforts. Goals focus on the end results the organization seeks. Starbucks' mission statement, for example, incorporates the company's goals of striving for a high-quality product, a sound financial position, and community responsibility.

A **marketing objective** states what is to be accomplished through marketing activities. A marketing objective of Ritz-Carlton Hotels, for example, is to have more than 90 percent of its customers indicate they had a memorable experience at the hotel. Marketing objectives should be based on a careful study of the SWOT analysis and should relate to matching strengths to opportunities and/or converting weaknesses or threats. These objectives can be stated in terms of product introduction, product improvement or innovation, sales volume, profitability, market share, pricing, distribution, advertising, or employee training activities.

Marketing objectives should possess certain characteristics. First, a marketing objective should be expressed in clear, simple terms so that all marketing personnel understand exactly what they are trying to achieve. Second, an objective should be written so that it can be measured accurately. This allows the organization to determine if and when the objective has been achieved. If an objective is to increase market share by 10 percent, the firm should be able to measure market share changes accurately. Third, a marketing objective should specify a time frame for its accomplishment. A firm that sets an objective of introducing a new product should state the time period in which to do this. Finally, a marketing objective should be consistent with both business-unit and corporate strategy. This ensures that the firm's mission is carried out at all levels of the organization.

Developing Corporate, Business-Unit, and Marketing Strategies

In any organization, strategic planning begins at the corporate level and proceeds downward to the business-unit and marketing levels. Corporate strategy is the broadest of these three levels and should be developed with the organization's overall mission in mind. Business-unit strategy should be consistent with the corporate strategy, and marketing strategy should be consistent with both the business-unit and corporate strategies. Figure 2.3 shows the relationships among these planning levels.

Figure 2.3 Levels of Strategic Planning

◆ Corporate Strategy

corporate strategy A strategy that determines the means for utilizing resources in the various functional areas to reach the organization's goals

Corporate strategy determines the means for utilizing resources in the functional areas of marketing, production, finance, research and development, and human resources to reach the organization's goals. A corporate strategy determines not only the scope of the business but also its resource deployment, competitive advantages, and overall coordination of functional areas. In particular, top management's marketing expertise and deployment of resources for addressing markets contribute to sales growth and profitability.[15] Corporate strategy addresses the two questions posed in the organization's mission statement: Who are our customers? and What is our core

Corporate Strategy
General Motors used a corporate strategy of revitalizing its brand by offering twenty new models in twenty months, including the Chevy Colorado.

competency? The term *corporate* in this context does not apply solely to corporations; corporate strategy is used by all organizations, from the smallest sole proprietorship to the largest multinational corporation.

Corporate strategy planners are concerned with broad issues such as corporate culture, competition, differentiation, diversification, interrelationships among business units, and environmental and social issues. They attempt to match the resources of the organization with the opportunities and threats in the environment. Nike, for example, is attempting to capitalize on its strong brand appeal by expanding beyond athletic shoes and sports clothing into women's casual apparel. The company has also opened several NIKEgoddess boutique stores to sell Nike athletic and casual products.[16] Corporate strategy planners are also concerned with defining the scope and role of the firm's business units so that the units are coordinated to reach the ends desired.

◆ Business-Unit Strategy

After analyzing corporate operations and performance, the next step in strategic planning is to determine future business directions and develop strategies for individual business units. A **strategic business unit (SBU)** is a division, product line, or other profit center within the parent company. Borden's strategic business units, for example, consist of dairy products, snacks, pasta, niche grocery products like ReaLemon juice and Cremora coffee creamer, and other units such as glue and paints. Each of these units sells a distinct set of products to an identifiable group of customers, and each competes with a well-defined set of competitors. The revenues, costs, investments, and strategic plans of each SBU can be separated from those of the parent company and evaluated. SBUs operate in a variety of markets, all with differing growth rates, opportunities, degrees of competition, and profit-making potential.

Strategic planners should recognize the strategic performance capabilities of each SBU and carefully allocate scarce resources among those divisions. This requires market-focused flexibility in considering changes in the environment.[17] Several tools allow a firm's portfolio of strategic business units, or even individual products, to be classified and visually displayed according to the attractiveness of various markets and the business's relative market share within those markets. A **market** is a group of individuals and/or organizations that have needs for products in a product class and have the ability, willingness, and authority to purchase those products. The percentage of a market that actually buys a specific product from a particular company is referred to as that product's (or business unit's) **market share.** Hershey Foods, for example, controls 43 percent of the market for chocolate candy in the United States, while its rivals Mars Inc. and Nestlé command 27 percent and 9 percent, respectively.[18]

One of the most helpful tools is the **market growth/market share matrix**, the Boston Consulting Group (BCG) approach, which is based on the philosophy that a product's market growth rate and its market share are important considerations in determining its marketing strategy. All the firm's SBUs and products should be integrated into a single, overall matrix and evaluated to determine appropriate strategies for individual products and overall portfolio strategies. Managers can use this model to determine and classify each product's expected future cash contributions and future cash requirements. The BCG analytical approach is more of a diagnostic tool than a guide for making strategy prescriptions.

Figure 2.4, which is based on work by the BCG, enables the strategic planner to classify a firm's products into four basic types: stars, cash cows, dogs, and question marks.[19] *Stars* are products with a dominant share of the market and good prospects for growth. However, they use more cash than they generate to finance growth, add capacity, and increase market share. An example of a star might be Apple's iPod MP3 player. *Cash cows* have a dominant share of the market but low prospects for growth; typically they generate more cash than is required to maintain market share. Bounty, the best-selling paper towels in the United States, represents a cash cow for Procter & Gamble. *Dogs* have a subordinate share of the market and

strategic business unit (SBU)
A division, product line, or other profit center within the parent company

market A group of individuals and/or organizations that have needs for products in a product class and have the ability, willingness, and authority to purchase those products

market share The percentage of a market that actually buys a specific product from a particular company

market growth/market share matrix A strategic planning tool based on the philosophy that a product's market growth rate and market share are important considerations in its determining marketing strategy

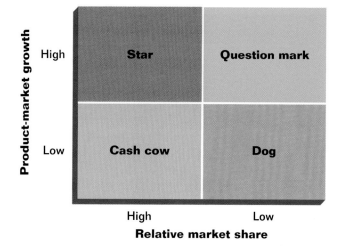

Figure 2.4 Growth Share Matrix Developed by the Boston Consulting Group
Source: Perspectives, No. 66, "The Product Portfolio." Reprinted by permission from The Boston Consulting Group, Inc., Boston, MA. Copyright © 1970.

low prospects for growth; these products are often found in established markets. The Oldsmobile brand may be considered a dog at General Motors; its declining profits and market share contributed to GM's decision to eliminate the brand. *Question marks,* sometimes called "problem children," have a small share of a growing market and generally require a large amount of cash to build market share. Mercedes mountain bikes, for example, are a question mark relative to Mercedes' automobile products.

The long-term health of an organization depends on having some products that generate cash (and provide acceptable profits) and others that use cash to support growth. Among the indicators of overall health are the size and vulnerability of the cash cows; the prospects for the stars, if any; and the number of question marks and dogs. Particular attention should be paid to those products with large cash appetites. Unless the company has an abundant cash flow, it cannot afford to sponsor many such products at one time. If resources, including debt capacity, are spread too thin, the company will end up with too many marginal products and will be unable to finance promising new-product entries or acquisitions in the future.

◆ Marketing Strategy

The next phase in strategic planning is the development of sound strategies for each functional area of the organization. Within the marketing area, a strategy is typically designed around two components: (1) the selection of a target market and (2) the creation of a marketing mix that will satisfy the needs of the chosen target market. A marketing strategy articulates the best use of the firm's resources and tactics to achieve its marketing objectives. It should also match customers' desire for value with the organization's distinctive capabilities. Internal capabilities should be used to maximize external opportunities. The planning process should be guided by a marketing-oriented organizational culture and processes.[20] When properly implemented, a sound marketing strategy also enables a company to achieve its business-unit and corporate objectives. Although corporate, business-unit, and marketing strategies all overlap to some extent, the marketing strategy is the most detailed and specific of the three.

NET SIGHTS

Corporate executives and marketing managers must stay informed to develop successful corporate, business-unit, and marketing strategies. In addition to regularly reading local, national, and international industry-related newspapers and journals, many busy executives turn to CEO Express. This website, **www. ceoexpress.com,** *provides online access to daily newspapers from all over the nation and beyond. It has links to alternative weekly newspapers, local and regional business journals, special-interest publications, and syndicated news services. Visitors to the site can also track stocks and sports teams, access government agencies, and search the Web for the latest industry news.*

THE ONLY THING THAT WILL GROW FASTER
IS THE COST OF A COLLEGE EDUCATION.

Kids grow up fast, and soon it's time for college. State Farm® can help you plan for the cost of your child's education. With investment choices such as education savings plans and mutual funds, your State Farm agent is ready to help. So call today. WE LIVE WHERE YOU LIVE.™

LIKE A GOOD NEIGHBOR STATE FARM IS THERE.™

Providing Insurance and Financial Services

Securities offered by registered representatives of State Farm VP Management Corp., Bloomington, IL. State Farm VP Management Corp. is a separate entity from those State Farm entities that provide insurance products. Consult your tax or legal advisor for specific advice.

ML2003-39 05/03

Target Market Selection
State Farm targets parents for its financial services.

Target Market Selection. Selecting an appropriate target market may be the most important decision a company has to make in the planning process because the target market must be chosen before the organization can adapt its marketing mix to meet this market's needs and preferences. Defining the target market and developing an appropriate marketing mix are the keys to strategic success. Consider that there are 72 million consumers in "Generation Y"—those born between 1977 and 1994—in the United States, and they command about $187 billion a year in spending power. These "Ys" are skeptical and resourceful, and more comfortable with cell phones, instant messaging, and Internet shopping than any other market. This represents a significant opportunity for marketers willing to adapt their marketing mixes to satisfy the needs of this important target market.[21] If a company selects the wrong target market, all other marketing decisions will be a waste of time. Ford Motor, for example, experienced poor sales of its reintroduced Thunderbird, in part because its $35,000 to $40,000 price tag was too steep for the retro-styled convertible's target market of younger baby boomers and older Generation Xers. However, the Thunderbird could not compete with luxury high-performance vehicles like the BMW Z4 and the Audi TT, which offer greater horsepower and more features.[22]

Accurate target market selection is crucial to productive marketing efforts. Products and even companies sometimes fail because marketers do not identify appropriate customer groups at whom to aim their efforts. Organizations that try to be all things to all people rarely satisfy the needs of any customer group very well. An organization's management therefore should designate which customer groups the firm is trying to serve and gather adequate information about those customers. Identification and analysis of a target market provide a foundation on which the firm can develop a marketing mix.

When exploring possible target markets, marketing managers try to evaluate how entering them would affect the company's sales, costs, and profits. Marketing information should be organized to facilitate a focus on the chosen target customers. Accounting and information systems, for example, can be used to track revenues and costs by customer (or group of customers). In addition, managers and employees need to be rewarded for focusing on profitable customers. Teamwork skills can be developed with organizational structures that promote a customer orientation that allows quick responses to changes in the marketing environment.[23]

Marketers should also assess whether the company has the resources to develop the right mix of product, price, promotion, and distribution to meet the needs of a particular target market. In addition, they should determine if satisfying those needs is consistent with the firm's overall objectives and mission. When Amazon.com, the number one Internet bookseller, began selling electronics on its website, it made the decision that efforts to target this market would increase profits and be consistent with its objective to be the largest online retailer. The size and number of competitors already marketing products in potential target markets are concerns as well.

Creating the Marketing Mix. The selection of a target market serves as the basis for creating a marketing mix to satisfy the needs of that market. The decisions made in creating a marketing mix are only as good as the organization's understanding of its target market. This understanding typically comes from careful, in-depth research into the characteristics of the target market. Thus, while demographic information is important, the organization should also analyze customer needs, preferences, and behavior with respect to product design, pricing, distribution, and promotion. For example, Toyota's marketing research about Generation Y drivers found that they practically live in their cars, and many even keep a change of clothes handy in their vehicles. As a result of this research, Toyota designed its Scion as a "home on wheels," with a 15-volt outlet for plugging in a computer, reclining front seats for napping, and a powerful audio system for listening to MP3 music files, all for a $12,500 price tag.[24]

Marketing mix decisions should have two additional characteristics: consistency and flexibility. All marketing mix decisions should be consistent with the business-unit and corporate strategies. Such consistency allows the organization to achieve its objectives on all three levels of planning. Flexibility, on the other hand, permits the organization to alter the marketing mix in response to changes in market conditions, competition, and customer needs. Marketing strategy flexibility has a positive influence on organizational performance. Marketing orientation and strategic flexibility complement each other to help the organization manage varying environmental conditions.[25]

The concept of the four marketing mix variables has stood the test of time, providing marketers with a rich set of questions for the four most important decisions in strategic marketing. Consider the efforts of Harley-Davidson to improve its competitive position. The company worked to improve its product by eliminating oil leaks and other problems, and set prices that customers consider fair. The firm used promotional tools to build a community of Harley riders renowned for their camaraderie. Harley-Davidson also fostered strong relationships with the dealers that distribute the company's motorcycles and related products and that reinforce the firm's promotional messages. Even the Internet has not diminished the importance of finding the right marketing mix, although it has affected specific marketing mix elements. Amazon.com, for example, has exploited information technology to facilitate sales promotion by offering product feedback from other customers to help shoppers make purchase decisions.[26]

Competitive Advantage
Hewlett-Packard has manufactured high quality printers for over twenty years.

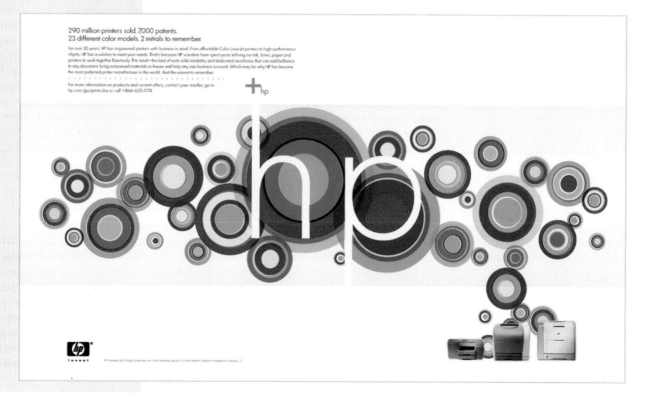

At the marketing mix level, a firm can detail how it will achieve a competitive advantage. To gain an advantage, the firm must do something better than its competition. In other words, its products must be of higher quality, its prices must be consistent with the level of quality (value), its distribution methods must be efficient and cost as little as possible, and its promotion must be more effective than the competition's. It is also important that the firm attempt to make these advantages sustainable. A **sustainable competitive advantage** is one that the competition cannot copy. Wal-Mart, for example, maintains a sustainable competitive advantage over Kmart because of its highly efficient and low-cost distribution system. This advantage allows Wal-Mart to offer lower prices.

sustainable competitive advantage An advantage that the competition cannot copy

Creating the Marketing Plan

marketing planning The process of assessing marketing opportunities and resources, determining marketing objectives, defining marketing strategies, and establishing guidelines for implementation and control of the marketing program

A major concern in the strategic planning process is **marketing planning**, the systematic process of assessing marketing opportunities and resources, determining marketing objectives, defining marketing strategies, and establishing guidelines for implementation and control of the marketing program. The outcome of marketing planning is the development of a marketing plan. As noted earlier, a marketing plan is a written document that outlines and explains all the activities necessary to implement marketing strategies. It describes the firm's current position or situation, establishes marketing objectives for the product or product group, and specifies how the organization will attempt to achieve those objectives.

Developing a clear, well-written marketing plan, though time consuming, is important. The plan is the basis for internal communication among employees. It covers the assignment of responsibilities and tasks, as well as schedules for implementation. It presents objectives and specifies how resources are to be allocated to achieve those objectives. Finally, it helps marketing managers monitor and evaluate the performance of a marketing strategy.

Marketing planning and implementation are inextricably linked in successful companies. The marketing plan provides a framework to stimulate thinking and provide strategic direction, while implementation occurs as an adaptive response to day-to-day issues, opportunities, and unanticipated situations—for example, increasing interest rates or an economic slowdown—that cannot be incorporated into marketing plans. Implementation-related adaptations directly affect an organization's marketing orientation, rate of growth, and strategic effectiveness.[27]

Organizations use many different formats when devising marketing plans. Plans may be written for strategic business units, product lines, individual products or brands, or specific markets. Most plans share some common ground, however, by including many of the same components. Table 2.1 describes the major parts of a typical marketing plan.

Implementing Marketing Strategies

marketing implementation The process of putting marketing strategies into action

intended strategy The strategy the company decided on during the planning phase and wants to use

realized strategy The strategy that actually takes place

Marketing implementation is the process of putting marketing strategies into action. Although implementation is often neglected in favor of strategic planning, the implementation process itself can determine whether a marketing strategy succeeds. It is also important to recognize that marketing strategies almost always turn out differently than expected. In essence, all organizations have two types of strategy: intended strategy and realized strategy.[28] The **intended strategy** is the strategy the organization decided on during the planning phase and wants to use, whereas the **realized strategy** is the strategy that actually takes place. The difference between the two is often the result of how the intended strategy is implemented. For example,

Table 2.1	Components of the Marketing Plan		
Plan Component	**Component Summary**	**Highlights**	
Executive Summary	One- to two-page synopsis of the entire marketing plan		
Environmental Analysis	Information about the company's current situation with respect to the marketing environment	1. Assessment of marketing environment factors 2. Assessment of target market(s) 3. Assessment of current marketing objectives and performance	
SWOT Analysis	Assessment of the organization's strengths, weaknesses, opportunities, and threats	1. Strengths 2. Weaknesses 3. Opportunities 4. Threats	
Marketing Objectives	Specification of the firm's marketing objectives	Qualitative measures of what is to be accomplished	
Marketing Strategies	Outline of how the firm will achieve its objectives	1. Target market(s) 2. Marketing mix	
Marketing Implementation	Outline of how the firm will implement its marketing strategies	1. Marketing organization 2. Activities and responsibilities 3. Implementation timetable	
Evaluation and Control	Explanation of how the firm will measure and evaluate the results of the implemented plan	1. Performance standards 2. Financial controls 3. Monitoring procedures (audits)	

Chrysler's PT Cruiser was originally marketed to young drivers, but the retro-styled vehicle ultimately proved more popular with their nostalgic baby boomer parents. Just 4 percent of the PT Cruiser's buyers were from the car's intended target market of drivers under 25.[29] The realized strategy, though not necessarily any better or worse than the intended strategy, often does not live up to planners' expectations.

◆ Approaches to Marketing Implementation

Just as organizations can achieve their goals by using different marketing strategies, they can implement their marketing strategies by using different approaches. In this section, we discuss two general approaches to marketing implementation: internal marketing and total quality management. Both approaches represent mindsets that marketing managers may adopt when organizing and planning marketing activities. These approaches are not mutually exclusive; indeed, many companies adopt both when designing marketing activities.

external customers Individuals who patronize a business

internal customers A company's employees

Internal Marketing. **External customers** are the individuals who patronize a business—the familiar definition of customers—whereas **internal customers** are the company's employees. For implementation to succeed, the needs of both groups of customers must be met. If internal customers are not satisfied, it is likely external customers will not be satisfied either. Thus, in addition to targeting marketing activities at

internal marketing A management philosophy that coordinates internal exchanges between the organization and its employees to achieve successful external exchanges between the organization and its customers

external customers, a firm uses internal marketing to attract, motivate, and retain qualified internal customers by designing internal products (jobs) that satisfy their wants and needs. **Internal marketing** is a management philosophy that coordinates internal exchanges between the organization and its employees to achieve successful external exchanges between the organization and its customers.[30]

Generally speaking, internal marketing refers to the managerial actions necessary to make all members of the marketing organization understand and accept their respective roles in implementing the marketing strategy. This means everyone, from the president of the company down to the hourly workers on the shop floor, must understand the role they play in carrying out their jobs and implementing the marketing strategy. In short, anyone invested in the firm, both marketers and those who perform other functions, must recognize the tenet of customer orientation and service that underlies the marketing concept.

Like external marketing activities, internal marketing may involve market segmentation, product development, research, distribution, and even public relations and sales promotion.[31] For example, an organization may sponsor sales contests to inspire sales personnel to boost their selling efforts. This helps employees (and ultimately the company) to understand customers' needs and problems, teaches them valuable new skills, and heightens their enthusiasm for their regular jobs. In addition, many companies use planning sessions, websites, workshops, letters, formal reports, and personal conversations to ensure that employees comprehend the corporate mission, the organization's goals, and the marketing strategy. The ultimate results are more satisfied employees and improved customer relations.

total quality management (TQM) A philosophy that uniform commitment to quality in all areas of the organization will promote a culture that meets customers' perceptions of quality

Total Quality Management.   Quality has become a major concern in many organizations, particularly in light of intense foreign competition, more demanding customers, and poorer profit performance owing to reduced market share and higher costs. To regain a competitive edge, a number of firms have adopted a total quality management approach. **Total quality management (TQM)** is a philosophy that uniform commitment to quality in all areas of the organization will promote a culture that meets customers' perceptions of quality. It involves coordinating efforts to improve customer satisfaction, increase employee participation and empowerment, form and strengthen supplier partnerships, and facilitate an organizational culture of continuous quality improvement. TQM requires continuous quality improvement and employee empowerment.

Continuous improvement of an organization's goods and services is built around the notion that quality is free; in contrast, *not* having high-quality goods and services can be very expensive, especially in terms of dissatisfied customers.[32] A primary tool of the continuous improvement process is **benchmarking**, comparing the quality of the organization's goods, services, or processes with that of the best-performing companies in the industry.[33] Benchmarking lets the organization know where it stands competitively in its industry, thus giving it a goal to aim for over time.

benchmarking Comparing the quality of the firm's goods, services, or processes with that of its best-performing competitors

Ultimately TQM succeeds or fails because of the efforts of the organization's employees. Thus, employee recruitment, selection, and training are critical to the success of marketing implementation. **Empowerment** gives customer-contact employees the authority and responsibility to make marketing decisions without seeking the approval of their supervisors.[34] Although employees at any level in an organization can be empowered to make decisions, empowerment is used most often at the frontline, where employees interact daily with customers.

empowerment Giving customer-contact employees authority and responsibility to make marketing decisions without seeking approval of their supervisors

One characteristic of empowerment is that employees can perform their jobs the way they see fit, as long as their methods and outcomes are consistent with the organization's mission. However, empowering employees is successful only if the organization is guided by an overall corporate vision, shared goals, and a culture that supports the TQM effort.[35] For example, Ritz-Carlton hotels give each customer-contact employee permission to take care of customer needs as he or she observes issues. A great deal of time, effort, and patience is needed to develop and sustain a quality-oriented culture in an organization.

◆ Organizing Marketing Activities

The structure and relationships of a marketing unit, including lines of authority and responsibility that connect and coordinate individuals, strongly affect marketing activities. Firms that truly adopt the marketing concept develop a distinct organizational culture: a culture based on a shared set of beliefs that makes the customer's needs the pivotal point of the firm's decisions about strategy and operations.[36] Instead of developing products in a vacuum and then trying to persuade customers to purchase them, companies using the marketing concept begin with an orientation toward their customers' needs and desires. Recreational Equipment, Inc. (REI), for example, gives customers a chance to try out sporting goods in conditions that approximate how the products will actually be used. Customers can try out hiking boots on a simulated hiking path with a variety of trail surfaces and inclines or test climbing gear on an indoor climbing wall. In addition, REI offers clinics to customers, such as "Rock Climbing Basics," "Basic Backpacking," and "REI's Outdoor School."

If the marketing concept serves as a guiding philosophy, the marketing

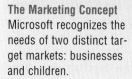

The Marketing Concept
Microsoft recognizes the needs of two distinct target markets: businesses and children.

unit will be closely coordinated with other functional areas such as production, finance, and human resources. Marketing must interact with other departments in a number of key areas. It needs to work with manufacturing in determining the volume and variety of the company's products. Those in charge of production rely on marketers for accurate sales forecasts. Research and development departments depend heavily on information gathered by marketers about product features and benefits consumers desire. Decisions made by the physical distribution department hinge on information about the urgency of delivery schedules and cost/service trade-offs. Information technology is often a crucial ingredient in effectively managing customer relationships, but successful customer relationship management (CRM) programs must include every department involved in customer relations.[37]

How effectively a firm's marketing management can plan and implement marketing strategies also depends on how the marketing unit is organized. Organizing marketing activities in ways that mesh with the implementation requirements of the firm's strategy enhances performance.[38] Effective organizational planning can give the firm a competitive advantage. The organizational structure of a marketing department establishes the authority relationships among marketing personnel and specifies who is responsible for making certain decisions and performing particular activities. This internal structure helps direct marketing activities.

centralized organization
A structure in which top-level managers delegate little authority to lower levels

decentralized organization A structure in which decision-making authority is delegated as far down the chain of command as possible

One crucial decision regarding structural authority is centralization versus decentralization. In a **centralized organization**, top-level managers delegate little authority to lower levels. In a **decentralized organization**, decision-making authority is delegated as far down the chain of command as possible. The decision to centralize or decentralize the organization directly affects marketing. Most traditional organizations are highly centralized. In these organizations, most, if not all, marketing decisions are made at the top levels. However, as organizations become more marketing oriented, centralized decision making proves somewhat ineffective. In these organizations, decentralized authority allows the company to respond to customer needs more quickly.

No single approach to organizing a marketing unit works equally well in all businesses. The best approach or approaches depends on the number and diversity of the firm's products, the characteristics and needs of the people in the target market, and many other factors. A marketing unit can be organized according to (1) functions, (2) products, (3) regions, or (4) types of customers. Firms often use some combination of these organizational approaches. Product features may dictate that the marketing unit be structured by products, whereas customer characteristics may require that it be organized by geographic region or by types of customers. By using more than one type of structure, a flexible marketing unit can develop and implement marketing plans to match customers' needs precisely.

Organizing by Functions. Some marketing departments are organized by general marketing functions, such as marketing research, product development, distribution, sales, advertising, and customer relations. The personnel who direct these functions report directly to the top-level marketing executive. This structure is fairly common because it works well for some businesses with centralized marketing operations, such as Ford and General Motors. In more decentralized firms, such as grocery store chains, functional organization can cause serious coordination problems. However, the functional approach may suit a large, centralized company whose products and customers are neither numerous nor diverse.

Organizing by Products. An organization that produces and markets diverse products may find the functional approach inadequate. The decisions and problems related to a single marketing function for one product may be quite different from those related to the same marketing function for another product. As a result, businesses that produce diverse products sometimes organize their marketing units according to product groups. Organizing by product groups gives a firm the flexibility to develop special marketing mixes for different products. Procter & Gamble, like many firms in the consumer packaged goods industry, is organized by product group. Although organizing by products allows a company to remain flexible, this approach can be rather expensive unless efficient categories of products are grouped together to reduce duplication and improve coordination of product management.

Organizing by Regions. A large company that markets products nationally (or internationally) may organize its marketing activities by geographic regions. Managers of marketing functions for each region report to their regional marketing manager; all the regional marketing managers report directly to the executive marketing manager. Frito-Lay, for example, is organized into four regional divisions, allowing the company to get closer to its customers and respond more quickly and efficiently to regional competitors. This form of organization is especially effective for a firm whose customers' characteristics and needs vary greatly from one region to another. Firms that try to penetrate the national market intensively may divide regions into subregions.

Organizing by Types of Customers. Sometimes a company's marketing unit is organized according to types of customers. This form of internal organization works well for a firm that has several groups of customers whose needs and problems differ significantly. For example, Bic may sell pens to large retail stores, wholesalers, and institutions. Retailers may want more rapid delivery of small shipments and more personal selling by the producer than do either wholesalers or institutional buyers. Because the marketing decisions and activities required for these two groups of customers differ considerably, the company may find it efficient to organize its marketing unit by types of customers.

◆ Controlling Marketing Activities

marketing control process
Establishing performance standards, evaluating actual performance by comparing it with established standards, and reducing the differences between desired and actual performance

To achieve both marketing and general organizational objectives, marketing managers must effectively control marketing efforts. The **marketing control process** consists of establishing performance standards, evaluating actual performance by comparing it with established standards, and reducing the differences between desired and actual performance.

   Although the control function is a fundamental management activity, it has received little attention in marketing. Organizations have both formal and informal control systems. The formal marketing control process, as mentioned earlier, involves performance standards, evaluation of actual performance, and corrective action to remedy shortfalls (see Figure 2.5). The informal control process involves self-control, social or group control, and cultural control through acceptance of the firm's value system. Which type of control system dominates depends on the

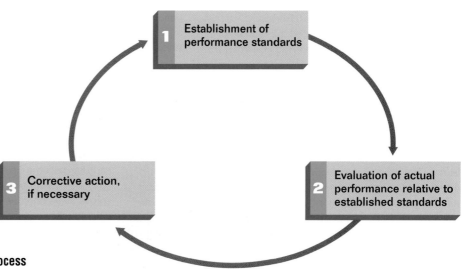

Figure 2.5 The Marketing Control Process

environmental context of the firm.[39] We now discuss these steps in the formal control process and consider the major problems they involve.

Establishing Performance Standards. Planning and controlling are closely linked because plans include statements about what is to be accomplished. For purposes of control, these statements function as performance standards. A **performance standard** is an expected level of performance against which actual performance can be compared. A performance standard might be a 20 percent reduction in customer complaints, a monthly sales quota of $150,000, or a 10 percent increase per month in new-customer accounts. As stated earlier, performance standards should be tied to organizational goals. For example, if General Motors had a goal of selling more than 250,000 Saabs in the United States in 2005, the introduction of new car models may help them make this objective possible.[40]

Evaluating Actual Performance. To compare actual performance with performance standards, marketing managers must know what employees within the company are doing and have information about the activities of external organizations that

> **performance standard** An expected level of performance against which actual performance can be compared

---

BUILDING CUSTOMER RELATIONSHIPS

Red Bull Energizes Sales with Stimulating Marketing Strategy

Many consumers find Red Bull energizing thanks to the trendy drink's caffeine, vitamins, carbohydrates, taurine, and amino acids. An 8.3-ounce can of Red Bull has 80 milligrams of caffeine—about the same as a cup of coffee. Red Bull International contends that the caffeine reacts with amino acids in the product to revitalize the drinker and enhance performance and endurance. The product has been warmly embraced by twenty-somethings looking for an after-work lift before hitting the clubs; some also like to use Red Bull as a mixer with their favorite liquor so they can dance all night. Word-of-mouth promotion and strong demand have helped push the Austrian export into 70 countries, including the United States. Red Bull International essentially pioneered the market for energy drinks when it developed Red Bull in 1987, and the high-energy drink now commands 65 percent of the $1.6 billion U.S. market.

Red Bull is available at almost every supermarket, convenience store, gas station, bar, and night club in the United States. The product is intensively distributed through aggressive recruiting of small distributors; in some markets, the company has set up warehouses and hired young people to handle and deliver the product. At $2 a can, the retail price yields a healthy margin for retailers and distributors of the product. The company relies on strong personal selling efforts by its young sales force, who visit trendy clubs and bars and pass out samples, counting on the clubs' hip customers to pass the word about Red Bull. Only when a market has matured does the company employ more traditional television advertisements, which feature an animated bull touting the theme that "Red Bull gives you wings." The company also sponsors alternative and extreme sporting events that 16-to-29-year-olds are likely to frequent. Red Bull's popularity has also benefited from some unusual publicity: rumors abound that the drink contains "liquid Viagra," or a secret ingredient from bull's testicles—rumors the company denies on its website.

Red Bull's dramatic success has spawned competition looking to cash in on the hot, new energy-drink market. In addition to Coca-Cola's KMX and Anheuser-Busch's 180, Red Bull is competing with offerings from smaller, regional firms such as Go Fast, Roaring Lion, and Rockstar, as well as more traditional sports drinks such as Gatorade. With global sales of $1 billion, Red Bull appears to have developed an effective marketing strategy for targeting 16-to-29-year-olds looking for a quick pick-me-up and willing to pay a premium price. Will Red Bull prove to be another fad, or will Red Bull International adapt its marketing strategy to maintain its marketing dominance against such marketing powerhouses as Coca-Cola?

provide the firm with marketing assistance. For example, Saturn, like many automakers, evaluates its product and service levels by how well it ranks on the J. D. Power & Associates Customer Service Index. In 2003, Saturn ranked number two among all automakers, behind Infiniti but ahead of Acura, Lexus, and Lincoln.[41] Records of actual performance are compared with performance standards to determine whether and how much of a discrepancy exists. For example, if General Motors had determined that only 225,000 Saabs were sold in 2005, a discrepancy would have existed because its goal for Saab was 250,000 vehicles.

Taking Corrective Action. Marketing managers have several options for reducing a discrepancy between established performance standards and actual performance. They can take steps to improve actual performance, reduce or totally change the performance standard, or do both. To improve actual performance, the marketing manager may have to use better methods of motivating marketing personnel or find more effective techniques for coordinating marketing efforts.

Problems in Controlling Marketing Activities. In their efforts to control marketing activities, marketing managers frequently run into several problems. Often the information required to control marketing activities is unavailable or is available only at a high cost. Although marketing controls should be flexible enough to allow for environmental changes, the frequency, intensity, and unpredictability of such changes may hamper control. In addition, the time lag between marketing activities and their results limits a marketing manager's ability to measure the effectiveness of specific marketing activities. This is especially true for all advertising activities. Companies that market trendy products, such as the one profiled in the Building Customer Relationships box (on p. 46), need to constantly evaluate and adjust their marketing strategy.

Because marketing and other business activities overlap, marketing managers cannot determine the precise costs of marketing activities. Without an accurate measure of marketing costs, it is difficult to know if the outcome of marketing activities is worth the expense. Finally, marketing control may be difficult because it is very hard to develop exact performance standards for marketing personnel.

SUMMARY

Through the process of strategic planning, a firm identifies or establishes an organizational mission and goals, corporate strategy, marketing goals and objectives, marketing strategy, and a marketing plan. To achieve its marketing objectives, an organization must develop a marketing strategy, which includes identifying a target market and developing a plan of action for developing, distributing, promoting, and pricing products that meet the needs of customers in that target market. The strategic planning process ultimately yields the framework for a marketing plan, a written document that specifies the activities to be performed for implementing and controlling an organization's marketing activities.

The marketing environment, including economic, competitive, political, legal and regulatory, sociocultural, and technological forces, can affect the resources a firm can acquire and create favorable opportunities. Resources may include core competencies, which are things that a firm does extremely well, sometimes so well that it gives the company an advantage over its competition. When the right combination of circumstances and timing permit an organization to take action toward reaching a particular target market, a market opportunity exists. Strategic windows are temporary periods of optimal fit between the key requirements of a market and the particular capabilities of a firm competing in that market. When a company matches a core competency to opportunities it has discovered in the marketplace, it is said to have a competitive advantage.

An organization's goals should be derived from its mission statement, a long-term view, or vision, of what the organization wants to become. A well-formulated mission statement helps give an organization a clear purpose and direction, distinguish it from competitors, provide direction for strategic planning, and foster a focus on customers. An organization's goals and objectives, which focus on the end results sought, guide the remainder of its planning efforts.

Corporate strategy determines the means for utilizing resources in the areas of production, finance, research and development, human resources, and marketing to reach the organization's goals. Business-unit strategy focuses on strategic business units (SBUs)—divisions, product lines, or other profit centers within the parent company used to define areas for consideration in a specific strategic market plan. The Boston Consulting Group's market growth/market share matrix integrates a firm's products or SBUs into a single, overall matrix for evaluation to determine appropriate strategies for individual products and business units. Marketing strategies, the most detailed and specific of the three levels of strategy, are composed of two elements: the selection of a target market and the creation of a marketing mix that will satisfy the needs of the chosen target market. The selection of a target market serves as the basis for the creation of the marketing mix to satisfy the needs of that market. Marketing mix decisions should also be consistent with business-unit and corporate strategies and be flexible enough to respond to changes in market conditions, competition, and customer needs. Different elements of the marketing mix can be changed to accommodate different marketing strategies.

The outcome of marketing planning is the development of a marketing plan, which outlines all the activities necessary to implement marketing strategies. The plan fosters communication among employees, assigns responsibilities and schedules, specifies how resources are to be allocated to achieve objectives, and helps marketing managers monitor and evaluate the performance of a marketing strategy.

Marketing implementation is the process of executing marketing strategies. Marketing strategies do not always turn out as expected. Realized marketing strategies often differ from the intended strategies because of issues related to implementation. Proper implementation requires efficient organizational structures and effective control and evaluation.

One major approach to marketing implementation is internal marketing, a management philosophy that coordinates internal exchanges between the organization and its employees to achieve successful external exchanges between the organization and its customers. For strategy implementation to be successful, the needs of both internal and external customers must be met. Another approach is total quality management (TQM), which relies heavily on the talents of employees to continually improve the quality of the organization's goods and services.

 Please visit the student website at **www.prideferrell.com** for ACE Self-Test questions that will help you prepare for exams.

IMPORTANT TERMS

Strategic planning
Marketing strategy
Marketing plan
Core competencies
Market opportunity
Strategic window
Competitive advantage
SWOT analysis
Mission statement
Marketing objective
Corporate strategy
Strategic business unit
  (SBU)
Market
Market share
Market growth/market
  share matrix
Sustainable competitive
  advantage
Marketing planning
Marketing implementation
Intended strategy
Realized strategy

External customers
Internal customers
Internal marketing
Total quality management
  (TQM)
Benchmarking
Empowerment
Centralized organization
Decentralized organization
Marketing control process
Performance standard

DISCUSSION & REVIEW QUESTIONS

1. Identify the major components of strategic planning, and explain how they are interrelated.
2. What are the two major parts of a marketing strategy?
3. What are some issues to consider in analyzing a firm's resources and opportunities? How do these issues affect marketing objectives and marketing strategy?
4. How important is the SWOT analysis to the marketing planning process?
5. How should organizations set marketing objectives?
6. Explain how an organization can create a competitive advantage at the corporate, business-unit, and marketing strategy levels.
7. Refer to question 6. How can an organization make its competitive advantages sustainable over time? How difficult is it to create sustainable competitive advantages?
8. What benefits do marketing managers gain from planning? Is planning necessary for long-run survival? Why or why not?
9. Why does an organization's intended strategy often differ from its realized strategy?

10. Why might an organization use multiple bases for organizing its marketing unit?
11. What are the major steps of the marketing control process?

APPLICATION QUESTIONS

1. Contact three organizations that appear to be successful. Ask one of the company's managers or executives if he or she would share with you the company's mission statement or organizational goals. Obtain as much information as possible about the statement and organizational goals. Discuss how the statement matches the criteria outlined in the text.
2. Assume you own a new, family-style restaurant that will open for business in the coming year. Formulate a long-term goal for the company, and then develop short-term goals to help you achieve the long-term goal.
3. Amazon.com identified an opportunity to capitalize on a desire of many consumers to shop at home. This strategic window gave Amazon.com a very competitive position in a new market. Consider the opportunities that may be present in your city, region, or the United States as a whole. Identify a strategic window, and discuss how a company could take advantage of this opportunity. What kind of core competencies are necessary?
4. Marketing units may be organized according to functions, products, regions, or types of customers. Describe how you would organize the marketing units for the following:
   a. A toothpaste with whitener; a toothpaste with extra-strong nicotine cleaners; a toothpaste with bubble-gum flavor
   b. A national line offering all types of winter and summer sports clothing for men and women
   c. A life insurance company that provides life, health, and disability insurance

Internet Exercise & Resources

Visit **www.prideferrell.com** for resources to help you master the material in this chapter, plus materials that will help you expand your marketing knowledge, including Internet exercise updates, ACE self-tests, hotlinks to companies featured in this chapter, and much more.

Sony

Internet analysts have praised Sony's website as one of the best organized and most informative on the Internet. See why by accessing **www.sony.com.**

1. Based on the information provided on the website, describe Sony's strategic business units.
2. Based on your existing knowledge of Sony as an innovative leader in the consumer electronics industry, describe the company's primary competitive advantage. How does Sony's website support this competitive advantage?
3. Assess the quality and effectiveness of Sony's website. Specifically, perform a preliminary SWOT analysis comparing Sony's website with other high-quality websites you have visited.

Video Case 2.1

The Global Expansion of Subway Sandwich Shops

The Subway story began in 1965 when Dr. Peter Buck loaned Fred DeLuca $1,000 to open a sandwich shop in Bridgeport, Connecticut, which DeLuca hoped would help fund his college education. Since that time, Subway Sandwich Shops has grown to more than 20,000 restaurants in 71 countries, ranking it first in number of outlets in the United States and making its founder a billionaire. Subway remains a 100 percent franchised organization, and all Subway restaurants are individually owned and operated. Opening a Subway franchise store requires a $12,500 franchise fee to acquire the Subway name and $75,000 to $200,000 to build a store, depending on location. The company has been named the number one franchise opportunity in every category by *Entrepreneur* magazine, won a Restaurants and Institutions (Choice and Chains) Gold Award in the sandwich category, and received a *Nation's Restaurant News* Menu Masters Award for the best menu/line extension.

More than 3,700 Subway stores have opened outside the United States. Initially Subway did not seek to expand internationally, but when an entrepreneur from Bahrain approached the company about opening a sandwich shop on the Persian Gulf island, Subway decided to accept the challenge of global expansion. Expanding a food venture into a foreign country involves many issues, such as finding quality supplies for use in making sandwiches. Subway insists on a "gold standard of quality" when adapting to international environments. To properly train new franchise owners in locations around the globe, Subway has had to adapt to different languages and cultures. Initially international franchisees were trained in English in the United States; now the company has training facilities in Puerto Rico, Australia, and China.

When Subway enters a new market, the first issues it faces are building brand awareness and learning about potential customers' eating preferences and customs. Rather than second-guessing cultural differences, Subway attempts to adapt quickly to a new restaurant's immediate service area. In Israel, for example, the company omits pork items from its menu to avoid violating religious dietary customs. In other countries where people are not used to eating sandwiches, Subway has had to educate consumers about this uniquely American product.

In addition to established markets, Subway is expanding into developing nations. In 2001, Subway opened its first restaurant in Croatia. Located in a 1929 building shared with the Capital Hotel Dubrovnik, the restaurant's entrance faces a busy pedestrian street with many shops and open terraces in one of the most beautiful areas of Zagreb. The franchisees chose to open a Subway because they wanted to offer Croatians something new and recognized an opportunity in the dynamic Croatian market to serve a need for affordable fast food with friendly service. The company plans to open additional shops in other major Croatian cities.

Subway also opened its first restaurant in Oman in 2001, where it joins other fast-food restaurants such as Fuddruckers, McDonald's, and Pizza Hut. Oman is one of the fastest-growing economies in the Middle East, with many international businesses in operation. Subway hopes to fill a void for those in the market for health-conscious food. In Oman, Subway offers its traditional menu and plans to include specialized items to meet local preferences.

France became the twenty-third European country to have a Subway sandwich shop in 2001. France's first Subway is situated near the Bastille in Paris. By day, the area's rich history attracts many tourists; at night, the area is renowned for its night life. The French are passionate about food, and they like submarine sandwiches. Although both Oman and France were slow to embrace the Subway concept, the brand's healthy attributes appear to have been a major factor in this expansion.

Subway had begun to position its menu as a more health-conscious alternative to fast food when it learned about the unique weight loss plan of one of its customers. Jared S. Fogle had been a regular Subway customer, but after reaching 425 pounds, he noticed the store's "7 under 6" promotion, which highlighted seven sandwiches with fewer than 6 grams of fat. Fogle began to eat a 6-inch turkey sandwich (no oil, mayo, condiments, or cheese) for lunch and a 12-inch veggie sandwich (no condiments or cheese) for dinner every day. His initial weight loss reinforced his commitment to eating more of the low-fat sandwiches. Jared Fogle ultimately lost 245 pounds on his "Subway diet." His story turned Fogle into a national celebrity, with appearances on *Oprah* and NBC's *Today* with Katie Couric, an article in *USA Today*, and numerous TV commercials for Subway. Subway's TV ads make it clear that Fogle's diet was his own creation and may not be appropriate for everyone. Fogle, who has maintained his weight loss, continues to do TV commercials and make special appearances for Subway.

Subway has translated the Jared Fogle commercials into other languages for some international markets. The message is that Subway sandwiches are not only tasty but also healthier than offerings from competing fast-food restaurants. For example, one quarter-pound hamburger at another leading fast-food restaurant contains more than 62 grams of fat, whereas Subway offers a number of items with fewer than 10 grams of fat. Promoting the healthy benefits of its products has helped Subway develop its concept into the largest submarine sandwich franchise in the world.[42]

QUESTIONS FOR DISCUSSION

1. What market opportunities and strategic windows has Subway been able to capitalize on?
2. Based on the facts presented in the case, conduct a brief SWOT analysis for Subway.
3. Describe Subway's apparent marketing mix and target market.

Case 2.2

Saturn: "A Different Kind of Company. A Different Kind of Car."

In 1990, after seven years of incubation, Saturn, a division of General Motors Corporation, debuted in the crowded market of compact cars. Since 1985, GM's share of the U.S. passenger car market had fallen 11 points to 33 percent. Moreover, a J. D. Power & Associates study revealed that 42 percent of all new-car shoppers wouldn't even consider a GM car. Saturn's mission, then, was to sell 80 percent of its cars to drivers who would not otherwise have bought a GM car. GM believed Saturn was the key to its long-term competitiveness and survival. Saturn managers spent years developing the new company from scratch. They viewed partnerships as a key element of Saturn's future relationships between management and labor and between company and supplier, with everyone sharing the risks and rewards. To truly separate Saturn from the traditional Detroit auto-building mentality, GM built Saturn in Spring Hill, Tennessee.

The story of Saturn is inseparable from its advertising history, because Saturn involved all marketing entities, from the advertising agency to the dealers, in all decisions from the very beginning. A straight-talk, people-oriented philosophy in consumer advertising was used, stressing Saturn, the company, rather than the car. "A different kind of company. A different kind of car." was the theme line. The first commercials told stories about the Spring Hill heartland and about Saturn employees. The ads had a down-home feeling and featured ordinary people talking about the cars and the Saturn concept. They told about how employees took a risk and left Detroit for something new and exciting: to start from the drawing board and "build cars again . . . but in a brand new way." The ads stressed that by recapturing the USA's can-do spirit, Saturn knows how to make cars. Later ads featured stories of Saturn customers, focusing on Saturn buyers' lifestyles and playing up product themes that baby boomers hold dear, such as safety, utility, and value. One commercial highlighted a recall order Saturn had issued to fix a seat problem and showed a Saturn representative traveling to Alaska to fix the Saturn owned by Robin Millage, an actual customer who had ordered her car, sight unseen, from a dealer in the continental United States. The result of the folksy, straight-talk campaign was a sharply focused brand image for Saturn.

The revolutionary ideas employed at Saturn continued with its pricing strategy. Today base prices for Saturn models range from $10,995 for an Ion sedan to $24,535 for a Vue all-wheel drive with a V6 engine.

For most dealers, there are no rebates or promotions and no haggling or dealing. A price tag of $15,225 on an Ion quad coupe (base price plus a transportation charge) means the customer pays $15,225—period. Saturn cannot set prices or control the one-price policy because of legal considerations. However, dealers have found the one-price policy very desirable because of tight profit margins and the high-integrity sales approach that is part of Saturn's marketing strategy. Potential buyers can also visit Saturn's website (www.saturn.com) to obtain pricing information for all models, as well as "build" their own Saturns, starting with a base car and adding options. Monthly payments can be estimated and financing options chosen.

Initially Saturn offered only four products: the Saturn SC1 and SC2 coupes and the Saturn SL1 and SL2 sedans. An SW1 and SW2 station wagon and entry-level coupe (SL) were introduced in 1993, followed by the EV1 (a limited-production electric car) in 1996 and an innovative three-door version of the SC1 and SC2 in 1998. The long-awaited introduction of a mid-size sedan and station wagon, known as the L-Series, took place in mid-1999. Initially the ad agency/dealer advisory panel believed the cars should not be given descriptive names (such as Chevrolet Camaro) because they did not want anything to dilute the Saturn name. However, the most recent additions to Saturn's product lineup—the Vue, the Ion, and the Relay, the last a minivan expected to arrive in showrooms in 2005—have been given more descriptive brand names.

The Vue, a sport-utility vehicle, arrived in dealer showrooms in 2001. With a base price of just over $17,000, the Vue is less expensive than competing models such as the Honda CR-V, Jeep Liberty, Ford Escape, and Hyundai Santa Fe. Saturn has positioned the Vue as an entry-level SUV for 18-to-45 year-old drivers.

The Ion replaced the reliable but conservatively styled S Series in 2002. Available in sedan and coupe models, the Ion has a considerably more modern look than the S Series, as well as more interior room and a longer wheelbase. Another design improvement for the Ion is the use of hydraulic engine mounts that reduce engine noise and vibration inside the vehicle. Ion models have base prices of $11,000 to $16,000, making them competitively priced with rivals such as the Ford Focus and Toyota Echo.

With marketing and distribution of new cars accounting for 30 to 35 percent of a car's cost, Saturn planned its distribution very carefully. Dealers are given large territories so that each competes with rival brands rather than with one another. Saturn generally has only one dealership in a metropolitan area. The first dealerships were set up in areas where import-car sales are high, and most were located on the East and West coasts to avoid cannibalizing sales of other GM cars. In addition, Saturn chose dealers who know how to appeal to import-car buyers. Most Saturn dealers have salespeople work in teams and avoid high-pressure sales techniques. Usually salespeople split commissions and cooperate in providing a relaxed, inviting showroom environment, allowing customers to browse and offering service and advice only as customers seek it.

Despite the excitement surrounding the new automobile marquis, Saturn has never sold more than 286,000 vehicles in a year and continues to struggle to be profitable. However, the company still has many positives on which to build. Customers love the firm's no-haggle policy, and satisfaction with Saturn vehicles remains high. In 2002, Saturn ranked first in a J. D. Power & Associates survey of satisfaction with dealer service departments. It marked the first time a non-luxury brand took top honors. Moreover, 70 percent of Saturn buyers are new to General Motors, helping the automaker better compete with import brands. Although Saturn parted ways with its original ad agency, Publicis & Hal Riney, in 2002, its new agency, Goodby, Silverstein & Partners, won a prestigious Golden Lion Award at the 2003 International Advertising Festival for "Sheet Metal," a commercial depicting people in car-related situations without their cars. Saturn dealers credited the $300 million ad campaign with increasing customer traffic in showrooms. Accomplishments such as these give Saturn a foundation for continuing a tradition of innovation in designing, building, and marketing automobiles.[43]

QUESTIONS FOR DISCUSSION

1. Have Saturn's strategic marketing planning efforts been successful? Why or why not?
2. What should Saturn do as competitors attempt to copy its unique brand image and pricing and dealer service policies?
3. Briefly describe the target market and marketing mix used by Saturn.

USA Today: The Nation's Newspaper

USA Today debuted in 1982 as the first national general-interest daily newspaper in the United States. The paper was the brainchild of Allen H. Neuharth, then chairman of Gannett Company, Inc., a diversified global news and communications company that owns newspapers and television stations and operates commercial printing, newswire, data, and news programming services. Gannett is the largest U.S. newspaper firm, with 100 daily newspapers with a combined daily paid circulation of nearly 8 million newspapers.

The Launch of *USA Today*   In February 1980, Neuharth met with members of a task force to discuss his vision for a unique nationally distributed daily newspaper. He believed a national newspaper could capitalize on two seemingly disparate trends: an increasingly short attention span among a generation nurtured on television and a growing public hunger for more information. Thus, *USA Today*'s primary mission would be to provide more news about more subjects in less time. Research suggested that *USA Today* should target primarily achievement-oriented men in professional and managerial positions who are heavy newspaper readers and frequent travelers. Whereas newspapers like *The New York Times* and *The Wall Street Journal* are targeted at the nation's intellectual elite and business leaders, *USA Today* would be edited for "Middle America": young, well-educated Americans who are on the move and care about what is going on in the world.

By early 1982, a team of news, advertising, and production personnel from Gannett's daily newspapers had developed and printed three different prototypes, which were sent to nearly 5,000 professional people. Although the prototypes had similar content, they differed in layout and graphic presentations. Readers were also sent response cards asking what they liked best and least about the proposed paper and whether or not they would buy it. After receiving a positive response, Gannett's board of directors unanimously approved the paper's launch.

On September 15, 1982, 155,000 copies of the first edition of *USA Today* hit the newsstands. On page one, Neuharth summarized *USA Today*'s mission statement, explaining that he wanted to make the newspaper enlightening and enjoyable to the public, informative to national leaders, and attractive to advertisers. The first issue sold out. Barely a month after its debut, *USA Today*'s circulation hit 362,879, double the original year-end projection, and topped the 1 million mark just seven months after its introduction. The typical reader turned out to be a well-educated, 40-year-old professional, usually a manager, with an annual income of about $60,000.

For a newspaper, *USA Today* was truly unique. It was a paper created for the TV generation, an idea reflected in its distinctive coin box, designed to look like a television set. The paper's motto was "An economy of words. A wealth of information." Each issue included four sections: News, Money, Life, and Sports. A prospective reader could grasp the top news of the day on page one just by viewing it in the coin box. For time-pressed readers, *USA Today* layered news for easy access and quick comprehension, and it made extensive use of briefs columns, secondary headlines, subheads, breakouts, at-a-glance boxes, and informational graphics.

After research indicated that many readers brought the paper home instead of reading it on their commute or at work, Gannett launched a home delivery subscription service in 1984. Home delivery caused problems at first, because the in-house computer technology could not handle subscription mailing lists efficiently, and the postal service did not always deliver the paper on its publication day. Nevertheless, subscriptions grew, and by 1991 nearly half of *USA Today*'s distribution was via home and office delivery.

Critics were quick to pan the unconventional paper. Some labeled it "McPaper"—the fast food of the newspaper business—due to its terse, brash writing style and short coverage of complex issues. Among their criticisms were that the paper was loaded with "gimmicks," such as tight, short stories that did not jump from page to page (except for the cover story); splashy, colorful graphics, including a national weather map; a distinctive, casual writing style; a brief roundup of news items from each state; summary boxes; charts and statistics-laden sports coverage; and a focus on celebrities and sports, with more detailed sports stories than almost any other paper in the nation. There was no foreign staff and little coverage of the world beyond the United States. Nevertheless, readers seemed to admire the paper for its balance and focus on brevity and clarity. Circulation surpassed 1.4 million by late 1985.

By the end of its third year, *USA Today* had become the second-largest paper in the country, with a circulation topped only by *The Wall Street Journal*. However, Neuharth's early predictions that *USA Today* would turn a profit within a few years of launch proved overly optimistic. It took about five years to move from the red to the black, but by 1993 profits were approximately $5 million, and the following year they doubled to about $10 million.

Marketing Mix Changes Although *USA Today* competed primarily against weekly newsmagazines and business newspapers rather than with daily local papers, many dailies began to borrow from *USA Today*'s style. Even old-line newspapers, such as *The New York Times*, began to add more color, shorten their stories, and beef up circulation campaigns to compete with "The Nation's Newspaper." In the face of this increasing competition, along with a recognition of changing reader needs, it was time for *USA Today* to respond to those needs and evolve in the late 1980s.

To stay ahead of imitators, *USA Today* continued to innovate and began a move toward becoming a more serious newspaper with improved journalism. The shift to harder news began with the space shuttle *Challenger* disaster in 1986, when major coverage of the tragedy helped circulation skyrocket. Starting in the late 1980s, Gannett also began incorporating less traditional value-added features to keep readers interested. The paper added 1–800 and 1–900 hotline numbers that readers could call for expert information on financial planning, college admissions, minority business development, taxes, and other subjects. Thousands of readers responded to opinion polls and write-in surveys on political and current-event issues. In 1991, the editorial pages were redesigned to provide more room for guest columnists and to encourage debate. Gannett also initiated a high school Academic All Star program that it later expanded to include colleges and universities. The year 2000 saw the first major redesign in *USA Today*'s history as the paper moved from a 54-inch to a 50-inch width to make it easier to read and cleaner in design. The pages were slimmer and easier to handle, especially in tight spaces like airplanes, trains, buses, and subways, and it fit more readily into briefcases, a need Gannett had learned about from focus groups.

USA Today has also been innovative in its promotional activities. Historically the paper limited its promotions primarily to outdoor advertising and television. In the late 1980s, however, Neuharth launched a BusCapade promotion tour, traveling to all 50 states and talking with all kinds of people,

including the governors of each state, to raise public awareness of the paper. Encouraged by the tour's success, Neuharth soon followed up with a JetCapade promotion in which he and a small news team traveled to 30 countries in 7 months, stimulating global demand for the paper. During a visit to the troops of Operation Desert Storm in the Persian Gulf in 1991, General Norman Schwarzkopf expressed a need for news from home, and *USA Today* arranged for delivery of 18,000 copies a day. The overseas success of *USA Today* led to the publication of *USA Today International*, now available in more than 90 countries in Western Europe, the Middle East, North Africa, and Asia.

Gannett's first strategy for enlisting advertisers was called the Partnership Plan, which offered six months of free space to those who purchased six months of paid advertising. In 1987, *USA Today* began to accept regional advertising for a wide variety of categories, including regional travel, retailing, tourism, and economic development. The paper also moved aggressively into "blue-chip circulation," offering bulk quantities of *USA Today* at discounted prices to hotels, airlines, and restaurants, which in turn provided the paper free to their customers. Today more than 500,000 copies of *USA Today* are distributed through blue-chip circulation every day.

In 1991, *USA Today* broke one of the most sacred practices of daily newspapers when it began offering advertising space on page one. The company sold 1-inch color strips across the entire width of the bottom of the page through one-year contracts for $1 million to $1.2 million each, with each advertiser taking one day a week. As has been true for so many of *USA Today*'s innovations, critics were quick to criticize this move, claiming the paper had "besmirched" its front page with advertising.

Rapid delivery has always been crucial to *USA Today*'s success. By the mid-1990s, the paper was earning kudos for its ability to deliver timely news, thanks to its late deadlines. For instance, in many parts of the country, *USA Today* prints later sports scores than local or regional papers. To speed distribution, the paper added printing sites around the world. Additional technological advances allowed Gannett to make production of *USA Today* totally digital, providing newsrooms with later deadlines and readers with earlier delivery times.

USA Today Online A decade after its launch, *USA Today* had become the most widely read newspaper in the country, with daily readership of more than 6.5 million. In an era when nearly all major national media were experiencing declines in readership or viewing audience, *USA Today* continued to grow.

Rising distribution and promotion costs, however, were beginning to cut into the newspaper's profits. To reverse this trend, *USA Today* created several spinoffs, including its first special-interest publication, *Baseball Weekly*. *USA Today* also joined with Cable News Network to produce a football TV program, and it launched SkyRadio to provide live radio on commercial airline flights. In 2000, Gannett launched a new broadcast and Internet initiative known as *USA Today Live* to provide news stories to Gannett television stations.

The major spinoff, however, was USA Today Online, which the company introduced in 1995. Like its print sibling, the website (**www.usatoday.com**) is organized into News, Sports, Money, and Life sections that allow readers to receive up-to-the-moment news with colorful graphics and crisp audio. Now renamed USAToday.com, it represents one of the most extensive sites on the World Wide Web, with more than 140,000 pages of up-to-the-minute general, sports, business, and technology news, as well as 5-day weather forecasts and travel information, all available free 24 hours a day.

Although the website's daily news content is free, Gannett has left open the option to charge site users in the future. Currently advertising provides revenue streams. Another revenue generator, launched in response to frequent reader requests for archived material, was a pay-per-view archive service (**http://archives.usatoday.com**) launched in 1998. This service allows readers to conduct a free, unlimited search of all the paper's articles that have run since April 1987. Articles may be downloaded for $1 per story, with payments handled by credit card.

Like its print sibling, USAToday.com has evolved to meet consumers' changing desires. In 1997 the website launched an online classifieds area, giving readers the opportunity to buy the goods and services of 24 companies in 6 online Marketplaces: Classifieds, Travel, Financial, Technology, Entertainment, and Flowers and Gifts. Since its inception, the website has studied computer logs to make decisions about editorial content, staff, and even budgetary expenditures. In 1998, it adopted custom software developed by Intelligent Environments to create a real-time system for surveying online readers. The resulting Quick Question gauges the opinions of USAToday.com readers on newsworthy events and issues.

Looking Ahead *USA Today* has been remarkably successful, with 20 years of continuous circulation growth in a time when overall newspaper readership was on the decline. More than 5.6 million consumers read *USA Today* daily, and approximately 2.3 million

subscribe to the paper. USA Today Online, one of the few profitable websites, was the world's most visited website, according to Media Metrix, with more than 15 million visitors each month. At the corporate level, Gannett took in approximately $6.4 billion in revenues in 2002, fueled by rising advertising demand, the war in Iraq, election-related ad spending, and strategic acquisitions.

To remain competitive, *USA Today* continues to upgrade and innovate, keeping several priorities in mind. One priority is to hold the price at 50 cents despite cost pressures. Another is to continue updating both the print and web products to ensure they are providing a complete "read" that people can trust. A third priority is to push technology so the print product can provide the latest sports scores and news ahead of competitors. Adopting a value-added strategy can help *USA Today* continue to differentiate itself from other national news providers. In the future, the key will be to ensure that both the print and online versions of *USA Today* provide content that readers cannot find anywhere else.

QUESTIONS FOR DISCUSSION

1. Describe Gannett's target market for *USA Today*. How did the firm's marketing strategy appeal to this market?
2. What forces in the marketing environment created opportunities for a successful national daily newspaper? What forces have created challenges for the newspaper?
3. Evaluate *USA Today*'s decision to enter the online news market. In light of this decision, should Gannett change the marketing strategy for the print version of *USA Today*?

Part Two

The Global Environment and Social and Ethical Responsibilities

Part Two deals with the marketing environment, examining concepts, influences, and trends both in the United States and abroad. **Chapter 3** examines competitive, economic, political, legal and regulatory, technological, and sociocultural forces in the marketing environment, which can have profound effects on marketing strategies. **Chapter 4** explores the role of ethical and social responsibility issues in marketing decisions.

Chapter 5 focuses on the nature, involvement, and strategy of marketing in a global economy.

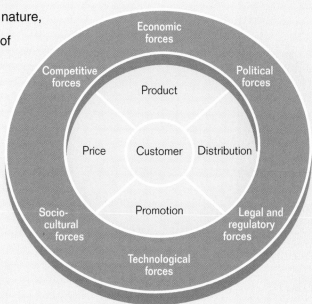

3 The Marketing Environment

OBJECTIVES

1. To recognize the importance of environmental scanning and analysis

2. To understand how competitive and economic factors affect organizations' ability to compete and customers' ability and willingness to buy products

3. To identify the types of political forces in the marketing environment

4. To understand how laws, government regulations, and self-regulatory agencies affect marketing activities

5. To explore the effects of new technology on society and on marketing activities

6. To analyze sociocultural issues marketers must deal with as they make decisions

Porsche Adapts to the Marketing Environment

Porsche AG, headquartered in Stuttgart, Germany, has long been one of the most profitable carmakers in the world, building on the popularity of its luxury sports cars. But the company was left at the starting line when the sports-utility vehicle revolution swept through North America and other markets. It had redesigned its 911 sports car and launched the Boxster to boost sales, but competitors were steadily introducing new cars and SUVs geared to the changing tastes of the same high-income buyers that Porsche wanted to reach.

CEO Wendelin Wiedeking decided Porsche needed something entirely different to fuel growth in an increasingly crowded competitive field—and this something would be an upscale four-wheel-drive vehicle. He sent the product development team across the United States, Europe, and Asia to research the SUV market in person. Drawing on internal resources and the expertise of key suppliers, the team designed the Cayenne, an SUV with the powerful performance and sleek styling for which Porsche is famed. Wiedeking himself supplied the name Cayenne, based on a pepper he grows at home: "It is spicy and adventurous, just like the car, and it is a name we can use everywhere in the world."

Not everyone welcomed the announcement of Cayenne's introduction. Some long-time customers were concerned that adding an SUV would dilute the brand's exclusivity. By the time the Cayenne actually made its debut, economic recession was dampening demand in many countries. However, once the Cayenne went on sale in Europe and North America, customers raced to buy the entire first year's output of 25,000 vehicles. In fact, the company had difficulty meeting unexpectedly strong demand for certain optional features. As a result, some customers waited up to a year for delivery. Thanks to the Cayenne, Porsche is meeting Wiedeking's sales and profitability goals despite lower sales of the 911 and Boxster. The company has also introduced slightly less expensive versions of the Cayenne to reach a broader customer group.

Competition remains a major global challenge. BMW is pitting its Z4 model against the Boxster, and Aston Martin, Lamborghini, and Mercedes-Benz are developing high-end sports cars to rival Porsche's 911. The Cayenne is competing with luxury SUVs from Cadillac, Mercedes, BMW, and Volkswagen. Nevertheless, if sales of the Cayenne continue to rise, Porsche will soon be selling more than 80,000 vehicles per year—and, just as important, it will be making its mark in a fast-growing vehicle category.[1] ∎

Companies like Porsche are modifying marketing strategies in response to changes in the marketing environment. Because recognizing and addressing such changes in the marketing environment are crucial to marketing success, we will focus in detail on the forces that contribute to these changes.

This chapter explores the competitive, economic, political, legal and regulatory, technological, and sociocultural forces that constitute the marketing environment. First, we define the marketing environment and consider why it is critical to scan and analyze it. Next, we discuss the effects of competitive forces and explore the influence of general economic conditions: prosperity, recession, depression, and recovery. We also examine buying power and look at the forces that influence consumers' willingness to spend. We then discuss the political forces that generate government actions affecting marketing activities and examine the effects of laws and regulatory agencies on these activities. After analyzing the major dimensions of the technological forces in the environment, we consider the impact of sociocultural forces on marketing efforts.

Examining and Responding to the Marketing Environment

The marketing environment consists of external forces that directly or indirectly influence an organization's acquisition of inputs (human, financial, and natural resources and raw materials, and information) and creation of outputs (goods, services, or ideas). As we saw in Chapter 1, the marketing environment includes six such forces: competitive, economic, political, legal and regulatory, technological, and sociocultural.

Whether fluctuating rapidly or slowly, environmental forces are always dynamic. Changes in the marketing environment create uncertainty, threats, and opportunities for marketers. Although the future is not very predictable, marketers try to forecast what may happen. We can say with certainty that marketers continue to modify their marketing strategies and plans in response to dynamic environmental forces. Consider how technological changes have affected the products offered by computer companies and how the public's growing concern with health and fitness has influenced the products of clothing, food, exercise equipment, and health care companies. Marketing managers who fail to recognize changes in environmental forces leave their firms unprepared to capitalize on marketing opportunities or cope with threats created by those changes. Monitoring the environment is crucial to an organization's survival and to the long-term achievement of its goals.

◆ Environmental Scanning and Analysis

environmental scanning The process of collecting information about forces in the marketing environment

To monitor changes in the marketing environment effectively, marketers engage in environmental scanning and analysis. **Environmental scanning** is the process of collecting information about forces in the marketing environment. Scanning involves observation; secondary sources such as business, trade, government, and general-interest publications; and marketing research. The Internet has become a popular scanning tool, since it makes data more accessible and allows companies to gather needed information quickly. Environmental scanning gives companies an edge over competitors in allowing them to take advantage of current trends. However, simply gathering information about competitors and customers is not enough; companies must know *how* to use that information in the strategic planning process. Managers must be careful not to gather so much information that sheer volume makes analysis impossible.

environmental analysis The process of assessing and interpreting the information gathered through environmental scanning

Environmental analysis is the process of assessing and interpreting the information gathered through environmental scanning. A manager evaluates the information for accuracy, tries to resolve inconsistencies in the data, and, if warranted, assigns significance to the findings. Evaluating this information should enable the manager to identify potential threats and opportunities linked to environmental changes. Understanding the current state of the marketing environment and recognizing threats and opportunities arising from changes within it help companies in their strategic planning. In particular, it can help marketing managers assess the performance of current marketing efforts and develop future marketing strategies.

◆ Responding to Environmental Forces

Marketing managers take two general approaches to environmental forces: accepting them as uncontrollable or attempting to influence and shape them. An organization that views environmental forces as uncontrollable remains passive and reactive toward the environment. Instead of trying to influence forces in the environment, its marketing managers adjust current marketing strategies to environmental changes. They approach with caution market opportunities discovered through environmental scanning and analysis. On the other hand, marketing managers who believe environmental forces can be shaped adopt a more proactive approach. For example, if a market is blocked by traditional environmental constraints, proactive marketing managers may apply economic, psychological, political, and promotional skills to gain access to and operate within it. Once they identify what is constraining a market opportunity, they assess the power of the various parties involved and develop strategies to overcome the obstructing environmental forces. Microsoft and Intel, for example, have responded to political, legal, and regulatory concerns about their power in the computer industry by communicating the value of their competitive approaches to various publics. The computer giants contend that their competitive success results in superior products for their customers.

A proactive approach can be constructive and bring desired results. To influence environmental forces, marketing managers seek to identify market opportunities or

Responding to Environmental Forces
Both Honda and Toyota are producing hybrid (gas and electric) powered cars in response to both customer demand and their own desires to exceed regulatory agency emissions standards.

I ♥ CLEAN AIR

Sticking it on a Honda LEV would be redundant.

When it comes to a clean environment, there's nothing wrong with repetition. Fortunately, we're not alone in this thinking. Over one million Hondas have been sold with low-emission technology, and every car we build is now LEV-rated or cleaner.

This commitment to clean air took off in 1975. That's when our Civic CVCC became the first car without a catalytic converter to comply with the emission standards set by the 1970 U.S. Clean Air Act. However, we didn't stop there. In 1995, we voluntarily reduced smog-contributing hydrocarbons by 70% and became the first to meet California's strict Low-Emission Vehicle (LEV) standard. And in 2001, the Civic became an Ultra-Low-Emission Vehicle (ULEV).

Not too long ago, the California Air Resources Board issued an even stricter emissions standard for 2004: Super-Ultra-Low-Emission Vehicle (SULEV). Naturally, we've decided there's no reason to wait. The 2000 Accord SULEV¹ was the first gasoline-powered vehicle to meet this standard. And our dedication to the environment was recently recognized by the Union of Concerned Scientists, who named Honda Motor Co. the cleanest car company in the world.¹

HONDA
The power of dreams:

*Accord EX Sedan with Leather only available in California. ¹Based on a U.S. emissions study (2000) by the Union of Concerned Scientists. The Union of Concerned Scientists is an independent organization. Results do not imply endorsement of Honda or its products. ©2001 American Honda Motor Co., Inc. honda.com

Introducing high performance technology that's also good for the environment. Now you can hug corners while you hug Mother Nature.

Toyota's revolutionary new Hybrid Synergy Drive® combines a gasoline engine with a powerful electric motor that never needs to be plugged in. The result? Super-efficient, super-charged performance. This groundbreaking yet affordable technology has already hit the roads in the all-new Prius. Prius achieves nearly 2.5 times the average fuel efficiency of conventional vehicles and close to 90% fewer smog-forming emissions – all while accelerating from 0 to 60 mph in 20% less time than its competitor.

Beyond Prius, Hybrid Synergy Drive will be available in more and more Toyota products – including SUVs.

With Hybrid Synergy Drive, we're helping save the planet. Faster.

toyota.com/tomorrow

*Based on 2004 EPA est. city & combined mpg. 0-60 mph for comparison only. Obtained with prototype vehicle by professional using special procedures. Do not attempt. ©2003

 HYBRID SYNERGY DRIVE

 TODAY  TOMORROW **TOYOTA**

to extract greater benefits relative to costs from existing market opportunities. For example, a firm losing sales to competitors with lower-priced products develops a technology that makes its production processes more efficient, thus allowing it to lower prices of its own products. Political action is another way to affect environmental forces. The pharmaceutical industry, for example, has lobbied very effectively for fewer restrictions on prescription drug marketing. However, managers must recognize that there are limits on how much environmental forces can be shaped. Although an organization may be able to influence legislation through lobbying, it is unlikely that a single organization can significantly increase the national birthrate or move the economy from recession to prosperity.

We cannot say whether a reactive or a proactive approach to environmental forces is better. For some organizations the passive, reactive approach is more appropriate, but for others the aggressive approach leads to better performance. Selection of a particular approach depends on an organization's managerial philosophies, objectives, financial resources, customers, and human skills, as well as on the environment within which the organization operates. Both organizational factors and managers' personal characteristics affect the variety of responses to changing environmental conditions. Microsoft, for example, can take a proactive approach because of its financial resources and the highly visible image of its founder, Bill Gates.

In the remainder of this chapter, we explore in greater detail each of the six environmental forces—competitive, economic, political, legal and regulatory, technological, and sociocultural—that interact to create opportunities and threats that must be considered in strategic planning.

Competitive Forces

competition Other organizations that market products that are similar to or can be substituted for a marketer's products in the same geographic area

brand competitors Firms that market products with similar features and benefits to the same customers at similar prices

product competitors Firms that compete in the same product class but market products with different features, benefits, and prices

generic competitors Firms that provide very different products that solve the same problem or satisfy the same basic customer need

total budget competitors Firms that compete for the limited financial resources of the same customers

Few firms, if any, operate free of competition. In fact, for most goods and services, customers have many alternatives from which to choose. Thus, when marketing managers define the target market(s) their firm will serve, they simultaneously establish a set of competitors.[2] In addition, marketing managers must consider the type of competitive structure in which the firm operates. In this section, we examine types of competition and competitive structures, as well as the importance of monitoring competitors' actions.

◆ Types of Competition

Broadly speaking, all firms compete with one another for customers' dollars. More practically, however, a marketer generally defines **competition** as other firms that market products that are similar to or can be substituted for its products in the same geographic area. These competitors can be classified into one of four types. **Brand competitors** market products with similar features and benefits to the same customers at similar prices. For example, a thirsty, calorie-conscious customer may choose a diet soda, such as Diet Coke, Diet Pepsi, or Diet RC, from the soda machine. However, these sodas face competition from other types of beverages. **Product competitors** compete in the same product class but market products with different features, benefits, and prices. The thirsty dieter, for instance, might purchase iced tea, juice, or bottled water instead of a soda. **Generic competitors** provide very different products that solve the same problem or satisfy the same basic customer need. Our dieter, for example, might simply have a glass of water from the kitchen tap to satisfy her thirst. **Total budget competitors** compete for the limited financial resources of the same customers.[3] Total budget competitors for Diet Coke, for example, might include gum, a newspaper, and bananas. Although all four types of competition can affect a firm's marketing performance, brand competitors are the most significant because buyers typically see the different products of these firms as direct substitutes

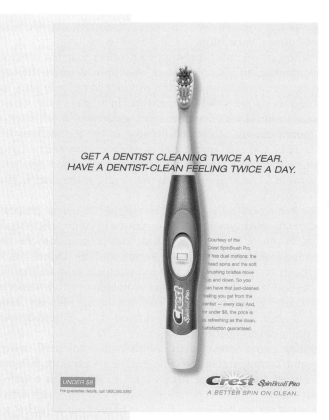

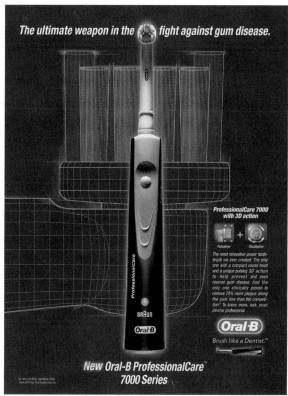

Brand Competitors
Crest SpinBrush Pro
toothbrush and the Oral-B
Professional Care 7000
Series toothbrush are brand
competitors in the tooth-
brush market.

for one another. Consequently marketers tend to concentrate environmental analyses on brand competitors.

◆ Types of Competitive Structures

The number of firms that supply a product may affect the strength of competitors.
When just one or a few firms control supply, competitive factors exert a different form
of influence on marketing activities than when many competitors exist. Table 3.1

Table 3.1	Selected Characteristics of Competitive Structures			
Type of Structure	**Number of Competitors**	**Ease of Entry into Market**	**Product**	**Example**
Monopoly	One	Many barriers	Almost no substitutes	Fort Collins (Colorado) Water Utilities
Oligopoly	Few	Some barriers	Homogeneous or differentiated (with real or perceived differences)	General Motors (autos)
Monopolistic competition	Many	Few barriers	Product differentiation, with many substitutes	Levi Strauss (jeans)
Pure competition	Unlimited	No barriers	Homogeneous products	Vegetable farm (sweet corn)

presents four general types of competitive structures: monopoly, oligopoly, monopolistic competition, and pure competition.

A **monopoly** exists when an organization offers a product that has no close substitutes, making that organization the sole source of supply. Because the organization has no competitors, it controls supply of the product completely and, as a single seller, can erect barriers to potential competitors. In reality, most monopolies surviving today are local utilities, which are heavily regulated by local, state, or federal agencies. These monopolies are tolerated because of the tremendous financial resources needed to develop and operate them. For example, few organizations can obtain the financial or political resources to mount any competition against a local water supplier. On the other hand, competition is increasing in the electric and cable television industries.

monopoly A competitive structure in which an organization offers a product that has no close substitutes, making that organization the sole source of supply

An **oligopoly** exists when a few sellers control the supply of a large proportion of a product. In this case, each seller considers the reactions of other sellers to changes in marketing activities. Products facing oligopolistic competition may be homogeneous, such as aluminum, or differentiated, such as automobiles. Usually barriers of some sort make it difficult to enter the market and compete with oligopolies. For example, because of the enormous financial outlay required, few companies or individuals could afford to enter the oil-refining or steel-producing industry. Moreover, some industries demand special technical or marketing skills, a qualification that deters entry of many potential competitors.

oligopoly A competitive structure in which a few sellers control the supply of a large proportion of a product

Monopolistic competition exists when a firm with many potential competitors attempts to develop a marketing strategy to differentiate its product. For example, Levi Strauss has established an advantage for its blue jeans through a well-known trademark, design, advertising, and a reputation for quality. Although many competing brands of blue jeans are available, this firm has carved out a market niche by emphasizing differences in its products.

monopolistic competition
A competitive structure in which a firm has many potential competitors and tries to develop a marketing strategy to differentiate its product

Pure competition, if it existed at all, would entail a large number of sellers, none of which could significantly influence price or supply. Products would be homogeneous, and entry into the market would be easy. The closest thing to an example of pure competition is an unregulated farmers' market, where local growers gather to sell their produce.

pure competition A market structure characterized by an extremely large number of sellers, none strong enough to significantly influence price or supply

Pure competition is an ideal at one end of the continuum; monopoly is at the other end. Most marketers function in a competitive environment somewhere between these two extremes.

◆ Monitoring Competition

Marketers need to monitor the actions of major competitors to determine what specific strategies competitors are using and how those strategies affect their own. Price is one marketing strategy variable that most competitors monitor. When AirTran or Southwest Airlines lowers its fare on a route, most major airlines attempt to match the price. Monitoring guides marketers in developing competitive advantages and in adjusting current marketing strategies and planning new ones.

In monitoring competition, it is not enough to analyze available information; the firm must develop a system for gathering ongoing information about competitors. Understanding the market and what customers want, as well as what the competition is providing, will help the firm maintain a marketing orientation.[4] Information about competitors allows marketing managers to assess the performance of their own marketing efforts and to recognize the strengths and weaknesses in their own marketing strategies. In addition, organizations are rewarded for taking risks and dealing with the uncertainty created by inadequate information.[5] Data about market shares, product movement, sales volume, and expenditure levels can be useful. However, accurate information on these matters is often difficult to obtain. We explore how marketers collect and organize such data in Chapter 6.

Economic Forces

Economic forces in the marketing environment influence both marketers' and customers' decisions and activities. In this section, we examine the effects of general economic conditions as well as buying power and the factors that affect people's willingness to spend.

◆ Economic Conditions

business cycle A pattern of economic fluctuations that has four stages: prosperity, recession, depression, and recovery

The overall state of the economy fluctuates in all countries. Changes in general economic conditions affect (and are affected by) supply and demand, buying power, willingness to spend, consumer expenditure levels, and the intensity of competitive behavior. Therefore, current economic conditions and changes in the economy have a broad impact on the success of organizations' marketing strategies.

Fluctuations in the economy follow a general pattern, often referred to as the **business cycle**. In the traditional view, the business cycle consists of four stages: prosperity, recession, depression, and recovery. From a global perspective, different regions of the world may be in different stages of the business cycle during the same period. Throughout much of the last decade, for example, the United States experienced booming growth (prosperity). The U.S. economy began to slow in 2000, with a brief recession, especially in high-technology industries, in 2001. Japan, however, endured a recession during most of the last decade and into the 2000s. Economic

Adverse Economic Conditions While individuals and companies both want to control costs under any type of economic condition, they are especially interested in controlling costs during adverse economic conditions.

variation in the global marketplace creates a planning challenge for firms that sell products in multiple markets around the world.

prosperity A stage of the business cycle characterized by low unemployment and relatively high total income, which together ensure high buying power (provided the inflation rate stays low)

During **prosperity**, unemployment is low and total income is relatively high. Assuming a low inflation rate, this combination ensures high buying power. If the economic outlook remains prosperous, consumers generally are willing to buy. In the prosperity stage, marketers often expand their product offerings to take advantage of increased buying power. They can sometimes capture a larger market share by intensifying distribution and promotion efforts.

recession A stage of the business cycle during which unemployment rises and total buying power declines, stifling both consumer and business spending

Because unemployment rises during a **recession**, total buying power declines. These factors, usually accompanied by consumer pessimism, often stifle both consumer and business spending. As buying power decreases, many customers may become more price and value conscious, and look for basic, functional products. During a recession, some firms make the mistake of drastically reducing their marketing efforts, thus damaging their ability to survive. Obviously, however, marketers should consider some revision of their marketing activities during a recessionary period. Because consumers are more concerned about the functional value of products, a company should focus its marketing research on determining precisely what functions buyers want and make sure those functions become part of its products. Promotional efforts should emphasize value and utility. For example, KeepMedia, an online periodical content archive, discovered consumers wanted to pay for quality periodical content on the Internet but were unwilling to pay a separate fee for each title across the Web as they do for magazines offline. The company CEO put together recent editorial materials from recognizable publications at one flat fee.[6]

depression A stage of the business cycle when unemployment is extremely high, wages are very low, total disposable income is at a minimum, and consumers lack confidence in the economy

A prolonged recession may become a **depression**, a period in which unemployment is extremely high, wages are very low, total disposable income is at a minimum, and consumers lack confidence in the economy. A depression usually lasts for an extended period, often years, and has been experienced by Russia, Mexico, and Brazil in the last decade. During the economic turmoil in Mexico, Coca-Cola Company chose to continue its marketing efforts, whereas most of its competitors cut back or even abandoned the Mexican market. By maintaining a high level of marketing, Coca-Cola increased its share of the Mexican market by 4 to 6 percent. Although evidence supports maintaining or even increasing spending during economic slowdowns, marketing budgets are more likely to be cut in the face of an economic downturn.[7]

recovery A stage of the business cycle in which the economy moves from recession or depression toward prosperity

During **recovery**, the economy moves from recession or depression toward prosperity. During this period, high unemployment begins to decline, total disposable income increases, and the economic gloom that reduced consumers' willingness to buy subsides. Both the ability and the willingness to buy rise. Marketers face some problems during recovery; for example, it is difficult to ascertain how quickly and to what level prosperity will return. In this stage, marketers should maintain as much flexibility in their marketing strategies as possible so they can make the needed adjustments.

◆ Buying Power

buying power Resources, such as money, goods, and services, that can be traded in an exchange

The strength of a person's **buying power** depends on economic conditions and the size of the resources—money, goods, and services that can be traded in an exchange—that enable the individual to make purchases. The major financial sources of buying power are income, credit, and wealth. For an individual, **income** is the amount of money received through wages, rents, investments, pensions, and subsidy payments for a given period, such as a month or a year. Normally this money is allocated among taxes, spending for goods and services, and savings. The median annual household income in the United States is approximately $42,409.[8] However, because of differences in people's educational levels, abilities, occupations, and wealth, income is not equally distributed in this country.

income For an individual, the amount of money received through wages, rents, investments, pensions, and subsidy payments for a given period

disposable income After-tax income

Marketers are most interested in the amount of money left after payment of taxes because this **disposable income** is used for spending or saving. Because disposable income is a ready source of buying power, the total amount available in a nation is important to marketers. Several factors determine the size of total disposable income. One is the total amount of income, which is affected by wage levels, the rate of unemployment, interest rates, and dividend rates. Because disposable income is income left after taxes are paid, the number and amount of taxes directly affect the size of total disposable income. When taxes rise, disposable income declines; when taxes fall, disposable income increases.

discretionary income
Disposable income available for spending and saving after an individual has purchased the basic necessities of food, clothing, and shelter

Disposable income that is available for spending and saving after an individual has purchased the basic necessities of food, clothing, and shelter is called **discretionary income**. People use discretionary income to purchase entertainment, vacations, automobiles, education, pets, furniture, appliances, and so on. Changes in total discretionary income affect sales of these products, especially automobiles, furniture, large appliances, and other costly durable goods.

Credit enables people to spend future income now or in the near future. However, credit increases current buying power at the expense of future buying power. Several factors determine whether people use or forgo credit. First, credit must be available. Interest rates too affect buyers' decisions to use credit, especially for expensive purchases such as homes, appliances, and automobiles. When interest rates are low, the total cost of automobiles and houses becomes more affordable. In the United States, low interest rates over the past ten years induced many buyers to take on the high level of debt necessary to own a home, fueling a tremendous boom in the construction of new homes and the sale of older homes. In contrast, when interest rates are high, consumers are more likely to delay buying such expensive items. Use of credit is also affected by credit terms, such as size of the down payment and amount and number of monthly payments.

wealth The accumulation of past income, natural resources, and financial resources

Wealth is the accumulation of past income, natural resources, and financial resources. It exists in many forms, including cash, securities, savings accounts, jewelry, and real estate. Like income, wealth is unevenly distributed. A person can have a high income and very little wealth. It is also possible, but not likely, for a person to have great wealth but little income. The significance of wealth to marketers is that as people become wealthier, they gain buying power in three ways: they can use their wealth to make current purchases, to generate income, and to acquire large amounts of credit.

Income, credit, and wealth equip consumers with buying power to purchase goods and services. Marketing managers need to be aware of current levels and expected changes in buying power in their own markets because buying power directly affects the types and quantities of goods and services customers purchase. Information about buying power is available from government sources, trade associations, and research agencies. One of the most current and comprehensive sources of buying power data is the *Sales & Marketing Management Survey of Buying Power*, published annually by *Sales & Marketing Management* magazine. Having buying power, however, does not mean consumers will buy. They must also be willing to use their buying power.

◆ Willingness to Spend

willingness to spend An inclination to buy because of expected satisfaction from a product, influenced by the ability to buy and numerous psychological and social forces

People's **willingness to spend**—their inclination to buy because of expected satisfaction from a product—is, to some degree, related to their ability to buy. That is, people are sometimes more willing to buy if they have the buying power. However, a number of other elements also influence willingness to spend. Some elements affect specific products; others influence spending in general. A product's price and value influence almost all of us. Cross pens, for example, appeal to customers who are willing to spend more for fine writing instruments even when lower-priced pens are readily available. The amount of satisfaction received from a product already owned may also influence customers' desire to buy other products. Satisfaction depends not only on the quality of the currently owned product but also on numerous psychological and social forces. The American Customer Satisfaction Index, computed by

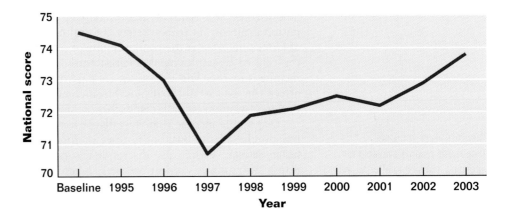

Figure 3.1 American Customer Satisfaction Index
Source: "American Customer Satisfaction Index," University of Michigan Business School, Nov. 2003, **http://www.theacsi.com/ April 2004**

the National Quality Research Center at the University of Michigan (see Figure 3.1) offers an indicator of customer satisfaction with a wide variety of businesses. Among other things, the index suggests that if customers become more dissatisfied, they may curtail their overall spending, which could stifle economic growth.[9]

Factors that affect consumers' general willingness to spend are expectations about future employment, income levels, prices, family size, and general economic conditions. Willingness to spend ordinarily declines if people are unsure whether or how long they will be employed, and usually increases if people are reasonably certain of higher incomes in the future. Expectations of rising prices in the near future may also increase willingness to spend in the present. For a given level of buying power, the larger the family, the greater the willingness to spend. One reason for this relationship is that as the size of a family increases, more dollars must be spent to provide the basic necessities to sustain family members.

Political Forces

Political, legal, and regulatory forces of the marketing environment are closely interrelated. Legislation is enacted, legal decisions are interpreted by courts, and regulatory agencies are created and operated, for the most part, by elected or appointed officials. Legislation and regulations (or their lack) reflect the current political outlook. Consequently the political forces of the marketing environment have the potential to influence marketing decisions and strategies.

Marketing organizations strive to maintain good relations with elected political officials for several reasons. Political officials well disposed toward particular firms or industries are less likely to create or enforce laws and regulations unfavorable to those companies. For example, political officials who believe oil companies are making honest efforts to control pollution are unlikely to create and enforce highly restrictive pollution control laws. In addition, governments are big buyers, and political officials can influence how much a government agency purchases and from whom. Finally, political officials can play key roles in helping organizations secure foreign markets.

Many marketers view political forces as beyond their control and simply adjust to conditions arising from those forces. Some firms, however, seek to influence the political process. In some cases, organizations publicly protest the actions of legislative bodies. More often, organizations help elect to political offices individuals who regard them positively. Much of this help is in the form of campaign contributions. Although laws restrict direct corporate contributions to campaign funds, corporate influence may be channeled into campaigns through executives' or stockholders' personal contributions. Such actions violate the spirit of corporate campaign contribution laws. A sizable donation to a campaign fund may carry an implicit understanding that the elected official will perform political favors for the executive's firm. Occasionally some businesses find it so important to ensure favorable treatment that they make illegal corporate contributions to campaign funds.

Although laws limit corporate contributions to campaign funds for specific candidates, it is legal for businesses and other organizations to contribute to political parties. Some companies even choose to donate to more than one party. Marketers can also influence the political process through political action committees (PACs) that solicit donations from individuals and then contribute those funds to candidates running for political office. Companies are barred by federal law from donating directly to candidates for federal offices or to political action committees, but they can organize PACs to which their executives, employees, and stockholders can make significant donations as individuals. Companies can also participate in the political process through lobbying to persuade public and/or government officials to favor a particular position in decision making. Many organizations concerned about the threat of legislation or regulation that may negatively affect their operations employ lobbyists to communicate their concerns to elected officials. For example, World Health Organization (WHO), did a study suggesting a relationship between food advertising and childhood obesity prompted the U.S. advertising industry to mount lobbying and public relations efforts to influence the regulation of food advertising.[10]

Legal and Regulatory Forces

A number of federal laws influence marketing decisions and activities. Table 3.2 (on p. 70) lists some of the most important laws. In addition to discussing these laws, which deal with competition and consumer protection, this section examines the effects of regulatory agencies and self-regulatory forces on marketing efforts.

◆ Procompetitive Legislation

Procompetitive laws are designed to preserve competition. Most of these laws were enacted to end various antitrade practices deemed unacceptable by society. The Sherman Antitrust Act, for example, was passed in 1890 to prevent businesses from restraining trade and monopolizing markets. Examples of illegal anticompetitive practices include stealing trade secrets or obtaining other confidential information from a competitor's employees, trademark and copyright infringement, price fixing, false advertising, and deceptive selling methods such as "bait and switch" and false representation of products. For example, the Lanham Act (1946) and the Federal Trademark Dilution Act (1995) help companies protect their trademarks (brand names, logos, and other registered symbols) against infringement. The latter also requires users of names that match or parallel existing trademarks to relinquish them to prevent confusion among consumers. Antitrust laws also authorize the government to punish companies that engage in such anticompetitive practices. For example, Rhône-Poulenc Bochimie S.A. paid a $5 million fine for participating in a conspiracy to fix prices and allocate customers for pharmaceutical-grade methyl glucamine sold in the United States and elsewhere.[11]

◆ Consumer Protection Legislation

Consumer protection legislation is not a recent development. During the mid-1800s, lawmakers in many states passed laws to prohibit adulteration of food and drugs. However, consumer protection laws at the federal level mushroomed in the mid-1960s and early 1970s. A number of them deal with consumer safety, such as the food and drug acts, designed to protect people from actual and potential physical

Table 3.2	Major Federal Laws Affecting Marketing Decisions
(Date Enacted)	**Purpose**
Sherman Antitrust Act (1890)	Prohibits contracts, combinations, or conspiracies to restrain trade; establishes as a misdemeanor monopolizing or attempting to monopolize
Clayton Act (1914)	Prohibits specific practices such as price discrimination, exclusive-dealer arrangements, and stock acquisitions whose effect may noticeably lessen competition or tend to create a monopoly
Federal Trade Commission Act (1914)	Created the Federal Trade Commission; also gives the FTC investigatory powers to be used in preventing unfair methods of competition
Robinson-Patman Act (1936)	Prohibits price discrimination that lessens competition among wholesalers or retailers; prohibits producers from giving disproportionate services of facilities to large buyers
Wheeler-Lea Act (1938)	Prohibits unfair and deceptive acts and practices regardless of whether competition is injured; places advertising of foods and drugs under the jurisdiction of the FTC
Lanham Act (1946)	Provides protections for and regulation of brand names, brand marks, trade names, and trademarks
Celler-Kefauver Act (1950)	Prohibits any corporation engaged in commerce from acquiring the whole or any part of the stock or other share of the capital assets of another corporation when the effect would substantially lessen competition or tend to create a monopoly
Fair Packaging and Labeling Act (1966)	Prohibits unfair or deceptive packaging or labeling of consumer products
Magnuson-Moss Warranty (FTC) Act (1975)	Provides for minimum disclosure standards for written consumer product warranties; defines minimum consent standards for written warranties; allows the FTC to prescribe interpretive rules in policy statements regarding unfair or deceptive practices
Consumer Goods Pricing Act (1975)	Prohibits the use of price maintenance agreements among manufacturers and resellers in interstate commerce
Antitrust Improvements Act (1976)	Requires large corporations to inform federal regulators of prospective mergers or acquisitions so these arrangements can be studied for any possible violations of the law
Trademark Counterfeiting Act (1980)	Imposes civil and criminal penalties against those who deal in counterfeit consumer goods or any counterfeit goods that can threaten health or safety
Trademark Law Revision Act (1988)	Amends the Lanham Act to allow brands not yet introduced to be protected through registration with the Patent and Trademark Office
Nutrition Labeling and Education Act (1990)	Prohibits exaggerated health claims; requires all processed foods to contain labels with nutritional information
Telephone Consumer Protection Act (1991)	Establishes procedures to avoid unwanted telephone solicitations; prohibits marketers from using an automated telephone dialing system or an artificial or prerecorded voice to certain telephone lines
Federal Trademark Dilution Act (1995)	Grants trademark owners the right to protect trademarks and requires relinquishment of names that match or parallel existing trademarks

(continued)

Table 3.2	*(continued)*
Digital Millennium Copyright Act (1996)	Refined copyright laws to protect digital versions of copyrighted materials, including music and movies
Children's Online Privacy Protection Act (2000)	Regulates the collection of personally identifiable information (name, address, e-mail address, hobbies, interests, or information collected through cookies) online from children under age 13
Do Not Call Implementation Act (2003)	Directs the FCC and FTC to coordinate so that their rules are consistent regarding telemarketing call practices including the Do Not Call Registry and other lists, as well as call abandonment

harm caused by adulteration or mislabeling. Other laws prohibit the sale of various hazardous products, such as flammable fabrics and toys that may injure children. Others concern automobile safety. Congress has also passed several laws concerning information disclosure. Some require that information about specific products, such as textiles, furs, cigarettes, and automobiles, be provided on labels. Other laws focus on particular marketing activities: product development and testing, packaging, labeling, advertising, and consumer financing. For example, concerns about companies' online collection and use of personal information, especially about children, resulted in the passage of the Children's Online Privacy Protection Act of 2000, which prohibits websites and Internet providers from seeking personal information from children under age 13 without parental consent.[12]

◆ Encouraging Compliance with Laws and Regulations

Marketing activities are sometimes at the forefront of organizational misconduct, with fraud and antitrust violations the most frequently sentenced organizational crimes. Legal violations usually begin when marketers develop programs that unwittingly overstep legal bounds. Many marketers lack experience in dealing with complex legal actions and decisions. Some test the limits of certain laws by operating in a legally questionable way to see how far they can get with certain practices before being prosecuted. Other marketers interpret regulations and statutes very strictly to avoid violating a vague law. When marketers interpret laws in relation to specific marketing practices, they often analyze recent court decisions both to better understand what the law is intended to do and to predict future court interpretations. The flip side of this issue—consumers engaging in legally questionable use of certain products—is explored in Ethics and Social Responsibility (on p. 72).

To ensure that marketers comply with the law, the federal government is moving toward greater organizational accountability for misconduct. The U.S. Sentencing Commission (USSC) introduced a detailed set of guidelines to regulate the sentencing of companies convicted of breaking the law. The basic philosophy of the Federal Sentencing Guidelines for Organizations is that companies are responsible for crimes committed by their employees. These guidelines

Snapshot

Most frequent consumer fraud complaints

Complaints received by the Federal Trade Commission:

ID theft — 43%

Internet auctions — 13%

Internet services/computer — 6%

Shop-at-home catalog sales — 5%

Advance-fee loans and credit protection — 5%

Source: Data from Federal Trade Commission's Consumer Sentinel database.

were designed not only to hold companies as well as employees accountable for illegal actions but also to streamline sentencing and fine structures for offenses. (Previously laws punished only those employees directly responsible for an offense, not the company.) The underlying assumption is that "good citizen corporations" maintain compliance systems and internal controls to prevent misconduct and educate employees about questionable activities. Thus, the new guidelines focus on crime prevention and detection by mitigating penalties for firms that have chosen to develop such compliance programs should one of their employees engage in misconduct.

The bottom line is that unless a marketer works in a company with an effective compliance program that meets the minimum requirements of the U.S. Sentencing Commission's recommendations, both the individual(s) and the company face severe penalties if the marketer violates the law. For example, Daiwa Bank was hit with a $340 million fine for misrepresenting financial information, and Archer Daniels Midland received a $100 million fine for price fixing. Further, the Federal Sentencing Guidelines for individuals often mandate substantial prison sentences even for first-time offenders convicted of a felony such as antitrust, fraud, import/export violations, or environmental crimes.

ETHICS AND SOCIAL RESPONSIBILITY

Is Sharing Digital Music and Movie Files Ethical?

Is it ethical to download and swap digital music and movie files with friends? Almost anyone with a computer and an Internet connection can find and trade MP3 and movie clips for free—and an estimated 60 million people do so. This upsets the entertainment industry, which argues that peer-to-peer file sharing of copyrighted materials constitutes "piracy" and is therefore illegal. Some performers also complain about losing money when people trade rather than buy songs. In fact, the recording companies report that sales of music CDs dropped more than 30 percent in two years because of file sharing. Supported by court rulings requiring Internet service providers to identify subscribers suspected of sharing files, the companies are fighting back.

The Recording Industry Association of America (RIAA), which represents Warner Music, EMI, BMG, and other major music labels, has sued hundreds of people for file sharing and subpoenaed thousands more. "We're trying to send a strong message that you are not anonymous when you participate in peer-to-peer file sharing and that the illegal distribution of copyrighted music has consequences," explains RIAA's CEO. For its part, the Motion Picture Association of America (MPAA) has launched an antipiracy campaign stressing that "if you haven't paid for it, you've stolen it."

File swappers see the issue differently. Some insist that music CDs are priced too high and that performers are making plenty of money from concert tickets and T-shirt sales. Some say they like being able to sample different songs, pick their favorites, and make a custom-tailored CD compilation. Many believe file sharing helps performers reach a wider audience of potential CD buyers. Above all, file sharers insist they are trading files for personal use, not for profit.

This controversy has opened the door to a potentially lucrative marketing opportunity. Apple Computer started its now popular iTunes Music Store to sell downloads of 500,000 songs, priced per song. Other online music stores let customers choose between paying a monthly subscription fee and paying for each song downloaded. Will file sharers choose to buy instead of swapping for free? Is file sharing unethical?

◆ Regulatory Agencies

Federal regulatory agencies influence many marketing activities, including product development, pricing, packaging, advertising, personal selling, and distribution. Usually these bodies have the power to enforce specific laws, as well as some discretion in establishing operating rules and regulations to guide certain types of industry practices. Because of this discretion and overlapping areas of responsibility, confusion or conflict regarding which agencies have jurisdiction over which marketing activities is common.

Federal Trade Commission (FTC) An agency that regulates a variety of business practices and curbs false advertising, misleading pricing, and deceptive packaging and labeling

Of all the federal regulatory units, the **Federal Trade Commission (FTC)** most heavily influences marketing activities. Although the FTC regulates a variety of business practices, it allocates a large portion of resources to curbing false advertising, misleading pricing, and deceptive packaging and labeling. When it receives a complaint or otherwise has reason to believe a firm is violating a law, the commission issues a complaint stating that the business is in violation. For example, the FTC filed formal complaints against Stock Value 1 Inc. and Comstar Communications Inc. for making unsubstantiated claims that their radiation-protection patches block the electromagnetic energy emitted by cellular telephones. The FTC's complaint charged that the companies "made false statements that their products had been significantly 'proven' and tested when in fact that was not the case."[13] If the company continues the questionable practice, the FTC can issue a cease-and-desist order demanding that the business stop doing whatever caused the complaint. The firm can appeal to the federal courts to have the order rescinded. However, the FTC can seek civil penalties in court, up to a maximum penalty of $10,000 a day for each infraction if a cease-and-desist order is violated.

The commission can also require companies to run corrective advertising in response to previous ads deemed misleading. This mandated corrective advertising is proving to be costly to some companies. The FTC has emerged as the leading enforcement agency for consumer protection issues on the Internet.[14] For example, the FTC is taking action against D Squared Solutions LLC, alleging the firm sells software that exploits a security hole in Microsoft's Messenger Service utility to send full-screen ads to consumers, then advertises software that would block the pop-up ads. "It's an unfair practice to [send] advertisements that create a problem and then charge consumers for the solution," said Howard Beales, director of the FTC's Bureau of Consumer Protection.[15]

The FTC also assists businesses in complying with laws and evaluates new marketing methods every year. For example, the agency has held hearings to help firms establish guidelines for avoiding charges of price fixing, deceptive advertising, and questionable telemarketing practices. It has also held conferences and hearings on electronic (Internet) commerce. When general sets of guidelines are needed to improve business practices in a particular industry, the FTC sometimes encourages firms within that industry to establish a set of trade practices voluntarily. The FTC may even sponsor a conference bringing together industry leaders and consumers for this purpose.

Unlike the FTC, other regulatory units are limited to dealing with specific products, services, or business activities. For example, the Food and Drug Administration (FDA) enforces regulations prohibiting the sale and distribution of adulterated, misbranded, or hazardous food and drug products. Table 3.3 (on p. 74) outlines the areas of responsibility of six federal regulatory agencies.

In addition, all states, as well as many cities and towns, have regulatory agencies that enforce laws and regulations regarding marketing practices within their states or municipalities. State and local regulatory agencies try not to establish regulations that conflict with those of federal regulatory agencies. They generally enforce laws dealing with the production and sale of particular goods and services. The utility, insurance, financial, and liquor industries are commonly regulated by state agencies. Among these agencies' targets are misleading advertising and pricing. Recent legal actions suggest that states are taking a firmer stance against perceived deceptive pricing practices and are using basic consumer research to define deceptive pricing.

Table 3.3	Major Federal Regulatory Agencies
Agency	**Major Areas of Responsibility**
Federal Trade Commission (FTC)	Enforces laws and guidelines regarding business practices; takes action to stop false and deceptive advertising, pricing, packaging, and labeling
Food and Drug Administration (FDA)	Enforces laws and regulations to prevent distribution of adulterated or misbranded foods, drugs, medical devices, cosmetics, veterinary products, and potentially hazardous consumer products
Consumer Product Safety Commission (CPSC)	Ensures compliance with the Consumer Product Safety Act; protects the public from unreasonable risk of injury from any consumer product not covered by other regulatory agencies
Federal Communications Commission (FCC)	Regulates communication by wire, radio, and television in interstate and foreign commerce
Environmental Protection Agency (EPA)	Develops and enforces environmental protection standards and conducts research into the adverse effects of pollution
Federal Power Commission (FPC)	Regulates rates and sales of natural gas producers, thereby affecting the supply and price of gas available to consumers; also regulates wholesale rates for electricity and gas, pipeline construction, and U.S. imports and exports of natural gas and electricity

◆ Self-Regulatory Forces

In an attempt to be good corporate citizens and prevent government intervention, some businesses try to regulate themselves. A number of trade associations have developed self-regulatory programs. Though these programs are not a direct outgrowth of laws, many were established to stop or stall the development of laws and governmental regulatory groups that would regulate the associations' marketing practices. Sometimes trade associations establish ethics codes by which their members must abide or risk censure or exclusion from the association. For example, the Water Quality Association has developed a comprehensive code of ethics to help companies that sell water purification equipment avoid illegal and unethical activities.

Better Business Bureau (BBB)
A local, nongovernmental regulatory agency, supported by local businesses, that helps settle problems between customers and specific business firms

Perhaps the best-known nongovernmental regulatory group is the **Better Business Bureau (BBB)**, a local regulatory agency supported by local businesses. More than 140 bureaus help settle problems between consumers and specific business firms. Each bureau also acts to preserve good business practices in a locality, although it usually lacks strong enforcement tools for dealing with firms that employ questionable practices. When a firm continues to violate what the Better Business Bureau believes to be good business practices, the bureau warns consumers through local newspapers or broadcast media. If the offending organization is a BBB member, it may be expelled from the local bureau. For example, Debtco, a credit repair organization, had its membership revoked by the San Diego Better Business Bureau for failing to eliminate the underlying cause of multiple complaints on file.[16]

It's a cleaner, greener power machine.

The H System™ turbine from GE is designed to produce more power for more people. But, for every unit of that power, it will use less fuel and produce fewer greenhouse gas emissions compared to other large gas turbines. No wonder, in the power industry, it's generating so much excitement.

imagination at work

When Mr. Belding remodeled his home, he included an addition for a little buddy

Owls, like this screech owl, can be found throughout North America, but their habitats are quickly disappearing. Urban sprawl and deforestation are threatening the natural living space for these attractive predators. You can help the owl population by placing nesting boxes in your yard to provide shelter. This will also provide you with the pleasure of observing these stately animals.

National Wildlife Federation's® Backyard Habitat™ program teaches ways to make your backyard more inviting to owls and other wildlife. Through a partnership with The Home Depot®, NWF is deploying its Habitat Ambassadors™ to several Home Depot locations nationwide to teach customers how home improvement can be habitat improvement, too. To learn more visit www.nwf.org/homedepot/.

NATIONAL WILDLIFE FEDERATION® www.nwf.org®

photo credit © Bob & Ann Simpson/VIREO
©2004, HOMER TLC, Inc. All rights reserved. AE86040A

Regulatory Forces
A number of companies such as GE and The Home Depot seek to meet customer needs with products that reduce emmisions and energy use and otherwise minimize or improve environmental impact.

National Advertising Review Board (NARB) A self-regulatory unit that considers challenges to issues raised by the National Advertising Division (an arm of the Council of Better Business Bureaus) about an advertisement

The Council of Better Business Bureaus is a national organization composed of all local Better Business Bureaus. The National Advertising Division (NAD) of the Council of Better Business Bureaus operates a self-regulatory program that investigates claims regarding alleged deceptive advertising. For example, after receiving complaints from a rival firm, the NAD asked the Federal Trade Commission and Bureau of Alcohol, Tobacco, and Firearms to investigate whether Diageo PLC's labeling, packaging, and promotion for Smirnoff Ice misleads consumers into thinking the malt-based beverage contains vodka.[17]

Another self-regulatory entity, the **National Advertising Review Board (NARB)**, considers cases in which an advertiser challenges issues raised by the National Advertising Division about an advertisement. Cases are reviewed by panels drawn from NARB members representing advertisers, agencies, and the public. The NARB, sponsored by the Council of Better Business Bureaus and three advertising trade organizations, has no official enforcement powers. However, if a firm refuses to comply with its decision, the NARB may publicize the questionable practice and file a complaint with the FTC. For example, Sidney Frank Importing Company appealed to the NARB an NAD order to abandon its claim that the company's Grey Goose Vodka is "rated the No. 1 Tasting Vodka in the World." The NARB concurred with the NAD on the issue. Frank refused to comply with the NARB, and the NARB referred the case to the FTC and the Alcohol and Tobacco Tax and Trade Bureau.[18]

Self-regulatory programs have several advantages over governmental laws and regulatory agencies. Establishment and implementation are usually less expensive, and guidelines are generally more realistic and operational. In addition, effective self-regulatory programs reduce the need to expand government bureaucracy. However, these programs have several limitations. When a trade association creates a set of industry guidelines for its members, nonmember firms do not have to abide by them. Furthermore, many self-regulatory programs lack the tools or authority to enforce guidelines. Finally, guidelines in self-regulatory programs are often less strict than those established by government agencies.

Technological Forces

The word *technology* brings to mind scientific advances such as computers, DVDs, cellular phones, cloning, robots, lifestyle drugs, lasers, space shuttles, the Internet, and more. Such developments allow marketers to operate ever more efficiently and to provide an exciting array of products for consumers. However, even though these innovations are outgrowths of technology, none of them *is* technology. **Technology** is the application of knowledge and tools to solve problems and perform tasks more efficiently. Technology grows out of research performed by businesses, universities, government agencies, and nonprofit organizations. More than half of this research is paid for by the federal government, which supports research in such diverse areas as health, defense, agriculture, energy, and pollution.

The rapid technological growth of the last several decades is expected to accelerate. It has transformed the U.S. economy into the most productive in the world and provided Americans with an ever-higher standard of living and tremendous opportunities for sustained business expansion. Technology and technological advancements clearly influence buyers' and marketers' decisions, so let's take a closer look at the impact of technology and its use in the marketplace.

technology The application of knowledge and tools to solve problems and perform tasks more efficiently

◆ Impact of Technology

Technology determines how we, as members of society, satisfy our physiological needs. In various ways and to varying degrees, eating and drinking habits, sleeping patterns, sexual activities, health care, and work performance are all influenced by both existing technology and changes in technology. Because of the technological revolution in communications, for example, marketers can now reach vast numbers of people more efficiently through a variety of media. Electronic mail, voice mail, cellular phones, pagers, and notebook computers help marketers stay in touch with clients, make appointments, and handle last-minute orders or cancellations. Telecommuting—using telecommunications technology to work from home or other nontraditional areas—is an increasingly popular use of computer technology. About 28 million employees telecommute for at least part of their workweek, and marketing has become a significant telecommuting job.[19]

Personal computers are now in about 75 percent of U.S. consumers' homes, and millions of PCs include broadband or modems for accessing the Internet. Although we enjoy the benefits of communicating through the Internet, we are increasingly concerned about protecting our privacy and intellectual property. Likewise, although health and medical research has created new drugs that save lives, cloning and genetically modified foods have become controversial issues in many segments of society. In various ways and to varying degrees, home environments, health care, leisure, and work performance are all influenced by both current technology and advances in technology.[20] FCC implementation of wireless portability rules means most phone customers can keep the same number when they switch from regular landline to wireless phones. Within five years, 20 percent of U.S. households may use a cellular phone as their primary phone.[21]

Impact of Technology
Diverse companies like Dell, through research and development, create technologically advanced products.

The effects of technology relate to such characteristics as dynamics, reach, and the self-sustaining nature of technological progress. The *dynamics* of technology involve the constant change that often challenges the structures of social institutions, including social relationships, the legal system, religion, education, business, and leisure. *Reach* refers to the broad nature of technology as it moves through society. Consider the impact of cellular and wireless telephones. The ability to call from almost any location has many benefits but also negative side effects, including increases in traffic accidents, increased noise pollution, and fears about potential health risks.[22]

The *self-sustaining* nature of technology relates to the fact that technology acts as a catalyst to spur even faster development. As new innovations are introduced, they stimulate the need for more advancements to facilitate further development. For example, the Internet has created the need for ever-faster transmission of signals through broadband connections such as high-speed phone lines (DSL), satellites, and cable. Technology initiates a change process that creates new opportunities for new technologies in every industry segment or personal life experience that it touches. At some point, there is a multiplier effect that causes still greater demand for more change to improve performance.[23]

The expanding opportunities for e-commerce, the sharing of business information, and the ability to maintain business relationships and conduct business transactions via telecommunications networks are already changing the relationship between businesses and consumers.[24] More and more people are turning to the Internet to purchase computers and related peripherals, software, books, music, and even furniture. Consumers are increasingly using the Internet to book travel reservations, transact banking business, and trade securities. The forces unleashed by the Internet are particularly important in business-to-business relationships, where uncertainties are being reduced by improving the quantity, reliability, and timeliness of information. Consider the alliance among Ford, General Motors, DaimlerChrysler, Renault, Nissan, Oracle, and Commerce One, which makes parts from suppliers available through a competitive online auction, compacting months of negotiations into a single day. The goal of the alliance is to reduce the time required to bring a new vehicle to market from 54 months to 18.[25] Numerous companies are moving toward making most of their purchases online. Business-to-business Internet sales are more than $5 trillion.[26]

◆ Adoption and Use of Technology

Many companies lose their status as market leaders because they fail to keep up with technological changes. It is important for firms to determine when a technology is changing the industry and to define the strategic influence of the new technology. For example, wireless devices in use today include radios, cellphones, TVs, pagers, and car keys. Figure 3.2 depicts the most popular activities on wireless web devices. In the future, refrigerators, medicine cabinets, and

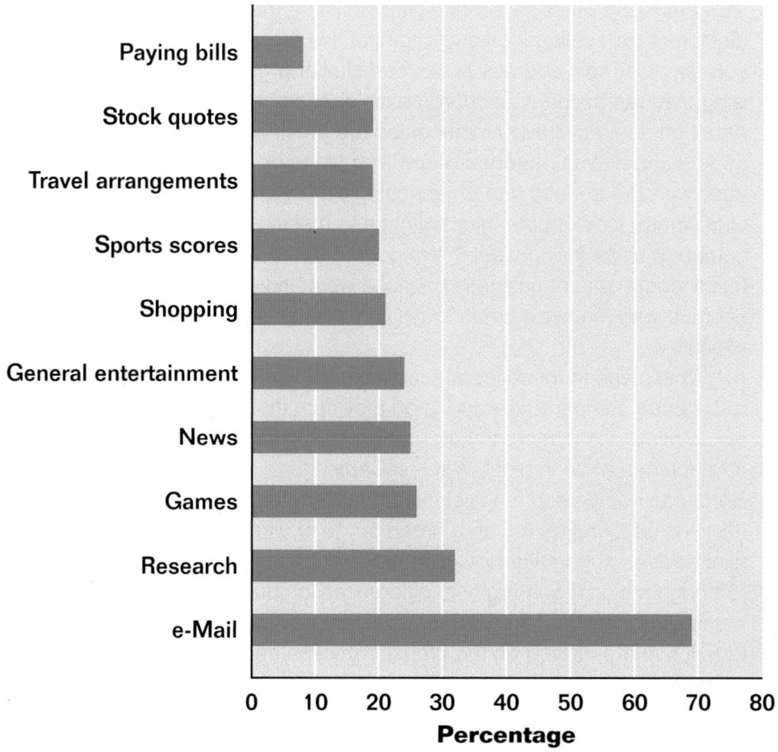

Figure 3.2 Top Ten Activities for Wireless Web Device Users

Source: "New Survey Indicates Wireless Web Penetration Highest Among Young Affluent Males," TNS Intersearch, press release, Feb. 7, 2001, **www.intersearch.tnsofres.com/**.

even product packaging may contain wireless micro devices that broadcast product characteristics, features, expiration dates, and other information.[27] To remain competitive, companies today must keep up with and adapt to technological advances.

The extent to which a firm can protect inventions stemming from research also influences its use of technology. How secure a product is from imitation depends on how easily others can copy it without violating its patent. If ground-breaking products and processes cannot be protected through patents, a company is less likely to market them and make the benefits of its research available to competitors. The challenge of doing this in the cellphone industry is examined in Tech Know.

Through a procedure known as *technology assessment,* managers try to foresee the effects of new products and processes on their firm's operations, on other business organizations, and on society in general. With information obtained through a technology assessment, management tries to estimate whether benefits of adopting a specific technology outweigh costs to the firm and to society at large. The degree to which a business is technologically based also influences its managers' response to technology.

TECH KNOW

Cellphones: Technology Fuels Competition

One day your cellphone is state of the art, the next day it's "so yesterday." Welcome to the cellphone industry, where ever-changing technology is creating almost boundless opportunity as well as intense global competition. The first cellphone marketed by U.S.-based Motorola was both heavy (28 ounces) and expensive ($4,000). Now, 20 years later, Motorola's cellphones weigh a mere 2.8 ounces and sell for a fraction of the original price. In those 20 years, many competitors have entered the $60 billion market on the strength of innovative technology and many have exited because the technology was evolving so rapidly.

The world's top cellphone makers compete by developing new technology to make handsets smaller, lighter, more attractive, and packed with more features and functions. They are also becoming expert in moving technology from market to market according to demand. After Korea's Samsung Electronics began selling cellphones with color screens in Asia,

response was so favorable that the company quickly put the technology into handsets for Europe and the United States. Meanwhile, rivals Motorola and Finland's Nokia had to scramble to catch up.

Competition has become even more intense as cellphone companies race to develop new cellphone technology for wireless web access and e-mail, built-in cameras, electronic games, music players, and video recorders and players. In addition, Palm and other personal digital assistant manufacturers are feeling increased competitive pressure as electronic address books and similar organizing features become standard on cellphones. Although some cellphone companies are thriving through innovation, others are unwilling to keep pace with the frenetic rate of technological change. Qualcomm, for example, has switched to making computer chips for handsets. "We got out of the [cellphone] handset business because we couldn't keep up with the cycle times," says a company executive.

What's ahead for cellphone technology? AirCell, a Colorado company, is working on a system that would allow passengers to safely use a cellphone on airplanes while in flight. WirelessCabin, its European competitor, is developing a system for allowing passengers to use a broad range of wireless devices during flights. Cellphones will be able to bridge national and regional differences in communication network technologies so users can stay in touch in the air and on the ground, anytime and anywhere.

Sociocultural Forces

sociocultural forces The influences in a society and its culture(s) that change people's attitudes, beliefs, norms, customs, and lifestyles

Sociocultural forces are the influences in a society and its culture(s) that bring about changes in people's attitudes, beliefs, norms, customs, and lifestyles. Profoundly affecting how people live, these forces help determine what, where, how, and when people buy products. Like the other environmental forces, sociocultural forces present marketers with both challenges and opportunities. For a closer look at sociocultural forces, we examine three major issues: demographic and diversity characteristics, cultural values, and consumerism.

◆ Demographic and Diversity Characteristics

Changes in a population's demographic characteristics—age, gender, race, ethnicity, marital and parental status, income, and education—have a significant bearing on relationships and individual behavior. These shifts lead to changes in how people live and ultimately in their consumption of such products as food, clothing, housing, transportation, communication, recreation, education, and health services. We look at a few of the changes in demographics and diversity that are affecting marketing activities.

One demographic change affecting the marketplace is the increasing proportion of older consumers. According to the U.S. Census Bureau, the number of people age 65 and older is expected to more than double by the year 2050, reaching 82 million.[28] Consequently, marketers can expect significant increases in the demand for health care services, recreation, tourism, retirement housing, and selected skin care products. Del Webb Development Company is one firm taking advantage of this opportunity by creating several Sun City retirement communities for mature adults. In addition to providing housing, facilities, and activities designed for older residents, Del Webb's newest Sun City is located to take advantage of the scenic beauty and moderate climate of the Texas Hill country, as well as close proximity to cultural events in nearby Austin. To reach older customers effectively, of course, marketers must understand the diversity within the mature market with respect to geographic location, income, marital status, and limitations in mobility and self-care.

The number of singles is also on the rise. Nearly 40 percent of U.S. adults are single, and many plan to remain that way. Moreover, single men living alone comprise 11 percent of all households (up from 3.5 percent in 1970), and single women living alone make up nearly 15 percent (up from 7.3 percent in 1970).[29] Single people have quite different spending patterns than couples and families with children. They are less likely to own homes and thus buy less furniture and fewer appliances. They spend more heavily on convenience foods, restaurants, travel, entertainment, and recreation. In addition, they tend to prefer smaller packages, whereas families often buy bulk goods and products packaged in multiple servings.

The United States is entering another baby boom, with 74 million Americans age 18 or younger. The new baby boom represents 29 percent of the total population; the original baby boomers, born between 1946 and 1964, account for nearly 30 percent.[30] The children of the original baby boomers differ from one another radically in terms of race, living arrangements, and socioeconomic status. Thus, the newest baby boom is much more diverse than previous generations.

Another noteworthy population trend is the increasingly multicultural nature of U.S. society. The number of immigrants into the United States has steadily risen during the last 40 years. In the 1960s, 3.3 million people immigrated to the United States; in the 1970s, 4.5 million came here; in the 1980s, 7.6 million arrived; and in the 1990s, the United States received 7.3 million legal immigrants.[31]

In contrast to earlier immigrants, very few recent ones are of European origin. Another reason for the increasing cultural diversification of the United States is that most recent immigrants are relatively young, whereas U.S. citizens of

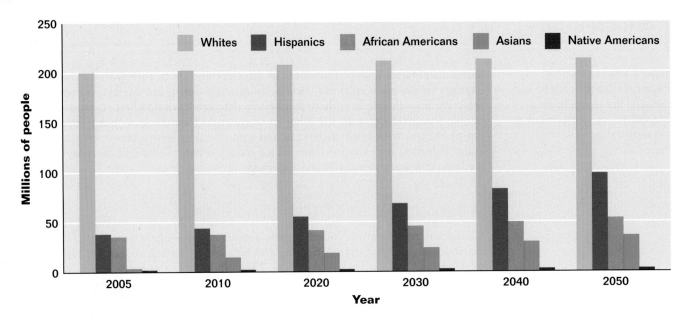

Figure 3.3 U.S. Population Projections by Race

Source: Bureau of the Census, *Statistical Abstract of the United States, 2000* (Washington, DC: Government Printing Office, 2002), p. 16.

NET SIGHTS

The U.S. government compiles a staggering amount of demographic data on American citizens that marketers can mine for information about specific target markets. Much of this information is available in the annual Statistical Abstract of the United States (**www.census.gov/statab/www/**). *In addition, marketers eagerly await the latest results of the decennial U.S. census survey, much of which is accessible at* **www.census.gov**.

European origin are growing older. These younger immigrants tend to have more children than their older counterparts, further shifting the population balance. By the turn of the twentieth century, the U.S. population had shifted from one dominated by whites to one consisting largely of three racial and ethnic groups: whites, blacks, and Hispanics. The U.S. government projects that by the year 2025, nearly 61 million Hispanics, 47 million blacks, 22 million Asians, and 3 million Native Americans will call the United States home.[32] Figure 3.3 depicts how experts believe the U.S. population will change over the next 50 years.

Marketers recognize that these profound changes in the U.S. population bring unique problems and opportunities. Hispanics, for example, generate nearly $653 billion in annual buying power.[33] But a diverse population means a more diverse customer base, and marketing practices must be modified—and diversified—to meet its changing needs. Home and personal care product company Unilever researched what messages appeal to Hispanic women and launched *"Secretos de belleza,"* a beauty secrets campaign honoring Latin women who serve their communities. Burger King sponsored the Latin Grammy Awards, and an "Empowering Latinas" tour by *Catlina* magazine during Hispanic Heritage Month.[34] General Motors increased its minority marketing budget from $70 million to $140 million in 2002 and boosted it more than 50 percent for 2003, recognizing the growing buying power of ethnically diverse customers.[35]

◆ **Cultural Values**

Changes in cultural values have dramatically influenced people's needs and desires for products. Although cultural values do not shift overnight, they do change at varying speeds. Marketers try to monitor these changes, knowing this information can equip them to predict changes in consumers' needs for products at least in the near future.

Starting in the late 1980s, issues of health, nutrition, and exercise grew in importance. People today are more concerned about the foods they eat and thus are choosing more low-fat, nonfat, and no-cholesterol products. Compared to those in the previous two decades, Americans today are more likely to favor smoke-free environments and reduced consumption of alcohol. They have also altered their sexual behavior to reduce the risk of contracting sexually transmitted diseases. Marketers have responded with a proliferation of foods, beverages, and exercise products that fit this new lifestyle, as well as with programs to help people quit smoking and contraceptives that are safer and more effective. Americans are also becoming increasingly open to alternative medicines and nutritionally improved foods. As a result,

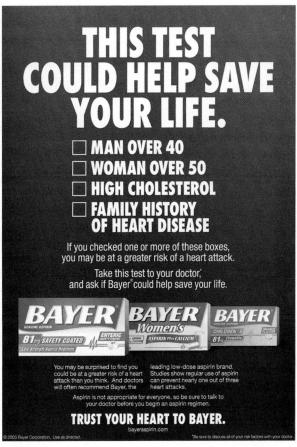

Cultural Values
A number of companies have created products that are consistent with changes in cultural values such as greater emphasis on easy and quick food preparation and preventative medicine.

sales of herbs and herbal remedies, vitamins, and dietary supplements have escalated. More marketers are investing in research into traditional herbal medicines and fortified foods to take advantage of this market opportunity. Celestial Seasonings, for example, has developed herbal teas like Mama Bear's Cold Care, with echinacea and mint, and Sleepytime, with chamomile.

The major source of cultural values is the family. For years, when asked about the most important aspects of their lives, adults specified family issues and a happy marriage. Today, however, only one out of three marriages are predicted to last. Values regarding the permanence of marriage are changing. Because a happy marriage is prized so highly, more people are willing to give up an unhappy one and seek a different marriage partner or opt to stay single. Children remain important, however. Marketers have responded with safer, upscale baby gear and supplies, children's electronics, and family entertainment products. Marketers are also aiming more marketing efforts directly at children because children often play pivotal roles in purchasing decisions.

Children and family values are also a factor in the trend toward more eat-out and take-out meals. Busy families in which both parents work are usually eager to spend less time in the kitchen and more time together enjoying themselves. Beneficiaries of this trend have primarily been fast-food and casual restaurants like McDonald's, Taco Bell, Boston Market, and Applebee's, but 75 percent of grocery stores have added more ready-to-cook or ready-to-serve meal components to meet the needs of busy customers.

Today's consumers are more and more concerned about the natural environment. One of society's environmental hurdles is proper disposal of waste, especially of nondegradable materials such as disposable diapers and polystyrene packaging. Companies have responded by developing more environmentally sensitive products and packaging. Procter & Gamble, for example, uses recycled materials in some of its packaging and sells environment-friendly refills. Raytheon has developed a new Amana refrigerator that does not use chlorofluorocarbons (CFCs), which harm the earth's ozone layer. A number of marketers sponsor recycling programs and encourage their customers to take part in them. Many organizations, including America's Electric Utility Companies and Phillips Petroleum, take pride in their efforts to protect the environment.

◆ Consumerism

consumerism Organized efforts by individuals, groups, and organizations to protect consumers' rights

Consumerism involves organized efforts by individuals, groups, and organizations to protect consumers' rights. The movement's major forces are individual consumer advocates, consumer organizations and other interest groups, consumer education, and consumer laws.

To achieve their objectives, consumers and their advocates write letters or send e-mail to companies, lobby government agencies, broadcast public service announcements, and boycott companies whose activities they deem irresponsible. For example, several organizations evaluate children's products for safety, often announcing dangerous products before Christmas so parents can avoid them. Other actions by the consumer movement have resulted in seat belts and air bags in automobiles, dolphin-safe tuna, the banning of unsafe three-wheel motorized vehicles, and numerous laws regulating product safety and information. We take a closer look at consumerism in the next chapter.

SUMMARY

The marketing environment consists of external forces that directly or indirectly influence an organization's acquisition of inputs (personnel, financial resources, raw materials, and information) and generation of outputs (goods, services, and ideas). The marketing environment includes competitive, economic, political, legal and regulatory, technological, and sociocultural forces.

Environmental scanning is the process of collecting information about forces in the marketing environment; environmental analysis is the process of assessing and interpreting information obtained in scanning. This information helps marketing managers predict opportunities and threats associated with environmental fluctuation. Marketing managers may assume either a passive, reactive approach or a proactive, aggressive approach in responding to these environmental fluctuations. The choice depends on the organization's structures and needs and on the composition of environmental forces that affect it.

All businesses compete for customers' dollars. A marketer, however, generally defines competition as other firms that market products that are similar to or can be substituted for its products in the same geographic area. These competitors can be classified into one of four types: brand competitors, product competitors, generic competitors, and total budget competitors. The number of firms controlling the supply of a product may affect the strength of competitors. The four general types of competitive structures are monopoly, oligopoly, monopolistic competition, and pure competition. Marketers

monitor what competitors are currently doing and assess changes occurring in the competitive environment.

General economic conditions, buying power, and willingness to spend can strongly influence marketing decisions and activities. The overall state of the economy fluctuates in a general pattern known as the business cycle, which consists of four stages: prosperity, recession, depression, and recovery. Consumers' goods, services, and financial holdings make up their buying power, or ability to purchase. Financial sources of buying power are income, credit, and wealth. After-tax income used for spending or saving is disposable income. Disposable income left after an individual has purchased the basic necessities of food, clothes, and shelter is discretionary income. Factors affecting buyers' willingness to spend include product price; level of satisfaction obtained from currently used products; family size; and expectations about future employment, income, prices, and general economic conditions.

The political, legal, and regulatory forces of the marketing environment are closely interrelated. The political environment may determine what laws and regulations affecting specific marketers are enacted and how much the government purchases and from which suppliers. It can also be important in helping organizations secure foreign markets.

Federal legislation affecting marketing activities can be divided into procompetitive legislation—laws designed to preserve and encourage competition—and consumer protection laws, which generally relate to product safety and information disclosure. Actual effects of legislation are determined by how marketers and courts interpret the laws. Federal guidelines for sentencing violations of these laws represent an attempt to force marketers to comply with the laws.

Federal, state, and local regulatory agencies usually have power to enforce specific laws and some discretion in establishing operating rules and drawing up regulations to guide certain types of industry practices. Industry self-regulation represents another regulatory force; marketers view this type of regulation more favorably than government action because they have more opportunity to take part in creating guidelines. Self-regulation may be less expensive than government regulation, and its guidelines are generally more realistic. However, such regulation generally cannot ensure compliance as effectively as government agencies.

Technology is the application of knowledge and tools to solve problems and perform tasks more efficiently. Consumer demand, product development, packaging, promotion, prices, and distribution systems are all influenced directly by technology.

Sociocultural forces are the influences in a society and its culture that result in changes in attitudes, beliefs, norms, customs, and lifestyles. Major sociocultural issues directly affecting marketers include demographic and diversity characteristics, cultural values, and consumerism. Changes in a population's demographic characteristics, such as age, income, race, and ethnicity, can lead to changes in that population's consumption of products. Changes in cultural values, such as those relating to health, nutrition, family, and the natural environment, have had striking effects on people's needs for products and therefore are closely monitored by marketers. Consumerism involves the efforts of individuals, groups, and organizations to protect consumers' rights. Consumer rights organizations inform and organize other consumers, raise issues, help businesses develop consumer-oriented programs, and pressure lawmakers to enact consumer protection laws.

Please visit the student website at **www.prideferrell.com** for ACE Self-Test questions that will help you prepare for exams.

IMPORTANT TERMS

Environmental scanning
Environmental analysis
Competition
Brand competitors
Product competitors
Generic competitors
Total budget competitors
Monopoly
Oligopoly
Monopolistic competition
Pure competition
Business cycle
Prosperity
Recession
Depression

Recovery
Buying power
Income
Disposable income
Discretionary income
Wealth
Willingness to spend
Federal Trade Commission
 (FTC)
Better Business Bureau
National Advertising
 Review Board (NARB)
Technology
Sociocultural forces
Consumerism

DISCUSSION & REVIEW QUESTIONS

1. Why are environmental scanning and analysis important to marketers?
2. What are the four types of competition? Which is most important to marketers?
3. In what ways can each of the business cycle stages affect consumers' reactions to marketing strategies?
4. What business cycle stage are we experiencing currently? How is this stage affecting business firms in your area?

5. Define *income, disposable income,* and *discretionary income.* How does each type of income affect consumer buying power?
6. How do wealth and consumer credit affect consumer buying power?
7. What factors influence a buyer's willingness to spend?
8. Describe marketers' attempts to influence political forces.
9. What types of problems do marketers experience as they interpret legislation?
10. What are the goals of the Federal Trade Commission? List the ways in which the FTC affects marketing activities. Do you think a single regulatory agency should have such broad jurisdiction over so many marketing practices? Why or why not?
11. Name several nongovernmental regulatory forces. Do you believe self-regulation is more or less effective than governmental regulatory agencies? Why?
12. What does the term *technology* mean to you? Do the benefits of technology outweigh its costs and potential dangers? Defend your answer.
13. Discuss the impact of technology on marketing activities.
14. What factors determine whether a business organization adopts and uses technology?
15. What evidence exists that cultural diversity is increasing in the United States?
16. In what ways are cultural values changing? How are marketers responding to these changes?
17. Describe consumerism. Analyze some active consumer forces in your area.

APPLICATION QUESTIONS

1. Assume you are opening one of the following retail stores. Identify publications at the library or online that provide information about the environmental forces likely to affect the store. Briefly summarize the information each source provides.
   a. Convenience store
   b. Women's clothing store
   c. Grocery store
   d. Fast-food restaurant
   e. Furniture store

2. For each of the following products, identify brand competitors, product competitors, generic competitors, and total budget competitors.
   a. Dodge Caravan minivan
   b. Levi's jeans
   c. America Online

3. Technological advances and sociocultural forces have a great impact on marketers. Identify at least one technological advance and one sociocultural change that has affected you as a consumer. Explain the impact of each change on your needs as a customer.

Internet Exercise & Resources

Visit **www.prideferrell.com** for resources to help you master the material in this chapter, plus materials that will help you expand your marketing knowledge, including Internet exercise updates, ACE self-tests, hotlinks to companies featured in this chapter, and much more.

The Federal Trade Commission

To learn more about the Federal Trade Commission and its functions, look at the FTC's website at **www.ftc.gov.**

1. Based on information on the website, describe the FTC's impact on marketing.
2. Examine the sections entitled News Room and Formal Actions. Describe three recent incidents of illegal or inappropriate marketing activities and the FTC's response to those actions.
3. How could the FTC's website assist a company in avoiding misconduct?

Video Case 3.1

Netscape Navigates a Changing Environment

One of the earliest players in the Internet-driven "New Economy" was Netscape Communications. Its best-known product was web-browsing software, but it also offered business software solutions and operated Netscape NetCenter, a popular web portal. Netscape was the fastest-growing software company in history until a bitter fight with Microsoft forced the company to reinvent itself.

Marc Andreessen and Jim Clark founded Netscape in 1994. While a computer science student at the University of Illinois, Andreessen had come up with the idea for a web browser with a graphical user interface (GUI). The Internet was then in its infancy and essentially accessible only to scientists, researchers, government engineers, and a few students with strong computer skills using text-based software. Together with a team of UI students, Andreessen translated his vision into Mosaic, the first GUI web browser, which the university distributed for noncommercial use. Mosaic represented a major technological breakthrough that not only permitted multimedia applications but, for the first time, allowed people with limited computer skills to access the Internet. After Andreessen left the university, he joined forces with Jim Clark to start Netscape.

Within months, the startup firm launched its first product, a new GUI browser called Netscape Navigator. Because of its ease of use and ability to tap into the volume and variety of web information, Navigator became an overnight success and a media star. In Netscape's first year, the number of Internet users grew from 2 million to 15 million and the company earned $45 million in revenues from licensing the browser technology to other companies.

The Web's dramatic growth attracted Microsoft, which saw its potential for commercial uses. By 1995, Microsoft had developed its own web browser, Internet Explorer, and bundled it into the popular Windows operating system. Microsoft executives saw

Netscape as a serious threat because of Navigator's success. According to Netscape's CEO Microsoft's strategy for Windows and Internet Explorer involved nothing short of eliminating Netscape. Together with executives from other firms, Netscape's CEO complained that Microsoft's strategy was anticompetitive and violated federal antitrust laws because it bundled Windows with Internet Explorer, restricted computer manufacturers' ability to install competing browsers (e.g., Netscape Navigator), and offered Internet service providers financial incentives to make Internet Explorer their "preferred" browser.

The effect of Microsoft's strategy was dramatic. In early 1996, Netscape held a 70 percent share of the web browser market and derived about 70 percent of its revenue from licenses. By the fall of 1998, Netscape's share of the market had declined to less than 50 percent, and the company had to literally give the product away to compete with Microsoft. These figures were cited as evidence of "Microsoft's Monopoly" in a lawsuit the federal government and 20 states filed against the software giant in 1998. Microsoft was eventually found guilty of violating federal antitrust laws.

Before Microsoft's trial ended, Netscape was acquired by America Online (AOL), the largest U.S. Internet service provider, as part of AOL's plan to expand its e-commerce profits. AOL then merged with the media giant Time Warner, and, when Microsoft and AOL finally settled their legal differences, Netscape was no longer a major player in browsers. Under the terms of the settlement, Microsoft paid AOL $750 million, and AOL agreed to use Microsoft's Internet Explorer—rather than its own Netscape—as the service's main web browser. At this point, Internet Explorer enjoyed a commanding 96 percent share of the browser market.

Netscape lives on, however, and not just in the operation of the Netscape.com portal. It has also collaborated with Powered Inc. to develop the Netscape Learning Center, which markets fee-based online courses covering such subjects as home videos, entertainment, and money and business. Moreover, high-speed broadband service is becoming more popular in spite of its higher prices, while dial-up customers are clamoring for lower-priced service. Therefore, part of AOL's response to this high-pressure competitive situation has been to put the Netscape brand on a low-priced, basic dial-up Internet service. "The brand still has incredibly strong awareness, very strong positive attributes with consumers," notes one AOL official.

Clearly Netscape is not the high-tech star it once was, thanks to the combination of profound technological changes, powerful legal forces, and shifting corporate priorities. AOL not only has cut the size of Netscape's browser development staff but it has helped fund a new organization, the Mozilla Foundation, to coordinate the work of volunteer programmers on an open-source web browser and software in the Linux tradition. Mozilla promises to bring about yet another evolution in web technology that will profoundly alter the marketing environment in much the same way Netscape's first GUI browser revolutionized the Internet. In this ever-changing environment, what will Netscape do to reinvent itself and serve customers in new ways?[36]

QUESTIONS FOR DISCUSSION

1. What factors in the marketing environment helped Netscape achieve success in such a short time? What factors later harmed the company?

2. What are the advantages and disadvantages of AOL's decision to apply the Netscape brand to a basic dial-up Internet service?

3. Describe the current competitive structure of the web browser industry. What are the implications of this structure for Netscape's future in web browsers?

Case 3.2

Frito-Lay Adapts to Changes in the Environment

Frito-Lay knows that yesterday's recipe for success is not necessarily tomorrow's. Owned by PepsiCo, Frito-Lay sells 15 billion bags of salty snacks every year under such well-known brands as Lay's, Doritos, Cheetos, Tostitos, and Ruffles. The snack food industry has been feeling the effects of concerns about widespread obesity and the health consequences of certain fats. The resulting changes in customer attitudes and regulatory guidelines have prompted Frito-Lay to reformulate both its recipes and its marketing efforts.

Food manufacturers began using partially hydrogenated oils to enhance snack taste and texture after health experts linked saturated fats such as butter and palm oil to higher cholesterol levels and coronary heart disease. Then experts determined that partially hydrogenated vegetable oils, known as trans fats, were also linked to the risk of heart disease and diabetes. In Europe, Unilever took the early initiative in

responding to these concerns by voluntarily reducing or eliminating trans fats. In fact, the success of Unilever's trans-fat-free margarine encouraged competing food manufacturers to introduce margarines made without trans fats.

In the United States, the Food and Drug Administration deliberated for ten years before requiring that the amount of trans fats be identified on food labels. As long as they did not have to change their labels, most major food manufacturers resisted reducing or eliminating trans fats because of the expense of developing new products and changing processing systems. Meanwhile, customers were learning more about the dangers of trans fats, and some were switching to healthier snack alternatives. This benefited companies marketing "all-natural" snacks without trans fats but put more pressure on companies marketing snacks containing trans fats.

Frito-Lay was already offering some low-fat, reduced-fat, and no-fat snacks. For example, it made Lay's potato chips with corn oil rather than trans fats. Parent PepsiCo's senior management also recognized that customers' attitudes toward health and diet were changing. In 2002, PepsiCo invited prominent doctors to a health and wellness conference attended by representatives of Frito-Lay and the other divisions. Frito-Lay's CEO remembers that after the doctors told the group, "The single biggest thing you could do is to eliminate trans fats," he decided to do just that. Although this meant investing in new production technologies and finding substitute ingredients, the CEO was convinced that the reformulated snacks would be more appealing to customers. Moreover, he believed the decision would demonstrate Frito-Lay's leadership within the industry, an important competitive consideration.

Based on this decision, Frito-Lay product developers came up with trans-fat-free recipes, and the company announced the changeover with a $2 million ad campaign during 2003. The headline was clear and to the point: "Great News! America's Favorite Snacks Have 0 Grams of Trans Fats." In addition, the company worked with a doctor to create a special Smart Snack label for products that meet certain nutritional guidelines for calorie, fat, trans fat, and sodium content. Eyeing the growing demand for natural products, it also created a line of natural,

reduced-fat potato chips. "Today's consumers are more aware of what they eat, and we know they want better snack choices," explained Frito-Lay's vice president of North American marketing.

The company was the first in the industry to list trans-fat information on snack food labels, more than two years ahead of the January 2006 deadline for the new labeling set by the Food and Drug Administration. Kraft and other Frito-Lay competitors also prepared for the change by revamping their products to reduce or replace trans fats and adding label information to comply with the new regulations. Nutrition experts agree that eliminating trans fats is a step in the right direction, but some express reservations about promoting chips and similar snacks on the basis of diet and health. "A no-trans-fat potato chip has just as many calories as a trans-fat chip," stresses a spokesperson at the Center for Science in the Public Interest.

Because Frito-Lay had addressed the trans-fat challenge in advance of new food labeling rules, it could seize the opportunity to introduce new flavors and new snacks based on feedback from marketing research. The vice president of potato chip marketing commented, "We're going back to basics with an emphasis on flavor. Consumers told us that flavor is the number one driver for eating chips." Other studies indicated that customers were choosing Procter & Gamble's Pringles crisps over Lay's chips because they wanted a "clean-eating snack." Therefore, after five years of research, development, and testing, the company introduced Lay's Stax, uniform, scoop-shaped potato crisps in a resealable plastic container, to compete head-on with Pringles.

Thanks to the new labeling requirement and increased public awareness of the health risks of trans fats, the snack category will never be the same. Some customers will go out of their way to find snacks without trans fats, and some will use label information to compare the amount of trans fats when choosing among competing brands. Either way, Frito-Lay is in a position to benefit.[37]

QUESTIONS FOR DISCUSSION

1. How did competition affect Frito-Lay's responses to the changes in the marketing environment?
2. How did cultural values affect the decisions made by food manufacturers in the snack food industry?
3. Why would Frito-Lay make a point of being the first food manufacturer to eliminate trans fats from its best-selling snack products years before the new labeling requirement took effect?

Social Responsibility and Ethics in Marketing

4

OBJECTIVES

1. To understand the concept and dimensions of social responsibility

2. To define and describe the importance of marketing ethics

3. To become familiar with ways to improve ethical decisions in marketing

4. To understand the role of social responsibility and ethics in improving marketing performance

If It Sounds Too Good to Be True . . .

The Better Business Bureau (BBB), one of the best-known self-regulatory associations in the United States, works to promote good business practices within communities and is supported by local member businesses. When a company violates bureau standards, the BBB warns consumers through the media. One recent nationwide alert warned college students, high school students, and other young people to beware of potentially fraudulent offers from modeling/talent agencies. Some students who were approached on college campuses and targeted at sporting events and shopping venues have responded to enticing ads promising a glamorous career as a model or an actor. The BBB hopes to educate young people about the potential pitfalls of such offers.

Requests to local BBBs for reports on various modeling/talent agencies have more than tripled during the past two years, an indication that more young people are being approached by such agencies. Many of the 200,000 people who check with the BBB this year will find that the modeling/talent agency they are inquiring about has an unsatisfactory record; unfortunately, some of them will have already signed a contract or paid an upfront fee of $1,000 or more. The number of such complaints processed by the BBB rose by 50 percent in one year alone.

The BBB recommends that anyone considering an offer or advertisement to be a model or an actor take the time to research the business and check references to come to a sensible decision. High-pressure sales tactics may indicate a scam artist: A reputable agency will give interested parties plenty of time and information to make an informed decision. To avoid being conned, the BBB recommends that anyone considering such offers (1) obtain all verbal promises, claims, and agency information in writing; (2) check the complaint history with the local BBB office, as well as the Consumer Protection Agency and the state attorney general; (3) research state laws regarding such agencies and verify any licensing/bonding information; (4) ask for a blank copy of any contract to review before signing; (5) be wary of claims about high salaries, especially in smaller cities or towns; (6) use common sense; (7) avoid giving in to demands for cash; and (8) be wary of promises that a deposit is totally refundable.

BBB records indicate that fewer than half of all complaints against modeling/talent agencies are resolved to the customer's satisfaction, suggesting that the industry has more than a few unsavory operators employing misleading claims and promises to entice unsuspecting consumers. According to the BBB, the quickest way to verify an agency's reliability is to ask for proof of its success. A reputable agency should be willing to provide contact information for models or actors who have secured successful work based on the agency's efforts, as well as information for companies that have hired models or actors trained by the agency. This information should be used to research the agency and determine whether a successful experience is likely.[1] ∎

Most marketers operate responsibly and within the limits of the law. However, some companies, like the fraudulent modeling/talent agencies, choose to engage in activities that customers, other marketers, and society in general deem unacceptable. Such activities include questionable selling practices, bribery, price discrimination, deceptive advertising, misleading packaging, and marketing defective products. For example, 37 percent of the software programs used by businesses worldwide are illegally pirated copies.[2] Practices of this kind raise questions about marketers' obligations to society. Inherent in these questions are the issues of social responsibility and marketing ethics.

Because social responsibility and ethics can have a profound impact on the success of marketing strategies, we devote this chapter to their role in marketing decision making. We begin by defining social responsibility and exploring its dimensions. We then discuss social responsibility issues, such as the natural environment and the marketer's role as a member of the community. Next, we define and examine the role of ethics in marketing decisions. We consider ethical issues in marketing, the ethical decision-making process, and ways to improve ethical conduct in marketing. Finally, we incorporate social responsibility and ethics into strategic market planning.

The Nature of Social Responsibility

social responsibility An organization's obligation to maximize its positive impact and minimize its negative impact on society

In marketing, **social responsibility** refers to an organization's obligation to maximize its positive impact and minimize its negative impact on society. Social responsibility thus deals with the total effect of all marketing decisions on society. Ample evidence demonstrates that ignoring society's demands for responsible marketing can destroy customers' trust and even prompt government regulations. Irresponsible actions that anger customers, employees, or competitors may not only jeopardize a marketer's financial standing but have legal repercussions as well. For instance, after an investigation into mutual fund trading improprieties resulted in civil fraud charges against Putnam Investments, customers withdrew $14 billion from Putnam mutual funds in one week. Although Putnam denied any wrongdoing, CEO Lawrence J. Lasser resigned and the firm remained under investigation in the growing mutual fund scandal.[3] In contrast, socially responsible activities can generate positive publicity and boost sales. The Breast Cancer Awareness Crusade sponsored by Avon Products, for example, has helped raise nearly $250 million to fund community-based breast cancer education and early detection services. Within the first few years of the Awareness Crusade, hundreds of stories about Avon's efforts appeared in major media, which contributed to an increase in company sales. Avon, a marketer of women's cosmetics, is also known for employing a large number of women and promoting them to top management; the firm has more female top managers (86 percent) than any other Fortune 500 company.[4]

AVEDA
the art and science of pure flower and plant essences

beauty rooted in environmentalism.

For more than two decades, Aveda has synergized beauty and well-being with environmental activism. That's why so many of our products, including our new Scalp Benefits™ Balancing Shampoo and Conditioner, are formulated using a richly foaming cleanser and luscious conditioning ingredient derived from certified organic Brazilian babassu nuts—hand-collected and -processed by women's collectives in the eastern Amazon. Our collaboration with these *quebradeiras de coco*, or "coconut breakers," helps them to preserve their traditional livelihood while helping rebuild a biologically rich region of Brazil. And it allows us to find harmony in pleasing our customers while caring for the world.
To find your own balance, find Aveda stores, salons and spas at 800.000.0000 toll-free or www.aveda.com. Ask for Scalp Benefits™—the healthy foundation for healthy hair.

The Nature of Social Responsibility
Aveda recognizes its responsibility to protect the natural environment by gathering the ingredients for its products naturally and sustainably.

Table 4.1	Best Corporate Citizens
1	General Mills
2	Cummins Inc.
3	Intel
4	Procter & Gamble
5	IBM
6	Hewlett-Packard
7	Avon Products
8	Green Mountain Coffee Roasters
9	John Nuveen
10	St. Paul
11	AT&T
12	Fannie Mae
13	Bank of America
14	Motorola
15	Herman Miller
16	Expedia
17	Autodesk
18	Cisco Systems
19	Wild Oats Markets
20	Deluxe

Source: Peter Asmus, with Sandra Waddock and Samuel Graves, "100 Best Corporate Citizens of 2003," *Business Ethics,* **www.business-ethics.com/100best.htm** (accessed Oct. 24, 2003).

Socially responsible efforts like Avon's have a positive impact on local communities; at the same time, they indirectly help the sponsoring organization by attracting goodwill, publicity, and potential customers and employees. Thus, while social responsibility is certainly a positive concept in itself, most organizations embrace it in the expectation of indirect long-term benefits. Our own research suggests that an organizational culture that is conducive to social responsibility engenders greater employee commitment and improved business performance.[5] Table 4.1 provides a sampling of companies that have chosen to make social responsibility a strategic long-term objective.

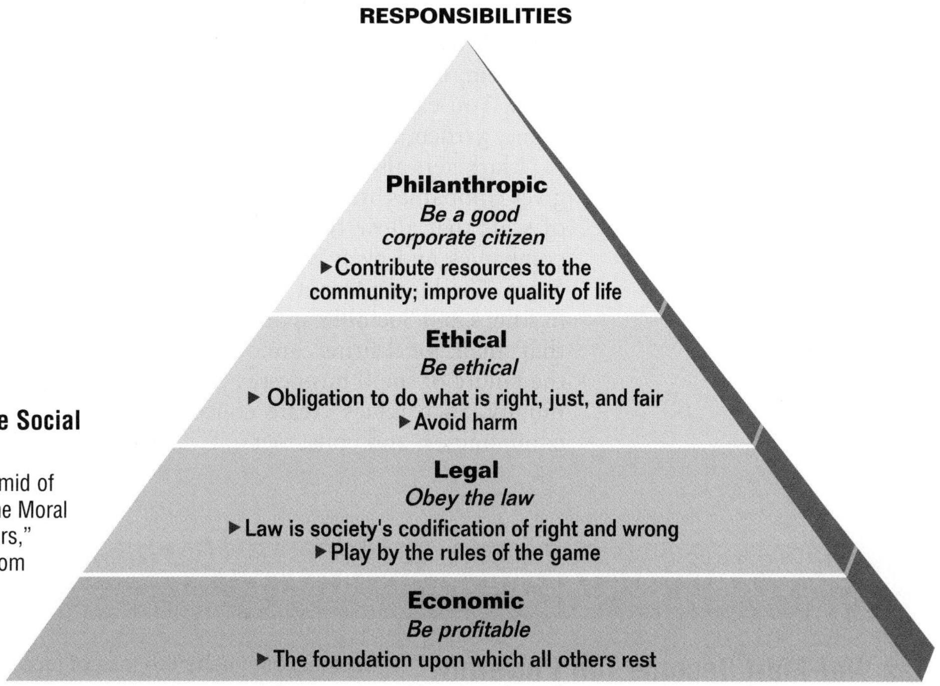

RESPONSIBILITIES

Figure 4.1 The Pyramid of Corporate Social Responsibility
Source: From Archie B. Carroll, "The Pyramid of Corporate Social Responsibility: Toward the Moral Management of Organizational Stakeholders," adaptation of Figure 3, p. 42. Reprinted from *Business Horizons,* July/Aug. 1991. Copyright © 1991 by the Foundation for the School of Business at Indiana University. Reprinted with permission.

marketing citizenship The adoption of a strategic focus for fulfilling the economic, legal, ethical, and philanthropic social responsibilities expected by stakeholders

stakeholders Constituents who have a "stake," or claim, in some aspect of a company's products, operations, markets, industry, and outcomes

◆ The Dimensions of Social Responsibility

Socially responsible organizations strive for **marketing citizenship** by adopting a strategic focus for fulfilling the economic, legal, ethical, and philanthropic social responsibilities that their stakeholders expect of them. **Stakeholders** include those constituents who have a "stake," or claim, in some aspect of the company's products, operations, markets, industry, and outcomes; these include customers, employees, investors and shareholders, suppliers, governments, communities, and many others. Companies that consider the diverse perspectives of stakeholders in their daily operations and strategic planning are said to have a *stakeholder orientation,* an important element of social responsibility.[6] For example, British home improvement retailer B&Q secured stakeholder input on issues ranging from child labor, fair wages, and equal opportunity to environmental impact. Based on consultations with store managers, employees, suppliers, and government representatives, the retailer now recognizes and measures its progress on all four dimensions of corporate social responsibility.[7] As Figure 4.1 shows, these dimensions can be viewed as a pyramid.[8] The economic and legal aspects have long been acknowledged, whereas philanthropic and ethical issues have gained recognition more recently.

At the most basic level, all companies have an economic responsibility to be profitable so they can provide a return on investment to their owners and investors, create jobs for the community, and contribute goods and services to the economy. How organizations relate to stockholders, employees, competitors, customers, the community, and the natural environment affects the economy. When economic downturns or poor decisions lead companies to lay off employees, communities often suffer as they attempt to absorb the displaced employees. Customers may experience diminished levels of service as a result of fewer experienced employees. Stock prices often decline when layoffs are announced, affecting the value of stockholders' investment portfolios. Moreover, stressed-out employees facing demands to reduce expenses may make poor decisions that affect the natural environment, product quality, employee rights, and customer service. An organization's sense of economic responsibility is especially significant for employees, raising such issues as equal job opportunities, workplace diversity, job safety, health, and employee privacy. Economic responsibilities require finding a balance between society's demand for social responsibility and investors' desire for profits. Aaron Lamstein, founder and CEO of WorldWise, says, "You can't put one in front of the other. You can't be successful if you can't do both." Lamstein's company markets home, garden, and pet care products made of recycled or organic materials.[9]

Marketers also have an economic responsibility to compete fairly. Size frequently gives companies an advantage over rivals. Large firms can often generate economies of scale that allow them to put smaller firms out of business. Consequently small companies and even whole communities may resist the efforts of firms like Wal-Mart, The Home Depot, and Best Buy to open stores in their vicinity, as described in Ethics and Social Responsibility. These firms are able to operate at such low costs that small, local firms cannot compete. Though consumers appreciate lower prices, the failure of small businesses creates unemployment for some members of the community. Such issues create concerns about social responsibility for organizations, communities, and consumers.

ETHICS AND SOCIAL RESPONSIBILITY

Has Wal-Mart Become Too Powerful?

When you purchased school supplies or shopped for items for your home or dorm room, did you consider where to go for the lowest prices? If you did, chances are you went to Wal-Mart, a company that lives rigorously by its low-price mantra and, as a result, has come to dominate sales in a number of product categories, including home textiles and personal care items. Wal-Mart is often called a "retail giant" or "retail king," but some argue that these are understatements given the enormous influence the company wields. After all, Wal-Mart is not only the largest retailer, with 4,750 stores around the world, but the world's largest company, with $245 billion in revenues in 2002. A basic issue is that Wal-Mart has gotten so big that it is able to do virtually anything it wants in some areas, and this kind of power has enormous ethical and social implications.

Suppliers report that Wal-Mart is able to dictate almost every aspect of their operations—from product design to pricing—in an effort to deliver maximum savings to the consumer. To meet Wal-Mart's demands for lower prices, some suppliers have been forced to lay off employees or move operations to countries where production costs are lower. Companies that balk risk losing their most lucrative outlet and will find their products quickly replaced by a competitor's on Wal-Mart's shelves.

Wal-Mart stores can also wreak havoc on businesses and workers in communities. After Wal-Mart entered the Oklahoma City market, 30 supermarkets closed their doors. The demise of local businesses means the loss of jobs, and although Wal-Mart may rehire some workers, Wal-Mart employees generally receive lower pay and fewer benefits than workers at other retail stores. Because of the vast Wal-Mart work force, these policies have been blamed for driving down retail wages across America. Other employment issues that have significant ethical and legal ramifications are allegations that Wal-Mart workers have been forced to work "off the clock" and that the company has discriminated against women and minorities in promotions to management positions.

Another consequence of Wal-Mart's dominance is that the company has become, in essence, an arbiter of culture. The retailer is famous for banning music and videos with what it deems objectionable content; it is nonetheless the biggest seller of CDs, videos, and DVDs. Consequently record companies are producing "sanitized" versions of albums exclusively for Wal-Mart. Other products Wal-Mart has chosen not to sell are racy, male-oriented magazines, such as *Maxim,* and the "morning-after" pill that prevents unwanted pregnancy.

Unquestionably there are benefits to Wal-Mart's philosophy: it has compelled suppliers to concentrate on efficiency and to innovate with new products (to become more competitive), revived more than one floundering company, and directly and indirectly saved consumers an estimated $100 billion a year. But the real costs of Wal-Mart's philosophy have yet to be tallied up. As the world's largest company, it must accept the public scrutiny and social responsibilities that come with the territory.

Marketers are also expected, of course, to obey laws and regulations. The efforts of elected representatives and special-interest groups to promote responsible corporate behavior have resulted in laws and regulations designed to keep U.S. companies' actions within the range of acceptable conduct. When customers, interest groups, or businesses become outraged over what they perceive as irresponsibility on the part of a marketing organization, they may urge their legislators to draft new legislation to regulate the behavior or engage in litigation to force the organization to "play by the rules." For example, a California consumer filed suit against J. M. Smucker Company, arguing that the firm's jam labels touting "simply 100 percent" fruit are misleading and in violation of state and federal labeling regulations. Although the company has not commented on the pending litigation, tests found just 30 percent strawberries in the company's strawberry jam and 43 percent blueberries in its blueberry jam. The company's website also indicates that its upscale jams contain fruit syrup, lemon juice concentrate, fruit pectin, grape juice concentrate, and natural flavors. A similar case was filed in Wisconsin.[10]

Economic and legal responsibilities are the most basic levels of social responsibility for a good reason: failure to consider them may mean that a marketer is not around long enough to engage in ethical or philanthropic activities. Beyond these dimensions is **marketing ethics**, principles and standards that define acceptable conduct in marketing as determined by various stakeholders, including the public, government regulators, private-interest groups, consumers, industry, and the organization itself. The most basic of these principles have been codified as laws and regulations to encourage marketers to conform to society's expectations for conduct. However, marketing ethics goes beyond legal issues. Ethical marketing decisions foster trust, which helps build long-term marketing relationships. We take a more detailed look at the ethical dimension of social responsibility later in this chapter.

At the top of the pyramid of corporate responsibility (see Figure 4.1) are philanthropic responsibilities. These responsibilities, which go beyond marketing ethics, are not required of a company, but they promote human welfare or goodwill, as do the economic, legal, and ethical dimensions of social responsibility. That many companies have demonstrated philanthropic responsibility is evidenced by the more than $12 billion in annual corporate donations and contributions to environmental and social causes.[11] For example, Safeway, the nation's fourth-largest grocer, has donated millions of dollars to organizations involved in medical research, such as Easter Seals and the Juvenile Diabetes Research Foundation International. The company's employees have also raised funds to support social causes of interest.[12] Even small companies participate in philanthropy through donations and volunteer support of local causes and national charities, such as the Red Cross and the United Way.

More companies than ever are adopting a strategic approach to corporate philanthropy. Many firms link their products to a particular social cause on an ongoing or short-term basis. One of the first companies to apply this practice, known as **cause-related marketing**, was American Express, which donated to the Statue of Liberty restoration fund every time customers used their American Express card. The promotion was extraordinarily successful, generating new customers and dramatically increasing the use of the company's credit cards. Such cause-related programs tend to appeal to consumers because they provide an additional reason to "feel good" about a particular purchase. Marketers like the programs because well-designed ones increase sales and create feelings of respect and admiration for the companies involved. Some companies are beginning to extend the concept of corporate philanthropy beyond financial contributions by adopting a **strategic philanthropy** approach, the synergistic use of organizational core competencies and resources to address key stakeholders' interests and achieve both organizational and social benefits. Strategic philanthropy involves employees, organizational resources and expertise, and the ability to link those assets to the concerns of key stakeholders, including employees, customers, suppliers, and social needs. Strategic philanthropy involves both financial and nonfinancial contributions to stakeholders

marketing ethics Principles and standards that define acceptable marketing conduct as determined by various stakeholders

cause-related marketing The practice of linking products to a particular social cause on an ongoing or short-term basis

strategic philanthropy The synergistic use of organizational core competencies and resources to address key stakeholders' interests and achieve both organizational and social benefits

Philanthropic Responsibilities
Paul Newman donates all of his profits from his Newman's Own line of products to charity.

(employee time, goods and services, and company technology and equipment, as well as facilities), but it also benefits the company.[13] The Home Depot, for example, has been progressive in aligning its expertise and resources to address community needs. Its relationship with Habitat for Humanity gives employees a chance to improve their skills and bring direct knowledge back into the workplace to benefit customers. It also enhances Home Depot's image of expertise as the "do-it-yourself" center. Home Depot also responds to customers' needs during disasters such as hurricanes. Many home building supply and hardware stores have taken advantage of customers by inflating prices on emergency materials, but Home Depot opens its stores 24 hours a day and makes materials available at reduced costs to help customers survive the disaster.[14]

◆ Social Responsibility Issues

Although social responsibility may seem to be an abstract ideal, managers make decisions related to social responsibility every day. To be successful, a business must determine what customers, government regulators, and competitors, as well as society in general, want or expect in terms of social responsibility. Table 4.2 summarizes three major categories of social responsibility issues: the natural environment, consumerism, and community relations.

Table 4.2	Social Responsibility Issues	
Issue	**Description**	**Major Social Concerns**
Natural environment	Consumers insisting not only on a good quality of life but on a healthful environment so they can maintain a high standard of living during their lifetimes	Conservation Water pollution Air pollution Land pollution
Consumerism	Activities undertaken by independent individuals, groups, and organizations to protect their rights as consumers	The right to safety The right to be informed The right to choose The right to be heard
Community relations	Society eager to have marketers contribute to its well-being, wishing to know what marketers do to help solve social problems	Equality issues Disadvantaged members of society Safety and health Education and general welfare

The Natural Environment. One of the more common ways marketers demonstrate social responsibility is through programs designed to protect and preserve the natural environment. One survey indicated that 83.5 percent of Fortune 500 companies have a written environmental policy, 74.7 percent engage in recycling activities, and 69.7 percent have made investments in waste reduction efforts.[15] Many companies are making contributions to environmental protection organizations, sponsoring and participating in clean-up events, promoting recycling, retooling manufacturing processes to minimize waste and pollution, and generally reevaluating the effects of their products on the natural environment. Wal-Mart, for example, provides on-site recycling for customers and encourages its suppliers to reduce wasteful packaging. Procter & Gamble uses recycled materials in some of its packaging and markets refills for some products, which reduces packaging waste. Such efforts generate positive publicity and often increase sales for the companies involved.

green marketing The specific development, pricing, promotion, and distribution of products that do not harm the natural environment

Green marketing refers to the specific development, pricing, promotion, and distribution of products that do not harm the natural environment. Toyota and Honda, for example, have succeeded in marketing "hybrid" cars that use electric motors to augment their internal-combustion engines, improving the vehicles' fuel economy without reducing their power. Ford Motor introduced the first hybrid SUV, the Escape, in 2005.[16] Herman Miller, Inc., has replaced a number of the glues and finishes used in its ergonomic furniture with more environmentally friendly compounds and chooses woods carefully to ensure they come from renewable sources. The company also encourages its suppliers to switch to reusable packaging materials and designs its production facilities to function as efficiently as possible, thereby reducing waste and energy use.[17]

Many products have been certified as "green" by environmental organizations such as Green Seal and carry a special logo identifying their organization as green marketers. Lumber products at The Home Depot, for example, may carry a seal from the Forest Stewardship Council to indicate they were harvested from sustainable forests using environmentally friendly methods.[18] Likewise, most Chiquita bananas are certified through the Rainforest Alliance's Better Banana Project as having been grown with more environmentally and labor-friendly practices.[19] In Europe, companies can voluntarily apply for an Eco-label to indicate that their products are less harmful to the environment than competing products, based on scientifically determined criteria (see Figure 4.2).

Green Marketing
Hitachi addresses environmental issues such as the reduction of atmospheric CO_2 in efforts to preserve the environment.

Figure 4.2 **The European Eco-label**

Snapshot

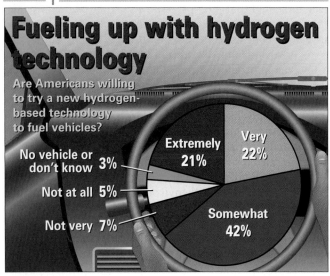

Fueling up with hydrogen technology

Are Americans willing to try a new hydrogen-based technology to fuel vehicles?

- No vehicle or don't know 3%
- Not at all 5%
- Not very 7%
- Extremely 21%
- Very 22%
- Somewhat 42%

Source: Data from Harris Interactive for Millennium Cell and U.S. Borax.

Although demand for economic, legal, and ethical solutions to environmental problems is widespread, the environmental movement in marketing includes many different groups whose values and goals often conflict. Some environmentalists and marketers believe companies should work to protect and preserve the natural environment by implementing the following goals:

1. *Eliminate the concept of waste.* Recognizing that pollution and waste usually stem from inefficiency, the question is not what to do with waste but how to make things without waste.

2. *Reinvent the concept of a product.* Products should be reduced to only three types and eventually just two. The first type is consumables, which are eaten or, when placed in the ground, turn into soil with few harmful side effects. The second type is durable goods—such as cars, televisions, computers, and refrigerators—which should be made, used, and returned to the manufacturer within a closed-loop system. Such products should be designed for disassembly and recycling. The third category is unsalables and includes such products as radioactive materials, heavy metals, and toxins. These products should always belong to the original makers, who should be responsible for the products and their full life cycle effects. Reclassifying products in this way encourages manufacturers to design products more efficiently.

Recycling
EnergyConservationPosters.com makes promotional materials to encourage recycling.

RECYCLE FOR A BRIGHT FUTURE

3. *Make prices reflect the cost.* Every product should reflect or at least approximate its actual cost—not only the direct cost of production but also the cost of air, water, and soil. For example, the cost of a gallon of gasoline, according to the World Resources Institute in Washington, DC, is approximately $4.50 when pollution, waste disposal, health effects, and defense expenditures like those of the Persian Gulf War are factored in.

4. *Make environmentalism profitable.* Consumers are beginning to recognize that competition in the marketplace should not occur between companies harming the environment and those trying to save it.[20]

Consumerism. Another significant issue in socially responsible marketing is consumerism, which we defined in Chapter 3 as the efforts of independent individuals, groups, and organizations to protect the rights of consumers. A number of interest groups and individuals have taken action against companies they consider irresponsible by lobbying government officials and agencies, engaging in letter-writing campaigns and boycotts, and making public service announcements. Indeed, research suggests that angry consumers not only fail to make repeat purchases but may retaliate against the source of their dissatisfaction.[21] The consumer movement has been helped by news-format television programs, such as *Dateline, 60 Minutes,* and *Prime Time Live,* as well as by 24-hour news coverage from CNN and MSNBC. The Internet too has changed the way consumers obtain information about companies' goods, services, and activities.

Ralph Nader, one of the best-known consumer activists, continues to crusade for consumer rights. Consumer activism by Nader and others has resulted in legislation requiring many features that make cars safer: seat belts, air bags, padded dashboards, stronger door latches, head restraints, shatterproof windshields, and collapsible steering columns. Activists' efforts have also facilitated the passage of several consumer protection laws, including the Wholesome Meat Act of 1967, the Radiation Control for Health and Safety Act of 1968, the Clean Water Act of 1972, and the Toxic Substance Act of 1976.

Also of great importance to the consumer movement are four basic rights spelled out in a consumer "bill of rights" drafted by President John F. Kennedy. These rights include the right to safety, the right to be informed, the right to choose, and the right to be heard.

Ensuring consumers' *right to safety* means marketers are obligated not to market a product that they know could harm consumers. This right can be extended to imply that all products must be safe for their intended use, include thorough and explicit instructions for proper and safe use, and have been tested to ensure reliability and quality.

Consumers' *right to be informed* means consumers should have access to and the opportunity to review all relevant information about a product before buying it. Many laws require specific labeling on product packaging to satisfy this right. In addition, labels on alcoholic and tobacco products must inform consumers that these products may cause illness and other problems.

The *right to choose* means consumers should have access to a variety of products and services at competitive prices. They should also be assured of satisfactory quality and service at a fair price. Activities that reduce competition among businesses in an industry might jeopardize this right.

The *right to be heard* ensures that consumers' interests will receive full and sympathetic consideration in the formulation of government policy. The right to be heard also promises consumers fair treatment when they complain to marketers about products. This right benefits marketers too, because when consumers complain about a product, the manufacturer can use this information to modify the product and make it more satisfying.

Community Relations. Social responsibility also extends to marketers' roles as community members. Individual communities expect marketers to make philanthropic contributions to civic projects and institutions and to be "good corporate citizens."

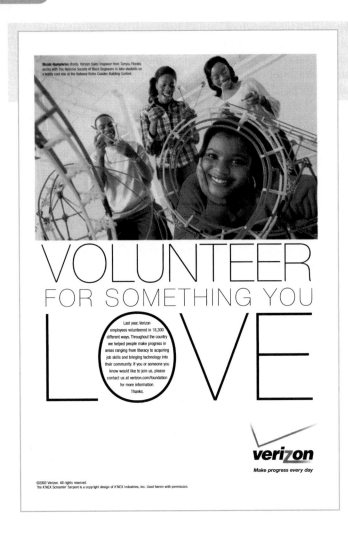

©2003 Verizon. All rights reserved.
The K'NEX Screamin' Serpent is a copyright design of K'NEX Industries, Inc. Used herein with permission.

Corporate Citizenship
Verizon contributes to local communities by encouraging employees to volunteer in areas ranging from literacy to job skills training.

While most charitable donations come from individuals, corporate philanthropy is on the rise. Target, for example, contributes significant resources to education, including direct donations of $100 million to schools as well as fund-raising and scholarship programs that assist teachers and students. Through the retailer's Take Charge of Education program, customers using a Target Guest Card can designate a specific school to which Target donates 1 percent of their total purchase. This program is designed to make customers feel their purchases are benefiting their community while increasing the use of Target Guest Cards.[22]

Smaller firms can also make positive contributions to their communities. For example, Colorado-based New Belgium Brewing Company donates $1 for every barrel of beer brewed to charities within the markets it serves. The brewery divides the funds among states in proportion to interests and needs, considering environmental, social, drug and alcohol awareness, and cultural issues.[23] From a positive perspective, a marketer can significantly improve its community's quality of life through employment opportunities, economic development, and financial contributions to educational, health, cultural, and recreational causes.[24]

The Nature of Ethics

As noted earlier, marketing ethics is a dimension of social responsibility involving principles and standards that define acceptable conduct in marketing. Acceptable standards of conduct in making individual and group decisions in marketing are determined by various stakeholders and by an organization's ethical climate.

Marketers should be aware of ethical standards for acceptable conduct from several viewpoints: company, industry, government, customers, special-interest groups, and society at large. When marketing activities deviate from accepted standards, the exchange process can break down, resulting in customer dissatisfaction, lack of trust, and lawsuits. In recent years, a number of ethical scandals have resulted in a massive loss of confidence in the integrity of American businesses.[25] In fact, 76 percent of consumers say they would boycott the products of a socially irresponsible company, and 91 percent would consider switching to a competitor's products.[26] For example, after 174 deaths and more than 700 injuries resulted from traffic accidents involving Ford Explorers equipped with Firestone tires, Bridgestone/Firestone and Ford Motor Company faced numerous lawsuits and much negative publicity. Ford claimed that defective Firestone tires were to blame for the accidents, while Bridgestone/Firestone contended that design flaws in Ford's best-selling Explorer made it more likely to roll over than other sport-utility vehicles. Many consumers, concerned more for their own safety than with the corporate blame game, lost confidence in both companies and turned to competitors' products.[27] Ethics and Social

Responsibility looks at another scandal-plagued firm. When managers engage in activities that deviate from accepted principles, continued marketing exchanges become difficult, if not impossible. The best time to deal with such problems is during the strategic planning process, not after major problems materialize.

As we already noted, marketing ethics goes beyond legal issues. Marketing decisions based on ethical considerations foster mutual trust in marketing relationships. Although we often try to draw a boundary between legal and ethical issues, the distinction between the two is frequently blurred in decision making. Marketers operate in an environment in which overlapping legal and ethical issues color many decisions. To separate legal and ethical decisions, one must assume that marketing managers can instinctively differentiate legal and ethical issues. However, while the legal ramifications of some issues and problems may be obvious, others are not. Questionable decisions and actions often result in disputes that must be resolved through litigation. The legal system therefore provides a formal venue for marketers to resolve ethical disputes as well as legal ones. Hasbro, for example, filed suit

ETHICS AND SOCIAL RESPONSIBILITY

Qwest Struggles with Legal Issues

Qwest Communications is the local telephone company for 14 states extending from Minnesota west to Washington and southwest to Arizona and New Mexico. Four former executives of the company—the chief financial officer, a senior vice president, the assistant controller, and a vice president—were indicted on criminal charges of fraud. The four were accused of devising a scheme to create more than $33 million in revenue, violating Securities and Exchange Commission (SEC) rules by incorrectly reporting a purchase order with the Arizona School Facilities Board. According to the government, Qwest sold equipment to the statewide school computer network, billed the customer, but then held the merchandise for later delivery. According to government officials, the executives took this action to help Qwest meet its numbers during a difficult time for the company. According to the chairman of the SEC, "Simply put, the defendants couldn't make the numbers work, so they cheated." The Justice Department said the company knowingly filed false documents to hide its actions. The SEC also sought civil penalties against a total of eight former employees, including the loss of salaries and bonuses during the time of the alleged misdeed.

This was not the first time the company has been in trouble.

In 2002, Qwest chief executive Joseph Nacchio resigned under pressure. In his public testimony, Nacchio said he had talked with founder and director Philip Anschutz about all major decisions. Congressional investigators then interviewed Anschutz about his role in the company's day-to-day affairs. Qwest had been investigated by the Justice Department and the Securities and Exchange Commission and was the subject of congressional hearings into its financial practices. The investigations probed whether Qwest artificially inflated its revenues by swapping network capacity with another scandal-plagued company, Global Crossing Ltd. The company restated its financial reports for 1999 to 2001 because of accounting errors and said it would erase $950 million from improperly booked swaps. Still attempting to clean up its image and its books, Qwest announced in February 2003 that $531 million in revenue that was booked prematurely in the last two years would be deferred.

In 2003, Qwest was fined $20.3 million by California regulators for switching customers' long-distance accounts without their permission (a practice known as "slamming") and adding unauthorized charges to their bills (known as "cramming"). At that time, it was the largest fine ever levied against Qwest by a regulatory agency, but Minnesota officials were considering an even larger one. The administrative judge in California cited 3,583 cases of slamming and 4,871 cases of cramming. Qwest said it had disciplined sales agencies that committed the unlawful practices and introduced new procedures to prevent them in the future. California utilities commissioners took Qwest's efforts into consideration before levying the fine, but the commission president said, "This company fixed its systems only after regulators began investigating." The commission also required the company to provide refunds to the affected customers within 90 days.

against a Pennsylvania man who marketed a board game called Ghettopoly. Hasbro's suit accused David Chang's game of unlawfully copying the packaging and logo of Hasbro's long-selling Monopoly board game and causing "irreparable injury" to Hasbro's reputation and goodwill. After minority-rights activists complained that Ghettopoly promoted negative stereotypes of African Americans, some retailers stopped selling the game.[28] Indeed, most ethical disputes reported in the media involve the legal system at some level. In many cases, however, settlements are reached without requiring the decision of a judge or jury.

Before we proceed with our discussion of ethics in marketing, it is important to state that it is not our purpose to question anyone's ethical beliefs or personal convictions. Nor is it our purpose to examine the conduct of consumers, although some do behave unethically (engaging, for instance, in coupon fraud, shoplifting, returning clothing after wearing it, and other abuses). Instead, our goal here is to underscore the importance of resolving ethical issues in marketing and to help you learn about marketing ethics.

◆ Ethical Issues in Marketing

ethical issue An identifiable problem, situation, or opportunity requiring a choice among several actions that must be evaluated as right or wrong, ethical or unethical

An **ethical issue** is an identifiable problem, situation, or opportunity requiring an individual or organization to choose from among several actions that must be evaluated as right or wrong, ethical or unethical. Any time an activity causes marketing managers or customers in their target market to feel manipulated or cheated, a marketing ethical issue exists, regardless of the legality of that activity. For example, organizational objectives that call for increased profits or market share may pressure marketers to knowingly bring an unsafe product to market. Such pressures represent ethical issues. Regardless of the reasons behind specific ethical issues, marketers must be able to identify those issues and decide how to resolve them. To do so requires familiarity with the many kinds of ethical issues that may arise in marketing. Some examples of ethical issues related to product, promotion, price, and distribution (the marketing mix) appear in Table 4.3.

Product-related ethical issues generally arise when marketers fail to disclose risks associated with a product or information regarding the function, value, or use of a product. Most automobile companies have experienced negative publicity associated with design or safety issues that resulted in a government-required recall of specific models. Pressures can build to substitute inferior materials or product components to reduce costs. Ethical issues also arise when marketers fail to inform

Table 4.3	Typical Ethical Issues Related to the Marketing Mix
Product Issue Product information	Covering up defects in products that could cause harm to a consumer; withholding critical performance information that could affect a purchase decision.
Distribution Issue Counterfeiting	Counterfeit products are widespread, especially in the areas of computer software, clothing, and audio and video products. The Internet has facilitated the distribution of counterfeit products.
Promotion Issue Advertising	Deceptive advertising or withholding important product information in a personal selling situation.
Pricing Issue Pricing	Indicating that an advertised sale price is a reduction below the regular list price when in fact that is not the case.

customers about existing conditions or changes in product quality; such failure is a form of dishonesty about the nature of the product. Consider the introduction of a new size of candy bar, labeled with a banner touting its "new larger size." However, when placed in vending machines alongside older candy bars of the same brand, it was apparent that the product was actually slightly *smaller* than the candy bar it replaced. Although this could have been a mistake, the firm still has to defend and deal with the consequences of its actions.

Promotion can create ethical issues in a variety of ways, among them false or misleading advertising and manipulative or deceptive sales promotions, tactics, and publicity. A major ethical issue in promotion pertains to the marketing of video games that allegedly promote violence and weapons to children. Many other ethical issues are linked to promotion, including the use of bribery in personal selling situations. Even a bribe that is offered to benefit the organization is usually considered unethical. Because it jeopardizes trust and fairness, it hurts the organization in the long run.

In pricing, common ethical issues are price fixing, predatory pricing, and failure to disclose the full price of a purchase. The emotional and subjective nature of price creates many situations in which misunderstandings between the seller and buyer cause ethical problems. Marketers have the right to price their products to earn a reasonable profit, but ethical issues may crop up when a company seeks to earn high profits at the expense of its customers. Some pharmaceutical companies, for example, have been accused of pricing products at exorbitant levels and taking advantage of customers who must purchase the medicine to survive or to maintain their quality of life. Another issue relates to quantity surcharges that occur when consumers are effectively overcharged for buying a larger package size of the same grocery product.[29]

Ethical issues in distribution involve relationships among producers and marketing middlemen. Marketing middlemen, or intermediaries (wholesalers and retailers), facilitate the flow of products from the producer to the ultimate customer. Each intermediary performs a different role and agrees to certain rights, responsibilities, and rewards associated with that role. For example, producers expect wholesalers and retailers to honor agreements and keep them informed of inventory needs. Other serious ethical issues with regard to distribution include manipulating a product's availability for purposes of exploitation and using coercion to force intermediaries to behave in a specific manner.

◆ The Ethical Decision-Making Process

To grasp the significance of ethics in marketing decision making, it is helpful to examine the factors that influence the ethical decision-making process. As Figure 4.3 shows, individual factors, organizational relationships, and opportunity interact to determine ethical decisions in marketing.

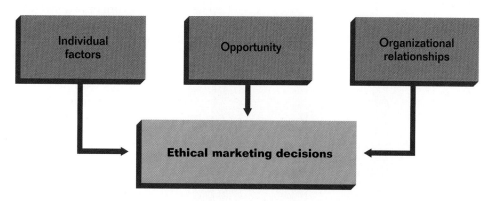

Figure 4.3 **Factors That Influence the Ethical Decision-Making Process in Marketing**

Individual Factors. When people need to resolve ethical conflicts in their daily lives, they often base their decisions on their own values and principles of right or wrong. For example, a study by the Josephson Institute of Ethics reported that seven out of ten students admitted to cheating on a test at least once in the past year, and 92 percent admitted to lying to their parents in the past year. One out of six students confessed to showing up for class drunk in the same period.[30] People learn values and principles through socialization by family members, social groups, religion, and formal education. In the workplace, however, research has established that an organization's values often have more influence on marketing decisions than do a person's own values.[31]

Organizational Relationships. Although people can and do make ethical choices pertaining to marketing decisions, no one operates in a vacuum.[32] Ethical choices in marketing are most often made jointly, in work groups and committees or in conversations and discussions with coworkers. Marketing employees resolve ethical issues based not only on what they learned from their own backgrounds but also on what they learn from others in the organization. The outcome of this learning process depends on the strength of each individual's personal values, opportunity for unethical behavior, and exposure to others who behave ethically or unethically. Superiors, peers, and subordinates in the organization influence the ethical decision-making process. Although people outside the organization, such as family members and friends, also influence decision makers, organizational culture and structure operate through organizational relationships to influence ethical decisions.

Organizational, or **corporate, culture** is a set of values, beliefs, goals, norms, and rituals that members of an organization share. These values also help shape employees' satisfaction with their employer, which may affect the quality of the service they provide to customers. Figure 4.4 indicates that at least 92 percent of surveyed employees who see trust, respect, and honesty applied frequently in their organizations express satisfaction with their employers.[33] A firm's culture may be expressed formally through codes of conduct, memos, manuals, dress codes, and ceremonies, but it is also conveyed informally through work habits, extracurricular activities, and anecdotes. An organization's culture gives its members meaning and suggests rules for how to behave and deal with problems within the organization.

With regard to organizational structure, most experts agree that the chief executive officer or vice president of marketing sets the ethical tone for the entire marketing organization. Lower-level managers obtain their cues from top managers, but they too impose some of their personal values on the company. This interaction between corporate culture and executive leadership helps determine the firm's ethical value system.

organizational (corporate) culture A set of values, beliefs, goals, norms, and rituals that members of an organization share

Figure 4.4 The Relationship of Organizational Values to Employee Satisfaction
Source: Ethics Resource Center, *The Ethics Resource Center's 2000 National Business Ethics Survey: How Employees Perceive Ethics at Work* (Washington, DC: Ethics Resource Center, 2000), p. 85. Reprinted with permission.

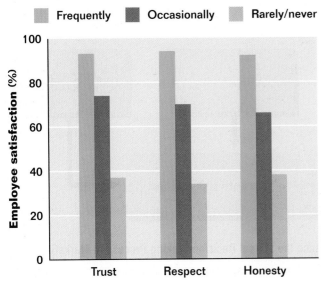

Coworkers' influence on an individual's ethical choices depends on the person's exposure to unethical behavior. Especially in gray areas, the more a person is exposed to unethical activity by others in the organizational environment, the more likely he or she is to behave unethically. Most marketing employees take their cues from coworkers in learning how to solve problems, including ethical problems.[34] Moreover, research suggests that marketing employees who perceive their work environment as ethical experience less role conflict and ambiguity, are more satisfied with their jobs, and are more committed to their employer.[35]

Organizational pressure plays a key role in creating ethical issues. For example, because of pressure to meet a schedule, a superior may ask a salesperson to lie to a customer over the phone about a late product shipment. Similarly, pressure to meet a sales quota may result in overly aggressive sales tactics. Research in this area indicates that superiors and

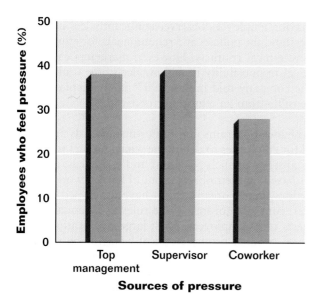

Figure 4.5 Sources of Pressure to Compromise Ethics Standards at Work

Source: Ethics Resource Center, *The Ethics Resource Center's 2000 National Business Ethics Survey: How Employees Perceive Ethics at Work* (Washington, DC: Ethics Resource Center, 2000), p. 38. Reprinted with permission.

coworkers can generate organizational pressure, which plays a key role in creating ethical issues. In a study by the Ethics Resource Center, 60 percent of respondents said they had experienced pressure from superiors or coworkers to compromise ethical standards to achieve business objectives.[36] Figure 4.5 shows the sources of pressure reported by employees. Nearly all marketers face difficult issues whose solutions are not obvious or that present conflicts between organizational objectives and personal ethics.

Opportunity. Another factor that may shape ethical decisions in marketing is opportunity, that is, conditions that limit barriers or provide rewards. A marketing employee who takes advantage of an opportunity to act unethically and is rewarded or suffers no penalty may repeat such acts as other opportunities arise. For example, a salesperson who receives a raise after using a deceptive sales presentation to increase sales is being rewarded and thus will probably continue the behavior. Indeed, opportunity to engage in unethical conduct is often a better predictor of unethical activities than are personal values.[37] Beyond rewards and the absence of punishment, other elements in the business environment may create opportunities. Professional codes of conduct and ethics-related corporate policy also influence opportunity by prescribing what behaviors are acceptable, as we will see later. The larger the rewards and the milder the punishment for unethical conduct, the greater the likelihood that unethical behavior will occur.

However, just as the majority of people who go into retail stores do not try to shoplift at each opportunity, most marketing managers do not try to take advantage of every opportunity for unethical behavior in their organizations. Although marketing managers often perceive many opportunities to engage in unethical conduct in their companies and industries, research suggests that most refrain from taking advantage of such opportunities. Moreover, most marketing managers do not believe unethical conduct in general results in success.[38] Individual factors as well as organizational culture may influence whether an individual becomes opportunistic and tries to take advantage of situations unethically.

◆ Improving Ethical Conduct in Marketing

It is possible to improve ethical conduct in an organization by hiring ethical employees and eliminating unethical ones, and by improving the organization's ethical standards. One way to approach improvement of an organization's ethical standards is to use a "bad apple–bad barrel" analogy. Some people always do things in their own self-interest, regardless of organizational goals or accepted moral standards; they are sometimes called "bad apples." To eliminate unethical conduct, an organization must rid itself of bad apples through screening techniques and enforcement of the firm's ethical standards. However, organizations sometimes become "bad barrels" themselves, not because the individuals within them are unethical but because the pressures to survive and succeed create conditions (opportunities) that reward unethical behavior. One way to resolve the problem of the bad barrel is to redesign the organization's image and culture so that it conforms to industry and societal norms of ethical conduct.[39]

If top management develops and enforces ethical and legal compliance programs to encourage ethical decision making, it becomes a force to help individuals make better decisions. The 2003 National Business Ethics Survey found that ethics programs that include written standards of conduct, ethics training, ethics advice lines or offices, and systems for anonymous reporting increase the likelihood that employees will report misconduct observed in the workplace. The survey results also suggest that when top managers talk about the importance of ethics, inform employees, keep promises, and model ethical behavior, employees observe significantly less unethical conduct.[40] When marketers understand the policies and requirements for ethical conduct, they can more easily resolve ethical conflicts. However, marketers can never fully abdicate their personal ethical responsibility in making decisions. Claiming to be an agent of the business ("the company told me to do it") is unacceptable as a legal excuse and is even less defensible from an ethical perspective.[41]

Codes of Conduct. Without compliance programs and uniform standards and policies regarding conduct, it is hard for employees to determine what conduct is acceptable within the company. In the absence of such programs and standards, employees will generally make decisions based on their observations of how coworkers and superiors behave. To improve ethics, many organizations have developed **codes of conduct** (also called *codes of ethics*) consisting of formalized rules and standards that describe what the company expects of its employees. Most large corporations have formal codes of conduct. Codes of conduct promote ethical behavior by reducing opportunities for unethical behavior; employees know both what is expected of them and what kind of punishment they face if they violate the rules. Codes help marketers deal with ethical issues or dilemmas that develop in daily operations by prescribing or limiting specific activities. Codes of conduct have also made companies that subcontract manufacturing operations abroad more aware of the ethical issues associated with supporting facilities that underpay and even abuse their work force. The American Apparel & Footwear Association, for example, has endorsed the principles and certification program of Worldwide Responsible Apparel Production (WRAP), a nonprofit organization dedicated to promoting and certifying "lawful, humane, and ethical manufacturing throughout the world." Companies that endorse the principles are expected to allow independent monitoring to ensure their contractors are complying with the principles.[42]

Codes of conduct do not have to be so detailed that they take every situation into account, but they should provide guidelines that enable employees to achieve organizational objectives in an ethical, acceptable manner. The American Marketing Association Code of Ethics, reprinted in Table 4.4, does not cover every possible ethical issue, but it provides a useful overview of what marketers believe are sound principles for guiding marketing activities. This code serves as a helpful model for structuring an organization's code of conduct.

codes of conduct Formalized rules and standards that describe what the company expects of its employees

Table 4.4	**Code of Ethics of the American Marketing Association**

ETHICAL NORMS AND VALUES FOR MARKETERS

Preamble
The American Marketing Association commits itself to promoting the highest standard of professional ethical norms and values for its members. Norms are established standards of conduct expected and maintained by society and/or professional organizations. Values represent the collective conception of what people find desirable, important and morally proper. Values serve as the criteria for evaluating the actions of others. Marketing practitioners must recognize that they serve not only their enterprises but also act as stewards of society in creating, facilitating and executing the efficient and effective transactions that are part of the greater economy. In this role, marketers should embrace the highest ethical norms of practicing professionals as well as the ethical values implied by their responsibility toward stakeholders (e.g., customers, employees, investors, channel members, regulators and the host community).

General Norms
1. Marketers must first do no harm. This means doing work for which they are appropriately trained or experienced so that they can actively add value to their organizations and customers. It also means adhering to all applicable laws and regulations as well as embodying high ethical standards in the choices they make.

(continued)

Table 4.4	*(continued)*

2. Marketers must foster trust in the marketing system. This means that products are appropriate for their intended and promoted uses. It requires that marketing communications about goods and services are not intentionally deceptive or misleading. It suggests building relationships that provide for the equitable adjustment and/or redress of customer grievances. It implies striving for good faith and fair dealing so as to contribute toward the efficacy of the exchange process.
3. Marketers should embrace, communicate and practice the fundamental ethical values that will improve consumer confidence in the integrity of the marketing exchange system. These basic Values are intentionally aspirational and include: Honesty, Responsibility, Fairness, Respect, Openness and Citizenship.

Ethical Values

Honesty—this means being truthful and forthright in our dealings with customers and stakeholders.
- We will tell the truth in all situations and at all times.
- We will offer products of value that do what we claim in our communications.
- We will stand behind our produts if they fail to deliver their claimed benefits.
- We will honor our explicit and implicit commitments and promises.

Responsibility—this involves accepting the consequences of our marketing decisions and strategies.
- We will make strenuous efforts to serve the needs of our customers.
- We will avoid using coercion with all stakeholders.
- We will acknowledge the social obligations to stakeholders that come with increased marketing and economic power.
- We will recognize our special commitments to economically vulnerable segments of the market such as children, the elderly and others who may be substantially disadvantaged.

Fairness—this has to do with justly trying to balance the needs of the buyer with the interests of the seller.
- We will clearly represent our products in selling, advertising and other forms of communication; this includes the avoidance of false, misleading and deceptive promotion.
- We will reject manipulations and sales tactics that harm customer trust.
- We will not engage in price fixing, predatory pricing, price gouging or 'bait and switch' tactics.
- We will not knowingly participate in material conflicts of interest.

Respect—this addresses the basic human dignity of all stakeholders.
- We will value individual differences even as we avoid customer stereotyping or depicting demographic groups (e.g., gender, race, sexual) in a negative or dehumanizing way in our promotions.
- We will listen to the needs of our customers and make all reasonable efforts to monitor and improve their satisfaction on an on-going basis.
- We will make a special effort to understand suppliers, intermediaries and distributors from other cultures.
- We will appropriately acknowledge the contributions of others, such as consultants, employees and co-workers, to our marketing endeavors.

Openness—this focuses on creating transparency in our marketing operations.
- We will strive to communicate clearly with all our constituencies.
- We will accept constructive criticism from our customers and other stakeholders.
- We will explain significant product or service risks, component substitutions or other foreseeable eventualities affecting the customer or their perception of the purchase decision.
- We will fully disclose list prices and terms of financing as well as available price deals and adjustments.

Citizenship—this involves a strategic focus on fulfilling the economic, legal, philanthropic and societal responsibilities that serve stakeholders.
- We will strive to protect the natural environment in the execution of marketing campaigns.
- We will give back to the community through volunteerism and charitable donations.
- We will work to contribute to the overall betterment of marketing and its reputation.
- We will encourage supply chain members to ensure that trade is fair for all participants, including producers in developing countries.

Implementation

Finally, we recognize that every industry sector and marketing sub-discipline (e.g., marketing research, e-commerce, direct selling, direct marketing, advertising, etc.) has its own specific ethical issues that require policies and commentary. An array of such codes can be accessed via links on the AMA website. We encourage all such groups to develop and/or refine their industry and discipline-specific codes of ethics in order to supplement these general norms and values.

Source: Copyright © 2004 by the American Marketing Association.

Ethics Officers. Organizational compliance programs must also have oversight by high-ranking persons in the organization known to respect legal and ethical standards. Ethics officers are typically responsible for creating and distributing a code of conduct, enforcing the code, and meeting with organizational members to discuss or provide advice about ethical issues. At MCI, for example, chief ethics officer Nancy Higgins is in the process of revamping the firm's ethics program, after an accounting scandal forced the company—previously known as WorldCom—into bankruptcy. In addition to revising the company's "honor code," Higgins, who reports directly to MCI's CEO, is responsible for providing ethics training for 55,000 employees and identifying regional "ethics advisors" to help employees address ethics issues.[43]

Many ethics officers also employ toll-free telephone "hotlines" to provide advice, anonymously when desired, to employees who believe they face an ethical issue. Since the passage of the 2002 Sarbanes-Oxley Act, more companies have implemented anonymous hotlines for employees to report misconduct; many companies, including Halliburton and Coca-Cola, have contracted the operation of these hotlines to third parties, such as National Hotline Services and Pinkerton Consulting & Investigations. Although the majority of incidents reported to these hotlines have been minor infractions, one caller identified kickbacks from suppliers, and another reported on a multimillion-dollar falsified contract.[44]

Implementing Ethical and Legal Compliance Programs. To nurture ethical conduct in marketing, open communication and coaching on ethical issues are essential. This requires providing employees with ethics training, clear channels of communication, and follow-up support throughout the organization.

Implementing Ethics Programs
Business Ethics magazine makes annual awards to organizations that have excellent ethical performance.

It is important that companies consistently enforce standards and impose penalties or punishment on those who violate codes of conduct. In addition, companies must take reasonable steps in response to violations of standards and, as appropriate, revise their compliance programs to diminish the likelihood of future misconduct. To succeed, a compliance program must be viewed as a part of the overall marketing strategy implementation. If ethics officers and other executives are not committed to the principles and initiatives of marketing ethics and social responsibility, the program's effectiveness will be in question. On the other hand, ethics officers still must focus most of their attention on the development of the organization's culture. While the Federal Sentencing Guidelines for Organizations may have been the chief motivating factor in the creation of ethics offices, a survey of ethics officers reported that 76 percent believe the purpose of their ethics office is to "ensure commitment to corporate values," and 68 percent said they were motivated by the need to establish a better corporate culture. Today the purpose of most compliance programs is not to check off boxes corresponding to the Federal Sentencing Guidelines' seven requirements for a compliance program but to create a values-based corporate culture.[45]

Although the virtues of honesty, fairness, and openness are often assumed to be self-evident and universally accepted, marketing strategy decisions involve complex and detailed matters in which correctness may not be so clear-cut. A high level of personal morality may not be sufficient to prevent an individual from violating the law in an organizational context in which even experienced lawyers debate the exact meaning of the law. Because it is impossible to train all members of an organization as lawyers, the identification of ethical issues and implementation of compliance programs and codes of conduct that incorporate both legal and ethical concerns constitute the best approach to preventing violations and avoiding litigation. Codifying ethical standards into meaningful policies that spell out what is and is not acceptable gives marketers an opportunity to reduce the probability of behavior that could create legal problems. Without proper ethical training and guidance, it is impossible for the average marketing manager to understand the exact boundaries of illegality in the areas of price fixing, copyright violations, fraud, export/import violations, and so on. A corporate focus on ethics helps create a buffer zone around issues that could trigger serious legal complications for the company.

NET SIGHTS

The E-Center for Business Ethics (http://e-businessethics.com) offers a wealth of information about business ethics, corporate citizenship, organizational compliance, and related topics. In addition to specific resources on Internet privacy and corporate codes of conduct, this comprehensive site offers articles, case studies, and games, as well as links to numerous organizations and agencies that support ethics and compliance in business.

Incorporating Social Responsibility and Ethics into Strategic Planning

Although the concepts of marketing ethics and social responsibility are often used interchangeably, it is important to distinguish between them. *Ethics* relates to individual and group decisions—judgments about what is right or wrong in a particular decision-making situation—whereas *social responsibility* deals with the total effect of marketing decisions on society. The two concepts are interrelated because a company that supports socially responsible decisions and adheres to a code of conduct is likely to have a positive effect on society. Because ethics and social responsibility programs can be profitable as well, an increasing number of companies are incorporating them into their overall strategic market planning.

Table 4.5	Organizational Audit of Social Responsibility and Ethics Control Mechanisms

Answer True or False for each statement.

T	F	1. No mechanism exists for top management to detect social responsibility and ethical issues relating to employees, customers, the community, and society.
T	F	2. There is no formal or informal communication within the organization about procedures and activities that are considered acceptable behavior.
T	F	3. The organization fails to communicate its ethical standards to suppliers, customers, and groups that have a relationship with the organization.
T	F	4. There is an environment of deception, repression, and cover-ups concerning events that could be embarrassing to the company.
T	F	5. Compensation systems are totally dependent on economic performance.
T	F	6. The only concerns about environmental impact are those that are legally required.
T	F	7. Concern for the ethical value systems of the community with regard to the firm's activities is absent.
T	F	8. Products are described in a misleading manner, with no information on negative impact or limitations communicated to customers.

True answers indicate a lack of control mechanisms, which, if implemented, could improve ethics and social responsibility.

As we have emphasized throughout this chapter, ethics is one dimension of social responsibility. Being socially responsible relates to doing what is economically sound, legal, ethical, and socially conscious. One way to evaluate whether a specific activity is ethical and socially responsible is to ask other members of the organization if they approve of it. Contact with concerned consumer groups and industry or government regulatory groups may be helpful. A check to see whether there is a specific company policy about an activity may help resolve ethical questions. If other organization members approve of the activity and it is legal and customary within the industry, chances are the activity is acceptable from both an ethical and a social responsibility perspective. Table 4.5 provides an audit of mechanisms to help control ethics and social responsibility in marketing.

A rule of thumb for resolving ethical and social responsibility issues is that if an issue can withstand open discussion that results in agreement or limited debate, an acceptable solution may exist. Nevertheless, even after a final decision is reached, different viewpoints on the issue may remain. Openness is not the end-all solution to the ethics problem. However, it creates trust and facilitates learning relationships.[46]

◆ Being Socially Responsible and Ethical Is Not Easy

To promote socially responsible and ethical behavior while achieving organizational goals, marketers must monitor changes and trends in society's values. In response to the increasing popularity of low-carbohydrate diets, for example, a number of companies have developed and marketed "low-carb" products ranging from bread and tortillas to beer.[47] Likewise, when consumers began to demand greater transparency, or openness, from companies in the wake of a number of ethics scandals, transparency became a factor in most marketing and management decisions.[48] An organization's top management must assume some responsibility for employees' conduct by establishing and enforcing policies that address society's desires.

After determining what society wants, marketers must attempt to predict the long-term effects of decisions pertaining to those wants. Specialists outside the company, such as doctors, lawyers, and scientists, are often consulted, but sometimes there is a lack of agreement within a discipline as to what is an acceptable marketing decision. Forty years ago, for example, tobacco marketers promoted cigarettes as being good for one's health. Today, years after the discovery that cigarette smoking is linked to cancer and other medical problems, society's attitude toward smoking has changed, and marketers face new social responsibilities, such as providing a smoke-free atmosphere for customers. Most major hotel chains allocate at least some of their rooms to nonsmokers, many rental car companies provide smoke-free cars, and most other businesses within the food, travel, and entertainment industries provide smoke-free environments or sections.

Many of society's demands impose costs. For example, society wants a cleaner environment and the preservation of wildlife and their habitats, but it also wants low-priced products. Consider the plight of the gas station owner who asked his customers if they would be willing to spend an additional 1 cent per gallon if he instituted an air filtration system to eliminate harmful fumes. The majority indicated they supported his plan. However, when the system was installed and the price increased, many customers switched to a lower-cost competitor across the street. Thus, companies must carefully balance the costs of providing low-priced products against the costs of manufacturing, packaging, and distributing their products in an environmentally responsible manner.

In trying to satisfy the desires of one group, marketers may dissatisfy others. Regarding the smoking debate, for example, marketers must balance nonsmokers' desire for a smoke-free environment against smokers' desire, or need, to continue to smoke. Some anti-tobacco crusaders call for the complete elimination of tobacco products to ensure a smoke-free world. However, this attitude fails to consider the difficulty smokers have in quitting (now that tobacco marketers have admitted their product is addictive) and the impact on U.S. communities and states that depend on tobacco crops for their economic survival. Thus, this issue, like most ethical and social responsibility issues, cannot be viewed in black and white.

Balancing society's demands to satisfy all members of society is difficult, if not impossible. Marketers must evaluate the extent to which members of society are willing to pay for what they want. For instance, customers may want more information about a product but be unwilling to pay the costs the firm incurs in providing the data. Marketers who want to make socially responsible decisions may find the task a challenge because, ultimately, they must ensure their economic survival.

◆ Social Responsibility and Ethics Improve Marketing Performance

Do not think, however, that the challenge is not worth the effort. On the contrary, increasing evidence indicates that being socially responsible and ethical pays off. Research suggests that a relationship exists between a marketing orientation and an organizational climate that supports marketing ethics and social responsibility. This relationship implies that being ethically and socially concerned is consistent with meeting the demands of customers and other stakeholders. By encouraging employees to understand their markets, companies can help them respond to stakeholders' demands.[49]

You see kids waiting for a bus.

We see a neighborhood waiting for a dentist.

So we brought the dentist to them. Working in partnership with dental programs from across the country, Crest is reaching out to kids and neighborhoods with a fleet of vans that are actual traveling dentist offices. These vans have kept over 73,000 appointments since October 2001, and that's just a start. Because we'll go to any length to get kids on the road to healthy, beautiful smiles for life.

Crest

Healthy, beautiful smiles for life.

Planning for Social Responsibility Crest responds to the need for better dental care in some neighborhoods across the country by providing a fleet of vans with traveling dental offices.

A survey of marketing managers found a direct association between corporate social responsibility and profits.[50] In a survey of consumers, nearly 90 percent indicated that when quality, service, and price are equal among competitors, they would be more likely to buy from the company with the best reputation for social responsibility. In addition, 54 percent would pay more for a product that supports a cause they care about, 66 percent would switch brands to support such a cause, and 62 percent would switch retailers.[51]

Thus, recognition is growing that the long-term value of conducting business in a socially responsible manner far outweighs short-term costs.[52] Companies that fail to develop strategies and programs to incorporate ethics and social responsibility into their organizational culture may pay the price with poor marketing performance and the potential costs of legal violations, civil litigation, and damaging publicity when questionable activities are made public. Because marketing ethics and social responsibility are not always viewed as organizational performance issues, many managers do not believe they need to consider them in the strategic planning process. Individuals also have different ideas as to what is ethical or unethical, leading them to confuse the need for workplace ethics and the right to maintain their own personal values and ethics. While the concepts are undoubtedly controversial, it is possible—and desirable—to incorporate ethics and social responsibility into the planning process.

SUMMARY

Social responsibility refers to an organization's obligation to maximize its positive impact and minimize its negative impact on society. It deals with the total effect of all marketing decisions on society. Although social responsibility is a positive concept, most organizations embrace it in the expectation of indirect long-term benefits.

Marketing citizenship involves adopting a strategic focus for fulfilling the economic, legal, ethical, and philanthropic social responsibilities expected of organizations by their stakeholders, those constituents who have a stake, or claim, in some aspect of the company's products, operations, markets, industry, and outcomes. At the most basic level, companies have an economic responsibility to be profitable so they can provide a return on investment to their stockholders, create jobs for the community, and contribute goods and services to the economy. Marketers are also expected to obey laws and regulations. Marketing ethics refers to principles and standards that define acceptable conduct in marketing as determined by various stakeholders, including the public, government regulators, private-interest groups, industry, and the organization itself. Philanthropic responsibilities go beyond marketing ethics; they are not required of a company, but they promote human welfare or goodwill. Many firms use cause-related marketing, the practice of linking products to a social cause on an ongoing or short-term basis. Strategic philanthropy is the synergistic use of organizational core competencies and resources to address key stakeholders' interests and achieve both organizational and social benefits.

Three major categories of social responsibility issues are the natural environment, consumerism, and community relations. One of the more common ways marketers demonstrate social responsibility is through programs designed to protect and preserve the natural environment. Green marketing refers to the specific development, pricing, promotion, and distribution of products that do not harm the environment. Consumerism consists of the efforts of independent individuals, groups, and organizations to protect the rights of consumers. Consumers expect to have the right to safety, the right to be informed, the right to choose, and the right to be heard. Many marketers view social responsibility as including contributions of resources (money, products, and time) to community causes such as the natural environment, arts and recreation, disadvantaged members of the community, and education.

Whereas social responsibility is achieved by balancing the interests of all stakeholders in the organization, ethics relates to acceptable standards of conduct in making individual and group decisions. Marketing ethics goes beyond legal issues. Ethical marketing decisions foster mutual trust in marketing relationships.

An ethical issue is an identifiable problem, situation, or opportunity requiring an individual or organization to choose from among several actions that must be evaluated as right or wrong, ethical or unethical. A number of ethical issues relate to the marketing mix (product, promotion, price, and distribution).

Individual factors, organizational relationships, and opportunity interact to determine ethical decisions in marketing. Individuals often base their decisions on their own values and principles of right or wrong. However, ethical choices in marketing are most often made jointly, in work groups and committees or in conversations and discussions with coworkers. Organizational culture and structure operate through organizational relationships (with superiors, peers, and subordinates) to influence ethical decisions. Organizational, or corporate, culture is a set of values, beliefs, goals, norms, and rituals that members of an organization share. The more a person is exposed to unethical activity by others in the organizational environment, the more likely he or she is to behave unethically. Organizational pressure plays a key role in creating ethical issues, as does opportunity, conditions that limit barriers or provide rewards.

It is possible to improve ethical behavior in an organization by hiring ethical employees and eliminating unethical ones, and by improving the organization's ethical standards. If top management develops and enforces ethics and legal compliance programs to encourage ethical decision making, it becomes a force to help individuals make better decisions. To improve company ethics, many organizations have developed codes of conduct, formalized rules and standards that describe what the company expects of its employees. A marketing compliance program must have oversight by a high-ranking organization member known to abide by legal and common ethical standards; this person is usually called an ethics officer. To nurture ethical conduct in marketing, open communication and coaching on ethical issues are essential. This requires providing employees with ethics training, clear channels of communication, and follow-up support throughout the organization. Companies must consistently enforce standards and impose penalties or punishment on those who violate codes of conduct.

An increasing number of companies are incorporating ethics and social responsibility programs into their overall strategic market planning. To promote socially responsible and ethical behavior while achieving organizational goals, marketers must monitor changes and trends in society's values. They must determine what society wants and attempt to predict the long-term effects of their decisions. Costs are associated with many of society's demands, and balancing those demands to satisfy all of society is difficult. However, increasing evidence indicates that being socially responsible and ethical results in valuable benefits: an enhanced public reputation (which can increase market share) costs savings, and profits.

Please visit the student website at **www.prideferrell.com** for ACE Self-Test questions that will help you prepare for exams.

IMPORTANT TERMS

Social responsibility
Marketing citizenship
Stakeholders
Marketing ethics
Cause-related marketing
Strategic philanthropy

Green marketing
Ethical issue
Organizational
 (corporate) culture
Codes of conduct

DISCUSSION & REVIEW QUESTIONS

1. What is social responsibility? Why is it important?
2. What are stakeholders? What role do they play in strategic marketing decisions?
3. What are four dimensions of social responsibility? What impact do they have on marketing decisions?
4. What is strategic philanthropy? How does it differ from more traditional philanthropic efforts?
5. What are some major social responsibility issues? Give an example of each.
6. What is the difference between ethics and social responsibility?
7. Why is ethics an important consideration in marketing decisions?
8. How do the factors that influence ethical or unethical decisions interact?
9. What ethical conflicts may exist if business employees fly on certain airlines just to receive benefits for their personal "frequent flier" programs?
10. Give an example of how ethical issues can affect each component of the marketing mix.
11. How can the ethical decisions involved in marketing be improved?
12. How can people with different personal values work together to make ethical decisions in organizations?

13. What tradeoffs might a company have to make to be socially responsible and responsive to society's demands?
14. What evidence exists that being socially responsible and ethical is worthwhile?

APPLICATION QUESTIONS

1. Some organizations promote their social responsibility. These companies often claim that being ethical is good business and that it pays to be a "good corporate citizen." Identify an organization in your community that has a reputation for being ethical and socially responsible. What activities account for this image? Is the company successful? Why or why not?
2. If you had to conduct a social audit of your organization's ethics and social responsibility, what information would most interest you? What key stakeholders would you want to communicate with? How could such an audit assist the company in improving its ethics and social responsibility?
3. Suppose that in your job you face situations that require you to make decisions about what is right or wrong and then act on these decisions. Describe such a situation. Without disclosing your actual decision, explain what you based it on. What and whom did you think of when you were considering what to do? Why did you consider them?
4. Consumers interact with many businesses daily and weekly. Not only do companies in an industry acquire a reputation for being ethical or unethical; entire industries also become known as ethical or unethical. Identify two types of businesses with which you or others you know have had the most conflict involving ethical issues. Describe those ethical issues.

Internet Exercise & Resources

Visit **www.prideferrell.com** for resources to help you master the material in this chapter, plus materials that will help you expand your marketing knowledge, including Internet exercise updates, ACE self-tests, hotlinks to companies featured in this chapter, and much more.

Business for Social Responsibility

Business for Social Responsibility (BSR) is a nonprofit organization for companies desiring to operate responsibly and demonstrate respect for ethical values, people, communities, and the natural environment. Founded in 1992, BSR offers members practical information, research, educational programs, and technical assistance as well as the opportunity to network with peers on current social responsibility issues. To learn more about this organization and access its many resources, visit **www.bsr.org**.

1. What types of businesses join BSR, and why?
2. Describe the services available to member companies. How can these services help companies improve their performance?
3. Peruse the "Issue Briefs" and find the reports on ethics codes and training. Using these reports, list some examples of corporate codes of ethics and training.

Video Case 4.1

New Belgium Brewing Company

The idea for New Belgium Brewing Company (NBB) began with a bicycling trip through Belgium, where some of the world's finest ales have been brewed for centuries. As Jeff Lebesch, an American electrical engineer, cruised around the country on a fat-tired mountain bike, he wondered if he could produce such high-quality ales in his home state of Colorado. After returning home, Lebesch began to experiment in his Fort Collins basement. When his home-brewed experiments earned rave reviews from friends, Lebesch and his wife, Kim Jordan, decided to open the New Belgium Brewing Company in 1991. They named their first brew Fat Tire Amber Ale in honor of Lebesch's Belgian biking adventure.

Today New Belgium markets a variety of permanent and seasonal ales and pilsners. The standard line includes Sunshine Wheat, Blue Paddle Pilsner, Abbey Ale, Trippel Ale, and 1554 Black Ale, as well as the firm's number one seller, the original Fat Tire Amber Ale. NBB also markets seasonal beers, such as Frambozen and Abbey Grand Cru, released at Thanksgiving, and Christmas and Farmhouse Ale, sold during the early fall months. The firm also occasionally offers one-time-only brews—such as LaFolie, a wood-aged beer—that are sold only until the batch runs out. Bottle label designs employ "good ol' days" nostalgia. The Fat Tire label, for example, features an old-style cruiser bike with wide tires, a padded seat, and a basket hanging from the handlebars. All the label and packaging designs were created by the same watercolor artist, Jeff Lebesch's next-door neighbor.

Although Fat Tire was initially sold only in Fort Collins, distribution quickly expanded throughout the rest of Colorado. Customers can now find Fat Tire and other New Belgium offerings in 13 western states, including Washington, Montana, Texas, New Mexico, and Arizona. The brewery regularly receives e-mails and telephone inquiries as to when New Belgium beers will be available elsewhere.

Since its founding, NBB's most effective promotion has been via word-of-mouth advertising by devoted customers. The company avoids mass advertising because it doesn't fit the image NBB wants to project. Instead the brewery relies on small-scale, local promotions, such as print advertisements in alternative magazines, participation in local festivals, and sponsorship of alternative sports events. Through event sponsorships, such as the Tour de Fat and Ride the Rockies, NBB has raised thousands of dollars for various environmental, social, and cycling nonprofit organizations.

New Belgium beers are priced to reflect their quality at about $7 per six-pack. This pricing strategy conveys the message that the products are special and of consistently higher quality than macrobrews, such as Budweiser and Coors, but also keeps them competitive with other microbrews, such as Pete's Wicked Ale, Pyramid Pale Ale, and Sierra Nevada. To demonstrate its appreciation for its retailers and business partners, New Belgium does not sell beer to consumers on-site at the brewhouse for less than the retailers charge.

NBB's marketing strategy involves pairing the quality of its products, as well as their names and looks, with a concern for how the company's activities affect the natural environment. The brewery looks for cost-efficient, energy-saving alternatives to conducting business and reducing its impact on the environment. Thus, the company's employee-owners unanimously agreed to invest in a wind turbine, making NBB the first fully wind-powered brewery in the United States. Since the switch from coal power, NBB has reduced its CO_2 emissions by 1,800 metric tons per year. The company further reduces its energy use with a steam condenser that captures and reuses the hot water from boiling the barley and hops in the production process to start the next brew; the steam is redirected to heat the floor tiles and de-ice the loading docks in cold weather. NBB also strives to recycle as many supplies as possible, including cardboard boxes, keg caps, office materials, and the amber glass used in bottling. New Belgium has recycled tons of amber glass, cardboard, and shrink-wrap. The brewery also stores spent barley and hop grains in an on-premise silo and invites local farmers to pick up the grains, free of charge, to feed their pigs. Another way NBB conserves energy is through the use of "sun tubes," which provide natural daytime lighting throughout the brewhouse all year long. NBB also encourages employees to reduce air pollution through alternative transportation. As an incentive, NBB gives each employee a "cruiser bike"—just like the one on the Fat Tire Amber Ale label—after one year of employment to encourage biking to work.

Beyond its use of environment-friendly technologies and innovations, New Belgium Brewing Company strives to improve communities and enhance lives through corporate giving, event sponsorship, and philanthropic involvement. The company donates $1 per barrel of beer sold to various cultural, social, environmental, and drug and alcohol awareness programs across the 13 western states in which it distributes beer. Typical grants range from $2,500 to $5,000. Involvement is spread equally among the 13 states, unless a special need requires greater participation or funding. The brewhouse also maintains a community board where organizations can post community involvement activities and proposals. This board allows tourists and employees to see opportunities to help out the community and provides nonprofit organizations with a forum for making their needs known. Organizations can also apply for grants through the New Belgium Brewing Company website, which has a link designated for this purpose.

New Belgium's commitment to quality, the environment, and its employees and customers is clearly expressed in its stated purpose: "To operate a profitable brewery which makes our love and talent manifest." This dedication has been well rewarded with loyal customers and industry awards. It was one of three winners of *Business Ethics* magazine's 2002 Business Ethics Awards for its "dedication to environmental excellence in every part of its innovative brewing process." It also won an honorable mention in the Better Business Bureau's 2002 Torch Award for Outstanding Marketplace Ethics competition. The company has also earned awards for best mid-size

brewing company of the year and best mid-size brewmaster at the Great American Beer Festival, while Jeff Lebesch and Kim Jordan were named the recipients of the Rocky Mountain Region Entrepreneur of the Year Award for manufacturing. New Belgium also took home medals for three different brews: Abbey Belgian Style Ale, Blue Paddle Pilsner, and LaFolie specialty ale.

From cutting-edge environmental programs and high-tech industry advancements to employee-ownership programs and a strong belief in giving back to the community, New Belgium demonstrates its desire to create a living, learning community. According to David Edgar, director of the Institute for Brewing Studies, "They've created a very positive image for their company in the beer-consuming public with smart decision making." Although some members of society do not believe a brewery can be socially responsible, New Belgium has set out to prove that for those who make the choice to drink responsibly, the company can do everything possible to contribute to society.[53]

QUESTIONS FOR DISCUSSION

1. What steps has New Belgium Brewing Company taken to be socially responsible?

2. As a smaller business, how can New Belgium justify donating $1 per barrel of beer sold to environmental and community causes?

3. Some segments of society contend that companies that sell alcoholic beverages cannot be socially responsible organizations because of the inherent nature of their products. Do you believe New Belgium Brewing Company's actions and initiatives make it a socially responsible business? Why or why not?

Case 4.2

Scandal at Martha Stewart Living Omnimedia Inc.

Martha Stewart is one of the latest chief executive officers to become embroiled in a series of corporate scandals across the United States. Born Martha Kostyra, she developed a passion for cooking, gardening, and homemaking. She

became Martha Stewart when she married in her sophomore year. Although she became a successful stockbroker on Wall Street, she left to open a gourmet-food shop that later became a catering business in Westport, Connecticut. In 2001, America's most famous homemaker and one of its richest women executives became the center of headlines, talk-show fodder, and ultimately a federal investigation and indictment on charges related to her sale of nearly 4,000 shares of ImClone stock one day before that firm's stock price plummeted.

Stewart's natural business instincts and leadership skills helped her make smart choices as she transformed her small business into a media empire and her name into a well-recognized brand. She founded Martha Stewart Living Omnimedia Inc. and eventually took her rapidly growing business public in 1999. Her company now owns three magazines, a TV and cable program, 34 books, a newspaper column, a radio program, a website, and a merchandising line, as well as the Martha by Mail catalog business. The company earns 65 percent of its revenues from publishing, and its media properties reach 88 million people a month around the world.

Despite her reputation and business successes, Stewart was indicted in 2003 on criminal charges and faced several civil lawsuits related to her sale of the ImClone stock. Stewart sold the stock on December 27, 2001, one day before the Food and Drug Administration refused to review ImClone System's cancer drug Erbitux; the company's stock tumbled following the FDA's announcement. Stewart denied that she had engaged in any improper trading when she sold her shares of ImClone stock. Stewart claimed she was flying in her private jet to Mexico for a vacation with two friends on December 27. En route, she called her office to check her messages, which included one from her broker, Peter Bacanovic, with news that her ImClone stock had dropped below $60 per share. Stewart claimed she had previously issued a stop-loss order to sell the ImClone stock if it fell below $60 per share. Stewart called Bacanovic and asked him to sell her 3,928 shares. She also called her friend Sam Waksal, but could not reach him. Stewart's assistant left a message for Waksal: "Something's going on with ImClone, and she wants to know what it is. She's staying at Los Ventanos." Waksal did not call her back. However, Stewart's explanation that she unloaded her stock because of a prearranged sell order fell apart when Douglas Faneuil, Bacanovic's assistant who handled the sale of the ImClone stock for Stewart, told Merrill Lynch lawyers that Bacanovic had pressured him to lie about a stop-loss order.

On June 4, 2003, a federal grand jury indicted Stewart on charges of securities fraud, conspiracy (together with Peter Bacanovic), making false statements, and obstruction of justice. The 41-page indictment alleged that she had lied to federal investigators about the stock sale, attempted to cover up her activities, and defrauded Martha Stewart Living Omnimedia shareholders by misleading them about the gravity of the situation and thereby keeping the stock price from falling. The indictment further accused Stewart of deleting a computer log of the telephone message from Bacanovic informing her that he thought ImClone's stock "was going to start trading downward." Bacanovic was also indicted on charges of making false statements, making and using false documents, perjury, and obstruction of justice. The indictment alleged that Bacanovic had altered his personal notes to create the impression of a prior agreement to sell Stewart's ImClone shares if the price fell below $60 per share. Both Stewart and Bacanovic pleaded "not guilty" to all charges. At her trial, the indictment for securities fraud was dropped, but the other indictments were prosecuted. In addition, the Securities and Exchange Commission filed a civil lawsuit accusing both Stewart and Bacanovic of insider trading, demanding more than $45,000 in recompensation and seeking to bar Stewart from being an officer or a director of a public company. Federal law bars officers of public corporations from knowingly making false statements that are material in effect, meaning they have the potential to shape a reasonable investor's decision to buy or sell stock in a particular company. Prosecutors intend to prove that Stewart made a deceptive statement to repair her credibility and keep her firm's stock price from falling. Already one shareholder has filed suit against Stewart. Although Stewart denied the charges, she resigned her positions as chief executive officer and chairman of the board of Martha Stewart Living Omnimedia just hours after the indictment.

After her indictment and resignation, Stewart took out a full-page newspaper ad in which she reiterated her innocence and appealed to her customers to remain loyal. The indictment and 2004 guilty verdict for obstruction of justice have affected Stewart's company: its stock price has fallen by more than 70 percent, and magazine revenues and subscription renewals have declined. According to one estimate, the scandal washed away more than a quarter of Stewart's net worth, estimated at $650 million.

Many wonder whether the firm can recover without Stewart's presence. Separating Martha Stewart from Omnimedia, the company she personifies, would be no simple task. Her most important role in the company is as its highly recognizable spokesperson, brand, and television personality. Finding someone to fill that role would be far more difficult than finding a replacement chairperson and CEO.

The scandal occurred at an unfortunate time for Martha Stewart Living Omnimedia. The company's publishing arm was in its mature stage, its television show was suffering declining ratings, and its Internet operation was taking heavy losses. Moreover, some market analysts have expressed concern that the company depends too heavily on the name and image of its celebrated founder. Stewart personifies the brand that is associated with her credibility and honesty—traits the public and investors now question. Market analysts agree that Stewart needs to take steps to ensure that the brand can go beyond the person. Although Stewart has taken steps to make her company more independent, doubts about the long-term effects of the scandal remain.

Some observers, however, believe Martha Stewart's drive and spirit will help her overcome this setback. Jerry Della Femina, an advertising executive, said, "The brand will survive because Martha has gone beyond being a person who represents a brand." Before the scandal broke, Stewart was asked about her close ties with her brand. She replied, "I think that my role is Walt Disney. There are very few brands that were really started by a person, with a person's name, that have survived as nicely as that. Estée Lauder has

certainly survived beautifully, despite Mrs. Lauder's absence from the business in the last, maybe, 15 years. I would like to engender that same kind of spirit and same kind of high quality."[54]

QUESTIONS FOR DISCUSSION

1. How has Martha Stewart's involvement in the insider-trading scandal (despite her denial of wrongdoing) affected her company and branded products?

2. When Martha Stewart took out a full-page newspaper ad to proclaim her innocence and appeal to her customers, were her actions ethical? What level of corporate social responsibility does Stewart have to her company and its stakeholders?

3. Will Martha Stewart Living Omnimedia survive in spite of Stewart's 2004 conviction for obstruction of justice? To survive, what changes will need to be made at the company?

Global Markets and International Marketing

5

OBJECTIVES

1. To understand the nature of global markets and international marketing

2. To analyze the environmental forces affecting international marketing efforts

3. To identify several important regional trade alliances, markets, and agreements

4. To examine methods of involvement in marketing activities

5. To recognize that international marketing strategies fall along a continuum from customization to globalization

Starbucks Energizes Consumers Around the World

Starbucks Coffee Company markets gourmet coffees, pastries, and premium coffee beans and blends in more than 6,000 shops around the globe. Since its startup in 1971, the company has done things its own way, becoming an industry pioneer in employee management and social responsibility. Starbucks extends health benefits to all employees, including part-timers, and provides a stock option program worth 12 percent of each employee's base pay. This policy has kept employee turnover rates well below those of competitors and granted the company a spot on *Fortune* magazine's annual list of the "Best Places to Work." The company enjoys an excellent reputation in Latin America as a result of its focus on environmental conservation and the welfare of farmers who grow its coffee beans. Starbucks pays better-than-market-value prices for coffee beans so that Latin American farmers can afford to treat their laborers well. Its efforts have been well rewarded with annual sales in excess of $1 billion, as well as growing acceptance around the world.

Starbucks is now cashing in on its reputation by expanding internationally at an accelerated pace. The company already has more than 1,500 shops in 30 countries outside the U.S., and opens an average of three new stores every day somewhere in the world. In Japan alone, it serves more than 2 million customers a week. Starbucks exceeded its goal of opening 4,000 stores by 2001, and has since altered that goal to 10,000 shops by 2005. The company recently opened its first stores in Turkey, Oman, and Chile.

Starbucks eschews marketing research when entering new international markets. Founder and chairman Howard Schultz says, "Our consultants told us before we went to Japan that there was no way Japanese would be caught dead with takeout coffee on the street. Now, you can't walk five minutes in Tokyo without seeing somebody with a Starbucks cup." Instead the company focuses on doing what it does best: providing a variety of high-quality coffees and a generous selection of pastries in clean, smoking-free shops with plenty of seating. Only time will tell whether this strategy will continue to propel sales in countries where coffee shops are already a way of life.[1] ∎

Before picking up an Egg McMuffin at McDonald's this morning, a young woman in Hong Kong may have brightened her smile with Colgate toothpaste and highlighted her eyes with Avon eye shadow. Her brother, on business that same day in Frankfurt, may cash a check in a local Citicorp branch bank. Elsewhere that day, a Polish office worker may lunch on a pizza from Pizza Hut, fried chicken from KFC, or a taco from Taco Bell. An Australian mother shopping for a birthday present in Melbourne may drop in at Daimaru, a Japanese department store, while a New Yorker in Syracuse may shop for a train set for his 2-year-old at the Lost Forest, an Australian toy boutique. The earth is now populated by more than 6.3 billion people whose lives are intertwined in one tremendous global marketplace. In fact, global trade in goods and services reached $9 trillion in 2002, up from $5.5 trillion in 1999.[2]

In deference to the increasingly global nature of marketing, we devote this chapter to the unique features of global markets and international marketing. We begin by exploring the environmental forces that create opportunities and threats for international marketers. Next, we consider several regional trade alliances, markets, and agreements. Finally, we examine the levels of commitment by U.S. firms to international marketing and their degree of involvement in it. These critical factors must be considered in any marketing plan that includes an international component.

The Nature of International Marketing

international marketing
Developing and performing marketing activities across national boundaries

Technological advances and rapidly changing political and economic conditions are making it easier than ever for companies to market their products overseas as well as at home. **International marketing** involves developing and performing marketing activities across national boundaries. For example, Wal-Mart has nearly 1.5 million employees and operates 4,750 stores in ten countries, including the United States, Canada, and Mexico, while Starbucks serves 20 million customers a week at more than 6,000 shops in 30 countries.[3]

Many U.S. firms are finding that international markets provide tremendous opportunities for growth. For example, Amazon.com, an online retailer, has nine distribution centers from Nevada to Germany that fill 1.7 million orders a day and ship them to customers in every corner of the world.[4] Indeed, most of the world's population and two-thirds of its total purchasing power are outside the United States. Accessing these markets can promote innovation, while intensifying global competition spurs companies to market better, less expensive products. Most automobile marketers, for instance, are developing products for use by customers worldwide. In the future, just ten auto brands may be recognized globally. Some of these are likely to be from General Motors, whose many globally recognized brands include Saab, Opel, Chevrolet, and Cadillac. Others may come from Japan's Toyota Motors, which aggressively markets automobiles and trucks around the world and commands 11.2 percent of the U.S. market.[5]

Environmental Forces in International Markets

Firms that enter foreign markets often find they must make significant adjustments in their marketing strategies. The environmental forces that affect foreign markets may differ dramatically from those affecting domestic markets. Thus, a successful international marketing strategy requires a careful environmental analysis. Conducting research to understand the needs and desires of foreign customers is crucial to international marketing success. Many firms have demonstrated that such efforts can generate tremendous financial rewards, increase market share, and heighten customer awareness of their products around the world. In this section, we explore how differences in the sociocultural, economic, political, legal, and technological forces of the marketing environment in other countries can profoundly affect marketing activities.

◆ Cultural, Social, and Ethical Forces

Cultural, social, and ethical differences among nations can have significant effects on marketing activities. Because marketing activities are primarily social in purpose, they are influenced by beliefs and values regarding family, religion, education, health, and recreation. For example, in Greece, where sunbathing is a common form of recreation, American products such as Johnson & Johnson Baby Sunblock have a large target market. By identifying major sociocultural variations among countries, marketers lay the groundwork for an effective adaptation of marketing strategy. For instance, when Little Caesars opened new franchise pizza outlets abroad, it made some menu changes to accommodate local tastes and social norms. In Japan, Little Caesars' pizzas are garnished with asparagus, potatoes, squid, or seaweed. Turkish menus include a local pastry for dessert, while Middle Eastern menus exclude pork.[6] Although football is a popular sport in the United States and a major opportunity for many television advertisers, soccer is the most popular televised sport in Europe. And, of course, marketing communications often must be translated into other languages. For example, New Horizons Computer Learning Centers, the world's largest computer training firm, has translated course materials into 14 languages and adapted marketing campaigns to serve customers in 45 countries.[7]

It can be difficult to transfer marketing symbols, trademarks, logos, and even products to international markets, especially if they are associated with objects that have profound religious or cultural significance in a particular culture. For example, when Big Boy opened a new restaurant in

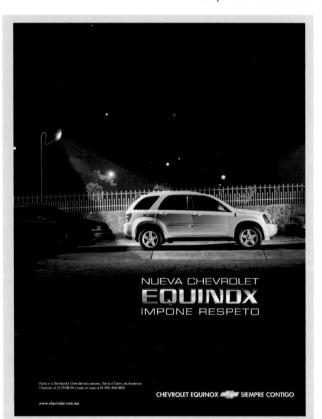

Cultural Differences
GM markets its new Equinox in Mexico and the U.S.

Bangkok, it quickly became popular with European and American tourists, but the local Thais refused to eat there. Instead they placed gifts of rice and incense at the feet of the Big Boy statue—a chubby boy holding a hamburger—which reminded them of Buddha. In Japan, customers were forced to tiptoe around a logo painted on the floor at the entrance to an Athlete's Foot store because in Japan it is taboo to step on a crest. On the other hand, A&W's Great Root Beer is an American icon that has been successfully translated around the world: it appeals to customers everywhere.[8]

Cultural differences may also affect marketing negotiations and decision-making behavior. For example, consumers in Russia found the American-style energetic happiness of McDonald's employees insincere and offensive when the company opened its first stores there.[9] Although Americans and Taiwanese sales agents are equally sensitive to customer interests, research suggests that Taiwanese are more sensitive to the interests of their companies and competitors and less attuned to the interests of colleagues. Identifying such differences in work-related values of employees across different nationalities helps companies design more effective sales management practices.[10] However, the use of American sales management techniques among Polish retail salespeople has been successful despite many cultural, economic, and political differences in the environments.[11] Table 5.1 offers a sampling of behaviors that may be viewed as rude, insensitive, or offensive in global business negotiations. Cultural differences in the emphasis placed on personal relationships, status, and decision-making styles have been known to complicate dealings between Americans and businesspeople from other countries. In the Far East, a gift may be considered a necessary introduction before negotiation, whereas in the United States or Canada, a gift may be misconstrued as an illegal bribe.

Buyers' perceptions of other countries can influence product adoption and use. For example, research indicates that Japanese consumers evaluate products from Japan more favorably than those from other countries regardless of product superiority. Americans, however, evaluate domestic products more favorably than foreign ones only when the U.S. products are superior to products from other countries.[12] When people are unfamiliar with products from another country, their perceptions of the country itself may affect their attitude toward the product and help determine whether they will buy it. If a country has a reputation for producing quality products and therefore has a positive image in consumers' minds, marketers of products from that country will want to make the country of origin well

Table 5.1	A Sampling of Cross-Cultural Behavioral Differences
Country	**Behaviors Viewed as Rude or Otherwise Unacceptable**
Japan	Talking about price during negotiations
Finland	Standing with your arms folded across your chest
Belgium	Talking with your hands in your pockets
Egypt	Showing the sole of your shoe (as when legs are crossed)
Zambia	Pointing directly at someone or something
France	Chewing gum, yawning, or conversing loudly in public
Hong Kong	Blinking conspicuously during conversation
India	Expressing anger
New Zealand	Using toothpicks or chewing gum in public
England	Pushing your way in front of others standing in a line
Sri Lanka	Touching, leaning on, or sitting on an image of Buddha
Thailand	Stepping on a doorsill when entering a building

Source: "Gestures Around the World," Web of Culture, **www.webofculture.com/worldsmart/gestures.html**, July 5, 2001.

known. For example, a generally favorable image of Western computer technology has fueled sales of American personal computers and Microsoft software in Japan. On the other hand, marketers may want to dissociate themselves from a particular country. For example, because the world has not always viewed Mexico as producing quality products, Volkswagen may not want to advertise that some of the models it sells in the United States, including the Beetle, are made in Mexico.

When products are introduced from one nation into another, acceptance is far more likely if similarities exist between the two cultures. Due to a new global sensitivity about food, middle-class U.S. families are eating more like their counterparts in Japan, France, and Canada. On the other hand, Europeans are eating more like Americans, as highlighted in Global Marketing. For international marketers, cultural

GLOBAL MARKETING

Supersizing Europeans

The American trend toward obesity has spread to Europe. Europeans are now eating more foods high in fat, sugar, and salt. In England, consumption of carbonated, or "fizzy," drinks has almost doubled in the past 15 years, with young adults now consuming an average of six cans each week. Fast-food consumption is also on the rise: in 2001, around 2 billion meals were eaten at "quick-service" catering outlets in the United Kingdom. Likewise, in Greece, there has been a shift from traditional Mediterranean cooking to fast food.

American eating habits are having a growing influence on European cultures. Obesity task force spokesperson Neville Rigby reports, "The Americanization of diet and the Americanization of lifestyle is how (obesity) is exported." Eating fast food is very trendy to Europeans. Luca Biagi, a 28-year-old Italian, says, "Everything comes from America: clothes, music, fat." Italian officials fear the "Americanization" of eating is threatening their culture.

However, the change in Italian culture may be influenced not only by Americans but by Western society in general. There are more working mothers in Italy, which has contributed to a change in eating patterns. Most stores and businesses have traditionally closed from 1:00 P.M. to 4:00 P.M. so that people can go home for the traditional main meal, *pranzo*. This custom is slowly disappearing, however. Although 72 percent of workers went home for lunch ten years ago, today just over half do, according to the National Institute of Statistics. Traditionally Italian snacks, *merendine*, contain cheese and fruit. Today stores package snacks for convenience, gaining them appeal among busy Italians, including working mothers.

In addition, Europeans, like Americans, have become more sedentary. Four out of ten boys and six out of ten girls are not meeting the hour-a-day physical activity for children recommended by the Health Education Authority in the United Kingdom. In England, children spend an average 11.4 hours a week watching TV or video, 7.5 hours on sport/exercise, and 4.4 hours playing computer games. Eighteen percent of English parents do not encourage their children to partake in any physical activity. And in Italy, many apartment complexes have banned children from playing in courtyards to deter noise.

European authorities are concerned about the long-term costs of this trend, particularly chronic health problems linked to obesity such as heart disease, Type 2 diabetes, high blood pressure, and osteoarthritis. Although some costs are direct, others are indirect to a society. Many European governments are therefore searching for ways to respond to this growing issue. Sweden, for example, negotiated voluntary restrictions on TV advertising for soft drinks, snacks, and junk food aimed at children. Italy's health minister, Girolamo Sirchia, has asked restaurants to reduce portion sizes and institute Friday as a day of fasting. The Rome City Council has even suggested a reduction in taxes on apartment buildings where children are allowed to play outside.

The United Kingdom is also trying to find solutions to obesity. A member of Parliament introduced a bill to ban advertising of foods containing high levels of sugar, fat, and salt during preschool TV programs. A British medical journal published an editorial appealing for a prohibition on celebrity endorsements of junk food. The British Medical Association called for 17.5 percent "fat tax" on junk foods.

differences have implications for product development, advertising, packaging, and pricing. Schlotzsky's, for example, experienced slower-than-expected sales when it opened a new restaurant in Beijing. Although the Texas-based sandwich chain has enjoyed great success in the United States, Chinese consumers are less accustomed to eating foods with their hands, and they often like to share their meals with companions, which is difficult to do with a sandwich. The company hopes that training staff and placing pictures on restaurant tables to demonstrate how to hold and eat its large sandwiches will help Chinese customers appreciate them and thus increase sales.[13]

Differences in ethical standards can also affect marketing efforts. For example, there are significant differences between the expectations of American versus French and German consumers regarding the social responsibilities of business.[14] In China and Vietnam, standards regarding intellectual property differ from those in the United States, creating potential conflicts for marketers of computer software, music CDs, and books. Because of differences in cultural and ethical standards, many companies are working both individually and collectively to establish ethics programs and standards for international business conduct.[15] Levi Strauss's code of ethics, for example, bars the firm from manufacturing in countries where workers are known to be abused. Starbucks' global code of ethics strives to protect agricultural workers who harvest coffee beans. Many companies are choosing to standardize their ethical behavior across national boundaries to maintain a consistent and well-integrated corporate culture.

◆ Economic Forces

Global marketers need to understand the international trade system, particularly the economic stability of individual nations, as well as trade barriers that may stifle marketing efforts. Economic differences among nations—differences in standards of living, credit, buying power, income distribution, national resources, exchange rates, and the like—dictate many of the adjustments firms must make in marketing abroad.

The United States and Western Europe are more stable economically than many other regions of the world. In recent years, a number of countries, including Russia, Korea, Thailand, and Singapore, have experienced economic problems such as depression, high unemployment, corporate bankruptcies, instability in currency markets, trade imbalances, and financial systems that need major reforms. Even more stable developing countries, such as Mexico and Brazil, tend to have greater fluctuations in their business cycles than the United States does. Economic instability can disrupt the markets for U.S. products in places that otherwise might be excellent marketing opportunities.

Beyond assessing the stability of a nation's economy, marketers should consider whether that nation imposes trade restrictions, such as tariffs. An **import tariff** is any duty levied by a nation on goods bought outside its borders and brought in. Because they raise the prices of foreign goods, tariffs impede free trade between nations. Tariffs are usually designed either to raise revenue for a country or to protect domestic products.

Nontariff trade barriers include quotas and embargoes. A **quota** is a limit on the amount of goods an importing country will accept for certain product categories in a specific time period. An **embargo** is a government's suspension of trade in a particular product or with a given country. Embargoes are generally directed at specific goods or countries and are established for political, health, or religious reasons. For example, the United States forbids the importation of cigars from Cuba for political reasons. However, demand for Cuban cigars is so strong that many enter the U.S. market illegally. Laws regarding pricing policies may also serve as trade barriers. Great Britain, for example, has weaker antitrust laws than the United States and is generally more accepting of price collusion. Consequently many products cost much more in Britain than in the United States. Because customers may be unable to afford the higher prices of imported products, such policies effectively create barriers to foreign trade.

import tariff A duty levied by a nation on goods bought outside its borders and brought in

quota A limit on the amount of goods an importing country will accept for certain product categories in a specific time period

embargo A government's suspension of trade in a particular product or with a given country

exchange controls Government restrictions on the amount of a particular currency that can be bought or sold

balance of trade The difference in value between a nation's exports and its imports

gross domestic product (GDP) The market value of a nation's total output of goods and services for a given period; an overall measure of economic standing

Economic and Political Differences
Companies such as Ernst & Young assist business customers in dealing with economic and political differences.

Exchange controls, government restrictions on the amount of a particular currency that can be bought or sold, may also limit international trade. They can force businesspeople to buy and sell foreign products through a central agency, such as a central bank. On the other hand, to promote international trade, some countries have joined together to form free trade zones, multinational economic communities that eliminate tariffs and other trade barriers. Such regional trade alliances are discussed later in the chapter. Foreign currency exchange rates also affect the prices marketers can charge in foreign markets. Fluctuations in the international monetary market can change the prices charged across national boundaries on a daily basis. Thus these fluctuations must be considered in any international marketing strategy.

Countries may limit imports to maintain a favorable balance of trade. The **balance of trade** is the difference in value between a nation's exports and its imports. When a nation exports more products than it imports, a favorable balance of trade exists because money is flowing into the country. The United States has a negative balance of trade for goods and services of $418 billion, the largest deficit since 1988.[16] A negative balance of trade is considered harmful because it means U.S. dollars are supporting foreign economies at the expense of U.S. companies and workers.

In terms of the value of all products produced by a nation, the United States has the largest gross domestic product in the world, nearly $10 trillion.[17] **Gross domestic product (GDP)** is an overall measure of a nation's economic standing; it is the market value of a nation's total output of goods and services for a given period. However, it does not take into account the concept of GDP in relation to population (GDP per capita). The United States has a GDP per capita of $35,619. Switzerland is roughly 230 times smaller than the United States—a little larger than the state of Maryland—but its population density is six times greater than that of the United States.

Although Switzerland's GDP is about one-fortieth the size of the U.S. GDP, its GDP per capita is about the same. Even Canada, which is comparable in size to the United States, has a lower GDP and GDP per capita.[18] Table 5.2 provides a comparative economic analysis of Switzerland, Canada, and the United States. Knowledge about per capita income, credit, and the distribution of income provides general insights into market potential.

Opportunities for international trade are not limited to countries with the highest incomes. Some nations are progressing at a much faster rate than they were a few years ago, and these countries—especially in Latin America, Africa, Eastern Europe, and the Middle East—have great market potential. However, marketers must understand the political and legal environments before they can convert buying power of customers in these countries into actual demand for specific products.

◆ **Political and Legal Forces**

A nation's political system, laws, regulatory bodies, special-interest groups, and courts all have great impact on international marketing. A government's policies toward public and private enterprise, consumers, and foreign firms influence marketing across national boundaries. Some countries have established import barriers. Many nontariff barriers, such as quotas and minimum price levels set on imports, port-of-entry taxes, and stringent health and safety requirements, still make it difficult for American

Where else can you find so many foreign tax professionals under one roof?

In whatever country you do business, you can benefit from the objective advice of Ernst & Young's foreign tax professionals. From M&A to transfer pricing, from business realignment to exploring the capital markets, our professionals do more than just advise on the tax implications of doing international business—they deliver integrated solutions that help you realize your goals. Visit our international tax Web site today. It will make a world of difference.

ey.com/internationaltax

ERNST & YOUNG
Quality In Everything We Do

Table 5.2	A Comparative Economic Analysis of Canada, Switzerland, and the United States		
	Canada	**Switzerland**	**United States**
Land area (sq. mi.)	3,560,219	15,355	3,539,227
Population (millions)	31.59	7.28	278.06
Population density (persons per sq. mi.)	9	474	79
GDP, 2000 ($ billions)	$701	$239	$9,810
GDP per capita	$22,783	$33,326	$35,619

Source: Bureau of the Census, *Statistical Abstract of the United States, 2002* (Washington, DC: Government Printing Office, 2003), pp. 824–826, 834.

companies to export their products. For example, the collectivistic nature of Japanese culture and the high-context nature of Japanese communication make some types of direct marketing messages less effective there and may predispose many Japanese to support greater regulation of direct marketing practices.[19] A government's attitude toward importers has a direct impact on the economic feasibility of exporting to that country.

Differences in national standards of ethics are illustrated by what the Mexicans call *la mordida*, "the bite." The use of payoffs and bribes is deeply entrenched in many governments. Because U.S. trade and corporate policy, as well as U.S. law, prohibits direct involvement in payoffs and bribes, American companies may have a hard time competing with foreign firms that engage in these practices. Some U.S. businesses that refuse to make payoffs are forced to hire local consultants, public relations firms, or advertising agencies, which results in indirect payoffs. The ultimate decision about whether to give small tips or gifts where they are customary must be based on a company's code of ethics. However, under the Foreign Corrupt Practices Act of 1977, it is illegal for U.S. firms to attempt to make large payments or bribes to influence policy decisions of foreign governments. Nevertheless, facilitating payments, or small payments to support the performance of standard tasks, are often acceptable. The Foreign Corrupt Practices Act also subjects all publicly held U.S. corporations to rigorous internal controls and recordkeeping requirements for their overseas operations.

◆ Technological Forces

Advances in technology have made international marketing much easier. Voice mail, e-mail, fax, cellular phones, and the Internet make international marketing activities more affordable and convenient. Internet use has accelerated dramatically within the United States and abroad. In Europe, 50 percent of households have Internet access at home or work, pushing e-commerce revenues to $16.4 billion.[20] In Japan, 56 million are logging on to the Internet, and 18 million Russians have Internet access.[21]

Information Technology
Pitney Bowes provides web-based software and information technology to facilitate global shipping.

In many developing countries that lack the level of technological infrastructure found in the United States and Japan, marketers are beginning to capitalize on opportunities to "leapfrog" existing technology. For example, cellular and wireless phone technology is reaching many countries at less expense than traditional hard-wired telephone systems. Consequently opportunities for growth in the cellphone market remain strong in Southeast Asia, Africa, and the Middle East. In war-torn Iraq, many firms are fiercely competing for opportunities to rebuild the nation's telecommunications infrastructure, and MCI and Motorola have already won contracts to develop cellphone networks there.[22] Hewlett-Packard also hopes to bring new technologies to less developed countries. The company has launched World e-Inclusion, an economic development initiative that seeks to apply technology-based solutions to empower people in developing countries. Pilot programs for the initiative have already yielded high-speed Internet connections for remote villages in Central America and specialized software for coffee growers in Sumatra.[23]

Regional Trade Alliances, Markets, and Agreements

Although many more firms are beginning to view the world as one huge marketplace, various regional trade alliances and specific markets affect companies engaging in international marketing: some create opportunities, and others impose constraints. In this section we examine several regional trade alliances, markets, and changing conditions affecting markets, including the North American Free Trade Agreement among the United States, Canada, and Mexico; the European Union; the Common Market of the Southern Cone; Asia-Pacific Economic Cooperation; the General Agreement on Tariffs and Trade; and the World Trade Organization.

◆ The North American Free Trade Agreement (NAFTA)

North American Free Trade Agreement (NAFTA) An alliance that merges Canada, Mexico, and the United States into a single market

The **North American Free Trade Agreement (NAFTA)**, implemented in 1994, effectively merged Canada, Mexico, and the United States into one market of more than 421 million consumers.[24] NAFTA will eliminate virtually all tariffs on goods produced and traded among Canada, Mexico, and the United States to create a free trade area by 2009. The estimated annual output for this trade alliance is $11 trillion.[25]

NAFTA makes it easier for U.S. businesses to invest in Mexico and Canada; provides protection for intellectual property (of special interest to high-technology and entertainment industries); expands trade by requiring equal treatment of U.S. firms in both countries; and simplifies country-of-origin rules, hindering Japan's use of Mexico as a staging ground for further penetration into U.S. markets. Although most tariffs on products coming to the United States will be lifted, duties on more sensitive products, such as household glassware, footware, and some fruits and vegetables, will be phased out over a 15-year period.

Canada's 31.6 million consumers are relatively affluent, with a per capita GDP of $22,783.[26] Trade between the United States and Canada totals approximately $411 billion.[27] Currently exports to Canada support approximately 1.5 million U.S. jobs. Canadian investments in U.S. companies are also increasing, and various markets, including air travel, are opening as regulatory barriers dissolve.[28]

With a per capita GDP of $5,903, Mexico's 102 million consumers are less affluent than Canadian consumers. However, they bought $107 billion worth of U.S. products last year. In fact, Mexico has become the United States' second-largest trading market, after Canada.[29] Many U.S. companies, including Hewlett-Packard, IBM, and General Motors, have taken advantage of Mexico's low labor costs and close proximity to the United States to set up production facilities, sometimes called *maquiladoras*. Production at the *maquiladoras*, especially in the automotive, electronics, and apparel industries, tripled between 1994 and 2000 as companies as diverse as Ford, John Deere, Motorola, Sara Lee, Kimberly-Clark, and VF Corpo-

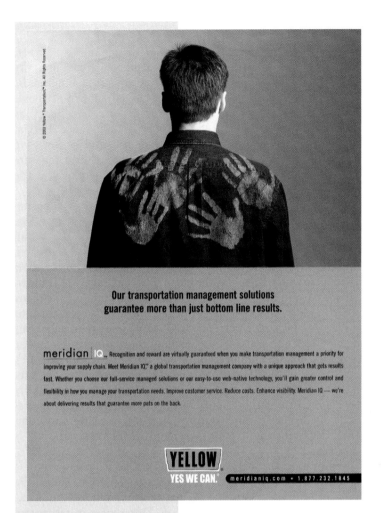

Our transportation management solutions guarantee more than just bottom line results.

meridian IQ ™ Recognition and reward are virtually guaranteed when you make transportation management a priority for improving your supply chain. Meet Meridian IQ,™ a global transportation management company with a unique approach that gets results fast. Whether you choose our full-service managed solutions or our easy-to-use web-native technology, you'll gain greater control and flexibility in how you manage your transportation needs. Improve customer service. Reduce costs. Enhance visibility. Meridian IQ — we're about delivering results that guarantee more pats on the back.

YELLOW
YES WE CAN.®   meridianiq.com • 1.877.232.1845

NAFTA Creates Opportunities
Yellow Transportation helps companies ship from the U.S. to Canada, where it reaches more than 85 percent of the population.

ration set up facilities in north-central Mexican states. With the *maquiladoras* accounting for roughly half of Mexico's exports, Mexico has risen to become the world's ninth-largest economy.[30] Although Mexico experienced financial instability throughout the 1990s, privatization of some government-owned firms and other measures instituted by the Mexican government and businesses, along with a booming U.S. economy, have helped Mexico's economy. Moreover, increasing trade between the United States and Canada constitutes a strong base of support for the ultimate success of NAFTA.

Mexico's membership in NAFTA links the United States and Canada with other Latin American countries, providing additional opportunities to integrate trade among all the nations in the Western Hemisphere. Indeed, efforts to create a free trade agreement among the 34 nations of North and South America are expected to be completed by 2005. Like NAFTA, the Free Trade Area of the Americas (FTAA) will progressively eliminate trade barriers and create the world's largest free trade zone, with 800 million people.[31] However, a trade dispute between the United States and Brazil over investment, intellectual property rights, antidumping tariffs, and agriculture subsidies may delay the final agreement.[32]

Despite its benefits, NAFTA has been controversial and disputes continue to arise over its implementation. Archer Daniels Midland, for example, filed a claim against the Mexican government for losses resulting from a tax on soft drinks containing high-fructose corn syrup, which the company believes violates the provisions of NAFTA.[33] While many Americans feared the agreement would erase jobs in the United States, Mexicans have been disappointed that it failed to create more jobs. Moreover, Mexico's rising standard of living has increased the cost of doing business there; some 850 *maquiladoras* have closed their doors and transferred work to China and other nations where labor costs are lower. Indeed, China has become the United States' second-largest source of imported goods.[34]

Although NAFTA has been controversial, it has become a positive factor for U.S. firms wishing to engage in international marketing. Because licensing requirements have been relaxed under the pact, smaller businesses that previously could not afford to invest in Mexico and Canada will be able to do business in those markets without having to locate there. NAFTA's long phase-in period provides ample time for adjustment for those firms affected by reduced tariffs on imports. Furthermore, increased competition should lead to a more efficient market, and the long-term prospects of including most Western Hemisphere countries in the alliance promise additional opportunities for U.S. marketers.

NET SIGHTS

One excellent source for country-specific information may be somewhat surprising: the U.S. Central Intelligence Agency (CIA). For years, the CIA has published an annual World Fact Book **(www.cia.gov/cia/publications/factbook/index.html)**, *which profiles every country in the world. This useful guide offers detailed information on each country's geography (including maps and climate information), population, government and military, economy, infrastructure, and significant transnational issues. Before doing business in a specific country, marketers will need to conduct further research, and* The World Fact Book *can be an excellent place to begin.*

◆ The European Union (EU)

European Union (EU) An alliance that promotes trade among its member countries in Europe

The **European Union (EU)**, also called the *European Community* or *Common Market*, was established in 1958 to promote trade among its members, which initially included Belgium, France, Italy, West Germany, Luxembourg, and the Netherlands. In 1991 East and West Germany united, and by 1995 the United Kingdom, Spain, Denmark, Greece, Portugal, Ireland, Austria, Finland, and Sweden had joined as well. (Cyprus, Poland, Hungary, the Czech Republic, Slovenia, Estonia, Latvia, Lithuania, Slovakia, and Malta joined in 2004; Romania, Bulgaria, and Turkey have requested membership as well.[35]) Until 1993 each nation functioned as a separate market, but at that time the members officially unified into one of the largest single world markets, which today includes 390 million consumers.

To facilitate free trade among members, the EU is working toward standardizing business regulations and requirements, import duties, and value-added taxes; eliminating customs checks; and creating a standardized currency for use by all members. Many European nations (Austria, Belgium, Finland, France, Germany, Ireland, Italy, Luxembourg, the Netherlands, Portugal, and Spain) link their exchange rates together to a common currency, the *euro;* however, several EU members have rejected use of the euro in their countries. Although the common currency requires many marketers to modify their pricing strategies and will subject them to increased competition, the use of a single currency frees companies that sell goods among European countries from the nuisance of dealing with complex exchange rates.[36] The long-term goals are to eliminate all trade barriers within the EU, improve the economic efficiency of the EU nations, and stimulate economic growth, thus making the union's economy more competitive in global markets, particularly against Japan and other Pacific Rim nations, and North America. However, several disputes and debates still divide the member nations, and many barriers to completely free trade remain. Consequently it may take many years before the EU is truly one deregulated market.

As the EU nations attempt to function as one large market, consumers in the EU may become more homogeneous in their needs and wants. Marketers should be aware, however, that cultural differences among the nations may require modifications in the marketing mix for customers in each nation. Differences in tastes and preferences in these diverse markets are significant for international marketers. But there is evidence that such differences may be diminishing. Gathering information about these distinct tastes and preferences is likely to remain a very important factor in developing marketing mixes that satisfy the needs of European customers.

◆ The Common Market of the Southern Cone (MERCOSUR)

Common Market of the Southern Cone (MERCOSUR) An alliance that promotes the free circulation of goods, services, and production factors, and has a common external tariff and commercial policy among member nations in South America

The **Common Market of the Southern Cone (MERCOSUR)**, was established in 1991 under the Treaty of Asunción to unite Argentina, Brazil, Paraguay, and Uruguay as a free trade alliance; Bolivia and Chile joined as associates in 1996. The alliance represents two-thirds of South America's population and has a combined gross domestic product of (US) $800 billion, making it the third-largest trading bloc behind NAFTA and the European Union. Like NAFTA, MERCOSUR promotes "the free circulation of goods, services and production factors among the countries" and established a common external tariff and commercial policy.[37]

◆ Asia-Pacific Economic Cooperation (APEC)

Asia-Pacific Economic Cooperation (APEC) An alliance that promotes open trade and economic and technical cooperation among member nations throughout the world

The **Asia-Pacific Economic Cooperation (APEC)**, established in 1989, promotes open trade and economic and technical cooperation among member nations, which initially included Australia, Brunei Darussalam, Canada, Indonesia, Japan, Korea, Malaysia, New Zealand, the Philippines, Singapore, Thailand, and the United States. Since then the alliance has grown to include China, Hong Kong, Chinese Taipei, Mexico, Papua New Guinea, Chile, Peru, Russia, and Vietnam. The 21-member alliance represents 2.5 billion consumers, has a combined gross domestic product of (US) $19 trillion, and accounts for nearly 47 percent of global trade. APEC differs from other international trade alliances in its commitment to facilitating business and its practice of allowing the business/private sector to participate in a wide range of APEC activities.[38]

Despite economic turmoil and a recession in Asia in recent years, companies of the APEC have become increasingly competitive and sophisticated in global business in the last three decades. Moreover, the markets of the APEC offer tremendous opportunities to marketers who understand them.

Japanese firms in particular have made tremendous inroads on world markets for automobiles, motorcycles, watches, cameras, and audio and video equipment. Products from Sony, Sanyo, Toyota, Mitsubishi, Canon, Suzuki, and Toshiba are sold all over the world and have set standards of quality by which other products are often judged. Despite the high volume of trade between the United States and Japan, the two economies are less integrated than the U.S. economy is with Canada's and Western Europe's. If Japan imported goods at the same rate as other major nations, the United States would sell billions of dollars more each year to Japan. The United States and Japan continually struggle with cultural and political differences and are, in general, at odds over how to do business with each other.

The People's Republic of China, a country of 1.3 billion people, has launched a program of economic reform to stimulate its economy by privatizing many industries, restructuring its banking system, and increasing public spending on infrastructure (including railways and telecommunications).[39] As a result, China has become a manufacturing powerhouse, with an economy growing at a rate of 7 percent a year.[40] Many foreign companies, including General Motors, Volkswagen, and Toyota, are opening factories in China to take advantage of its low labor costs.[41] Nike and Adidas have shifted most of their shoe production to China, and recently China has become a major producer of compact disc players, cellular phones, portable stereos, and personal computers. The potential of China's consumer market is so vast that it is almost impossible to measure, but doing business in China also entails many risks. Political and economic instability, especially inflation, corruption, and erratic policy shifts, have undercut marketers' efforts to stake a claim in what could become the world's largest market. Moreover, piracy is a major issue, and protecting a brand name in China is difficult. Because copying is a tradition in China and laws protecting copyrights and intellectual property are weak and minimally enforced, the country is flooded with counterfeit videos, movies, compact discs, computer software, furniture, and clothing.

Pacific Rim regions, such as South Korea, Thailand, Singapore, Taiwan, and Hong Kong, have become major manufacturing and financial centers. Even before Korean brand names such as Samsung, Daewoo, and Hyundai became household words, these products prospered under U.S. company labels, including GE, GTE, RCA, and JCPenney. Singapore boasts huge global markets for rubber goods and pharmaceuticals. Hong Kong is still a strong commercial center after being transferred to Chinese control. Vietnam is becoming one of Asia's fastest-growing markets for U.S. businesses, but Taiwan may have the most promising future of all the Pacific Rim nations as a strong local economy and low import barriers draw increasing imports. Firms from Thailand and Malaysia are also thriving, carving out niches in the world markets for a variety of products from toys to automobile parts.

◆ General Agreement on Tariffs and Trade (GATT) and World Trade Organization (WTO)

General Agreement on Tariffs and Trade (GATT) An agreement among nations to reduce worldwide tariffs and increase international trade

Like NAFTA and the European Union, the **General Agreement on Tariffs and Trade (GATT)** is based on negotiations among member countries to reduce worldwide tariffs and increase international trade. Originally signed by 23 nations in 1947, GATT provides a forum for tariff negotiations and for discussion and resolution of international trade problems. GATT sponsors rounds of negotiations aimed at reducing

dumping Selling products at unfairly low prices

World Trade Organization (WTO) An entity that promotes free trade among member nations by eliminating trade barriers and educating individuals, companies, and governments about trade rules around the world

trade restrictions. The most recent round, the Uruguay Round (1988–1994), further reduced trade barriers for most products and provided new rules to prevent **dumping**, the selling of products at unfairly low prices. The most significant outcome of the Uruguay Round was the establishment of the **World Trade Organization (WTO)** to promote free trade among member nations. Fulfilling this purpose requires eliminating trade barriers; educating individuals, companies, and governments about trade rules around the world; and assuring global markets that no sudden changes of policy will occur. At the heart of the WTO are agreements that provide legal ground rules for international commerce and trade policy. Based in Geneva, Switzerland, the WTO also serves as a forum for trade negotiations and dispute resolution.[42] For example, after the European Union and seven countries protested a U.S. tariff on imported steel, the World Trade Organization investigated and ultimately ruled the U.S. duties illegal under international trade rules. The United States had imposed the tariffs to protect domestic steel producers from less expensive imported steel, but the WTO found that the United States had failed to prove that its steel industry had been harmed by dumping.[43] Facing the prospect of retaliatory sanctions against American goods, the United States dropped the tariffs 16 months early after the ruling.[44]

International Involvement

Marketers engage in international marketing activities at several levels of involvement covering a wide spectrum, as Figure 5.1 shows. Domestic marketing involves marketing strategies aimed at markets within the home country; at the other extreme, global marketing entails developing marketing strategies for major regions or for the entire world. Many firms with an international presence start out as small companies serving local and regional markets and expand to national markets before considering opportunities in foreign markets. Limited exporting may occur even if a firm makes little or no effort to obtain foreign sales. Foreign buyers may seek out the company and/or its products, or a distributor may discover the firm's products and export them. The level of commitment to international marketing is a

Figure 5.1 **Levels of Involvement in Global Marketing**

Domestic marketing
All marketing strategies focus on the market in the country of origin.

Limited exporting
The firm develops no international marketing strategies, but international distributors or foreign firms purchase some of its products.

International marketing
International markets are a consideration in the marketing strategy.

Globalized marketing
Marketing strategies are developed for major regions or the entire world so firms can compete globally.

Snapshot

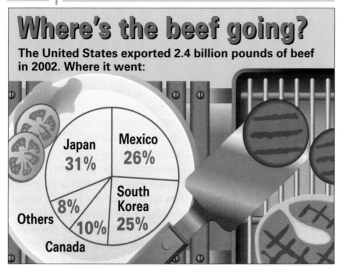

Where's the beef going?

The United States exported 2.4 billion pounds of beef in 2002. Where it went:

Japan 31%
Mexico 26%
South Korea 25%
Canada 10%
Others 8%

Source: USDA Economic Research Service, "Background Statistics on U.S. Beef and Cattle Industry," January 13, 2004, **www.ers.usda.gov/new/BSEcoverage.htm,** accessed February 20, 2004.

importing The purchase of products from a foreign source

exporting The sale of products to foreign markets

trading company A company that links buyers and sellers in different countries

major variable in global marketing strategies. In this section, we examine importing and exporting, trading companies, licensing and franchising, contract manufacturing, joint ventures, direct ownership, and some of the other approaches to international involvement.

◆ Importing and Exporting

Importing and exporting require the least amount of effort and commitment of resources. **Importing** is the purchase of products from a foreign source. **Exporting**, the sale of products to foreign markets, enables firms of all sizes to participate in global business. A firm may find an exporting intermediary to take over most marketing functions associated with selling to other countries. This approach entails minimal effort and cost. Modifications in packaging, labeling, style, or color may be the major expenses in adapting a product for the foreign market.

Export agents bring together buyers and sellers from different countries and collect a commission for arranging sales. Export houses and export merchants purchase products from different companies and then sell them abroad. They are specialists at understanding foreign customers' needs. Using exporting intermediaries involves limited risk because no direct investment in the foreign country is required.

Buyers from foreign companies and governments provide a direct method of exporting and eliminate the need for an intermediary. These buyers encourage international exchange by contacting overseas firms about their needs and the opportunities available in exporting to them. Indeed, research suggests that many small firms tend to rely heavily on such native contacts, especially in developed markets, and remain production oriented rather than marketing oriented in their approach to international marketing.[45] Domestic firms that want to export with minimal effort and investment should seek out export intermediaries. Once a company becomes involved in exporting, it usually develops a more positive image of its country and becomes more confident in its competitiveness.[46]

◆ Trading Companies

Marketers sometimes employ a **trading company**, which links buyers and sellers in different countries but is not involved in manufacturing and does not own assets related to manufacturing. Trading companies buy goods in one country at the lowest price consistent with quality and sell them to buyers in another country. For instance, Sci Net (**www.scinet-corp.com**) offers an online world trade system that connects 17 million companies in 245 countries, offering more than 50 million products and services. The Sci Net system offers online payments and handles customs, tariffs, and inspections of goods for their clients. A trading company acts like a wholesaler, taking on much of the responsibility of finding markets while facilitating all marketing aspects of a transaction. An important function of trading companies is taking title to products and performing all the activities necessary to move the products from the domestic country to a foreign country. For example, large grain-trading companies operating out of home offices in both the United States and overseas control a major portion of the world's trade in basic food commodities. These trading companies sell homogeneous agricultural commodities that can be stored and moved rapidly in response to market conditions.

Trading companies reduce risk for firms seeking to get involved in international marketing. A trading company provides producers with information about products that meet quality and price expectations in domestic and international markets. Additional services a trading company may provide include consulting, marketing research, advertising, insurance, product research and design, legal assistance, warehousing, and foreign exchange.

◆ Licensing and Franchising

licensing An alternative to direct investment requiring a licensee to pay commissions or royalties on sales or supplies used in manufacturing

When potential markets are found across national boundaries, and when production, technical assistance, or marketing know-how is required, **licensing** is an alternative to direct investment. The licensee (the owner of the foreign operation) pays commissions or royalties on sales or supplies used in manufacturing. The licensee may also pay an initial down payment or fee when the licensing agreement is signed. Exchanges of management techniques or technical assistance are primary reasons for licensing agreements. Yoplait, for example, is a French yogurt that is licensed for production in the United States; the Yoplait brand tries to maintain a French image.

Licensing is an attractive alternative to direct investment when the political stability of a foreign country is in doubt or when resources are unavailable for direct investment. Licensing is especially advantageous for small manufacturers wanting to launch a well-known brand internationally. For example, Questor Corporation owns the Spalding name but produces not a single golf club or tennis ball itself; all Spalding sporting products are licensed worldwide.

franchising A form of licensing in which a franchiser, in exchange for a financial commitment, grants a franchisee the right to market its product in accordance with the franchiser's standards

Franchising is a form of licensing in which a company (the franchiser) grants a franchisee the right to market its product, using its name, logo, methods of operation, advertising, products, and other elements associated with the franchiser's business, in return for a financial commitment and an agreement to conduct business in accordance with the franchiser's standard of operations. This arrangement allows franchisers to minimize the risks of international marketing in four ways: (1) the franchiser does not have to put up a large capital investment; (2) the franchiser's revenue stream is fairly consistent because franchisees pay a fixed fee and royalties; (3) the franchiser retains control of its name and increases global penetration of its product; and (4) franchise agreements ensure a certain standard of behavior from

Licensing and Franchising
7-Eleven franchisees in Hong Kong carry some brands that would be familiar in the U.S. market and others that would not be familiar.

7-Eleven, Inc. is the trademark owner of 7-Eleven®. All materials on this site are directed solely at persons accessing this site from the Special Administration Region of Hong Kong. The Dairy Farm Company Ltd. reserves all right of materials. Reprinted with permission.

Table 5.3	The Ten Largest Global Franchisers
Rank	**Company**
1	Subway
2	Curves
3	McDonald's
4	GNC Franchising
5	Jani-King
6	Baskin-Robbins USA
7	Taco Bell Corp.
8	The UPS Store
9	Quizno's Franchise
10	Burger King

Source: "Top 10 Global Franchises for 2003," *Entrepreneur,* **www.entrepreneur.com/franzone/listings/topglobal/0,5835,,00.html** (accessed Nov. 3, 2003).

franchisees, which protects the franchise name.[47] KFC, Wendy's, McDonald's, Holiday Inn, and Marriott are well-known franchisers with international visibility. Table 5.3 lists the world's leading franchisers.

◆ Contract Manufacturing

Contract manufacturing occurs when a company hires a foreign firm to produce a designated volume of the firm's product to specification and the final product carries the domestic firm's name. The Gap, for example, relies on contract manufacturing for some of its apparel; Reebok uses Korean contract manufacturers to produce many of its athletic shoes. Marketing may be handled by the contract manufacturer or by the contracting company.

◆ Joint Ventures

In international marketing, a **joint venture** is a partnership between a domestic firm and a foreign firm or government. Joint ventures are especially popular in industries that call for large investments, such as natural resources extraction or automobile manufacturing. Control of the joint venture may be split equally, or one party may control decision making. Joint ventures are often a political necessity because of nationalism and government restrictions on foreign ownership. They may occur when acquisition or internal development is not feasible or when the risks and constraints leave no other alternative. They also provide legitimacy in the eyes of the host country's citizens. Local partners have firsthand knowledge of the economic and sociopolitical environment and of distribution networks, and they may have privileged access to local resources (raw materials, labor management, and so on). However, joint venture relationships require trust throughout the relationship to provide a foreign partner with a ready means of implementing its own marketing strategy.[48] Joint ventures are assuming greater global importance because of cost advantages and the number of inexperienced firms entering foreign markets. They may be the result of a tradeoff between a firm's desire for completely unambiguous control of an enterprise and its quest for additional resources.

Strategic alliances, the newest form of international business structure, are partnerships formed to create competitive advantage on a worldwide basis. They are very similar to joint ventures. What distinguishes international strategic alliances from other business structures is that partners in the alliance may have been traditional rivals competing for the same market. An example of such an alliance is New United Motor Manufacturing, Inc. (NUMMI), formed by Toyota and General Motors to make automobiles for both firms. This alliance united the quality engineering of Japanese cars with the marketing expertise and market access of General Motors. Today NUMMI manufactures the popular Toyota Tacoma compact pickup truck, as well as the Toyota Corolla, Pontiac Vibe, and a right-hand-drive Toyota Voltz for sale in Japan.[49] Partners in international strategic alliances often retain their distinct identities, and each brings a core competency to the union.

The success rate of international alliances could be higher if there were a better fit between the companies. A strategic alliance should focus on a joint market opportunity from which all partners can benefit.[50] In the automobile, computer, and airline industries, strategic alliances are becoming the predominant means of competing. International competition in these industries is so fierce and the costs of competing on a global basis are so high that few firms have all the resources needed to do it alone. Firms that lack the internal resources essential for international

contract manufacturing The practice of hiring a foreign firm to produce a designated volume of the domestic firm's product to specification; the final product carries the domestic firm's name

joint venture A partnership between a domestic firm and a foreign firm or government

strategic alliance A partnership formed to create a competitive advantage on a worldwide basis

Leadership. Reliability.
Commitment to clients.

A winning combination in
Latin America.

With local offices throughout Latin America, and over
100 years of experience in the region, JPMorgan is
dedicated to providing advice, capital and a complete
range of global products to meet the needs of
corporations, financial institutions and sovereigns.
If you seek global strength, local expertise and
proven commitment, turn to JPMorgan.

jpmorgan.com

JPMorgan

JPMorgan is a marketing name for investment banking businesses of J.P. Morgan Chase & Co. and its subsidiaries worldwide. Investment banking activities are performed
by securities affiliates of J.P. Morgan Chase & Co., including J.P. Morgan Securities Inc., member NYSE/SIPC. Lending, derivative, and commercial banking activities are
performed by banking affiliates of J.P. Morgan Chase & Co. ©2003 J.P. Morgan Chase & Co. All rights reserved.

Direct Ownership
J. P. Morgan Chase is a leading global financial services firm with operations in over 50 countries. As such, it offers local expertise in many regions where its clients might want to do business.

success may seek to collaborate with other companies. A shared mode of leadership among partner corporations combines joint abilities and allows collaboration from a distance. Focusing on customer value and implementing innovative ways to compete create a winning strategy.[51] One such collaboration is a partnership of Northwest Airlines, KLM, Air China, Alitalia, Japan Air System, Kenya Airways, and Malaysia Airlines, designed to improve customer service among the seven firms.

◆ Direct Ownership

Once a company makes a long-term commitment to marketing in a foreign nation that has a promising political and economic environment, **direct ownership** of a foreign subsidiary or division is a possibility. Mexico's Gigante gro-

direct ownership A situation in which a company owns subsidiaries or other facilities overseas

cery chain, for example, has opened stores in Los Angeles and southern California, where it hopes its name will appeal to the large Hispanic population there.[52] Most foreign investment covers only manufacturing equipment or personnel because the expenses of developing a separate foreign distribution system can be tremendous. The opening of retail stores in Europe, Canada, or Mexico can require a staggering financial investment in facilities, research, and management.

multinational enterprise A firm that has operations or subsidiaries in many countries

The term **multinational enterprise** refers to a firm that has operations or subsidiaries in many countries. Often the parent company is based in one country and carries on production, management, and marketing activities in other countries. The firm's subsidiaries may be mostly autonomous so they can respond to the needs of individual international markets. Table 5.4 lists the ten largest global corporations.

A wholly owned foreign subsidiary may be allowed to operate independently of the parent company to give its management more freedom to adjust to the local environment. Cooperative arrangements are developed to assist in marketing efforts, production, and management. A wholly owned foreign subsidiary may export products to the home country. Some U.S. automobile manufacturers, for example, import cars built by their foreign subsidiaries. A foreign subsidiary offers important tax, tariff, and other operating advantages. One of the greatest advantages is the cross-cultural approach. A subsidiary usually operates under foreign management so that it can develop a local identity. The greatest danger in such an arrangement comes from political uncertainty: it is possible for a firm to lose its foreign investment.

Rank	Company	Country	Industry	Revenues (in millions)
	Table 5.4 **The Ten Largest Global Corporations**			
1	Wal-Mart Stores	U.S.	General merchandiser	$246,525
2	General Motors	U.S.	Motor vehicles	$186,763
3	Exxon Mobil	U.S.	Petroleum refining	$182,466
4	Royal Dutch/Shell Group	Netherlands/Britain	Petroleum refining	$179,431
5	BP	Britain	Petroleum refining	$178,721
6	Ford Motor	U.S.	Motor vehicles	$163,871
7	DaimlerChrysler	Germany	Motor vehicles	$141,421
8	Toyota Motor	Japan	Motor vehicles	$131,754
9	General Electric	U.S.	Diversified financials	$131,698
10	Mitsubishi	Japan	Trading	$109,386

Source: "Global 500: The World's Largest Corporations," *Fortune,* July 15, 2003, p. 106.

Customization Versus Globalization of International Marketing Strategies

globalization The development of marketing strategies that treat the entire world (or its major regions) as a single entity

Like domestic marketers, international marketers develop marketing strategies to serve specific target markets. Traditionally international marketing strategies have customized marketing mixes according to cultural, regional, and national differences. Many soap and detergent manufacturers, for example, adapt their products to local water conditions, equipment, and washing habits. Colgate-Palmolive even devised an inexpensive, plastic, hand-powered washing machine for use in households that have no electricity in less developed countries. Coca-Cola markets distinct versions of its soft drinks for the tastes of different regions of the world; it also contributes to local causes and customizes promotion to feature local people, humor, and sports teams in its advertising.[53] Global Marketing (on p. 136) highlights a Spanish firm that tailors products for different cultures.

At the other end of the spectrum, **globalization** of marketing involves developing marketing strategies as though the entire world (or its major regions) were a single entity: a globalized firm markets standardized products in the same way everywhere.[54] Nike and Adidas shoes, for example, are standardized worldwide. Other examples of globalized products include electronic communications equipment, Western American clothing, movies, soft drinks, rock and alternative music CDs, cosmetics, and toothpaste. Sony televisions, Levi jeans, and American cigarette brands post year-to-year gains in the world market.

For many years, organizations have attempted to globalize their marketing mixes as much as possible by employing standardized products, promotion campaigns, prices, and distribution channels for all markets. The economic and competitive payoffs for globalized marketing strategies are certainly great. Brand name, product characteristics, packaging, and labeling are among the easiest marketing mix variables to standardize; media allocation, retail outlets, and price may be more difficult. In the end, the degree of similarity among the various environmental and market conditions determines the feasibility and degree of globalization. A successful globalization strategy often depends on the extent to which a firm is able to implement the idea of "think globally, act locally."[55] Even take-out food lends itself to globalization: McDonald's, KFC, and Taco Bell restaurants seem to satisfy hungry customers in every hemisphere, although menus may be customized to some degree to satisfy local tastes.

International marketing demands some strategic planning if a firm is to incorporate foreign sales into its overall marketing strategy. International marketing activities often require customized marketing mixes to achieve the firm's goals. Globalization requires a total commitment to the world, regions, or multinational areas as an integral part of the firm's markets; world or regional markets become as important as domestic ones. Regardless of the extent to which a firm chooses to globalize its marketing strategy, extensive environmental analysis and marketing research are necessary to understand the needs and desires of the target market(s) and successfully implement the chosen marketing strategy. A global presence does not automatically result in a global competitive advantage. However, a global presence generates five opportunities for creating value: (1) to adapt to local market differences, (2) to exploit economies of global scale, (3) to exploit economies of global scope, (4) to mine optimal locations for activities and resources, and (5) to maximize the transfer of knowledge across locations.[56] To exploit these opportunities, marketers need to conduct marketing research, the topic of the next chapter.

GLOBAL MARKETING

Chupa Chups: Sweetening the World, One Country at a Time

What's your favorite flavor of lollipop? Cherry? Root beer? How about blue raspberry? These are viable options—if you live in the United States. But if you live in the Netherlands, you might have picked licorice as your favorite flavor. In China lichee nut and tea are favorite flavors, while *tarte tatin,* a type of apple pie, is popular in France. Like many companies, Chupa Chups Group is working to serve more markets around the world.

In 1958, Barcelona-based Chupa Chups decided to drop more than 200 products and focus exclusively on lollipops. Now the company produces more than 4 billion suckers annually and distributes them in 170 countries. With more than $455 million in sales, it is the sixth largest seller of hard candy in the world. Sales have been increasing as much as 40 percent a year, and 92 percent of sales now come from outside Spain.

Chupa Chups' international success can be attributed to two key marketing strategies: tailoring its product to meet different flavor preferences and understanding and respecting the various cultures to which it markets. This explains why the company markets so many different and seemingly unusual flavors: to satisfy different consumer taste preferences in each country. In an advertising campaign in Germany, the company successfully used *leck mich,* which means "lick me." However, a similar campaign, in partnership with M&M/Mars in the United States, was rejected because of its risqué nature. In China, research indicated that eating candy without offering to share with other children is considered rude. Chupa Chups addressed the issue so children could feel comfortable eating suckers in public. The firm is also looking to take advantage of the Chinese cultural practice of handing out candy at weddings.

Chupa Chups also faced difficulty marketing lollipops to teenage girls in Middle Eastern countries, where eating a sucker in public is viewed as an attempt to be seductive and therefore frowned on within the Muslim culture. Thus, the company is emphasizing lollipop consumption in private places such as homes, movie theaters, and cafés. Chupa Chups achieved great publicity in Europe by giving free candy to a well-known soccer coach who was trying to quit smoking. The coach was shown on television pacing the field during stressful moments and sucking on a Chupa Chups lollipop. The company is also working to adapt this concept to an American lifestyle. Although most Americans are not soccer fans, many may appreciate the need to cope with stress and cravings while trying to quit smoking. Marketing lollipops as a nicotine substitute may prove an effective strategy in a country that is increasingly frowning on the consumption of tobacco.

By striving to understand the cultures in which it does business, Chupa Chups has successfully entered many foreign countries and gained market share. In Spain, Chupa Chups has practically become synonymous with the word *lollipop.* The company hopes that its customized marketing efforts will make the brand name a household term around the world.

SUMMARY

International marketing involves developing and performing marketing activities across national boundaries. International markets can provide tremendous opportunities for growth.

A detailed analysis of the environment is essential before a company enters a foreign market. Environmental aspects of special importance include cultural, social, ethical, economic, political, legal, and technological forces. Because marketing activities are primarily social in purpose, they are influenced by beliefs and values regarding family, religion, education, health, and recreation. Cultural differences may affect marketing negotiations, decision-making behavior, and product adoption and use. A nation's economic stability and trade barriers can affect marketing efforts. Significant trade barriers include import tariffs, quotas, embargoes, and exchange controls. Gross domestic product (GDP) and GDP per capita are common measures of a nation's economic standing. Political and legal forces include a nation's political system, laws, regulatory bodies, special-interest groups, and courts. Advances in technology have greatly facilitated international marketing.

Various regional trade alliances and specific markets create both opportunities and constraints for companies engaged in international marketing. These include the North American Free Trade Agreement, the European Union, the Common Market of the Southern Cone, Asia-Pacific Economic Cooperation, the General Agreement on Tariffs and Trade, and the World Trade Organization.

There are several ways to get involved in international marketing. Importing (the purchase of products from a foreign source) and exporting (the sale of products to foreign markets) are the easiest and most flexible methods. Marketers may employ a trading company, which links buyers and sellers in different countries but is not involved in manufacturing and does not own assets related to manufacturing. Licensing and franchising are arrangements whereby one firm pays fees to another for the use of its name, expertise, and supplies. Contract manufacturing occurs when a company hires a foreign firm to produce a designated volume of the domestic firm's product to specification and the final product carries the domestic firm's name. Joint ventures are partnerships between a domestic firm and a foreign firm or government. Strategic alliances are partnerships formed to create competitive advantage on a worldwide basis. Finally, a firm can build its own marketing or production facilities overseas. When companies have direct ownership of facilities in many countries, they may be considered multinational enterprises.

Although most firms adjust their marketing mixes for differences in target markets, some firms standardize their marketing efforts worldwide. Traditional full-scale international marketing involvement is based on products customized according to cultural, regional, and national differences. Globalization, however, involves developing marketing strategies as if the entire world (or regions of it) were a single entity; a globalized firm markets standardized products in the same way everywhere. International marketing demands some strategic planning if a firm is to incorporate foreign sales into its overall marketing strategy.

Please visit the student website at **www.prideferrell.com** for ACE Self-Test questions that will help you prepare for exams.

IMPORTANT TERMS

International marketing
Import tariff
Quota
Embargo
Exchange controls
Balance of trade
Gross domestic product (GDP)
North American Free Trade Agreement (NAFTA)
European Union (EU)
Common Market of the Southern Cone (MERCOSUR)
Asia-Pacific Economic Cooperation (APEC)
General Agreement on Tariffs and Trade (GATT)
Dumping
World Trade Organization (WTO)
Importing
Exporting
Trading company
Licensing
Franchising
Contract manufacturing
Joint venture
Strategic alliance
Direct ownership
Multinational enterprise
Globalization

DISCUSSION & REVIEW QUESTIONS

1. How does international marketing differ from domestic marketing?
2. What factors must marketers consider as they decide whether to engage in international marketing?
3. Why are the largest industrial corporations in the United States so committed to international marketing?
4. Why do you think this chapter focuses on an analysis of the international marketing environment?
5. A manufacturer recently exported peanut butter with a green label to a nation in the Far East. The product failed because it was associated with jungle sickness. How could this mistake have been avoided?
6. If you were asked to provide a small tip (or bribe) to have a document approved in a foreign nation where this practice is customary, what would you do?

7. How will NAFTA affect marketing opportunities for U.S. products in North America (the United States, Mexico, and Canada)?

8. In marketing dog food to Latin America, what aspects of the marketing mix would a U.S. firm need to alter?

9. What should marketers consider as they decide whether to license or enter into a joint venture in a foreign nation?

10. Discuss the impact of strategic alliances on marketing strategies.

11. Contrast globalization with customization of marketing strategies. Is one practice better than the other? Explain.

APPLICATION QUESTIONS

1. To successfully implement marketing strategies in the international marketplace, a marketer must understand the complexities of the global marketing environment. Which environmental forces (sociocultural, economic, political/legal, or technological) might a marketer need to consider when marketing the following products in the international marketplace, and why?
   a. Barbie dolls   c. Financial services
   b. Beer   d. Television sets

2. Many firms, including Procter & Gamble, FedEx, and Occidental Petroleum, wish to do business in Eastern Europe and in the countries that were once part of the Soviet Union. What events could occur that would make marketing in these countries more difficult? What events might make it easier?

3. This chapter discusses various organizational approaches to international marketing. Which would be the best arrangements for international marketing of the following products, and why?
   a. Construction equipment
   b. Cosmetics
   c. Automobiles

4. Procter & Gamble has made a substantial commitment to foreign markets, especially in Latin America. Its actions may be described as a "globalization of marketing." Describe how a shoe manufacturer would go from domestic marketing, to limited exporting, to international marketing, and finally to a globalization of marketing. Give examples of some activities that might be involved in this process.

Internet Exercise & Resources

Visit **www.prideferrell.com** for resources to help you master the material in this chapter, plus materials that will help you expand your marketing knowledge, including Internet exercise updates, ACE self-tests, hotlinks to companies featured in this chapter, and much more.

FTD

Founded in 1910 as "Florists' Telegraph Delivery," FTD was the first company to offer a "flowers-by-wire" service. FTD does not itself deliver flowers but depends on local florists to provide this service. In 1994, FTD expanded its toll-free telephone-ordering service by establishing a website. Visit the site at **www.ftd.com.**

1. Click on International. Select a country to which you would like to send flowers. Summarize the delivery and pricing information that would apply to that country.

2. Determine the cost of sending fresh-cut seasonal flowers to Germany.

3. What are the benefits of this global distribution system for sending flowers worldwide? What other consumer products could be distributed globally through the Internet?

Video Case 5.1

BMW International

Bayerische Motoren Werke (better known as BMW) is one of Europe's top automakers. The Munich-based company manufactures vehicles under several brand names, including BMW, Mini, and Rolls-Royce Motor Cars, as well as BMW Motorcycles, which also offers a line of motorcycling apparel such as leather suits, gloves, and boots. The company sold more than 1 million vehicles in 2003.

In the United States, the BMW Group has grown to include marketing, sales, and financial service organizations for the BMW and Mini brands and Rolls-Royce Motor Cars; DesignworksUSA, an industrial design firm in California; and a technology office in Silicon Valley and various other operations throughout the country. BMW Manufacturing Corporation in South Carolina is part of BMW Group's global manufacturing network and is the exclusive manufacturer for all Z4 roadster and X5 Sports Activity Vehicles, supplying these products to more than 100 countries. The BMW Group sales organization markets vehicles in the United States through networks of 340 BMW car, 327 BMW Sports Activity Vehicle, 148 BMW Motorcycle, and 70 Mini dealers. BMW (US) Holding Corporation, the BMW Group's sales headquarters for North, Central, and South America, is located in Woodcliff Lake, New Jersey.

In Germany, the United States, and abroad, BMW concentrates exclusively on selected premium segments in the automobile market, making it the only multibrand automobile manufacturer in the world that is not active in the mass market. With the BMW, Mini, and (since 2003) Rolls Royce brands, BMW covers the premium segments ranging from the small car to the absolute-luxury category. BMW's premium brand strategy allows it to focus on achieving higher revenues per vehicle on the basis of a high value and a distinctive brand profile. The premium brand strategy therefore positions BMW for further profitable growth. The company expects the premium segments of the automobile market to grow worldwide by about 50 percent in the next ten years, while the mass volume automobile segments will increase by about 25 percent. The BMW Group is aiming to exploit this growth by assessing consumer behavior and meeting consumers' expectations for premium-branded automobiles.

Consumers are increasingly status and brand conscious. They are willing to pay more than $3 for a latté at Starbucks, yet clip coupons for the grocery store and shop at wholesale clubs for discounted household items. According to Michael Silverstrein and Neil Fiske in their book *Trading Up,* people are willing to pay more for quality products that matter to them, even if that requires making sacrifices in other areas. Mercedes recognized this in the early 1990s and responded by introducing less expensive, "entry-level" luxury autos—such as the M class and C class automobiles, which sold for $26,000 to $40,000—with the hope that buyers would "trade up" to more expensive vehicles as they matured. The phenomenon of trading up affects a variety of income levels—from $50,000 to $200,000—and all demographics—singles, seniors, families, and so on. Part of Mercedes' strategy stemmed from its recognition that the average age of its customers was over 50, but it wanted to reach a younger target market. BMW has also benefited from customers' desire for status and quality. BMW recognized the lifetime value of its customers and sought to encourage them to get into BMW-branded vehicles as

early as possible. Thus, BMW introduced the 318i, which, at a retail price in the mid-$20,000s, reached a whole new market for the company.

Luxury goods can be broken down into several categories, including "accessible superpremium" and "old luxury brand extensions." Accessible superpremium products are priced at the high end of their category (e.g., high-end liquors, pet foods, cosmetics), while old luxury extensions reflect the strategic orientation that BMW has adopted in global markets. This strategy involves offering lower-priced versions of existing products, which previously were accessible only to affluent buyers, to attract new market segments.

The best example of making a luxury brand accessible is the Mini. The brand's association with BMW makes it a premium small-car product, while its $17,000 entry price in the United States makes it affordable. The car also appeals to the nostalgia for small British roadsters and fun cars. Publicity from the film *The Italian Job* may also have helped the car reach record sales of 170,000 in 2003. The Mini will gain a competitor in 2006 when DaimlerChrysler launches the Smart minicar brand. DaimlerChrysler hopes to sell about 60,000 Smart-brand vehicles once the brand is established.

The BMW Group is following a worldwide strategy that can best be described as mass customization: tailoring products, prices, and distribution for customers' personal selection in the premium brand market. Although such customizing is more complex than mass producing computers and cars, BMW, as well as other automakers, desires to custom-build more vehicles to match specific customer needs.

The best example of success through product diversification is the various BMW product lines. The 3-series is available in the mid-$20,000 to $50,000 range and includes sedans, coupes, and convertibles as well as the X3 All-Activity vehicle. The 5-series caters to the core luxury market with prices beginning in the low $40,000s to mid-$50,000s. This series is complemented by the X5 All-Activity vehicle. The 6-series is a luxury coupe that sells in the $60,000 to $70,000 range. It is considered a "grand turismo," which represents the combination of sports car spirit and luxury-salon comfort. The high-tech car

of the future, the 7-series, embodies all the features of the ultimate luxury brand. But for those who might not consider the 7-series sufficiently luxurious, BMW's recently purchased Rolls-Royce brand should certainly satisfy their desire for the best in an automobile.

As a German company, BMW has developed an international brand and reputation that has become a role model for other organizations engaging in global marketing. Its key to success is acquiring an understanding of its demanding target market and developing a marketing mix to create a marketing strategy that provides customer satisfaction. Consumers around the world aspire to the pride of owning and driving a BMW.[57]

QUESTIONS FOR DISCUSSION

1. How has BMW developed such a successful international marketing strategy?
2. How would you compare BMW's worldwide marketing strategy with that of American car manufacturers, such as Ford and General Motors?
3. Do you think BMW's global marketing strategy meets the requirements of the concept of globalization as described in this chapter?

Case 5.2

Gillette Company

Founded in 1901 by King C. Gillette, Gillette Company was one of the first great multinational organizations and, some would say, a marvel of marketing effectiveness. Just four years after founding the firm in Boston, King Gillette opened a branch office in London, and the company quickly gained sales and profits throughout Western Europe. About 20 years later, Gillette said of his safety razor, "There is no other article for individual use so universally known or widely distributed. In my travels, I have found it in the most northern town in Norway and in the heart of the Sahara Desert." From the beginning, Gillette set out to offer consumers high-quality shaving products that would satisfy their basic grooming needs at a fair price. Having gained more than half of the entire razor and blades market, Gillette's manufacturing efficiency allowed it to implement marketing programs on a large scale, which helped the company gain both profits and market leadership.

Today Gillette Company is the world leader in male grooming products, a category that includes blades, razors, and shaving preparations, and in selected female grooming products, such as wet-shaving products and hair removal devices. In addition, the company holds the number one position worldwide in alkaline batteries and in manual and power toothbrushes. Gillette's manufacturing operations are conducted at 32 facilities in 15 countries, and products are distributed through wholesalers, retailers, and agents in more than 200 countries and territories.

Gillette's Mach3 and Mach3 Turbo shaving systems, which reap $2 billion in sales, remain the best-selling men's shavers, and its line of Venus razors leads the women's shaver market. "Gillette's blade and razor business is the single most valuable franchise in the household products and cosmetics industries," said William H. Steele, an analyst at Bank of America Securities. The blade and razor segment accounts for roughly 40 percent of Gillette's sales and more than 70 percent of the company's profits. Sales in this segment have more than doubled since 1989, and the outlook for this segment is promising as the shaving population increases, particularly in such locations as Asia, Eastern Europe, and Latin America. The company's progress in its principal line of business reflects the success of its technologically advanced products, including the Sensor family of shaving systems and, more recently, the Mach3 system.

Toiletries are now considered part of the grooming products business segment. At one time, this segment included hair care products, as well as the more familiar deodorants, antiperspirants, and shaving preparations. Intense competition and slow growth for certain products prompted Gillette to pare its toiletries portfolio. In 1998, Gillette sold its Jafra cosmetics line to narrow its focus. The company further refined its focus in 2000 when it sold its hair care brands to Diamond Products Company, a private-label marketer. Sales and profits in this category peaked in 1997 and have been declining steadily since that time.

Gillette's current strategy in the personal care market is to focus resources on core grooming products such as deodorants/antiperspirants and shaving preparations while providing supporting products in key markets. The premier brand in this product mix is the Gillette Series, which includes both shaving gels and foams, as well as Gillette Series antiperspirants and deodorants. The personal care segment also includes many of Gillette's best-known and most respected brands, including Foamy shaving cream and Right Guard, Soft & Dri, and Dry Idea deodorants/antiperspirants.

Gillette Company also owns Braun, which turned in a record performance in 1997 but has since struggled to contribute profits. As a result, Braun is no longer considered one of the company's primary business segments. However, Gillette still values Braun's shaving products, oral care products, and hair removal (epilation) devices, which fit well with the company's emphasis on product innovation and with its other business segments. Other Braun products— namely kitchen appliances, personal care products, and health care instruments—do not fit as well with Gillette's focus. As a result, the company has contemplated selling most of the Braun line but keeping the key products in shaving, oral care, and hair removal.

Another brand in Gillette's stable is Oral-B, which develops and markets a broad range of superior oral care products worldwide in a strong and well-established partnership with dental professionals. Led by toothbrushes, the Oral-B line also includes interdental products, specialty toothpastes, mouth rinses, and professional dental products. Sales and profits continue to increase in this segment as a result of technological developments and product innovations. For example, the Oral-B CrossAction toothbrush features innovative technology that is clinically proven to provide a greater level of manual plaque removal.

With the acquisition of Duracell International, Gillette instantly achieved worldwide leadership in the alkaline battery market. This segment is key to Gillette's portfolio, with Duracell products generating a sizable share of the company's sales and profits. Duracell is an excellent fit with Gillette's focus on technologically driven consumer products. Also, Duracell and Gillette share many characteristics,

including global brand franchises, common distribution channels, and geographic expansion potential. With Gillette's backing, Duracell enjoys significant economies of scale and greater market penetration through Gillette's worldwide distribution network.

Perhaps the most attractive aspect of Duracell for Gillette was and still is the market potential of alkaline batteries. Duracell leads this market with approximately a 40 percent share. Among the reasons for this growth is the booming popularity of portable electronic products, aggressive merchandising by battery manufacturers, and constant performance improvements, especially in battery life.

Though the prospects for growth are tremendous, sales of Duracell products have declined slightly in recent years due to increasing competition. Competitors such as Kodak's Photolife and Energizer have been investing in their own research and development processes. Energizer's e^2 batteries are clearly the dominant competitor for Duracell's Ultra. Long-time competitor Rayovac has experienced a resurgence in recent years. Although Rayovac's aggressive marketing appears to have taken more market share away from Energizer than from Duracell, Rayovac's growth and lower pricing point to a potential vulnerability in Duracell's strategy. Additional price competition for alkaline batteries is coming from private-label batteries, particularly Wal-Mart's EvrActiv line.

From its headquarters in Boston, Massachusetts, Gillette Company touches the lives of consumers around the globe. Each day, more than 1 billion people interact with a Gillette product. In the more than 100 years since the company was founded, Gillette has gained a leadership position through its strategy of managing its business with a long-term, global perspective. This ability to generate long-term, profitable growth in a changing global marketplace rests on several fundamental strengths, including a constantly increasing accumulation of scientific knowledge, innovative products that embody meaningful technological advances, and an immense manufacturing capability to produce billions of products every year reliably, efficiently, and cost effectively. Gillette's fundamental strengths have created strong and enduring consumer brand loyalty around the world.[58]

QUESTIONS FOR DISCUSSION

1. What environmental factors have contributed to Gillette's success in global markets? What forces may have created challenges for the company?
2. What strategy does Gillette appear to have adopted for international marketing?
3. How can Gillette continue to compete effectively in the battery and grooming markets?

Mattel Takes on Global Challenges

Mattel, Inc., with $4.7 billion in annual revenues, is the world leader in the design, manufacture, and marketing of children's toys. The company's major toy brands include Barbie (with more than 120 different Barbie dolls), Fisher-Price, Disney entertainment lines, Hot Wheels and Matchbox cars, Tyco Toys, American Girl, and games such as UNO. In addition, Mattel promotes international sales by tailoring toys for specific global markets instead of simply modifying favorites from the United States. Headquartered in El Segundo, California, Mattel also has offices in 36 countries and markets its products in more than 155 nations.

Mattel's marketing prowess and reach have paid off. In a poll conducted by the annual Power Brands study, Mattel had strong popularity among consumers. As many as four out of ten people said that if they were shopping for toys, Mattel would be the brand they most prefer. Retailers also singled out Mattel as the number one performer, with more than six out of ten mentions. This survey proved that both children and adults are enthused about Mattel and its line of products. In 2002, the Mattel and Fisher-Price names topped a survey of consumers who were asked about their brand preferences when buying toys in discount stores or superstores. The same consumers mentioned Barbie and Hot Wheels repeatedly. Mattel, Inc., owns all the leaders in this survey's report of top toy brands.

Customer Orientation at Mattel Mattel's management philosophy focuses on satisfying customers' needs and wants. For example, Mattel redesigned Barbie to more naturally reflect a "normal" athletic woman in an attempt to meet the demand for a more realistic doll. Barbie has also taken on many different professions to reach a wider audience. These product modifications and extensions are designed to meet consumer and social demands while still accomplishing company objectives. Some Hot Wheels cars now sport NASCAR logos to meet consumer demand for more merchandise related to this popular televised sport.

Mattel's pursuit of interactive multimedia is an attempt to adapt to the shorter span of time young girls spend playing with Barbie and other dolls and more traditional toys. Increasingly children are turning to more interactive toys, and Mattel acquired The Learning Company to meet and capitalize on this demand. This acquisition, however, did not prove profitable for Mattel, and the company eventually sold the division.

As another indicator of its commitment to customers, Mattel employs market research to ensure that its strategy and tactics match customer desires. This is combined with research and development in an effort to release new products yearly based on these consumer needs and wants. A recent addition to the Mattel product lines includes the construction and activity set called Ello. The product is meant to compete with Lego AG and draw girls to building toys, which traditionally have been geared almost exclusively to boys. Mattel research teams watched girls play with pipe cleaners, scissors, glue, paper, and cardboard, and concluded that girls wanted to make panels and tell stories about the space. The idea behind Ello is to build a house or figures using interconnecting plastic shapes, allowing girls to build and create while engaging in social play. Mattel hopes Ello will be a globally recognized brand with a unique name that does not require translation.

Mattel's Core Products—*Barbie*   The first Barbie doll sported open-toed shoes, a ponytail, sunglasses, earrings, and a zebra-striped bathing suit. Fashions and accessories were also available for the doll. While buyers at the annual Toy Fair in New York City took no interest in Barbie, little girls of the time certainly did. The intense demand seen at the retail stores was insufficiently met for several years; Mattel just could not produce the Barbie dolls fast enough. Barbie is one of Mattel's major product lines, accounting for more than 50 percent of its total sales.

March 1999 marked the fortieth anniversary of Barbie. It also heralded a new Barbie campaign called "Be Anything," which encourages girls to be anything from athletes to computer experts to dreamers. A Barbie doll is barely present in the ads, and not one of Barbie's accessories appears. The campaign is an attempt to retain the interest of girls for another two years after the usual post-Barbie age of 7 by making Barbie more "real" to older girls.

By August 2002, Barbie's popularity had slipped and Barbie failed to make the list of the five top-selling dolls. Mattel reacted by introducing a line of My Scene dolls, which includes a multicultural Barbie, aimed at older girls referred to as "tweens." The tween market consists of girls ages 8 to 12 who would rather watch MTV than play with dolls. The website **www.myscene.com** engages girls in the lives of four friends living in the Big City through short "shows" and music videos. Other efforts targeted at tweens include the Mystery Squad (a crime-solving crew) and the Barbie doll as Elle Woods, which is a tribute to the blonde character in the film *Legally Blonde 2: Red, White and Blonde.*

Hot Wheels   With more than 15 million boys ages 5 to 15 collecting Hot Wheels cars, this line of small die-cast vehicles is now involved with almost every racing circuit in the world, including NASCAR (National Association for Stock Car Auto Racing), Formula One, NHRA (National Hot Rod Association), CART (Championship Auto Racing Teams), AMA (American Motorcycle Association), and many others. This immense popularity has created a group of young collectors: the average boy collector owns more than 41 Hot Wheels.

Hot Wheels celebrated its thirty-fifth anniversary in 2003, with a massive marketing campaign called the Hot Wheels Highway 35 World Race. Mattel created a story- and character-based package that included collectible cars, racetracks, comic books, home videos, a video game, a television network special, and an online race. The idea was to appeal to the many age groups of collectors Mattel has acquired in recent years.

Fisher-Price   Acquired in 1993 as a wholly owned subsidiary, Fisher-Price is the umbrella brand for all of Mattel's infant and preschool lines. The brand is trusted by parents all over the world and appears on everything from children's software to eyewear and books to bicycles. Some of the more classic products include the Rock-a-Stack and Little People play sets. New favorites include Power Wheels vehicles and Rescue Heroes, a line of firefighter action figures that has been in great demand since September 11, 2001. Through licensing agreements, the brand also develops character-based toys such as Sesame Street's Elmo and Big Bird and Disney's Winnie the Pooh and Mickey Mouse.

Fisher-Price has built trust with parents by creating products that are educational, safe, and useful. For example, during recent years, the brand has earned high regard for innovative car seats and nursery monitors. One project includes collaboration with Microsoft to develop an activity table that teaches infants through preschoolers with "smart technology." Fisher-Price keeps pace with the interests of today's families through innovative learning toys and award-winning baby gear.

International Sales   Under current CEO Robert A. Eckert's leadership, Mattel has maintained its strategy of strong expansion overseas with a goal of raising

international sales to 50 percent. International sales increased 13 percent from 2000 to 2001 and another 11 percent from 2001 to 2002. Of the 34 percent of sales in 2002, two-thirds are in Europe, one-third in Latin America, and a small percentage in the Asia-Pacific region. The international segment has benefited from Mattel's strategic focus on globalization of brands, including improved product availability, better alignment of worldwide marketing and sales plans, and strong product launches.

Worldwide, Mattel's most recognized product continues to be Barbie. In a study conducted by Interbrand and published in *Business Week*, Barbie was the only Mattel brand that made the list of the 2002 "100 Best Global Brands." However, the traditional Barbie doll is receiving a cool welcome in some international markets. The Malaysian Consumers' Association of Penanghas tried to ban Barbie because of her non-Asian appearance and the lack of creativity needed to play with her. The public and media soon protested against the ban. But government agencies in other countries, such as Iran, are carrying out similar campaigns against Barbie.

Ethics and Responsibility at Mattel   Like most organizations, Mattel has recognized the different responsibilities it has to various stakeholders, including customers, employees, investors, suppliers, and the community, in its products, markets, and business outcomes. Mattel demonstrates a commitment to economic, legal, ethical, and philanthropic responsibilities.

Mattel's core products and business environment can present ethical issues. For example, since its products are designed primarily for children, the company must be sensitive to societal concerns about children's rights. In addition, the international environment often complicates business transactions, especially in the areas of employee rights and safety in manufacturing facilities. Different legal systems and cultural expectations about business can create ethical conflict. Finally, the use of technology may present ethical dilemmas, especially with regard to consumer privacy. Mattel has recognized these potential issues and

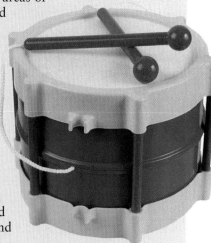

has taken steps to strengthen its commitment to business ethics and social responsibility.

Advances in technology have created special issues for Mattel's marketing efforts. Mattel recognizes that because it markets to children, it has the responsibility to communicate with parents about corporate marketing strategy. The company has taken special steps to inform both children and adults about its philosophy regarding Internet-based marketing tools, such as the Hot Wheels website.

At the Barbie.com website, parents are encouraged to read and follow Mattel's suggestions on Internet safety. This parents' page provides tips for creating rules and regulations for their children's use of the Internet. There is also a sample Internet Safety Promise for children and parents to complete, forming a "contract" to engage in smart, safe, and responsible behavior when surfing the Web.

Today Mattel faces many market opportunities and threats, including the rate at which children are maturing and abandoning toys, the role of technology in consumer products, and purchasing power and consumer needs in global markets. Mattel's sales growth potential, especially in the international markets, continues to grow. For a company that began with two friends making picture frames, Mattel has demonstrated marketing dexterity. But the next few years will test the firm's resolve and strategy within the highly competitive but lucrative toy market.

QUESTIONS FOR DISCUSSION

1. Describe Mattel's target market for Barbie and Hot Wheels. How did the firm's marketing strategy appeal to this market?
2. How has Mattel tried to be a socially responsible firm in its numerous world markets?
3. What environmental forces have created challenges for Mattel as it continues expansion into global markets? Which markets have created opportunities?

Part Three

Using Technology and Information to Build Customer Relationships

Part Three expands the marketing environment by examining how marketers use technology and information about customers in greater detail. **Chapter 6** explores how marketers use information technology to build long-term relationships with customers by targeting them more precisely than ever before. Both e-marketing and customer relationship management are presented in the context of building an effective marketing strategy. **Chapter 7** provides a foundation for analyzing buyers through a discussion of marketing information systems and the basic steps in the marketing research process. Understanding elements that affect buying decisions enables marketers to better analyze customers' needs and evaluate how specific marketing strategies can satisfy those needs.

6

E-Marketing and Customer Relationship Management

OBJECTIVES

1. To define *electronic marketing* and *electronic commerce* and recognize their increasing importance in strategic planning

2. To understand the characteristics of electronic marketing—addressability, interactivity, memory, control, accessibility, and digitalization—and how they differentiate electronic marketing from traditional marketing activities

3. To examine how the characteristics of electronic marketing affect marketing strategy

4. To understand how electronic marketing and information technology can facilitate customer relationship management

5. To identify legal and ethical considerations in electronic marketing

Google Finds Success with Technology and Positive Relationships

Google, Inc., has created one of the most successful—some would say indispensable—websites by providing a search engine with an uncanny knack for generating relevant results. The company derived its name from the term *googol*, which refers to the number represented by 1 followed by 100 zeros, to reflect its mission to organize the seemingly infinite amount of information available on the World Wide Web. Google accounts for approximately 75 percent of all Internet searches, providing results for more than 200 million searches a day in 88 languages. Founded by Sergey Brin and Larry Page in 1998, the company employs 1,000 and rings up an estimated $600 million to $800 million in annual revenues from licensing fees and advertising. Google has succeeded where so many other dot-coms have failed by following a conservative strategy: providing a simple, easy-to-use website and developing effective relationships with advertisers.

From the beginning, the firm refused to follow the pack of free-spending Internet startups and instead focused on what it does best: providing efficient access to information on the Internet. Google can search more than 3.1 billion online documents and return results in a fifth of a second. Although most search engines generate results based on the number of times the search criteria appear in a website's content, Google looks for hyperlinks pointing to a webpage from other websites to create a more reliable search result.

Half the firm's revenues stem from the sale of text-based advertisements that searchers see with their search results. However, Google doesn't permit banner and pop-up ads, which many Internet users find annoying, or accept payment for giving advertisers better placement in the search result. Instead, Google's advertising clients benefit from web surfers' appreciation of the firm's ability to generate relevant results as well as an advertisement click-through rate that is five times higher than the industry standard. The company continually collects and analyzes data to identify popular search topics and phrases, and then solicits advertisers in relevant industries. Google emphasizes the importance of establishing strong advertising client relationships and works to find beneficial matches with each client.

In addition to providing an award-winning search engine for web surfers, Google has agreements to provide search services for hundreds of corporate websites, including Sony and Cingular Wireless. The company plans to expand this and related search services to more corporate clients around the globe. The company is also considering offering a new service that will permit Internet users to browse online through print catalogs scanned into Google's servers. By maintaining a conservative strategy, Google has grown into the world's largest search engine.[1] ■

The phenomenal growth of the Internet presents exciting opportunities for companies such as Google to forge interactive relationships with consumers and business customers. The interactive nature of the Internet, particularly the World Wide Web, has made it possible to target markets more precisely and even reach markets that previously were inaccessible. It also facilitates customer relationship management, allowing companies to network with manufacturers, wholesalers, retailers, suppliers, and outsource firms to serve customers more efficiently. Because of its ability to enhance the exchange of information between customer and marketer, the Internet has become an important component of most firms' marketing strategies.

We devote this chapter to exploring this exciting frontier. We begin by defining *electronic marketing* and exploring its context within marketing strategies. Next, we examine the characteristics that differentiate electronic marketing activities from traditional ones and explore how marketers are using the Internet strategically to build competitive advantage. Then we take a closer look at the role of the Internet and electronic marketing in managing customer relationships. Finally, we consider some of the ethical and legal implications that affect Internet marketing.

Marketing on the Internet

electronic commerce (e-commerce) Sharing business information, maintaining business relationships, and conducting business transactions by means of telecommunications networks

electronic marketing (e-marketing) The strategic process of creating, distributing, promoting, and pricing products for targeted customers in the virtual environment of the Internet

A number of terms have been coined to describe marketing activities and commercial transactions on the Internet. One of the most popular terms is **electronic commerce (or e-commerce)**, defined as "the sharing of business information, maintaining business relationships, and conducting business transactions by means of telecommunications networks."[2] In this chapter, we focus on how the Internet, especially the World Wide Web, relates to all aspects of marketing, including strategic planning. Thus, we use the term **electronic marketing (or e-marketing)** to refer to the strategic process of creating, distributing, promoting, and pricing products for targeted customers in the virtual environment of the Internet.

One of the most important benefits of e-marketing is the ability of marketers and customers to share information. Through company websites, consumers can learn about a firm's products, including features, specifications, and even prices. Many websites also provide feedback mechanisms through which customers can ask questions, voice complaints, indicate preferences, and otherwise communicate about their needs and desires. The Internet has changed the way marketers communicate and develop relationships not only with their customers but also with their employees and suppliers. Lockheed Martin, for example, created a global network linking 80 suppliers to help build a new stealth fighter jet. The company expects the project to save about $25 million a year during product development.[3] Many companies use e-mail, groupware (software that allows people in different locations to access and work on the same file or document over the Internet), instant messaging, videoconferencing, and other technologies to coordinate activities and communicate with employees. Because such technology facilitates and lowers the cost of communications, the Internet can contribute significantly to any industry or activity that depends on the flow of information, such as software, entertainment, health care, education, travel services, and government services.[4] The Homeland Security Department, for example, created a secure web-based network that lets emergency services share information and coordinate responses to disasters. The Disaster Management Interoperability Services system facilitates vital communications during disasters and may benefit the country in the event of a terrorist attack.[5] Indeed, research has found that using the Internet for communication and administration activities has a greater effect on business performance than higher-profile activities such as order taking and procurement.[6]

Telecommunications technology offers additional benefits to marketers, including rapid response, expanded customer service capability (e.g., 24 hours a day,

Item# FJV016 – **$18**

Uncommon Jellies
Looking for something a little different?
Try some of our favorite hard-to-find flavors.
Once you taste them, they're sure to become your favorites
too! Enjoy six 12 oz. jars of Smucker's jelly: Curant, Mixed
Fruit, Elderberry, Guava, Apple, and Black Raspberry.

Shop Online at www.Smuckers.com
Call Toll-Free 1-800-742-6729

® Registered trademarks of The J.M. Smucker Company.

Electronic Marketing
Through the Internet, an online store can provide hard-to-find products. Smucker's provides jellies that may not be in local stores.

7 days a week, or 24/7), decreased operating costs, and reduced geographic barriers. Data networks have decreased cycle and decision times and permitted companies to treat customers more efficiently.[7] In today's fast-paced world, the ability to shop for books, clothes, and other merchandise at midnight, when traditional stores are usually closed, is a benefit for both buyers and sellers. Indeed, research by comScore Networks found that 20 percent of online shopping occurs between 9 P.M. and 9 A.M.[8] The Internet allows even small firms to reduce the impact of geography on their operations. For example, Coastal Tool & Supply, a small power tool and supply store in Connecticut, has generated sales from around the world through its website.

Despite these benefits, many companies that chose to make the Internet the core of their marketing strategies—often called "dot-coms"—failed to earn profits or acquire sufficient resources to remain in business. Many dot-coms went bankrupt because they thought the only thing that mattered was brand awareness. In reality, however, Internet markets are more similar to traditional markets than they are different.[9] Thus, successful e-marketing strategies, like traditional marketing strategies, depend on creating, distributing, promoting, and pricing products that customers need or want, not merely developing a brand name or reducing the costs associated with online transactions. In fact, traditional retailers continue to do quite well in some areas that many people thought the Internet would dominate just a few years ago. For example, although many marketers believed there would be a shift to buying cars online, experts estimate that just 5.4 percent of all new cars will be sold via the Internet in 2008. Research suggests that online shoppers are very concerned about price, and a firm's profits can vanish quickly as competition drives prices down. Few consumers are willing to spend $30,000 online to purchase a new automobile. However, consumers are increasingly making car-buying decisions on the basis of information found online.[10]

Indeed, e-marketing has not changed all industries, although it has had more of an impact in some industries in which the costs of business and customer transactions are very high. For example, trading stock has become significantly easier and less expensive for customers who can go online and execute their own orders. Firms such as E*Trade and Charles Schwab have been innovators in this area, and traditional brokerage firms such as Merrill Lynch have had to introduce online trading for their customers to remain competitive. In many other industries, however, the impact of e-marketing may be incremental.

◆ Basic Characteristics of Electronic Marketing

Although e-marketing is similar to traditional marketing, it is helpful to understand the basic characteristics that distinguish this environment from the traditional marketing environment. These characteristics include addressability, interactivity, memory, control, accessibility, and digitalization.

Addressability. The technology of the Internet makes it possible for visitors to a website to identify themselves and provide information about their product needs and wants before making a purchase. The ability of a marketer to identify customers before they make a purchase is called **addressability.** Many websites encourage visitors to register to maximize their use of the site or to gain access to premium areas; some even require it. Registration forms typically ask for basic information, such as

addressability A marketer's ability to identify customers before they make a purchase

Addressability
At usairways.com visitors can register to receive weekly e-mails about discount last-minute air fares.

© US Airways, Inc. Reprinted with permission.

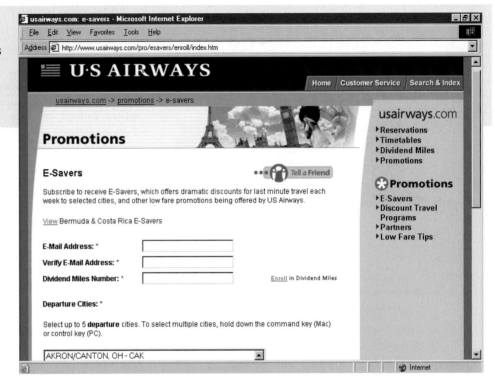

name, e-mail address, age, and occupation, from which marketers can build user profiles to enhance their marketing efforts. CDNow (a partner of Amazon.com), for example, asks music lovers to supply information about their listening tastes so the company can recommend new releases. Some websites even offer contests and prizes to encourage users to register. Marketers can also conduct surveys to learn more about the people who access their websites, offering prizes as motivation to participate.

Addressability represents the ultimate expression of the marketing concept. With the knowledge about individual customers garnered through the Web, marketers can tailor marketing mixes more precisely to target customers with narrow interests, such as recorded blues music or golf. Addressability also facilitates tracking website visits and online buying activity, which makes it easier for marketers to accumulate data about individual customers to enhance future marketing efforts. Amazon.com, for example, stores data about customers' purchases and uses that information to make recommendations the next time they visit the site.

cookie An identifying string of text stored on a website visitor's computer

Some website software can store a **cookie**, an identifying string of text, on a visitor's computer. Marketers use cookies to track how often a particular user visits the website, what he or she may look at while there, and in what sequence. Cookies also permit website visitors to customize services, such as virtual shopping carts, as well as the particular content they see when they log onto a webpage. CNN, for example, allows visitors to its website to create a custom news page tailored to their particular interests. The use of cookies to store customer information can be an ethical issue, however, depending on how the data are used. If a website owner can use cookies to link a visitor's interests to a name and address, that information could be sold to advertisers and other parties without the visitor's consent or even knowledge. The potential for misuse of cookies has made many consumers wary of this technology. Because technology allows access to large quantities of data about customers' use of websites, companies must carefully consider how the use of such information affects individuals' privacy, as we discuss in more detail later in this chapter.

interactivity The ability to allow customers to express their needs and wants directly to the firm in response to the firm's marketing communications

Interactivity. Another distinguishing characteristic of e-marketing is **interactivity**, which allows customers to express their needs and wants directly to the firm in response to its marketing communications. This means marketers can interact with prospective customers in real time (or at least a close approximation of it). Of course, salespeople have always been able to do this, but at a much greater cost. The Web provides the advantages of a virtual sales representative, with broader market coverage and at lower cost.

Interactivity helps marketers maintain high-quality relationships with existing customers by shaping customer expectations and perceptions. Customers with a higher expectation of continuing a relationship with a marketer are more likely to maintain that relationship even after a less than satisfactory experience with that firm.[11] To help build such relationships, companies are using the Internet to share increasing levels of information with customers. Amazon.com, for example, launched Search Inside the Book, which enables customers to search for a word or phrase in 120,000 books. After the new feature was introduced, sales for searchable books rose by 9 percent over books not included in the service.[12]

One implication of interactivity is that a firm's customers can also communicate with other customers (and noncustomers). For this reason, differences in the amount and type of information possessed by marketers and their customers are less pronounced than in the past. One result is that the new- and used-car businesses have become considerably more competitive because buyers are coming into dealerships armed with more complete product and cost information obtained through comparison shopping on the Net. By providing information, ideas, and a context for interacting with other customers, e-marketers can enhance customers' interest in and involvement with their products.

community A sense of group membership or feeling of belonging by individual members

Interactivity also enables marketers to capitalize on the concept of community to help customers derive value from the firm's products and website. **Community** refers to a sense of group membership or feeling of belonging by individual members of a group.[13] One such community is Tripod, a website where Generation Xers can create their own webpages and chat or exchange messages on bulletin boards about topics ranging from cars and computers to health and careers. Another example is

Interactivity
iVillage facilitates customer feedback through over 300 online quizzes related to personal issues.

Reprinted with permission from iVillage.com. iVillage.com is a registered trademark of iVillage, Inc.

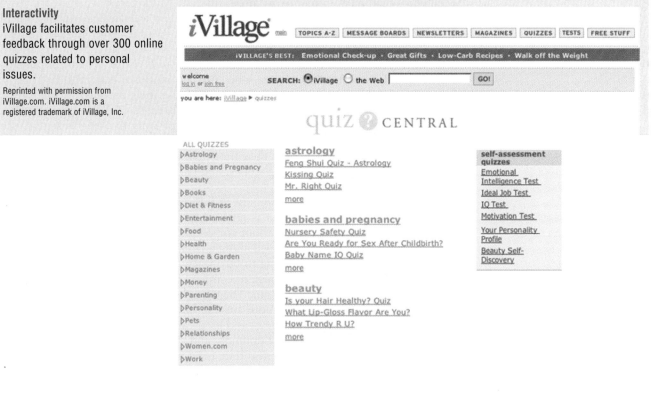

iVillage, a website targeted at women. Because such communities have well-defined demographics and share common interests, they represent a valuable audience for marketers, which typically fund the sites through advertising.

Memory. **Memory** refers to a firm's ability to access databases or data warehouses containing individual customer profiles and purchase histories and use these data in real time to customize its marketing offer to a specific customer. A **database** is a collection of information arranged for easy access and retrieval. Although companies have had database systems for many years, the information these systems contain did not become available on a real-time basis until fairly recently. Current software technology allows a marketer to identify a specific visitor to its website instantaneously, locate that customer's profile in its database, and then display the customer's past purchases or suggest new products based on past purchases while he or she is still at the site. For example, Bluefly, an online clothing retailer, asks visitors to provide their e-mail addresses, clothing preferences, brand preferences, and sizes so it can create a customized online catalog of clothing that matches the customer's specified preferences. The firm uses customer purchase profiles to manage its merchandise buying. Whenever it adds new clothing items to its inventory, it checks them against its database of customer preferences and, if it finds a match, alerts the individual in an e-mail message. Applying memory to large numbers of customers represents a significant advantage when a firm uses it to learn more about individual customers each time they visit the firm's website.

Control. In the context of e-marketing, **control** refers to customers' ability to regulate the information they view and the rate and sequence of their exposure to that information. The Web is sometimes referred to as a *pull* medium because users determine what they view at websites; website operators' ability to control the content users look at and in what sequence is limited. In contrast, television can be characterized as a *push* medium because the broadcaster determines what the viewer sees once she or he has selected a particular channel. Both television and radio provide "limited exposure control" (you see or hear whatever is broadcast until you change the station).

For e-marketers, the primary implication of control is that attracting—and retaining—customers' attention is more difficult. Marketers have to work harder and more creatively to communicate the value of their websites clearly and quickly, or the viewer may lose interest and move on to another site. With literally hundreds of millions of unique pages of content available to any web surfer, simply putting a website on the Internet does not guarantee anyone will visit it or make a purchase. Publicizing the website may require innovative promotional activities. For this reason, many firms pay millions of dollars to advertise their products or websites on high-traffic sites such as America Online (AOL). Because of AOL's growing status as a **portal** (a multiservice website that serves as a gateway to other websites), firms are eager to link to it and other such sites to help draw attention to their own sites. Indeed, consumers spend most of their time online on portal sites such as MSN and Yahoo!, checking e-mail, tracking stocks, and perusing news, sports, and weather.

Accessibility. An extraordinary amount of information is available on the Internet. The ability to obtain information is referred to as **accessibility**. Because customers can access in-depth information about competing products, prices, reviews, and so forth, they are much better informed about a firm's products and their relative value than ever before. Someone looking to buy a new truck, for example, can go to the websites of Ford, Toyota, and Dodge to compare the features of the Ford F-150, the Toyota Tundra, and the Dodge Ram. The truck buyer can also access online magazines and pricing guides to get more specific information about product features, performance, and prices. Many new- and used-car buyers turn to independent websites such as Kelley Blue Book, Edmunds, and Autobytel for pricing information before they go to a dealership to negotiate for a new vehicle.

Accessibility dramatically increases competition for Internet users' attention. Without substantial promotion, such as advertising on portals like America Online,

memory The ability to access databases or data warehouses containing individual customer profiles and purchase histories and use these data in real time to customize a marketing offer

database A collection of information arranged for easy access and retrieval

control Customers' ability to regulate the information they view and the rate and sequence of their exposure to that information

portal A multiservice website that serves as a gateway to other websites

accessibility The ability to obtain information available on the Internet

Accessibility
Through Expedia.com customers can access in-depth information about competing products and prices, and make reservations for travel and entertainment.

MSN, Yahoo!, and other high-traffic sites, it is becoming increasingly difficult to attract a visitor's attention to a particular website. Consequently e-marketers are having to become increasingly creative and innovative to attract visitors to their sites.

Accessibility also relates to making information available for employees to service customers. Krispy Kreme, for example, has a network that provides store managers with a wealth of information, ranging from instructional videos and ordering recommendations based on each store's order history to weather forecasts, because consumers are more likely to buy donuts when the temperature falls. Having so much information readily accessible allows employees to focus on customers instead of paperwork.[14]

digitalization The ability to represent a product, or at least some of its benefits, as digital bits of information

Digitalization. **Digitalization** is the ability to represent a product, or at least some of its benefits, as digital bits of information. Digitalization allows marketers to use the Internet to distribute, promote, and sell those features apart from the physical item itself. FedEx, for example, has developed web-based software that allows consumers and business customers to track their own packages from starting point to destination. Distributed over the Web at very low cost, the online tracking system adds value to FedEx's delivery services. Digitalization can be enhanced for users who have broadband access to the Internet, because broadband's faster connections allow streaming audio and video and other new technologies.

In addition to providing distribution efficiencies, digitizing part of a product's features allows new combinations of features and services to be created quickly and inexpensively. For example, a service station that keeps a customer's history of automotive oil changes in a database can e-mail that customer when the next oil change is due and at the same time suggest other types of preventive maintenance, such as

Napster is a safe, reliable and totally legal way to discover, download and collect music. Listen to over 500,000 tracks for less than 10 bucks per month. Quickly find new tracks that match your independent taste. Then share them with your friends. GO TO NAPSTER.COM.

Digitalization
Napster.com provides downloads of over 500,000 songs for a fee.

tire rotation or a tune-up. Digital features are easy to mix and match to meet the demands of individual customers.

◆ E-Marketing Strategies

Now that we have examined some distinguishing characteristics of doing business on the Internet, let's consider how these characteristics affect marketing strategy. Marketing strategy involves identifying and analyzing a target market and creating a marketing mix to satisfy individuals in that market, regardless of whether those individuals are accessible online, as in Building Customer Relationships, or through more traditional avenues. However, there are significant differences in how the marketing mix components are developed and combined into a marketing strategy in the electronic environment of the Web. As we continue this discussion, keep in mind that the Internet is a very dynamic environment, and therefore e-marketing strategies may need to be modified frequently to keep pace.

BUILDING CUSTOMER RELATIONSHIPS

Harris Poll Uses Internet to Survey Consumers

Conducting marketing research the old-fashioned way has become, well, old-fashioned. Marketers are increasingly finding the Internet to be a quick and inexpensive source of information about customer interests and preferences. Internet users, in turn, are finding marketing researchers increasingly willing to offer rewards for simply providing their opinions.

The Harris Poll Online gives Internet users a chance to sound off on a variety of topics, ranging from upcoming movies and television shows to the latest fashions for teenagers. At Harris Poll, Internet users can sign up for a "subpanel" about a particular topic in which they have some interest and knowledge and receive discounts, free merchandise, or other compensation in exchange for their participation. A teenager, for example, might be offered discounts toward purchases at her favorite clothing outlet if she is willing to view pictures of models wearing particular items and then rate her probability of buying those products. The resulting survey data can help marketers better understand the desires of their target markets and thus tailor their product offerings more effectively.

Harris Poll Online also offers Internet surfers a unique opportunity to influence decision makers by participating in opinion polls about controversial topics. Through such participation, respondents can let politicians, lobbyists, and other decision makers know their personal views. In other circumstances, users can enter sweepstakes, win prizes, or receive some other compensation for their time and opinions about potential goods and services. Harris Poll Online even offers a reward program, somewhat like frequent flier miles, that benefits the most opinionated participants. The more respondents sound off, the more points they earn and can redeem for prizes.

These methods allow the Harris Poll, one of the oldest and most prestigious polling institutions in America, to gather up-to-date information in the Internet age. The information is valuable to businesses looking to study their target markets and offers them the opportunity to conduct a virtual test of their product with a specified target market before releasing it. The opinion polls also tell companies whether they might commit a social *faux pas* with their upcoming products if they fail to conform to popular opinion.

Table 6.1	Internet Use Around the World, by Selected Country	
Country	**Users (in Millions)**	**Estimated Percentage of Population**
Australia	13.1	66.1
United States	185.9	64.0
Canada	20.5	63.5
Japan	78.0	63.3
United Kingdom	34.1	56.7
Germany	41.9	50.8
Israel	3.0	49.8
Chile	5.2	33.5
Russia	22.3	15.4
South Africa	5.2	11.8
Mexico	11.1	10.6
Argentina	4.0	10.3
China	95.8	7.5
India	39.2	3.8
Iraq	0.0125	0.05

Source: "Population Explosion!" CyberAtlas, May 10, 2004, **http://cyberatlas.internet.com/big_ picture/geographics/article/0,1323,5911_151151,00.html.**

Target Markets. Marketing strategy involves identifying and analyzing a target market and creating a marketing mix to satisfy individuals in that market. With more than half of Americans online, the Internet has become an important medium for reaching consumers. Although Internet access outside the United States has lagged behind, people around the world are rapidly discovering the Web's potential for communication and e-marketing, as shown in Table 6.1.

Although Internet usage statistics have long been dominated by men, American women are turning to the Internet in greater numbers for work and to save time and money. About 52 percent of Internet users in the United States are women, compared to only 42 percent of European Internet users.[15] About 45 percent of Americans use e-mail, and one-third search for product information online.[16] More than half (53 percent) of U.S. Internet users have made a purchase online. Increasing numbers of Americans are using the Internet for online banking and other financial transactions. As Lee Rainie, director of the Pew Internet & American Life Project, says, "The Internet has gone from novelty to utility for many Americans."[17] Most Americans (66.2 percent of residential users) continue to access the Internet through a telephone modem. Broadband access (primarily via DSL or cable modem) accounts for 25 percent of residential access.[18]

NET SIGHTS

*Anything associated with the Internet seems to move at the speed of light; thus, statistics on Internet access and usage are obsolete almost as soon as they appear in print. One valuable source of up-to-date statistics for marketers is CyberAtlas (**http://cyberatlas. Internet.com/**), which provides an easily accessible clearinghouse of Internet data from leading research firms such as Forrester Research, Jupiter Research, Gartner Dataquest, and Nielsen/NetRatings. The award-winning site offers the latest demographic and geographic, usage, and traffic statistics, as well as articles about Internet advertising, business-to-business markets, retailing, and more.*

Product Considerations. The growth of the Internet and the World Wide Web presents exciting opportunities for marketing products to both consumers and organizations. Computers and computer peripherals, industrial supplies, and packaged software are the leading business purchases online. According to International Data Corporation (IDC), the total value of goods and services purchased by businesses worldwide through e-commerce will climb from $282 billion in 2000 to $4.3 trillion by 2005, an annual rate of 73 percent.[19] Consumer products account for a small but growing percentage of Internet transactions, with food and beverage, sporting goods, and home goods among the fastest-growing online consumer purchases. Online retail sales are expected to grow from $95.7 billion in 2003 to $229 billion in 2008 and account for 10 percent of total retail sales.[20] Through e-marketing, companies can provide products, including goods, services, and ideas, that offer unique benefits and improve customer satisfaction.

The online marketing of goods such as computer hardware and software, books, videos, DVDs, CDs, toys, automobiles, and even groceries is accelerating rapidly. For example, Internet grocers such as FreshDirect and Peapod expect to see online sales of food and beverages grow from $3.7 billion to $17.4 billion in five years.[21] Based in New York City, FreshDirect uses technology to provide made-to-order meat, produce, bakery items, and other grocery products at prices up to 35 percent less than competitors.[22] Autobytel has established an effective model for online auto sales by helping consumers find the best prices on their preferred models and then arranging for local delivery. However, low profit margins due to customized deliveries have challenged the ability of firms to deliver tangible goods.

Services may have the greatest potential for online marketing success. Many websites offer or enhance services ranging from home- and car-buying assistance to travel reservations and stock trading. At Century 21's website, consumers can search for the home of their dreams anywhere in the United States, get information about mortgages and credit and tips on buying real estate, and learn about the

Products
Ebay provides a wide choice of new, used, and collectible products.

Snapshot

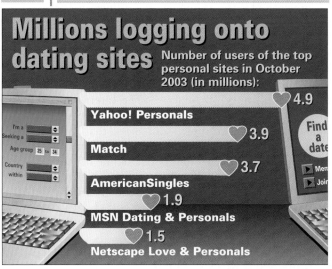

Millions logging onto dating sites Number of users of the top personal sites in October 2003 (in millions):

Yahoo! Personals — 4.9
Match — 3.9
AmericanSingles — 3.7
MSN Dating & Personals — 1.9
Netscape Love & Personals — 1.5

Source: Data from Nielsen/NetRatings.

company's relocation services. Airlines are increasingly booking flights via their websites. Southwest Airlines, for example, booked more than $2.5 billion worth of airplane tickets online last year.[23]

The proliferation of information on the World Wide Web has itself spawned new services. Web search engines and directories such as Google, Yahoo!, Lycos, and Excite are among the most heavily accessed sites on the Internet. Without these services, which track and index the vast quantity of information available on the Web, the task of finding something of interest would be tantamount to searching for the proverbial needle in a haystack. Many of these services, most notably Yahoo!, have evolved into portals by offering additional services, including news, weather, chat rooms, free e-mail accounts, and shopping.

Even ideas have potential for success on the Internet. Web-based distance learning and educational programs are becoming increasingly popular. Corporate employee training is a $55 billion industry, and online training modules are growing rapidly. Kinko's, for example, replaced 51 employee-training centers with a web-based training network that lets workers take online courses on the company's products and policies.[24] Additional ideas being marketed online include marriage and personal counseling; medical, tax, and legal advice; and even psychic services.

Distribution Considerations. The role of distribution is to make products available at the right time at the right place in the right quantities. The Internet can be viewed as a new distribution channel. Physical distribution is especially compatible with e-marketing. The ability to process orders electronically and increase the speed of communications via the Internet reduces inefficiencies, costs, and redundancies throughout the marketing channel. Most trucking firms now accept orders through the Internet, for example, but Yellow Transportation feeds order data from the Internet and the firm's call centers into a custom program to determine how many drivers it needs to schedule at each of its 335 facilities across the nation. By helping Yellow schedule 19,300 Teamsters and 8,250 trucks, the system saves the company approximately $100 million a year.[25]

More firms are exploiting advances in information technology to synchronize the relationships between their manufacturing or product assembly and their customer contact operations. This increase in information sharing among the firm's various operations makes product customization easier to accomplish. Marketers can use their websites to query customers about their needs and then manufacture products that exactly fit those needs. Gateway and Dell, for example, help customers build their own computers by asking them to

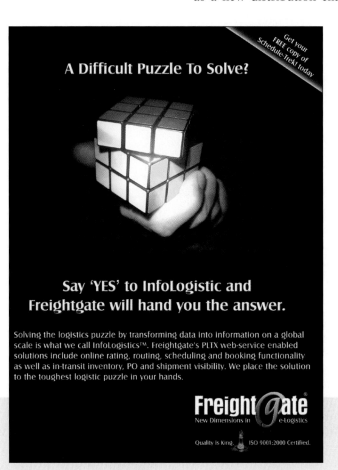

A Difficult Puzzle To Solve?

Get your FREE copy of Schedule-Trek! today

Say 'YES' to InfoLogistic and Freightgate will hand you the answer.

Solving the logistics puzzle by transforming data into information on a global scale is what we call InfoLogistics™. Freightgate's PLTX web-service enabled solutions include online rating, routing, scheduling and booking functionality as well as in-transit inventory, PO and shipment visibility. We place the solution to the toughest logistic puzzle in your hands.

Freightgate
New Dimensions in e-Logistics

Quality is King.   ISO 9001:2000 Certified.

Distribution Considerations
Freightgate provides online routing, scheduling, and tracking for in-transit inventory shipments.

specify what components to include; the firms then assemble and ship the customized products directly to the customers in a few days. Imperial Sugar lets customers place orders, check stock, and track shipments via its website, which now accounts for 10 percent of the firm's sales.[26]

One of the most visible members of any marketing channel is the retailer, and the Internet is increasingly becoming a retail venue. Although just 1 percent of all retail purchases occur online, Jupiter Media Metrix projects that by 2006 the percentage of the population shopping online will grow to 71 percent and online retail sales in the United States will climb to $130 billion.[27] The Internet provides an opportunity for marketers of everything from computers to travel reservations to encourage exchanges. Amazon.com, for example, sold more than $5 billion of books, CDs, DVDs, videos, toys, games, and electronics directly from its website in 2003.[28] Indeed, Amazon.com's success at marketing books online has been so phenomenal that many imitators have adopted its retailing model for everything from CDs to toys. Another retailing venture is online auctioneers, such as eBay and Haggle Online, which auction everything from fine wines and golf clubs to computer goods and electronics.

Promotion Considerations. The Internet is an interactive medium that can be used to inform, entertain, and persuade target markets to accept an organization's products. In fact, gathering information about goods and services is one of the main reasons people use the Internet. The accessibility and interactivity of the Internet allow marketers to complement their traditional media usage for promotional efforts. The control characteristic of e-marketing means that customers who visit a firm's website are there because they choose to be, indicating they are interested in the firm's products and therefore can be at least somewhat involved in its website's message and dialog. For these reasons, the Internet represents a highly cost-effective communication tool for small businesses. Results of Verizon's Annual Small Business Internet Survey suggest that 37 percent of small businesses now have a website, and these marketers use the Internet primarily as a tool to foster customer relations, advertising, and communications.[29]

Promotion
Kraftfoods.com provides online recipes to promote its products.

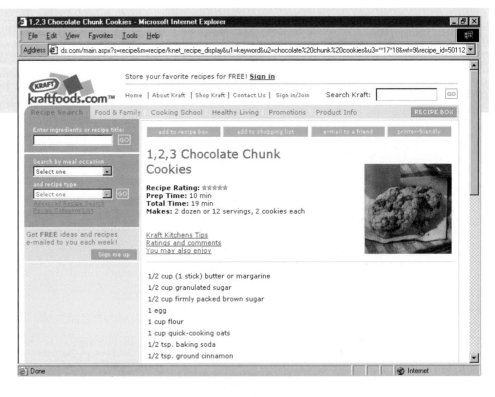

Table 6.2	Types of Advertising on Websites
Banner ads	Small, rectangular, static, or animated ads that typically appear at the top of a webpage
Keyword ads	Ads that relate to text or subject matter specified in a web search
Button ads	Small, square or rectangular ads bearing a corporate or brand name or logo and usually appearing at the bottom or side of a webpage
Pop-up ads	Large ads that open in a separate web browser window on top of the website being viewed
Pop-under ads	Large ads that open in a new browser window underneath the website being viewed
Sponsorship ads	Ads that integrate companies' brands and products with the editorial content of certain websites

Many companies augment their TV and print advertising campaigns with web-based promotions. Both Kraft and Ragu, for example, have created websites with recipes and entertaining tips to help consumers get the most out of their products. Many movie studios have set up websites at which visitors can view clips of their latest releases, and television commercials for new movies often encourage viewers to visit these sites. In addition, many companies choose to advertise their goods, services, and ideas on portals, search engines, and even other firms' websites. Table 6.2 describes the most common types of advertisements found on websites.

Many marketers are also offering buying incentives and adding value to their products online through the use of sales promotions, especially coupons. Several websites, including coolsavings.com, valupage.com, and valpak.com, offer online coupons for their members. Val-pak, for example, offers about 30,000 coupons through its site, and its (free) membership has grown to 600,000. Val-pak has succeeded by offering coupons for a variety of local merchants, including restaurants, dry cleaners, video stores, fitness centers, and carwashes.[30]

The characteristics of e-marketing make promotional efforts on the Internet significantly different from those using more traditional media. First, because Internet users can control what they see, customers who visit a firm's website are there because they choose to be, which implies, as pointed out previously, that they are interested in the firm's products and therefore may be more involved in the message and dialog provided at the site. Second, the interactivity characteristic allows marketers to enter into dialogs with customers to learn more about their interests and needs. This information can then be used to tailor promotional messages to individual customers. In fact, customized communications can help reduce information overload and improve buying decisions, which can enhance customer relationships.[31] Finally, addressability can make marketing efforts directed at specific customers more effective. Indeed, direct marketing combined with effective analysis of customer databases may become one of e-marketing's most valuable promotional tools.

Pricing Considerations. Pricing relates to perceptions of value and is the most flexible element of the marketing mix. Electronic marketing facilitates both price and nonprice competition because the accessibility characteristic of e-marketing gives consumers access to more information about the costs and prices of products than has ever been available to them before. As mentioned earlier, car shoppers can access automakers' webpages, configure an ideal vehicle, and get instant feedback on its cost. They can also visit Autobytel, Edmund's, and other websites to obtain comparative pricing information on both new and used cars to help them find the best value.

Customer Relationship Management

One characteristic of companies engaged in e-marketing is a renewed focus on relationship marketing by building customer loyalty and retaining customers—in other words, on customer relationship management (CRM). As we noted in Chapter 1, CRM focuses on using information about customers to create marketing strategies that develop and sustain desirable long-term customer relationships. A focus on customer relationship management is possible in e-marketing because of marketers' ability to target individual customers. This effort is enhanced over time as customers invest time and effort into "teaching" the firm what they want. This investment in the firm also increases the costs a customer would incur by switching to another company. Once a customer has learned to trade stocks online through Charles Schwab, for example, there is a cost associated with leaving to find a new brokerage firm: another firm may offer less service, and it may take time to find a new firm and learn a new system. Any time a marketer can learn more about its customers to strengthen the match between its marketing mix and target customers' desires and preferences, it increases the perceived costs of switching to another firm. Strong customer identification with a company can also help build meaningful relationships and even turn customers into "champions" of those companies and their products.[32]

E-marketing permits companies to target customers more precisely and accurately than ever before. The addressability, interactivity, and memory characteristics of e-marketing allow marketers to identify specific customers, establish interactive dialogs with them to learn about their needs, and combine this information with their purchase histories to customize products to meet those needs. Like many online retailers, Amazon.com stores and analyzes purchase data to understand each customer's interests. This information helps the retailer improve its ability to satisfy individual customers and thereby increase sales of books, music, movies, and other products to each customer. The ability to identify individual customers allows marketers to shift their focus from targeting groups of similar customers to increasing their share of an individual customer's purchases. Thus, the emphasis shifts from *share of market* to *share of customer*. However, improving share of customer by maximizing customer loyalty can be difficult.[33] Thus, a firm should ensure that individual target customers have sufficient potential to justify such specialized efforts. Indeed, one benefit arising from the

Customer Relationship Management
Amazon.com uses advanced software from SAS to provide a unique online shopping experience.

addressability characteristic of e-marketing is that firms can track and analyze individual customers' purchases and identify the most profitable and loyal customers.

Focusing on share of customer requires recognizing that all customers have different needs and that all customers do not have equal value to a firm. The most basic application of this idea is the 80/20 rule: 80 percent of business profits come from 20 percent of customers. Although this idea is not new, advances in technology and data collection techniques now permit firms to profile customers in real time. The goal is to assess the worth of individual customers and thus estimate their lifetime value (LTV) to the firm. Some customers—those who require considerable hand holding or return products frequently—may simply be too expensive to retain given the low level of profits they generate. Companies can discourage these unprofitable customers by requiring them to pay higher fees for additional services. For example, many banks and brokerages charge hefty maintenance fees on small accounts. Such practices allow firms to focus their resources on developing and managing long-term relationships with more profitable customers.[34] Developing systematic CRM procedures is thus one of the most important steps in managing relationships.[35]

◆ Technology Drives CRM

Customer relationship management focuses on building satisfying exchange relationships between buyers and sellers by gathering useful data at all customer-contact points—telephone, fax, online, and personal—and analyzing those data to better understand customers' needs and desires. Companies are increasingly automating and managing customer relationships through technology. Indeed, one fast-growing area of CRM is customer support and call center software, which helps companies capture information about all interactions with customers and provides a profile of the most important aspects of the customer experience on the Web and on the phone. Using technology, marketers can analyze interactions with customers to identify performance issues and even build a library of "best practices" for customer interaction.[36] Customer support and call center software can focus on those aspects of customer interaction that are most relevant to performance, such as how long customers have to wait on the phone to ask a question of a service representative or how long they must wait to receive a response from an online request. This technology can also help marketers determine whether call center personnel are missing opportunities to promote additional products or provide better service. For example, after buying a new Saab automobile, the customer is supposed to meet a service mechanic who can answer any technical questions about the car during the first service visit. Saab follows up this visit with a telephone survey to determine whether the new-car buyer met the Saab mechanic and to learn about the buyer's experience with the first service call.

Sales automation software can link a firm's sales force to e-marketing applications that facilitate selling and providing service to customers. Often these applications enable customers to assist themselves instead of using traditional sales and service organizations. At Cisco, for example, 80 percent of all customer support questions can be answered online through the firm's website, eliminating 75,000 phone calls a month.[37] In addition, CRM systems can provide sales managers with information that helps them develop the best product solutions for customers and thus maximize service. Dell Computer, for example, employs CRM data to identify those customers with the greatest need for computer hardware and then provides these select customers with additional value in the form of free, secure, customized websites. These "premier pages" allow customers—typically large companies—to check their order status, arrange deliveries, and troubleshoot problems. Although Dell collects considerable data about its customers from its online sales transactions, the company avoids selling customer lists to outside vendors.[38] CRM applications such as that used by Dell include software for marketing automation, sales automation, and customer support and call centers. The market for CRM applications is expected to reach $17.7 billion in the United States by 2006.[39]

◆ Customer Satisfaction Is the End Result of CRM

Although technology drives CRM and can help companies build relationships with desirable customers, it is too often used as a cost reduction tactic or a tool for selling, with little thought toward developing and sustaining long-term relationships. Some companies spend millions to develop CRM systems, yet fail to achieve the associated benefits. These companies often see themselves as sophisticated users of technology to manage customers, but they do not view customers as assets. Customer relationship management is effective only when it is developed as a relationship-building tool. CRM is a process of reaching out to customers and building trust, not a technology solution for customer sales.[40] In addition, service quality and satisfaction depend on customer contact employees' commitment to their company and its customers as well as technology.[41]

Perhaps because of the software and information technology associated with collecting information from consumers and responding to their desires, some critics view CRM as a form of manipulation. It is possible to use information about customers at their expense to obtain quick results—for example, charging higher prices whenever possible and using available data to maximize profits. However, using CRM to foster customer loyalty does not require collecting every conceivable piece of data from consumers or trying to sell customers products they don't want. Marketers should not try to control customers; they should try to develop relationships that derive from the trust gained over many transactions and are sustained by customers' belief that the company genuinely desires their continued patronage.[42] Trust reduces the costs associated with worrying about whether expectations will be honored and simplifies customers' buying efforts in the future.

What marketers can do with CRM technology is identify their most valuable customers so they can make an investment in building long-term relationships with those customers.[43] To be successful, marketers must measure the effectiveness of their CRM systems in terms of their progress toward developing satisfactory customer relationships. Fewer than 20 percent of companies track customer retention, but developing and assessing customer loyalty is important in managing long-term customer relationships. At **www.loyaltyeffect.com**, a survey asks customers whether a company is worthy of their loyalty. Companies that rank high in customer loyalty on the survey include Enterprise Rent-a-Car, Harley-Davidson, L. L. Bean, and Northwestern Mutual.[44]

The most important component of customer relationship management is remembering that it is not about technology but about relationships with customers. It has proven useful for business-to-business, business-to-customer, and nonprofit marketing. In all cases, high-contact relationships may require greater effort in developing organizational identity.[45] Customer relationship management systems should ensure that marketers listen to customers and then respond to their needs and concerns to build long-term relationships. The Internet can provide a valuable listening post and serve as a medium to manage customer relationships.[46]

Legal and Ethical Issues in E-Marketing

How marketers use technology to gather information—both online and offline—to foster long-term relationships with customers has raised numerous legal and ethical issues. The popularity and widespread use of the Internet grew so quickly that global legal systems have been unable to keep pace with advances in technology. Among the issues of concern are personal privacy, unsolicited e-mail, and misappropriation of copyrighted intellectual property.

One of the most significant privacy issues involves the personal information companies collect from website visitors. A survey by the Progress and Freedom Foundation found that 96 percent of popular commercial websites collect personally identifying information from visitors.[47] Several companies, including Qwest

Communications International Inc. and Comcast Corporation, have been criticized for improperly using personal data, both online and offline.[48] Cookies are the most common means of obtaining such information. Some people fear the collection of personal information from website users may violate users' privacy, especially if done without their knowledge.

In response to privacy concerns, some companies are cutting back on the amount of information they collect. The 96 percent of websites identified by the Progress and Freedom Foundation survey as collectors of personal information was down from 99 percent two years before, and 84 percent of the surveyed sites indicated they are collecting fewer data than previously.[49] Public concerns about online privacy remain, however, and many professionals in the industry are urging self-policing on this issue to head off potential regulation. One effort toward self-policing is the online privacy program developed by the BBBOnLine subsidiary of the Council of Better Business Bureaus (see Figure 6.1). The program awards a privacy seal to companies that clearly disclose to their website visitors what information they are collecting and how they are using it.[50]

Figure 6.1 The BBBOnLine Privacy Seal and Program Explanation
Reprinted by permission of the Council of Better Business, Inc.

Few laws specifically address personal privacy in the context of e-marketing, but the standards for acceptable marketing conduct implicit in other laws and regulations can generally be applied to e-marketing. Personal privacy is protected by the U.S. Constitution; various Supreme Court rulings; and laws such as the 1971 Fair Credit Reporting Act, the 1978 Right to Financial Privacy Act, and the 1974 Privacy Act, which deals with the release of government records. However, with few regulations on how businesses use information, companies can legally buy and sell information about customers to gain competitive advantage. Some have suggested that if personal data were treated as property, customers would have greater control over their use.

The most serious strides toward regulating privacy issues associated with e-marketing are emerging in Europe, as examined in Ethics and Social Responsibility. The 1998 European Union Directive on Data Protection specifically requires companies to explain how the personal information they collect will be used and to obtain the individual's permission. Companies must make customer data files available on request, just as U.S. credit reporting firms must grant customers access to their personal credit histories. The law also bars website operators from selling e-mail addresses and using cookies to track visitors' movements and preferences without first obtaining permission. Because of this legislation, no company may deliver personal information about EU citizens to countries whose privacy laws do not meet EU standards.[51] The directive may ultimately establish a precedent for Internet privacy that other nations emulate.

ETHICS AND SOCIAL RESPONSIBILITY

Europe Takes the Lead in Privacy Protection

When General Motors decided to update its electronic corporate phone book, the U.S. automaker learned that Europe's strict privacy laws defined office telephone numbers as "personal information." It took General Motors six months of legal documentation and other paperwork expenses to obtain an internal global electronic company phone book. Tough privacy rules like those established in the European Union (EU) have become the norm in Canada, South America, Australia, and parts of Asia. These laws dictate how companies can transmit personal data to countries that the EU claims lack "adequate" privacy laws, including the United States. The European Union Directive on Data Protection specifically requires companies to explain how collected personal information will be used, obtain the individual's permission to collect and use the information, and make customer data files available on request.

Fundamental differences separate U.S. and European regulation of privacy issues. While Europe has defined privacy as a human right, U.S. data protection laws are often diminished by the free-speech protec-

tions granted by the U.S. Constitution. The result has been specific federal laws addressing sensitive areas such as medical and financial records and children's personal data. Some states have sought to go beyond federal regulation. California, for example, passed a law requiring businesses to keep records of all California customers' data shared with third parties—online or offline—for direct marketing purposes. The law requires businesses to tell California customers about all the data, including information relating to income and purchases, that they have shared, as well as the names of the third-party users, within 30 days of a consumer request for this information. Most U.S. companies set their own standards, whereas in Europe there is a coordinated comprehensive system for data protection.

In Canada, private industry has taken the lead in creating and developing privacy policies through the Direct Marketing Association of Canada (DMAC). The DMAC's policies resulted in additional Canadian legislation to protect personal privacy. This legislation was inspired by the EU Directive on Data Protection. The challenge for the future is whether the United States will continue employing a patchwork of state, federal, and industry-specific legislation or match the EU's initiatives on privacy.

spam Unsolicited commercial e-mail

Spam, or unsolicited commercial e-mail (UCE), is likely to be the next target of government regulation in the United States. Many Internet users believe spam violates their privacy and steals their resources. Spam has been likened to receiving a direct-mail promotional piece with postage due. Some angry recipients of spam have organized boycotts against companies that advertise in this manner. Other recipients, however, appreciate the opportunity to learn about new products. Table 6.3 lists common reactions to spam.

Most commercial online services (e.g., America Online) and Internet service providers offer their subscribers the option to filter out e-mail from certain Internet addresses that generate a large volume of spam. Many reputable companies are cutting back on unsolicited bulk e-mailings designed to acquire new customers in favor of more targeted e-mail campaigns aimed at retaining customers who have indicated their willingness to receive such mailings. L. L. Bean, for example, e-mails customized offers, coupons, and information about new products to customers based on their purchase history.[52] Nonetheless, the debate over spam is far from over, and legislation to regulate it has been enacted in 36 states. Those laws may be preempted by the federal Controlling the Assault of Non-Solicited Pornography and Marketing (CAN-SPAM) Law, which went into effect in 2004. This law bans fraudulent or deceptive unsolicited commercial e-mail and requires senders to provide information on how recipients can opt out of receiving additional messages.[53]

The Internet has also created issues associated with intellectual property, the copyrighted or trademarked ideas and creative materials developed to solve problems, carry out applications, and educate and entertain others. Intellectual property losses in the United States total more than $11 billion a year in lost revenue from the illegal copying of computer programs, movies, compact discs, and books. This issue has become a global concern because of disparities in enforcement of laws throughout the world. The software industry estimates that worldwide piracy costs its companies roughly $12 billion every year.[54] The Digital Millennium Copyright Act (DMCA) was passed to protect copyrighted materials on the Internet.

Protecting trademarks can also be problematic. For example, some companies have discovered that another firm has registered a URL that duplicates or is very similar to their own trademarks. The "cyber-squatter" then attempts to sell the right to use the URL to the legal trademark owner. Companies such as Taco Bell, MTC, and KFC have paid thousands of dollars to gain control of domain names that

Table 6.3	Common Reactions to Spam
Action	**Percent Reporting**
Deleted without opening	86%
Clicked "remove me"	67
Clicked to get more information	33
Reported to e-mail provider	21
Ordered product	7
Reported to consumer or government agency	7
Provided requested personal information	4
Gave money in response	1

Source: Pew Internet & American Life Project, in Robyn Greenspan, "Spam: Always Annoying, Often Offensive," CyberAtlas, Oct. 22, 2003, **http://cyberatlas.internet.com/big_picture/applications/article/0,,1301_3097351,00.html**.

match or parallel their company trademarks.[55] To help companies address this conflict, Congress passed the Federal Trademark Dilution Act of 1995, which gives trademark owners the right to protect their trademarks, prevents the use of trademark-protected entities, and requires the relinquishment of names that duplicate or closely parallel registered trademarks.

As the Internet continues to evolve, more legal and ethical issues will certainly arise. Recognizing this, the American Marketing Association has developed a Code of Ethics for Marketing on the Internet (see Table 6.4). Such self-regulatory policies may help head off government regulation of electronic marketing and commerce. Marketers and all other users of the Internet should make an effort to learn and abide by basic "netiquette" (Internet etiquette) to ensure they get the most out of the resources available on this growing medium. Fortunately, most marketers recognize the need for mutual respect and trust when communicating in any public medium. They know that doing so will allow them to maximize the tremendous opportunities the Internet offers to foster long-term relationships with customers.

Table 6.4	American Marketing Association Code of Ethics for Marketing on the Internet

Preamble

The Internet, including online computer communications, has become increasingly important to marketers' activities, as they provide exchanges and access to markets worldwide. The ability to interact with stakeholders has created new marketing opportunities and risks that are not currently specifically addressed in the American Marketing Association Code of Ethics. The American Marketing Association Code of Ethics for Internet marketing provides additional guidance and direction for ethical responsibility in this dynamic area of marketing. The American Marketing Association is committed to ethical professional conduct and has adopted these principles for using the Internet, including online marketing activities utilizing network computers.

General Responsibilities

Internet marketers must assess the risks and take responsibility for the consequences of their activities. Internet marketers' professional conduct must be guided by:
1. Support of professional ethics to avoid harm by protecting the rights of privacy, ownership and access.
2. Adherence to all applicable laws and regulations with no use of Internet marketing that would be illegal, if conducted by mail, telephone, fax or other media.
3. Awareness of changes in regulations related to Internet marketing.
4. Effective communication to organizational members on risks and policies related to Internet marketing, when appropriate.
5. Organizational commitment to ethical Internet practices communicated to employees, customers and relevant stakeholders.

Privacy

Information collected from customers should be confidential and used only for expressed purposes. All data, especially confidential customer data, should be safeguarded against unauthorized access. The expressed wishes of others should be respected with regard to the receipt of unsolicited e-mail messages.

Ownership

Information obtained from the Internet sources should be properly authorized and documented. Information ownership should be safeguarded and respected. Marketers should respect the integrity and ownership of computer and network systems.

(continued)

Table 6.4	*(continued)*

Access

Marketers should treat access to accounts, passwords, and other information as confidential, and only examine or disclose content when authorized by a responsible party. The integrity of others' information systems should be respected with regard to placement of information, advertising or messages.

Source: From the American Marketing Association, **www.ama.org/about/ama/ethcode.asp**. Reprinted with permission.

SUMMARY

Electronic commerce (e-commerce) refers to sharing business information, maintaining business relationships, and conducting business transactions by means of telecommunications networks. Electronic marketing (e-marketing) is the strategic process of creating, distributing, promoting, and pricing products for targeted customers in the virtual environment of the Internet. The Internet has changed the way marketers communicate and develop relationships with their customers, employees, and suppliers. Telecommunications technology offers marketers potential advantages, including rapid response, expanded customer service capability, reduced costs of operation, and diminished geographic barriers. Despite these benefits, many Internet companies failed because they did not realize Internet markets are more similar to traditional markets than they are different and thus require the same marketing principles.

Addressability is a marketer's ability to identify customers before they make a purchase. One way websites achieve addressability is through the use of cookies, strings of text placed on a visitor's computer. Interactivity allows customers to express their needs and wants directly to a firm in response to its marketing communications. It also enables marketers to capitalize on the concept of community and customers to derive value from the use of the firm's products and websites. Memory refers to a firm's ability to access collections of information in databases or data warehouses containing individual customer profiles and purchase histories. Firms can then use these data in real time to customize their marketing offers to specific customers. Control refers to customers' ability to regulate the information they view, as well as the rate and sequence of their exposure to that information. Accessibility refers to customers' ability to obtain the vast amount of information available on the Internet. Digitalization is the representation of a product, or at least the representation of some of its benefits, as digital bits of information.

The addressability, interactivity, and memory characteristics of e-marketing enable marketers to identify specific customers, establish interactive dialogs with them to learn their needs, and combine this information with their purchase histories to customize products to meet their needs. Thus, e-marketers can focus on building customer loyalty and retaining customers.

The growth of the Internet and the World Wide Web presents opportunities for marketing products (goods, services, and ideas) to both consumers and organizations. The Internet can also be viewed as a new distribution channel. The ability to process orders electronically and to increase the speed of communications via the Internet reduces inefficiencies, costs, and redundancies throughout the marketing channel. The Internet is an interactive medium that can be used to inform, entertain, and persuade target markets to accept an organization's products. The accessibility of the Internet presents marketers with an opportunity to expand and complement their traditional media promotional efforts. The Internet gives consumers access to more information about the costs and prices of products than has ever been available to them before.

One characteristic of companies engaged in e-marketing is a focus on customer relationship management (CRM), which employs information about customers to create marketing strategies that develop and sustain desirable long-term customer relationships. The addressability, interactivity, and memory characteristics of e-marketing allow marketers to identify specific customers, establish interactive dialogs with them to learn about their needs, and combine this information with customers' purchase histories to tailor products that meet those needs. It also permits marketers to shift their focus from share of market to share of customer. Although technology drives CRM and can help companies build relationships with desirable customers, customer relationship management cannot be effective unless it is developed as a relationship-building tool.

One of the most controversial issues in e-marketing is personal privacy, especially the personal information companies collect from website visitors, often through the use of cookies. Additional issues relate to spam, or unsolicited commercial e-mail (UCE), and misappropriation of copyrighted or trademarked intellectual property. More issues are likely to emerge as the Internet and e-marketing continue to evolve.

Please visit the student website at **www.prideferrell.com** for ACE Self-Test questions that will help you prepare for exams.

IMPORTANT TERMS

Electronic commerce
  (e-commerce)
Electronic marketing
  (e-marketing)
Addressability
Cookie
Interactivity
Community

Memory
Database
Control
Portal
Accessibility
Digitalization
Spam

DISCUSSION & REVIEW QUESTIONS

1. How does addressability differentiate e-marketing from the traditional marketing environment? How do marketers use cookies to achieve addressability?
2. Define *interactivity* and explain its significance. How can marketers exploit this characteristic to improve relations with customers?
3. Memory gives marketers quick access to customers' purchase histories. How can a firm use this capability to customize its product offerings?
4. Explain the distinction between *push* and *pull* media. What is the significance of control in terms of using websites to market products?
5. What is the significance of digitalization?
6. How can marketers exploit the characteristics of the Internet to improve the product element of their marketing mixes?
7. How do the characteristics of e-marketing affect the promotion element of the marketing mix?
8. How does e-marketing facilitate customer relationship management?

9. How can technology help marketers improve their relationships with customers?
10. Electronic marketing has raised several ethical questions related to consumer privacy. How can cookies be misused? Should the government regulate the use of cookies by marketers?

APPLICATION QUESTIONS

1. Amazon.com is one of the Web's most recognizable marketers. Visit the company's site at **www.amazon.com,** and describe how the company adds value to its customers' buying experience.
2. Some products are better suited than others to electronic marketing activity. For example, Art.com specializes in selling art prints via its online store. The ability to display a variety of prints in many different categories gives customers a convenient and efficient way to search for art. On the other hand, General Electric has a website displaying its appliances, but customers must visit a retailer to purchase them. Visit **www.art.com** and **www.geappliances.com,** and compare how each firm uses the electronic environment of the Internet to enhance its marketing efforts.
3. Visit the website **www.covisint.com** and evaluate the nature of the business customers attracted. Who is the target audience for this business marketing site? Describe the types of firms currently doing business through this exchange. What other types of organizations might be attracted? Is it appropriate to sell any banner advertising on a site such as this? What other industries might benefit from developing similar e-marketing exchange hubs?

Internet Exercise & Resources

Visit **www.prideferrell.com** for resources to help you master the material in this chapter, plus materials that will help you expand your marketing knowledge, including Internet exercise updates, ACE self-tests, hotlinks to companies featured in this chapter, and much more.

iVillage.com

iVillage is an example of an online community. Explore the content of this website at **www.ivillage.com.**

1. What target market can marketers access through iVillage?
2. How can marketers target this community to market their goods and services?
3. Based on your understanding of the characteristics of e-marketing, analyze the advertisements you observe on this website.

Video Case 6.1

4SURE.com Targets Business Customers

One company that has succeeded in the dot-com arena is 4SURE.com, which rang up $200 million in sales in 2000. Founded in 1998 by Bruce Martin and Linwood Lacy, 4SURE.com markets technology products online primarily to business customers through two distinct websites: solutions4SURE.com and computers4SURE.com. Solutions4SURE.com caters to the needs of large businesses and of government and educational customers, while computers4SURE.com targets individuals and small office and home office (SOHO) customers. Both websites serve as online technology superstores featuring more than 60,000 brand name products, including computers, hardware, software, and supplies. Among the characteristics that distinguish these sites from competitors are a powerful search engine, fast checkout, the ability to pay with credit cards and wire transfers, and a bill-when-shipped policy.

4SURE.com is committed to offering customers an extensive selection of products at competitive prices with first-rate customer service. Its easy-to-navigate website is backed by well-trained, knowledgeable customer service representatives, hassle-free exchanges and returns, and guaranteed secure transactions. The company alerts customers about sale prices and new items via e-mail and provides technical customer service for more knowledgeable buyers. To foster a close working relationship with customer contact personnel the company has kept sales and customer service teams in-house. The firm even installed giant digital clocks to count down the time customers are kept on hold. The company is also linked electronically to all of its major distributors and partners, which include Compaq Computer and Sony Electronics. Although the company outsources much of its logistics needs, it has built its own warehouse to ensure that it can supply customers quickly—even overnight when necessary. By leveraging extensive relationships with manufacturers and suppliers, 4SURE.com grants customers the opportunity to "buy with confidence—guaran-

teed." To reinforce business customers' confidence, the company's websites carry the TRUSTe trustmark logo, as well as certifications from Bizrate.com, VeriSign, and the BBBOnline Reliability Program.

Thanks to the company's strong focus on customer service, computers4SURE.com has received three prestigious awards—from Bizrate.com, Gomez.com, and RatingWonders.com—for its site's product selection, ease of use, privacy policy, and customer support. Bizrate.com, which rates online stores on the basis of customer feedback, gave the computers4SURE.com site 4.5 stars out of a potential 5, the highest rating achieved by any company reviewed by that site. RatingWonders.com also gave computers4SURE.com a score of 4.5 out of 5.

In 2001, 4SURE.com was acquired by Office Depot, the world's largest retailer of office products. Office Depot's own websites, including nine international sites, have already been recognized as industry leaders in the online retailing of office products. Office Depot hopes that 4SURE.com's brand name and success will help the firm reach new markets and achieve its goal of being the industry leader in providing knowledge, solutions, and products through multiple channels. According to Office Depot's CEO, Bruce Nelson, "This acquisition strategically positions Office Depot to grow in an online customer/product segment we have not successfully reached."[56]

QUESTIONS FOR DISCUSSION

1. How does 4SURE.com exploit the characteristics of electronic marketing to serve its customers? Which of these characteristics are most important to 4SURE.com's success?
2. Describe 4SURE.com's marketing mix. How does this mix differ from that of a more traditional, "brick-and-mortar" office supply store?
3. 4SURE.com has focused primarily on business markets, but it markets to consumers through its computers4SURE.com site. Assess this strategy in light of the firm's apparent success at a time when so many other dot-coms have failed.

Case 6.2

eBay Auctions Everything

One of the best-known Internet companies is eBay, whose stated mission is "to provide a global platform where practically anyone can trade practically anything." The leading online auction site has grown into a community of 62 million

registered users around the world who can buy or sell literally anything from automobiles, boats, and furniture to jewelry, musical instruments, electronics, and collectibles. The auction site, described by CEO Meg Whitman as a "dynamic self-regulating economy," transacts nearly $15 billion in merchandise a year, more than the gross domestic product of many countries, giving it 80 percent of the online auction market. The firm sells more used vehicles than the nation's number one dealer, Auto-Nation. Unlike many high-tech dot-com companies, eBay has been profitable almost from the beginning. The company's revenues topped $1 billion in 2002, and its 50 percent annual growth rate is expected to continue for the foreseeable future.

Why has eBay been so successful when so many other Internet startups have failed? Many people believe the company's success is due largely to the leadership of Whitman, who ranked second on a recent *Fortune* list of the most powerful women in business. Whitman, who gained experience at Hasbro, FTD, Stride Rite, Disney, and Procter & Gamble before taking the reins at eBay, keeps the company focused on the "big-picture" objectives and key priorities, such as keeping company expenses down and building a world-class executive team to keep the company on its fast-growing profitable pace. She expects to meet company objectives by making smart acquisition decisions; reaching new customers, including more corporate ones; and opening a fixed-price bazaar. Whitman believes her most valuable contribution to eBay's success is the development of a work ethic and an organizational culture that focuses on a fun, open, and trusting environment, which she hopes will help the firm achieve $3 billion in revenues by 2005.

Another reason for the company's success is its responsiveness to its users. For example, eBay's Voice of the Customer program brings in a dozen buyers and sellers every month to question about how they work and what else eBay could do to improve. In addition, the firm holds hour-long teleconferences at least twice a week to survey users on new features and policies.

Although eBay is known primarily for consumer-to-consumer actions, many small businesses have discovered they can sell older equipment and excess inventory through eBay. After a downturn in the aerospace industry, Reliable Tools Inc. sold a few items on eBay, including a $7,000, 2,300-pound milling machine. The California machine tool shop now sells about $1 million a month, accounting for 75 percent of its business. Increasingly, larger, multinational firms are setting up shop on eBay as well. Sun Microsystems and IBM, for example, have their own webpages within eBay's computer category from which they market products, primarily to small and mid-size business customers.

For many small businesses, eBay serves as their retail outlet. An estimated 150,000 individuals sell products full time on the auction site; eBay has also spawned a number of "Trading Assistants," independent companies that act as intermediaries to help consumers and businesses sell goods on its site. AuctionDrop, for example, provides six sites in San Francisco where sellers can drop off goods for the small business to auction on eBay, after which it collects 40 percent of the sales price as a commission, on top of the transaction fee charged by eBay. The company, which handles up to 1,000 items per day, plans to expand to four more locations around the U.S.

To maintain customer confidence in auction transactions, eBay has taken numerous steps to avoid fraud. Although fraud occurs in only 0.01 percent of all eBay transactions, even a few fraudulent activities generate negative publicity and ill will, and could jeopardize the firm's reputation for quality transactions. To battle the potential for fraud, the company modified its user agreement to permit the barring of any user from the auction site and established feedback forms that allow buyers and sellers to rate each other based on their experience. The company also offers escrow, payment processing, and credit card protection services through PayPal, Billpoint, and other providers, which further reduce the potential for fraud. The firm also established the Trust & Safety Department to look for suspicious activities and assist law enforcement agents in battling fraud.

By providing an easy-to-use site for consumers and businesses to buy and sell goods and remaining proactive, eBay has essentially become the poster child for a successful Internet venture. With strong leadership from Meg Whitman, Internet insiders believe the company will continue to serve as a model for electronic commerce.[57]

QUESTIONS FOR DISCUSSION

1. Which of the basic characteristics of e-marketing is most important to eBay?
2. Describe eBay's marketing mix. How does this mix differ from that of a more traditional, "brick-and-mortar" discount store?
3. Online fraud has been a factor in some consumers' reluctance to use auction sites by eBay (and perhaps in the rise in intermediary companies). Has eBay done enough to prevent fraud on its site? What else could the company do to improve its services?

Marketing Research and Information Systems

7

OBJECTIVES

1. To describe the basic steps in conducting marketing research

2. To explore the fundamental methods of gathering data for marketing research

3. To describe the nature and role of information systems in marketing decision making

4. To understand how such tools as databases, decision support systems, and the Internet facilitate marketing research

5. To identify key ethical and international considerations in marketing research

The World's Largest Marketing Research Company

VNU, Inc., a publishing company founded in the Netherlands in 1964, became the largest marketing research firm after acquiring ACNielsen and Nielsen Media in 2001. Originally called Verenigde Nederlandse Uitgeversbedrijven (United Dutch Publishers), the company now serves clients in more than 100 countries, answering questions such as "What is happening in the marketplace?" "Why is it happening?" "What will happen next?" and "What is the best way to grow my business?"

Through the ACNielsen group, VNU provides retail measurement information on competitive sales volume, market share, distribution, pricing, merchandising, and promotional activities to manufacturers and retailers of fast-moving consumer goods. Its consumer panel services provide marketers with insights based on actual consumer purchase information for more than 155,000 households in 22 countries. To provide customized research services in more than 60 countries, VNU conducts hundreds of thousands of consumer surveys, interviews, and focus groups every year to offer its clients greater understanding of consumer attitudes and purchase behavior. The firm's modeling and analytical services integrate and analyze information from a variety of sources to improve marketing decisions on pricing, promotion, product, and media use and placement.

Although most marketing firms rely on outside sources such as VNU to gain insight into key marketing questions, it is crucial that marketing managers know what questions to ask and be able to recognize effective marketing research and information system development. It is important that companies acquire the data that provide them with the insights necessary to develop effective marketing strategies.[1] ∎

The marketing research conducted by VNU enables marketers to implement the marketing concept by helping them acquire information about the characteristics, needs, and desires of target market customers. In fact, U.S. companies spend more than $6 billion annually on services provided by major marketing research firms such as VNU.[2] When used effectively, such information facilitates relationship marketing by helping marketers focus their efforts on meeting and even anticipating the needs of their customers. Marketing research and information systems that can provide practical and objective information to help firms develop and implement marketing strategies therefore are essential to effective marketing.

In this chapter, we focus on how marketers gather information needed to make marketing decisions. First, we define marketing research and examine the individual steps of the marketing research process, including various methods of collecting data. Next, we look at how technology aids in collecting, organizing, and interpreting marketing research data. Finally, we consider ethical and international issues in marketing research.

The Importance of Marketing Research

marketing research The systematic design, collection, interpretation, and reporting of information to help marketers solve specific marketing problems or take advantage of marketing opportunities

Marketing research is the systematic design, collection, interpretation, and reporting of information to help marketers solve specific marketing problems or take advantage of marketing opportunities. As the word *research* implies, it is a process for gathering information not currently available to decision makers. The purpose of marketing research is to inform an organization about customers' needs and desires, marketing opportunities for particular goods and services, and changing attitudes and purchase patterns of customers. Detecting shifts in buyers' behaviors and attitudes helps companies stay in touch with the ever-changing marketplace. Marketers of automobiles and related accessories, for example, would be interested to know that young women are increasingly buying and customizing compact cars such as the Honda Civic, Ford Focus, and Mitsubishi Eclipse. Wielding their own tools, women now comprise 18 percent of the market for customized cars, and more than a few of them have set their sights on breaking records on the racetrack. The $2.3 billion consumers spend to turn their cars into customized speed machines represents a tremendous opportunity for those companies willing to invest the resources to understand this market. One firm that is capitalizing on the trend is **GirlieGirlracing.com**, which markets clothing and car accessories to young female car enthusiasts.[3] Strategic planning requires marketing research to facilitate the process of assessing such opportunities or threats.

Marketing research can help a firm better understand market opportunities, ascertain the potential for success for new products, and determine the feasibility of a particular marketing strategy. Pizza Hut, for example, conducted research to learn more about its most profitable group of customers: high school and college

The Value of Marketing Research
Decision Analyst assists companies in developing new products, services, and promotions.

students. The research involved asking a carefully selected group of 350 students to refrain from consuming pizza products for 30 days and record their cravings for pizza and feelings about going without it during the study period. The company, owned by Yum! Brands, hopes this research will help it better understand the effects of "pizza deprivation," food cravings, and food desires among this desirable market, which may result in modifications in its marketing strategy.[4]

All sorts of organizations use marketing research to help them develop marketing mixes to match the needs of customers. Supermarkets, for example, have learned from marketing research that roughly half of all Americans prefer to have their dinners ready in 15 to 30 minutes. Such information highlights a tremendous opportunity for supermarkets to offer high-quality "heat and eat" meals to satisfy this growing segment of the food market. Political candidates also depend on marketing research to understand the scope of issues their constituents view as important. National political candidates may spend millions surveying voters to better understand issues and craft their images accordingly.

The real value of marketing research is measured by improvements in a marketer's ability to make decisions. Marketers should treat information in the same manner they use other resources, and they must weigh the costs of obtaining information against the benefits. Information should be judged worthwhile if it results in marketing activities that better satisfy the firm's target customers, lead to increased sales and profits, or help the firm achieve some other goal.

The Marketing Research Process

To maintain the control needed to obtain accurate information, marketers approach marketing research as a process with logical steps: (1) locating and defining problems or issues, (2) designing the research project, (3) collecting data, (4) interpreting research findings, and (5) reporting research findings (see Figure 7.1). These steps should be viewed as an overall approach to conducting research rather than as a rigid set of rules to be followed in each project. In planning research projects, marketers must consider each step carefully and determine how they can best adapt the steps to resolve the particular issues at hand.

◆ Locating and Defining Problems or Research Issues

The first step in launching a research study is problem or issue definition, which focuses on uncovering the nature and boundaries of a situation or question related to marketing strategy or implementation. The first sign of a problem is typically a departure from some normal function, such as failure to attain objectives. If a corporation's objective is a 12 percent sales increase and the current marketing strategy resulted in a 6 percent increase, this discrepancy should be analyzed to help guide future marketing strategies. Declining sales, increasing expenses, and decreasing profits also signal problems. Customer relationship management (CRM) is frequently based on analysis of existing customers. However, research indicates that this information could be biased and therefore misleading when making decisions

Figure 7.1 The Five Steps of the Marketing Research Process

| 1 Locating and defining problems or issues | 2 Designing the research project | 3 Collecting data | 4 Interpreting research findings | 5 Reporting research findings |

related to identifying and acquiring new customers.[5] Armed with this knowledge, a firm could define a problem as finding a way to adjust for biases stemming from existing customers when gathering data or to develop methods for gathering information to help find new customers. Conversely, when an organization experiences a dramatic rise in sales or some other positive event, it may conduct marketing research to discover the reasons and maximize the opportunities stemming from them.

NET SIGHTS

Perhaps one of the best-known pollsters and research firms, the Gallup Organization, has been conducting public opinion surveys and providing other management consulting services since 1935. The company is frequently called on to survey the public about political issues—especially during election campaigns—as well as business and economic issues, social issues, and lifestyle topics. To view the company's latest survey results, visit **www.gallup.com/**.

Marketing research often focuses on identifying and defining market opportunities or changes in the environment. When a firm discovers a market opportunity, it may need to conduct research to understand the situation more precisely so it can craft an appropriate marketing strategy. For example, Lowe's Companies, Inc., the second-largest home improvement retail chain, discovered that 75 percent of its sales come from retail customers, who account for 50 percent of the home improvement market. On the other hand, 25 percent of Lowe's sales come from contractors and other commercial business customers, whose spending accounts for about 44 percent of the market. Armed with this information, the company can focus its efforts on specific target markets and refine its marketing strategy to maximize its customer orientation.[6]

To pin down the specific boundaries of a problem or an issue through research, marketers must define the nature and scope of the situation in a way that requires probing beneath the superficial symptoms. The interaction between the marketing manager and the marketing researcher should yield a clear definition of the research need. Researchers and decision makers should remain in the problem or issue definition stage until they have determined precisely what they want from marketing research and how they will use it. Deciding how to refine a broad, indefinite problem or issue into a precise, researchable statement is a prerequisite for the next step in the research process.

◆ Designing the Research Project

research design An overall plan for obtaining the information needed to address a research problem or issue

Once the problem or issue has been defined, the next step is creating a **research design**, an overall plan for obtaining the information needed to address it. This step requires formulating a hypothesis and determining what type of research is most appropriate for testing the hypothesis to ensure the results are reliable and valid.

hypothesis An informed guess or assumption about a certain problem or set of circumstances

Developing a Hypothesis. The objective statement of a marketing research project should include hypotheses based on both previous research and expected research findings. A **hypothesis** is an informed guess or assumption about a certain problem or set of circumstances. It is based on all the insight and knowledge available about the problem or circumstances from previous research studies and other sources. As information is gathered, the researcher can test the hypothesis. For example, a food marketer such as H. J. Heinz might propose the hypothesis that children today have considerable influence on their families' buying decisions regarding ketchup and other grocery products. A marketing researcher would then gather data, perhaps through surveys of children and their parents, and draw conclusions as to whether the hypothesis is correct. Volkswagen might hypothesize that its new Phaeton luxury sedan, which sells for more than $65,000, would be purchased by individuals with an average age of 45 years. The carmaker could test this hypothesis on the basis of the cars' first year's purchase data. Sometimes several hypotheses are developed during an actual research project; the hypotheses that are accepted or rejected become the study's chief conclusions.

Snapshot

Popularity of sports drinks

Percentage of teenagers 13–19 who say they drink sports drinks (Gatorade, Powerade, etc.) during an average week:

Boys 43%

Girls 20%

Source: Data from BuzzBack Market Research.

exploratory research Research conducted to gather more information about a problem or to make a tentative hypothesis more specific

descriptive research Research conducted to clarify the characteristics of certain phenomena to solve a particular problem

causal research Research in which it is assumed that a particular variable X causes a variable Y

reliability A condition existing when a research technique produces almost identical results in repeated trials

validity A condition existing when a research method measures what it is supposed to measure

Types of Research. The hypothesis being tested determines whether an exploratory, descriptive, or causal approach will be used to gather data. When marketers need more information about a problem or want to make a tentative hypothesis more specific, they may conduct **exploratory research**. For instance, they may review the information in the firm's own records or examine publicly available data. Questioning knowledgeable people inside and outside the organization may yield new insights into the problem. Information about industry trends or demographics may also be an excellent source for exploratory research. For example, finding data indicating that inner-city household incomes grew by 20 percent to $35,000 a year between 1990 and 2000 while the national median household income grew by just 14 percent could be useful to consider in marketing plans to serve specific market segments.[7]

If marketers need to understand the characteristics of certain phenomena to solve a particular problem, **descriptive research** can aid them. Descriptive studies may range from general surveys of customers' education, occupation, or age to specifics on how often teenagers consume sports drinks or how often customers buy new pairs of athletic shoes. For example, if Nike and Reebok want to target more young women, they might ask 15- to 35-year-old females how often they work out, how frequently they wear athletic shoes for casual use, and how many pairs of athletic shoes they buy in a year. Such descriptive research can be used to develop specific marketing strategies for the athletic-shoe market. Descriptive studies generally demand much prior knowledge and assume the problem or issue is clearly defined. For example, a survey of automobile buyers found that those who use the Internet to search for vehicles are more likely to be younger and more educated and to spend more time searching in general.[8] Some descriptive studies require statistical analysis and predictive tools. The marketer's major task is to choose adequate methods for collecting and measuring data.

Hypotheses about causal relationships call for a more complex approach than a descriptive study. In **causal research**, it is assumed that a particular variable X causes a variable Y. Marketers must plan the research so that the data collected prove or disprove that X causes Y. To do so, marketers must try to hold constant all variables except X and Y. For example, to determine whether new carpeting, pet-friendly policies, or outside storage increases the number of rentals in an apartment complex, researchers need to keep all variables, except one of these three variables, constant in a specific time period.

Research Reliability and Validity. In designing research, marketing researchers must ensure that research techniques are both reliable and valid. A research technique has **reliability** if it produces almost identical results in repeated trials. However, a reliable technique is not necessarily valid. To have **validity**, the research method must measure what it is supposed to measure, not something else. For example, although a group of customers may express the same level of satisfaction based on a rating scale, as individuals they may not exhibit the same repurchase behavior because of different personal characteristics. This result may cause the researcher to question the validity of the satisfaction scale if the purpose of rating satisfaction was to estimate potential repurchase behavior.[9] A study to measure the effect of advertising on sales would be valid if advertising could be isolated from other factors or variables that affect sales. The study would be reliable if replications of it produced the same results.

◆ Collecting Data

The next step in the marketing research process is collecting data to help prove (or disprove) the research hypothesis. The research design must specify what types of data to collect and how they will be collected.

primary data Data observed and recorded or collected directly from respondents

secondary data Data compiled both inside and outside the organization for some purpose other than the current investigation

Types of Data. Marketing researchers have two types of data at their disposal. **Primary data** are observed and recorded or collected directly from respondents. This type of data must be gathered by observing phenomena or surveying people of interest. **Secondary data** are compiled both inside and outside the organization for some purpose other than the current investigation. Secondary data include general reports supplied to an enterprise by various data services and internal and online databases. Such reports might concern market share, retail inventory levels, and customers' buying behavior. Commonly, secondary data are already available in private or public reports or have been collected and stored by the organization itself. Due to the opportunity to obtain data via the Internet, more than half of all marketing research now comes from secondary sources.

Sources of Secondary Data. Marketers often begin the data collection phase of the marketing research process by gathering secondary data. They may use available reports and other information from both internal and external sources to study a marketing problem.

Internal sources of secondary data can contribute tremendously to research. An organization's own database may contain information about past marketing activities, such as sales records and research reports, which can be used to test hypotheses and pinpoint problems. From sales reports, for example, a firm may be able to determine not only which product sold best at certain times of the year but also which colors and sizes customers preferred. Such information may have been gathered for management or financial purposes.[10] Table 7.1 lists some commonly available internal company information that may be useful for marketing research purposes.

Accounting records are also an excellent source of data but, surprisingly, are often overlooked. The large volume of data an accounting department collects does not automatically flow to other departments. As a result, detailed information about costs, sales, customer accounts, or profits by product category may not be easily accessible to the marketing area. This condition develops particularly in organizations that do not store marketing information on a systematic basis.

External sources of secondary data include periodicals, government publications, unpublished sources, and online databases. Periodicals such as *Business Week, The Wall Street Journal, Sales & Marketing Management, American Demographics, Marketing Research,* and *Industrial Marketing* publish general information that can help marketers define problems and develop hypotheses. *Survey of Buying Power,* an annual supplement to *Sales & Marketing Management,* contains sales data for major industries on a county-by-county basis. Many marketers also consult federal government publications such as the *Statistical Abstract of the United States,* the *Census of Business,* the *Census of Agriculture,* and the *Census of Population;* some of these government publications are available through online

Table 7.1	Internal Sources of Secondary Data

- Sales data, which may be broken down by geographical area, product type, or even type of customer
- Accounting information, such as costs, prices, and profits, by product category
- Competitive information gathered by the sales force

Table 7.2	**External Sources of Secondary Data**

- Trade associations (e.g., American Marketing Association)
- Industry publications and databases (e.g., *Inbound Logistics, Sales & Marketing Management*)
- Government databases (e.g., Census Bureau, Department of Commerce)
- Sales, volume, and brand market share from marketing research firms (e.g., ACNielsen Company, Information Resources, Inc.)

information services or the Internet. Data from the 2000 U.S. census helped Hyundai Motor America pinpoint communities and neighborhoods with specific demographics matching Hyundai vehicle buyer profiles. This information allowed the company to target its promotional efforts at specific zip codes with promising demographics rather than at entire cities. As a result, the number of customers taking test drives and ultimately purchasing Hyundai vehicles like the Sonata and Santa Fe jumped, and the company's costs per vehicle were slashed by half.[11]

In addition, companies may subscribe to services, such as ACNielsen or Information Resources, Inc. (IRI), that track retail sales and other information. For example, IRI tracks consumer purchases using in-store, scanner-based technology. Marketing firms can purchase information from IRI about a product category, such as frozen orange juice, as secondary data.[12] Although smaller firms may be unable to afford such services, they can still find a wealth of information through industry publications and trade associations. Table 7.2 summarizes the major external sources of secondary data, excluding syndicated services.

Methods of Collecting Primary Data. Collection of primary data is a lengthier, more expensive, and more complex process than collection of secondary data. To gather primary data, researchers use sampling procedures, survey methods, observation, and experimentation. These efforts can be handled in-house by the firm's own research department or contracted to a private research firm such as ACNielsen, Information Resources, Inc., or IMS International.

Sampling Because the time and resources available for research are limited, it is almost impossible to investigate all the members of a target market or other population. A **population**, or "universe," includes all the elements, units, or individuals of interest to researchers for a specific study. For example, for a Gallup poll designed to predict the results of a presidential election, all registered voters in the United States would constitute the population. By systematically choosing a limited number of units—a **sample**—to represent the characteristics of a total population, researchers can project the reactions of a total market or market segment. (In the case of the presidential poll, a representative national sample of several thousand registered voters would be selected and surveyed to project the probable voting outcome.) **Sampling** in marketing research, therefore, is the process of selecting representative units from a total population. Sampling techniques allow marketers to predict buying behavior fairly accurately on the basis of the responses from a representative portion of the population of interest. Most types of marketing research employ sampling techniques.

There are two basic types of sampling: probability sampling and nonprobability sampling. With **probability sampling**, every element in the population being studied has a known chance of being selected for study. Random sampling is a form of probability sampling. When marketers employ **random sampling**, all the units in a population have an equal chance of appearing in the sample. The various events that can occur have an equal or known chance of taking place. For example, a specific card in a regulation deck should have a 1/52 probability of being drawn at any one time.

population All the elements, units, or individuals of interest to researchers for a specific study

sample A limited number of units chosen to represent the characteristics of a total population

sampling The process of selecting representative units from a total population

probability sampling A sampling technique in which every element in the population being studied has a known chance of being selected for study

random sampling A type of probability sampling in which all units in a population have an equal chance of appearing in the sample

Sample units are ordinarily chosen by selecting from a table of random numbers statistically generated so that each digit, 0 through 9, will have an equal probability of occurring in each position in the sequence. The sequentially numbered elements of a population are sampled randomly by selecting the units whose numbers appear in the table of random numbers.

stratified sampling A type of probability sampling in which the population of interest is divided into groups according to a common attribute and a random sample is then chosen within each group

Another type of probability sampling is **stratified sampling**, in which the population of interest is divided into groups according to a common attribute and a random sample is then chosen within each group. The stratified sample may reduce some of the error that could occur in a simple random sample. By ensuring that each major group or segment of the population receives its proportionate share of sample units, investigators avoid including too many or too few sample units from each group. Samples are usually stratified when researchers believe there may be variations among different types of respondents. For example, many political opinion surveys are stratified by gender, race, age, and/or geographic location.

nonprobability sampling A sampling technique in which there is no way to calculate the likelihood that a specific element of the population being studied will be chosen

The second type of sampling, **nonprobability sampling**, is more subjective than probability sampling because there is no way to calculate the likelihood that a specific element of the population being studied will be chosen. Quota sampling, for example, is highly judgmental because the final choice of participants is left to the researchers. In **quota sampling**, researchers divide the population into groups and then arbitrarily choose participants from each group. A study of people who wear eyeglasses, for example, may be conducted by interviewing equal numbers of men and women who wear eyeglasses. In quota sampling, there are some controls—usually limited to two or three variables, such as age, gender, or race—over the selection of participants. The controls attempt to ensure that representative categories of respondents are interviewed. Because quota samples are not probability samples, not everyone has an equal chance of being selected, and sampling error therefore cannot be measured statistically. Quota samples are used most often in exploratory studies, when hypotheses are being developed. Often a small quota sample will not be projected to the total population, although the findings may provide valuable insights into a problem. Quota samples are useful when people with some common characteristic are found and questioned about the topic of interest. A probability sample used to study people allergic to cats, for example, would be highly inefficient.

quota sampling A nonprobability sampling technique in which researchers divide the population into groups and then arbitrarily choose participants from each group

Survey Methods   Marketing researchers often employ sampling to collect primary data through mail, telephone, online, or personal interview surveys. The results of such surveys are used to describe and analyze buying behavior. Selection of a survey method depends on the nature of the problem or issue; the data needed to test the hypothesis; and the resources, such as funding and personnel, available to the researcher. Table 7.3 (on p. 180) summarizes and compares the advantages of the various survey methods.

Gathering information through surveys is becoming increasingly difficult because fewer people are willing to participate. Many people believe responding to surveys takes up too much scarce personal time, especially as surveys become longer and more detailed. Others have concerns about how much information marketers

Table 7.3	Comparison of the Four Basic Survey Methods			
	Mail Surveys	**Telephone Surveys**	**Online Surveys**	**Personal Interview Surveys**
Economy	Potentially lower in cost per interview than telephone or personal surveys if there is an adequate response rate.	Avoids interviewers' travel expenses; less expensive than in-home interviews.	The least expensive method if there is an adequate response rate.	The most expensive survey method; shopping mall and focus-group interviews have lower costs than in-home interviews.
Flexibility	Inflexible; questionnaire must be short and easy for respondents to complete.	Flexible because interviewers can ask probing questions, but observations are impossible.	Less flexible; survey must be easy for online users to receive and return; short, dichotomous, or multiple-choice questions work best.	Most flexible method; respondents can react to visual materials; demographic data are more accurate; in-depth probes are possible.
Interviewer bias	Interviewer bias is eliminated; questionnaires can be returned anonymously.	Some anonymity; may be hard to develop trust in respondents.	Interviewer bias is eliminated, but e-mail address on the return eliminates anonymity.	Interviewers' personal characteristics or inability to maintain objectivity may result in bias.
Sampling and respondents' cooperation	Obtaining a complete mailing list is difficult; nonresponse is a major disadvantage.	Sample limited to respondents with telephones; devices that screen calls, busy signals, and refusals are a problem.	Sample limited to respondents with computer access; the available e-mail address list may not be a representative sample for some purposes.	Not-at-homes are a problem, which may be overcome by focus-group and shopping mall interviewing.

are gathering and whether their privacy is being invaded. The unethical use of selling techniques disguised as marketing surveys has also led to decreased cooperation. These factors contribute to nonresponse rates for any type of survey.

mail survey A research method in which respondents answer a questionnaire sent through the mail

In a **mail survey**, questionnaires are sent to respondents, who are encouraged to complete and return them. Mail surveys are used most often when the individuals in the sample are spread over a wide area and funds for the survey are limited. A mail survey is less expensive than a telephone or personal interview survey as long as the response rate is high enough to produce reliable results. The main disadvantages of this method are the possibility of a low response rate and of misleading results if respondents differ significantly from the population being sampled.

Premiums or incentives that encourage respondents to return questionnaires have been effective in developing panels of respondents who are interviewed regularly by mail. Such mail panels, selected to represent a target market or market segment, are especially useful in evaluating new products and providing general information about customers, as well as records of their purchases (in the form of purchase diaries). Mail panels and purchase diaries are much more widely used than custom mail surveys, but both panels and purchase diaries have shortcomings.

Telephone Surveys
The National Do Not Call Registry is having a negative impact on the telephone surveying industry.

Farewell, Old Friend.

There are now more than 50 million consumer phone numbers in the National Do Not Call Registry – and it's growing every day. To complicate matters, almost half* of all Americans incorrectly believe that telephone survey calls are now banned by the Do Not Call rules.

The future of telephone survey work is in doubt. But there is no doubt that viable, accurate data collection alternatives exist.

Call Harris Interactive today to learn more – we'll be happy to answer the phone.

42% of all U.S. adults think that the registry applies to calls to conduct surveys about products and services – The Harris Poll – September 4, 2003

HarrisInteractive®
MARKET RESEARCH
The Harris Poll® PEOPLE

www.harrisinteractive.com/DNC Tel 877.919.4765
©2003. Harris Interactive Inc. All rights reserved. 36USC220506 EOE M/F/D/V 12.03

telephone survey A research method in which respondents' answers to a questionnaire are recorded by an interviewer on the phone

online survey A research method in which respondents answer a questionnaire via e-mail or on a website

People who take the time to fill out a diary may differ from the general population based on income, education, or behavior, such as the time available for shopping activities.

In a **telephone survey**, an interviewer records respondents' answers to a questionnaire over a phone line. A telephone survey has some advantages over a mail survey. The rate of response is higher because it takes less effort to answer the telephone and talk than to fill out and return a questionnaire. If there are enough interviewers, a telephone survey can be conducted very quickly. Thus, political candidates or organizations seeking an immediate reaction to an event may choose this method. In addition, a telephone survey permits interviewers to gain rapport with respondents and ask probing questions.

However, only a small proportion of the population likes to participate in telephone surveys. Just one-third of Americans are willing to participate in telephone interviews, down from two-thirds 20 years ago.[13] This poor image can significantly limit participation and distort representation in a telephone survey. Moreover, telephone surveys are limited to oral communication; visual aids or observation cannot be included. Interpreters of results must make adjustments for individuals who are not at home or do not have telephones. Many households are excluded from telephone directories by choice (unlisted numbers) or because the residents moved after the directory was published. Potential respondents often use telephone answering machines, voice mail, or caller ID to screen or block calls. Moreover, an increasing number of younger Americans are giving up their fixed telephone lines in favor of cellular or wireless phones.[14] These issues have serious implications for the use of telephone samples in conducting surveys. Some adjustment must be made for groups of respondents that may be undersampled because of a smaller-than-average incidence of telephone listings. Nondirectory telephone samples can overcome such bias. Various methods are available, including random-digit dialing (adding random numbers to the telephone prefix) and plus-one telephone sampling (increasing the last digit of a directory number by 1). These methods make it feasible to dial any working number, whether or not it is listed in a directory. However, these methods do not address the fact that younger Americans are increasingly favoring their cellphones, which marketing researchers may not call.[15]

Online surveys are evolving as an alternative to telephone surveys. In an **online survey**, questionnaires can be transmitted to respondents who have agreed to be contacted and have provided their e-mail addresses. Because e-mail is semi-interactive, recipients can ask for clarification of specific questions or pose questions of their own. The potential advantages of e-mail surveys are quick response and lower cost than traditional mail, telephone, and personal interview surveys if the response rate is adequate. In addition, more firms are using their websites to conduct surveys. Evolving technology and the interactive nature of the Internet allow for considerable flexibility in designing online questionnaires.

Given the growing number of households that have computers with Internet access, marketing research is likely to rely heavily on online surveys in the future. Indeed, experts predict that Internet-based marketing research will account for about 50 percent, or around $3 billion, of marketing research spending by 2005 compared to just 2 percent of marketing research revenues in 1998.[16] Furthermore, as negative attitudes toward telephone surveys render that technique less representative and more expensive, the integration of e-mail, fax, and voice mail functions into one computer-based system provides a promising alternative for survey research. E-mail surveys have especially strong potential within organizations whose employees are networked and for associations that publish members' e-mail addresses. College students in particular are often willing to provide their e-mail addresses and other personal information in exchange for incentives such as T-shirts and other giveaways.[17] However, there are some ethical issues to consider when using e-mail for marketing research, such as spam (unsolicited e-mail) and privacy.

In a **personal interview survey**, participants respond to questions face to face. Various audiovisual aids—pictures, products, diagrams, or prerecorded advertising copy—can be incorporated into a personal interview. Rapport gained through direct interaction usually permits more in-depth interviewing, including probes, follow-up questions, or psychological tests. In addition, because personal interviews can be longer, they may yield more information. Finally, respondents can be selected more carefully, and reasons for nonresponse can be explored.

One such research technique is the **in-home (door-to-door) interview**. The in-home interview offers a clear advantage when thoroughness of self-disclosure and elimination of group influence are important. In an in-depth interview of 45 to 90 minutes, respondents can be probed to reveal their real motivations, feelings, behaviors, and aspirations.

The object of a **focus-group interview** is to observe group interaction when members are exposed to an idea or a concept. The state of Nebraska used focus groups as part of its effort to develop a formal marketing campaign. Among other things, focus groups suggested the state promote its history and natural beauty.[18] Focus-group interviews are often conducted informally, without a structured questionnaire, in small groups of 8 to 12 people. They allow customer attitudes, behaviors, lifestyles, needs, and desires to be explored in a flexible and creative manner. Questions are open-ended and stimulate respondents to answer in their own words. Researchers can ask probing questions to clarify something they do not fully understand or something unexpected and interesting that may help explain buying behavior. On the other hand, focus-group participants do not always tell the truth. Some participants may be less than honest in an effort to be sociable or to receive money and/or food in exchange for their participation. Research has found a poor correlation between stated intent

personal interview survey
A research method in which participants respond to survey questions face to face

in-home (door-to-door) interview A personal interview that takes place in the respondent's home

focus-group interview
A research method involving observation of group interaction when members are exposed to an idea or a concept

Collecting Survey Data
Delve provides extensive data collection techniques including web surveys.

and actual purchase behavior.[19] It may be necessary to use separate focus groups for each major market segment studied—men, women, and age groups—and experts recommend the use of at least two focus groups per segment in case one group is unusually idiosyncratic.[20]

telephone depth interview
An interview that combines the traditional focus group's ability to probe with the confidentiality provided by telephone surveys

Still another option is the **telephone depth interview**, which combines the traditional focus group's ability to probe with the confidentiality provided by a telephone survey. This type of interview is most appropriate for qualitative research projects among a small targeted group that is difficult to bring together for a traditional focus group because of members' professions, locations, or lifestyles. Respondents can choose the time and day for the interview. Although this method is difficult to implement, it can yield revealing information from respondents who otherwise would be unwilling to participate in marketing research.[21]

The nature of personal interviews has changed. In the past, most personal interviews, which were based on random sampling or prearranged appointments, were conducted in the respondent's home. Today most personal interviews are conducted in shopping malls. **Shopping mall intercept interviews** involve interviewing a percentage of individuals passing by certain "intercept" points in a mall. Like any face-to-face interviewing method, mall intercept interviewing has many advantages. The interviewer is in a position to recognize and react to respondents' nonverbal indications of confusion. Respondents can be shown product prototypes, videotapes of commercials, and the like, and asked for their reactions. The mall environment lets the researcher deal with complex situations. For example, in taste tests, researchers know that all the respondents are reacting to the same product, which can be prepared and monitored from the mall test kitchen. In addition to the ability to conduct tests requiring bulky equipment, lower cost and greater control make shopping mall intercept interviews popular.

shopping mall intercept interview   A research method that involves interviewing a percentage of individuals passing by "intercept" points in a mall

An **on-site computer interview** is a variation of the mall intercept interview in which respondents complete a self-administered questionnaire displayed on a computer monitor. A computer software package can be used to conduct such interviews in shopping malls. After a brief lesson on how to operate the software, respondents can proceed through the survey at their own pace. Questionnaires can be adapted so that respondents see only those items (usually a subset of an entire scale) that may provide useful information about their attitudes.[22]

on-site computer interview
A variation of the shopping mall intercept interview in which respondents complete a self-administered questionnaire displayed on a computer monitor

Questionnaire Construction   A carefully constructed questionnaire is essential to the success of any survey. Questions must be clear, easy to understand, and directed toward a specific objective; that is, they must be designed to elicit information that meets the study's data requirements. Researchers need to define the objective before trying to develop a questionnaire because the objective determines the substance of the questions and the amount of detail. A common mistake in constructing questionnaires is to ask questions that interest the researchers but do not yield information useful in deciding whether to accept or reject a hypothesis. Finally, the most important rule in composing questions is to maintain impartiality.

The questions are usually of three kinds: open-ended, dichotomous, and multiple-choice.

Open-Ended Question

How do you feel about broadband Internet access for your computer?

_____

_____

_____

Dichotomous Question

Do you presently have broadband access at home, work, or school?

Yes _____   No _____

Multiple-Choice Question

What age group are you in?

Under 20 _____

20–29 _____

30–39 _____

40–49 _____

50–59 _____

60 and over _____

Problems may develop in the analysis of dichotomous or multiple-choice questions when responses for one outcome outnumber others. For example, a dichotomous question asking respondents to choose between "buy" or "not buy" might require additional sampling from the disproportionately smaller group if there were not enough responses to analyze.[23]

Researchers must also be very careful about questions that a respondent might consider too personal or that might require an admission of activities that other people are likely to condemn. Questions of this type should be worded to make them less offensive.

Observation Methods   In using observation methods, researchers record individuals' overt behavior, taking note of physical conditions and events. Direct contact with them is avoided; instead, their actions are examined and noted systematically. For instance, researchers might use observation methods to answer the question "How long does the average McDonald's restaurant customer have to wait in line before being served?" Observation may include the use of ethnographic techniques, such as watching customers interact with a product in a real-world environment. Bissell employed ethnographic techniques when it observed how a very small sample of consumers used its Steam Gun, a hot-water-based cleaning appliance, in the home. Based on this research, the company made a number of changes to the product, including its name, before launching the Steam N Clean.[24] Building Customer Relationships explores how Procter & Gamble uses observational methods.

Observation may also be combined with interviews. For example, during a personal interview, the condition of a respondent's home or other possessions may be observed and recorded. The interviewer can also directly observe and confirm such demographic information as race, approximate age, and gender.

Data gathered through observation can sometimes be biased if the person is aware of the observation process. However, an observer can be placed in a natural market environment, such as a grocery store, without influencing shoppers' actions. If the presence of a human observer is likely to bias the outcome or if human sensory abilities are inadequate, mechanical means may be used to record behavior. Mechanical observation devices include cameras, recorders, counting machines, scanners, and equipment that records physiological changes. A special camera can be used to record the eye movements of people as they look at an advertisement; the camera detects the sequence of reading and the parts of the advertisement that receive greatest attention. The electronic scanners used in supermarkets are very useful in marketing research: they provide accurate data on sales and customers' purchase patterns, and marketing researchers may buy such data from the supermarkets.

Observation is straightforward and avoids a central problem of survey methods: motivating respondents to state their true feelings or opinions. However, observation tends to be descriptive. When it is the only method of data collection, it may not provide insights into causal relationships. Another drawback is that analyses based on observation are subject to the observer's biases or the limitations of the mechanical device.

experiment A research method that attempts to maintain certain variables while measuring the effects of experimental variables

Experimentation   Another method for gathering primary data is experimentation. In an **experiment**, marketing researchers attempt to maintain certain variables while measuring the effects of experimental variables. Experimentation requires that an independent variable (one not influenced by or dependent on other variables) be manipulated and the resulting changes in a dependent variable (one contingent on, or restricted to, one value or set of values assumed by the independent variable) be measured. For example, when Apple introduced its iPod MP3 player, it needed to estimate the number of players it could sell at various levels of advertising expenditure and price. The dependent variable would be sales, and the independent variable would be advertising expenditure and price. Researchers would design the experiment so that other independent variables that might influence sales, such as distribution and variations of the product, would be controlled. Experimentation is used in marketing research to improve hypothesis testing.

BUILDING CUSTOMER RELATIONSHIPS

Reality TV or Marketing Research?

Imagine waking up in the morning, stumbling to the bathroom sink, loading your toothbrush with Crest toothpaste, and looking up to see the fuzzy reflection of a video camera in the mirror. Forget that you signed up for MTV's *The Real World*? No, it's just the Procter & Gamble (P&G) research crew you allowed into your home to observe how you perform your daily activities. Although marketing research has traditionally focused on problems consumers already recognize, P&G researchers hope this direct observation approach will help them identify and address problems that consumers don't even know they have.

Although 98 percent of U.S. consumers purchase Crest, Charmin, Comet, and many other P&G brands, just 33 percent of the world population buys products made by the Cincinnati-based firm. With sales growth languishing at 2.5 percent a year, P&G hopes to boost its revenues by capitalizing on growth opportunities overseas. To achieve this goal, many of P&G's marketing research efforts are now targeted toward international markets such as the United Kingdom, Italy, Germany, and China.

Compared to other research methods, direct observation of consumers provides several benefits. Video clips can be placed on a secure website for viewing by 150 P&G employees. A bigger audience gives the company greater potential for valuable feedback. More problems can be identified and solutions found to address those issues. Direct observation can also generate information that participants normally might forget or choose not to disclose when being interviewed or surveyed. For example, many people say they brush their teeth twice a day because they believe that is the correct and expected response. But in reality, many people don't brush twice daily because of interference from external sources. Direct observation of consumers can uncover such information. Another advantage of this approach is that it contributes to insights gained through coordinated and integrated research efforts.

P&G can cross-reference these results with any of 4,000 to 5,000 research studies it conducts annually or to its existing database of 50,000 studies. Finally, P&G can get a global perspective on the wants and needs of its target market.

This new form of research also has some drawbacks, especially concerns about privacy. Although participants in these studies willingly allow themselves to be videotaped, the company must avoid recording certain behaviors, inform any visitors about the situation, and guarantee the videos will be viewed only internally for research purposes. Another issue is reactivity, which occurs when participants modify normal behaviors because they know they are being observed. For example, a participant might increase his or her daily intake of vegetables during the observation period to appear more in line with social norms or expectations. Another drawback is that it is not practical to pore through hours of videotape for just a few clues about human behavior. Although the information gained may be interesting, not all of it will be useful or result in a successful new product. Finally, such research doesn't guarantee that any new product innovation will result.

Recently P&G conducted a study to determine why consumers dread washing dishes after cooking meals at home. More than 42 percent said the reason they dislike it is that it is time consuming. Such research will become more valuable if P&G can confirm it through direct observation studies. The company also runs a research project in Cincinnati at a local laundromat that allows P&G researchers to conduct interviews while consumers wash their clothes. Comparing the behaviors at a public laundromat with how consumers use products at home will likely yield valuable insights.

Put better, faster decision-making
in your sights.

Get a single view of your business with Teradata.

With Teradata®, it's all right there in front of you. We consolidate all your data from throughout
your organization into an enterprise data warehouse to give you one, integrated view of your
business. So, you have all the information you need—readily available—to uncover new
opportunities and make better decisions, fast. Which, quite clearly, will help your business
grow. Bring your company's future into focus. *See it all with Teradata.*

Teradata
a division of ⊙NCR

You've never seen your business like this before.   *Teradata.com*

Interpreting Data
Teradata interprets consumer data to help businesses make full use of their information.

statistical interpretation
Analysis of what is typical or what deviates from the average

◆ Interpreting Research Findings

After collecting data to test their hypotheses, marketers need to interpret the research findings. Interpretation of the data is easier if marketers carefully plan their data analysis methods early in the research process. They should also allow for continual evaluation of the data during the entire collection period. They can then gain valuable insights into areas that should be probed during the formal interpretation.

The first step in drawing conclusions from most research is to display the data in table format. If marketers intend to apply the results to individual categories of the things or people being studied, cross-tabulation may be useful, especially in tabulating joint occurrences. For example, using the two variables gender and purchase rates of automobile tires, a cross-tabulation could show how men and women differ in purchasing automobile tires.

After the data are tabulated, they must be analyzed. **Statistical interpretation** focuses on what is typical or what deviates from the average. It indicates how widely responses vary and how they are distributed in relation to the variable being measured. When marketers interpret statistics, they must take into account estimates of expected error or deviation from the true values of the population. The analysis of data may lead researchers to accept or reject the hypothesis being studied.

Data require careful interpretation by the marketer. If the results of a study are valid, the decision maker should take action; if a question has been incorrectly or poorly worded, however, the results may produce poor decisions. Consider the research conducted for a food marketer that asked respondents to rate a product on criteria such as "hearty flavor," as well as how important each criterion was to the respondent. Although such results may have had utility for advertising purposes, they were less helpful in product development because it was not possible to discern respondents' meaning of "hearty flavor."[25] Likewise, knowing that a majority of consumers support cause-related marketing does not provide enough information to guide marketing strategy decisions. Further research, however, found that at least 65 percent of surveyed consumers had participated in a cause-related marketing campaign. Of those, three-quarters indicated they had either switched brands, tried a product, or increased their product usage, and four out of five said they felt more positive about these purchases, more loyal to the company or brand, and more inclined to seek out future cause-related campaigns.[26] Managers must understand the research results and relate them to a context that permits effective decision making.

◆ Reporting Research Findings

The final step in the marketing research process is to report the research findings. Before preparing the report, the marketer must take a clear, objective look at the findings to see how well the gathered facts answer the research question or support or negate the initial hypotheses. In most cases, it is extremely doubtful that the study can provide everything needed to answer the research question. Thus, the researcher must point out the deficiencies, and the reasons for them, in the report.

The report of research results is usually a formal, written document. Researchers must allow time for the writing task when they plan and schedule the project. Because the report is a means of communicating with the decision makers who will use the research findings, researchers need to determine beforehand how much detail and supporting data to include. They should keep in mind that corporate executives prefer reports that are short, clear, and simply expressed. Researchers often give their summary and recommendations first, especially if decision makers do not have time to study how the results were obtained. A technical report allows its users to analyze data and interpret recommendations because it describes the research methods and procedures and the most important data gathered. Thus, researchers must recognize the needs and expectations of the report user and adapt to them.

Bias and distortion can be a major problem if the researcher is intent on obtaining favorable results. For example, research analyzing consumers' reports of their frequency of using long-distance telephone calls, letters, cards, and visits for personal communication found that some groups underreport their usage, whereas other groups overreport it. In particular, researchers found that consumers underestimate the duration of lengthy telephone calls but overestimate the length of short ones; in general, people tend to overestimate both the frequency and duration of their telephone calls. Without this information, companies relying on survey results may get a distorted view of the market for long-distance telephone services by mistakenly judging it to be larger and more homogeneous than it really is.[27]

Marketing researchers want to know about behavior and opinions, and they want accurate data to help them in making decisions. Careful wording of questions is very important because a biased or emotional word can dramatically change the results. Marketing research and marketing information systems can provide an organization with accurate and reliable customer feedback, which a marketer must have to understand the dynamics of the marketplace. As managers recognize the benefits of marketing research, they assign it a much larger role in decision making.

Using Technology to Improve Marketing Information Gathering and Analysis

Technology is making information for marketing decisions increasingly accessible. The ability of marketers to track customer buying behavior and to better discern what buyers want is changing the nature of marketing. Customer relationship management is being enhanced by integrating data from all customer contacts and combining that information to improve customer retention. Information technology permits internal research and quick information gathering to help marketers better understand and satisfy customers. For example, company responses to e-mail complaints as well as to communications through mail, telephone, and personal contact can be used to improve customer satisfaction, retention, and value.[28] Armed with such information, marketers can fine-tune marketing mixes to satisfy their customers' needs.

The integration of telecommunications and computer technologies is allowing marketers to access a growing array of valuable information sources related to industry forecasts, business trends, and customer buying behavior. Electronic communication tools can be effectively utilized to gain accurate information with minimal customer interaction. Most marketing researchers have e-mail, voice mail, teleconferencing, and fax machines at their disposal. In fact, many firms use marketing information systems to network all these technologies and organize all the marketing data available to them. In this section, we look at marketing information systems and specific technologies that are helping marketing researchers obtain and manage marketing research data.

◆ Marketing Information Systems

A **marketing information system (MIS)** is a framework for the day-to-day management and structuring of information gathered regularly from sources both inside and outside the organization. As such, an MIS provides a continuous flow of information about prices, advertising expenditures, sales, competition, and distribution expenses. Kraft General Foods, for example, operates one of the largest marketing information systems in the food industry, maintaining, using, and sharing information with others to increase the value of its product offerings. Kraft seeks to develop a dialog with customers by providing toll-free numbers. It receives hundreds of thousands of calls annually from customers who ask questions and express concerns about its products.

The main focus of the marketing information system is on data storage and retrieval, as well as on computer capabilities and management's information requirements. Regular reports of sales by product or market categories, data on inventory levels, and records of salespeople's activities are examples of information that is useful in making decisions. In the MIS, the means of *gathering* data receive less attention than do the procedures for expediting the *flow* of information.

An effective marketing information system starts by determining the objective of the information, that is, by identifying decision needs that require certain information. The firm can then specify an information system for continuous monitoring to provide regular, pertinent information on both the external and internal environment. FedEx, for example, has developed interactive marketing systems to provide instantaneous communication between the company and its customers. Via either telephone or the Internet, customers can track their packages and receive immediate feedback concerning delivery. The company's website provides valuable information about customer usage and allows customers to express directly what they think about company services. The evolving telecommunications and computer technology is allowing marketing information systems to cultivate one-to-one relationships with customers.

◆ Databases

Most marketing information systems include internal databases. As mentioned in Chapter 6, a database is a collection of information arranged for easy access and retrieval. Databases allow marketers to tap into an abundance of information useful in making marketing decisions: internal sales reports, newspaper articles, company news releases, government economic reports, bibliographies, and more, often accessed through a computer system. Information technology has made it possible to develop databases to guide strategic planning and help improve customer services. Wal-Mart maintains one of the largest corporate databases in the United States, with data about sales and inventory levels as well as data mined from customer receipts from all its stores. These data help Wal-Mart pinpoint purchasing patterns, which helps the firm manage inventory levels and determine effective product placement. Many commercial websites require consumers to register and provide personal information to access the site or make a purchase. Frequent flier programs permit airlines to ask loyal customers to participate in surveys about their needs and desires, and to track their best customers' flight patterns by time of day, week, month, and year. Supermarkets gain a significant amount of data through checkout scanners tied to store discount cards.

Marketing researchers can also use commercial databases developed by information research firms, such as LEXIS-NEXIS, to obtain useful information for marketing decisions. Many of these commercial databases are accessible online for a fee. They can also be obtained in printed form or on computer compact discs (CD-ROMs). With most commercial databases, the user typically conducts a computer search by key word, topic, or company, and the database service generates abstracts, articles, or reports that can then be printed out. Accessing multiple reports or a complete article may cost extra.

single-source data Information provided by a single marketing research firm

Information provided by a single firm on household demographics, purchases, television viewing behavior, and responses to promotions such as coupons and free samples is called **single-source data**.[29] For example, Behavior Scan, offered by Information Resources, Inc., screens about 60,000 households in 26 U.S. markets. This single-source information service monitors consumer household televisions and records the programs and commercials watched. When buyers from these households shop in stores equipped with scanning registers, they present Hotline cards (similar to credit cards) to cashiers. This enables each customer's identification to be electronically coded so the firm can track each product purchased and store the information in a database. It is important to gather longitudinal (long-term) information on customers to maximize the usefulness of single-source data.[30]

◆ Marketing Decision Support Systems

marketing decision support system (MDSS) Customized computer software that aids marketing managers in decision making

A **marketing decision support system (MDSS)** is customized computer software that aids marketing managers in decision making by helping them anticipate the effects of certain decisions. Some decision support systems have a broader range and offer greater computational and modeling capabilities than spreadsheets; they let managers explore a greater number of alternatives. For example, a decision support system can determine how sales and profits might be affected by higher or lower interest rates or how sales forecasts, advertising expenditures, production levels, and the like might affect overall profits. For this reason, decision support system software is often a major component of a company's marketing information system. For example, both Oracle and Ford Motor Company use a software product called NeuroServer that acts as a customer interface to solve problems and answer questions for customers. Based on customized parameters, it allows marketers to acquire specific information on customers that can go into the decision support system.[31] Some decision support systems incorporate artificial intelligence and other advanced computer technologies.

◆ The Internet and Online Information Services

The Internet has evolved as a most powerful communication medium, linking customers and companies around the world in computer networks via e-mail, forums, webpages, and more. Growth of the Internet, and especially the World Wide Web, has launched an entire industry that is working to make marketing information easily accessible to both marketing firms and customers.

Table 7.4 lists a number of websites that can be valuable resources for marketing research. The Census Bureau, for example, uses the World Wide Web to disseminate information that may be useful to marketing researchers, particularly through the *Statistical Abstract of the United States* and data from the most recent census. Among the companies that exploit census data for marketing decisions are Starbucks, which analyzes the data to assess potential coffee shop sites, and Blockbuster, which mines the data to help determine how many copies of a particular movie or video game to offer at each store.[32]

Companies can also mine their own websites for useful information. Amazon.com, for example, has built a relationship with its customers by tracking the types of books and music they purchase. Each time a customer logs on to the website, the company can offer recommendations based on the customer's previous purchases. Such a marketing system helps the company track the changing desires and buying habits of its most valued customers.

Marketing researchers can also subscribe to online services such as CompuServe, MSN, Prodigy, DIALOG, and NEXIS. These services typically offer their subscribers such specialized services as databases, news services, and forums, as well as access to the Internet itself. Marketers can subscribe to "mailing lists" that periodically deliver electronic newsletters to their computer screens, and they can participate in on-screen discussions with thousands of network users. This enhanced communication with a firm's customers, suppliers, and employees provides a high-speed link that boosts the capabilities of the firm's marketing information system.

While most webpages are open to anyone with Internet access, big companies like Cisco Systems also maintain internal webpages, called "intranets," that allow employees to access such internal data as customer profiles and product inventory—information once hidden in databases only technicians could unlock. Such sensitive corporate information can be protected from outside users of the World Wide Web by special security software called *firewalls*.

Table 7.4	Resources for Marketing Information
Government Sources	
U.S. Census Bureau	**www.census.gov**
U.S. Department of State	**www.state.gov**
FedWorld	**www.fedworld.gov**
Commercial Sources	
ACNielsen	**www.acnielsen.com**
Information Resources, Inc.	**www.infores.com**
Gallup	**www.gallup.com**
Arbitron	**www.arbitron.com**
Periodicals and Books	
American Demographics	**www.americandemographics.com**
Advertising Age	**www.adage.com**
Sales & Marketing Management	**www.salesandmarketing.com**
Fortune	**www.fortune.com**
Inc.	**www.inc.com**
Business Week	**www.businessweek.com**
Bloomberg Report	**www.bloomberg.com**

IBM uses its intranets to help its 300,000 employees around the world collaborate on projects. In addition to improving communications, the system has helped the company slash training and travel expenses by nearly $400 million.[33]

Issues in Marketing Research

◆ The Importance of Ethical Marketing Research

Marketing managers and other professionals are relying more and more on marketing research, marketing information systems, and new technologies to make better decisions. It is therefore essential that professional standards be established by which to judge the reliability of marketing research. Such standards are necessary because gathering marketing research data often generates ethical and legal issues as illustrated in Ethics and Social Responsibility. In addition, the relationships between research suppliers, such as marketing research agencies, and the marketing managers who make strategy decisions require ethical behavior. Organizations such as the Marketing Research Association have developed codes of conduct and guidelines to

ETHICS AND SOCIAL RESPONSIBILITY

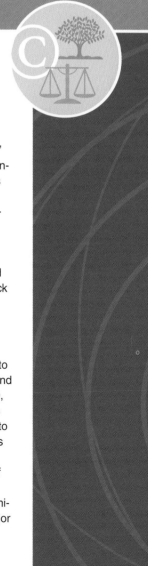

Burger King's Relationship with Coke Fizzles After Marketing Research Debacle

Sometimes businesspeople perceive such strong pressures to succeed that they engage in less than ethical activities, such as manipulating research data. Coca-Cola Company recognized three years ago that its fountain drink business with Burger King was not meeting sales expectations. To boost sales, Coca-Cola suggested that Burger King invest in and promote Frozen Coke as a kid's snack. The fast-food chain arranged to test market the product for three weeks in Richmond, Virginia, and evaluate the results before agreeing to roll out the new product nationally. The test marketing involved customers receiving a coupon for a free Frozen Coke when they purchased a Combo Meal (sandwich, fries, and drink). Burger King executives wanted to be cautious about the new product because of the enormous investment each restaurant would require to distribute and promote it nationally. Restaurants would need to purchase equipment to make the frozen drink, buy extra syrup, and spend advertising funds to promote the product.

When results of the test marketing began coming into Coca-Cola, sales of Frozen Coke were grim. Coca-Cola then gave an individual $10,000 to take hundreds of children to Burger King to purchase Value Meals, thus moving an exaggerated number of Frozen Cokes. Coca-Cola's action netted just 700 additional Value Meals out of nearly 100,000 sold during the entire promotion. It also

netted an investigation by the U.S. attorney general for the North District of Georgia.

Authorities learned about the fraud after Matthew Whitley, an 11-year Coca-Cola employee, filed a lawsuit exposing the $65 million marketing fraud as well as accusing the firm of overstating revenue and profit, using "slush funds" to hide losses of the company's computerized fountain drink dispensing system, selling frozen drinks with metal residue inside, and discriminating against minority employees. Although senior management acknowledged that the results of the Burger King market test had been manipulated, it did not fire the vice president in charge of the Burger King account. Instead, Coca-Cola withheld 50 percent of his bonus in 2000 and all of his stock options in 2001. The vice president was not fired until after word of the manipulation surfaced; Matthew Whitley was fired soon after he blew the whistle on the company.

Coca-Cola is now spending about $21 million to repair its damaged relationship with Burger King and has settled Matthew Whitley's lawsuit for $100,000, a $140,000 severance package, and his attorney's fees of $300,000. The soft-drink giant has agreed to cooperate with the U.S. attorney general as well as the Securities and Exchange Commission in their investigations of its business practices. The cost of manipulating the Frozen Coke research has been considerable for Coca-Cola: negative publicity, criminal investigations, a soured relationship with a major customer, and a loss of stakeholder trust.

Table 7.5	Guidelines for Questionnaire Introduction

Questionnaire introduction should:

- Allow interviewers to introduce themselves by name.
- State the name of the research company.
- Indicate this is a marketing research project.
- Explain there will be no sales involved.
- Note the general topic of discussion (if this is a problem in a "blind" study, a statement such as "consumer opinion" is acceptable).
- State the likely duration of the interview.
- Assure the anonymity of the respondent and confidentiality of all answers.
- State the honorarium if applicable (for many business-to-business and medical studies this is done up front for both qualitative and quantitative studies).
- Reassure the respondent with a statement such as, "There are no right or wrong answers, so please give thoughtful and honest answers to each question" (recommended by many clients).

Source: Reprinted with permission of The Marketing Research Association, P.O. Box 230, Rocky Hill, CT 06067-0230, (860)257-4008.

promote ethical marketing research. To be effective, such guidelines must instruct marketing researchers on how to avoid misconduct. Table 7.5 recommends explicit steps interviewers should follow when introducing a questionnaire.

◆ International Issues in Marketing Research

As we saw in Chapter 5, sociocultural, economic, political, legal, and technological forces vary in different regions of the world. These variations create challenges for organizations attempting to understand foreign customers through marketing research. The marketing research process we described in this chapter is used globally, but to ensure the research is valid and reliable, data-gathering methods may have to be modified to allow for regional differences. For example, the annual Global Airline Performance (GAP) study, which surveys 240,000 air travelers every year about their opinions on 22 airlines departing from 30 North American, European, and Asian airports, can be conducted in English, French, Dutch, German, Swedish, Chinese, or Japanese.[34] To ensure that global and regional differences are satisfactorily addressed, many companies retain a research firm with experience in the country of interest. Most of the largest marketing research firms derive a significant share of their revenues from research conducted outside the United States. As Table 7.6 indicates, VNU, Inc., the largest marketing research firm in the world, received 46 percent of its revenues from outside the United States.[35]

Table 7.6	Top Marketing Research Firms	
Company	Global Revenues (millions)	Percentage Revenues from Outside the U.S.
1. VNU, Inc.	$2,814	45.8
2. IMS Health Inc.	1,220	60.0
3. Information Resources Inc.	555	25.8
4. Westat Inc.	342	0.0
5. The Kantar Group	987	68.3

Source: "Top 50 U.S. Research Organizations," *Marketing News,* June 9, 2003, p. H4.

Experts recommend a two-pronged approach to international marketing research. The first phase involves a detailed search for and analysis of secondary data to gain greater understanding of a particular marketing environment and to pinpoint issues that must be taken into account in gathering primary research data. Secondary data can be particularly helpful in building a general understanding of the market, including economic, legal, cultural, and demographic issues, as well as in assessing the risks of doing business in that market and in forecasting demand.[36] Marketing researchers often begin by studying country trade reports from the U.S. Department of Commerce as well as country-specific information from local sources, such as a country's website, and trade and general business publications such as *The Wall Street Journal*. These sources can offer insights into the marketing environment in a particular country and can even indicate untapped market opportunities abroad.

The second phase involves field research using many of the methods described earlier, including focus groups and telephone surveys, to refine a firm's understanding of specific customer needs and preferences. Specific differences among countries can have a profound influence on data gathering. For example, in-home (door-to-door) interviews are illegal in some countries. In China, few people have regular telephone lines, making telephone surveys both impractical and nonrepresentative of the total population. Primary data gathering may have a greater chance of success if the firm employs local researchers who better understand how to approach potential respondents and can do so in their own language.[37] Regardless of the specific methods used to gather primary data, whether in the United States or abroad, the goal is to better understand the needs of specific target markets to craft the best marketing strategy to satisfy the needs of customers in each market, as we will see in the next chapter.

SUMMARY

To implement the marketing concept, marketers need information about the characteristics, needs, and wants of target market customers. Marketing research and information systems that furnish practical, unbiased information help firms avoid assumptions and misunderstandings that could lead to poor marketing performance.

Marketing research is the systematic design, collection, interpretation, and reporting of information to help marketers solve specific marketing problems or take advantage of marketing opportunities. It is a process for gathering information not currently available to decision makers. The value of marketing research is measured by improvements in a marketer's ability to make decisions.

To maintain the control needed to obtain accurate information, marketers approach marketing research as a process with logical steps: (1) locating and defining problems or issues, (2) designing the research project, (3) collecting data, (4) interpreting research findings, and (5) reporting research findings.

The first step in launching a research study, problem or issue definition, focuses on uncovering the nature and boundaries of a situation or question related to marketing strategy or implementation. In the second step, marketing researchers design a research project to obtain the information needed to address it. This step requires formulating a hypothesis and determining what type of research to employ to test the hypothesis so the results are reliable and valid. A hypothesis is an informed guess or assumption about a problem or set of circumstances. The type of hypothesis being tested dictates whether an exploratory, descriptive, or causal approach will be used to gather data. Research is considered reliable if it produces almost identical results in repeated trials; it is valid if it measures what it is supposed to measure.

For the third step of the research process, collecting data, two types of data are available. Primary data are observed and recorded or collected directly from respondents; secondary data are compiled inside or outside the organization for some purpose other than the current investigation. Sources of secondary data include an organization's own database and other internal sources, periodicals, government publications, unpublished sources, and online databases. Methods of collecting primary data include sampling, surveys, observation, and experimentation. Sampling involves selecting representative units from a total population. In probability sampling, every element in the population being studied has a known chance of being selected for study. Nonprobability sampling is more subjective than probability sampling because there is no way to calculate the likelihood that a specific element of the population being studied will be chosen. Marketing researchers employ sampling to collect primary data through mail, telephone, online, or personal interview surveys. A carefully constructed questionnaire is essential to the success of any survey. In using observation

methods, researchers record respondents' overt behavior and take note of physical conditions and events. In an experiment, marketing researchers attempt to maintain certain variables while measuring the effects of experimental variables.

To apply research data to decision making, marketers must interpret and report their findings properly—the final two steps in the marketing research process. Statistical interpretation focuses on what is typical or what deviates from the average. After interpreting the research findings, the researchers must prepare a report on the findings that the decision makers can understand and use. Researchers must also take care to avoid bias and distortion.

Many firms use computer technology to create a marketing information system (MIS), a framework for managing and structuring information gathered regularly from sources both inside and outside the organization. A database is a collection of information arranged for easy access and retrieval. A marketing decision support system (MDSS) is customized computer software that aids marketing managers in decision making by helping them anticipate the effects of certain decisions. Online information services and the Internet also enable marketers to communicate with customers and obtain information.

Eliminating unethical marketing research practices and establishing generally acceptable procedures for conducting research are important goals of marketing research. Both domestic and international marketing use the same marketing research process, but international marketing may require modifying data-gathering methods to address regional differences.

Please visit the student website at **www.prideferrell.com** for ACE Self-Test questions that will help you prepare for exams.

IMPORTANT TERMS

Marketing research
Research design
Hypothesis
Exploratory research
Descriptive research
Causal research
Reliability
Validity
Primary data
Secondary data

Population
Sample
Sampling
Probability sampling
Random sampling
Stratified sampling
Nonprobability sampling
Quota sampling
Mail survey
Telephone survey

Online survey
Personal interview survey
In-home (door-to-door) interview
Focus-group interview
Telephone depth interview
Shopping mall intercept interview
On-site computer interview
Experiment

Statistical interpretation
Marketing information system (MIS)
Single-source data
Marketing decision support system (MDSS)

DISCUSSION & REVIEW QUESTIONS

1. What is marketing research? Why is it important?
2. Describe the five steps in the marketing research process.
3. What is the difference between defining a research problem and developing a hypothesis?
4. Describe the different types of approaches to marketing research and indicate when each should be used.
5. Where are data for marketing research obtained? Give examples of internal and external data.
6. What is the difference between probability sampling and nonprobability sampling? In what situation would random sampling be best? Stratified sampling? Quota sampling?
7. Suggest some ways to encourage respondents to cooperate in mail surveys.
8. If a survey of all homes with listed telephone numbers is to be conducted, what sampling design should be used?
9. Describe some marketing problems that could be solved through information gained from observation.
10. What is a marketing information system, and what should it provide?
11. Define a database. What is its purpose, and what does it include?
12. How can marketers use online services and the Internet to obtain information for decision making?
13. What role does ethics play in marketing research? Why is it important that marketing researchers be ethical?
14. How does marketing research in other countries differ from marketing research in the United States?

APPLICATION QUESTIONS

1. After observing customers' traffic patterns, Bashas' Markets repositioned the greeting card section in its stores, and card sales increased substantially. To increase sales for the following types of companies, what information might marketing researchers want to gather from customers?
   a. Furniture stores
   b. Gasoline outlets/service stations
   c. Investment companies
   d. Medical clinics
2. When a company wants to conduct research, it must first identify a problem or possible opportunity to market its goods or services. Choose a company in your city that you think might benefit from a research project. Develop a research question and outline a method to approach this question. Explain why you think the research question is relevant to the organization and why the particular methodology is suited to the question and the company.
3. Input for marketing information systems can come from internal or external sources. ACNielsen Corporation is the largest provider of single-source marketing research in the world. Identify two firms in your city that might benefit from internal sources and two that might benefit from external sources. Explain why these sources would be useful to these companies. Suggest the type of information each company should gather.
4. Suppose you are opening a health insurance brokerage firm and want to market your services to small businesses with fewer than 50 employees. Determine which database for marketing information you will use in your marketing efforts, and explain why you will use it.

Internet Exercise & Resources

Visit **www.prideferrell.com** for resources to help you master the material in this chapter, plus materials that will help you expand your marketing knowledge, including Internet exercise updates, ACE self-tests, hotlinks to companies featured in this chapter, and much more.

World Association of Opinion and Marketing Research Professionals

The World Association of Opinion and Marketing Research Professionals (ESOMAR, founded as the European Society for Opinion and Marketing Research in 1948) is a nonprofit association for marketing research professionals. ESOMAR promotes the use of opinion and marketing research to improve marketing decisions in companies worldwide and works to protect personal privacy in the research process. Visit the association's website at **www.esomar.nl/.**

1. How can ESOMAR help marketing professionals conduct research to guide marketing strategy?
2. How can ESOMAR help marketers protect the privacy of research subjects when conducting marketing research in other countries?
3. ESOMAR introduced the first professional code of conduct for marketing research professionals in 1948. The association continues to update the document to address new technology and other changes in the marketing environment. According to ESOMAR's code, what are the specific professional responsibilities of marketing researchers?

Video Case 7.1

IRI Provides Marketing Research Data from Multiple Sources

Marketing research is a crucial marketing activity because it informs companies about customers' needs, desires, and changes in attitudes and purchase patterns, and helps marketers identify opportunities for particular goods and services. One of today's leading marketing research firms is Information Resources, Inc. (IRI), which provides sales data to customers indicating how much of their products have been sold, where, and at what price. Such information is critical to strategic market planning and managing the movement of products through the supply chain. The Chicago-based firm's customers include manufacturers, retailers, and sales/marketing agencies in the United States and throughout the world. With annual revenues in excess of $550 million, the firm offers these customers vital marketing intelligence to help them make sound strategic marketing decisions.

One of IRI's most renowned research tools is the InfoScan store-tracking service. Through InfoScan, IRI collects sales data from a system of checkout scanners in supermarkets, drugstores, and mass merchandisers. Every week, data collected from more than 20,000 stores are input into IRI's huge database for analysis. IRI then breaks this information down into client-specific databases. The company then sells the analyzed information to customers, which include manufacturers such as Nestlé, Procter & Gamble, PepsiCo, and Lever Bros., and retailers such as Kroger's, Albertson's, Walgreen's, and Target.

Databases developed by IRI allow these marketers to tap into a wealth of information on sales, market share, distribution, pricing, and promotion for hundreds of consumer product categories. For example, InfoScan can track new products to assess their performance and gauge competitors' reactions to their marketing strategy. Once new products are on store shelves, IRI monitors related information such as prices and market share of competing products. This information helps the products' marketers determine the effects of competitors' tactics so they can adjust their marketing strategies as necessary. InfoScan can also help marketers assess customers' reactions to changes in a product's price, packaging, display, and other marketing mix elements. By tracking a product's sales in relation to promotional efforts, InfoScan data also help marketers assess the effects of their own advertising as well as that of competitors.

Another IRI product, Behavior Scan, provides single-source data on household demographics, television viewing behavior, purchases, and responses to promotions such as coupons and free samples. Through Behavior Scan, IRI screens about 70,000 households in 26 U.S. markets. The company also has data on households in Europe through its alliance with Europanel. Behavior Scan monitors participating households' television viewing habits, recording the programs and commercials each household watches. When consumers from these households shop in a store equipped with scanning registers, they present credit card–size hotline cards that allow the store to electronically identify them so IRI can track their purchases and store the information in a database for analysis. With this information, IRI can relate the purchases of a household to the commercials viewed on television, further allowing the companies to assess the effects of their promotional strategies.

Although IRI specializes primarily in scanner-based data collection that documents what consumers buy under certain conditions–that is, behavioral research–the company also recognizes the value of attitudinal research to explain the "why behind the buy." To this end, IRI sought an alliance with Sorensen Associates to observe and interview shoppers at the point of purchase in supermarkets and other retail outlets. These in-store research methods provide valuable insights into shopping behavior and attitudes in a real-life retail environment. To further expand its portfolio of client services, IRI has also partnered with Mosaic Group to conduct field surveys. By providing survey research, IRI can introduce new services to help clients make better and timelier marketing decisions. As companies develop databases, the various data sources can be merged to improve efficiency and develop and improve customer satisfaction.

All of IRI's services facilitate customer relationship management using marketing research and information technology to provide profiles of consumers, including behavior and attitudes. IRI is also employing information technology to deliver information over the Internet. In 2000 the company launched CPGNetwork.com, through which customers can access marketing intelligence in the form of data-driven analyses, alerts, key performance indicators, "best practices," and case studies via the Web.

In addition to its services to client customers, IRI occasionally provides public relations information to the retail industry. For example, the company recently released a study indicating that 23 percent of online consumers have purchased consumer packaged goods online, and 99 percent of those customers planned to maintain or increase their online spending levels over the next year. Although just 12 percent of online consumer packaged goods shoppers spent more than 25 percent of their budgets online, that number is expected to increase by 35 percent. Such information is important to retailers because it indicates that Internet purchases of consumer packaged goods are increasing and represent an opportunity for online retailers.

IRI tailors its information services to the unique information needs of each customer. The research it provides arms these companies with marketing intelligence to help them match their marketing mixes to the needs of their own customers. With timely and accurate information about what products are selling, where they are selling, the most effective prices, and competitors' activities, marketers can make sound decisions about the marketing strategy for specific products.[38]

QUESTIONS FOR DISCUSSION

1. How are the data gathered by IRI useful in customer relationship management?
2. What is the advantage of integrating scanner data with television viewing behavior?
3. Compare the usefulness of behavioral scanner data with data conducted through surveys.

Case 7.2

A Look-Look at Youth Trends

Teenagers and young adults have become the trendsetters and taste makers for American society. However, these trends are dynamic, seeming to change overnight, so today's "cool" fashion item quickly becomes "so yesterday." Moreover, the nation's 60 million teenagers command some $140 billion in buying power, and this figure is expected to grow 5 to 10 percent annually. Keeping up with this lucrative yet dynamic market is a challenge that few marketing research firms have been able to meet with both accuracy and speed. One firm, however, has been able to peer into the minds of today's youth with startling clarity: Look-Look.com, an online information and research firm that offers information, news, and photographs about trends among the 14- to 30-year-old demographic group in near real time. The firm's reputation has grown rapidly, and its revenues are projected to reach $20 million to $50 million in the next five years.

Look-Look was founded in 1999 by DeeDee Gordon and Sharon Lee, who met while working at Lambesis, a Del Mar, California, advertising agency. Gordon became an astute observer of youth trends while running a Boston store. Lee is the strategist who turns Gordon's observations into successful marketing plans. The two have been labeled "urban archaeologists" because they are able to uncover trends and opportunities that marketers can tap into to satisfy this challenging market.

To understand the constantly changing trends among 14- to 30–year-olds, Look-Look hand-picked and prescreened more than 20,000 young people from all over the world. The firm chooses forward-thinking trendsetters who are innovative and influential among their peers and pays them to answer surveys; report on their opinions, ideas, styles, and trends; and even photograph fashion trends with digital cameras. Although such trendsetters account for only about 20 percent of youths, they influence the other 80 percent. Gordon and Lee believe that understanding today's young people requires a continuing "e-dialog," not just once- or twice-a-year focus groups or market surveys. Gordon and Lee also make frequent trips to Tokyo and London, which are often breeding grounds for the next hot trend.

Look-Look clients pay $20,000 a year to gain instant access to the results of the firm's online surveys and other research. These clients include firms representing the apparel, cosmetics, beverage, video game, and movie industries. Look-Look provides these clients with information about the latest trends in youth fashion, entertainment, technology, leisure activities, foods and beverages, health and beauty, mindset, and more. Look-Look delivers fast, accurate, and timely information through the Internet and the company's own intranet and database. Clients can even get almost immediate responses to research questions the firm poses to its 10,000 respondents 24 hours a day.

The firm's website offers a variety of information to help clients better understand the tastes and interests of today's young people, including photo spreads; news stories and "youth correspondent" reports; survey results; graphics; and top-ten lists of respondents' favorite gadgets, books, celebrities, and music. For example, one recent survey reported that most young people are willing to pay a monthly fee to use websites that allow music downloads, such as the iTunes Music Store, and that their use of these sites has little effect on the number of CDs they actually purchase. Other Look-Look research suggests that young people are sophisticated enough to distinguish between make-believe violence and real-life violence. Indeed, Look-Look's success may stem from the fact that the company respects the increasing sophistication of today's young people and does not treat them condescendingly. As Sharon Lee says, "Teen consumers have gotten sophisticated about companies and style. Trends move so quickly, and there are so many choices. Manufacturers and retailers have to listen to get the competitive edge."

The "living research" Look-Look provides continuously listens to and observes young people to ensure the information it supplies is authentic and up to date. Whether it's cropped, cherry-red hair, skin-tight leather hip-hugger pants, tattoos, or body piercing, Look-Look knows what young people like and, for a fee, helps marketers stay on top of these trends to satisfy this very lucrative market.[39]

QUESTIONS FOR DISCUSSION

1. How does the information Look-Look.com supplies help marketers appeal to teenagers and young adults?
2. What advantages do the methods Look-Look employs have over traditional marketing research methods?
3. Some critics claim that Look-Look's core of trend-setting respondents are "too hip" to reflect the tastes of mainstream teens and young adults. How might this be a problem for a company using Look-Look data to develop a marketing strategy?

Strategic Case 3

FedEx Corporation

In 1973, Frederick W. Smith founded Federal Express Corporation with part of an $8 million inheritance. At the time, the U.S. Postal Service and United Parcel Service (UPS) provided the only means of delivering letters and packages, and they often took several days or more to get packages to their destinations. While a student at Yale in 1965, Smith wrote a paper proposing an independent, overnight delivery service. Although he received a C on the paper, Smith never lost sight of his vision. He believed many businesses would be willing to pay more to get letters, documents, and packages delivered overnight. He was right.

Federal Express began shipping packages overnight from Memphis, Tennessee, on April 17, 1973. On that first night of operations, the company handled six packages, one of which was a birthday present sent by Smith himself. Today FedEx Corporation handles more than 3 million overnight packages and documents a day, and more than 5 million shipments a day around the world. FedEx controls more than 50 percent of the overnight delivery market, with total operating income of $1.47 billion on an astounding $22.4 billion in total revenue. FedEx does not view itself as being in the package and document transport business; rather, it describes its business as delivering "certainty" by connecting the global economy with a wide range of transportation, information, and supply chain services.

Although most people are familiar with FedEx's overnight delivery services, the company is actually divided into seven major divisions:

- **FedEx Express®** The world's largest express transportation company, serving 214 countries, including every address in the United States

- **FedEx Ground®** North America's second-largest ground carrier for small package shipments

- **FedEx Freight®** The largest U.S. regional less-than-truckload freight company, which provides next-day and second-day delivery of heavy freight in both the United States and international markets

- **FedEx Custom Critical®** Provides 24/7 nonstop, door-to-door delivery of urgent shipments in the United States, Canada, and Europe

- **FedEx Trade Networks®** Facilitates international trade, customs brokerage, and freight forwarding

- **FedEx Services®** Consolidated sales, marketing, information technology, and supply chain services that support all FedEx global brands

- **Kinko's®** A chain of more than 1,200 retail stores providing business services such as copying, publishing, and shipping operations

FedEx purchased Kinko's in 2004 to provide new business services and to expand FedEx shipping options at Kinko's 1,200 retail stores. The purchase followed rival UPS's acquisition of 3,000 Mail Boxes Etc. stores. Renamed the UPS Store, that acquisition put UPS closer to small to medium-size customers and high-profit infrequent shippers. FedEx's purchase of Kinko's, which operates 110 stores in 10 countries, is expected to help the company reach new customers and expand in Asia and Europe.

FedEx Express and FedEx Ground provide the bulk of the company's business, offering valuable services to anyone who needs to deliver letters, documents, and packages. Whether dropped off at one of 43,000 drop boxes or more than 1,000 world service centers, or picked up by FedEx courier, each package is taken to a local FedEx office, where it is trucked to the nearest airport. The package is flown to one of the company's distribution "hubs" for sorting and then flown to the airport nearest its destination. The package is then trucked to another FedEx office, where a courier picks it up and hand-delivers it to the correct recipient. All of this takes place overnight, with many packages delivered before 8:00 A.M. the next day. FedEx confirms that roughly 99 percent of its deliveries are made on time.

To achieve this successful delivery rate, FedEx maintains an impressive infrastructure of equipment and processes. The company owns more than 70,000 vehicles, and its 643 aircraft fly more than 500,000 miles every day. FedEx operates its own weather forecasting service, ensuring that most of its flights arrive within 15 minutes of schedule. Most packages shipped within the United States are sorted at the company's Memphis superhub, where FedEx takes over control of Memphis International Airport at roughly 11 P.M. each night. FedEx planes land side by side on parallel runways every minute or so for well over one hour each night. After the packages are sorted, all FedEx planes take off in time to reach their destinations. Not all packages are shipped via air: whenever possible, FedEx uses ground transportation to save on expenses. For international deliveries, FedEx uses a combination of direct services and independent contractors.

FedEx services are priced using a zone system in which the distance a package must travel to reach its final destination determines the price. FedEx offers FedEx SameDay® Delivery for $173 for packages up to 25 pounds. FedEx Ground rates vary widely by package weight and shipping zone. For an extra $4, customers can have a courier pick up their packages rather than dropping them off at a drop box. Saturday pickup and delivery is also available for an additional $12.50. Prices vary for larger packages and international shipments.

In 2001, FedEx Express expanded its reach with the announcement of two 7-year service agreements with the U.S. Postal Service. In the first agreement, FedEx Express provides air transportation for certain postal services, including Priority Mail. The second agreement gives FedEx Express the option to place a drop box in every U.S. post office. FedEx did not get the exclusive rights to drop boxes, which left open the potential for UPS to negotiate its own agreement with the postal service. Both FedEx and the postal service operate competitively and maintain separate services in all other categories.

FedEx Maintains Leadership Information Technology

Despite its tremendous successes, FedEx has faced some difficult times in its efforts to grow and compete against strong rivals. The overnight delivery market matured very rapidly as intense competition from the U.S. Postal Service, UPS, Emery, DHL, RPS, and electronic document delivery (i.e., fax machines and e-mail) forced FedEx to search for viable means of expansion. In 1984, facing a growing threat from electronic document delivery, FedEx introduced its ZapMail service for customers who could not afford expensive fax machines. For $35, FedEx would fax up to 10 pages of text to any FedEx site around the world. The document was then hand-delivered to its recipient. Soon after the service was introduced, the price of fax machines plummeted, ultimately forcing FedEx to drop ZapMail after losing more than $190 million. Many analysts still argue that the overnight delivery market could eventually lose as much as 30 percent of its letter business to electronic document delivery, especially e-mail.

FedEx constantly strives to improve its services by enhancing its distribution networks, transportation infrastructure, information technology, and employee performance. FedEx also continues to invest heavily in information technology by installing computer terminals at customers' offices and giving away its proprietary tracking software. Today the vast majority of FedEx customers—more than 70 percent—electronically generate their own pickup and delivery requests. FedEx has also moved more aggressively into e-commerce with respect to order fulfillment for business-to-business and business-to-consumer merchants. For example, FedEx's Home Delivery network has grown rapidly and now reaches virtually every U.S. residential address.

FedEx offers a wealth of electronic tools, applications, and online interfaces for customers to integrate into their processes to shorten response time, reduce inventory costs, and generate better returns, and to simplify their shipping. FedEx InSight is the first web-based application to offer proactive, real-time status information on inbound, outbound, and third-party shipments. It enables customers to identify issues instantly and address them before they become problems. In addition, FedEx InSight allows customers to see the progress of their shipments without requiring a tracking number, giving them convenient and unprecedented data visibility critical to effective management of their supply chain systems. FedEx technology enables customers, couriers, and contract delivery personnel to wirelessly access the company's information systems networks anytime, anywhere. In fact, FedEx was the first transportation company to embrace wireless technology—more than two decades ago—and continues to be a leader in the use of innovative wireless solutions.

The Future for FedEx Corporation   As FedEx moves ahead, the company has a lot going for it. No other carrier can match FedEx's global capabilities or one-stop shopping—at least not yet. To increase its competitiveness, FedEx is focusing on increasing revenue and reducing costs through tighter integration and consolidation, improved productivity, and reduced capital expenditures. Five themes frame FedEx's efforts to fully leverage the strong franchise of the FedEx brand:

- *Vision:* It's the foundation of any successful business, and it starts with the management team. Our core strategy is clear and reinforced throughout the organization through effective communications.
- *Service:* We must continue to streamline all our internal processes that touch the customer to deliver a flawless experience every time. We are delighted at being ranked highest in the J. D. Power and Associates 2002 Small Package Delivery Service Business Customer Satisfaction

Study℠ for air, ground and international delivery services, and we look forward to raising the service bar even higher.

- *People:* Our diverse and talented employees around the world are united in their absolutely, positively, whatever-it-takes spirit. No matter which operating company they work for, their teamwork and their commitment run purple.
- *Innovation:* We will continue to invest in new technologies such as a real-time wireless pocket PC that gives our FedEx Express couriers fast wireless access to the FedEx network.
- *Value:* As we add more value to our customers' businesses, we believe we can also create more value for our shareowners.

Why has FedEx been so successful? A major reason is the company's enviable corporate culture and work force. Because employees are critical to the company's success, FedEx strives to hire the best people and offers them the best training and compensation in the industry. FedEx employees are loyal, highly efficient, and extremely effective in delivering good service. In fact, FedEx employees claim to have "purple blood" to match the company's official color. It is not surprising that FedEx has been named one of the "100 Best Companies to Work For" six consecutive years.

Another reason for FedEx's success is its leadership in information technology and customer relationship management. The company's focus on "delivering certainty" has allowed it to hone in on opportunities that give FedEx additional capabilities in innovative information technology solutions.

A final reason for FedEx's success is outstanding marketing: FedEx is a master at recognizing untapped customer needs and building relationships. FedEx is also never content to sit on its laurels as it constantly strives to improve service and offer more options to its customers. After 30 years of success, there is little doubt that Fred Smith's C paper has become an indispensable part of the business world.

QUESTIONS FOR DISCUSSION

1. Evaluate the methods used by FedEx to grow, both domestically and internationally.
2. Picture a world without FedEx. How would business be different? How would your life be different?
3. What has been the role of information technology and customer relationship management in the success of FedEx Corporation?

Part Four

Target Markets and Customer Behavior

Part Four focuses on the buyer. The development of a marketing strategy begins with the customer. Understanding elements that affect buying decisions enables marketers to better analyze customers' needs and evaluate how specific marketing strategies can satisfy those needs. **Chapter 8** focuses on one of the major steps in marketing strategy development: selecting and analyzing target markets. **Chapter 9** examines consumer buying decision processes and factors that influence buying decisions. **Chapter 10** explores business markets, business customers, the buying center, and the business buying decision process.

8

Target Markets: Segmentation and Evaluation

OBJECTIVES

1. To learn what a market is

2. To understand the differences among general targeting strategies

3. To become familiar with the major segmentation variables

4. To know what segment profiles are and how they are used

5. To understand how to evaluate market segments

6. To identify the factors that influence the selection of specific market segments for use as target markets

7. To become familiar with sales forecasting methods

The Disney Channel Targets Tweens

The Disney Channel's audience is too young for MTV and too old for the Wiggles, but just the right age for family-oriented shows featuring middle school and high school characters. With more than $1 billion in annual revenues, the Disney Channel enjoys an impressive 50 percent profit margin and contributes roughly half of parent company Walt Disney's annual operating income. How does the Disney Channel do it?

When Anne Sweeney became president of the Disney Channel, she investigated what her 10-year-old son and his friends liked to watch on cable television. MTV seemed inappropriate for their age, and she observed that "they weren't enjoying shows for much younger kids." At the time, the Disney Channel aired a lot of cartoons but few shows specifically for 8- to 14-year-olds. Sweeney knew, however, that the 29 million U.S. tweens were loyal to their favorite shows and asked parents to buy show-related merchandise. If the Disney Channel could develop shows that appealed to tweens and earned their parents' approval, it would significantly strengthen its position against cable competitors Nickelodeon and the Cartoon Network.

The Disney Channel implemented this strategy by casting newcomer preteen and young-teen actors in situation comedies and other shows created specifically for the tween lifestyle. *Lizzie McGuire,* an early tweens series, was an instant hit for the Disney Channel. It was followed by *That's So Raven, The Cheetah Girls,* and a succession of other shows and television movies that have captured tweens' imaginations.

Just as important, the shows have helped other Disney divisions profit from tweens' buying power and influence on family spending. At the height of *Lizzie McGuire's* popularity, Walt Disney Pictures released *The Lizzie McGuire Movie* and earned $50 million in box office revenues. Disney's Buena Vista division has done extremely well marketing compact discs with music from the movie and the series, CDs of *Lizzie* tunes for tween karaoke parties, and DVDs of episodes from the series. Disney Press has sold several million copies of *Lizzie McGuire* novels, with more titles being published every year.

Disney Consumer Products has put the *Lizzie* brand on a wide array of products, from dolls and games to blankets and pencils. It has also licensed *Lizzie* for a girls' apparel line distributed nationwide by Kohl's Department Stores. By one estimate, Walt Disney has earned nearly $100 million in revenues from *Lizzie* merchandise sales and licensing fees.

Thanks to savvy shows that reflect a keen understanding of the tween target market, Disney Channel cable television shows now reach 83 million households and, in some months, draw more prime-time viewers than either Nickelodeon or the Cartoon Network. *Lizzie* was a hit in its day, but as tween tastes change, Sweeney and her staff are ready with new shows and new stars for this important market segment.[1] ■

To compete effectively, the Disney Channel has singled out specific customer groups toward which it will direct its marketing efforts. Any organization that wants to succeed must identify its customers and develop and maintain marketing mixes that satisfy the needs of those customers.

In this chapter, we explore markets and market segmentation. Initially we define the term *market* and discuss the major requirements of a market. Then we examine the steps in the target market selection process, including identifying the appropriate targeting strategy, determining which variables to use for segmenting consumer and business markets, developing market segment profiles, evaluating relevant market segments, and selecting target markets. Finally, we discuss various methods for developing sales forecasts.

What Are Markets?

The word *market* has a number of meanings. People sometimes use it to refer to a specific location where products are bought and sold—for example, a flea market. A large geographic area may also be called a market. Sometimes *market* refers to the relationship between supply and demand of a specific product, as in the question "How is the market for digital cameras?" *Market* may also be used as a verb, meaning to sell something.

A market is a group of people who, as individuals or as organizations, have needs for products in a product category and have the ability, willingness, and authority to purchase such products. In general use, the term *market* sometimes refers to the total population, or mass market, that buys products. However, our definition is more specific: it refers to groups of people seeking products in a specific product category. For example, students are part of the market for textbooks, as well as the markets for software, pens, paper, food, music, and other products. Obviously our complex economy has many different markets.

◆ Requirements of a Market

As stated in our definition, for a market to exist, the people in the aggregate must meet the following four requirements:

1. They must need or desire a particular product. If they do not, that aggregate is not a market.
2. They must have the ability to purchase the product. Ability to purchase is a function of buying power, which consists of resources such as money, goods, and services that can be traded in an exchange situation.
3. They must be willing to use their buying power.
4. They must have the authority to buy the specific products

Individuals can have the desire, the buying power, and the willingness to purchase certain products but may not be authorized to do so. For example, teenagers may have the desire, the money, and the willingness to buy liquor, but a liquor producer does not consider them a market because teenagers are prohibited by law from buying alcoholic beverages. An aggregate of people that lacks any one of the four requirements thus does not constitute a market.

◆ Types of Markets

consumer market Purchasers and household members who intend to consume or benefit from the purchased products and do not buy products to make profits

Markets fall into one of two categories: consumer markets and business markets (also called business-to-business, industrial, or organizational markets). These categories are based on the characteristics of the individuals and groups that make up a specific market and the purposes for which they buy products. A **consumer market**

Consumer and Business Markets
Mars is aiming this Dove Bar advertisement at consumer markets. Ricoh promotes its products to business markets.

business market Individuals or groups that purchase a specific kind of product for resale, direct use in producing other products, or use in general daily operations

consists of purchasers and individuals in their households who intend to consume or benefit from the purchased products and do not buy products for the main purpose of making a profit. Each of us belongs to numerous consumer markets. The millions of individuals with the ability, willingness, and authority to buy make up a multitude of consumer markets for such products as housing, food, clothing, vehicles, personal services, appliances, furniture, and recreational equipment.

A **business market** consists of individuals or groups that purchase a specific kind of product for one of three purposes: resale, direct use in producing other products, or use in general daily operations. For example, a lamp producer that buys electrical wire to use in the production of lamps is a part of a business market for electrical wire. This same firm purchases dust mops to clean its office areas. Although the mops are not used in the direct production of lamps, they are used in the firm's operations; thus, this manufacturer is part of a business market for dust mops. The four categories of business markets are producer, reseller, government, and institutional.

Target Market Selection Process

In Chapter 1, we point out that the first of two major components of developing a marketing strategy is to select a target market. Although marketers may employ several methods for target market selection, generally they use a five-step process. This process is shown in Figure 8.1, and we discuss it in the following sections.

Figure 8.1 Target Market Selection Process

1 Identify the appropriate targeting strategy	2 Determine which segmentation variables to use	3 Develop market segment profiles	4 Evaluate relevant market segments	5 Select specific target markets

Step 1: Identify the Appropriate Targeting Strategy

Recall from Chapter 1 that a target market is a group of people or organizations for which a business creates and maintains a marketing mix specifically designed to satisfy the needs of group members. The strategy used to select a target market is affected by target market characteristics, product attributes, and the organization's objectives and resources. Figure 8.2 illustrates the three basic targeting strategies: undifferentiated, concentrated, and differentiated.

◆ Undifferentiated Strategy

undifferentiated targeting strategy A strategy in which an organization defines an entire market for a particular product as its target market, designs a single marketing mix, and directs it at that market

An organization sometimes defines an entire market for a particular product as its target market. When a company designs a single marketing mix and directs it at the entire market for a particular product, it is using an **undifferentiated targeting strategy.** As Figure 8.2 shows, the strategy assumes that all customers in the target market for a specific kind of product have similar needs, and thus the organization can satisfy most customers with a single marketing mix. This mix consists of one type of product with little or no variation, one price, one promotional program aimed at everybody, and one distribution system to reach most customers in the total market. Products marketed successfully through the undifferentiated strategy include staple food items, such as sugar and salt, and certain kinds of farm produce.

homogeneous market A market in which a large proportion of customers have similar needs for a product

The undifferentiated targeting strategy is effective under two conditions. First, a large proportion of customers in a total market must have similar needs for the product, a situation termed a **homogeneous market**. A marketer using a single marketing mix for a total market of customers with a variety of needs would find that the marketing mix satisfies very few people. A "universal car" meant to satisfy everyone would satisfy very few customers' needs for cars because it would not provide the specific attributes a particular person wants. Second, the organization must be able to develop and maintain a single marketing mix that satisfies customers' needs. The company must be able to identify a set of needs common to most customers in a total market and have the resources and managerial skills to reach a sizable portion of that market.

Although customers may have similar needs for a few products, for most products their needs decidedly differ. In such instances, a company should use a concentrated or a differentiated strategy.

◆ Concentrated Strategy Through Market Segmentation

heterogeneous market A market made up of individuals or organizations with diverse needs for products in a specific product class

market segmentation The process of dividing a total market into groups with relatively similar product needs to design a marketing mix that matches those needs

market segment Individuals, groups, or organizations sharing one or more similar characteristics that cause them to have similar product needs

Markets made up of individuals or organizations with diverse product needs are called **heterogeneous markets**. Not everyone wants the same type of car, furniture, or clothes. For example, some individuals want an economical car, others desire a status symbol, and still others seek a roomy and comfortable vehicle. The automobile market thus is heterogeneous.

For such heterogeneous markets, market segmentation is appropriate. **Market segmentation** is the process of dividing a total market into groups, or segments, consisting of people or organizations with relatively similar product needs. The purpose is to enable a marketer to design a marketing mix that more precisely matches the needs of customers in the selected market segment. A **market segment** consists of individuals, groups, or organizations sharing one or more similar characteristics that cause them to have relatively similar product needs. For instance, the cola market could be divided into segments consisting of diet cola drinkers and regular cola drinkers. The main rationale for segmenting heterogeneous markets is that a company is better able to develop a satisfying marketing mix for a relatively small portion of a total market than to develop a mix that meets the needs of all people. Market segmentation is widely used. Fast-food chains, soft-drink companies, magazine publishers, hospitals, and banks are just a few types of organizations that employ market segmentation.

Figure 8.2 **Targeting Strategies**
The letters in each target market represent potential customers. Customers with the same letters have similar characteristics and similar product needs.

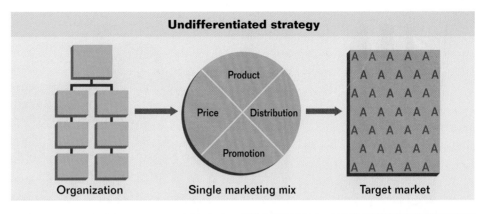

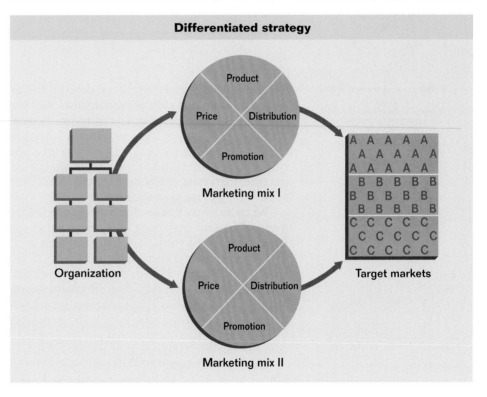

For market segmentation to succeed, five conditions must exist. First, customers' needs for the product must be heterogeneous; otherwise there is little reason to segment the market. Second, segments must be identifiable and divisible. The company must find a characteristic or variable for effectively separating individuals in a total market into groups containing people with relatively uniform needs for the product.

concentrated targeting strategy
A market segmentation strategy in which an organization targets a single market segment using one marketing mix

Third, the total market should be divided so that segments can be compared with respect to estimated sales potential, costs, and profits. Fourth, at least one segment must have enough profit potential to justify developing and maintaining a special marketing mix for that segment. Finally, the company must be able to reach the chosen segment with a particular marketing mix. Some market segments may be difficult or impossible to reach because of legal, social, or distribution constraints. For instance, marketers of Cuban rum and cigars cannot sell to U.S. consumers because of political and trade restrictions.

When an organization directs its marketing efforts toward a single market segment using one marketing mix, it is employing a **concentrated targeting strategy.** Porsche focuses on the luxury sports car segment and directs all its marketing efforts toward high-income individuals who want to own high-performance sports cars. Cross Pen Company aims its products at the upscale gift segment of the pen market and does not compete with Bic, which focuses on the inexpensive, disposable-pen segment. Notice in Figure 8.2 that the organization using the concentrated strategy is aiming its marketing mix only at "B" customers. Similarly, Lionel targets the segment of the toy train market that prefers detailed, large-scale trains—a $250 million segment, but only 25 percent of the overall market for toy trains.[2]

The chief advantage of the concentrated strategy is that it allows a firm to specialize. The firm analyzes characteristics and needs of a distinct customer group and then focuses all its energies on satisfying that group's needs. A firm may generate a large sales volume by reaching a single segment. Also, concentrating on a single segment permits a firm with limited resources to compete with larger organizations that may have overlooked smaller segments.

Specialization, however, means that a company puts all its eggs in one basket, which can be hazardous. If a company's sales depend on a single segment and the segment's demand for the product declines, the company's financial strength also deteriorates. Moreover, when a firm penetrates one segment and becomes well entrenched, its popularity may keep it from moving into other segments. For example, it is very unlikely that Cross could or would want to compete with Bic in the low-end, disposable-pen market segment.

◆ Differentiated Strategy Through Market Segmentation

differentiated targeting strategy A strategy in which an organization targets two or more segments by developing a marketing mix for each segment

With a **differentiated targeting strategy**, an organization directs its marketing efforts at two or more segments by developing a marketing mix for each segment (see Figure 8.2). After a firm uses a concentrated strategy successfully in one market segment, it sometimes expands its efforts to include additional segments. For example, Fruit of the Loom underwear has traditionally been aimed at one segment: men. However, the company now markets underwear for women and children as well. Marketing mixes for a differentiated strategy may vary as to product features, distribution methods, promotion methods, and prices.

A firm may increase sales in the aggregate market through a differentiated strategy because its marketing mixes are aimed at more people. For example, the Gap, which established its retail apparel reputation by targeting people under 25, now targets several age groups, from infants to people over 60. A company with excess production capacity may find a differentiated strategy advantageous because the sale of products to additional segments may absorb excess capacity. On the other hand, a differentiated strategy often demands more production processes, materials, and people. Thus, production costs may be higher than with a concentrated strategy.

Step 2: Determine Which Segmentation Variables to Use

segmentation variables Characteristics of individuals, groups, or organizations used to divide a market into segments

Segmentation variables are the characteristics of individuals, groups, or organizations used to divide a market into segments. For example, location, age, gender, or rate of product usage can all be bases for segmenting markets.

To select a segmentation variable, several factors are considered. The segmentation variable should relate to customers' needs for, uses of, or behavior toward the product. Stereo marketers might segment the stereo market based on income and age, but not on religion, because people's stereo needs do not differ due to religion. Furthermore, if individuals or organizations in a total market are to be classified accurately, the segmentation variable must be measurable. Age, location, and gender are measurable because such information can be obtained through observation or questioning. In contrast, segmenting a market on the basis of, say, intelligence is extremely difficult because this attribute is harder to measure accurately.

A company's resources and capabilities affect the number and size of segment variables used. The type of product and degree of variation in customers' needs also dictate the number and size of segments targeted. In short, there is no best way to segment markets.

Choosing a segmentation variable or variables is a critical step in targeting a market. Selecting an inappropriate variable limits the chances of developing a successful marketing strategy. To help you better understand potential segmentation variables, we next examine the major types of variables used to segment consumer markets and the types used to segment business markets.

◆ Variables for Segmenting Consumer Markets

A marketer using segmentation to reach a consumer market can choose one or several variables from an assortment of possibilities. As Figure 8.3 (on p. 210) shows, segmentation variables can be grouped into four categories: demographic, geographic, psychographic, and behavioristic.

Figure 8.3 Segmentation Variables for Consumer Markets

Demographic variables
- Age
- Gender
- Race
- Ethnicity
- Income
- Education
- Occupation
- Family size
- Family life cycle
- Religion
- Social class

Geographic variables
- Region
- Urban, suburban, rural
- City size
- County size
- State size
- Market density
- Climate
- Terrain

Psychographic variables
- Personality attributes
- Motives
- Lifestyles

Behavioristic variables
- Volume usage
- End use
- Benefit expectations
- Brand loyalty
- Price sensitivity

Demographic Variables. Demographers study aggregate population characteristics such as the distribution of age and gender, fertility rates, migration patterns, and mortality rates. Demographic characteristics that marketers commonly use in segmenting markets include age, gender, race, ethnicity, income, education, occupation, family size, family life cycle, religion, and social class. Marketers rely on these demographic characteristics because they are often closely linked to customers' needs and purchasing behavior and can be readily measured. Like demographers, a few marketers even use mortality rates. Service Corporation International (SCI), the largest

Gender-Based Segmentation As shown in these two advertisements, some brands of razors are aimed at women, whereas others are aimed at men.

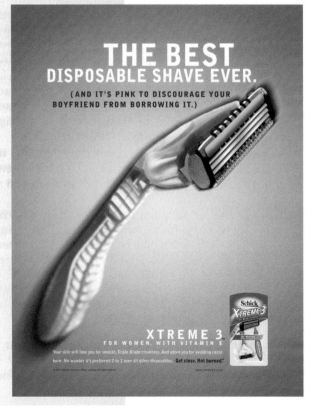

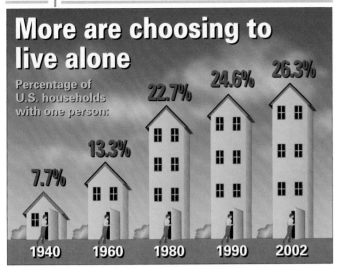

Snapshot

Source: Data from U.S. Census Bureau.

U.S. funeral services company, attempts to locate its facilities in higher-income suburban areas with high mortality rates. SCI operates more than 3,070 funeral service locations, cemeteries, and crematoriums.[3]

Age is a commonly used variable for segmentation purposes. For example, Norwegian Coastal Voyage runs luxury cruises to the Norwegian fjords, Chile, Spitzbergen, and Antarctica, and developed its own special age segmentation. Called "Gray Rainbow," the cruise line's management determined that its customers are not typical cruise passengers; they are more active and adventurous. Targeting the cruise line's message to this older crowd has doubled response rates. The company changed its approach to selling the value of the destination rather than concentrating on discounting.[4] Marketers need to be aware of age distribution and how that distribution is changing. All age groups under 55 are expected to decrease by the year 2025, and all age categories 55 and older are expected to increase. In 1970, the average age of a U.S. citizen was 27.9; currently it is about 35.7. As Figure 8.4 shows, Americans 65 and older spend as much or more on food, housing, and health care compared to Americans in the two younger age groups.

Many marketers recognize the purchase influence of children and are targeting more marketing efforts at them. As a group, children ages 4 to 12 have annual incomes in excess of $40 billion. Numerous products are aimed specifically at

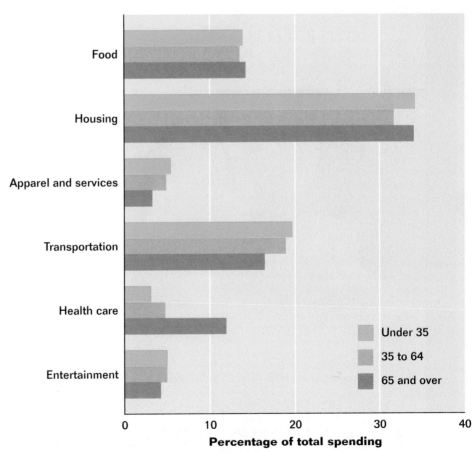

Figure 8.4 **Spending Levels of Three Age Groups for Selected Product Categories**
Source: U.S. Department of Labor, Bureau of Labor Statistics. August 2000.

children—toys, clothing, food and beverages, and entertainment such as movies and TV cable channels. In addition, children in this age group influence $500 billion of parental spending yearly.[5] In households with only one parent or those in which both parents work, children often take on additional responsibilities such as cooking, cleaning, and grocery shopping, and thus influence the types of products and brands these households purchase.

Gender is another demographic variable commonly used to segment markets, including the markets for clothing, soft drinks, nonprescription medications, toiletries, magazines, and even cigarettes. The Census Bureau reports that girls and women account for 50.9 percent and boys and men for 49.1 percent of the total U.S. population.[6] Some deodorant marketers utilize gender segmentation: Secret deodorant is marketed specifically to women, whereas Old Spice deodorant is directed toward men. A number of websites are aimed at females, including Girl Tech, Moms Online, Women.com, and Online Women's Business Center. Effective online targeting of women relies heavily on personalization, sense of community, and trust.[7] Food and beverage companies are paying close attention to women and have determined that all important food marketing trends are partially the result of women's influence in the home. Foods offering convenience, portability, and easy preparation have a good chance of success. For example, cereal maker Kellogg Company spun off its Rice Krispie Treats from its Rice Krispies line, and its convenience makes it the most popular snack bar in the country, with annual sales topping $140 million. Its easy portability and convenience, which appeals to women consumers, is a factor.[8]

Marketers also use race and ethnicity as variables for segmenting markets for such products as food, music, clothing, and cosmetics and for services such as banking and insurance. The U.S. Hispanic population

WE SEE JUST HOW QUICKLY
THEY GO FROM BABIES TO BABYSITTERS.
WE LIVE WHERE YOU LIVE.™

It's amazing. Kids grow up so fast. Is your life insurance keeping pace? To help you be absolutely sure your family's growing financial needs aren't outgrowing your coverage, talk to someone who understands you and your life. For life insurance, call your neighborhood State Farm agent, or visit statefarm.com®

LIKE A GOOD NEIGHBOR   STATE FARM   STATE FARM IS THERE.™

Providing Insurance and Financial Services

illustrates the importance of ethnicity as a segmentation variable. Made up of people of Mexican, Cuban, Puerto Rican, and Central and South American heritage, this ethnic group is growing five times faster than the general population. Consequently Campbell Soup, Procter & Gamble, and other companies are targeting Hispanic consumers, viewing this segment as attractive because of its size and growth potential. However, targeting Hispanic customers is not an easy task. For example, although marketers have long believed Hispanic consumers are exceptionally brand loyal and prefer Spanish-language broadcast media, research does not consistently support these assumptions.

Because income strongly influences people's product needs, it often provides a way to divide markets. Income affects people's ability to buy and their desires for certain lifestyles. Product markets segmented by income include sporting goods, housing, furniture, cosmetics, clothing, jewelry, home appliances, automobiles, and electronics.

Among the factors influencing household income and product needs are marital status and the presence and age of children. These characteristics, often combined and called the *family life cycle,* affect needs for housing, appliances, food and beverages, automobiles, and recreational equipment. Using the information in Table 8.1, consider how life cycle stages affect the purchase of beverages.

Table 8.1	Life Cycle Stages Influence Beverage Purchases

Percent of All Dollars Spent Annually in Each Beverage Category, by Life Stage

	Carbonated Beverages	Coffee	Juices, Refrigerated	Soft Drinks, Non-carb.	Bottled Water	All Remaining Carb. Bev/Diet	All Remaining Carb. Bev/Reg	Coffee, Liquid
Young singles (age 18–34)	2%	1%	2%	2%	2%	2%	1%	3%
Childless younger couples (two adults, 18–34)	4%	3%	4%	4%	6%	4%	4%	8%
New families (2 adults, 1 or more children <6)	5%	3%	5%	8%	6%	4%	5%	4%
Maturing families (2 adults, 1 or more children, not all <6 or +12)	26%	19%	22%	36%	22%	21%	30%	19%
Established families (1 or more children, all +12)	12%	9%	10%	10%	10%	9%	14%	12%
Middle-aged singles (35–54)	7%	5%	7%	4%	9%	9%	7%	7%
Middle-aged childless couples (2 adults, 35–54)	18%	17%	16%	14%	18%	19%	16%	18%
Empty-nesters (2 adults, +55, no children at home)	20%	32%	24%	17%	20%	24%	17%	21%
Older singles (55+)	7%	11%	10%	6%	7%	8%	6%	8%
Total	100%	100%	100%	100%	100%	100%	100%	100%

Source: American Demographics, "Drink Me" by Matthew Grimm. February 2000, pp. 62–63. Copyright © 2000. Reprinted with permission from *American Demographics.*

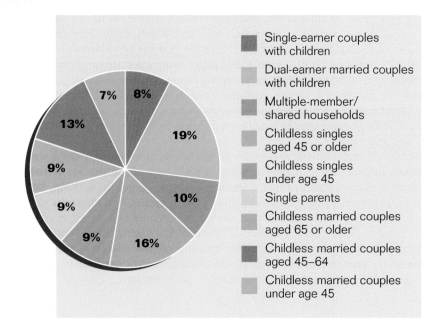

- Single-earner couples with children
- Dual-earner married couples with children
- Multiple-member/shared households
- Childless singles aged 45 or older
- Childless singles under age 45
- Single parents
- Childless married couples aged 65 or older
- Childless married couples aged 45–64
- Childless married couples under age 45

Figure 8.5 Family Life Cycle Stages as a Percentage of All Households
Source: Bureau of the Census, *Current Population Survey.*

Family life cycles can be broken down in various ways. Figure 8.5 shows a breakdown into nine categories. The composition of the American household in relation to family life cycle has changed. The "typical" American family of a single-earner married couple with children dropped from 21 percent of all households in 1970 to about 7 percent today, and the number of households in which one person lives alone or with unrelated people has increased from 23 percent to about 38 percent. Childless singles under age 45 headed just 3 percent of households in 1970, but their share has increased to about 10 percent today. People in a particular life cycle stage may have very specific needs that can be satisfied by precisely designed marketing mixes. For more information about how American families are changing, see the Building Customer Relationships boxed feature.

BUILDING CUSTOMER RELATIONSHIPS

The New American Household

The American household has never had so many different faces. Of all U.S. households, only half consist of traditional married couples, a sharp decline from the 80 percent tallied by the U.S. census in 1950. The other half includes an ever-increasing number of single-person households, unmarried adults living together, and nontraditional families. This demographic diversity is a challenge for marketers that want to initiate or maintain relationships with people in these market segments.

Both men and women are delaying marriage until their late 20s, choosing instead to live alone or with a partner. According to government projections, more than 25 percent of all households will contain one person by the time the next census is conducted in 2010. Still, 85 percent of single Americans are likely to walk down the aisle once (perhaps more than once), compared to 95 percent 50 years ago.

Among unmarried couples living together, more than 43 percent have children in their households versus 46 percent of married couples. The number of same-sex partners raising children continues to grow as well. Households consisting of married couples with children are no longer the norm. By 2010, just 20 percent of U.S. households will fit this description.

Mixed-race families comprise a small but steadily rising percentage of American households. In 1990, husbands and wives in 1 out of 23 married couples were of different races. Ten years later, husbands and wives in 1 out of 15 married couples were of different races. Moreover, 17 percent of the children adopted into American families are not the same race as their adoptive parents.

Looking ahead, American households will only get more diverse, forcing companies to find new ways to segment the market and connect with targeted consumer groups. Clearly, fewer and fewer U.S. families will fit the traditional model of working father and stay-at-home mother raising two school-age children. New households means new targeting strategies and new marketing mixes designed for particular target markets, from vacation packages designed for same-sex couples to commercials showing single women test-driving new cars.

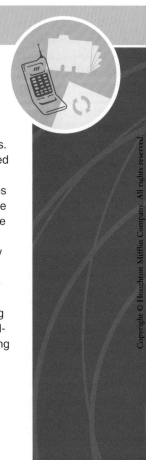

Marketers also use many other demographic variables. For instance, dictionary publishing companies segment markets by education level. Some insurance companies segment markets using occupation, targeting health insurance at college students and at younger workers with small employers that do not provide health coverage.

Geographic Variables. Geographic variables—climate, terrain, city size, population density, and urban/rural areas—also influence consumer product needs. Markets may be divided into regions because one or more geographic variables can cause customers to differ from one region to another. A company selling products to a national market might divide the United States into the following regions: Pacific, Southwest, Central, Midwest, Southeast, Middle Atlantic, and New England. A firm operating in one or several states might regionalize its market by counties, cities, zip code areas, or other units.

City size can be an important segmentation variable. Some marketers focus efforts on cities of a certain size. For example, one franchised restaurant organization will not locate in cities of fewer than 200,000 people. It concluded that a smaller population base would result in inadequate profits. Other firms actively seek opportunities in smaller towns. A classic example is Wal-Mart, which initially located only in small towns.

Because cities often cut across political boundaries, the U.S. Census Bureau developed a system to classify metropolitan areas (any area with a city or urbanized area of at least 50,000 population and a total metropolitan population of at least 100,000). Metropolitan areas are categorized as one of the following: a metropolitan statistical area (MSA), a primary metropolitan statistical area (PMSA), or a consolidated metropolitan statistical area (CMSA). An MSA is an urbanized area encircled by nonmetropolitan counties and is neither socially nor economically dependent on any other metropolitan area. A metropolitan area within a complex of at least 1 million inhabitants can elect to be named a PMSA. A CMSA is a metropolitan area of at least 1 million consisting of two or more PMSAs. Of the 20 CMSAs, the 5 largest—New York, Los Angeles, Chicago, San Francisco, and Philadelphia—account for 20 percent of the U.S. population. The federal government provides a considerable amount of socioeconomic information about MSAs, PMSAs, and CMSAs that can aid in market analysis and segmentation.

market density The number of potential customers within a unit of land area

Market density refers to the number of potential customers within a unit of land area, such as a square mile. Although market density relates generally to population density, the correlation is not exact. For example, in two different geographic markets of approximately equal size and population, market density for office supplies would be much higher in one area if it contained a much greater proportion of business customers than the other area. Market density may be a useful segmentation variable because low-density markets often require different sales, advertising, and distribution activities than do high-density markets.

geodemographic segmentation A method of market segmentation that clusters people in zip code areas and smaller neighborhood units based on lifestyle and demographic information

A number of marketers are using geodemographic segmentation. **Geodemographic segmentation** clusters people in zip code areas and even smaller neighborhood units based on lifestyle information and especially demographic data such as income, education, occupation, type of housing, ethnicity, family life cycle, and level of urbanization. These small, precisely described population clusters help marketers isolate demographic units as small as neighborhoods where the demand for specific products is strongest. Information companies such as Donnelley Marketing Information Services, Claritas, and C.A.C.I., Inc., provide geodemographic data services called Prospect Zone, PRIZM, and Acorn, respectively. PRIZM is based on a classification of the more than 500,000 U.S. neighborhoods into one of 40 cluster types, such as "shotguns and pickups," "money and brains," and "gray power."

micromarketing An approach to market segmentation in which organizations focus precise marketing efforts on very small geographic markets

Geodemographic segmentation allows marketers to engage in micromarketing. **Micromarketing** is the focusing of precise marketing efforts on very small geographic markets, such as community and even neighborhood markets. Providers of financial and health care services, retailers, and consumer products companies use micromarketing. Special advertising campaigns, promotions, retail site location analyses, special pricing, and unique retail product offerings are a few examples of micro-marketing facilitated through geodemographic segmentation.

Climate is commonly used as a geographic segmentation variable because of its broad impact on people's behavior and product needs. Product markets affected by climate include air-conditioning and heating equipment, clothing, gardening equipment, recreational products, and building materials.

Psychographic Variables. Marketers sometimes use psychographic variables, such as personality characteristics, motives, and lifestyles, to segment markets. A psychographic dimension can be used by itself to segment a market or combined with other types of segmentation variables.

Personality characteristics can be useful for segmentation when a product resembles many competing products and consumers' needs are not significantly related to other segmentation variables. However, segmenting a market according to personality traits can be risky. Although marketing practitioners have long believed consumer choice and product use vary with personality, until recently marketing research had indicated only weak relationships. It is hard to measure personality traits accurately, especially since most personality tests were developed for clinical use, not for segmentation purposes.

When appealing to a personality characteristic, a marketer almost always selects one that many people view positively. Individuals with this characteristic, as well as those who would like to have it, may be influenced to buy that marketer's brand. Marketers taking this approach do not worry about measuring how many people have the positively valued characteristic; they assume a sizable proportion of people in the target market either have it or want to have it.

Lifestyle Segmentation
Recreation-related products are often segmented on the basis of lifestyle, as illustrated in this advertisement.

When motives are used to segment a market, the market is divided according to consumers' reasons for making a purchase. Personal appearance, affiliation, status, safety, and health are examples of motives affecting the types of products purchased and the choice of stores in which they are bought. Marketing efforts based on health motives can be a point of competitive advantage, as illustrated by the ad campaign launched by sandwich retailer Subway. The marketing of the "Subway Diet" and its spokesperson, Jared Fogle, transformed its sandwiches into a popular diet plan.[9]

Lifestyle segmentation groups individuals according to how they spend their time, the importance of things in their surroundings (homes or jobs, for example), beliefs about themselves and broad issues, and some demographic characteristics, such as income and education.[10] Lifestyle analysis provides a broad view of buyers because it encompasses numerous characteristics related to people's activities (work, hobbies, entertainment, sports), interests (family, home, fashion, food, technology), and opinions (politics, social issues, education, the future). For example, homeownership is valued by most income and age segments. Among Generation Xers (born between 1964 and 1973), homeownership by unmarried couples is increasing, as is homeownership by single women. Unlike baby boomers (born 1946–1963), Generation X home buyers tend to view their homes as expressions of their individuality and prefer housing located close to work, schools, and shopping over size.[11] Several lifestyle dimensions of baby boomers and pre-boomers are discussed in the Building Customer Relationships boxed feature.

One of the most popular consumer lifestyle frameworks is SRI Consulting Business Intelligence's VALS™ Program. VALS classifies consumers into eight basic

BUILDING CUSTOMER RELATIONSHIPS

Understanding Mature Customers

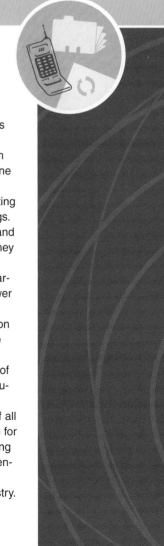

Demographically speaking, because America is making more older people than younger people, many companies are targeting mature customers. Seniors tend to have considerable disposable income, especially if they continue working while receiving social security or pension benefits. By 2025, at least 100 million Americans will have passed their fiftieth birthday, representing huge opportunity marketing for many companies.

Consider the psychographic variable of lifestyle. Research shows that today's seniors think and feel young—about seven to ten years younger than their real ages. Knowing this, car advertisements rarely feature people who appear to be near retirement age. For example, the average age of consumers who buy new Lincoln Town Cars is 67. Yet the brand is projecting a more youthful image through its spokesperson, Magic Johnson, a 40-something former basketball star turned successful businessman.

Family lifestyle is another important psychographic variable. Many adults over 50 are grandparents (or great-grandparents) and enjoy indulging younger family members with gifts of toys and other products. In fact, seniors buy 25 percent of toys sold during any given year. The influence of lifestyle extends to major purchases as well. As an example, minivan commercials showing families with young children appeal to seniors because, says one expert, grandparents realize that minivans are perfect for transporting grandchildren and their belongings.

Today's seniors are healthier and more active than ever before, and they are seeking specific benefits from the products they buy. Retired seniors in particular have the time and spending power to play sports, travel, attend cultural events, go back to school, buy a vacation home, and pursue other interests. To be able to afford an active lifestyle during retirement, seniors need a wide variety of financial services, creating more opportunity for insurance firms, banks, brokers, and financial planners. Finally, seniors of all ages want to stay as healthy as possible for as long as possible. Therefore, segmenting this market in terms of specific health benefits is a top priority for pharmaceutical firms and others in the health care industry.

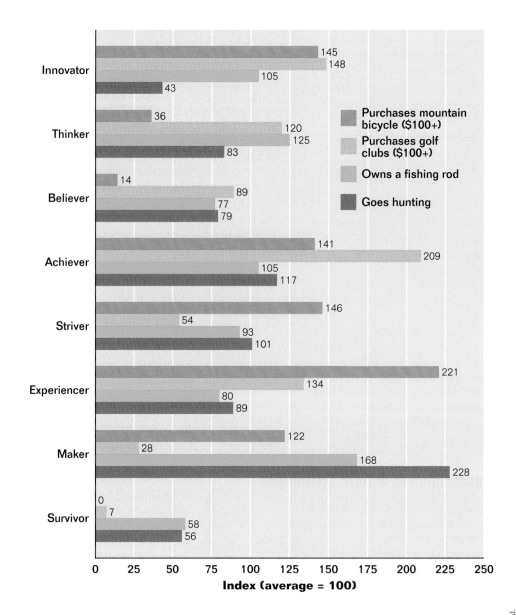

Figure 8.6 VALS™ Types and Sports Preferences

Source: VALS™ Program. SRI Consulting Business Intelligence. Reprinted with permission.

groups based on psychological characteristics that are correlated with purchase behavior and four key demographics. The VALS is used to identify the group that a respondent belongs to. This VALS questionnaire is then attached to larger surveys that focus on particular products, services, leisure activities, or media preferences to learn about the lifestyles of the eight groups. The eight groups are: Innovators, Thinkers, Achievers, Experiencers, Believers, Strivers, Makers, and Survivors. An example of VALS data is shown in Figure 8.6. This figure shows the proportion of each VALS group that purchased a mountain bike, purchased golf clubs, owns a fishing rod, and goes hunting. Marketers of reasonably priced, American made hunting equipment might target Makers, whereas marketers of products relating to mountain biking would do better to target Experiencers[12]. VALS research is also used to create new products as well as to segment existing markets. VALS systems have been developed for the United States, Japan, and the United Kingdom.

Many other lifestyle classification systems exist. Several companies, such as Experían's BehaviorBank, collect lifestyle data on millions of consumers.

Behavioristic Variables.   Firms can divide a market according to some feature of consumer behavior toward a product, commonly involving some aspect of product use. For example, a market may be separated into users—classified as heavy, moderate, or light—and nonusers. To satisfy a specific group, such as heavy users, marketers may create a distinctive product, set special prices, or initiate special promotion and distribution activities. Per capita consumption data help identify different levels of usage. For example, the Beverage Market Index of 2003 shows that per capita consumption of bottled water varies from 9.0 gallons in the East Central states (Illinois, Indiana, Kentucky, Michigan, Ohio, West Virginia, and Wisconsin) to 34.5 gallons in the Southwest (Arizona, New Mexico, Oklahoma, and Texas).[13]

How customers use or apply products may also determine the method of segmentation. To satisfy customers who use a product in a certain way, some feature—say, packaging, size, texture, or color—may be designed precisely to make the product easier to use, safer, or more convenient.

benefit segmentation The division of a market according to benefits that customers want from the product

Benefit segmentation is the division of a market according to benefits that consumers want from the product. Although most types of market segmentation assume a relationship between the variable and customers' needs, benefit segmentation differs in that the benefits customers seek *are* their product needs. For example, a customer who purchases over-the-counter cold relief medication may be specifically interested in two benefits: stopping a runny nose and relieving chest congestion. Thus, individuals are segmented directly according to their needs. By determining the desired benefits, marketers may be able to divide people into groups seeking certain sets of benefits. The effectiveness of such segmentation depends on three conditions: (1) the benefits sought must be identifiable; (2) using these benefits, marketers must be able to divide people into recognizable segments; and (3) one or more of the resulting segments must be accessible to the firm's marketing efforts. Both Timberland and Avia, for example, segment the foot apparel market based on benefits sought.

As this discussion shows, consumer markets can be divided according to numerous characteristics. Business markets are segmented using different variables, as we will see in the following section.

◆ Variables for Segmenting Business Markets

Like consumer markets, business markets are frequently segmented. Marketers segment business markets according to geographic location, type of organization, customer size, and product use.

Geographic Location. Earlier we noted that the demand for some consumer products can vary considerably among geographic areas because of differences in climate, terrain, customer preferences, and similar factors. Demand for business products also varies according to geographic location. For example, producers of certain types of lumber divide their markets geographically because their customers' needs vary from region to region. Geographic segmentation may be especially appropriate for reaching industries concentrated in certain locations. Furniture and textile producers, for example, are concentrated in the Southeast.

Type of Organization. A company sometimes segments a market by types of organizations within that market. Different types of organizations often require different product features, distribution systems, price structures, and selling strategies. Given these variations, a firm may either concentrate on a single segment with one marketing mix (a concentration targeting strategy) or focus on several groups with multiple mixes (a differentiated targeting strategy). A carpet producer, for example, could segment potential customers into several groups, such as automobile makers, commercial carpet contractors (firms that carpet large commercial buildings), apartment complex developers, carpet wholesalers, and large retail carpet outlets.

Customer Size. An organization's size may affect its purchasing procedures and the types and quantities of products it wants. Size can thus be an effective variable for segmenting a business market. To reach a segment of a particular size, marketers may have to adjust one or more marketing mix components. For example, customers that buy in extremely large quantities are sometimes offered discounts. In addition, marketers often must expand personal selling efforts to serve large organizational buyers properly. Because the needs of large and small buyers tend to be quite distinct, marketers frequently use different marketing practices to reach various customer groups.

Product Use. Certain products, especially basic raw materials like steel, petroleum, plastics, and lumber, are used in numerous ways. How a company uses products affects the types and amounts of products purchased, as well as the purchasing method. For example, computers are used for engineering purposes, basic scientific research, and business operations such as word processing, accounting, and telecommunications. A computer maker therefore may segment the computer market by types of use because organizations' needs for computer hardware and software depend on the purpose for which products are purchased.

Step 3: Develop Market Segment Profiles

A market segment profile describes the similarities among potential customers within a segment and explains the differences among people and organizations in different segments. A profile may cover such aspects as demographic characteristics, geographic factors, product benefits sought, lifestyles, brand preferences, and usage rates. Individuals and organizations within segments should be relatively similar with respect to several characteristics and product needs, and differ considerably from those within other market segments. Marketers use market segment profiles to assess the degree to which their possible products can match or fit potential customers' product needs. Market segment profiles help marketers understand how a business can use its capabilities to serve potential customer groups.

The use of market segment profiles benefits marketers in several ways. Such profiles help a marketer determine which segment or segments are most attractive to the organization relative to the firm's strengths, weaknesses, objectives, and resources. While marketers may initially believe certain segments are quite attractive, development of market segment profiles may yield information that indicates the opposite. For the market segment or segments chosen by the organization, the information included in market segment profiles can be highly useful in making marketing decisions.

Step 4: Evaluate Relevant Market Segments

After analyzing the market segment profiles, a marketer is likely to identify several relevant market segments that require further analysis and eliminate certain segments from consideration. To further assess relevant market segments, several important factors, including sales estimates, competition, and estimated costs associated with each segment, should be analyzed.

◆ Sales Estimates

Potential sales for a market segment can be measured along several dimensions, including product level, geographic area, time, and level of competition.[14] With respect to product level, potential sales can be estimated for a specific product item (for example, Diet Coke) or an entire product line (Coca-Cola Classic, Caffeine-Free Coke, Diet Coke, Caffeine-Free Diet Coke, Vanilla Coke, Diet Vanilla Coke, Cherry Coca-Cola, and Diet Cherry Coca-Cola comprise one product line). A manager must also determine the geographic area to include in the estimate. In relation to time, sales estimates can be short range (one year or less), medium range (one to five years), or long range (longer than five years). The competitive level specifies whether sales are being estimated for a single firm or for an entire industry.

market potential The total amount of a product that customers will purchase within a specified period at a specific level of industrywide marketing activity

Market potential is the total amount of a product that customers will purchase within a specified period at a specific level of industrywide marketing activity. Market potential can be stated in terms of dollars or units. A segment's market potential is affected by economic, sociocultural, and other environmental forces. Marketers must assume a certain general level of marketing effort in the industry when they estimate market potential. The specific level of marketing effort varies from one firm to another, but the sum of all firms' marketing activities equals industrywide marketing efforts. A marketing manager must also consider whether and to what extent industry marketing efforts will change.

company sales potential The maximum percentage of market potential that an individual firm can expect to obtain for a specific product

Company sales potential is the maximum percentage of market potential that an individual firm within an industry can expect to obtain for a specific product. Several factors influence company sales potential for a market segment. First, the market potential places absolute limits on the size of the company's sales potential. Second, the magnitude of industrywide marketing activities has an indirect but definite impact on the company's sales potential. Those activities have a direct bearing on the size of the market potential. When Domino's Pizza advertises home-delivered pizza, for example, it indirectly promotes pizza in general; its commercials may indirectly help sell Pizza Hut's and other competitors' home-delivered pizza. Third, the intensity and effectiveness of a company's marketing activities relative to competitors' affect the size of the company's sales potential. If a company spends twice as much as any of its competitors on marketing efforts and if each dollar spent is more effective in generating sales, the firm's sales potential will be quite high compared to competitors'.

breakdown approach Measuring company sales potential based on a general economic forecast for a specific period and the market potential derived from it

buildup approach Measuring company sales potential by estimating how much of a product a potential buyer in a specific geographic area will purchase in a given period, multiplying the estimate by the number of potential buyers, and adding the totals of all the geographic areas considered

There are two general approaches to measuring company sales potential: breakdown and buildup. In the **breakdown approach**, the marketing manager first develops a general economic forecast for a specific time period. Next, the manager estimates market potential based on this economic forecast. Then the manager derives the company's sales potential from the general economic forecast and estimate of market potential. In the **buildup approach**, the marketing manager begins by estimating how much of a product a potential buyer in a specific geographic area, such as a sales territory, will purchase in a given period. The manager then multiplies that amount by the total number of potential buyers in that area. The manager performs the same calculation for each geographic area in which the firm sells products and then adds the totals for each area to calculate market potential. To determine company sales potential, the manager must estimate, based on planned levels of company marketing activities, the proportion of the total market potential the company can obtain.

◆ Competitive Assessment

Besides obtaining sales estimates, it is crucial to assess competitors already operating in the segments being considered. Without competitive information, sales estimates may be misleading. A market segment that seems attractive based on sales estimates may prove much less so following a competitive assessment. Such an assessment should ask several questions about competitors: How many exist? What are their strengths and weaknesses? Do several competitors have major market shares and together dominate the segment? Can our company create a marketing mix to compete effectively against competitors' marketing mixes? Is it likely that new competitors will enter this segment? If so, how will they affect our firm's ability to compete successfully? Answers to such questions are important for proper assessment of the competition in potential market segments.

The actions of a national food company that considered entering the dog food market illustrate the importance of competitive assessment. Through a segmentation study, the company determined that dog owners could be divided into three segments according to how they viewed their dogs and dog foods. One group saw their dogs as performing a definite utilitarian function, such as protecting family members, playing with children, guarding the property, or herding farm animals. These people wanted a low-priced, nutritious dog food and were not interested in a wide variety of flavors. The second group treated their dogs as companions and family members. These individuals were willing to pay relatively high prices for dog foods and wanted a variety of types and flavors so their dogs would not get bored. Dog owners in the third segment were found to actually hate their dogs. These people wanted the cheapest dog food they could buy and were not concerned with nutrition, flavor, or variety. The food company examined the extent to which competitive brands were serving all these dog owners and found that each segment contained at least three well-entrenched competing brands, which together dominated the segment. The company's management decided not to enter the dog food market because of the strength of the competing brands.

◆ Cost Estimates

To fulfill the needs of a target segment, an organization must develop and maintain a marketing mix that precisely meets the wants and needs of individuals and organizations in that segment. Developing and maintaining such a mix can be expensive. Distinctive product features, attractive package design, generous product warranties, extensive advertising, attractive promotional offers, competitive prices, and high-quality personal service consume considerable organizational resources. Indeed, to reach certain segments, the costs may be so high that a marketer concludes the segment is inaccessible. Another cost consideration is whether the organization can effectively reach a segment at costs equal to or below competitors' costs. If the firm's costs are likely to be higher, it will be unable to compete in that segment in the long run.

Step 5: Select Specific Target Markets

An important initial consideration in selecting a target market is whether customers' needs differ enough to warrant the use of market segmentation. If segmentation analysis shows customer needs to be fairly homogeneous, the firm's management may decide to use the undifferentiated approach, discussed earlier. However, if customer needs are heterogeneous, which is much more likely, one or more target markets must be selected. On the other hand, marketers may decide not to enter and compete in any of the segments.

Assuming one or more segments offer significant opportunities to achieve organizational objectives, marketers must decide in which segments to participate. Ordinarily information gathered in the previous step—about sales estimates, competitors, and cost estimates—requires careful consideration in this final step to determine long-term profit opportunities. Also, the firm's management must investigate whether the organization has the financial resources, managerial skills, employee expertise, and facilities to enter and compete effectively in selected segments. Furthermore, the requirements of some market segments may be at odds with the firm's overall objectives, and the possibility of legal problems, conflicts with interest groups, and technological advancements could make certain segments unattractive. In addition, when prospects for long-term growth are taken into account, some segments may appear very attractive and others less desirable.

Selecting appropriate target markets is important to an organization's adoption and use of the marketing concept philosophy. Identifying the right target market is the key to implementing a successful marketing strategy, whereas failure to do so can lead to low sales, high costs, and severe financial losses. A careful target market analysis places an organization in a better position to both serve customers' needs and achieve its objectives.

Developing Sales Forecasts

sales forecast The amount of a product a company expects to sell during a specific period at a specified level of marketing activities

A **sales forecast** is the amount of a product the company expects to sell during a specific period at a specified level of marketing activities. The sales forecast differs from the company sales potential. It concentrates on what actual sales will be at a certain level of company marketing effort, whereas the company sales potential assesses what sales are possible at various levels of marketing activities assuming certain environmental conditions will exist. Businesses use the sales forecast for planning, organizing, implementing, and controlling their activities. The success of numerous activities depends on this forecast's accuracy. Common problems in failing companies are improper planning and lack of realistic sales forecasts. Overly ambitious sales forecasts can lead to overbuying, overinvestment, and higher costs.

executive judgment A sales forecasting method based on the intuition of one or more executives

To forecast sales, a marketer can choose from a number of forecasting methods, some arbitrary and others more scientific, complex, and time consuming. A firm's choice of method or methods depends on the costs involved, type of product, market characteristics, time span of the forecast, purposes of the forecast, stability of the historical sales data, availability of required information, managerial preferences, and forecasters' expertise and experience.[15] Common forecasting techniques fall into five categories: executive judgment, surveys, time series analysis, regression analysis, and market tests.

◆ Executive Judgment

At times, a company forecasts sales chiefly on the basis of **executive judgment**, the intuition of one or more executives. This approach is unscientific but expedient and inexpensive. Executive judgment may work reasonably well when product demand is relatively stable and the forecaster has years of market-related experience. However, because intuition is swayed most heavily by recent experience, the forecast may be overly optimistic or overly pessimistic. Another drawback to intuition is that the forecaster has only past experience as a guide for deciding where to go in the future.

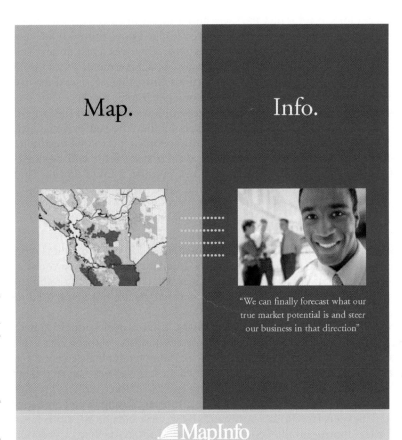

Map.   Info.

"We can finally forecast what our true market potential is and steer our business in that direction"

◢ MapInfo

MapInfo gives you innovative ways to determine true market potential and helps guide better and more profitable business decisions.

To learn more about innovative business intelligence solutions and receive a free Market Potential information kit, call MapInfo at 888-889-0136 or e-mail us at acrm@mapinfo.com

Developing Sales Forecasts
A number of products are available that assist organizations in developing sales forecasts.

◆ Surveys

customer forecasting survey
A survey of customers regarding the quantities of products they intend to buy during a specific period

Another way to forecast sales is to question customers, sales personnel, or experts regarding their expectations about future purchases. In a **customer forecasting survey**, marketers ask customers what types and quantities of products they intend to buy during a specific period. This approach may be useful to a business with relatively few customers. For example, Intel, which markets to a limited number of companies (primarily computer manufacturers), could conduct customer forecasting surveys effectively. PepsiCo, in contrast, has millions of customers and could not feasibly use a customer survey to forecast future sales.

Customer surveys have several drawbacks. Customers must be able and willing to make accurate estimates of future product requirements. Although some organizational buyers can estimate their anticipated purchases accurately from historical buying data and their own sales forecasts, many cannot make such estimates. In addition, customers may not want to take part in a survey. Occasionally a few respondents give answers they know are incorrect, making survey results inaccurate. Moreover, customer surveys reflect buying intentions rather than actual purchases. Customers' intentions may not be well formulated, and even when potential purchasers have definite buying intentions, they do not necessarily follow through on them. Finally, customer surveys consume much time and money.

sales force forecasting survey
A survey of a firm's sales force regarding anticipated sales in their territories for a specified period

In a **sales force forecasting survey**, the firm's salespeople estimate anticipated sales in their territories for a specified period. The forecaster combines these territorial estimates to arrive at a tentative forecast. A marketer may survey the sales staff for several reasons. The most important is that the sales staff is closer to customers on a daily basis than other company personnel and therefore should know more about customers' future product needs. Moreover, when sales representatives assist in developing the forecast, they are more likely to work toward its achievement. In addition, forecasts can be prepared for single territories, divisions consisting of several territories, regions made up of multiple divisions, and the total geographic market. Thus, the method provides sales forecasts from the smallest geographic sales unit to the largest.

A sales force survey also has limitations. Salespeople may be too optimistic or pessimistic due to recent experiences. In addition, salespeople tend to underestimate sales potential in their territories when they believe their sales goals will be determined by their forecasts. They also dislike paperwork because it takes up time that could be spent selling. If preparation of a territorial sales forecast is time consuming, the sales staff may not do the job adequately.

Nonetheless, sales force surveys can be effective under certain conditions. The salespeople as a group must be accurate, or at least consistent, estimators. If the aggregate forecast is consistently over or under actual sales, the individual who develops the final forecast can make the necessary adjustments. Assuming the survey is well administered, the sales force can have the satisfaction of helping to establish reasonable sales goals and the assurance that its forecasts are not being used to set sales quotas.

expert forecasting survey Sales forecasts prepared by experts outside the firm, such as economists, management consultants, advertising executives, or college professors

When a company wants an **expert forecasting survey**, it hires professionals to help prepare the sales forecast. These experts are usually economists, management consultants, advertising executives, college professors, or other individuals outside the firm with solid experience in a specific market. Drawing on this experience and their analyses of available information about the company and the market, experts prepare and present forecasts or answer questions regarding a forecast. Using experts is expedient and relatively inexpensive. However, because they work outside the firm, these forecasters may be less motivated than company personnel to do an effective job.

Delphi technique A procedure in which experts create initial forecasts, submit them to the company for averaging, and then refine the forecasts

A more complex form of the expert forecasting survey incorporates the Delphi technique. In the **Delphi technique**, experts create initial forecasts, submit them to the company for averaging, and have the results returned to them so they can make individual refined forecasts. The premise is that the experts will use the averaged results when making refined forecasts and these forecasts will be in a narrower range. The procedure may be repeated several times until the experts, each working separately, reach a consensus on the forecasts. The ultimate goal in using the Delphi technique is to develop a highly accurate sales forecast.

◆ Time Series Analysis

time series analysis A forecasting method that uses historical sales data to discover patterns in the firm's sales over time and generally involves trend, cycle, seasonal, and random factor analyses

With **time series analysis**, the forecaster uses the firm's historical sales data to discover a pattern or patterns in the firm's sales over time. If a pattern is found, it can be used to forecast sales. This forecasting method assumes that past sales patterns will continue in the future. The accuracy, and thus usefulness, of time series analysis hinges on the validity of this assumption.

trend analysis An analysis that focuses on aggregate sales data over a period of many years to determine general trends in annual sales

In a time series analysis, a forecaster usually performs four types of analysis: trend, cycle, seasonal, and random factor. **Trend analysis** focuses on aggregate sales data, such as the company's annual sales figures, covering a period of many years to determine whether annual sales are generally rising, falling, or staying about the same. Through **cycle analysis**, a forecaster analyzes sales figures (often monthly sales data) from a period of three to five years to ascertain whether sales fluctuate in a consistent, periodic manner. When performing a **seasonal analysis**, the analyst studies daily, weekly, or monthly sales figures to evaluate the degree to which seasonal factors, such as climate and holiday activities, influence sales. In a **random factor analysis**, the forecaster attempts to attribute erratic sales variations to random, nonrecurrent events, such as a regional power failure, a natural disaster, or political unrest in a foreign market. After performing each of these analyses, the forecaster combines the results to develop the sales forecast. Time series analysis is an effective forecasting method for products with reasonably stable demand, but not for products with highly erratic demand.

cycle analysis An analysis of sales figures for a period of three to five years to ascertain whether sales fluctuate in a consistent, periodic manner

seasonal analysis An analysis of daily, weekly, or monthly sales figures to evaluate the degree to which seasonal factors influence sales

random factor analysis An analysis attempting to attribute erratic sales variations to random, nonrecurrent events

◆ Regression Analysis

regression analysis A method of predicting sales based on finding a relationship between past sales and one or more independent variables, such as population or income

Like time series analysis, regression analysis requires the use of historical sales data. In **regression analysis**, the forecaster seeks to find a relationship between past sales (the dependent variable) and one or more independent variables, such as population, per capita income, or gross domestic product. Simple regression analysis uses one independent variable, whereas multiple regression analysis includes two or more independent variables. The objective of regression analysis is to develop a mathematical formula that accurately describes a relationship between the firm's sales and one or more variables; however, the formula indicates only an association, not a causal relationship. Once an accurate formula is established, the analyst plugs the necessary information into the formula to derive the sales forecast.

Regression analysis is useful when a precise association can be established. However, a forecaster seldom finds a perfect correlation. Furthermore, this method can be used only when available historical sales data are extensive. Thus, regression analysis is futile for forecasting sales of new products.

◆ Market Tests

market test Making a product available to buyers in one or more test areas and measuring purchases and consumer responses to marketing efforts

A **market test** involves making a product available to buyers in one or more test areas and measuring purchases and consumer responses to distribution, promotion, and price. Test areas are often cities with populations of 200,000 to 500,000, but can be larger metropolitan areas or towns with populations of 50,000 to 200,000. For example, ACNielsen Market Decisions, a marketing research firm, conducts market tests for client firms in Boise, Tucson, Colorado Springs, Peoria, Evansville, Charleston, and Portland, in addition to custom test markets in cities chosen by clients.[16] A market test provides information about consumers' actual rather than intended purchases. In addition, purchase volume can be evaluated in relation to the intensity of other marketing activities such as advertising, in-store promotions, pricing, packaging, and distribution. Forecasters base their sales estimate for larger geographic units on customer response in test areas.

Because it does not require historical sales data, a market test is effective for forecasting sales of new products or sales of existing products in new geographic areas. A market test also gives a marketer an opportunity to test various elements of the marketing mix. However, these tests are often time consuming and expensive.

In addition, a marketer cannot be certain that consumer response during a market test represents the total market response or that such a response will continue in the future.

◆ Using Multiple Forecasting Methods

Although some businesses depend on a single sales forecasting method, most firms use several techniques. Sometimes a company is forced to use multiple methods when marketing diverse product lines, but even a single product line may require several forecasts, especially when the product is sold to different market segments. Thus, a producer of automobile tires may rely on one technique to forecast tire sales for new cars and on another to forecast sales of replacement tires. Variation in the length of needed forecasts may call for several forecasting methods. A firm that employs one method for a short-range forecast may find it inappropriate for long-range forecasting. Sometimes a marketer verifies results of one method by using one or more other methods and comparing outcomes.

SUMMARY

A market is an aggregate of people who, as individuals or as organizations, have needs for products in a product class and have the ability, willingness, and authority to purchase such products.

In general, marketers employ a five-step process when selecting a target market. Step 1 is to identify the appropriate targeting strategy. When a company designs a single marketing mix and directs it at the entire market for a particular product, it is using an undifferentiated targeting strategy. The undifferentiated strategy is effective in a homogeneous market, whereas a heterogeneous market needs to be segmented through a concentrated targeting strategy or a differentiated targeting strategy. Both these strategies divide markets into segments consisting of individuals, groups, or organizations that have one or more similar characteristics and thus can be linked to similar product needs. When using a concentrated strategy, an organization directs marketing efforts toward a single market segment through one marketing mix. With a differentiated targeting strategy, an organization directs customized marketing efforts at two or more segments.

Certain conditions must exist for effective market segmentation. First, customers' needs for the product should be heterogeneous. Second, the segments of the market should be identifiable and divisible. Third, the total market should be divided so that segments can be compared with respect to estimated sales, costs, and profits. Fourth, at least one segment must have enough profit potential to justify developing and maintaining a special marketing mix for that segment. Fifth, the firm must be able to reach the chosen segment with a particular marketing mix.

Step 2 is determining which segmentation variables to use. Segmentation variables are the characteristics of individuals, groups, or organizations used to divide a total market into segments. The segmentation variable should relate to customers' needs for, uses of, or behavior toward the product. Segmentation variables for consumer markets can be grouped into four categories: demographic (e.g., age, gender, income, ethnicity, family life cycle), geographic (population, market density, climate), psychographic (personality traits, motives, lifestyles), and behavioristic (volume usage, end use, expected benefits, brand loyalty, price sensitivity). Variables for segmenting business markets include geographic location, type of organization, customer size, and product use.

Step 3 in the target market selection process is to develop market segment profiles. Such profiles describe the similarities among potential customers within a segment and explain the differences among people and organizations in different market segments. Step 4 is evaluating relevant market segments, which requires that several important factors—including sales estimates, competition, and estimated costs associated with each segment—be determined and analyzed. Step 5 involves the actual selection of specific target markets. In this final step, the company considers whether customers' needs differ enough to warrant segmentation and which segments to target.

A sales forecast is the amount of a product the company actually expects to sell during a specific period at a specified level of marketing activities. To forecast sales, marketers can choose from a number of methods. The choice depends on various factors, including the costs involved, type of product, market characteristics, and time span and purposes of the forecast. There are five categories of forecasting techniques: executive judgment, surveys, time series analysis, regression analysis, and market tests. Executive judgment is based on the intuition of one or more executives. Surveys include customer, sales force, and expert forecasting surveys. Time series analysis uses the firm's historical sales data to discover patterns in the firm's sales over time and employs four major types of analyses: trend, cycle, seasonal, and random factor. With regression analysis, forecasters attempt to find a relationship between past sales and one or more independent variables. Market testing involves making a product available to buyers in one or more test areas and measuring purchases and consumer responses to distribution, promotion, and price. Many companies employ multiple forecasting methods.

 Please visit the student website at **www.prideferrell.com** for ACE Self-Test questions that will help you prepare for exams.

IMPORTANT TERMS

Consumer market
Business market
Undifferentiated targeting strategy
Homogeneous market
Heterogeneous market
Market segmentation
Market segment
Concentrated targeting strategy
Differentiated targeting strategy
Segmentation variables
Market density
Geodemographic segmentation
Micromarketing
Benefit segmentation
Market potential
Company sales potential
Breakdown approach
Buildup approach
Sales forecast
Executive judgment
Customer forecasting survey
Sales force forecasting survey
Expert forecasting survey
Delphi technique
Time series analysis
Trend analysis
Cycle analysis
Seasonal analysis
Random factor analysis
Regression analysis
Market test

DISCUSSION & REVIEW QUESTIONS

1. What is a market? What are the requirements for a market?
2. In your local area, identify a group of people with unsatisfied product needs who represent a market. Could this market be reached by a business organization? Why or why not?
3. Outline the five major steps in the target market selection process.
4. What is an undifferentiated strategy? Under what conditions is it most useful? Describe a present market situation in which a company is using an undifferentiated strategy. Is the business successful? Why or why not?
5. What is market segmentation? Describe the basic conditions required for effective segmentation. Identify several firms that use market segmentation.
6. List the differences between concentrated and differentiated strategies, and describe the advantages and disadvantages of each.

7. Identify and describe four major categories of variables that can be used to segment consumer markets. Give examples of product markets that are segmented by variables in each category.
8. What dimensions are used to segment business markets?
9. Define *geodemographic segmentation*. Identify several types of firms that might employ this type of market segmentation, and explain why.
10. What is a market segment profile? Why is it an important step in the target market selection process?
11. Describe the important factors that marketers should analyze to evaluate market segments.
12. Why is a marketer concerned about sales potential when trying to select a target market?
13. Why is selecting appropriate target markets important for an organization that wants to adopt the marketing concept philosophy?
14. What is a sales forecast? Why is it important?
15. What are the two primary types of surveys a company might use to forecast sales? Why would a company use an outside expert forecasting survey?
16. Under what conditions are market tests useful for sales forecasting? What are the advantages and disadvantages of market tests?
17. Under what conditions might a firm use multiple forecasting methods?

APPLICATION QUESTIONS

1. MTV Latino targets the growing Hispanic market in the United States. Identify another product marketed to a distinct target market. Describe the target market, and explain how the marketing mix appeals specifically to that group.
2. Generally marketers use one of three basic targeting strategies to focus on a target market: (1) undifferentiated, (2) concentrated, or (3) differentiated. Locate an article that describes the targeting strategy of a particular organization. Describe the target market, and explain the strategy being used to reach that market.

3. The stereo market may be segmented according to income and age. Discuss two ways the market for each of the following products might be segmented.
   a. Candy bars
   b. Travel agency services
   c. Bicycles
   d. Hair spray
4. If you were using a time series analysis to forecast sales for your company for the next year, how would you use the following sets of sales figures?

a.

1995	$145,000	2000	$149,000
1996	$144,000	2001	$148,000
1997	$147,000	2002	$180,000
1998	$145,000	2003	$191,000
1999	$148,000	2004	$227,000

b.

	2002	2003	2004
Jan.	$12,000	$14,000	$16,000
Feb.	$13,000	$14,000	$15,500
Mar.	$12,000	$14,000	$17,000
Apr.	$13,000	$15,000	$17,000
May	$15,000	$17,000	$20,000
June	$18,000	$18,000	$21,000
July	$18,500	$18,000	$21,500
Aug.	$18,500	$19,000	$22,000
Sep.	$17,000	$18,000	$21,000
Oct.	$16,000	$15,000	$19,000
Nov.	$13,000	$14,000	$19,000
Dec.	$14,000	$15,000	$18,000

c. 2002 sales increased 21.2 percent (opened an additional store in 2002)
   2004 sales increased 18.8 percent (opened another store in 2004)

Internet Exercise & Resources

Visit **www.prideferrell.com** for resources to help you master the material in this chapter, plus materials that will help you expand your marketing knowledge, including Internet exercise updates, ACE self-tests, hotlinks to companies featured in this chapter, and much more.

iExplore

iExplore is an Internet company that offers a variety of travel and adventure products. Learn more about its goods, services, and travel advice through its website at **www.iexplore.com.**

1. Based on the information provided at the website, what are some of iExplore's basic products?
2. What market segments does iExplore appear to be targeting with its website? What segmentation variables is the company using to segment these markets?
3. How does iExplore appeal to comparison shoppers?

Video Case 8.1

BuyandHold.com Is Bullish on Smaller Investors

Whether the financial markets go up or down, BuyandHold.com's strategy of targeting smaller, more cost-conscious investors is paying dividends. BuyandHold.com launched its online brokerage site in 1999 with the goal of offering consumers affordable access to stocks and mutual funds. "Wall Street put up a lot of different barriers for people," the CEO notes. "BuyandHold.com came along and took all those barriers down."

Now a division of Freedom Investments in New Jersey, BuyandHold.com offers pricing that seems low even when compared with the commissions charged by deep-discount, web-only brokers. Customers pay as little as $6.99 per month, including two trades. Moreover, they can buy securities according to the amount they have to invest, even if this means buying a fraction of a share. In contrast, traditional brokerages prefer trades made in 100-share blocks or at least full-share lots.

Pricing isn't the only difference between Buyand-Hold.com and other brokerage firms. The company also focuses on an unusual target market. Merrill Lynch and other full-service firms generally target investors with larger portfolios who want considerable investment advice and personal assistance; DirecTrade and competing online brokers target day traders and other active investors who frequently buy and sell. In contrast, BuyandHold.com aims for lower-income consumers who can afford to build a portfolio only little by little and who see investing as a way to meet a long-term need such as financing a child's college education or saving for retirement. "Most of our customers embrace the BuyandHold philosophy of investing," explains the CEO. "They invest regularly, adding to their portfolios weekly, monthly, or quarterly, regardless of market conditions."

The only way BuyandHold.com can offer rock-bottom pricing to serve its target segment is to keep costs as low as possible. One way it does this is by bundling all the orders it receives and going into the market to buy and sell just three times a day. Although this process minimizes trading costs, it also limits the customer's ability to take advantage of changing market conditions and place trades at specific prices. Another way BuyandHold.com keeps costs down is by limiting its selection of stocks and mutual funds. In contrast, mainstream brokers generally allow investors to choose from a much wider selection of securities. Finally, BuyandHold.com opens accounts online and uses cost-efficient e-mail for most customer communications.

However, low cost doesn't mean no service. BuyandHold.com maintains an online library for customers who want to learn more about investing and to investigate particular securities. It also promotes an automated plan that enables customers to electronically transfer funds and make small investments on a set schedule throughout the year. In addition, the company has won several "Best of the Web" awards from business and financial services publications.

By targeting just one consumer segment, BuyandHold.com's managers have the opportunity to learn a great deal about their market. For example, they found that many cost-conscious investors looked to save money by buying shares directly from public companies rather than through brokers. In response, the firm established the Virtual Direct Stock Purchase Plan. Under this plan, participating companies post an online link to a special BuyandHold.com webpage where consumers can set up accounts and buy stock. The companies save money because they don't have to prepare and mail customer statements, and consumers can stick with their investment choices or trade in additional securities at a low price through BuyandHold.com.

Through careful targeting and ongoing innovation, BuyandHold.com attracted 200,000 accounts in its first 15 months of operation. However, the firm now faces increased competitive pressures. ShareBuilder.com, which also targets buy-and-hold investors, offers buying commissions as low as $4 per trade and a wider selection of securities. Customers who trade infrequently can choose to pay by the trade, while more active investors can choose a flat monthly fee that includes a set number of trades. Like BuyandHold.com, ShareBuilder.com courts investors who want to buy investments on a regular basis and maintain their holdings for the long term.

What does the future hold for BuyandHold.com? The brokerage industry is changing. Some of the smaller firms have been merged into or acquired by larger brokerage firms. In recent years, BuyandHold.com's parent company has bought a number of other brokerage firms. Meanwhile, rivals continue introducing or enhancing their own versions of affordable investment services. In the coming years, BuyandHold.com will have to use all its marketing savvy to continue attracting cost-conscious consumers who want to invest for the long term.[17]

QUESTIONS FOR DISCUSSION

1. What type of general targeting strategy does BuyandHold.com use? Explain.
2. What segmentation variables does BuyandHold.com use?
3. As more competitors start marketing to the cost-conscious segment, would you recommend that BuyandHold.com change its targeting strategy? Why or why not?

Case 8.2

IKEA Targets Do-It-Yourselfers

For more than 60 years, the Swedish firm IKEA has marketed simple but stylish home furnishings for cost-conscious customers who don't mind assembling their purchases to save money. Traditional furniture stores display beautiful home furnishings for high-end customers with deep pockets and little inclination to attach legs to a table or bolt together a bed frame. In contrast, IKEA's strategy is "to offer a wide range of home furnishings with good design and function at prices so low that as many people as possible will be able to afford them." Its products serve a wide range of functions—from frying pans and lamps to entire kitchens and living rooms—and come in different styles that can be coordinated easily.

To keep prices low for its thrifty customers, IKEA looks for ways to cut costs in manufacturing, marketing, warehousing, raw materials, and sales so it can pass the savings along to customers. For example, it buys raw materials in bulk and searches the world for efficient suppliers to keep per-unit costs low. It uses a special software package to collect price quotes from suppliers and streamline the purchasing process. For a company that buys from 1,700 suppliers, including some that are thousands of miles from company headquarters, even small efficiencies quickly add up to significant savings.

In addition to welcoming shoppers in its stores, the company invites customers to shop online or order from its catalogs, which saves on warehouse and retail expenses. More cost savings come from shipping furniture unassembled in flat boxes and having customers pick up their purchases for assembly at home. Low cost is not the only consideration, however. IKEA also requires its suppliers to abide by a code of conduct that forbids child labor, sets minimum standards for working conditions, and protects the environment.

Although IKEA's customers are frugal, they want to buy fashionable furniture that fits their personalities and lifestyles. In fact, the store's appeal cuts across demographic lines. Some customers who can well afford to shop at the poshest emporiums come to IKEA because they like the combination of chic design, down-to-earth functionality, and speedy assembly. Not every item must be assembled, but those that do are accompanied by simple, step-by-step instructions, which reassures even the most inexperienced do-it-yourselfer.

If customers get hungry as they walk through one of IKEA's cavernous stores, they can drop into the informal store restaurant for a quick snack or a light meal of delicacies from IKEA's home country. The most popular dish is Swedish meatballs: customers devour 155 tons of these tiny meatballs every year.

Customers in many countries have responded enthusiastically to IKEA's formula of fashionable, affordable, and functional furniture. After expanding beyond Sweden to Norway and Denmark, the company opened stores in Europe, Australia, Canada and, in 1985, the United States. More recently, IKEA has opened stores in Russia, Japan, and China, with additional U.S. outlets on the way.

Product names such as Leksvik bookcases and Klippan sofas are standard throughout the world and reflect IKEA's Swedish origins. However, the company translates its catalogs into 36 languages and distributes 130 million copies every year. Here again, IKEA looks for ways to minimize expenses. It has all products photographed at one of Europe's largest studios and transmits the images electronically to printing facilities in the different regions where the catalogs will be distributed, saving on shipping and mailing costs. Every detail, from paper quality to type size, is scrutinized to identify new cost efficiencies.

IKEA's targeting strategy has proven very successful. Every year, 286 million people go shopping in IKEA stores. The combined annual sales of home furnishings (and restaurant meals) in all of its 187 stores is nearly $11 billion. North America is one of IKEA's most important markets because it accounts for $2 billion in annual sales. No matter how large and fast IKEA grows, its focus will remain on keeping costs low to continue satisfying its target market's need for reasonably priced, well-designed assemble-it-yourself home furnishings.[18]

QUESTIONS FOR DISCUSSION

1. Is IKEA's targeting strategy concentrated or undifferentiated? Explain your answer.
2. Which of the variables for segmenting consumer markets is IKEA using, and why are these variables appropriate?
3. What combination of techniques might IKEA apply when preparing sales forecasts for North America?

Consumer Buying Behavior

9

OBJECTIVES

1. To understand consumers' level of involvement with a product and describe the types of consumer problem-solving processes

2. To recognize the stages of the consumer buying decision process

3. To explore how situational influences may affect the consumer buying decision process

4. To understand the psychological influences that may affect the consumer buying decision process

5. To examine the social influences that may affect the consumer buying decision process

Marketing "Cool"— Right Now

Cool today, gone tomorrow. The quest for cool drives much of the buying done by teenagers and young adults. However, marketers that target these segments have to act quickly, because products based on the newest trend or the latest pop culture development can go out of style suddenly and without warning. "Cycles of newness and novelty are paramount to capturing the interest and loyalty of the teen market," observes a Maybelline cosmetics executive. For this reason, many companies hire trend consultants or specialized researchers to help them spot the new, new thing before it becomes the old, old thing.

Often what teenagers think is cool is heavily influenced by media. "Each season, teens get more fashionable," says Erin Conroy of Brown Shoe, a fashion shoe company. "They are tuned in to MTV and Hollywood, and follow celebrities and other trend-setters rather than setting the trends." Yet media coverage contributes to the speedy death of trends as well as to their birth. One expert notes that her job of identifying the next trend in cool is more difficult "because the minute we spot a trend, we've got about four seconds to tell our clients." Almost immediately after a celebrity wears a new style, the word spreads through the Internet, television, magazines, and newspapers. Teens jump into trends right away—and jump out again just as quickly. Long-time trend analyst Irma Zandl stresses the importance of timing: being the first to introduce a product in the hope of making it trendy is just as risky as being the last to market.

Moreover, teen tastes are key influences on what preteens and young adults will buy. As other groups start to buy what teens in the vanguard are buying, trendy products move into the mainstream and become much less appealing to the superhip. This is when style-oriented companies put once-cool items on sale and gear up for the next trend. Firms that cater to trendy teens cannot afford the luxury of waiting months for items to be produced and shipped from the Far East or other distant sources, because the window of opportunity closes much sooner these days. When teens want a cool product, they want it *now*—next week is simply too late. Price is a secondary consideration.

From cars to colas, jeans to jerseys, music to mobile phones, soft drinks to snacks, cool makes a difference in many product categories. Teens may be loyal to a cool brand in one category but readily sample cool new brands in another. The bottom line for marketers is that the quest for cool never ends. Now more than ever, companies need to know their customers and look carefully for clues to the next cool thing.[1]

Successful marketers go to great lengths to understand their customers' needs and gain a better grasp of customers' buying behavior. A firm's ability to establish and maintain satisfying customer relationships requires an understanding of buying behavior. **Buying behavior** is the decision processes and acts of people involved in buying and using products. **Consumer buying behavior** refers to the buying behavior of ultimate consumers, those who purchase products for personal or household use and not for business purposes. Marketers attempt to understand buying behavior for several reasons. First, buyers' reactions to a firm's marketing strategy have a great impact on the firm's success. Second, as we saw in Chapter 1, the marketing concept stresses that a firm should create a marketing mix that satisfies customers. To find out what satisfies buyers, marketers must examine the main influences on what, where, when, and how consumers buy. Third, by gaining a deeper understanding of the factors that affect buying behavior, marketers are in a better position to predict how consumers will respond to marketing strategies.

We begin this chapter by examining how the customer's level of involvement with a product affects the type of problem solving employed and discussing the types of consumer problem-solving processes. Then we analyze the major stages of the consumer buying decision process, beginning with problem recognition, information search, and evaluation of alternatives and proceeding through purchase and postpurchase evaluation. Next, we examine situational influences—surroundings, time, purchase reason, and buyer's mood and condition—that affect purchasing decisions. We go on to consider psychological influences on purchasing decisions: perception, motives, learning, attitudes, personality and self-concept, and lifestyles. We conclude with a discussion of social influences that affect buying behavior, including roles, family, reference groups and opinion leaders, social classes, and culture and subcultures.

buying behavior The decision processes and acts of people involved in buying and using products

consumer buying behavior Buying behavior of people who purchase products for personal or household use and not for business purposes

Level of Involvement and Consumer Problem-Solving Processes

level of involvement An individual's intensity of interest in a product and the importance of the product for that person

Consumers generally try to acquire and maintain an assortment of products that satisfy their current and future needs. To do so, consumers engage in problem solving. When purchasing such products as food, clothing, shelter, medical care, education, recreation, and transportation, people engage in different types of problem-solving processes. The amount of effort, both mental and physical, that buyers expend in solving problems varies considerably. A major determinant of the type of problem-solving process employed depends on the customer's **level of involvement**, the degree of interest in a product and the importance the individual places on that product. High-involvement products tend to be those that are visible to others (such as clothing, furniture, or automobiles) and are expensive. Expensive bicycles, for example, are usually high-involvement products. High-importance issues, such as health care, are associated with high levels of involvement. Low-involvement products tend to be those that are less expensive and have less associated social risk, such as many grocery items. A person's interest in a product category that is ongoing and long term is referred to as *enduring involvement*. In contrast, *situational involvement* is temporary and dynamic, and results from a particular set of circumstances. Involvement level, as well as other factors, affects a person's selection of one of three types of consumer problem solving: routinized response behavior, limited problem solving, or extended problem solving.

routinized response behavior A consumer problem-solving process used when buying frequently purchased, low-cost items that require very little search-and-decision effort

A consumer uses **routinized response behavior** when buying frequently purchased, low-cost items needing very little search-and-decision effort. When buying such items, a consumer may prefer a particular brand but is familiar with several brands in the product class and views more than one as acceptable. Typically, low-involvement products are bought through routinized response behavior, that is, almost

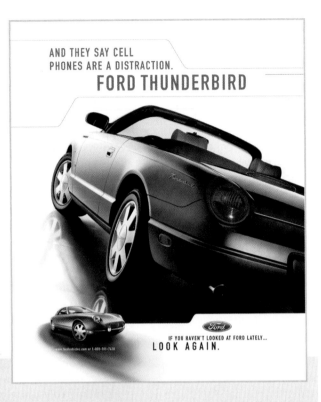

Levels of Involvement
Buying decisions about numerous grocery products, such as olives, are associated with low levels of involvement. Buying decisions regarding automobiles, such as the Ford Thunderbird, are associated with high levels of involvement.

automatically. For example, most buyers spend little time or effort selecting soft drinks or cereals.

Buyers engage in **limited problem solving** when buying products occasionally or when they need to obtain information about an unfamiliar brand in a familiar product category. This type of problem solving requires a moderate amount of time for information gathering and deliberation. For example, if Procter & Gamble introduces an improved Tide laundry detergent, buyers will seek additional information about the new product, perhaps by asking a friend who has used it or watching a commercial about it, before making a trial purchase.

The most complex type of problem solving, **extended problem solving**, occurs when purchasing unfamiliar, expensive, or infrequently bought products—for instance, a car, home, or college education. The buyer uses many criteria to evaluate alternative brands or choices and spends much time seeking information and deciding on the purchase. Extended problem solving is frequently used for purchasing high-involvement products.

Purchase of a particular product does not always elicit the same type of problem-solving process. In some instances, we engage in extended problem solving the first time we buy a certain product but find that limited problem solving suffices when we buy it again. If a routinely purchased, formerly satisfying brand no longer satisfies us, we may use limited or extended problem solving to switch to a new brand. Thus, if we notice that the brand of pain reliever we normally buy is not working, we may seek out a different brand through limited problem solving. Most consumers occasionally make purchases solely on impulse and not on the basis of any of these three problem-solving processes. **Impulse buying** involves no conscious planning but results from a powerful urge to buy something immediately.

limited problem solving
A consumer problem-solving process used when purchasing products occasionally or needing information about an unfamiliar brand in a familiar product category

extended problem solving A consumer problem-solving process employed when purchasing unfamiliar, expensive, or infrequently bought products

impulse buying An unplanned buying behavior resulting from a powerful urge to buy something immediately

Consumer Buying Decision Process

The **consumer buying decision process**, shown in Figure 9.1, includes five stages: problem recognition, information search, evaluation of alternatives, purchase, and postpurchase evaluation. Before we examine each stage, consider these important points. First, the actual act of purchasing is only one stage in the process, and usually not the first stage. Second, even though we indicate that a purchase occurs, not all decision processes lead to a purchase; individuals may end the process at any stage. Finally, not all consumer decisions include all five stages. People engaged in extended problem solving usually go through all stages of this decision process, whereas those engaged in limited problem solving and routinized response behavior may omit some stages.

◆ Problem Recognition

Problem recognition occurs when a buyer becomes aware of a difference between a desired state and an actual condition. Consider a student who owns a nonprogrammable calculator and learns she needs a programmable one for her math course. She recognizes that a difference exists between the desired state—having a programmable calculator—and her actual condition. She therefore decides to buy a new calculator.

The speed of consumer problem recognition can be quite rapid or rather slow. Sometimes a person has a problem or need but is unaware of it. Marketers use sales personnel, advertising, and packaging to help trigger recognition of such needs or problems. For example, a university bookstore may advertise programmable calculators in the school newspaper at the beginning of the term. Students who see the advertisement may recognize that they need these calculators for their course work.

Figure 9.1 Consumer Buying Decision Process and Possible Influences on the Process

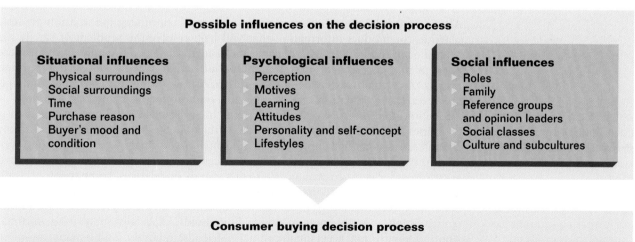

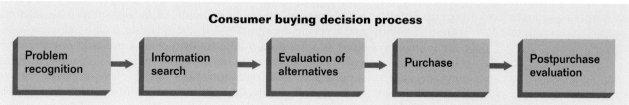

Problem Recognition
Culligan Water uses this advertisement to stimulate problem recognition, the first stage in the consumer buying decision process.

◆ **Information Search**

After recognizing the problem or need, a buyer (if continuing the decision process) searches for product information that will help resolve the problem or satisfy the need. For example, after recognizing her need for a programmable calculator, the above-mentioned student may search for information about different types and brands of calculators. She acquires information over time from her surroundings. However, the information's impact depends on how she interprets it.

An information search has two aspects. In an **internal search**, buyers search their memories for information about products that might solve their problem. If they cannot retrieve enough information from memory to make a decision, they seek additional information from outside sources in an **external search**. The external search may focus on communication with friends or relatives, comparison of available brands and prices, marketer-dominated sources, and/or public sources. For example, a recent survey reports that the Internet is the most preferred information source among car shoppers in online households, especially for pricing information.[2] An individual's personal contacts—friends, relatives, and associates—often are influential sources of information because the person trusts and respects them. Utilizing marketer-dominated sources of information, such as salespeople, advertising, package labeling, and in-store demonstrations and displays, typically requires little effort on the consumer's part. Buyers also obtain information from public sources—for instance, government reports, news presentations, publications such as *Consumer Reports*, and reports from product-testing organizations. Consumers

internal search An information search in which buyers search their memories for information about products that might solve their problem

external search An information search in which buyers seek information from sources other than memory

Chapter 9 Consumer Buying Behavior   237

frequently view information from public sources as highly credible because of its factual and unbiased nature.

Repetition, a technique well known to advertisers, increases consumers' learning of information. When seeing or hearing an advertising message for the first time, recipients may not grasp all its important details, but they learn more details as the message is repeated. Nevertheless, even when commercials are initially effective, repetition eventually may cause wearout, meaning consumers pay less attention to the commercial and respond to it less favorably than they did at first.

Information can be presented verbally, numerically, or visually. Marketers pay great attention to the visual components of their advertising materials.

◆ Evaluation of Alternatives

A successful information search within a product category yields a group of brands that a buyer views as possible alternatives. This group of brands is sometimes called a **consideration set** (also called an *evoked set*). For example, a consideration set of calculators might include those made by Texas Instruments, Hewlett-Packard, Sharp, and Casio.

To assess the products in a consideration set, the buyer uses **evaluative criteria**, objective (such as an EPA mileage rating) and subjective (such as style) characteristics that are important to the buyer. For example, one calculator buyer may want a rechargeable unit with a large display and large buttons, whereas another may have no size preferences but dislikes rechargeable calculators. The buyer also assigns a certain level of importance to each criterion: some features and characteristics carry more weight than others. Using the criteria, the buyer rates and eventually ranks brands in the consideration set. The evaluation stage may yield no brand the buyer is willing to purchase. In that case, a further information search may be necessary.

Marketers may influence consumers' evaluations by *framing* the alternatives, that is, describing the alternatives and their attributes in a certain manner. Framing can make a characteristic seem more important to a consumer and facilitate its recall from memory. For example, by stressing a car's superior comfort and safety features over those of a competitor's, a carmaker can direct consumers' attention toward these points of superiority. Framing probably influences the decision processes of inexperienced buyers more than those of experienced ones. If the evaluation of alternatives yields one or more brands the consumer is willing to buy, he or she is ready to move on to the next stage of the decision process: the purchase.

consideration set A group of brands within a product category that a buyer views as alternatives for possible purchase

evaluative criteria Objective and subjective characteristics that are important to a buyer

Copyright © Houghton Mifflin Company. All rights reserved.

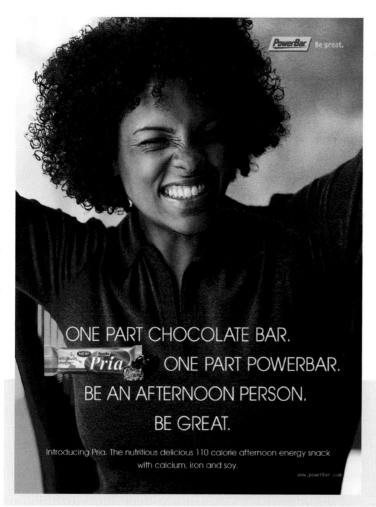

ONE PART CHOCOLATE BAR.
Pria ONE PART POWERBAR.
BE AN AFTERNOON PERSON.
BE GREAT.

Introducing Pria. The nutritious delicious 110 calorie afternoon energy snack with calcium, iron and soy.

www.powerbar.com

PowerBar Be great.

Framing Product Attributes
PowerBar helps to frame product attributes of its Pria bar by advertising features such as "nutritious," "delicious," "110 calories," and an "energy snack with calcium, iron, and soy."

◆ Purchase

In the purchase stage, the consumer chooses the product or brand to be bought. Selection is based on the outcome of the evaluation stage and on other dimensions. Product availability may influence which brand is purchased. For example, if the brand ranked highest in evaluation is unavailable, the buyer may purchase the brand ranked second. If a consumer wants a pair of black Nikes and cannot find them in his size, he may buy a pair of black Reeboks.

During this stage, buyers also pick the seller from which they will buy the product. The choice of seller may affect final product selection and therefore the terms of sale, which, if negotiable, are determined at this stage. Other issues, such as price, delivery, warranties, maintenance agreements, installation, and credit arrangements, are also settled. Finally, the actual purchase takes place during this stage, unless the consumer decides to terminate the buying decision process.

◆ Postpurchase Evaluation

After the purchase, the buyer begins evaluating the product to ascertain if its actual performance meets expected levels. Many criteria used in evaluating alternatives are applied again during postpurchase evaluation. The outcome of this stage is either satisfaction or dissatisfaction, which influences whether the consumer complains, communicates with other possible buyers, and repurchases the brand or product.

cognitive dissonance A buyer's doubts shortly after a purchase about whether the decision was the right one

Shortly after purchase of an expensive product, evaluation may result in **cognitive dissonance**, doubts in the buyer's mind about whether purchasing the product was the right decision. For example, after buying a pair of $169 inline skates, the consumer may feel guilty about the purchase or wonder whether she purchased the right brand and quality. Cognitive dissonance is most likely to arise when a person has recently bought an expensive, high-involvement product that lacks some of the desirable features of competing brands. A buyer experiencing cognitive dissonance may attempt to return the product or seek positive information about it to justify choosing it. Marketers sometimes attempt to reduce cognitive dissonance by having salespeople telephone recent purchasers to make sure they are satisfied with their new purchases. At times, recent buyers are sent results of studies showing that other consumers are very satisfied with the brand.

As Figure 9.1 shows, three major categories of influences are believed to affect the consumer buying decision process: situational, psychological, and social. In the remainder of this chapter, we focus on these influences. Although we discuss each major influence separately, their effects on the consumer decision process are interrelated.

Marketers employ a number of marketing research techniques, some of which were discussed in Chapter 7, to better understand their customers' buying decision processes and factors that influence those buying decision processes. Both conventional, and at times, unconventional marketing research methods are used. The Building Customer Relationships boxed feature describes ethnography and examines a less conventional approach.

Situational Influences on the Buying Decision Process

situational influences Influences resulting from circumstances, time, and location that affect the consumer buying decision process

Situational influences result from circumstances, time, and location that affect the consumer buying decision process. For example, buying an automobile tire after noticing while washing your car that the tire is badly worn is a different experience from buying a tire right after a blowout on the highway derails your vacation. Situational factors can influence the buyer during any stage of the consumer buying decision process and may cause the individual to shorten, lengthen, or terminate the process.

Situational factors can be classified into five categories: physical surroundings, social surroundings, time perspective, reason for purchase, and the buyer's momen-

Snapshot

When do Americans shop?

Percentage of Americans shopping on weekdays and weekends:

Time	Weekdays	Weekends
8 am–10 am	1.6%	2.9%
10 am–noon	5.2%	7.7%
Noon–2 pm	6.2%	11.2%
2 pm–4 pm	6.1%	11.6%
4 pm–6 pm	4.7%	7.3%
6 pm–8 pm	4.1%	4.6%
8 pm–10 pm	2.3%	1.9%

Source: Data from Simmons Market Research.

tary mood and condition.[3] Physical surroundings include location, store atmosphere, aromas, sounds, lighting, weather, and other factors in the physical environment in which the decision process occurs. Marketers at some banks, department stores, and specialty stores go to considerable effort and expense to create physical settings conducive to making purchase decisions. Numerous restaurant chains, such as Olive Garden and Chili's, invest heavily in facilities, often building from the ground up, to provide special surroundings that enhance customers' dining experiences.

In some settings, dimensions, such as weather, traffic sounds, and odors, are clearly beyond marketers' control; instead marketers must try to make customers more comfortable. General climatic conditions, for example, may influence a customer's decision to buy a specific type of vehicle (such as an SUV) and certain accessories (such as four-wheel drive). Current weather conditions, depending on whether they are favorable or unfavorable, may either encourage or discourage consumers to go shopping to seek out specific products.

Social surroundings include characteristics and interactions of others who are present when during a purchase decision, such as friends, relatives, salespeople, and other customers. Buyers may feel pressured to behave in a certain way because they are in a public place such as a restaurant, store, or sports arena. Thoughts about who will be around when the product is used or consumed is also a dimension of the social

BUILDING CUSTOMER RELATIONSHIPS

Observing Customers in Their Native Habitats

How do consumers really make their buying decisions? More marketers are finding out through the use of *ethnography,* observing and interviewing consumers in action in stores or at home. Although surveys and other techniques are valuable marketing research tools, consumers are not always able to express their needs, nor do they always make buying decisions exactly the way they describe to researchers. Through ethnography, marketers such as Frontier Airlines and Microsoft are examining actual consumer behavior in everyday settings, then using what they learn to create an appropriate marketing mix for each targeted segment.

For example, researchers for Frontier Airlines went to Denver International Airport and observed passengers' behavior. They were surprised to see that the carrier's jets were drawing enthusiastic crowds because of the cats, foxes, and rabbits painted on the tailfins. Capitalizing on this appeal, Frontier changed its advertising and created a lighthearted campaign with the animals as the centerpiece of the ads.

Microsoft's researchers used ethnography to study how families use the company's MSN online service. They discovered that many parents avoided the tracking features labeled as "parental controls" because they did not want to "police" their children's use of the Internet. Microsoft used this insight to group such tools under the label of "safety and security," which more clearly explains the parental benefits of monitoring children's web browsing.

A growing number of marketers are using ethnography to catch customers in the act of shopping. One Minneapolis advertising agency operates a small store called Once Famous. The store carries an eclectic merchandise mix because at any one time the agency may be testing reactions to baby clothes, candles, furniture, and more. To avoid invading shoppers' privacy, the store has a prominent sign notifying consumers that they will be videotaped if they enter. Inside, trained interviewers ask selected shoppers about their motivations and decisions regarding the products, yielding information that helps marketers do an even better job of satisfying customers.

setting. An overcrowded store or an argument between a customer and a salesperson may cause consumers to stop shopping or even leave the store.

The time dimension, too, influences the buying decision process in several ways, such as the amount of time required to become knowledgeable about a product, to search for it, and to buy and use it. For instance, more parents are visiting websites such as Fandango's to buy advance tickets for movies they want to see with their children, despite an added service charge. "If you are going to pile three kids and mom and dad into the minivan to go to the theater, you want to make sure you have tickets for the show," says a Fandango executive.[4] Time plays a major role in that the buyer considers the possible frequency of product use, the length of time required to use the product, and the length of the overall product life. Other time dimensions that influence purchases include time of day, day of the week or month, seasons, and holidays. The amount of time pressure a consumer is under affects how much time is devoted to purchase decisions. A customer under severe time constraints is likely either to make a quick purchase decision or to delay a decision.

The purchase reason raises the questions of what exactly the product purchase should accomplish and for whom. Generally, consumers purchase an item for their own use, for household use, or as a gift. For example, people who are buying a gift may buy a different product from one they would buy for themselves. If you own a Cross pen, for example, it is unlikely that you bought it for yourself.

The buyer's momentary moods (such as anger, anxiety, contentment) or momentary conditions (fatigue, illness, being flush with cash) may have a bearing on the consumer buying decision process. These moods or conditions immediately precede the current situation and are not chronic. Any of these moods or conditions can affect a person's ability and desire to search for information, receive information, or seek and evaluate alternatives. They can also significantly influence a consumer's postpurchase evaluation.

Psychological Influences on the Buying Decision Process

psychological influences
Factors that in part determine people's general behavior, thus influencing their behavior as consumers

Psychological influences partly determine people's general behavior and thus influence their behavior as consumers. Primary psychological influences on consumer behavior are perception, motives, learning, attitudes, personality and self-concept, and lifestyles. Even though these psychological factors operate internally, they are very much affected by social forces outside the individual.

◆ Perception

perception The process of selecting, organizing, and interpreting information inputs to produce meaning

information inputs Sensations received through the sense organs

selective exposure The process of selecting inputs to be exposed to the person's awareness while ignoring others

Different people perceive the same thing at the same time in different ways. When you first look at the illustration below, do you see the fish changing into birds or the birds changing into fish? Similarly, an individual may perceive the same item in a number of ways at different times. **Perception** is the process of selecting, organizing, and interpreting information inputs to produce meaning. **Information inputs** are sensations received through sight, taste, hearing, smell, and touch. When we hear an advertisement, see a friend, smell polluted air or water, or touch a product, we receive information inputs.

As the definition indicates, perception is a three-step process. Although we receive numerous pieces of information at once, only a few reach our awareness. We select some inputs and ignore others because we cannot be conscious of all inputs at one time. This phenomenon is sometimes called **selective exposure** because an individual selects which inputs will reach awareness. If you are concentrating on this paragraph, you probably are not aware that cars outside are making noise, that the room light is on, or that you are touching this page. Even though you receive these inputs, they do not reach your awareness until they are pointed out.

Fish or Birds?
Do you see fish changing into birds or birds changing into fish?

selective distortion An individual's changing or twisting of information that is inconsistent with personal feelings or beliefs

selective retention Remembering information inputs that support personal feelings and beliefs and forgetting inputs that do not

An individual's current set of needs affects selective exposure. Information inputs that relate to one's strongest needs at a given time are more likely to be selected to reach awareness. It is not by random chance that many fast-food commercials are aired near mealtimes. Customers are more likely to tune in to these advertisements at these times.

The selective nature of perception may result not only in selective exposure but also in two other conditions: selective distortion and selective retention. **Selective distortion** is changing or twisting currently received information; it occurs when a person receives information inconsistent with personal feelings or beliefs. For example, on seeing an advertisement promoting a disliked brand, a viewer may distort the information to make it more consistent with prior views. This distortion substantially lessens the effect of the advertisement on the individual. In **selective retention**, a person remembers information inputs that support personal feelings and beliefs and forgets inputs that do not. After hearing a sales presentation and leaving a store, for example, a customer may forget many selling points if they contradict personal beliefs.

The second step in the process of perception is perceptual organization. Information inputs that reach awareness are not received in an organized form. To produce meaning, an individual must mentally organize and integrate new information with what is already stored in memory. People use several methods to organize. One method, called *closure*, occurs when a person mentally fills in missing elements in a pattern or statement. In an attempt to draw attention to its brand, an advertiser will capitalize on closure by using incomplete images, sounds, or statements in its advertisements.

Interpretation, the third step in the perceptual process, is the assignment of meaning to what has been organized. A person bases interpretation on what he or she expects or what is familiar. For this reason, a manufacturer that changes a product or its package faces a major problem: when people are looking for the old, familiar product or package, they may not recognize the new one. For instance, when Smucker's redesigned its packaging, marketers told designers that although they wanted a more contemporary package design, they also wanted a classic look so that customers would perceive the products to be the familiar ones they had been buying for years. Unless a product or package change is accompanied by a promotional program that makes people aware of the change, an organization may suffer a sales decline.

Although marketers cannot control buyers' perceptions, they often try to influence them through information. Several problems may arise from such attempts, however. First, a consumer's perceptual process may operate such that a seller's information never reaches that person. For example, a buyer may block out a salesperson's presentation. Second, a buyer may receive a seller's information but perceive it differently than was intended. For example, when a toothpaste producer advertises that "35 percent of the people who use this toothpaste have fewer cavities," a customer might infer that 65 percent of users have more cavities. Third, a buyer who perceives information inputs to be inconsistent with prior beliefs is likely to forget the information quickly.

◆ Motives

motive An internal energizing force that directs a person's behavior toward satisfying needs or achieving goals

A **motive** is an internal energizing force that orients a person's activities toward satisfying needs or achieving goals. Buyers' actions are affected by a set of motives rather than by just one motive. At a single point in time, some of a person's motives are stronger than others. For example, a person's motives for having a cup of coffee are much stronger right after waking up than just before going to bed. Motives also affect the direction and intensity of behavior. Some motives may help an individual achieve his or her goals, whereas others create barriers to goal achievement.

Abraham Maslow, an American psychologist, conceived a theory of motivation based on a hierarchy of needs. According to Maslow, humans seek to satisfy five levels of needs, from most important to least important, as shown in Figure 9.2. This sequence is known as **Maslow's hierarchy of needs**. Once needs at one level are met, humans seek to fulfill needs at the next level up in the hierarchy.

Maslow's hierarchy of needs The five levels of needs that humans seek to satisfy, from most to least important

At the most basic level are *physiological needs*, requirements for survival such as food, water, sex, clothing, and shelter, which people try to satisfy first. Food and beverage marketers often appeal to physiological needs. Marketers of whitening toothpastes, such as Ultrabrite, sometimes promote their brands based on sex appeal.

At the next level are *safety needs*, which include security and freedom from physical and emotional pain and suffering. Life insurance, automobile air bags, carbon monoxide detectors, vitamins, and decay-fighting toothpastes are products that consumers purchase to meet safety needs.

Next are *social needs*, the human requirements for love and affection and a sense of belonging. Advertisements frequently appeal to social needs. Ads for cosmetics and other beauty products, jewelry, and even cars often suggest that purchasing these products will bring love. Certain types of trendy clothing, such as Gap cargoes, Nike athletic shoes, or T-shirts imprinted with logos or slogans, appeal to the customer's need to belong.

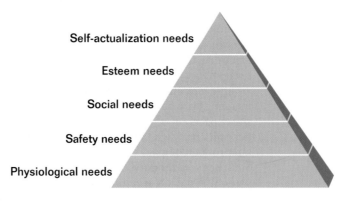

Figure 9.2 Maslow's Hierarchy of Needs   Maslow believed that people seek to fulfill five categories of needs.

At the level of *esteem needs,* people require respect and recognition from others as well as self-esteem, a sense of one's own worth. Owning a Lexus automobile, having a beauty makeover, or flying first class can satisfy esteem needs. Slim-Fast Foods uses motivational research to design more effective marketing programs. After learning that dieters who regularly received encouraging e-mail messages lost weight more quickly than those who did not, the company designed a Buddy Program to match dieters according to age, food preferences, and other characteristics. More than 14,000 dieters signed up, an indication of the motivational power of recognition and respect from others. "Our club members wanted someone they could share stories with—about their successes, their hurdles, how they prepare menus," says a Slim-Fast spokesperson.[5]

At the top of the hierarchy are *self-actualization needs.* These refer to people's need to grow and develop and to become all they are capable of becoming. Some products that satisfy these needs include fitness center memberships, education, self-improvement workshops, and skiing lessons. In its recruiting advertisements, the U.S. Army told potential enlistees to "be all that you can be in the Army." These messages imply that people can reach their full potential by enlisting in the U.S. Army.

Motives that influence where a person purchases products on a regular basis are called **patronage motives.** A buyer may shop at a specific store because of such patronage motives as price, service, location, product variety, or friendliness of salespeople. To capitalize on patronage motives, marketers try to determine why regular customers patronize a particular store and to emphasize these characteristics in the store's marketing mix.

patronage motives Motives that influence where a person purchases products on a regular basis

◆ Learning

learning Changes in an individual's thought processes and behavior caused by information and experience

Learning refers to changes in a person's thought processes and behavior caused by information and experience. Consequences of behavior strongly influence the learning process. Behaviors that result in satisfying consequences tend to be repeated. For example, a consumer who buys a Snickers candy bar and enjoys the taste is more likely to buy a Snickers again. In fact, the individual will probably continue to purchase that brand until it no longer provides satisfaction. When effects of the behavior are no longer satisfying, the person may switch brands or stop eating candy bars altogether.

When making purchasing decisions, buyers process information. Individuals' abilities in this regard differ. The type of information inexperienced buyers use may differ from the type used by experienced shoppers familiar with the product and purchase situation. Thus, two potential purchasers of an antique desk may use different types of information in making their purchase decisions. The inexperienced buyer may judge the desk's value by price, whereas the more experienced buyer may seek information about the manufacturer, period, and place of origin to judge the desk's quality and value. Consumers lacking experience may seek information from others when making a purchase and even take along an informed "purchase pal." More experienced buyers have greater self-confidence and more knowledge about the product and can recognize which product features are reliable cues to product quality. For example, Safeway decided to launch its Safeway.com online grocery shopping service in Portland, Oregon, and Vancouver, Washington, because consumers in those two cities were already familiar with the operation and offerings of web-based grocery stores. As a result, these consumers had the experience and knowledge, and thus were more likely to understand and use Safeway.com.[6]

Marketers help customers learn about their products by helping them gain experience with them. Free samples, sometimes coupled with coupons, can successfully encourage trial and reduce purchase risk. For example, because some consumers may be wary of exotic menu items, restaurants sometimes offer free samples. In-store demonstrations foster knowledge of product uses. A software producer may use point-of-sale product demonstrations to introduce a new product. Test drives give potential new-car purchasers some experience with the automobile's features.

Consumers also learn by experiencing products indirectly through information from salespeople, advertisements, friends, and relatives. Through sales personnel and advertisements, marketers offer information before (and sometimes after) purchases to influence what consumers learn and to create more favorable attitudes toward the product. However, their efforts are seldom fully successful. Marketers encounter problems in attracting and holding consumers' attention, providing consumers with important information for making purchase decisions, and convincing them to try the product.

◆ Attitudes

attitude An individual's enduring evaluation of feelings about and behavioral tendencies toward an object or idea

An **attitude** is an individual's enduring evaluation of feelings about and behavioral tendencies toward an object or idea. The objects toward which we have attitudes may be tangible or intangible, living or nonliving. For example, we have attitudes toward sex, religion, politics, and music, just as we do toward cars, football, and breakfast cereals. Although attitudes can change, they tend to generally remain stable and do not vary from moment to moment. However, all of a person's attitudes do not have equal impact at any one time; some are stronger than others. Individuals acquire attitudes through experience and interaction with other people.

An attitude consists of three major components: cognitive, affective, and behavioral. The cognitive component is the person's knowledge and information about the object or idea. The affective component comprises the individual's feelings and emotions toward the object or idea. The behavioral component manifests itself in the person's actions regarding the object or idea. Changes in one of these components may or may not alter the other components. Thus, a consumer may become more knowledgeable about a specific brand without changing the affective or behavioral components of his or her attitude toward that brand.

Consumer attitudes toward a company and its products greatly influence success or failure of the firm's marketing strategy. When consumers have strong negative attitudes toward one or more aspects of a firm's marketing practices, they may not only stop using its products but also urge relatives and friends to do likewise.

Because attitudes play such an important part in determining consumer behavior, marketers should measure consumer attitudes toward prices, package designs, brand names, advertisements, salespeople, repair services, store locations, features of existing or proposed products, and social responsibility efforts. Several methods help marketers gauge these attitudes. One of the simplest ways is to question people directly. Press Ganey Associates, in South Bend, Indiana, researches patient opinions about their hospitalization, one of the factors being hospital food. Marion General Hospital in Marion, Indiana, found satisfaction with its food service ranked in the 40th percentile. To help increase its score, the hospital consulted with a Fort Wayne hospital whose food service ranked in the 90th percentile. Instituting several

Attempting to Change Attitudes
A number of organizations attempt to convince smokers to quit smoking and to inform them about the effects of secondhand smoke.

attitude scale A means of measuring consumer attitudes by gauging the intensity of individuals' reactions to adjectives, phrases, or sentences about an object

ideas from the consultation, Marion General's score rose to the 70th percentile and eventually reached a rating in the 90s.[7] Marketers also evaluate attitudes through attitude scales. An **attitude scale** usually consists of a series of adjectives, phrases, or sentences about an object. Respondents indicate the intensity of their feelings toward the object by reacting to the adjectives, phrases, or sentences in a certain way. For example, a marketer measuring people's attitudes toward shopping might ask respondents to indicate the extent to which they agree or disagree with a number of statements, such as "Shopping is more fun than watching television." By using an attitude scale, a marketing research company was able to identify and classify six major types of clothing purchasers. The scale was based on such attributes as demographics, media use, and purchase behavior.

When marketers determine that a significant number of consumers have negative attitudes toward an aspect of a marketing mix, they may try to change those attitudes to make them more favorable. This task is generally lengthy, expensive, and difficult, and may require extensive promotional efforts. For example, the California Prune Growers, an organization of prune producers, has tried to use advertising to change consumers' attitudes toward prunes by presenting them as a nutritious snack high in potassium and fiber. To alter consumers' responses so that more of them buy a given brand, a firm might launch an information-focused campaign to change the cognitive component of a consumer's attitude or a persuasive (emotional) campaign to influence the affective component. Distributing free samples might help change the behavioral component. Both business and nonbusiness organizations try to change people's attitudes about many things, from health and safety to prices and product features.

◆ Personality and Self-Concept

personality A set of internal traits and distinct behavioral tendencies that result in consistent patterns of behavior

Personality is a set of internal traits and distinct behavioral tendencies that result in consistent patterns of behavior in certain situations. An individual's personality arises from hereditary characteristics and personal experiences that make the person unique. Personalities typically are described as having one or more characteristics, such as compulsiveness, ambition, gregariousness, dogmatism, authoritarianism, introversion, extroversion, and competitiveness. Marketing researchers look for relationships between such characteristics and buying behavior. Even though a few links between several personality traits and buyer behavior have been determined, results of many studies have been inconclusive. The weak association between personality and buying behavior may be the result of unreliable measures rather than a lack of a relationship. A number of marketers are convinced that consumers' personalities do influence types and brands of products purchased. For example, the type of clothing, jewelry, or automobile a person buys may reflect one or more personality characteristics.

At times marketers aim advertising at certain types of personalities. For example, ads for certain cigarette brands are directed toward specific personality types. Marketers focus on positively valued personality characteristics, such as security consciousness, sociability, independence, or competitiveness, rather than on negatively valued ones, such as insensitivity or timidity.

self-concept A perception or view of oneself

A person's self-concept is closely linked to personality. **Self-concept** (sometimes called *self-image*) is a perception or view of oneself. Individuals develop and alter their self-concepts based on an interaction between psychological and social dimensions. Research shows that buyers purchase products that reflect and enhance their self-concepts and that purchase decisions are important to the development and maintenance of a stable self-concept. Consumers' self-concepts may influence whether they buy a product in a specific product category and may affect brand selection as well as where they buy. For example, home improvement retailer Lowe's is targeting women—who make 90 percent of household decisions about home decor and home improvement—using self-concept as the basis of its advertising message. "Only Lowe's has everything and everyone to help your house tell the story about who you really are," says the company's advertising tag line.[8]

Lifestyles
A variety of purchasing decisions are partially influenced by lifestyles.

◆ Lifestyles

lifestyle An individual's pattern of living expressed through activities, interests, and opinions

A **lifestyle** is an individual's pattern of living expressed through activities, interests, and opinions. Lifestyle patterns include the ways people spend time, the extent of their interaction with others, and their general outlook on life and living. People partially determine their own lifestyles, but the pattern is also affected by personality and by demographic factors such as age, education, income, and social class. Lifestyles are measured through a lengthy series of questions.

Lifestyles have a strong impact on many aspects of the consumer buying decision process, from problem recognition to postpurchase evaluation. Lifestyles influence consumers' product needs, brand preferences, types of media used, and how and where they shop.

Social Influences on the Buying Decision Process

social influences The forces other people exert on one's buying behavior

Forces that other people exert on buying behavior are called **social influences**. As Figure 9.1 shows, they are grouped into five major areas: roles, family, reference groups and opinion leaders, social classes, and culture and subcultures.

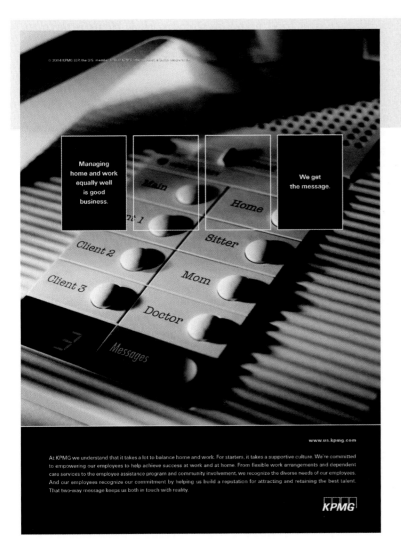

Role Influences
Some organizations, such as KPMG, recognize the existence of multiple role influences and express sensitivity toward them.

◆ Roles

All of us occupy positions within groups, organizations, and institutions. Associated with each position is a **role**, a set of actions and activities a person in a particular position is supposed to perform based on expectations of both the individual and surrounding persons. Because people occupy numerous positions, they have many roles. For example, a man may perform the roles of son, husband, father, employee or employer, church member, civic organization member, and student in an evening college class. Thus, multiple sets of expectations are placed on each person's behavior.

An individual's roles influence both general behavior and buying behavior. The demands of a person's many roles may be diverse and even inconsistent. Consider the various types of clothes that you buy and wear depending on whether you are going to class, to work, to a party, or to an aerobics class. You and others involved in these settings have expectations about what is acceptable clothing for these events. Thus, the expectations of those around us affect our purchases of clothing and many other products.

role Actions and activities that a person in a particular position is supposed to perform based on expectations of the individual and surrounding persons

◆ Family Influences

Family influences have a very direct impact on the consumer buying decision process. Parents teach children how to cope with a variety of problems, including those dealing with purchase decisions. **Consumer socialization** is the process through which a person acquires the knowledge and skills to function as a consumer. Often children gain this knowledge and set of skills by observing parents and older siblings in purchase situations, as well as through their own purchase experiences. Children observe brand preferences and buying practices in their families and, as adults, retain some of these brand preferences and buying practices as they establish and raise their own families. Buying decisions made by a family are a combination of group and individual decision making.

consumer socialization The process through which a person acquires the knowledge and skills to function as a consumer

Although female roles continue to change, women still make buying decisions related to many household items, including health care products, laundry supplies, paper products, and foods. Spouses participate jointly in the purchase of a variety of products, especially durable goods. Due to changes in men's roles, a significant proportion of men are major grocery shoppers. Children make many purchase decisions and influence numerous household purchase decisions. Knowing that children wield considerable influence over food brand preferences, H. J. Heinz is targeting them with EZ Squirt green ketchup in a squeeze bottle. Kids like squeezing squiggly green patterns on their hamburgers, and parents like the ketchup's extra vitamin C. Demand has been so strong that the company achieved its initial year's sales projections in the first 90 days after launching the product.[9] Also, many advertising messages are targeted at teens. For example, Britney Spears speaks for Pepsi, Brandy for CoverGirl, Jennifer Love Hewitt for Neutrogena, and Jessica Biel for L'Oreal.[10]

The extent to which either one or both of the two adult family members take part in family decision making varies among families and product categories. Traditionally family decision-making processes have been grouped into four categories: autonomic, husband-dominant, wife-dominant, and syncratic. In autonomic decision making, each adult household member makes an equal number of decisions. In husband-dominant or wife-dominant decision making, the husband or the wife makes most of the family decisions. Syncratic decision making means both partners jointly make most decisions concerning purchases. The type of family decision making employed depends on the values and attitudes of family members.

When two or more family members participate in a purchase, their roles may dictate that each is responsible for performing certain purchase-related tasks, such as initiating the idea, gathering information, determining if the product is affordable, deciding whether to buy the product, or selecting the specific brand. The specific purchase tasks performed depend on the types of products being considered, the kind of family purchase decision process typically employed, and the amount of influence children have in the decision process. Thus, different family members may play different roles in the family buying process. To develop a marketing mix that precisely meets the needs of target market members, marketers must know not only who does the actual buying but also which other family members perform purchase-related tasks.

The family life cycle stage affects individual and joint needs of family members. (Family life cycle stages are discussed in Chapter 8.) For example, consider how the car needs of recently married "twenty-somethings" differ from those of the same couple when they are "forty-somethings" with a 13-year-old daughter and a 17-year-old son. Family life cycle changes can affect which family members are involved in purchase decisions and the types of products purchased.

◆ Reference Groups and Opinion Leaders

reference group Any group that positively or negatively affects a person's values, attitudes, or behavior

A **reference group** is any group that positively or negatively affects a person's values, attitudes, or behavior. Reference groups can be large or small. Most people have several reference groups, such as families, work-related groups, fraternities or sororities, civic clubs, professional organizations, or church-related groups.

In general, there are three major types of reference groups: membership, aspirational, and disassociative. A membership reference group is one to which an individual actually belongs; the individual identifies with group members strongly enough to take on the values, attitudes, and behaviors of people in that group. An aspirational reference group is a group to which a person aspires to belong; the individual desires to be like those group members. A group that a person does not wish to be associated with is a disassociative reference group; the individual does not want to take on the values, attitudes, and behavior of group members.

A reference group may serve as an individual's point of comparison and source of information. A customer's behavior may change to be more in line with actions and beliefs of group members. For example, a person may stop buying one brand of shirts and switch to another based on reference group members' advice. An individual may also seek information from the reference group about other factors regarding a prospective purchase, such as where to buy a certain product.

The extent to which a reference group affects a purchase decision depends on the product's conspicuousness and on the individual's susceptibility to reference group influence. Generally, the more conspicuous a product, the more likely that the purchase decision will be influenced by reference groups. A product's conspicuousness is determined by whether others can see it and whether it can attract attention. Reference groups can affect whether a person does or does not buy a product at all, buys a type of product within a product category, or buys a specific brand.

A marketer sometimes tries to use reference group influence in advertisements by suggesting that people in a specific group buy a product and are highly satisfied with it. In this type of appeal, the advertiser hopes that many people will accept the suggested group as a reference group and buy (or react more favorably to) the product. Whether this kind of advertising succeeds depends on three factors: how effectively the advertisement communicates the message, the type of product, and the individual's susceptibility to reference group influence.

In most reference groups, one or more members stand out as opinion leaders. An **opinion leader** provides information about a specific sphere of interest to reference group participants who seek information. Opinion leaders are viewed by other group members as being well informed about a particular area and as easily accessible. An opinion leader is not the foremost authority on all issues. However, because such individuals know they are opinion leaders, they feel a responsibility to remain informed about their sphere of interest and thus seek out advertisements, manufacturers' brochures, salespeople, and other sources of information.

An opinion leader is likely to be most influential when consumers have high product involvement but low product knowledge, when they share the opinion leader's values and attitudes, and when the product details are numerous or complicated.

opinion leader A reference group member who provides information about a specific sphere of interest to reference group participants

◆ Social Classes

In all societies, people rank others into higher or lower positions of respect. This ranking results in social classes. A **social class** is an open group of individuals with similar social rank. For example, a class is referred to as *open* because people can move into and out of it. Criteria for grouping people into classes vary from one society to another. In the United States, we take into account many factors, including occupation, education, income, wealth, race, ethnic group, and possessions. A person who is ranking someone does not necessarily apply all of a society's criteria. Sometimes, too, the role of income in social class determination tends to be overemphasized. Although income does help determine social class, the other factors also play a role. Within social classes, both incomes and spending habits differ significantly among members.

social class An open group of individuals with similar social rank

Analyses of social class in the United States commonly divide people into three to seven categories. Social scientist Richard P. Coleman suggests that for purposes of consumer analysis the population be divided into the four major status groups shown in Table 9.1 (on p. 250). However, he cautions marketers that considerable diversity exists in people's life situations within each status group.

To some degree, individuals within social classes develop and assume common behavioral patterns. They may have similar attitudes, values, language patterns, and possessions. Social class influences many aspects of people's lives. For example, it affects their chances of having children and their children's chances of surviving infancy. It influences their childhood training, choice of religion, selection of occupation, and leisure time activities. Because social class has a bearing on so many aspects of a person's life, it also affects buying decisions.

Social class influences people's spending, saving, and credit practices. It determines to some extent the type, quality, and quantity of products a person buys and uses. For example, it affects purchases of clothing, foods, financial and health care services, travel, recreation, entertainment, and home furnishings. Social class also affects an individual's shopping patterns and types of stores patronized. In some instances, marketers attempt to focus on certain social classes through store location and interior design, product design and features, pricing strategies, personal sales efforts, and advertising.

Table 9.1	Social Class Behavioral Traits and Purchasing Characteristics	
Class (% of Population)	**Behavioral Traits**	**Buying Characteristics**
Upper (14%); includes upper-upper, lower-upper, upper-middle	Income varies among the groups, but goals are the same Various lifestyles: preppy, conventional, intellectual, etc. Neighborhood and prestigious schooling important	Prize quality merchandise Favor prestigious brands Products purchased must reflect good taste Invest in art Spend money on travel, theater, books, tennis, golf, and swimming clubs
Middle (32%)	Often in management Considered white collar Prize good schools in a nice, well-maintained neighborhood Often emulate the upper class Enjoy travel and physical activity Often very involved in children's school and sports activities	Like fashionable items Consult experts via books, articles, etc., before purchasing Spend for experiences they consider worthwhile for their children (e.g., ski trips, college education) Tour packages, weekend trips Attractive home furnishings
Working (38%)	Emphasis on family, and especially for economic and emotional supports (e.g., job opportunity tips, help in times of trouble) Blue collar Earn good incomes Enjoy mechanical items and recreational activities Enjoy leisure time after working hard	Buy vehicles and equipment related to recreation, camping, and selected sports Strong sense of value Shop for best bargains at off-price and discount stores Purchase automotive equipment for making repairs Enjoy local travel, recreational parks
Lower (16%)	Often unemployed due to situations beyond their control (e.g., layoffs, company takeovers) Can include individuals on welfare and homeless individuals Often have strong religious beliefs May be forced to live in less desirable neighborhoods In spite of their problems, often good-hearted toward others Enjoy everyday activities when possible	Most products purchased are for survival Ability to convert good discards into usable items

Source: Adapted with permission from Richard P. Coleman, "The Continuing Significance of Social Class to Marketing," *Journal of Consumer Research,* Dec. 1983, pp. 265–280, with data from J. Paul Peter and Jerry C. Olson, *Consumer Behavior: Marketing Strategy Perspective* (Homewood, IL: Irwin, 1987), p. 433.

◆ Culture and Subcultures

culture The values, knowledge, beliefs, customs, objects, and concepts of a society

Culture is the accumulation of values, knowledge, beliefs, customs, objects, and concepts that a society uses to cope with its environment and passes on to future generations. Examples of objects are foods, furniture, buildings, clothing, and tools. Concepts include education, welfare, and laws. Culture also includes core values and the degree of acceptability of a wide range of behaviors in a specific society. For example, in our culture customers as well as businesspeople are expected to behave ethically.

Culture influences buying behavior because it permeates our daily lives. Our culture determines what we wear and eat and where we reside and travel. Society's interest in the healthfulness of food affects food companies' approaches to developing and promoting their products. Culture also influences how we buy and use products and our satisfaction from them. In the U.S. culture, makers of furniture, cars, and clothing strive to understand how people's color preferences are changing.

Because culture determines product purchases and uses to some degree, cultural changes affect product development, promotion, distribution, and pricing. Food marketers, for example, have made a multitude of changes in their marketing efforts. Thirty years ago, most U.S. families ate at least two meals a day together, and the mother spent four to six hours a day preparing those meals. Today more than 75 percent of women between ages 25 and 54 work outside the home, and average family incomes have risen considerably. These shifts, along with scarcity of time, have resulted in dramatic changes in the national per capita consumption of certain food products, such as take-out foods, frozen dinners, and shelf-stable foods.

When U.S. marketers sell products in other countries, they realize the tremendous impact those cultures have on product purchases and use. Global marketers find that people in other regions of the world have different attitudes, values, and needs, which call for different methods of doing business as well as different types of marketing mixes. Some international marketers fail because they do not or cannot adjust to cultural differences.

A culture consists of various subcultures. **Subcultures** are groups of individuals whose characteristic values and behavior patterns are similar and differ from those of the surrounding culture. Subcultural boundaries are usually based on geographic designations and demographic characteristics, such as age, religion, race, and ethnicity. Our culture is marked by a number of different subcultures, among them West Coast, teenage, Asian American, and college students. Within subcultures, greater similarities exist in people's attitudes, values, and actions than within the broader culture. Relative to other subcultures, individuals in one subculture may have stronger preferences for specific types of clothing, furniture, or foods. It is important to understand that a person can be a member of more than one subculture and that the behavioral patterns and values attributed to specific subcultures do not necessarily apply to all group members.

The percentage of the American population comprising ethnic and racial subcultures is expected to grow. By 2050, about one-half of the U.S. population will be members of racial and ethnic minorities. The U.S. Census Bureau reports that the three largest and fastest-growing ethnic U.S. subcultures are African Americans, Hispanics, and Asians. The population growth of these subcultures interests marketers. As illustrated in Building Customer Relationships (on p. 252), marketers are striving to become increasingly sensitive to and knowledgeable about group differences to target these subcultures more precisely. Businesses recognize that to succeed, their marketing strategies will have to take into account the

subculture A group of individuals whose characteristic values and behavior patterns are similar and differ from those of the surrounding culture

Subcultures Based on Age
Marketers sometimes aim marketing mixes at age-based subcultures.

values, needs, interests, shopping patterns, and buying habits of various subcultures. Consider how several companies are marketing their products to specific subcultures as explained in the Building Customer Relationships boxed feature.

African American Subculture. In the United States the African American subculture represents 12 percent of the population.[11] Like all subcultures, African American consumers possess distinct buying patterns. For example, African American consumers spend more money on telephone service, electricity, shoes, children's apparel, groceries, and housing than do white consumers.[12] Conversely, African Americans tend to spend much less on health insurance, health care, entertainment, education, alcoholic beverages, and eating out.[13]

Recently, Procter and Gamble Company began an initiative to increase marketing aimed at the African American community.[14] By including African American actors in their ads, the company believes it can encourage a positive response to its products, increasing sales among African American consumers, while still main-

---

BUILDING CUSTOMER RELATIONSHIPS

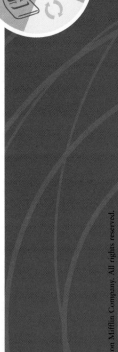

One Nation, Many Subcultures

America is one nation with many subcultures—and many opportunities for marketers that celebrate the differences as well as the similarities. PepsiCo's director of multicultural marketing emphasizes that "the multicultural mind-set is more about your interests, like music, than whether you're African American or Latino." PepsiCo uses music as a way to appeal to what it calls "the multicultural heart." Pepsi commercials featuring Shakira and Beyoncé Knowles cross cultural boundaries and link the brand with two of the music world's hottest stars.

The company has developed specific products for particular subcultures, such as Gatorade Xtremo geared to Hispanic tastes. However, it often promotes Pepsi soft drinks and Doritos snacks in one campaign, adjusting the tone and the product mix for different subcultures. As an example, its advertisements for Hispanic audiences create a fiestalike atmosphere, whereas its ads for African American audiences highlight barbecue-flavored snacks.

Fast-food marketer McDonald's is known for its promotional efforts targeting individual subcultures, including the subculture shared by urban youth. "Today's younger generation is far more aware of diversity," notes one of

McDonald's ad agency executives. Therefore, he says, companies should "offer a multicultural connection in order to be relevant, with people from different ethnic backgrounds having fun and playing together." In one commercial created for the Big Mac sandwich, a diverse group of actors sang hip-hop music in English and Spanish. This multicultural approach worked: Big Mac sales rose more than 30 percent during the six weeks this commercial appeared on ABC, CBS, NBC, network television, Univision, Telemundo, and Black Entertainment Television.

Shell Oil is also moving toward subculturally targeted advertising. "You just need to look in the newspapers and magazines to see the growing trends and how ethnically diverse the environment is getting," says the manager of national advertising and brands for Shell Oil in the United States. "You can't treat your customers as one homogeneous group because they're very diverse." After studying how Hispanic and African American customers make buying decisions about gasoline, Shell came up with magazine advertising and radio commercials for these two important groups. Later campaigns will promote products such as coffee and groceries, which many Shell dealers offer in their convenience stores.

taining ties with white consumers.[15] For example, if an African American family is featured in an ad, the white consumers will see a heartwarming bond between family members. The African American viewers will note the inclusion of their race, and feel a stronger connection to the product.[16]

Other corporations are reaching out to the African American community by celebrating Black History Month. Chrysler Group, partnering with DaimlerChrysler African American Network, organized an assortment of festivities to commemorate Black History Month. Exhibits, concerts, and guest speakers helped increase awareness about the African American community and their vital contributions to present-day society.[17] Hawaiian Punch also supports Black History Month with a national contest inviting schoolchildren to learn about historical African American figures.[18] In 2002, McDonalds launched 365Black™, a program that celebrates Black History all year round. The following year, they introduced 365Black™ Awards. At these annual awards, modern-day African Americans are honored for their outstanding achievements.

NET SIGHTS

Consumerworld.org offers a variety of free information to those interested in consumer buying behavior. Articles and other resources make this an interesting and helpful site for marketers. Visit www.consumerworld.org.

Hispanic Subculture. Hispanics represent 13 percent of the United States population.[19] Because of the group's growth and purchasing power, understanding the Hispanic subculture is critical to marketers. In general, Hispanics have strong family values, concern for product quality, and strong brand loyalty.[20] Studies reveal that the majority of Hispanic consumers not only are brand loyal but also will pay more for a well-known brand.[21] Like African American consumers, Hispanics spend more on groceries, telephone services, and children's apparel and shoes. But they also spend more on small appliances and houseware.[22]

White consumers, especially between the ages of 12 and 34, continue to be influenced by minority cultures, especially in areas such as fashion, entertainment, dining, sports, and music.[23] Thanks to this increasing appeal, advertisers have made a beneficial discovery. They can target both white and Hispanic consumers by hiring famous Hispanic people to appear in their ad campaigns.[24] Pepsi put Latina pop star Shakira in their ads. Bell South telephone company hired actress Daisy Fuentes to appear in a commercial discussing the importance of friends and family.[25] The ad was aired both in English and Spanish. This is crucial, as 61 percent of bilingual households are Spanish speaking.[26]

When considering the buying behavior of Hispanics, marketers must keep in mind that this subculture is really composed of nearly two dozen nationalities, including Cuban, Mexican, Puerto Rican, Caribbean, Spanish, and Dominican. Each has its own history and unique culture that affect consumer preferences and buying behavior.

To attract this powerful subculture, marketers are taking Hispanic values and preferences into account when developing products and creating advertising and promotions. Kmart focuses major marketing efforts on Hispanics; and it expects Hispanics to emerge as its number one core shoppers by 2020.[27] The company launched a monthly Spanish magazine and a Sunday advertising circular. Kmart has roughly one-third of its stores in urban markets.[28]

Asian American Subculture. The term *Asian American* includes people from more than 15 ethnic groups, including Filipinos, Chinese, Japanese, Asian Indians, Koreans, and Vietnamese. Asian Americans are the fastest-growing American subculture. They also have the most money, the best education, and the largest percentage of professionals and managers of all U.S. minorities.[29] The individual language, religion, and value system of each group influences its members' purchasing decisions. Some traits of this subculture, however, carry across ethnic divisions, including an emphasis on hard work, strong family ties, and a high value placed on education.[30]

Retailers with a large population of Chinese shoppers have begun to capitalize on this group's celebration of the Lunar New Year. For example, during this period in the Los Angeles area, supermarkets stock traditional Chinese holiday foods and items used in the celebration, such as candles, greeting cards, and party goods. The McDonalds website features a link about the Chinese New Year, and traditional ways of celebrating the important holiday. The website also features an extensive assortment of facts about different Asian cultures, and the holidays they celebrate. Catering to the tastes of Asians living in America, Maria's Bakery (based in Hong Kong), Ten Ren (based in Taiwan), and Woo Lae Oak (based in South Korea) have opened restaurants in Washington, DC, and other areas. With a few menu changes, they are also successfully introducing their foods to other U.S. customers.[31]

SUMMARY

Buying behavior consists of the decision processes and acts of people involved in buying and using products. Consumer buying behavior is the buying behavior of ultimate consumers.

An individual's level of involvement—the importance and intensity of interest in a product in a particular situation—affects the type of problem-solving process used. Enduring involvement is an ongoing interest in a product class because of personal relevance, whereas situational involvement is a temporary interest stemming from the particular circumstance or environment in which buyers find themselves. There are three kinds of consumer problem solving: routinized response behavior, limited problem solving, and extended problem solving. Consumers rely on routinized response behavior when buying frequently purchased, low-cost items requiring little search-and-decision effort. Limited problem solving is used for products purchased occasionally or when buyers need to acquire information about an unfamiliar brand in a familiar product category. Consumers engage in extended problem solving when purchasing an unfamiliar, expensive, or infrequently bought product. Purchase of a certain product does not always elicit the same type of decision making. Impulse buying is not a consciously planned buying behavior but involves a powerful urge to buy something immediately.

The consumer buying decision process includes five stages: problem recognition, information search, evaluation of alternatives, purchase, and postpurchase evaluation. Not all decision processes culminate in a purchase, nor do all consumer decisions include all five stages. Problem recognition occurs when buyers become aware of a difference between a desired state and an actual condition. After recognizing the problem or need, buyers search for information about products to help resolve the problem or satisfy the need. In the internal search, buyers search their memories for information about products that might solve the problem. If they cannot retrieve from memory enough information for a decision, they seek additional information through an external search. A successful search yields a group of brands, called a consideration set, that a buyer views as possible alternatives. To evaluate the products in the consideration set, the buyer establishes certain criteria by which to compare, rate, and rank different products. Marketers can influence consumers' evaluations by framing alternatives.

In the purchase stage, consumers select products or brands on the basis of results from the evaluation stage and on other dimensions. Buyers also choose the seller from whom they will buy the product. After the purchase, buyers evaluate the product to determine if its actual performance meets expected levels. Shortly after the purchase of an expensive product, for example, the postpurchase evaluation may result in cognitive dissonance, dissatisfaction brought on by the consumer's doubts as to whether he or she should have bought the product in the first place or would have been better off buying another desirable brand.

Three major categories of influences affect the consumer buying decision process: situational, psychological, and social. Situational influences are external circumstances or conditions existing when a consumer makes a purchase decision. Situational influences include surroundings, time, reason for purchase, and the buyer's mood and condition.

Psychological influences partly determine people's general behavior, thus influencing their behavior as consumers. The primary psychological influences on consumer behavior are perception, motives, learning, attitudes, personality and self-concept, and lifestyles. Perception is the process of selecting, organizing, and interpreting information inputs (sensations received through sight, taste, hearing, smell, and touch) to produce meaning. The three steps in the perceptual process are selection, organization, and interpretation. Individuals have numerous perceptions of packages, products, brands, and organizations that affect their buying decision processes. A motive is an internal energizing force that orients a person's activities toward satisfying needs or achieving goals. Learning refers to changes in a person's thought processes and behavior caused by information and experience. Marketers try to shape what consumers learn to influence what they buy. An attitude is an individual's enduring evaluation, feelings, and behavioral tendencies toward an object or idea and consists of three major components: cognitive, affective, and behavioral.

Personality is the set of traits and behaviors that make a person unique. Self-concept, closely linked to personality, is one's perception or view of oneself. Research indicates that buyers purchase products that reflect and enhance their self-concepts. Lifestyle is an individual's pattern of living expressed through activities, interests, and opinions. Lifestyles influence consumers' needs, brand preferences, and how and where they shop.

Social influences are forces that other people exert on buying behavior. They include roles, family, reference groups and opinion leaders, social class, and culture and subcultures. Everyone occupies positions within groups, organizations, and institutions, and each position has a role, a set of actions and activities that a person in a particular position is supposed to perform based on expectations of both the individual and surrounding persons. In a family, children learn from parents and older siblings how to make decisions, such as purchase decisions. Consumer socialization is the process through which a person acquires the knowledge and skills to function as a consumer. The consumer socialization process is partially accomplished through family influences. A reference group is any group that positively or negatively affects a person's values, attitudes, or behavior. The three major types of reference groups are membership, aspirational, and disassociative. In most reference groups, one or more members stand out as opinion leaders by furnishing requested information to reference group participants. A social class is an open group of individuals with similar social rank. Social class influences people's spending, saving, and credit practices. Culture is the accumulation of values, knowledge, beliefs, customs, objects, and concepts that a society uses to cope with its environment and passes on to future generations. A culture is made up of subcultures, groups of individuals whose characteristic values and behavior patterns are similar and differ from those of the surrounding culture. U.S. marketers focus on three major ethnic subcultures: African American, Hispanic, and Asian American.

Please visit the student website at **www.prideferrell.com** for ACE Self-Test questions that will help you prepare for exams.

IMPORTANT TERMS

Buying behavior
Consumer buying behavior
Level of involvement
Routinized response behavior
Limited problem solving
Extended problem solving
Impulse buying
Consumer buying decision process
Internal search
External search
Consideration set
Evaluative criteria
Cognitive dissonance
Situational influences
Psychological influences
Perception
Information inputs
Selective exposure

Selective distortion
Selective retention
Motive
Maslow's hierarchy of needs
Patronage motives
Learning
Attitude
Attitude scale
Personality
Self-concept
Lifestyle
Social influences
Role
Consumer socialization
Reference group
Opinion leader
Social class
Culture
Subculture

DISCUSSION & REVIEW QUESTIONS

1. How does a consumer's level of involvement affect his or her choice of problem-solving process?
2. Name the types of consumer problem-solving processes. List some products you have bought using each type. Have you ever bought a product on impulse? If so, describe the circumstances.
3. What are the major stages in the consumer buying decision process? Are all these stages used in all consumer purchase decisions? Why or why not?
4. What are the categories of situational factors that influence consumer buying behavior? Explain how each of these factors influences buyers' decisions.
5. What is selective exposure? Why do people engage in it?
6. How do marketers attempt to shape consumers' learning?
7. Why are marketers concerned about consumer attitudes?
8. In what ways do lifestyles affect the consumer buying decision process?
9. How do roles affect a person's buying behavior? Provide examples.
10. What are family influences, and how do they affect buying behavior?
11. What are reference groups? How do they influence buying behavior? Name some of your own reference groups.
12. How does an opinion leader influence the buying decision process of reference group members?
13. In what ways does social class affect a person's purchase decisions?
14. What is culture? How does it affect a person's buying behavior?
15. Describe the subcultures to which you belong. Identify buying behavior that is unique to one of your subcultures.

APPLICATION QUESTIONS

1. Consumers use one of three problem-solving processes when purchasing goods or services: routinized response behavior, limited problem solving, or extended problem solving. Describe three buying experiences you have had (one for each type of problem solving), and identify which problem-solving type you used. Discuss why that particular process was appropriate.

2. The consumer buying process consists of five stages: problem recognition, information search, evaluation of alternatives, purchase, and postpurchase evaluation. Not every buying decision goes through all five stages, and the process does not necessarily conclude in a purchase. Interview a classmate about the last purchase he or she made. Report the stages used and those skipped, if any.

3. Attitudes toward products or companies often affect consumer behavior. The three components of an attitude are cognitive, affective, and behavioral. Briefly describe how a beer company might alter the cognitive and affective components of consumer attitudes toward beer products and toward the company.

4. An individual's roles influence that person's buying behavior. Identify two of your roles and give an example of how they have influenced your buying decisions.

5. Select five brands of toothpaste and explain how the appeals used in advertising these brands relate to Maslow's hierarchy of needs.

Internet Exercise & Resources

Visit **www.prideferrell.com** for resources to help you master the material in this chapter, plus materials that will help you expand your marketing knowledge, including Internet exercise updates, ACE self-tests, hotlinks to companies featured in this chapter, and much more.

Amazon.com

Some mass market e-commerce sites, such as Amazon.com Inc., have extended the concept of customization to their customer base. Amazon has created an affinity group by drawing on certain users' likes and dislikes to make product recommendations to other users. Check out this pioneering online retailer at **www.amazon.com.**

1. What might motivate some consumers to read a "Top Selling" list?
2. Is the consumer's level of involvement with online book purchase likely to be high or low?
3. Discuss the consumer buying decision process as it relates to a decision to purchase from Amazon.com.

Video Case 9.1

Building Customer Experiences at Build-A-Bear

How many retail empires are built by chief executive bears—especially CEBs with a keen sense of consumer behavior? So far, just one: the Build-A-Bear Workshop, a store chain that turns the point-of-sale buying process into a hands-on, interactive experience.

The CEB behind Build-A-Bear is Maxine Clark, who spent 25 years as an executive with May Department Stores before leaving the corporate world in 1997 to become an entrepreneur. Thinking back to her much-loved teddy bear and to the magic she remembered in special shopping trips as a child, Clark focused her new business on a very smart niche: entertainment retailing designed to please children of all ages. Today her idea has blossomed into a chain of more than 130 North American stores, ringing up $170 million in annual sales, plus franchised operations in Europe and Japan.

Clark was determined to make memories, not simply sell an everyday, off-the-shelf product. So she created a store-based workshop environment and invited buyers to actively participate in crafting their own stuffed animals. Master Bear Builders (store employees) help buyers choose the types of animals they want. Bears, bunnies, dogs, ponies, and frogs, available in small or large sizes, are just some of the choices. Next, buyers select the fake-fur color and the amount of stuffing, insert the heart, help stitch the seams, gently fluff the fur, and name their new friends.

Finally, they get to dress their animals in miniature cowboy gear, angel wings, or dozens of other whimsical outfits and pick out cute accessories to create one-of-a-kind, personalized stuffed animals that express their interests and dreams. Each animal goes home in a house-shaped package, complete with a birth certificate signed by Clark as CEB.

As part of the buying procedure, customers enter their animals' names and their own names and addresses, e-mail addresses, gender, and birth dates at computer stations in each store. This information is used to generate a birth certificate for every bear. Then the information is pooled with sales data and other details, carefully analyzed, and used to plan newsletters and other communications and promotions. In addition, because each animal contains a unique bar-coded tag, the company can send lost bears back to their owners by consulting the database to determine ownership.

Before opening the first Build-A-Bear store—in St. Louis, Missouri—Clark tested the idea on the 10-year-old daughter of a friend, who was enthusiastic about the concept. As the business grows, she continues to stay in touch with changes in her market's needs and behavior through a Cub Advisory Board composed of 20 children, ages 6 to 14. The group meets every three months to discuss new programs and review proposals for new stuffed animals, fur colors, accessories, and fashions. Between meetings, Clark requests feedback from the board on specific questions via mail and e-mail, and combs through customer letters and e-mail messages to learn more about what customers like and don't like. The CEB has also formed a web-based advisory board to tap the ideas of a broader cross-section of customers in preparation for further expansion.

The special retail atmosphere Clark is creating requires lots of behind-the-scenes planning. Build-A-Bear's retail employees must complete an intensive three-week training course at World Bearquarters in St. Louis before they start work in a store. Yet the company doesn't take itself too seriously. The organization weaves a "bear" theme throughout its official activities. For example, managers hold titles such as "bearitory leader," and employees are entitled to "honey days," 15 days of paid vacation and personal time off every year.

Although Build-A-Bear began as a one-store business, it has quickly grown into a bear-size success story. Each store rings up about $700 per square foot in annual sales, an impressive achievement for a relatively new retail concept. Clark also realizes that her business has many rivals for the customer's time and attention. "We compete with anything that involves a family doing something together, whether it's a baseball game, going to the movies, or ice skating," she says.

Clark is working to expand her chain to 400 stores within a few years and to offer a variety of multimedia products such as books and videos. Customers can already buy CDs and audiocassettes featuring fun songs like "Ready Teddy." No matter what innovations Clark implements, she will continue to put on a great show for her customers. "Retail is entertainment, and the store is a stage," Clark says. "When customers have fun, they spend more money."[32]

QUESTIONS FOR DISCUSSION

1. Which situational influences would you expect to be most important for customers in a Build-A-Bear Workshop?

2. What role does learning play in shaping the buying behavior of Build-A-Bear's customers?

3. How does Build-A-Bear influence the level of involvement that customers might attach to stuffed animals? Does the level of involvement depend on whether the customer is a child or a parent? Explain.

Case 9.2

AutoTrader.com Fuels Online Buying of Used Cars

AutoTrader.com operates the largest virtual used-car lot in the United States. Founded in 1997, this fast-growing company has accelerated beyond competitors eBay and cars.com to capture a dominant share of the online used-car market. At any one time, the AutoTrader website (**www.autotrader.com**) features classified ads for more than 2 million cars, both new and used. Buyers and sellers make contact through the site to negotiate the final terms for purchases. Today AutoTrader's customers can choose from vehicles offered by 40,000 dealers and 250,000 individuals across the United States.

When AutoTrader first opened its online business, few people had ever bought or sold a vehicle on the Internet. Therefore, the company's initial challenge was to change the habits of consumers and dealers who were accustomed to using newspaper classified advertising for used-car transactions. Instead of charging dealers for every listing, as newspapers did, AutoTrader decided to set a flat monthly fee for posting any number of descriptions and photos. Because dealers did not have to pay separately for every car listed, they could afford to post information about every vehicle in their inventory.

As more dealers signed up and listed cars for sale, the website became more attractive to consumers who wanted to choose from a large selection of vehicles. However, the company still had to educate its primary target market, 25- to 49-year-old men, about an unfamiliar buying process. AutoTrader's solution was to run informative television commercials showing step by step how to use its site. Its policy of charging buyers no fee to browse or buy was a plus. Soon the site was drawing more than 5.5 million visitors every month.

Next, AutoTrader targeted a slightly younger segment of 18- to 24-year-olds because research showed that these first-time buyers account for a significant percentage of used-car purchasers. The company hired a video game specialist to adapt the look of its fast-paced television commercials to an online promotion titled "Slide into Your Ride." Players earned prizes for correctly lining up three cars by matching their colors and were entered in a sweepstakes to win a $25,000 AutoTrader shopping spree and other prizes.

Knowing that students typically search for used cars before heading off for college in the fall, AutoTrader scheduled this promotional game for August and September. The company placed banner ads on popular websites and sent e-mail announcements to its online newsletter subscribers, as well as to people on a *Sports Illustrated* list. Although this promotion cost $1 million, it was a good investment because it raised brand awareness and drew an additional 500,000 visitors to the site during the first month alone.

More than half the visitors who played the game were women, and about one-third of the players were in the 18- to 24-year-old age group. More than 60 percent of the players signed up to receive AutoTrader's monthly online newsletter, enabling the company to continue building relationships with these potential buyers. Equally important, several hundred thousand players searched for used cars on the AutoTrader site during the promotional period.

Meanwhile AutoTrader noticed that online auctions were becoming more popular. At one time it cooperated with eBay, the world's best-known auction site, to link the two sites so consumers could search for cars on either one. After monitoring buyer behavior for two years, AutoTrader ended the agreement and created its own vehicle auction operation, going into direct competition with eBay. "We did a lot of research and studied very closely the behavior of auction style users on our site," says Chip Perry, AutoTrader's CEO. He acknowledges that eBay is the "current major player in an extremely small niche segment of the car business." At the same time, he sees plenty of room for AutoTrader to profitably serve customers in this $2 billion market segment.

As its annual vehicle sales accelerate past $100 million, AutoTrader is not putting on the brakes. The company continues to reinforce brand recognition through television advertising, especially during the weeks leading up to the busy fall buying season. And it constantly introduces new features to draw new visitors and serve the more than 7 million consumers who use the site every month to check the listings, compare prices, and buy or bid on vehicles.[33]

QUESTIONS FOR DISCUSSION

1. In what ways has AutoTrader helped potential car buyers learn how to buy cars online?
2. In which stage of the consumer buying decision process would AutoTrader's television commercials be most likely to influence potential car buyers to use AutoTrader's website? Why?
3. Why is it important for AutoTrader to influence first-time buyers' perceptions of its site through online promotions such as "Slide into Your Ride"?

Business Markets and Buying Behavior

10

1. To become familiar with the various types of business markets

2. To identify the major characteristics of business customers and transactions

3. To understand several attributes of demand for business products

4. To become familiar with the major components of a buying center

5. To understand the stages of the business buying decision process and the factors that affect this process

6. To describe industrial classification systems and explain how they can be used to identify and analyze business markets

Brighton Provides Strong Marketing Support to Its Business Customers

What a bright idea! Brighton treats its business customers—6,000 independent retailers—like "valued customers." Brighton is an accessories manufacturer based in City of Industry, California, that produces coordinating head-to-toe accessories for women as well as some men's accessories. The company started out making fashion leather goods such as belts, handbags, and wallets. Then Brighton added a succession of new product lines, from footwear and fragrances to sunglasses and jewelry. Its newest additions are gifts and home accessories.

What makes Brighton really stand out from its competitors is CEO Jerry Kohl's decision to do business almost exclusively with smaller specialty stores. Many accessories firms prefer to market their products through department stores. Having owned a small store at one time, Kohl was convinced that Brighton would prosper if it focused on building enduring relationships with independent stores. Since then, he and his management team have frequently researched what retailers need to satisfy customers and boost profits. Studying in-store buying behavior has led to fresh product ideas for attracting new shoppers and selling more to current customers. It has also helped Brighton design special promotions to heighten brand awareness and encourage shopper loyalty.

Equally important, Brighton gives its retailers the tools they need

to serve their customers more effectively. For example, Brighton sales representatives travel the country visiting retailers and educating their sales staffs about Brighton products—how a handbag or belt is made, why it lasts longer, and why customers will benefit. They update store owners on the latest sales promotions for customers and sales personnel. Brighton representatives also gather retailers' sales tips and success stories, then share the information with the entire retailer network.

In addition, retailers receive useful reference books such as *M.I.S.S. (Marketing Is Simply Smart)* and a subscription to the colorful *Brighton View* newsletter. Each newsletter offers insights into customer behavior, describes new products, and gives step-by-step instructions for analyzing sales of Brighton products and setting appropriate inventory levels. Finally, owners of stores that sell at least $150,000 worth of Brighton products in a year receive a free trip to the company's annual convention in Hawaii.

By choosing to market through small specialty stores and providing excellent marketing support to them, Kohl has built Brighton into a major accessories company. The retailers also prosper. Many enjoy above-average gross profit margins from sales of Brighton products. "I have close to 60 different vendors and I would put Brighton right at the top because of the support from its sales representatives, the product quality, the value, and the overall assistance in helping me build my business," says the owner of Morgan Fitzgerald's, a Brighton retailer in Bryan, Texas. "Brighton treats us as their customers and this helps us learn how to better treat our customers."[1]

erving business markets effectively requires understanding those markets. Marketers at Brighton go to considerable lengths to understand their customers so they can provide better services and develop and maintain long-term customer relationships. Like consumer marketers, business marketers are concerned about satisfying their customers.

In this chapter, we look at business markets and business buying decision processes. We first discuss various kinds of business markets and the types of buyers making up those markets. Next, we explore several dimensions of business buying, such as characteristics of transactions, attributes and concerns of buyers, methods of buying, and distinctive features of demand for products sold to business purchasers. We then examine how business buying decisions are made and who makes the purchases. Finally, we consider how business markets are analyzed.

Business Markets

business market Individuals or groups that purchase a specific kind of product for resale, direct use in producing other products, or use in general daily operations

A **business market** (also called a *business-to-business market*) consists of individuals or groups that purchase a specific kind of product for one of three purposes: resale, direct use in producing other products, or use in general daily operations. The four categories of business markets are producer, reseller, government, and institutional. In the remainder of this section, we discuss each of these types of markets.

◆ Producer Markets

producer markets Individuals and business organizations that purchase products to make profits by using them to produce other products or using them in their operations

Individuals and business organizations that purchase products for the purpose of making a profit by using them to produce other products or using them in their operations are classified as **producer markets.** Producer markets include buyers of raw materials, as well as purchasers of semifinished and finished items, used to produce other products. For example, manufacturers buy raw materials and component parts for direct use in product production. Grocery stores and supermarkets are part of producer markets for numerous support products such as paper and plastic bags, counters, and scanners. Farmers are part of producer markets for farm machinery, fertilizer, seed, and livestock. Producer markets include a broad array of industries ranging from agriculture, forestry, fisheries, and mining to construction, transportation, communications, and utilities. As Table 10.1 indicates, the number of business establishments in national producer markets is enormous.

Table 10.1	Number of Establishments in Industry Groups
Industry	**Number of Establishments**
Agriculture, forestry, fishing	27,000
Mining	24,000
Construction	699,000
Manufacturing	360,000
Transportation, public utilities	187,000
Finance, insurance, real estate	418,000
Services	2,077,000

Source: Bureau of the Census, *Statistical Abstract of the United States* (Washington, DC: Government Printing Office, 2002), p. 544.

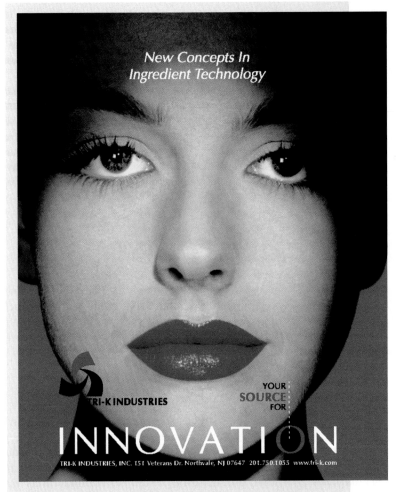

Producer Markets
TRI-K Industries makes ingredients for skin care products and hair care products. These ingredients are sold to manufacturers.

Manufacturers are geographically concentrated. More than half are located in only seven states: New York, California, Pennsylvania, Illinois, Ohio, New Jersey, and Michigan. This concentration sometimes enables businesses that sell to producer markets to serve them more efficiently. Within certain states, production in a specific industry may account for a sizable proportion of that industry's total production.

◆ Reseller Markets

reseller market Intermediaries that buy finished goods and resell them for profit

Reseller markets consist of intermediaries, such as wholesalers and retailers, that buy finished goods and resell them for profit. Aside from making minor alterations, resellers do not change the physical characteristics of the products they handle. Except for items producers sell directly to consumers, all products sold to consumer markets are first sold to reseller markets.

Wholesalers purchase products for resale to retailers, to other wholesalers, and to producers, governments, and institutions. Of the 446,000 wholesalers in the United States, a large percentage are located in New York, California, Illinois, Texas, Ohio, Pennsylvania, and New Jersey.[2] Although some products are sold directly to end users, many manufacturers sell their products to wholesalers, which in turn sell the products to other firms in the distribution system. Thus, wholesalers

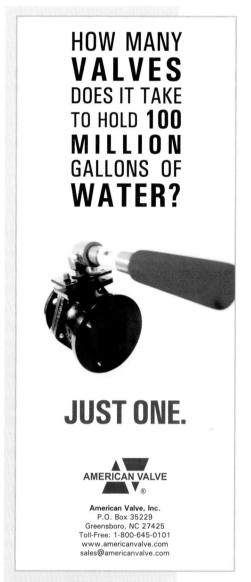

HOW MANY VALVES DOES IT TAKE TO HOLD 100 MILLION GALLONS OF WATER?

JUST ONE.

AMERICAN VALVE
®

American Valve, Inc.
P.O. Box 35229
Greensboro, NC 27425
Toll-Free: 1-800-645-0101
www.americanvalve.com
sales@americanvalve.com

Reseller Markets
American Valve produces valves and sells them through wholesalers and industrial distributors, which are resellers.

government market A federal, state, county, or local government that buys goods and services to support its internal operations and provide products to its constituencies

are very important in helping producers get a product to customers. Professional buyers and buying committees make wholesalers' initial purchase decisions. Reordering is often automated.

Retailers purchase products and resell them to final customers. There are approximately 1.1 million retailers in the United States, employing more than 15 million people and generating more than $3.1 trillion in annual sales.[3] Some retailers carry a large number of items. Supermarkets may handle as many as 30,000 different products. In small, individually owned retail stores, owners or managers make purchasing decisions. In chain stores, a central office buyer or buying committee frequently decides whether a product will be made available for selection by store managers. For most products, however, local management makes the actual buying decisions for a particular store.

When making purchase decisions, resellers consider several factors. They evaluate the level of demand for a product to determine in what quantity and at what prices the product can be resold. Retailers assess the amount of space required to handle a product relative to its potential profit, sometimes on the basis of sales per square foot of selling area. Because customers often depend on resellers to have products available when needed, resellers typically appraise a supplier's ability to provide adequate quantities when and where wanted. Resellers also take into account the ease of placing orders and the availability of technical assistance and training programs from producers. When resellers consider buying a product not previously carried, they try to determine whether the product competes with or complements products they currently handle. These types of concerns distinguish reseller markets from other markets.

◆ Government Markets

Federal, state, county, and local governments make up **government markets**. These markets spend billions of dollars annually for a variety of goods and services to support their internal operations and provide citizens with such products as highways, education, water, energy, and national defense. The federal government spends about $348 billion annually on national defense alone.[4] Government expenditures annually account for about 19 percent of the U.S. gross domestic product.

As of this writing, besides the federal government, there are 50 state governments, 3,043 county governments, and 84,410 local governments.[5] The amount spent by federal, state, and local units during the last 30 years has increased rapidly because the total number of government units and the services they provide have both increased. Costs of providing these services have also risen. As Table 10.2 (on p. 264) notes, the federal government spends more than half the total amount spent by all governments except in 2002.

The types and quantities of products bought by government markets reflect societal demands on various government agencies. As citizens' needs for government services change, so does demand for products by government markets. For example, Identix now sells its fingerprint security systems to government agencies and airports around the United States, including Oakland Metropolitan Airport and Des Moines International Airport.[6] Although it is common to hear of large corporations being awarded government contracts, in fact businesses of all sizes market to government agencies. For example, over the last five years, Infinity Technologies, a small firm in Huntsville, Alabama, has been awarded government contracts with the U.S. Army, the U.S. Navy, NASA, the U.S. Air Force, and the General Services Administration.[7]

Because government agencies spend public funds to buy the products needed to provide services, they are accountable to the public. This accountability explains their relatively complex set of buying procedures. Some firms do not even try to sell to government buyers because they want to avoid the tangle of red tape. However,

Table 10.2	Annual Expenditures by Government Units for Selected Years (in billions of dollars)		
Year	Total Government Expenditures	Federal Government Expenditures	State and Local Expenditures
1975	560	292	268
1980	959	526	432
1985	1,581	1,032	658
1990	2,369	1,393	976
1995	2,820	1,704	1,116
2002	3,669	1,779	1,890

Source: Bureau of the Census, *Statistical Abstract of the United States* (Washington, D.C.: Government Printing Office, 2002), and Bureau of the Census, Governments Division, August 18, 2003.

many marketers have learned to deal efficiently with government procedures and do not find them a stumbling block. For certain products, such as defense-related items, the government may be the only customer. The U.S. Government Printing Office publishes and distributes several documents explaining buying procedures and describing the types of products various federal agencies purchase.

Governments make purchases through bids or negotiated contracts. Although companies may be reluctant to approach government markets because of the complicated bidding process, once they understand the rules of this process, some firms routinely penetrate government markets. To make a sale under the bid system, firms must apply for and be approved to be placed on a list of qualified bidders. When a government unit wants to buy, it sends out a detailed description of the products to qualified bidders. Businesses wishing to sell such products submit bids. The government unit is usually required to accept the lowest bid.

When buying nonstandard or highly complex products, a government unit often uses a negotiated contract. Under this procedure, the government unit selects only a few firms and then negotiates specifications and terms; it eventually awards the contract to one of the negotiating firms. Most large defense-related contracts, once held by such companies as McDonnell Douglas and General Dynamics, traditionally were negotiated in this fashion. However, as the number and size of such contracts have declined, these companies have had to strengthen their marketing efforts and look to other markets. Although government markets can impose intimidating requirements, they can also be very lucrative.

◆ Institutional Markets

institutional market Organizations with charitable, educational, community, or other nonbusiness goals

Organizations with charitable, educational, community, or other nonbusiness goals constitute **institutional markets**. Members of institutional markets include churches, some hospitals, fraternities and sororities, charitable organizations, and private colleges. Institutions purchase millions of dollars' worth of products annually to provide goods, services, and ideas to congregations, students, patients, and others. Because institutions often have different goals and fewer resources than other types of organizations, marketers may use special marketing efforts to serve them. For example, Hussey Seating in Maine sells bleacher stadium seating to schools, colleges, and other institutions, as well as to sports arenas. The family-owned business shows its support for institutional customers through assistance with school funding and reduced-cost construction of local economic development projects.[8]

Dimensions of Marketing to Business Customers

Now that we have considered different types of business customers, we look at several dimensions of marketing to business customers. We examine characteristics of transactions with business customers and then discuss attributes of business customers and some of their primary concerns when making purchase decisions. Next, we consider buying methods and major types of purchases. Finally, we discuss the characteristics of demand for business products.

◆ Characteristics of Transactions with Business Customers

Transactions between businesses differ from consumer sales in several ways. Orders by business customers tend to be much larger than individual consumer sales. Suppliers often must sell products in large quantities to make profits; consequently they prefer not to sell to customers who place small orders. For example, Airborne Express competes successfully against FedEx and UPS by providing low-cost overnight delivery services primarily to businesses that buy such services in high volume.

reciprocity An arrangement unique to business marketing in which two organizations agree to buy from each other

Some business purchases involve expensive items, such as computers. Other products, such as raw materials and component items, are used continuously in production, and their supply may need frequent replenishing. The contract regarding terms of sale of these items is likely to be a long-term agreement.

Discussions and negotiations associated with business purchases can require considerable marketing time and selling effort. Purchasing decisions are often made by committee, orders are frequently large and expensive, and products may be custom built. Several people or departments in the purchasing organization will probably be involved. For example, one department expresses a need for a product, a second department develops the specifications, a third stipulates maximum expenditures, and a fourth places the order.

One practice unique to business markets is **reciprocity**, an arrangement in which two organizations agree to buy from each other. Reciprocal agreements that threaten competition are illegal. The Federal Trade Commission and the Justice Department take actions to stop anticompetitive reciprocal practices. Nonetheless, a certain amount of reciprocal activity occurs among small businesses and, to a lesser extent, among larger companies. Because reciprocity influences purchasing agents to deal only with certain suppliers, it can lower morale among agents and lead to less than optimal purchases.

Building Long-Term Relationships with Customers
Like many other companies, ERB Industries attempts to build long-term customer relationships. In this advertisement, the company states "our mission at ERB Safety is to develop and maintain long-term customer relationships by providing exceptional service and value."

◆ Attributes of Business Customers

Business customers differ from consumers in their purchasing behavior in that they are better informed about the products they purchase. They demand detailed information about products' functional features and technical specifications to ensure that the products meet their needs. Personal goals, however, may also influence business buying behavior. Most purchasing agents seek the psychological satisfaction that comes with organizational advancement and financial rewards. Agents who consistently exhibit rational business buying behavior are likely to attain these personal goals because they help their firms achieve organizational objectives. Today many suppliers and their customers build and maintain mutually beneficial relationships, sometimes called *partnerships*.

◆ Primary Concerns of Business Customers

When making purchasing decisions, business customers take into account a variety of factors. Among their chief considerations are price, product quality, and service. Price matters greatly to business customers because it influences operating costs and costs of goods sold, which in turn affect selling price, profit margin, and ultimately the ability to compete. When purchasing major equipment, a business customer views price as the amount of investment necessary to obtain a certain level of return or savings. A business customer is likely to compare the price of a product with the benefits the product will yield to the organization.

Most business customers try to achieve and maintain a specific level of quality in the products they buy. To achieve this goal, most firms establish standards (usually stated as a percentage of defects allowed) for these products and buy them on the basis of a set of expressed characteristics, commonly called *specifications*. A customer evaluates the quality of the products being considered to determine whether they meet specifications. If a product fails to meet specifications or malfunctions for the ultimate consumer, the customer may drop that product's supplier and switch to a different one. On the other hand, customers are ordinarily cautious about buying products that exceed specifications because such products often cost more, thus increasing the organization's overall costs. Specifications are designed to meet a customer's wants, and anything that does not contribute to meeting those wants is considered wasteful.

Business buyers value service. Services offered by suppliers directly and indirectly influence customers' costs, sales, and profits. In some instances, the mix of customer services is the major means by which marketers gain a competitive advantage. Typical services customers desire are market information, inventory maintenance, on-time delivery, and repair services. Business buyers are likely to need technical product information, data regarding demand, information about general economic conditions, or supply and delivery information. Maintaining adequate inventory is critical because it helps make products accessible when a customer needs them and reduces the customer's inventory

Primary Concerns of Business Customers
This United States Postal Service ad for Priority Mail focuses on two primary concerns of business customers—service and price.

requirements and costs. Since business customers are usually responsible for ensuring that products are on hand and ready for use when needed, on-time delivery is crucial. Furthermore, reliable, on-time delivery saves business customers money because it enables them to carry less inventory. Purchasers of machinery are especially concerned about obtaining repair services and replacement parts quickly because inoperable equipment is costly. Caterpillar Inc., manufacturer of earth-moving, construction, and materials-handling machinery, has built an international reputation, as well as a competitive advantage, by providing prompt service and replacement parts for its products around the world.

Quality of service is a critical issue because customer expectations about service have broadened. Using traditional service quality standards based only on traditional manufacturing and accounting systems is not enough. Communication channels that allow customers to ask questions, voice complaints, submit orders, and trace shipments are indispensable components of service. Marketers should strive for uniformity of service, simplicity, truthfulness, and accuracy. They should also develop customer service objectives and monitor customer service programs. Firms can monitor service by formally surveying customers or informally calling on customers and asking questions about the service they receive. Expending the time and effort to ensure that customers are happy can greatly benefit marketers by increasing customer retention. One study found that boosting customer retention by 5 percent could double a small firm's profitability.[9]

As in a number of areas associated with business transactions, occasionally ethical issues arise that are associated with businesses doing business with other organizations. One of these ethical issues is discussed in the Ethics and Social Responsibility boxed feature.

ETHICS AND SOCIAL RESPONSIBILITY

Is It Ethical to Buy Business from Your Customers?

When does a gift or rebate become a bribe to buy a customer's business? This is a growing concern in business markets, where companies want to build goodwill, educate customers, and encourage them to buy or recommend certain products. Therefore, many companies give small gifts such as pens and pencils to keep their brand names in front of customers. However, giving more expensive gifts may be construed as crossing the line into bribery. Still, more than 23 percent of the salespeople and managers responding to a survey by *Sales and Marketing Management* had felt pressured to give a gift worth more than $100 in exchange for a customer's business. Moreover, 88 percent said they actually had given such gifts.

The line between gift and bribe is becoming clearer in the pharmaceutical industry, where new drugs cost millions of dollars to develop. Traditionally many representatives gave away concert tickets, golf bags with logos, steak dinners, and even cash, in addition to free drug samples, to encourage doctors to prescribe new drugs. At one point, drug companies were spending $8 billion annually on doctors' perks.

All this gift giving attracted the attention of industry leaders and government officials. To clarify which gifts are appropriate and when, the Pharmaceutical Research and Manufacturers of America recently adopted a voluntary ethics code. Salespeople can buy meals for doctors in educational settings, but they cannot give golf bags with logos, tickets, cash, or other lavish gifts in exchange for an agreement to prescribe medications.

Vermont now requires pharmaceutical firms to report gifts valued at $25 or more. The U.S. Office of the Inspector General warns that pharmaceutical firms may face legal action for giving lavish gifts, paying doctors to switch patients to their drugs, or paying doctors to participate in marketing or educational efforts. Also, some medical professionals are questioning the ethics of allowing pharmaceutical firms to sponsor continuing education programs for doctors.

Experts emphasize that buying business is ineffective in the long run. "It really diminishes what you're doing," says one critic. "Even people accepting such perks will start to figure that your service or pricing must not be very good if you have to resort to such things."

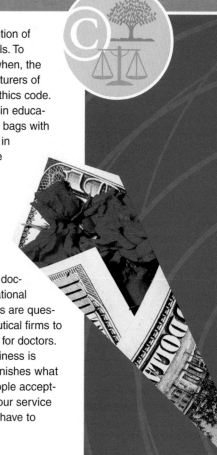

◆ Methods of Business Buying

Although no two business buyers do their jobs the same way, most use one or more of the following purchase methods: *description, inspection, sampling,* and *negotiation.* When products are standardized according to certain characteristics (such as size, shape, weight, and color) and graded using such standards, a business buyer may be able to purchase simply by describing or specifying quantity, grade, and other attributes. Agricultural products often fall into this category. Sometimes buyers specify a particular brand or its equivalent when describing the desired product. Purchases on the basis of description are especially common between a buyer and seller with an ongoing relationship built on trust.

Certain products, such as industrial equipment, used vehicles, and buildings, have unique characteristics and may vary with regard to condition. For example, a particular used truck may have a bad transmission. Consequently, business buyers of such products must base purchase decisions on inspection.

Sampling entails taking a specimen of the product from the lot and evaluating it on the assumption that its characteristics represent the entire lot. This method is appropriate when the product is homogeneous—for instance, grain—and examining the entire lot is not physically or economically feasible.

Some purchases by businesses are based on negotiated contracts. In certain instances, buyers describe exactly what they need and ask sellers to submit bids. They then negotiate with the suppliers that submit the most attractive bids. This approach may be used when acquiring commercial vehicles, for example. In other cases, the buyer may be unable to identify specifically what is to be purchased and can provide only a general description, as might be the case for a piece of custom-made equipment. A buyer and seller might negotiate a contract that specifies a base price and provides for the payment of additional costs and fees. These contracts are most commonly used for one-time projects such as buildings, capital equipment, and special projects.

A number of business organizations purchase products through online auctions. The Tech Know boxed feature provides additional details on business purchases through online auctions.

Purchases Through Negotiated Contracts
Customized technology products such as the security solutions offered by Pitney Bowes are often purchased through negotiated contracts.

◆ Types of Business Purchases

new-task purchase An initial purchase by an organization of an item to be used to perform a new job or solve a new problem

straight rebuy purchase A routine purchase of the same products by a business buyer

modified rebuy purchase A new-task purchase that is changed on subsequent orders or when the requirements of a straight rebuy purchase are modified

Most business purchases are one of three types: new-task, straight rebuy, or modified rebuy purchase. In a **new-task purchase**, an organization makes an initial purchase of an item to be used to perform a new job or solve a new problem. A new-task purchase may require development of product specifications, vendor specifications, and procedures for future purchases of that product. To make the initial purchase, the business buyer usually needs much information. New-task purchases are important to suppliers, because if business buyers are satisfied with the products, suppliers may be able to sell buyers large quantities of them for many years.

A **straight rebuy purchase** occurs when buyers purchase the same products routinely under approximately the same terms of sale. Buyers require little information for these routine purchase decisions and tend to use familiar suppliers that have provided satisfactory service and products in the past. These suppliers try to set up automatic reordering systems to make reordering easy and convenient for business buyers. A supplier may even monitor the business buyer's inventories and indicate to the buyer what should be ordered and when.

In a **modified rebuy purchase**, a new-task purchase is changed the second or third time it is ordered or requirements associated with a straight rebuy purchase are modified. A business buyer might seek faster delivery, lower prices, or a different quality level of product specifications. A modified rebuy situation may cause regular suppliers to become more competitive to keep the account, since other suppliers could obtain the business. For example, when a firm buys a slightly different set of communication services, it has made a modified purchase.

TECH KNOW

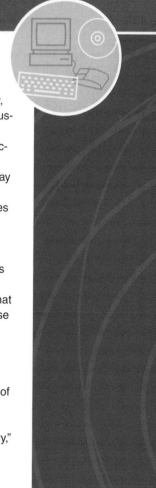

Online Auctions Click with Businesses

Going, going, gone—to the Internet! Instead of shipping products to an auction site and waiting for the auctioneer to lower the gavel, businesses are increasingly using online auctions to find new business customers and sell more products. The process is cost effective and connects buyers and sellers who might be unable to find each other otherwise.

Before a business-to-business (B2B) auction starts, bidders can inspect online digital photos or video files of the products being sold. Some auctions accept bids over the course of several hours or days. Others take place at a specified time, with participants logging on to bid against one another for a few minutes. Sellers can serve far-flung customers, and customers can find bargains on numerous products, from computers and dental supplies to commercial refrigerators and cattle.

Kentucky cattle farmers with small herds, for example, used to attract a limited group of bidders when they auctioned cattle locally. Now they videotape their herds and auction them through Cattleinfonet.com and other sites. Because more buyers participate, the competition yields slightly higher

winning bids than the bids at local auctions.

Major auction sites such as eBay and Yahoo! host hundreds of B2B auctions every day. The eBay site has an extensive listing of new, discontinued, and used products arranged by industry and type of equipment, which helps business buyers find what they want quickly. Mitsubishi Electric Automation auctions outdated inventory of industrial systems and other products through eBay auctions. In addition, businesses can offer goods and services through industry-specific auction sites such as those in construction, landscaping, and aviation.

The rise of online B2B auctions has led to higher demand for software that helps businesses manage bidding and fulfillment. Atlanta-based Auctionworks, for example, makes the systems that The Home Depot, IBM, and other corporations use to track auction sales of their products. Richland Equipment, which sells John Deere agricultural machinery, also relies on Auctionworks software. Within 18 months of its first foray into online auctions, the retailer was ringing up nearly one-third of its revenues through auctions. "It pretty much opens up a new client base for us because I'm able to get in front of people all across the country," says Richland's CEO.

Types of Business Purchases
The purchase of a Brother multifunction machine likely would be a modified rebuy purchase or a new-task purchase. The purchase of consulting services offered by Everest most likely would be a new-task purchase.

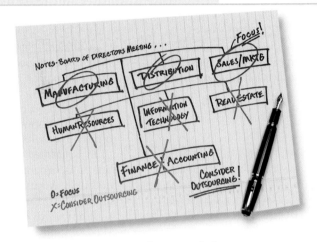

◆ Demand for Business Products

Unlike consumer demand, demand for business products (also called *industrial demand*) can be characterized as (1) derived, (2) inelastic, (3) joint, or (4) fluctuating.

Derived Demand. Because business customers, especially producers, buy products for direct or indirect use in the production of goods and services to satisfy consumers' needs, the demand for business products derives from the demand for consumer products; it is therefore called **derived demand**. In the long run, no demand for business products is totally unrelated to the demand for consumer products. The derived nature of demand is usually multilevel. Business marketers at different levels are affected by a change in consumer demand for a particular product. For instance, consumers have become concerned with health and good nutrition, and as a result are purchasing more products with less fat, cholesterol, and sodium. When consumers reduced their purchases of high-fat foods, a change occurred in the demand for products marketed by food processors, equipment manufacturers, and suppliers of raw materials associated with these products. When consumer

derived demand Demand for industrial products that stems from demand for consumer products

Bread is strictly optional.

A friendly reminder from America's Peanut Farmers

www.nationalpeanutboard.org

A two-tablespoon serving of peanut butter contains 12.2 grams of unsaturated fat and 3.3 grams of saturated fat, and 0 cholesterol.

Derived Demand
The National Peanut Board promotes additional uses of peanut butter beyond the traditional peanut butter and jelly sandwich, because a portion of the demand for peanuts derives from the consumer demand for peanut butter.

demand for a product changes, a wave is set in motion that affects demand for all firms involved in the production of that product.

Inelastic Demand. With **inelastic demand**, a price increase or decrease will not significantly alter demand for a business product. Because some business products contain a number of parts, price increases affecting only one or two parts may yield only a slightly higher per-unit production cost. When a sizable price increase for a component represents a large proportion of the product's cost, demand may become more elastic because the price increase in the component causes the price at the consumer level to rise sharply. For example, if aircraft engine manufacturers substantially increase the price of engines, forcing Boeing to raise the prices of the aircraft it manufactures, the demand for airliners may become more elastic as airlines reconsider whether they can afford to buy new aircraft. An increase in the price of windshields, however, is unlikely to greatly affect either the price of or the demand for airliners.

Inelasticity applies only to industry demand for business products, not to the demand curve an individual firm faces. Suppose a spark plug producer increases the price of spark plugs sold to manufacturers of small engines, but its competitors continue to maintain lower prices. The spark plug company will probably experience reduced unit sales because most small-engine producers will switch to lower-priced brands. A specific firm is vulnerable to elastic demand, even if industry demand for a specific business product is inelastic.

Joint Demand. Demand for certain business products, especially raw materials and components, is subject to joint demand. **Joint demand** occurs when two or more items are used in combination to produce a product. For example, a firm that manufactures axes needs the same number of ax handles as it does ax blades. These two products thus are demanded jointly. If a shortage of ax handles exists, the producer buys fewer ax blades. Understanding the effects of joint demand is particularly important for a marketer selling multiple jointly demanded items. Such a marketer realizes that when a customer begins purchasing one of the jointly demanded items, a good opportunity exists to sell related products.

Fluctuating Demand. Because it is derived from consumer demand, the demand for business products may fluctuate enormously. In general, when particular consumer products are in high demand, their producers buy large quantities of raw materials and components to ensure meeting long-run production requirements. In addition, these producers may expand production capacity, which entails acquiring new equipment and machinery, more workers, and more raw materials and component

inelastic demand Demand that is not significantly altered by a price increase or decrease

joint demand Demand involving the use of two or more items in combination to produce a product

parts. Conversely, a decline in demand for certain consumer goods significantly reduces demand for business products used to produce those goods.

Marketers of business products may notice changes in demand when customers alter inventory policies, perhaps because of expectations about future demand. For example, if several dishwasher manufacturers that buy timers from one producer increase their inventory of timers from a two-week to a one-month supply, the timer producer will have a significant, immediate increase in demand.

Sometimes price changes lead to surprising temporary changes in demand. A price increase for a business product may initially cause business customers to buy more of the item because they expect the price to rise further. Similarly, demand for a business product may decrease significantly following a price cut because buyers are waiting for further price reductions. Fluctuations in demand can be substantial in industries in which prices change frequently.

Business Buying Decisions

business (organizational) buying behavior The purchase behavior of producers, government units, institutions, and resellers

Business (organizational) buying behavior refers to the purchase behavior of producers, government units, institutions, and resellers. Although several factors affecting consumer buying behavior (discussed in the previous chapter) also influence business buying behavior, a number of factors are unique to the latter. In this section, we first analyze the buying center to learn who participates in business purchase decisions. Then we focus on the stages of the buying decision process and the factors that affect it.

◆ The Buying Center

buying center The people within an organization, including users, influencers, buyers, deciders, and gatekeepers, who make business purchase decisions

Relatively few business purchase decisions are made by just one person; mostly they are made through a buying center. The **buying center** is the group of people within the organization who make business purchase decisions. They include users, influencers, buyers, deciders, and gatekeepers.[10] One person may perform several roles. These participants share some goals and risks associated with their decisions.

Users are the organization members who actually use the product being acquired. They frequently initiate the purchase process and/or generate purchase specifications. After the purchase, they evaluate product performance relative to the specifications.

Influencers are often technical personnel, such as engineers, who help develop the specifications and evaluate alternative products. Technical personnel are especially important influencers when products being considered involve new, advanced technology.

Buyers select suppliers and negotiate terms of purchase. They may also become involved in developing specifications. Buyers are sometimes called purchasing agents or purchasing managers. Their choices of vendors and products, especially for new-task purchases, are heavily influenced by people occupying other roles in the buying center. For straight rebuy purchases, the buyer plays a major role in vendor selection and negotiations.

Deciders actually choose the products. Although buyers may be deciders, it is not unusual for different people to occupy these roles. For routinely purchased items, buyers are commonly deciders. However, a buyer may not be authorized to make purchases exceeding a certain dollar limit, in which case higher-level management personnel are deciders.

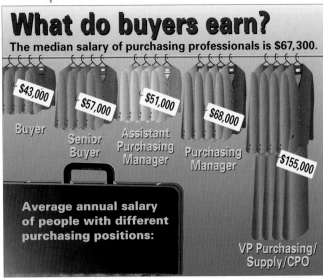

Snapshot

What do buyers earn?

The median salary of purchasing professionals is $67,300.

$43,000 — Buyer
$57,000 — Senior Buyer
$51,000 — Assistant Purchasing Manager
$68,000 — Purchasing Manager
$155,000 — VP Purchasing/ Supply/CPO

Average annual salary of people with different purchasing positions:

Source: The World Almanac and Book of Facts 2003, World Almanac Books, p. 709.

Finally, gatekeepers, such as secretaries and technical personnel, control the flow of information to and among people occupying other roles in the buying center. Buyers who deal directly with vendors also may be gatekeepers because they can control information flows. The flow of information from a supplier's sales representatives to users and influencers is often controlled by personnel in the purchasing department.

The number and structure of an organization's buying centers are affected by the organization's size and market position, the volume and types of products being purchased, and the firm's overall managerial philosophy regarding exactly who should be involved in purchase decisions. The size of a buying center is influenced by the stage of the buying decision process and by the type of purchase. The size of the buying center likely would be larger for a new-task purchase than for a straight rebuy. For example, when Siebel Systems began talking with Fleetwood Enterprises about purchasing its customer relationship management software—a new-task buy—Siebel personnel had to consider the needs and influence of the executives who would make the final buying decision as well as those of the influencers (including Fleetwood's information technology experts) and the actual users (Fleetwood's marketing, sales, and customer service personnel).[11] Varying goals among members of a buying center can have both positive and negative effects on the purchasing process.

A marketer attempting to sell to a business customer should determine who is in the buying center, the types of decisions each individual makes, and which individuals are most influential in the decision process. Because in some instances many people make up the buying center, marketers cannot feasibly contact all participants. Instead, they must be certain to contact a few of the most influential.

◆ Stages of the Business Buying Decision Process

Like consumers, businesses follow a buying decision process. This process is summarized in the lower portion of Figure 10.1. In the first stage, one or more individuals recognize that a problem or need exists. Problem recognition may arise under a variety of circumstances, for instance, when machines malfunction

Figure 10.1 Business (Organizational) Buying Decision Process and Factors That May Influence It

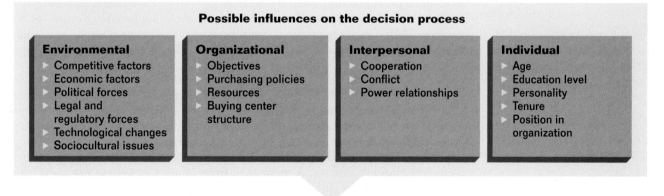

Possible influences on the decision process

Environmental	Organizational	Interpersonal	Individual
▸ Competitive factors ▸ Economic factors ▸ Political forces ▸ Legal and regulatory forces ▸ Technological changes ▸ Sociocultural issues	▸ Objectives ▸ Purchasing policies ▸ Resources ▸ Buying center structure	▸ Cooperation ▸ Conflict ▸ Power relationships	▸ Age ▸ Education level ▸ Personality ▸ Tenure ▸ Position in organization

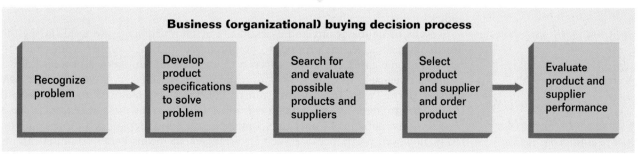

Business (organizational) buying decision process

Recognize problem → Develop product specifications to solve problem → Search for and evaluate possible products and suppliers → Select product and supplier and order product → Evaluate product and supplier performance

Read the IT chart. You've got serious problems.

Porn may be the most visible, but it's only one of your worries. See more clearly with Websense Enterprise, the most comprehensive solution for protecting your network from threats that appear as employee computing and the Internet converge. You don't have to rely on 20/20 hindsight.

For a **free white paper** on *Emerging Threats in Employee Computing* or to assess your risks visit **www.websense.com/checkup.**

WEBSENSE.

FILTER | PROTECT | OPTIMIZE

Problem Recognition
Websense is attempting to stimulate problem recognition among its potential customers.

or a firm modifies an existing product or introduces a new one. Individuals in the buying center, such as users, influencers, or buyers, may be involved in problem recognition, but it may be stimulated by external sources, such as sales representatives or advertisements.

The second stage of the process, development of product specifications, requires that buying center participants assess the problem or need and determine what is necessary to resolve or satisfy it. During this stage, users and influencers, such as engineers, often provide information and advice for developing product specifications. By assessing and describing needs, the organization should be able to establish product specifications.

Searching for and evaluating potential products and suppliers is the third stage in the decision process. Search activities may involve looking in company files and trade directories; contacting suppliers for information; soliciting proposals from known vendors; and examining websites, catalogs, and trade publications. To facilitate a vendor search, some organizations, such as Wal-Mart, advertise their desire to build partnerships with specific types of vendors, such as those owned by women or by minorities. During this stage some organizations engage in **value analysis**, an evaluation of each component of a potential purchase. Value analysis examines quality, design, materials, and possibly item reduction or deletion to acquire the product in the most cost-effective way. Some vendors may be deemed unacceptable because they are not large enough to supply needed quantities; others may be excluded because of poor delivery and service records. Sometimes the product is not available from any existing vendor and the buyer must find an innovative company, such as 3M, to design and make it. Products are evaluated to make sure they meet or exceed product specifications developed in the second stage. Usually suppliers are judged according to multiple criteria. A number of firms employ **vendor analysis**, a formal, systematic evaluation of current and potential vendors focusing on such characteristics as price, product quality, delivery service, product availability, and overall reliability.

Results of deliberations and assessments in the third stage are used during the fourth stage to select the product to be purchased and the supplier from which to buy it. In some cases, the buyer selects and uses several suppliers, a process known as **multiple sourcing**. In others, only one supplier is selected, a situation called **sole sourcing**. Firms with federal government contracts are required to have several sources for an item. Sole sourcing has traditionally been discouraged except when a product is available from only one company. Sole sourcing is much more common today, however, partly because such an arrangement means better communications

value analysis An evaluation of each component of a potential purchase, including quality, design, or materials, to acquire the most cost-effective product

vendor analysis A formal, systematic evaluation of current and potential vendors

multiple sourcing An organization's decision to use several suppliers

sole sourcing An organization's decision to use only one supplier

Diversity + Inclusion = Innovation + Opportunity

The Altria family of companies encourages diversity in every part of our business. For over thirty years, our family of companies has built partnerships with thousands of minority-owned and women-owned firms. We believe that we couldn't be as successful without their support and we're proud to partner with them.

Diversity and innovation are hallmarks of the community-based programs sponsored by the Altria family of companies. Through contributions supporting hunger relief, domestic violence prevention, the arts, and the battle against AIDS, we've been making a difference in communities around the world for more than forty-five years.

The people of Altria are committed to helping those in need, and to supporting visionary individuals and organizations

Altria
Kraft Foods
Philip Morris International
Philip Morris USA
altria.com

Vendor Search
Altria has a vendor diversity program focused on partnering with minority- and women-owned businesses.

between buyer and supplier, stability and higher profits for suppliers, and often lower prices for buyers. However, many organizations still prefer multiple sourcing because this approach lessens the possibility of disruption caused by strikes, shortages, or bankruptcies. The actual product is ordered in this fourth stage, and specific details regarding terms, credit arrangements, delivery dates and methods, and technical assistance are finalized.

During the fifth stage, the product's performance is evaluated by comparing it with specifications. Sometimes the product meets the specifications, but its performance fails to adequately solve the problem or satisfy the need recognized in the first stage. In that case, product specifications must be adjusted. The supplier's performance is also evaluated during this stage. If supplier performance is inadequate, the business purchaser seeks corrective action from the supplier or searches for a new one. Results of the evaluation become feedback for the other stages in future business purchase decisions.

This business buying decision process is used in its entirety primarily for new-task purchases. Several stages, but not necessarily all, are used for modified rebuy and straight rebuy situations.

◆ Influences on the Business Buying Decision Process

Figure 10.1 also lists four major categories of factors that influence business buying decisions: environmental, organizational, interpersonal, and individual.

Environmental factors include competitive and economic factors, political forces, legal and regulatory forces, technological changes, and sociocultural issues. These factors generate considerable uncertainty for an organization, which can make individuals in the buying center apprehensive about certain types of purchases. Changes in one or more environmental forces can create new purchasing opportunities and threats. For example, changes in competition and technology can make buying decisions difficult for products such as software, computers, and telecommunications equipment.

Organizational factors influencing the buying decision process include the company's objectives, purchasing policies, and resources, as well as the size and composition of its buying center. An organization may have certain buying policies to which buying center participants must conform. For instance, a firm's policies may mandate long-term contracts, perhaps longer than most sellers desire. An organization's financial resources may require special credit arrangements. Any of these conditions could affect purchase decisions.

Interpersonal factors are the relationships among people in the buying center. Use of power and level of conflict among buying center participants influence business buying decisions. Certain individuals in the buying center may be better communicators and more persuasive than others. Often these interpersonal dynamics are hidden, making them difficult for marketers to assess.

Individual factors are personal characteristics of participants in the buying center, such as age, education, personality, and tenure and position in the organization. For example, a 55-year-old manager who has been in the organization for 25 years may affect decisions made by the buying center differently than a 30-year-old person employed only two years. How influential these factors are depends on the buying situation, the type of product being purchased, and whether the purchase is new-task, modified rebuy, or straight rebuy. Negotiating styles of people vary within an organization and from one organization to another. To be effective, marketers must know customers well enough to be aware of these individual factors and their potential effects on purchase decisions.

Using Industrial Classification Systems

Marketers have access to a considerable amount of information about potential business customers, since much of this information is available through government and industry publications and websites. Marketers use this information to identify potential business customers and to estimate their purchase potential.

◆ Identifying Potential Business Customers

Standard Industrial Classification (SIC) system The federal government's system for classifying selected economic characteristics of industrial, commercial, financial, and service organizations

North American Industry Classification System (NAICS) An industry classification system that will generate comparable statistics among the United States, Canada, and Mexico

Much information about business customers is based on industrial classification systems. In the United States, marketers traditionally have relied on the **Standard Industrial Classification (SIC) system**, which the federal government developed to classify selected economic characteristics of industrial, commercial, financial, and service organizations. However, the SIC system is being replaced by a new industry classification system called the **North American Industry Classification System (NAICS)**. NAICS is a single industry classification system that all three NAFTA partners (the United States, Canada, and Mexico) will use to generate comparable statistics among all three countries. The NAICS classification is based on the types of production activities performed.[12] NAICS is similar to the International Standard Industrial Classification (ISIC) system used in Europe and many other parts of the world. Whereas the SIC system divides industrial activity into 10 divisions, NAICS divides it into 20 sectors. NAICS contains 1,172 industry classifications, compared with 1,004 in the SIC system. NAICS is more comprehensive and will be more up to date; all three countries have agreed to update it every five years. In addition, NAICS will provide considerably more information about service industries and high-tech products. A comparison of the SIC system and NAICS appears in Table 10.3. Over the next few years, all three NAFTA countries will convert from previously used industrial classification systems to NAICS.

Industrial classification systems are ready-made tools that allow marketers to divide organizations into groups based mainly on the types of goods and services provided. Although an industrial classification system is a vehicle for segmentation, it is most appropriately used in conjunction with other types of data to determine exactly how many and which customers a marketer can reach.

input-output data Information that identifies what types of industries purchase the products of a particular industry

Input-output analysis works well in conjunction with an industrial classification system. This type of analysis is based on the assumption that the output, or sales, of one industry are the input, or purchases, of other industries. **Input-output data** identify what types of industries purchase the products of a particular industry. A major source of national input-output data is the *Survey of Current Business*, published by the Office of Business Economics, U.S. Department of Commerce. After learning which industries purchase the major portion of an industry's output, the next step is to find the industrial classification numbers for those industries. Because firms are grouped differently in input-output tables and industrial classification systems, ascertaining industrial classification numbers can be difficult. However, the Office of Business Economics provides some limited conversion tables with input-output

Table 10.3	Comparison of the SIC System and NAICS for Manufacturers of Magnetic and Optical Media

SIC Hierarchy		NAICS Hierarchy	
Division D	Manufacturing	Sector 31–33	Manufacturing
Major Group 36	Manufacturers of electronic and other electrical equipment,except computer equipment	Subsector 334	Computer and electronic manufacturing
Industry Subgroup 369	Manufacturers of miscellaneous electrical machinery, equipment, and supplies	Industry Group 3346	Manufacturing and reproduction of magnetic and optical media
Detailed Industry 3695	Manufacturers of magnetic and optical recording media	Industry 33461	Manufacturing and reproduction of magnetic and optical media
		U.S. Industry 334611	U.S. specific—reproduction of software

Source: Copyright © 1998, Manufacturers' Agents National Association, 23016 Mill Creek Road, P.O. Box 3467, Laguna Hills, CA 92654-3467. Phone (949) 859-4040; fax (949) 855-2973. All rights reserved. Reproduction without permission is strictly prohibited.

data. These tables can help marketers assign classification numbers to industry categories used in input-output analysis.

After determining the classification numbers of industries that buy the firm's output, a marketer is in a position to ascertain the number of organizations that are potential buyers. Government sources, such as the *Census of Business,* the *Census of Manufacturers,* and *County Business Patterns,* report the number of establishments, the value of industry shipments, the number of employees, the percentage of imports and exports, and industry growth rates within classifications. Commercial sources also provide information about organizations categorized by industrial classifications.

A marketer can take several approaches to determine the identities and locations of organizations in specific groups. One approach is to use state directories or commercial industrial directories, such as *Standard & Poor's Register* and Dun & Bradstreet's *Million Dollar Directory.* These sources contain such information about a firm as its name, industrial classification, address, phone number, and annual sales. By referring to one or more of these sources, marketers isolate business customers with industrial classification numbers, determine their locations, and develop lists of potential customers by desired geographic area.

A more expedient, although more expensive, approach is to use a commercial data service. Dun & Bradstreet, for example, can provide a list of organizations that fall into a particular industrial classification group. For each company on the list, Dun & Bradstreet gives the name, location, sales volume, number of employees, type of products handled, names of chief executives, and other pertinent information. Either method can effectively identify and locate a group of potential customers. However, a marketer probably cannot pursue all organizations on the list. Because some companies have greater purchasing potential than others, marketers must determine which customer or customer group to pursue.

NET SIGHTS

The Thomas Register of Manufacturers (**www.thomasregister.com**) *is an online database of nearly 160,000 U.S. and Canadian manufacturers. This website allows quick searches by company name, product, or brand name. Results include links to company websites, fax-back literature, and online commerce when available. Registration is required and free.*

◆ Estimating Purchase Potential

To estimate the purchase potential of business customers or groups of customers, a marketer must find a relationship between the size of potential customers' purchases and a variable available in industrial classification data, such as the number of employees. For example, a paint manufacturer might attempt to determine the average number of gallons purchased by a specific type of potential customer relative to the number of employees. A marketer with no previous experience in this market segment will probably have to survey a random sample of potential customers to establish a relationship between purchase sizes and numbers of employees. Once this relationship is established, it can be applied to potential customer groups to estimate their purchases. After deriving these estimates, the marketer is in a position to select the customer groups with the most sales and profit potential.

Despite their usefulness, industrial classification data pose several problems. First, a few industries do not have specific designations. Second, because a transfer of products from one establishment to another is counted as a part of total shipments, double counting may occur when products are shipped between two establishments within the same firm. Third, because the Census Bureau is prohibited from providing data that identify specific business organizations, some data, such as value of total shipments, may be understated. Finally, because government agencies provide industrial classification data, a significant lag usually exists between data collection time and the time the information is released.

SUMMARY

Business markets consist of individuals and groups that purchase a specific kind of product for resale, direct use in producing other products, or use in day-to-day operations. Producer markets include those individuals and business organizations that purchase products for the purpose of making a profit by using them to produce other products or as part of their operations. Intermediaries that buy finished products and resell them to make a profit are classified as reseller markets. Government markets consist of federal, state, county, and local governments, which spend billions of dollars annually for goods and services to support internal operations and to provide citizens with needed services. Organizations with charitable, educational, community, or other not-for-profit goals constitute institutional markets.

Transactions involving business customers differ from consumer transactions in several ways. Such transactions tend to be larger, and negotiations occur less frequently, though they are often lengthy. They frequently involve more than one person or department in the purchasing organization. They may also involve reciprocity, an arrangement in which two organizations agree to buy from each other. Business customers are usually better informed than ultimate consumers and more likely to seek information about a product's features and technical specifications.

When purchasing products, business customers are particularly concerned about quality, service, and price. Quality is important because it directly affects the quality of products the buyer's firm produces. To achieve an exact level of quality, organizations often buy products on the basis of a set of expressed characteristics, called specifications. Because services have such a direct influence on a firm's costs, sales, and profits, factors such as market information, on-time delivery, and availability of parts are crucial to a business buyer. Although business customers do not depend solely on price to decide which products to buy, price is of primary concern because it directly influences profitability.

Business buyers use several purchasing methods, including description, inspection, sampling, and negotiation. Most organizational purchases are new-task, straight rebuy, or modified rebuy. In a new-task purchase, an organization makes an initial purchase of items to be used to perform new jobs or solve new problems. In a modified rebuy purchase, a new-task purchase is changed the second or third time it is ordered or requirements associated with a straight rebuy purchase are modified. A straight rebuy purchase occurs when a buyer purchases the same products routinely under approximately the same terms of sale.

Industrial demand differs from consumer demand along several dimensions. Industrial demand derives from demand for consumer products. At the industry level, industrial demand is inelastic. If an industrial item's price changes, product demand will not change as much proportionally. Some industrial products are subject to joint demand, which occurs when two or more items are used in combination to make a product. Finally, because organizational demand derives from consumer demand, the demand for business products can fluctuate widely.

Business (or organizational) buying behavior refers to the purchase behavior of producers, resellers, government units, and institutions. Business purchase decisions are made through a buying center, the group of people involved in making such purchase decisions. Users are those in the organization who actually use the product. Influencers help develop specifications and evaluate alternative products for possible use. Buyers select suppliers and negotiate purchase terms. Deciders choose the products. Gatekeepers control the flow of information to and among individuals occupying other roles in the buying center.

The stages of the business buying decision process are problem recognition, development of product specifications to solve problems, search for and evaluation of products and suppliers, selection and ordering of the most appropriate product, and evaluation of the product's and supplier's performance.

Four categories of factors influence business buying decisions: environmental, organizational, interpersonal, and individual. Environmental factors include political forces, laws and regulations, sociocultural factors, economic conditions, competitive forces, and technological changes. Business factors include the company's objectives, purchasing policies, and resources, as well as the size and composition of its buying center. Interpersonal factors are the relationships among people in the buying center. Individual factors are personal characteristics of members of the buying center, such as age, education,

personality, tenure, and position in the organization.

Business marketers have a considerable amount of information available for use in planning marketing strategies. Much of this information is based on an industrial classification system, which categorizes businesses into major industry groups, industry subgroups, and detailed industry categories. An industrial classification system provides marketers with information needed to identify business customer groups. Currently the United States is converting from the traditional SIC system to NAICS. It can best be used for this purpose in conjunction with other information, such as input-output data. After identifying target industries, a marketer can obtain the names and locations of potential customers by using government and commercial data sources. Marketers then must estimate potential purchases of business customers by finding a relationship between a potential customer's purchases and a variable available in industrial classification data.

 Please visit the student website at **www.prideferrell.com** for ACE Self-Test questions that will help you prepare for exams.

IMPORTANT TERMS

Business market
Producer markets
Reseller market
Government market
Institutional market
Reciprocity
New-task purchase
Straight rebuy purchase
Modified rebuy purchase
Derived demand
Inelastic demand
Joint demand
Business (organizational)
  buying behavior

Buying center
Value analysis
Vendor analysis
Multiple sourcing
Sole sourcing
Standard Industrial
  Classification (SIC)
  system
North American Industry
  Classification System
  (NAICS)
Input-output data

DISCUSSION & REVIEW QUESTIONS

1. Identify, describe, and give examples of the four major types of business markets.
2. Why might business customers generally be considered more rational in their purchasing behavior than ultimate consumers?
3. What are the primary concerns of business customers?
4. List several characteristics that differentiate transactions involving business customers from consumer transactions.

5. What are the commonly used methods of business buying?
6. Why do buyers involved in a straight rebuy purchase require less information than those making a new-task purchase?
7. How does demand for business products differ from consumer demand?
8. What are the major components of a firm's buying center?
9. Identify the stages of the business buying decision process. How is this decision process used when making straight rebuys?
10. How do environmental, business, interpersonal, and individual factors affect business purchases?
11. What function does an industrial classification system help marketers perform?
12. List some sources that a business marketer can use to determine the names and addresses of potential customers.

APPLICATION QUESTIONS

1. Identify organizations in your area that fit each business market category: producer, reseller, government, and institutional. Explain your classifications.
2. Indicate the method of buying (description, inspection, sampling, or negotiation) an organization would be most likely to use when purchasing each of the following items. Defend your selections.

a. A building for the home office of a light bulb manufacturer

b. Wool for a clothing manufacturer

c. An Alaskan cruise for a company retreat, assuming a regular travel agency is used

d. One-inch nails for a building contractor

3. Purchases by businesses may be described as new-task, modified rebuy, or straight rebuy. Categorize the following purchase decisions and explain your choices.

a. Bob has purchased toothpicks from Smith Restaurant Supply for 25 years and recently placed an order for yellow toothpicks rather than the usual white ones.

b. Jill's investment company has been purchasing envelopes from AAA Office Supply for a year and now needs to purchase boxes to mail year-end portfolio summaries to clients. Jill calls AAA to purchase these boxes.

c. Reliance Insurance has been supplying its salespeople with small personal computers to assist in their sales efforts. The company recently agreed to begin supplying them with faster, more sophisticated computers.

4. Identifying qualified customers is important to the survival of any organization. NAICS provides helpful information about many different businesses. Find the NAICS manual at the library and identify the NAICS code for the following items.

a. Chocolate candy bars

b. Automobile tires

c. Men's running shoes

Internet Exercise & Resources

Visit **www.prideferrell.com** for resources to help you master the material in this chapter, plus materials that will help you expand your marketing knowledge, including Internet exercise updates, ACE self-tests, hotlinks to companies featured in this chapter, and much more.

General Electric Company

General Electric Company is a highly diversified, global corporation with many divisions. GEPolymerland.com is the online site for GE's resins business. Visit the site at **www.GEPolymerland.com**.

1. At what types of business markets are GE's resin products targeted?
2. How does GEPolymerland address some of the concerns of business customers?
3. What environmental factors do you think affect demand for GE resin products?

Video Case 10.1

VIPdesk Brings Concierge Services to Business Markets

Imagine having a concierge on call to make restaurant reservations, obtain sports tickets, arrange for home repairs, or find that perfect gift—at any hour of the day. MasterCard's platinum cardholders have immediate access to round-the-clock concierge services through VIPdesk, a web-based business headed by CEO Mary Naylor. VIPdesk evolved from Naylor's years of experience providing on-site concierge services for the employees of corporations in major office complexes around metropolitan Washington, DC. Recognizing the opportunity to cost-effectively serve a wider corporate customer base through technology, Naylor established her first concierge website in 1996 and upgraded it to VIPdesk in 2000.

Today VIPdesk specializes in handling concierge services for 10 million users in two segments of the U.S. business market. Companies such as Van Kampen offer VIPdesk's services as a reward for outstanding employees. In addition, corporate clients such as MasterCard, Citibank, and JP Morgan arrange for VIPdesk to provide concierge services for their customers. For example, when MasterCard was planning the launch of its platinum World Card, management realized that VIPdesk's high-tech yet very personalized service would be a good way to help member banks differentiate the new credit card. Alice Droogan, vice president of worldwide cardholder services, notes that VIPdesk's services cost MasterCard "pennies a card, and as enhancements go, that's quite valuable." Seventeen financial institutions are using the service to attract new cardholders and reinforce cardholder loyalty, and Droogan expects demand to increase.

MasterCard is particularly enthusiastic about VIPdesk's flexibility in responding to just about any request rather than simply offering a limited menu of preset options. Although "most of the other companies we looked at were just basically travel assistance services," Droogan was impressed with VIPdesk's wider capabilities. Given the highly competitive environment in the credit card field, where MasterCard must battle Visa, American Express, Discover, and Diner's Club, VIPdesk is playing an important role because it helps MasterCard "support our initiatives to offer more services to our issuers," says Droogan.

Depending on her business customers' requirements, Naylor offers access to her company's services in many ways. Users can search the VIPdesk website for information, initiate a live text chat with a concierge, send e-mail messages requesting assistance, call to talk with a concierge, obtain customized information via web-enabled cellphones, or contact a concierge via a handheld computer such as a Palm. In addition to maintaining two call centers staffed with dozens of concierges, VIPdesk hires former hotel concierges to work part time from home during periods of peak demand. These part-timers bring an in-depth knowledge of local resources they can tap to satisfy requests from callers in their area.

The price that businesses pay depends on the level of service provided to their employees or customers. The least expensive level is Instant Answer, which gives users access to VIPdesk's website for basic services such as finding restaurant recommendations and arranging reservations. The next level is Quick Assist, which allows each user to submit a question and receive a prompt response from one of the concierges on staff. At the most expensive level, Full Concierge, users can communicate directly with a concierge to receive personalized attention for such requests as making travel plans and shopping for special gifts.

Regardless of the level or the specific request, all users get fast, free, professional help. "In effect, what we provide to the customer is a virtual personal assistant," CEO Naylor says.

Instead of paying for each use of VIPdesk's services, business customers pay a flat annual fee. This means companies can set a definite budget for the expense rather than worrying about being billed different amounts every month if usage varies. The price, says Naylor, may range "anywhere from $25 a person a year to as low as 25 cents per person per year." In exchange, the business customer benefits "by decommoditizing its products and extending the relationship well beyond the core products to the everyday life of the customer." Naylor adds, "It can cost less than a key chain or some token item that a corporation may give as a gift to a customer, and yet it keeps giving every day and keeps that brand identity in front of that end user."[13]

QUESTIONS FOR DISCUSSION

1. Are VIPdesk's business customers members of producer markets, reseller markets, government markets, or institutional markets?

2. What would be the primary concerns of a credit card company that is considering the use of VIPdesk's services for its cardholders? What is VIPdesk doing to address these concerns?

3. How might a credit card company use methods of description, inspection, sampling, and negotiation when making a buying decision about offering VIPdesk's services to its customers?

Case 10.2

WebMD Delivers Online Services to Health Care Providers

How do doctors, hospitals, pharmaceutical firms, laboratories, health insurers, pharmacies, and medical suppliers stay connected to deliver quality health care services to consumers? The divisions of WebMD (www.webmd.com) aim to provide the common connection. For physicians and clinics, WebMD Practice Services offers office management systems to manage appointments, handle billing, maintain patient files, and track insurance claims. These systems help medical practitioners streamline their office procedures for higher productivity. Doctors can also use WebMD Practice Services to access a patient's medical records, insurance coverage, and treatment options using handheld computers. This convenience not only saves time but allows the doctor to check patient information while the patient waits on the examination table and replaces reams of paperwork.

Each medical visit sparks a tidal wave of transactions among doctors, insurers, pharmacies, hospitals, laboratories, and others—an area where WebMD Envoy can bring expertise. As the market leader in electronic health care transaction processing, WebMD Envoy reduces paperwork by putting claims and payments in digital form, arranging online prescriptions, and transmitting laboratory test orders and reports. This service is especially important as the U.S. medical industry works to comply with federally mandated standards for electronic exchange of information.

WebMD Envoy was already processing 2.5 billion digital transactions annually before WebMD acquired Medifax-EDI, a company that checks a patient's health insurance coverage and determines eligibility for medical services. The combination makes WebMD Envoy a more powerful competitor, in part because Medifax-EDI's customer base, mainly hospitals and Medicaid providers, complements WebMD Envoy's customer base of doctors, dentists, and insurers. In addition, the combined company offers a much wider array of services and can therefore expedite processing of nearly any medical visit's administrative and financial details, from start to finish. Its business customers save a lot of money when they convert from manual to electronic claims processing. A doctor's office might spend up to $6 to process a claim by hand, but the cost drops below $1 when the office processes a claim electronically. WebMD's CEO estimates that customers pay an average of 21 cents for each digital transaction processed.

Every participant in the health care network needs timely medical information, especially patients and doctors. On the business side, health care professionals can use WebMD's Medscape website to obtain articles from medical journals, follow presentations at recent medical conferences, look up the latest medical developments, and take continuing medical education courses. More than 2 million medical professionals use this site to stay current in their areas of expertise. On the consumer side, WebMD Health is one of the best-known online sources of information about the latest medical breakthroughs, health news, specific diseases and conditions, support communities, and medical education. This popular website draws 20 million consumers every month and provides medical news to millions more through deals with America Online and other Internet portals.

Despite its promise, WebMD's high-tech strategy faces several challenges. First, the competition is becoming more intense. Rivals such as NDCHealth and ProxyMed are active in some of the same business markets WebMD serves. The company will feel even more pressure if IBM, Electronic Data Systems, and other giants start offering transaction and information

services to health care service providers.

Second, WebMD may wind up with lower transaction volumes or be forced to cut prices if health insurers choose to strengthen their ties with doctors by providing electronic transaction processing for free. The company will face similar threats if many hospitals and clinics create their own electronic processing systems rather than paying WebMD or other firms to handle digital transactions. Some hospitals have made the transition to software that connects their systems for processing purposes, sharply reducing the need for outside processing services. For example, Sharp HealthCare, based in California, now processes the majority of its claims through an internal system, although it still pays WebMD to handle a small number of transactions.

Third, health care providers are particularly interested in goods and services tailored to their specialties. However, they are reluctant to sign up for fee-based services, such as a monthly subscription for accessing medical information through a handheld device, unless they believe they will get a solid payback. They value short-term benefits such as improving productivity but also want to know they will enjoy long-term benefits that make the cost worthwhile. Therefore, as medical knowledge expands and government regulations evolve, WebMD will have to stay tuned to its customers' needs and priorities and add innovations to remain ahead of competitors.[14]

QUESTIONS FOR DISCUSSION

1. Which of the environmental influences that can affect the business buying process are creating opportunities for WebMD?
2. Which of the organizational influences that can affect the business buying process could pose threats for WebMD?
3. Would a customer that prefers multiple sourcing welcome WebMD's acquisition of Medifax-EDI if the customer previously contracted for services from both companies? Explain.

Strategic Case 4

Reebok Races into the Urban Market

Reebok wants to give front-runner Nike a run for its money in the race for market share in athletic footwear, apparel, and equipment. Reebok, based in Canton, Massachusetts, gained speed from the 1980s into the early 1990s by marketing special aerobics shoes for women. Then Nike pulled way ahead with new clothing and equipment endorsed by high-profile athletes such as Michael Jordan and Tiger Woods. Nike has remained the market leader, completely outdistancing all competitors to dominate the industry with $10.7 billion in annual sales and a 35 percent share of the U.S. sportswear market.

In contrast, Reebok's U.S. market share is about one-half that of Nike, and its $3.5 billion in annual sales is about one-third of Nike's. Now Reebok is seeking to close the distance by changing its selection of target markets. In the process, it is aiming to change consumers' perceptions of and attitudes toward its brand and its products with the objective of boosting both sales and profits.

Breaking Tradition with Hip-Hop Traditionally sneaker manufacturers have captured market attention by signing successful or fast-rising sports stars to promote their shoes.

Reebok still likes to link its brand to popular sports. Its multimillion-dollar contract with basketball's Yao Ming is one of the industry's most expensive deals, and it has many other sports figures under contract, including tennis star Venus Williams. The fierce rivalry with Nike continues on the playing field. Reebok has lucrative contracts to make branded hats for the National Basketball Association and to supply the National Football League with uniforms and equipment. Nike has an exclusive contract to provide performance apparel to all 30 major league baseball teams.

Looking beyond sports, Reebok's marketers investigated the urban market, where fashion rather than performance is the deciding factor in buying decisions. Urban teens tend to be extremely style conscious, buying as many as ten pairs of athletic-style shoes a year so they can be seen in the very latest thing. Many are also fans of hip-hop music and buy clothing designed by hip-hop celebrities such as Jay-Z, Sean "P. Diddy" Combs, and Russell Simmons.

Reebok's marketing research confirmed this market's considerable buying power and the influence of hip-hop artists. To effectively reach this market, Reebok needed a new brand, new products, and new promotional efforts. First, the company took the focus off its mainstream Reebok brand by creating Rbk as a new brand specifically for the urban market. Next, it partnered with hip-hop artists such as Jay-Z and 50 Cent to develop special footwear collections, backed by targeted promotional efforts emphasizing style with attitude.

New Street Credibility   Reebok found it was tapping into a significant market opportunity. Right after Reebok introduced soft-leather, flat-soled S. Carter shoes (after Jay-Z's original name, Shawn Carter), the line sold out. Demand for the $100 shoes quickly spiked so high that eager buyers bid up to $250 for one pair on the eBay auction site. Within eight months, the company had shipped 500,000 pairs to retailers around the country and was preparing to launch a second S. Carter shoe.

On the heels of this success, Reebok introduced G-Unit footwear, named after a hit song by the rapper 50 Cent, who says, "Reebok's Rbk Collection is the real thing when it comes to connecting with the street and hip-hop culture." Hip-hop's Eve was also asked to design a shoe. "She is one of the first artists in the campaign who has male and female appeal, urban and suburban," observes Reebok's director of global advertising. "She is as much a fashion icon as a music icon."

Moreover, the company found a way to bring sports and hip-hop together by launching the 13 Collection line of shoes by basketball star Allen Iverson. Iverson promoted the line by appearing in a series of fast-paced commercials filmed in rap-video style. Although he was shown playing basketball for a second or two, the commercials focused more on his off-court style than his on-court technique.

Despite the added credibility that such celebrities bring to the Rbk brand, the strategy entails some risks. Fads in street fashion and music can come and go at a dizzying pace, which means a shoe that is red-hot one day may be ice-cold the next. Moreover, Reebok could feel the repercussions if one of its celebrities gets into trouble. Still, the company's chief marketing officer is committed to the strategy. "With athletes, they wear the shoes for the length of a basketball season," he comments. "With hip-hop, the publicity is intense but short, just like movies." The advantage, he says, is that "You'll know very quickly whether you hit or miss."

Targeting Urban Markets in China   In pursuit of growth, Reebok is also targeting promising global markets. China is high on its list of priorities. Interest in sports is skyrocketing there, thanks in part to Chinese basketball star Yao Ming's move to the NBA. According to company research, 93 percent of Chinese males ages 13 to 25—a prime market for athletic shoes—watch NBA broadcasts on a regular basis. Reebok's Asia Pacific general manager cites one projection showing 50 percent annual growth in footwear sales. His prediction: "It's hard to say what the [actual sales] numbers are going to be, but they are going to be huge."

To make the most of this opportunity, Reebok has set up "Yao's House" basketball courts around central Shanghai. Each features the Reebok trademark and a giant *Sports Illustrated* cover showing the basketball star. By giving teens and young adults a place to hone their slam-dunks, Reebok hopes to shape their attitudes toward its products. "The trends are made in the urban areas and on street basketball courts, just like in the United States," says one Reebok executive.

Reebok is not the only athletic-shoe manufacturer entering this market. Nike sponsors a basketball court in Beijing, New Balance is building awareness of its shoes, and Pony is selling sneakers in Beijing, Shanghai, and Guandong. With the Summer Olympics coming to Beijing in 2008, sports fever is likely to spread throughout the major cities.

Reebok's New Vector   Nike has its Swoosh, one of the most recognized trademarks in the world. Now Reebok has its Vector, a streamlined trademark designed to communicate the brand's attributes in a fast, fun way. The idea is to make the Vector synonymous with Reebok, just as the Swoosh is synonymous with Nike. "Our research suggests that consumers react better to logos than words, and it's a very effective marketing tool," stresses Reebok's head of marketing.

In addition, the company is giving its brand a touch of glamour with showcase stores in major U.S. cities. In New York City, for example, Reebok opened a new men's store right next to its women's store. Both feature footwear, apparel, and accessories, and both share the building with the Reebok Sport Club/NY. The displays are as stylish as the products, showing a mix of cashmere sweaters, varsity jackets, wristwatches, and sunglasses along with shoes. "We want people to say, 'I didn't know Reebok made that,'" notes Reebok's vice president of retail. CEO Paul Fireman sums things up as follows: "The ultimate thing we are striving for is not brand recognition, but how people perceive us."

QUESTIONS FOR DISCUSSION

1. What segmentation variables is Reebok using for its products? Why are these variables appropriate?
2. Which of the three targeting strategies is Reebok applying? Explain.
3. What influences on the consumer buying decision process appear to have the most impact on Reebok's customers' purchase decisions?
4. In terms of segmentation and buying behavior, explain the meaning of this statement by a Reebok executive: "The trends are made in the urban areas and on street basketball courts, just like in the United States."

Part Five

Product Decisions

We are now prepared to analyze the decisions and activities associated with developing and maintaining effective marketing mixes. In Parts Five through Eight, we focus on the major components of the marketing mix: product, distribution, promotion, and price. **Part Five** explores the product component of the marketing mix. **Chapter 11** introduces basic concepts and relationships that must be understood to make effective product decisions. **Chapter 12** analyzes a variety of dimensions regarding product management, including line extensions and product modification, new-product development, and product deletions. **Chapter 13** discusses branding, packaging, and labeling. **Chapter 14** explores the nature, importance, and characteristics of services.

11

Product Concepts

OBJECTIVES

1. To understand the concept of a product

2. To explain how to classify products

3. To examine the concepts of product item, product line, and product mix and understand how they are connected

4. To understand the product life cycle and its impact on marketing strategies

5. To describe the product adoption process

6. To understand why some products fail and some succeed

McGriddle Sweetens Breakfast Sales at McDonald's

Move over, Egg McMuffin—McDonald's has a second breakfast sandwich for the fast-food crowd. The McGriddle consists of two soft, maple-flavored griddle cakes wrapped around a center of sausage, sausage plus egg and cheese, or bacon plus egg and cheese. Why expand the morning menu when the savory Egg McMuffin has been successful since 1973? "We found that there was a real demand for sweeter breakfast foods," says Gerald Tomlinson, McDonald's executive chef. Responding to this research, Tomlinson came up with the idea of combining the sweet taste of pancakes with the salty taste of sausage or bacon. He knew that any new menu item would have to be as convenient as the Egg McMuffin to accommodate McDonald's customers who buy breakfast at the drive-through window and eat on the go. The new sandwich would also have to be fast to prepare in keeping with the chain's goal of serving customers quickly.

The challenge was to translate any sandwich concept into an actual breakfast food. Initially Tomlinson considered stirring specks of sausage into pancake batter baked in a muffin tin. He saw two problems, however. First, would McDonald's customers be confused by pancakes in the form of muffins? Second, how could the sandwich contain maple syrup without being too sticky for one-hand nibbling? Tomlinson and his team kept experimenting. After rejecting the muffin-shaped product, he tested a sandwich of flat, round pancakes with a sausage filling and syrup topping. Customers would recognize the pancake shape, but the sandwich proved too messy for easy eating.

Finally, the executive chef invited some of the company's suppliers to a new-product meeting and explained what he wanted to do. Coincidentally, one supplier had recently developed a method of turning syrup into crystals that could be stirred into batter. As the batter heated on the griddle, the syrup crystals would infuse the pancake with maple flavor. The process seemed straightforward but actually required many tests and adjustments to perfect the right ingredients in the right proportions. To make the new product look appealing, Tomlinson's team pinpointed the exact time needed to grill the sandwich until golden brown.

Before introducing the McGriddle in all its U.S. restaurants, McDonald's tested the new sandwich in parts of Ohio, Texas, California, and New York. Customer response was so positive that after only a few weeks the company launched the McGriddle nationwide with an advertising campaign describing it as "bizarre but yummy." The taste combination intrigued customers who were tired of the usual breakfast routine and boosted both sales and profits. "We're actually growing the category instead of simply engaging in a share war," observes a McDonald's executive.[1] ■

The product is an important variable in the marketing mix. Products such as the McGriddle can be a firm's most important asset. If a company's products do not meet customers' desires and needs, the firm will fail unless it makes adjustments. Developing successful products such as the McGriddle requires knowledge of fundamental marketing and product concepts.

In this chapter, we first define *product* and discuss how buyers view products. Next, we examine the concepts of product line and product mix. We then explore the stages of the product life cycle and the effect of each life cycle stage on marketing strategies. Next, we outline the product adoption process. Finally, we discuss the factors that contribute to a product's failure or success.

What Is a Product?

good A tangible physical entity

service An intangible result of the application of human and mechanical efforts to people or objects

idea A concept, philosophy, image, or issue

As defined in Chapter 1, a *product* is a good, a service, or an idea received in an exchange. It can be either tangible or intangible and includes functional, social, and psychological utilities or benefits. It also includes supporting services, such as installation, guarantees, product information, and promises of repair or maintenance. Thus, the 5-year/60,000-mile warranty that covers most new automobiles is part of the product itself. A **good** is a tangible physical entity, such as a Dell personal computer or a Subway sandwich. A **service**, in contrast, is intangible; it is the result of the application of human and mechanical efforts to people or objects. Examples of services include a performance by Britney Spears, online travel agencies, medical examinations, child day care, real estate services, and martial arts lessons. (Chapter 14 provides a detailed discussion of services.) An **idea** is a concept, philosophy, image, or issue. Ideas provide the psychological stimulation that aids in solving problems or adjusting to the environment. For example, MADD (Mothers Against Drunk Driving) promotes safe consumption of alcohol and stricter enforcement of laws against drunk driving.

What Is a Product?
A product can be a good, a service, or an idea. The entertainment events provided by athletic teams, such as the Washington Wild Things in Washington, Pennsylvania, are services. Similarly, the Central Philadelphia Transportation Management Association is marketing the service of public transportation.

When buyers purchase a product, they are really buying the benefits and satisfaction they think the product will provide. A Rolex watch, for example, is purchased to make a statement of success, not just for telling time. Services in particular are purchased on the basis of expectations. Expectations, suggested by images, promises, and symbols, as well as processes and delivery, help consumers make judgments about tangible and intangible products. Products are formed by the activities and processes that help satisfy expectations. CNN, for example, did not invent network news, but it did make national and international news available worldwide 24 hours a day. Likewise, Starbucks did not originate the coffee shop, but it did develop standardized and inviting stores with high-quality coffee beverages that became a stylish way to enjoy what traditionally was a commodity product.[2] Often symbols and cues are used to make intangible products more tangible, or real, to the consumer. Allstate Insurance Company, for example, uses giant hands to symbolize security, strength, and friendliness.

Classifying Products

consumer products Products purchased to satisfy personal and family needs

business products Products bought to use in an organization's operations, to resell, or to make other products

Products fall into one of two general categories. Products purchased to satisfy personal and family needs are **consumer products**. Products bought to use in a firm's operations, to resell, or to make other products are **business products**. Consumers buy products to satisfy their personal wants, whereas business buyers seek to satisfy the goals of their organizations.

The same item can be both a consumer product and a business product. For example, when a consumer buys a 100-watt light bulb for lighting a closet, it is classified as a consumer product. However, when an organization purchases a 100-watt light bulb for lighting a reception area, it is considered a business product because it is used in daily operations. Thus, the buyer's intent—or the ultimate use of the product—determines whether an item is classified as a consumer or business product.

Product classifications are important because classes of products are aimed at particular target markets, which affects distribution, promotion, and pricing decisions. Furthermore, appropriate marketing strategies vary among the classes of consumer and business products. In short, how a product is classified can affect the entire marketing mix. In this section, we examine the characteristics of consumer and business products and explore the marketing activities associated with some of these products.

◆ Consumer Products

The most widely accepted approach to classifying consumer products is based on characteristics of consumer buying behavior. It divides products into four categories: convenience, shopping, specialty, and unsought products. However, not all buyers behave in the same way when purchasing a specific type of product. Thus, a single product can fit into several categories. To minimize this problem, marketers think in terms of how buyers *generally* behave when purchasing a specific item. In addition, they recognize that the "correct" classification can be determined only by considering a particular firm's intended target market. Examining the four traditional categories of consumer products can provide further insight.

convenience products Relatively inexpensive, frequently purchased items for which buyers exert minimal purchasing effort

Convenience Products. **Convenience products** are relatively inexpensive, frequently purchased items for which buyers exert only minimal purchasing effort. They range from bread, soft drinks, and chewing gum to gasoline and newspapers. The buyer spends little time planning the purchase or comparing available brands or sellers. Even a buyer who prefers a specific brand will readily choose a substitute if the preferred brand is not conveniently available.

Causes separation anxiety
in furniture delivery guys.

The Byron Chair

L A Z B O Y
The new look of comfort

©2003 La-Z-Boy Incorporated www.lazboy.com

Convenience and Shopping Products

Most consumer cleaning products, such as CLOROX® READYMOP®, are convenience products. Most consumer furniture products, such as the La-Z-Boy chair, are shopping products.

shopping products Items for which buyers are willing to expend considerable effort in planning and making purchases

Classifying a product as a convenience product has several implications for a firm's marketing strategy. A convenience product is normally marketed through many retail outlets. Because sellers experience high inventory turnover, per-unit gross margins can be relatively low. Producers of convenience products, such as Altoid mints, expect little promotional effort at the retail level and thus must provide it themselves with advertising and sales promotion. Packaging is also an important element of the marketing mix for convenience products. The package may have to sell the product because many convenience items are available only on a self-service basis at the retail level.

Shopping Products. **Shopping products** are items for which buyers are willing to expend considerable effort in planning and making the purchase. Buyers spend much time comparing stores and brands with respect to prices, product features, qualities, services, and perhaps warranties. Appliances, bicycles, furniture, stereos, cameras, and shoes exemplify shopping products. These products are expected to last a fairly long time and thus are purchased less frequently than convenience items. Although shopping products are more expensive than convenience products, few buyers of shopping products are particularly brand loyal. Most consumers, for example, are not brand loyal for computers and clothing. If they were, they would be unwilling to shop and compare among brands. Even when they are brand loyal, they may still spend considerable time comparing the features of different models of a brand. A consumer looking for a new Maytag washing machine, for example, may explore the company's website to compare the features of different washers before talking to a salesperson. Regardless of the number of brands of interest, buyers may also consult buying guides such as *Consumer Reports* or visit consumer information websites such as opinions.com to view others' opinions or ratings of brands and models before making an actual purchase.

To market a shopping product effectively, a marketer considers several key issues. Shopping products require fewer retail outlets than convenience products. Because shopping products are purchased less frequently, inventory turnover is lower, and marketing channel members expect to receive higher gross margins. Although large sums of money may be required to advertise shopping products, an even larger percentage of resources is likely to be used for personal selling. Usually the producer and the marketing channel members expect some cooperation from one another with respect to providing parts and repair services and performing promotional activities.

specialty products Items with unique characteristics that buyers are willing to expend considerable effort to obtain

Specialty Products. **Specialty products** possess one or more unique characteristics, and generally buyers are willing to expend considerable effort to obtain them. Buyers actually plan the purchase of a specialty product; they know exactly what they want and will not accept a substitute. Examples of specialty products include a Mont Blanc pen and a one-of-a-kind piece of baseball memorabilia, such as a ball signed by Babe Ruth. When searching for specialty products, buyers do not compare alternatives; they are concerned primarily with finding an outlet that has the preselected product available. Bentley automobiles, for example, are very expensive, ranging from $215,000 to $360,000. Suppose a Bentley dealer invites a prospective buyer to test-drive a vehicle at a racetrack. If the prospect decides to make a purchase, he or she has a Bentley "personally commissioned" and typically flies to the automaker's plant in Crewe, England, to observe its manufacture.[3]

The fact that an item is a specialty product can affect a firm's marketing efforts in several ways. Specialty products are often distributed through a limited number of retail outlets. Like shopping products, they are purchased infrequently, causing lower inventory turnover and thus requiring relatively high gross margins.

unsought products Products purchased to solve a sudden problem, products of which customers are unaware, and products that people do not necessarily think of buying

Unsought Products. **Unsought products** are products purchased when a sudden problem must be solved, products of which customers are unaware, and products that people do not necessarily think of purchasing. Emergency medical services and automobile repairs are examples of products needed quickly to solve a problem. A consumer who is sick or injured has little time to plan to go to an emergency medical center or a hospital. Likewise, in the event of a broken fan belt on the highway, a consumer will likely seek out the nearest auto repair facility to get back on the road as quickly as possible. In such cases, speed and problem resolution are far more important than price and other features buyers might consider if they had more time for decision making.

◆ **Business Products**

Business products are usually purchased on the basis of an organization's goals and objectives. Generally the functional aspects of the product are more important than the psychological rewards sometimes associated with consumer products. Business products can be classified into seven categories according to their characteristics and intended uses: installations, accessory equipment, raw materials, component parts, process materials, MRO supplies, and business services.

installations Facilities and nonportable major equipment

Installations. **Installations** include facilities, such as office buildings, factories, and warehouses, and major equipment that is nonportable, such as production lines and very large machines. Major equipment usually is used for production purposes. Some major equipment is custom made to perform specific functions for a particular organization; other items are standardized and perform similar tasks for many types of firms. Normally installations are expensive and intended to be used for a considerable length of time. Because they are so expensive and typically involve a long-term investment of capital, purchase decisions are often made by high-level management. Marketers of installations frequently must provide a variety of services, including training, repairs, maintenance assistance, and even financial assistance.

accessory equipment Equipment used in production or office activities that does not become a part of the final physical product but is used in production or office activities

Accessory Equipment. **Accessory equipment** does not become a part of the final physical product but is used in production or office activities. Examples include file cabinets, fractional-horsepower motors, calculators, and tools. Compared with major equipment, accessory items are usually much cheaper, purchased routinely with less negotiation, and treated as expense items rather than capital items because they are not expected to last as long. Accessory products are standardized items that can be used in several aspects of a firm's operations. More outlets are required for distributing accessory equipment than for installations, but sellers do not have to provide the numerous services expected of installations marketers.

raw materials Basic natural materials that become part of a physical product

Raw Materials. **Raw materials** are the basic natural materials that actually become part of a physical product. They include minerals, chemicals, agricultural products, and materials from forests and oceans. They are usually bought and sold according to grades and specifications, and in relatively large quantities. Rose oil and jasmine are examples of raw materials in making perfume.

component parts Items that become part of the physical product and are either finished items ready for assembly or items that need little processing before assembly

Component Parts. **Component parts** become a part of the physical product and are either finished items ready for assembly or products that need little processing before assembly. Although they become part of a larger product, component parts often can be easily identified and distinguished. Spark plugs, tires, clocks, and switches are all component parts of an automobile. Buyers purchase such items according to their own specifications or industry standards. They expect the parts to be of specified quality and delivered on time so that production is not slowed or stopped. Producers that are primarily assemblers, such as most lawn mower and computer manufacturers, depend heavily on suppliers of component parts.

Business Products
A vise, such as the one shown here, is classified as accessory equipment since it would be used in the production of other goods. The botanicals promoted in the Bioland advertisement are process materials since they would be mixed with other ingredients to make skin care products.

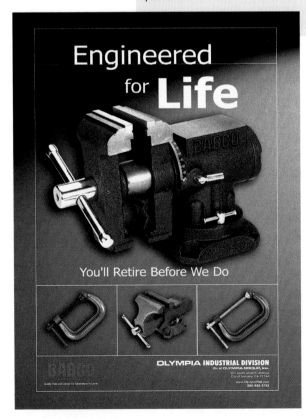

process materials Materials that are used directly in the production of other products but are not readily identifiable

MRO supplies Maintenance, repair, and operating items that facilitate production and operations but do not become part of the finished product

business services Intangible products that many organizations use in their operations

Process Materials. **Process materials** are used directly in the production of other products. Unlike component parts, however, process materials are not readily identifiable. For example, a salad dressing manufacturer includes vinegar in its salad dressing. The vinegar is a process material because it is included in the salad dressing but is not identifiable. As with component parts, process materials are purchased according to industry standards or the purchaser's specifications.

MRO Supplies. **MRO supplies** are maintenance, repair, and operating items that facilitate production and operations but do not become part of the finished product. Paper, pencils, oils, cleaning agents, and paints are in this category. MRO supplies are commonly sold through numerous outlets and are purchased routinely. To ensure supplies are available when needed, buyers often deal with more than one seller.

Business Services. **Business services** are the intangible products that many organizations use in their operations. They include financial, legal, marketing research, information technology, and janitorial services. Firms must decide whether to provide their own services internally or obtain them from outside the organization. This decision depends on the costs associated with each alternative and how frequently the services are needed.

Product Line and Product Mix

product item A specific version of a product

product line A group of closely related product items viewed as a unit because of marketing, technical, or end-use considerations

Marketers must understand the relationships among all the products of their organization to coordinate the marketing of the total group of products. The following concepts help describe the relationships among an organization's products.

A **product item** is a specific version of a product that can be designated as a distinct offering among an organization's products. An L. L. Bean flannel shirt represents a product item. A **product line** is a group of closely related product items that are considered to be a unit because of marketing, technical, or end-use considerations. For example, there are 9 kinds of Kleenex tissue, 16 flavors of Eggo waffles, and 19 varieties of Colgate toothpaste. Each year more than 31,000 new consumer products come out with multiple items for almost every product line.[4] The exact boundaries of a product line (although sometimes blurred) are usually indicated by using descriptive terms such as "frozen dessert" product line or "shampoo" product line. To come up with the optimal product line, marketers must understand buyers' goals. In the personal computer industry, for example, companies are likely to expand their product lines when industry barriers are low or perceived market opportunities exist. Firms with high market share are likely to expand their product lines aggressively, as are marketers with relatively high prices or limited product lines.[5] Specific product items in a product line usually reflect the desires of different target markets or the different needs of consumers.

Product Line
Shoe care products and shoe laces represent two of the product lines offered by Penguin.

Laundry detergents	Toothpastes	Bar soaps	Deodorants	Shampoos	Tissue/Towel
Ivory Snow 1930	Gleem 1952	Ivory 1879	Old Spice 1948	Pantene 1947	Charmin 1928
Dreft 1933	Crest 1955	Camay 1926	Secret 1956	Head & Shoulders 1961	Puffs 1960
Tide 1946		Zest 1952	Sure 1972	Vidal Sassoon 1974	Bounty 1965
Cheer 1950		Safeguard 1963		Pert Plus 1979	
Bold 1965		Oil of Olay 1993		Ivory 1983	
Gain 1966				Infusium 23 1986	
Era 1972				Physique 2000	
Febreze Clean Wash 2000				Herbal Essence 2001	

Depth

Width

Figure 11.1 The Concepts of Product Mix Width and Depth Applied to Selected United States Procter & Gamble Products   *Source:* Reprinted by permission of The Procter and Gamble Company.

product mix The total group of products that an organization makes available to customers

width of product mix The number of product lines a company offers

depth of product mix The average number of different products offered in each product line

A **product mix** is the composite, or total, group of products that an organization makes available to customers. For example, all the health care, beauty care, laundry and cleaning, food and beverage, paper, cosmetic, and fragrance products that Procter & Gamble manufactures constitute its product mix. The **width of product mix** is measured by the number of product lines a company offers. For example, Coleman recently widened its product mix beyond camping lanterns and stoves by introducing a new line of gas grills—in green, the brand's signature color—for backyard use.[6] The **depth of product mix** is the average number of different products offered in each product line. Figure 11.1 shows the width and depth of a part of Procter & Gamble's product mix. Procter & Gamble is known for using distinctive branding, packaging, and consumer advertising to promote individual items in its detergent product line. Tide, Bold, Gain, Cheer, and Era—all Procter & Gamble detergents—share the same distribution channels and similar manufacturing facilities, but each is promoted as a distinctive product, adding depth to the product line.

Product Life Cycles and Marketing Strategies

product life cycle The progression of a product through four stages: introduction, growth, maturity, and decline

Just as biological cycles progress from birth through growth and decline, so do product life cycles. As Figure 11.2 shows, a **product life cycle** has four major stages: introduction, growth, maturity, and decline. As a product moves through its life cycle, the strategies relating to competition, promotion, distribution, pricing, and market information must be periodically evaluated and possibly changed. Astute marketing managers use the life cycle concept to make sure the introduction, alteration, and termination of a product are timed and executed properly. By understanding the typical life cycle pattern, marketers are better able to maintain profitable products and drop unprofitable ones.

◆ Introduction

introduction stage The initial stage of a product's life cycle; its first appearance in the marketplace when sales start at zero and profits are negative

The **introduction stage** of the product life cycle begins at a product's first appearance in the marketplace, when sales start at zero and profits are negative. Profits are below zero because initial revenues are low, and the company generally must cover large expenses for promotion and distribution. Notice in Figure 11.2 how sales should move upward from zero, and profits should also move upward from a position in which they are negative because of high expenses.

Figure 11.2 The Four Stages of the Product Life Cycle

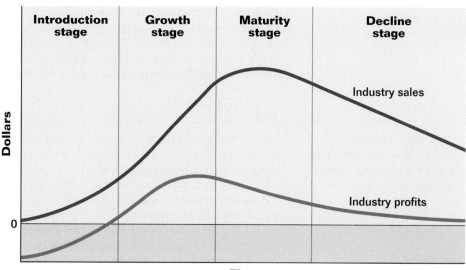

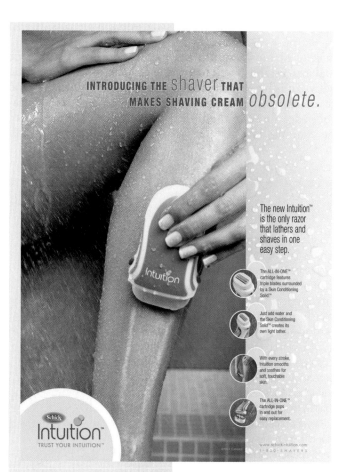

INTRODUCING THE *shaver* THAT MAKES SHAVING CREAM *obsolete.*

The new Intuition™ is the only razor that lathers and shaves in one easy step.

The ALL-IN-ONE™ cartridge features triple blades surrounded by a Skin Conditioning Solid.™

Just add water and the Skin Conditioning Solid™ creates its own light lather.

With every stroke, Intuition smooths and soothes for soft, touchable skin.

The ALL-IN-ONE™ cartridge pops in and out for easy replacement.

Schick Intuition™
TRUST YOUR INTUITION™

www.schickintuition.com
1-800-SHAVERS

Introduction Stage
The Schick Intuition all-in-one shaver is the first shaving instrument that combines lathering and shaving in one step. This new product category is in the introduction stage of the product life cycle.

Developing and introducing a new product can mean an outlay of $100 million or more. Colgate-Palmolive derives 38 percent of its global revenues from products introduced within the last five years. For revenues from the U.S. market, the figure is even higher: 61 percent.[7] Although the importance of new products is significant, the risk of new-product failure is quite high, depending on the industry. For example, Polaroid Corporation was forced into bankruptcy protection for more than a year after repeated new-product offerings failed to replace its outdated instant-photography camera.[8] Because of high risks and costs, few product introductions represent revolutionary inventions. More typically, product introductions involve a new packaged convenience food, a new model of automobile, or a new fashion in clothing rather than a major product innovation. The more marketing oriented the firm, the more likely it will be to launch innovative, new-to-the-market products.[9]

Potential buyers must be made aware of the new product's features, uses, and advantages. Two difficulties may arise at this point. First, sellers may lack the resources, technological knowledge, and marketing know-how to launch the product successfully. Second, the initial product price may have to be high to recoup expensive marketing research or development costs. Given these difficulties, it is not surprising that many products never get beyond the introduction stage.

Most new products start off slowly and seldom generate enough sales to bring immediate profits.

NET SIGHTS

Founded in 1976, the Product Development & Management Association (PDMA) is a nonprofit organization of product developers, academics, and service providers dedicated to the support of product development research. PDMA sponsors an annual international conference on new-product development, highlighting the latest academic research, and offers members several publications devoted to product innovation. Many of these publications and other information related to new-product development and management are available on the organization's website at **www.pdma.org.**

As buyers learn about the new product, marketers should be alert for product weaknesses and make corrections quickly to prevent the product's early demise. Marketing strategy should be designed to attract the segment that is most interested in the product and has the fewest objections. As the sales curve moves upward and the break-even point is reached, the growth stage begins.

◆ Growth

growth stage The product life cycle stage when sales rise rapidly and profits reach a peak, then start to decline

During the **growth stage**, sales rise rapidly and profits reach a peak, then start to decline (see Figure 11.2). The growth stage is critical to a product's survival because competitive reactions to the product's success during this period will affect the product's life expectancy. For example, Palm successfully marketed the first personal digital assistant (PDA), the PalmPilot, but today competes against numerous other brands such as Handspring, Casio, and Hewlett-Packard.

Profits begin to decline late in the growth stage as more competitors enter the market, driving prices down and creating the need for heavy promotional expenses. At this point, a typical marketing strategy encourages strong brand loyalty and competes with aggressive emulators of the product. During the growth stage, the organization tries to strengthen its market share and develop a competitive niche by emphasizing the product's benefits. Aggressive pricing, including price cuts, is also typical during this stage.

As sales increase, management must support the momentum by adjusting the marketing strategy. The goal is to establish and fortify the product's market position by encouraging brand loyalty. To achieve greater market penetration, segmentation may have to be used more intensely. That would require developing product variations to satisfy the needs of people in several different market segments. Be sure to read about the cell phone example in the Tech Know boxed feature. Palm, for

TECH KNOW

Nokia: Phone Fun and Games

Calling all game players: Nokia's N-Gage multifunction cellphone packs a lot of fun into one small handset. Users can make phone calls and send text messages, but the main attraction is the phone's ability to play popular video games such as *Tomb Raider* and *Tony Hawk's Pro Skater,* alone or with other players. Adding to the appeal, the N-Gage can play MP3 music files and pick up FM radio signals.

What is Finland's Nokia, the leader in mobile communications, doing in the video game market? The company commands 39 percent of the global market and sells 170 million handsets annually. However, it is facing more competition as Asian and U.S. manufacturers launch a steady stream of new handsets. This rivalry has driven down handset prices and profits, prompting Nokia to expand into video games for future growth. The $30 billion video game industry is largely driven by demand from teenagers and young adults, a key segment of the cellphone market.

The N-Gage takes phone-based gaming to an entirely new level. Earlier, users were limited to downloading basic games (for a small fee) from mobile phone carriers. In contrast, the Nokia phone is equipped to run more sophisticated 3D video games stored on memory cards. Users simply switch memory cards when they want to play a different game. Perhaps the biggest innovation is the option for multiplayer gaming. The N-Gage incorporates Bluetooth wireless communication, allowing people in one room to play against each other. It also serves as a gateway to the Nokia Game, a website where thousands of people register to play interactively and win prizes. During the introduction of the N-Gage, Nokia started the Nokia Game, an annual multimedia gaming challenge that attracted 1 million players in 25 countries. Players raced to complete the game by checking for clues on the website, in text messages, in newspapers, and in other media. The prize: next-generation Nokia phones, of course.

Now Nokia must keep the momentum going as it pits the N-Gage against two formidable opponents in the video game world, Nintendo's Game Boy and Sony's PlayStation Portable. Can Nokia keep the fun and games rolling?

example, markets many versions of its PalmPilot personal digital assistant, as well as related software and accessories, to satisfy different customer groups. Marketers should also analyze competing brands' product positions relative to their own brands and take corrective actions.

Gaps in geographic market coverage should be filled during the growth period. As a product gains market acceptance, new distribution outlets usually become easier to obtain. Marketers sometimes move from an exclusive or a selective exposure to a more intensive network of dealers to achieve greater market penetration. Marketers must also make sure the physical distribution system is running efficiently so that customers' orders are processed accurately and delivered on time.

Promotion expenditures may be slightly lower than during the introductory stage, but are still quite substantial. As sales increase, promotion costs should drop as a percentage of total sales. A falling ratio between promotion expenditures and sales should contribute significantly to increased profits. The advertising messages should stress brand benefits. Coupons and samples may be used to increase market share.

After recovering development costs, a business may be able to lower prices. As sales volume increases, efficiencies in production can result in lower costs. These savings may be passed on to buyers. For example, when satellite navigation systems for cars were initially introduced, the price was $5,000 or more. As demand soared, manufacturers were able to take advantage of economies of scale to reduce production costs and lower prices to less than $2,000 within several years.[10] If demand remains strong and there are few competitive threats, prices tend to remain stable. If price cuts are feasible, they can help a brand gain market share and discourage new competitors from entering the market.

◆ Maturity

maturity stage The stage of a product's life cycle when the sales curve peaks and starts to decline, and profits continue to fall

During the **maturity stage**, the sales curve peaks and starts to decline and profits continue to fall (see Figure 11.2). This stage is characterized by intense competition, as many brands are now in the market. Competitors emphasize improvements and differences in their versions of the product. As a result, during the maturity stage, weaker competitors are squeezed out or lose interest in the product. For example, some brands of DVDs will perish as the DVD reaches the maturity stage.

During the maturity phase, the producers who remain in the market are likely to change their promotional and distribution efforts. Advertising and dealer-oriented promotions are typical during this stage of the product life cycle. Marketers must also take into account that as the product reaches maturity, buyers' knowledge of it attains a high level. Consumers of the product are no longer inexperienced generalists; instead they are experienced specialists. Marketers of mature products sometimes expand distribution into global markets. Often the products have to be adapted to more precisely fit differing needs of global customers.

Because many products are in the maturity stage of their life cycles, marketers must know how to deal with these products and be prepared to adjust their marketing strategies. As Table 11.1 (on p. 298) shows, there are many approaches to altering marketing strategies during the maturity stage. As noted in the table, to increase the sales of mature products, marketers may suggest new uses for them. Arm & Hammer has boosted demand for its baking soda with this method. Likewise, as AOL's subscription growth leveled off in the United States, the Internet service provider's life cycle was extended through aggressive expansion into Europe as well as Asia and Latin America.[11] As customers become more experienced and knowledgeable about products during the maturity stage (particularly about business products), the benefits they seek may change as well, necessitating product modifications.

Three general objectives can be pursued during the maturity stage:

1. *Generate cash flow.* This is essential for recouping the initial investment and generating excess cash to support new products.

2. *Maintain share of market.* Companies with marginal market share must decide whether they have a reasonable chance to improve their position or whether they should drop out.

Table 11.1   Selected Approaches for Managing Products in the Maturity Stage

Approach	Examples
Develop new product uses	Knox gelatin used as a plant food Arm & Hammer baking soda marketed as a refrigerator deodorant Cheez Whiz promoted as a microwavable cheese sauce
Increase product usage among current users	Multiple packaging used for products in which a larger supply at the point of consumption actually increases consumption (such as for soft drinks or beer)
Increase number of users	Global markets or small niches in domestic markets pursued
Add product features	Cellphones that can access the Internet Global positioning systems in automobiles
Change package sizes	Single-serving sizes introduced Travel-size packages of personal care products introduced
Increase product quality	Life of light bulbs increased Reliability and durability of U.S.-made automobiles increased
Change nonproduct marketing mix variables—promotion, price, distribution	Focus of Dr Pepper advertisements shifted from teenagers to people ages 18 to 54 A package of dishwasher detergent containing one-third more product offered for the same price Computer hardware marketed through mail-order outlets

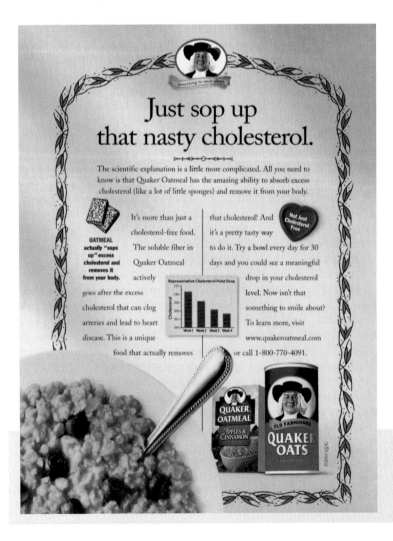

3. *Increase share of customer.* Whereas *market share* refers to the percentage of total customers a firm holds, *share of customer* relates to the percentage of each customer's needs that the firm is meeting. For example, many banks have added new services (brokerage, financial planning, auto leasing, etc.) to gain more of each customer's financial services business. Likewise, many supermarkets are seeking to increase share of customer by adding services such as restaurants, movie rentals, and dry cleaning to provide one-stop shopping for their customers' household needs.[12]

During the maturity stage, marketers actively encourage dealers to support the product. Dealers may be offered promotional assistance in lowering their inventory costs. In general, marketers go to great lengths to serve dealers and provide incentives for selling their brands.

Maintaining market share during the maturity stage requires moderate, and sometimes large, promotion expenditures. Advertising messages focus on differentiating a brand from

Maturity Stage
Oatmeal is in the maturity stage of the product life cycle. The Quaker Oats Company is using an effective marketing strategy to promote its well-respected brand in this stage.

the field of competitors, and sales promotion efforts are aimed at both consumers and resellers.

A greater mixture of pricing strategies is used during the maturity stage. Strong price competition is likely and may ignite price wars. Firms also compete in ways other than price, such as through product quality or service. In addition, marketers develop price flexibility to differentiate offerings in product lines. Markdowns and price incentives are common. Prices may have to be increased, however, if distribution and production costs rise.

◆ Decline

decline stage The stage of a product's life cycle when sales fall rapidly

During the **decline stage**, sales fall rapidly (see Figure 10.2). When this happens, the marketer considers pruning items from the product line to eliminate those not earning a profit. The marketer may also cut promotion efforts, eliminate marginal distributors, and, finally, plan to phase out the product. Although Procter & Gamble's Oxydol detergent had been around for almost 90 years, the company phased it out and sold the brand name to Redox Brands for $7 million. Sales had declined from $64 million in 1950 to $5.5 million when the product was terminated.[13]

An organization can justify maintaining a product as long as the product contributes to profits or enhances the overall effectiveness of a product mix. Unilever, which markets diverse products ranging from Dove soap to Lipton tea, has slashed its product mix from 1,600 to 970 items and plans to eliminate another 250. The firm believes too many choices can frustrate consumers. Other marketers are cutting back on the number of items carried in a product category.[14]

In this stage, marketers must determine whether to eliminate the product or try to reposition it to extend its life. Usually a declining product has lost its distinctiveness because similar competing products have been introduced. Competition engenders increased substitution and brand switching as buyers become insensitive to minor product differences. For these reasons, marketers do little to change a product's style, design, or other attributes during its decline. New technology or social trends, product substitutes, or environmental considerations may also indicate that the time has come to delete the product.

During a product's decline, outlets with strong sales volumes are maintained and unprofitable outlets are weeded out. An entire marketing channel may be eliminated if it does not contribute adequately to profits. An outlet not previously used, such as a factory outlet, is sometimes used to liquidate remaining inventory of an obsolete product. As sales decline, the product becomes more inaccessible, but loyal buyers seek out dealers who still carry it.

Spending on promotion efforts is usually reduced considerably. Advertising of special offers may slow the rate of decline. Sales promotions, such as coupons and premiums, may temporarily regain buyers' attention. As the product continues to decline, the sales staff shifts its emphasis to more profitable products.

The marketing manager has two options during the decline stage: attempt to postpone the decline or accept its inevitability. Many firms lack the resources to renew a product's demand and are forced to consider harvesting or divesting the product or the strategic business unit (SBU). The *harvesting* approach employs a gradual reduction in marketing expenditures and a less resource-intensive marketing mix. A company adopting the *divesting* approach withdraws all marketing support from the declining product or SBU. It may continue to sell the product until losses are sustained or arrange for another firm to acquire the product. The Home Depot, for example, made the

Snapshot

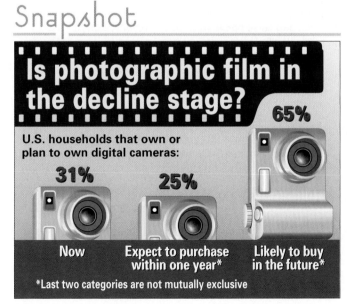

Is photographic film in the decline stage?

U.S. households that own or plan to own digital cameras:

31% — Now

25% — Expect to purchase within one year*

65% — Likely to buy in the future*

*Last two categories are not mutually exclusive

Source: Data from eBrain Market Research for the Consumer Electronics Association.

tough decision to divest its Crossroads stores for farm dwellers and move human and financial resources to Home Depot Expo, a chain for upscale consumers engaged in major renovations or remodeling projects.[15]

Because most businesses have a product mix consisting of multiple products, a firm's destiny is rarely tied to one product. A composite of life cycle patterns forms when various products in the mix are at different cycle stages: as one product is declining, other products are in the introduction, growth, or maturity stage. Marketers must deal with the dual problem of prolonging the lives of existing products and introducing new products to meet organizational sales goals.

Product Adoption Process

product adoption process
The five-stage process of buyer acceptance of a product: awareness, interest, evaluation, trial, and adoption

Acceptance of new products—especially new-to-the-world products—usually doesn't happen overnight. In fact, it can take a very long time. People are sometimes cautious or even skeptical about adopting new products, as indicated by some of the remarks quoted in Table 11.2. Customers who eventually accept a new product do so through an adoption process. The stages of the **product adoption process** are as follows:

1. *Awareness.* The buyer becomes aware of the product.

2. *Interest.* The buyer seeks information and is receptive to learning about the product.

3. *Evaluation.* The buyer considers the product's benefits and decides whether or not to try it.

Table 11.2	**Most New Ideas Have Their Skeptics**

"I think there is a world market for maybe five computers."
—Thomas Watson, chairman of IBM, 1943

"This 'telephone' has too many shortcomings to be seriously considered as a means of communication. The device is inherently of no value to us."
—Western Union internal memo, 1876

"The wireless music box has no imaginable commercial value. Who would pay for a message sent to nobody in particular?"
—David Sarnoff's associates in response to his urgings for investment in the radio in the 1920s

"The concept is interesting and well-formed, but in order to earn better than a 'C,' the idea must be feasible."
—A Yale University management professor in response to Fred Smith's paper proposing reliable overnight delivery service (Smith went on to found Federal Express Corporation)

"Who the hell wants to hear actors talk?"
—H. M. Warner, Warner Brothers, 1927

"A cookie store is a bad idea. Besides, the market research reports say America likes crispy cookies, not soft and chewy cookies like you make."
—Banker's response to Debbie Fields's idea of starting Mrs. Fields' Cookies

"We don't like their sound, and guitar music is on the way out."
—Decca Recording Company rejecting the Beatles, 1962

4. *Trial.* The buyer examines, tests, or tries the product to determine if it meets his or her needs.

5. *Adoption.* The buyer purchases the product and can be expected to use it again whenever the need for this general type of product arises.[16]

In the first stage, when individuals become aware that the product exists, they have little information about it and are not concerned about obtaining more. Consumers enter the interest stage when they are motivated to get information about the product's features, uses, advantages, disadvantages, price, or location. During the evaluation stage, individuals consider whether the product will satisfy certain criteria that are crucial to meeting their specific needs. In the trial stage, they use or experience the product for the first time, possibly by purchasing a small quantity, taking advantage of free samples, or borrowing the product from someone. Supermarkets, for instance, frequently offer special promotions to encourage consumers to taste products. During this stage, potential adopters determine the usefulness of the product under the specific conditions for which they need it.

Individuals move into the adoption stage by choosing a specific product when they need a product of that general type. However, entering the adoption process does not mean the person will eventually adopt the new product. Rejection may occur at any stage, including the adoption stage. Both product adoption and product rejection can be temporary or permanent. As discussed in the Building Customer Relationships boxed feature, production adoption of digital photography is quickly occurring.

BUILDING CUSTOMER RELATIONSHIPS

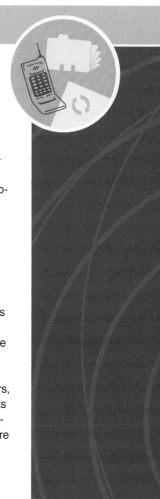

Kodak Pictures a Digital Future

Although its bright-yellow packages of film will not disappear from store shelves any time soon, Eastman Kodak pictures a much brighter future in digital photography. Because traditional film and photography products bring in 70 percent of Kodak's revenue, making the decision to commit to a digital future was far from easy. The company had been watching and waiting as more consumers became aware of digital cameras, took an interest, investigated the benefits, tested one of the new cameras, and adopted the product. However, Kodak executives were surprised by how quickly consumers embraced digital photography—and how drastically its film sales dropped as a result of this rapid adoption.

Kodak has had both good and bad experiences launching products for the digital imaging market. Several years ago, it worked with a partner to create a photo ink-jet printer for home use. The key feature was a direct camera-printer connection for downloading and printing photos. The product did not sell well because digital camera users typically transfer images to their personal computers and tinker with them before printing the photos they want. On the other hand, Kodak's affordable EasyShare digital cameras were immediately successful, giving the company a firm foundation for marketing higher-priced, more sophisticated digital cameras.

The fast-growing consumer market for digital photography has also created lucrative opportunities on the business side. Kodak entered this market by partnering with a manufacturer to make a digital minilab machine for stores to use in developing and printing consumers' digital and traditional photos. While similar equipment from competitor Fuji steadily gained retail acceptance, the original Kodak machine was plagued by repair problems. After the company changed manufacturing partners, its new minilab machine gained more success.

Eyeing strong demand for home ink-jet printers designed to print digital photos, Kodak is about to introduce a new line for consumers. In addition, the company is moving deeper into the business market by purchasing Scitex Digital Printing. Between its digital cameras, minilab products, ink-jet printers, and commercial printing equipment, Kodak expects to double the amount of revenue derived from digital photography within three years. The digital future is almost here.

This adoption model has several implications when launching a new product. First, the company must promote the product to create widespread awareness of its existence and its benefits. Samples or simulated trials should be arranged to help buyers make initial purchase decisions. At the same time, marketers should emphasize quality control and provide solid guarantees to reinforce buyer opinion during the evaluation stage. Finally, production and physical distribution must be linked to patterns of adoption and repeat purchases.

When an organization introduces a new product, people do not begin the adoption process at the same time, nor do they move through the process at the same speed. Of those who eventually adopt the product, some enter the adoption process rather quickly, whereas others start considerably later. For most products, there is also a group of nonadopters who never begin the process.

Depending on the length of time it takes them to adopt a new product, consumers fall into one of five major adopter categories: innovators, early adopters, early

innovators First adopters of new products

early adopters Careful choosers of new products

early majority Individuals who adopt a new product just prior to the average person

majority, late majority, and laggards.[17] Figure 11.3 illustrates each adopter category and the percentage of total adopters it typically represents. **Innovators** are the first to adopt a new product; they enjoy trying new products and tend to be venturesome. **Early adopters** choose new products carefully and are viewed as "the people to check with" by those in the remaining adopter categories. People in the **early majority** adopt a new product just prior to the average person; they are deliberate and cautious in

Figure 11.3 Distribution of Product Adopter Categories
Source: Reprinted with permission of The Free Press, a division of Simon & Schuster Adult Publishing Group, from *Diffusion of Innovation,* Fourth Edition, by Everett M. Rogers. Copyright © 1995 by Everett M. Rogers. Copyright © 1962, 1971, 1983 by The Free Press. All rights reserved.

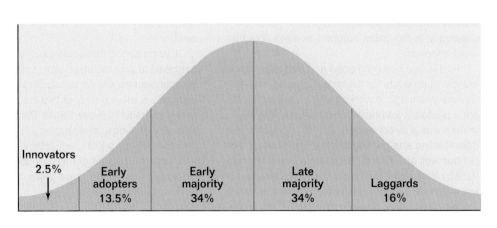

late majority Skeptics who adopt new products when they feel it is necessary

laggards The last adopters, who distrust new products

trying new products. Individuals in the **late majority** are quite skeptical of new products, but eventually adopt them because of economic necessity or social pressure. **Laggards**, the last to adopt a new product, are oriented toward the past. They are suspicious of new products, and when they finally adopt the innovation, it may already have been replaced by a new product.

Why Some Products Fail and Others Succeed

Thousands of new products are introduced annually, and many fail. Statistical bureaus, consulting firms, and trade publications estimate that one in three new products fails each year; others report an annual new-product failure rate as high as 80 to 90 percent. The annual cost of product failures to American firms can reach $100 billion. Failure and success rates vary from organization to organization, but in general consumer products fail more often than business products. Being one of the first brands launched in a product category is no guarantee of success. Table 11.3 shows examples of recent product successes and failures.

Products fail for many reasons. One of the most common reasons is the company's failure to match product offerings to customer needs. When products do not offer value and lack the features customers want, they fail in the marketplace. For example, Thirsty Cat! and Thirsty Dog! bottled waters for pets failed because consumers saw no reason to buy fish- or beef-flavored bottled water for their pets.[18] Ineffective or inconsistent branding has also been blamed for product failures. Examples of products that failed due to failure to convey the right message or image include Gerber Singles (gourmet food for adults packaged in baby food jars), Microsoft's Bob (a "social interface" cartoon character that many users perceived as juvenile), and Gillette's For Oily Hair Only shampoo.[19] Other reasons cited for new-product failure include technical or design problems, poor timing, overestimation of market size, ineffective promotion, and insufficient distribution.

When examining the problem of product failure, it is important to distinguish the degree of failure. Absolute failure occurs when an organization loses money on a new product because it is unable to recover development, production, and marketing costs. This product usually is deleted from the product mix. Relative prod-

Table 11.3	Product Successes and Failures
Product Successes	**Product Failures**
Smith Kline Beecham	R. J. Reynolds Premier smokeless
Nicoderm CQ	cigarettes
Canon Elph digital camera	Cadillac Allante luxury cars
Palm PDAs	Apple Lisa personal computer
Coca-Cola Dasani water	Heinz Ketch Salsa
Starbucks coffee shops	Nestlé Panache coffee
Procter & Gamble Pantene shampoos	Gillette For Oily Hair shampoo
Tide High Efficiency laundry detergent	Drel Home Dry Cleaning Kits
Procter & Gamble Swiffer mop and	S. C. Johnson Allercare aerosol spray,
dusting cloths	carpet powder, and dust mite powder
Bacardi Breezers	Bud and Michelob Dry Beer

uct failure occurs when a product returns a profit but does not meet a company's profit or market share objectives. If a company repositions or improves a relative product failure, that product may become a successful member of the product line. Some products experience relative product failure after years of success. Campbell Soup, for example, has been growing slowly for many years. The company continues to focus on its condensed-soup product line but has done little to improve packaging, promotion, or distribution. This leaves Campbell Soup with a core product whose market share has fallen 21 percent during a recent four-year period.[20]

In contrast to this gloomy picture of new-product failure, some new products are very successful. Perhaps the most important ingredient for success is the product's ability to provide a significant and perceivable benefit to a sizable number of customers. New products with an observable advantage over similar available products, such as more features, ease of operation, or improved technology, have a greater chance to succeed. The Nintendo GameBoy Advance, for example, which has a screen that is 50 percent larger and has greater resolution than previous GameBoy versions, has proven very popular among preteens. Critical to launching a product that will achieve market success is effective planning and management. Companies that follow a systematic, customer-focused plan for new-product development, such as Procter & Gamble, Gillette, and 3M, are well positioned to launch successful products.

SUMMARY

A product is a good, a service, or an idea received in an exchange. It can be either tangible or intangible and includes functional, social, and psychological utilities or benefits. When consumers purchase a product, they are buying the benefits and satisfaction they think the product will provide.

Products can be classified on the basis of the buyer's intentions. Consumer products are those purchased to satisfy personal and family needs. Business products are purchased for use in a firm's operations, to resell, or to make other products. Consumer products can be subdivided into convenience, shopping, specialty, and unsought products. Business products can be classified as installations, accessory equipment, raw materials, component parts, process materials, MRO supplies, or business services.

A product item is a specific version of a product that can be designated as a distinct offering among an organization's products. A product line is a group of closely related product items that are viewed as a unit because of marketing, technical, or end-use considerations. The product mix is the composite, or total, group of products that an organization makes available to customers. The width of the product mix is measured by the number of product lines the company offers. The depth of the product mix is the average number of different products offered in each product line.

The product life cycle describes how product items in an industry move through four stages: introduction, growth, maturity, and decline. The life cycle concept is used to ensure that the introduction, alteration, and termination of a product are timed and executed properly. The sales curve is at zero at introduction, rises at an increasing rate during growth, peaks at maturity, and then declines. Profits peak toward the end of the growth stage of the product life cycle. The life expectancy of a product is based on buyers' wants, the availability of competing products, and other environmental conditions. Most businesses have a composite of life cycle patterns for various products. It is important to manage existing products and develop new ones to keep the overall sales performance at a desired level.

When customers accept a new product, they usually do so through a five-stage adoption process. The first stage is awareness, when buyers become aware that a product exists. Interest, the second stage, occurs when buyers seek information about the product. In the third stage, evaluation, buyers consider the product's benefits and decide whether to try it. The fourth stage is trial, when buyers examine, test, or try the product to determine if it meets their needs. The last stage is adoption, when buyers actually purchase the product and use it whenever a need for this general type of product arises.

Of the thousands of new products introduced every year, many fail. Absolute failure occurs when an organization loses money on a new product. Absolute failures are usually removed from the product mix. Relative failure occurs when a product returns a profit but fails to meet a company's objectives. Reasons for product failure include failure to match product offerings to customer needs, poor timing, and ineffective or inconsistent branding. New products that succeed provide significant and observable benefits to customers. Products that have perceivable advantages over similar products also have a better chance to succeed. Effective marketing planning and product management are important factors in a new product's chances of success.

 Please visit the student website at **www.prideferrell.com** for ACE Self-Test questions that will help you prepare for exams.

IMPORTANT TERMS

Good	Product mix
Service	Width of product mix
Idea	Depth of product mix
Consumer products	Product life cycle
Business products	Introduction stage
Convenience products	Growth stage
Shopping products	Maturity stage
Specialty products	Decline stage
Unsought products	Product adoption process
Installations	Innovators
Accessory equipment	Early adopters
Raw materials	Early majority
Component parts	Late majority
Process materials	Laggards
MRO supplies	
Business services	
Product item	
Product line	

DISCUSSION & REVIEW QUESTIONS

1. List the tangible and intangible attributes of a pair of Nike athletic shoes. Compare its benefits with those of an intangible product such as a hairstyling in a salon.
2. A product has been referred to as a "psychological bundle of satisfaction." Is this a good definition of a product? Why or why not?
3. Is a personal computer sold at a retail store a consumer product or a business product? Defend your answer.
4. How do convenience products and shopping products differ? What are the distinguishing characteristics of each type of product?
5. In the category of business products, how do component parts differ from process materials?
6. How does an organization's product mix relate to its development of a product line? When should an enterprise add depth to its product lines rather than width to its product mix?

7. How do industry profits change as a product moves through the four stages of its life cycle?
8. What is the relationship between the concepts of product mix and product life cycle?
9. What are the stages in the product adoption process, and how do they affect the commercialization phase?
10. What are the five major adopter categories describing the length of time required for a consumer to adopt a new product, and what are the characteristics of each?
11. In what ways does the marketing strategy for a mature product differ from the marketing strategy for a growth product?
12. What are the major reasons for new-product failure?

APPLICATION QUESTIONS

1. Choose a familiar clothing store. Describe its product mix, including its depth and width. Evaluate the mix and make suggestions to the owner.
2. Tabasco pepper sauce is a product that has entered the maturity stage of the product life cycle. Name products that would fit into each of the four stages: introduction, growth, maturity, and decline. Describe each product and explain why it fits in that stage.
3. Generally buyers go through a product adoption process before becoming loyal customers. Describe your experience in adopting a product you now use consistently. Did you go through all the stages of the process?
4. Identify and describe a friend or family member who fits into each of the following adopter categories. How would you use this information if you were product manager for a fashion-oriented, medium-priced clothing retailer such as J. Crew or JCPenney?
   a. Innovator
   b. Early adopter
   c. Early majority
   d. Late majority
   e. Laggard

Internet Exercise & Resources

Visit **www.prideferrell.com** for resources to help you master the material in this chapter, plus materials that will help you expand your marketing knowledge, including Internet exercise updates, ACE self-tests, hotlinks to companies featured in this chapter, and much more.

Goodyear Tire & Rubber Company

In addition to providing information about the company's products, Goodyear's website helps consumers find the exact products they want and will even direct them to the nearest Goodyear retailer. Visit the Goodyear site at **www.goodyear.com**.

1. How does Goodyear use its website to communicate information about the quality of its tires?
2. How does Goodyear's website demonstrate product design and features?
3. Based on what you learned at the website, describe what Goodyear has done to position its tires.

Video Case 11.1

 ### Sony's PlayStation Plays On and On

Stoked by advancing computer technology and consumer demand for better, more realistic animation and higher-quality games, the $13 billion video game industry has become more competitive over the years. Sony has long been the dominant player, thanks to its hugely successful PlayStation game platform. Between sales of the original PlayStation, introduced in the mid-1990s, and sales of PlayStation 2, introduced in 2000, Sony holds 74 percent of the worldwide video game market. With each introduction, Sony has increased the product's sophistication. PlayStation 1 featured 64-bit graphics, PlayStation 2 offered 128-bit graphics, and PlayStation 3 will feature 256-bit graphics, giving players an even more vivid and realistic video game experience. Most important, PlayStation 2 and 3 consoles are compatible with older games created for the earlier models. As a result, players who upgrade to PlayStation 2 (or 3) can still use the games they bought for PlayStation 1 (or 2).

Sony's PlayStation faces challenges from two main rivals: Nintendo's GameCube console and Microsoft's Xbox console. The GameCube came to market a year after PlayStation 2 with a retail price $100 lower than the Sony system. Although Nintendo's GameBoy devices have been best sellers for years—with more than 100 million units sold since 1989—the company had not competed directly with Sony before launching the GameCube. In its first two years, GameCube sold about 15 million units, just a fraction of the 60 million PlayStation 2 units sold to date and fewer than

half of the 37.5 million PlayStation 1 units sold.

Microsoft launched its Xbox game console late in 2001 and has sold approximately 15 million units since that time. The Xbox was developed to challenge Sony's PlayStation 2 on price, speed, and other features. The Xbox has twice the graphics and processing power of PlayStation 2. However, unlike the Sony unit, it cannot play DVDs and CDs without a separate remote control. Microsoft, famed for its software, is focusing its marketing efforts on the Xbox's games and user-friendly interface. It has also started Xbox Live, a subscription-only online gaming platform that is now played by more than 500,000 gamers in 11 countries. Users can play the latest version of 100 different video games by logging on to the Xbox Live site rather than paying to buy each game individually.

Fueled by new game console technology and more lifelike graphics, consumers are snatching up next-generation video games such as *Snake Eater, Mario Kart, Project Gotham Racing 2*, and *Halo 2*. Video games represent a product that is more intangible than tangible. Buyers search for performance and functional benefits. Every time they play a game, they have a different experience. The experience and excitement associated with playing the game are the ultimate product. Marketers can make video games more tangible and demonstrate their value through clever advertising, eye-popping packaging, consistent branding, and special hints for gamers.

On average, video games cost $50, including a fee of roughly $10 that the game publisher pays to the console maker (Sony, Nintendo, or Microsoft). Sony's decision to make future PlayStations compatible with older video games allows players to keep their favorites instead of being forced to invest in newer versions when they buy a new console. This is a key benefit that Sony emphasizes when communicating the features, benefits, and uses of its PlayStation consoles. Moreover, it puts pressure on Microsoft and Nintendo to ensure that new versions of their game consoles can accept video games purchased for older versions. This adds another layer of complexity and expense to the product development process.

Sony continues to set the industry standard by developing innovative new products that incorporate PlayStation technology. The PSX home entertainment center, for example, can play video games but also has a television tuner, a DVD player and recorder, a digital video recorder and storage, an MP3 music player and storage, and a digital photo album. The company also has brought out a variety of accessories, including larger hard drives, network connectors, LCD monitors, and multimedia software. The original PlayStation remains available, now called PSOne and downsized with a lower price tag to match. When PlayStation 3 comes on the market, Sony will price it higher than previous models and back it with a multimillion-dollar marketing campaign. At the same time, the company will reposition its older consoles and cut their prices to inject new life into sales as it did when launching the PlayStation 2. Watch for the PlayStation to play on and on.[21]

QUESTIONS FOR DISCUSSION

1. As a consumer product, how can PlayStation 2 be classified? Defend your classification.
2. To which product adopter groups would Sony be most likely to promote PlayStation 3? Why?
3. Where in their life cycles are PSOne and PlayStation 2? What are the implications for Sony's marketing strategy backing these products?

Case 11.2

Dell Mixes It Up with Computers, Electronics, and More

From MP3 music players and an online music store to flat-screen televisions to home theater projectors, Dell is filling out its product mix with goods and services for the entire household. The company formerly known as Dell Computer wants to build on its dominance of the personal computer market by making inroads into the lucrative, $100 billion world of consumer electronics. Based in Austin, Texas, Dell made its name selling computers directly to customers through its dell.com website. In the future, the company expects to derive an ever-larger portion of revenues and profits from a wider mix of products for use beyond the home office.

This drive for diversification started with the introduction of the Dell Axim handheld computer—in direct competition with Palm and other established rivals—followed one year later by a second Axim model. Because the Axims are priced lower than most comparable products, Dell's entry has forced Hewlett-Packard and other competitors to lower prices to protect their market share. The company used the same approach when it began selling printers and ink cartridges on its website, again competing directly with Hewlett-Packard. Even some Dell insiders were surprised when printer sales in the first six months were two times higher than forecasted sales.

Now the stage was set for a more comprehensive move into electronics designed for the digital home. Founder Michael Dell and his team envisioned consumers using a personal computer (from Dell, of course) to control televisions, music players, and other products all around the house. They began the planning process by carefully examining electronics products made by nearly 90 manufacturers. They also analyzed consumers' needs, buying patterns, and

complaints about incompatibility problems between new and older products. Based on all of this research, they developed an ultra-bright, flat-screen LCD television, a Dell Digital Jukebox (DJ) to store and play music files, and a home theater projector for viewing DVDs and other entertainment. These new products were introduced in time for the holiday buying season, along with the Dell Music Store (selling downloadable music files) and software preloaded on Dell computers to help consumers manage digital entertainment files.

These new products, like the printers and handheld computers before them, put Dell squarely in the middle of a competitive battle with well-established rivals. The Dell DJ competes with Apple's iPod digital music player. The Dell Music Store sells downloadable music files in competition with Apple's iTunes store and other online retailers of digital music. The LCD television not only challenges Sony's television business but sets up a different kind of confrontation about which appliance will serve as the control center of home entertainment. Dell is putting its brand and money behind the computer as the controlling appliance, whereas Sony is putting its resources behind the television as the controlling appliance. "Now is the time for TVs to be reborn," comments a Sony spokesperson.

Although Dell started with only a product or two in each new line, it is gradually adding depth and expanding the width of its product mix. The company is not looking to pioneer new lines; it specializes in applying new technology, adding new features, and making production more efficient. As Dell gains experience with consumer electronics products, it finds ways to lower costs while enhancing each new model.

Meanwhile Hewlett-Packard is focusing more on consumer products with the introduction of more than 150 new products, including digital cameras designed for compatibility with its color printers. Samsung and Sony are aggressively targeting segments of the home entertainment market with plasma televisions, home theater projectors, and other products.

Can Dell triumph in such a dynamic and competitive environment? The company certainly knows how to keep prices low by wringing the most productivity out of its direct distribution method. It also knows how to stay close to customers and find out what they want. Finally, with a 20-year history of marketing technology-based products, Dell is among the best-known brands in the country. "We've come out of nowhere to be the number-three consumer brand in the U.S. in less than five years, while Coca-Cola has been doing it for 100 years," says Dell's general manager of consumer business for the United States. "We're not in this to be number three. Number one is the only target around here."[22]

QUESTIONS FOR DISCUSSION

1. As a product, how can the Dell DJ music player be classified? Why?
2. While Dell has successfully marketed computers directly to customers, are customers likely to be willing to purchase consumer electronics such as home theater systems direct from Dell?
3. How far can Dell widen its product mix without hurting the company's credibility? For example, what might be the impact of new products such as Dell motorcycles or Dell frozen pastries?

Developing and Managing Products

12

OBJECTIVES

1. To understand how companies manage existing products through line extensions and product modifications

2. To describe how businesses develop a product idea into a commercial product

3. To understand the importance of product differentiation and the elements that differentiate one product from another

4. To explore how products are positioned and repositioned in the customer's mind

5. To examine how product deletion is used to improve product mixes

6. To describe organizational structures used for managing products

Segway: Introducing a New Product

Dean Kamen was trying to reinvent the wheelchair when he had an insight that led him to create an entirely new product: the Segway Human Transporter. Kamen is an experienced inventor whose company holds hundreds of patents and has developed dozens of ideas into commercially viable products. More than a decade ago, he was searching for a way to keep a wheelchair upright while its occupant went up or down the stairs and rolled over bumps. Kamen examined a number of wheelchair designs and then decided to study the human angle—specifically, how the inner ear helps people maintain their balance. Through trial and error, he devised a wheelchair equipped with a set of electronic gyroscopes that, like the inner ear, automatically adjusts to ensure stability even on rough or uneven ground.

Although Kamen needed more time to perfect the self-balancing wheelchair (now called the iBot), he saw other commercial possibilities for gyroscope-stabilized products. "Once we were able to make devices that essentially mimic human balance and walking," he recalls, "it wasn't that big a leap to take the seat off." With more tinkering, Kamen and his engineers came up with the Segway Human Transporter, a compact, battery-powered two-wheeled scooter.

The Segway rider stands on a platform between the chair's wheels, leans forward to move forward, leans back to reverse course, and stands straight to brake. Onboard electronic sensors constantly check the device's balance, and five gyroscopes make any adjustments needed to maintain the rider's stability. Early Segway models had a top speed of 10 to 12 miles per hour and a range of 11 to 17 miles between battery charges.

Because the Segway runs on battery power and has no emissions, it is an efficient, environmentally friendly mode of travel—just right for getting around cities, in Kamen's view. In fact, some municipal police departments and post offices have purchased fleets of Segways for their workers, and a Florida company is selling two-hour tours of Sarasota conducted on Segways. Still, with price tags of up to $5,000, Segway models are not flying out of stores even with all the media attention. Moreover, 6,000 Segways sold during the first year were recalled to fix a problem that caused some riders to tumble off when battery power was low. And, fearing collisions with pedestrians, San Francisco and a few other cities have banned the use of Segways on sidewalks.

How long will it take for the Segway to graduate from being a novelty to becoming an everyday product? "I think the jury's still out," its inventor notes. He adds, "In the Internet age, can education and knowledge spread more quickly and increase the rate at which good ideas get accepted? I don't know the answer to that question."[1] ■

To compete effectively and achieve their goals, organizations, like the maker of the Segway, must be able to adjust their product mixes in response to changes in customers' needs. A firm often has to introduce new products, modify existing products, or delete products that were successful perhaps only a few years ago. To provide products that satisfy target markets and achieve the organization's objectives, a marketer must develop, alter, and maintain an effective product mix. An organization's product mix may need several types of adjustments. Because customers' attitudes and product preferences change over time, their desire for certain products may wane.

In some cases, a company needs to alter its product mix for competitive reasons. A marketer may have to delete a product from the mix because a competitor dominates the market for that product. Similarly, a firm may have to introduce a new product or modify an existing one to compete more effectively. A marketer may expand the firm's product mix to take advantage of excess marketing and production capacity.

In this chapter, we examine several ways to improve an organization's product mix, including management of existing products, development of new products, product differentiation, positioning and repositioning of products, and elimination of weak products from the product mix. First, we discuss managing existing products through effective line extension and product modification. Next, we examine the stages of new-product development. Then we look at the ways companies differentiate their products in the marketplace and discuss product positioning and repositioning. Next, we examine the importance of deleting weak products and the methods companies use to eliminate them. Finally, we look at the organizational structures used to manage products.

Managing Existing Products

An organization can benefit by capitalizing on its existing products. By assessing the composition of the current product mix, a marketer can identify weaknesses and gaps. This analysis can then lead to improvement of the product mix through line extension and product modification.

◆ Line Extensions

line extension Development of a product that is closely related to existing products in the line but meets different customer needs

A **line extension** is the development of a product closely related to one or more products in the existing product line but designed specifically to meet somewhat different customer needs. For example, Nabisco extended its cookie line to include Reduced Fat Oreos and Double Stuffed Oreos.

Many of the so-called new products introduced each year are in fact line extensions. Line extensions are more common than new products because they are a less expensive, lower-risk alternative for increasing sales. A line extension may focus on a different market segment or be an attempt to increase sales within the same market segment by more precisely satisfying the needs of people in that segment. Line extensions are also used to take market share from competitors. However, one side effect of employing a line extension is that it may result in a more negative evaluation of the core product.[2]

◆ Product Modifications

product modifications Changes in one or more characteristics of a product

Product modification means changing one or more characteristics of a product. A product modification differs from a line extension in that the original product does not remain in the line. For example, U.S. automakers use product modifications annually when they create new models of the same brand. Once the new models are

'Half-Caf'

While you might think this refers to milk made from really small cows, 'Half-Caf' actually means half regular and half decaf. **Customize Your Cup.**

Line Extensions
Through the management of their existing products, both Doritos and Starbucks have expanded their mixes through the use of line extensions.

introduced, the manufacturers stop producing last year's model. Like line extensions, product modifications entail less risk than developing new products.

Product modification can indeed improve a firm's product mix, but only under certain conditions. First, the product must be modifiable. Second, customers must be able to perceive that a modification has been made. Third, the modification should make the product more consistent with customers' desires so it provides greater satisfaction. There are three major ways to modify products: quality, functional, and aesthetic modifications.

quality modifications Changes relating to a product's dependability and durability

Quality Modifications. **Quality modifications** are changes relating to a product's dependability and durability. The changes usually are executed by altering the materials or the production process. For example, Energizer increased its product's durability by using better materials—a larger cathode and anode interface—that make batteries last longer.

Reducing a product's quality may allow an organization to lower its price and direct the item at a different target market. In contrast, increasing the quality of a product may give a firm an advantage over competing brands. Higher quality may enable a company to charge a higher price by creating customer loyalty and lowering customer sensitivity to price. However, higher quality may require the use of more expensive components and processes, thus forcing the organization to cut costs in other areas. Some firms, such as Caterpillar, are finding ways to increase quality while reducing costs.

functional modifications
Changes affecting a product's versatility, effectiveness, convenience, or safety

Functional Modifications. Changes that affect a product's versatility, effectiveness, convenience, or safety are called **functional modifications**; they usually require redesign of the product. Product categories that have undergone considerable functional modification include office and farm equipment, appliances, cleaning products, and telecommunications services. For example, for more than ten years, telephone

Only the new Ford F-150 has rear shocks placed beyond the frame rails, outboard of the leaf springs. Nobody else builds their trucks like that. Our geometry provides superior control of axle movement and gives you a more surefooted stance. In turn, even while towing on washboard roads, your truck remains on track and in control.

Why did we go to the trouble to move our shocks to a place past all others? Easy, it makes your truck handle better.

Call 1-800-301-7430 or go to fordvehicles.com and find out how this truck earned the right to be the next Ford F-150.

WHY DOESN'T EVERY TRUCK HAVE ITS REAR SHOCKS MOUNTED TO THE OUTSIDE OF THE FRAME?

THE NEXT F-150

Product Modifications
Automakers are major users of product modifications in order to manage their product mixes. In this advertisement, Ford is promoting a feature modification. The rear shock absorbers on the Ford F-150 are mounted to the outside of the frame.

companies have offered caller ID services. However, customers still complain that many calls show up as "unknown" or "out of area." In response, some telephone companies have enhanced the service to allow customers to screen out such unidentified calls. Other companies offer Privacy Manager, a caller ID add-on service that requires unidentified callers to record their names so the recipient can decide whether to answer the call.[3]

Functional modifications can make a product useful to more people and thus enlarge its market. They can place a product in a favorable competitive position by providing benefits that competing brands do not offer. They can also help an organization achieve and maintain a progressive image. Finally, functional modifications are sometimes made to reduce the possibility of product liability lawsuits.

aesthetic modifications
Changes relating to the sensory appeal of a product

Aesthetic Modifications. **Aesthetic modifications** change the sensory appeal of a product by altering its taste, texture, sound, smell, or appearance. A buyer making a purchase decision is swayed by how a product looks, smells, tastes, feels, or sounds. Procter & Gamble, for example, added a new Caribbean flavor to its Sunny Delight orange beverage product line. Thus, an aesthetic modification may strongly affect purchases. For years, automobile makers have relied on quality and aesthetic modifications.

Aesthetic modifications can help a firm differentiate its product from competing brands and thus gain a sizable market share. For example, DaimlerChrysler introduced its Crossfire two-seat roadster as a combination of sporty Chrysler styling and quality Mercedes engineering.[4] DaimlerChrysler management hoped that the sporty aesthetic appeal plus quality image by Mercedes would be well received by customers. The major drawback in using aesthetic modifications is that their value is determined subjectively. Although a firm may strive to improve the product's sensory appeal, customers may actually find the modified product less attractive.

Developing New Products

A firm develops new products as a means of enhancing its product mix and adding depth to a product line. However, developing and introducing new products is frequently expensive and risky. For example, Kellogg's management decided to discontinue Kellogg's Cereal Mates after two years of being in the marketplace. Cereal Mates, available in Corn Flakes, Fruit Loops, Mini Wheats, and Frosted Flakes, consisted of two components: cereal and aseptically packaged milk. The product failed because Americans do not care for warm milk on cereal and found the aseptically

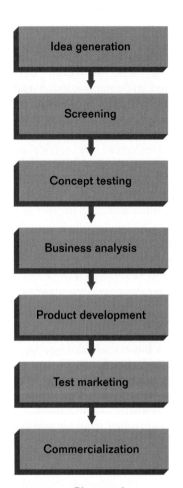

Figure 12.1 **Phases of New-Product Development**

packaged milk unappealing; some customers viewed the product as slightly overpriced.[5] As we discussed in the previous chapter, new-product failures occur frequently and can create major financial problems for organizations, sometimes even causing them to go out of business.

Failure to introduce new products is also risky. For example, the makers of Timex watches gained a large share of the U.S. watch market through effective marketing strategies during the 1960s and early 1970s. In the 1980s, Timex's market share slipped considerably, in part because Timex had failed to introduce new products. In recent years, however, Timex has introduced new, technologically advanced products and has regained market share.

The term *new product* can have more than one meaning. A genuinely new product offers innovative benefits. However, products that are different and distinctly better are often viewed as new. The following items are product innovations of the last 30 years: Post-it® Notes, fax machines, cell phones, personal computers, PDAs, disposable razors, caller ID, and DVDs. Thus, a new product can be an innovative product that has never been sold by any organization, such as the digital camera was when introduced for the first time. A radically new product involves a complex developmental process, including an extensive business analysis to determine the potential for success.[6] It can also be a product that a given firm has not marketed previously although similar products have been available from other companies, such as Crayola School Glue. Eddie Bauer, best known for its rugged outdoor wear, extended this image with the introduction of a new line of men's cologne. It was considered a new product because Eddie Bauer had not previously marketed cologne or cosmetics. Finally, a product can be viewed as new when it is brought to one or more markets from another market. For example, making the Saturn VUE SUV available in Japan was viewed as a new-product introduction in Japan.

Before a product is introduced, it goes through the seven phases of the **new-product development process** shown in Figure 12.1: (1) idea generation, (2) screening, (3) concept testing, (4) business analysis, (5) product development, (6) test marketing, and (7) commercialization. A product may be dropped (and many are) at any stage of development. In this section, we look at the process through which products are developed, from idea inception to fully commercialized product.

new-product development process A seven-phase process for introducing products: idea generation, screening, concept testing, business analysis, product development, test marketing, and commercialization

◆ Idea Generation

idea generation Seeking product ideas to achieve organizational objectives

Businesses and other organizations seek product ideas that will help them achieve their objectives. This activity is **idea generation**. The fact that only a few ideas are good enough to be commercially successful underscores the difficulty of the task.

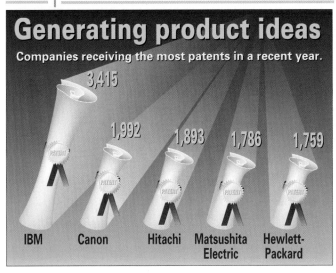

Snapshot

Generating product ideas
Companies receiving the most patents in a recent year.

3,415 1,992 1,893 1,786 1,759

IBM   Canon   Hitachi   Matsushita Electric   Hewlett-Packard

Source: Data from United States Patent and Trademark Office and IBM.

Although some organizations get their ideas almost by chance, firms that try to manage their product mixes effectively usually develop systematic approaches for generating new-product ideas. Indeed, in organizations there is a relationship between the amount of market information gathered and the number of ideas generated by work groups.[7] At the heart of innovation is a purposeful, focused effort to identify new ways to serve a market.

New-product ideas can come from several sources. They may stem from internal sources: marketing managers, researchers, sales personnel, engineers, or other organizational personnel. Brainstorming and incentives or rewards for good ideas are typical intrafirm devices for stimulating development of ideas. For example, the idea for 3M Post-it adhesive-backed notes came from an employee. As a church choir member, he used slips of paper to mark songs in his hymnal. Because the pieces of paper kept falling out, he suggested developing an adhesive-backed note. New-product ideas may also arise from sources outside the firm, such as customers, competitors, advertising agencies, management consultants, and private research organizations. For instance, Goodmark foods and other companies have obtained new-product ideas from the U.S Army, which researches technologies to solve problems such as how to feed soldiers in the field. After the army developed a way to keep bread fresh for three years, Goodmark Foods created sandwiches with a long shelf life.[8] Consultants are often used as sources for stimulating new-product ideas. The Eureka Ranch, also known as the "idea factory," charges clients as much as $150,000 for a three-day creativity session.[9] Developing new-product alliances with other firms has also been found to enhance the acquisition and use of information useful for creating new-product ideas.[10] A significant portion of this money is used to assess customers' needs. Asking customers what they want from products and organizations has helped many firms become successful and remain competitive.

◆ Screening

screening Choosing the most promising ideas for further review

In the process of **screening**, the ideas with the greatest potential are selected for further review. During screening, product ideas are analyzed to determine whether they match the organization's objectives and resources. If a product idea results in a product similar to the firm's existing offerings, marketers must assess the degree to which the new product could cannibalize the sales of current products. The company's overall abilities to produce and market the product are also analyzed. Other aspects of an idea to be weighed are the nature and wants of buyers and possible environmental changes. At times a checklist of new-product requirements is used when making screening decisions. This practice encourages evaluators to be systematic and thus reduces the chances of overlooking some pertinent fact. The largest number of new-product ideas are rejected during the screening phase.

◆ Concept Testing

concept testing Seeking potential buyers' responses to a product idea

To evaluate ideas properly, it may be necessary to test product concepts. In **concept testing**, a small sample of potential buyers is presented with a product idea through a written or oral description (and perhaps a few drawings) to determine their attitudes and initial buying intentions regarding the product. For a single product idea, an organization can test one or several concepts of the same product. Concept testing is a low-cost procedure that lets the organization determine customers' initial reactions to a product idea before it invests considerable resources in research and

Product description

An insecticide company is considering the development and introduction of a new tick and flea control product for pets. This product would consist of insecticide and a liquid dispensing brush for applying the insecticide to dogs and cats. The insecticide is in a cartridge that is installed in the handle of the brush. The insecticide is dispensed through the tips of the bristles when they touch the pet's skin (which is where most ticks and fleas are found). The actual dispensing works very much like a felt-tip pen. Only a small amount of insecticide actually is dispensed on the pet because of this unique dispensing feature. Thus, the amount of insecticide that is placed on your pet is minimal compared to conventional methods of applying a tick and flea control product. One application of insecticide will keep your pet free from ticks and fleas for fourteen days.

Please answer the following questions:

1. In general, how do you feel about using this type of product on your pet?

2. What are the major advantages of this product compared with the existing product that you are currently using to control ticks and fleas on your pet?

3. What characteristics of this product do you especially like?

4. What suggestions do you have for improving this product?

5. If it is available at an appropriate price, how likely are you to buy this product?

   Very likely   Semi-likely   Not likely

6. Assuming that a single purchase would provide 30 applications for an average-size dog or 48 applications for an average-size cat, approximately how much would you pay for this product?

Figure 12.2 Concept Test for a Tick and Flea Control Product

development. The results of concept testing can help product development personnel better understand which product attributes and benefits are most important to potential customers.

Figure 12.2 shows a concept test for a proposed tick and flea control product. Notice that the concept is briefly described, then a series of questions is presented. The questions vary considerably depending on the type of product being tested. Typical questions are: In general, do you find this proposed product attractive? Which benefits are especially attractive to you? Which features are of little or no interest to you? Do you feel this proposed product would work better for you than the product you currently use? Compared with your current product, what are the primary advantages of the proposed product? If this product were available at an appropriate price, would you buy it? How often would you buy this product? How could this proposed product be improved?

◆ Business Analysis

business analysis Assessing the potential of a product idea for the firm's sales, costs, and profits

During the **business analysis** stage, the product idea is evaluated to determine its potential contribution to the firm's sales, costs, and profits. In the course of a business analysis, evaluators ask a variety of questions: Does the product fit in with the organization's existing product mix? Is demand strong enough to justify entering the market, and will the demand endure? What types of environmental and competitive changes can be expected, and how will these changes affect the product's future sales, costs, and profits? Are the organization's research, development, engineering, and production capabilities adequate to develop the product? If new facilities must be constructed, how quickly can they be built and how much will they cost? Is the necessary financing for development and commercialization on hand or obtainable at terms consistent with a favorable return on investment?

In the business analysis stage, firms seek market information. The results of customer surveys, along with secondary data, supply the specifics needed to estimate potential sales, costs, and profits.

For many products in this stage (when they are still just product ideas), forecasting sales accurately is difficult. This is especially true for innovative and completely new products. Organizations sometimes employ break-even analysis to determine how many units they would have to sell to begin making a profit. At times an organization also uses payback analysis, in which marketers compute the time period required to recover the funds that would be invested in developing the new product. Because break-even and payback analyses are based on estimates, they are usually viewed as useful but not particularly precise during this stage.

◆ Product Development

product development Determining if producing a product is feasible and cost effective

Product development is the phase in which the organization determines if it is technically feasible to produce the product and if it can be produced at costs low enough to make the final price reasonable. To test its acceptability, the idea or concept is converted into a prototype, or working model. The prototype should reveal tangible and intangible attributes associated with the product in consumers' minds. The product's design, mechanical features, and intangible aspects must be linked to wants in the marketplace. Through marketing research and concept testing, product attributes important to buyers are identified. These characteristics must be communicated to customers through the design of the product.

After a prototype is developed, its overall functioning must be tested. Its performance, safety, convenience, and other functional qualities are tested both in a laboratory and in the field. Functional testing should be rigorous and lengthy enough to test the product thoroughly.

A crucial question that arises during product development is how much quality to build into the product. For example, a major dimension of quality is durability. Higher quality often calls for better materials and more expensive processing, which increase production costs and, ultimately, the product's price. In determining the specific level of quality, a marketer must ascertain approximately what price the target market views as acceptable. In addition, a marketer usually tries to set a quality level consistent with that of the firm's other products. Obviously the quality of competing brands is also a consideration. For example, Nike's market share has declined to 42 percent from 48 percent in 1997, in part because the firm focused on high-quality but high-end traditional athletic shoes while competitors such as Skechers and New Balance introduced trendier and more mid-priced shoes, which account for the majority of domestic athletic shoe sales.[11]

The development phase of a new product is frequently lengthy and expensive; thus, a relatively small number of product ideas are put into development. If the product appears sufficiently successful during this stage to merit test marketing, then, during the latter part of the development stage, marketers begin to make decisions regarding branding, packaging, labeling, pricing, and promotion for use in the test marketing stage.

◆ Test Marketing

test marketing Introducing a product on a limited basis to measure the extent to which potential customers will actually buy it

Test marketing is a limited introduction of a product in geographic areas chosen to represent the intended market. Its aim is to determine the extent to which potential customers will buy the product. Test marketing is not an extension of the development stage; it is a sample launching of the entire marketing mix. Test marketing should be conducted only after the product has gone through development and initial plans have been made regarding the other marketing mix variables.

Companies use test marketing to lessen the risk of product failure. The dangers of introducing an untested product include undercutting already profitable products and, should the new product fail, loss of credibility with distributors and customers. Anheuser-Busch, for example, historically has test marketed a number of nonalcoholic and trace-alcoholic beverages and did not launch them nationally. Recently the company test marketed another nonalcoholic energy drink, 180 Degrees, which will compete directly with Red Bull and other "New Age" beverages.[12]

Test marketing provides several benefits. It lets marketers expose a product in a natural marketing environment to measure its sales performance. While the product is being marketed in a limited area, the company can strive to identify weaknesses in the product or in other parts of the marketing mix. A product weakness discovered after a nationwide introduction can be expensive to correct. Moreover, if consumers' early reactions are negative, marketers may be unable to persuade consumers to try the product again. Thus, making adjustments after test marketing can be crucial to the success of a new product. On the other hand, test marketing results may be positive enough to warrant accelerating the product's introduction. Test marketing also allows marketers to experiment with variations in advertising, pricing, and packaging in different test areas and to measure the extent of brand awareness, brand switching, and repeat purchases resulting from these alterations in the marketing mix.

Selection of appropriate test areas is very important because the validity of test marketing results depends heavily on selecting test sites that provide accurate representation of the intended target market. Table 12.1 lists some of the most popular test market cities. The criteria used for choosing test market cities depend on the product's attributes, the target market's characteristics, and the firm's objectives and resources.

Test marketing is not without risks. It is expensive, and competitors may try to interfere. A competitor may attempt to "jam" the test program by increasing its own advertising or promotions, lowering prices, and offering special incentives, all to combat recognition and purchase of the new brand. Any such tactics can invalidate test results. Sometimes, too, competitors copy the product in the testing stage and rush to introduce a similar product. It is therefore desirable to move to the commercialization phase as soon as possible after successful testing. On the other hand, some firms have been known to heavily promote new products long before they are ready for the market to discourage competitors from developing similar new products. When the product introduction is delayed to the point where the public begins to doubt its existence, such products may become known as "vaporware," particularly in the computer software industry.[13]

Because of these risks, many companies use alternative methods to measure customer preferences. One such method is simulated test marketing. Typically consumers at shopping centers are asked to view an advertisement for a new product and are given a free sample to take home. These consumers are subsequently interviewed

Table 12.1	Popular Test Markets in the United States	
Tulsa, OK	Grand Junction, CO	Longview, TX
Ft. Wayne, IN	Bloomington, IL	Lafayette, LA
Midland, TX	Oklahoma City, OK	Omaha, NE
Tucson, AZ	South Bend, IN	Evansville, IN
Peoria, IL	Erie, PA	Rockford, IL
Portland, ME	Binghamton, NY	Albany, NY
Wichita, KS	Syracuse, NY	Des Moines, IA

Source: Marketing Research Association, December 2003.

over the phone and asked to rate the product. The major advantages of simulated test marketing are greater speed, lower costs, and tighter security, which reduce the flow of information to competitors and reduce jamming. Gillette's Personal Care Division, for example, spends less than $200,000 for a simulated test that lasts three to five months. A live test market costs Gillette $2 million, counting promotion and distribution, and takes one to two years to complete. Several marketing research firms, such as ACNielsen Company, offer test marketing services to provide independent assessment of proposed products.

Clearly not all products that are test marketed are launched. At times, problems discovered during test marketing cannot be resolved. Procter & Gamble, for example, test marketed a new plastic wrap product called Impress in Grand Junction, Colorado, but decided not to launch the brand nationally based on the results of test marketing.[14]

◆ Commercialization

commercialization Refining and finalizing plans and budgets for full-scale manufacturing and marketing of a product

During the **commercialization** phase, plans for full-scale manufacturing and marketing must be refined and finalized and budgets for the project prepared. Early in the commercialization phase, marketing management analyzes the results of test marketing to find out what changes in the marketing mix are needed before introducing the product. The results of test marketing may tell marketers to change one or more of the product's physical attributes, modify the distribution plans to include more retail outlets, alter promotional efforts, or change the product's price. However, as more and more changes are made based on test marketing findings, the test marketing projections may become less valid.

During the early part of this stage, marketers must not only gear up for larger-scale production but also make decisions about warranties, repairs, and replacement parts. The type of warranty a firm provides can be a critical issue for buyers, especially when expensive, technically complex goods such as appliances are involved. Maytag, for example, provides a money-back guarantee on its refrigerators. Establishing an effective system for providing repair services and replacement parts is necessary to maintain favorable customer relationships. Although the producer may furnish these services directly to buyers, it is more common for the producer to provide such services through regional service centers. Regardless of how services are provided, it is important to customers that they be performed quickly and correctly.

The product enters the market during the commercialization phase. When introducing a product, a firm may spend enormous sums for advertising, personal selling, and other types of promotion, as well as for plant and equipment. Such expenditures may not be recovered for several years. Smaller organizations may find product commercialization especially difficult.

Usually products are not launched nationwide overnight but are introduced through a process called a *roll-out*. With a roll-out, a product is introduced in stages, starting in one set of geographic areas and gradually expanding into adjacent areas. It may take several years to market the product nationally. Sometimes the test cities are used as initial marketing areas, and the introduction of the product becomes a natural extension of test marketing. A product test marketed in Sacramento, Fort Collins, Abilene, Springfield, and Jacksonville, as the map in Figure 12.3 (on p. 320) shows, could be introduced first in those cities. After the stage 1 introduction is complete, stage 2 could include market coverage of the states where the test cities are located. In stage 3, marketing efforts might be extended into adjacent states. All remaining states would then be covered in stage 4. Gradual product introductions do not always occur state by state; other geographic combinations, such as groups of counties that overlap across state borders, are sometimes used. Products destined for multinational markets may also be rolled out one country or region at a time. Procter & Gamble test marketed its Circ line of men's hair coloring products in several cities in the United Kingdom, gradually expanding the areas for the product's distribution.[15]

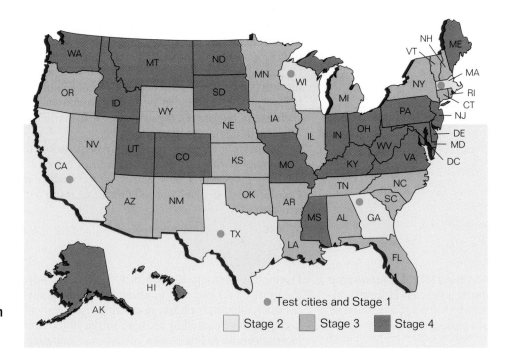

Figure 12.3 Stages of Expansion into a National Market During Commercialization

Gradual product introduction is desirable for several reasons. First, it reduces the risks of introducing a new product. If the product fails, the firm will experience smaller losses if it introduced the item in only a few geographic areas than if it marketed the product nationally. Second, a company cannot introduce a product nationwide overnight because a system of wholesalers and retailers to distribute the product cannot be established so quickly; developing a distribution network may take considerable time. Third, if the product is successful, the number of units needed to satisfy nationwide demand for it may be too large for the firm to produce in a short time.

Despite the good reasons for introducing a product gradually, marketers realize this approach creates some competitive problems. A gradual introduction allows competitors to observe what the firm is doing and to monitor results just as the firm's own marketers are doing. If competitors see that the newly introduced product is successful, they may quickly enter the same target market with similar products. In addition, as a product is introduced region by region, competitors may expand their marketing efforts to offset promotion of the new product.

Product Differentiation Through Quality, Design, and Support Services

product differentiation Creating and designing products so that customers perceive them as different from competing products

Some of the most important characteristics of products are the elements that distinguish them from one another. **Product differentiation** is the process of creating and designing products so that customers perceive them as different from competing products. Customer perception is critical in differentiating products. Perceived differences might include quality, features, styling, price, or image. A crucial element used to differentiate one product from another is the brand, discussed in the next chapter. In this section, we examine three aspects of product differentiation that companies must consider when creating and offering products for sale: product quality, product design and features, and product support services. These aspects involve the company's attempt to create real differences among products. Later in this chapter, we discuss how companies position their products in the marketplace based on these three aspects.

◆ Product Quality

quality The overall characteristics of a product that allow it to perform as expected in satisfying customer needs

Quality refers to the overall characteristics of a product that allow it to perform as expected in satisfying customer needs. The words *as expected* are very important to this definition because quality usually means different things to different customers. For some, durability signifies quality. Among the most durable products on the market today is the Craftsman line of tools at Sears; indeed, Sears provides a lifetime guarantee on the durability of its tools. For other consumers, a product's ease of use may indicate quality.

The concept of quality also varies between consumer and business markets. Consumers consider high-quality products to be reliable, durable, and easy to maintain. For business markets, technical suitability, ease of repair, and company reputation are important characteristics. Unlike consumers, most organizations place far less emphasis on price than on product quality.

level of quality The amount of quality a product possesses

One important dimension of quality is **level of quality**, the amount of quality a product possesses. The concept is a relative one; that is, the quality level of one product is difficult to describe unless it is compared with that of other products. For example, most consumers would consider the quality level of Timex watches to be good, but when they compare Timex with Rolex, most consumers would say a Rolex's level of quality is higher. How high should the level of quality be? It depends on the product and the costs and consequences of a product failure.

consistency of quality The degree to which a product has the same level of quality over time

A second important dimension is consistency. **Consistency of quality** refers to the degree to which a product has the same level of quality over time. Consistency means giving consumers the quality they expect every time they purchase the product. Like level of quality, consistency is a relative concept; however, it implies a quality comparison within the same brand over time. The quality level of McDonald's French fries is generally consistent from one location to another. If FedEx delivers more than 99 percent of overnight packages on time, its service has consistent quality.

The consistency of product quality can also be compared across competing products. It is at this stage that consistency becomes critical to a company's success. Companies that can provide quality on a consistent basis have a major competitive advantage over rivals. FedEx, for example, is viewed as more consistent in delivery schedules than the U.S. Postal Service. In simple terms, no company has ever succeeded by creating and marketing low-quality products. Many companies have taken major steps, such as implementing total quality management (TQM), to improve the quality of their products.

By and large, higher product quality means marketers will charge a higher price for the product. This fact forces marketers to consider quality carefully in their product-planning efforts. Not all customers want or can afford the highest-quality products available. Thus, some companies offer products with moderate quality.

newbalance.com/W745   N is for mileage, not image. achieve new balance

Differentiation Through Product Quality
New Balance athletic shoes are being differentiated from competitors based on product quality.

◆ Product Design and Features

product design How a product is conceived, planned, and produced

Product design refers to how a product is conceived, planned, and produced. Design is a very complex topic because it involves the total sum of all the product's physical characteristics. Many companies are known for the outstanding designs of their products: Sony for personal electronics, Hewlett-Packard for laser printers, Levi Strauss for clothing, and JanSport for backpacks. Good design is one of the best competitive advantages any brand can possess.

styling The physical appearance of a product

One component of design is **styling**, or the physical appearance of the product. The style of a product is one design feature that can allow certain products to sell very rapidly. Good design, however, means more than just appearance; it also involves a product's functioning and usefulness. For example, a pair of jeans may look great, but if they fall apart after three washes, clearly the design was poor. Most consumers seek out products that both look good and function well.

product features Specific design characteristics that allow a product to perform certain tasks

Product features are specific design characteristics that allow a product to perform certain tasks. By adding or subtracting features, a company can differentiate its products from those of the competition. Chrysler promotes its line of minivans as having more features related to passenger safety—dual air bags, steel-reinforced doors, and integrated child safety seats—than any other auto company. Product features can also be used to differentiate products within the same company. For example, Nike offers both a walking shoe and a run-walk shoe for specific consumer needs. In these cases, the company's products are sold with a wide range of features, from low-priced "base" or "stripped-down" versions to high-priced, prestigious "feature-packed" ones. The automotive industry regularly sells products with a wide range of features. In general, the more features a product has, the higher its price and, often, the higher the perceived quality.

Differentiation Through Product Features
As shown in this advertisement, Glastron differentiates its boats based on product features.

For a brand to have a sustainable competitive advantage, marketers must determine the product designs and features that customers desire. Information from marketing research efforts and from databases can help in assessing customers' product design and feature preferences. Being able to meet customers' desires for product design and features at prices they can afford is crucial to a product's long-term success. Marketers must be careful not to misrepresent or over promise regarding product features or product performance, as discussed in the Ethics and Social Responsibility boxed feature.

◆ Product Support Services

customer services Human or
mechanical efforts or activities that
add value to a product

Many companies differentiate their product offerings by providing support services. Usually referred to as **customer services**, these services include any human or mechanical efforts or activities a company provides that add value to a product.[16] Examples of customer services include delivery and installation, financing arrangements, customer training, warranties and guarantees, repairs, layaway plans, convenient

---

ETHICS AND SOCIAL RESPONSIBILITY

Lying to Customers

Should a company or its employees resort to lying about goods or services? A surprising number do. In a survey of managers by *Sales & Marketing Management* magazine, 45 percent of the respondents had heard their companies' salespeople lie about product delivery times, 20 percent had heard their salespeople lie about the company's service, and more than 77 percent said competitors were spreading lies about the respondents' companies.

Employees who misrepresent product quality, features, delivery, or some other element often do so to clinch a sale. When they lie, however, they not only act unethically but hurt their companies' reputations. Recently six salespeople and the general manager of a Los Angeles car dealership were indicted for lying about pricing. They failed to disclose certain costs and overcharged more than 1,000 buyers. Although the salespeople and general manager no longer work there, the incident undoubtedly had long-lasting negative effects on the dealership's image.

In many cases, lying violates the law, whether the misrepresentations are made in person, by mail, or online. "All sellers are obligated to keep their promises to consumers about when their products will be delivered," says the director of the Federal Trade Commission's Bureau of Consumer

Protection. "Real-time promises demand real-time performance." For example, the office supply retailer Staples paid $850,000 to settle FTC charges that its website misled customers about product availability and delivery. Under the settlement, Staples agreed to notify customers if products would be shipped late and allow customers to cancel orders if they were dissatisfied with the delay.

Lying can also be costly, as Household International found out. This financial services firm owns mortgage lending operations that target homeowners who have imperfect credit histories. After officials in 20 states found that Household employees had not disclosed certain costs and had overcharged customers, the firm agreed to pay $484 million in restitution. It also agreed to place limits on the fees it can charge and is required to accurately disclose all pricing—with an independent monitor enforcing these rules.

Finally, lying is poor business. Customers who realize they have been misled rarely buy from that company or employee again. "In relationship selling you can't lie—if you mess up you'll never hear from the client again," stresses Professor Andy Zoltners of the Kellogg School of Management. By telling the truth, employees build trust and encourage customer loyalty. Still, for their own protection, customers should always remember the old adage of caveat emptor: buyer beware.

Audi Assured
Certified Pre-Owned Cars

We gave it the once-over. 300 times.

Audi Assured
Certified Pre-Owned Cars   Backed by an Audi 2 year or 100,000 mile limited warranty.

Winner of *Car and Driver's* 10Best Award 1996, 1997 and 1998 • Available with legendary quattro® all-wheel drive • Extensive multi-point inspection • Luxurious interior of fine fabrics, leather, wood and aluminum • A rare opportunity to drive an Audi A4 at a remarkable price.

Visit your Audi dealer or www.audiusa.com/preowned to search our national vehicle locator.

hours of operation, adequate parking, and information through toll-free numbers. For example, many hotel chains, including Marriott International, Hilton Hotels, and Starwood Hotels & Resorts Worldwide, offer web-based reservation services for their customers' convenience. The companies' websites also provide information on the hotels' prices, amenities, and frequent-guest programs.[17]

Whether as a major or minor part of the total product offering, all marketers of goods sell customer services. Providing good customer service may be the only way a company can differentiate its products when all products in a market have essentially the same quality, design, and features. This is especially true in the computer industry. When buying a laptop computer, for example, consumers shop more for fast delivery, technical support, warranties, and price than for product quality and design. Through research, a company can discover the types of services customers want and need. For example, some customers are more interested in financing, whereas others are more concerned with installation and training. The level of customer service a company provides can profoundly affect customer satisfaction. The American Customer Satisfaction Index, compiled by the National Quality Research Center at the University of Michigan, ranks customer satisfaction among a wide variety of businesses. Recent surveys suggest that dissatisfied customers may curtail their overall spending, which could stifle economic growth.[18] Among the industries rated low on customer satisfaction are phone companies, airlines, and utilities.[19]

Product Positioning and Repositioning

product positioning Creating and maintaining a certain concept of a product in customers' minds

Product positioning refers to the decisions and activities intended to create and maintain a certain concept of the firm's product (relative to competitive brands) in customers' minds. When marketers introduce a product, they try to position it so that it seems to possess the characteristics the target market most desires. This projected image is crucial. For example, Crest is positioned as a fluoride toothpaste that fights cavities, and Close-Up is positioned as a whitening toothpaste that enhances the user's sex appeal.

Product position is the result of customers' perceptions of a product's attributes relative to those of competitive brands. Buyers make numerous purchase decisions on a regular basis. To avoid a continuous reevaluation of numerous products, buyers tend to group, or "position," products in their minds to simplify buying decisions. Rather than allowing customers to position products independently, marketers often try to influence and shape consumers' concepts or perceptions of products through advertising. Marketers sometimes analyze product positions by developing perceptual maps, as shown in Figure 12.4. Perceptual maps are created by questioning a sample of consumers about their perceptions of products, brands, and organizations with respect to two or more dimensions. To develop a perceptual map such as the one in Figure 12.4, respondents would be asked how they perceive selected pain relievers in regard to price and type of pain for which the products are

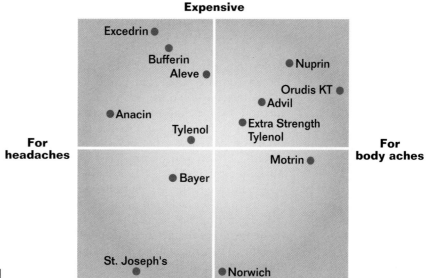

Expensive

Excedrin
Bufferin
Aleve
Nuprin
Orudis KT
Advil
Anacin
Extra Strength Tylenol
Tylenol
Motrin
Bayer
St. Joseph's
Norwich

For headaches   **For body aches**

Inexpensive

Figure 12.4 **Hypothetical Perceptual Map for Pain Relievers**

Product Positioning
Red Bull is positioned as the drink that improves performance, increases endurance, increases concentration, and improves reaction speed. Stonyfield Farm positions its yogurt as the yogurt made from only natural and organic ingredients.

used. Also, respondents would be asked about their preferences for product features to establish "ideal points" or "ideal clusters," which represent a consensus about what a specific group of customers desires in terms of product features. Then marketers can compare how their brand is perceived compared with the ideal points.

A firm can position a product to compete head-on with another brand, as PepsiCo has done against Coca-Cola, or to avoid competition, as 7Up has done relative to other soft-drink producers. Head-to-head competition may be a marketer's positioning objective if the product's performance characteristics are at least equal to

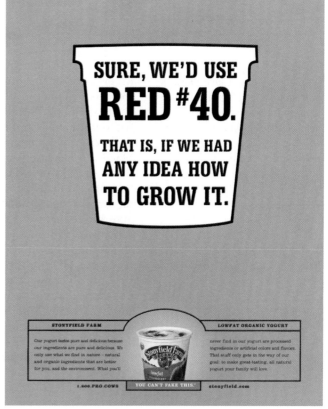

those of competitive brands and if the product is priced lower. Head-to-head positioning may be appropriate even when the price is higher if the product's performance characteristics are superior. Conversely, positioning to avoid competition may be best when the product's performance characteristics do not differ significantly from competing brands. Moreover, positioning a brand to avoid competition may be appropriate when that brand has unique characteristics that are important to some buyers. Volvo, for example, has for years positioned itself away from competitors by focusing on the safety characteristics of its cars. Whereas some auto companies mention safety issues in their advertisements, many are more likely to focus on style, fuel efficiency, performance, or terms of sale. Avoiding competition is critical when a firm introduces a brand into a market in which it already has one or more brands. Marketers usually want to avoid cannibalizing sales of their existing brands, unless the new brand generates substantially larger profits.

If a product has been planned properly, its features and brand image will give it the distinct appeal needed. Style, shape, construction, quality of work, and color help create the image and the appeal. If buyers can easily identify the benefits, they are, of course, more likely to purchase the product. When the new product does not offer certain preferred attributes, there is room for another new product.

Positioning decisions are not just for new products. Evaluating the positions of existing products is important because a brand's market share and profitability may be strengthened by product repositioning. For example, several years ago Kraft was on the verge of discontinuing Cheez Whiz because its sales had declined considerably. After Kraft marketers repositioned Cheez Whiz as a fast, convenient, microwavable cheese sauce, its sales rebounded to new heights. When introducing a new product into a product line, one or more existing brands may have to be repositioned to minimize cannibalization of established brands and ensure a favorable position for the new brand.

Repositioning can be accomplished by physically changing the product, its price, or its distribution. Rather than making any of these changes, marketers sometimes reposition a product by changing its image through promotional efforts.

Product Deletion

product deletion Eliminating a product from the product mix when it no longer satisfies a sufficient number of customers

Generally a product cannot satisfy target market customers and contribute to the achievement of the organization's overall goals indefinitely. **Product deletion** is the process of eliminating a product from the product mix, usually because it no longer satisfies a sufficient number of customers. A declining product reduces an organization's profitability and drains resources that could be used to modify other products or develop new ones. A marginal product may require shorter production runs, which can increase per-unit production costs. Finally, when a dying product completely loses favor with customers, the negative feelings may transfer to some of the company's other products. Consider how General Motors has strengthened its product mix through product deletion, as discussed in the Building Customer Relationships boxed feature.

Most organizations find it difficult to delete a product. A decision to drop a product may be opposed by managers and other employees who believe the product is necessary to the product mix. Salespeople who still have some loyal customers are especially upset when a product is dropped. In such cases, companies may spend considerable resources and effort to change a slipping product's marketing mix to improve its sales and thus avoid having to eliminate it.

Some organizations delete products only after the products have become heavy financial burdens. A better approach is some form of systematic review in which each product is evaluated periodically to determine its impact on the overall effectiveness of the firm's product mix. Such a review should analyze the product's contribution to the firm's sales for a given period, as well as estimate future sales, costs, and profits associated with the product. It should also gauge the value of making changes in the marketing strategy to improve the product's performance. A systematic review allows an organization to improve product performance and ascertain when to delete products. Procter & Gamble, for example, discontinued its White Cloud brand of toilet tissue in the early 1990s after determining the product did not match customer needs. However, after Wal-Mart acquired the rights to the name, White Cloud was repositioned as a premium private-label brand and expanded to include laundry detergent, fabric softener, and dryer sheets. Ironically, these products now compete head to head with Procter & Gamble's Tide laundry detergent and Downy fabric softener in Wal-Mart stores.[20]

Basically there are three ways to delete a product: phase it out, run it out, or drop it immediately (see Figure 12.5 on p. 328). A *phase-out* allows the product to decline without a change in the marketing strategy; no attempt is made to give the product new life. A *run-out* exploits any strengths left in the product. Intensifying marketing efforts in core markets or eliminating some marketing expenditures, such as advertising, may cause a sudden jump in profits. This approach is commonly taken for technologically obsolete products, such as older models of computers and calculators. Often the price is reduced to generate a sales spurt. The third alternative, an *immediate drop* of an unprofitable product, is the best strategy when losses are too great to prolong the product's life.

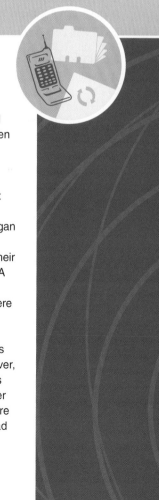

BUILDING CUSTOMER RELATIONSHIPS

General Motors Takes Slow-Selling Products Off the Road

General Motors has permanently parked the car that inspired the century-old song "In My Merry Oldsmobile." It has also taken the Pontiac Grand Am, Chevrolet Cavalier, Cadillac Catera, and Cadillac Eldorado off the road. Deleting one car is a momentous decision, yet GM has deleted five in the past few years and could delete others as it systematically reassesses each product in its mix. What do these deletions mean for GM, its customers, and its dealers?

GM's market share, a critical measure of competitive success, has been only slightly affected by the deletions. By its final year of production, Oldsmobile's share had plummeted below 1 percent. The Catera's sales were so disappointing that GM deleted it just six years after introduction. The once-popular Eldorado and Grand Am had become slow sellers and were shunted aside in favor of new models with updated styling. Sales of the Cavalier spiked after GM's announcement that the car would be replaced by the Cobalt, but the deletion decision stood.

The Oldsmobile deletion was a run-out supported by direct-mail advertising, price incentives,

and other marketing activities. Still, GM was concerned about whether customers would buy the car in its final months on the market. To encourage purchasing, the company promised that it would honor all Oldsmobile warranties and make parts and service available for at least seven more years. Nonetheless, as the deletion date approached, fewer dealers carried the cars and some Oldsmobile dealers went out of business.

Once GM made the deletion decision public, it launched an aggressive customer retention campaign to counter the efforts of competitors that began approaching Oldsmobile customers. One million-piece mailing thanked Oldsmobile customers for their loyalty and promoted other cars in the GM family. A later mailing to 300,000 customers highlighted the specific features and benefits of GM's Buicks. Where Oldsmobile dealers had closed, GM dealers contacted Oldsmobile owners to offer other GM cars.

Initial results show that Oldsmobile customers are not leaving GM in significant numbers. However, the long-term effect of deleting all five products is not yet clear. As it introduces the Cobalt and other replacements, GM is monitoring both market share and customer retention to get a picture of the road ahead.

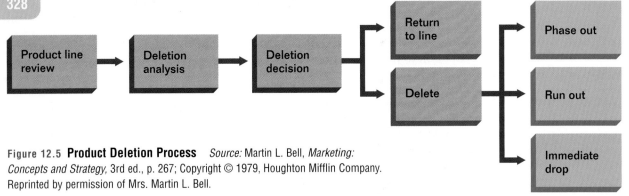

Figure 12.5 Product Deletion Process *Source:* Martin L. Bell, *Marketing: Concepts and Strategy,* 3rd ed., p. 267; Copyright © 1979, Houghton Mifflin Company. Reprinted by permission of Mrs. Martin L. Bell.

Organizing to Develop and Manage Products

After reviewing the concepts of product line and mix, life cycles, positioning, and repositioning, it should be obvious that managing products is a complex task. Often the traditional functional form of organization, in which managers specialize in such business functions as advertising, sales, and distribution, does not fit a company's needs. In this case, management must find an organizational approach that accomplishes the tasks necessary to develop and manage products. Alternatives to functional organization include the product or brand manager approach, the market manager approach, and the venture team approach.

A **product manager** is responsible for a product, a product line, or several distinct products that make up an interrelated group within a multiproduct organization. A **brand manager** is responsible for a single brand. General Foods, for example, has one brand manager for Maxim coffee and one for Maxwell House coffee. A product or brand manager operates cross-functionally to coordinate the activities, information, and strategies involved in marketing an assigned product. Product managers and brand managers plan marketing activities to achieve objectives by coordinating a mix of distribution, promotion (especially sales promotion and advertising), and price. They must consider packaging and branding decisions, and work closely with personnel in research and development, engineering, and production. Marketing research helps product managers understand consumers and find target markets. The product or brand manager approach to organization is used by many large, multiple-product companies. General Motors, for example, supports new-vehicle introductions by assigning brand managers who previously worked on successful launches: "We've got some people who are good at launches, and we'll move them where the launches are going on for some additional expertise," says a GM executive.[21]

A **market manager** is responsible for managing the marketing activities that serve a particular group of customers. This organizational approach is particularly effective when a firm engages in different types of marketing activities to provide products to diverse customer groups. A company might have one market manager for business markets and another for consumer markets. These broad market categories might be broken down into more limited market responsibilities.

A **venture team** creates entirely new products that may be aimed at new markets. Unlike a product or market manager, a venture team is responsible for all aspects of developing a product: research and development, production and engineering, finance and accounting, and marketing. Venture team members are brought together from different functional areas of the organization. In working outside of established divisions, venture teams have greater flexibility to apply inventive approaches to develop new products that can take advantage of opportunities in highly segmented markets. Companies are increasingly using such cross-functional teams for product development in an effort to boost product quality. Quality may be positively related to information integration within the team, customers' influence on the product development process, and a quality orientation within the

product manager The person within an organization responsible for a product, a product line, or several distinct products that make up a group

brand manager The person responsible for a single brand

market manager The person responsible for managing the marketing activities that serve a particular group of customers

venture team A cross-functional group that creates entirely new products that may be aimed at new markets

firm.[22] When a new product has demonstrated commercial potential, team members may return to their functional areas, or they may join a new or existing division to manage the product.

SUMMARY

Organizations must be able to adjust their product mixes to compete effectively and achieve their goals. A product mix can be improved through line extension and product modification. A line extension is the development of a product closely related to one or more products in the existing line but designed specifically to meet different customer needs. Product modification is the changing of one or more characteristics of a product. This approach can be effective when the product is modifiable, when customers can perceive the change, and when customers want the modification. Quality modifications relate to a product's dependability and durability. Functional modifications affect a product's versatility, effectiveness, convenience, or safety. Aesthetic modifications change the sensory appeal of a product.

Developing new products can enhance a firm's product mix and add depth to the product line. A new product may be an innovation that has never been sold by any organization; a product that a given firm has not marketed previously, although similar products have been available from other organizations; or a product brought from one market to another.

Before a product is introduced, it goes through a seven-phase new-product development process. In the idea generation phase, new-product ideas may come from internal or external sources. In the process of screening, ideas are evaluated to determine whether they are consistent with the firm's overall objectives and resources. Concept testing, the third phase, involves having a small sample of potential customers review a brief description of the product idea to determine their initial perceptions of the proposed product and their early buying intentions. During the business analysis stage, the product idea is evaluated to determine its potential contribution to the firm's sales, costs, and profits. In the product development stage, the organization determines if it is technically feasible to produce the product and if it can be produced at a cost low enough to make the final price reasonable. Test marketing is a limited introduction of a product in areas chosen to represent the intended market. Finally, in the commercialization phase, full-scale production of the product begins and a complete marketing strategy is developed.

Product differentiation is the process of creating and designing products so that customers perceive them as different from competing products. Product quality, product design and features, and product support services are three aspects of product differentiation that companies consider when creating and marketing products.

Product quality includes the overall characteristics of a product that allow it to perform as expected in satisfying customer needs. The level of quality is the amount of quality a product possesses. Consistency of quality is the degree to which a product has the same level of quality over time. Product design refers to how a product is conceived, planned, and produced. Components of product design include styling (the physical appearance of the product) and product features (the specific design characteristics that allow a product to perform certain tasks). Companies often differentiate their products by providing support services, usually called customer services. Customer services are human or mechanical efforts or activities that add value to a product.

Product positioning entails the decisions and activities that create and maintain a certain concept of the firm's product in customers' minds. Product position is the result of customers' perceptions of the product's attributes relative to competitive brands. Product positioning plays a role in market segmentation. Organizations can position a product to compete head to head with another brand if the product's performance is at least equal to the competitive brand's and is priced lower. When a brand possesses unique characteristics that are important to some buyers, positioning it to avoid competition is appropriate. It is important to avoid positioning a product so that it competes with sales of the company's existing products. Companies can also increase an existing brand's market share and profitability through product repositioning. Repositioning can be accomplished by making physical changes in the product, changing its price or distribution, or changing its image.

Product deletion is the process of eliminating a product that no longer satisfies a sufficient number of customers. Although a firm's personnel may oppose product deletion, weak products are unprofitable, consume too much time and effort, may require shorter production runs, and can create an unfavorable impression of the firm's other products. A product mix should be systematically reviewed to determine when to delete products. Products to be deleted can be phased out, run out, or dropped immediately.

Often the traditional functional form of organization does not lend itself to the complex task of developing and managing products. Alternative organizational forms include the product or brand manager approach, the market manager approach, and the venture team approach. A product manager is responsible for a product, a product line, or several distinct products that make up an interrelated group within a multiproduct organization. A brand manager is responsible for a single brand. A market manager is responsible for managing the marketing activities that serve a particular group or class of customers. A venture team is sometimes used to create entirely new products that may be aimed at new markets.

Please visit the student website at **www.prideferrell.com** for ACE Self-Test questions that will help you prepare for exams.

IMPORTANT TERMS

Line extension
Product modifications
Quality modifications
Functional modifications
Aesthetic modifications
New-product development
  process
Idea generation
Screening
Concept testing
Business analysis
Product development
Test marketing
Commercialization

Product differentiation
Quality
Level of quality
Consistency of quality
Product design
Styling
Product features
Customer services
Product positioning
Product deletion
Product manager
Brand manager
Market manager
Venture team

DISCUSSION & REVIEW QUESTIONS

1. What is a line extension, and how does it differ from a product modification?
2. Compare and contrast the three major approaches to modifying a product.
3. Identify and briefly explain the seven major phases of the new-product development process.
4. Do small companies that manufacture just a few products need to be concerned about developing and managing products? Why or why not?
5. Why is product development a cross-functional activity—involving finance, engineering, manufacturing, and other functional areas—within an organization?
6. What is the major purpose of concept testing, and how is it accomplished?
7. What are the benefits and disadvantages of test marketing?
8. Why can the process of commercialization take a considerable amount of time?
9. What is product differentiation, and how can it be achieved?
10. Explain how the term *quality* has been used to differentiate products in the automobile industry in recent years. What are some makes and models of automobiles that come to mind when you hear the terms *high quality* and *poor quality?*
11. What is product positioning? Under what conditions would head-to-head product positioning be appro-

priate? When should head-to-head positioning be avoided?
12. What types of problems does a weak product cause in a product mix? Describe the most effective approach for avoiding such problems.
13. What type of organization might use a venture team to develop new products? What are the advantages and disadvantages of such a team?

APPLICATION QUESTIONS

1. When developing a new product, a company often test markets the proposed product in a specific area or location. Suppose you wish to test market your new, revolutionary SuperWax car wax, which requires only one application for a lifetime finish. Where and how would you test market your new product?
2. Product positioning aims to create a certain concept of a product in consumers' minds relative to its competition. For example, Pepsi is positioned in direct competition with Coca-Cola, whereas Volvo has traditionally positioned itself away from competitors by emphasizing its cars' safety features. Following are several distinct positions in which an organization may place its product. Identify a product that would fit into each position.
   a. High price/high quality
   b. Low price
   c. Convenience
   d. Uniqueness
3. Select an organization that you think should reposition itself in the consumer's eye. Identify where it is currently positioned, and make recommendations for repositioning. Explain and defend your suggestions.
4. A product manager may make quality, functional, or aesthetic modifications when modifying a product. Identify a familiar product that recently was modified, categorize the modification (quality, functional, or aesthetic), and describe how you would have modified it differently.
5. Phasing out a product from the product mix often is difficult for an organization. Visit a retail store in your area, and ask the manager what products he or she has had to discontinue in the recent past. Find out what factors influenced the decision to delete the product and who was involved in the decision. Ask the manager to identify any products that should be but have not been deleted, and try to ascertain the reason.

Internet Exercise & Resources

Merck & Company

Merck, a leading global pharmaceutical company, develops, manufactures, and markets a broad range of health care products. In addition, the firm's Merck-Medco Managed Care Division manages pharmacy benefits for more than 40 million Americans. The company has established a website to serve as an educational and informational resource for Internet users around the world. To learn more about the company and its research, visit its award-winning site at **www.merck.com**.

1. What products has Merck developed and introduced recently?
2. What role does research play in Merck's success? How does research facilitate new-product development at Merck?
3. Find Merck's mission statement. Is Merck's focus on research consistent with the firm's mission and values?

Video Case 12.1

Cali Cosmetics Positions Products with Olive Oil

Competition in the $32 billion global market for skin care products is extremely intense. Any newcomer to this industry must confront the brand power and marketing muscle of international beauty giants such as L'Oréal, Procter & Gamble, Unilever, Shiseido, and Estée Lauder. Thousands of new skin care products arrive on store shelves every year in the United States, and these are as likely to have been launched by lesser-known firms such as Hearts and Roses, Love Thy Hair, and Matahari as by the market leaders.

In this highly competitive industry, product differentiation is crucial. Typically companies accomplish this through brand name, product design, and styling, as well as specific product features and ingredients. For example, cosmetics companies have incorporated fruits, vegetables, herbs, vitamins, and just about anything else imaginable that can be safely applied to skin. Yet formulating beauty products with olive oil—the same ingredient favored by professional chefs and home cooks alike—is a relatively recent innovation. The ancient Romans called olive oil

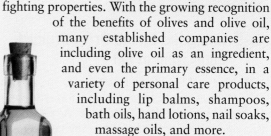

"liquid gold" and "nectar of the gods." The healthful benefits of olive oil for human skin and hair have long been recognized: ancient Egyptians used it as a moisturizer, Roman gladiators as a salve for wounds, and the Spanish as a primary ingredient of Castile soap.

Olive oil has recently experienced a resurgence in the cosmetics industry as part of a trend toward using more botanical ingredients in beauty products. Experts believe the olive offers many cosmetic benefits: the skin, pulp, and oil contain glycerides and fatty acids that clean and moisturize, while the pits and bark make excellent exfoliants. Research also suggests that olive oil may have anti-aging and cancer-fighting properties. With the growing recognition of the benefits of olives and olive oil, many established companies are including olive oil as an ingredient, and even the primary essence, in a variety of personal care products, including lip balms, shampoos, bath oils, hand lotions, nail soaks, massage oils, and more.

Some companies offer just one item infused with olive extracts, such as Philosophy's Amazing Grace perfumed olive oil body scrub and Bibo's O-live a Little hand and body lotion. Australia's Aesop line now includes an olive facial cleanser, Greece's Korres Athens offers an olive pit scrub, and Britain's Body Shop markets an olive moisturizer. Other companies are marketing entire collections of olive oil–based cosmetics, including The Thymes, which introduced Olive Leaf, a product line that incorporates every part of the olive into products designed to improve the skin's texture and protect it from environmental damage.

An Italian firm, Cali Cosmetics, has entered the industry with its Oliva line of beauty products. Founded by Italy's Baronessa Consuelo Cali, Cali offers beauty products with vitamin-enriched extracts of Italian olive oil designed to protect and soften skin. Cali Cosmetics grew out of the Cali family's olive orchard and spa. Legend has it that the area, on the outskirts of Rome overlooking the Mediterranean Sea, was discovered by Roman nobles who enjoyed olive oil treatments there in the nineteenth century. The Cali Beauty Farm, housed in the Cali family's ancestral castle, has attracted customers ever since with olive-based food recipes and beauty treatments.

Baronessa Cali became the spa's primary owner in the late 1980s. In the late 1990s, she began to adapt generations-old family recipes and use modern technology to perfect them for home use. The process involves extracting all the vitamins from olive oil to create skin-pampering products that do not feel greasy. Now the line includes cleansers, moisturizers, and scrubs for the hair, face, body, and feet. Over time, the baronessa expects to introduce up to 100 new products based on her family's recipes.

In a market saturated with beauty products that smell good, feel good, and claim to promote healthy skin, Cali can succeed only by making its products stand out. To do this, the company focuses on linking its brand and image to the health and beauty benefits of its olive oil-based skin care products. Customers are already responding: Cali achieved annual sales of more than $1 million a year during its first three years in the U.S. market. Cali products are also available in Belgium, Canada, Germany, Hong Kong, Saudi Arabia, Singapore, Switzerland, and the United Kingdom. Experts see a bright future for skin care products, with demand especially strong in Europe and Asia. Cali is counting on its brand's distinctive appeal and the beauty benefits of olive oil ingredients to keep Oliva sales growing in the coming years.[23]

QUESTIONS FOR DISCUSSION

1. Are Oliva beauty products line extensions, modified products, or new products for the Cali family?
2. Describe the positioning of Oliva beauty products.
3. Assess Cali Cosmetics' strategy for differentiating its products from those of competitors.

Case 12.2

Using the 3Rs to Drive Product Innovation at 3M

3M, the $16 billion company formerly known as Minnesota Mining and Manufacturing, drives new-product development by carefully managing the 3Rs: risk, reward, and responsibility. 3M has more than a century of experience in successfully developing and managing a diverse mix of consumer and business products. Post-it Notes and Scotch-Brite scouring pads are just two of 3M's well-known brand names. The company also creates products for very specific uses, such as light-reflective coatings for street signs and medicinal creams for fighting skin-based viruses.

Day in and day out, 6,500 employees follow the 3R system as they search for new technologies and applications that could conceivably become 3M's next blockbuster product. The first R, risk, is a vital element in decisions about whether a product idea is promising enough to be developed into a prototype, test marketed, and ultimately brought to market through commercialization. Rather than take the safer path of incrementally improving existing products, 3M is taking calculated risks in its search for major breakthroughs. Its ambitious goals are to introduce twice the number of new products and triple the number of successful products, that it has in the past.

Risks are evaluated relative to the second R, reward. Through the 3M Acceleration system, managers filter out ideas with lower profit potential and concentrate company resources on the few hundred ideas with higher profit potential. The point is to more productively support corporate growth by bringing high-potential products to market faster. Executives monitor all the ideas that make it into the Acceleration program to ensure speedy progress toward commercialization and measure the rewards in terms of revenue and profits.

With respect to the third *R*, responsibility, Lead User Teams—cross-functional groups of up to six employees—are responsible for new-product development. In addition to technical and marketing staff, a team may have members from manufacturing, finance, procurement, or other departments, depending on its focus. Each team investigates product ideas to satisfy the unspoken or unrecognized needs of its customer segment. "They are taught to set their sights on exploring the areas where the possibilities for discovery are greatest because the pre-existing knowledge is most slim," says one 3M manager. This entails systematically examining trends that barely register today to consider products so advanced that "even the 'early adopters' have not yet arrived."

In addition to team responsibility, 3M has a long-standing tradition of nurturing independent research into potential new products. This encourages innovation from within and has led to new products and processes that benefited the company as well as its customers. Staff scientists are allowed to spend up to 15 percent of their time on self-directed projects that they think will blossom into commercially feasible products. They can request funding from their own business units or any other 3M unit to pursue the best ideas. If they are unable to obtain funding from a business unit, they can apply for a company-sponsored independent research grant of up to $100,000. Employees are also eligible for awards that honor outstanding achievement in new-product development, technology, and quality.

Along with the 3Rs, 3M is relying on DFSS—Design for Six Sigma—to boost product quality and development efficiency. The Six Sigma program takes quality far beyond simple error measurement and reduction: it teaches employees to incorporate the customer perspective early in the development process. More than 20,000 managers and scientists around the world have already received training in Six Sigma. These techniques "allow us to be more closely connected to the market and give us a much higher probability of success in our new-product designs," says 3M's vice president of research and development. The program has been so successful that the company is teaching its customers to apply Six Sigma techniques to improve their processes and products.

Finally, 3M is expediting new-product development by transferring 400 scientists from the corporate research and development department to specific business units. "By bringing more of our technical people into 3M businesses, we are strengthening our ability

to commercialize new products now and well into the future," explains the CEO. "Now technical people can play more of a role in transforming pipeline projects into marketplace realities."[24]

QUESTIONS FOR DISCUSSION

1. Why would 3M apply quality improvement techniques to the design of new products?

2. What effect is the 3M Acceleration program likely to have on each stage of the new-product development process?

3. Evaluate 3M's goals of launching twice the number of new products and triple the number of successful products compared with previous years. Are these goals practical and attainable? How might these goals affect the efforts of 3M's Lead User Teams?

Branding and Packaging

13

OBJECTIVES

1. To explain the value of branding

2. To understand brand loyalty

3. To analyze the major components of brand equity

4. To recognize the types of brands and their benefits

5. To understand how to select and protect brands

6. To examine three types of branding policies

7. To understand co-branding and brand licensing

8. To describe the major packaging functions and design considerations and how packaging is used in marketing strategies

9. To examine the functions of labeling and describe some legal issues pertaining to labeling

Making Brands More Alive Through Brand Mascots

Who are Red and Yellow? M&M lovers may not know these names, but they know what brand the animated candies represent. The list of well-known brand mascots goes on and on, from the Ronald McDonald clown and the Pillsbury Dough Boy to the Energizer Bunny and the Kellogg's Rice Crispies Snap, Crackle, and Pop. Some mascots have a long history: the Michelin Man, for example, dates back to 1898. At the other extreme, the insurance company AFLAC first used its duck mascot in 2000.

To successfully make a brand come alive, a mascot should symbolize the brand's strengths and evoke positive feelings. Consider Maytag's dilemma. Customers buy dishwashers and other appliances on the basis of reliability and performance, but advertisements conveying these attributes through statistics would be dull and unappealing. Instead, the company's advertising agency came up with the idea for Ol' Lonely, a likable Maytag repairman who never sees customers because the brand is so reliable. "Our consumer research shows time and again the character humanizes our brand and that's a huge point for us," stresses Maytag's brand manager.

Brand mascots can be effective in business markets as well as consumer markets. The Concoman is a superhero mascot who appears in direct-mail campaigns for Conco Systems, a company that repairs and maintains power plants. "Concoman is an action figure that demonstrates the type of heroic activities our field technicians perform on a daily basis for clients," says the vice president of sales and marketing. "When customers are faced with difficult tasks, we want to demonstrate strength, responsiveness, and superior technology."

Another important principle is to refresh mascots over time so they remain relevant. For example, the Buddy Lee kewpie doll first appeared in Lee Jeans advertisements several decades ago. When the company's advertising experts began planning a new campaign a few years ago, they remembered the mascot. By researching the target market of 18- to 24-year-olds, they learned that the mascot needed "a new archetype of coolness." The update worked: jeans sales among this target market rose more than 20 percent in the campaign's first year.

Finally, the mascot needs the right amount of exposure. Red Dog beer ads originally featured the Red Dog mascot talking about individuality. The dog became such a big hit that it popped up on clothing, key chains, and many other products, threatening the brand's individuality message. In contrast, some companies give their mascots time off or lend them to other marketers. Ol' Lonely appeared in a Chevrolet commercial, reinforcing how much free time he has. Kellogg replaced its traditional mascots for a summer with Cartoon Network characters such as the Power Puff Girls. The idea was to refresh connections with children by building on the cartoon characters' popularity. Afterward the reappearance of Kellogg's familiar mascots attracted children's attention, as well.[1] ■

Packages, brands, and components of brands, such as the popular brand mascots, are part of a product's tangible features, the verbal and physical cues that help customers identify the products they want and influence their choices when they are unsure. As such, branding and packaging play an important role in marketing strategy. A successful brand is distinct and memorable; without one, a firm could not differentiate its products, and shoppers' choices would essentially be arbitrary. A good package design is cost effective, safe, environmentally responsible, and valuable as a promotional tool.

In this chapter, we first discuss branding, its value to customers and marketers, brand loyalty, and brand equity. Next, we examine the various types of brands. We then consider how companies choose and protect brands, the various branding policies employed, co-branding, and brand licensing. We look at packaging's critical role as part of the product. Next, we explore the functions of packaging, issues to consider in packaging design, how the package can be a major element in marketing strategy, and packaging criticisms. Finally, we discuss the functions of labeling and relevant legal issues.

Branding

brand A name, term, design, symbol, or other feature that identifies a seller's products and differentiates them from competitors' products

brand name The part of a brand that can be spoken, including letters, words, and numbers

brand mark The part of a brand not made up of words, such as a symbol or design

Marketers must make many decisions about products, including choices about brands, brand names, brand marks, trademarks, and trade names. A **brand** is a name, term, design, symbol, or any other feature that identifies one seller's good or service as distinct from those of other sellers. A brand may identify one item, a family of items, or all items of that seller.[2] A **brand name** is the part of a brand that can be spoken—including letters, words, and numbers—such as 7Up. A brand name is often a product's only distinguishing characteristic. Without the brand name, a firm could not differentiate its products. To consumers, a brand name is as fundamental as the product itself. Indeed, many brand names have become synonymous with the product, such as Scotch Tape and Xerox copiers. Through promotional activities, the owners of these brand names try to protect them from being used as generic names for tape and photocopiers.

The element of a brand that is not made up of words—often a symbol or design— is a **brand mark**. One example is the Golden Arches, which identify McDonald's

A NEW OATMEAL BAR MADE WITH OLD FASHIONED KNOW-HOW.

Brand Mark
The portrait of the Quaker man is an example of a brand mark.

trademark A legal designation of exclusive use of a brand

trade name The full legal name of an organization

restaurants and can be seen on patches worn by athletic teams—from U.S. Olympic teams to Little League softball teams—sponsored by McDonald's. A **trademark** is a legal designation indicating that the owner has exclusive use of a brand or a part of a brand and others are prohibited by law from using it. To protect a brand name or brand mark in the United States, an organization must register it as a trademark with the U.S. Patent and Trademark Office. In 2000, the Patent and Trademark Office registered 133,225 trademarks.[3] Finally, a **trade name** is the full legal name of an organization, such as Ford Motor Company, rather than the name of a specific product.

◆ Value of Branding

Both buyers and sellers benefit from branding. Brands help buyers identify specific products that they do and do not like, which in turn facilitates the purchase of items that satisfy their needs and reduces the time required to purchase the product. Without brands, product selection would be quite random because buyers would have no assurance they were purchasing what they preferred. The purchase of certain brands can be a form of self-expression. For example, clothing brand names are important to many teenage boys; names such as Tommy Hilfiger, Polo, Champion, Guess, and Nike give manufacturers an advantage in the marketplace. A brand also helps buyers evaluate the quality of products, especially when they are unable to judge a product's characteristics; that is, a brand may symbolize a certain quality level to a customer, and in turn the person lets that perception of quality represent the quality of the item. A brand helps reduce a buyer's perceived risk of purchase. In addition, a psychological reward may come from owning a brand that symbolizes status. The Mercedes-Benz brand in the United States is an example.

Sellers benefit from branding because each company's brands identify its products, which makes repeat purchasing easier for customers. Branding helps a firm introduce a new product that carries the name of one or more of its existing products because buyers are already familiar with those brands. Branding also facilitates promotional efforts because the promotion of each branded product indirectly promotes all other similarly branded products. Branding also fosters brand loyalty. To the extent that buyers become loyal to a specific brand, the company's market share for that product achieves a certain level of stability, allowing the firm to use its resources more efficiently. Once a firm develops some degree of customer loyalty for a brand, it can maintain a fairly consistent price rather than continually cutting the price to attract customers. A brand is as much of an asset as the company's building or machinery. When marketers increase their brand's value, they also raise the total asset value of the organization. (We discuss brand value in more detail later in this chapter.) At times, marketers must decide whether to change a brand name. This is a difficult decision because the value in the existing brand name must be given up to gain the potential to build a higher value in a new brand name.

◆ Brand Loyalty

brand loyalty A customer's favorable attitude toward a specific brand and likelihood of consistent purchase

As we just noted, creating and maintaining customer loyalty toward a brand is a major benefit of branding. **Brand loyalty** is a customer's favorable attitude toward a specific brand. If brand loyalty is strong enough, customers may consistently purchase this brand when they need a product in that product category. Although brand loyalty may not result in a customer's purchasing a specific brand all the time, the brand is at least viewed as a potentially viable choice in the set of brands being considered for purchase. Development of brand loyalty in a customer reduces his or her risks and shortens the time spent buying the product. However, the degree of brand loyalty for products varies from one product category to another. For example, it is challenging to develop brand loyalty for most products because customers can usually judge a product's quality and do not need to refer to a brand as an indicator of quality. Brand loyalty also varies by country. Customers in France, Germany, and the United Kingdom tend to be less brand-loyal than U.S. customers.

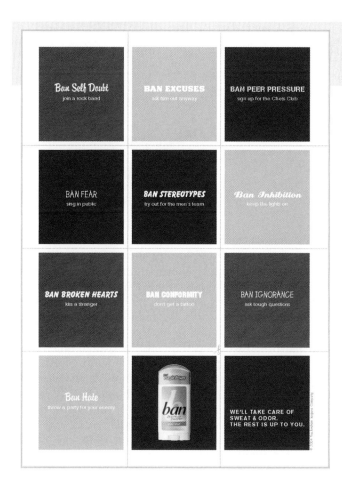

Brand Insistence
A number of consumers are brand insistent regarding their deodorant.

Three degrees of brand loyalty exist: recognition, preference, and insistence. **Brand recognition** occurs when a customer is aware that the brand exists and views it as an alternative purchase if the preferred brand is unavailable or if the other available brands are unfamiliar. This is the mildest form of brand loyalty. The term *loyalty* clearly is used very loosely here. One of the initial objectives when introducing a new brand is to create widespread awareness of the brand to generate brand recognition.

Brand preference is a stronger degree of brand loyalty: a customer definitely prefers one brand over competitive offerings and will purchase this brand if available. However, if the brand is not available, the customer will accept a substitute brand rather than expending additional effort finding and purchasing the preferred brand. A marketer is likely to be able to compete effectively in a market when a number of customers have developed brand preference for its specific brand.

When **brand insistence** occurs, a customer strongly prefers a specific brand, will accept no substitute, and is willing to spend a great deal of time and effort to acquire that brand. If a brand-insistent customer goes to a store and finds the brand unavailable, he or she will seek the brand elsewhere rather than purchase a substitute brand. Brand insistence is the strongest degree of brand loyalty; it is a brander's dream. However, it is the least common type of brand loyalty. Customers vary considerably regarding the product categories for which they may be brand-insistent. Can you think of products for which you are brand-insistent? Perhaps it's a brand of deodorant, soft drink, jeans, or even pet food (if your pet is brand-insistent).

Brand loyalty in general seems to be declining, partly because of marketers' increased reliance on sales, coupons, and other short-term promotions and partly because of the sometimes overwhelming array of similar new products from which customers can choose. Several recent studies indicate that brand loyalty is declining for all age groups and especially among consumers age 50 and older.[4]

Building brand loyalty is a major challenge for many marketers. It is an extremely important issue. The creation of brand loyalty significantly contributes to an organization's ability to achieve a sustainable competitive advantage.

brand recognition Awareness that a brand exists and is an alternative purchase

brand preference The degree of brand loyalty in which a customer prefers one brand over competitive offerings

brand insistence The degree of brand loyalty in which a customer strongly prefers a specific brand and will accept no substitute

brand equity The marketing and financial value associated with a brand's strength in a market

◆ Brand Equity

A well-managed brand is an asset to an organization. The value of this asset is often referred to as brand equity. **Brand equity** is the marketing and financial value associated with a brand's strength in a market. Besides the actual proprietary brand assets, such as patents and trademarks, four major elements underlie brand equity: brand name awareness, brand loyalty, perceived brand quality, and brand associations (see Figure 13.1 on p. 340).[5]

Awareness of a brand leads to brand familiarity, which in turn results in a level of comfort with the brand. A familiar brand is more likely to be selected than an unfamiliar brand because the familiar brand is often viewed as more reliable and of more acceptable quality. The familiar brand is likely to be in a customer's consideration set, whereas the unfamiliar brand is not.

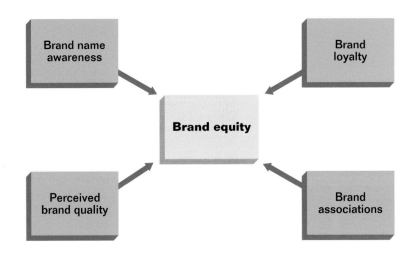

Figure 13.1 Major Elements of Brand Equity *Source:* Adapted with the permission of The Free Press, a division of Simon & Schuster Adult Publishing Group, from *Managing Brand Equity: Capitalizing on the Value of a Brand Name* by David A. Aaker. Copyright © 1991 by David A. Aaker. All rights reserved.

Brand loyalty is an important component of brand equity because it reduces a brand's vulnerability to competitors' actions. Brand loyalty allows an organization to keep its existing customers and avoid spending an enormous amount of resources gaining new ones. Loyal customers provide brand visibility and reassurance to potential new customers. Because customers expect their brands to be available when and where they shop, retailers strive to carry the brands known for their strong customer following.

Customers associate a particular brand with a certain level of overall quality. A brand name may be used as a substitute for judgment of quality. In many cases, customers can't actually judge the quality of the product for themselves and instead must rely on the brand as a quality indicator. Perceived high brand quality helps support a premium price, allowing a marketer to avoid severe price competition. Also, favorable perceived brand quality can ease the introduction of brand extensions, since the high regard for the brand will likely translate into high regard for the related products.

Brand Awareness
Numerous companies employ advertising aimed at building brand awareness, which in turn builds brand equity.

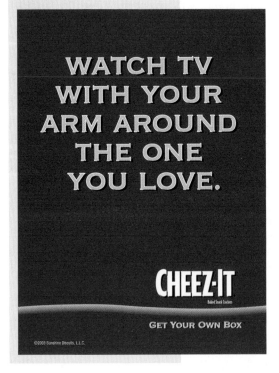

Stimulating Brand Associations
Some organizations use trade characters, such as Tony the Tiger, to stimulate favorable brand associations.

The set of associations linked to a brand is another key component of brand equity. At times a marketer works to connect a particular lifestyle or, in some instances, a certain personality type with a specific brand. For example, customers associate Michelin tires with protecting family members, a De Beers diamond with a loving, long-lasting relationship ("A Diamond Is Forever"), and Dr Pepper with a unique taste. These types of brand associations contribute significantly to the brand's equity. Brand associations are sometimes facilitated by using trade characters, such as the Jolly Green Giant, the Pillsbury Dough Boy, and Charlie the Tuna. Placing these trade characters in advertisements and on packages helps consumers link the ads and packages to the brands.

Although difficult to measure, brand equity represents the value of a brand to an organization. An organization may buy a brand from another company at a premium price because outright brand purchase may be less expensive and less risky than creating and developing a brand from scratch. For example, PepsiCo purchased Quaker Oats Company for $13.4 billion primarily to acquire the Gatorade brand, which at that time had 78 percent of the sports-drink market.[6] Brand equity helps give a brand the power to capture and maintain a consistent market share, which provides stability to the organization's sales volume.

Table 13.1 lists the 25 brands with the highest economic value. Any company that owns a brand listed in Table 13.1 would agree that the economic value of that

Table 13.1   The World's Most Valuable Brands

Rank	Brand	Country	Brand Value (in Millions $)
1	Coca-Cola	U.S.	70.45
2	Microsoft	U.S.	65.17
3	IBM	U.S.	51.77
4	GE	U.S.	42.34
5	Intel	U.S.	31.11
6	Nokia	Finland	29.44
7	Disney	U.S.	28.04
8	McDonald's	U.S.	24.70
9	Marlboro	U.S.	22.18
10	Mercedes	Germany	21.37
11	Toyota	Japan	20.78
12	Hewlett-Packard	U.S.	19.86
13	Citibank	U.S.	18.57
14	Ford	U.S.	17.07
15	American Express	U.S.	16.83
16	Gillette	U.S.	15.98
17	Cisco	U.S.	15.79
18	Honda	Japan	15.63
19	BMW	Germany	15.11
20	Sony	Japan	13.15
21	Nescafé	Switzerland	12.34
22	Budweiser	U.S.	11.89
23	Pepsi	U.S.	11.78
24	Oracle	U.S.	11.26
25	Samsung Electronics	South Korea	10.85

Source: "Business Week Reports Interbrand's Annual Ranking of 'The Best Global Brands,'" PR Newswire, July 24, 2003.

Types of Brands
Shown here are examples of store brands, generic brands, and manufacturer brands.

manufacturer brand A brand initiated by its producer

private distributor brand A brand initiated and owned by a reseller

Snapshot

Consumers often choose the store brand

Percentage of total product sales derived from store brand products:

57.8% Sugar
50.9% Powdered milk
51.7% Dry beans/vegetables
53.4% Marshmallows
45.4% Coffee creamer

Source: PLMA's 2003 Private Label Yearbook: A Statistical Guide to Today's Store Brands, p. 63.

brand is likely to be the greatest single asset the organization possesses. A brand's overall economic value rises and falls with the brand's profitability, brand awareness, brand loyalty, and perceived brand quality and with the strength of positive brand associations.

◆ Types of Brands

There are three categories of brands: manufacturer, private distributor, and generic. **Manufacturer brands** are initiated by producers and ensure that producers are identified with their products at the point of purchase—for example, Green Giant, Compaq Computer, and Levi's jeans. A manufacturer brand usually requires a producer to become involved in distribution, promotion, and, to some extent, pricing decisions. Brand loyalty is encouraged by promotion, quality control, and guarantees; it is a valuable asset to a manufacturer. The producer tries to stimulate demand for the product, which tends to encourage sellers and resellers to make the product available.

Private distributor brands (also called *private brands, store brands,* or *dealer brands*) are initiated and owned by resellers, that is, wholesalers or retailers. The major characteristic of private brands is that the manufacturers are not identified on the products. Retailers and wholesalers use private distributor brands to develop more efficient promotion, generate higher gross margins, and change store image. Safeway stores, for example, use private brands to compete against deep discounters and have a magazine to promote their brands. There are private-label products at every price point and in every category from trash bags to ice cream.[7] Private distributor brands give retailers or wholesalers freedom to purchase products of a specified quality at the lowest cost without disclosing the identities of the manufacturers. Wholesaler brands include IGA (Independent Grocers' Alliance) and Topmost (General Grocer). Familiar retailer brand names include Sears' Kenmore and JCPenney's Arizona. Many successful private brands are distributed nationally. Kenmore washers are as well known as most manufacturer brands. Sometimes retailers with successful private distributor brands start manufacturing their own products to gain more control over product costs, quality, and design in the hope of increasing profits. Private brands account for more than 16 percent of dollar volume sales and comprise approximately 21 percent of unit volume sales in supermarkets.[8] Supermarket private brands are popular globally, too. In the United Kingdom, private brand products generate more than 30 percent of supermarket revenues; in France, 25 percent; in Belgium and Germany, more than 22 percent; in Holland, 18 percent; and in Spain, 10 percent. Boots, the largest drugstore chain in Great Britain, has earned such a wide reputation for high-quality store brands that its private-label suntan lotion and painkiller are the nation's top sellers in their product categories.[9]

Competition between manufacturer brands and private distributor brands (sometimes called "the battle of the brands") is ongoing. To compete against manufacturer brands, retailers have tried to strengthen consumer confidence in private brands. Results of a recent study on consumer perceptions of private and manufacturer brands appear in Figure 13.2. For manufacturers, developing multiple manufacturer brands and distribution systems has been an effective means of combating the increased competition from private brands. By developing a new brand name, a producer can adjust various elements of its marketing mix to appeal to a different target market.

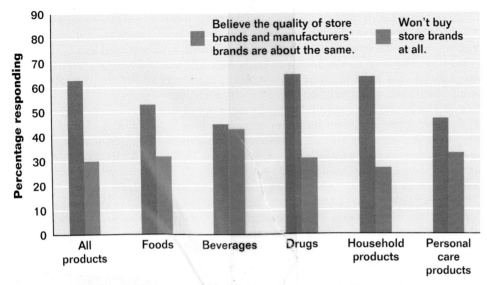

Figure 13.2 Consumers' Perceptions of Store and Manufacturers' Brands for Selected Product Groups *Source:* "Store Brands at the Turning Point," Consumer Research Network, 3624 Market Street, Philadelphia, PA.

generic brand A brand indicating only the product category

The growth of private brands has been steady. One reason is that retailers advertise the manufacturer brands, which brings customers to their stores, but sell the private brands, especially to price-sensitive customers. Another reason is that retailers with private labels negotiate better prices from producers of manufacturer brands.[10] To compete against private brands, some manufacturer brand makers have stopped increasing prices or even cut their prices, which has narrowed the price gap—the major advantage of buying a private brand. Traditionally private brands have appeared in packaging that directly imitates the packaging of competing manufacturers' brands without significant legal ramifications. However, the legal risks of using look-alike packaging are increasing for private branders. For additional information and illustrations of how private brands and manufacturer brands compete, take a look at the Building Customer Relationships boxed features (on p. 344).

Some private distributor brands are produced by companies that specialize in making only private distributor brands; others are made by producers of manufacturer brands. At times, producers of both types of brands find it difficult to ignore the opportunities that arise from producing private distributor brands. If a producer decides not to produce a private brand for a reseller, a competitor probably will. Moreover, the production of private distributor brands allows the producer to use excess capacity during periods when its own brands are at nonpeak production. The ultimate decision of whether to produce a private or a manufacturer brand depends on a company's resources, production capabilities, and goals.

Some marketers of traditionally branded products have embarked on a policy of not branding, often called *generic branding*. **Generic brands** indicate only the product category (such as aluminum foil) and do not include the company name or other identifying terms. Generic brands are usually sold at lower prices than comparable branded items. Although at one time generic brands may have represented as much as 10 percent of all retail grocery sales, today they account for less than half of 1 percent.

◆ Selecting a Brand Name

Marketers consider a number of factors in selecting a brand name. First, the name should be easy for customers (including foreign buyers, if the firm intends to market its products in other countries) to say, spell, and recall. Short, one-syllable names, such as Cheer, often satisfy this requirement. Second, the brand name should indicate the product's major benefits and, if possible, suggest in a positive way the product's uses and special characteristics; negative or offensive references should be avoided. For example, the brand names of such household cleaning products as Ajax dishwashing liquid, Vanish toilet bowl cleaner, Formula 409 multipurpose cleaner, Cascade dishwasher detergent, and Wisk laundry detergent connote strength and effectiveness. Third, to set it apart from competing brands, the brand should be distinctive. If a marketer intends to use a brand for a product line, that brand must be compatible with all products in the line. Finally, a brand should be designed so that it can be used and recognized in all types of media. Finding the right brand name has become a challenging task because many obvious product names have already been used.

How are brand names devised? Brand names can be created from single or multiple words—for example, Bic or Dodge Grand Caravan. Letters and numbers are used to create such brands as IBM PC or Z71. Words, numbers, and letters are combined to yield brand names such as Mazda MX-5 Miata or BMW Z4 Roadster. To avoid terms that have negative connotations, marketers sometimes use fabricated words that have absolutely no meaning when created—for example, Kodak and Exxon. Occasionally a brand is simply brought out of storage and used as is or modified. Firms often maintain banks of registered brands, some of which may have been used in the past. Cadillac, for example, has a bank of approximately 360 registered trademarks. The LaSalle brand, used in the 1920s and 1930s, could be called up for a new Cadillac model in the future. Possible brand names sometimes are tested in focus groups or other settings to assess customers' reactions.

Who actually creates brand names? Brand names can be created internally by the organization. Sometimes a name is suggested by individuals who are close to the product's development. Some organizations have committees that participate in brand name creation and approval. Large companies that introduce numerous new products annually are likely to have a department that develops brand names. At times, outside consultants and companies that specialize in brand name development are used. For example, Philip Morris hired Landor Associates to develop its new name, Altria Group.[11]

Although most of the important branding considerations apply to both goods and services, branding a service has some additional dimensions. The service brand is usually the same as the company name. Financial companies, such as Fidelity

BUILDING CUSTOMER RELATIONSHIPS

The Power of Private Distributor Brands

In the battle of the brands, private distributor brands such as Ol' Roy dog food and Charles Shaw are gaining power every day. Wal-Mart owns the Ol' Roy brand, a worldwide market leader that has surpassed sales of competing manufacturer brands. The gourmet grocery chain Trader Joe's markets the popular Charles Shaw brand of wine, nicknamed "Two-Buck Chuck" after the $2-per-bottle price. Clearly the price is right—but Charles Shaw and many other retailer brands also offer the quality and image that value-conscious customers want. "It's a mistake to think that store brands are not 'real' brands," Procter & Gamble's CEO has told employees. "In some categories these brands are tougher competitors than traditional brands."

Already, private distributor brands account for 20 percent of the merchandise purchased in U.S. stores every year.

They are even more powerful in Europe, where they account for 40 percent of store merchandise purchased. Some manufacturers are adjusting to this power shift by agreeing to make goods for retailers to market under store brands. For example, Campbell Soup produces canned soups for European retailers, and Chef Boyardee produces canned pasta for Save-a-Lot stores.

Although private distributor brands are not new, many have considerably higher brand equity than at any time in the past. In part, this is because retailers are putting more emphasis on memorable brand names and marks, boosting product quality, creating more aesthetically pleasing packaging, and guaranteeing customer satisfaction. In turn, as customers have good experiences with a retailer's brand, they develop loyalty and are more willing to at least try other private distributor brands.

Procter & Gamble, Kraft, Unilever, and other manufacturing giants are fighting back by giving their best brands a stronger promotional push. They are also searching more aggressively for innovative product ideas that can launch a new brand or extend an established one. Given the profitability cushion that private distributor brands deliver to retailers, the battle of the brands is likely to become even more intense.

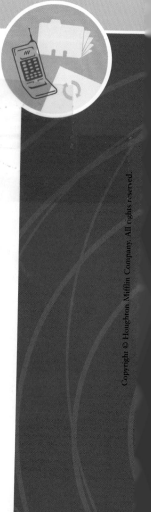

Investments and Charles Schwab Discount Brokerage, have established strong brand recognition. These companies have used their names to create an image of value and friendly, timely, responsible, accurate, and knowledgeable customer assistance. Service providers (such as United Air Lines) are perceived by customers as having one brand name, even though they offer multiple products (first class, business class, and coach). Because the service brand name and company name are so closely interrelated, a service brand name must be flexible enough to encompass a variety of current services, as well as new ones the company may offer in the future. Geographical references such as *western* and descriptive terms such as *trucking* limit the scope of possible associations with the brand name. Because Southwest Airlines now flies to many parts of the country, its name has become too limited in its scope of associations. *Humana*, with its connotations of kindness and compassion, is flexible enough to encompass all services that a hospital, insurance plan, or health care facility offers. Frequently a service marketer employs a symbol along with its brand name to make the brand distinctive and communicate a certain image.

◆ Protecting a Brand

A marketer should also design a brand so that it can be protected easily through registration. A series of court decisions has created a broad hierarchy of protection based on brand type. From most protectable to least protectable, these brand types are fanciful (Exxon), arbitrary (Dr Pepper), suggestive (Spray 'n Wash), descriptive (Minute Rice), and generic (aluminum foil). Generic brands are not protectable. Surnames and descriptive, geographic, or functional names are difficult to protect.[12] However, research shows that overall, consumers prefer descriptive and suggestive brand names and find them easier to recall than fanciful and arbitrary brand names.[13] Because of their designs, some brands can be legally infringed on more easily than others. Although registration protects trademarks domestically for ten years and trademarks can be renewed indefinitely, a firm should develop a system for ensuring that its trademarks are renewed as needed.

To protect its exclusive rights to a brand, a company must make certain the brand is not likely to be considered an infringement on any brand already registered with the U.S. Patent and Trademark Office. This task may be complex because infringement is determined by the courts, which base their decisions on whether a brand causes consumers to be confused, mistaken, or deceived about the source of the product. McDonald's is one company that aggressively protects its trademarks against infringement; it has brought charges against a number of companies with *Mc* names because it fears the use of that prefix will give consumers the impression that these companies are associated with or owned by McDonald's. Auto Shack changed its name to AutoZone when faced with legal action from Tandy Corporation, owner of Radio Shack. Tandy maintained that it owned the name *Shack*. After research showed that virtually every auto supply store in the country used *auto* in its name, *zone* was deemed the best word to pair with *auto*.

A marketer should guard against allowing a brand name to become a generic term used to refer

Protecting a Brand
Through this advertisement, the maker of Kleenex® brand tissues points out that Kleenex® is an adjective and not a noun. It's always spelled with a capital *K*, followed by the registered trademark symbol, and then followed by the word *tissue*. Note also on the package that the word *brand* appears with the term Kleenex®.

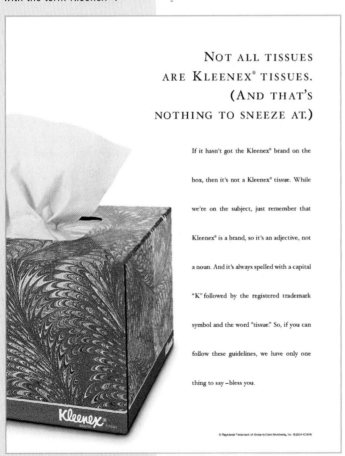

NOT ALL TISSUES
ARE KLEENEX® TISSUES.
(AND THAT'S
NOTHING TO SNEEZE AT.)

If it hasn't got the Kleenex® brand on the

box, then it's not a Kleenex® tissue. While

we're on the subject, just remember that

Kleenex® is a brand, so it's an adjective, not

a noun. And it's always spelled with a capital

"K" followed by the registered trademark

symbol and the word "tissue." So, if you can

follow these guidelines, we have only one

thing to say – bless you.

to a general product category. Generic terms cannot be protected as exclusive brand names. For example, *aspirin, escalator,* and *shredded wheat*—all brand names at one time—eventually were declared generic terms that refer to product classes. Thus, they could no longer be protected. To keep a brand name from becoming a generic term, the firm should spell the name with a capital letter and use it as an adjective to modify the name of the general product class, as in Kool-Aid Brand Soft Drink Mix.[14] Including the word *brand* just after the brand name is also helpful. An organization can deal with this problem directly by advertising that its brand is a trademark and should not be used generically. The firm can also indicate that the brand is a registered trademark by using the symbol ®.

In the interest of strengthening trademark protection, Congress enacted the Trademark Law Revision Act in 1988, the only major federal trademark legislation since the Lanham Act of 1946. The purpose of this more recent legislation is to increase the value of the federal registration system for U.S. firms relative to foreign competitors and to better protect the public from counterfeiting, confusion, and deception.

A U.S. firm that tries to protect a brand in a foreign country frequently encounters problems. In many countries, brand registration is not possible; the first firm to use a brand in such a country automatically has the rights to it. In some instances, U.S. companies actually have had to buy their own brand rights from a firm in a foreign country because the foreign firm was the first user in that country.

Marketers trying to protect their brands must also contend with brand counterfeiting. In the United States, for instance, one can purchase counterfeit General Motors parts, Cartier watches, Louis Vuitton handbags, Walt Disney character dolls, Warner Brothers clothing, Mont Blanc pens, and a host of other products illegally marketed by manufacturers that do not own the brands. Annual losses caused by counterfeit products are estimated at between $250 billion and $350 billion annually. Many counterfeit products are manufactured overseas—in Turkey, China, Thailand, Italy, and Colombia, for example—but some are counterfeited in the United States. Counterfeit products are often hard to distinguish from the real brands. Products most likely to be counterfeited are well-known brands that appeal to a mass market and products whose physical materials are inexpensive relative to the products' prices. Microsoft estimates that its revenues would double if counterfeiting of its brand name products were eliminated. Some $40 billion a year are lost in the computer software business because of counterfeit and pirated products. Brand fraud not only results in lost revenue for the brand's owner; it also results in a low-quality product for customers, distorts competition, affects investment levels, reduces tax revenues and legitimate employment, creates safety risks, and affects international relations. It also likely affects customers' perceptions of the brand due to the counterfeit product's inferior quality.

◆ Branding Policies

Before establishing branding policies, a firm must decide whether to brand its products at all. If a company's product is homogeneous and similar to competitors' products, it may be difficult to brand. Raw materials such as coal, sand, and farm produce are hard to brand because of the homogeneity and physical characteristics of such products.

individual branding A branding policy in which each product is given a different name

If a firm chooses to brand its products, it may opt for one or more of the following branding policies: individual, family, or brand extension branding. **Individual branding** is a policy of giving each product a different name. For example, Unilever relies on an individual branding policy for its line of detergents, which includes Wisk, Persil, and All. The company has organized its products into three branding tiers: "power" brands marketed across national borders, products marketed under different brands in different countries, and local brands sold only in specific markets.[15] A major advantage of individual branding is that if an organization introduces a poor product, the negative images associated with it do not contaminate

At Inter-American Foods, we produce products for more than 30 categories. Let us help you customize a program that consolidates your vendor opportunities. You talk, we listen. We're as good as your name. We guarantee it.

We Are.
INTER-AMERICAN FOODS, INC.
1-800-645-2233

Individual Branding
Inter-American Foods, Inc., as shown in its advertisement, uses an individual branding policy.

the company's other products. An individual branding policy may also facilitate market segmentation when a firm wishes to enter many segments of the same market. Separate, unrelated names can be used and each brand aimed at a specific segment. Sara Lee utilizes individual branding among its many divisions, which include Hanes underwear, L'eggs pantyhose, Champion sportswear, Jimmy Dean, Bali, Ball Park, and other vastly diverse brands.

In **family branding**, all of a firm's products are branded with the same name or part of the name, such as Kellogg's Frosted Flakes, Kellogg's Rice Krispies, and Kellogg's Corn Flakes. In some cases, a company's name is combined with other words to brand items. Arm & Hammer uses its name on all its products, along with a generic description of the item, such as Arm & Hammer Heavy Duty Detergent, Arm & Hammer Pure Baking Soda, and Arm & Hammer Carpet Deodorizer. Unlike individual branding, family branding means the promotion of one item with the family brand promotes the firm's other products. Other major companies that use

family branding Branding all of a firm's products with the same name or part of the name

brand extension branding Using an existing brand name for an improved or new product

family branding include Mitsubishi, Kodak, and Fisher-Price.

In **brand extension branding**, a firm uses one of its existing brand names as part of a brand for an improved or new product, which is often in the same product category as the existing brand. McNeil Consumer Products, makers of Tylenol and Extra Strength Tylenol, also introduced Extra Strength Tylenol P.M., thus extending the Tylenol brand. Marketers share a common concern that if a brand is extended too many times or extended too far outside its original product category, the brand can be significantly weakened. For example, Miller Brewing Company has extended its brand to Miller Lite, Genuine Draft, Draft Lite, Ice, Ice Lite, Milwaukee's Best, Ice House, and Red Dog, but so many extensions may confuse customers and encourage them to engage in considerable brand switching. The Nabisco Snackwell brand initially appeared only on crackers, cookies, and snack bars, all of which fall into the baked-snack category. However, extending the brand to yogurts and gelatin mixes goes further afield. Although some experts might caution Nabisco against extending the Snackwell brand to this degree, some evidence suggests that brands can be successfully extended to less closely related product categories through the use of advertisements that extend customers' perceptions of the original product category. For example, Waterford, an upscale Irish brand of crystal, extended its name to writing instruments when seeking sales growth beyond closely related product categories such as china, cutlery, and table linens.[16]

An organization is not limited to a single branding policy. A company that uses primarily individual branding for many of its products may also use brand extensions. Branding policy is influenced by the number of products and product lines the company produces, the characteristics of its target markets, the number and types of competing products available, and the size of the firm's resources.

◆ Co-Branding

co-branding Using two or more brands on one product

Co-branding is the use of two or more brands on one product. Marketers employ co-branding to capitalize on the brand equity of multiple brands. Co-branding is popular in a number of processed food categories and in the credit card industry. The brands used for co-branding can be owned by the same company. For example, Kraft's Lunchables product teams the Kraft cheese brand with Oscar Mayer lunchmeats, another Kraft-owned brand. The brands may also be owned by different companies. Credit card companies such as American Express, Visa, and Master-Card, for instance, team up with other brands such as General Motors, AT&T, and many airlines. It is predicted that in just a few years, credit card purchases will outstrip flying as the number one way to earn frequent flier miles.[17]

Effective co-branding capitalizes on the trust and confidence customers have in the brands involved. The brands should not lose their identities, and it should be clear to customers which brand is the main brand. For example, it is fairly obvious that Kellogg owns the brand and is the main brander of Kellogg's Healthy Choice Cereal. (The Choice brand is owned by ConAgra.) It is important for marketers to understand that when a co-branded product is unsuccessful, both brands are implicated in the product failure. To gain customer acceptance, the brands involved must represent a complementary fit in the minds of buyers. Trying to link a brand like Harley-Davidson with a brand like Healthy Choice will not achieve co-branding objectives because customers are not likely to perceive these brands as compatible.

Co-branding can help an organization differentiate its products from those of competitors. By using the product development skills of a co-branding partner, an organization can create a distinctive product. For example, fashion designer Giorgio Armani and carmaker Mercedes-Benz have teamed up to produce a Mercedes cabriolet with leather seats, dashboard, and leather steering wheel designed by Armani. The two are considering joint marketing events and advertising.[18] Co-branding can also allow the partners to take advantage of each other's distribution capabilities.

While co-branding has been used for a number of years, it began to grow in popularity in the 1980s when Monsanto aggressively promoted its NutraSweet product as an ingredient in such well-known brands as Diet Coke. The company also used this approach with lesser-known brands to instill trust and confidence in buyers' minds. Intel, too, has capitalized on ingredient co-branding through its "Intel Inside" program. The effectiveness of ingredient co-branding relies heavily on continued promotional efforts by the ingredient's producer.

With Residence Inn and AT&T, you can keep up with all the news from home.

Sure you miss the family. But you won't miss the news. Because every suite has reliable AT&T communications to help you keep in touch on extended business trips. It's just what you'd expect from Marriott's flagship all-suite hotel. Where you earn Marriott Rewards points or miles toward a free vacation. To learn more or make a reservation, visit residenceinn.com, call your travel agent or call us at 800-331-3131.

*Available at most locations.

Room to work, room to relax, room to breathe.

Co-Branding
This advertisement promotes co-branded products.

◆ Brand Licensing

brand licensing An agreement whereby a company permits another organization to use its brand on other products for a licensing fee

A popular branding strategy involves **brand licensing**, an agreement in which a company permits another organization to use its brand on other products for a licensing fee. Royalties may be as low as 2 percent of wholesale revenues or higher than 10 percent. Mattel, for example, licensed Warner Brothers' Harry Potter brand for use on board games and toys to tie in with the first movie based on the wildly popular book series. Warner was guaranteed royalties of $20 million from Mattel's licensing fee of 15 percent of gross revenues earned on these branded products.[19] The licensee is responsible for all manufacturing, selling, and advertising functions, and bears the costs if the licensed product fails. Not long ago only a few firms licensed their corporate trademarks, but today licensing is a multibillion-dollar business. The top U.S. licensing company is Walt Disney Company. The NFL, the NCAA, NASCAR, and Major League Baseball are all in the top ten in retail sales of licensed products.

The advantages of licensing range from extra revenues and low-cost or free publicity to new images and trademark protection. For example, Coca-Cola has licensed its trademark for use on glassware, radios, trucks, and clothing in the hope of protecting its trademark. However, brand licensing has drawbacks. The major disadvantages are a lack of manufacturing control, which could hurt the company's name, and bombarding consumers with too many unrelated products bearing the same name. Licensing arrangements can also fail because of poor timing, inappropriate distribution channels, or mismatching of product and name.

Packaging

Packaging involves the development of a container and a graphic design for a product. A package can be a vital part of a product, making it more versatile, safer, and easier to use. Like a brand name, a package can influence customers' attitudes toward a product and thus affect their purchase decisions. For example, several producers of jellies, sauces, and ketchups have packaged their products in squeezable containers to make use and storage more convenient. Package characteristics help shape buyers' impressions of a product at the time of purchase or during use. In this section, we examine the main functions of packaging and consider several major packaging decisions. We also analyze the role of the package in a marketing strategy.

◆ Packaging Functions

Effective packaging means more than simply putting products in containers and covering them with wrappers. First, packaging materials serve the basic purpose of protecting the product and maintaining its functional form. Fluids such as milk, orange juice, and hair spray need packages that preserve and protect them. The packaging should prevent damage that could affect the product's usefulness and thus lead to higher costs. Since product tampering has become a problem, several packaging techniques have been developed to counter this danger. Some packages are also designed to deter shoplifting.

Another function of packaging is to offer convenience to consumers. For example, small aseptic packages—individual-size boxes or plastic bags that contain liquids and do not require refrigeration—strongly appeal to children and young adults with active lifestyles. The size or shape of a package may relate to the product's storage, convenience of use, or replacement rate. Small, single-serving cans of vegetables, for instance, may prevent waste and make storage easier.

A third function of packaging is to promote a product by communicating its features, uses, benefits, and image. Sometimes a reusable package is developed to make the product more desirable. For example, the Cool Whip package doubles as a food storage container.

◆ Major Packaging Considerations

In developing packages, marketers must take many factors into account. Obviously one major consideration is cost. Although a variety of packaging materials, processes, and designs are available, costs vary greatly. In recent years, buyers have shown a willingness to pay more for improved packaging, but there are limits. Marketers should conduct research to determine exactly how much customers are willing to pay for effective and efficient package designs.

As already mentioned, developing tamper-resistant packaging is very important for certain products. Although no package is tamperproof, marketers can develop packages that are difficult to tamper with. At a minimum, all packaging must comply with the Food and Drug Administration's packaging regulations. However, packaging should also make any product tampering evident to resellers and consumers. Although effective tamper-resistant packaging may be expensive to develop, when balanced against the costs of lost sales, loss of consumer confidence and company reputation, and potentially expensive product liability lawsuits, the costs of ensuring consumer safety are minimal.

Marketers should also consider how much consistency is desirable among an organization's package designs. No consistency may be the best policy, especially if a firm's products are unrelated or aimed at vastly different target markets. To promote an overall company image, a firm may decide that all packages should be similar or include one major element of the design. This approach is called **family packaging**. Sometimes it is used only for lines of products, such as Campbell's soups, Weight Watchers' foods, and Planter's nuts.

A package's promotional role is an important consideration. Through verbal and nonverbal symbols, the package can inform potential buyers about the product's content, features, uses, advantages, and hazards. A firm can create desirable images and associations by its choice of color, design, shape, and texture. Many cosmetics manufacturers, for example, design their packages to create impressions of richness, luxury, and exclusivity. A package performs a promotional function when it is designed to be safer or more convenient to use if such characteristics help stimulate demand.

To develop a package that has a definite promotional value, a designer must consider size, shape, texture, color, and graphics. Beyond the obvious limitation that the package must be large enough to hold the product, a package can be designed to appear taller or shorter. Light-colored packaging may make a package appear larger, whereas darker colors may minimize the perceived size.

Colors on packages are often chosen to attract attention, and color can positively influence customers' emotions. People associate specific colors with certain feelings and experiences. For example,

- Blue is soothing; it is also associated with wealth, trust, and security.
- Gray is associated with strength, exclusivity, and success.
- Orange often signifies low cost.
- Red connotes excitement and stimulation.
- Purple is associated with dignity and stateliness.
- Yellow connotes cheerfulness and joy.
- Black is associated with being strong and masterful.[20]

When opting for color on packaging, marketers must judge whether a particular color will evoke positive or negative feelings when linked to a specific product. Rarely, for example, do processors package meat or bread in green materials because customers may associate green with mold. Marketers must also determine whether a specific target market will respond favorably or unfavorably to a particular color. Cosmetics for women are more likely to be sold in pastel packaging than are personal care products

family packaging Using similar packaging for all of a firm's products or packaging that has one common design element

Distinctive Package Shapes and Colors
Distinctive package shapes and colors provide enhanced brand identity.

for men. Packages designed to appeal to children often use primary colors and bold designs. A relatively recent trend in packaging is colorless packages. Clear products and packaging connote a pure, natural product.

Packaging must also meet the needs of resellers. Wholesalers and retailers consider whether a package facilitates transportation, storage, and handling. Concentrated versions of laundry detergents and fabric softeners, for example, enable retailers to offer more product diversity within the existing shelf space. Resellers may refuse to carry certain products if their packages are cumbersome.

A final consideration is whether to develop packages that are environmentally responsible. Nearly one-half of all garbage consists of discarded plastic packaging, such as polystyrene containers, plastic soft-drink bottles, and carry-out bags. Plastic packaging material does not biodegrade, and paper requires the destruction of valuable forests. Consequently a number of companies have changed to environmentally sensitive packaging; they are also recycling more materials. Procter & Gamble markets several cleaning products in a concentrated form, which requires less packaging than the ready-to-use version. H. J. Heinz is looking for alternatives to its plastic ketchup squeeze bottles. Other companies are also searching for alternatives to environmentally harmful packaging. In some instances, however, customers have objected to such switches because the newer environmentally responsible packaging may be less effective or more inconvenient. Therefore, marketers must carefully balance society's desire to preserve the environment against customers' desire for convenience. The Tech Know boxed feature details how marketers are using advanced technology to improve the color and graphics of their packages.

NET SIGHTS

The Institute of Packaging Professionals is a global resource for information about packaging and the packaging industry. The organization's website (**www.packinfo-world.org**) includes online discussions about packaging issues, news and press releases, contact information for packaging organizations around the world, and past and present winners of Worldstar, an international award in packaging.

TECH KNOW

Technology Brings Eye-Catching Colors to Packaging

Thanks to technology, more companies are attracting more attention to more products. Before Smartfood put its cheddar-coated popcorn into bold, black, flavor-sealing packages, few snacks came in black containers. Now the snack food aisles are bursting with packages in black and in nearly every other hue and tint imaginable. Given black's mystique and its association with sophistication and power, the trend toward black packaging is not surprising.

With today's improved technology, marketers can create packaging in intense colors or subtle shadings to help a product stand out on the shelf, communicate or change an image, and evoke an emotional response. Many create packages using yellow, the first color babies reach for, because of its warmth and optimistic associations. For example, Yoo-hoo's marketers used yellow to create a more youthful packaging for the chocolate drink. The original Yoo-hoo bottle was clear with a yellow label. The new Yoo-hoo bottle, redesigned to appeal to teenage boys, is a vivid yellow with a large brand logo on the label.

Age affects how consumers perceive color. For example, teens cite baby blue as their favorite shade of blue, whereas seniors favor sky blue. Children are exposed to more colors at an earlier age, thanks to computer graphics and larger boxes of subtly hued crayons. As a result, they develop more sophisticated preferences and enjoy novel colors in packaging and products. Parkay has taken advantage of this shift by creating bright pink margarine, and Heinz's green and purple ketchups, packaged in see-through containers with colorful labels, have been big hits.

Firms are also using the latest color-printing technology to link packaging to a specific theme or holiday. Welch's has experimented with red, white, and blue wrapping to promote its sparkling grape juices during the Fourth of July period. Customers responded so enthusiastically that the company began using colored packaging to tie in with Valentine's Day, Easter, Halloween, and the May–June wedding–graduation period. In the coming years, Welch's expects this packaging innovation to boost sales of its sparkling juices by 40 percent, thus making more green for the company.

Table 13.2	Companies That Spend the Most on Packaging
Anheuser-Busch	Kraft General Foods
Campbell Soup	Kraft USA
Coca-Cola	Miller Brewing
Coca-Cola Foods	PepsiCo
General Mills	Procter & Gamble

◆ Packaging and Marketing Strategy

Packaging can be a major component of a marketing strategy. A new cap or closure, a better box or wrapper, or a more convenient container may give a product a competitive advantage. The right type of package for a new product can help it gain market recognition very quickly. In the case of existing brands, marketers should reevaluate packages periodically. Marketers should view packaging as a major strategic tool, especially for consumer convenience products. For instance, in the food industry, jumbo and large package sizes for such products as hot dogs, pizzas, English muffins, frozen dinners, and biscuits have been very successful. When considering the strategic uses of packaging, marketers must also analyze the cost of packaging and package changes. Table 13.2 lists the biggest packaging spenders. In this section, we examine several ways to use packaging strategically.

Altering the Package. At times, a marketer changes a package because the existing design is no longer in style, especially when compared with the packaging of competitive products. Arm & Hammer now markets a refillable plastic shaker for its baking soda. Quaker Oats hired a package design company to redesign its Rice-A-Roni package to give the product the appearance of having evolved with the times while retaining its traditional taste appeal. Rice-A-Roni had been experiencing a lag in sales because of increased competition. An overhaul of the product packaging to a refreshing and more up-to-date look was credited with a 20 percent increase in sales over the previous year. Similarly, Del Monte introduced a contemporary look for its tomato products and experienced a double-digit gain in the first year.

A package may be redesigned because new product features need to be highlighted or because new packaging materials have become available. An organization may decide to change a product's packaging to reposition the product or to make the product safer or more convenient to use. Nestlé USA, for example, changed its Coffee Mate package to a new, easy-to-grip plastic container that features a portable spout, eliminating the need to unscrew the lid and spoon out the creamer. Nestlé expects the

So easy, this could be the only can opener you'll ever need.

NEW! EASY OPEN TOP

Chef BOYARDEE
BEEF
Ravioli
in Tomato & Meat Sauce

Convenience
Con-Agra Foods, the maker of Chef Boyardee, altered its packaging to make Chef Boyardee Ravioli more convenient to use.

new, more convenient package to give its powdered-creamer product a boost in the marketplace.[21]

Secondary-Use Packaging. A secondary-use package can be reused for purposes other than its initial function. For example, a margarine container can be reused to store leftovers, and a jelly container can serve as a drinking glass. Customers often view secondary-use packaging as adding value to products, in which case its use should stimulate unit sales.

Category-Consistent Packaging. With category-consistent packaging, the product is packaged in line with the packaging practices associated with a particular product category. Some product categories—for example, mayonnaise, mustard, ketchup, and peanut butter—have traditional package shapes. Other product categories are characterized by recognizable color combinations, such as red and white for soup and red, white, and blue for Ritz-like crackers. When an organization introduces a brand in one of these product categories, marketers will often use traditional package shapes and color combinations to ensure customers will recognize the new product as being in that specific product category.

Innovative Packaging. Sometimes a marketer employs a unique cap, design, applicator, or other feature to make a product distinctive. Such packaging can be effective when the innovation makes the product safer or easier to use, or provides better protection for the product. In some instances, marketers use innovative or unique packages that are inconsistent with traditional packaging practices to make the brand stand out from competitors. To distinguish their products, marketers in the beverage industry have long used innovative shapes and packaging materials. Unusual packaging sometimes requires expending considerable resources, not only on package design but also on making customers aware of the unique package and its benefit.

Multiple Packaging. Rather than packaging a single unit of a product, marketers sometimes use twin packs, tri-packs, six-packs, or other forms of multiple packaging. For certain types of products, multiple packaging may increase demand because it increases the amount of the product available at the point of consumption (in one's house, for example). It may also increase consumer acceptance of the product by encouraging the buyer to try the product several times. Multiple packaging can make products easier to handle and store, as in the case of six-packs for soft drinks; it can also facilitate special price offers, such as two-for-one sales. However, multiple packaging does not work for all types of products. One would not use additional table salt, for example, simply because an extra box is in the pantry.

WAKE UP TO FRESH AROMA MORNING AFTER MORNING.

INTRODUCING THE ALL NEW FOLGERS® AROMASEAL™ CANISTER.

Wake up to a unique lid that seals in that Mountain Grown® aroma and helps seal air out.

Wake up to delicious coffee.

Wake up to a convenient new handle that's easy to hold.

THE BEST PART OF WAKIN' UP IS FOLGERS IN YOUR CUP.®

Innovative Packaging
The maker of Folgers Coffee adds value to its brand by using a new canister design that keeps coffee fresh and is easier to hold.

Handling-Improved Packaging. A product's packaging may be changed to make it easier to handle in the distribution channel—for example, by changing the outer carton or using special bundling, shrink-wrapping, or pallets. In some cases, the shape of the package is changed. An ice cream producer, for instance, may change from a cylindrical package to a rectangular one to facilitate handling. In addition, at the retail level, the ice cream producer may be able to get more shelf facings with a rectangular package than with a round one. Outer containers for products are sometimes changed so they will proceed more easily through automated warehousing systems.

◆ Criticisms of Packaging

The last several decades have brought a number of improvements in packaging. However, some packaging problems still need to be resolved. Some packages suffer from functional problems in that they simply do not work well. The packaging for flour and sugar is, at best, poor. Both grocers and consumers are very much aware that these packages leak and tear easily. Can anyone open and close a bag of flour without spilling at least a little bit? Certain packages, such as refrigerated biscuit cans, milk cartons with fold-out spouts, and potato chip bags, are frequently difficult to open. The traditional shapes of packages for products such as ketchup and salad dressing make the product inconvenient to use. Have you ever wondered when tapping on a ketchup bottle why the producer didn't put the ketchup in a mayonnaise jar?

Although many steps have been taken to make packaging safer, critics still focus on the safety issues. Containers with sharp edges and breakable glass bottles are sometimes viewed as a threat to safety. Certain types of plastic packaging and aerosol containers represent possible health hazards.

At times, packaging is viewed as deceptive. Package shape, graphic design, and certain colors may be used to make a product appear larger than it actually is. The inconsistent use of certain size designations, such as giant, economy, family, king, and super, can lead to customer confusion.

Finally, although customers in this country traditionally prefer attractive, effective, convenient packaging, the cost of such packaging is high.

Labeling

labeling Providing identifying, promotional, or other information on package labels

universal product code (UPC) A series of electronically readable lines identifying a product and containing inventory and pricing information

Labeling is very closely interrelated with packaging and is used for identification, promotional, and informational and legal purposes. Labels can be small or large relative to the size of the product and carry varying amounts of information. The sticker on a Chiquita banana, for example, is quite small and displays only the brand name of the fruit. A label can be part of the package itself or a separate feature attached to the package. The label on a can of Coke is actually part of the can, whereas the label on a two-liter bottle of Coke is separate and can be removed. Information presented on a label may include the brand name and mark, the registered trademark symbol, package size and content, product features, nutritional information, type and style of the product, number of servings, care instructions, directions for use and safety precautions, the name and address of the manufacturer, expiration dates, seals of approval, and other facts.

For many products, the label includes a **universal product code (UPC)**, a series of electronically readable lines identifying the product and providing inventory and pricing information for producers and resellers. The UPC is electronically read at the retail checkout counter.

Labels can facilitate the identification of a product by displaying the brand name in combination with a unique graphic design. For example, Heinz ketchup is easy to identify on a supermarket shelf because the brand name is easy to read and the label has a distinctive crownlike shape. By drawing attention to products and their benefits, labels can strengthen an organization's promotional efforts. Labels may contain such promotional messages as the offer of a discount or a larger package size at the same price, or information about a new or improved product feature.

A number of federal laws and regulations specify information that must be included on the labels of certain products. Garments must be labeled with the name of the manufacturer, country of manufacture, fabric content, and cleaning instructions. Labels on nonedible items such as shampoos and detergents must include both safety precautions and directions for use. In 1966, Congress passed the Fair Packaging and Labeling Act, one of the most comprehensive pieces of labeling and packaging legislation. This law focuses on mandatory labeling requirements, voluntary adoption of packaging standards by firms within industries, and the provision of power to the Federal Trade Commission and the Food and Drug Administration to establish and enforce packaging regulations.

The Nutrition Labeling Act of 1990 requires the FDA to review food labeling and packaging, focusing on nutrition content, label format, ingredient labeling, food descriptions, and health messages. This act regulates much of the labeling on more than 250,000 products made by some 17,000 U.S. companies. Any food product for which a nutritional claim is made must have nutrition labeling that follows a standard format. Food product labels must state the number of servings per container, serving size, number of calories per serving, number of calories derived from fat, number of carbohydrates, and amounts of specific nutrients such as vitamins. In addition, new nutritional labeling requirements focus on the amounts of trans-fatty acids in food products. Although consumers have responded favorably to this type of information on labels, evidence as to whether they actually use it has been mixed.

The use of new technology in the production and processing of food has led to additional food labeling issues. The FDA now requires that a specific irradiation logo be used when labeling irradiated food products. In addition, the FDA has issued voluntary guidelines for food companies to follow if they choose to label foods as biotech-free or promote biotech ingredients.[22]

Despite legislation to make labels as accurate and informative as possible, questionable labeling practices persist. The Center for Science in the Public Interest questions the practice of naming a product "Strawberry Frozen Yogurt Bars" when it contains strawberry flavoring but no strawberries, or of calling a breakfast cereal "lightly sweetened" when sugar makes up 22 percent of its ingredients. Many labels on vegetable oils say "no cholesterol," but many of these oils contain saturated fats that can raise cholesterol levels. The Food and Drug Administration amended its regulations to forbid producers of vegetable oil from making "no cholesterol" claims on their labels.

Another area of concern is "green labeling." Consumers who are committed to making environmentally responsible purchasing decisions are sometimes fooled by labels. The U.S. Public Interest Research Group accused several manufacturers of "greenwashing" customers, using misleading claims to sell products by playing on customers' concern for the environment. For example, some manufacturers put a recycling symbol on labels for products made of polyvinyl chloride plastic, which cannot be recycled in the vast majority of American communities.

Of concern to many manufacturers are the Federal Trade Commission's guidelines regarding "Made in U.S.A." labels, a growing problem due to the increasingly global nature of manufacturing. The FTC requires that "all or virtually all" of a product's components be made in the United States if the label says "Made in U.S.A." Although the FTC recently considered changing its guidelines to read "substantially all," it rejected this idea and maintains the "all or virtually all" standard. In light of this decision, the FTC ordered New Balance to stop using the "Made in U.S.A." claim on its athletic-shoe labels because some components (rubber soles) are made in China. The "Made in U.S.A." labeling issue has not been totally resolved. The FTC criteria for using "Made in U.S.A." are likely to be challenged and subsequently changed.[23]

SUMMARY

A brand is a name, term, design, symbol, or any other feature that identifies one seller's good or service and distinguishes it from those of other sellers. A brand name is the part of a brand that can be spoken. A brand mark is the element not made up of words. A trademark is a legal designation indicating that the owner has exclusive use of the brand or part of the brand and others are prohibited by law from using it. A trade name is the legal name of an organization. Branding helps buyers identify and evaluate products, helps sellers facilitate product introduction and repeat purchasing, and fosters brand loyalty.

Brand loyalty is a customer's favorable attitude toward a specific brand. If brand loyalty is strong enough, customers may consistently purchase a particular brand when they need a product in this product category. The three degrees of brand loyalty are brand recognition, brand preference, and brand insistence. Brand recognition occurs when a customer is aware that the brand exists and views it as an alternative purchase if the preferred brand is unavailable. With brand preference, a customer prefers one brand over competing brands and will purchase it if available. Brand insistence occurs when a customer will accept no substitute.

Brand equity is the marketing and financial value associated with a brand's strength. It represents the value of a brand to an organization. The four major elements underlying brand equity include brand name awareness, brand loyalty, perceived brand quality, and brand associations.

A manufacturer brand, initiated by the producer, ensures that the firm is associated with its products at the point of purchase. A private distributor brand is initiated and owned by a reseller, sometimes taking on the name of the store or distributor. Manufacturers combat growing competition from private distributor brands by developing multiple brands. A generic brand indicates only the product category and does not include the company name or other identifying terms.

When selecting a brand name, a marketer should choose one that is easy to say, spell, and recall and that alludes to the product's uses, benefits, or special characteristics. Brand names can be devised from words, letters, numbers, nonsense words, or a combination of these. Brand names are created inside an organization by individuals, committees, or branding departments and by outside consultants. Services as well as products are branded, often with the company name and an accompanying symbol that makes the brand distinctive or conveys a desired image.

Producers protect ownership of their brands through registration with the U.S. Patent and Trademark Office. A company must make certain the brand name it selects does not infringe on an already registered brand by confusing or deceiving consumers about the source of the product. In most foreign countries, brand registration is on a first-come, first-serve basis, making protection more difficult. Brand counterfeiting is becoming increasingly common and can undermine consumers' confidence in a brand.

Companies brand their products in several ways. Individual branding designates a unique name for each of a company's products, family branding identifies all of a firm's products with a single name, and brand extension branding applies an existing name to a new or improved product. Co-branding is the use of two or more brands on one product. It is a popular branding method in a number of processed food categories and in the credit card industry. The brands may be owned by the same company or by different companies. Effective co-branding profits from the trust and confidence customers have in the brands involved. To avoid confusion, marketers must ensure that customers understand which brand is the main brand. Co-brands must have a complementary fit in buyers' minds. Co-branding sometimes allows an organization to differentiate its products from those of competitors. The co-branding partners can also take advantage of each other's distribution capabilities. Finally, through a licensing agreement and for a licensing fee, a firm may permit another organization to use its brand on other products. Brand licensing enables producers to earn extra revenue, receive low-cost or free publicity, and protect their trademarks.

Packaging involves development of a container and a graphic design for a product. Effective packaging offers protection, economy, safety, and convenience. It can influence a customer's purchase decision by promoting features, uses, benefits, and image. When developing a package, marketers must consider the value to the customer of efficient and effective packaging, offset by the price the customer is willing to pay. Other considerations include making the package tamper resistant, whether to use multiple packaging and family packaging, how to design the package as an effective promotional tool, how best to accommodate resellers, and whether to develop environmentally responsible packaging. Firms choose particular colors, designs, shapes, and textures to create desirable images and associations. Packaging can be an important part of an overall marketing strategy and can be used to target certain market segments. Modifications in packaging can revive a mature product and extend its product life cycle. Producers alter packages to convey new features or to make them safer or more convenient. If a package has a secondary use, the product's value to the consumer may increase. Category-consistent packaging makes products more easily recognizable to consumers. Innovative packaging enhances a product's distinctiveness. Consumers may criticize packaging that does not work well, poses health or safety problems, is deceptive in some way, or is not biodegradable or recyclable.

Labeling is closely interrelated with packaging and is used for identification, promotional, and informational and legal purposes. The labels of many products include a universal product code, a series of electronically readable lines identifying a product and containing inventory and pricing information. Various federal laws and regulations require that certain products be labeled or marked with warnings, instructions, nutritional informa-

tion, manufacturer's identification, and the like. Despite legislation, questionable labeling practices persist, including misleading information about fat content and cholesterol, freshness, and recyclability of packaging.

Please visit the student website at **www.prideferrell.com** for ACE Self-Test questions that will help you prepare for exams.

IMPORTANT TERMS

Brand	Private distributor brand
Brand name	Generic brand
Brand mark	Individual branding
Trademark	Family branding
Trade name	Brand extension branding
Brand loyalty	Co-branding
Brand recognition	Brand licensing
Brand preference	Family packaging
Brand insistence	Labeling
Brand equity	Universal product code
Manufacturer brand	(UPC)

DISCUSSION & REVIEW QUESTIONS

1. What is the difference between a brand and a brand name? Compare and contrast a brand mark and a trademark.
2. How does branding benefit consumers and marketers?
3. What are the three major degrees of brand loyalty?
4. What is brand equity? Identify and explain the major elements of brand equity.
5. Compare and contrast manufacturer brands, private distributor brands, and generic brands.
6. Identify the factors a marketer should consider in selecting a brand name.
7. The brand name Xerox is sometimes used generically to refer to photocopiers, and Kleenex is used to refer to tissues. How can the manufacturers protect their brand names, and why would they want to do so?
8. What is co-branding? What major issues should be considered when using co-branding?
9. What are the major advantages and disadvantages of brand licensing?
10. Describe the functions a package can perform. Which function is most important? Why?
11. What are the main factors a marketer should consider when developing a package?

12. In what ways can packaging be used as a strategic tool?
13. What are the major criticisms of packaging?
14. What are the major functions of labeling?
15. In what ways do regulations and legislation affect labeling?

APPLICATION QUESTIONS

1. Identify two brands for which you are brand insistent. How did you begin using these brands? Why do you no longer use other brands?
2. General Motors introduced the subcompact Geo with a name that appeals to a world market. Invent a brand name for a line of luxury sports cars that also would appeal to an international market. Suggest a name that implies quality, luxury, and value.
3. When a firm decides to brand its products, it may choose one of several strategies. Name one company that utilizes each of the following strategies. How does each strategy help the company?
   a. Individual branding
   b. Family branding
   c. Brand extension branding
4. For each of the following product categories, choose an existing brand. Then, for each selected brand, suggest a co-brand and explain why the co-brand would be effective.
   a. Cookies
   b. Pizza
   c. Long-distance telephone service
   d. A sports drink
5. Packaging provides product protection; customer convenience; and promotion of image, key features, and benefits. Identify a product that utilizes packaging in each of these ways, and evaluate the effectiveness of the package for that function.
6. Identify a package that you believe is inferior. Explain why you think the package is inferior, and discuss your recommendations for improving it.

Internet Exercise & Resources

Visit **www.prideferrell.com** for resources to help you master the material in this chapter, plus materials that will help you expand your marketing knowledge, including Internet exercise updates, ACE self-tests, hotlinks to companies featured in this chapter, and much more.

Pillsbury

Like other marketers of consumer products, Pillsbury has set up a website to inform and entertain consumers. Catering to the appeal of its most popular product spokesperson, Pillsbury has given its Dough Boy his own site. Visit him at **www.doughboy.com**.

1. What branding policy does Pillsbury seem to be using with regard to the products it presents on this site?
2. How does this Pillsbury website promote brand loyalty?
3. What degree of consistency exists in Pillsbury's packaging of its products displayed on the website?

Video Case 13.1

PlumpJack Winery Pours Out Cork Controversy

PlumpJack Winery has embarked on a highly public and controversial experiment in wine packaging. Instead of using corks to seal its $150 Napa Valley Reserve Cabernet Sauvignon wine bottles, the winery is sealing half the bottles with metal screw-tops. To call attention to this unusual method of closing bottles of premium wines, the winery is packaging the bottles in a twin-pack, one with a cork and one with a screw-top. This unorthodox packaging approach may not necessarily sell more wine, but it certainly generates media coverage and provides a distinctive marketing angle for the brand.

PlumpJack is owned by composer Gordon Getty, his son Bill Getty, and San Francisco politician Gavin Newsom. Named after an opera that the elder Getty wrote, which features the Jack Falstaff character from Shakespeare's *Henry IV*, the winery is set on 50 acres in Oakville, deep in California's Napa Valley wine country. The vineyards of Robert Mondavi and other famous wine brands are nearby, but so far PlumpJack is the only one to embrace screw-tops for high-end wines.

Gordon Getty devised the screw-top idea out of concern for the environmental impact of the dwindling worldwide supply of cork. He also disliked the musty character that natural cork occasionally imparts to bottled wine and the tiny bits of broken cork that often fall into newly uncorked bottles. Getty knew that a few wineries were testing synthetic corks as replacements for natural corks. Even though synthetic corks have been available for more than a decade, they have managed to replace only 2 percent of the world's 14 billion corks. So Getty and his partners, working with winery management, decided to explore other alternatives.

"In researching the idea, we found that there are premium Swiss and European wines with screw-tops," recalls John Conover, the winery's general manager. Despite some European acceptance of the new packaging, wine lovers in the United States generally associate screw-top bottles with cheap wines. Even the experts disagree on whether screw-tops or any other cork substitute can maintain wine quality during long-term storage. So the PlumpJack team needed a good explanation—and good media coverage—to educate buyers about the benefits of screw-tops.

Their first step was to invite the University of California at Davis to study the quality of the wine from both corked and screw-top bottles. This close scrutiny by a respected institution would, over time, confirm or disprove the winery's theory that screw-top packaging was at least as effective as natural cork for maintaining wine quality. Simply announcing the university study showed wine buyers (and competitors) how serious PlumpJack's owners were about their innovative packaging. Next, the partners came up with the twin-pack concept as a way to encourage buyers to personally compare the wines from the corked bottle and the screw-top bottle.

Once their packaging plans were in place, the PlumpJack partners kicked off a media campaign to announce the screw-top innovation. CNN picked up the story, a national morning television program showcased the wine, and reporters from Europe and Asia interviewed the winery's management. Meanwhile industry publications debated the appeal and effectiveness of screw-tops and quoted the views of different experts.

The globalization of wine marketing is also working in PlumpJack's favor. "The marketplace for premium California wine is now global," remarks Conover. "Where we once had a market that was basically west of the Rockies, we are now selling wine into Germany, Japan, New York, and other places where California wines were not featured before. The playing field for premium wines is now bigger than it has ever been." Because wine buyers outside the United States may be more familiar with screw-top bottles, they may be more willing to give the screw-top PlumpJack wine an objective taste test.

Another trend is helping PlumpJack, according to Mary Pisor, the winery's associate winemaker. "The consumer's ability to buy ultra-premium wines has increased dramatically since the early 1990s," she says. "As I travel around the country, I find wine collectors in their 20s and 30s who have the fiscal ability to pay the kind of prices we now see for our wines."

PlumpJack's luxury wines usually retail for $100-plus per bottle, even without the added expense of capping with screw-tops.

Now other premium wineries are exchanging corks for screw-tops. One New Zealand winemaker said he would switch after having to discard most of the 630,000 corks he tested during one recent year. Gordon Getty sees slow but steady movement in the direction of screw-tops. "The technology is in place, we believe the market is prepared, and all that remains is for someone to break the barrier of tradition," he says.[24]

QUESTIONS FOR DISCUSSION

1. Can PlumpJack's screw-top bottles be considered category-consistent packaging? Explain.
2. PlumpJack is using screw-top caps to improve the quality of its premium wine and perhaps make it more distinctive. But since screw-top caps are used mainly for inexpensive wines in the United States, will customers view PlumpJack wines as cheaper, lower-quality wines even though the screw-top cap may actually improve the quality? Explain.
3. Should PlumpJack sell its screw-top wines as singles instead of in a twin-pack with corked wines? Why or why not?
4. How might PlumpJack use labeling to promote its innovative packaging?

Case 13.2

The Harley-Davidson Brand Roars into Its Second Century

Harley-Davidson has roared up and down the fast track in its time. Named for the two founders, the company was started with one motorcycle built in a shed in 1903. Now Harley-Davidson annually sells more than 290,000 motorcycles across the United States, Japan, and Europe. During the 1970s, however, product quality suffered as Harley-Davidson expanded too quickly. The company was nearly out of business by the mid-1980s when management decided to reduce manufacturing output, focus on improving quality, and redesign its basic motorcycle engine. Customers noticed the difference, and sales began to accelerate.

Soon Harley-Davidson was well on the road to reclaiming the brand's market dominance in the United States and beating back competition from Yamaha, Honda, Suzuki, and Kawasaki. Despite higher demand, management was careful to increase production only slightly from year to year. This allowed closer control over quality, but it also meant dealers never had enough inventory on hand. As a result, eager customers sometimes waited one or two years for the more popular models and paid thousands of dollars over the regular price when a particularly desirable bike became available. Demand soared higher still when Harley-Davidson sold special limited-edition models to celebrate its centennial in 2003.

The motorcycle experience is central to Harley-Davidson's culture and marketing. Nearly half of the company's 8,000 employees own one of the firm's motorcycles—purchased from local dealers—so they know a great deal about how their products are used.

In addition, hundreds of employees attend cycling rallies around the country to mingle with customers, applying what they learn when developing new products and new marketing programs. After observing how riders personalized their bikes with unusual handlebars and unique paint jobs, Harley-Davidson launched a line of custom bikes complete with special accessories. These motorcycles sell for around $25,000 and are more profitable than regular sport and touring models, which fetch $8,000 to $17,000.

To its customers, the Harley-Davidson brand represents more than just two-wheeled transportation. When they line up to buy Harley-Davidson bikes, wear branded apparel, and participate in cross-country tours benefiting charities, customers are making a lifestyle choice. Nonmotorcycle products with the Harley-Davidson brand are so popular that they bring in revenues exceeding $10 million monthly. Customers snap up T-shirts in sizes from newborn to XXXL. They also buy leather jackets, teddy bears, blankets, drinking glasses, collectible pins, and hundreds of other branded items. In fact, some customers start out wearing Harley-Davidson clothing and then progress to buying Harley-Davidson motorcycles.

Owning a Harley-Davidson makes customers part of a brand-oriented motorcycle community. The Harley Owners Group—640,000 members strong—allows enthusiasts to connect with one another and with the brand. Annual rallies such as those held at Sturgis, South Dakota, and Daytona Beach, Florida, routinely draw 100,000 or more Harley-Davidson owners. When the company threw a weeklong 100th birthday bash in Milwaukee, 250,000 bikers showed up to celebrate and shop for all manner of Harley-Davidson merchandise.

Nevertheless, the company may face a bumpy ride as it searches for ways to appeal to younger customers and fend off rivals. Fifteen years ago, the average age of a Harley-Davidson buyer was 35; today the average age is 46. Moreover, market share is beginning to slip as customers buy high-performance models from competitors. In response, Harley-Davidson is introducing sleek new models with liquid-cooled engines. Some of these new models can reach speeds up to 140 miles per hour. It has also opened a new factory to keep up with demand. Through the Rider's Edge program, the company is teaching a new generation of customers how to ride and care for their motorcycles.

Harley-Davidson remains on top of the North American market and has reported record sales for more than 17 consecutive years. One of the co-founder's grandsons, Willie G. Davidson, serves as senior vice president and rides his Harley to customer gatherings. What he calls "the rebel thing" is an integral part of the brand image. Harley owners may enjoy this image when they ride, and a large number change their leathers for business suits during the workweek. To stay on the road to higher sales and profits, Harley-Davidson will have to stay attuned to its customers' perceptions of this century-old brand.[25]

QUESTIONS FOR DISCUSSION

1. What might Harley-Davidson's employees do to measure brand equity as they mingle with customers at motorcycle rallies?

2. Should the company continue family branding or move to individual branding for new models of motorcycles? Explain.

3. What questions should Harley-Davidson ask of an apparel company that wants to license the Harley-Davidson brand to place on its clothing?

Services Marketing

14

OBJECTIVES

1. To understand the nature and importance of services

2. To identify the characteristics of services that differentiate them from goods

3. To describe how the characteristics of services influence the development of marketing mixes for services

4. To understand the importance of service quality and explain how to deliver exceptional service quality

5. To explore the nature of nonprofit marketing

Keeping TV Sets and Wallets Tuned to Nickelodeon

The cable television network Nickelodeon—Nick for short—has to satisfy a number of tough audiences. Toddlers want fun, engaging programs such as *Blue's Clues* and *Dora the Explorer*. School-age viewers enjoy slightly wacky cartoons such as *SpongeBob SquarePants*. Younger teens tune in for programs like *All That*, while older teens watch the celebrity specials. And parents want to be sure that Nick's programs entertain without violence or sex when a child is holding the remote control. Nick delivers for all these audiences, with ratings that top the list of basic cable networks and annual revenues exceeding $1 billion.

Every program presents new opportunities to give viewers a good experience and encourage them to tune in again—and again. Nick is known for its in-depth marketing research and its careful control of animation and production. Because no one can predict precisely which characters and shows will resonate with viewers, the network has had both tremendous successes and big disappointments. Management was surprised by the immediate and immense popularity of *SpongeBob SquarePants*. Sponge-Bob first aired as a weekend series and, as the audience grew, became a regular part of the Saturday-morning schedule and the prime-time weekday schedule. However, children did not take to either the *Animorphs* series or the *Noah*

Knows Best series. One Nick executive says these programs were "too talky and a little too old."

With millions of children tuning in every week, Nick has been able to profit from selling advertising time and from licensing its brand for an ever-widening mix of goods and services. Retail sales of its branded products total $3 billion annually. Seeing the problems that Warner Brothers and Walt Disney have had in operating their own retail chains, Nick instead licensed its brand for Nick Zone departments within JCPenney stores.

One of Nick's newest licensing ventures involves a theme resort in Florida, the Nickelodeon Family Suites by Holiday Inn. In addition to waterslides, pools, and game rooms, the hotel will be decorated with Nick-character furnishings, offer breakfast with Nick characters, and stage live shows starring Nick characters. This deal will present entirely different service challenges compared with Nick's television business. Still, Nick believes that viewers who enjoy its characters will look forward to staying at a Nick-themed hotel and is working with Holiday Inn to open several more resorts soon. Can the resort deliver the kind of service that is consistent with the Nick brand? Stay tuned.[1] ■

The products offered by Nickelodeon are services rather than tangible goods. This chapter presents concepts that apply specifically to products that are services. The organizations that market service products include for-profit firms, such as those offering financial, personal, and professional services, and nonprofit organizations, such as educational institutions, churches, charities, and governments.

We begin this chapter with a focus on the growing importance of service industries in our economy. We then address the unique characteristics of services. Next, we deal with the challenges these characteristics pose in developing and managing marketing mixes for services. We then discuss customers' judgment of service quality and the importance of delivering high-quality services. Finally, we define nonprofit marketing and examine the development of nonprofit marketing strategies.

The Nature and Importance of Services

service An intangible product involving a deed, a performance, or an effort that cannot be physically possessed

All products, whether goods, services, or ideas, are to some extent intangible. A **service** is an intangible product involving a deed, a performance, or an effort that cannot be physically possessed.[2] Services are usually provided through the application of human and/or mechanical efforts directed at people or objects. For example, a service such as education involves the efforts of service providers (teachers) directed at people (students), whereas janitorial and interior decorating services direct their efforts at objects. Services can also involve the use of mechanical efforts directed at people (air transportation) or objects (freight transportation). A wide variety of services, such as health care and landscaping, involve both human and mechanical efforts. Although many services entail the use of tangibles such as tools and machinery, the primary difference between a service and a good is that a service is dominated by the intangible portion of the total product.

Services as products should not be confused with the related topic of customer services. Customer service involves any human or mechanical activity that adds value to the product.[3] While customer service is a part of the marketing of goods, service marketers also provide customer services. For example, many service companies offer guarantees to their customers in an effort to increase value. Hampton Inns, a national chain of mid-price hotels, gives its guests a free night if they are not 100 percent satisfied with their stay (fewer than one-half of 1 percent of Hampton customers ask for a refund). In some cases, a 100 percent satisfaction guarantee or similar service commitment may motivate employees to provide high-quality service, not because failure to do so leads to personal penalties but because they are proud to be part of an organization that is so committed to good service.

The increasing importance of services in the U.S. economy has led many people to call the United States the world's first service economy. Service industries account for about 80 percent of the country's gross domestic product (GDP). More than one-half of new businesses are service businesses, and service employment is expected to continue to grow. These industries have absorbed much of the influx of women and minorities into the work force.

One major catalyst in the growth of consumer services has been long-term economic growth (slowed only by a few recessions) in the United States, which has led to increased interest in financial services, travel, entertainment, and personal care. Lifestyle changes have similarly encouraged expansion of the service sector. In the past 40 years, the number of women in the work force has more than doubled. With a high proportion of women now working, the need for child care, domestic services, and other time-saving services has increased. Many consumers want to avoid such tasks as meal preparation, house cleaning, yard maintenance, and tax preparation; consequently, franchise operations such as Subway, Merry Maids, Chem-Lawn, and H&R Block have experienced rapid growth. Also, because Americans have become more fitness and recreation oriented, the demand for exercise and recreational facilities has escalated. In terms of demographics, the U.S. population is growing older, a fact that has promoted tremendous expansion of health care services. Finally, the increasing number and complexity of high-tech goods have spurred demand for repair services.

Business services have prospered as well. Business services include repairs and maintenance, consulting, installation, equipment leasing, marketing research, advertising, temporary office personnel, and janitorial services. Expenditures for business services have risen even faster than expenditures for consumer services. A contributing factor has been the recent trend in downsizing among many U.S. companies, which has dramatically raised demand for temporary office personnel. The growth in business services has been attributed to the increasingly complex, specialized, and competitive business environment.

Characteristics of Services

The issues associated with marketing service products differ somewhat from those associated with marketing goods. To understand these differences, we need to look at the distinguishing characteristics of services. Services have six basic characteristics: intangibility, inseparability of production and consumption, perishability, heterogeneity, client-based relationships, and customer contact.[4]

◆ Intangibility

intangibility Unable to be perceived by the senses or to be possessed

As already noted, the major characteristic that distinguishes a service from a good is intangibility. **Intangibility** means a service is not physical and therefore cannot be perceived by the senses. For example, it is impossible to touch the education that students derive from attending classes; the intangible benefit is becoming more knowledgeable. In addition, services cannot be physically possessed. Students obviously cannot physically possess knowledge as they can a stereo or a car.

Figure 14.1 depicts a tangibility continuum from pure goods (tangible) to pure services (intangible). Pure goods, if they exist at all, are rare since practically all

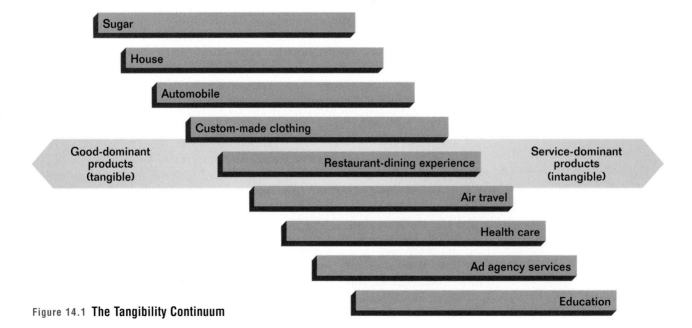

Figure 14.1 The Tangibility Continuum

marketers of goods also provide customer services. Even a tangible product such as sugar must be delivered to the store, priced, and placed on a shelf before a customer can purchase it. Intangible, service-dominant products such as education or health care are clearly service products. But what about products near the center of the continuum? Is a restaurant such as Chili's a goods marketer or a service marketer? Services like airline flights have something tangible to offer, such as drinks and meals. Knowing where the product lies on the continuum is important in creating marketing strategies for service-dominant products.

◆ Inseparability of Production and Consumption

Another important characteristic of services that creates challenges for marketers is **inseparability**, which refers to the fact that the production of a service cannot be separated from its consumption by customers. For example, air passenger service is produced and consumed simultaneously. In other words, services are often produced, sold, and consumed at the same time. In goods marketing, a customer can purchase a good, take it home, and store it until ready to use it. The manufacturer of the good may never see an actual customer. Customers, however, often must be present at the production of a service (such as investment consulting or surgery) and cannot take the service home. For instance, customers who use coin-counting machines in their local supermarkets must pour in their coins and then wait until all change is tallied. Coinstar machines tally $1.4 billion worth of coins every year.[5] Because of inseparability, customers not only want a specific type of service but expect it to be provided in a specific way by a specific individual. For example, the production and consumption of a medical exam occur simultaneously, and the patient knows in advance who the physician is and generally understands how the exam will be conducted.

Inseparability of Production and Consumption

The services provided by hospitals are characterized by the inseparability of production and consumption. As hospital services are produced, they simultaneously are consumed.

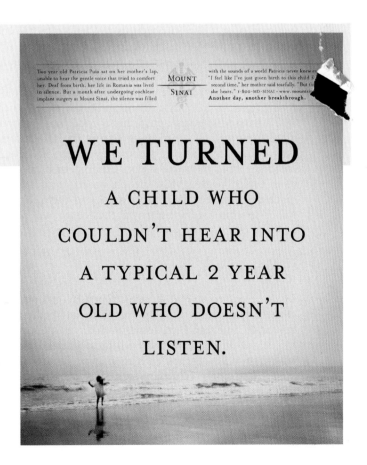

Two year old Patricia Puia sat on her mother's lap, unable to hear the gentle voice that tried to comfort her. Deaf from birth, her life in Romania was lived in silence. But a month after undergoing cochlear implant surgery at Mount Sinai, the silence was filled with the sounds of a world Patricia never knew... "I feel like I've just given birth to this child a second time," her mother said tearfully. "But the she hears." 1-800-MD-SINAI • www.mountsi

MOUNT SINAI

Another day, another breakthrough.

WE TURNED
A CHILD WHO
COULDN'T HEAR INTO
A TYPICAL 2 YEAR
OLD WHO DOESN'T
LISTEN.

◆ Perishability

Services are characterized by **perishability** in that the unused service capacity of one time period cannot be stored for future use. For example, empty seats on an airline flight today cannot be stored and sold to passengers at a later date. Other examples of service perishability include unsold basketball tickets, unscheduled dentists' appointment times, and empty hotel rooms. Although some goods, such as meat, milk, and produce, are perishable, goods generally are less perishable than services. If a pair of jeans has been sitting on a department store shelf for a week, someone can still buy them the next day. Goods marketers can handle the supply-demand problem through production scheduling and inventory techniques. Service marketers do not have the same advantage and face several hurdles in trying to balance supply and demand. They can, however, plan for demand that fluctuates according to day of the week, time of day, or season.

◆ Heterogeneity

Services delivered by people are susceptible to **heterogeneity**, or variation in quality. Quality of manufactured goods is easier to control with standardized procedures, and mistakes are easier to isolate and correct. Because of the nature of human behavior, however, it is very difficult for service providers to maintain a consistent quality of service delivery. This variation in quality can occur from one organization to another, from one service person to another within the same service facility, and from one service facility to another within the same organization. For example, one bank may provide more convenient hours and charge fewer fees than the one next door, or the retail clerks in one bookstore may be more knowledgeable and therefore more helpful than those in another bookstore owned by the same chain. In addition, the service a single employee provides can vary from customer to customer, day to day, or even hour to hour. Although many service problems are one-time events that cannot be predicted or controlled ahead of time, training and establishment of standard procedures can help increase consistency and reliability.

Heterogeneity usually increases as the degree of labor intensiveness increases. Many services, such as auto repair, education, and hairstyling, rely heavily on human labor. Other services, such as telecommunications, health clubs, and public transportation, are more equipment intensive. People-based services are often prone to fluctuations in quality from one time period to the next. For example, the fact that a hairstylist gives a customer a good haircut today does not guarantee that customer a haircut of equal quality from the same hairstylist at a later date or even a later hour. A morning customer may receive a better haircut than an end-of-the-day customer from the same stylist. Equipment-based services suffer from this problem to a lesser degree than people-based services. For instance, automated teller machines have reduced inconsistency in the quality of teller services at banks, and bar-code scanning has improved the accuracy of service at checkout counters in grocery stores.

◆ Client-Based Relationships

The success of many services depends on creating and maintaining **client-based relationships**, interactions that result in satisfied customers who use a service repeatedly over time.[6] In fact, some service providers, such as lawyers, accountants, and financial advisers, call their customers *clients* and often develop and maintain close, long-term relationships with them. For such service providers, it is not enough to attract customers. They are successful only to the degree to which they can maintain a group of clients who use their services on an ongoing basis. For example, an accountant may serve a family in his or her area for decades. If the members of this family like the quality of the accountant's services, they are likely to recommend the accountant to other families. If several families repeat this positive word-of-mouth

Yes, the world does revolve around you.

THE GRAND HOTEL

MINNEAPOLIS

Level of Customer Contact
At a high service hotel, such as The Grand Hotel in Minneapolis, there is a considerable amount of customer contact in order to provide valued services. For the United States Postal Service, there is a very low level of customer contact necessary to provide and receive the service.

communication, the accountant will likely acquire a long list of satisfied clients before long. This process is the key to creating and maintaining client-based relationships. To ensure that it actually occurs, the service provider must take steps to build trust, demonstrate customer commitment, and satisfy customers so well that they become very loyal to the provider and unlikely to switch to competitors.

◆ Customer Contact

Not all services require a high degree of customer contact, but many do. **Customer contact** refers to the level of interaction between the service provider and the customer necessary to deliver the service. High-contact services include health care, real estate, and legal and hair care services. Examples of low-contact services are tax preparation, auto repair, and dry cleaning. Note that high-contact services generally involve actions directed toward people, who must be present during production. A hairstylist's customer, for example, must be present during the styling process. Because the customer must be present, the process of production may be just as important as its final outcome. Although it is sometimes possible for the service provider to go to the customer, high-contact services typically require that the customer go to the production facility. Thus, the physical appearance of the facility may be a major component of the customer's overall evaluation of the service. While low-contact services do not require the customer's physical presence during delivery, the customer will likely need to be present to initiate and terminate the service. For example, customers of tax preparation services must bring in all necessary documents but often do not remain during the preparation process.

Employees of high-contact service providers are a very important ingredient in creating satisfied customers. A fundamental precept of customer contact is that satisfied employees lead to satisfied customers. In fact, research indicates that employee satisfaction is the single most important factor in providing high service quality. Thus, to minimize the problems customer contact can create, service organizations must take steps to understand and meet the needs of employees by adequately

customer contact The level of interaction between provider and customer needed to deliver the service

training them, empowering them to make more decisions, and rewarding them for customer-oriented behavior.[7] To provide the quality of customer service that has made it the fastest-growing coffee retailer in the world, Starbucks provides extensive employee training. Employees receive about 25 hours of initial training, which includes memorizing recipes and learning the differences among a variety of coffees, proper coffee-making techniques, and many other skills that stress Starbucks' dedication to customer service. Starbucks has approximately 6,500 coffee shops and about 74,000 employees worldwide.[8]

Developing and Managing Marketing Mixes for Services

The characteristics of services discussed in the previous section create a number of challenges for service marketers (see Table 14.1). These challenges are especially evident in the development and management of marketing mixes for services. Although such mixes contain the four major marketing mix variables—product, distribution,

Table 14.1	Service Characteristics and Marketing Challenges
Service Characteristics	**Resulting Marketing Challenges**
Intangibility	Difficult for customer to evaluate
	Customer does not take physical possession
	Difficult to advertise and display
	Difficult to set and justify prices
	Service process is usually not protectable by patents
Inseparability of production and consumption	Service provider cannot mass produce services
	Customer must participate in production
	Other consumers affect service outcomes
	Services are difficult to distribute
Perishability	Services cannot be stored
	Balancing supply and demand is very difficult
	Unused capacity is lost forever
	Demand may be very time sensitive
Heterogeneity	Service quality is difficult to control
	Service delivery is difficult to standardize
Client-based relationships	Success depends on satisfying and keeping customers over the long term
	Generating repeat business is challenging
	Relationship marketing becomes critical
Customer contact	Service providers are critical to delivery
	Requires high levels of service employee training and motivation
	Changing a high-contact service into a low-contact service to achieve lower costs is difficult to achieve without reducing customer satisfaction

Sources: K. Douglas Hoffman and John E. G. Bateson, *Essentials of Services Marketing* (Mason, OH: Southwestern, 2001); Valarie A. Zeithaml, A. Parasuraman, and Leonard L. Berry, *Delivering Quality Service: Balancing Customer Perceptions and Expectations* (New York: Free Press, 1990); Leonard L. Berry and A. Parasuraman, *Marketing Services: Competing through Quality* (New York: Free Press, 1991), p. 5.

promotion, and price—the characteristics of services require that marketers consider additional issues. The challenges of having distinctive marketing mixes for services are highlighted in the Building Customer Relationships boxed feature.

◆ Development of Services

A service offered by an organization generally is a package, or bundle, of services consisting of a core service and one or more supplementary services. A core service is the basic service experience or commodity that a customer expects to receive. A supplementary service is a supportive one related to the core service and is used to differentiate the service bundle from competitors'. For example, Hampton Inns provides a room as a core service. Bundled with the room are such supplementary services as free local phone calls, cable television, and a complimentary continental breakfast.

As discussed earlier, heterogeneity results in variability in service quality and makes it difficult to standardize service delivery. However, heterogeneity provides one advantage to service marketers: it allows them to customize their services to match the specific needs of individual customers. Health care is an example of an extremely customized service; the services provided differ from one patient to the

BUILDING CUSTOMER RELATIONSHIPS

Segmentation Blurred by Combining Marketing Efforts in Car Rental Services

Two service firms with combined marketing strategies—can it work? National Car Rental targets corporate travelers, and Alamo Rent-a-Car targets price-sensitive vacationers. However, under owner ANC Rental Car, the two companies shared one distribution strategy. Customers of either company waited in the same line to talk with the same employees at the same airport counter. They rode the same airport shuttle buses (bearing both companies' brands) to shared rental lots and picked up cars from a shared fleet. ANC's idea was to cut costs by combining distribution and service delivery, putting both brands on rental agents' uniforms, shuttle buses, and rental lots. In the process, it blurred the distinctions between the two brands and alienated some customers in each segment.

National's road-warrior customers want to fly into a city, pick up their rental cars, and be on their way to the next appointment—fast. The company promises speedy service and charges 10 to 20 percent more than Alamo for this important benefit. Alamo's customers travel for leisure and are willing to wait a bit in exchange for saving a lot on rental fees. Despite these clearly defined needs and expectations, customers in neither segment perceived significant differences in service distribution or delivery when ANC owned National and Alamo.

Satisfaction surveys showed customers were displeased with the shared distribution strategy. The number of customer complaints rose, nearly doubling in a few major markets. National responded by running shuttle buses more frequently and allowing corporate travelers to skip the rental counter and go directly to the rental lot. According to company research, customers continued to believe service quality was declining, and National lost market share in some key locations.

Then Vanguard Car Rental USA bought National and Alamo, and began phasing out dual branding to better match each company's distribution strategy with its targeted customer segment. "Our job is to restore the confidence the high-frequency business traveler had in National and to make sure that Alamo is positioned as the value brand," said Vanguard's CEO. Customers are taking notice. The number of complaints has dropped and satisfaction levels are improving as Vanguard has implemented separate marketing strategies for each car rental service.

Snapshot

Source: Data from Answer Financial survey.

next. Such customized services can be expensive for both provider and customer, and some service marketers therefore face a dilemma: how to provide service at an acceptable level of quality in an efficient and economic manner and still satisfy individual customer needs. To cope with this problem, some service marketers offer standardized packages. For example, a lawyer may offer a divorce package at a specified price for an uncontested divorce. When service bundles are standardized, the specific actions and activities of the service provider usually are highly specified. Automobile quick-lube providers frequently offer a service bundle for a single price; the specific work to be done on a customer's car is spelled out in detail. Various other equipment-based services are also often standardized into packages. For instance, cable television providers frequently offer several packages, such as "Basic," "Standard," "Premier," and "Hollywood."

The characteristic of intangibility makes it difficult for customers to evaluate a service prior to purchase. A customer who is shopping for a pair of jeans can try them on before buying them, but how does she or he evaluate a haircut before receiving the service? Intangibility requires service marketers such as hairstylists to market promises to customers. The customer is forced to place some degree of trust in the service provider to perform the service in a manner that meets or exceeds those promises. Service marketers must guard against making promises that raise customer expectations beyond what they can provide.

To cope with the problem of intangibility, marketers employ tangible cues, such as well-groomed, professional-appearing contact personnel and clean, attractive physical facilities, to help assure customers about the quality of the service. Life insurance companies sometimes try to make the quality of their policies more tangible by printing them on premium-quality paper and enclosing them in leather sheaths. Since customers often rely on brand names as an indicator of product quality, service marketers at organizations whose names are the same as their service brand names should strive to build a strong national image for their companies. For example, American Express, McDonald's, American Life, and America Online try to maintain strong, positive national company images because these names are the brand names of the services they provide.

The inseparability of production and consumption and the level of customer contact also influence the development and management of services. The fact that customers take part in the production of a service means other customers can affect the outcome of the service. For instance, if a nonsmoker dines in a restaurant without a no-smoking section, the overall quality of service experienced by the non-smoking customer declines. For this reason, many restaurants have no-smoking sections and some prohibit smoking anywhere on their premises. Service marketers can reduce these problems by encouraging customers to share the responsibility of maintaining an environment that allows all participants to receive the intended benefits of the service.

Some of the challenges of service design may be overcome by relying on the behavioral sciences. Using the results of behavioral studies, Richard Chase and Sriram Dasu have identified five major guidelines to consider when designing a service. The first guideline is to segment the pleasure and combine the pain. For example, when gambling, people prefer to win $5 twice rather than $10 just one time and to lose only one time rather than twice. Cruise lines have picked up on this idea: a look at any cruise's agenda will reveal a vacation packed with fun events, yet cruise customers pay only one time. The second guideline is to get the bad experiences out of the way as soon as possible. For example, during a doctor's appointment,

For people who love to drive.

Hertz rents Fords and other fine cars. ® Reg. U.S. Pat. Off. © 2003 Hertz System, Inc.

Rent with Hertz on your next golf outing.

Grab your clubs and your driving gloves – and head for the course with Hertz. Choose from a wide selection of vehicles, Driving Directions and 24-Hour Emergency Roadside Assistance. You can also take advantage of NeverLost,® our in-car navigation system. Products and services that add up to convenience and peace of mind (sure to come in handy while putting). For reservations, visit us at hertz.com or call your travel agent or Hertz at 1-800-654-3131. At Hertz, we know exactly how you feel. So we have exactly what you need.

Maintaining a Positive National Image
Companies such as Hertz use a significant amount of advertising in order to maintain a strong, favorable image.

unpleasant events such as injections should be completed quickly because the patient usually dreads them. The third guideline is to build commitment through choice. When a physician allows patients to participate in decisions about their treatments, patients feel as though they have some control over their lives and are more likely to come back to the same clinic. Choice seems to ease the pain and discomfort of unpleasant events. The fourth guideline is to give customers rituals and stick to them. Since people are creatures of habit, they include many rituals in their daily lives. Rituals are especially significant in longer-term professional services; deviation from them can even be considered a sign of failure. Finally, service providers should finish strong. For example, the final evenings of most cruises include lavish meals with extravagant desserts and spectacular shows.[9]

◆ Distribution of Services

Marketers deliver services in a variety of ways. In some instances, customers go to a service provider's facility. For example, most health care, dry cleaning, hair care, and tanning services are delivered at the provider's facilities. Some services are provided at the customer's home or business. Lawn care, air conditioning and heating repair, and carpet cleaning are examples. Other services are delivered primarily at "arm's length," meaning no face-to-face contact occurs between the customer and the service provider. A number of equipment-based services are delivered at arm's length, including electric, online, cable television, and telephone services. Providing high-quality customer service at arm's length can be costly but essential in keeping customers satisfied and maintaining market share. AT&T, for example, is paying the consulting firm Accenture $2.6 billion to develop technology and training for the personnel who serve the firm's 60 million customers. The goal is to improve efficiency while providing faster service.[10]

Marketing channels for services are usually short and direct, meaning the producer delivers the service directly to the end user. Some services, however, use intermediaries. For example, travel agents facilitate the delivery of airline services, independent insurance agents participate in the marketing of a variety of insurance policies, and financial planners market investment services.

Service marketers are less concerned with warehousing and transportation than are goods marketers. They are, however, very concerned about inventory management, especially balancing supply and demand for services. The service characteristics of inseparability and level of customer contact contribute to the challenges of demand management. In some instances, service marketers use appointments and reservations as approaches for scheduling delivery of services. Health care providers, attorneys, accountants, auto mechanics, and restaurants often use appointments or reservations to plan and pace delivery of their services. To increase the supply of a service, marketers use multiple service sites and also increase the number of contact service providers at each site. National and regional eye care and hair care services are examples.

To make delivery more accessible to customers and increase the supply of a service, as well as reduce labor costs, some service providers have replaced some contact personnel with equipment. In other words, they have changed a high-contact service into a low-contact one. The banking industry is an example. By installing ATMs, banks have increased production capacity and reduced customer contact. In addition, a number of automated banking services are now available by telephone 24 hours a day. Such services have helped lower costs by reducing the need for customer service representatives. Changing the delivery of services from human to equipment has created some problems, however. Some customers complain that automated services are less personal. When designing service delivery, marketers must pay attention to the degree of personalization customers desire.

◆ Promotion of Services

The intangibility of services results in several promotion-related challenges to service marketers. Since it may not be possible to depict the actual performance of a service in an advertisement or display it in a store, explaining a service to customers can be a difficult task. Promotion of services typically includes tangible cues that symbolize the service. For example, Trans America uses its pyramid-shaped building to symbolize strength, security, and reliability, important features associated with insurance and other financial services. Similarly, the hands Allstate uses in its ads symbolize personalized service and trustworthy, caring representatives. Although these symbols have nothing to do with the actual services, they make it much easier for customers to understand the intangible attributes associated with insurance services. To make a service more tangible, advertisements for services often show pictures of facilities, equipment, and service personnel. Marketers may also promote their services as a tangible expression of consumers' lifestyles.

Compared with goods marketers, service providers are more likely to promote price, guarantees, performance documentation, availability, and training and certification of contact personnel. The International Smart Tan Network, a trade association for indoor tanning salons, offers a certification course in professional standards for tanning facility operators. The association encourages salons to promote their "Smart Tan Certification" in advertising and throughout the salon as a measure of quality training.[11] When preparing advertisements, service marketers are careful to use concrete, specific language to help make services more tangible in customers' minds. They are also careful not to promise too much regarding their services so that customer expectations do not rise to unattainable levels.

Through their actions, service contact personnel can be directly or indirectly involved in the personal selling of services. Personal selling is often important because personal influence can help the customer visualize the benefits of a given service. Because service contact personnel may engage in personal selling, some companies invest heavily in training. For example, Kinko's developed Knowledge Network, a virtual learning environment for the company's 20,000 employees in all 50 states. The Knowledge Network combines e-learning and instruction-led training, and replaces the 51 employee training sites located throughout the United States. The company has found that this program not only reduces time to market for training on new products but also has resulted in savings of about $10 million a year in training costs.[12]

As noted earlier, intangibility makes experiencing a service prior to purchase difficult, if not impossible in some cases. A car can be test driven, a snack food can be sampled in a supermarket, and a new brand of bar soap can be mailed to customers as a free sample. Some services also can be offered on a trial basis at little or no risk to the customer, but a number of services cannot be sampled before purchase. Promotional programs that encourage trial use of insurance, health care, or auto repair are difficult to design because even after purchase of such services, assessing their quality may require a considerable length of time. For example, an individual may purchase auto insurance from the same provider for ten years before filing a claim, but the quality of the coverage is based primarily on how the customer is treated and protected when a claim is made.

Because of the heterogeneity and intangibility of services, word-of-mouth communication is important in service promotion. What other people say about a service provider can have a tremendous impact on whether an individual decides to use that provider. Some service marketers attempt to stimulate positive word-of-mouth communication by asking satisfied customers to tell their friends and associates about the service and may even provide incentives for doing so.

◆ Pricing of Services

Prices for services can be established on several different bases. The prices of pest control services, dry cleaning, carpet cleaning, and a physician's consultation are usually based on the performance of specific tasks. Other service prices are based on time. For example, attorneys, consultants, counselors, piano teachers, and plumbers often charge by the hour or day.

Some services use demand-based pricing. When demand for a service is high, the price also is high; when demand for a service is low, so is the price. The perishability of services means that when demand is low, the unused capacity cannot be stored and therefore is lost forever. Every empty seat on an airline flight or in a movie theater represents lost revenue. Some services are very time sensitive in that a significant number of customers desire the service at a particular time. This point in time is called *peak demand*. A provider of time-sensitive services brings in most of its revenue during peak demand. For an airline, peak demand is usually early and late in the day; for cruise lines, peak demand occurs in the winter for Caribbean cruises and in the summer for Alaskan cruises. Providers of time-sensitive services often use demand-based pricing to manage the problem of balancing supply and demand. They charge top prices during peak demand and lower prices during off-peak demand to encourage more customers to use the service. This is why the price of a matinee movie is often half the price of the same movie shown at night. Major airlines maintain sophisticated databases to help them adjust ticket prices to fill as many seats as possible on every flight. On a single day, each airline makes thousands of fare changes to maximize the use of its seating capacity and thus maximize its revenues. To accomplish this objective, many airlines have to overbook flights and discount fares.

When services are offered to customers in a bundle, marketers must decide whether to offer the services at one price, price them separately, or use a combination of the two methods. For example, some hotels offer a package of services at one price, while others charge separately for the room, phone service, breakfast, and even in-room safes. Some service providers offer a one-price option for a specific bundle of services and make add-on bundles available at additional charges. For example, a number of cable television companies offer a standard package of channels for one price and offer add-on channel packages for additional charges. Telephone services, such as call waiting and caller ID, are frequently bundled and sold as a package for one price.

Because of the intangible nature of services, customers sometimes rely heavily on price as an indicator of quality. If customers perceive the available services in a service category as being similar in quality, and if the quality of such services is difficult to judge even after these services are purchased, customers may seek out the lowest-priced provider. For example, many customers seek

Pricing Services
The price for hotel rooms is sometimes based on the level of demand. When demand for a specific hotel is higher, then its room prices will be higher. When demand is lower on particular evenings, then the room prices will be lower.

auto insurance providers with the lowest rates. If the quality of different service providers is likely to vary, customers may rely heavily on the price-quality association. For example, if you have to have an appendectomy, will you choose the surgeon who charges an average price of $1,500 or the surgeon who will take your appendix out for $399?

For certain types of services, market conditions may limit how much can be charged for a specific service, especially if the services in this category are perceived as generic in nature. For example, the prices charged by a self-serve laundromat are likely to be limited by the going price for laundromat services in a given community. Also, state and local government regulations may reduce price flexibility. Such regulations may substantially control the prices charged for auto insurance, utilities, cable television service, and even housing rentals.

Service Quality

service quality Customers' perception of how well a service meets or exceeds their expectations

Delivery of high-quality services is one of the most important and most difficult tasks any service organization faces. Because of their characteristics, services are very difficult to evaluate. Hence customers must look closely at service quality when comparing services. **Service quality** is defined as customers' perceptions of how well a service meets or exceeds their expectations.[13] Note that customers, not the organization, evaluate service quality. This distinction is critical because it forces service marketers to examine quality from the customer's viewpoint. For example, a bank may view service quality as having friendly and knowledgeable employees. However, the bank's customers may be more concerned with waiting time, ATM access, security, and statement accuracy. Thus, it is important for service organizations to determine what customers expect and then develop service products that meet or exceed those expectations.

◆ Customer Evaluation of Service Quality

search qualities Tangible attributes that can be judged before the purchase of a product

experience qualities Attributes that can be assessed only during purchase and consumption of a service

credence qualities Attributes that customers may be unable to evaluate even after purchasing and consuming a service

The biggest obstacle for customers in evaluating service quality is the intangible nature of the service. How can customers evaluate something they cannot see, feel, taste, smell, or hear? Evaluation of a good is much easier because all goods possess **search qualities**, tangible attributes such as color, style, size, feel, or fit that can be evaluated prior to purchase. Trying on a new coat and taking a car for a test drive are examples of how customers evaluate search qualities. Services, on the other hand, have very few search qualities; instead, they abound in experience and credence qualities. **Experience qualities** are attributes, such as taste, satisfaction, or pleasure, that can be assessed only during the purchase and consumption of a service.[14] Restaurants and vacations are examples of services high in experience qualities. **Credence qualities** are attributes that customers may be unable to evaluate even after the purchase and consumption of the service. Examples of services high in credence qualities are surgical operations, automobile repairs, consulting, and legal representation. Most consumers lack the knowledge or skills to evaluate the quality of these types of services. Consequently they must place a great deal of faith in the integrity and competence of the service provider.

Despite the difficulties in evaluating quality, service quality may be the only way customers can choose one service over another. For this reason, service marketers live or die by understanding how consumers judge service quality. Table 14.2 defines five dimensions consumers use when evaluating service quality: tangibles, reliability, responsiveness, assurance, and empathy. Note that all of these dimensions have links to employee performance. Of the five, reliability is the most important in determining customer evaluations of service quality.[15]

Table 14.2   Dimensions of Service Quality

Dimension	Evaluation Criteria	Examples
Tangibles: Physical evidence of the service	Appearance of physical facilities Appearance of service personnel Tools or equipment used to provide the service	A clean and professional-looking doctor's office A clean and neatly attired repairperson The quality of food in a restaurant The equipment used in a medical exam
Reliability: Consistency and dependability in performing the service	Accuracy of billing or recordkeeping Performing services when promised	An accurate bank statement A confirmed hotel reservation An airline flight departing and arriving on time
Responsiveness: Willingness or readiness of employees to provide the service	Returning customer phone calls Providing prompt service Handling urgent requests	A server refilling a customer's cup of tea without being asked An ambulance arriving within 3 minutes
Assurance: Knowledge/competence of employees and ability to convey trust and confidence	Knowledge and skills of employees Company name and reputation Personal characteristics of employees	A highly trained financial adviser A known and respected service provider A doctor's bedside manner
Empathy: Caring and individual attention provided by employees	Listening to customer needs Caring about customers' interests Providing personalized attention	A store employee listening to and trying to understand a customer's complaint A nurse counseling a heart patient

Sources: Adapted from Leonard L. Berry and A. Parasuraman, *Marketing Services: Competing through Quality* (New York: Free Press, 1991); Valarie A. Zeithaml, A. Parasuraman, and Leonard L. Berry, *Delivering Quality Service: Balancing Customer Perceptions and Expectations* (New York: Free Press, 1990); A. Parasuraman, Leonard L. Berry, and Valarie A. Zeithaml, "An Empirical Examination of Relationships in an Extended Service Quality Model," *Marketing Science Institute Working Paper Series,* Report no. 90-112 (Cambridge, MA: Marketing Science Institute, 1990), p. 29.

Service marketers pay a great deal of attention to the tangibles of service quality. Tangible elements, such as the appearance of facilities and employees, are often the only aspects of a service that can be viewed before purchase and consumption. Therefore, service marketers must ensure that these tangible elements are consistent with the overall image of the service.

Except for the tangibles dimension, the criteria customers use to judge service quality are intangible. For instance, how does a customer judge reliability? Since dimensions such as reliability cannot be examined with the senses, customers must rely on other ways of judging service. One of the most important factors in customer judgments of service quality is service expectations. Service expectations are influenced by past experiences with the service, word-of-mouth communication from other customers, and the service company's own advertising. For example, customers are usually eager to try a new restaurant, especially when friends recommend it. These same customers may have also seen advertisements placed by the restaurant. As a result, they have an idea of what to expect when they visit the restaurant for the first time. When they finally dine there, the quality they experience will change the expectations they have for their next visit. That is why providing consistently high service quality is important. If the quality of a restaurant, or of any service, begins to deteriorate, customers will alter their own expectations and change their word-of-mouth communication to others accordingly.

Service Quality
Smith Barney Financial Consultants establish trusting relationships with their clients through a shared identification of a strong work ethic, innovative thinking, and never being satisfied.

◆ Delivering Exceptional Service Quality

Providing high-quality service on a consistent basis is very difficult. All consumers have experienced examples of poor service: late flight departures and arrivals, inattentive restaurant servers, rude bank employees, long lines. Obviously it is impossible for a service organization to ensure exceptional service quality 100 percent of the time. However, an organization can take many steps to increase the likelihood of providing high-quality service. First, though, the service company must consider the four factors that affect service quality: (1) analysis of customer needs, (2) service quality specifications, (3) employee performance, and (4) management of service expectations (see Figure 14.2).[16]

Analysis of Customer Expectations. Providers need to understand customer expectations when designing a service to meet or exceed those expectations. Only then can they deliver good service. Customers usually have two levels of expectations: desired and acceptable. The desired level of expectations is what the customer really wants. If this level of expectations is provided, the customer will be very satisfied. The acceptable level of expectations is what the customer views as adequate. The difference between these two levels of expectations is called the customer's *zone of tolerance*.[17]

Service companies sometimes use marketing research, such as surveys and focus groups, to discover customer needs and expectations. For instance, Ritz-Carlton Hotels conducted focus-group research to find out the level of service expected by high-tech executives and entrepreneurs, the target audience for its Silicon Valley resort hotel. Based on this analysis, the resort began offering guests around-the-clock tech support as well as high-speed web access, in-room video game consoles, safes to store laptop computers, and cellphone rentals.[18] Other service marketers,

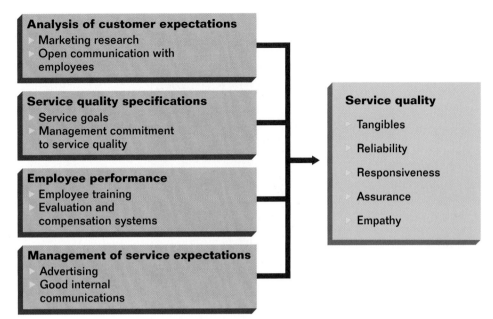

Figure 14.2 **Service Quality Model**   *Source:* Adapted from A. Parasuraman, Leonard L. Berry, and Valarie A. Zeithaml, "An Empirical Examination of Relationships in an Extended Service Quality Model," *Marketing Science Institute Working Paper Series,* Report no. 90-112 (Cambridge, MA: Marketing Science Institute, 1990). Used with permission.

especially restaurants, use comment cards on which customers can complain or provide suggestions. Still another approach is to ask employees. Because customer contact employees interact daily with customers, they are in a good position to know what customers want from the company. Service managers should regularly interact with their employees by asking their opinions on the best way to serve customers.

Service Quality Specifications. Once an organization understands its customers' needs, it must establish goals to help ensure good service delivery. These goals, or service specifications, are typically set in terms of employee or machine performance. For example, a bank may require its employees to conform to a dress code. Likewise, the bank may require that all incoming phone calls be answered by the third ring. Specifications such as these can be very important in providing quality service as long as they are tied to the needs expressed by customers.

Perhaps the most critical aspect of service quality specifications is managers' commitment to service quality. Service managers who are committed to quality become role models for all employees in the organization. Such commitment motivates customer contact employees to comply with service specifications. It is crucial that all managers within the organization embrace this commitment, especially frontline managers, who are much closer to customers than higher-level managers.

Employee Performance. Once an organization sets service quality standards and managers are committed to them, the organization must find ways to ensure that customer contact employees perform their jobs well. Contact employees in most service industries (bank tellers, flight attendants, servers, sales clerks, etc.) are often the least trained and lowest-paid members of the organization. Service organizations must realize that contact employees are the most important link to the customer, and thus their performance is critical to customer perceptions of service quality. The way to ensure that employees perform well is to train them well so they understand how to do their jobs. Providing information about customers, service specifications, and the organization itself during the training promotes this understanding. The year-old company When Pigs Fly helps managers equip frontline workers at amusement parks, fairs, carnivals, and other amusement-related facilities with the training, tools, encouragement, and motivation they need to do their jobs well. Much of their training is targeted at the GenXers who staff these facilities. "Hospitality, customer service, safety—these things don't come naturally to kids," says company co-owner Patty Beazley.[19]

TRUE REDEMPTION™ DEFINED:

No Blackouts. No Limits. No Hassles.

Starwood Preferred Guest™ offers you the most award-winning hotels any time you want to go.
Redeem your Starpoints™ instantly and enjoy any of our 750 hotels and resorts worldwide.

BECOME A STARWOOD PREFERRED GUEST AT SPG.COM

WESTIN   Sheraton   Four Points Sheraton   ST. REGIS   LUXURY COLLECTION   W HOTELS

VOTED BEST FREQUENT GUEST PROGRAM 4 YEARS IN A ROW — FREDDIE AWARDS 1999-2002

Building Service Expectations
Starwood Preferred Guest is building and managing customers' service expectations through this advertisement.

The evaluation and compensation system the organization uses also plays a part in employee performance. Many service employees are evaluated and rewarded on the basis of output measures, such as sales volume (automobile salespeople) or a low error rate (bank tellers). But systems using output measures overlook other major aspects of job performance, including friendliness, teamwork, effort, and customer satisfaction. These customer-oriented measures of performance may be a better basis for evaluation and reward. In fact, a number of service marketers use customer satisfaction ratings to determine a portion of service employee compensation.

Management of Service Expectations. Because expectations are so significant in customer evaluations of service quality, service companies recognize they must set realistic expectations about the service they can provide. They can set these expectations through advertising and good internal communication. In their advertisements, service companies make promises about the kind of service they will deliver. As already noted, a service company is forced to make promises because the intangibility of services prevents the organization from showing the benefits in the advertisement. However, the advertiser should not promise more than it can deliver. Doing so will likely mean disappointed customers.

To deliver on promises made, a company needs to have thorough internal communication among its departments, especially management, advertising, and store operations. Assume, for example, that a restaurant's radio advertisements guarantee service within five minutes or the meal is free. If top management or the advertising department fails to inform store operations about the five-minute guarantee, the restaurant will very likely fail to meet its customers' service expectations. Even though customers might appreciate a free meal, the restaurant will lose some credibility as well as revenue.

As mentioned earlier, word-of-mouth communication from other customers also shapes customer expectations. However, service companies cannot manage this "advertising" directly. The best way to ensure positive word-of-mouth communication is to provide exceptional service quality. It has been estimated that customers tell four times as many people about bad service as they do about good service.

Nonprofit Marketing

nonprofit marketing Marketing activities conducted to achieve some goal other than ordinary business goals such as profit, market share, or return on investment

Nonprofit marketing includes marketing activities conducted by individuals and organizations to achieve some goal other than ordinary business goals such as profit, market share, or return on investment. Nonprofit marketing is divided into two categories: nonprofit-organization marketing and social marketing. Nonprofit-organization marketing is the use of marketing concepts and techniques by organizations whose goals do not include making profits. Social marketing promotes social causes, such as AIDS research and recycling.

Most of the previously discussed concepts and approaches to service products also apply to nonprofit organizations. Indeed, many nonprofit organizations provide mainly service products. In this section, we examine the concept of nonprofit marketing to determine how it differs from marketing activities in for-profit business organizations. We also explore the marketing objectives of nonprofit organizations and the development of their product strategies.

◆ How Is Nonprofit Marketing Different?

Many nonprofit organizations strive for effective marketing activities. Charitable organizations and supporters of social causes are major nonprofit marketers in this country. Political parties, unions, religious sects, and fraternal organizations also perform marketing activities, but they are not considered businesses. Whereas the chief beneficiary of a business enterprise is whoever owns or holds stock in it, in theory the only beneficiaries of a nonprofit organization are its clients, its members, or the public at large. The American Museum of Natural History, for example, is a nonprofit service organization.

Nonprofit organizations have greater opportunities for creativity than most for-profit business organizations, but trustees or board members of nonprofit organizations are likely to have difficulty judging the performance of the trained professionals they oversee. It is harder for administrators to evaluate the performance of professors or social workers than it is for sales managers to evaluate the performance of salespeople in a for-profit organization.

NET SIGHTS

Nonprofit organizations often face unique challenges as they attempt to market their services to clients, volunteers, and donors. The Internet Nonprofit Center has a webpage devoted to marketing issues important to nonprofit organizations. Visit **www.nonprofits.org/npofaq/ keywords/2n.html** *to learn more about nonprofit services marketing.*

Nonprofit Organizations that Provide Services
Both The Hole in the Wall Gang Camp and Earth Share are nonprofit organizations engaged in services marketing.

The Hole in The Wall Gang Camp, opened by Paul Newman in 1988, is a nonprofit residential summer camp and year-round center designed to serve children and families coping with cancer, sickle cell anemia, HIV/AIDS and other blood diseases.

FOR INFORMATION ON THE CAMP AND HOW YOU CAN HELP, PLEASE CONTACT US AT 555 LONG WHARF DRIVE, NEW HAVEN, CT 06511, (203)772.0522, OR VISIT OUR WEB SITE AT WWW.HOLEINTHEWALLGANG.ORG

How can you help protect the prairie and the penguin?

Simple. Visit www.earthshare.org and learn how the world's leading environmental groups are working together under one name. And how easy it is for you to help protect the prairies and the penguins and the planet.

www.earthshare.org

One environment. One simple way to care for it.   Earth Share

Another way nonprofit marketing differs from for-profit marketing is that non-profit marketing is sometimes quite controversial. Nonprofit organizations such as Greenpeace, the National Rifle Association, and the National Organization for Women spend lavishly on lobbying efforts to persuade Congress, the White House, and even the courts to support their interests, in part because not all of society agrees with their aims. However, marketing as a field of study does not attempt to state what an organization's goals should be or to debate the issue of nonprofit versus for-profit business goals. Marketing tries only to provide a body of knowledge and concepts to help further an organization's goals. Individuals must decide whether they approve or disapprove of a particular organization's goal orientation. Most marketers would agree that profit and consumer satisfaction are appropriate goals for business enterprises, but would probably disagree considerably about the goals of a controversial nonprofit organization.

◆ Nonprofit Marketing Objectives

The basic aim of nonprofit organizations is to obtain a desired response from a target market. The response could be a change in values, a financial contribution, the donation of services, or some other type of exchange. Nonprofit marketing objectives are shaped by the nature of the exchange and the goals of the organization. These objectives should state the rationale for the organization's existence. An organization that defines its marketing objective as providing a product can be left without a purpose if the product becomes obsolete. However, servicing and adapting to the perceived needs and wants of a target public, or market, enhances an organization's chance to survive and achieve its goals.

◆ Developing Nonprofit Marketing Strategies

target public People interested in or concerned about an organization, a product, or a social cause

Nonprofit organizations develop marketing strategies by defining and analyzing a target market and creating and maintaining a total marketing mix that appeals to that market.

Target Markets. We must revise the concept of target markets slightly to apply it to nonprofit organizations. Whereas a business seeks out target groups that are potential purchasers of its product, a nonprofit organization may attempt to serve many diverse groups. For our purposes, a **target public** is a collective of individuals who have an interest in or a concern about an organization, a product, or a social cause. The terms *target market* and *target public* are difficult to distinguish for many nonprofit organizations. The target public of the Partnership for a Drug Free America consists of parents, adults, and concerned teenagers. However, the target market for the organization's advertisements consists of potential and current drug users. When an organization is concerned

Promotion of a Nonprofit Organization
The Pan-Massachusetts Challenge, as a part of its marketing strategy, appeals for support in its efforts to raise money for The Jimmy Fund and cancer research.

about changing values or obtaining a response from the public, it views the public as a market.[20]

client publics Direct consumers of a product of a nonbusiness organization

general publics Indirect consumers of a product of a nonbusiness organization

In nonprofit marketing, direct consumers of the product are called **client publics** and indirect consumers are called **general publics**.[21] For example, the client public for a university is its student body, and its general public includes parents, alumni, and trustees. The client public usually receives most of the attention when an organization develops a marketing strategy.

Developing a Marketing Mix. A marketing mix strategy limits alternatives and directs marketing activities toward achieving organizational goals. The strategy should include a blueprint for making decisions about product, distribution, promotion, and price. These decision variables should be blended to serve the target market.

In developing the product, nonprofit organizations usually deal with ideas and services. Problems may evolve when an organization fails to define what it is providing. What product, for example, does the Peace Corps provide? Its services include vocational training, health services, nutritional assistance, and community development. It also markets the ideas of international cooperation and the implementation of U.S. foreign policy. The product of the Peace Corps is more difficult to define than the average business product. As indicated in the first part of this chapter, services are intangible and therefore need special marketing efforts. The marketing of ideas and concepts is likewise more abstract than the marketing of tangibles, and much effort is required to present benefits. To gain a better understanding of the importance of branding for nonprofit organizations, read the Ethics and Social Responsibility boxed feature.

ETHICS AND SOCIAL RESPONSIBILITY

Nonprofits Benefit from Brand Savvy

Nonprofit organizations own some of the most trusted brands in the world and are becoming increasingly savvy about the value of their brands. Universities earn money by allowing MBNA and other banks to put their brand names on Visa and MasterCard credit cards marketed to students and alumni. The National Geographic Society is partnering with Lowe's home improvement centers to sell the nonprofit's branded bird feeders and bird houses. Tyson Foods underwrites the nonprofit Share Our Strength's nutrition education program and contributes food products to local food banks. The participating businesses benefit by enhancing their corporate reputations. Nonprofit organizations gain wider awareness of their brands and good works, and receive cash or product donations from their corporate partners.

One of the more unusual deals involving a nonprofit brand is the arrangement between entrepreneur Sam Mulgrew and the Trappist monks at New Melleray Abbey in Peosta, Iowa. Mulgrew had created an affordable line of basic wooden caskets but was having difficulty marketing them without an established brand name. Then he heard about the

financial problems of the abbey, which is not far from Mulgrew's home. The abbey needs $480,000 annually to feed the 30 monks in residence, heat the buildings, pay for health care, and fund retirement accounts. Mulgrew approached the abbot with a business proposition to put the Trappist brand on a line of caskets. The abbot agreed, with the condition that the abbey retain full ownership of the Trappist Caskets company. Mulgrew agreed.

Today 12 monks work with 12 nonabbey employees to produce the caskets from Mulgrew's designs. Although Mulgrew draws a salary and receives bonuses, he is the entrepreneurial heart of the operation. In addition to establishing a website (**www.trappistcaskets.com**) to sell the caskets directly to customers, he buys advertising space in Catholic newspapers and newsletters across the country. Trappist Caskets has been so successful, with annual revenues exceeding $1 million, that expansion plans are under way. The monks are pleased with the profits, the entrepreneur is proud of the company's growth, and customers are able to buy reasonably priced wooden caskets that bear a trusted brand name.

Distribution decisions in nonprofit organizations relate to how ideas and services will be made available to clients. If the product is an idea, selecting the right media to communicate the idea will facilitate distribution. By nature, services consist of assistance, convenience, and availability. Availability is thus part of the total service. Making a product such as health services available calls for knowledge of such retailing concepts as site location analysis.

Developing a channel of distribution to coordinate and facilitate the flow of nonprofit products to clients is a necessary task, but in a nonprofit setting the traditional concept of the marketing channel may need to be revised. The independent wholesalers available to a business enterprise do not exist in most nonprofit situations. Instead, a very short channel—nonprofit organization to client—is the norm because production and consumption of ideas and services are often simultaneous.

Making promotional decisions may be the first sign that a nonprofit organization is performing marketing activities. Nonprofit organizations use advertising and publicity to communicate with clients and the public. Direct mail remains the primary means of fund-raising for social services, such as those provided by the Red Cross and Special Olympics. Some nonprofits use the immediacy of the Internet to reach fund-raising and promotional goals. Nonprofits use the Internet as a form of e-commerce to accept online gifts and conduct online auctions, and many use application service providers to maintain software and save money.[22] Many nonprofit organizations also use personal selling, although they may call it by another name. Churches and charities rely on personal selling when they send volunteers to recruit new members or request donations. The U.S. Army uses personal selling when its recruiting officers attempt to persuade men and women to enlist. Special events to obtain funds, communicate ideas, or provide services are also effective promotional activities. Amnesty International, for example, has held worldwide concert tours featuring well-known musical artists to raise funds and increase public awareness of political prisoners around the world.

Although product and promotional techniques may require only slight modification when applied to nonprofit organizations, pricing is generally quite different and decision making is more complex. The different pricing concepts the nonprofit organization faces include pricing in user and donor markets. Two types of monetary pricing exist: *fixed* and *variable*. There may be a fixed fee for users, or the price may vary depending on the user's ability to pay. When a donation-seeking organization will accept a contribution of any size, it is using variable pricing.

The broadest definition of price (valuation) must be used to develop nonprofit marketing strategies. Financial price, an exact dollar value, may or may not be charged for a nonprofit product. Economists recognize the giving up of alternatives as a cost. **Opportunity cost** is the value of the benefit given up by selecting one alternative over another. According to this traditional economic view of price, if a nonprofit organization persuades someone to donate time to a cause or to change his or her behavior, the alternatives given up are a cost to (or a price paid by) the individual. Volunteers who answer phones for a university counseling service or a suicide hotline, for example, give up the time they could spend studying or doing other things and the income they might earn from working at a for-profit business organization.

For other nonprofit organizations, financial price is an important part of the marketing mix. Nonprofit organizations today are raising money by increasing the prices of their services or are starting to charge for services if they have not done so before. They are using marketing research to determine what kinds of products people will pay for. Pricing strategies of nonprofit organizations often stress public and client welfare over equalization of costs and revenues. If additional funds are needed to cover costs, the organization may solicit donations, contributions, or grants.

opportunity cost The value of the benefit given up by choosing one alternative over another

SUMMARY

Services are intangible products involving deeds, performances, or efforts that cannot be physically possessed. They are the result of applying human or mechanical efforts to people or objects. Services are a growing part of the U.S. economy. They have six fundamental characteristics: intangibility, inseparability of production and consumption, perishability, heterogeneity, client-based relationships, and customer contact. Intangibility means that a service cannot be seen, touched, tasted, or smelled. Inseparability refers to the fact that the production of a service cannot be separated from its consumption by customers. Perishability means unused service capacity of one time period cannot be stored for future use. Heterogeneity is variation in service quality. Client-based relationships are interactions with customers that lead to the repeated use of a service over time. Customer contact is the interaction between providers and customers needed to deliver a service.

Core services are the basic service experiences customers expect; supplementary services are those that relate to and support core services. Because of the characteristics of services, service marketers face several challenges in developing and managing marketing mixes. To address the problem of intangibility, marketers use cues that help assure customers about the quality of their services. The development and management of service products are also influenced by the service characteristics of inseparability and level of customer contact. Some services require that customers come to the service provider's facility; others are delivered with no face-to-face contact. Marketing channels for services are usually short and direct, but some services employ intermediaries. Service marketers are less concerned with warehousing and transportation than are goods marketers, but inventory management and balancing supply and demand for services are important issues. The intangibility of services poses several promotion-related challenges. Advertisements with tangible cues that symbolize the service and depict facilities, equipment, and personnel help address these challenges. Service providers are likely to promote price, guarantees, performance documentation, availability, and training and certification of contact personnel. Through their actions, service personnel can be involved directly or indirectly in the personal selling of services.

Intangibility makes it difficult to experience a service before purchasing it. Heterogeneity and intangibility make word-of-mouth communication an important means of promotion. The prices of services are based on task performance, time required, or demand. Perishability creates difficulties in balancing supply and demand because unused capacity cannot be stored. The point in time when a significant number of customers desire a service is called peak demand; demand-based pricing results in higher prices charged for services during peak demand. When services are offered in a bundle, marketers must decide whether to offer them at one price, price them separately, or use a combination of the two methods. Because services are intangible, customers may rely on price as a sign of quality. For some services, market conditions may dictate the price; for others, state and local government regulations may limit price flexibility.

Service quality is customers' perception of how well a service meets or exceeds their expectations. Although one of the most important aspects of service marketing, service quality is very difficult for customers to evaluate because the nature of services renders benefits impossible to assess before actual purchase and consumption. These benefits include experience qualities, such as taste, satisfaction, or pleasure, and credence qualities, which customers may be unable to evaluate even after consumption. When competing services are very similar, service quality may be the only way for customers to distinguish among them. Service marketers can increase the quality of their services by following the four-step process of understanding customer needs, setting service specifications, ensuring good employee performance, and managing customers' service expectations.

Nonprofit marketing is marketing aimed at nonbusiness goals, including social causes. It uses most of the same concepts and approaches that apply to business situations. Whereas the chief beneficiary of a business enterprise is whoever owns or holds stock in it, the beneficiary of a nonprofit enterprise should be its clients, its members, or its public at large. The goals of a nonprofit organization reflect its unique philosophy or mission. Some nonprofit organizations have very controversial goals, but many organizations exist to further generally accepted social causes.

The marketing objective of nonprofit organizations is to obtain a desired response from a target market. Developing a nonprofit marketing strategy consists of defining and analyzing a target market and creating and maintaining a marketing mix. In nonprofit marketing, the product is usually an idea or a service. Distribution is aimed at the communication of ideas and the delivery of services. The result is a very short marketing channel. Promotion is very important to nonprofit marketing. Nonprofit organizations use advertising, publicity, and personal selling to communicate with clients and the public. Direct mail remains the primary means of fund-raising for social services, but some nonprofits use the Internet for fund-raising and promotional activities. Price is more difficult to define in nonprofit marketing because of opportunity costs and the difficulty of quantifying the values exchanged.

Please visit the student website at **www.prideferrell.com** for ACE Self-Test questions that will help you prepare for exams.

IMPORTANT TERMS

Service
Intangibility
Inseparability
Perishability
Heterogeneity
Client-based relationships
Customer contact
Service quality

Search qualities
Experience qualities
Credence qualities
Nonprofit marketing
Target public
Client publics
General publics
Opportunity cost

DISCUSSION & REVIEW QUESTIONS

1. How important are services in the U.S. economy?
2. Identify and discuss the major characteristics of services.
3. For each marketing mix element, which service characteristics are most likely to have an impact? Explain.
4. What is service quality? Why do customers find it difficult to judge service quality?
5. Identify and discuss the five components of service quality. How do customers evaluate these components?
6. What is the significance of tangibles in service marketing?
7. How do search, experience, and credence qualities affect the way customers view and evaluate services?
8. What steps should a service company take to provide exceptional service quality?
9. How does nonprofit marketing differ from marketing in for-profit organizations?

10. What are the differences among clients, publics, and customers? What is the difference between a target public and a target market?
11. Discuss the development of a marketing strategy for a university. What marketing decisions must be made as the strategy is developed?

APPLICATION QUESTIONS

1. Imagine you are the owner of a new service business. What is your service? Be creative. What are some of the most important considerations in developing the service, training salespeople, and communicating about your service to potential customers?
2. As discussed in this chapter, the characteristics of services affect the development of marketing mixes for services. Choose a specific service and explain how each marketing mix element could be affected by these service characteristics.
3. In advertising services, a company must often use symbols to represent the offered product. Identify three service organizations you have seen in outdoor, television, or magazine advertising. What symbols do these organizations use to represent their services? What message do the symbols convey to potential customers?
4. Delivering consistently high-quality service is difficult for service marketers. Describe an instance when you received high-quality service and an instance when you experienced low-quality service. What contributed to your perception of high quality? Of low quality?

Internet Exercise & Resources

Visit **www.prideferrell.com** for resources to help you master the material in this chapter, plus materials that will help you expand your marketing knowledge, including Internet exercise updates, ACE self-tests, hotlinks to companies featured in this chapter, and much more.

Matchmaker.com

The Internet abounds with dating sites, but few offer as much information about their members as Matchmaker.com. Matchmaker profiles are gleaned from a survey of some 60 question and essay responses. Check out the site at **www.matchmaker.com**.

1. Classify Matchmaker.com's product in terms of its position on the service continuum.
2. How does Matchmaker.com enhance customer service and foster better client-based relationships through its Internet marketing efforts?
3. Discuss the degree to which experience and credence qualities exist in the services offered by Matchmaker.com and other dating websites.

Video Case 14.1

The New Wave of Marketing at New England Aquarium

From sea turtles and seals to penguins and porpoises, the nonprofit New England Aquarium houses an incredibly diverse array of creatures. Its 200,000-gallon tank, situated on a busy Boston wharf, serves as an underwater microcosm of the world's sea life. The Aquarium wants to appeal to the broadest possible client and general publics. Its mission is "to present, promote, and protect the world of water." In line with this mission, the organization's products are both ideas (education and research) and services (conservation efforts and museum exhibits).

More than 1 million visitors annually stream through the Aquarium's doors to see the sharks, watch divers feed the fish, listen to a lecture about penguins, or enjoy a special feature at the IMAX theater. Some visit the Aquarium Medical Center, an onsite hospital where specialists care for the facility's marine animals and treat sick or stranded animals from nearby beaches. Others opt for one of the Science at Sea boat rides or the half-day whale-watching cruises. The organization also maintains an aquatic exploration center in Rhode Island and a porpoise rehabilitation facility south of Boston.

Marketing brings in the money needed to support all these activities. In addition to admission fees and sales of branded merchandise, the Aquarium operates a café, rents its premises for private parties, and solicits donations from individuals and businesses. Corporate sponsorships help pay for a wide range of educational activities. For example, EMC Corporation sponsors the Penguin Outreach Program, paying for Roast Beef the penguin to travel to local institutions in a special temperature-controlled van. It is also the sponsor of the Blue Lobster Bowl, a fast-paced quiz show in which high school students compete to show their knowledge of ocean-related subjects.

The Internet is an important and cost-effective marketing tool for the Aquarium. Members of the public can browse its website (**www.neaq.org**) to find out about current exhibits, scan the calendar of upcoming programs, donate money, become a member, or check the hours of operation and ticket prices. The website also explains the organization's many volunteer opportunities. Its staff of 1,000 volunteers, one of the nonprofit world's largest, contributes 100,000 hours of service yearly working with animals, exhibits, and programs. Many high school and college students volunteer so they can try out possible career choices. Hundreds of adults volunteer part time as well.

The Aquarium markets itself to volunteers because it needs assistance in nearly every department and has a very limited payroll budget. Therefore, Maureen C. Hentz, director of volunteer programs, is always looking for volunteers to supplement the paid staff in education, administration, animal rescue, and other areas. Hentz and her staff maintain an active schedule, going out into the community to build awareness of the Aquarium's services and encouraging people to volunteer their time.

Admission fees help offset the cost of expanding the marine life collection, rehabilitating injured whales, and other expenses. However, the Aquarium faces a delicate balancing act when pricing tickets. If admission fees seem too high, people may not visit or may visit less often. On the other hand, if admission fees are too low, the organization may not generate the revenue needed to cover ongoing operating costs and repay its considerable debt. The Aquarium recently decided to raise its adult admission fees after attendance fell below expected levels because of a sluggish local economy and a drop in tourism. Financial concerns also caused the organization to cancel a $125 million expansion project that would have added 100,000 square feet of exhibit space to the Boston location.

Although the Aquarium welcomes publicity about its services, it sometimes asks for special cooperation from media representatives. When the organization planned to release rescued seals into the ocean after rehabilitation, for example, it invited media representatives to cover the event. However, it requested that reporters not reveal the exact location in advance because of concerns that crowds would gather, jeopardizing a successful release.

Thanks to its new wave of marketing, the Aquarium is fulfilling its mission. It is now Boston's top-drawing attraction. The IMAX theater remains one of its most popular features, and the whale-watching cruises usually depart with a full passenger load. Weekends are the busiest time, when neighborhood families and out-of-town visitors alike enjoy the world of water brought to life. The Aquarium continues its leadership position in protecting marine life and conserving the aquatic environment.[23]

QUESTIONS FOR DISCUSSION

1. Who can be considered the Aquarium's client public?
2. In addition to using the Web and attending community meetings, what other marketing efforts would help Maureen Hentz attract new Aquarium volunteers?
3. How could the Aquarium use pricing to manage its attendance?

Case 14.2

AARP Strengthens Its Brand and Services

Formerly known as the American Association of Retired Persons, AARP is a membership and advocacy organization for people in the 50-and-over age group. The organization, founded in 1958, offers group discount programs, consumer education, and other services, in addition to lobbying on behalf of its 35 million members. However, AARP is not just for retired people anymore, which is why the organization changed its name and gave its services a major makeover.

The first of 78 million U.S. baby boomers turned 50 years old in 1996, but many are determined to remain youthful regardless of chronological age. One of AARP's challenges is to show this new generation of seniors that its services are relevant and valuable. Fewer than one in three baby boomers join AARP when they first receive its invitation during the year they turn 50, although some join when they are a bit older. Nearly half of AARP's members have passed their 60th birthday. Although 48 percent of members are retired, 45 percent are still working when they join.

The decision to give special attention to baby boomers has led to AARP's second challenge: to balance its outreach to 50-year-olds with its commitment to older members. The message here is that the association is doing more for more people, not changing its focus. "I don't want to say that AARP is new," emphasizes William Novelli, the association's executive director. "We're building on the past." He has three goals for AARP: to push for "positive social change," to help members "make the most of life after 50," and to "be a world leader in global aging."

Before making any changes to its services, AARP conducted extensive marketing research to learn what baby boomers thought of the organization. Based on data collected in 33 focus groups, 2 national surveys, and various other studies, one AARP official notes, "Boomers right now think of AARP as more for their parents, but we think we can change this." In fact, when AARP researchers explained the organization's services, potential members responded positively. "So we don't need to reinvent AARP and come up with a bunch of new programs," concludes an AARP executive. "We have things they value."

With this background, AARP started its makeover by adopting the association's acronym as its name. This softened any negative reaction baby boomers might have to joining a group for "retired persons." Then management launched a $100 million, five-year advertising campaign to position AARP as the organization for active boomers and older seniors, using the tag line "Today's AARP: Your choice. Your voice. Your attitude." The association later fine-tuned the campaign to stress AARP's role as a force for change.

Not all AARP members agree with all of its activist positions. For example, the organization aggressively supported a legislative proposal to change Medicare. It spent $7 million promoting the bill's benefits, including prescription drug coverage for 40 million seniors and increased competition between Medicare and private health care plans. This position drew criticism from hundreds of members, who complained the bill would not halt the rising cost of drugs and might weaken the Medicare program. In protest, 1,000 members withdrew from the organization in a single weekend. Novelli acknowledges that the bill—now law—is not perfect. He also believes it "does a lot more good than it does harm. We need to get it into place now and then build on it."

As part of its service makeover, AARP also revamped its publications. "We realized that there are real challenges in producing a lifestyle magazine that is appropriate for everybody who is age 50 and above," says the director of publications. The association changed the name of its monthly magazine from *Modern Maturity* to *AARP The Magazine* and created three tailored editions: one for members in their 50s, one for members in their 60s, and one for members age 70 and up. In addition, it launched a Spanish-language publication, *Segunda Juventud,* as part of its outreach to Hispanic American seniors.

Novelli notes that the organization's long-term marketing objective is to attract half of all Americans age 50 and older as members. Although approximately 47 percent are currently members, achieving the overall goal will not be easy because the senior segment continues to grow quite rapidly: more than 10,000 baby boomers turn 50 every day. The redesigned marketing has started to increase membership among people in the baby boomer segment. Still, as AARP moves toward its fiftieth year of operation, it continues reexamining its services to be sure it is working on behalf of members of all ages.[24]

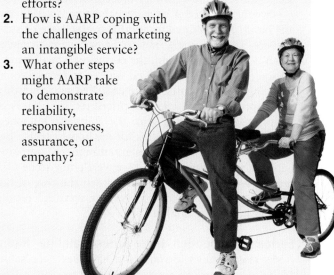

QUESTIONS FOR DISCUSSION

1. What dimensions of service quality are being addressed by AARP's marketing efforts?
2. How is AARP coping with the challenges of marketing an intangible service?
3. What other steps might AARP take to demonstrate reliability, responsiveness, assurance, or empathy?

Strategic Case 5

Radio Goes Sky-High at XM Satellite Radio

XM Satellite Radio is changing the world of radio with 2 satellites, 101 channels, and 2 state-of-the-art performance studios in its Washington, DC, headquarters. The company started on the road to static-free radio in 1997, when it paid more than $80 million for a federal license to broadcast digital radio. Until then, AM and FM radio stations had been free to all listeners, mainly because of commercial sponsorship. However, XM believed that commuters—and anyone traveling by car for long periods—would be willing to pay for perfect 24-hour radio reception and dozens of channel choices anywhere in the United States. After all, millions of viewers were paying for cable television service, even though in many geographic areas they could watch broadcast television for free.

Getting Ready for the Launch   Turning the concept of digital radio into reality cost XM more than $1 billion. First, the company had to design and launch two satellites into orbit over the United States. It set up satellite dishes to beam radio signals to the satellites and erected antennas on 800 buildings in major cities to reach local listeners across the country. In addition,

XM created a vast library of digital recordings and built two performance studios to broadcast and record live musical performances.

Another big challenge was developing the radio equipment for customers' cars. XM planned to encode its satellite signals to prevent noncustomers from listening to its channels. The radio had to be capable of receiving and decoding the satellite signals, yet compact enough to fit in a car. After building and testing prototypes, XM began manufacturing a radio about the size of a suitcase, to be connected to an antenna on the car's roof for proper reception. Initially customers had to retrofit their cars with XM radios. In time, the company arranged for General Motors, Honda, Audi, Nissan, and several other big automakers to offer factory-installed XM radios as options in their new cars.

What to Broadcast, What to Charge?

At the same time the company was getting its technology in order, XM was conducting marketing research to determine the target market's listening tastes. Based on this research, the company decided to devote most of its radio stations to specific types of music, such as country, rap, jazz, blues, rock and roll, classic rock, international pop, instrumental classical music, and movie soundtracks. For more variety, it planned news-only, sports-only, talk-only, comedy-only, and children's stations, among other special-interest stations.

Pricing involved a delicate balancing act. On the one hand, XM wanted to build a sizable base of subscribers, so its pricing had to be within customers' reach. On the other hand, the company was planning for long-term profitability and wanted to recoup some of its high startup costs. In the end, XM set a monthly subscription fee of $9.95 and priced its first radios at $300 or less. Within a year, the company launched smaller, less expensive radios for the home and for listening on the go. "We are an entertainment company, but we also recognized that if we were going to be successful, we had to rapidly drive down the cost of the equipment people needed to get our service," recalls an XM marketing analyst.

Serious Competition from Sirius Satellite Radio

XM's new-product introduction has been successful. More than 1 million customers signed up in the first two years, and the company is preparing for even greater expansion, with profitability expected in the near future. In contrast, its only competitor, New York-based Sirius Satellite Radio, began operating a year after XM and has a much smaller customer base of 260,000 customers. Like XM, Sirius paid millions for a digital radio broadcast license, launched sophisticated satellites, and created specialized programming for 100 stations.

Sirius charges a monthly subscription fee of $12.95 with discounts for multiyear contracts, but its channels are entirely commercial free, whereas some XM channels broadcast commercials as well as music. Sirius also sees drivers as the highest-opportunity customer segment, so it has arranged for its radios to be preinstalled as options in cars manufactured by DaimlerChrysler, Ford, BMW, and several other automakers not covered by XM's deals.

Tuning into Satellite Radio's Future

Satellite radio is gaining popularity at a much faster rate than cable television, VCRs, and CDs did after their introductions. As early majority adopters start tuning into satellite radio, the industry could be serving an estimated 25 million customers by 2010. A Sirius official sees even bigger numbers ahead once the late majority group and the laggards get interested in the product: "We believe there are 350 million potential subscribers in the United States alone." Responding to critics who doubt that pay-radio will become big business, Sirius's CEO observes, "People said no one would ever pay for satellite television, and now it has 21 million subscribers. The same thing is going to be true here."

One of XM's recent innovations is a $50 radio that can be connected to a personal computer, complete with software for switching between channels. It also began broadcasting weather and traffic reports for the 21 largest U.S. cities to draw listeners who otherwise would have tuned into local AM or FM stations for this information. Today XM customers must have the company's radio equipment to receive XM channels, just as Sirius customers must have its equipment to receive Sirius channels. That will change in a few months, when new radios capable of receiving either company's channels become available. Still, XM's CEO expects to maintain his company's market dominance by putting the emphasis on program content. "The technology is only the facilitator," he says. "Music connects so personally to people. We're putting the passion back into radio."

QUESTIONS FOR DISCUSSION

1. How is XM Satellite Radio differentiating its product from that of Sirius?
2. What role has quality played in XM's product development and management?
3. At what stage of the product life cycle is satellite radio? How is the rate of adoption affecting the product's progression through the life cycle?
4. Evaluate the brand names of XM Satellite Radio and Sirius Satellite Radio. What are the strengths and weaknesses of each brand name? Which is the better brand name? Why?

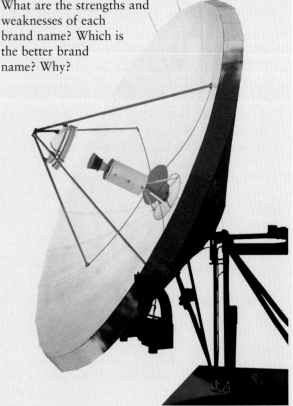

Part Six

Distribution Decisions

Developing products that satisfy customers is important, but it is not enough to guarantee successful marketing strategies. Products must also be available in adequate quantities in accessible locations at the times when customers desire them. **Part Six** deals with the distribution of products and the marketing channels and institutions that help make products available. **Chapter 15** discusses the structure and functions of marketing channels and presents an overview of institutions that make up these channels. **Chapter 16** analyzes the types of wholesalers and their functions, as well as the decisions and activities associated with the physical distribution

of products, such as order processing, materials handling, warehousing, inventory management, and transportation. **Chapter 17** focuses on retailing and direct marketing, including types of retailers, nonstore retailing, franchising, and strategic retailing issues.

15 Marketing Channels and Supply Chain Management

OBJECTIVES

1. To describe the nature and functions of marketing channels

2. To explain how supply chain management can facilitate distribution for the benefit of all channel members, especially customers

3. To identify the types of marketing channels

4. To examine the major levels of marketing coverage

5. To explore the concepts of leadership, cooperation, and conflict in channel relationships

6. To specify how channel integration can improve channel efficiency

7. To examine the legal issues affecting channel management

The Hard Rock Café Serves Up Food, Music, Memorabilia, and More

The Hard Rock Café rocks on. Every year, 30 million customers around the world and high in the sky are enjoying the Hard Rock Café's casual American meals and rock-and-roll theme. The first Hard Rock Café opened in London in 1971. Today, Hard Rock Café International operates more than 100 restaurants in dozens of cities worldwide, from Boston and Bangkok to Berlin and Beirut, as well as hotels, casinos, and a website (**www.hardrock.com**).

The company also sells its sandwiches and salads on United Airlines flights. "We saw this as an opportunity to put our food and product in front of business and leisure travelers," explains Hard Rock's CEO. "Some of them may have never been to one of our restaurants." United Airlines is enthusiastic because "we want to offer our customers quality-branded meals that they'll recognize," according to a spokesperson. "Hard Rock is certainly one of these brands."

Along with burgers and beer, Hard Rock Cafés offer branded merchandise, live and recorded music, and rock music memorabilia. Arranging for branded merchandise to be shipped to every café in the right quantities and at the right times is a complex undertaking. Therefore, Hard Rock Café International has hired outside experts to help with supplier contacts, inventory management, transportation, and storage. As a result, the company will need 44 percent less warehouse space in the United States, cut its operational costs by 20 percent, and boost service to the restaurants by 22 percent.

The company also arranges to rotate its $32 million collection of rock music artifacts between restaurants to draw repeat business. Each restaurant's design reflects the local rock scene, enhanced by the ever-changing memorabilia. On the stage of the Detroit café, for example, a garage door stands as a tribute to garage-band music. The original London café has showcased guitars from Eric Clapton and Pete Townsend, among other British rock artists. Other cafés display costumes, instruments, posters, and photos of Eminem, Elvis Presley, Madonna, John Lennon, Jimi Hendrix, the Goo Goo Dolls, and hundreds of other stars.

Many customers are tourists who eat at a Hard Rock Café and then buy T-shirts or other items as souvenirs. Some branded, city-specific items can be purchased only in person, which encourages customers to visit other Hard Rock Cafés when they travel. In all, the cost of outfitting a new café can exceed $3 million. This does not include the cost of all the food and merchandise that must be ready for customers on opening day. By making its distribution system more efficient, the company can rock on with continued expansion and added profits.[1] ∎

distribution The activities that make products available to customers when and where they want to purchase them

The Hard Rock Café is increasing its profits by making decisions that cut costs and improve efficiencies. Some of these decisions relate to the **distribution** component of the marketing mix, which focuses on the decisions and actions involved in making products available to customers when and where they want to purchase them. Choosing which channels of distribution to use is a major decision in the development of marketing strategies.

In this chapter, we focus on marketing channels. First, we discuss the nature of marketing channels and the need for intermediaries and then analyze the primary functions they perform. Next, we outline the types of marketing channels and explore how marketers determine the appropriate intensity of market coverage for a product. We then consider supply chain management, including behavioral patterns within marketing channels and forms of channel integration. Finally, we look at several legal issues affecting channel management.

The Nature of Marketing Channels

marketing channel A group of individuals and organizations that direct the flow of products from producers to customers

marketing intermediary A middleman linking producers to other middlemen or ultimate consumers through contractual arrangements or through the purchase and resale of products

A **marketing channel** (also called a *channel of distribution* or *distribution channel*) is a group of individuals and organizations that direct the flow of products from producers to customers. The major role of marketing channels is to make products available at the right time at the right place in the right quantities. Providing customer satisfaction should be the driving force behind marketing channel decisions. Buyers' needs and behavior are therefore important concerns of channel members.

Some marketing channels are direct—from producer straight to customer—but most channels have marketing intermediaries. A **marketing intermediary** (or *middleman*) links producers to other intermediaries or to ultimate consumers through contractual arrangements or through the purchase and reselling of products. Marketing intermediaries perform the activities described in Table 15.1. Wholesalers and retail-

Table 15.1	Marketing Channel Activities Performed by Intermediaries	
Category of Marketing Activities	**Possible Activities Required**	
Marketing information	Analyze sales data and other information in databases and information systems	
	Perform or commission marketing research	
Marketing management	Establish strategic plans for developing customer relationships and organizational productivity	
Facilitating exchanges	Choose product assortments that match the needs of customers	
	Cooperate with channel members to develop partnerships	
Promotion	Set promotional objectives	
	Coordinate advertising, personal selling, sales promotion, publicity, and packaging	
Price	Establish pricing policies and terms of sales	
Physical distribution	Manage transportation, warehousing, materials handling, inventory control, and communication	

ers are examples of intermediaries. Wholesalers buy and resell products to other wholesalers, to retailers, and to industrial customers. Retailers purchase products and resell them to ultimate consumers. For example, your local supermarket probably purchased the Tylenol or Advil on its shelves from a wholesaler, which purchased that product, along with other over-the-counter and prescription drugs, from manufacturers such as McNeil Consumer Labs and Whitehall-Robins. Chapters 16 and 17 discuss the functions of wholesalers and retailers in marketing channels in greater detail.

Marketing channel members share certain significant characteristics. Each member has different responsibilities within the overall structure of the channel. Mutual profit and success for channel members are attained most readily when channel members cooperate to deliver satisfying products to customers.

Although distribution decisions need not precede other marketing decisions, they are a powerful influence on the rest of the marketing mix. Channel decisions are critical because they determine a product's market presence and the product's accessibility to buyers. For example, because small businesses are more likely to purchase computers from office supply stores such as Office Depot or warehouse clubs such as Sam's, computer companies may be at a disadvantage without distribution through these outlets. Channel decisions have additional strategic significance because they entail long-term commitments. Thus, it is usually easier to change prices or promotional strategies than to change marketing channels.

Marketing channels serve many functions, including creating utility and facilitating exchange efficiencies. Although some of these functions may be performed by a single channel member, most functions are accomplished through both independent and joint efforts of channel members. When managed effectively, the relationships among channel members can also form supply chains that benefit all members of the channel, including the ultimate consumer.

Creating Utility
Marketing channel members, like Motion Industries, make sure that products are delivered when they are needed and that orders are filled accurately.

◆ Marketing Channels Create Utility

Marketing channels create three types of utility: time, place, and possession. *Time utility* is having products available when customers want them. *Place utility* is created by making products available in locations where customers wish to purchase them. *Possession utility* means customers have access to the product to use or store for future use. Possession utility can occur through ownership or through arrangements that give the customer the right to use the product, such as a lease or rental agreement. Channel members sometimes create utility by assembling, preparing, or otherwise refining the product to suit individual customer needs.

◆ Marketing Channels Facilitate Exchange Efficiencies

Marketing intermediaries can reduce the costs of exchanges by efficiently performing certain services or functions. Even if producers and buyers are located in the same city, exchanges have associated costs. As Figure 15.1 (on p. 394) shows, when 4 buyers seek products from 4 producers, 16 transactions are possible. If one intermediary serves both producers and buyers, the number of transactions can be reduced to 8. Intermediaries are specialists in facilitating exchanges. They provide valuable

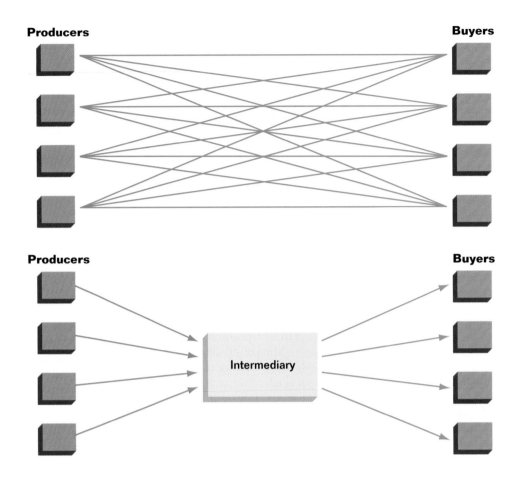

Figure 15.1 Efficiency in Exchanges Provided by an Intermediary

assistance because of their access to and control over important resources used in the proper functioning of marketing channels.

Nevertheless, the media, consumers, public officials, and other marketers freely criticize intermediaries, especially wholesalers. Critics accuse wholesalers of being inefficient and parasitic. Buyers often wish to make the distribution channel as short as possible, assuming the fewer the intermediaries, the lower the price will be. Because suggestions to eliminate them come from both ends of the marketing channel, wholesalers must be careful to perform only those marketing activities that are truly desired. To survive, they must be more efficient and more customer focused than other marketing institutions.

Critics who suggest that eliminating wholesalers would lower customer prices do not recognize that this would not eliminate the need for services wholesalers provide. Although wholesalers can be eliminated, the functions they perform cannot. Other channel members would have to perform those functions, and customers would still have to pay for them. In addition, all producers would have to deal directly with retailers or customers, meaning every producer would have to keep voluminous records and hire enough personnel to deal with a multitude of customers. Customers might end up paying a great deal more for products because prices would reflect the costs of less efficient channel members.

To illustrate the efficiency of wholesalers' services, assume all wholesalers have been eliminated. Because more than 1.5 million retail stores exist, a widely purchased consumer product—say, candy—would require an extraordinary number of sales contacts, possibly more than a million, to maintain the current level of product exposure. For example, Mars, Inc., would have to deliver candy, purchase and service thousands of vending machines, establish warehouses all over the country, and maintain fleets of trucks. Selling and distribution costs for candy would skyrocket. Instead of a few contacts with food brokers, large retail organizations, and merchant wholesalers, candy manufacturers would have to make thousands of expensive contacts with and shipments to smaller retailers. Such an operation would be highly inefficient, and costs would be passed on to consumers. Candy bars would cost more and be harder to find. Clearly wholesalers are often more efficient and less expensive.

◆ Marketing Channels Form a Supply Chain

supply chain management
Long-term partnerships among marketing channel members that reduce inefficiencies, costs, and redundancies and develop innovative approaches to satisfy customers

An important function of the marketing channel is the joint effort of all channel members to create a supply chain, a total distribution system that serves customers and creates a competitive advantage. **Supply chain management** refers to long-term partnerships among marketing channel members that reduce inefficiencies, costs, and redundancies in the marketing channel and develop innovative approaches to satisfy customers. Worldwide spending on supply-chain management systems is over $19 billion.[2]

Supply chain management involves manufacturing, research, sales, advertising, shipping, and—most of all—cooperation and understanding of tradeoffs throughout the whole channel to achieve optimal levels of efficiency and service. Table 15.2 (on p. 396) outlines the key tasks involved in supply chain management. Whereas traditional marketing channels tend to focus on producers, wholesalers, retailers, and customers, the supply chain is a broader concept that includes facilitating agencies such as shipping companies, communication companies, and other organizations that indirectly take part in marketing exchanges. Thus, the supply chain includes all entities that facilitate product distribution and benefit from cooperative efforts. Toyota, for example, had long relied on a hand-picked group of 213 suppliers to provide low-cost parts and components. Under the pressure of increased global competition, the automaker began encouraging some of its suppliers to work more closely by combining manufacturing operations, attracting more orders to improve economies of scale, and cooperating to create less expensive but high-quality standardized parts.[3]

Technology Facilitates Supply Chain Management
There are numerous technology-based tools that assist supply chain managers in improving efficiency and coordination.

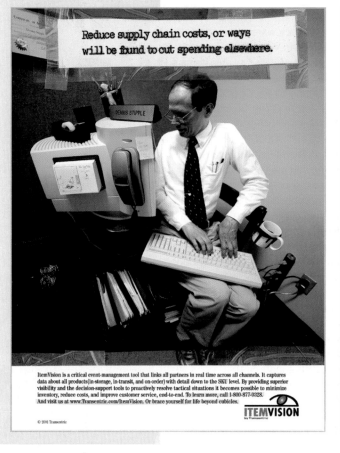

Table 15.2	Key Tasks in Supply Chain Management
Planning	Organizational and systemwide coordination of marketing channel partnerships to meet customers' product needs
Sourcing	Purchasing of necessary resources, goods, and services from suppliers to support all supply chain members
Facilitating delivery	All activities designed to move the product through the marketing channel to the end user
Relationship building	All marketing activities related to selling, service, and the development of long-term customer relationships

Supply chain management is helping more firms realize that optimizing supply chain costs through partnerships will improve all members' profits. All parties should focus on cooperating to reduce the costs of all affected channel members. Supply chains start with the customer and require the cooperation of channel members to satisfy customer requirements. When the buyer, the seller, marketing intermediaries, and facilitating agencies work together, the cooperative relationship results in compromise and adjustments that meet customers' needs regarding delivery, scheduling, packaging, or other requirements.

Most companies do not set out to develop a supply chain. Typically they see a need to rework the way they serve their customers. Often they need to increase the quality of a good or service, which results in such goals as reducing the time from production to customer purchase, decreasing transportation costs, or lowering information management or administrative costs. Achieving these goals to attain a more competitive position often requires that channel members cooperate and share information as well as accommodate one another's needs. As discussed in the Tech Know boxed feature, U.S. armed forces are adopting practices associated with supply chain management in order to achieve greater efficiencies.

TECH KNOW

U.S. Armed Forces Revamp Their Supply-Chain Management Strategies

The U.S. Marine Corps needed a few good parts in a lot less time. A few years ago, when a marine requisitioned a spare part, it might not arrive for a week, even if it came from the other side of the same base. Most of the Marines' computer systems worldwide couldn't communicate, forcing soldiers to rely on the less efficient telephone or fax to place orders. With the nature of global conflict changing, the corps needed a faster, more flexible process for deploying huge volumes of materials to military sites around the world. After studying the supply-chain management successes of businesses such as Wal-Mart, UPS, and Swissair, the corps developed a ten-year plan to revamp its supply-chain system.

With advice from Sapient, a consulting firm, and Pennsylvania State University's Center for Logistics Research, the U.S. Marine Corps began by pruning its inventory, saving $200 million and allowing 2,000 marines to be shifted from distribution tasks to military duties. The corps also streamlined the processes required to move 10,000 different items to 450 units through 35 distribution centers, cutting through layers of paperwork, inspections, and approvals. Next, it brought in high-tech tools like handheld wireless

scanners to track warehouse contents and to strengthen relationships with suppliers to ensure access to less readily available items such as tanks. This successful program has earned the corps a Supply Chain Operational Excellence Award from the Supply Chain Council.

Now other branches of the U.S. armed forces are reinventing their supply-chain management processes. The Military Transportation Management Command and the U.S. Transportation Command developed a sophisticated system to expedite the distribution of supplies to U.S. military sites worldwide. This system eliminates the expensive process of assembling smaller orders and shipping each individually. Instead, large quantities of supplies are packed into large containers, sealed, and loaded onto commercial ships. Each container is matched to a computerized inventory document so the contents can be split quickly into individual orders at the destination port. Then the orders are trucked to the military sites that requisitioned the supplies. This supply-chain management system not only saves time and money, it reassures commanders that they will receive their supplies as ordered.

Technology has dramatically improved the capability of supply chain management on a global basis. The information technology revolution in particular has created a virtually seamless distribution process for matching inventory needs to customers' requirements. With integrated information sharing among channel members, costs can be reduced, service improved, and value provided to the customer enhanced. For example, one key to Wal-Mart's success is the use of bar code and electronic data interchange (EDI) technology, extending from the firm's suppliers to the warehouse to the customer at the store checkout. Tools such as electronic billing, purchase order verification, bar code technology, and image processing integrate needed data into the supply chain and improve overall performance. Intensely competitive industries operate the most sophisticated systems of supply chain management. Several companies provide supply chain management software to assist customers in managing sales orders, procurement, warehousing, transportation, and customer service. For example, Manhattan Associates is a U.S. company specializing in supply chain management software. Jeff Baum, senior vice president of international operations, said the newest tool to increase supply chain efficiency is the radio frequency identification tag. The RFID emits a signal containing detailed information about a product, which is expected to eclipse the barcode and cut labor-intensive intervention in retail logistics.[4]

Supply chain management should not be considered just a buzzword. Reducing inventory and transportation costs, speeding order cycle times, cutting administrative and handling costs, and improving customer service are all improvements that provide rewards for *all* channel members. The rewards will come as companies determine their positions in the supply chain, identify their partners and their roles, and establish partnerships that focus on customer relationships.

Types of Marketing Channels

Because marketing channels appropriate for one product may be less suitable for others, many different distribution paths have been developed. The various marketing channels can be classified generally as channels for consumer products and channels for business products.

◆ Channels for Consumer Products

Figure 15.2 (on p. 398) illustrates several channels used in the distribution of consumer products. Channel A depicts the direct movement of goods from producer to consumers. Producers that sell goods directly from their factories to end users use direct marketing channels, as do companies that sell their own products via the Internet, such as Dell Computer. In fact, because Internet purchases have increased significantly, direct marketing via Internet has become an important part of some companies' distribution strategies. Although direct marketing channels are the simplest, they are not necessarily the most effective distribution method. Faced with the strategic choice of going directly to the customer or using intermediaries, a firm must evaluate the benefits to customers of going direct versus the transaction costs involved in using intermediaries.

Channel B, which moves goods from the producer to a retailer and then to customers, is a frequent choice of large retailers, since it allows them to buy in quantity from manufacturers. Retailers such as Kmart and Wal-Mart sell clothing, stereos, and many other items purchased directly from producers. New automobiles and new college textbooks are also sold through this type of marketing channel. Primarily nonstore retailers, such as L. L. Bean and J. Crew, also use this type of channel.

A long-standing distribution channel, especially for consumer products, channel C takes goods from the producer to a wholesaler, then to a retailer, and finally to consumers. It is a practical option for producers that sell to hundreds of thousands

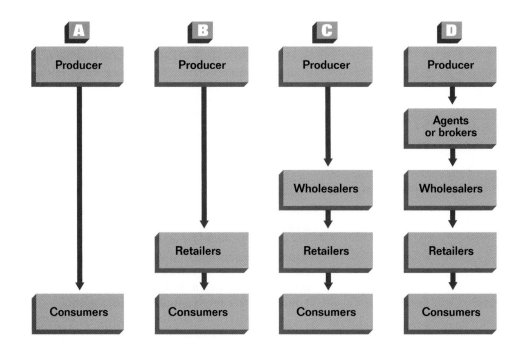

Figure 15.2 **Typical Marketing Channels for Consumer Products**

of customers through thousands of retailers. A single producer finds it hard to do business directly with thousands of retailers. Consider the number of retailers marketing Wrigley's chewing gum. It would be extremely difficult, if not impossible, for Wrigley to deal directly with each retailer that sells its brand of gum. Manufacturers of tobacco products, some home appliances, hardware, and many convenience goods sell their products to wholesalers, which then sell to retailers, which in turn do business with individual consumers.

Channel D, through which goods pass from producer to agents to wholesalers to retailers and then to consumers, is frequently used for products intended for mass distribution, such as processed foods. For example, to place its cracker line in specific retail outlets, a food processor may hire an agent (or a food broker) to sell the crackers to wholesalers. Wholesalers then sell the crackers to supermarkets, vending machine operators, and other retail outlets.

Contrary to popular opinion, a long channel may be the most efficient distribution channel for some consumer goods. When several channel intermediaries perform specialized functions, costs may be lower than when one channel member tries to perform them all.

◆ Channels for Business Products

Figure 15.3 shows four of the most common channels for business products. As with consumer products, manufacturers of business products sometimes work with more than one level of wholesalers.

Channel E illustrates the direct channel for business products. In contrast to consumer goods, more than half of all business products, especially expensive equipment, are sold through direct channels. Business customers prefer to communicate directly with producers, especially when expensive or technically complex products are involved. For this reason, business buyers prefer to purchase expensive and highly complex mainframe computers directly from IBM and other mainframe producers. Intel has established direct marketing channels for selling its microprocessor chips to computer manufacturers. In these circumstances, a customer wants the technical assistance and personal assurances that only a producer can provide.

In the second business products channel, channel F, an industrial distributor facilitates exchanges between producer and customer. An **industrial distributor** is an

industrial distributor An independent business organization that takes title to industrial products and carries inventories

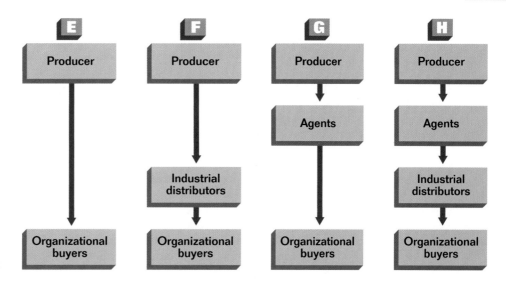

Figure 15.3 **Typical Marketing Channels for Business Products**

independent business that takes title to products and carries inventories. Industrial distributors usually sell standardized items such as maintenance supplies, production tools, and small operating equipment. Some industrial distributors carry a wide variety of product lines. Others specialize in one or a small number of lines. Industrial distributors are carrying an increasing percentage of business products. Due to mergers and acquisitions, they have become larger and more powerful.[5] Industrial distributors can be most effectively used when a product has broad market appeal, is easily stocked and serviced, is sold in small quantities, and is needed on demand to avoid high losses.

Industrial distributors offer sellers several advantages. They can perform the needed selling activities in local markets at a relatively low cost to a manufacturer and reduce a producer's financial burden by providing customers with credit services. Also, because industrial distributors usually maintain close relationships with their customers, they are aware of local needs and can pass on market information to producers. By holding adequate inventories in their local markets, industrial distributors reduce producers' capital requirements.

Using industrial distributors has several disadvantages, however. Industrial distributors may be difficult to control since they are independent firms. Because they often stock competing brands, a producer cannot depend on them to sell its brand aggressively. Furthermore, since industrial distributors maintain inventories, they incur numerous expenses; consequently they are less likely to handle bulky or slow-selling items or items that need specialized facilities or extraordinary selling efforts. In some cases, industrial distributors lack the technical knowledge necessary to sell and service certain products.

Industrial Distributor
Baldor is an industrial distributor.

The third channel for business products, channel G, employs a *manufacturers' agent,* an independent businessperson who sells complementary products of several producers in assigned territories and is compensated through commissions. Unlike an industrial distributor, a manufacturers' agent does not acquire title to the products and usually does not take possession. Acting as a salesperson on behalf of the producers, a manufacturers' agent has little or no latitude in negotiating prices or sales terms.

Using manufacturers' agents can benefit an organizational marketer. These agents usually possess considerable technical and market information and have an established set of customers. For an organizational seller with highly seasonal demand, a manufacturers' agent can be an asset because the seller does not have to support a year-round sales force. The fact that manufacturers' agents are paid on a commission basis may also be an economical alternative for a firm that has highly limited resources and cannot afford a full-time sales force.

Certainly the use of manufacturers' agents is not problem free. Even though straight commissions may be cheaper, the seller may have little control over manufacturers' agents. Because of the compensation method, manufacturers' agents generally prefer to concentrate on their larger accounts. They are often reluctant to spend time following up sales, putting forth special selling efforts, or providing sellers with market information when such activities reduce the amount of productive selling time. Because they rarely maintain inventories, manufacturers' agents have a limited ability to provide customers with parts or repair services quickly.

Finally, channel H includes both a manufacturers' agent and an industrial distributor. This channel may be appropriate when the producer wishes to cover a large geographic area but maintains no sales force due to highly seasonal demand or because it cannot afford a sales force. This type of channel can also be useful for a business marketer that wants to enter a new geographic market without expanding its existing sales force.

◆ Multiple Marketing Channels and Channel Alliances

To reach diverse target markets, manufacturers may use several marketing channels simultaneously, with each channel involving a different group of intermediaries. For example, a manufacturer uses multiple channels when the same product is directed to both consumers and business customers. When Del Monte markets ketchup for household use, the product is sold to supermarkets through grocery wholesalers or, in some cases, directly to retailers, whereas ketchup going to restaurants or institutions follows a different distribution channel. In some instances, a producer may prefer **dual distribution**, the use of two or more marketing channels to distribute the same products to the same target market. An example of dual distribution is a firm that sells products through retail outlets and its own mail-order catalog or website. For example, the upscale cosmetics manufacturer Estée Lauder is diversifying its marketing channels to fuel growth. In addition to selling through department stores, the company is selling via online retailers such as Gloss.com and selling its Aveda, MAC, and Origins products through single-brand cosmetics stores and websites.[6] Gateway sells its computers through a toll-free number and a website. Kellogg sells its cereals directly to large retail grocery chains and to food wholesalers that, in turn, sell them to retailers. Dual distribution, however, can cause dissatisfaction among wholesalers and smaller retailers when they must compete with large retail grocery chains that make direct purchases from manufacturers such as Kellogg. The practice of dual distribution has been challenged as being anticompetitive. We discuss the legal dimensions of dual distribution later in this chapter.

A **strategic channel alliance** exists when the products of one organization are distributed through the marketing channels of another. The products of the two firms are often similar with respect to target markets or uses, but they are not direct

dual distribution The use of two or more marketing channels to distribute the same product to the same target market

strategic channel alliance An agreement whereby the products of one organization are distributed through the marketing channels of another

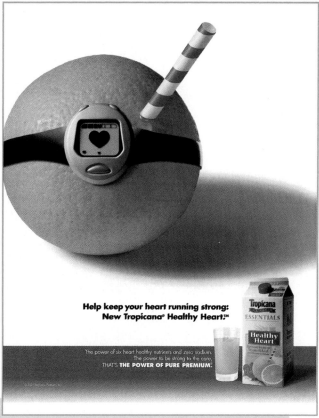

Using Multiple Marketing Channels
A number of food products, such as those shown in these advertisements, are marketed through multiple distribution channels.

competitors. For example, a brand of bottled water might be distributed through a marketing channel for soft drinks, or a domestic cereal producer might form a strategic channel alliance with a European food processor. Alliances can provide benefits for both the organization that owns the marketing channel and the company whose brand is being distributed through the channel.

Intensity of Market Coverage

In addition to deciding which marketing channels to use to distribute a product, marketers must determine the intensity of coverage that a product should get, that is, the number and kinds of outlets in which it will be sold. This decision depends on the characteristics of the product and the target market. To achieve the desired intensity of market coverage, distribution must correspond to behavior patterns of buyers. In Chapter 11, we divided consumer products into four categories—convenience products, shopping products, specialty products, and unsought products—according to how consumers make purchases. In considering products for purchase, consumers take into account replacement rate, product adjustment (services), duration of consumption, time required to find the product, and similar factors.[7] These variables directly affect the intensity of market coverage. Three major levels of market coverage are intensive, selective, and exclusive distribution.

Intensive and Exclusive Distribution
A few brands of cosmetics, such as Cover Girl, are sold through intensive distribution. Green Design Furniture, made in Maine, is marketed through exclusive distribution.

◆ Intensive Distribution

intensive distribution Using all available outlets to distribute a product

Snap/hot

Intensive distribution of sports drinks

Which sells the most?

- Supermarkets **28%**
- Convenience stores **44%**
- Mass merchandisers **9%**
- Vending **9%**
- Club stores **6%**
- Drug stores **6%**
- Food service **2%**

Source: Data from Beverage Marketing Corporation.

Intensive distribution uses all available outlets for distributing a product. Intensive distribution is appropriate for convenience products such as bread, chewing gum, soft drinks, and newspapers. Convenience products have a high replacement rate and require almost no service. To meet these demands, intensive distribution is necessary, and multiple channels may be used to sell through all possible outlets. For example, soft drinks, snacks, laundry detergent, and aspirin are available at convenience stores, service stations, supermarkets, discount stores, and other types of retailers. To consumers, availability means a store is located nearby and minimum time is necessary to search for the product at the store. Sales may have a direct relationship to product availability. The successful sale of such products as bread and milk at service stations or of gasoline at convenience grocery stores illustrates that availability of these products is more important than the nature of the outlet. Producers of consumer packaged items, such as Procter & Gamble, rely on intensive distribution for many of their products (for example, soaps, detergents, food and juice products, and personal care products) because consumers want ready availability.

◆ Selective Distribution

selective distribution Using only some available outlets to distribute a product

Selective distribution uses only some available outlets in an area to distribute a product. Selective distribution is appropriate for shopping products; durable goods such as televisions and stereos usually fall into this category. These products are more expensive than convenience goods, and consumers are willing to spend more time visiting several retail outlets to compare prices, designs, styles, and other features. For example, Hermes Parfums is launching Eau des Merveilles, an exclusive new scent, and related products, only to selected high-end retailers. It expects to generate more than $25 million in retail volume its first year.[8]

Selective distribution is desirable when a special effort, such as customer service from a channel member, is important. Shopping products require differentiation at the point of purchase. To motivate retailers to provide adequate presale service, selective distribution and company-owned stores are often used. Many business products are sold on a selective basis to maintain some control over the distribution process. For example, agricultural herbicides are distributed on a selective basis because dealers must offer services to buyers such as instructions about how to apply herbicides safely or the option to have the dealer apply the herbicide. Evinrude outboard motors are also sold by dealers on a selective basis.

◆ Exclusive Distribution

exclusive distribution Using a single outlet in a fairly large geographic area to distribute a product

Exclusive distribution uses only one outlet in a relatively large geographic area. Exclusive distribution is suitable for products purchased infrequently, consumed over a long period of time, or requiring service or information to fit them to buyers' needs. It is also used for expensive, high-quality products, such as Porsche automobiles. It is not appropriate for convenience products and many shopping products.

Exclusive distribution is often used as an incentive to sellers when only a limited market is available for products. For example, automobiles such as the Bentley, made by Rolls-Royce, are sold on an exclusive basis, and Patek Philippe watches, which may sell for $10,000 or more, are available in only a few select locations. A producer using exclusive distribution generally expects dealers to carry a complete inventory, send personnel for sales and service training, participate in promotional programs, and provide excellent customer service. Some products are appropriate for exclusive distribution when first introduced, but as competitors enter the market and the product moves through its life cycle, other types of market coverage and distribution channels often become necessary. A problem that can arise with exclusive distribution (and selective distribution) is that unauthorized resellers acquire and sell products, violating the agreement between a manufacturer and its exclusive authorized dealers. This has been a problem for Rolex, another manufacturer of prestige watches.

Supply Chain Management

To fulfill the potential of effective supply chain management and ensure customer satisfaction, marketing channels require leadership, cooperation, and management of channel conflict. They may also require consolidation of marketing channels through channel integration.

◆ Channel Leadership, Cooperation, and Conflict

Each channel member performs a different role in the distribution system and agrees (implicitly or explicitly) to accept certain rights, responsibilities, rewards, and sanctions for nonconformity. Moreover, each channel member holds certain expectations of other channel members. Retailers, for instance, expect wholesalers to maintain

channel captain The dominant member of a marketing channel or supply chain

channel power The ability of one channel member to influence another member's goal achievement

adequate inventories and deliver goods on time. Wholesalers expect retailers to honor payment agreements and keep them informed of inventory needs.

Channel partnerships facilitate effective supply chain management when partners agree on objectives, policies, and procedures for physical distribution efforts associated with the supplier's products. Such partnerships eliminate redundancies and reassign tasks for maximum systemwide efficiency. One of the best-known partnerships is that between Wal-Mart and Procter & Gamble. Procter & Gamble locates some of its staff near Wal-Mart's purchasing department in Bentonville, Arkansas, to establish and maintain the supply chain. Sharing information through a cooperative computer system, Procter & Gamble monitors Wal-Mart's inventory and additional data to determine production and distribution plans for its products. The results are increased efficiency, decreased inventory costs, and greater satisfaction for the customers of both companies. At this time, some suppliers have been unwilling or unable to make this level of commitment. In this section we discuss channel member behavior, including leadership, cooperation, and conflict, that marketers must understand to make effective channel decisions.

Channel Leadership. Many marketing channel decisions are determined by consensus. Producers and intermediaries coordinate efforts for mutual benefit. Some marketing channels, however, are organized and controlled by a single leader, or **channel captain** (also called *channel leader*). The channel captain may be a producer, wholesaler, or retailer. Channel captains may establish channel policies and coordinate development of the marketing mix. Wal-Mart, for example, dominates the supply chain for its retail stores by virtue of the magnitude of its resources (especially information management) and strong, nationwide customer base. To become a captain, a channel member must want to influence overall channel performance. To attain desired objectives, the captain must possess **channel power**, the ability to influence another channel member's goal achievement. The member that becomes the channel captain will accept the responsibilities and exercise the power associated with this role.

When a manufacturer's large-scale production efficiency demands increasing sales volume, the manufacturer may exercise power by giving channel members financing, business advice, ordering assistance, advertising, sales and service training, and support materials. For example, U.S. automakers provide these services to retail automobile dealerships. However, these manufacturers also place numerous requirements on their retail dealerships with respect to sales volume, sales and service training, and customer satisfaction.

As already noted, retailers may also function as channel captains. With the rise in power of national chain stores and private-brand merchandise, many large retailers such as Wal-Mart are doing so. Small retailers too may assume leadership roles when they gain strong customer loyalty in local or regional markets. These retailers control many brands and sometimes replace uncooperative producers. Increasingly, leading retailers are concentrating their buying power with fewer suppliers and, in the process, improving their marketing effectiveness and efficiency. Single-source supply relationships are often successful, whereas multiple-source

Channel Leadership
The manufacturer of Benjamin Moore Paints provides channel leadership in the distribution channels for its products.

supply relationships based on price competition are decreasing. Long-term commitments enable retailers to place smaller and more frequent orders as needed rather than waiting for large volume discounts or placing huge orders early in the season and assuming the risks associated with carrying a larger inventory.

Wholesalers assume channel leadership roles as well, although they were more powerful decades ago, when many manufacturers and retailers were smaller, underfinanced, and widely scattered. Today wholesaler leaders may form voluntary chains with several retailers, which they supply with bulk buying or management services; these chains may also market their own brands. In return, the retailers shift most of their purchasing to the wholesaler leader. The Independent Grocers' Alliance (IGA) is one of the best-known wholesaler leaders in the United States. IGA's power is based on its expertise in advertising, pricing, and purchasing knowledge that it makes available to independent business owners. Other wholesaler leaders help retailers with store layouts, accounting, and inventory control.

Channel Cooperation. Channel cooperation is vital if each member is to gain something from other members. Cooperation enables retailers, wholesalers, and suppliers to speed up inventory replenishment, improve customer service, and cut the costs of bringing products to the consumer.[9] Without cooperation, neither overall channel goals nor member goals can be realized. All channel members must recognize that the success of one firm in the channel depends in part on other member firms. Thus, marketing channel members should make a coordinated effort to satisfy market requirements. Channel cooperation leads to greater trust among channel members and improves the overall functioning of the channel. It also leads to more satisfying relationships among channel members. The Building Customer Relationships boxed feature focuses on the advantages of partnering among the channel members.

BUILDING CUSTOMER RELATIONSHIPS

Partnering with Channel Members

Seeking to do a better job of reaching and satisfying customers through improved channel efficiencies, many companies are forging closer partnerships with key channel members. As in any relationship, the companies and channel members must choose their partners carefully, communicate clearly, and agree on the expectations and obligations of both sides.

"Channel partners are an extension of your company," says the channel manager for Hoffman Enclosures, which manufactures industrial equipment. This is why Hoffman is extremely picky about its channel partners, seeking out distributors that demonstrate in-depth product knowledge and provide top-notch customer service. Companies that target the institutional market must also choose distributors with care. Because of intense competition, distributors like Gulf South Medical Supply stand ready to help nursing homes and other customers plan inventory or solve other problems. In turn, their closer connection with institutional customers opens the door to higher sales for the companies that Gulf South represents.

Companies that do business globally face the challenge of partnering with hundreds or thousands of channel members, sometimes spread across immense distances. Consider Microsoft, which sells software products in almost every country. Channel partnerships are vital to Microsoft's success, because many businesses and consumers depend on retailers and computer specialists to recommend software, install it, and provide training. The software giant spends millions of dollars annually to train and support 800,000 channel partners around the world. If problems at the channel level interfere with customer service, then even though "we think we've engineered something well for the customer," says Microsoft CEO Steve Ballmer, "we've screwed it up."

Computer Associates, an information technology company, starts every channel partnership by outlining what it will do and what it wants its distributors to do. "Too many times you recruit channel partners and promise the world, and then the expectations are far different from reality," says the general manager of its North American channel group. To prevent misunderstandings, Computer Associates delineates the training and assistance it will provide and asks distributors to submit plans showing how they will reach the agreed-upon sales levels. Then, if a channel relationship doesn't work out, Milford believes "it was a bad job of setting expectations up front."

There are several ways to improve channel cooperation. If a marketing channel is viewed as a unified supply chain competing with other systems, individual members will be less likely to take actions that create disadvantages for other members. Similarly, channel members should agree to direct efforts toward common objectives so channel roles can be structured for maximum marketing effectiveness, which in turn can help members achieve individual objectives. A critical component in cooperation is a precise definition of each channel member's tasks. This provides a basis for reviewing the intermediaries' performance and helps reduce conflicts because each channel member knows exactly what is expected of it.

Channel Conflict. Although all channel members work toward the same general goal—distributing products profitably and efficiently—members may sometimes disagree about the best methods for attaining this objective. However, if self-interest creates misunderstanding about role expectations, the end result is frustration and conflict for the whole channel. For individual organizations to function together, each channel member must clearly communicate and understand role expectations. Communication difficulties are a potential form of channel conflict because ineffective communication leads to frustration, misunderstandings, and ill-coordinated strategies, jeopardizing further coordination.

The increased use of multiple channels of distribution, driven partly by new technology, has increased the potential for conflict between manufacturers and intermediaries. For example, Hewlett-Packard makes products available directly to consumers through its website (**www.hewlett-packard.com**), thereby directly competing with existing distributors and retailers.[10] Channel conflicts also arise when intermediaries overemphasize competing products or diversify into product lines traditionally handled by other intermediaries. Sometimes conflict develops because producers strive to increase efficiency by circumventing intermediaries. Such conflict is occurring in marketing channels for computer software. A number of software-only stores are establishing direct relationships with software producers, bypassing wholesale distributors altogether.

When a producer that has traditionally used franchised dealers broadens its retailer base to include other types of retail outlets, considerable conflict can arise. When Goodyear intensified its market coverage by allowing Sears and Discount Tire to market Goodyear tires, its action antagonized 2,500 independent Goodyear dealers.

Although there is no single method for resolving conflict, partnerships can be reestablished if two conditions are met. First, the role of each channel member must be specified. To minimize misunderstanding, all members must be able to expect unambiguous, agreed-on performance levels from one another. Second, members of channel partnerships must institute certain measures of channel coordination, which requires leadership and benevolent exercise of control. To prevent channel conflict from arising, producers or other channel members may provide competing resellers with different brands, allocate markets among resellers, define policies for direct sales to avoid potential conflict over large accounts, negotiate territorial issues among regional distributors, and provide recognition to certain resellers for their importance in distributing to others.

◆ **Channel Integration**

Channel members can either combine and control most activities or pass them on to another channel member. Channel functions may be transferred between intermediaries and to producers and even to customers. However, a channel member cannot eliminate functions; unless buyers themselves perform the functions, they must pay for the labor and resources needed to perform them.

Various channel stages may be combined under the management of a channel captain either horizontally or vertically. Such integration may stabilize supply, reduce costs, and increase coordination of channel members.

vertical channel integration
Combining two or more stages of the marketing channel under one management

Vertical Channel Integration. **Vertical channel integration** combines two or more stages of the channel under one management. This may occur when one member of a marketing channel purchases the operations of another member or simply performs the functions of another member, eliminating the need for that intermediary.

Whereas members of conventional channel systems work independently, participants in vertical channel integration coordinate efforts to reach a desired target market. In this more progressive approach to distribution, channel members regard other members as extensions of their own operations. Vertically integrated channels are often more effective against competition because of increased bargaining power and sharing of information and responsibilities. At one end of a vertically integrated channel, a manufacturer might provide advertising and training assistance, and the retailer at the other end might buy the manufacturer's products in large quantities and actively promote them.

Integration has been successfully institutionalized in marketing channels called **vertical marketing systems (VMSs)**, in which a single channel member coordinates or manages channel activities to achieve efficient, low-cost distribution aimed at satisfying target market customers. Vertical integration brings most or all stages of the marketing channel under common control or ownership. The Limited, a retail clothing chain, uses a wholly owned subsidiary, Mast Industries, as its primary supply source. Radio Shack operates as a vertical marketing system, encompassing both wholesale and retail functions. Because efforts of individual channel members are combined in a VMS, marketing activities can be coordinated for maximum effectiveness and economy, without duplication of services. Vertical marketing systems are competitive, accounting for a significant share of retail sales in consumer goods.

vertical marketing system (VMS) A marketing channel managed by a single channel member to achieve efficient, low-cost distribution aimed at satisfying target market customers

Most vertical marketing systems take one of three forms: corporate, administered, or contractual. A *corporate VMS* combines all stages of the marketing channel, from producers to consumers, under a single owner. For example, The Limited established a corporate VMS that operates corporate-owned production facilities and retail stores. Supermarket chains that own food-processing plants and large retailers that purchase wholesaling and production facilities are other examples of corporate VMSs.

In an *administered VMS*, channel members are independent but a high level of interorganizational management is achieved through informal coordination. Members of an administered VMS may, for example, adopt uniform accounting and ordering procedures and cooperate in promotional activities for the benefit of all partners. Although individual channel members maintain autonomy, as in conventional marketing channels, one channel member (such as a producer or large retailer) dominates the administered VMS so that distribution decisions take the whole system into account. Because of its size and power, Intel exercises a strong influence over distributors and manufacturers in its marketing channels, as do Kellogg (cereal) and Magnavox (televisions and other electronic products).

Under a *contractual VMS*, the most popular type of vertical marketing system, channel members are linked by legal agreements spelling out each member's rights and obligations. Franchise organizations, such as McDonald's and KFC, are contractual VMSs. Other contractual VMSs include wholesaler-sponsored groups, such as IGA (Independent Grocers' Alliance) stores, in which independent retailers band together under the contractual leadership of a wholesaler. Retailer-sponsored cooperatives, which own and operate their own wholesalers, are a third type of contractual VMS.

horizontal channel integration
Combining organizations at the same level of operation under one management

Horizontal Channel Integration. Combining organizations at the same level of operation under one management constitutes **horizontal channel integration**. An organization may integrate horizontally by merging with other organizations at the same level in the marketing channel. The owner of a dry cleaning firm, for example, might buy and combine several other dry cleaning establishments. Horizontal integration may enable a firm to generate sufficient sales revenue to integrate vertically as well.

Although horizontal integration permits efficiencies and economies of scale in purchasing, marketing research, advertising, and specialized personnel, it is not always the most effective method of improving distribution. Problems of size often follow, resulting in decreased flexibility, difficulties in coordination, and the need for additional marketing research and large-scale planning. Unless distribution functions for the various units can be performed more efficiently under unified management than under the previously separate managements, horizontal integration will neither reduce costs nor improve the competitive position of the integrating firm.

Legal Issues in Channel Management

The multitude of federal, state, and local laws governing channel management are based on the general principle that the public is best served by protecting competition and free trade. Under the authority of such federal legislation as the Sherman Antitrust Act and the Federal Trade Commission Act, courts and regulatory agencies determine under what circumstances channel management practices violate this underlying principle and must be restricted. Although channel managers are not expected to be legal experts, they should be aware that attempts to control distribution functions may have legal repercussions. The following practices are among those frequently subject to legal restraint.

◆ Dual Distribution

Earlier we noted that some companies may use dual distribution by utilizing two or more marketing channels to distribute the same products to the same target market. Compaq, for example, sells computers directly to consumers through a toll-free telephone line and a website, as well as through electronics retailers such as Best Buy. Courts do not consider this practice illegal when it promotes competition. A manufacturer can also legally open its own retail outlets. But the courts view as a threat to competition a manufacturer that uses company-owned outlets to dominate or drive out of business independent retailers or distributors that handle its products. In such cases, dual distribution violates the law. To avoid this interpretation, producers should use outlet prices that do not severely undercut independent retailers' prices.

◆ Restricted Sales Territories

To tighten control over distribution of its products, a manufacturer may try to prohibit intermediaries from selling its products outside designated sales territories. Intermediaries themselves often favor this practice because it gives them exclusive territories, allowing them to avoid competition for the producer's brands within these territories. In recent years, the courts have adopted conflicting positions in regard to restricted sales territories. Although the courts have deemed restricted sales territories a restraint of trade among intermediaries handling the same brands (except for small or newly established companies), they have also held that exclusive territories can actually promote competition among dealers handling different brands. At present, the producer's intent in establishing restricted territories and the overall effect of doing so on the market must be evaluated for each individual case.

tying agreement An agreement in which a supplier furnishes a product to a channel member with the stipulation that the channel member must purchase other products as well

◆ Tying Agreements

When a supplier (usually a manufacturer or franchiser) furnishes a product to a channel member with the stipulation that the channel member must purchase other products as well, a **tying agreement** exists. Suppliers may institute tying agreements to move weaker products along with more popular items, or a franchiser may tie purchase of equipment and supplies to the sale of franchises, justifying the policy as necessary for quality control and protection of the franchiser's reputation.

A related practice is *full-line forcing,* in which a supplier requires that channel members purchase the supplier's entire line to obtain any of the supplier's products. Manufacturers sometimes use full-line forcing to ensure that intermediaries accept new products and that a suitable range of products is available to customers.

The courts accept tying agreements when the supplier alone can provide products of a certain quality, when the intermediary is free to carry competing products as well, and when a company has just entered the market. Most other tying agreements are considered illegal.

◆ Exclusive Dealing

exclusive dealing A situation in which a manufacturer forbids an intermediary to carry products of competing manufacturers

When a manufacturer forbids an intermediary to carry products of competing manufacturers, the arrangement is called **exclusive dealing**. Manufacturers receive considerable market protection in an exclusive-dealing arrangement and may cut off shipments to intermediaries that violate the agreement.

The legality of an exclusive-dealing contract is generally determined by applying three tests. If the exclusive dealing blocks competitors from as much as 10 percent of the market, if the sales revenue involved is sizable, and if the manufacturer is much larger (and thus more intimidating) than the dealer, the arrangement is considered anticompetitive.[11] If dealers and customers in a given market have access to similar products or if the exclusive-dealing contract strengthens an otherwise weak competitor, the arrangement is allowed.

◆ Refusal to Deal

For more than 75 years, the courts have held that producers have the right to choose channel members with which they will do business (and the right to reject others). Within existing distribution channels, however, suppliers may not legally refuse to deal with wholesalers or dealers merely because these wholesalers or dealers resist policies that are anticompetitive or in restraint of trade. Suppliers are further prohibited from organizing some channel members in refusal-to-deal actions against other members that choose not to comply with illegal policies.

SUMMARY

A marketing channel, or channel of distribution, is a group of individuals and organizations that direct the flow of products from producers to customers. The major role of marketing channels is to make products available at the right time at the right place and in the right amounts. In most channels of distribution, producers and consumers are linked by marketing intermediaries, or middlemen. The two major types of intermediaries are retailers, which purchase products and resell them to ultimate consumers, and wholesalers, which buy and resell products to other wholesalers, retailers, and business customers.

Marketing channels serve many functions. They create time, place, and possession utility by making products available when and where customers want them and providing customers with access to product use through sale or rental. Marketing intermediaries facilitate exchange efficiencies, often reducing the costs of exchanges by performing certain services and functions. Although critics suggest eliminating wholesalers, someone must perform their functions in the marketing channel. Because intermediaries serve both producers and buyers, they reduce the total number of transactions that otherwise would be needed to move products from producer to ultimate users.

Marketing channels also form a supply chain, a total distribution system that serves customers and creates a competitive advantage. Supply chain management refers to long-term partnerships among channel members working together to reduce inefficiencies, costs, and redundancies and to develop innovative approaches to satisfy customers. The supply chain includes all entities—

shippers and other firms that facilitate distribution, as well as producers, wholesalers, and retailers—that distribute products and benefit from cooperative efforts. Supply chains start with the customer and require the cooperation of channel members to satisfy customer requirements.

Channels of distribution are broadly classified as channels for consumer products and channels for business products. Within these two broad categories, different marketing channels are used for different products. Although consumer goods can move directly from producer to consumers, consumer product channels that include wholesalers and retailers are usually more economical and efficient. Distribution of business products differs from that of consumer products in the types of channels used. A direct distribution channel is common in business marketing. Also used are channels containing industrial distributors, manufacturers' agents, and a combination of agents and distributors. Most producers have multiple or dual channels so the distribution system can be adjusted for various target markets.

A marketing channel is managed such that products receive appropriate market coverage. In choosing intensive distribution, producers strive to make a product available to all possible dealers. In selective distribution, only some outlets in an area are chosen to distribute a product. Exclusive distribution usually gives a single dealer rights to sell a product in a large geographic area.

Each channel member performs a different role in the system and agrees to accept certain rights, responsibilities, rewards, and sanctions for nonconformance. Although many marketing channels are determined by consensus, some are organized and controlled by a single leader, or channel captain. A channel captain may be a producer, wholesaler, or retailer. Channels function most effectively when members cooperate; when they deviate from their roles, channel conflict can arise.

Integration of marketing channels brings various activities under one channel member's management. Vertical integration combines two or more stages of the channel under one management. The vertical marketing system (VMS) is managed centrally for the mutual benefit of all channel members. Vertical marketing systems may be corporate, administered, or contractual. Horizontal integration combines institutions at the same level of channel operation under a single management.

Federal, state, and local laws regulate channel management to protect competition and free trade. Courts may prohibit or permit a practice depending on whether it violates this underlying principle. Various procompetitive legislation applies to distribution practices. Channel management practices frequently subject to legal restraint include dual distribution, restricted sales territories, tying agreements, exclusive dealing, and refusal to deal. When these practices strengthen weak competitors or increase competition among dealers, they may be permitted; in most other cases, when competition may be weakened considerably, they are deemed illegal.

Please visit the student website at **www.prideferrell.com** for ACE Self-Test questions that will help you prepare for exams.

IMPORTANT TERMS

Distribution	Channel captain
Marketing channel	Channel power
Marketing intermediary	Vertical channel
Supply chain management	integration
Industrial distributor	Vertical marketing system
Dual distribution	(VMS)
Strategic channel alliance	Horizontal channel
Intensive distribution	integration
Selective distribution	Tying agreement
Exclusive distribution	Exclusive dealing

DISCUSSION & REVIEW QUESTIONS

1. Describe the major functions of marketing channels. Why are these functions better accomplished through combined efforts of channel members?

2. Can one channel member perform all the channel functions? Explain your answer.

3. "Shorter channels are usually a more direct means of distribution and therefore are more efficient." Comment on this statement.

4. List several reasons consumers often blame intermediaries for distribution inefficiencies.

5. Compare and contrast the four major types of marketing channels for consumer products. Through which type of channel is each of the following products most likely to be distributed?
   a. New automobiles
   b. Saltine crackers
   c. Cut-your-own Christmas trees
   d. New textbooks
   e. Sofas
   f. Soft drinks

6. Outline the four most common channels for business products. Describe the products or situations that lead marketers to choose each channel.

7. Describe an industrial distributor. What types of products are marketed through an industrial distributor?

8. Under what conditions is a producer most likely to use more than one marketing channel?

9. Explain the differences among intensive, selective, and exclusive methods of distribution.

10. "Channel cooperation requires that members support the overall channel goals to achieve individual goals." Comment on this statement.

11. Name and describe firms that use (a) vertical integration and (b) horizontal integration in their marketing channels.

12. Explain the major characteristics of each of the three types of vertical marketing systems (VMSs): corporate, administered, and contractual.

13. Under what conditions are tying agreements, exclusive dealing, and dual distribution judged illegal?

APPLICATION QUESTIONS

1. *Supply chain management* refers to long-term partnerships among channel members working together to reduce inefficiencies, costs, and redundancies and to develop innovative approaches to satisfy customers. Select one of the following companies and explain how supply chain management could increase marketing productivity.
   a. Dell Computer
   b. FedEx
   c. Nike
   d. Taco Bell

2. Organizations often form strategic channel alliances when they find it more profitable or convenient to distribute their products through the marketing channel of another organization. Find an article in a newspaper or on the Internet that describes such a strategic channel alliance. Briefly summarize the article and indicate the benefits each organization expects to gain.

3. Marketers can select from three major levels of market coverage when determining the number and kinds of outlets in which to sell a product: intensive, selective, or exclusive distribution. Characteristics of the product and its target market determine the intensity of coverage a product should receive. Indicate the intensity level best suited for the following products, and explain why it is appropriate.
   a. Personal computer
   b. Deodorant
   c. Canon digital cameras
   d. Nike athletic shoes

4. Describe the decision process you might go through if you were attempting to determine the most appropriate distribution channel for one of the following:
   a. Shotguns for hunters
   b. Women's lingerie
   c. Telephone systems for small businesses
   d. Toy trucks for 2-year-olds

Internet Exercise & Resources

Visit **www.prideferrell.com** for resources to help you master the material in this chapter, plus materials that will help you expand your marketing knowledge, including Internet exercise updates, ACE self-tests, hotlinks to companies featured in this chapter, and much more.

iSupply

Distribution bottlenecks can be an expensive problem for any business. Trying to prevent such problems is iSupply, an Internet supply chain management tool that links all members of a supply chain from the supplier's system to the retailer's storefront system. Learn more about this innovative tool at **www.ie.com.my/html/isupply.html**.

1. Does iSupply represent a new type of marketing channel? Why or why not?
2. Why would firms be cautious when deciding whether to use iSupply?
3. Do you think iSupply represents the future of supply chain management? Why or why not?

Video Case 15.1

Smarter Channel Management at SmarterKids

Marketing through online retailing, catalogs, and directly to institutional customers can be a difficult juggling act for any company, but Excelligence Learning Corporation is up to the challenge of channel management. One of the stars of its Early Childhood division is SmarterKids, a website targeting parents who want to buy quality educational toys. Other Excelligence divisions develop new educational toys, market supplies and furniture to schools through printed catalogs, and offer products for schools to buy for resale during fund-raising drives.

Excelligence maintains a sales force of 51 representatives who visit schools and child care facilities to sell the full array of company products. In addition, it publishes a magazine and maintains a website for educators who work with preschool and elementary school students. Because Excelligence has so many businesses focused on children and education, it is in a unique position to effectively manage the flow of products to each of its target markets.

Consider the SmarterKids site (**www.smarterkids.com**), which serves as a consumer marketing channel for products made by the parent company as well as by outside manufacturers. Many toy retailers try to compete with industry giants such as Toys "R" Us by stocking a huge number of products. SmarterKids takes a different approach. Rather than compete on the basis of an extensive product mix, SmarterKids narrows the choices by having a team of teachers individually test each product. The teachers even watch every video and play every computer game being considered for the website. Then they rate the products using hundreds of criteria, including ease of use, creativity, educational approach, and durability. The result is a smaller but much more focused selection of approximately 4,000 products that meet SmarterKids' extremely demanding criteria for advancing children's development and education.

SmarterKids' marketers know that parents have limited time and do not want to wander endlessly through cavernous stores looking at a dizzying array of toys that may or may

not be right for their children. Ideally parents want to buy products that their children—newborns to teenagers—will enjoy for more than a few days. And they want to buy products that will help children develop their skills and build their knowledge. Customers may well be impressed by the number of toys a retailer stocks. However, many will find more value in buying from SmarterKids because it helps narrow the choices to a manageable subset of toys, games, movies, and books that make sense for a particular child.

When customers log onto the colorful SmarterKids website, they can search for toys in four ways. First, they can search according to age categories (such as birth to 1 year old or preschool age). Second, they can choose a particular toy category (such as puzzles, music, or books). Third, they can search by developmental area (such as language, creative expression, or sensory development). Fourth, they can enter a keyword (such as a brand name or type of toy). In addition, the homepage highlights toys that are sold exclusively by SmarterKids, toys that are best sellers in their category, and discounted toys featured in the site's clearance section. Then, instead of pushing a shopping cart through endless miles of cramped aisles, customers simply point and click to browse and buy. Thus, SmarterKids makes the online shopping experience more efficient and more productive for its time-pressured customers.

Parents can also access special sections of the SmarterKids site to learn more about six child developmental areas. The site explains why each area of development is important and posts a number of fun, easy activities for home use. No SmarterKids toys are needed. Instead, the activities are designed to bring parents and children together for a few minutes of educational playtime involving simple household items such as pots and pans or sponges. These sections represent an evolution from the detailed, personalized assessments that SmarterKids once offered on the site.

SmarterKids has found through research that customers who take full advantage of the site's information and activities wind up purchasing twice as much as those who don't. More data means the retailer can do a better job of buying the

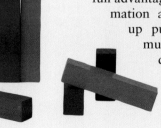

most appropriate toys and planning e-mail newsletters and other targeted promotions. The idea is to establish and strengthen connections with customers by showing that SmarterKids is dedicated to satisfying their needs and the needs of their children. Big stores may have bigger inventories, but SmarterKids believes its retailing strategy is smarter for long-term customer loyalty. "If you are able to develop a trusting relationship with consumers, they're going to come back time and time again," says the CEO.[12]

QUESTIONS FOR DISCUSSION

1. What is Excelligence's approach to channel integration?
2. Some toys are sold to parents through the direct selling "party plan." Should SmarterKids use this channel in addition to online retailing? Explain.
3. Under what conditions would a toy manufacturer be as interested in marketing its products through SmarterKids as it would through Toys "R" Us?

Case 15.2

Grainger Wires the Channel for Business Products

Need an electric motor or a hard hat? W. W. Grainger has dozens for sale among the many thousands of products showcased in its voluminous catalogs and on its website. Grainger is an industrial distributor offering virtually one-stop shopping for producer, government, and institutional markets seeking to buy a wide range of maintenance, repair, and operating (MRO) supplies. With more than 560 distribution branches spread across North America, the company can time shipments to arrive quickly when business customers place orders.

William W. Grainger founded the Illinois-based company in the 1920s as a wholesaler of electric motors. To build sales, Grainger mailed out postcards about his offerings and compiled a catalog titled *MotorBook*. In less than a decade, he was operating 15 U.S. sales branches to serve business customers from coast to coast. By 1949, he had expanded his branch network to 30 states.

Son David Grainger, now senior chairperson, continued the founder's expansion strategy. In the 1980s and 1990s, the company opened high-tech regional distribution centers in Kansas, Georgia, and Texas to supplement its Chicago-area facilities and slash fulfillment time for orders placed by customers around the country. Grainger also expanded its geographic reach by buying Acklands Ltd., a Canadian distributor of automotive and industrial safety products.

By the mid-1990s, Grainger was getting wired. Recognizing that the Internet could bring in many more business customers at a lower cost, management

created Grainger.com as a comprehensive online catalog site. Over the years, the company continued to refine its web presence by posting informative resources, adding live-chat customer assistance, a virtual tour of the site for new customers, special international services, and web-only price promotions to bring customers back to the site again and again. Within the first three years of operation, annual web sales grew from $3 million to $267 million as customers flocked to the online catalog, which features many more items than the 80,000 products shown in a typical printed Grainger catalog.

Not all of Grainger's Internet initiatives have been as successful, however. The company had high hopes for its Material Logic division covering three web-based distribution sites. TotalMRO.com was designed as an industrywide portal with catalogs from Grainger and competing distributors. MROverstocks.com was created as an auction site for discontinued or excess industrial products. FindMRO.com was designed as a search site for specialized and hard-to-find industrial products. After launching the three sites, Grainger tried to interest competing distributors and outside investors in buying a stake in Material Logic. The company had spent more than $100 million on its web operations and sought outside funding to support its aggressive movement into electronic procurement. But when no one stepped forward to invest, Grainger quickly shut down the unprofitable division. At the same time, FindMRO.com was becoming popular, so it was merged into the existing Grainger.com operation.

Today Grainger sells $5 billion worth of industrial products every year. Approximately 10 percent of total sales revenues come from the profitable Grainger.com site, and the percentage continues to rise as more customers switch from paper-based to electronic purchasing. Despite its Internet success, Grainger is not abandoning its branch system. In line with the changing demographics of its customer base, the company is reassessing the intensity of its market coverage in major metropolitan areas. It has closed two older branches, opened three new branches, expanded or relocated seven branches, and hired more sales staff. The company has also opened convenient on-site branches for two big customers, Florida State University and Langley Air Force Base. "Grainger's multi-channel model is what distinguishes us from our competition," the CEO emphasizes. "No other company has as broad a product line with tens of thousands of items immediately available all across the country."

To handle future volume more productively, Grainger is opening an additional nine automated distribution centers and implementing a new logistics network. The added efficiency will allow the company to lower its inventory investment by $100 million while profitably serving more customers. Grainger is also showing major customers such as the U.S. Postal Service how to better manage their supply chains and cut costs throughout the procurement process. More efficiencies are ahead as the company, already the largest industrial distributor in North America, aggressively pursues higher market share and higher profits.[13]

QUESTIONS FOR DISCUSSION

1. Why would a competing industrial distributor even consider investing in a portal designed by Grainger?
2. Is Grainger in a position to be a channel captain? Explain.
3. Why would a hospital buy from Grainger instead of buying directly from producers?

Wholesaling and Physical Distribution

16

OBJECTIVES

1. To understand the nature of wholesaling in the marketing channel

2. To explain wholesalers' functions

3. To understand how wholesalers are classified

4. To recognize how physical distribution activities are integrated into marketing channels and overall marketing strategies

5. To examine the major physical distribution functions of order processing, inventory management, materials handling, warehousing, and transportation

6. To discuss the strategic implications of physical distribution systems

Skechers Manages Inventory the Wireless Way

How can a fashion footwear firm manage the flow of 60,000 individual products to thousands of retail stores around the world? This is the challenge facing Skechers, a California company known for making stylish men's, women's, and children's shoes. In its early years, the company relied on a network of wholesalers to service retail accounts outside the United States. Then it began handling its own distribution in Canada and 11 western European countries. To do this, it opened a huge distribution center in Belgium, supplementing its distribution center in California.

Because the popularity of specific fashion footwear can be brief and unpredictable, the company must have inventory ready to ship to stores at a moment's notice. Skechers holds extra inventory in outside warehouses and shifts products between facilities as needed to fill orders in each distribution center. Searching the 1.5 million square feet of warehouse space to find a pair of shoes in a particular style, color, and size would be a major headache if not for the company's state-of-the-art inventory management system.

Skechers has put wireless computer terminals into the hands of warehouse employees and installed them in warehouse vehicles, docks, and doorways. When a case of shoes arrives from a Skechers factory, the wireless system picks up information about the contents and records where all items are transported and stored. As stores submit orders, the wireless system identifies each item's location, notes which products are being shipped to which store, deducts the products from current inventory levels, prepares shipping documents, and arranges for invoicing. Even rush orders are no problem now that employees can find every pair of shoes instantly—even those in the process of being shifted from one part of the warehouse to another—by consulting one of the wireless terminals.

Thanks to this wireless system, Skechers can count all of its inventory in less than two days instead of the five days required before the company went wireless. The system automatically issues a warning if it detects any errors or discrepancies. This puts Skechers in a better position to fill store orders completely and correctly. Moreover, employees no longer have the tedious task of manually entering every shipment that enters or leaves the warehouse. "Now we're able to track all of our merchandise throughout all of our buildings in real time, without a piece of paper and without any kind of data entry going on," says the company's vice president of distribution.[1] ∎

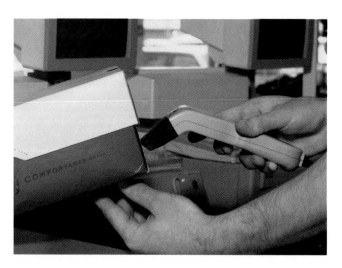

ompanies such as Sketchers rely heavily on physical distribution, a crucial set of functions in supply chain management because it includes those activities associated with handling and moving products through the marketing channel. Wholesalers help make products available to customers when and where they want them. Wholesalers often play a key role in supply chain management and physical distribution.

In this chapter, we explore the role of wholesaling and physical distribution in supply chain management. First, we examine the importance of wholesalers in marketing channels, including their functions and classifications. Next, we consider critical physical distribution concepts, including order processing, inventory management, materials handling, warehousing, and transportation.

The Nature of Wholesaling

wholesaling Transactions in which products are bought for resale, for making other products, or for general business operations

wholesaler An individual or organization that facilitates and expedites wholesale transactions

Wholesaling refers to all transactions in which products are bought for resale, for making other products, or for general business operations. It does not include exchanges with ultimate consumers. A **wholesaler** is an individual or organization that facilitates and expedites exchanges that are primarily wholesale transactions. In other words, wholesalers buy products and resell them to reseller, government, and institutional users. For example, SYSCO, the nation's number one food service distributor, supplies restaurants, hotels, schools, industrial caterers, and hospitals with everything from frozen and fresh food and paper products to medical and cleaning supplies. There are approximately 446,000 wholesaling establishments in the United States,[2] and more than half of all products sold in this country pass through these firms.

Table 16.1 lists the major activities wholesalers perform, but individual wholesalers may perform more or fewer functions than the table shows. Distribution of all

Table 16.1	Major Wholesaling Functions
Supply chain management	Creating long-term partnerships among channel members
Promotion	Providing a sales force, advertising, sales promotion, and publicity
Warehousing, shipping, and product handling	Receiving, storing, and stockkeeping Packaging Shipping outgoing orders Materials handling Arranging and making local and long-distance shipments
Inventory control and data processing	Processing orders Controlling physical inventory Recording transactions Tracking sales data for financial analysis
Risk taking	Assuming responsibility for theft, product obsolescence, and excess inventories
Financing and budgeting	Extending credit Borrowing Making capital investments Forecasting cash flow
Marketing research and information systems	Providing information about markets Conducting research studies Managing computer networks to facilitate exchanges and relationships

goods requires wholesaling activities whether or not a wholesaling firm is involved. Wholesaling activities are not limited to goods; service companies, such as financial institutions, also use active wholesale networks. For example, some banks buy loans in bulk from other financial institutions as well as making loans to their own retail customers.

Wholesalers perform services for other organizations in the marketing channel. They bear primary responsibility for the physical distribution of products from manufacturers to retailers. In addition, they may establish information systems that help producers and retailers better manage the supply chain from producer to customer. Many wholesalers are using information technology and the Internet to allow their employees, customers, and suppliers to share information between intermediaries and facilitating agencies such as trucking companies and warehouse firms. For example, FedEx, which serves as a facilitating agency in providing overnight or even same-day delivery of packages, provides online tracking of packages for the benefit of its customers. Other firms are making their databases and marketing information systems available to their supply chain partners to facilitate order processing, shipping, and product development and to share information about changing market conditions and customer desires. As a result, some wholesalers play a key role in supply chain management decisions.

Meeting Customer Service Standards
Organizations like Merit Abrasive Products set customer service standards associated with filling a high percentage of orders from their inventories and shipping the orders on time.

◆ Services Provided by Wholesalers

Wholesalers provide essential services to both producers and retailers. By initiating sales contacts with a producer and selling diverse products to retailers, wholesalers serve as an extension of the producer's sales force. Wholesalers also provide financial assistance. They often pay for transporting goods; they reduce a producer's warehousing expenses and inventory investment by holding goods in inventory; they extend credit and assume losses from buyers who turn out to be poor credit risks; and when they buy a producer's entire output and pay promptly or in cash, they are a source of working capital. Wholesalers also serve as conduits for information within the marketing channel, keeping producers up to date on market developments and passing along the manufacturers' promotional plans to other intermediaries. Using wholesalers therefore gives producers a distinct advantage because the specialized services wholesalers perform allow producers to concentrate on developing and manufacturing products that match customers' needs and wants.

Many producers would prefer more direct interaction with retailers. Wholesalers, however, are more likely to have closer contact with retailers because of their strategic position in the marketing channel. Although a producer's own sales force is probably more effective at selling, the costs of maintaining a sales force and performing functions normally done by wholesalers are sometimes higher than the benefits received from an independent sales staff. Wholesalers can spread sales costs over many more products than can most producers, resulting in lower costs per product unit. For these reasons, many producers shift informational, financing, and physical distribution activities, such as transportation and warehousing, to wholesalers. Thus, the wholesaler often becomes a major link in the supply chain, creating an optimal level of efficiency and customer service.

98% On-Time delivery on all stock items.

we know abrasives

Wholesalers support retailers by assisting with marketing strategy, especially the distribution component. Wholesalers also help retailers select inventory. They are often specialists on market conditions and experts at negotiating final purchases. In industries in which obtaining supplies is important, skilled buying is indispensable. For example, Atlanta-based Genuine Parts Company (GPC), the nation's top automotive parts wholesaler, has more than 70 years of experience in the auto parts business. This experience helps the company serve its customers effectively. GPC supplies more than 300,000 replacement parts to 6,000 NAPA Auto Parts stores.[3] Effective wholesalers make an effort to understand the businesses of their customers. They can reduce a retailer's burden of looking for and coordinating supply sources. If the wholesaler purchases for several buyers, all customers can share expenses. Furthermore, whereas a manufacturer's salesperson offers retailers only a few products at a time, independent wholesalers always have a wide range of products available. Thus, through partnerships, wholesalers and retailers can forge successful relationships for the benefit of customers.

Buying in large quantities and delivering to customers in smaller lots enable wholesalers to perform physical distribution activities efficiently. These activities (discussed later in this chapter) include order processing, transportation, materials handling, inventory planning, and warehousing. Wholesalers furnish greater service than might be feasible for a producer's or retailer's own physical distribution system. Furthermore, wholesalers offer quick and frequent delivery even when demand fluctuates and can do so at low cost, which lets the producer and the wholesalers' customers avoid risks associated with holding large inventories.

The distinction between services performed by wholesalers and those provided by other businesses has blurred in recent years. Changes in the competitive nature of business, especially the growth of strong retail chains such as Wal-Mart, The Home Depot, and Best Buy, are changing supply chain relationships. In many product categories, such as electronics, furniture, and even food products, retailers have discovered they can deal directly with producers, performing wholesaling activities themselves at a lower cost. An increasing number of retailers are relying on computer technology to expedite ordering, delivery, and handling of goods. Technology is thus allowing retailers to take over many wholesaling functions. When a wholesaler is eliminated from a marketing channel, the functions, listed in Table 16.1, still have to be performed by a member of the marketing channel, whether a producer, retailer, or facilitating agency. These wholesaling activities are critical components of supply chain management.

◆ Types of Wholesalers

Wholesalers are classified according to several criteria. Whether a wholesaler is independently owned or owned by a producer influences how it is classified. Wholesalers can also be grouped according to whether they take title to (own) the products they handle. The range of services provided is another criterion used for classification. Finally, wholesalers are classified according to the breadth and depth of their product lines. Using these criteria, we discuss three general types of wholesaling establishments: merchant wholesalers, agents and brokers, and manufacturers' sales branches and offices.

merchant wholesaler An independently owned business that takes title to goods, assumes ownership risks, and buys and resells products to other wholesalers, business customers, or retailers

Merchant Wholesalers.   **Merchant wholesalers** are independently owned businesses that take title to goods, assume risks associated with ownership, and generally buy and resell products to other wholesalers, business customers, or retailers. A producer is likely to rely on merchant wholesalers when selling directly to customers would be economically unfeasible. Merchant wholesalers are also useful for providing market coverage, making sales contacts, storing inventory, handling orders, collecting market information, and furnishing customer support. Some merchant wholesalers are even involved in packaging and developing private brands to help retail customers be competitive. Merchant wholesalers go by various names, including *wholesaler,*

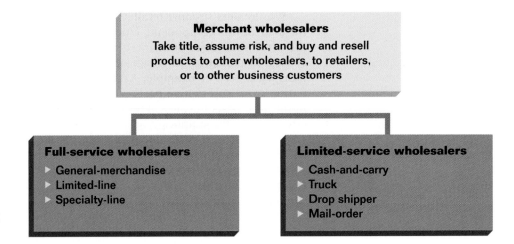

Figure 16.1 **Types of Merchant Wholesalers**

jobber, distributor, assembler, exporter, and *importer.* They fall into one of two broad categories: full-service and limited-service (see Figure 16.1).

full-service wholesaler A merchant wholesaler that performs the widest range of wholesaling functions

Full-service wholesalers perform the widest possible range of wholesaling functions. Customers rely on them for product availability, suitable assortments, breaking large quantities into smaller lots, financial assistance, and technical advice and service. Universal Corporation, the world's largest buyer and processor of leaf tobacco, is an example of a full-service wholesaler. Based in Richmond, Virginia, the firm buys, resells, packs, and ships tobacco, and provides financing for its customers, which include cigarette manufacturers such as Philip Morris (which accounts for a significant portion of Universal's sales). Universal is also involved in sales of lumber, rubber, tea, nuts, dried fruit, and other products, and has operations in 40 countries.[4] Full-service wholesalers handle either consumer or business products and provide numerous marketing services to their customers. Many large grocery wholesalers help retailers with store design, site selection, personnel training, financing, merchandising, advertising, coupon redemption, and scanning. Although full-service wholesalers often earn higher gross margins than other wholesalers, their operating expenses are also higher because they perform a wider range of functions.

general-merchandise wholesaler A full-service wholesaler with a wide product mix but limited depth within product lines

Full-service wholesalers are categorized as general-merchandise, limited-line, and specialty-line wholesalers, and as rack jobbers. **General-merchandise wholesalers** carry a wide product mix but offer limited depth within product lines. They deal in such products as drugs, nonperishable foods, cosmetics, detergents, and tobacco. **Limited-line wholesalers** carry only a few product lines, such as groceries, lighting fixtures, or oil-well drilling equipment, but offer an extensive assortment of products within those lines. Bergen Brunswig Corporation, for example, is a limited-line wholesaler of pharmaceuticals and health and beauty aids. Limited-line wholesalers provide a range of services similar to those of general-merchandise wholesalers. **Specialty-line wholesalers** offer the narrowest range of products, usually a single product line or a few items within a product line. Wholesalers that specialize in shellfish, fruit, or other food delicacies are specialty-line wholesalers. Red River Floods, for example, is the leading importer (specialty-line wholesaler) of nuts, seeds, and dried fruits in the United States.[5] **Rack jobbers** are full-service, specialty-line wholesalers that own and maintain display racks in supermarkets, drugstores, and discount and variety stores. They set up displays, mark merchandise, stock shelves, and keep billing and inventory records; retailers need to furnish only space. Rack jobbers specialize in nonfood items with high profit margins, such as health and beauty aids, books, magazines, hosiery, and greeting cards.

limited-line wholesaler A full-service wholesaler that carries only a few product lines but many products within those lines

specialty-line wholesaler A full-service wholesaler that carries only a single product line or a few items within a product line

rack jobber A full-service, specialty-line wholesaler that owns and maintains display racks in stores

limited-service wholesaler A merchant wholesaler that provides some services and specializes in a few functions

Limited-service wholesalers provide fewer marketing services than full-service wholesalers and specialize in just a few functions. Producers perform the remaining functions or pass them on to customers or to other intermediaries. Limited-service wholesalers take title to merchandise but often do not deliver merchandise, grant

Table 16.2   Services That Limited-Service Wholesalers Provide

	Cash-and-Carry	Truck	Drop Shipper	Mail-Order
Physical possession of merchandise	Yes	Yes	No	Yes
Personal sales calls on customers	No	Yes	No	No
Information about market conditions	No	Some	Yes	Yes
Advice to customers	No	Some	Yes	No
Stocking and maintenance of merchandise in customers' stores	No	No	No	No
Credit to customers	No	No	Yes	Some
Delivery of merchandise to customers	No	Yes	No	No

credit, provide marketing information, store inventory, or plan ahead for customers' future needs. Because they offer restricted services, limited-service wholesalers are compensated with lower rates and have smaller profit margins than full-service wholesalers. The decision about whether to use a limited-service or a full-service wholesaler depends on the structure of the marketing channel and the need to manage the supply chain to provide competitive advantage. Although certain types of limited-service wholesalers are few in number, they are important in the distribution of such products as specialty foods, perishable items, construction materials, and coal. Table 16.2 summarizes the services provided by four typical limited-service wholesalers: cash-and-carry wholesalers, truck wholesalers, drop shippers, and mail-order wholesalers.

Cash-and-carry wholesalers are intermediaries whose customers—usually small businesses—pay cash and furnish transportation. Cash-and-carry wholesalers typically handle a limited line of products with a high turnover rate, such as groceries, building materials, and electrical or office supplies. Many small retailers whose accounts are refused by other wholesalers survive because of cash-and-carry wholesalers. **Truck wholesalers**, sometimes called *truck jobbers,* transport a limited line of products directly to customers for on-the-spot inspection and selection. They are often small operators who own and drive their own trucks. They usually have regular routes, calling on retailers and other institutions to determine their needs. **Drop shippers**, also known as *desk jobbers,* take title to goods and negotiate sales but never actually take possession of products. They forward orders from retailers, business buyers, or other wholesalers to manufacturers and arrange for carload shipments of items to be delivered directly from producers to these customers. They assume responsibility for products during the entire transaction, including the costs of any unsold goods. **Mail-order wholesalers** use catalogs instead of sales forces to sell products to retail and business buyers. Wholesale mail-order houses generally feature cosmetics, specialty foods, sporting goods, office supplies, and automotive parts. Mail-order wholesaling enables buyers to choose and order particular catalog

cash-and-carry wholesaler A limited-service wholesaler whose customers pay cash and furnish transportation

truck wholesaler A limited-service wholesaler that transports products directly to customers for inspection and selection

drop shipper A limited-service wholesaler that takes title to products and negotiates sales but never actually takes possession of products

mail-order wholesaler A limited-service wholesaler that sells products through catalogs

Snapshot

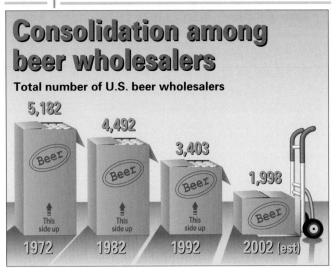

Consolidation among beer wholesalers

Total number of U.S. beer wholesalers

5,182 — 1972
4,492 — 1982
3,403 — 1992
1,998 — 2002 (est)

Source: Data from National Beer Wholesalers Association.

agent A functional intermediary that represents either buyers or sellers on a permanent basis

broker A functional intermediary that brings buyers and sellers together temporarily

manufacturers' agent An independent intermediary that represents more than one seller and offers complete product lines

items for delivery through United Parcel Service, the U.S. Postal Service, or other carriers. This is a convenient and effective method of selling small items to customers in remote areas that other wholesalers might find unprofitable to serve. The Internet has enabled mail-order wholesalers to sell products via their own websites and have the products shipped by the manufacturers.

Agents and Brokers. Agents and brokers negotiate purchases and expedite sales but do not take title to products (see Figure 16.2). Sometimes called *functional middlemen*, they perform a limited number of services in exchange for a commission, which is generally based on the product's selling price. **Agents** represent either buyers or sellers on a permanent basis, whereas **brokers** are intermediaries that buyers or sellers employ temporarily.

Although agents and brokers perform even fewer functions than limited-service wholesalers, they are usually specialists in particular products or types of customers and can provide valuable sales expertise. They know their markets well and often form long-lasting associations with customers. Agents and brokers enable manufacturers to expand sales when resources are limited, to benefit from the services of a trained sales force, and to hold down personal selling costs. Despite the advantages they offer, agents and brokers face increased competition from merchant wholesalers, manufacturers' sales branches and offices, and direct-sales efforts through manufacturer-owned websites. We look here at three types of agents—manufacturers' agents, selling agents, and commission merchants—and at the broker's role in bringing about exchanges between buyers and sellers. Table 16.3 summarizes the services agents and brokers provide.

Manufacturers' agents, which account for more than half of all agent wholesalers, are independent intermediaries that represent two or more sellers and usually offer customers complete product lines. They sell and take orders year-round, much as a manufacturer's sales force does. Restricted to a particular territory, a manufacturers' agent handles noncompeting and complementary products. The relationship between the agent and the manufacturer is governed by written contracts that outline territories, selling price, order handling, and terms of sale related to delivery,

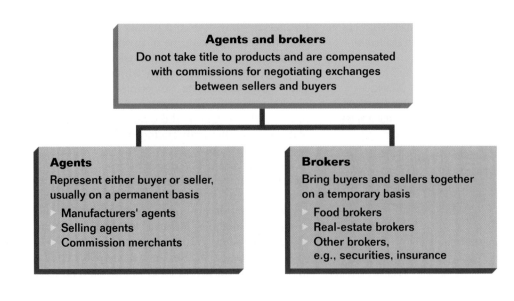

Agents and brokers
Do not take title to products and are compensated with commissions for negotiating exchanges between sellers and buyers

Agents
Represent either buyer or seller, usually on a permanent basis
- Manufacturers' agents
- Selling agents
- Commission merchants

Brokers
Bring buyers and sellers together on a temporary basis
- Food brokers
- Real-estate brokers
- Other brokers, e.g., securities, insurance

Figure 16.2 Types of Agents and Brokers

Table 16.3	Services That Agents and Brokers Provide			
	Manufacturers' Agents	Selling Agents	Commission Merchants	Brokers
Physical possession of merchandise	Some	Some	Yes	No
Long-term relationship with buyers or sellers	Yes	Yes	Yes	No
Representation of competing product lines	No	No	Yes	Yes
Limited geographic territory	Yes	No	No	No
Credit to customers	No	Yes	Some	No
Delivery of merchandise to customers	Some	Yes	Yes	No

service, and warranties. Manufacturers' agents have little or no control over producers' pricing and marketing policies. They do not extend credit and may be unable to provide technical advice. They do occasionally store and transport products, assist producers with planning and promotion, and help retailers advertise. Some maintain a service organization; the more services offered, the higher the agent's commission. Manufacturers' agents are commonly used in sales of apparel, machinery and equipment, steel, furniture, automotive products, electrical goods, and certain food items.

selling agent An intermediary that markets a whole product line or a manufacturer's entire output

Selling agents market either all of a specified product line or a manufacturer's entire output. They perform every wholesaling activity except taking title to products. Selling agents usually assume the sales function for several producers simultaneously and are often used in place of marketing departments. In fact, selling agents are used most often by small producers or by manufacturers that have difficulty maintaining a marketing department because of seasonal production or other factors. In contrast to manufacturers' agents, selling agents generally have no territorial limits and have complete authority over prices, promotion, and distribution. To avoid conflicts of interest, selling agents represent noncompeting product lines. They play a key role in advertising, marketing research, and credit policies of the sellers they represent, at times even advising on product development and packaging.

commission merchant An agent that receives goods on consignment from local sellers and negotiates sales in large, central markets

Commission merchants receive goods on consignment from local sellers and negotiate sales in large, central markets. Sometimes called *factor merchants*, these agents have broad powers regarding prices and terms of sale. They specialize in obtaining the best price possible under market conditions. Most often found in agricultural marketing, commission merchants take possession of truckloads of commodities, arrange for necessary grading or storage, and transport the commodities to auctions or markets where they are sold. When sales are completed, the agents deduct commissions and sales expenses, and then turn over the remaining revenue to the producer. Commission

NET SIGHTS

U.S. Business Reporter devotes a section of its website to wholesaling. Visitors can find a variety of concise, informative articles on the wholesaling environment, relevant statistics, and industry issues, characteristics, and trends. At **www.activemedia-guide.com/ wholesaling_industry.htm,** *users can search by company name or by industry.*

merchants also offer planning assistance and sometimes extend credit, but usually do not provide promotional support.

A broker's primary purpose is to bring buyers and sellers together. Thus, brokers perform fewer functions than other intermediaries. They are not involved in financing or physical possession, have no authority to set prices, and assume almost no risks. Instead they offer customers specialized knowledge of a particular commodity and a network of established contacts. Brokers are especially useful to sellers of certain types of products, such as supermarket products and real estate. Food brokers, for example, sell food and general merchandise to retailer-owned and merchant wholesalers, grocery chains, food processors, and business buyers.

sales branch A manufacturer-owned intermediary that sells products and provides support services to the manufacturer's sales force

Manufacturers' Sales Branches and Offices. Sometimes called *manufacturers' wholesalers,* manufacturers' sales branches and offices resemble merchant wholesalers' operations. **Sales branches** are manufacturer-owned intermediaries that sell products and provide support services to the manufacturer's sales force. Situated away from the manufacturing plant, they are usually located where large customers are concentrated and demand is high. They offer credit, deliver goods, give promotional assistance, and furnish other services. In many cases, they carry inventory (although this practice often duplicates functions of other channel members and is now declining). Customers include retailers, business buyers, and other wholesalers. Manufacturers of electrical supplies, such as Westinghouse Electric, and of plumbing supplies, such as American Standard, often have branch operations. Sales branches are also common in the lumber and automotive parts industries.

sales office A manufacturer-owned operation that provides services normally associated with agents

Sales offices are manufacturer-owned operations that provide services normally associated with agents. Like sales branches, they are located away from manufacturing plants; unlike branches, they carry no inventory. A manufacturer's sales office (or branch) may sell products that enhance the manufacturer's own product line. Companies such as Campbell Soup provide diverse services to their wholesale and retail customers. Hiram Walker, a liquor producer, imports wine from Spain to increase the number of products its sales offices can offer wholesalers.

Manufacturers may set up these branches or offices to reach their customers more effectively by performing wholesaling functions themselves. A manufacturer may also set up such a facility when specialized wholesaling services are not available through existing intermediaries. A manufacturer's performance of wholesaling and physical distribution activities through its sales branch or office may strengthen supply chain efficiency. In some situations, though, a manufacturer may bypass its sales office or branches entirely—for example, if the producer decides to serve large retailer customers directly.

The Nature of Physical Distribution

physical distribution Activities used to move products from producers to consumers and other end users

Physical distribution, also known as *logistics,* refers to the activities used to move products from producers to consumers and other end users. These activities include order processing, inventory management, materials handling, warehousing, and transportation. Planning an efficient physical distribution system is crucial to developing an effective marketing strategy because it can decrease costs and increase customer satisfaction. Speed of delivery, service, and dependability are often as important to customers as costs. Companies that have the right goods in the right place, at the right time, in the right quantity, and with the right support services are able to sell more than competitors that do not. For example, a construction equipment dealer with a low inventory of replacement parts requires fast, dependable service from component suppliers when it needs parts not in stock. Even when the demand for products is unpredictable, suppliers must be able to respond quickly to inventory needs. In such cases, physical distribution costs may be a minor consideration when compared with service, dependability, and timeliness.

Physical distribution deals with the physical movement and storage of products and supplies both within and among marketing channel members. Physical distribution systems must meet the needs of both the supply chain and customers. Distribution activities are thus an important part of supply chain planning and require the cooperation of all partners. Often one channel member manages physical distribution for all channel members.

Within the marketing channel, physical distribution activities may be performed by a producer, a wholesaler, or a retailer, or they may be outsourced. In the context of distribution, **outsourcing** is the contracting of physical distribution tasks to third parties that do not have managerial authority within the marketing channel. Most physical distribution activities can be outsourced to third-party firms that have special expertise in such areas as warehousing, transportation, and information technology. Cooperative relationships with third-party organizations, such as trucking companies, warehouses, and data-service providers, can help reduce marketing channel costs and boost service and customer satisfaction for all supply chain partners. For example, a number of e-businesses, as well as some traditional brick-and-mortar ones, have outsourced physical distribution activities, including shipping and warehousing, to build a supply chain of strategic partners to maximize customer service. Such relationships are increasingly being integrated in the supply chain to achieve physical distribution objectives. When choosing companies through which to outsource, marketers take care to use efficient firms that will help the outsourcing company provide excellent customer service.

outsourcing Contracting physical distribution tasks to third parties that do not have managerial authority within the marketing channel

◆ Physical Distribution Objectives

For most companies, the main objectives of physical distribution are to decrease costs and transit time while increasing customer service. However, few distribution systems achieve these goals in equal measure. The large inventories and rapid transportation necessary for good customer service drive up costs. Supply chain managers therefore strive for a reasonable balance among service, costs, and resources. They determine what level of customer service is acceptable and realistic, and then develop a "system" outlook to minimize total distribution costs and cycle time.

Meeting Standards of Customer Service. In physical distribution, availability, timeliness, and accuracy are important dimensions of customer service. Companies set customer service standards based on one or a combination of these three dimensions. *Availability* refers to the percentage of orders that can be filled directly from a company's existing inventory. For example, on average, catalog retailers fill 90.8 percent of their orders from their existing inventories. *Timeliness* refers to how quickly the product is shipped out to the customer. For example, some organizations set a service standard of shipping the product within 24 hours. *Accuracy* refers to whether the product the customer ordered is the product that is shipped to the customer. Some organizations have achieved better than a 99 percent order accuracy rate.[6]

Customers seeking a high level of customer service may also want sizable inventories, efficient order processing, availability of emergency shipments, progress reports, postsale services, prompt replacement of defective items, and warranties. Customers' inventory requirements influence the expected level of physical distribution service. Business customers seeking to reduce their inventory storage and shipping costs may expect wholesalers or third-party firms to take responsibility for maintaining inventory in the marketing channel or to assume the cost of premium transportation. Because service needs vary from customer to customer, companies must analyze, and adapt to, customer preferences. Attention to customer needs and preferences is crucial to increasing sales and obtaining repeat orders. Failure to provide the desired level of service may mean loss of customers.

Companies must also examine the service levels competitors offer and match or exceed those standards when the costs of providing the services are justified by the sales generated. Many companies guarantee service performance to win customers. Services are provided most effectively when service standards are developed and

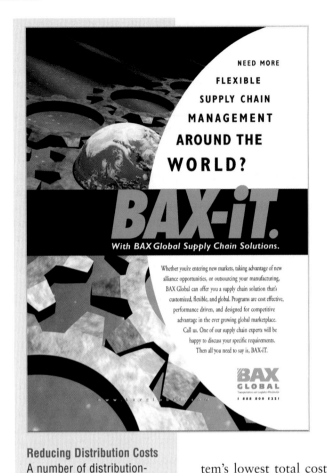

Reducing Distribution Costs
A number of distribution-related organizations help companies to improve efficiencies and to reduce costs.

stated in measurable terms, for example, "98 percent of all orders filled within 48 hours." Standards should be communicated clearly to both customers and employees, and diligently enforced. Many service standards outline delivery times and specify provisions for back-ordering, returning goods, and obtaining emergency shipments.

Reducing Total Distribution Costs. Although physical distribution managers try to minimize the costs associated with order processing, inventory management, materials handling, warehousing, and transportation, decreasing costs in one area often raises costs in another. Figure 16.3 shows the percentage of total costs that physical distribution functions represent. A total-cost approach to physical distribution enables managers to view physical distribution as a system rather than a collection of unrelated activities. This approach shifts the emphasis from lowering the separate costs of individual activities to minimizing overall distribution costs.

The total-cost approach involves analyzing the costs of all distribution alternatives, even those considered too impractical or expensive. Total-cost analyses weigh inventory levels against warehousing expenses, materials costs against various modes of transportation, and all distribution costs against customer service standards. Costs of potential sales losses from lower performance levels must also be considered. In many cases, accounting procedures and statistical methods are used to figure total costs. When hundreds of combinations of distribution variables are possible, computer simulations are helpful. A distribution system's lowest total cost is never the result of using a combination of the cheapest functions. Instead, it is the lowest overall cost compatible with the company's stated service objectives. For example, in the mid-1990s, Federated Department Stores created a separate division called Federated Logistics and Operations to coordinate merchandise distribution, logistics, and vendor technology across the company, including online retail operations and brick-and-mortar retail operations such as Burdine's, Macy's, Rich's/Lazarus, Bloomingdale's, Goldsmith's, Sterns, and The Bon Marché. Through this integrated physical distribution system, Federated has saved more than $150 million over the last five years.[7]

Figure 16.3 Proportional Cost of Each Physical Distribution Function as a Percentage of Total Distribution Costs
Source: Herbert W. Davis and Company/Establish, Inc., Ft. Lee. NJ. *Davis Database*, June 2004, **www.establishinc.com**. Reprinted by permission of Herbert W. Davis and Company/Establish, Inc. *Davis Database*, Copyright © 2004 by Herbert W. Davis and Company/Establish, Inc.

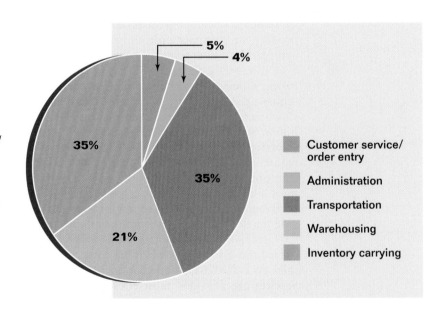

5%
4%
35%
35%
21%

Customer service/order entry
Administration
Transportation
Warehousing
Inventory carrying

Physical distribution managers must be sensitive to the issue of cost tradeoffs. Higher costs in one functional area of a distribution system may be necessary to achieve lower costs in another. Tradeoffs are strategic decisions to combine (and recombine) resources for greatest cost effectiveness. When distribution managers regard the system as a network of integrated functions, tradeoffs become useful tools in implementing a unified, cost-effective distribution strategy.

cycle time The time needed to complete a process

Reducing Cycle Time. Another important goal of physical distribution involves reducing **cycle time**, the time needed to complete a process. Doing so can reduce costs and/or increase customer service. Many companies, particularly manufacturers, overnight delivery firms, major news media, and publishers of books of current interest, are using cycle time reduction to gain a competitive advantage. FedEx believes so strongly in this concept that, in the interest of being the fastest provider of overnight delivery, it conducts research on reducing cycle time and identifying new management techniques and procedures for its employees. Seattle's Boeing Company is considering the construction of a plant to be run by two major suppliers and built next to Boeing's proposed 7E7 assembly plant. The plant would assemble about 75 percent of the 7E7's fuselage and deliver it to Boeing's final assembly plant next door. This arrangement not only would reduce cycle time but would save transportation costs on large pieces.[8]

◆ Functions of Physical Distribution

As we saw earlier, physical distribution includes the activities necessary to get products from producers to customers. In this section we take a closer look at these activities, which include order processing, inventory management, materials handling, warehousing, and transportation.

order processing The receipt and transmission of sales order information

Order Processing. **Order processing** is the receipt and transmission of sales order information. Although management sometimes overlooks the importance of these activities, efficient order processing facilitates product flow. Computerized order processing provides a database for all supply chain members to increase their productivity. When carried out quickly and accurately, order processing contributes to customer satisfaction, decreased costs and cycle time, and increased profits.

Order processing entails three main tasks: order entry, order handling, and order delivery. Order entry begins when customers or salespeople place purchase orders via telephone, mail, e-mail, or website. Electronic ordering is less time consuming than a manual, paper-based ordering system and reduces costs. In some companies, sales representatives receive and enter orders personally, handle complaints, prepare progress reports, and forward sales order information.

Order accuracy: up
Fulfillment time: down

"Voice directed picking combined with a smart conveying and sorting network speeds up the fulfillment process and dramatically increases order accuracy."

Tim Beauchamp, Senior Vice President of Distribution Operations for Corporate Express

When Corporate Express needed a high productivity order fulfillment system, Siemens provided an integrated solution consisting of a conveying and sorting system, powerful zone routing software and voice directed picking. The system allows Corporate Express to ship 100,000 orders overnight with greater than 99.95% accuracy.

One Source system solutions:
· Supply Chain Management Services
· WMS, WCS and Material Flow Software
· RFID Integration
· Voice and Light directed Order Fulfillment
· Package Conveyor and Sortation
· Pallet Conveyor and Robotic Palletizing
· AS/RS and AGVS
· Assembly Conveyor
· 24/7 Technical Support

Siemens
Logistics and Assembly Systems
1-877-725-7500
www.usa.siemens-dematic.com

SIEMENS

Improving Order Processing
A number of organizations provide both hardware and software to improve order processing by making it more accurate and efficient.

Order handling involves several tasks. Once an order is entered, it is transmitted to a warehouse, where product availability is verified, and to the credit department, where prices, terms, and the customer's credit rating are checked. If the credit department approves the purchase, warehouse personnel (sometimes assisted by automated equipment) pick and assemble the order. If the requested product is not in stock, a production order is sent to the factory or the customer is offered a substitute.

When the order has been assembled and packed for shipment, the warehouse schedules delivery with an appropriate carrier. If the customer pays for rush service, overnight delivery by FedEx, UPS, or another overnight carrier is used. The customer is sent an invoice, inventory records are adjusted, and the order is delivered.

Whether to use a manual or an electronic order-processing system depends on which method provides the greater speed and accuracy within cost limits. Manual processing suffices for small-volume orders and is more flexible in certain situations. Most companies, however, use **electronic data interchange (EDI)**, which uses computer technology to integrate order processing with production, inventory, accounting, and transportation. Within the supply chain, EDI functions as an information system that links marketing channel members and outsourcing firms together. It reduces paperwork for all members of the supply chain and allows them to share information on invoices, orders, payments, inquiries, and scheduling. Consequently many companies have pushed their suppliers toward EDI to reduce distribution costs and cycle times. For example, Dobbs, an airline food service company, has all its merchandising vendors on EDI systems and requests that all other suppliers be EDI-capable. FedEx uses EDI systems to develop innovative solutions to resolve some of its complex business problems. In addition, a large proportion of FedEx's major business customers carry out transactions via EDI.[9]

electronic data interchange (EDI) A computerized means of integrating order processing with production, inventory, accounting, and transportation

inventory management Developing and maintaining adequate assortments of products to meet customers' needs

Inventory Management. **Inventory management** involves developing and maintaining adequate assortments of products to meet customers' needs. Because a firm's investment in inventory usually represents a significant portion of its total assets, inventory decisions have a major impact on physical distribution costs and the level of customer service provided. When too few products are carried in inventory, the result is *stockouts*, or shortages of products, which in turn result in brand switching, lower sales, and loss of customers. When too many products (or too many slow-moving products) are carried, costs increase, as do risks of product obsolescence, pilferage, and damage. The objective of inventory management is to minimize inventory costs while maintaining an adequate supply of goods to satisfy customers. To achieve this objective, marketers focus on two major issues: when to order and how much to order. As discussed in the Tech Know boxed feature, some organizations, like JC Penney, contract with other organizations to help them achieve this inventory management objective.

To determine when to order, a marketer calculates the *reorder point*, the inventory level that signals the

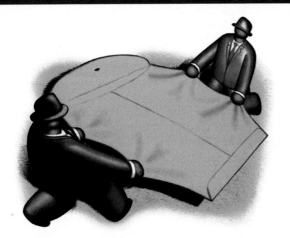

Jump to Better Inventory Control

The Paradies Shops turns inventory 25% faster with GERS

GERS' Enterprise1 merchandising application facilitates more defined merchandising strategies, enabling The Paradies Shops to maximize profits by geographic area. Analytical inventory and sales information provides views to high volume movers and profitable items, ensuring in-stock positions, high margins, and optimal returns on their inventory investment.

Over 400 retailers have implemented GERS to improve their business performance.

So, what are you waiting for?
www.gers.com / 800.854.2263

GERS
The Right Decision
RIGHT NOW

Inventory Management
GERS is a software program that helps retail organizations to more effectively manage their inventories.

need to place a new order. To calculate the reorder point, the marketer must know the order lead time, the usage rate, and the amount of safety stock required. The *order lead time* refers to the average time lapse between placing the order and receiving it. The *usage rate* is the rate at which a product's inventory is used or sold during a specific time period. *Safety stock* is the amount of extra inventory a firm keeps to guard against stockouts resulting from above-average usage rates and/or longer-than-expected lead times. The reorder point can be calculated using the following formula:

$$\text{Reorder Point} = (\text{Order Lead Time} \times \text{Usage Rate}) + \text{Safety Stock}$$

Thus, if order lead time is 10 days, usage rate is 3 units per day, and safety stock is 20 units, the reorder point is 50 units.

just-in-time (JIT) An inventory management approach in which supplies arrive just when needed for production or resale

Efficient inventory management with accurate reorder points is crucial for firms that use a **just-in-time (JIT)** approach, in which supplies arrive just as they are needed for use in production or for resale. When using JIT, companies maintain low inventory levels and purchase products and materials in small quantities whenever they need them. Usually there is no safety stock, and suppliers are expected to provide consistently high-quality products. Just-in-time inventory management requires a high level of coordination between producers and suppliers, but it eliminates waste and reduces inventory costs significantly. This approach has been used successfully by many well-known firms, including DaimlerChrysler, Harley-Davidson, and Dell Computer, to reduce costs and boost customer satisfaction. When a JIT approach is used in a supply chain, suppliers often move close to their customers.

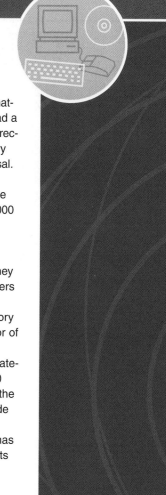

TECH KNOW

TAL Manages JCPenney Shirt Inventory

At one time, JCPenney was so concerned about stockouts of its private-brand men's dress shirts that the department store held nine months of safety stock. If customer demand for its shirts suddenly skyrocketed, Penney would be ready. On the other hand, if one or more shirt styles fell out of fashion, Penney would still have plenty of inventory to sell. In short, the retailer's management of dress-shirt inventory was both inefficient and expensive.

Then Harry Lee of TAL Apparel stepped up with a bold suggestion. Lee is managing director of the Hong Kong manufacturer that supplies Penney with private-brand clothing. TAL's factories turn out 50 million apparel products every year under private brands for retailers such as Penney, Brooks Brothers, and L. L. Bean. They also produce garments under manufacturers' brands such as Liz Claiborne, Tommy Hilfiger, and Calvin Klein. In fact, 12 percent of all dress shirts sold in the United States come from TAL's factories.

Lee's proposal was to have TAL manage Penney's dress-shirt inventory on a just-in-time basis. He suggested shipping shirts directly to each store instead of sending large shipments to the retailer's warehouses. His argument was that TAL could respond quickly to store sales trends and keep costs down by eliminating the need for safety stock. Because Penney had a long-standing relationship with the company and recognized the potential savings from better inventory management, it eventually accepted Lee's proposal. TAL worked for a year to develop an automated reordering system. After a successful test with one store, the system was expanded to more than 1,000 Penney stores.

Next, Lee suggested that his company take over responsibility for forecasting sales of the retailer's private-brand shirts, and Penney again agreed. Now TAL programmers analyze a steady stream of sales data to determine the best inventory level for each style, size, and color of shirt in every store. Penney also relies on TAL to develop new private-brand shirt styles, test them in 50 Penney stores, and choose only the best-selling products for chainwide introduction. With TAL effectively managing its inventory, Penney has the right assortment of dress shirts in stock at the right time.

materials handling Physical handling of products

Materials Handling. **Materials handling,** the physical handling of products, is an important factor in warehouse operations, as well as in transportation from points of production to points of consumption. Efficient procedures and techniques for materials handling minimize inventory management costs, reduce the number of times a good is handled, improve customer service, and increase customer satisfaction. Systems for packaging, labeling, loading, and movement must be coordinated to maximize cost reduction and customer satisfaction.

Product characteristics often determine handling. For example, the characteristics of bulk liquids and gases determine how they can be moved and stored. Internal packaging is also an important consideration in materials handling; goods must be packaged correctly to prevent damage or breakage during handling and transportation. Most companies employ packaging consultants to help them decide which packaging materials and methods will result in the most efficient handling.

Unit loading and containerization are two common methods used in materials handling. With *unit loading,* one or more boxes are placed on a pallet or skid; these units can then be efficiently loaded by mechanical means such as forklifts, trucks, or conveyer systems. *Containerization* is the consolidation of many items into a single large container, which is sealed at its point of origin and opened at its destination. Containers are usually 8 feet wide, 8 feet high, and 10 to 40 feet long. They can be conveniently stacked and shipped via train, barge, or ship. Once containers reach their destinations, wheel assemblies can be added to make them suitable for ground transportation. Because individual items are not handled in transit, containerization greatly increases efficiency and security in shipping.

warehousing The design and operation of facilities for storing and moving goods

Warehousing. **Warehousing,** the design and operation of facilities for storing and moving goods, is another important physical distribution function. Warehousing provides time utility by enabling firms to compensate for dissimilar production and consumption rates. When mass production creates a greater stock of goods than can be sold immediately, companies may warehouse the surplus until customers are ready to buy. Warehousing also helps stabilize prices and availability of seasonal items.

Warehousing is not simply the storage of products. The basic distribution functions warehouses perform include receiving, identifying, sorting, and dispatching goods to storage; holding goods in storage until needed; recalling and assembling stored goods for shipment; and dispatching shipments. When warehouses receive goods by carloads or truckloads, they break down the shipments into smaller quantities for individual customers.

The choice of warehouse facilities is an important strategic consideration. The right type of warehouse allows a company to reduce transportation and inventory costs or improve service to customers. The wrong type of warehouse may drain company resources. Beyond deciding how many facilities to operate and where to locate them, a company must determine which type of warehouse is most appropriate. Warehouses fall into two general categories: private and public. In many cases, a combination of private and public facilities provides the most flexible warehousing approach.

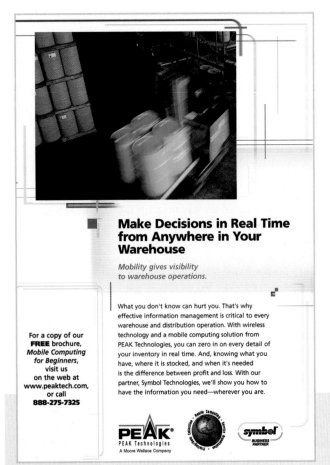

Make Decisions in Real Time from Anywhere in Your Warehouse

Mobility gives visibility to warehouse operations.

What you don't know can hurt you. That's why effective information management is critical to every warehouse and distribution operation. With wireless technology and a mobile computing solution from PEAK Technologies, you can zero in on every detail of your inventory in real time. And, knowing what you have, where it is stocked, and when it's needed is the difference between profit and loss. With our partner, Symbol Technologies, we'll show you how to have the information you need—wherever you are.

For a copy of our **FREE** brochure, *Mobile Computing for Beginners,* visit us on the web at www.peaktech.com, or call **888-275-7325**

PEAK®
PEAK Technologies
A Moore Wallace Company

symbol®
BUSINESS PARTNER

Warehousing
Specialized information technology is helping managers to operate warehouses more efficiently.

private warehouse A company-operated facility for storing and shipping products

Companies operate **private warehouses** for storing and shipping their own products. A firm usually leases or purchases a private warehouse when its warehousing needs in a given geographic market are substantial and stable enough to warrant a long-term commitment to a fixed facility. Private warehouses are also appropriate for firms that require special handling and storage and that want control of warehouse design and operation. Retailers such as Sears, Radio Shack, and Kmart find it economical to integrate private warehousing with purchasing and distribution for their retail outlets. When sales volumes are fairly stable, ownership and control of a private warehouse may provide benefits such as property appreciation. Private warehouses, however, face fixed costs such as insurance, taxes, maintenance, and debt expense. They also limit flexibility when firms wish to move inventories to more strategic locations. Before tying up capital in a private warehouse or entering into a long-term lease, a company should consider its resources, level of expertise in warehouse management, and the role of the warehouse in its overall marketing strategy. Many private warehouses are being eliminated by direct links between producers and customers, reduced cycle times, and outsourcing to public warehouses.

public warehouse A business that leases storage space and related physical distribution facilities to other firms

Public warehouses lease storage space and related physical distribution facilities as an outsource service to other companies. They sometimes provide such distribution services as receiving, unloading, inspecting, and reshipping products; filling orders; providing financing; displaying products; and coordinating shipments. Unified Facilities, Inc., for example, offers a wide range of services, including mixing inventory received from different places to consolidate shipments to customers as well as packaging, filling, painting, assembly, and in-store setup, and corporate services such as purchasing, programming, writing, and order fulfillment.[10] Public warehouses are especially useful to firms that have seasonal production or low-volume storage needs, have inventories that must be maintained in many locations, are testing or entering new markets, or own private warehouses but occasionally require additional storage space. Public warehouses also serve as collection points during product recall programs. Whereas private warehouses have fixed costs, public warehouses offer variable (and often lower) costs because users rent space and purchase warehousing services only as needed.

Many public warehouses furnish security for products being used as collateral for loans, a service provided at either the warehouse or the site of the owner's inventory. *Field public warehouses* are established by public warehouses at the owner's inventory location. The warehouser becomes custodian of the products and issues a receipt that can be used as collateral for a loan. Public warehouses also provide *bonded storage*, a warehousing arrangement in which imported or taxable products are not released until the products' owners pay U.S. customs duties, taxes, or other fees. Bonded warehouses enable firms to defer tax payments on such items until they are delivered to customers.

distribution center A large, centralized warehouse that focuses on moving rather than storing goods

Distribution centers are large, centralized warehouses that receive goods from factories and suppliers, regroup them into orders, and ship them to customers quickly; their focus is on movement of goods rather than storage.[11] Distribution centers are specially designed for rapid flow of products. They are usually one-story buildings (to eliminate elevators) with access to transportation networks such as major highways or railway lines. Many distribution centers are highly automated, with computer-directed robots, forklifts, and hoists that collect and move products to loading docks. Although some public warehouses offer such specialized services, most distribution centers are privately owned. They serve customers in regional markets and, in some cases, function as consolidation points for a company's branch warehouses. Distribution centers typically are located within 500 miles of half of a company's market.

Distribution centers offer several benefits, the most important being improved customer service. Distribution centers ensure product availability by maintaining full product lines, and the speed of their operations cuts delivery time to a minimum. Distribution centers also reduce costs. Instead of making many smaller shipments to scattered warehouses and customers, factories ship large quantities of goods directly to distribution centers at bulk rates, thus lowering transportation costs. Furthermore, rapid inventory turnover lessens the need for warehouses and cuts storage costs. Federated Department Stores serves more than 400 stores through seven distribution centers, including two in New Jersey, two in California, and one each in Florida, Georgia, and Washington.[12] Some distribution centers facilitate production by receiving and consolidating raw materials and providing final assembly for certain products.

transportation The movement of products from where they are made to where they are used

Transportation. **Transportation,** the movement of products from where they are made to where they are used, is the most expensive physical distribution function. Because product availability and timely deliveries depend on transportation functions, transportation decisions directly affect customer service. A firm may even build its distribution and marketing strategy around a unique transportation system if that system can ensure on-time deliveries and thereby give the firm a competitive edge. Companies may build their own transportation fleets (private carriers) or outsource the transportation function to a common or contract carrier.

Transportation Modes   There are five basic transportation modes for moving physical goods: railroads, trucks, waterways, airways, and pipelines. Each mode offers distinct advantages. Many companies adopt physical handling procedures that facilitate the use of two or more modes in combination. Figure 16.4 indicates the percentage of intercity freight carried by each transportation mode; Table 16.4 shows typical transportation modes for various products.

Railroads such as Union Pacific and Canadian National carry heavy, bulky freight that must be shipped long distances overland. Railroads commonly haul minerals, sand, lumber, chemicals, and farm products, as well as low-value manufactured goods and an increasing number of automobiles. They are especially efficient for transporting full carloads, which can be shipped at lower rates than smaller quantities because they require less handling. Many companies locate factories or warehouses near major rail lines or on spur lines for convenient loading and unloading.

Trucks provide the most flexible schedules and routes of all major transportation modes because they can go almost anywhere. Because trucks have a unique ability to move goods directly from factory or warehouse to customer, they are often used in conjunction with other forms of transport that cannot provide door-to-door deliveries. Although trucks usually travel much faster than trains, they are more expensive and somewhat more vulnerable to bad weather. They are also subject to size and weight restrictions on the products they carry. Trucks are sometimes criticized for

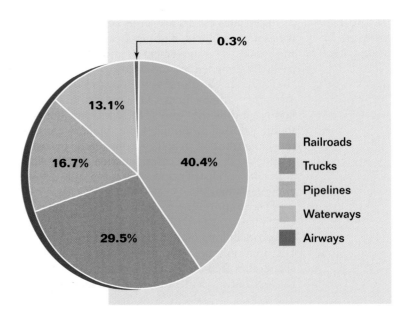

Figure 16.4 Proportion of Intercity Freight Carried by Various Transportation Modes
Source: Bureau of the Census, *Statistical Abstract of the United States* (Washington, DC: Government Printing Office, 2002), p. 658.

Table 16.4	**Typical Transportation Modes for Various Products**			
Railroads	**Trucks**	**Waterways**	**Airways**	**Pipelines**
Coal	Clothing	Petroleum	Flowers	Oil
Grain	Paper goods	Chemicals	Perishable food	Processed coal
Chemicals	Computers	Iron ore	Instruments	Natural gas
Lumber	Books	Bauxite	Emergency parts	Water
Automobiles	Livestock	Grain	Overnight mail	Chemicals
Steel				

high levels of loss and damage to freight and for delays caused by rehandling small shipments. In response, the trucking industry has turned to computerized tracking of shipments and the development of new equipment to speed loading and unloading. Marten Transport Ltd. in Wisconsin charges its customers for the time drivers have to wait and rewards clients that help keep things moving. Using a satellite-tracking system, the company can track when a driver arrives at a site and how long it takes to load and unload freight. The data are shared with customers, and Marten and its customers work together to eliminate wasteful practices. Marten has lost customers, but has also reduced rates to others who have expedited loading and unloading.[13]

Waterways are the cheapest method of shipping heavy, low-value, nonperishable goods such as ore, coal, grain, and petroleum products. Water carriers offer considerable capacity. Powered by tugboats and towboats, barges that travel along intercoastal canals, inland rivers, and navigation systems can haul at least ten times the weight of one rail car, and oceangoing vessels can haul thousands of containers. However, many markets are inaccessible by water transportation unless supplemented by rail or truck. Furthermore, water transport is extremely slow and sometimes comes to a standstill during freezing weather. Companies depending on waterways may ship their entire inventory during the summer and then store it for winter use. Droughts and floods also create difficulties for users of inland waterway transportation. Nevertheless, the extreme fuel efficiency of water transportation and the continuing globalization of marketing will likely increase its use in the future.

Air transportation is the fastest but most expensive form of shipping. It is used most often for perishable goods; for high-value, low-bulk items; and for products requiring quick delivery over long distances, such as emergency shipments. Some air carriers transport combinations of passengers, freight, and mail. Despite its expense, air transit can reduce warehousing and packaging costs and losses from theft and damage, thus helping to lower total costs (but truck transportation needed for pickup and final delivery adds to cost and transit time). Although air transport accounts for less than 1 percent of total ton-miles carried, its importance as a mode of transportation is growing. In fact, the success of many businesses is now based on the availability of overnight air delivery service provided by such organizations as UPS, DHL Airborne, FedEx, RPS Air, and the U.S. Postal Service. Amazon.com, for example, ships via UPS many products ordered online within a day of order. In addition, a number of companies are turning to air freight because they are ordering smaller quantities more frequently and requiring high-speed transportation in an effort to reduce inventory costs.[14]

Trucking
A number of transportation services are provided through trucks.

Pipelines, the most highly automated transportation mode, usually belong to the shipper and carry the shipper's products. Most pipelines carry petroleum products or chemicals. The Trans-Alaska Pipeline, owned and operated by a consortium of oil companies that includes Exxon, Mobil, and BP-Amoco, transports crude oil from remote oil-drilling sites in central Alaska to shipping terminals on the coast. Slurry pipelines carry pulverized coal, grain, or wood chips suspended in water. Pipelines move products slowly but continuously and at relatively low cost. They are dependable and minimize the problems of product damage and theft. However, contents are subject to as much as 1 percent shrinkage, usually from evaporation. Pipelines have also been a concern to environmentalists, who fear installation and leaks could harm plants and animals.

Choosing Transportation Modes   Distribution managers select a transportation mode based on the combination of cost, speed, dependability, load flexibility, accessibility, and frequency that is most appropriate for their products and generates the desired level of customer service. Table 16.5 shows relative ratings of each transportation mode by these selection criteria.

Marketers compare alternative transportation modes to determine whether benefits from a more expensive mode are worth higher costs. Air freight carriers such as FedEx promise many benefits, such as speed and dependability, but at much higher costs than other transportation modes. When such benefits are less important, marketers prefer lower costs. Bicycles, for instance, are often shipped by rail because an unassembled bicycle can be shipped more than 1,000 miles on a train for as little as $3.60. Bicycle wholesalers plan purchases far enough in advance to capitalize on this cost advantage. Companies such as Accuship can assist marketers in analyzing a variety of transportation options. This Internet firm's software gives corporate users, such as Coca-Cola and the Home Shopping Network, information about the speed and cost of different transportation modes and allows them to order shipping and then track shipments online. Accuship processes nearly 1 million shipments every day.[15]

Speed is measured by the total time a carrier has possession of goods, including the time required for pickup and delivery, handling, and movement between points of origin and destination. Speed obviously affects a marketer's ability to provide service, but other, less obvious implications are important as well. Marketers take advantage of transit time to process orders for goods en route, a capability especially important to agricultural and raw materials shippers. Some railroads also let carloads in transit be redirected for maximum flexibility in selecting markets. A carload of peaches, for instance, may be shipped to a closer destination if the fruit is in danger of ripening too quickly.

Dependability of a transportation mode is determined by the consistency of service provided. Marketers must be able to count on carriers to deliver goods on time and in an acceptable condition. Along with speed, dependability affects a marketer's inventory costs, including sales lost when merchandise is not available. Undependable transportation necessitates higher inventory levels to avoid stockouts, whereas

Table 16.5	Relative Ratings of Transportation Modes by Selection Criteria					
Mode	**Cost**	**Speed**	**Dependability**	**Load Flexibility**	**Accessibility**	**Frequency**
Railroads	Moderate	Average	Average	High	High	Low
Trucks	High	Fast	High	Average	Very high	High
Waterways	Very low	Very slow	Average	Very high	Limited	Very low
Airways	Very high	Very fast	High	Low	Average	Average
Pipelines	Low	Slow	High	Very low	Very limited	Very high

reliable delivery service enables customers to carry smaller inventories at lower cost. Security problems vary considerably among transportation modes and are a major consideration in carrier selection. A firm does not incur costs directly when goods are lost or damaged because the carrier is usually held liable. Nevertheless, poor service and lack of security indirectly lead to increased costs and lower profits because damaged or lost goods are unavailable for immediate sale or use.

Load flexibility is the degree to which a transportation mode can provide appropriate equipment and conditions for moving specific kinds of goods and can be adapted for moving other products. Many products must be shipped under controlled temperature and humidity. Other products, such as liquids or gases, require special equipment or facilities for shipment. A marketer with unusual transport needs can consult the *Official Railway Equipment Register,* which lists the various types of cars and equipment each railroad owns. As Table 16.5 shows, waterways and railroads have the highest load flexibility, whereas pipelines have the lowest.

Accessibility refers to a carrier's ability to move goods over a specific route or network. For example, marketers evaluating transportation modes for reaching Great Falls, Montana, would consider rail lines, truck routes, and scheduled airline service but would eliminate water-borne carriers because Great Falls is inaccessible by water. Some carriers differentiate themselves by serving areas their competitors do not. After deregulation, many large railroad companies sold off or abandoned unprofitable routes, making rail service inaccessible to facilities located on spur lines. Some marketers were forced to buy or lease their own truck fleets to get their products to market. In recent years, small, short-line railroad companies have started buying up track and creating networks of low-cost feeder lines to reach underserved markets.

Frequency refers to how often a company can send shipments by a specific transportation mode. When using pipelines, shipments can be continuous. A marketer shipping by railroad or waterway is limited by the carriers' schedules.

intermodal transportation
Two or more transportation modes used in combination

freight forwarder An organization that consolidates shipments from several firms into efficient lot sizes

Coordinating Transportation   To take advantage of the benefits offered by various transportation modes and compensate for deficiencies, marketers often combine and coordinate two or more modes. In recent years, **intermodal transportation**, as this integrated approach is sometimes called, has been facilitated by new developments within the transportation industry.

Several kinds of intermodal shipping are available. All combine the flexibility of trucking with the low cost or speed of other forms of transport. Containerization facilitates intermodal transportation by consolidating shipments into sealed containers for transport by *piggyback* (shipping that uses both truck trailers and railway flatcars), *fishyback* (truck trailers and water carriers), and *birdyback* (truck trailers and air carriers). As transportation costs have increased, intermodal shipping has gained popularity.

Specialized outsource agencies provide other forms of transport coordination. Known as **freight forwarders**, these firms combine shipments from several organizations into efficient lot sizes. Small loads (less than 500 pounds) are much more expensive to ship than full carloads or truckloads, which frequently requires consolidation. Freight

FedEx ships ocean?
Absolutely.

Wherever in the world you trade, FedEx Trade Networks can get you there with competitive ocean transportation. Whether it is full-container-load or less-than-container-load, FedEx Trade Networks connects you to major world markets with a complete line of transportation solutions. Worried about competitive ocean rates and flexible transit times? **Relax, it's FedEx..**

ftn.fedex.com   1.800.715.4045

©2003 FedEx

FedEx
Trade Networks

Intermodal Transportation
A number of organizations, like FedEx, have intermodal transportation capabilities.

forwarders take small loads from various marketers, buy transport space from carriers, and arrange for goods to be delivered to buyers. Freight forwarders' profits come from the margin between the higher, less-than-carload rates they charge each marketer and the lower carload rates they themselves pay. Because large shipments require less handling, use of freight forwarders can speed delivery. Freight forwarders can also determine the most efficient carriers and routes. They are useful for shipping goods to foreign markets because freight forwarders know how to clear customs, pay duties, and handle the necessary paperwork. Some companies prefer to outsource their shipping to freight forwarders because the latter provide door-to-door services.

megacarrier A freight transportation firm that provides several modes of shipment

Another transportation innovation is the development of **megacarriers**, freight transportation companies that offer several shipment methods, including rail, truck, and air service. CSX, for example, has trains, barges, container ships, trucks, and pipelines, thus offering a multitude of transportation services. In addition, air carriers have increased their ground transportation services. As they expand the range of transportation alternatives, carriers too put greater stress on customer service.

◆ Strategic Issues in Physical Distribution

The physical distribution functions discussed in this chapter—order processing, inventory management, materials handling, warehousing, and transportation—account for about half of all marketing costs. Whether performed by a producer, wholesaler, or retailer, or outsourced to some other firm, these functions have a significant impact on customer service and satisfaction, which are of primary importance to all members of the supply chain.

Strategic Physical Distribution
Many organizations incorporate physical distribution functions into their marketing strategies. These efforts are facilitated by a number of information technology-related software and hardware products.

The strategic importance of physical distribution is evident in all elements of the marketing mix. Product design and packaging must allow for efficient stacking, storage, transport, and tracking. Differentiating products by size, color, and style must take into account additional demands placed on warehousing and shipping facilities. Competitive pricing may depend on a firm's ability to provide reliable delivery or emergency shipments of replacement parts. Firms trying to lower inventory costs may offer quantity discounts to encourage large purchases. Promotional campaigns must be coordinated with distribution functions so that advertised products are available to buyers and order-processing departments can handle additional sales orders efficiently. Channel members must consider warehousing and transportation costs, which may influence a firm's policy on stockouts or its decision to centralize (or decentralize) inventory. Consider how OshKosh B'Gosh improved its inventory management and reduced its costs, as discussed in the Global Marketing boxed feature.

Improving physical distribution starts by closing the gap with customers. The entire supply chain must understand and meet customers' requirements. An effective way to improve physical distribution is to integrate processes across the boundaries of all members of the supply chain. The full scope of the physical distribution process includes suppliers, manufacturers, wholesalers, retailers, transportation firms, and warehouses. To work well, the process requires a formal, integrated plan to balance supply and demand within a defined time period. Physical distribution can also be improved by developing cooperative relationships with suppliers of component parts and services. These relationships should emphasize joint improvement. Cooperation can be enhanced through information technology that allows channel partners to work together to plan production and physical distribution activities; improve the efficiency and safety of product handling and movement; and reduce waste and costs for the benefit of all channel members, including the customer.

No single distribution system is ideal for all situations, and any system must be evaluated continually and adapted as necessary. Pressures to adjust service levels or to reduce costs may lead to a total restructuring of supply chain relationships. The ensuing changes in transportation, warehousing, materials handling, and inventory may affect speed of delivery, reliability, and economy of service. Recognizing that changes in any major distribution function may affect all other functions, marketing strategists consider customers' changing needs and preferences. Customer-oriented marketers analyze the characteristics of their target markets and plan distribution systems to provide products in the right place, at the right time, and at acceptable costs.

GLOBAL MARKETING

How OshKosh B'Gosh Brings Bib Overalls from Abroad

OshKosh B'Gosh has been known for making sturdy bib overalls since 1895. Employees originally cut and assembled the overalls in the company's hometown of OshKosh, Wisconsin. In recent years, however, OshKosh B'Gosh, like many U.S.-based apparel firms, has reduced domestic production in favor of clothing made in overseas factories. This shift has caused the company to rethink how it coordinates the different modes of transportation used to bring bib overalls (and more) from abroad.

When OshKosh B'Gosh first began importing, it had clothing packed into containers, loaded onto ships, and sent to U.S. ports. An outside logistics firm then ushered the sealed containers through customs and put them on trucks bound for the company's distribution centers. Between crowded ports and weekday-only working hours, containers that arrived by ship on a Thursday might sit untouched until Monday. However, especially during periods of peak demand, OshKosh B'Gosh needed stock replenished as quickly as possible. Even a few days' delay in getting products to distribution centers and into the store network could be costly in terms of lost sales and profits.

As its volume of imports increased, the company hired a logistics specialist, Averitt Express, to speed shipments from the ports to the distribution centers. Averitt learned that the shipping lines had crews available to offload containers both nights and weekends, although they rarely publicized the

service. Therefore, Averitt arranged a Thursday-to-Sunday schedule for offloading OshKosh B'Gosh's containers at three ports: Charleston, South Carolina; Gulfport, Mississippi; and Long Beach, California. Rather than transport the containers intact from the ports, Averitt began sorting the contents into separate trailers for each distribution center and sending them on by truck.

Now OshKosh B'Gosh receives its imported products six days sooner and pays less for water transportation because the containers remain at the port. Moreover, it can check the status of every container immediately to find out which are still at sea, which have arrived at the port, which have been cleared through customs, and which have been emptied. With millions of dollars in global sales at stake, OshKosh B'Gosh is in a better position to manage the flow of goods into its distribution centers and, ultimately, to the racks in retail locations.

SUMMARY

Wholesaling consists of all transactions in which products are bought for resale, for making other products, or for general business operations. Wholesalers are individuals or organizations that facilitate and expedite exchanges that are primarily wholesale transactions. For producers, wholesalers are a source of financial assistance and information; by performing specialized accumulation and allocation functions, they allow producers to concentrate on manufacturing products. Wholesalers provide retailers with buying expertise, wide product lines, efficient distribution, and warehousing and storage.

Merchant wholesalers are independently owned businesses that take title to goods and assume ownership risks. They are either full-service wholesalers, offering the widest possible range of wholesaling functions, or limited-service wholesalers, providing only some marketing services and specializing in a few functions. Full-service merchant wholesalers include general-merchandise wholesalers, which offer a wide but relatively shallow product mix; limited-line wholesalers, which offer extensive assortments within a few product lines; specialty-line wholesalers, which carry only a single product line or a few items within a line; and rack jobbers, which own and service display racks in supermarkets and other stores. Limited-service merchant wholesalers include cash-and-carry wholesalers, which sell to small businesses, require payment in cash, and do not deliver; truck wholesalers, which sell a limited line of products from their own trucks directly to customers; drop shippers, which own goods and negotiate sales but never take possession of products; and mail-order wholesalers, which sell to retail and business buyers through direct-mail catalogs.

Agents and brokers, sometimes called functional middlemen, negotiate purchases and expedite sales in exchange for a commission, but they do not take title to products. Usually specializing in certain products, they can provide valuable sales expertise. Whereas agents represent buyers or sellers on a permanent basis, brokers are intermediaries that buyers and sellers employ on a temporary basis to negotiate exchanges. Manufacturers' agents offer customers the complete product lines of two or more sellers. Selling agents market a complete product line or a producer's entire output and perform every wholesaling function except taking title to products. Commission merchants are agents that receive goods on consignment from local sellers and negotiate sales in large, central markets.

Manufacturers' sales branches and offices are owned by manufacturers. Sales branches sell products and provide support services for the manufacturer's sales force in a given location. Sales offices carry no inventory and function much as agents do.

Physical distribution, or logistics, refers to the activities used to move products from producers to customers and other end users. These activities include order processing, inventory management, materials handling, warehousing, and transportation. An efficient physical distribution system is an important component of an overall marketing strategy because it can decrease costs and increase customer satisfaction. Within the marketing channel, physical distribution activities are often performed by a wholesaler, but they may be performed by a producer or retailer, or outsourced to a third party.

The main objectives of physical distribution are to decrease costs and transit time while increasing customer service. Physical distribution managers strive to balance service, distribution costs, and resources. Because customers' service needs vary, companies must adapt to them. They must also offer service comparable to or better than competitors' and develop and communicate desirable customer service policies. Costs of providing service are minimized most effectively through the total-cost approach, which evaluates costs of the distribution system as a whole rather than as a collection of separate activities. Reducing cycle time, the time required to complete a process, is also important.

Order processing is the receipt and transmission of sales order information. It consists of three main tasks. Order entry begins when customers or salespeople place purchase orders by mail, e-mail, telephone, or computer. Order handling involves verifying product availability, checking customer credit, and preparing products for shipping. Order delivery is provided by the carrier most suitable for a desired level of customer service. Order processing can be done manually, but it is usually accomplished through electronic data interchange (EDI), a computerized system that integrates order processing with production, inventory, accounting, and transportation.

The objective of inventory management is to minimize inventory costs while maintaining a supply of goods adequate for customers' needs. To avoid stockouts without tying up too much capital in inventory, firms must have systematic methods for determining a reorder point, the inventory level that signals the need to place a new order. When firms use the just-in-time approach, products arrive just as they are needed for use in production or resale.

Materials handling, the physical handling of products, is an important factor in warehouse operations, as well as in transportation from points of production to points of consumption. Systems for packaging, labeling, loading, and movement must be coordinated to maximize cost reduction and customer satisfaction. Basic handling systems include unit loading, which entails placing boxes on pallets or skids and using mechanical devices to move them, and containerization.

Warehousing involves the design and operation of facilities for storing and moving goods. Private warehouses are operated by companies for the purpose of distributing their own products. Public warehouses are businesses that lease storage space and related physical distribution facilities to other firms. Distribution centers are large, centralized warehouses specially designed for rapid movement of goods to customers. In many cases, a combination of private and public facilities is the most flexible warehousing approach.

Transportation adds time and place utility to a product by moving it from where it is made to where it is purchased and used. The basic modes of transporting goods are railroads, trucks, waterways, airways, and pipelines. The criteria marketers use when selecting a transportation mode are cost, speed, dependability, load flexibility, accessibility, and frequency. Intermodal transportation allows marketers to combine advantages of two or more modes of transport. Freight forwarders coordinate transport by combining small shipments from several organi-

zations into efficient lot sizes, while megacarriers offer several shipment methods.

Physical distribution functions account for about half of all marketing costs and have a significant impact on customer satisfaction. Effective marketers are therefore actively involved in the design and control of physical distribution systems. Physical distribution affects every element of the marketing mix: product, price, promotion, and distribution. To satisfy customers, marketers consider customers' changing needs and shifts within major distribution functions. They then adapt existing physical distribution systems for greater effectiveness.

Please visit the student website at **www.prideferrell.com** for ACE Self-Test questions that will help you prepare for exams.

IMPORTANT TERMS

Wholesaling
Wholesaler
Merchant wholesaler
Full-service wholesaler
General-merchandise
  wholesaler
Limited-line wholesaler
Specialty-line wholesaler
Rack jobber
Limited-service wholesaler
Cash-and-carry wholesaler
Truck wholesaler
Drop shipper
Mail-order wholesaler
Agent
Broker
Manufacturers' agent
Selling agent
Commission merchant

Sales branch
Sales office
Physical distribution
Outsourcing
Cycle time
Order processing
Electronic data interchange
  (EDI)
Inventory management
Just-in-time (JIT)
Materials handling
Warehousing
Private warehouse
Public warehouse
Distribution center
Transportation
Intermodal transportation
Freight forwarder
Megacarrier

DISCUSSION & REVIEW QUESTIONS

1. What is wholesaling?
2. What services do wholesalers provide to producers and retailers?
3. What is the difference between a full-service merchant wholesaler and a limited-service merchant wholesaler?
4. Drop shippers take title to products but do not accept physical possession of them, whereas commis-

sion merchants take physical possession of products but do not accept title. Defend the logic of classifying drop shippers as wholesale merchants and commission merchants as agents.
5. Why are manufacturers' sales offices and branches classified as wholesalers? Which independent wholesalers are replaced by manufacturers' sales branches? Which independent wholesalers are replaced by manufacturers' sales offices?
6. Discuss the cost and service tradeoffs involved in developing a physical distribution system.
7. What factors must physical distribution managers consider when developing a customer service mix?
8. What are the main tasks involved in order processing?
9. Discuss the advantages of using an electronic order-processing system. Which types of organizations are most likely to utilize electronic order processing?
10. Explain the tradeoffs inventory managers face when reordering products or supplies. How is the reorder point computed?
11. How does a product's package affect materials handling procedures and techniques?
12. What is containerization? Discuss its major benefits.
13. Explain the major differences between private and public warehouses. What is a field public warehouse?
14. Distribution centers focus on the movement of goods. Describe how distribution centers are designed for the rapid flow of products.
15. Compare and contrast the five major transportation modes in terms of cost, speed, dependability, load flexibility, accessibility, and frequency.
16. Discuss ways marketers can combine or coordinate two or more modes of transportation. What is the advantage of doing so?

APPLICATION QUESTIONS

1. Contact a local retailer with which you do business, and ask the manager to describe the store's relationship with one of its wholesalers. Using Table 15.1 as a guide, identify the activities the wholesaler performs. Are any of the functions shared by both the retailer and the wholesaler?

2. Assume you are responsible for the physical distribution of computers at a mail-order company. What would you do to ensure product availability, timely delivery, and quality service for your customers?

3. The type of warehouse facilities used has important strategic implications for a firm. What type of warehouse would be most appropriate for the following situations, and why?

a. A propane gas company recently entered the market in the state of Washington. The company's customers need varied quantities of propane on a timely basis and, at times, on short notice.

b. A suntan lotion manufacturer has little expertise in managing warehouses and needs storage space in several locations in the Southeast.

c. A book publisher must have short cycle time to get its products to customers quickly and needs to send the products to many different retailers.

4. Marketers select a transportation mode based on cost, speed, dependability, load flexibility, accessibility, and frequency (see Table 15.5). Identify a product and then select a mode of transportation based on these criteria. Explain your choice.

Internet Exercise & Resources

Visit **www.prideferrell.com** for resources to help you master the material in this chapter, plus materials that will help you expand your marketing knowledge, including Internet exercise updates, ACE self-tests, hotlinks to companies featured in this chapter, and much more.

FedEx

FedEx has become a critical link in the distribution network of both small and large firms. With its efficient and strategically located superhub in Memphis, FedEx has truly revolutionized the shipping industry. View the company's website at **www.fedex.com**.

1. Comment on how the website's overall design reflects the services the site promotes.
2. Why does FedEx so prominently display a "News" area on its website?
3. Does FedEx differentiate between small and large customers on its website? Why or why not?

Video Case 16.1

Quick International Courier Delivers Time-Sensitive Shipments

From delicate biomedical supplies to state-of-the-art integrated circuit boards, Quick International Courier has been speeding time-sensitive shipments to global destinations for more than 20 years. The company, based in New York City, offers round-the-clock pickup of virtually any kind of shipment. Different divisions focus on rapid delivery logistics for specific industries. The QuickSTAT division handles time-sensitive deliveries of biomedical materials, while QuickAerospace transports aircraft components. Quick Medical Devices Transportation Services safely delivers sensitive equipment such as diagnostic instruments and nuclear imaging machines. Quick Legal Services guar-

antees secure, on-time shipment of legal documents. QT Priority Service serves the delivery needs of the entertainment industry.

Depending on the type of product and the urgency of the delivery, Quick and its subsidiaries can arrange for shipment on the very next flight or on a later flight for same-day delivery nationally and internationally. If necessary, Quick will charter a plane for the fastest possible point-to-point shipment. When the company is unable to ship by air because of bad weather or other problems, it has a courier drive the most urgent packages to their destinations. Quick's offices are open around the clock every day of the year and have back-up systems in place so they can continue operating even if surrounding areas lose electrical power or telephone service. Business customers value the company's expedited service because they save precious time and, in turn, are able to offer a higher level of service to their customers.

Starting with a location near the two New York City airports, Quick expanded over the years to better serve the needs of business customers all over North America. The company currently operates in 15 cities across the United States and Canada, and has additional facilities in Europe. Over time, some of these offices have developed special services geared to the needs of particular industries. The Los Angeles office, for example, offers custom deliveries for the movie and music businesses. The New York office specializes in deliveries for the financial industry. The Virginia office handles speedy medical shipments to hospitals around the country.

Some shipments may be large, some small, but all are urgently needed hundreds or thousands of miles away. On any given day, Quick may be arranging for a manufacturer, such as Photronics, to send a new semiconductor photomask from the East Coast to Manchester, England, or helping to rush bone marrow from a donor in Germany to a transplant patient in a Texas medical center.

Michael Montagano, a sourcing specialist in logistics at Photronics, says that Quick's speedy, to-the-minute deliveries spare his customers the expensive downtime they would face if products failed to arrive as scheduled. But on-time delivery is just part of the reason Photronics uses Quick: "Because rapid delivery is integral to our clients' success, they need to know exactly where a particular shipment is once it leaves any one of our thirteen manufacturing sites," Montagano says. Quick makes it easy for shippers and their customers to monitor the progress of deliveries at every point from pickup, to cargo loading, to customs processing, to delivery at the final destination.

Now customers can use the company's QuickOnline website to electronically manage all aspects of their urgent shipments. The site allows customers to request courier pickup within 60 minutes, reserve cargo space on a particular airline flight, review cargo specifications from different airlines, arrange for insurance and documentation, track shipments in progress, look at proof of delivery for shipments already received, request e-mail notification of delivery status, and order specialized shipping supplies. Day or night, customers can log on and find out where and when shipments are moving. "Our goal on track and trace is to update the whereabouts of shipments every thirty minutes all the way, even in the Third World," says Quick's CEO. Customers can also read about new service enhancements, get shipping tips, and find other information on Quick's latest online newsletter.

Thanks to the worldwide boom in e-commerce, specialized delivery services are in even higher demand today. Quick competes with Sonic Air (owned by shipping giant United Parcel Service) and Sky Courier (owned by UPS rival Airborne Express). Despite this intense competition, Quick's reputation for on-time delivery has attracted some 3,000 business customers, including 75 percent of the largest U.S. companies. Annual revenues top $100 million and continue to grow as the company expands its personalized delivery services for business customers with shipments that cannot wait until tomorrow.[16]

QUESTIONS FOR DISCUSSION

1. Is it possible for a company that pays extra for urgent air shipments through Quick International Courier to actually reduce its total distribution costs? Explain.
2. What details about materials handling might Quick have to consider before arranging to pick up specialized cargo such as a shipment of bone marrow or a package of computer chips?
3. Should Quick expand into air delivery for businesses that serve consumer markets? Why or why not?

Case 16.2

Wal-Mart Competes Using Efficient, Low-Cost Physical Distribution

How does the world's largest retailer keep the shelves stocked at 4,750 stores while keeping prices low enough to attract 138 million shoppers worldwide every week? Physical distribution is the key. Since the first Wal-Mart opened in Rogers, Arkansas, in 1962, management has carefully balanced its inventory levels, delivery schedules, and transportation costs to ensure products arrive at the right stores at the right time and at the right price. Today the company uses information technology to coordinate the movement of products from suppliers to the loading docks of its 62 distribution centers and on to the company's Wal-Mart discount stores,

SuperCenter combination food/general merchandise outlets, Sam's Club warehouse stores, and Neighborhood Market grocery stores.

Through its Retail Link network, Wal-Mart collaborates with suppliers to forecast sales, plan future orders, and replenish stock automatically. Here is how the system works. The point-of-sale scanning equipment in each store captures item-by-item, brand-by-brand sales data. Using sophisticated database technology, Wal-Mart analyzes the sales patterns and historical results for the previous 65 weeks with all of its suppliers. Next, Wal-Mart and its suppliers agree on forecasts for future sales. Then they jointly decide on an order and delivery schedule to ensure inventory levels at each distribution center are appropriate for the forecasted store sales. Wal-Mart makes the system available to suppliers free of charge. In exchange, suppliers share detailed analyses of results and forecasts with Wal-Mart officials.

Retail Link works. During a pilot test with the maker of Listerine, Wal-Mart was able to boost its in-stock position from 87 percent to 98 percent while cutting the order fulfillment cycle time from 21 to 11 days. The supplier also benefited because it sold Wal-Mart an additional $8.5 million of Listerine and was able to better manage its production and delivery activities. Customers benefited because they were able to pick up bottles of Listerine from store shelves when they wanted, and they saved money because low costs allow Wal-Mart to set everyday low prices.

Another technology that helps Wal-Mart streamline its physical distribution system is radio frequency identification (RFID). Wal-Mart requires its 100 largest suppliers to attach an RFID tag (bearing a computer chip, radio antenna, and identification number) to each case or pallet of merchandise. Using readers in its distribution centers, Wal-Mart picks up radio signals indicating which products are being received and in what quantities. Now the company can track inbound inventory on conveyer belts traveling 540 feet per minute without individually counting each container—and with complete accuracy. Next-generation RFID technology will enable Wal-Mart to track shipments on much faster-moving conveyer belts.

Despite a global roster of 20,000 suppliers, Wal-Mart is always looking for ways to improve its supply chain management and gain flexibility, slash costs, and identify new supply sources around the world. For example, the company imports $12 billion worth of merchandise from China every year. It also maintains a private procurement website to request and receive supplier bids on contracts, centrally negotiate purchasing, and arrange shipping.

As the most powerful channel captain on the planet, Wal-Mart can command ever-higher efficiencies from its suppliers, squeeze additional costs from physical distribution due to economies of scale, and pass the savings on to consumers in the form of lower retail prices. Consider its private-brand George jeans, which were originally priced at $26.67. Wal-Mart reduced costs by purchasing in high volume directly from suppliers in Asia rather than working through wholesalers. It cut costs even further by refining materials handling and transportation. Now George jeans sell for $7.85—less than one-third of the old price.

As Wal-Mart spreads farther from its Arkansas base, management continues opening distribution centers and arranging transportation to ship merchandise to clusters of stores in the area. The company operates a huge truck fleet to transfer products from distribution centers to stores, but it also contracts with independent trucking firms to transport food and other specialized products. In the Northeast, for example, Wal-Mart receives and stores grocery products at an 868,000-square-foot food distribution center in Johnstown, New York. From there, trucks operated by Clarksville Refrigerated Lines bring orders to Wal-Mart stores across New England, New York, and Pennsylvania. Similarly, a fleet of refrigerated trucks operated by M.S. Carriers transports perishable food products from Wal-Mart's food distribution center in Monroe, Georgia, to Sam's Club warehouse stores in five surrounding states.

Rather than reinvent the wheel for every distribution center and store in North America, Argentina, Brazil, Germany, the United Kingdom, Japan, China, and Korea, the company encourages each region to share its best distribution practices. As a result, Wal-Mart's German stores are benefiting from the U.S. stores' experience in reducing inventory levels and restocking more rapidly. Its Korean stores are replicating the Mexican operation's popular and profitable web-based grocery delivery program. The world's largest retailer is not finished expanding. As it opens hundreds of new stores in the coming years, it will keep honing its distribution skills to keep shelves stocked at the lowest possible cost.[17]

QUESTIONS FOR DISCUSSION

1. Why is physical distribution so important to Wal-Mart's marketing strategy?
2. Why does Wal-Mart prefer to deal directly with suppliers rather than buying from wholesalers?
3. How does Retail Link help Wal-Mart better control order processing and inventory management?

Retailing and Direct Marketing

17

OBJECTIVES

1. To understand the purpose and function of retailers in the marketing channel

2. To identify the major types of retailers

3. To understand direct marketing and two other forms of nonstore retailing

4. To examine the major types of franchising and the benefits and weaknesses of franchising

5. To explore strategic issues in retailing

443

Krispy Kreme Turns Doughnuts into Dollars

When a Krispy Kreme store lights up its "hot doughnuts now" sign, customers line up. With just 330 stores, Krispy Kreme is a fraction of the size of the Dunkin' Donuts chain, but it is growing rapidly. Starting from the original site in Winston-Salem, North Carolina, the chain has expanded through company-owned and franchised stores across the United States and into Canada, the United Kingdom, Australia, and Mexico. The company sells 2.7 billion doughnuts every year under a brand name that is as hot as its freshly made fluffy, glazed doughnuts.

One reason for Krispy Kreme's success is its emphasis on the store as "doughnut theater." The production area is arranged so customers can watch (and smell) as the yeast doughnuts are dunked briefly into sizzling vegetable shortening, covered with sugar glaze, and moved by conveyor belt into bins behind the sales counter. Behind the scenes, store managers have their hands full taking care of all the tasks needed to operate a Krispy Kreme outlet. Thanks to a recently installed web-based system, store managers can monitor their inventory of supplies and place orders online. Moreover, the system has vastly reduced the number of ordering errors. If a store manager happens to order 400 bags of doughnut mix instead of the usual 4 bags, the system flags the discrepancy for special attention.

Krispy Kreme has built its brand using cost-effective public relations and cause-related marketing. When a new store opens, management sends free boxes of fresh doughnuts to local reporters, radio personalities, and television news anchors. Every store invites charities to buy doughnuts at a discount and resell them for fund-raising. Doughnut lovers tell their friends about Krispy Kreme's great taste, and the store is off to a good start. Today 65 percent of Krispy Kreme's revenue comes from retail sales of doughnuts and coffee. Another 31 percent comes from distributing doughnut mix, equipment, and related supplies to franchisees. Only 4 percent of revenue comes from franchisee payments.

Eyeing Krispy Kreme's sweet success, several celebrities have become franchisees. Baseball home run champ Hank Aaron owns a franchised store in Atlanta and plans two more. Dick Clark, long-running host of the *New Year's Rockin' Eve* broadcast from Times Square, is a partner in several franchised stores in the United Kingdom. Jimmy Buffett, known for his hit song *Margaritaville,* owns a franchise in Palm Beach, Florida. As more franchisees sign up, Krispy Kreme's revenues and profits will climb even higher in the coming years.[1] ■

R etailers such as Krispy Kreme, JCPenney, The Home Depot, and Old Navy are the most visible and accessible channel members to consumers. They are an important link in the marketing channel because they are both marketers for and customers of producers and wholesalers. They perform many marketing functions, such as buying, selling, grading, risk taking, and developing and maintaining information databases about customers. Retailers are in a strategic position to develop relationships with consumers and partnerships with producers and intermediaries in the marketing channel.

In this chapter, we examine the nature of retailing and its importance in supplying consumers with goods and services. We discuss the major types of retail stores. Then we describe direct marketing and two other types of nonstore retailing. Next, we look at franchising, a retailing form that continues to grow in popularity. Finally, we explore several strategic issues in retailing, including location, retail positioning, store image, scrambled merchandising, and the wheel of retailing.

The Nature of Retailing

retailing Transactions in which ultimate consumers are the buyers

retailer An organization that purchases products for the purpose of reselling them to ultimate consumers

Retailing includes all transactions in which the buyer intends to consume the product through personal, family, or household use. Buyers in retail transactions are therefore the ultimate consumers. A **retailer** is an organization that purchases products for the purpose of reselling them to ultimate consumers. Although most retailers' sales are directly to the consumer, nonretail transactions occasionally occur when retailers sell products to other businesses. Retailing often takes place in stores or service establishments, but it also occurs through direct selling, direct marketing, and vending machines outside stores.

Retailing is important to the national economy. Approximately 1.1 million retailers operate in the United States.[2] This number has remained relatively constant for the past 25 years, but sales volume has increased more than fourfold. Most personal income is spent in retail stores, and nearly one out of seven people employed in the United States works in a retail operation.

Retailers add value, provide services, and assist in making product selections. They can enhance the value of the product by making the shopping experience more convenient, as in home shopping. Through its location, a retailer can facilitate comparison shopping; for example, car dealerships often cluster in the same general vicinity. Product value is also enhanced when retailers offer services, such as technical advice, delivery, credit, and repair services. Finally, retail sales personnel can demonstrate to customers how a product can help address their needs or solve a problem.

The value added by retailers is significant for both producers and ultimate consumers. Retailers are the critical link between producers and ultimate consumers because they provide the environment in which exchanges with ultimate consumers occur. Ultimate consumers benefit through retailers' performance of marketing functions that result in availability of broader arrays of products. Retailers play a major role in creating time, place, and possession utility and, in some cases, form utility.

Leading retailers such as Wal-Mart, The Home Depot, Taco Bell, Macy's, and Toys "R" Us offer consumers a place to browse and compare merchandise to find exactly what they need. However, such traditional retailing is being challenged by direct marketing channels that provide home shopping through catalogs, television, and the Internet. Traditional retailers are responding to this change in the retail environment in various ways. Wal-Mart has joined forces with fast-food giants McDonald's and KFC to attract consumers and offer them the added convenience of eating where they shop. In response to competition from Amazon.com, Barnes & Noble developed a website to sell books via the Internet.

New store formats and advances in information technology are making the retail environment highly dynamic and competitive. Instant-messaging technology is helping online retailers converse with customers so they don't click away to another site. Rather than e-mail a retail site and wait for a response, shoppers on Lands' End's website simply click to chat, via keyboard, directly with a customer service representative about sizes, colors, or other product details.[3] This technology has helped the company triple its online sales in just three years. The key to success in retailing is to have a strong customer focus with a retail strategy that provides the level of service, product quality, and innovation that consumers desire. Partnerships among noncompeting retailers and other marketing channel members are providing new opportunities for retailers. For example, airports are leasing space to retailers such as Sharper Image, McDonald's, Sunglass Hut, and The Body Shop. Kroger and Nordstrom have developed joint co-branded credit cards that offer rebates to customers at participating stores.

Retailers are also finding global opportunities. For example, The Gap is now opening more international stores than domestic ones, a trend that is likely to continue for the foreseeable future. Wal-Mart and The Home Depot are opening stores in Canada, Mexico, and South America. McDonald's is growing faster outside the United States than domestically.

Major Types of Retail Stores

Many types of retail stores exist. One way to classify them is by the breadth of products offered. Two general categories include general-merchandise retailers and specialty retailers.

general-merchandise retailer A retail establishment that offers a variety of product lines that are stocked in depth

department store A large retail organization characterized by wide product mixes and organized into separate departments to facilitate marketing efforts and internal management

◆ General-Merchandise Retailers

A retail establishment that offers a variety of product lines stocked in considerable depth is referred to as a **general-merchandise retailer.** The types of product offerings, mixes of customer services, and operating styles of retailers in this category vary considerably. The primary types of general-merchandise retailers are department stores, discount stores, supermarkets, superstores, hypermarkets, warehouse clubs, and warehouse and catalog showrooms (see Table 17.1).

Department Stores. **Department stores** are large retail organizations characterized by wide product mixes and employing at least 25 people. To facilitate marketing efforts and internal management in these stores, related product lines are organized into separate departments, such as cosmetics, housewares, apparel, home furnishings, and appliances. Often each department functions as a self-contained business, and buyers for individual departments are fairly autonomous.

Department stores are distinctly service oriented. Their total product may include credit, delivery, personal assistance, merchandise returns, and a pleasant atmosphere. Although some so-called department stores are actually large, departmentalized

Department Stores
As a department store, Sears offers numerous product lines and a number of customer services.

Table 17.1	General-Merchandise Retailers	
Type of Retailer	**Description**	**Examples**
Department store	Large organization offering a wide product mix and organized into separate departments	Macy's, JCPenney, Sears
Discount store	Self-service, general-merchandise store offering brand name and private-brand products at low prices	Wal-Mart, Target, Kmart
Supermarket	Self-service store offering a complete line of food products and some nonfood products	Kroger, Albertson's, Winn-Dixie
Superstore	Giant outlet offering all food and nonfood products found in supermarkets, as well as most routinely purchased products	Wal-Mart Supercenters
Hypermarket	Combination supermarket and discount store; larger than a superstore	Carrefour
Warehouse club	Large-scale, members-only establishment combining cash-and-carry wholesaling and discount retailing	Sam's Club, Costco
Warehouse showroom	Facility in a large, low-cost building with large on-premises inventories and minimal service	Ikea
Catalog showroom	Warehouse showroom in which consumers use catalogs to place orders for products, which are then filled directly in the warehouse area and picked up by buyers in the showroom	Service Merchandise

specialty stores, most department stores are shopping stores: consumers can compare price, quality, and service at one store with those at competing stores. Along with large discount stores, department stores are often considered retailing leaders in a community and are found in most places with populations of more than 50,000.

Typical department stores, such as Macy's, Sears, Marshall Field's, Dillard's, and Neiman Marcus, obtain a large proportion of sales from apparel, accessories, and cosmetics. Other products these stores carry include gift items, luggage, electronics, home accessories, and sports equipment. Some department stores offer such services as automobile insurance, hair care, income tax preparation, and travel and optical services. In some cases, space for these specialized services is leased out, with proprietors managing their own operations and paying rent to the store.

discount store A self-service, general-merchandise store offering brand name and private-brand products at low prices

Discount Stores. **Discount stores** are self-service, general-merchandise outlets that regularly offer brand name and private-brand products at low prices. Discounters accept lower margins than conventional retailers in exchange for high sales volume. To keep inventory turnover high, they carry a wide but carefully selected assortment of products, from appliances to housewares and clothing. Major discount establishments also offer food products, toys, automotive services, garden supplies, and sports equipment. Wal-Mart, Target, and Kmart are the three largest discount stores. Many discounters are regional organizations, such as Venture, Bradlees, and

Meijer. Most operate in large (50,000 to 80,000 square feet), no-frills facilities. Discount stores usually offer everyday low prices rather than relying on sales events.

Discount retailing developed on a large scale in the early 1950s, when postwar production began catching up with consumer demand for appliances, home furnishings, and other hard goods. Discount stores were often cash-only operations in warehouse districts, offering goods at savings of 20 to 30 percent over conventional retailers. Facing increased competition from department stores and other discount stores, some discounters have improved store services, atmosphere, and location, raising prices and sometimes blurring the distinction between discount store and department store. Other discounters continue to focus on price alone.

supermarket A large, self-service store that carries a complete line of food products, along with some nonfood products

Supermarkets. **Supermarkets** are large, self-service stores that carry a complete line of food products, as well as some nonfood products such as cosmetics and nonprescription drugs. Supermarkets are arranged in departments for maximum efficiency in stocking and handling products, but have central checkout facilities. They offer lower prices than smaller neighborhood grocery stores, usually provide free parking, and may also cash checks. Supermarkets must operate efficiently because net profits after taxes are usually less than 1 percent of sales. Supermarkets may be independently owned but are often part of a chain operation. Top U.S. supermarket chains include Kroger, Albertson's, Safeway, and A&P.

Today consumers make more than three-quarters of all grocery purchases in supermarkets. Even so, supermarkets' total share of the food market is declining because consumers now have widely varying food preferences and buying habits. Furthermore, in many communities shoppers can choose from a number of convenience stores, discount stores, and specialty food stores, as well as a wide variety of restaurants.

superstore A giant retail outlet that carries food and nonfood products found in supermarkets, as well as most routinely purchased consumer products

Superstores. **Superstores**, which originated in Europe, are giant retail outlets that carry not only food and nonfood products ordinarily found in supermarkets but also routinely purchased consumer products. Besides a complete food line, superstores sell housewares, hardware, small appliances, clothing, personal care products, garden products, and tires—about four times as many items as supermarkets. Services available at superstores include dry cleaning, automotive repair, check cashing, bill paying, and snack bars.

Superstore
Wal-Mart Super Centers combine the features of a discount store and a complete supermarket.

Superstores combine features of discount stores and supermarkets. Examples include Wal-Mart Supercenters, some Kroger stores, and Super Kmart Centers. To cut handling and inventory costs, superstores use sophisticated operating techniques and often have tall shelving that displays entire assortments of products. Superstores can have an area of as much as 200,000 square feet (compared with 20,000 square feet in traditional supermarkets). Sales volume is two to three times that of supermarkets, partly because locations near good transportation networks help generate the in-store traffic needed for profitability.

hypermarket A store that combines supermarket and discount store shopping in one location

Hypermarkets. **Hypermarkets** combine supermarket and discount store shopping in one location. Larger than superstores, they range from 225,000 to 325,000 square feet and offer 45,000 to 60,000 different types of low-priced products. They commonly allocate 40 to 50 percent of their space to grocery products and the remainder to general merchandise, including athletic shoes, designer jeans, and other apparel; refrigerators, televisions, and other appliances; housewares; cameras; toys; jewelry; hardware; and automotive supplies. Many lease space to noncompeting businesses such as banks, optical shops, and fast-food restaurants. All hypermarkets focus on low prices and vast selections. Although Kmart, Wal-Mart, and Carrefour (a French retailer) have operated hypermarkets in the United States, most of these stores have been unsuccessful and have closed. Such stores are too big for time-constrained U.S. shoppers. However, hypermarkets are successful in Europe and South America.

warehouse club A large-scale, members-only establishment that combines features of cash-and-carry wholesaling with discount retailing

Warehouse Clubs. **Warehouse clubs,** a rapidly growing form of mass merchandising, are large-scale, members-only selling operations combining cash-and-carry wholesaling with discount retailing. For a nominal annual fee (usually about $35), small retailers purchase products at wholesale prices for business use or for resale. Warehouse clubs also sell to ultimate consumers affiliated with government agencies, credit unions, schools, hospitals, and banks, but instead of paying a membership fee, individual consumers may pay about 5 percent more on each item than do business customers.

Sometimes called *buying clubs,* warehouse clubs offer the same types of products as discount stores, but in a limited range of sizes and styles. Whereas most discount stores carry around 40,000 items, a warehouse club handles only 3,500 to 5,000 products, usually acknowledged brand leaders. Sam's Club stores, for example, stock a little more than 4,000 items, with 1,400 available most of the time and the rest being one-time buys. Costco leads the warehouse club industry with sales of $42.5 billion. Sam's Club is second with $31.7 billion in store sales. A third company, BJ's Wholesale Club, which operates in the Northeast and Florida, has a much smaller market.[4] All these establishments offer a broad product mix, including food, beverages, books, appliances, housewares, automotive parts, hardware, and furniture. Warehouse clubs appeal to many price-conscious consumers and small retailers unable to obtain wholesaling services from large distributors. The average warehouse club shopper has more education, a higher income, and a larger household than the average supermarket shopper.

To keep prices lower than those of supermarkets and discount stores, warehouse clubs provide few services. They generally do not advertise, except through direct mail. Their facilities, often located in industrial areas, have concrete floors and aisles wide enough for forklifts. Merchandise is stacked on pallets or displayed on pipe racks. Customers must transport purchases themselves.

warehouse showroom A retail facility in a large, low-cost building with large on-premise inventories and minimal services

Warehouse and Catalog Showrooms. **Warehouse showrooms** are retail facilities with five basic characteristics: large, low-cost buildings, warehouse materials handling technology, vertical merchandise displays, large on-premises inventories, and minimal services. IKEA, a Swedish company, sells furniture, household goods, and kitchen accessories in warehouse showrooms and through catalogs around the world. Wickes Furniture and Levitz Furniture also operate warehouse showrooms. These high-volume, low-overhead operations stress fewer personnel and services. Lower costs are possible because some marketing functions have been shifted to consumers, who must transport, finance, and perhaps store merchandise. Most consumers carry away purchases in the manufacturers' cartons, although stores will deliver for a fee.

catalog showroom A warehouse showroom in which consumers use catalogs to place orders for products, which are then filled directly in the warehouse area and picked up by buyers in the showroom

In **catalog showrooms**, one item of each product is displayed, often in a locked case, with remaining inventory stored out of the buyer's reach. Using catalogs that have been mailed to their homes or are on store counters, customers order products by phone or in person. Clerks fill orders from the warehouse area, and products are presented in the manufacturers' cartons. In contrast to traditional catalog retailers, which offer no discounts and require that customers wait for delivery, catalog showrooms regularly sell below list price and often provide goods immediately.

Catalog showrooms usually sell jewelry, luggage, photographic equipment, toys, small appliances and housewares, sporting goods, and power tools. They advertise extensively and carry established brands and models that are not likely to be discontinued. Because catalog showrooms have higher product turnover, fewer losses through shoplifting, and lower labor costs than department stores, they are able to feature lower prices. However, they offer minimal services and customers often have to stand in line to examine items or place orders. The rapid growth of discounters and warehouse clubs is also putting pressure on catalog showrooms.

Service Merchandise and Best Products are examples of catalog showroom retailers. Neiman Marcus Group Inc. is testing the concept of a catalog showroom inside two stores (one in Plano, Texas, and the other in suburban Chicago) as part of an effort to expand its retail formats.[5]

◆ Specialty Retailers

In contrast to general-merchandise retailers with their broad product mixes, specialty retailers emphasize narrow and deep assortments. Despite their name, specialty retailers do not sell specialty items (except when specialty goods complement the overall product mix). Instead, they offer substantial assortments in a few product lines. We examine three types of specialty retailers: traditional specialty retailers, off-price retailers, and category killers.

traditional specialty retailer A store that carries a narrow product mix with deep product lines

Traditional Specialty Retailers. **Traditional specialty retailers** are stores that carry a narrow product mix with deep product lines. Sometimes called *limited-line retailers*, they may be referred to as *single-line retailers* if they carry unusual depth in one main product category. Specialty retailers commonly sell such shopping products as apparel, jewelry, sporting goods, fabrics, computers, and pet supplies. The Limited, Radio Shack, Hickory Farms, The Gap, and Foot Locker are examples of retailers offering limited product lines but great depth within those lines.

Although the number of chain specialty stores is increasing, many specialty stores are independently owned. Florists, bakery shops, and bookstores are among the small, independent specialty retailers that appeal to local target markets, although these stores can be owned and managed by large corporations. Even if this kind of retailer adds a few supporting product lines, the store may still be classified as a specialty store.

Because they are usually small, specialty stores may have high costs in proportion to sales, and satisfying customers may require carrying some products with low turnover rates. However, these

Leave cookies and milk for Santa. Get sushi and dim sum in return.
Whether your shopping list is full of serious cooks or just serious food lovers, look to the Far East and Crate and Barrel for wisdom this year.
Our cast iron wok has a deep bowl that distributes heat beautifully for stir frying, sautéing, or even deep frying.
Our stoneware plates can be used to serve hors d'ouvres as well as sushi.
And our lacquered crimson trays and soup bowls will add a touch of Asian flair to anything from miso to matzo.
So stop in at a Crate and Barrel store this holiday season, or visit us online at crateandbarrel.com.
Crate&Barrel Holiday

For the store nearest you call 800.996.9960.

Traditional Specialty Stores
Crate & Barrel, as a traditional specialty store, focuses its marketing efforts on very specific product lines.

stores sometimes obtain lower prices from suppliers by purchasing limited lines of merchandise in large quantities. Successful specialty stores understand their customer types and know what products to carry, thus reducing the risk of unsold merchandise. Specialty stores usually offer better selections and more sales expertise than department stores, their main competitors. By capitalizing on fashion, service, personnel, atmosphere, and location, specialty retailers position themselves strategically to attract customers in specific market segments. For example, customers seeking fashion jeans likely would shop at specialty stores. About 21 percent of U.S. jeans purchases are made in traditional specialty stores.[6] Specialty stores may even become exclusive dealers in their markets for certain products. Through specialty stores, small-business owners provide unique services to match consumers' varied desires. For consumers dissatisfied with the impersonal nature of large retailers, the close, personal contact offered by a small specialty store can be a welcome change.

off-price retailer A store that buys manufacturers' seconds, overruns, returns, and off-season merchandise for resale to consumers at deep discounts

category killer A very large specialty store that concentrates on a major product category and competes on the basis of low prices and enormous product availability

Off-Price Retailers. **Off-price retailers** buy manufacturers' seconds, overruns, returns, and off-season production runs at below-wholesale prices for resale to consumers at deep discounts. Unlike true discount stores, which pay regular wholesale prices for goods and usually carry second-line brand names, off-price retailers offer limited lines of national-brand and designer merchandise, usually clothing, shoes, and/or housewares. The number of off-price retailers has grown since the mid-1980s. Ross Dress For Less is an off-price clothing retailer frequently found near other off-price specialty stores such as T.J. Maxx, Marshalls, Stein Mart, and Burlington Coat Factory. Ross keeps inventory lean in an attempt to keep selections fresh, new, and exciting, says a company spokesperson. Individual stores typically receive shipments of new clothing five times a week.[7]

Off-price stores charge 20 to 50 percent less than department stores for comparable merchandise but offer few customer services. They often feature community dressing rooms and central checkout counters. Some of these stores do not take returns or allow exchanges. Off-price stores may or may not sell goods with original labels intact. They turn over their inventory nine to twelve times a year, three times as often as traditional specialty stores. They compete with department stores for the same customers: price-conscious customers who are knowledgeable about brand names.

Category Killers
Some stores, like The Home Depot, are referred to as category killers. As specialty retailers, category killers are large stores with enormous product mixes and low prices.

Another form of off-price retailer is the manufacturer's outlet mall, which makes available manufacturer overstocks and unsold merchandise from other retail outlets at discounted prices. Diverse manufacturers are represented in these malls.

To ensure a regular flow of merchandise into their stores, off-price retailers establish long-term relationships with suppliers that can provide large quantities of goods at reduced prices. Manufacturers may approach retailers with samples, discontinued products, or items that have not sold well. Also, retailers may seek out manufacturers, offering to pay cash for goods produced during the manufacturers' off season. Although manufacturers benefit from such arrangements, they also risk alienating their specialty and department store customers. Department stores tolerate off-price stores as long as they do not advertise brand names, limit merchandise to lower-quality items, and are located away from the department stores. When off-price retailers obtain large stocks of in-season, top-quality merchandise, tension builds between department stores and manufacturers.

Category Killers. Over the last two decades, a new breed of specialty retailer, the category killer, has evolved. A **category killer** is a very large specialty store that concentrates on a major product category and competes on the basis of low prices and enormous product availability. These stores are referred to as category killers because they expand rapidly and gain sizable market shares, taking business away from smaller, high-cost retail outlets. Examples of category killers include The Home Depot (building materials), Office Depot (office supplies and equipment), Toys "R" Us (toys), and Best Buy (electronics).

Direct Marketing

direct marketing The use of the telephone, Internet, and nonpersonal media to introduce products to customers, who can then purchase them via mail, telephone, or the Internet

nonstore retailing The selling of products outside the confines of a retail facility

catalog marketing A type of marketing in which an organization provides a catalog from which customers make selections and place orders by mail, telephone, or the Internet

Direct marketing is the use of the telephone, Internet, and nonpersonal media to communicate product and organizational information to customers, who can then purchase products via mail, telephone, or the Internet. Direct marketing is one type of nonstore retailing. **Nonstore retailing** is the selling of products outside the confines of a retail facility. This form of retailing accounts for an increasing percentage of total sales. Direct marketing can occur through catalog marketing, direct-response marketing, telemarketing, television home shopping, and online retailing.

◆ Catalog Marketing

In **catalog marketing**, an organization provides a catalog from which customers make selections and place orders by mail, telephone, or the Internet. Catalog marketing began in 1872, when Montgomery Ward issued its first catalog to rural families. Today there are more than 7,000 catalog marketing companies in the United States, as well as a number of retail stores, such as JCPenney, that engage in catalog marketing. Some organizations, including Spiegel and JCPenney, offer a broad array of products spread over multiple product lines. Catalog companies such as Lands' End, Pottery Barn, and J. Crew offer considerable depth in one major line of products. Still other catalog companies specialize in only a few products within a single line. Some catalog retailers—for instance, Crate and Barrel and Sharper Image—have stores in major metropolitan areas. When Sears, Roebuck and Company acquired Lands' End, it continued to operate both entities separately, but found ways to incorporate Lands' End into Sears by opening mini Lands' End stores within Sears stores.[8]

The advantages of catalog retailing include efficiency and convenience for customers. The retailer benefits by being able to locate in remote, low-cost areas, save on expensive store fixtures, and reduce both personal selling and store operating expenses. On the other hand, catalog retailing is inflexible, provides limited service, and is most effective only for a selected set of products.

Catalog sales are about $132 billion annually and are expected to grow to $177 billion by 2008.[9] Even though the cost of mailing catalogs continues to rise, catalog sales are growing at double the rate of in-store retailing. Williams-Sonoma, for example, sells kitchenware and home and garden products through five catalogs, including Pottery Barn and Gardeners' Eden.

How does the Marinac stop wind, defy rain and blow other jackets away?

Catalog Marketing
Lands' End is a catalog marketer. It also engages in direct marketing through online retailing.

Catalog sales have been increasing due to the convenience of catalog shopping. Product quality is often high, and because consumers can call toll free 24 hours a day, charge purchases to a credit card, and have the merchandise delivered to their door in one to two days, such shopping is much easier than going to a store. In addition, three-fourths of catalog retailers provide the convenience of shopping online.

◆ Direct-Response Marketing

direct-response marketing A type of marketing in which a retailer advertises a product and makes it available through mail or telephone orders

Direct-response marketing occurs when a retailer advertises a product and makes it available through mail or telephone orders. Generally a purchaser may use a credit card, but other forms of payment are acceptable. Examples of direct-response marketing include a television commercial offering a recording artist's musical collection available through a toll-free number, a newspaper or magazine advertisement for a series of children's books available by filling out the form in the ad or calling a toll-free number, and even a billboard promoting floral services available by calling 1-800-Flowers. Direct-response marketing is also conducted by sending letters, samples, brochures, or booklets to prospects on a mailing list and asking that they order the advertised products by mail or telephone. In general, products must be priced above $20 to justify the advertising and distribution costs associated with direct-response marketing.

Source: Data from Cable & Telecommunications Association for Marketing.

◆ Telemarketing

A number of organizations use the telephone to strengthen the effectiveness of traditional marketing methods. **Telemarketing** is the performance of marketing-related activities by telephone. Some organizations use a prescreened list of prospective clients. Telemarketing can help generate sales leads, improve customer service, speed up payments on past-due accounts, raise funds for nonprofit organizations, and gather marketing data.

telemarketing The performance of marketing-related activities by telephone

Currently the laws and regulations regarding telemarketing, while in a state of flux, are becoming more restrictive. Several states have established do-not-call lists of customers who do not want to receive telemarketing calls from companies operating in their state. On October 1, 2003, the U.S. Congress implemented the national do-not-call registry for consumers who do not wish to receive telemarketing calls. By the end of 2003, more than 54 million phone numbers were listed on the registry, nearly one-third of the 166 million residential phone numbers in the United States. Companies are subject to a fine of up to $12,000 for each call made to a consumer listed on the national do-not-call registry.[10] The national registry is enforced by the Federal Trade Commission and the Federal Communications Commission.[11] Certain exceptions apply to no-call lists. A company can still use telemarketing to communicate with existing customers. In addition, charitable, political, and telephone survey organizations are not restricted by the national registry.

◆ Television Home Shopping

television home shopping A form of selling in which products are presented to television viewers, who can buy them by calling a toll-free number and paying with a credit card

Television home shopping presents products to television viewers, encouraging them to order through toll-free numbers and pay with credit cards. Home Shopping Network in Florida originated and popularized this format. There are several home shopping cable channels. A few of these channels specialize in certain product categories. The most popular products sold through television home shopping are jewelry (40 percent of total sales), clothing, housewares, and electronics.

Home shopping channels have grown so rapidly in recent years that more than 60 percent of U.S. households have access to home shopping programs. Home Shopping Network and QVC are two of the largest home shopping networks. Approximately 60 percent of home shopping sales revenues come from repeat purchasers.

The television home shopping format offers several benefits. Products can be easily demonstrated, and an adequate amount of time can be spent showing the product so to make viewers well informed. The length of time a product is shown depends not only on the time required for doing demonstrations but also on whether the product is selling. Once the calls peak and begin to decline, a new product is shown. Another benefit is that customers can shop at their convenience from the comfort of their homes.

◆ Online Retailing

online retailing Retailing that makes products available to buyers through computer connections

Online retailing makes products available to buyers through computer connections. The phenomenal growth of Internet use and online information services such as AOL has created new retailing opportunities. Many retailers have set up websites to disseminate information about their companies and products. Although most retailers with websites use them primarily to promote products, a number of companies, including Barnes & Noble, REI, Lands' End, and OfficeMax, sell goods online. Consumers can purchase hard-to-find items, such as Pez candy dispensers and Elvis memorabilia, on eBay. They can buy upscale items for their dogs at SitStay.com, a web retailer specializing in high-end dog supplies that carries a carefully screened selection of 1,500 products. "We don't have 10,000 products," explains co-founder Kent Krueger. "We have the best of the best."[12] Banks and brokerage firms have established websites to give customers direct access to manage their accounts and enable them to trade online. With advances in computer technology continuing and consumers ever more pressed for time, online retailing will

Online Retailing
Orbitz is an online retailer of travel-related services.

continue to escalate. The Tech Know boxed feature focuses on Dell, one of the most successful online retailers.

Although online retailing represents a major retailing venue, security remains an issue. In a recent survey conducted by the Business Software Alliance, about 75 percent of Internet users expressed concerns about shopping online. The major issues are identity theft and credit card theft.

Other Types of Nonstore Retailing

Besides direct marketing, there are two other major types of nonstore retailing: direct selling and automatic vending.

◆ Direct Selling

direct selling Marketing products to ultimate consumers through face-to-face sales presentations at home or in the workplace

Direct selling is the marketing of products to ultimate consumers through face-to-face sales presentations at home or in the workplace. Traditionally called *door-to-door selling*, direct selling in the United States began with peddlers more than a century ago and has since grown into a sizable industry of several hundred firms. Although direct sellers historically used a cold-canvass, door-to-door approach to finding prospects, many companies today, such as World Book, Kirby, Amway, Mary Kay, and Avon, use other approaches. They initially identify customers through the mail, the telephone, the Internet, or shopping mall intercepts and set up appointments.

Direct selling sometimes uses the "party plan," which can occur in the customer's home or workplace. With a party plan, the customer acts as a host and

---

TECH KNOW

Dell Builds PCs and Profits Through Direct Marketing

Michael Dell, founder and CEO of Dell, realized early in the life of his business that he could bypass the traditional distribution network through which personal computers (PCs) are sold and market directly to customers. Customers simply log onto the company's website, specify the features they want, and arrange for payment. The new, built-to-order PC arrives via FedEx within a few days. If they prefer, customers can browse Dell's printed catalog and call toll free to place an order. Building 150,000 PCs a day, Dell's use of direct marketing allows the company to keep costs low and profits at an acceptable level.

Instead of developing every component in-house, Dell saves time and money by choosing among the best components available on the market. "We didn't grow to be a $40 billion company in 19 years by trying to do everything ourselves," says the founder. The company strengthens relationships with suppliers by guaranteeing certain purchasing volumes in exchange for on-time delivery and expedited transactions. Because parts are available pre-

cisely when needed, Dell can maintain ultra-low inventory levels of components and minimize warehousing costs.

Dell's build-to-order business model eliminates excess inventory, which in the highly dynamic personal computer industry can become obsolete overnight. In contrast, competitors that market through retailers must assemble PCs in advance, ship them to stores, and have sufficient inventory to fill reorders quickly. Moreover, Dell's control over its marketing channel gives it more flexibility to try different marketing ideas. For example, the company recently borrowed a share-building idea from the automotive industry by offering zero percent financing on products costing $500 or more.

Dell's efficient and effective direct marketing strategy has paid off handsomely. In many cases, Dell can book an order, build the PC, and receive payment before it must pay suppliers for the components in that product. When PC sales are slow, Dell's low costs allow it to compete on price and increase its market share. When PC sales are strong, Dell can introduce new models at attractive prices to keep the orders—and the profits—rolling in.

invites a number of friends and associates to view merchandise in a group setting, where a salesperson demonstrates products. The congenial party atmosphere helps to overcome customers' reluctance and encourages them to buy. Direct selling through the party plan requires effective salespeople who can identify potential hosts and provide encouragement and incentives for them to organize a gathering of friends and associates. Companies that commonly use the party plan include Tupperware, Stanley Home Products, and Sarah Coventry.

Direct selling has both benefits and limitations. It gives the marketer an opportunity to demonstrate the product in an environment—usually customers' homes—where it would most likely be used. The door-to-door seller can give the customer personal attention, and the product can be presented to the customer at a convenient time and location. Personal attention to the customer is the foundation on which some direct sellers, such as Mary Kay, have built their businesses. Because commissions for salespeople are so high, ranging from 30 to 50 percent of the sales price, and great effort is required to isolate promising prospects, overall costs of direct selling make it the most expensive form of retailing. Furthermore, some customers view direct selling negatively, owing to unscrupulous and fraudulent practices used by some direct sellers in the past. Some communities even have local ordinances that control or, in some cases, prohibit direct selling.

◆ Automatic Vending

automatic vending The use of machines to dispense products

Automatic vending is the use of machines to dispense products. It accounts for less than 2 percent of all retail sales. Video game machines provide an entertainment service, and many banks offer automatic teller machines (ATMs), which dispense cash and perform other services.

Automatic vending is one of the most impersonal forms of retailing. Small, standardized, routinely purchased products (e.g., chewing gum, candy, newspapers, cigarettes, soft drinks, coffee) can be sold in machines because consumers usually buy them at the nearest available location. Machines in areas of heavy traffic provide efficient and continuous service to consumers. Such high-volume areas may have more diverse product availability—for example, hot and cold sandwiches, and even cameras. To market its one-time-use Max Cameras, Eastman Kodak is rolling out 10,000 vending machines that allow credit card transactions, are refrigerated to protect the film, and are connected to the Internet. The vending machine's Internet connection will inform Eastman Kodak about who bought each camera, where customers live, the specific location of the machine, and the machine's inventory level. These machines will be located at zoos, stadiums, parks, hotels, and resorts.[13]

Since vending machines need only a small amount of space and no sales personnel, this retailing method has some advantages over stores. The advantages are partly offset, however, by the high costs of equipment and frequent servicing and repairs.

Franchising

franchising An arrangement in which a supplier (franchiser) grants a dealer (franchisee) the right to sell products in exchange for some type of consideration

Franchising is an arrangement in which a supplier, or franchiser, grants a dealer, or franchisee, the right to sell products in exchange for some type of consideration. The franchiser may receive some percentage of total sales in exchange for furnishing equipment, buildings, management know-how, and marketing assistance to the franchisee. The franchisee supplies labor and capital, operates the franchised business, and agrees to abide by the provisions of the franchise agreement. Table 17.2 lists the top 20 U.S. franchises, type of product, and startup costs.

Because of changes in the international marketplace, shifting employment options in the United States, the expanding U.S. service economy, and corporate interest in more joint venture activity, franchising is rapidly increasing. In 2000,

Franchising
This relatively low-cost franchise provides a large number of services and support materials to its franchisees.

franchising companies and their franchisees accounted for an estimated $1 trillion in annual U.S. retail sales from 320,000 franchised small businesses in 75 industries. Franchising accounted for more than 40 percent of all U.S. retail sales and employed more than 8 million people. A new franchise outlet opens somewhere in the United States every 8 minutes, and approximately 8 percent of retail business establishments are franchised businesses.[14] In this section, we look at major types of retail franchises and the advantages and disadvantages of franchising.

◆ Major Types of Retail Franchises

Retail franchise arrangements fall into three general categories. In one arrangement, a manufacturer authorizes a number of retail stores to sell a certain brand name item. This franchise arrangement, one of the oldest forms, is common in sales of cars and trucks, farm equipment, shoes, paint, earth-moving equipment, and petroleum. In the second type of

Table 17.2	Top 20 Franchises and Their Startup Costs		
Rank*	**Franchise**	**Description**	**Startup Costs**
1	Subway	Sandwiches, salads	$86,000–$213,000
2	Curves	Women's fitness and weight loss	$35,600–$41,100
3	Quizno's	Sandwiches, soups, salads	$208,400–$243,800
4	7-Eleven	Convenience store	Varies
5	Jackson-Hewitt	Tax preparation services	$47,400–$75,200
6	UPS Store	Postal, business, communications services	$141,100–$239,700
7	McDonald's	Fast food	$506,000–$1,600,000
8	Jani-King	Commercial cleaning	$11,300–$34,100
9	Dunkin' Donuts	Doughnuts, baked goods	$255,700–$1,100,000
10	Baskin-Robbins	Ice cream, yogurt	$145,700–$527,800
11	Jiffy Lube	Fast oil change	$174,000–$194,000
12	InterContinental Hotels	Hotels	Varies
13	Sonic Drive-In Restaurants	Drive-in fast food	$710,000–$2,300,000
14	Domino's	Pizza	$141,400–$415,100
15	Super 8 Motels	Economy motels	$291,000–$2,300,000
16	Kumon Math & Reading Centers	Supplemental education	$8,000–$30,000
17	Chem-Dry Carpet Drapery & Upholstery Cleaning	Carpet, drapery, and upholstery cleaning	$23,600–$82,800
18	ServiceMaster Clean	Commercial/residential cleaning and disaster restoration	$26,600–$90,500
19	RE/MAX	Real estate	$20,000–$200,000
20	Snap-on Tools	Professional tools and equipment	$17,600–$254,700

*Ranking is based primarily on financial strength and stability, growth rate, size of the system, number of years in business, startup costs, litigation, percentage of terminations, and whether the company provides financing.
Source: "Franchise 500® 2004 Rankings," **www.entrepreneur.com**, accessed Mar. 26, 2004.

retail franchise, a producer licenses distributors to sell a given product to retailers. This arrangement is common in the soft-drink industry. Most national manufacturers of soft-drink syrups, including Coca-Cola, Dr Pepper, and PepsiCo, grant franchises to bottlers, which in turn serve retailers. In the third type of retail franchise, a franchiser supplies brand names, techniques, or other services instead of complete products. The franchiser may provide certain production and distribution services, but its primary role in the arrangement is careful development and control of marketing strategies. This approach to franchising is very common today and is used by such organizations as Holiday Inn, AAMCO, McDonald's, Dairy Queen, KFC, and H&R Block.

◆ Advantages and Disadvantages of Franchising

Franchising offers several advantages to both the franchisee and the franchiser. It enables a franchisee to start a business with limited capital and benefit from the business experience of others. Moreover, nationally advertised franchises, such as ServiceMaster and Burger King, are often assured of customers as soon as they open. If business problems arise, the franchisee can obtain guidance and advice from the franchiser at little or no cost. Franchised outlets are generally more successful than independently owned businesses. Fewer than 10 percent of franchised retail businesses fail during the first two years of operation, compared to approximately 50 percent of independent retail businesses. As discussed in the Global Marketing boxed feature, franchising operations also are increasing in selected other countries.

GLOBAL MARKETING

Fueling Customers in Thailand with Gas, Coffee, and Convenience

Jet Stations, owned by Conoco (Thailand) Ltd., is the fastest-growing retail gasoline brand among Thai motorists. The company has experienced steady market share growth and achieved the highest fuel sales per service station in Thailand. Each of the 139 Jet Stations contains a Jiffy convenience store as well as a franchised Ban Rai Coffee House bar. Jiffy's sales have been growing at an even faster rate than that of Jet fuel since Conoco opened the first convenience store inside its Thai service stations in 1993. A survey by ACNielsen (Thailand) found that 56 percent of new Jet customers became regular customers. One reason for this high customer retention rate is the convenience of having a Ban Rai Coffee House bar inside every Jiffy store.

Plantation and Farm Design Company, Ltd. owns the franchise to operate Ban Rai Coffee Houses at Jet Stations. The founder noticed that many Thai drivers like to drink coffee to stay alert while driving. To satisfy this market, Ban Rai brews freshly roasted, strong Thai coffee on-site for take-out at each convenience store. At a time when "buy Thai" sentiments are growing, Ban Rai's emphasis on supporting products from local communities, such as coffee and cookies, is proving quite effective. Also, Ban Rai serves the coffee in clay cups instead of paper cups to bring out the flavor and to differentiate its brand. Customers enjoy the clay cups because they can reuse them. Thanks to the clear brand differentiation and customer preference for Ban Rai, the company can charge premium prices for its coffee.

By placing franchised outlets in Conoco's Jet Stations, Ban Rai has been able to expand distribution to cover most highways throughout Thailand. Whenever customers see a Jet Station, they know they will find a Ban Rai Coffee House inside. This relationship allows both companies to leverage their brands. Conoco's strategy of standardizing the quality of service stations and offering clean restrooms, Jiffy convenience stores, and Ban Rai Coffee Houses has made Jet Stations and Ban Rai a very welcome sight to Thai drivers on the road.

Also, the franchisee receives materials to use in local advertising and can benefit from national promotional campaigns sponsored by the franchiser.

Through franchise arrangements, the franchiser gains fast and selective product distribution without incurring the high cost of constructing and operating its own outlets. The franchiser therefore has more capital for expanding production and advertising. It can also ensure, through the franchise agreement, that outlets are maintained and operated according to its own standards. The franchiser benefits from the fact that the franchisee, being a sole proprietor in most cases, is likely to be very highly motivated to succeed. Success of the franchise means more sales, which translate into higher income for the franchiser.

Franchise arrangements also have several drawbacks. The franchiser can dictate many aspects of the business: decor, design of employees' uniforms, types of signs, and numerous details of business operations. In addition, franchisees must pay to use the franchiser's name, products, and assistance. Usually there is a one-time franchise fee and continuing royalty and advertising fees, often collected as a percentage of sales. For example, Subway requires franchisees to come up with $30,000 to $90,000 in startup costs. Franchisees often must work very hard, putting in 10- to 12-hour days 6 days a week. In some cases, franchise agreements are not uniform; one franchisee may pay more than another for the same services. Finally, the franchiser gives up a certain amount of control when entering into a franchise agreement. Consequently individual establishments may not be operated exactly according to the franchiser's standards.

Strategic Issues in Retailing

Consumers often have vague reasons for making retail purchases. Whereas most business purchases are based on economic planning and necessity, consumer purchases may result from social and psychological influences. Because consumers shop for a variety of reasons—to search for specific items, escape boredom, or learn about something new—retailers must do more than simply fill space with merchandise. They must make desired products available, create stimulating shopping environments, and develop marketing strategies that increase store patronage. In this section, we discuss how store location, retail positioning, store image, scrambled merchandising, and the wheel of retailing affect retailing objectives.

◆ Location of Retail Stores

Location, the least flexible of the strategic retailing issues, is one of the most important because location dictates the limited geographic trading area from which a store draws its customers. Retailers consider a variety of factors when evaluating potential locations, including location of the firm's target market within the trading area, kinds of products being sold, availability of public transportation, customer characteristics, and competitors' locations.

In choosing a location, a retailer evaluates the relative ease of movement to and from the site, including such factors as pedestrian and vehicular traffic, parking, and transportation. Most retailers prefer sites with high pedestrian traffic. Preliminary site investigations often include a pedestrian count to determine how many passersby are prospective customers. The nature of the area's vehicular traffic is also analyzed. Because customers of certain retailers, such as service stations and many convenience stores, drive to these retail sites, overly congested locations should be avoided. Parking space must be adequate for projected demand, and transportation networks (major thoroughfares and public transit) must accommodate customers and delivery vehicles.

Retailers also evaluate the characteristics of the site itself: types of stores in the area; size, shape, and visibility of the lot or building under consideration; and rental, leasing, or ownership terms. Retailers look for compatibility with nearby retailers because stores that complement one another draw more customers for everyone. When making site location decisions, retailers select from among several general types of locations: freestanding structures, traditional business districts, traditional shopping centers, or nontraditional shopping centers.

Freestanding Structures. Freestanding structures are buildings unconnected to other buildings. Organizations may build such structures or lease or buy them. A retailer, for example, may find that its most successful stores are in freestanding structures close to a shopping mall but not in the mall. Use of freestanding structures allows retailers to physically position themselves away from or close to competitors. Quick-service oil change dealers and fast-food restaurants frequently use freestanding structures and locate close to each other. Toys "R" Us and The Home Depot also tend to locate in freestanding structures.

Traditional Business Districts. A traditional business district—the "downtown shopping district"—usually consists of structures attached to one another and located in a central part of a town or city. Often these structures are aging and, in some cities, traditional business districts are decaying and are viewed as nonviable locations for retailers. However, many towns and cities are preserving or revitalizing their traditional business districts, thus making them attractive locations for certain types of retailers. Some cities have enclosed walkways, shut off streets from traffic, and provided free parking and trolley systems to help traditional business districts compete with shopping malls more effectively.

neighborhood shopping center
A shopping center usually consisting of several small convenience and specialty stores

Traditional Shopping Centers. Traditional shopping centers include neighborhood, community, and regional shopping centers. **Neighborhood shopping centers** usually consist of several small convenience and specialty stores, such as small grocery stores, gas stations, and fast-food restaurants. Many of these retailers consider their target markets to be consumers who live within two to three miles of their stores, or ten minutes' driving time. Because most purchases are based on convenience or personal contact, there is usually little coordination of selling efforts within a neighborhood shopping center. Generally product mixes consist of essential products, and depth of product lines is limited. Convenience stores are most successful when they are closer to consumers than, for example, supermarkets. A good strategy for neighborhood centers is to locate near hotels or interstate highways, or on the route to regional shopping centers.

community shopping center
A shopping center with one or two department stores, some specialty stores, and convenience stores

Community shopping centers include one or two department stores and some specialty stores, as well as convenience stores. They draw consumers looking for shopping and specialty products not available in neighborhood shopping centers. Because these centers serve larger geographic areas, consumers must drive longer distances to community shopping centers than to neighborhood centers. Community shopping centers are planned and coordinated to attract shoppers. Special events, such as art exhibits, automobile shows, and sidewalk sales, stimulate traffic. Overall management of a community shopping center looks for tenants that complement the center's total assortment of products. Such centers have wide product mixes and deep product lines.

regional shopping center
A type of shopping center with the largest department stores, the widest product mix, and the deepest product lines of all shopping centers

Regional shopping centers usually have the largest department stores, the widest product mixes, and the deepest product lines of all shopping centers. Many shopping malls are regional shopping centers, although some are community shopping centers. Regional shopping centers carry most products found in a downtown shopping district. With 150,000 or more consumers in their target market, regional shopping centers must have well-coordinated management and marketing activities. Target markets may include consumers traveling from a distance to find products and prices not available in their hometowns.

Because of the expense of leasing space in regional shopping centers, tenants are more likely to be national chains than small, independent stores. Large centers usually advertise, have special events, furnish transportation to some consumer groups, maintain their own security forces, and carefully select the mix of stores. Mall of America, in the Minneapolis area, is one of the largest shopping malls in the world. It contains about 500 stores, including Nordstrom and Bloomingdale's, and 100 restaurants and nightclubs. The shopping center features Camp Snoopy, a theme park based on Charlie Brown's famous dog, as well as hotels, miniature golf courses, and water slides.

Recently concern has been expressed regarding the possible decline of regional shopping malls. Some regional shopping centers are viewed as being out of touch with the needs of an aging population, struggling with massive debt accumulation, and in need of significant structural repair.[15]

Nontraditional Shopping Centers. Three relatively recent types of shopping centers have emerged that differ significantly from traditional shopping centers. Factory outlet malls feature discount and factory outlet stores carrying traditional manufacturer brands, such as Van Heusen, Levi Strauss, HealthTex, and Wrangler. Some outlet malls feature upscale products. Manufacturers own these stores and make a special effort to avoid conflict with traditional retailers of their products. Manufacturers claim their stores are in noncompetitive locations; indeed, most factory outlet malls are located outside metropolitan areas. Not all factory outlets stock close-outs and irregulars, but most avoid comparison with discount houses. Factory outlet malls attract value-conscious customers seeking quality and major brand names. They operate in much the same way as regional shopping centers, but usually draw customers, some of which may be tourists, from a larger shopping radius. Promotional activity is at the heart of these shopping centers. Craft and antique shows, contests, and special events attract a great deal of traffic.

Another nontraditional shopping center is the miniwarehouse mall. These loosely planned centers sell space to retailers, which operate essentially retail stores out of warehouse bays. Developers of the miniwarehouse mall may also sell space to wholesalers or to light manufacturers that maintain a retail facility in their warehouse bays. Some miniwarehouses are located in high-traffic areas and provide ample customer parking, as well as display windows visible from the street. Home improvement materials, specialty foods, pet supplies, and garden and yard supplies are often sold in these malls. Unlike traditional shopping centers, miniwarehouse malls usually do not have coordinated promotional programs and store mixes. This type of nontraditional shopping center comes closest to a neighborhood or community shopping center.

A third type of nontraditional shopping center is one that does not include a traditional anchor department store. Most malls have one to three main anchor department stores to ensure a continuous stream of mall traffic. With traditional mall sales declining, this more recent type of shopping mall may be anchored by a store such as The Gap. Other likely stores for such malls include Toys "R" Us, Circuit City, PETsMART, and The Home Depot. Shopping center developers are combining off-price stores with category killers in "power center" formats. Off-price centers are growing, resulting in a variety of formats vying for the same retail dollar. To compete, existing region malls may have to adapt by changing their store mixes.

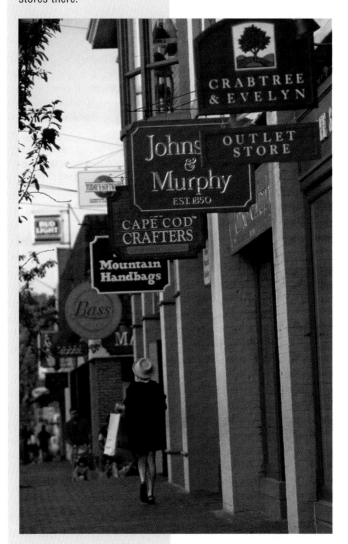

Shopping Centers
Freeport, Maine, home to L.L.Bean, is a popular destination for outlet shoppers. Numerous organizations have set up outlet stores there.

◆ Retail Positioning

The emergence of new types of stores and expansion of product offerings by traditional stores have intensified retailing competition. Retail positioning is therefore an important consideration. **Retail positioning** involves identifying an unserved or underserved market segment and serving it through a strategy that distinguishes the retailer from others in the minds of those customers. For example, Hot Topic, a specialty store chain, has carved out a unique retail position by stocking "alternative" merchandise such as glow-in-the-dark tongue rings, hair dye, gothic boots, and other apparel and accessories that appeal to teens who dislike trendy stores such as the Gap, Abercrombie & Fitch, and Wet Seal.[16]

Retailers position themselves. A retailer may position itself as a seller of high-quality, premium-priced products and provide many services. Neiman Marcus, for example, specializes in expensive, high-fashion clothing and jewelry, sophisticated electronics, and exclusive home furnishings, and provides wrapping and delivery, valet parking, and personal shopping consultants. Another type of retail organization may be positioned as a marketer of reasonable-quality products at everyday low prices. Pizza Hut, for example, has positioned itself as the value alternative by offering a variety of large pizzas at low prices. Its rival, Papa John's, has established a product quality position with the slogan "Better ingredients. Better pizza." The Albertson's supermarket chain is changing its retail positioning from its produce-centric positioning using a $145 million campaign touting its stores as the place for busy moms to shop.[17]

◆ Store Image

To attract customers, a retail store must project an image—a functional and psychological picture in the consumer's mind—that appeals to its target market. Store environment, merchandise quality, and service quality are key determinants of store image.

Atmospherics, the physical elements in a store's design that appeal to consumers' emotions and encourage buying, help to create an image and position a retailer. McDonald's, for example, is opening McCafés complete with special café decor and menu items such as gourmet coffee and desserts. McDonald's has about 300 McCafés in 17 countries and plans to open several in the U.S. soon.[18]

Exterior atmospheric elements include the appearance of the storefront, display windows, store entrances, and degree of traffic congestion. Exterior atmospherics are particularly important to new customers, who tend to judge an unfamiliar store by its outside appearance and may not enter if they feel intimidated by the building or inconvenienced by the parking lot. Interior atmospheric elements include aesthetic considerations such as lighting, wall and floor coverings, dressing facilities, and store fixtures. Interior sensory elements contribute significantly to atmosphere. Color can attract shoppers to a retail display. Many fast-food restaurants use bright colors, such as red and yellow, because these have been shown to make customers feel hungrier and eat faster, which increases turnover. Sound is another important sensory component of atmosphere and may range from silence to subdued background sounds to music. One study indicated that retail customers shop for a longer period when exposed to unfamiliar music than they do when exposed to familiar music.[19] Many retailers believe shoppers who remain in their stores longer will, in fact, purchase more. A store's layout—arrangement of departments, width of aisles, grouping of products, and location of checkout areas—is another determinant of atmosphere. Department stores, restaurants, hotels, service stations, and specialty stores combine these elements in different ways to create specific atmospheres that may be perceived as warm, fresh, functional, or exciting.

Retailers must assess the atmosphere the target market seeks and then adjust atmospheric variables to encourage desired consumer awareness and action. High-fashion boutiques generally strive for an atmosphere of luxury and novelty. Ralph Lauren's Polo Shops offer limited merchandise in large, open areas with props such as saddles or leather chairs adding to the exclusive look and image. On the other hand, discount department stores strive *not* to seem too exclusive and expensive. To

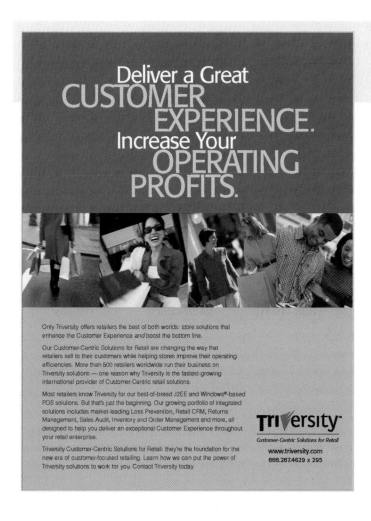

Deliver a Great
CUSTOMER EXPERIENCE.
Increase Your
OPERATING PROFITS.

Only Triversity offers retailers the best of both worlds: store solutions that enhance the Customer Experience *and* boost the bottom line.

Our Customer-Centric Solutions for Retail are changing the way that retailers sell to their customers while helping stores improve their operating efficiencies. More than 500 retailers worldwide run their business on Triversity solutions — one reason why Triversity is the fastest-growing international provider of Customer-Centric retail solutions.

Most retailers know Triversity for our best-of-breed J2EE and Windows®-based POS solutions. But that's just the beginning. Our growing portfolio of integrated solutions includes market-leading Loss Prevention, Retail CRM, Returns Management, Sales Audit, Inventory and Order Management and more, all designed to help you deliver an exceptional Customer Experience throughout your retail enterprise.

Triversity Customer-Centric Solutions for Retail: they're the foundation for the new era of customer-focused retailing. Learn how we can put the power of Triversity solutions to work for you. Contact Triversity today.

TriVersity
Customer-Centric Solutions for Retail
www.triversity.com
888.287.4629 x 295

Store Image
Triversity helps retailers improve service quality—one dimension of store image—by offering technology solutions to help manage returns and inventory, among other things.

appeal to multiple market segments, a retailer may create different atmospheres for different operations within the store; for example, the discount basement, the sports department, the housewares department, and the women's shoe department may each have a unique atmosphere.

Although heavily dependent on atmospherics, a store's image is also shaped by its reputation for integrity, number of services offered, location, merchandise assortments, pricing policies, promotional activities, and community involvement. Characteristics of the target market—social class, lifestyle, income level, and past buying behavior—help form store image as well. How consumers perceive the store can be a major determinant of store patronage. Consumers from lower socioeconomic groups tend to patronize small, high-margin, high-service food stores and prefer small, friendly loan companies over large, impersonal banks, even though the former charge higher interest. Affluent consumers tend to look for exclusive establishments offering high-quality products and prestigious labels. Retailers should be aware of the multiple factors contributing to store image and recognize that perceptions of image vary.

◆ Scrambled Merchandising

scrambled merchandising The addition of unrelated products and product lines to an existing product mix, particularly fast-moving items that can be sold in volume

When retailers add unrelated products and product lines—particularly fast-moving items that can be sold in volume—to an existing product mix, they are practicing **scrambled merchandising.** Retailers adopting this strategy hope to accomplish one or more of the following: (1) convert stores into one-stop shopping centers, (2) generate more traffic, (3) realize higher profit margins, and (4) increase impulse purchases. In scrambled merchandising, retailers must deal with diverse marketing channels. Scrambled merchandising can also blur a store's image in consumers' minds, making it more difficult for a retailer to succeed in today's highly competitive, saturated markets. Finally, scrambled merchandising intensifies competition among traditionally distinct types of stores and forces suppliers to adjust distribution systems to accommodate new channel members.

◆ The Wheel of Retailing

wheel of retailing A hypothesis holding that new retailers usually enter the market as low-status, low-margin, low-price operators but eventually evolve into high-cost, high-price merchants

As new types of retail businesses evolve, they strive to fill niches in a dynamic retailing environment. One hypothesis regarding the evolution and development of new types of retail stores is the **wheel of retailing**. According to this theory, new retailers enter the marketplace with low prices, margins, and status. Their low prices are usually the result of innovative cost-cutting procedures and soon attract imitators. Gradually, as these businesses attempt to broaden their customer base and increase sales, their operations and facilities become more elaborate and more expensive. They may move to more desirable locations, begin to carry higher-quality merchandise, or add services. Eventually they emerge at the high end of the price, cost, and service scales, competing with newer discount retailers following the same evolutionary process.[20]

Figure 17.1 The Wheel of Retailing If the "wheel" is considered to be turning slowly in the direction of the arrows, then the department stores around 1900 and the discounters that came later can be viewed as coming on the scene at the low end of the wheel. As it turns slowly, they move with it, becoming higher-price operations and leaving room for lower-price firms to gain entry at the low end of the wheel.
Source: Adapted from Robert F. Hartley, *Retailing: Challenge and Opportunity,* 3rd ed., p. 42. Copyright © 1984 by Houghton Mifflin Company. Used by permission.

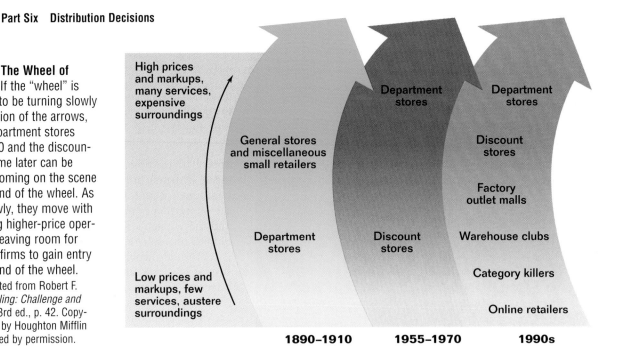

Supermarkets, for example, have undergone many changes since their introduction in 1921. Initially they offered limited services and low food prices. Over time they developed a variety of new services, including free coffee, gourmet food sections, and children's play areas. Today supermarkets are being challenged by superstores, which offer more product choices and undercut supermarket prices.

Consider the evolution of department stores, discount stores, warehouse clubs, category killers, and online retailers, shown in Figure 17.1. Department stores such as Sears started out as high-volume, low-cost merchants competing with general stores and other small retailers. Discount stores developed later in response to rising expenses of services in department stores. Many discount outlets now appear to be following the wheel of retailing by offering more services, better locations, quality inventories, and therefore higher prices. Some discount stores are almost indistinguishable from department stores. In response have emerged category killers, such as PETsMART and Office Depot, which concentrate on a major product category and offer enormous product depth, in many cases at lower prices than discount stores. Even these retailers, however, seem to be following the wheel. Lowe's, a home improvement retailer, has added big-ticket items and more upscale brands, such as Laura Ashley.

The wheel of retailing, along with other changes in the marketing environment and in buying behavior itself, requires that retailers adjust to survive and compete. Consumers have less time than ever to shop. Shopping today centers on "needs fulfillment" and thus is more utilitarian and work oriented, a fact that many major retailing executives have noticed. As consumers have less time to shop and greater access to more sophisticated technology, retailing venues such as catalog retailing, television home shopping, and online retailing will take on greater importance. New retailers will evolve to capitalize on these opportunities, while those that cannot adapt will not survive.

SUMMARY

Retailing includes all transactions in which buyers intend to consume products through personal, family, or household use. Retailers, organizations that sell products primarily to ultimate consumers, are important links in the marketing channel because they are both marketers for and customers of wholesalers and producers. Retailers add value, provide services, and assist in making product selections.

Retail stores can be classified according to the breadth of products offered. Two broad categories are general-merchandise retailers and specialty retailers. The primary types of general-merchandise retailers include department stores, discount stores, supermarkets, super-stores, hypermarkets, warehouse clubs, and warehouse and catalog showrooms. Department stores are large retail organizations employing at least 25 people and characterized by wide product mixes of considerable depth for most product lines. Their products are organized into separate departments that function like self-contained businesses. Discount stores are self-service, low-price, general-merchandise outlets. Supermarkets are large, self-service food stores that also carry some nonfood products. Superstores are giant retail outlets that carry all the products found in supermarkets and most consumer products purchased on a routine basis. Hypermarkets offer supermarket and discount store shopping at one location. Warehouse clubs are large-scale, members-only discount operations. Warehouse and catalog showrooms are low-cost operations characterized by warehouse methods of materials handling and display, large inventories, and minimal services.

Specialty retailers offer substantial assortments in a few product lines. They include traditional specialty retailers, which carry narrow product mixes with deep product lines; off-price retailers, which sell brand name manufacturers' seconds and production overruns at deep discounts; and category killers, large specialty stores that concentrate on a major product category and compete on the basis of low prices and enormous product availability.

Direct marketing is the use of telephone and nonpersonal media to communicate product and organizational information to consumers, who can then purchase products by mail or telephone. Direct marketing is a type of nonstore retailing, the selling of goods or services outside the confines of a retail facility. Forms of direct marketing include catalog marketing, direct-response marketing, telemarketing, television home shopping, and online retailing. Two other types of nonstore retailing are direct selling and automatic vending. Direct selling is the marketing of products to ultimate consumers through face-to-face sales presentations at home or in the workplace. Automatic vending is the use of machines to dispense products.

Franchising is an arrangement in which a supplier grants a dealer the right to sell products in exchange for some type of consideration. Retail franchises are of three general types. A manufacturer may authorize a number of retail stores to sell a certain brand name item; a producer may license distributors to sell a given product to retailers; or a franchiser may supply brand names, techniques, or other services instead of a complete product. Franchise arrangements have a number of advantages and disadvantages over traditional business forms, and their use is increasing.

To increase sales and store patronage, retailers must consider strategic issues. Location determines the trading area from which a store draws its customers and should be evaluated carefully. When evaluating potential sites, retailers take into account a variety of factors, including the location of the firm's target market within the trading area, kinds of products sold, availability of public transportation, customer characteristics, and competitors' locations. Retailers can choose among several types of locations, including freestanding structures, traditional business districts, traditional shopping centers, or nontraditional shopping centers.

Retail positioning involves identifying an unserved or underserved market segment and serving it through a strategy that distinguishes the retailer from others in those customers' minds. Store image, which various customers perceive differently, derives not only from atmosphere but also from location, products offered, customer services, prices, promotion, and the store's overall reputation. Atmospherics refers to the physical elements of a store's design that can be adjusted to appeal to consumers' emotions and thus induce them to buy. Scrambled merchandising adds unrelated product lines to an existing product mix and is being used by a growing number of stores to generate sales.

The wheel of retailing hypothesis holds that new retail institutions start out as low-status, low-margin, and low-price operations. As they develop, they increase services and prices, and eventually become vulnerable to newer organizations, which enter the market and repeat the cycle.

Please visit the student website at **www.prideferrell.com** for ACE Self-Test questions that will help you prepare for exams.

IMPORTANT TERMS

Retailing
Retailer
General-merchandise
  retailer
Department store
Discount store
Supermarket
Superstore
Hypermarket
Warehouse club

Warehouse showroom
Catalog showroom
Traditional specialty
  retailer
Off-price retailer
Category killer
Direct marketing
Nonstore retailing
Catalog marketing
Direct-response marketing

Telemarketing
Television home shopping
Online retailing
Direct selling
Automatic vending
Franchising
Neighborhood shopping
  center
Community shopping
  center

Regional shopping center
Retail positioning
Atmospherics
Scrambled merchandising
Wheel of retailing

DISCUSSION & REVIEW QUESTIONS

1. What value do retailers add to a product? What value do retailers add for producers and ultimate consumers?
2. Differentiate between the two general categories of retail stores based on breadth of product offering.
3. What are the major differences between discount stores and department stores?
4. How does a superstore differ from a supermarket?
5. In what ways are traditional specialty stores and off-price retailers similar? How do they differ?
6. Describe direct marketing and the other two major types of nonstore retailing. List some products you have purchased through these types of nonstore retailing in the last six months. Why did you choose this method for making your purchases instead of going to a retail outlet?
7. How is door-to-door selling a form of retailing? Some consumers believe direct-response orders bypass the retailer. Is this true? Explain.
8. Evaluate the following statement: "Telemarketing, television home shopping, and online retailing will eventually eliminate the need for traditional forms of retailing."
9. If you were opening a retail business, would you prefer to open an independent store or own a store under a franchise arrangement? Explain your preference.
10. What major issues should be considered when determining a retail site location?
11. Describe the three major types of traditional shopping centers. Give an example of each type in your area.
12. Discuss the major factors that help determine a retail store's image.

13. How does atmosphere add value to products sold in a store? How important is atmospherics for convenience stores?
14. Is it possible for a single retail store to have an overall image that appeals to sophisticated shoppers, extravagant buyers, and bargain hunters? Why or why not?
15. In what ways does the use of scrambled merchandising affect a store's image?

APPLICATION QUESTIONS

1. Juanita wants to open a small retail store that specializes in high-quality, high-priced children's clothing. With what types of competitors should she be concerned in this competitive retail environment? Why?
2. Location of retail outlets is a primary issue in strategic planning. What initial steps would you recommend to Juanita (see question 1) when she considers a location for her store?
3. Different types of stores offer varying breadth and depth of assortments. Godiva Chocolate stores, for example, offer a very narrow assortment of products but provide great depth. Visit a discount store, a specialty store, or a department store, and report on the number of different product lines offered and the depth within each line.
4. Atmospherics is an important tool used by retailers in their efforts to position stores. Visit a retail store you shop in regularly. Identify the store and describe its atmospherics. Be specific about both exterior and interior elements, and indicate how the store is being positioned through its use of atmospherics.

Internet Exercise & Resources

Visit **www.prideferrell.com** for resources to help you master the material in this chapter, plus materials that will help you expand your marketing knowledge, including Internet exercise updates, ACE self-tests, hotlinks to companies featured in this chapter, and much more.

Walmart.com

Wal-Mart provides a website where customers can shop for products, search for a nearby store, and even pre-order new products. The website lets browsers see what's on sale and view company information. Access Wal-Mart's website at **www.walmart.com**.

1. How does Wal-Mart attempt to position itself on its website?
2. Compare the atmospherics of Wal-Mart's website to the atmospherics of a traditional Wal-Mart store. Are they consistent? If not, should they be?
3. Read the "Wal-Mart Story" on the website. Relate the firm's history to the wheel of retailing concept.

Video Case 17.1

REI Scales New Heights in Retailing

In 1938, 25 mountain climbers founded Recreational Equipment Inc. (REI) to pool their buying power for a better deal on ice axes and other climbing gear. From the start, REI was a consumer cooperative: a retail business that shares some of its profits with members. Today the retailer sells a vast array of outdoor sporting goods and apparel through 66 stores in 24 states, a printed catalog, and 2 websites. It also operates a travel service, REI Adventures, for those who want to paddle, climb, cycle, ski, hike, or enjoy a combination of outdoor activities while on vacation.

REI's store atmospherics are unique, making the shopping experience an adventure in itself. Every store contains a two-story climbing wall that customers are invited to scale when trying out gear before buying. For example, the store in Sandy, Utah, features a 22-foot-high climbing wall modeled after the granite walls of a local canyon. Like other stores in the chain, the Sandy store has demonstration areas devoted to camp stoves, water filter testing, and hiking boots. Surrounding these special areas are acres and acres of items that one employee calls "grown-up toys," from kayaks and canteens to snow shoes and sleeping bags.

The store employees are enthusiastic about the merchandise they sell because they share their customers' love of the active life. "A passion for the outdoors comes first throughout REI and is a natural bond between employees and customers," observes REI's vice president of direct sales. "That passion and commitment to quality are reflected whether you're in an REI store, shopping online, or placing a catalog order on the phone." Employees are trained to determine their customers' needs, demonstrate appropriate products, and help customers make an informed buying decision. The emphasis is on educating and satisfying customers rather than on trying to close as many sales as possible.

This emphasis is reflected in the attractive, easy-to-navigate design of REI.com. Customers can log on, select a product category, and scroll through thousands of pages filled with product details, prod-

uct comparisons, and how-to articles about outdoor sports, recreation, and equipment. The company's discount website, REI-Outlet.com, also provides extensive information about its marked-down products. Each REI store has several web kiosks where customers can browse the company's two websites and order any of the 45,000 products in stock for home delivery. If they prefer, customers can eliminate shipping fees by having online orders sent to a nearby store for pickup—an option chosen by more than 30 percent of REI-Outlet.com's customers.

Customers can become REI members by paying a one-time fee of $15. Because the retailer operates as a cooperative, members are eligible for refund vouchers of up to 10 percent on their total annual purchases from REI stores, catalogs, and websites. They also pay lower prices for equipment rented or repaired in REI stores and for travel packages arranged through REI Adventures.

One of REI's core values is its ongoing commitment to protecting the natural environment through contributions and volunteerism. The company donates thousands of dollars to support nature centers, open-space projects, youth recreation programs, land conservation, and related activities in each community where it does business. In all, REI's annual contributions total nearly $2 million. Moreover, as REI's president notes, store employees invest a great deal of "sweat equity" in the local community by volunteering their time to maintain hiking trails, clean up rivers, and preserve the environment in many other ways.

REI is not the only retailer pursuing the market for outdoor sporting goods and apparel. Bass Pro Shops, headquartered in Missouri, targets customers who like fishing, hunting, and boating. Its 27 U.S. stores offer demonstration areas for fishing and other sports, creating a focal point for customers. Eastern Mountain Sports (EMS), headquartered in New Hampshire, operates 100 stores in eastern and midwestern states, including 22 spread across the state of New York. REI must also compete with many independent stores and chain retailers that carry clothing and gear for the active lifestyle.

In this increasingly competitive climate, REI is relying on its innovative and appealing atmospherics as a key differentiating factor. It is also bringing customers back again and again through in-store demonstrations and an informative e-mail newsletter. Currently REI generates more than $700 million in revenue and serves 2 million customers a year. More growth is on the way with new store openings, new website features, and new "grown-up toys."[21]

Case 17.2

Costco Offers Low Prices and a Unique Product Mix

More than 20 years after Costco opened its first warehouse club store in Seattle, the company's philosophy can still be summed up as "pile 'em high, price 'em low." Costco stores are anything but fancy; in fact, the first store was located inside a warehouse. Yet 42 million consumers and small-business owners pay $45 (fee may vary) annually so they can save on everything from mayonnaise and prescription medicines to handheld computers and truck-size snow tires. In fact, customers never really know what products they will find each time they visit one of the 735 Costco stores around the world. Surprises are all part of the shopping experience at Costco.

"The art form of our business is intuition," says CEO James D. Sinegal. His buyers must choose carefully, because the typical Costco carries less than 10 percent of the number of products displayed in a Wal-Mart store. Moreover, Costco aims for a profit margin of no more than 14 percent, which means inventory must sell quickly. If products sell slowly, they will tie up precious cash that could be better spent on newer or more popular merchandise. Therefore, Costco's buyers watch for particularly hot products and product categories. When the chief electronics buyer noticed the cost of plasma-screen televisions dropping, for example, he took what he calls "an educated gamble" and placed a sizable order. The gamble paid off: the televisions, priced below $5,000, sold out quickly even before the year-end holiday shopping season.

Costco carries a broad and varied merchandise assortment, all priced low to move quickly. It sells 55,000 rotisserie chickens every day and $600 million worth of fine wines every year. It also sells 45 million hot dogs and 60,000 carats of diamonds annually. The hot dogs retail for $1.50 each, while a single piece of jewelry can retail for as much as $100,000. Well-known manufacturers' brands share shelf space with Kirkland Signature, Costco's private brand. Members may walk past stacks of best-selling books on the right and color printers on the left as they push their shopping carts down the aisle. This variety enhances the store's appeal, says the CEO: "Our customers don't drive 15 miles to save on a jar of peanut butter. They come for the treasure hunt."

Despite the low prices, Costco offers a generous return policy. Customers can return anything at any time. If dissatisfied with their membership, they can even get a full refund on that. The sole exception is computers, which cannot be brought back after six months. No receipt? No problem at Costco. Customers have ample opportunity to exchange or return items because they visit the stores frequently. Research shows that, on average, members visit Costco stores more than 11 times a year and spend $94 on each visit.

Costco's main competitor is Sam's Club, owned by Wal-Mart. Given Wal-Mart's buying power and channel leadership, Sam's Club can buy products at very low prices and get them to stores with unusual efficiency.

Nonetheless, Costco tops Sam's Club in a number of ways. Each U.S. Costco store rings up, on average, $112 million worth of merchandise annually. By comparison, the average yearly sales of each U.S. Sam's Club store is $63 million. Whereas the average sales per square foot at Sam's Club is $497, Costco's equivalent figure is a whopping $797 per square foot. Although Sam's Club charges a lower membership fee, Costco's members are quite loyal, with a renewal rate of 86 percent.

In recent years, Costco has expanded by offering new services at low prices. For example, members can log onto the retailer's website (**www.costco.com**) and sign up for long-distance telephone service, apply for a mortgage, buy life insurance, or price a vacation trip. The company has also started a new chain of stores, Costco Home, which specializes in home furnishings. In warehouse retailing, however, Sam's Club remains the competitor to beat. Before Sam's Club opened stores in Canada, Costco prepared for the increased competition by remodeling some of its stores. And price wars sometimes break out when the two competitors battle for customers. The parent company of Sam's Club is by far the largest company in the world, but Costco is so adept at warehouse retailing that it continues to hold its own.[22]

QUESTIONS FOR DISCUSSION

1. How do Costco's atmospherics support its retail positioning?
2. Analyze the retail strategy represented by the new Costco Home chain.
3. How is Costco's retail positioning likely to be affected by its target profit margin of 14 percent?

Strategic Case 6

The Home Depot Reinforces Its Strong Channel Strategy

Got growth? North America's number one home improvement retailer, The Home Depot, is always looking for profitable growth. The company has 1,700 stores and $58 billion in annual sales, giving it a commanding lead over competitor Lowe's Companies, which rings up $26 billion annually and operates 1,000 stores. Home Depot built its reputation with category-killer stores that sell tens of thousands of home improvement products, from lumber and locks to faucets and flashlights. Consumers tackling do-it-yourself projects, as well as building contractors, come for the large selection and the low prices. Nobody minds the warehouselike ambiance.

Despite its industry dominance, Home Depot remains committed to growth by opening hundreds of new category-killer stores every year in the United States, Mexico, and Canada. The company also is opening new types of stores, adapting stores to local needs, moving deeper into the service business, and buying complementary firms with high-growth potential.

Going Upscale with Expo   In 1991, Home Depot launched an upscale chain, called Expo Design Center, to attract affluent consumers planning to remodel or redecorate their homes. Each Expo showcases a carefully chosen assortment of high-end products for kitchens, bathrooms, and every other room in the house, from professional-quality stoves and hand-painted ceramic tiles to high-tech lighting and colorful carpeting. The convenience of one-stop shopping is as important as the merchandise mix. Lowe's has no stores of this type, and Sears is not making its chain of home decorating stores, The Great Indoors, a priority.

Although the 54-store Expo chain is profitable, it has undergone a number of changes as management refines the retail strategy. The first Expo store was not a big hit because many of its products were already available in nearby Home Depot stores. Moreover, the store looked too much like any Home Depot outlet. The company decided to differentiate Expo by stocking more exclusive, higher-priced merchandise and rearranging the showrooms to create a new layout.

In a second change, the retailer conducted marketing research with an eye toward broadening the target market and boosting sales. Expo originally targeted homeowners with annual household incomes of $75,000 or more and was considering lowering the annual income threshold to $50,000. After months of research, however, the company discovered that the typical Expo customer's household income was $100,000. These customers were spending, on average, $40,000 to renovate a kitchen and $15,000 to redo a bathroom with products from Expo. This convinced management to raise rather than lower its income target and replace more of the lower-priced products with higher-priced offerings.

Adapting Stores for Different Markets By studying each area's buying patterns, the company has developed ways to adapt its Home Depot stores to local needs. For example, when a housing boom was increasing consumer and contractor demand in Anaheim Hills, California, the company replaced a much smaller Home Depot with a well-stocked store the size of four football fields. Landscaping is big business here, so the garden center is twice the size of those in most Home Depots, complete with a drive-through checkout for customers buying in bulk. Instead of 3 display areas of bathroom fixtures, the new store has 21 such displays. Moreover, products for consumers are shelved separately from products for contractors. This means consumers don't have to walk through aisles of cement and lumber to find household glue or lawn mowers, and contractors can readily find what they want and check out quickly.

Home Depot has opened several stand-alone Landscape Supply stores in markets where demand for such products is especially high. It has also developed a smaller type of Home Depot store for city locations, carrying only items appropriate to urban customers. Meanwhile the company is investing nearly $2 billion to make all of its stores more attractive through new lighting, new signs, upgraded flooring, and other improvements.

Online and Beyond Online retailing is an important part of Home Depot's growth strategy. The website (www.homedepot.com) acts as an online catalog for consumers and business customers to browse before buying via the Internet or visiting a neighborhood Home Depot store. It also contains extensive educational material to help consumers plan and implement home improvement projects and explains how the company works with building professionals.

Internet sales are increasing, but the stores remain the company's main focus. To enhance its differentiation, Home Depot is increasing its inventory of product lines not available elsewhere, such as Ridgid professional tools, and expanding its tool rental program. In addition, it is gearing up to become a major player in home improvement services. On the consumer side, Home Depot wants to offer services for many materials installation and home repair projects. On the business side, it wants to provide floor installation and other services to construction professionals. To accomplish this, Home Depot will be making more acquisitions such as its recent purchase of Creative Touch Interiors, a company that contractors hire to install flooring and counters.

Behind the Scenes Home Depot constantly reevaluates its physical distribution system to find ways to eliminate inefficiencies and give the stores

more support. At one time, it required suppliers to deliver ordered merchandise directly to individual Home Depot stores. Today the company has gained more control over the timing of inventory replenishment by having suppliers ship merchandise to its regional distribution centers. Once a shipment arrives, it is sorted and repacked according to each store's order, then loaded onto trucks for immediate delivery. This system allows Home Depot to restock sold-out merchandise within 24 hours.

The company has also found a solution for the potentially expensive problem of storing huge quantities of seasonal inventory. Rather than building warehouses that will stand empty when not storing snow blowers in the winter and grills in the spring, Home Depot rents space in public warehouses near its stores. Each company that rents space in this kind of warehouse has its own entrance and is responsible for managing the goods in its part of the building.

If Home Depot had thousands of small or perishable items to store in different quantities for different periods, it would need highly automated warehouses. However, because it holds a narrower range of large products for a limited time, the company can make do without the sophisticated technology and equipment that keep its distribution centers humming. Each store manager uses special PC software to check on what is available in the shared warehouses and place orders as needed. The company then arranges a speedy transfer of merchandise from the appropriate warehouse to the individual store. Now the distribution centers can concentrate on getting year-round goods to the stores as quickly as possible, and Home Depot can free up funds to fuel its ongoing growth.

QUESTIONS FOR DISCUSSION

1. What roles do physical distribution efforts play in Home Depot's retail success?
2. What are the advantages and disadvantages of using public warehouses for storing seasonal inventory?
3. What are the major strategic dimensions through which Home Depot competes and grows?
4. How does the positioning of the Expo store differ from the positioning of the regular Home Depot store?

Part Seven

Promotion Decisions

Part Seven focuses on communication with target market members and, at times, other groups. A specific marketing mix cannot satisfy people in a particular target market unless they are aware of the product and know where to find it. Some promotion decisions relate to a specific marketing mix; others are geared toward promoting the entire organization. **Chapter 18** discusses integrated marketing communications. It describes the communication process and the major promotional methods that can be included in promotion mixes. **Chapter 19** analyzes the major steps in developing an advertising campaign. It also explains what public relations is and how it can be used. **Chapter 20** deals with personal selling and the role it can play in a firm's promotional efforts. This chapter also explores the general characteristics of sales promotion and describes sales promotion techniques.

18

Integrated Marketing Communications

OBJECTIVES

1. To describe the nature of integrated marketing communications

2. To understand the role of promotion in the marketing mix

3. To examine the process of communication

4. To explain the objectives of promotion

5. To explore the elements of the promotion mix

6. To examine the major methods of promotion

7. To describe factors that affect the choice of promotional methods

8. To examine criticisms and defenses of promotion

Turkey & Gravy Brings Attention to Small Bottler

Seattle-based Jones Soda Company manufactures premium soft drinks known for creative flavors, labels, and promotions that clearly differentiate them from mass market offerings by Coca-Cola and PepsiCo. Jones Soda continuously promotes its premium brand and regularly changes flavors and labels, which may include photos sent in by customers. Customers can even suggest new flavors to Jones on the company's website.

Despite its reputation for curious flavors, Jones' management was surprised by the deluge of publicity generated by the release of a turkey- and gravy-flavored soft drink around Thanksgiving. The company produced just a few thousand bottles of the seasonal flavor as part of a promotional campaign to draw attention to its other soft drinks. Turkey & Gravy Soda sold out in a matter of hours, perhaps because it seemed fun, unique, and timely. Although product developers at Jones characterized the product as a sipping soda rather than a thirst-satisfying one, the timing of its holiday release helped fuel its success.

One thing is clear about Turkey & Gravy Soda: people loved talking about the soft drink that was purported to taste like "microwaved Thanksgiving leftovers." In the three weeks following its introduction, the company's president, Peter Van Stolks, was contacted more than 500 times by the media, resulting in nearly 100 radio interviews. Even *Business Week* acknowledged the product. Jones was particularly pleased with the radio publicity generated by Turkey & Gravy Soda because the company's target market is teenagers, who are known to be devoted radio listeners.

In the case of this novelty product, it is doubtful that paid advertising could have generated nearly as much interest in the curiously flavored soft drink as this buzz marketing approach did. Indeed, Turkey & Gravy Soda has been Jones's most successful promotion to date, exceeding the impact of previous promotions associated with flavors such as Ham and Fish-Taco. Van Stolks further maximized the public relations impact by mentioning in every radio interview that the company planned to donate all profits from Turkey & Gravy Soda to the Toys for Tots charity. Such creativity in marketing certainly seems to have paid off for Jones Soda: its sales have doubled over the last four years, from $11 million to $22 million.[1] ■

Organizations such as Jones Soda employ a variety of promotional methods to communicate with their target markets. Providing information to customers is vital to initiating and developing long-term customer relationships. This chapter looks at the general dimensions of promotion. First, we discuss the nature of integrated marketing communications. We then define and examine the role of promotion. Next, we analyze the meaning and process of communication and explore some of the reasons promotion is used. Then we consider major promotional methods and the factors that influence marketers' decisions to use particular methods. Finally, we examine criticisms and defenses of promotion.

The Nature of Integrated Marketing Communications

integrated marketing communications Coordination of promotion and other marketing efforts for maximum informational and persuasive impact

Integrated marketing communications refer to the coordination of promotion and other marketing efforts to ensure maximum informational and persuasive impact on customers. Coordinating multiple marketing tools to produce this synergistic effect requires a marketer to employ a broad perspective. A major goal of integrated marketing communications is to send a consistent message to customers. Because various units both inside and outside most companies have traditionally planned and implemented promotional efforts, customers have not always received consistent messages. Integrated marketing communications allow an organization a way to coordinate and manage its promotional efforts to ensure that customers receive consistent messages. Integrated marketing communications also enable synchronization of promotion elements and can reduce overspending on elements that may produce a smaller return on investment.[2] Thus, this approach fosters not only long-term customer relationships but also the efficient use of promotional resources.

The concept of integrated marketing communications has been increasingly accepted for several reasons. Mass media advertising, a very popular promotional method in the past, is used less frequently today because of its high cost and lower effectiveness in reaching some target markets.[3] Marketers can now take advantage of more precisely targeted promotional tools, such as cable TV, direct mail, CD-ROMs, the Internet, special-interest magazines, videocassettes, and DVDs. Database marketing is also allowing marketers to more precisely target individual customers. Until recently, suppliers of marketing communications were specialists. Advertising agencies provided advertising campaigns, sales promotion companies provided sales promotion activities and materials, and public relations organizations engaged in publicity efforts. Today a number of promotion-related companies provide one-stop shopping for the client seeking advertising, sales promotion, and public relations, thus reducing coordination problems for the sponsoring company. Because the overall cost of marketing communications has risen significantly, upper management demands systematic evaluations of communication efforts and a reasonable return on investment.

Change Motivation
with Behavior-Based Marketing.

Personalize your communications. Influence consumer behavior and attitude. Maximize marketing ROI. Now you can motivate consumers as individuals, not averages or composites. Behavior-based marketing allows you to target individual consumers – on a mass scale – with messages based on their actual purchase behavior. ▲ For 20 years, Catalina Marketing has innovated the art and science of behavior-based marketing for many of the world's leading manufacturers and retailers. Today, we offer the most advanced services in behavior-based marketing – incentives, promotional messaging, sampling, market research, direct mail and loyalty programs. ▲ Leverage the power of behavior-based marketing today. Contact a Catalina Marketing representative at (888) 322-3850 or www.catalinamarketing.com.

CATALINA MARKETING
Targeting Change

MANUFACTURER SERVICES | RETAIL SERVICES | DIRECT MARKETING SERVICES | RESEARCH SOLUTIONS | HEALTH RESOURCE

The Nature of Integrated Marketing Communications
Catalina Marketing uses access to customers and gives insight into their individual purchase behavior to help its clients develop more effective promotion programs.

Snapshot

Consumers prefer custom messages

Most customers say they prefer personalized e-mail marketing messages.

Prefer non-personalized messages and offers that everyone receives regardless of needs or interest — **22%**

Prefer highly-personalized messages and offers that are unique to my needs or interests — **78%**

Source: Data from Cable & Telecommunications Association for Marketing survey.

The specific communication vehicles employed and the precision with which they are used are changing as both information technology and customer interests become increasingly dynamic. For example, the *Bakersfield Californian* newspaper used text messaging on cellphones to target 15- to 24-year-olds in a cross-promotion with a local music store. The promotion allowed fans to vote for their favorite new CD listed in World Music's print ads, with participants gaining an opportunity to win gift certificates and other prizes.[4] Today marketers and customers have almost unlimited access to data about each other. Integrating and customizing marketing communications while protecting customer privacy has become a major challenge. However, research indicates that 75 percent of adult consumers want products customized to their personal needs, and 70 percent say they would be more loyal to companies that make an effort to discover their needs and tastes.[5] Through the Internet, companies can provide product information and services that are coordinated with traditional promotional activities. Communication relationships with customers can actually determine the nature of the product. For example, Reflect.com, an online cosmetics firm, mixes makeup for different skin types based on information exchanges with customers. Thus, consumers may be willing to exchange personal information for customized products.[6] The sharing of information and use of technology to facilitate communication between buyers and sellers are essential for successful customer relationship management.

The Role of Promotion

promotion Communication to build and maintain relationships by informing and persuading one or more audiences

Promotion is communication that builds and maintains favorable relationships by informing and persuading one or more audiences to view an organization positively and to accept its products. While a company may pursue a number of promotional objectives (discussed later in this chapter), the overall role of promotion is to stimulate product demand. Toward this end, many organizations spend considerable resources on promotion to build and enhance relationships with current and potential customers. For example, the lumber ("Be Constructive"), pork ("Pork: The Other White Meat"), and milk ("Got Milk?") industries promote the use of these products to stimulate demand.[7] Building Customer Relationships (on p. 476) looks at how rival companies teamed up to stimulate cereal demand. Marketers also indirectly facilitate favorable relationships by focusing information about company activities and products on interest groups (such as environmental and consumer groups), current and potential investors, regulatory agencies, and society in general. For example, some organizations promote responsible use of products criticized by society such as tobacco, alcohol, and violent movies. Companies sometimes promote programs that help selected groups. Yoplait, for

The Role of Promotion
The 3-A-Day of Dairy campaign promotes the health benefits of multiple dairy products.

instance, supports the Susan G. Komen Breast Cancer Research Foundation with its "Save Lids to Save Lives" campaign, which contributes 10 cents to the charity for every pink yogurt lid sent in by consumers.[8] Such cause-related marketing, as we discussed in Chapter 4, links the purchase of products to philanthropic efforts for one or more causes. By contributing to causes that its target markets support, cause-related marketing can help marketers boost sales and generate goodwill.

Marketers also sponsor special events, often leading to news coverage and positive promotion of organizations and their brands. Reebok, for example, held a star-studded party in Manhattan to promote Allen Iverson's Answer 7 and 50 Cent's G6 footwear. The event's highlight was a 6,000-pound half-court basketball court that floated down from the ceiling at midnight.[9]

For maximum benefit from promotional efforts, marketers strive for proper planning, implementation, coordination, and control of communications. Effective

---

BUILDING CUSTOMER RELATIONSHIPS

Rivals Team Up to Advertise Cereal

Although Kellogg, General Mills, Post, and Quaker are fierce rivals, they are banding together to combat a common enemy: soggy sales in the ready-to-eat cereal category. Cereal sales have plummeted more than $500 million since 1997, in part because today's hectic lifestyles leave little time for breakfast. In addition, people now have a much wider choice of breakfast foods, from bagels, yogurt, and toaster pastries to cereal bars and instant hot cereals. They can also grab breakfast on the go at many convenience stores, fast-food chains, and coffee shops. As a result, cereal marketers

face a difficult battle for share in a shrinking market, unless they can stimulate primary demand to give the entire category a boost.

The California Milk Processor Board approached the four cereal makers after recognizing that 25 percent of the milk industry's sales come from milk poured on breakfast cereals. The board's executives proposed an industrywide advertising campaign to boost cereal consumption, similar to the dairy industry's long-running "Got Milk?" campaign. The cereal makers agreed and pooled a total of $50 million to invest in the campaign.

The industry campaign is not intended to replace the promotional efforts of individual cereal makers. In fact, Kellogg, General Mills, Post, and

Quaker all reduced their advertising spending in the five years before the industry campaign began. During the same period, however, the rivals continued to launch new products and try different sales promotion efforts to improve sales.

One spinoff product, Kellogg's Rice Krispies Treats, has become the best-selling snack bar in the United States. Quaker's Fruit and Oatmeal bars are also popular, as are the cereal-and-milk bars offered by General Mills. The cereal makers have also highlighted health and nutrition in new products and promotions. Two notable successes are Smart Start (from Kellogg) and Harmony (from General Mills), both positioned as healthy cereals.

Kellogg, which recently lost its market leadership position to General Mills, previously tested promotional efforts designed to increase category sales. A few years ago, the company teamed up with two supermarket chains to try an in-store promotion called Breakfastland. Kellogg has also created ad campaigns encouraging people to include its healthy cereals as part of a nutritious weight loss diet. Quaker's ads have focused on convenience and nutrition, two key benefits for busy, health-conscious cereal customers.

Despite the cereal makers' individual promotional efforts, annual sales for the category as a whole fell from more than $72.5 billion to $6.7 billion in just five years. Although the industrywide campaign is aimed at reversing this downward trend, critics note that the "Got Milk?" campaign failed to increase overall milk sales. The dairy industry's ad agencies counter that sales would have dropped even further without the campaign to stimulate primary demand for milk. Kellogg, General Mills, Quaker, and Post hope their industry's campaign will whet consumers' appetites for ready-to-eat cereal at breakfast and beyond.

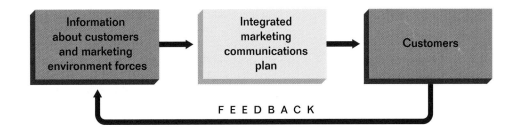

Figure 18.1 Information Flows Are Important in Integrated Marketing Communications

management of integrated marketing communications is based on information about and feedback from customers and the marketing environment, often obtained from an organization's marketing information system (see Figure 18.1). How successfully marketers use promotion to maintain positive relationships depends largely on the quantity and quality of information the organization receives. Because customers derive information and opinions from many different sources, integrated marketing communications planning also takes into account informal methods of communication such as word of mouth and independent information sources on the Internet. Because promotion is communication that can be managed, we now analyze what communication is and how the communication process works.

Promotion and the Communication Process

Communication is essentially the transmission of information. For communication to take place, both the sender and receiver of information must share some common ground. They must have a common understanding of the symbols, words, and pictures used to transmit information. An individual transmitting the following message may believe he or she is communicating with you:

$$在工廠吾人製造化粧品,在商店吾人銷售希望。$$

However, communication has not taken place if you don't understand the language in which the message is written.[10] Thus, we define **communication** as a sharing of meaning.[11] Implicit in this definition is the notion of transmission of information because sharing necessitates transmission.

As Figure 18.2 shows, communication begins with a source. A **source** is a person, group, or organization with a meaning it attempts to share with an audience. A source could be a salesperson wishing to communicate a sales message or an organization wanting to send a message to thousands of customers through an

communication A sharing of meaning through the transmission of information

source A person, group, or organization with a meaning it tries to share with a receiver or an audience

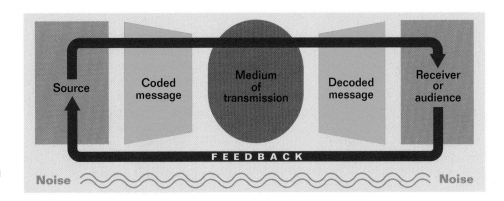

Figure 18.2 The Communication Process

receiver The individual, group, or organization that decodes a coded message

coding process Converting meaning into a series of signs or symbols

Beautiful woman in the latest mesh string bikini.

Face it, your customers would rather see the picture.

If your customers could use your site to search visually, they'd stay longer and come back more often.
Go to www.ditto.com/partners or call 650-231-1100 and find out how easy it is to turn your web site into a web sight.

ditto

Search visually.

Medium of Transmission
Ditto.com illustrates the visual benefits of a website in its advertising.

medium of transmission
The medium that carries the coded message from the source to the receiver

advertisement. Developing a strategy can enhance the effectiveness of the source's communication. For example, a strategy in which a salesperson attempts to influence a customer's decision by eliminating competitive products from consideration has been found to be effective.[12] A **receiver** is the individual, group, or organization that decodes a coded message, and an *audience* is two or more receivers. The intended receivers or audience of an advertisement for Nokia's 3300 cellphone, for example, might be younger consumers who appreciate the phone's MP3 and text messaging capabilities. Research suggests that 53 percent of the youth market—twice the national average—use their cellphones for text messaging.[13] Nokia could use this information to target receivers with integrated marketing communications about its products.

To transmit meaning, a source must convert the meaning into a series of signs or symbols representing ideas or concepts. This is called the **coding process**, or *encoding*. When coding meaning into a message, the source must consider certain characteristics of the receiver or audience. To share meaning, the source should use signs or symbols familiar to the receiver or audience. Marketers that understand this realize the importance of knowing their target market and ensuring that an advertisement, for example, uses language the target market understands. Thus, when General Mills advertises Cheerios, it does not mention all the ingredients used to make the cereal because some ingredients would have little meaning to consumers. Some notable problems have occurred in translating English advertisements into other languages to communicate with customers in global markets. For example, Budweiser has been advertised in Spain as the "Queen of Beers," and the Chinese have been encouraged to "eat their fingers off" when receiving KFC's slogan "Finger-Lickin' Good."[14] Clearly it is important that people understand the language used in promotion.

When coding a meaning, a source needs to use signs or symbols that the receiver or audience uses to refer to the concepts the source intends to convey. For this reason, marketers may need to offer instructions, warnings, and other product information in Spanish as well as English in some parts of the United States.[15] Marketers try to avoid signs or symbols that may have several meanings for an audience. For example, *soda* as a general term for soft drinks may not work well in national advertisements. Although in some parts of the United States the word means "soft drink," in other regions it may connote bicarbonate of soda, an ice cream drink, or something one mixes with Scotch whiskey.

To share a coded meaning with the receiver or audience, a source selects and uses a medium of transmission. A **medium of transmission** carries the coded message from the source to the receiver or audience. Transmission media include ink on paper, air wave vibrations produced by vocal cords, chalk marks on a chalkboard, and electronically produced vibrations of air waves (in radio and television signals, for example).

When a source chooses an inappropriate medium of transmission, several problems may arise. The coded message may reach some receivers, but the wrong ones. For example, dieters embracing the Atkins low-carbohydrate diet are more likely to focus on communications relating to their food concerns, such as "Eat Meat Not Wheat" T-shirts, QVC's Low-Carb Hour, and fast-food chain advertising that communicates information about carbohydrate content of menu items.[16] An advertiser attempting to reach this group would need to take this information into account when choosing an appropriate medium of transmission. Coded messages may also reach intended receivers in incomplete form because the intensity of the transmission is weak. For example, radio and broadcast television signals

decoding process Converting signs or symbols into concepts and ideas

noise Anything that reduces a communication's clarity and accuracy

feedback The receiver's response to a decoded message

channel capacity The limit on the volume of information a communication channel can handle effectively

are received effectively only over a limited range, which varies according to climatic conditions. Members of the target audience living on the fringe of the broadcast area may receive a weak signal; others well within the broadcast area may also receive an incomplete message if, for example, they listen to the radio while driving or studying.

In the **decoding process**, signs or symbols are converted into concepts and ideas. Seldom does a receiver decode exactly the same meaning the source coded. For example, recognizing that one-fourth of the U.S. population is nonwhite, marketers such as Cover Girl, Clairol, Avon, and PepsiCo realize the importance of advertising that includes African Americans and other minority groups, and thus are increasingly turning to African American models. To communicate effectively with black women, appropriate images need to be available in the decoding process.[17] When the result of decoding differs from what was coded, noise exists. **Noise** is anything that reduces the clarity and accuracy of the communication; it has many sources and may affect any or all parts of the communication process. Noise sometimes arises within the medium of transmission itself. Radio static, poor or slow Internet connections, and laryngitis are sources of noise. Noise also occurs when a source uses signs or symbols that are unfamiliar to the receiver or have a meaning different from the one intended. Noise may also originate in the receiver; a receiver may be unaware of a coded message when perceptual processes block it out.

The receiver's response to a decoded message is **feedback** to the source. The source usually expects and normally receives feedback, although perhaps not immediately. During feedback, the receiver or audience is the source of a message directed toward the original source, which then becomes a receiver. Feedback is coded, sent through a medium of transmission, and decoded by the receiver, the source of the original communication. Thus, communication is a circular process, as indicated in Figure 18.2.

During face-to-face communication, such as occurs in personal selling and product sampling, verbal and nonverbal feedback can be immediate. Instant feedback lets communicators adjust messages quickly to improve the effectiveness of their communications. For example, when a salesperson realizes through feedback that a customer does not understand a sales presentation, the salesperson adapts the presentation to make it more meaningful to the customer. This may be why face-to-face sales presentations create higher behavioral intentions to purchase services than do telemarketing sales contacts.[18] In interpersonal communication, feedback occurs through talking, touching, smiling, nodding, eye movements, and other body movements and postures.

When mass communication such as advertising is used, feedback is often slow and difficult to recognize. For example, Nickelodeon, a cable television network, is trying to expand its market by targeting "tweens," children ages 9 to 14, with advertising between programs and commercial-free Nick Jr. programs on CBS on Saturday mornings.[19] However, it may be several years before the effects of this promotion will be known. Feedback does exist for mass communication in the form of measures of changes in sales volume or in consumers' attitudes and awareness levels.

Each communication channel has a limit on the volume of information it can handle effectively. This limit, called **channel capacity**, is determined by the least efficient component of the communication process. Consider communications that depend on speech. An individual source can speak only so fast, and there is a limit to how much an individual receiver can take in aurally. Beyond that point, additional messages cannot be decoded; thus, meaning cannot be shared. Although a radio announcer can read several hundred words a minute, a one-minute advertising message should not exceed 150 words because most announcers cannot articulate words into understandable messages at a rate beyond 150 words per minute. Channel capacity can also relate to the types and amounts of information that can be communicated over the Internet. Broadband connections through cable modem, DSL, or satellite can increase the amount of information that can be sent and received.

Objectives of Promotion

Promotional objectives vary considerably from one organization to another and within organizations over time. Large firms with multiple promotional programs operating simultaneously may have quite varied promotional objectives. For the purpose of analysis, we focus on the eight promotional objectives shown in Table 18.1. Although the list is not exhaustive, one or more of these objectives underlie many promotional programs.

Table 18.1	Possible Objectives of Promotion

- Create awareness
- Stimulate demand
- Encourage product trial
- Identify prospects
- Retain loyal customers
- Facilitate reseller support
- Combat competitive promotional efforts
- Reduce sales fluctuations

◆ Create Awareness

A considerable amount of promotion focuses on creating awareness. For an organization introducing a new product or a line extension, making customers aware of the product is crucial to initiating the product adoption process. A marketer that has invested heavily in product development strives to create product awareness quickly to generate revenues to offset the high costs of product development and introduction. To create awareness of its new Nivea for Men's Revitalizing Lotion Q10, for example, Beiersdorf passed out samples of the new men's lotion along with coupons, CD samplers, and playing cards at 792 train and subway stations.[20]

Creating awareness is important for existing products, too. Promotional efforts may aim to increase awareness of brands, product features, image-related issues (such as organizational size or socially responsive behavior), or operational characteristics (such as store hours, locations, and credit availability). Some promotional programs are unsuccessful because marketers fail to generate awareness of critical issues among a significant portion of target market members. For example, Chrysler Group effectively dropped an expensive campaign to launch its new Pacifica when sales failed to meet expectations. Chrysler had hoped to target the new vehicle at younger, more affluent consumers. However, Celine Dion, the popular Canadian singer chosen to appear in television commercials for the campaign, appeals to a much older audience, with an average age of 52.[21]

◆ Stimulate Demand

primary demand Demand for a product category rather than for a specific brand

pioneer promotion Promotion that informs consumers about a new product

When an organization is the first to introduce an innovative product, it tries to stimulate **primary demand**—demand for a product category rather than for a specific brand of product—through pioneer promotion. **Pioneer promotion** informs potential customers about the product: what it is, what it does, how it can be used, and where it can be purchased. Because pioneer promotion is used in the introductory stage of the product life cycle, meaning there are no competing brands, it neither emphasizes brand names nor compares brands. The first company to introduce the DVD player, for instance, initially attempted to stimulate primary demand by

Stimulating Demand
The Almond Board of California promotes almonds to stimulate primary demand.

emphasizing the benefits of DVD players in general rather than the benefits of its specific brand.

Primary-demand stimulation is not just for new products. At times an industry trade association rather than a single firm uses promotional efforts to stimulate primary demand. Major League Baseball, for example, spent $250 million to get more consumers to watch major league baseball games. The campaign ranged from a Pepsi $100,000 Grand Slam under-the-cap promotion in 1 billion bottles and a Kraft Foods promotion featuring 56 million trading cards in Post cereals to neighborhood pickup games with Ken Griffey, Jr., and Derek Jeter. Stimulating demand among younger consumers is important because research indicates that of all the major sports, baseball attracts the oldest fans (median age 47), and TV ratings for baseball games have declined in recent years.[22]

selective demand Demand for a specific brand

To build **selective demand**, demand for a specific brand, a marketer employs promotional efforts that point out the strengths and benefits of a specific brand. Building selective demand also requires singling out attributes important to potential buyers. Selective demand can be stimulated by differentiating the product from competing brands in the minds of potential buyers. Microsoft, for example, spent $50 million to lure AOL subscribers to its MSN Internet service after AOL raised its price for Internet service, promising not to raise its own already lower rate.[23] Selective demand can also be stimulated by increasing the number of product uses and promoting them through advertising campaigns, as well as through price discounts, free samples, coupons, consumer contests and games, and sweepstakes. Promotions for large package sizes or multiple-product packages are directed at increasing consumption, which in turn can stimulate demand. In addition, selective demand can be stimulated by encouraging existing customers to use more of the product.

Encouraging Product Trial
Eastland Park Hotel in Portland, Maine, encourages trial by offering a second meal at half price.

◆ Encourage Product Trial

When attempting to move customers through the product adoption process, a marketer may successfully create awareness and interest, but customers may stall during the evaluation stage. In this case, certain types of promotion, such as free samples, coupons, test drives or limited free-use offers, contests, and games, are employed to encourage product trial. Rivals Gillette and Schick, for example, each gave out coupons and free razors that usually cost as much as $10 to promote the Gillette Mach 3 Turbo and Schick Quattro brands. The expensive promotion helped Schick achieve a 90 percent sales increase in replacement blades, giving the firm a significant boost in U.S. market share at Gillette's expense.[24] Whether a marketer's product is the first in a new product category, a new brand in an existing category, or simply an existing brand seeking customers, trial-inducing promotional efforts aim to make product trial convenient and low risk for potential customers.

◆ Identify Prospects

Certain types of promotional efforts aim to identify customers who are interested in the firm's product and are most likely to buy it. A marketer may use a magazine advertisement with a direct-response information form, requesting the reader to complete and mail the form to receive additional information. Some advertisements have toll-free numbers to facilitate direct customer response. Customers who fill out information blanks or call the organization usually have higher interest in the product, which makes them likely sales prospects. The organization can respond with phone calls, follow-up letters, or personal contact by salespeople. Dun & Bradstreet, for example, offered a free article on customer relationship management to businesses that mailed in a card or called a toll-free number. This helped the consulting firm identify prospects to sell data used to develop and maintain customer relationships.

◆ Retain Loyal Customers

Clearly, maintaining long-term customer relationships is a major goal of most marketers. Such relationships are quite valuable. For example, the value of a Taco Bell customer amounts to $12,000.[25] Promotional efforts directed at customer retention can help an organization control its costs because the costs of retaining customers are usually considerably lower than those of acquiring new ones. Frequent-user programs, such as those sponsored by airlines, car rental agencies, and hotels, aim to reward loyal customers and encourage them to remain loyal. Some organizations employ special offers that only their existing customers can use. To retain loyal customers, marketers not only advertise loyalty programs but also use reinforcement advertising, which assures current users they have made the right brand choice and tells them how to get the most satisfaction from the product.

◆ Facilitate Reseller Support

Reseller support is a two-way street: producers generally want to provide support to resellers to maintain sound working relationships, and in turn they expect resellers to support their products. When a manufacturer advertises a product to consumers, resellers should view this promotion as a form of strong manufacturer support. In some instances, a producer agrees to pay a certain proportion of retailers' advertising expenses for promoting its products. When a manufacturer is introducing a new consumer brand in a highly competitive product category, it may be difficult to persuade supermarket managers to carry this brand. However, if the manufacturer promotes the new brand with free sample and coupon distribution in the retailer's area, a supermarket manager views these actions as strong support and is much more likely to handle the product. To encourage wholesalers and retailers to increase their inventories of its products, a manufacturer may provide them with special offers and buying allowances. In certain industries, a producer's salesperson may provide support to a wholesaler by working with the wholesaler's customers (retailers) in the presentation and promotion of the products. Strong relationships with resellers are important to a firm's ability to maintain a sustainable competitive advantage. The use of various promotional methods can help an organization achieve this goal.

◆ Combat Competitive Promotional Efforts

At times a marketer's objective in using promotion is to offset or lessen the effect of a competitor's promotional program. This type of promotional activity does not necessarily increase the organization's sales or market share, but it may prevent a sales or market share loss. A combative promotional objective is used most often by firms in extremely competitive consumer markets, such as the fast-food and automobile industries. When some automakers began advertising their automobiles' ability to withstand collisions, as determined by crash tests conducted by various federal and private agencies, Volkswagen, BMW, Saturn, Mercedes-Benz, Toyota, and other firms quickly followed suit to combat their competitors' advertising. Although these ads were trying to promote safety records, the companies were also trying to prevent market share loss in a very competitive market.[26]

◆ Reduce Sales Fluctuations

Demand for many products varies from one month to another because of such factors as climate, holidays, and seasons. A business, however, cannot operate at peak efficiency when sales fluctuate rapidly. Changes in sales volume translate into changes in production, inventory levels, personnel needs, and financial resources. When promotional techniques reduce fluctuations by generating sales during slow periods, a firm can use its resources more efficiently.

Promotional techniques are often designed to stimulate sales during sales slumps. For example, advertisements promoting price reduction of lawn care equipment can increase sales during fall and winter months. During peak periods, a marketer may refrain from advertising to prevent stimulating sales to the point where the firm cannot handle all the demand. On occasion, an organization advertises that customers can be better served by coming in on certain days. A pizza outlet, for example, might distribute coupons that are valid only Monday through Thursday because on Friday through Sunday the restaurant is extremely busy.

To achieve the major objectives of promotion discussed here, companies must develop appropriate promotional programs. In the next section, we consider the basic components of such programs: the promotion mix elements.

The Promotion Mix

promotion mix A combination of promotional methods used to promote a specific product

Several promotional methods can be used to communicate with individuals, groups, and organizations. When an organization combines specific methods to manage the integrated marketing communications for a particular product, that combination constitutes the promotion mix for that product. The four possible elements of a **promotion mix** are advertising, personal selling, public relations, and sales promotion (see Figure 18.3). For some products, firms use all four ingredients; for others, they use only two or three.

◆ Advertising

Advertising is a paid nonpersonal communication about an organization and its products transmitted to a target audience through mass media, including television, radio, the Internet, newspapers, magazines, direct mail, outdoor displays, and signs on mass transit vehicles. One company even placed advertisements—in the form of temporary tattoos of company logos—on the foreheads of college students.[27] Individuals and organizations use advertising to promote goods, services, ideas, issues, and people. Being highly flexible, advertising can reach an extremely large target audience or focus on a small, precisely defined segment. For instance, Burger King's advertising focuses on a large audience of potential fast-food customers, ranging from children to adults, whereas advertising for Gulfstream jets aims at a much smaller and more specialized target market.

Advertising offers several benefits. It is extremely cost efficient when it reaches a vast number of people at a low cost per person. For example, the cost of a four-color, full-page advertisement in *Time* magazine is $223,000. Because the magazine reaches more than 4 million subscribers, the cost of reaching 1,000 subscribers is only about $56.[28] Advertising also lets the source repeat the message several times. Levi Strauss, for example, advertises on television, in magazines, and in outdoor displays. Advertising repetition has been found to be especially effective for brand name extensions beyond the original product category.[29] Furthermore, advertising a product a certain way can add to the product's value, and the visibility an organization gains from advertising can enhance its image. At times a firm tries to enhance its own or its product's image by including celebrity endorsers in advertisements. For example, the National Fluid Milk Processor Promotion Board's "milk moustache" campaign has featured Pete Sampras, Whoopi Goldberg, Britney Spears, and Elton John, as well as animated "celebrities" such as Garfield, the Rugrats, and Blues Clues.[30]

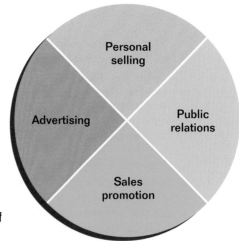

Figure 18.3 The Four Possible Elements of a Promotion Mix

TECHNOLOGY IN ACTION

It's nice to know your loved ones are safe at home. Wherever you are, you can monitor your home – even remotely control home appliances, temperatures and security devices. And in the ubiquitous networked society of the near future, you'll be connected to everyone and everything, anytime and anyplace. Even your cat. From broadband access networks, data storage solutions and hard disk drive technologies, to information devices like plasma displays and PDAs, Hitachi's technological expertise and services are making this a reality. Just one more example of technology not for its own sake but for the benefit of all. As an innovative global solutions company, Hitachi touches your life in many ways. Visit us on the Web and see technology in action.

INFRASTRUCTURE   IT   MEDICAL   ENVIRONMENT

HITACHI
Inspire the Next

www.hitachi.com/inspire/

Advertising
Hitachi uses the visual aspects of advertising to promote its efforts to use technology to address environmental issues.

kinesic communication
Communicating through the movement of head, eyes, arms, hands, legs, or torso

proxemic communication Communicating by varying the physical distance in face-to-face interactions

tactile communication
Communicating through touching

Advertising has disadvantages as well. Even though the cost per person reached may be low, the absolute dollar outlay can be extremely high, especially for commercials during popular television shows. High costs can limit, and sometimes preclude, use of advertising in a promotion mix. Moreover, advertising rarely provides rapid feedback. Measuring its effect on sales is difficult, and it is ordinarily less persuasive than personal selling. In most instances, the time available to communicate a message to customers is limited to seconds, since people look at a print advertisement for only a few seconds and most broadcast commercials are 30 seconds or less. Of course, the use of infomercials can increase exposure time for viewers.

◆ Personal Selling

Personal selling is a paid personal communication that seeks to inform customers and persuade them to purchase products in an exchange situation. The phrase *purchase products* is interpreted broadly to encompass acceptance of ideas and issues. Telemarketing, described in Chapter 17 as direct selling over the telephone, relies heavily on personal selling. However, negative consumer attitudes and legislation restricting telemarketing have lessened its effectiveness as a personal selling technique.

Personal selling has both advantages and limitations when compared with advertising. Advertising is general communication aimed at a relatively large target audience, whereas personal selling involves more specific communication directed at one or several individuals. Reaching one person through personal selling costs considerably more than through advertising, but personal selling efforts often have greater impact on customers. Personal selling also provides immediate feedback, allowing marketers to adjust their messages to improve communication. It helps them determine and respond to customers' information needs.

When a salesperson and a customer meet face to face, they use several types of interpersonal communication. The predominant communication form is language, both spoken and written. A salesperson and customer frequently use **kinesic communication**, or communication through the movement of head, eyes, arms, hands, legs, or torso. Winking, head nodding, hand gestures, and arm motions are forms of kinesic communication. A good salesperson often can evaluate a prospect's interest in a product or presentation by noting eye contact and head nodding. **Proxemic communication**, a less obvious form of communication used in personal selling situations, occurs when either person varies the physical distance separating them. When a customer backs away from a salesperson, for example, he or she may be displaying a lack of interest in the product or expressing dislike for the salesperson. Touching, or **tactile communication**, is also a form of communication, although less popular in the United States than in many other countries. Handshaking is a common form of tactile communication both in the United States and elsewhere.

Management of salespeople is very important in making this component of promotion effective. Salespeople who are directly involved in planning sales activities develop greater trust in their firm and experience increased sales performance.[31] Salespeople who have a positive influence on customers and who are more flexible in their selling techniques also have greater success.[32] More than any other aspect of promotion, the hiring, training, and motivation of the people involved determine its success. Satisfaction with assigned sales territories has also been linked to improved attitudes, motivation, and performance of salespeople.[33] Although many consumers do not hold salespeople in high regard, studies of complaints to government agencies suggest that it is the strategies used by companies rather than the practices of salespeople that generate the most complaints.[34]

◆ Public Relations

While many promotional activities focus on a firm's customers, other stakeholders—suppliers, employees, stockholders, the media, educators, potential investors, government officials, and society in general—are important to an organization as well. To communicate with customers and stakeholders, a company employs public relations. Public relations is a broad set of communication efforts used to create and maintain favorable relationships between an organization and its stakeholders. Maintaining a positive relationship with one or more stakeholders can affect a firm's current sales and profits, as well as its long-term survival.

Public relations uses a variety of tools, including annual reports, brochures, event sponsorship, and sponsorship of socially responsible programs aimed at protecting the environment or helping disadvantaged individuals. Other tools arise from the use of publicity, which is a component of public relations. Publicity is nonpersonal communication in news story form about an organization or its products, or both, transmitted through a mass medium at no charge. A few examples of publicity-based public relations tools are news releases, press conferences, and feature articles. When TiVo launched the personal video recorder, the company initially gave free devices to sports celebrities and select members of the entertainment industry to stimulate awareness and product trial. The company gained further publicity with news stories, product reviews, and strategic product placements in the mass media. TiVo may have chosen a public relations campaign over a more traditional advertising effort because its product enables consumers to bypass television commercials; use of personal video recorders is expected to reduce viewing of television advertisements by 19 percent by 2007.[35] Ordinarily public relations efforts are planned and implemented to be consistent with and support other elements of the promotion mix. Public relations efforts may be the responsibility of an individual or of a department within the organization, or the organization may hire an independent public relations agency.

Unpleasant situations and negative events such as product tampering or an environmental disaster may generate unfavorable public relations for an organization. For example, numerous lawsuits against Ford Motor Company over product quality and engineering issues created negative publicity for the firm. Many of the cases related to Ford's Crown Victoria police cars, Econoline passenger vans, and Ford Explorer sport-utility vehicles.[36] To minimize the damaging effects of unfavorable coverage, effective marketers have policies and procedures in place to help manage any public relations problems.

Public relations should not be viewed as a set of tools to be used only during crises. To get the most from public relations, an organization should have someone responsible for public relations either internally or externally, and should have an ongoing public relations program. Sears, for example, received positive publicity as an official sponsor of the 2002 Winter Olympics and for its initiative to provide home appliances for Olympics-related housing.[37]

◆ Sales Promotion

Sales promotion is an activity or material that acts as a direct inducement, offering added value or incentive for the product, to resellers, salespeople, or consumers.[38] Examples include free samples, games, rebates, sweepstakes, contests, premiums, and coupons. McDonald's, for example, teamed up with the Best Buy electronics retail chain in a joint promotion called Best Chance Monopoly, in which consumers collect game pieces from McDonald's meals to win prizes. Instant-win pieces

NET SIGHTS

Marketers that use television and radio commercials in their promotion mixes depend on organizations such as ACNielsen Corporation (http://acnielsen.com/), the world's leading provider of marketing research, information, and analysis. Although ACNielsen offers many research services, it is best known for its international television audience ratings. Another important rating service is Arbitron (www. arbitron.com/), which measures radio audiences in local markets across the United States; surveys retail, media, and product patterns of local market consumers; and provides software to analyze media audience and marketing information data. Find out where your favorite TV shows and radio stations rank by visiting these websites.

Expedia® Corporate Travel Incentive

A cup of coffee so strong it could save you 20%* on corporate travel.

Get a $25 premium coffee gift card free,

just for letting Expedia® Corporate Travel show you how we could save your company 20% annually on travel.

Thanks to our exclusive business model, we're able to offer substantial savings and provide the full service you expect.

To find out how we do it, call or visit us online for a demonstration. Give us a few minutes of your time and we'll give you a reason to believe, along with your free $25 coffee gift card.

Call 866-791-3479 or visit www.expediacorp.com/da3 today. Offer ends 4/30/04.

*20% savings off air ticket and transaction fees alone. Assumes 50% online booking and 50% agent-assisted booking of air travel at an average price of $453. For October 2003, the average ticket price for Expedia business travelers was $453 compared to the industry average of $543. This is a savings of $90 per ticket. Industry average for this period is based upon a study by Topaz International, Ltd. Call us or visit our website for more details. Copyright 2004, Expedia, Inc. All rights reserved. CST: 2029030-40 **This offer is exclusively for decision-makers, managers and those who influence choice in Corporate Travel Agencies.

Expedia® Corporate Travel

Sales Promotion
Expedia promotes the use of a coffee gift card as a sales promotion incentive.

awarded McDonald's products such as fries, while collectible prizes included cash, sport-utility vehicles, and Best Buy electronics. The promotion, intended to boost traffic at both retailers, issued 400 million game pieces.[39] *Sales promotion* should not be confused with *promotion;* sales promotion is just one part of the comprehensive area of promotion. Marketers spend more on sales promotion than on advertising, and sales promotion appears to be a faster-growing area than advertising. Coupons are especially important; Table 18.2 shows the product categories with the greatest distribution of coupons.

Generally, when companies employ advertising or personal selling, they depend on these activities continuously or cyclically. However, a marketer's use of sales promotion tends to be irregular. Many products are seasonal. A company such as Toro may offer more sales promotions in August than in the peak selling season of April or May, when more people buy tractors, lawn mowers, and other gardening equipment. Marketers frequently rely on sales promotion to improve the effectiveness of other promotion mix ingredients, especially advertising and personal selling. Decisions to cut sales promotion can have significant negative effects on a company. For example, Clorox decided to cut the promotion budget for Glad branded products two years in a row, in part to compensate for rising plastic resin prices. When competitors did not decrease their promotional budgets, Glad lost significant market share in trash bags (down 10.3 percent), food storage bags (down 10.6 percent), and lawn and leaf bags (down 23.2 percent).[40] In fact, research suggests that about one-third of a gain in sales from a sales promotion occurs at the expense of other brands in the same category.[41]

An effective promotion mix requires the right combination of components. To see how such a mix is created, we now examine the factors and conditions affecting the selection of promotional methods that an organization uses for a particular product.

Table 18.2	**Product Categories with the Greatest Distribution of Coupons**

1. Household cleaners
2. Prepared foods
3. Detergents
4. Medications, remedies, health aids
5. Paper products
6. Condiments and gravies
7. Personal soap and bath additives
8. Frozen prepared foods
9. Cereal
10. Skin care preparations

Source: "September Is National Coupon Month," Promotion Marketing Association, press release, Sep. 2, 2003, **www.couponmonth.com/pages/news.htm**. © Copyright 2004 by Promotion Marketing Association, Inc./PMA Educational Foundation, Inc. 257 Park Ave. South, New York, NY 10010. All rights reserved, including the right to disseminate in any format or media. Reproduction of this work in any form is forbidden without written permission of the publisher. See also **www.pmalink.org**.

Selecting Promotion Mix Elements

Marketers vary the composition of promotion mixes for many reasons. Although a promotion mix can include all four elements, frequently a marketer selects fewer than four. Many firms that market multiple product lines use several promotion mixes simultaneously.

When making decisions about the composition of promotion mixes, marketers should recognize that commercial messages, whether from advertising, personal selling, sales promotion, or public relations, are limited in the extent to which they can inform and persuade customers and move them closer to making purchases. Depending on the type of customers and the products involved, buyers to some extent rely on word-of-mouth communication from personal sources such as family members and friends. More than 67 percent of Americans are influenced by friends and family members when making purchases.[42] Such word-of-mouth communication is also very important when people are selecting restaurants and entertainment, and automotive, medical, legal, banking, and personal services such as hair care. Effective marketers that understand the importance of word-of-mouth communication attempt to identify advice givers and encourage them to try their products in the hope they will spread favorable word about them. Apple Computer, for example, relies on its devoted consumer following to spread the word about their satisfaction with Apple products such as PowerBooks and iPods by word of mouth. Apple has built an "army of evangelists," ranging from teenagers to middle-aged adults, not only because of its edgy advertising but also through an intense focus on the consumer.[43]

buzz marketing An attempt to create a trend or acceptance of a product through word-of-mouth communications

Buzz marketing is an attempt to create a trend or acceptance of a product through word-of-mouth communications. For example, Vespa Scooters paid models to ride and park its trendy motorbikes around the "in" cafés and fashionable retail establishments in Los Angeles in the hope of generating favorable word-of-mouth communication about the reissued European bikes. The idea behind buzz marketing is that an accepted member of a social group will always be more credible than any other form of paid communication.[44] Toyota parked its new Scions outside of raves and coffee shops, and offered hip-hop magazine writers test drives to get the "buzz" going about the new car.[45] Buzz marketing works best as a part of an integrated marketing communication program that also uses advertising, personal selling, sales promotion, and publicity. Marketers should not underestimate the importance of both word-of-mouth communication and personal influence, nor should they have unrealistic expectations about the performance of commercial messages.

Viral marketing is a term used to describe a strategy to get users of the Internet to pass on ads and promotions to others. In addition, consumers are increasingly turning to Internet sources for information and opinions about goods and services as well as about the companies. Users can go to a number of consumer-oriented websites, such as epinions.com and ConsumerReview.com, to learn about others' feelings toward and experiences with specific products. Buyers can also peruse local Internet-based newsgroups and forums to find word-of-mouth information. A consumer looking for a new cellphone service, for example, might inquire in local forums about other participants' experiences and level of satisfaction to gain more information before making a purchase decision.

◆ Promotional Resources, Objectives, and Policies

The size of an organization's promotional budget affects the number and relative intensity of promotional methods included in a promotion mix. If a company's promotional budget is extremely limited, the firm is likely to rely on personal selling because it is easier to measure a salesperson's contribution to sales than to measure the sales effectiveness of advertising. Businesses must have sizable promotional budgets to use regional or national advertising. Procter & Gamble, for example, spends $4.3 million a year on advertising its personal care and cleaning products around the world.[46] Organizations with extensive promotional resources generally include more elements in their promotion mixes, but having more promotional dollars to spend does not necessarily mean using more promotional methods.

An organization's promotional objectives and policies also influence the types of promotion selected. If a company's objective is to create mass awareness of a new convenience good, such as a breakfast cereal, its promotion mix probably leans heavily toward advertising, sales promotion, and possibly public relations. If a company hopes to educate consumers about the features of a durable good, such as a home appliance, its promotion mix may combine a moderate amount of advertising, possibly some sales promotion designed to attract customers to retail stores, and a great deal of personal selling because this method is an efficient way to inform customers about such products. If a firm's objective is to produce immediate sales of nondurable services, the promotion mix will probably stress advertising and sales promotion. For example, dry cleaners and carpet-cleaning firms are more likely to use advertising with a coupon or discount rather than personal selling.

◆ Characteristics of the Target Market

Size, geographic distribution, and demographic characteristics of an organization's target market help dictate the methods to include in a product's promotion mix. To some degree, market size determines composition of the mix. If the size is limited, the promotion mix will probably emphasize personal selling, which can be very effective for reaching small numbers of people. Organizations selling to industrial markets and firms marketing products through only a few wholesalers frequently make personal selling the major component of their promotion mixes. When a product's market consists of millions of customers, organizations rely on advertising and sales promotion because these methods reach masses of people at a low cost per person.

Geographic distribution of a firm's customers also affects the choice of promotional methods. Personal selling is more feasible if a company's customers are concentrated in a small area than if they are dispersed across a vast region. When the company's customers are numerous and dispersed, advertising may be more practical.

Distribution of a target market's demographic characteristics, such as age, income, or education, may affect the types of promotional techniques a marketer selects, as well as the messages and images employed. The 2000 U.S. census found that so-called traditional families—those composed of married couples with children—account for fewer than one-quarter of all U.S. households, down from 30 percent in 1980 and 45 percent in 1960. To reach the three-quarters of households consisting of single parents, unmarried couples, singles, and "empty nesters" (whose children have left home), more companies are modifying the images used in their promotions. Charles Schwab, for example, featured celebrity single mother Sarah Ferguson, the Duchess of York, in commercials for its financial services.

◆ Characteristics of the Product

Generally promotion mixes for business products concentrate on personal selling, whereas advertising plays a major role in promoting consumer goods. This generalization should be treated cautiously, however. Marketers of business products use some advertising to promote products. Advertisements for computers, road-building equipment, and aircraft are fairly common, and some sales promotion is also used occasionally to promote business products. Personal selling is used extensively for consumer durables, such as home appliances, automobiles, and houses, whereas consumer convenience items are promoted mainly through advertising and sales promotion. Public relations appears in promotion mixes for both business and consumer products.

Business Advertising
Xerox promotes fast high-tech products.

Marketers of highly seasonal products often emphasize advertising, and sometimes sales promotion as well, because off-season sales generally will not support an extensive year-round sales force. Although most toy producers have sales forces to sell to resellers, many of these companies depend chiefly on advertising to promote their products.

A product's price also influences the composition of the promotion mix. High-priced products call for personal selling because consumers associate greater risk with the purchase of such products and usually want information from a sales-person. Few people, for example, are willing to purchase a refrigerator from a self-service establishment. For low-priced convenience items, marketers use advertising rather than personal selling. Research suggests that consumers visiting a store specifically to purchase a product on sale are more likely to have read flyers and to have purchased other sale-priced products than consumers visiting the same store for other reasons.[47]

Another consideration in creating an effective promotion mix is the stage of the product life cycle. During the introduction stage, much advertising may be necessary for both business and consumer products to make potential users aware of them. For many products, personal selling and sales promotion are also helpful in this stage. In the growth and maturity stages, consumer services require heavy emphasis on advertising, whereas business products often call for a concentration of personal selling and some sales promotion. In the decline stage, marketers usually decrease all promotional activities, especially advertising.

Intensity of market coverage is still another factor affecting composition of the promotion mix. When products are marketed through intensive distribution, firms depend strongly on advertising and sales promotion. Many convenience products, such as lotions, cereals, and coffee, are promoted through samples, coupons, and money refunds. When marketers choose selective distribution, promotion mixes vary considerably. Items handled through exclusive distribution, such as expensive watches, furs, and high-quality furniture, typically require a significant amount of personal selling.

A product's use also affects the combination of promotional methods. Manufacturers of highly personal products, such as laxatives, nonprescription contraceptives, and feminine hygiene products, depend on advertising because many customers do not want to talk with salespeople about these products.

◆ Costs and Availability of Promotional Methods

Costs of promotional methods are major factors to analyze when developing a promotion mix. National advertising and sales promotion require large expenditures. However, if these efforts succeed in reaching extremely large audiences, the cost per individual reached may be quite small, possibly a few pennies. Some forms of advertising are relatively inexpensive. Many small, local businesses advertise products through local newspapers, magazines, radio and television stations, outdoor displays, and signs on mass transit vehicles.

Another consideration marketers explore when formulating a promotion mix is availability of promotional techniques. Despite the tremendous number of media vehicles in the United States, a firm may find that no available advertising medium effectively reaches a certain target market. The problem of media availability becomes more pronounced when marketers advertise in foreign countries. Some media, such as television, simply may not be available, or advertising on television may be illegal. Available media may not be open to certain types of advertisements. In some countries, advertisers are forbidden to make brand comparisons on television. Other promotional methods also have limitations. For instance, a firm may wish to increase its sales force but be unable to find qualified personnel.

◆ Push and Pull Channel Policies

push policy Promoting a product only to the next institution down the marketing channel

Another element marketers consider when planning a promotion mix is whether to use a push policy or a pull policy. With a **push policy**, the producer promotes the product only to the next institution down the marketing channel. In a marketing channel with wholesalers and retailers, the producer promotes to the wholesaler because in this case, the wholesaler is the channel member just below the producer (see Figure 18.4). Each channel member in turn promotes to the next channel member. A push policy normally stresses personal selling. Sometimes sales promotion and advertising are used in conjunction with personal selling to push the products down through the channel.

pull policy Promoting a product directly to consumers to develop strong consumer demand that pulls products through the marketing channel

As Figure 18.4 shows, a firm using a **pull policy** promotes directly to consumers to develop strong consumer demand for its products. It does so primarily through advertising and sales promotion. Because consumers are persuaded to seek the products in retail stores, retailers in turn go to wholesalers or the producers to buy the products. This policy is intended to pull the goods down through the channel by creating demand at the consumer level. Consumers are told that if the stores don't have it, ask them to get it. For example, when PepsiCo introduced Mountain Dew Code Red, a high-caffeine soda, the product was positioned to appeal to young people, especially teenage boys who like skateboarding and snowboarding. The product launch employed a pull strategy, but instead of blitzing the TV and radio air waves with commercials, the strategy initially targeted convenience stores and gas stations using colorful banners to promote the new soft drink.[48] Stimulating demand at the consumer level for Mountain Dew Code Red caused the product to be pulled through the channel.

Push and pull policies are not mutually exclusive. At times an organization uses both simultaneously.

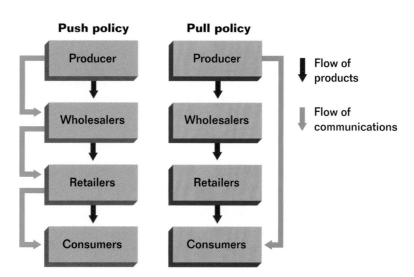

Figure 18.4 Comparison of Push and Pull Promotional Strategies

Criticisms and Defenses of Promotion

Even though promotional activities can help customers make informed purchasing decisions, social scientists, consumer groups, government agencies, and members of society in general have long criticized promotion. There are two main reasons for such criticism: promotion does have flaws, and it is a highly visible business activity that pervades our daily lives. Although complaints about too much promotional activity are almost universal, a number of more specific criticisms have been lodged. In this section, we discuss some of the criticisms and defenses of promotion.

◆ Is Promotion Deceptive?

One common criticism of promotion is that it is deceptive and unethical. During the nineteenth and early twentieth centuries, much promotion was blatantly deceptive. Although no longer widespread, some deceptive promotion still occurs. For example, Publishers Clearing House paid $34 million to settle lawsuits accusing the company of using deceptive sweepstake promotions to get consumers to buy magazines.[49] Questionable weight loss claims are made about various exercise devices and diet programs. Some promotions are unintentionally deceiving; for instance, when advertising to children, it is easy to mislead them because they are more naive than adults and less able to separate fantasy from reality. For this reason, the Federal Trade Commission monitors the ratings systems of the film, music, and electronic games industries as well as their advertising to children.[50] A promotion may also mislead some receivers because words can have diverse meanings for different people. However, not all promotion should be condemned because a small portion is flawed. Laws, government regulation, and industry self-regulation have helped decrease deceptive promotion. Ethics and Social Responsibility examines how one company has expanded the concept of cause-related marketing.

◆ Does Promotion Increase Prices?

Promotion is also criticized for raising prices, but in fact it often tends to lower them. The ultimate purpose of promotion is to stimulate demand. If it does, the business should be able to produce and market products in larger quantities and thus reduce per-unit production and marketing costs, which can result in lower prices. For example, as demand for flat-screen TVs and MP3 players has increased, their prices have dropped. When promotion fails to stimulate demand, the price of the promoted product increases because promotion costs must be added to other costs. Promotion also helps keep prices lower by facilitating price competition. When firms advertise prices, their prices tend to remain lower than when they are not promoting prices. Gasoline pricing illustrates how promotion fosters price competition. Service stations with the highest prices seldom have highly visible price signs.

◆ Does Promotion Create Needs?

Some critics of promotion claim that it manipulates consumers by persuading them to buy products they do not need, hence creating "artificial" needs. In his theory of motivation, Abraham Maslow (discussed in Chapter 9) indicates that an individual tries to satisfy five levels of needs: physiological needs, such as hunger, thirst, and sex; safety needs; needs for love and affection; needs for self-esteem and respect from others; and self-actualization needs, that is, the need to realize one's potential.[51] When needs are viewed in this context, it is difficult to demonstrate that promotion creates them. If there were no promotional activities, people would still have needs for food, water, sex, safety, love, affection, self-esteem, respect from others, and self-actualization.

Although promotion may not create needs, it does capitalize on them (which may be why some critics believe promotion creates needs). Many marketers base their appeals on these needs. For example, several mouthwash, toothpaste, and perfume advertisements associate these products with needs for love, affection, and respect. These advertisers rely on human needs in their messages, but they do not create the needs.

◆ Does Promotion Encourage Materialism?

Another frequent criticism of promotion is that it leads to materialism. The purpose of promoting goods is to persuade people to buy them; thus, if promotion works, consumers will want to buy more and more things. Marketers assert that values are instilled in the home and that promotion does not change people into materialistic consumers. However, the behavior of today's children and teenagers contradicts this view; many insist on high-priced, brand name apparel such as Gucci, Coach, Ralph Lauren, and Hummer.

ETHICS AND SOCIAL RESPONSIBILITY

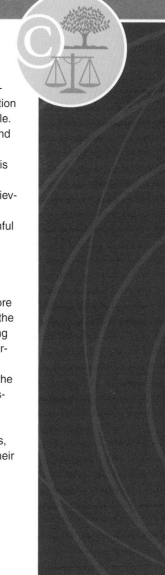

Truth in Advertising

What foods come to mind when you think of a healthy diet—whole grains, fresh vegetables, and . . . fried chicken? That's what a recent, short-lived advertising campaign from KFC, previously known as Kentucky Fried Chicken, wanted consumers to believe. The ads claimed the Colonel's chicken breast is less fatty than Burger King's Whopper and can work well as part of a healthy, balanced diet. In one ad, a young man tells a friend that the secret behind his weight loss is eating fried chicken. In another ad, a woman brings home a bucket of chicken and says, "Remember how we talked about eating better? Well, it starts today." Although the ads carried disclaimers that fried chicken is *not* low in fat, sodium, or cholesterol, the message was clear: fried chicken is good for you, so don't feel guilty about enjoying it.

Critics immediately lambasted the campaign, asserting the ads were misleading and irresponsible. Particularly strong criticism came from the Children's Advertising Review Unit, a watchdog group that condemned the airing of the ads during children's programming because they were likely to give kids the wrong idea about the overall nutritional value of fried chicken. After intense scrutiny from the Federal Trade Commission and other consumer interest groups, KFC pulled the ads.

KFC's campaign has fueled the ongoing debate surrounding the ethics of marketing the health value of foods to consumers who may be all too eager to believe claims. With the problem of obesity recognized as "epidemic" and with many more Americans trying to lose weight, it's no surprise that fast-food companies have tried to position their products as consistent with a healthy lifestyle. McDonald's has done so by promoting salads, and Subway adopted Jared Fogle as its "weight loss hero" in its advertising campaigns. The question is whether marketers that claim to offer "healthy" foods are helping or hindering consumers in achieving their goals to eat better.

Some evidence supports the benefits of truthful health food claims. For example, data from the ready-to-eat cereal market shows that allowing manufacturers to make truthful health claims resulted in greater health consciousness and improved diets among consumers, as well as more healthful product innovations in the industry. On the other hand, are manufacturers unfairly capitalizing on the health concerns of consumers or even perpetuating poor eating habits in some cases? Although KFC offered truthful statements about the fat content of its chicken breasts, the overall message was to promote fried chicken as a healthy product—a pretense that any dietician would be quick to debunk. To avoid legal and ethical pitfalls, marketers should ensure that health claims on their food products not only are truthful but also steer clear of the potential to mislead consumers.

DEAR BIG TOBACCO:

WE KNOW YOU'VE BEEN BURYING THE TRUTH.

Is Promotion Deceptive?
This ad, produced for the Iowa Department of Public Health, is intended to convince consumers that the tobacco industry is not honest about the harmful effects of tobacco products.

◆ Does Promotion Help Customers Without Costing Too Much?

Every year firms spend billions of dollars for promotion. The question is whether promotion helps customers enough to be worth the cost. Consumers do benefit because promotion informs them about product uses, features, advantages, prices, and locations where they can buy the products. Consumers thus gain more knowledge about available products and can make more intelligent buying decisions. Promotion also informs consumers about services—for instance, health care, educational programs, and day care—as well as about important social, political, and health-related issues. For example, several organizations, such as the California Department of Health Services, inform people about the health hazards associated with tobacco use.

◆ Should Potentially Harmful Products Be Promoted?

Finally, some critics of promotion, including consumer groups and government officials, suggest that certain products should not be promoted at all. Primary targets are products associated with violence and other possibly unhealthy activities, such as handguns, alcohol, and tobacco. Cigarette advertisements, for example, promote smoking, a behavior proven to be harmful and even deadly. Tobacco companies, which spend billions on promotion, have countered criticism of their advertising by pointing out that advertisements for red meat and coffee are not censured even though these products may also cause health problems. Those who defend such promotion assert that as long as it is legal to sell a product, promoting that product should be allowed.

SUMMARY

Integrated marketing communications is the coordination of promotion and other marketing efforts to ensure maximum informational and persuasive impact on customers. Promotion is communication to build and maintain relationships by informing and persuading one or more audiences.

Communication is a sharing of meaning. The communication process involves several steps. First, the source translates meaning into code, a process known as coding or encoding. The source should employ signs or symbols familiar to the receiver or audience. The coded message is sent through a medium of transmission to the receiver or audience. The receiver or audience then decodes the message and usually supplies feedback to the source. When the decoded message differs from the encoded one, a condition called noise exists.

Although promotional objectives vary from one organization to another and within organizations over time, eight primary objectives underlie many promotional programs. Promotion aims to create awareness of a new product, a new brand, or an existing product; to stimulate primary and selective demand; to encourage product trial through the use of free samples, coupons, limited free-use offers, contests, and games; to identify prospects; to retain loyal customers; to facilitate reseller support; to combat competitive promotional efforts; and to reduce sales fluctuations.

The promotion mix for a product may include four major promotional methods: advertising, personal selling, public relations, and sales promotion. Advertising is paid nonpersonal communication about an organization and its products transmitted to a target audience through a mass medium. Personal selling is paid personal communication that attempts to inform customers and persuade them to purchase products in an exchange situation. Public relations is a broad set of communication efforts used to create and maintain favorable relationships between an organization and its stakeholders. Sales promotion is an activity or material that acts as a direct inducement, offering added value or incentive for the product, to resellers, salespeople, or consumers.

Major determinants of which promotional methods to include in a product's promotion mix are the organization's promotional resources, objectives, and policies; characteristics of the target market; characteristics of the product; and cost and availability of promotional methods. Marketers also consider whether to use a push policy or a pull policy. With a push policy, the producer promotes the product only to the next institution down the marketing channel. Normally, a push policy stresses personal selling. Firms that use a pull policy promote directly to consumers, with the intention of developing strong consumer demand for the products. Once consumers are persuaded to seek the products in retail stores, retailers go to wholesalers or the producer to buy the products.

Promotional activities can help consumers make informed purchasing decisions, but they have also evoked many criticisms. Promotion has been accused of deception. Although some deceiving or misleading promotions do exist, laws, government regulation, and industry self-regulation minimize deceptive promotion.

Promotion has been blamed for increasing prices, but it usually tends to lower them. When demand is high, production and marketing costs decrease, which can result in lower prices. Moreover, promotion helps keep prices lower by facilitating price competition. Other criticisms of promotional activity are that it manipulates consumers into buying products they do not need, that it leads to a more materialistic society, and that consumers do not benefit sufficiently from promotional activity to justify its high cost. Finally, some critics of promotion suggest that potentially harmful products, especially those associated with violence, sex, and unhealthy activities, should not be promoted at all.

Please visit the student website at **www.prideferrell.com** for ACE Self-Test questions that will help you prepare for exams.

IMPORTANT TERMS

Integrated marketing communications	Channel capacity
	Primary demand
Promotion	Pioneer promotion
Communication	Selective demand
Source	Promotion mix
Receiver	Kinesic communication
Coding process	Proxemic communication
Medium of transmission	Tactile communication
Decoding process	Buzz marketing
Noise	Push policy
Feedback	Pull policy

DISCUSSION & REVIEW QUESTIONS

1. What does *integrated marketing communications* mean?
2. What is the major task of promotion? Do firms ever use promotion to accomplish this task and fail? If so, give several examples.
3. Define *communication* and describe the communication process. Is it possible to communicate without using all the elements in the communication process? If so, which elements can be omitted?
4. Identify several causes of noise. How can a source reduce noise?
5. Describe the possible objectives of promotion and discuss the circumstances under which each objective might be used.
6. Identify and briefly describe the four promotional methods an organization can use in its promotion mix.

7. What forms of interpersonal communication besides language can be used in personal selling?
8. How do target market characteristics determine which promotional methods to include in a promotion mix? Assume a company is planning to promote a cereal to both adults and children. Along what major dimensions would these two promotional efforts have to differ from each other?
9. How can a product's characteristics affect the composition of its promotion mix?
10. Evaluate the following statement: "Appropriate advertising media are always available if a company can afford them."
11. Explain the difference between a pull policy and a push policy. Under what conditions should each policy be used?
12. Which criticisms of promotion do you believe are the most valid? Why?
13. Should organizations be allowed to promote offensive, violent, sexual, or unhealthy products that can be legally sold and purchased? Support your answer.

APPLICATION QUESTIONS

1. The overall objective of promotion is to stimulate demand for a product. Through television advertising, the American Dairy Association promotes the benefits of drinking milk, a campaign that aims to stimulate primary demand. Advertisements for a specific brand of milk focus on stimulating selective demand. Identify two television commercials, one aimed at stimulating primary demand and one aimed at stimulating selective demand. Describe each commercial and discuss how each attempts to achieve its objective.

2. Developing a promotion mix is contingent on many factors, including the type of product and the product's attributes. Which of the four promotional methods—advertising, personal selling, public relations, or sales promotion—would you emphasize if you were developing the promotion mix for the following products? Explain your answers.
   a. Washing machine
   b. Cereal
   c. Halloween candy
   d. Compact disc
3. Suppose marketers at Falcon International Corporation have come to you for recommendations on how to promote their products. They want to develop a comprehensive promotional campaign and have a generous budget with which to implement their plans. What questions would you ask them, and what would you suggest they consider before developing a promotional program?
4. Marketers must consider whether to use a push or a pull policy when deciding on a promotion mix (see Figure 18.4). Identify a product for which marketers should use each policy and a third product that might best be promoted using a mix of the two policies. Explain your answers.

Internet Exercise & Resources

University of Iowa Alumni Association Hits the Net

As you will probably discover in a few years, university alumni associations are themselves marketing organizations. Thanks in large part to a popular course related to Internet marketing taught at the University of Iowa and to the Iowa City Chamber of Commerce and a local bank and bookstore, the University of Iowa Alumni Association is now online. Visit its website at **www.biz.uiowa.edu/Iowalum**.

1. Who are the target markets for the alumni association's Internet marketing efforts?
2. What is being promoted to these individuals?
3. What are the promotional objectives of the website?

Video Case 18.1

 Jordan's Furniture

Samuel Tatelman began selling furniture out of the back of his truck in Waltham, Massachusetts, in 1918. Today his great-grandsons, Eliot and Barry, sell more furniture per square foot at Jordan's Furniture than any other furniture retailer in the country and attract record numbers of guests each week. With just 5 stores, Jordan's Furniture has grown from 15 employees 25 years ago to more than 1,200 employees today. The company has broken just about all industry standards: inventory in stores turns over at a rate of 13 times a year (versus 1 to 2 times a year in average furniture stores); advertising and marketing expenditures are 2 percent (the industry average is 7 percent); and sales per square foot are $950 (most furniture stores average $150 per square foot). The company was purchased by Berkshire Hathaway Inc., Warren Buffet's holding company, in 1999.

The differences between Jordan's Furniture and its competitors strike consumers the moment they pull into the parking lot. The stores in Avon and Natick, Massachusetts, have 650 parking spaces and host more than 4,000 visitors on an average weekend. Inside the store, customers are greeted with a welcome map, although they can see clear, bright signs from the entry directing to points of interest. All

furniture in the store is tagged with a full product description, including the manufacturer, construction details, warranty information, product care, and physical dimensions. Although salespeople are present and attentive, they are not aggressive. In the bedding department, salespeople known as "Sleep Technicians" even wear white lab coats to reinforce their image. Unlike more "sales-oriented" furniture stores, Jordan's offers "underprices" and never has "sales."

At Jordan's Furniture, the sale is certainly important, but it is the follow-up after the sale that often determines whether customers will return. No matter the size or price of the purchase, customers are asked about their entire experience from entering the store to checking out, from delivery to product set-up. Results from these follow-up contacts are collected as part of the "Daily Report Card," which is sent directly to Barry and Eliot Tatelman. This gives them the opportunity to both correct any problems quickly and praise personnel who have done their jobs well. Barry Tatelman views such after-sale service as vital because everyone needs furniture, and "one satisfied customer can give you $300,000 worth of furniture over a lifetime."

With a slimmer advertising budget than its competitors, Jordan's employs "quirky" ads to gain consumers' attention in a saturated television market. The company has also sought ways to generate publicity, from supporting local and national causes, communicating about its employees and customers, or creating a unique retail experience. Jordan's Natick store features a 6-story, 262-seat, 3D IMAX Theater, a commercial venture run by AT&T. To enter the theater, patrons must walk through the furniture store. Riding the escalator to the theater gives customers the feeling of being a celebrity among the strobe lights, paparazzi murals, and crowd videos. David Grain, senior vice president for AT&T Broadband, states, "This partnership unites two companies that truly appreciate the value of entertainment for the American family." The

company has also benefited from a three-year Blue Cross Blue Shield of Massachusetts ad campaign that spotlights some of its endorsers, including Eliot and Barry Tatelman.

Jordan's also gains publicity from its support of local causes. Among the recipients of its largesse are Project Bread, which supports hungry people throughout Massachusetts; Furniture Bank, to which it donates 50 pieces of furniture a week to the MA Coalition for the Homeless; and M.O.M., a program that contributes to a group of charities including the American Cancer Society, AIDS Action Committee, American Red Cross, March of Dimes, Muscular Dystrophy Association, Children's Happiness Foundation, and Arthritis Foundation. Proceeds from Streetcar Named Dessert go to children's charities, as well as many others.

For its strong ethical and socially responsible business practices, Jordan's Furniture was recognized by the Better Business Bureau in 1997 with the National Torch Award for Marketplace Ethics and by Ernst & Young with the Entrepreneur of the Year/Social Responsibility award. The company was named "Retailer of the Year" by the National Home Furnishing Association and the GERS Retail System, and voted "The Most Unusual Furniture Store in the World" by *Home Furnishings Daily* and *Furniture Today*. Jordan's has also won Telly awards for many of its advertisements, as well as many other noteworthy awards.[52]

QUESTIONS FOR DISCUSSION

1. Describe the marketing mix of Jordan's Furniture.
2. How do the promotional efforts of Jordan's Furniture rise above the "noise" of regular furniture store promotions?
3. How does Jordan's promotional strategy illustrate integrated marketing communications?

Case 18.2

Carb Wars: New Diets Turn the Food Industry Upside Down

When changes occur in knowledge, attitudes, and consumer behavior, they may affect an entire industry if product acceptance patterns change as well. This is occurring in the food industry with the growing acceptance of low-carbohydrate diets as a means of losing weight more quickly and with fewer sacrifices than traditional diets. The Atkins, South Beach, and other diets have advanced the sales of protein-rich

foods while putting a dent in traditionally carbohydrate-rich foods such as breads, pastas, fruit, potatoes, and beans. During his life, Dr. Richard Atkins worked to encourage people to try his diet philosophy and discard misperceptions created by the so-called "food pyramid," which puts a premium on grains as well as fruits and vegetables. Now Atkins Nutritionals works to help consumers realize that protein is processed more quickly by the body and that consumption of carbohydrates often leads to fat accumulation because the body takes longer to process carbs than protein and fat.

Marketers can be quick to jump on marketing opportunities—sometimes fads, sometimes more long-term shifts in consumer buying patterns and product preferences. Food companies are now promoting low-carb bagels and tortillas, and even low-carb beers. In particular, the low-carb craze fostered by the popular diets has created an enormous opportunity for Atkins Nutritionals, which now markets 120 products and licenses numerous other products to dozens of companies. Restaurant chain TGIFriday's, for example, has introduced an Atkins-endorsed menu at restaurants across the United States. In recent years the food industry has seen little growth, and Atkins commands the lion's share of that growth. Consumers are getting their information on the merits of the Atkins diet from books, news stories, and word of mouth. Roughly 10 percent of the U.S. population follows the Atkins or other low-carb diets, fueling an increase in sales for marketers of eggs, cheese, and meat. The beef industry alone saw sales escalate by 10 percent in 2003. With beef prices at a 20-year high, even fast-food restaurants had to increase the prices of their hamburgers.

Another company exploiting the low-carb fad is Miller Brewing. Miller launched an advertising campaign directly attacking the taste of competitors' "light" beers with the message "I can't taste my beer." Since introducing the campaign, which compared the carbohydrate and calorie content of Miller Lite to those of brands offered by Coors and Budweiser, Miller Lite sales have been rising. Miller Brewing has been spending heavily on advertising to achieve this sales gain, rivaling much larger competitor Anheuser-Busch's spending over the same period last year. Coors responded to Miller's ads with an ad campaign pointing out that the difference between Coors Light and Miller Lite is just 1.8 carbohydrate grams, which consumers can easily burn off with a slow dance or by shopping online. Coors also introduced Aspen Edge, a super-premium, low-carb brand. Anheuser-Busch entered the low-carb fray with Michelob Ultra.

Although some companies have benefited from the low-carb phenomenon, other

industries have suffered, including the orange juice, tortilla, bread, pasta, and wheat industries. Negative publicity about the carbohydrate levels of these products has hurt sales. Orange juice marketers attribute a 2.7 percent drop in consumption to the low-carb trend, while the North American Millers Association blames it for dropping annual flour consumption to 137 pounds per person from its peak of 147 pounds per person in 1997. Dry pasta sales peaked in 2001 and have seen declines in recent years. Changing consumer diet preferences have prompted some companies to invest more heavily in advertising to counter the effects of the low-carb trend. One success story is Barilla pasta, the number-one-selling pasta in the United States after its entry in 1996. Barilla commands 17 percent of the dry pasta market, while its closest rival, Ronzoni, has just 7 percent. Al Ries, a marketing and branding expert, credits Barilla with offering great credentials for the pasta presented in the advertising. Barilla was touted as "Italy's No. 1 pasta," which evolved into "It must be good because it's Italy's No. 1 pasta" as the campaign went on. Effective advertising can be developed to support the carbohydrate-heavy segment of the market. As consumers become increasingly concerned about their weight and turn to trendy diets such as Atkins, more companies are likely to promote their low-carb products, while marketers of high-carb products may attempt to reposition their brands in consumers' minds as a healthful alternative.

Public relations has been a key tactic used by the beef industry as well as other low-carb food marketers to capitalize on the trend. Brochures, sponsorships, and scientific reports aim to increase consumers' awareness and acceptance of the benefits of these products as part of a low-carb diet. Indeed, publicity has been the main vehicle through which consumers have learned about low-carb food products. All the advertising and public relations have been enhanced by favorable word-of-mouth communication about the benefits and successes of the Atkins diet.[53]

QUESTIONS FOR DISCUSSION

1. Which of the promotion mix elements appear to be most effective in promoting the low-carb Atkins diet?
2. What are the key promotion objectives to overcome in dealing with a high-carbohydrate image and declining sales for pasta makers such as Barilla?
3. How can the coordination of promotion with other marketing efforts help industries under pressure due to the Atkins phenomenon, such as the fruit juice and wheat industries?

Advertising and Public Relations

19

OBJECTIVES

1. To describe the nature and types of advertising

2. To explore the major steps in developing an advertising campaign

3. To identify who is responsible for developing advertising campaigns

4. To examine the tools used in public relations

5. To analyze how public relations is used and evaluated

Apple Shines in a New Industry

Credit Steve Jobs with making Apple a brand name that once again turns heads—but this time in the music business. Apple, a pioneer in the computer industry in the 1980s, has long concentrated on developing products that people will want tomorrow and beyond. How did Apple regain its shine and gain *Advertising Age* magazine's 2003 Marketer of the Year honors? Thank the cutting-edge iPod portable digital music player, which runs on both the Macintosh and Microsoft Windows platforms. Indeed, Jobs has been acknowledged as the key person responsible for getting the music business moving in the right direction again.

Apple's iPod dominates the portable digital music player segment with 20 to 30 percent of the market. Although the company faces new competition from Wal-Mart, Microsoft, and other companies eager to cash in on the rising trend, Apple executives are optimistic that their product can maintain a leadership position. Apple has already sold more than 17 million songs through its iTunes Music Store at 99 cents each. Each downloaded song nets Apple just 10 cents in profits, but it helps sell iPods.

Advertising for the iPod has been more

strategic than sizable. The company spent just $10 million advertising iTunes and $9 million for iPods in the first eight months of 2003, a fraction of the $69 million Apple spent on promotions. However, Apple has leveraged its youthful brand image by entering into cooperative advertising arrangements with Volkswagen and PepsiCo, and a joint venture with McDonald's is in the works.

A great deal of Apple's rationale behind a more thoughtful, strategic approach to paid media is likely the result of the company's successful public relations campaign. More than 6,000 articles have been written about the iPod and iTunes service, enabling the company's advertising dollars to reinforce the highly successful publicity and buzz marketing campaigns. Apple has excelled at generating publicity for its products. In 2002, for example, the company gave free Apple computers to all seventh- and eighth-graders in the state of Maine.

The Apple brand has become so desirable that noncompeting firms are asking to link their products and brands with the Apple image. As Apple continues to craft its brand and image, it will likely continue to partner strategically with firms that can leverage their smaller advertising budgets while remaining sensitive to firms that "fit" with Apple's much valued brand name.[1] ■

Large organizations such as Apple, as well as smaller companies, use conventional and online promotional efforts, such as advertising, to change their corporate image, launch new products, or promote current brands. In this chapter, we explore several dimensions of advertising and public relations. First, we focus on the nature and types of advertising. Next, we examine the major steps in developing an advertising campaign and describe who is responsible for developing such campaigns. We then discuss the nature of public relations and how it is used. We examine various public relations tools and ways to evaluate the effectiveness of public relations. Finally, we focus on how companies deal with unfavorable public relations.

The Nature and Types of Advertising

advertising Paid nonpersonal communication about an organization and its products transmitted to a target audience through mass media

Advertising permeates our daily lives. At times, we view it positively; at other times, we avoid it. Some advertising informs, persuades, or entertains us; some bores, annoys, or even offends us.

As mentioned in Chapter 18, **advertising** is a paid form of nonpersonal communication transmitted through mass media, such as television, radio, the Internet, newspapers, magazines, direct mail, outdoor displays, and signs on mass transit vehicles. Organizations use advertising to reach a variety of audiences ranging from small, specific groups, such as stamp collectors in Idaho, to extremely large groups, such as all athletic-shoe purchasers in the United States.

When asked to name major advertisers, most people immediately mention business organizations. However, many nonbusiness types of organizations, including governments, churches, universities, and charitable organizations, take advantage of advertising. In 2002, the U.S. government was the twenty-fourth largest advertiser in the country, spending approximately $1.1 billion on advertising.[2] Although we analyze advertising in the context of business organizations here, much of the material applies to all types of organizations. For example, the Mexican Tourism Board developed an advertising campaign, tagged "Closer Than Ever," to encourage Americans and Canadians to continue spending their leisure time and money in Mexico. Tourism is Mexico's third-largest source of foreign currency, and visitors from the United States account for 90 percent of international tourists to Mexico.[3]

institutional advertising Advertising that promotes organizational images, ideas, and political issues

Advertising is used to promote goods, services, ideas, images, issues, people, and anything else advertisers want to publicize or foster. Depending on what is being promoted, advertising can be classified as institutional or product advertising. **Institutional advertising** promotes organizational images, ideas, and political issues. It can

Institutional Advertising
Budweiser promotes the importance of responsible drinking and using a designated driver.

advocacy advertising Advertising that promotes a company's position on a public issue

product advertising Advertising that promotes the uses, features, and benefits of products

pioneer advertising Advertising that tries to stimulate demand for a product category rather than a specific brand by informing potential buyers about the product

competitive advertising Advertising that points out a brand's special features, uses, and advantages relative to competing brands

be used to create or maintain an organizational image. Institutional advertisements may deal with broad image issues, such as organizational strength or the friendliness of employees. They may also aim to create a more favorable view of the organization in the eyes of noncustomer groups such as shareholders, consumer advocacy groups, potential stockholders, or the general public. When a company promotes its position on a public issue—for instance, a tax increase, abortion, gun control, or international trade coalitions—institutional advertising is referred to as **advocacy advertising**. Institutional advertising may be used to promote socially approved behavior such as recycling and moderation in consuming alcoholic beverages. Philip Morris, for example, has run television advertisements encouraging parents to talk to their children about not smoking. Research has identified a number of themes that advertisers can use to increase the effectiveness of antismoking messages for adolescents.[4] This type of advertising not only has societal benefits but also helps build an organization's image.

Product advertising promotes the uses, features, and benefits of products. There are two types of product advertising: pioneer and competitive. **Pioneer advertising** focuses on stimulating demand for a product category (rather than a specific brand) by informing potential customers about the product's features, uses, and benefits. This type of advertising is employed when the product is in the introductory stage of the product life cycle. **Competitive advertising** attempts to stimulate demand for a specific brand by promoting the brand's features, uses, and advantages, sometimes through indirect or direct comparisons with competing brands. Advertising effects on sales must reflect competitors' advertising activities. The type of competitive environment will determine the most effective industry approach.

Comparative Advertising
A visual comparison of Swanson's versus College Inn broth shows the difference between the two.

comparative advertising Advertising that compares two or more brands on the basis of one or more product characteristics

reminder advertising Advertising used to remind consumers about an established brand's uses, characteristics, and benefits

reinforcement advertising Advertising that assures users they chose the right brand and tells them how to get the most satisfaction from it

To make direct product comparisons, marketers use a form of competitive advertising called **comparative advertising**, which compares two or more brands on the basis of one or more product characteristics. Miller Brewing, for example, ran advertisements comparing Miller Lite's 96 calories and 3.2 grams of carbohydrates to the 110 calories and 6.6 grams of carbohydrates in Bud Light, owned by Anheuser-Busch.[5] Often the brands promoted through comparative advertisements have low market shares and are compared with competitors that have the highest market shares in the product category. Product categories that commonly use comparative advertising include soft drinks, toothpaste, pain relievers, foods, tires, automobiles, and detergents. Under the provisions of the 1988 Trademark Law Revision Act, marketers using comparative advertisements in the United States must not misrepresent the qualities or characteristics of competing products. Other countries may have laws that are stricter or less strict with regard to comparative advertising.

Other forms of competitive advertising include reminder and reinforcement advertising. **Reminder advertising** tells customers that an established brand is still around and still offers certain characteristics, uses, and advantages. **Reinforcement advertising** assures current users they have made the right brand choice and tells them how to get the most satisfaction from that brand.

Developing an Advertising Campaign

advertising campaign The creation and execution of a series of advertisements to communicate with a particular target audience

An **advertising campaign** involves designing a series of advertisements and placing them in various advertising media to reach a particular target audience. As Figure 19.1 indicates, the major steps in creating an advertising campaign are (1) identifying and analyzing the target audience, (2) defining the advertising objectives, (3) creating the advertising platform, (4) determining the advertising appropriation, (5) developing the media plan, (6) creating the advertising message, (7) executing the campaign, and (8) evaluating advertising effectiveness. The number of steps and the exact order in which they are carried out may vary according to the organization's resources, the nature of its product, and the type of target audience to be reached. Nevertheless, these general guidelines for developing an advertising campaign are appropriate for all types of organizations.

Figure 19.1 General Steps in Developing and Implementing an Advertising Campaign

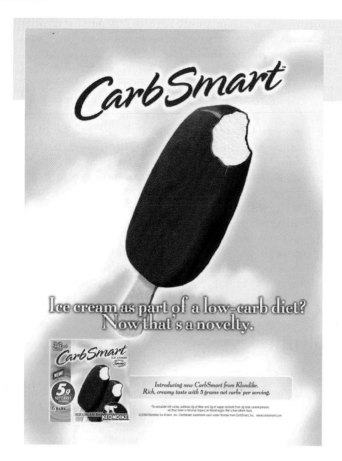

Target Audience
Klondike's CarbSmart ice cream bars target individuals who are interested in a low-carbohydrate diet.

◆ Identifying and Analyzing the Target Audience

The **target audience** is the group of people at whom advertisements are aimed. Advertisements for Barbie cereal are targeted toward young girls who play with Barbie dolls, whereas those for Special K cereal are directed at health-conscious adults. Identifying and analyzing the target audience are critical processes; the information yielded helps determine other steps in developing the campaign. The target audience may include everyone in the firm's target market. Marketers may, however, direct a campaign at only a portion of the target market. For example, Nissan, after recognizing that 10 to 12 percent of its buyers are Hispanic, expanded its advertising program to Spanish-language TV. The Japanese automaker ran its first Spanish ad for the Quest minivan after learning that one in two southwestern buyers of the van is Latino.[6]

Advertisers research and analyze advertising targets to establish an information base for a campaign. Information commonly needed includes location and geographic distribution of the target group; the distribution of demographic factors, such as age, income, race, gender, and education;

target audience The group of people at whom advertisements are aimed

lifestyle information; and consumer attitudes regarding purchase and use of both the advertiser's products and competing products. The exact kinds of information an organization finds useful depend on the type of product being advertised, the characteristics of the target audience, and the type and amount of competition. Generally, the more an advertiser knows about the target audience, the more likely the firm is to develop an effective advertising campaign. When the advertising target is not precisely identified and properly analyzed, the campaign may fail.

Snapshot

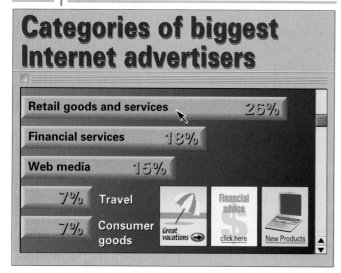

Categories of biggest Internet advertisers

Retail goods and services	25%
Financial services	18%
Web media	15%
Travel	7%
Consumer goods	7%

Source: Data from Nielsen//NetRatings.

◆ Defining the Advertising Objectives

The advertiser's next step is to determine what the firm hopes to accomplish with the campaign. Because advertising objectives guide campaign development, advertisers should define objectives carefully. Advertising objectives should be stated clearly, precisely, and in measurable terms. Precision and measurability allow advertisers to evaluate advertising success at the end of the campaign in terms of whether or not objectives have been met. To provide precision and measurability, advertising objectives should contain benchmarks and indicate how far the advertiser wishes to move from these standards. If the goal is to increase sales, the advertiser should state the current sales level (the benchmark) and the amount of sales increase sought through advertising. An advertising objective should also specify a time frame so that advertisers know exactly how long they have to accomplish the objective. An advertiser with average monthly sales of

$450,000 (the benchmark) might set the following objective: "Our primary advertising objective is to increase average monthly sales from $450,000 to $540,000 within 12 months."

If an advertiser defines objectives on the basis of sales, the objectives focus on increasing absolute dollar sales or unit sales, increasing sales by a certain percentage, or increasing the firm's market share. Even though an advertiser's long-run goal is to increase sales, not all campaigns are designed to produce immediate sales. Some campaigns aim to increase product or brand awareness, make consumers' attitudes more favorable, or heighten consumers' knowledge of product features. If the goal is to increase product awareness, the objectives are stated in terms of communication. A specific communication objective might be to increase product feature awareness from 0 to 40 percent in the target audience by the end of six months. For example, Curves, a women-only fitness center chain, set an objective of 120,000 phone calls to its toll-free line after it launched its first national advertising campaign. The response was actually twice the stated goal in the campaign's first nine months.[7]

◆ Creating the Advertising Platform

advertising platform Basic issues or selling points to be included in an advertising campaign

Before launching a political campaign, party leaders develop a political platform stating major issues that are the basis of the campaign. Like a political platform, an **advertising platform** consists of the basic issues or selling points that an advertiser wishes to include in the advertising campaign. PepsiCo, for example, launched a campaign to promote the consumption of Pepsi-Cola with food, such as hot dogs and pizza. The "It's the Cola" campaign featured television, radio, and outdoor advertising to help combat a decline in cola sales due to the increasing popularity of flavored teas, waters, and other noncarbonated drinks.[8] A single advertisement in an advertising campaign may contain one or several issues from the platform. Although the platform sets forth the basic issues, it does not indicate how to present them.

An advertising platform should consist of issues important to customers. One of the best ways to determine those issues is to survey customers about what they consider most important in the selection and use of the product involved. Selling features must not only be important to customers, they should also be strongly competitive features of the advertised brand. For example, in Argentina, where Coca-Cola has a 55 percent share of the soft-drink market, the company introduced Nativa, a new soft drink flavored with the country's yerba mate herbal tea. The advertising platform, with the tag line "Refresh your day with a flavor that is very much ours," focuses on Nativa's earthy qualities and the tea's status as a national icon.[9]

Although research is the most effective method for determining what issues to include in an advertising platform, it is expensive. Therefore, an advertising platform is most commonly based on opinions of personnel within the firm and of individuals in the advertising agency, if an agency is used. This trial-and-error approach generally leads to some successes and some failures.

Advertising Platform
Brown Cow's key selling point is that its yogurt is made in small batches using all-natural ingredients, not mass-produced.

Because the advertising platform is a base on which to build the advertising message, marketers should analyze this stage carefully. A campaign can be perfect in terms of selection and analysis of its target audience, statement of its objectives, media strategy, and the form of its message. But the campaign will ultimately fail if the advertisements communicate information that consumers do not deem important when selecting and using the product.

◆ Determining the Advertising Appropriation

advertising appropriation
The advertising budget for a specific time period

The **advertising appropriation** is the total amount of money a marketer allocates for advertising for a specific time period. It is difficult to determine how much to spend on advertising for a specific period because the potential effects of advertising are so difficult to measure precisely.

Many factors affect a firm's decision about how much to appropriate for advertising. Geographic size of the market and the distribution of buyers within the market have a great bearing on this decision. As Table 19.1 shows, both the type of product advertised and the firm's sales volume relative to competitors' sales volumes also play a part in determining what proportion of revenue to spend on advertising. Advertising appropriations for business products are usually quite small relative to product sales, whereas consumer convenience items, such as soft drinks, soaps, and cosmetics, generally have large advertising expenditures relative to sales.

Table 19.1	**Twenty Leading National Advertisers**		
Organization	**Advertising Expenditures ($ millions)**	**Sales ($ millions)**	**Advertising Expenditures as Percentage of Sales**
1. General Motors	3,652.2	138,692	2.6
2. AOL Time Warner	2,922.8	32,632	9.0
3. Procter & Gamble	2,673.4	21,198	12.6
4. Pfizer	2,566.2	20,762	12.4
5. Ford Motor	2,251.8	108,392	2.1
6. DaimlerChrysler	2,031.8	72,002	2.8
7. Walt Disney	1,803.0	20,770	8.7
8. Johnson & Johnson	1,799.0	22,455	8.0
9. Sears, Roebuck	1,661.2	37,180	4.5
10. Unilever*	1,640.0	11,535	14.2
11. Sony	1,621.1	19,748	8.2
12. GlaxoSmithKline	1,554.0	15,987	9.7
13. Toyota Motor*	1,552.7	51,488	3.0
14. Verizon	1,527.5	64,356	2.4
15. McDonald's	1,335.7	5,423	24.6
16. Viacom	1,259.8	20,577	6.1
17. Altria Group	1,206.0	44,725	2.7
18. Honda Motor*	1,192.8	38,708	3.1
19. Merck	1,158.4	43,500	2.7
20. L'Oreal*	1,117.7	4,114	27.2

*Based on North American sales.

Source: Reprinted with permission from the June 23, 2003 issue of *Advertising Age*. Copyright © Crain Communications Inc., 2003.

objective-and-task approach
Budgeting for an advertising campaign by first determining its objectives and then calculating the cost of all the tasks needed to attain them

percent-of-sales approach
Budgeting for an advertising campaign by multiplying the firm's past and expected sales by a standard percentage

competition-matching approach   Determining an advertising budget by trying to match competitors' advertising outlays

arbitrary approach   Budgeting for an advertising campaign as specified by a high-level executive in the firm

media plan   A plan that specifies the media vehicles to be used and the schedule for running advertisements

Of the many techniques used to determine the advertising appropriation, one of the most logical is the **objective-and-task approach**. Using this approach, marketers determine the objectives a campaign is to achieve and then attempt to list the tasks required to accomplish them. The costs of the tasks are calculated and added to arrive at the total appropriation. This approach has one main problem: marketers sometimes have trouble accurately estimating the level of effort needed to attain certain objectives. A coffee marketer, for example, may find it extremely difficult to determine how much of an increase in national television advertising is needed to raise a brand's market share from 8 to 10 percent.

In the more widely used **percent-of-sales approach**, marketers simply multiply the firm's past sales, plus a factor for planned sales growth or decline, by a standard percentage based on both what the firm traditionally spends on advertising and the industry average. This approach, too, has a major flaw: it is based on the incorrect assumption that sales create advertising rather than the reverse. A marketer using this approach during declining sales will reduce the amount spent on advertising, but such a reduction may further diminish sales. Though illogical, this technique has been favored because it is easy to use.

Another way to determine advertising appropriation is the **competition-matching approach**. Marketers following this approach try to match their major competitors' appropriations in absolute dollars or to allocate the same percentage of sales for advertising that their competitors do. Although a marketer should be aware of what competitors spend on advertising, this technique should not be used alone because the firm's competitors probably have different advertising objectives and different resources available for advertising. Many companies and advertising agencies review competitive spending on a quarterly basis, comparing competitors' dollar expenditures on print, radio, and television with their own spending levels. Competitive tracking of this nature occurs at both the national and regional levels.

At times marketers use the **arbitrary approach**, which usually means a high-level executive in the firm states how much to spend on advertising for a certain period. The arbitrary approach often leads to underspending or overspending. Although hardly a scientific budgeting technique, it is expedient.

Deciding how large the advertising appropriation should be is critical. If the appropriation is set too low, the campaign cannot achieve its full potential. When too much money is appropriated, overspending results and financial resources are wasted.

◆ Developing the Media Plan

As Table 19.2 (on p. 508) shows, advertisers spend tremendous amounts on advertising media. These amounts have grown rapidly during the past two decades. To derive maximum results from media expenditures, marketers must develop effective media plans. A **media plan** sets forth the exact media vehicles to be used (specific magazines, television stations, newspapers, and so forth) and the dates and times the advertisements will appear. The plan determines how many people in the target audience will be exposed to the message. It also determines, to some degree, the effects of the message on those individuals. Media planning is a

Media Plan
Automobile manufacturers know the importance of reaching their target market through auto magazines such as *Car and Driver*.

| Table 19.2 | Total Advertising Expenditures (in millions of dollars) |

	1990		1995		2000		2002	
	Total Dollar Amount	Percent of Total	Total Dollar Amount	Percent of Total	Total Dollar Amount	Percent of Total	Total Dollar Amount	Percent of Total
Newspapers	$32,281	25.1%	$36,317	22.6%	$49,050	20.1%	$44,030	18.6%
Magazines	5,803	5.3	8,580	5.3	12,370	5.1	11,000	4.6
Television	28,405	22.1	36,246	22.6	59,231	24.3	58,370	24.7
Radio	8,726	6.8	11,338	7.1	19,295	7.9	18,880	7.9
Yellow pages	8,926	6.9	10,236	6.4	13,228	5.4	13,780	5.8
Outdoor	1,084	0.8	1,263	0.8	1,758	0.7	5,180*	2.2*
Direct mail	23,370	18.2	32,866	20.5	44,591	18.3	46,070	19.4
Business press	2,875	2.2	3,559	2.2	4,915	2.0	3,980	1.7
Internet	NA	0.0	NA	0.0	4,333	1.8	4,880	2.1
Miscellaneous	16,170	12.6	20,232	12.5	34,919	14.4	30,730	13.0
TOTAL	$128,640	100.0%	$160,637	100.0%	$160,637	100.0%	$236,880	100.0%

*Category expanded to more inclusive "out of home."

Sources: "Coen Cuts Spending Forecast," *Advertising Age,* June 11, 2001, p. 47; Robert J. Coen, "Coen: Little Ad Growth," *Advertising Age,* May 6, 1991, pp. 1, 16; Robert J. Coen, "Coen's Spending Totals for 2002," *Advertising Age,* www.adage.com (accessed Dec. 2, 2003); Robert J. Coen, "U.S. Advertising Volume," *Advertising Age,* May 20, 1996, p. 24.

complex task requiring thorough analysis of the target audience. Sophisticated computer models have been developed to attempt to maximize the effectiveness of media plans.

To formulate a media plan, the planners select the media for the campaign and prepare a time schedule for each medium. The media planner's primary goal is to reach the largest number of people in the advertising target that the budget will allow. A secondary goal is to achieve the appropriate message reach and frequency for the target audience while staying within budget. *Reach* refers to the percentage of consumers in the target audience actually exposed to a particular advertisement in a stated period. *Frequency* is the number of times these targeted consumers are exposed to the advertisement.

Media planners begin with broad decisions but eventually make very specific ones. They first decide which kinds of media to use: radio, television, the Internet, newspapers, magazines, direct mail, outdoor displays, or signs on mass transit vehicles. They assess different formats and approaches to determine which are most effective. Some media plans are highly focused and use just one medium. The media plans of manufacturers of consumer packaged goods can be quite complex and dynamic.

Media planners take many factors into account when devising a media plan. They analyze location and demographic characteristics of consumers in the target audience because people's tastes in media differ according to demographic groups and locations. There are radio stations especially for teenagers, magazines for men ages 18 to 34, and television cable channels aimed at women in various age groups. Media planners also consider the sizes and types of audiences that specific media reach. Dillard's, for example, cut back on newspaper advertising because that medium reaches fewer target customers for its 329 department stores. The chain is experimenting with advertising through other media, such as magazines and direct mail.[10] Several data services collect and periodically provide information about circulations and audiences of various media. Building Customer Relationships examines a different way to use visual media to get promotional messages across.

The content of the message sometimes affects media choice. Print media can be used more effectively than broadcast media to present complex issues or numerous details in single advertisements. If an advertiser wants to promote beautiful colors, patterns, or textures, media offering high-quality color reproduction, such as magazines or television, should be used instead of newspapers. For example, food can be effectively promoted in full-color magazine advertisements but far less effectively in black and white.

The cost of media is an important but troublesome consideration. Planners try to obtain the best coverage possible for each dollar spent. The concept of integrated marketing communications stresses the benefits of coordinating and building synergy across various media to build brand equity. Overspending is less likely with an integrated approach to multimedia advertising.[11] However, there is no accurate way to compare the cost and impact of a television commercial with the cost and impact of

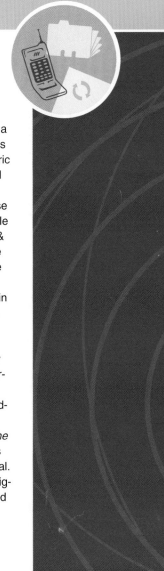

BUILDING CUSTOMER RELATIONSHIPS

Remodeling Advertising Messages

You may not have noticed it, but you are being bombarded with advertisements on the television shows you watch regularly. You may not have noticed because you skillfully maneuver around commercials using services such as TiVo or Replay TV, or by recording programs and fast forwarding through the commercials. In fact, consumers are routinely assailed by advertising commercials on outdoor billboards, radio, television, and the Internet; in magazines; in elevators; and even inside mass transit vehicles. To make their advertisements stand out among the crowd, companies are looking for more creative and effective ways to use their advertising dollars. One tactic gaining favor is the innovative use of product placements in movies and popular television programs.

Consumers seem more likely to attend to promotional messages when products are touted by "experts" or used by beloved characters in programs they watch every week. When James Bond drives a BMW in the latest movie episode, BMW arranges the product placement. The automaker even made a limited-edition James Bond version of the Z3 sports coupe available at Neiman Marcus to tie in with the movie placement. Bravo's hit show *Queer Eye for the Straight Guy* regularly promotes Disaronno liquor and Ecco Domani wines as well as numerous grooming, food, and home decor products. Bravo even offers a Shopping Guide for the products highlighted on *Queer Eye* episodes on its website.

Procter & Gamble—best known for brands such as Herbal Essences, Crest, Dawn, Infusium, Bounty, Pantene, Clairol, Olay, Cover Girl, Tide, Secret, Old Spice, Pepto-Bismol, Aussie, Charmin, Zest, Pur, Pringles, and Downey—recognized this advertising opportunity and inked a deal with CBS's *Survivor* series to place 20 brands in "Survivor 8." The sponsorship deal includes fabric and health products, home care, beauty care, oral care, and snack brands. The company also ran a contest giving consumers an opportunity to choose possible contestants for "Survivor 10." To be eligible to vote, consumers must purchase three Procter & Gamble products and answer questions about the program. A random drawing will yield five possible candidates for the program. To support Procter & Gamble's ambitious plans for double-digit growth in earnings per share, the company must engage in more aggressive and creative advertising than its competitors.

Home improvement and makeover shows may well be the best vehicle for advertisers to reach target audiences with focused messages about their products. When The Home Depot or Lowe's is credited for providing the merchandise for a home remodeling show such as HGTV's *Designing for the Sexes* or PBS's *This Old House,* the message has greater credibility than a traditional paid commercial.

So the next time you buy a shampoo or a refrigerator, you may want to think about how that brand came to your mind and whether you associate it with a television show or a movie.

cost comparison indicator
A means of comparing the costs of advertising vehicles in a specific medium in relation to the number of people reached

a newspaper advertisement. A **cost comparison indicator** lets an advertiser compare the costs of several vehicles within a specific medium (such as two magazines) in relation to the number of people each vehicle reaches. The *cost per thousand (CPM)* is the cost comparison indicator for magazines; it shows the cost of exposing 1,000 people to a one-page advertisement.

Table 19.2 shows that the extent to which each medium is used varies and the pattern of use has changed over the years. For example, the proportion of total advertising dollars spent on television has risen since 1990 and surpassed that spent on newspapers by 2000. The proportion of total advertising dollars spent on the Internet has also risen since 1990. Media are selected by weighing the various characteristics, advantages, and disadvantages of each (see Table 19.3 on pp. 512–513).

Like media selection decisions, media scheduling decisions are affected by numerous factors, such as target audience characteristics, product attributes, product seasonality, customer media behavior, and size of the advertising budget. There are three general types of media schedules: continuous, flighting, and pulsing. When a *continuous* schedule is used, advertising runs at a constant level with little variation throughout the campaign period. With a *flighting* schedule, advertisements run for set periods of time, alternating with periods in which no ads run. For example, an advertising campaign might have an ad run for two weeks, then suspend it for two weeks, and then run it again for two weeks. A *pulsing* schedule combines continuous and flighting schedules: during the entire campaign, a certain portion of advertising runs continuously, and during specific time periods of the campaign, additional advertising is used to intensify the level of communication with the target audience.

◆ Creating the Advertising Message

The basic content and form of an advertising message are a function of several factors. A product's features, uses, and benefits affect the content of the message. Characteristics of the people in the target audience—gender, age, education, race, income, occupation, lifestyle, and other attributes—influence both content and form. When Procter & Gamble promotes Crest toothpaste to children, the company emphasizes daily brushing and cavity control. When marketing Crest to adults, P&G stresses tartar and plaque control. To communicate effectively, advertisers use words, symbols, and illustrations that are meaningful, familiar, and appealing to people in the target audience.

An advertising campaign's objectives and platform also affect the content and form of its messages. If a firm's advertising objectives involve large sales increases, the message may include hard-hitting, high-impact language and symbols. When campaign objectives aim to increase brand awareness, the message may use much repetition of the brand name and words and illustrations associated with it. Thus, the advertising platform is the foundation on which campaign messages are built.

Choice of media obviously influences the content and form of the message. Effective outdoor displays and short broadcast spot

Black and White Versus Color
This example highlights the importance of using color in advertising.

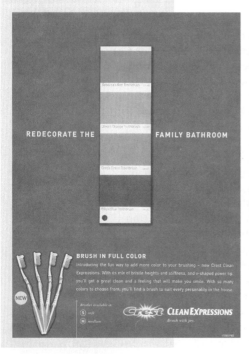

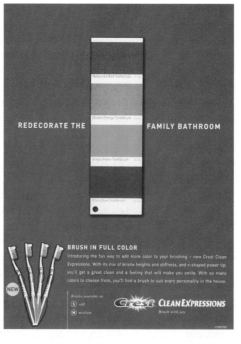

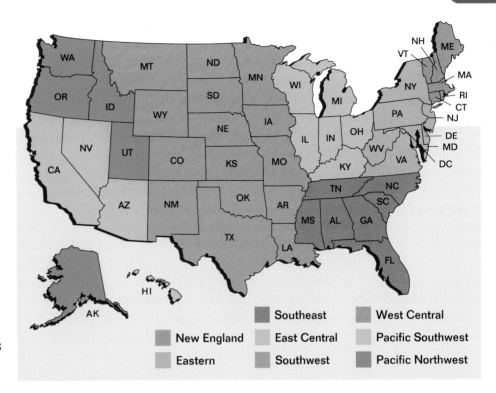

Figure 19.2 Geographic Divisions for *Time* Regional Issues
Source: Time magazine.

announcements require concise, simple messages. Magazine and newspaper advertisements can include considerable detail and long explanations. Because several kinds of media offer geographic selectivity, a precise message can be tailored to a particular geographic section of the target audience. Some magazine publishers produce **regional issues**, in which advertisements and editorial content of copies appearing in one geographic area differ from those appearing in other areas. As Figure 19.2 shows, *Time* magazine publishes eight regional issues. A company advertising in *Time* might decide to use one message in the New England region and another in the rest of the nation. A company may also choose to advertise in only one region. Such geographic selectivity lets a firm use the same message in different regions at different times.

regional issues Versions of a magazine that differ across geographic regions

Copy. **Copy** is the verbal portion of an advertisement and may include headlines, subheadlines, body copy, and signature. Not all advertising contains all of these copy elements. The headline is critical because often it is the only part of the copy that people read. It should attract readers' attention and create enough interest to make them want to read the body copy. The subheadline, if there is one, links the headline to the body copy and sometimes serves to explain the headline.

copy The verbal portion of advertisements

Body copy for most advertisements consists of an introductory statement or paragraph, several explanatory paragraphs, and a closing paragraph. Some copywriters have adopted guidelines for developing body copy systematically: (1) identify a specific desire or problem, (2) recommend the product as the best way to satisfy that desire or solve that problem, (3) state product benefits and indicate why the product is best for the buyer's particular situation, (4) substantiate advertising claims, and (5) ask the buyer to take action. When substantiating claims, it is important to present the substantiation in a credible manner. The proof of claims should help strengthen both the image of the product and company integrity.

The signature identifies the advertisement's sponsor. It may contain several elements, including the firm's trademark, logo, name, and address. The signature should be attractive, legible, distinctive, and easy to identify in a variety of sizes.

Because radio listeners often are not fully "tuned in" mentally, radio copy should be informal and conversational to attract listeners' attention, resulting in greater impact. Radio messages are highly perishable and should consist of short, familiar

Table 19.3   Characteristics, Advantages, and Disadvantages of Major Advertising Media

Medium	Types	Unit of Sale	Factors Affecting Rates
Newspaper	Morning Evening Sunday Sunday supplement Weekly Special	Agate lines Column inches Counted words Printed lines	Volume and frequency discounts Number of colors Position charges for preferred and guaranteed positions Circulation level Ad size
Magazine	Consumer Business Farm Regional	Pages Partial pages Column inches	Circulation level; Cost of publishing Type of audience; Volume discounts Frequency discounts Size of advertisement Position of advertisement (covers) Number of colors; Regional issues
Direct mail	Letters; catalogs; price lists; calendars; brochures; coupons; circulars; newsletters; postcards; booklets; broadsides; samplers	Not applicable	Cost of mailing lists Postage Production costs
Radio	AM FM	Programs: sole sponsor, co-sponsor, participative sponsor Spots: 5, 10, 20, 30, 60 seconds	Time of day Audience size Length of spot or program Volume and frequency discounts
Television	Network Local Cable	Programs: sole sponsor, co-sponsor, participative sponsor Spots: 5, 10, 15, 30, 60 seconds	Time of day Length of program Length of spot Volume and frequency discounts Audience size
Internet	Websites Banners; Buttons Sponsorships Pop-ups; Interstitials Classified ads	Not applicable	Length of time Complexity Type of audience Keywords Continuity
Inside transit	Buses Subways	Full, half, and quarter showings sold on monthly basis	Number of riders Multiple-month discounts Production costs Position
Outside transit	Buses Taxicabs	Full, half, and quarter showings; space also rented on per-unit basis	Number of advertisements Position; Size
Outdoor	Papered posters Painted displays Spectaculars	Papered posters; sold on monthly basis in multiples called "showings" Painted displays and spectaculars; sold on per-unit basis	Length of time purchased Land rental Cost of production Intensity of traffic Frequency and continuity discounts Location

Cost Comparison Indicator	Advantages	Disadvantages
Milline rate = Cost per agate line × 1,000,000 divided by circulation	Reaches large audience; purchased to be read; national geographic flexibility; short lead time; frequent publication; favorable for cooperative advertising; merchandising services	Not selective for socioeconomic groups; short life; limited reproduction capabilities; large advertising volume limits exposure to any one advertisement
Cost per thousand (CPM) = Cost per page × 1,000 divided by circulation	Demographic selectivity; good reproduction; long life; prestige; geographic selectivity when regional issues are available; read in leisurely manner	High absolute dollar cost; long lead time
Cost per contact	Little wasted circulation; highly selective; circulation controlled by advertiser; few distractions; personal; stimulates actions; use of novelty; relatively easy to measure performance; hidden from competitors	Expensive; no editorial matter to attract readers; considered junk mail by many; criticized as invasion of privacy
Cost per thousand (CPM) = Cost per minute × 1,000 divided by audience size	Reaches 95% of consumers age 12 and older; highly mobile; low-cost broadcast medium; message can be quickly changed; geographic selectivity; demographic selectivity	Provides only audio message; short life of message; listeners' attention limited because of other activities while listening
Cost per thousand (CPM) = Cost per minute × 1,000 divided by audience size	Reaches large audience; low cost per exposure; uses audio and video; highly visible; high prestige; geographic and demographic selectivity	High dollar costs; highly perishable message; size of audience not guaranteed; amount of prime time limited
Cost per thousand or by the number of click-throughs	Immediate response; potential to reach a precisely targeted audience; ability to track customers and build databases; very interactive medium	Costs of precise targeting are high; inappropriate ad placement; effects difficult to measure; concerns about security and privacy
Cost per thousand riders	Low cost; "captive" audience; geographic selectivity	Does not reach many professional persons; does not secure quick results
Cost per thousand exposures	Low cost; geographic selectivity; reaches broad, diverse audience	Lacks demographic selectivity; does not have high impact on readers
No standard indicator	Allows for repetition; low cost; message can be placed close to point of sale; geographic selectivity; operable 24 hours a day	Message must be short and simple; no demographic selectivity; seldom attracts readers' full attention; criticized as traffic hazard and blight on countryside

Sources: William F. Arens, *Contemporary Advertising* (Burr Ridge, IL: Irwin/McGraw-Hill, 2002); George E. Belch and Michael Belch, *Advertising and Promotion* (Burr Ridge, IL: Irwin/McGraw-Hill, 2001).

Components of a Print Ad
This Xerox ad contains all the major components of a print advertisement.

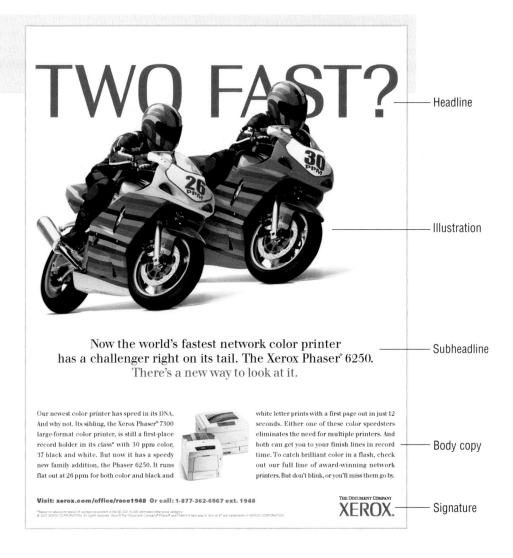

Headline

Illustration

Subheadline

Body copy

Signature

terms. The length should not require a rate of speech exceeding approximately two and one-half words per second.

In television copy, the audio material must not overpower the visual material, and vice versa. However, a television message should make optimal use of its visual portion, which can be very effective for product demonstrations. Copy for a television commercial is sometimes initially written in parallel script form. Video is described in the left column and audio in the right. When the parallel script is approved, the copywriter and artist combine copy with visual material by using a **storyboard**, which depicts a series of miniature television screens showing the sequence of major scenes in the commercial. Beneath each screen is a description of the audio portion to be used with that video segment. Technical personnel use the storyboard as a blueprint when producing the commercial.

storyboard A blueprint combining copy and visual material to show the sequence of major scenes in a commercial

artwork An advertisement's illustrations and layout

illustrations Photos, drawings, graphs, charts, and tables used to spark audience interest in an advertisement

Artwork. **Artwork** consists of an advertisement's illustrations and layout. **Illustrations** are often photographs but can also be drawings, graphs, charts, and tables. Illustrations are used to attract attention, encourage audiences to read or listen to the copy, communicate an idea quickly, or communicate ideas that are difficult to put into words.[12] They are especially important because consumers tend to recall the visual portions of advertisements better than the verbal portions. Advertisers use a variety of illustration techniques. They may show the product alone, in a setting, in use, or the results of its use. Illustrations can also take the form of comparisons, contrasts, diagrams, and testimonials.

layout The physical arrangement of an advertisement's illustration and copy

The **layout** of an advertisement is the physical arrangement of the illustration and the copy (headline, subheadline, body copy, and signature). These elements can be arranged in many ways. The final layout is the result of several stages of layout preparation. As it moves through these stages, the layout promotes an exchange of ideas among people developing the advertising campaign and provides instructions for production personnel.

◆ Executing the Campaign

Execution of an advertising campaign requires extensive planning and coordination because many tasks must be completed on time and several people and firms are involved. Production companies, research organizations, media firms, printers, photoengravers, and commercial artists are just a few of the people and firms contributing to a campaign.

Implementation requires detailed schedules to ensure that various phases of the work are done on time. Advertising management personnel must evaluate the quality of the work and take corrective action when necessary. In some instances, changes are made during the campaign so it meets objectives more effectively. Sometimes one firm develops a campaign and another executes it.

◆ Evaluating Advertising Effectiveness

A variety of ways exist to test the effectiveness of advertising. They include measuring achievement of advertising objectives; assessing effectiveness of copy, illustrations, or layouts; and evaluating certain media.

pretest Evaluation of advertisements performed before a campaign begins

consumer jury A panel of a product's existing or potential buyers who pretest ads

Advertising can be evaluated before, during, and after the campaign. An evaluation performed before the campaign begins is called a **pretest**. A pretest usually attempts to evaluate the effectiveness of one or more elements of the message. To pretest advertisements, marketers sometimes use a **consumer jury**, a panel of existing or potential buyers of the advertised product. Jurors judge one or several dimensions of two or more advertisements. Such tests are based on the belief that consumers are more likely than advertising experts to know what influences them. Companies can also solicit the assistance of marketing research firms to help assess ads. PepsiCo, for example, relies on Information Resources Inc.'s (IRI) BehaviorScan to pretest new commercials in Eau Claire, Wisconsin, and Cedar Rapids, Iowa. IRI sends different Pepsi product ads to participating households and then analyzes their purchasing activity to test the ads' effectiveness.[13]

To measure advertising effectiveness during a campaign, marketers usually rely on "inquiries." In a campaign's initial stages, an advertiser may use several advertisements simultaneously, each containing a coupon, form, or toll-free phone number through which potential customers can request information. The advertiser records the number of inquiries returned from each type of advertisement. If an advertiser receives 78,528 inquiries from advertisement A, 37,072 from advertisement B, and 47,932 from advertisement C, advertisement A is judged superior to advertisements B and C. Internet advertisers can also assess how many people "clicked" on an ad to obtain more product information. Before the launch of the Nissan 350Z, Nissan asked advertising agency TBWA/Chiat/Day to create an interactive Internet banner ad for the new sports car. In just 30 days, 50,000 clicked the ads, and Nissan ultimately saw 75,000 preorders for the car even before it went on sale.[14]

posttest Evaluation of advertising effectiveness after the campaign

Evaluation of advertising effectiveness after the campaign is called a **posttest**. Advertising objectives often determine what kind of posttest is appropriate. If the objectives focus on communication—to increase awareness of product features or brands or to create more favorable customer attitudes—the posttest should measure changes in these dimensions. Advertisers sometimes use consumer surveys or experiments to evaluate a campaign based on communication objectives. These methods are costly, however.

For campaign objectives stated in terms of sales, advertisers should determine the change in sales or market share attributable to the campaign. However, changes in sales or market share brought about by advertising cannot be measured precisely; many factors independent of advertisements affect a firm's sales and market share. Competitors' actions, regulatory actions, and changes in economic conditions, consumer preferences, and weather are only a few factors that might enhance or diminish a company's sales or market share. By using data about past and current sales and advertising expenditures, advertisers can make gross estimates of the effects of a campaign on sales or market share.

recognition test A posttest in which respondents are shown the actual ad and asked if they recognize it

Because it is difficult to determine the direct effects of advertising on sales, many advertisers evaluate print advertisements according to how well consumers can remember them. Posttest methods based on memory include recognition and recall tests. Such tests are usually performed by research organizations through surveys. In a **recognition test**, respondents are shown the actual advertisement and asked whether they recognize it. If they do, the interviewer asks additional questions to determine how much of the advertisement each respondent read. When recall is evaluated, respondents are not shown the actual advertisement but instead are asked about what they have seen or heard recently. For Internet advertising, research suggests that the longer a person is exposed to a website containing a banner advertisement, the more likely he or she is to recall the ad.[15]

unaided recall test A posttest in which respondents are asked to identify ads they have recently seen but are given no recall clues

aided recall test A posttest that asks respondents to identify recent ads and provides clues to jog their memories

Recall can be measured through either unaided or aided recall methods. In an **unaided recall test**, respondents identify advertisements they have seen recently but are not shown any clues to help them remember. A similar procedure is used with an **aided recall test**, but respondents are shown a list of products, brands, company names, or trademarks to jog their memories. For example, national advertisers such as Subway, CompUSA, KFC, and Kinko's are studying consumer reactions to messages delivered on web-capable wireless devices. In one test, these advertisers sent messages to participating cellular phone users who agreed to receive at least three advertisements per day. Advertisers found that wireless advertisements scored an encouraging 58 percent aided recall and that participants reacted positively to the products in messages they recalled.[16] Several research organizations, such as Daniel Starch, provide research services that test recognition and recall of advertisements.

The major justification for using recognition and recall methods is that people are more likely to buy a product if they can remember an advertisement about it than if they cannot. However, recalling an advertisement does not necessarily lead to buying the product or brand advertised. Researchers also use a sophisticated technique called *single-source data* to help evaluate advertisements. With this technique, individuals' behaviors are tracked from television sets to checkout counters. Monitors are placed in preselected homes, and microcomputers record when the television set is on and which station is being viewed. At the supermarket checkout, the individual in the sample household presents an identification card. Checkers then record the purchases by scanner, and data are sent to the research facility. Some single-source data companies provide sample households with scanning equipment for use at home to record purchases after returning from shopping trips. Single-source data provide information that links exposure to advertisements with purchase behavior.

Who Develops the Advertising Campaign?

An advertising campaign may be handled by an individual or by a few people within the firm, by the firm's own advertising department, or by an advertising agency.

In very small firms, one or two individuals are responsible for advertising (and for many other activities as well). Usually these individuals depend heavily on personnel at local newspapers and broadcast stations for copywriting, artwork, and advice about scheduling media.

In certain large businesses, especially large retail organizations, advertising departments create and implement advertising campaigns. Depending on the size of the advertising program, an advertising department may consist of a few multi-skilled individuals or a sizable number of specialists such as copywriters, artists, media buyers, and technical production coordinators. Advertising departments sometimes obtain the services of independent research organizations and hire free-lance specialists when a particular project requires it.

When an organization uses an advertising agency, the firm and the agency usually develop the advertising campaign jointly. How much each participates in the campaign's total development depends on the working relationship between the firm and the agency. Ordinarily a firm relies on the agency for copywriting, artwork, technical production, and formulation of the media plan.

Advertising agencies assist businesses in several ways. An agency, especially a large one, can supply the services of highly skilled specialists—not only copywriters, artists, and production coordinators but also media experts, researchers, and legal advisers. Agency personnel often have broad advertising experience and are usually more objective than a firm's employees about the organization's products.

Because an agency traditionally receives most of its compensation from a 15 percent commission paid by the media from which it makes purchases, firms can obtain some agency services at low or moderate costs. If an agency contracts for $400,000 of television time for a firm, it receives a commission of $60,000 from the television station. Although the traditional compensation method for agencies is changing and now includes other factors, media commissions still offset some costs of using an agency.

Like advertising, public relations can be a vital element in a promotion mix. We turn to this topic next.

Public Relations

public relations Communication efforts used to create and maintain favorable relations between an organization and its stakeholders

Public relations is a broad set of communication efforts used to create and maintain favorable relationships between an organization and its stakeholders. An organization communicates with various stakeholders, both internal and external, and public relations efforts can be directed toward any and all of them. A firm's stakeholders can include customers, suppliers, employees, stockholders, the media, educators, potential investors, government officials, and society in general.

Public relations can be used to promote people, places, ideas, activities, and even countries. It is often used by nonprofit organizations to achieve their goals. (Sometimes goals may run counter to those of particular companies, as shown in Building Customer Relationships on p. 518.) Public relations focuses on enhancing the image of the total organization. Assessing public attitudes and creating a favorable image are no less important than direct promotion of the organization's products. Because the public's attitudes toward a firm are likely to affect the sales of its products, it is very important for firms to maintain positive public perceptions. In addition, employee morale is strengthened if the public perceives the firm positively.[17] Although public relations can make people aware of a company's products, brands, or activities, it can also create specific company images, such as innovativeness or dependability. Companies such as Ben & Jerry's, Patagonia, Sustainable Harvest, and Honest Tea have reputations for being socially responsible not only because they engage in socially responsible behavior but because

Annual Report
Annual reports are an example of companies' public relations efforts.

their actions are reported through news stories and other public relations efforts.[18] By getting the media to report on a firm's accomplishments, public relations helps the company maintain positive public visibility. Some firms use public relations for a single purpose; others use it for several purposes.

◆ **Public Relations Tools**

Companies use a variety of public relations tools to convey messages and create images. Public relations professionals prepare written materials, such as brochures, newsletters, company magazines, news releases, and annual reports, that reach and influence their various stakeholders.

BUILDING CUSTOMER RELATIONSHIPS

PR Battles

Although many consumers welcome a new Wal-Mart Supercenter to their community or neighborhood, other consumers fear the impact of such "big-box" stores on the local economy. These stores often bring increased sales tax revenues and new jobs, but they may also threaten long-time "mom-and-pop" stores that make local communities unique. Driven by the growth of such supercenters, Wal-Mart has become the largest corporation in the world and accounts for 9 cents of every dollar spent in the United States. With more than 130 million customers visiting Wal-Mart stores worldwide weekly, Wal-Mart has also become the highest-volume grocery seller, surpassing traditional supermarket chains such as Safeway, Albertson's, and Kroger, which do not provide the complete product lines found in a Wal-Mart Supercenter.

Many residents fear the influx of big-box retailers such as Wal-Mart not only because they may jeopardize local businesses but also because they may stretch limited tax dollars available for infrastructure improvements for sprawling developments, such as roads, traffic lights, and water/sewer lines. In some areas, citizens have expressed concerns about potential effects on environmentally or historically sensitive sites. As a result, special-interest groups, ranging from environmentalists and cultural

preservationists to older citizens who don't want their small towns to mushroom into metropolises, often oppose the development of Wal-Mart Supercenters and other big-box stores.

Some small towns and city neighborhoods have successfully stopped new Wal-Marts by waging grass-roots public relations campaigns. For example, residents of the town of Old Saybrook, Connecticut, were able to ward off a Wal-Mart Supercenter. To protect their small-town culture, the citizens had to raise money to hire professional help and legal counsel, organize protests, circulate petitions, and raise awareness of the issue. Ultimately they convinced three local political bodies to block the supercenter; they have since established a website to help other small communities apply the public relations tactics they used in their fight. In Austin, Texas, environmental organizations and neighborhood associations organized demonstrations and mounted a vigorous e-mail campaign to successfully fend off a Wal-Mart Supercenter slated for a location atop the aquifer that supplies water for some central Texans. To help raise money to fund the public relations campaign, they held a special screening of *Store Wars: When Wal-Mart Comes to Town*, a documentary detailing a Virginia town's battle against the discount retailer, and invited local celebrities to speak.

As communities band together to share strategies for resisting big-box stores, Wal-Mart has turned to its own public relations arsenal to protect its reputation and ensure its plans for growth. The company used surveys and focus groups to identify problems with its image among many consumers. After hearing consumers voice concerns about issues such as job quality, store cleanliness, and community involvement and respect, as well as local economic issues, the retailer launched a public relations campaign of its own. It ran several television commercials presenting the discounter as a great place to work. The company plans to run additional commercials to improve its reputation.

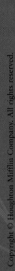

Public relations personnel also create corporate identity materials, such as logos, business cards, stationery, and signs, that make firms immediately recognizable. Speeches are another public relations tool. Because what a company executive says publicly at meetings or to the media can affect the organization's image, the speech must convey the desired message clearly.

Event sponsorship, in which a company pays for part or all of a special event, such as a benefit concert or a tennis tournament, is another public relations tool. Examples are The Home Depot's sponsorship of NASCAR and the U.S. Olympic team. Sponsoring special events can be an effective means of increasing company or brand recognition with relatively minimal investment. Event sponsorship can gain companies considerable amounts of free media coverage. An organization tries to ensure that its product and the sponsored event target a similar audience and that the two are easily associated in customers' minds. For example, United Parcel Service (UPS) has become the official express delivery company of Daytona International Speedway. Daytona International Speedway and the challenges of the Daytona 500 demand that NASCAR teams take speed, technology, and precision to the limit, making the speedway and its events a good match for UPS delivery service standards.[19] Public relations personnel also organize unique events to "create news" about the company. These may include grand openings with celebrities, prizes, hot-air balloon rides, and other attractions that appeal to a firm's publics.

Publicity is a part of public relations. **Publicity** is communication in news story form about the organization, its products, or both, transmitted through a mass medium at no charge. Although public relations has a larger, more comprehensive communication function than publicity, publicity is a very important aspect of public relations. Publicity can be used to provide information about goods or services; to announce expansions, acquisitions, research, or new-product launches; or to enhance a company's image.

The most common publicity-based public relations tool is the **news release**, sometimes called a *press release,* which is usually a single page of typewritten copy containing fewer than 300 words and describing a company event or product. A news release gives the firm's or agency's name, address, phone number, and contact person. Automakers and other manufacturers sometimes use news releases when introducing new products. When McDonald's introduced a new licensing initiative, including toys, clothing, videos, and books marketed under the McKids brand name, its public relations department sent out news releases to newspapers, magazines, television contacts, and suppliers, resulting in public relations in the form of magazine and newspaper articles and television coverage.[20] As

publicity A news story type of communication about an organization and/or its products transmitted through a mass medium at no charge

news release A short piece of copy publicizing an event or a product

Contact: Rick Stockwood
(617) 426-6500, ext. 213
Stockwood@BostonKids.org

NEW EXHIBIT HELPS CREATE POSITIVE AWARENESS OF PEOPLE LIVING WITH DISABILITIES

Boston Children's Museum to open access/Ability June 17, 2004

(Boston, MA) May 19, 2004...Boston Children's Museum will open *access/Ability June 17, 2004.* This exhibition is a highly interactive, yet sensitive disability awareness exhibit that delivers the message to children, parents and educators that as human beings, we are more alike than different.

This unique exhibit presents people living with disabilities as participants in the world and features fun and engaging activities that show the similarities and differences in how each of us, with or without disabilities, go places, communicate, have fun, and learn. Visitors will have a chance to learn phrases in American Sign Language, type their name in Braille, try a hand-pedaled bike and take part in a multi-sensory City Walk.

Throughout the exhibit, My Way kiosks introduce individuals living with disabilities who talk about themselves, their accomplishments, and how they overcome challenges in their lives. A resource area provides a quiet space where visitors can learn more about disabilities through books and computer resources.

This exhibition was created by the Boston Children's Museum and was funded in part by Lead Local Sponsor Liberty Mutual and with additional support provided by the Mitsubishi Electric America Foundation.

About Boston Children's Museum
Boston Children's Museum exists to help children understand and enjoy the world in which they live. It is a private, non-profit, educational institution that is recognized internationally as a research and development center and pacesetter for children's exhibitions, educational programs and curriculum. The Children's Museum focuses on three key areas of expertise: visitor programs, teacher resources and early childhood education. More information about The Children's Museum can be found at http://www.bostonkids.org.

Hours and Admission
The Museum is open daily from 10:00 a.m. – 5:00 p.m. and Fridays until 9:00 p.m. Children (2-15) and senior citizens, $7; other adults $9; one year olds, $2; Fridays 5:00pm – 9:00pm, all visitors $1. Infants under one and Museum members are always free. Special rates available for school and community groups; reservations required, call (617) 426-8433.

-end-

Example of a News Release
The Boston Children's Museum issued this information release to publicize an exhibit on positive awareness of people living with physical challenges.

Table 19.4	Possible Issues for Publicity Releases	
Changes in marketing personnel		Packaging changes
Support of a social cause		New products
Improved warranties		New slogan
Reports on industry conditions		Research developments
New uses for established products		Company's history and development
Product endorsements		Employment, production, and sales records
Quality awards		Award of contracts
Company name changes		Opening of new markets
Interviews with company officials		Improvements in financial position
Improved distribution policies		Opening of an exhibit
International business efforts		History of a brand
Athletic event sponsorship		Winners of company contests
Visits by celebrities		Logo changes
Reports on new discoveries		Speeches of top management
Innovative marketing activities		Merit awards
Economic forecasts		Anniversary of inventions

feature article A manuscript of up to 3,000 words prepared for a specific publication

captioned photograph A photograph with a brief description of its contents

press conference A meeting used to announce major news events

Table 19.4 shows, news releases tackle a multitude of specific issues. A **feature article** is a manuscript of up to 3,000 words prepared for a specific publication. A **captioned photograph** is a photograph with a brief description explaining its contents. Captioned photographs are effective for illustrating new or improved products with highly visible features.

There are several other kinds of publicity-based public relations tools. A **press conference** is a meeting called to announce major news events. Media personnel are invited to a press conference and are usually supplied with written materials and photographs. Letters to the editor and editorials are sometimes prepared and sent to newspapers and magazines. Videos and audiotapes may be distributed to broadcast stations in the hope they will be aired.

Publicity-based public relations tools offer several advantages, including credibility, news value, significant word-of-mouth communications, and a perception of media endorsement. The public may consider news coverage more truthful and credible than an advertisement because the media are not paid to provide the information. In addition, stories regarding a new-product introduction or a new environmentally responsible company policy, for example, are handled as news items and are likely to receive notice. Finally, the cost of publicity is low compared with the cost of advertising.[21]

Publicity-based public relations tools have some limitations. Media personnel must judge company messages to be newsworthy if the messages are to be published or broadcast at all. Consequently messages must be timely, interesting, accurate, and in the public interest. It may take a great deal of time and effort to convince media personnel of the news value of publicity releases, and many communications fail to qualify. Although public relations personnel usually encourage the media to air publicity releases at certain times, they control neither the content nor the timing of the communication. Media personnel alter length and content of publicity releases to fit publishers' or broadcasters' requirements and may even delete the parts of messages that company personnel view as most important. Furthermore, media personnel use publicity releases in time slots or positions most convenient for them. Thus, messages sometimes appear in locations or at times that may not reach the firm's target audiences. Although these limitations can be frustrating, properly managed publicity-based public relations tools offer an organization substantial benefits.

NET SIGHTS

Domestic and international corporate press releases are available at PR Newswire (www.prnewswire. com). Special subject areas highlight market segments, investor interests, and current news.

◆ Evaluating Public Relations Effectiveness

Because of the potential benefits of good public relations, it is essential that organizations evaluate the effectiveness of their public relations campaigns. Research can be conducted to determine how well a firm is communicating its messages or image to its target audiences. *Environmental monitoring* identifies changes in public opinion affecting an organization. A *public relations audit* is used to assess an organization's image among the public or to evaluate the effect of a specific public relations program. A *communications audit* may include a content analysis of messages, a readability study, or a readership survey. If an organization wants to measure the extent to which stakeholders view it as being socially responsible, it can conduct a *social audit*.

One approach to measuring the effectiveness of publicity-based public relations is to count the number of exposures in the media. To determine which releases are published in print media and how often, an organization can hire a clipping service, a firm that clips and sends news releases to client companies. To measure the effectiveness of television coverage, a firm can enclose a card with its publicity releases requesting that the television station record its name and the dates when the news item is broadcast (although station personnel do not always comply). Some television and radio tracking services exist, but they are extremely costly.

Counting the number of media exposures does not reveal how many people have actually read or heard the company's message or what they thought about the message afterward. However, measuring changes in product awareness, knowledge, and attitudes resulting from the publicity campaign helps yield this information. To assess these changes, companies must measure these levels before and after public relations campaigns. Although precise measures are difficult to obtain, a firm's marketers should attempt to assess the impact of public relations efforts on the organization's sales. For example, critics' reviews of films can affect the films' box office performance. Interestingly, negative reviews (publicity) harm revenue more than positive reviews help revenue in the early weeks of a film's release.[22]

◆ Dealing with Unfavorable Public Relations

Thus far, we have discussed public relations as a planned element of the promotion mix. However, companies may have to deal with unexpected and unfavorable public relations resulting from an unsafe product, an accident resulting from product use, controversial actions of employees, or some other negative event or situation. For example, an airline that experiences a plane crash faces a very tragic and distressing situation. Charges of anticompetitive behavior against Microsoft have raised public concern and generated unfavorable public relations for that organization. The public's image of The Body Shop as a socially responsible company diminished considerably when it was reported that the company's actions were less socially responsible than its promotion promised. Unfavorable coverage can have quick and dramatic effects. A single negative event that generates public relations can wipe out a company's favorable image and destroy positive customer attitudes established through years of expensive advertising campaigns and other promotional efforts. Moreover, today's mass media, including online services and the Internet, disseminate information faster than ever before, and bad news generally receives considerable media attention.

To protect its image, an organization needs to prevent unfavorable public relations or at least lessen its effect if it occurs. First and foremost, the organization should try to prevent negative incidents and events through safety programs, inspections, and effective quality control procedures. However, because negative events can befall even the most cautious firms, an organization should have predetermined plans in place to handle them when they do occur. Firms need to establish policies and procedures for reducing the adverse impact of news coverage of a crisis or controversy. In most cases, organizations should expedite news coverage of negative events rather than try to discourage or block them. If news coverage is suppressed, rumors and other misinformation may replace facts and be passed along anyway.

An unfavorable event can easily balloon into serious problems or public issues and become very damaging. By being forthright with the press and public and taking prompt action, a firm may be able to convince the public of its honest attempts to deal with the situation, and news personnel may be more willing to help explain complex issues to the public. Dealing effectively with a negative event allows an organization to lessen, if not eliminate, the unfavorable impact on its image.

SUMMARY

Advertising is a paid form of nonpersonal communication transmitted to consumers through mass media such as television, radio, the Internet, newspapers, magazines, direct mail, outdoor displays, and signs on mass transit vehicles. Both business and nonbusiness organizations use advertising. Institutional advertising promotes organizational images, ideas, and political issues. When a company promotes its position on a public issue such as taxation, institutional advertising is referred to as advocacy advertising. Product advertising promotes uses, features, and benefits of products. The two types of product advertising are pioneer advertising, which focuses on stimulating demand for a product category rather than a specific brand, and competitive advertising, which attempts to stimulate demand for a specific brand by indicating the brand's features, uses, and advantages. To make direct product comparisons, marketers use comparative advertising, which compares two or more brands. Two other forms of competitive advertising are reminder advertising, which reminds customers about an established brand's uses, characteristics, and benefits, and reinforcement advertising, which assures current users they have made the right brand choice.

Although marketers may vary in how they develop advertising campaigns, they should follow a general pattern. First, they must identify and analyze the target audience, the group of people at whom advertisements are aimed. Second, they should establish what they want the campaign to accomplish by defining advertising objectives. Objectives should be clear, precise, and presented in measurable terms. Third, marketers must create the advertising platform, which contains basic issues to be presented in the campaign. Advertising platforms should consist of issues important to consumers. Fourth, advertisers must decide how much money to spend on the campaign; they arrive at this decision through the objective-and-task approach, percent-of-sales approach, competition-matching approach, or arbitrary approach.

Advertisers must then develop a media plan by selecting and scheduling media to use in the campaign. Some factors affecting the media plan are location and demographic characteristics of the target audience, content of the message, and cost of the various media. The basic content and form of the advertising message are affected by product features, uses, and benefits; characteristics of the people in the target audience; the campaign's objectives and platform; and the choice of media. Advertisers use copy and artwork to create the message. The execution of an advertising campaign requires extensive planning and coordination.

Finally, advertisers must devise one or more methods for evaluating advertisement effectiveness. Pretests are evaluations performed before the campaign begins; posttests are conducted after the campaign. Two types of posttests are a recognition test, in which respondents are shown the actual advertisement and asked whether they recognize it, and a recall test. In aided recall tests, respondents are shown a list of products, brands, company names, or trademarks to jog their memories. In unaided tests, no clues are given.

Advertising campaigns can be developed by personnel within the firm or in conjunction with advertising agencies. A campaign created by the firm's personnel may be developed by one or more individuals or by an advertising department within the firm. Use of an advertising agency may be advantageous because an agency provides highly skilled, objective specialists with broad experience in advertising at low to moderate costs to the firm.

Public relations is a broad set of communication efforts used to create and maintain favorable relationships between an organization and its stakeholders. Public relations can be used to promote people, places, ideas, activities, and countries, and to create and maintain a positive company image. Some firms use public relations for a single purpose; others use it for several purposes. Public relations tools include written materials, such as brochures, newsletters, and annual reports; corporate identity materials, such as business cards and signs; speeches; event sponsorships; and special events. Publicity is communication in news story form about an organization, its products, or both, transmitted through a mass medium at no charge. Publicity-based public relations tools include news releases, feature articles, captioned photographs, and press conferences. Problems that organizations confront in using publicity-based public relations include reluctance of media personnel to print or air releases and lack of control over timing and content of messages.

To evaluate the effectiveness of their public relations programs, companies conduct research to determine how well their messages are reaching their audiences. Environmental monitoring, public relations audits, and counting the number of media exposures are all means of evaluating public relations effectiveness. Organizations should avoid negative public relations by taking steps to prevent negative events that result in unfavorable publicity. To diminish the impact of unfavorable public relations, organizations should institute policies and procedures for dealing with news personnel and the public when negative events occur.

 ACE self-test

Please visit the student website at **www.prideferrell.com** for ACE Self-Test questions that will help you prepare for exams.

IMPORTANT TERMS

Advertising	Cost comparison indicator
Institutional advertising	Regional issues
Advocacy advertising	Copy
Product advertising	Storyboard
Pioneer advertising	Artwork
Competitive advertising	Illustrations
Comparative advertising	Layout
Reminder advertising	Pretest
Reinforcement advertising	Consumer jury
Advertising campaign	Posttest
Target audience	Recognition test
Advertising platform	Unaided recall test
Advertising appropriation	Aided recall test
Objective-and-task approach	Public relations
	Publicity
Percent-of-sales approach	News release
Competition-matching approach	Feature article
	Captioned photograph
Arbitrary approach	Press conference
Media plan	

DISCUSSION & REVIEW QUESTIONS

1. What is the difference between institutional and product advertising?
2. What is the difference between competitive advertising and comparative advertising?
3. What are the major steps in creating an advertising campaign?
4. What is a target audience? How does a marketer analyze the target audience after identifying it?
5. Why is it necessary to define advertising objectives?
6. What is an advertising platform, and how is it used?
7. What factors affect the size of an advertising budget? What techniques are used to determine an advertising budget?
8. Describe the steps in developing a media plan.
9. What is the function of copy in an advertising message?
10. Discuss several ways to posttest the effectiveness of advertising.
11. What role does an advertising agency play in developing an advertising campaign?
12. What is public relations? Whom can an organization reach through public relations?

13. How do organizations use public relations tools? Give several examples you have observed recently.
14. Explain the problems and limitations associated with publicity-based public relations.
15. In what ways is the effectiveness of public relations evaluated?
16. What are some sources of negative public relations? How should an organization deal with unfavorable public relations?

APPLICATION QUESTIONS

1. An organization must define its objectives carefully when developing an advertising campaign. Which of the following advertising objectives would be most useful for a company, and why?
   a. The organization will spend $1 million to move from second in market share to market leader.
   b. The organization wants to increase sales from $1.2 million to $1.5 million this year to gain the lead in market share.
   c. The advertising objective is to gain as much market share as possible within the next 12 months.
   d. The advertising objective is to increase sales by 15 percent.
2. Copy, the verbal portion of advertising, is used to move readers through a persuasive sequence called AIDA: attention, interest, desire, and action. To achieve this, some copywriters have adopted guidelines for developing advertising copy. Select a print ad and identify how it (1) identifies a specific problem, (2) recommends the product as the best solution to the problem, (3) states the product's advantages and benefits, (4) substantiates the ad's claims, and (5) asks the reader to take action.
3. Advertisers use several types of publicity mechanisms. Look through some recent newspapers and magazines, and identify a news release, a feature article, and a captioned photograph used to publicize a product. Describe the type of product.
4. Negative public relations can harm an organization's marketing efforts if not dealt with properly. Identify a company that was recently the target of negative public relations. Describe the situation and discuss the company's response. What did marketers at this company do well? What, if anything, would you recommend that they change about their response?

Internet Exercise & Resources

Visit **www.prideferrell.com** for resources to help you master the material in this chapter, plus materials that will help you expand your marketing knowledge, including Internet exercise updates, ACE self-tests, hotlinks to companies featured in this chapter, and much more.

LEGO Company

LEGO Company has been making toys since 1932 and has become one of the most recognized brand names in the toy industry. With the company motto "Only the best is good enough," it is no surprise that LEGO Company has developed an exciting and interactive website. See how the company promotes LEGO products and encourages consumer involvement with the brand by visiting **www.lego.com**.

1. Which type of advertising is LEGO Company using on its website?
2. What target audience is LEGO attempting to reach through its website?
3. Identify the advertising objectives LEGO is attempting to achieve through its website.

Video Case 19.1

Vail Resorts Uses Public Relations to Put Out a Fire

Vail Resorts, Inc., is one of the leading resort operators in North America. The company operates four ski resorts in Colorado, including Vail, Keystone, Beaver Creek, and Breckenridge, as well as one in Lake Tahoe. Vail Mountain has become the most popular ski destination in the United States, with 1.6 million skier visits in the 2002–2003 season. *SKI* magazine has ranked Vail as the number one ski resort in North America 12 times since 1988.

Despite its success, the company experienced a very challenging year in 1998. In October of that year, just two weeks before the beginning of the ski season, the Vail Mountain resort suffered the largest "ecoterrorist" event in U.S. history. Several structures, including Patrol Headquarters, the Two Elk restaurant, and Camp One, were burned to the ground, and four chair lift operator buildings were damaged. Total damages exceeded $12 million. The deliberately and strategically set fires disabled three central lifts and the biggest restaurant and guest service center on the mountain.

Shortly after the fires, the Earth Liberation Front (ELF), a radical environmental organization, claimed responsibility. In an e-mail, ELF, which splintered off the better-known Earth First! organization, claimed to have set the fires to protest a planned expansion of the resort, which, the group argued, would threaten habitat needed to reintroduce the Canada lynx, an endangered wild cat. In the e-mail, ELF said, "Putting profits ahead of Colorado's wildlife will not be tolerated." ELF's communiqué also warned skiers to stay away from the resort "for your safety and convenience." However, Earth First! and many other environmental

groups, which had protested Vail's controversial plans to expand into lynx habitat, were quick to condemn ELF's firebombing at Vail.

As with most disasters, the mass media quickly swarmed the scene at Vail Mountain, and the resulting stories published around the country were not always beneficial to Vail Mountain and nearby Vail, Colorado—or accurate. Some newspapers reported that all ski lifts had been destroyed and that the resort would be unable to open for the season. A few reported that the nearby town of Vail was on fire, including hotels.

Vail Resorts responded to the misinformation by launching a direct-mail campaign to communicate with everyone who had made reservations for ski vacations through Vail Central Reservations, as well as to travel agents and individual hotels in town. The company reassured skiers that the resort would indeed open and would be a safe place for their families to vacation. Vail Resorts managed to salvage the season and make it successful, despite the havoc wreaked by the fires.

Vail Resorts, like many firms, had a generic crisis plan in place at the time of the incident. However, some analysts contend that the degree to which the company followed that plan was questionable. In hindsight, Vail management has stated that things might have gone more smoothly in the first 48 hours after the crisis if they had adhered more closely to that plan. For example, managers now recognize that they did not utilize their staff as effectively as possible. Instead of clearly defining responsibilities up front, staff members were called up somewhat randomly, adding to the confusion surrounding the event. The plan also failed to address communication with employees. Resort management quickly decided that keeping employees fully informed was a top priority, because they were the best ambassadors to the public.

Crisis management has been defined as preparation for low-probability or unexpected events that could threaten an organization's viability, reputation, or profitability. It has traditionally been viewed as "damage control," with little preplanning taking place. However, with the changing global political climate, events such as terrorist attacks and work-place violence have become more common, increasing the need for crisis management and disaster recovery planning for businesses. Even small companies are beginning to recognize the need to plan for the unexpected.

Crisis management and disaster recovery are critical for most organizations that deal with large numbers of customers, especially in the recreation and entertainment industries. The negative publicity resulting from a crisis can be potentially more devastating than a natural disaster such as an earthquake or a technological disruption such as a major power failure. The disruption of routine operations and paralysis of employees and customers in the face of crisis can reduce productivity, destroy long-established reputations, and erode public confidence in a company. Crisis planning can arm a company with tools and procedures to manage a crisis, protect a company's image, and reduce unfavorable publicity. By being forthright with the press and the public and taking prompt action, companies may be able to convince the public of their honest attempts to resolve the situation, and news media may be more willing to help explain complex issues to the public. Effectively dealing with a negative event allows an organization to reduce the unfavorable impact on its image.

In the case of Vail Resorts, managers believe they could have followed their previously established crisis management plan more closely. During the two days immediately following the fires, management was disorganized and employees and Vail residents were confused about the future of the resort. Ultimately Vail chose to be honest and open with the media and its employees, which helped the resort weather the crisis with its image intact. The company's direct-mail campaign to vacationers also helped preserve public trust in the company.

To prepare for unexpected events, all firms should develop a crisis management program, which includes four basic steps: conducting a crisis audit, making contingency plans, assigning a crisis management team, and practicing the plan. Conducting a crisis audit involves assessing the potential impacts of different events, such as the death of an executive or a natural disaster. *Contingency planning* refers to the development of backup plans for emergencies that specify actions to be taken and their expected consequences. Crisis management teams should also be designated so that key areas are covered in case of emergency, such as media relations and legal affairs. Finally, companies should practice the crisis management plan and update it as necessary on a regular basis so that all employees are familiar with the plan.[23]

QUESTIONS FOR DISCUSSION

1. What tools did Vail Resorts use to respond to the crisis?
2. Evaluate Vail Resorts' response to the crisis. What did the firm do right? What else could it have done to relieve public concerns about the safety of the resort as well as its controversial expansion into the habitat of an endangered species?
3. How can creating a crisis management and disaster recovery plan help a company protect its reputation, customer relationships, and profits?

Case 19.2

Microsoft: Crafting an Image Through Public Relations

A monopoly and a bully or a champion of free enterprise and high-tech innovation? Different people have different images of Microsoft, the largest and most successful software company in the world, and of Bill Gates, its founder and chair. Image is certainly important to Microsoft, which operates in a highly competitive, high-stakes industry. That's why the company has a team of 150 managers and outside experts dedicated to public relations. Their role is to shape and protect the image of Microsoft and its products, including the Windows operating system, the Internet Explorer web browser, the Xbox game console, and many other products for business and personal use.

Microsoft uses well-honed public relations skills to maintain favorable relationships with its stakeholders and support new-product introductions. For example, in the weeks leading up to the launch of every major update of Windows, computer users are bombarded by media coverage in newspapers, magazines, television, and radio. Many customers also receive newsletters and brochures in the mail or pick these up at local computer stores. By the time the new product finally arrives on store shelves, accompanied by special launch-day events, the enormous anticipatory buzz has created pent-up demand that boosts early sales and generates considerable word-of-mouth communication.

Giving Microsoft a "good-guy" image is another key public relations objective. Targeting students, the company has stepped up giveaways to get its products into grade schools, high schools, and colleges throughout the United States and around the globe. In addition, Bill Gates's charitable foundation has donated millions of dollars' worth of Microsoft software to U.S. public libraries. Such arrangements allow Microsoft to publicly display its strong support for education while simultaneously building brand equity. As the general manager of Microsoft's education consumer unit has observed, "Today's fifth-grader is tomorrow's business leader. The sooner we have them using our software, the more they carry that brand name forward."

Over time, Microsoft has developed a reputation for rather aggressive competitive tactics. This combative behavior has long been under regulatory scrutiny, culminating in a lawsuit brought against the company by the Department of Justice and investigations by state attorneys general into violations of antitrust law, which Microsoft vigorously denies. Throughout this protracted legal battle, Microsoft has had its public relations experts working to contain the damage to the company's image and present Microsoft's side most effectively.

Before the trial began, top Microsoft executives traveled around the United States making personal appearances and meeting with reporters. They stressed the message that Microsoft favored technological innovation and wanted customers to have more software choices. Brandishing the results of opinion polls, they also announced that U.S consumers and computer users were giving Microsoft its highest ratings ever.

The company also used the celebrity status of Bill Gates to its advantage during the pretrial period. Rather than keeping his private life private, Gates began talking more about his family life during media interviews. In addition, he scheduled visits to schools and made other public appearances, where he talked about Microsoft products and mingled with audiences. This higher visibility showed Gates's human side and allowed him to air his views on technology and related topics.

In addition, Microsoft conducted research to determine its standing with business decision makers and information technology professionals, two stakeholder groups that influence Microsoft purchases. Then, through informational ads in major newspapers, the company communicated its message that the antitrust case against Microsoft would stifle innovation and dampen free choice in the marketplace.

Even as these activities gained momentum, however, Microsoft came under fire after word leaked out about a proposed multimillion-dollar public relations plan targeting 12 states, including those where the company was under investigation. The proposal called for compiling statewide media lists, identifying potential supporters in the academic world, and having people write opinion pieces and letters for placement in local newspapers. A Microsoft spokesperson said the company would probably take some but not all of those actions. "We are particularly interested in telling our story in states where there have been questions about Microsoft," he said.

Ultimately Microsoft was convicted on antitrust violations, but appeals and other legal maneuvers continued for months afterward. Even as the company announced some conciliatory moves, a Microsoft-funded organization called Americans for Technology Leadership was at work behind the scenes. The organization hired professional telemarketers to contact consumers as part of an effort to pressure Congress to halt the Department of Justice's antitrust case. These telemarketers offered to write letters to congressional politicians in each consumer's name—and even pay the postage. "Microsoft's competitors do the same type of thing," explained the organization's president, who said the telemarketing initiative was just one element in "an ongoing effort to reach out to the general public and encourage them to let their opinions be known." Microsoft finally settled the suit in late 2002.

As Microsoft continues to introduce new products and pursue its marketing goals, its executives remain committed to using public relations to polish the company's image among its stakeholders and to keeping the Microsoft brand one of the best known in the world.[24]

QUESTIONS FOR DISCUSSION

1. What major public relations tools does Microsoft use?

2. Who are the stakeholders Microsoft wants to reach with its public relations efforts?

3. How should Microsoft evaluate the results of its public relations programs?

4. How do you think Microsoft should have used public relations to communicate its view during and after the antitrust trial? Explain.

Personal Selling and Sales Promotion

20

OBJECTIVES

1. To understand the major purposes of personal selling

2. To describe the basic steps in the personal selling process

3. To identify the types of sales force personnel

4. To understand sales management decisions and activities

5. To explain what sales promotion activities are and how they are used

6. To explore specific consumer and trade sales promotion methods

Sales Promotion Builds Share for McDonald's

uy a burger, get a toy. Toy giveaways are a major sales promotion weapon in McDonald's battle for fast-food market share. McDonald's has 13,000 U.S. restaurants, and its market share is approaching 43 percent. However, rival Burger King, with about 8,000 U.S. restaurants and nearly 18 percent of the market, is working hard to narrow the gap. To strengthen customer relationships in this high-stakes food fight, McDonald's is using a variety of promotional tools to target families as well as African American and Hispanic consumers.

Fast-food restaurants have long put toys in kids' meals to build traffic and encourage repeat visits from families. In recent years, however, the competition has gotten fiercer—and the budgets bigger—as the top chains develop promotional offers linked to new movies and hit television shows. Knowing that Disney films are generally big box office draws for families, McDonald's signed a ten-year, multimillion-dollar agreement to be the only fast-food restaurant promoting Disney movies. Typically the chain's movie-related sales promotions include colorful store displays, free toys, and a contest, giving families an incentive to return to McDonald's again and again. The deal is paying off. Already four of the ten

best-selling Happy Meals have featured Disney tie-ins such as toys from *Toy Story 2* and *The Haunted Mansion*. In addition, McDonald's is encouraging families to vary their food orders by tying specific menu items to movie and television promotions.

The family segment is just one of several market segments McDonald's has been targeting. Through research, the chain learned that African American and Hispanic consumers each account for 15 percent of its customer base. As a result, McDonald's has developed special promotional offers geared to these two segments. "McDonald's is doing bigger and better things to reach both African Americans and Hispanics with campaigns designed to be very specific to them," explains Mary Kay Eschbach, McDonald's U.S. media director. "Both communities are incredibly important to us."

One January, for example, McDonald's mounted a chainwide salute to Martin Luther King, followed by a February sweepstakes giving away a family vacation. In early fall, McDonald's promotional efforts carried an African American heritage theme. McDonald's has also been promoting its annual in-store Monopoly game and other promotions on the BET cable channel and website. To reach out to Hispanic consumers, McDonald's is airing a Spanish-language advertising campaign and spotlighting in-store promotions on Galavision. More sales promotion activities are ahead as McDonald's continues its battle to gain market share.[1] ∎

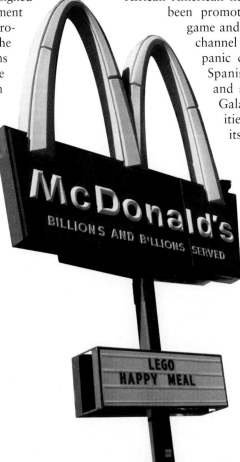

For many organizations, such as McDonald's, targeting customers with appropriate sales promotions can play a major role in maintaining long-term, satisfying customer relationships, which in turn contribute to the company's success. As we saw in Chapter 18, personal selling and sales promotion are two possible elements in a promotion mix. Sales promotion is sometimes a company's sole promotional tool, although it is generally used in conjunction with other promotion mix elements. It is playing an increasingly important role in marketing strategies. Personal selling is becoming more professional and sophisticated, with sales personnel acting more as consultants and advisers.

In this chapter, we focus on personal selling and sales promotion. We first consider the purposes of personal selling and then examine its basic steps. Next, we look at types of salespeople and how they are selected. We then discuss major sales force management decisions, including setting objectives for the sales force and determining its size; recruiting, selecting, training, compensating, and motivating salespeople; managing sales territories; and controlling and evaluating sales force performance. Then we examine several characteristics of sales promotion, reasons for using sales promotion, and sales promotion methods available for use in a promotion mix.

The Nature of Personal Selling

personal selling Paid personal communication that attempts to inform customers and persuade them to buy products in an exchange situation

Personal selling is paid personal communication that attempts to inform customers and persuade them to purchase products in an exchange situation. For example, a Hewlett-Packard (HP) salesperson describing the benefits of the company's servers, PCs, and printers to a small-business customer is engaging in personal selling. In fact, HP has a Small Business Initiative to reach more than 550,000 small businesses in the United States.[2] Personal selling gives marketers the greatest freedom to adjust a message to satisfy customers' information needs. Personal selling is the most precise of all promotion methods, enabling marketers to focus on the most promising sales prospects. Other promotion mix elements are aimed at groups of people, some of whom may not be prospective customers. However, personal selling is generally the most expensive element in the promotion mix. The average cost of a sales call is about $170.[3]

Millions of people, including increasing numbers of women, earn their living through personal selling. Sales careers can offer high income, a great deal of freedom, a high level of training, and a high degree of job satisfaction. Although personal selling is sometimes viewed negatively, major corporations, professional sales associations, and academic institutions are changing unfavorable stereotypes of salespeople.

Personal selling goals vary from one firm to another. However, they usually involve finding prospects, persuading prospects to buy, and keeping customers satisfied. Identifying potential buyers interested in the organization's products is critical. Because most potential buyers seek information before making purchases, salespeople can ascertain prospects' informational needs and then provide relevant information. To do so, sales personnel must be well trained regarding both their products and the selling process in general.

Salespeople must be aware of their competitors. They must monitor the development of new products and keep abreast of competitors' sales efforts in their sales territories, how often and when the competition calls on their accounts, and what the competition is saying about their product in relation to its own. For example, at PowerTV, a California firm that makes software and operating systems for digital cable television boxes, salespeople routinely collect information about competitors' activities and send it to the marketing department for posting on the firm's intranet. This steady flow allows all 240 employees to stay current on competitive developments so the company can respond quickly.[4] Salespeople must emphasize the benefits their products provide, especially when competitors' products do not offer those specific benefits.

Few businesses survive solely on profits from one-time customers. For long-run survival, most marketers depend on repeat sales and thus need to keep their customers satisfied. In addition, satisfied customers provide favorable word-of-mouth communications, thus attracting new customers. Although the whole organization is responsible for achieving customer satisfaction, much of the burden falls on salespeople, since they are almost always closer to customers than anyone else in the company and often provide buyers with information and service after the sale. Indeed, research shows that a firm's marketing orientation has a positive influence on salespeople's attitudes, commitment, and influence on customer purchasing intentions.[5] Such contact gives salespeople an opportunity to generate additional sales and offers them a good vantage point for evaluating the strengths and weaknesses of the company's products and other marketing mix components. Their observations help develop and maintain a marketing mix that better satisfies both the firm and its customers.

Elements of the Personal Selling Process

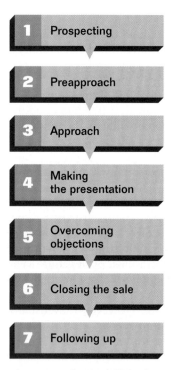

1. Prospecting
2. Preapproach
3. Approach
4. Making the presentation
5. Overcoming objections
6. Closing the sale
7. Following up

Figure 20.1 General Steps in the Personal Selling Process

prospecting Developing a list of potential customers

The specific activities involved in the selling process vary among salespeople and selling situations. No two salespeople use exactly the same selling methods. Nonetheless, many salespeople move through a general selling process as they sell products. This process consists of seven steps, outlined in Figure 20.1: prospecting, preapproach, approach, making the presentation, overcoming objections, closing the sale, and following up.

◆ Prospecting

Developing a list of potential customers is called **prospecting**. Salespeople seek names of prospects from company sales records, trade shows, commercial databases, newspaper announcements (of marriages, births, deaths, and so on), public records, telephone directories, trade association directories, and many other sources. Sales personnel also use responses to advertisements that encourage interested persons to send in information request forms. Seminars and meetings targeted at particular types of clients, such as attorneys or accountants, may also produce leads.

A number of salespeople prefer to use referrals—recommendations from current customers—to find prospects. Obtaining referrals requires that the salesperson have a good relationship with the current customer and therefore must have performed well before asking the customer for help. As might be expected, a customer's trust in and satisfaction with a salesperson influences his or her willingness to provide referrals.[6] Research shows that 1 referral is as valuable as 12 cold calls. Also, 80 percent of clients are willing to give referrals, but only 20 percent are ever asked. According to sales experts, the advantages of using referrals are that the resulting sales leads are highly qualified, sales rates are higher, initial transactions are larger, and the sales cycle is shorter.[7] Some companies even reward customers for referring their salespeople to new prospects by offering discounts off future purchases.[8]

Consistent activity is critical to successful prospecting. Salespeople must actively search the customer base for qualified prospects who fit the target market profile. After developing the prospect list, a salesperson evaluates whether each prospect is able, willing, and authorized to buy the product. Based on this evaluation, prospects are ranked according to desirability or potential.

◆ Preapproach

Before contacting acceptable prospects, a salesperson finds and analyzes information about each prospect's specific product needs, current use of brands, feelings about available brands, and personal characteristics. The most successful salespeople are thorough in their preapproach, which involves identifying key decision makers, reviewing account histories and problems, contacting other clients for information, assessing credit histories and problems, preparing sales presentations, identifying product needs, and obtaining relevant literature. Many companies employ information technology and customer relationship management (CRM) systems to scour their databases and thus identify the most profitable products and customers. These systems can also help sales departments manage leads, track customers, develop sales forecasts, and measure performance.[9] A salesperson with a lot of information about a prospect is better equipped to develop a presentation that precisely communicates with that prospect.

◆ Approach

approach The manner in which a salesperson contacts a potential customer

The **approach**, the manner in which a salesperson contacts a potential customer, is a critical step in the sales process. In more than 80 percent of initial sales calls, the purpose is to gather information about the buyer's needs and objectives. Creating a favorable impression and building rapport with prospective clients are important tasks in the approach because the prospect's first impressions of the salesperson are usually lasting ones. During the initial visit, the salesperson strives to develop a relationship rather than just push a product. Indeed, coming across as a "salesperson" may not be the best approach because some people are put off by strong selling tactics. Experts recommend using a neutral tone and normal conversational speech to improve the odds of making a sale.[10] The salesperson may have to call on a prospect several times before the product is considered. The approach must be designed to deliver value to targeted customers. If the sales approach is inappropriate, the salesperson's efforts are likely to have poor results.

One type of approach is based on referrals: the salesperson approaches the prospect and explains that an acquaintance, an associate, or a relative suggested the call. The salesperson who uses the "cold canvass" approach calls on potential customers without prior consent. Repeat contact is another common approach: when making the contact, the salesperson mentions a previous meeting. The exact type of approach depends on the salesperson's preferences, the product being sold, the firm's resources, and the prospect's characteristics. Ethics and Social Responsibility considers some ethical issues in personal selling.

ETHICS AND SOCIAL RESPONSIBILITY

Responsible Selling Improves Customer Relationships

Salespeople are trained about the products they sell so they can serve their customers and maximize sales revenues. Sometimes, however, it is not what a salesperson does but what he or she doesn't do that makes or breaks customer relationships. The six "deadly sins" for salespeople are (1) not being adequately prepared, (2) being overbearing or pushy, (3) going over a buyer's head to find a higher-ranking decision maker, (4) failing to follow up on a sale, (5) being rude, and (6) misleading customers about their products. Another increasingly frequent issue is offering extravagant gifts, bribes, and even kickbacks. During a slow economy, salespeople may resort to less than ethical tactics to close a deal, even back-stabbing their own colleagues. Such transgressions can result in inappropriate or unethical behavior, which can jeopardize relationships with customers.

For example, most customers prefer a salesperson who is confident but not pushy. Responsive salespeople can earn customers' trust, but pushy sales reps are often viewed as overly aggressive and even obnoxious. Salespeople also need to give a customer enough space so she or he doesn't feel pressured. Although giving a customer more time to make a decision may allow a competing salesperson time to make a presentation, it may help foster real customer loyalty. A salesperson should also focus on the individual who has the authority to make a purchase decision; if the salesperson chooses to go above that person to someone at a higher rank in the company, he or she risks insulting the decision maker and losing a sale. Another fine line sales reps must decide on is how much information to provide about their products. A customer who has been burned by a misleading or deceptive sales pitch most likely will refuse to do business with that salesperson or company again.

Research indicates that 60 percent of firms fail to follow up on prospective customers within 60 days, a trend attributed to increasing reliance on the Internet and other sales-related technologies instead of face-to-face contact between salespeople and customers. Salespeople who follow up on delivery, installation, warranty interpretation, product performance, and related customer service issues tend to have better performance. Word-of-mouth promotion is very important in sales, and a salesperson known for honesty and integrity will get many referrals.

Avoiding these "deadly sins" of personal selling can lead to a positive attitude toward sales presentations as well as long-term and lucrative customer relationships.

Enhancing Sales Presentations
Sales presentations are impacted by the quality of the technology used.

◆ Making the Presentation

During the sales presentation, the salesperson must attract and hold the prospect's attention, stimulate interest, and spark a desire for the product. The salesperson should have the prospect touch, hold, or use the product and, if possible, demonstrate the product or invite the prospect to use it. Automobile salespeople, for example, typically invite potential buyers to test drive the vehicle that interests them. Audiovisual equipment and software may also enhance the presentation.

During the presentation, the salesperson must not only talk but also listen. The sales presentation gives the salesperson the greatest opportunity to determine the prospect's specific needs by listening to questions and comments and observing responses. Even though the salesperson plans the presentation in advance, she or he must be able to adjust the message to meet the prospect's informational needs. Research demonstrates that adapting the message in response to the customer's needs generally enhances performance, particularly in new-task or modified-rebuy purchase situations.[11]

◆ Overcoming Objections

An effective salesperson usually seeks out a prospect's objections in order to address them. If they are not apparent, the salesperson cannot deal with them, and the prospect may not buy. One of the best ways to overcome objections is to anticipate and counter them before the prospect raises them. However, this approach can be risky because the salesperson may mention objections that the prospect would not have raised. If possible, the salesperson should handle objections as they arise. They can also be addressed at the end of the presentation.

◆ Closing the Sale

closing The stage in the personal selling process when the salesperson asks the prospect to buy the product

Closing is the stage in the personal selling process when the salesperson asks the prospect to buy the product. During the presentation, the salesperson may use a *trial close* by asking questions that assume the prospect will buy. The salesperson might ask the potential customer about financial terms, desired colors or sizes, or delivery arrangements. Reactions to such questions usually indicate how close the prospect is to buying. Properly asked questions may allow prospects to uncover their own problems and identify solutions themselves. One questioning approach uses broad questions (*what, how, why*) to probe or gather information and focused questions (*who, when, where*) to clarify and close the sale. A trial close allows prospects to indicate indirectly that they will buy the product without having to say those sometimes difficult words, "I'll take it."

Closing the Sale
WebEx online meeting and web conferencing services allow salespeople to make presentations and close sales.

A salesperson should try to close at several points during the presentation because the prospect may be ready to buy. An attempt to close the sale may result in objections. Thus, closing can uncover hidden objections, which the salesperson can then address. One closing strategy involves asking the potential customer to place a low-risk tryout order.

◆ Following Up

After a successful closing, the salesperson must follow up the sale. In the follow-up stage, the salesperson determines whether the order was delivered on time and installed properly, if installation was required. He or she should contact the customer to learn if any problems or questions regarding the product have arisen. The follow-up stage is also used to determine customers' future product needs.

Types of Salespeople

To develop a sales force, a marketing manager decides what kind of salesperson will sell the firm's products most effectively. Most business organizations use several different kinds of sales personnel. Based on the functions performed, salespeople can be classified into three groups: order getters, order takers, and support personnel. One salesperson can, and often does, perform all three functions.

◆ Order Getters

order getter A salesperson who sells to new customers and increases sales to current customers

To obtain orders, a salesperson informs prospects and persuades them to buy the product. The **order getter's** job is to increase sales by selling to new customers and increasing sales to present customers. This task is sometimes called *creative selling*. It requires that salespeople recognize potential buyers' needs and give them necessary information. Order getting is frequently divided into two categories: current-customer sales and new-business sales.

Current-Customer Sales. Sales personnel who concentrate on current customers call on people and organizations that have purchased products from the firm before. These salespeople seek more sales from existing customers by following up previous sales. Current customers can also be sources of leads for new prospects.

New-Business Sales. Business organizations depend to some degree on sales to new customers. New-business sales personnel locate prospects and convert them into buyers. In many organizations, salespeople help generate new business, but organizations that sell real estate, insurance, appliances, heavy industrial machinery, and automobiles depend in large part on new-customer sales.

◆ Order Takers

order taker A salesperson who primarily seeks repeat sales

Taking orders is a repetitive task salespeople perform to perpetuate long-lasting, satisfying customer relationships. **Order takers** primarily seek repeat sales. These salespeople generate the bulk of many firms' total sales. They are not passive functionaries who simply record orders in a machinelike manner. One major objective is to be certain customers have sufficient product quantities where and when needed. Most order takers handle orders for standardized products that are purchased routinely and do not require extensive sales efforts. The role of order takers is changing, however. In the future, they will probably serve more as identifiers and problem solvers to better meet the needs of their customers. There are two groups of order takers: inside order takers and field order takers.

Inside Order Takers. In many businesses, inside order takers, who work in sales offices, receive orders by mail, telephone, and the Internet. Certain producers, wholesalers, and retailers have sales personnel who sell from within the firm rather than in the field. This does not mean inside order takers never communicate with customers face to face. For example, retail salespeople are classified as inside order takers. As more orders are placed through the Internet, the role of the inside order taker will continue to change.

Field Order Takers. Salespeople who travel to customers are outside, or field, order takers. Often customers and field order takers develop interdependent relationships. The buyer relies on the salesperson to take orders periodically (and sometimes to deliver them), and the salesperson counts on the buyer to purchase a certain quantity of products periodically. Use of small computers has improved the field order taker's inventory and order-tracking capabilities.

Your customers need guidance. Your site needs LivePerson.
Offer real-time sales and customer service at critical moments.
www.liveperson.com/guidance 1.877.228.7984

Inside Order Takers
LivePerson provides real-time sales and customer service during Internet sales transactions.

◆ Support Personnel

support personnel Sales staff members who facilitate selling but usually are not involved solely with making sales

Support personnel facilitate selling but usually are not involved solely with making sales. They engage primarily in marketing industrial products, locating prospects, educating customers, building goodwill, and providing service after the sale. There are many kinds of sales support personnel; the three most common are missionary, trade, and technical salespeople.

missionary salesperson A support salesperson, usually employed by a manufacturer, who assists the producer's customers in selling to their own customers

Missionary Salespeople. **Missionary salespeople,** usually employed by manufacturers, assist the producer's customers in selling to their own customers. Missionary salespeople may call on retailers to inform and persuade them to buy the manufacturer's products. When they succeed, retailers purchase products from wholesalers, which are the producer's customers. Manufacturers of medical supplies and pharmaceuticals often use missionary salespeople, called *detail reps,* to promote their products to physicians, hospitals, and retail druggists.

trade salesperson A salesperson involved mainly in helping a producer's customers promote a product

Trade Salespeople. **Trade salespeople** are not strictly support personnel because they usually take orders as well. However, they direct much effort toward helping customers, especially retail stores, promote the product. They are likely to restock shelves, obtain more shelf space, set up displays, provide in-store demonstrations, and distribute samples to store customers. Food producers and processors commonly employ trade salespeople.

technical salesperson A support salesperson who gives technical assistance to a firm's current customers

Technical Salespeople. **Technical salespeople** give technical assistance to the organization's current customers, advising them on product characteristics and applications, system designs, and installation procedures. Because this job is often highly technical, the salesperson usually has formal training in one of the physical sciences or in engineering. Technical sales personnel often sell technical industrial products such as computers, heavy equipment, and steel.

When hiring sales personnel, marketers seldom restrict themselves to a single category because most firms require different types of salespeople. Several factors dictate how many of each type a particular company should have. Product use, characteristics, complexity, and price influence the kind of sales personnel used, as do the number and characteristics of customers. The types of marketing channels and the intensity and type of advertising also affect the composition of a sales force.

Managing the Sales Force

The sales force is directly responsible for generating one of an organization's primary inputs: sales revenue. Without adequate sales revenue, businesses cannot survive. In addition, a firm's reputation is often determined by the ethical conduct of its sales force. The morale and ultimately the success of a firm's sales force depend in large part on adequate compensation, room for advancement, sufficient training, and management support—all key areas of sales management. Salespeople who are not satisfied with these elements may leave. Evaluating the input of salespeople is an important part of sales force management because of its strong bearing on a firm's success.

We explore eight general areas of sales management: establishing sales force objectives, determining sales force size, recruiting and selecting salespeople, training sales personnel, compensating salespeople, motivating salespeople, managing sales territories, and controlling and evaluating sales force performance.

◆ Establishing Sales Force Objectives

To manage a sales force effectively, sales managers must develop sales objectives. Sales objectives tell salespeople what they are expected to accomplish during a specified time period. They give the sales force direction and purpose, and serve as standards for evaluating and controlling the performance of sales personnel. Sales objectives should be stated in precise, measurable terms and should specify the time period and geographic areas involved.

Sales objectives are usually developed for both the total sales force and individual salespeople. Objectives for the entire force are normally stated in terms of sales volume, market share, or profit. Volume objectives refer to dollar or unit sales. For example, the objective for an electric drill producer's sales force might be to sell $18 million worth of drills, or 600,000 drills annually. When sales goals are stated in terms of market share, they usually call for an increase in the proportion of the firm's sales relative to the total number of products sold by all businesses in that industry. When sales objectives are based on profit, they are generally stated in terms of dollar amounts or return on investment.

Sales objectives, or quotas, for individual salespeople are commonly stated in terms of dollar or unit sales volume. Other bases used for individual sales objectives include average order size, average number of calls per time period, and ratio of orders to calls.

NET SIGHTS

Sales & Marketing Management *magazine has a website* (**www.sales andmarketing.com**) *that focuses on weekly news and trends in the areas of personal selling and sales management. This site contains sales training tips, suggestions about what to read, and other content of interest to those in the field of sales management.*

◆ Determining Sales Force Size

Sales force size is important because it influences the company's ability to generate sales and profits. Moreover, size of the sales force affects the compensation methods used, salespeople's morale, and overall sales force management. Sales force size must be adjusted periodically because a firm's marketing plans change along with markets and forces in the marketing environment. One danger in cutting back the size of the sales force to increase profits is that the sales organization may lose strength and resiliency, preventing it from rebounding when growth occurs or better market conditions prevail.

Several analytical methods can help determine optimal sales force size. One method involves determining how many sales calls per year are necessary for the organization to serve customers effectively and then dividing this total by the average number of sales calls a salesperson makes annually. A second method is based on marginal analysis, in which additional salespeople are added to the sales force until the cost of an additional salesperson equals the additional sales generated by that person. Although marketing managers may use one or several analytical methods, they normally temper decisions with subjective judgments.

◆ Recruiting and Selecting Salespeople

To create and maintain an effective sales force, sales managers must recruit the right type of salespeople. In **recruiting**, the sales manager develops a list of qualified applicants for sales positions. Costs of hiring and training a salesperson are soaring, reaching more than $60,000 in some industries. Thus, recruiting errors are expensive.

To ensure the recruiting process results in a pool of qualified applicants, a sales manager establishes a set of qualifications before beginning to recruit. Although marketers have tried for years to identify a set of traits characterizing effective salespeople, no set of generally accepted characteristics yet exists. Experts agree that good salespeople exhibit optimism, flexibility, self-motivation, empathy, and the ability to network and maintain long customer relationships. One trait that may be useful in sensing customer reactions and generally being flexible is emotional intelligence: being in touch with one's own feelings and those of others.[12] Today companies are increasingly seeking applicants capable of employing relationship-building and consultative approaches.[13] Sales managers must determine what set of

recruiting Developing a list of qualified applicants for sales positions

Having a sales job.
Looking for one.
The only difference is what you're selling.

With thousands of available sales positions at CareerBuilder.com,™ you're sure to find
one that's perfect for you. And you always know your search is completely confidential.
To start your search, visit CareerBuilder.com today.

careerbuilder.com™
The smarter way to find a better job.

Recruiting and Selecting Salespeople
CareerBuilder.com assists companies
in recruiting and hiring salespeople.

traits best fits their companies' particular sales tasks. Two activities help establish this set of required attributes. First, the sales manager should prepare a job description listing specific tasks salespeople are to perform. Second, the manager should analyze characteristics of the firm's successful salespeople, as well as those of ineffective sales personnel. From the job description and analysis of traits, the sales manager should be able to develop a set of specific requirements and be aware of potential weaknesses that could lead to failure.

A sales manager generally recruits applicants from several sources: departments within the firm, other firms, employment agencies, educational institutions, respondents to advertisements, and individuals recommended by current employees. The specific sources depend on the type of salesperson required and the manager's experiences with particular sources.

The process of recruiting and selecting salespeople varies considerably from one company to another. Companies intent on reducing sales force turnover are likely to have strict recruiting and selection procedures. State Farm Life Insurance, for example, strives to retain customers by having low sales force turnover. Applicants for the job of State Farm Insurance agent must go through a year-long series of interviews, tests, and visits with agents before finding out if they have been hired. Approximately 80 percent of State Farm agents are still employed four years after being hired, compared with an industry average of only 30 percent.

Sales management should design a selection procedure that satisfies the company's specific needs. Some organizations use the specialized services of other companies to hire sales personnel. The process should include steps that yield the information required to make accurate selection decisions. However, because each step incurs a certain amount of expense, there should be no more steps than necessary. Stages of the selection process should be sequenced so that the more expensive steps, such as a physical examination, occur near the end. Fewer people will then move through higher-cost stages.

Recruitment should not be sporadic; it should be a continuous activity aimed at reaching the best applicants. The selection process should systematically and effectively match applicants' characteristics and needs with the requirements of specific selling tasks. Finally, the selection process should ensure that new sales personnel are available where and when needed.

◆ Training Sales Personnel

Many organizations have formal training programs; others depend on informal, on-the-job training. Some systematic training programs are quite extensive, whereas others are rather short and rudimentary. Whether the training program is complex or simple, developers must consider what to teach, whom to train, and how to train them. Building Customer Relationships examines an innovative sales training program.

A sales training program can concentrate on the company, its products, or selling methods. Training programs often cover all three. Such programs can be aimed at newly hired salespeople, experienced salespeople, or both. Training for experienced company salespeople usually emphasizes product information, although salespeople must also be informed about new selling techniques and changes in company plans, policies, and procedures. Ordinarily, new sales personnel require comprehensive training, whereas experienced personnel need both refresher courses on established products and training regarding new-product information.

Sales training may be done in the field, at educational institutions, in company facilities, and/or online using web-based technology. For many companies, online training saves time and money, and helps salespeople learn about new products quickly.[14] Some firms train new employees before assigning them to a specific sales position. Others put them into the field immediately, providing formal training only after they have gained some experience. Training programs for new personnel can be as short as several days or as long as three years; some are even longer. Sales training for experienced personnel is often scheduled when sales activities are not too demanding. Because experienced salespeople usually need periodic retraining, a firm's sales management must determine the frequency, sequencing, and duration of these efforts.

Sales managers, as well as other salespeople, often engage in sales training, whether daily on the job or periodically during sales meetings. Salespeople sometimes receive training from technical specialists within their own organizations. In addition, a number of outside companies specialize in providing sales training

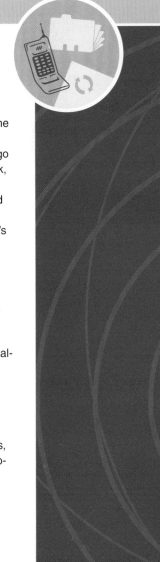

BUILDING CUSTOMER RELATIONSHIPS

Whirlpool Puts Salespeople in the "Real Whirled"

How can a multinational company train thousands of retail salespeople in the subtleties of selling 11 brands of household appliances to different customer segments in 170 countries? This was the challenge facing global appliance maker Whirlpool, the U.S. market leader and second in the world behind Electrolux of Sweden. The company manufactures appliances in 13 countries under such well-known brands as Kenmore, KitchenAid, SpeedQueen, and Whirlpool. Looking to build annual sales beyond the current $11 billion level, Whirlpool has created a unique training program for the trainers who work with store salespeople at Sears, The Home Depot, and other retailers.

The training program, called Real Whirled, puts a cadre of eight trainers together in a home equipped with Whirlpool appliances. The trainers live and work in the specially designed eight-bedroom home for eight weeks, doing daily chores such as laundry, cooking, cleaning, and baking with Whirlpool appliances. In between, they analyze product features and benefits, swap product use tips and frustrations, and critique one another's sales training talks. Whirlpool flies the trainers home twice during the two-month period so they don't lose touch with family and friends during the program.

Because the Real Whirled home is located close to Whirlpool's headquarters in Benton Harbor,

Michigan, the trainers sometimes have to show off their knowledge of company products by cooking impromptu dinners for senior managers who arrive without warning. Training directors are also apt to stop by to see how the trainers are progressing. After eight weeks of actually using the different appliances, the trainers sound more knowledgeable—and more credible—when they go on the road to train store salespeople. Brian Clark, a trainer who recently completed the program, found the experience intense but beneficial. "We'd spend a whole day learning about a dishwasher," he recalls, adding, "I have a confidence level that's making a difference in my client contacts."

The purpose of Real Whirled is to keep Whirlpool's trainers and their retail sales trainees focused squarely on how the appliances satisfy customer needs. "It seems like such a no-brainer, but we tend to get away from spending time with the consumer," comments Jackie Seib, the company's national training manager. "The biggest challenge in changing the retail culture is teaching salespeople what the consumer wants." Real Whirled gives the trainers firsthand experience in solving everyday problems using Whirlpool products. As a result, they have real anecdotes and solutions, not just product facts and specifications, to share with the salespeople they train. This innovative sales training program is moving the company closer to achieving its goal of "a Whirlpool product in every home, everywhere."

WE HAVE TO START MEETING LIKE THIS.

ANY HOTEL CAN GIVE YOU A PLACE TO MEET, BUT ONLY CAESARS CAN GIVE YOU AN ENTIRE EMPIRE. WITH 440 BEAUTIFUL ROOMS. 16,000 SQ. FT. OF FLEXIBLE MEETING SPACE. SUPERSTAR ENTERTAINMENT. A LUXURIOUS SPA. AWARD-WINNING RESTAURANTS. UNPARALLELED SERVICE. EXCITING RECREATION. AND A WORLD-CLASS CASINO. NO WONDER WE RECEIVED THE PARAGON AWARD FOR TWO CONSECUTIVE YEARS. ENJOY A FOUR STAR FOUR DIAMOND EXPERIENCE. SO IF YOU WANT TO START MEETING LIKE THIS, COME TO CAESARS MOUNTAIN EMPIRE ON THE BEAUTIFUL SOUTH SHORE OF LAKE TAHOE, NEVADA. THEN YOU'LL KNOW WHAT IT'S LIKE TO HAVE MET WITH SUCCESS. CALL CONVENTION SALES AT 1-800-367-4554.

CAESARS
TAHOE
caesars.com

Sales Training
Sales training can be conducted in formal environments in locations that bring the entire sales force together.

programs. Materials for sales training programs range from videos, texts, online materials, manuals, and cases to programmed learning devices and audio- and videocassettes. Lectures, demonstrations, simulation exercises, and on-the-job training can all be effective teaching methods. The choice of methods and materials for a particular sales training program depends on type and number of trainees, program content and complexity, length and location, size of the training budget, number of teachers, and teacher preferences.

◆ Compensating Salespeople

To develop and maintain a highly productive sales force, a business must formulate and administer a compensation plan that attracts, motivates, and retains the most effective individuals. The plan should give sales management the desired level of control and provide sales personnel with acceptable levels of income, freedom, and incentive. It should be flexible, equitable, easy to administer, and easy to understand. Good compensation programs facilitate and encourage proper treatment of customers. Obviously it is quite difficult to incorporate all of these requirements into a single program.

Developers of compensation programs must determine the general level of compensation required and the most desirable method of calculating it. In analyzing the required compensation level, sales management must ascertain a salesperson's value to the company on the basis of the tasks and responsibilities associated with the sales position. Sales managers may consider a number of factors, including salaries of other types of personnel in the firm, competitors' compensation plans, costs of sales force turnover, and nonsalary selling expenses. The average low-level salesperson earns about $56,000 annually (including commissions and bonuses), whereas a high-level, high-performing sales-

Table 20.1	Average Salaries for Sales Representatives and Executives		
	Base Salary	**Bonus + Commissions**	**Total Compensation**
Executives	$90,222	$46,181	$136,403
Top performers	$74,122	$65,704	$139,826
Mid-level reps	$49,542	$33,024	$82,566
Low-level reps	$36,740	$19,102	$55,842
Average	**$58,936**	**$38,161**	**$97,097**

Source: Christine Galea, "3rd Annual Compensation Survey," *Sales & Marketing Management,* May 2003, pp. 32–36. © 2003 VNU Business Media, Inc. Reprinted with permission from *Sales & Marketing Management.*

person can make as much as $140,000 a year.[15] Table 20.1 lists average salaries for sales personnel.

straight salary compensation plan Paying salespeople a specific amount per time period

Sales compensation programs usually reimburse salespeople for selling expenses, provide some fringe benefits, and deliver the required compensation level. To achieve this, a firm may use one or more of three basic compensation methods: straight salary, straight commission, or a combination of salary and commission. In a **straight salary compensation plan**, salespeople are paid a specified amount per time period. This sum remains the same until they receive a pay increase or decrease. In a **straight commission compensation plan**, salespeople's compensation is determined solely by sales for a given period. A commission may be based on a single percentage of sales or on a sliding scale involving several sales levels and percentage rates. In a **combination compensation plan**, salespeople receive a fixed salary plus a commission based on sales volume. Some combination programs require that a salesperson exceed a certain sales level before earning a commission; others offer commissions for any level of sales.

straight commission compensation plan Paying salespeople according to the amount of their sales in a given time period

combination compensation plan Paying salespeople a fixed salary plus a commission based on sales volume

Table 20.2 lists major characteristics of each sales force compensation method. Notice that the combination method is the most popular. When selecting a compensation method, sales management weighs the advantages and disadvantages listed in the table. Research suggests that sales managers may be moving away from individual performance-based commissions and toward salary- and team-based compensation methods.[16] For example, the Container Store, which markets do-it-yourself organizing and storage products, prefers to pay its sales staff salaries that are 50 to 100 percent higher than those offered by rivals instead of basing pay on commission plans.[17]

Table 20.2		**Characteristics of Sales Force Compensation Methods**		
Compensation Method	**Frequency of Use (%)***	**When Especially Useful**	**Advantages**	**Disadvantages**
Straight salary	17.5	Compensating new salespersons; firm moves into new sales territories that require developmental work; sales requiring lengthy presale and postsale services	Gives salesperson security; gives sales manager control over salespersons; easy to administer; yields more predictable selling expenses	Provides no incentive; necessitates closer supervision of salespersons; during sales declines, selling expenses remain constant
Straight commission	14.0	Highly aggressive selling is required; nonselling tasks are minimized; company uses contractors and part-timers	Provides maximum amount of incentive; by increasing commission rate, sales managers can encourage salespersons to sell certain items; selling expenses relate directly to sales resources	Salespersons have little financial security; sales manager has minimum control over sales force; may cause salespeople to give inadequate service to smaller accounts; selling costs less predictable
Combination	68.5	Sales territories have relatively similar sales potential; firm wishes to provide incentive but still control sales force activities	Provides certain level of financial security; provides some incentive; can move sales force efforts in profitable direction	Selling expenses less predictable; may be difficult to administer

*Figures computed from *Dartnell's 30th Sales Force Compensation Survey,* Dartnell Corporation, Chicago, 1999.

Source: Charles Futrell, *Sales Management* (Ft. Worth, TX: Dryden Press), 2001, pp. 307–316.

Increase Your Sales Force's Appetite

Is your team really hungry to meet, and even exceed their sales goals? An incentive like Omaha Steaks can really whet their appetite and make them hungry for more! Omaha Steaks offers quality products that will have real appeal and value. So give your sales force a reward worth sinking their teeth into and watch your profits grow.

PREMIUM HEARTLAND QUALITY
OMAHA STEAKS
SINCE 1917
OS SalesCo, Inc.

Call one of our Sales Incentive Experts today.
1-800-228-2480

Motivating Salespeople
Omaha Steaks provides sales incentives programs to companies to assist salespeople in achieving their goals.

◆ Motivating Salespeople

Although financial compensation is an important incentive, additional programs are necessary for motivating sales personnel. A sales manager should develop a systematic approach for motivating salespeople to be productive. Effective sales force motivation is achieved through an organized set of activities performed continuously by the company's sales management.

Sales personnel, like other people, join organizations to satisfy personal needs and achieve personal goals. Sales managers must identify those needs and goals and strive to create an organizational climate that allows each salesperson to fulfill them. Enjoyable working conditions, power and authority, job security, and opportunity to excel are effective motivators, as are company efforts to make sales jobs more productive and efficient. At the Container Store, for example, sales personnel receive hundreds of hours of training about the company's products every year so they can help customers solve organization and storage problems.[18] Sales contests and other incentive programs can also be effective motivators. Sales contests can motivate salespeople to increase sales or add new accounts, promote special items, achieve greater volume per sales call, and cover territories more thoroughly. Some companies find such contests powerful tools for motivating sales personnel to achieve company goals. In smaller firms lacking the resources for a formal incentive program, a simple but public "thank-you" from management at a sales meeting, along with a small-denomination gift card, can be rewarding.[19]

Properly designed incentive programs pay for themselves many times over, and sales managers are relying on incentives more than ever. Recognition programs that acknowledge outstanding performance with symbolic awards, such as plaques, can be very effective when carried out in a peer setting. Other common awards include travel, merchandise, gift cards, and cash. Travel reward programs can confer a high-profile honor, provide a unique experience that makes recipients feel special, and build camaraderie among award-winning salespeople. However, some recipients of travel awards may feel they already travel too much on the job. Cash rewards are easy to administer, are always appreciated by recipients, and appeal to all demographic groups. However, cash has no visible "trophy" value and provides few "bragging rights." The benefits of awarding merchandise are that the items have visible trophy value, recipients who are allowed to select the merchandise experience a sense of control, and merchandise awards can help build momentum for the sales force. The disadvantages of using merchandise include administrative complications and problems with perceived value on the part of recipients.[20] Some companies outsource their incentive programs to expert companies such as O. C. Tanner, which manufactures custom medals and jewelry for employee recognition programs and administers corporate recognition programs.[21]

◆ Managing Sales Territories

The effectiveness of a sales force that must travel to customers is somewhat influenced by management's decisions regarding sales territories. When deciding on territories, sales managers must consider size, shape, routing, and scheduling.

Creating Sales Territories. Several factors enter into the design of a sales territory's size and shape. First, sales managers must construct territories that allow sales potential to be measured. Sales territories often consist of several geographic units, such as census tracts, cities, counties, or states, for which market data are obtainable. Sales managers usually try to create territories with similar sales potential or requiring about the same amount of work. If territories have equal sales potential, they will almost always be unequal in geographic size. Salespeople with larger territories have to work longer and harder to generate a certain sales volume. Conversely, if sales territories requiring equal amounts of work are created, sales potential for those territories will often vary. If sales personnel are partially or fully compensated through commissions, they will have unequal income potential. Many sales managers try to balance territorial workloads and earning potential by using differential commission rates. At times sales managers use commercial programs to help them balance sales territories. Although a sales manager seeks equity when developing and maintaining sales territories, some inequities always prevail.

A territory's size and shape should also help the sales force provide the best possible customer coverage and should minimize selling costs. Customer density and distribution are important factors.

Routing and Scheduling Salespeople. The geographic size and shape of a sales territory are the most important factors affecting the routing and scheduling of sales calls. Next in importance are the number and distribution of customers within the territory, followed by sales call frequency and duration. Those in charge of routing and scheduling must consider the sequence in which customers are called on, specific roads or transportation schedules to be used, number of calls to be made in a given period, and time of day the calls will occur. In some firms, salespeople plan their own routes and schedules with little or no assistance from the sales manager; in others, the sales manager draws up the routes and schedules. No matter who plans the routing and scheduling, the major goals should be to minimize salespeople's nonselling time (time spent traveling and waiting) and maximize their selling time. Planners should try to achieve these goals so that a salesperson's travel and lodging costs are held to a minimum.

◈ Controlling and Evaluating Sales Force Performance

To control and evaluate sales force performance properly, sales management needs information. A sales manager cannot observe the field sales force daily and thus relies on salespeople's call reports, customer feedback, and invoices. Call reports identify the customers called on and present detailed information about interactions with those clients. Sales personnel often must file work schedules indicating where they plan to be during specific time periods. In addition, sales managers can keep abreast of a salesperson's activities through web-enabled mobile phones and personal digital assistants.[22] Data about a salesperson's interactions with customers and prospects can be included in the company's customer relationship management system. This information provides insights about the salesperson's performance.

Dimensions used to measure a salesperson's performance are determined largely by sales objectives, normally set by the sales manager. If an individual's sales objective is stated in terms of sales volume, that person should be evaluated on the basis of sales volume generated. Even if a salesperson is assigned a major objective, he or she is ordinarily expected to achieve several related objectives as well. Thus, salespeople are often judged along several dimensions. Sales managers evaluate many performance indicators, including average number of calls per day, average sales per customer, actual sales relative to sales potential, number of new-customer orders, average cost per call, and average gross profit per customer.

To evaluate a salesperson, a sales manager may compare one or more of these dimensions with predetermined performance standards. However, sales managers commonly compare a salesperson's performance with that of other employees operating under similar selling conditions or the salesperson's current performance with past performance. Sometimes management judges factors that have less direct bearing on sales performance, such as personal appearance, product knowledge, and ethical standards. One concern is the tendency to reprimand top sellers less severely than poor performers for engaging in unethical selling practices.[23]

After evaluating salespeople, sales managers take any needed corrective action to improve sales force performance. They may adjust performance standards, provide additional training, or try other motivational methods. Corrective action may demand comprehensive changes in the sales force.

The Nature of Sales Promotion

sales promotion An activity and/or material intended to induce resellers or salespeople to sell a product or consumers to buy it

Sales promotion is an activity or material, or both, that acts as a direct inducement, offering added value or incentive for the product, to resellers, salespeople, or consumers. It encompasses all promotional activities and materials other than personal selling, advertising, and public relations. In competitive markets, where products are very similar, sales promotion provides additional inducements that encourage product trial and purchase.

Marketers often use sales promotion to facilitate personal selling, advertising, or both. Companies also employ advertising and personal selling to support sales promotion activities. For example, marketers frequently use advertising to promote contests, free samples, and premiums. The most effective sales promotion efforts are highly interrelated with other promotional activities. Decisions regarding sales promotion often affect advertising and personal selling decisions, and vice versa.

Sales promotion can increase sales by providing extra purchasing incentives. Many opportunities exist to motivate consumers, resellers, and salespeople to take desired actions. Some kinds of sales promotion are designed specifically to stimulate resellers' demand and effectiveness, some are directed at increasing consumer demand, and some focus on both consumers and resellers. Regardless of the purpose, marketers must ensure that sales promotion objectives are consistent with the organization's overall objectives, as well as with its marketing and promotion objectives.

When deciding which sales promotion methods to use, marketers must consider several factors, particularly product characteristics (size, weight, costs, durability, uses, features, and hazards) and target market characteristics (age, gender, income, location, density, usage rate, and shopping patterns). How products are distributed and the number and types of resellers may determine the type of method used. The competitive and legal environment may also influence the choice.

The use of sales promotion has increased dramatically over the last 20 years, primarily at the expense of advertising. This shift in how promotional dollars are used has occurred for several reasons. Heightened concerns about value have made customers more responsive to promotional offers, especially price discounts and point-of-purchase displays. Thanks to their size and access to checkout scanner data, retailers have gained considerable power in the supply chain and are demanding greater promotional efforts from manufacturers to boost retail profits. Declines in brand loyalty have produced an environment in which sales promotions aimed at persuading customers to switch brands are more effective. Finally, the stronger emphasis placed on improving short-term performance results calls for greater use of sales promotion methods that yield quick (although perhaps short-lived) sales increases.[24]

In the remainder of this chapter, we examine several consumer and trade sales promotion methods, including what they entail and what goals they can help marketers achieve.

◆ Consumer Sales Promotion Methods

consumer sales promotion methods Sales promotion techniques that encourage consumers to patronize specific stores or try particular products

Consumer sales promotion methods encourage or stimulate consumers to patronize specific retail stores or try particular products. Consumer sales promotion methods initiated by retailers often aim to attract customers to specific locations, whereas those used by manufacturers generally introduce new products or promote established

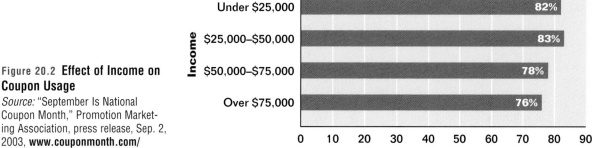

Figure 20.2 Effect of Income on Coupon Usage
Source: "September Is National Coupon Month," Promotion Marketing Association, press release, Sep. 2, 2003, **www.couponmonth.com/ pages/news.htm**.

brands. In this section we discuss coupons, cents-off offers, money refunds and rebates, frequent-user incentives, demonstrations, point-of-purchase displays, free samples, premiums, consumer contests and games, and consumer sweepstakes.

coupon A written price reduction used to encourage consumers to buy a specific product

Coupons and Cents-Off Offers. Coupons reduce a product's price and aim to prompt customers to try new or established products, increase sales volume quickly, attract repeat purchasers, or introduce new package sizes or features. Savings may be deducted from the purchase price or offered as cash. Coupons are the most widely used consumer sales promotion technique. In 2002, consumers redeemed 3.8 billion coupons, saving an estimated $3 billion. Nearly 80 percent of all consumers use coupons.[25] Figures 20.2 and 20.3 show that consumers' income and age have surprisingly little effect on coupon usage. Although some firms have tried to scale back their use of coupons and other sales promotion methods in favor of an everyday low price strategy, some groups of consumers have resisted these efforts, perhaps preferring the sense of achievement they experience from buying products on sale and/or with a coupon.[26]

For best results, the coupons should be easy to recognize and state the offer clearly. The nature of the product (seasonal demand for it, life cycle stage, frequency of purchase) is the prime consideration in setting up a coupon promotion. Paper coupons are distributed on and inside packages, through freestanding inserts (FSIs), in print advertising, and through direct mail. Electronic coupons are distributed online, via in-store kiosks, through shelf dispensers in stores, and at checkout counters.[27] When deciding on the distribution method for coupons, marketers should consider strategies and objectives, redemption rates, availability, circulation, and exclusivity. The coupon distribution and redemption arena has become very competitive. To draw customers to their stores, grocers double and sometimes even triple the value of customers' coupons.

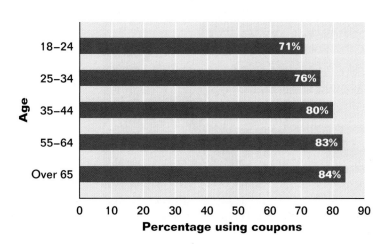

Figure 20.3 Effect of Age on Coupon Usage
Source: "September Is National Coupon Month," Promotion Marketing Association, press release, Sep. 2, 2003, **www. couponmonth.com/pages/news.htm**.

Not everything your child draws...

Before
After

...is a keeper!

Crayola Washable Markers truly wash off fabric and skin.
WASHABILITY YOU CAN TRUST!™

MANUFACTURER'S COUPON | EXPIRES 9/30/04
SAVE 75¢
off any 3 Crayola®
Washable products

VOID

Consumer Sales Promotion
Coupons should be easily recognized and should state the offer clearly.

cents-off offer A promotion that allows buyers to pay less than the regular price to encourage purchase

money refunds A sales promotion technique offering consumers a specified amount of money when they mail in a proof of purchase, usually for multiple product purchases

rebate A sales promotion technique in which a consumer receives a specified amount of money for making a single product purchase

Coupons offer several advantages. Print advertisements with coupons are often more effective at generating brand awareness than are print ads without coupons. Generally, the larger the coupon's cash offer, the better the recognition generated. Coupons reward present product users, win back former users, and encourage purchases in larger quantities. Because they are returned, coupons also let a manufacturer determine whether it reached the intended target market. The advantages of using electronic coupons over paper coupons include lower cost per redemption, greater targeting ability, improved data-gathering capabilities, and greater experimentation capabilities to determine optimal face values and expiration cycles.[28]

Drawbacks of coupon use include fraud and misredemption, which can be expensive for manufacturers. For example, counterfeit coupons circulated via the Internet are increasingly causing retailers that unwittingly accept them significant losses.[29] Another disadvantage, according to some experts, is that coupons are losing their value; because so many manufacturers offer them, consumers have learned not to buy without some incentive, whether a coupon, a rebate, or a refund. Furthermore, brand loyalty among heavy coupon users has diminished, and many consumers redeem coupons only for products they normally buy. It is believed that about three-fourths of coupons are redeemed by people already using the brand on the coupon. Thus, coupons have questionable success as an incentive for consumers to try a new brand or product. An additional problem with coupons is that stores often do not have enough of the coupon item in stock. This situation generates ill will toward both the store and the product.

With a **cents-off offer**, buyers pay a certain amount less than the regular price shown on the label or package. Similar to coupons, this method can be a strong incentive for trying products. It can stimulate product sales, yield short-lived sales increases, and promote products in off-seasons. It is an easy method to control and is often used for specific purposes. If used on an ongoing basis, however, cents-off offers reduce the price for customers who would buy at the regular price and may also cheapen a product's image. In addition, the method often requires special handling by retailers.

Copyright © Houghton Mifflin Company. All rights reserved.

Snapshot

What's in it for me?
Why consumers like rewards programs

Discounts — 60%
Cash back — 53%
Free merchandise — 42%
Special benefits or upgrades — 33%
Special members-only offers — 28%

Source: Data from Maritz Poll.

Refunds and Rebates. With **money refunds**, consumers submit proof of purchase and are mailed a specific amount of money. Usually manufacturers demand multiple product purchases before consumers qualify for refunds. With **rebates**, the consumer is sent a specified amount of money for making a single product purchase. Money refunds, used primarily to promote trial use of a product, are relatively low in cost, but because they sometimes generate a low response rate, they have limited impact on sales.

One problem with money refunds and rebates is that many people perceive the redemption process as too complicated. Only about half of individuals who purchase rebated products actually apply for the rebates.[30] Consumers may also have negative perceptions of manufacturers' reasons for offering rebates. They may believe the products are new, are untested, or have not sold well. If these perceptions are not changed, rebate offers may actually degrade the products' image and desirability. On the other hand,

Frequent User Incentives
Continental offers frequent fliers many incentives.

point-of-purchase (P-O-P) materials Signs, window displays, display racks, and similar devices used to attract customers

demonstration A sales promotion method a manufacturer uses temporarily to encourage trial use and purchase of a product or to show how a product works

free sample A sample of a product given out to encourage trial and purchase

rebates and low interest rates have been found to have a positive effect on car and truck sales.[31]

Frequent-User Incentives. Do you have a "Sub Club Card" from Subway? Many firms develop incentive programs to reward customers who engage in repeat (frequent) purchases. For example, most major airlines offer frequent flier programs that reward customers who have flown a specified number of miles with free tickets for additional travel. Frequent-user incentives foster customer loyalty to a specific company or group of cooperating companies. They are favored by service businesses such as airlines, auto rental agencies, hotels, and local coffee shops. Hilton Hotels, for example, uses its Hilton Honors program to reward travelers who stay at its hotels with points redeemable for stays at Hilton hotels and travel adventures such as African safaris. To encourage members to try its Hampton Inn chain, the company created a special program awarding 1 million Hilton Honors points to one Hampton Inn guest every month.[32]

Point-of-Purchase Materials and Demonstrations. **Point-of-purchase (P-O-P) materials** include outdoor signs, window displays, counter pieces, display racks, and self-service cartons. Innovations in P-O-P displays include sniff-teasers, which give off a product's aroma in the store as consumers walk within a radius of four feet, and computerized interactive displays. These items, often supplied by producers, attract attention, inform customers, and encourage retailers to carry particular products. A retailer is likely to use point-of-purchase materials if they are attractive, informative, well constructed, and in harmony with the store's image.

Demonstrations are excellent attention getters. Manufacturers offer them temporarily to encourage trial use and purchase of a product or to show how a product works. Because labor costs can be extremely high, demonstrations are not used widely. They can be highly effective for promoting certain types of products, such as appliances, cosmetics, and cleaning supplies. Even automobiles can be demonstrated, not only by a salesperson by also by the prospective buyer during a test drive. General Motors, for example, launched an advertising campaign to encourage more prospective buyers to test-drive new vehicles. The "Sleep on It" campaign resulted in more than 350,000 consumers taking GM vehicles home overnight and ultimately more than 100,000 sales.[33] Cosmetics marketers, such as Merle Norman and Clinique, sometimes offer potential customers "makeovers" to demonstrate product benefits and proper application.

Free Samples and Premiums. Marketers use **free samples** to stimulate trial of a product, increase sales volume in the early stages of a product's life cycle, and obtain desirable distribution. Sampling is the most expensive sales promotion method because production and distribution—at local events, by mail or door-to-door delivery, online, in stores, and on packages—entail high costs. Many consumers prefer to get their samples by mail. In designing a free sample, marketers should consider factors such as seasonal demand for the product, market characteristics, and prior advertising. Free samples usually are inappropriate for slow-turnover products. Despite high costs, use of sampling is increasing. PepsiCo, for example, used sampling to promote its Sierra Mist soft drink to reach more than 5 million potential consumers at well-traveled sites such as Times Square and Penn Station.[34] In a given year, almost three-fourths of consumer product companies may use sampling.

premium An item offered free or at a minimal cost as a bonus for purchasing a product

consumer contests and games Sales promotion methods in which individuals compete for prizes based on their analytical or creative skills

consumer sweepstakes A sales promotion in which entrants submit their names for inclusion in a drawing for prizes

Distribution of free samples through websites such as StartSampling.com and FreeSamples.com is growing. Consumers choose the free samples they would like to receive and request delivery. The online company manages the packaging and distribution of the samples. NSI, manufacturer of coffee flavorings called Flavour Creations, used a StartSampling.com online sample program to promote its products and expand their distribution. The owner of NSI was very impressed with consumer response to the StartSampling campaign. "We have never had a response like this," he said. "People liked our product and they called us and asked where they could buy it."[35]

Premiums are items offered free or at minimal cost as a bonus for purchasing a product. They are used to attract competitors' customers, introduce different sizes of established products, add variety to other promotional efforts, and stimulate consumer loyalty. Creativity is essential when using premiums; to stand out and achieve a significant number of redemptions, the premium must match both the target audience and the brand's image. To promote the independent British film *Bend It Like Beckham* in the United States, Fox Searchlight Pictures gave out 25,000 premium items, including soccer balls and stickers, in addition to holding 400 special screenings of the soccer-themed movie for soccer coaches and boys' and girls' organizations.[36] Premiums must also be easily recognizable and desirable. Premiums are placed on or inside packages and can also be distributed by retailers or through the mail. Examples include a service station giving a free carwash with a fill-up, a free toothbrush available with a tube of toothpaste, and a free plastic storage box given with the purchase of Kraft Cheese Singles.

Consumer Sweepstakes
Four Points Sheraton offers customers a chance to win bonus points in its sweepstakes.

trade sales promotion methods Methods intended to persuade wholesalers and retailers to carry a producer's products and market them aggressively

Consumer Games, Contests, and Sweepstakes. In **consumer contests and games**, individuals compete for prizes based on their analytical or creative skills. Entrants in a **consumer sweepstakes** submit their names for inclusion in a drawing for prizes. American Airlines, for example, held a regional sweepstakes in which the contest winner could invite 99 friends to fly from Chicago to Las Vegas, Miami, New York, or Los Angeles for a weekend.[37] Sweepstakes are employed more often than consumer contests and tend to attract a greater number of participants. However, contestants are usually more involved in consumer contests and games than in sweepstakes, even though total participation may be lower. Contests, games, and sweepstakes may be used in conjunction with other sales promotion methods, such as coupons.

◆ Trade Sales Promotion Methods

To encourage resellers, especially retailers, to carry their products and promote them effectively, producers use trade sales promotion methods. **Trade sales promotion methods** attempt to persuade wholesalers and retailers to carry a producer's products and market them more aggressively. These methods include buying allowances, buy-back allowances, scan-back allowances, merchandise allowances, cooperative advertising, dealer listings, free merchandise, premium or push money, dealer loaders, and sales contests.

buying allowance A temporary price reduction to resellers for purchasing specified quantities of a product

buy-back allowance A sum of money given to a reseller for each unit bought after an initial promotion deal is over

scan-back allowance A manufacturer's reward to retailers based on the number of pieces scanned

merchandise allowance A manufacturer's agreement to pay resellers certain amounts of money for providing special promotional efforts, such as setting up and maintaining a display

cooperative advertising An arrangement in which a manufacturer agrees to pay a certain amount of a retailer's media costs for advertising the manufacturer's products

dealer listing An advertisement that promotes a product and identifies the names of participating retailers that sell the product

free merchandise A manufacturer's reward given to resellers that purchase a stated quantity of products

dealer loader A gift, often part of a display, given to a retailer that purchases a specified quantity of merchandise

Trade Allowances. Many manufacturers offer trade allowances to encourage resellers to carry a product or stock more of it. One such trade allowance is a **buying allowance**, a temporary price reduction offered to resellers for purchasing specified quantities of a product. A soap producer, for example, might give retailers $1 for each case of soap purchased. Such offers provide an incentive for resellers to handle new products, achieve temporary price reductions, or stimulate purchase of items in larger-than-normal quantities. The buying allowance, which takes the form of money, yields profits to resellers and is simple and straightforward. There are no restrictions on how resellers use the money, which increases the method's effectiveness. One drawback of buying allowances is that customers may buy "forward," that is, buy large amounts that keep them supplied for many months. Another problem is that competitors may match (or beat) the reduced price, which can lower profits for all sellers.

A **buy-back allowance** is a sum of money that a producer gives to a reseller for each unit the reseller buys after an initial promotional deal is over. This method is a secondary incentive in which the total amount of money resellers receive is proportional to their purchases during an initial consumer promotion, such as a coupon offer. Buy-back allowances foster cooperation during an initial sales promotion effort and stimulate repurchase afterward. The main disadvantage of this method is expense.

A **scan-back allowance** is a manufacturer's reward to retailers based on the number of pieces moved through the retailers' scanners during a specific time period. To participate in scan-back programs, retailers are usually expected to pass along savings to consumers through special pricing. Scan-backs are becoming widely used by manufacturers because they link trade spending directly to product movement at the retail level.

A **merchandise allowance** is a manufacturer's agreement to pay resellers certain amounts of money for providing promotional efforts such as advertising or point-of-purchase displays. This method is best suited to high-volume, high-profit, easily handled products. A drawback is that some retailers perform activities at a minimally acceptable level simply to obtain allowances. Before paying retailers, manufacturers usually verify their performance. Manufacturers hope that retailers' additional promotional efforts will yield substantial sales increases.

Cooperative Advertising and Dealer Listings. **Cooperative advertising** is an arrangement in which a manufacturer agrees to pay a certain amount of a retailer's media costs for advertising the manufacturer's products. The amount allowed is usually based on the quantities purchased. As with merchandise allowances, a retailer must show proof that advertisements did appear before the manufacturer pays the agreed-on portion of the advertising costs. These payments give retailers additional funds for advertising. Some retailers exploit cooperative-advertising agreements by crowding too many products into one advertisement. Not all available cooperative-advertising dollars are used. Some retailers cannot afford to advertise, while others can afford it but do not want to advertise. A large proportion of all cooperative-advertising dollars is spent on newspaper advertisements.

Dealer listings are advertisements promoting a product and identifying participating retailers that sell the product. Dealer listings can influence retailers to carry the product, build traffic at the retail level, and encourage consumers to buy the product at participating dealers.

Free Merchandise and Gifts. Manufacturers sometimes offer **free merchandise** to resellers that purchase a stated quantity of products. Occasionally free merchandise is used as payment for allowances provided through other sales promotion methods. To avoid handling and bookkeeping problems, the "free" merchandise usually takes the form of a reduced invoice.

A **dealer loader** is a gift to a retailer that purchases a specified quantity of merchandise. Dealer loaders are often used to obtain special display efforts from retailers by offering essential display parts as premiums. For example, a manufacturer might design a display that includes a sterling silver tray as a major component and give the tray to the retailer. Marketers use dealer loaders to obtain new distributors and to push larger quantities of goods.

premium money Extra compensation to salespeople for pushing a line of goods

Premium (Push) Money. **Premium money** (or **push money**) is additional compensation to salespeople offered by the manufacturer as an incentive to push a line of goods. This method is appropriate when personal selling is an important part of the marketing effort; it is not effective for promoting products sold through self-service. Premium money often helps a manufacturer obtain a commitment from the sales force, but it can be very expensive.

sales contest A sales promotion method used to motivate distributors, retailers, and sales personnel through recognition of outstanding achievements

Sales Contests. A **sales contest** is designed to motivate distributors, retailers, and sales personnel by recognizing outstanding achievements. To be effective, this method must be equitable for all individuals involved. One advantage is that it can achieve participation at all distribution levels. Positive effects may be temporary, however, and prizes are usually expensive.

SUMMARY

Personal selling is the process of informing customers and persuading them to purchase products through paid personal communication in an exchange situation. The three general purposes of personal selling are finding prospects, persuading them to buy, and keeping customers satisfied.

Many salespeople, either consciously or unconsciously, move through a general selling process as they sell products. In prospecting, the salesperson develops a list of potential customers. Before contacting prospects, the salesperson conducts a preapproach that involves finding and analyzing information about prospects and their needs. The approach is the manner in which the salesperson contacts potential customers. During the sales presentation, the salesperson must attract and hold the prospect's attention to stimulate interest in and desire for the product. If possible, the salesperson should handle objections as they arise. During the closing, the salesperson asks the prospect to buy the product or products. After a successful closing, the salesperson must follow up the sale.

In developing a sales force, marketing managers consider which types of salespeople will sell the firm's products most effectively. The three classifications of salespeople are order getters, order takers, and support personnel. Order getters inform both current customers and new prospects and persuade them to buy. Order takers seek repeat sales and fall into two categories: inside order takers and field order takers. Sales support personnel facilitate selling, but their duties usually extend beyond making sales. The three types of support personnel are missionary, trade, and technical salespeople.

Sales force management is an important determinant of a firm's success because the sales force is directly responsible for generating the organization's sales revenue. Major decision areas and activities are establishing sales force objectives; determining sales force size; recruiting, selecting, training, compensating, and motivating salespeople; managing sales territories; and controlling and evaluating sales force performance.

Sales objectives should be stated in precise, measurable terms and specify the time period and geographic areas involved. The size of the sales force must be adjusted occasionally because a firm's marketing plans change along with markets and forces in the marketing environment.

Recruiting and selecting salespeople involves attracting and choosing the right type of salesperson to maintain an effective sales force. When developing a training program, managers must consider a variety of dimensions, such as who should be trained, what should be taught, and how training should occur. Compensation of salespeople involves formulating and administering a compensation plan that attracts, motivates, and retains the right types of salespeople. Motivated salespeople should translate into high productivity. Managing sales territories focuses on such factors as size, shape, routing, and scheduling. To control and evaluate sales force performance, sales managers use information obtained through salespeople's call reports, customer feedback, and invoices.

Sales promotion is an activity or a material (or both) that acts as a direct inducement, offering added value or incentive for the product to resellers, salespeople, or consumers. Marketers use sales promotion to identify and attract new customers, introduce new products, and increase reseller inventories. Sales promotion techniques fall into two general categories: consumer and trade. Consumer sales promotion methods encourage consumers to patronize specific stores or try a particular product. These sales promotion methods include coupons; cents-off offers; money refunds and rebates; frequent-user incentives; point-of-purchase displays; demonstrations; free samples and premiums; and consumer contests, games, and sweepstakes. Trade sales promotion techniques can motivate resellers to handle a manufacturer's products and market them aggressively.

These sales promotion techniques include buying allowances, buy-back allowances, scan-back allowances, merchandise allowances, cooperative advertising, dealer listings, free merchandise, dealer loaders, premium (or push) money, and sales contests.

Please visit the student website at **www.prideferrell.com** for ACE Self-Test questions that will help you prepare for exams.

IMPORTANT TERMS

Personal selling
Prospecting
Approach
Closing
Order getter
Order taker
Support personnel
Missionary salesperson
Trade salesperson
Technical salesperson
Recruiting
Straight salary
  compensation plan
Straight commission
  compensation plan
Combination
  compensation plan
Sales promotion
Consumer sales promotion
  methods
Coupon
Cents-off offer
Money refunds

Rebate
Point-of-purchase (P-O-P)
  materials
Demonstration
Free sample
Premium
Consumer contests and
  games
Consumer sweepstakes
Trade sales promotion
  methods
Buying allowance
Buy-back allowance
Scan-back allowance
Merchandise allowance
Cooperative advertising
Dealer listing
Free merchandise
Dealer loader
Premium money (or push
  money)
Sales contest

DISCUSSION & REVIEW QUESTIONS

1. What is personal selling? How does personal selling differ from other types of promotional activities?
2. What are the primary purposes of personal selling?
3. Identify the elements of the personal selling process. Must a salesperson include all these elements when selling a product to a customer? Why or why not?
4. How does a salesperson find and evaluate prospects? Do you consider any of these methods to be ethically questionable? Explain.
5. Are order getters more aggressive or creative than order takers? Why or why not?
6. Identify several characteristics of effective sales objectives.
7. How should a sales manager establish criteria for selecting sales personnel? What do you think are the general characteristics of a good salesperson?
8. What major issues or questions should management consider when developing a training program for the sales force?

9. Explain the major advantages and disadvantages of the three basic methods of compensating salespeople. In general, which method would you prefer? Why?
10. What major factors should be taken into account when designing the size and shape of a sales territory?
11. How does a sales manager, who cannot be with each salesperson in the field on a daily basis, control the performance of sales personnel?
12. What is sales promotion? Why is it used?
13. For each of the following, identify and describe three techniques and give several examples: (a) consumer sales promotion methods and (b) trade sales promotion methods.
14. What types of sales promotion methods have you observed recently? Comment on their effectiveness.

APPLICATION QUESTIONS

1. Briefly describe an experience you have had with a salesperson at a clothing store or an automobile dealership. Describe the steps the salesperson used. Did the salesperson skip any steps? What did the salesperson do well? Not so well? Would you describe the salesperson as an order getter, an order taker, or a support salesperson? Why? Did the salesperson perform more than one of these functions?
2. Leap Athletic Shoe, Inc., a newly formed company, is in the process of developing a sales strategy. Market research indicates sales management should segment the market into five regional territories. The sales potential for the North region is $1.2 million, for the West region $1 million, for the Central region $1.3 million, for the South Central region $1.1 million, and for the Southeast region $1 million. The firm wishes to maintain some control over the training and sales processes because of the unique features of its new product line, but Leap marketers realize the salespeople need to be fairly aggressive in their efforts to break into these markets. They would like to provide the incentive needed for the extra selling effort. What type of sales force compensation method would you recommend to Leap? Why?
3. Consumer sales promotions aim to increase sales of a particular retail store or product. Identify a familiar type of retail store or product. Recommend at least three sales promotion methods that could effectively promote the store or product. Explain why you would use these methods.

4. Producers use trade sales promotions to encourage resellers to promote their products more effectively. Identify which method or methods of sales promotion a producer might use in the following situations, and explain why the method would be appropriate.

a. A golf ball manufacturer wants to encourage retailers to add a new type of golf ball to current product offerings.

b. A life insurance company wants to increase sales of its universal life products, which have been lagging recently (the company has little control over sales activities).

c. A light bulb manufacturer with an overproduction of 100-watt bulbs wants to encourage its grocery store chain resellers to increase their bulb inventories.

Internet Exercise & Resources

Visit **www.prideferrell.com** for resources to help you master the material in this chapter, plus materials that will help you expand your marketing knowledge, including Internet exercise updates, ACE self-tests, hotlinks to companies featured in this chapter, and much more.

TerrAlign

TerrAlign offers consulting services and software products designed to help a firm maximize control and deployment of its field sales representatives. Review its website at **www.terralign.com**.

1. Identify three features of TerrAlign software that are likely to benefit salespeople.
2. Identify three features of TerrAlign software that are likely to benefit sales managers.
3. Why might field sales professionals object to the use of software from TerrAlign?

Video Case 20.1

Selling Bicycles and More at Wheelworks

From tricycles to tandems, Wheelworks sells just about every kind of bicycle. Founded in the 1970s, this three-store chain in suburban Boston has been named one of the top ten in the United States for more than a decade. The sales floor at each Wheelworks location boasts dozens of LeMond, Cannondale, Trek, and other brand name bicycles for mountain biking, triathlon, cyclocross, touring, fitness, and other cycling activities. The chain currently markets more than 10,000 bicycles and brings in $10.5 million in sales revenue every year, with a staff of 45 full-time employees plus 55 additional employees to handle seasonal sales spikes.

Wheelworks' salespeople are cycling enthusiasts who are extremely knowledgeable about the company's products and enjoy sharing what they know with customers. Some were recruited through referrals and personal contacts with store staff who participate in local cycling groups. Others were hired after replying to job openings posted on the Wheelworks website. New salespeople hired for the main store go through a formal training program. At the two branch stores, experienced salespeople act as mentors to new hires in an informal buddy system that supplements on-the-job training. All of the firm's salespeople have the opportunity to gain more product knowledge and ask questions when manufacturers' representatives visit. In addition, they can take classes to become certified in technical skills such as fitting bicycles.

Wheelworks doesn't believe in scripted sales pitches. Instead its salespeople focus on building relationships by asking questions, providing information, and making suggestions to match the right product to the right customer. Kurt Begemann, a competitive racer who sells at Wheelworks, says that "it's better to be seen as a teacher than to be seen as a salesperson." To keep their product knowledge updated, salespeople attend three to five in-store training clinics every month, each focusing on a particular product, product category, or manufacturer. From time to time, the sales manager appeals to his team's competitive spirit to spur higher closing rates as salespeople strive to match or exceed their colleagues' sales accomplishments.

Just as the salespeople work hard to match the right product to the right customer, Doug Shoemaker, the sales manager, works hard to match the right salesperson to the right customer. When a new Wheelworks customer begins browsing the sales floor, Shoemaker makes the initial approach, quickly sizes up the customer's needs and interests, and then brings in the salesperson he believes will work best with that customer. Even language poses no barrier, because staff members speak French, Italian, Spanish, and Chinese.

After a sale is closed, sales personnel add that customer's name and address to the firm's mailing list to receive announcements of upcoming special events and sales. The store also invites customers to bring their new bicycles back for a free tune-up after 30 days. This allows salespeople to follow up by checking on customer satisfaction and making any necessary adjustments.

Wheelworks sales personnel receive competitive retail wages and benefits such as health insurance coverage, vacation and

sick pay, profit sharing, and store discounts. They are also rewarded with seasonal bonuses tied to the company's sales achievements rather than to individual sales records. Sales manager Shoemaker stresses that this compensation method gives his salespeople the freedom to sell the right product for each customer's needs rather than trying to earn a special incentive by selling an item that's not right for the customer. The salespeople also prefer this compensation method. Salesperson Juliana Popper says Wheelworks customers "don't feel preyed upon" because they know the salespeople aren't trying to make more money by selling higher-priced bicycles.

Each salesperson sets goals for personal development as well as for store sales contributions. Store managers sit down to formally evaluate the performance of new salespeople six months after the salespeople are hired, and then on an annual basis. But sales personnel don't have to wait months to find out how they are doing. Because Wheelworks is not a huge organization, managers and peers constantly provide informal feedback and support. Salespeople who turn out to be stronger or more interested in nonsales activities can easily transfer, because at Wheelworks everybody, from the repair technicians to the graphic designer, has an important role to play in the personal selling process.[38]

QUESTIONS FOR DISCUSSION

1. Which of the three types of sales force compensation methods does Wheelworks use? Should Wheelworks change to another method? Explain.
2. How does Wheelworks motivate sales personnel?
3. What type of salesperson is Kurt Begemann? Evaluate his statement that "it's better to be seen as a teacher than to be seen as a salesperson."

Case 20.2

IBM Reorganizes to Improve Selling Solutions

International Business Machines (IBM), sometimes called "Big Blue," consistently maintained a position of leadership in the computer industry for most of the last three decades. For much of that time, the IBM name was nearly synonymous with the com-

puter industry as IBM's System/360 mainframe computer, the AS/400 minicomputer, and its line of personal computers set industry standards. For years, IBM's customer service was legendary. However, as the company fell on hard times in the early 1990s, customer confidence in Big Blue fell too. Despite the company's reputation for providing high-quality computers and strong customer service, intense competition and rapid changes in information technology challenged IBM's growth.

Today, with sales of more than $81 billion and 316,000 employees, IBM continues to strive to lead in the development, manufacture, and marketing of the most advanced information technologies, including computer systems, software, storage systems, and microelectronics. The company has reorganized to improve its decision-making time and responsiveness to changes in the marketing environment. IBM has also renewed its commitment to be *the* company for mainframe computers and to continue to provide solutions for its customers. With its increased emphasis on providing complete network management services to customers, organizing the company along industry lines, and restructuring its distribution system and sales organization to be more responsive to market needs, IBM appears poised to regain its sterling position in the computer industry.

For example, IBM's strategy for servers is to drive as many server shipments as possible through its business partners and derive maximum revenue from channel members marketing its products. With the exception of the largest accounts for IBM mainframe and mid-range servers and storage, the majority of IBM customer accounts are actually controlled by business partners rather than IBM itself. It is far less demanding to manage and predict the behavior of a few thousand key partners than that of 30,000 to 40,000 resellers. It's also more profitable to be a manufacturer that distributes through key business partners that train their own sales forces and sell further downstream to additional resellers, which in turn actually sell products to customers. This arrangement is similar to the kind of dealer network used by automakers, but with a few more layers. IBM gives up 20 to 40 percent of potential revenues on big-ticket items such as servers and storage—giving resellers some room to make money—in exchange for the resellers' commitment to achieve specific sales and customer contact targets. In effect, IBM has outsourced part of its sales organization in the belief that a diverse system of partners will more efficiently sell its products than a direct sales force.

New CEO Sam Palmisano, who rose to IBM's helm through sales, made wide changes to sales force strategies and the sales culture his first key initiative. He wanted to change everything from sales management, customer relationships, pricing authority, and even how much time people spend in sales meetings. He wanted salespeople interacting with customers, not talking to managers, staff members, or one another. His first move was to have IBM purchase PricewaterhouseCooper's consulting arm and Rational Software to offer staff and consulting expertise in addition to technology products. His goal was to have IBM's sales force sell both technology products and professional services.

Palmisano's next step was to restructure IBM's global sales organization from top to bottom. His only requirement was that members of the sales force have a single weekly sales meeting with their sales manager to get some coaching to help them sell. Indeed, individual and team coaching is a key part of IBM sales training. As with any sports team, coaching arms the sales force with the skills, tools, attitudes, and language they need to build trust and connect with customers effectively. Regular coaching develops the sales culture to be better prepared for sales performance.

These changes helped focus IBM salespeople on customers and their needs. They gave sales reps more time to become experts who can respond to customer needs without consulting other IBM staff or managers. Palmisano also created selling teams based on customer size, industry, and location. Because they work in teams, salespeople can offer a complete product portfolio without having to wade through a bureaucracy for help.

Finally, IBM's new organization helps the company focus on selling solutions rather than just products. This approach enables the salesperson or sales team to be proactive in going after business to solve a customer's problems. Working as a team begins with the customer and empowers salespeople to make decisions by giving them a voice. The sales staff adheres to a meeting schedule of only 30 minutes each week with their sales manager, which ensures a smooth flow of information, decisions, and training among the sales force, sales managers, and top executives.[39]

QUESTIONS FOR DISCUSSION

1. Why is it important for a company like IBM to focus on selling solutions rather than just products?
2. How have changes in the IBM sales force assisted in focusing on customers' needs?
3. Explain why you think that IBM's restructured sales force was only required to have a single weekly sales meeting to get some coaching help.

Strategic Case 7

Bass Pro Shops Reels Them in with Sales Promotion

John Morris's fishing tackle business has grown from an eight-foot-long display area in the back of one of his father's Brown Derby liquor stores in 1971 to one of the largest U.S. retailing chains of outdoor sporting goods, with 8,800 employees and estimated annual sales of $1.25 billion today. His privately owned company, Bass Pro Shops, is the corporate parent of Outdoor World, a chain of retail stores headquartered in Springfield, Missouri.

Outdoor World Stores   The company's flagship Springfield store, with $72 million in annual sales, is a 300,000-square-foot retail operation that in some ways resembles a mall because it includes a variety of entertainment and service offerings as well as sporting goods. The huge store, with 5 aquariums and a 4-story waterfall that thunders into a 64,000-gallon pool stocked with native Missouri fish, is the single greatest tourist attraction in Missouri. More than 4 million people visit Outdoor World in Springfield each year—more than the number who visit the famous Arch in St. Louis or the St. Louis Cardinals baseball team—and about half come from outside Missouri. Some people even plan their vacation schedules to permit a two- or three-day visit to the store. Eighty percent of visitors spend three and a half hours at the store; 10 percent spend all day.

The Springfield Outdoor World store is departmentalized, with a wide variety of merchandise and many choices within each line. For example, more than 7,000 fishing lures and about 200 bows and 100 handguns are available. Signs help customers find departments, merchandise lines, and clothing sizes, while promotional elements direct their attention to the merchandise. For example, ducks appear to descend over the Tracker Marine boat showroom, while a mounted bear and cub draw customers to the hunting department. Squirrels mounted as fencers decorate the workbench of a glass artist at the Wildlife Art Gallery entrance, while other mounted squirrels adorn the entrance counter to the store. Special in-store sales are announced with flyers; brochures provide maps to the departments and show the locations of various services.

Outdoor World offers useful product information brochures to help customers choose just the right items for their needs, ranging from baseball bats to sleeping bags, from camp foods to slalom water skies. Videotapes air near some products to demonstrate their use, while store displays show other products, such as camping equipment, set up as they should be used. Salespeople are trained not only to sell the products but to explain their proper use and maintenance to ensure that customers get the most from their purchases, even though Outdoor World backs everything with a 100 percent satisfaction guarantee.

Because Outdoor World customers often spend long hours in the store, a number of services are available. Hemingway's Blue Water Café, featuring a 29,000-gallon salt-water aquarium as well as mounted animal trophies and African ritual masks, provides an exotic family dining experience. Local businesspeople frequently dine there, and such notables as former president George Bush enjoy the café's biscuits and gravy. For those looking for simpler fare, a McDonald's is located across the top of the four-story waterfall from Hemingway's. Just past McDonald's is the Tall Tales Barbershop, which features real "fighting chairs" that fishers might use on a deep-sea fishing boat. The barbershop's location provides an excellent view of the many outdoor clothing choices below, and customers can have strands of their freshly cut hair made into a fishing lure. In addition, anglers can have a rod or reel repaired during their visit, and hunters can have their trophy animals mounted at the award-winning Wildlife Creations and Taxidermy shop. Guests can also have their favorite knife sharpened. With half its customers coming from outside Missouri, rifle, pistol, and archery ranges in the store enable customers to try out merchandise before taking it all the way back home. Golfers can test putters on an indoor putting green and test other clubs on an indoor driving range within the store.

Visitors can also watch SCUBA divers hand feed goldfish to large fresh-water game fish in one of the five in-store aquariums at Uncle Buck's 250-seat auditorium on the lower level of the store. They can visit a trout stream, see a 96-pound alligator snapping turtle (in the hunting department), and enjoy displays of antique fishing lures and mounted trophy fish and animals, including a lion that seems poised to leap with claws aimed at the visitor's chest. Many visitors can't resist posing by the cavernous jaws of a 3,247-pound great white shark and have a friend document their close encounter with a picture.

While the Springfield store is the operation's flagship, Bass Pro Shops began expanding in 1995, opening 12 stores under the Outdoor World banner, as well as 2 Sportsman's Warehouse stores and 2 World Wide Sportsman stores. The new Outdoor World stores are typically smaller than the Springfield store, ranging from about 100,000 to 200,000 square feet. They have similar merchandise, decorations, and entertainment qualities, giving them the look and feel of the flagship store, but with a regional flavor—for example, with displays featuring local native wildlife. However, some of the new stores' water features are smaller and less impressive than the Springfield store's, and their wildlife displays are less elaborate. At the Grapevine, Texas, store, for example, life-size mounted trophy animals are typically displayed in rows on ledges high above the merchandise racks. Bass Pro Shops also has additional stores in the planning stages.

Direct Marketing   Although Bass Pro Shops' retail store operation has taken on a life of its own, the company's telemarketing operation sells a high volume of merchandise from Outdoor World catalogs and thus indirectly encourages store visits. The direct marketing operation sends more than 34 million Bass Pro catalogs featuring some 30,000 items around the world every year, potentially attracting more customers to the store to try out a product before they buy it. Indeed, Outdoor World was originally intended to be a special store that would provide "red carpet" treatment for catalog customers who could see and buy products unavailable from other retailers. The 300-plus full-color pages of the 2004 Bass Pro Outdoor World Master Catalog lists more than 17,000 items, and the company also has specialty catalogs for sportsmen's clothing, hunting, fishing, and marine enthusiasts. About 34 percent of Bass Pro Shops' in-store and Internet sales have some connection to its catalog mailings. Since the typical Bass Pro customer is male and an avid outdoors enthusiast who dislikes shopping and crowds, this is a customer base ideally suited for catalog retailing.

The company employs about 500 operators who are busy every day around the clock, answering some 170 incoming WATS lines at the catalog operation. Thanks to a computerized distribution center, some 95 percent of orders are filled immediately and do not have to be back-ordered, a service record that has improved in the past several years. United Parcel Service (UPS) and the U.S. Postal Service handle 400,000 packages shipped to catalog customers monthly.

Special Events   Special events are an integral part of marketing at Outdoor World. The Spring Fishing Classic draws 50,000 people each of its four days to the Springfield store. Factory representatives from the nation's top fishing equipment manufacturers display and demonstrate the latest products, and renowned fishing pros present seminars on their techniques and strategies. Likewise, the Fall Hunting Classic draws a total of about 80,000 visitors to the Springfield store over its four-day run. In addition, the company sponsors a NASCAR race in Georgia.

Community Service   Bass Pro founder Johnny Morris tries to keep the Outdoor World name associated with community service and positive conservation efforts. He pledges large sums of money to support conservation in areas where Bass Pro conducts business, such as the $100,000 donated for habitat and conservation work to be done near the site of a new Outdoor World store in Texas. He has also donated $10 million to support a new wildlife museum and aquarium next door to the Springfield Outdoor World store.

The 400,000 packages mailed each month by the Bass Pro catalog division are shipped using environmentally friendly packing material. Coins tossed into Outdoor World fountains and aquariums in Springfield are donated to the Ronald McDonald House, which benefits critically ill children and their families.

Bass Pro Shops also offers safety education and hunter education classes through its Outdoor World stores, a service appreciated by parents of young hunters. It is also the sole corporate sponsor of Missouri's Operation Game Thief, intended to assist authorities in enforcing game laws and protecting game animal populations.

Bass Pro executives say their key operating philosophy has not been to add more and more to their organization. Rather, what they add is seen as important to outdoor enthusiasts in terms of providing them with a new experience or element of pleasure. The key idea for the executives seems to be the value-added notion of meeting the needs of the outdoor enthusiast right down to locational convenience, an idea at the very heart of the marketing concept.

QUESTIONS FOR DISCUSSION

1. What are some examples of the use of sales promotion tools at Bass Pro Shops?
2. How does the use of sales promotion tools at Bass Pro make shopping a better experience for customers?
3. What other elements of the promotion mix does Bass Pro use?

Part Eight

Pricing Decisions

To provide a satisfying marketing mix, an organization must set a price acceptable to target market members. Pricing decisions can have numerous effects on other parts of the marketing mix. For example, price can influence how customers perceive the product, what types of marketing institutions are used to distribute the product, and how the product is promoted. **Chapter 21** discusses the importance of price and looks at some characteristics of price and nonprice competition. It explores fundamental concepts such as demand, elasticity, marginal analysis, and break-even analysis. Then the chapter examines the major factors that affect marketers' pricing decisions. **Chapter 22** discusses six major stages in the process marketers use to establish prices.

21 Pricing Concepts

OBJECTIVES

1. To understand the nature and importance of price

2. To identify the characteristics of price and nonprice competition

3. To explore demand curves and price elasticity of demand

4. To examine the relationships among demand, costs, and profits

5. To describe key factors that may influence marketers' pricing decisions

6. To consider issues affecting the pricing of products for business markets

Universal Slashes CD Prices

n recent years, sales of music CDs have slumped in response to consumer perceptions of disproportionately high CD prices and increasing availability of music accessible from Internet file-sharing services. The decline in sales has started to slow, however, due in part to the success of breakthrough artists such as 50 Cent, whose CD *Get Rich or Die Tryin'* sold more than 6.5 million copies in one year. One factor contributing to the sales decline may be Warner Bros.' reduction in the prices of DVD movies several years ago to compete more effectively against rentals, broadening the price–value relationship between CDs and DVDs in consumers' minds. To deal with a maturing market, Universal Music Group—the largest music company, with a 30 percent market share in North America—slashed CD prices by as much as 32 percent. As a result, consumers can now find CDs by some best-selling artists for under $10.

Reducing prices is only part of Universal's broad strategy to breathe new life into music sales. To combat the illegal downloading of music and file swapping, the Vivendi Universal–owned company intends to take an aggressive legal stance against piracy. However, legal downloading is gaining in popularity through services such as Apple's iTunes, from which consumers downloaded 1 million songs in its first week of operation. Apple expects to sell 75 million songs a year at 99 cents per download. Dell, Hewlett-Packard, Wal-Mart, Amazon. com, Best Buy, and Microsoft have also launched competing online services.

In addition to reducing prices, Universal eliminated cooperative advertising with its retailers to support price margins. Cooperative advertising involves making direct payments to retailers to help offset some of the costs of local advertising. In many cases, the money was never used as designated and did not wind up funding CD advertisements for the retailer. Instead, Universal increased its own advertising budget to promote individual artists.

Universal used marketing research to determine the optimal price for CDs to restore consumer interest in buying music. After a year of testing various pricing strategies, Universal identified $12.98 as the best suggested retail price to trigger consumer buying while maintaining a reasonable profit margin for retailers. The new pricing strategy applies to all the company's releases except classical and Latin-music artists and boxed sets. Retailers are generally pleased with the new pricing strategy. Lloyd Greif, president of an investment banking firm handling the sale of Tower Records, explained, "Anything that brings customers through the door who wouldn't otherwise have come through the door is a positive development for a retailer like Tower." Grief also expects lower prices to spur impulse (unplanned) purchases. Other retailers have commented that Universal's new prices will help them compete more effectively against mass market retailers such as Best Buy and Wal-Mart.[1] ■

niversal Music Group uses pricing as a tool to compete against its major rivals and help boost sales industrywide. However, Universal's competitors may also employ pricing as a major competitive tool and match the firm's strategy. In other industries, however, many successful firms do not necessarily have the lowest prices; rather, they use various other pricing strategies.

In this chapter, we focus first on the nature of price and its importance to marketers. We then consider some characteristics of price and nonprice competition. Next, we discuss several pricing-related concepts such as demand, elasticity, and break-even analysis. Then we examine in some detail the numerous factors that can influence pricing decisions. Finally, we discuss selected issues related to pricing products for business markets.

The Nature of Price

price The value exchanged for products in a marketing transaction

The purpose of marketing is to facilitate satisfying exchange relationships between buyer and seller. **Price** is the value exchanged for products in a marketing exchange. Many factors may influence the assessment of value, including time constraints, price levels, perceived quality, and motivations to use available information about prices.[2] In most marketing situations, the price is apparent to both buyer and seller. However, price does not always take the form of money paid. In fact, trading of products, or **barter**, is the oldest form of exchange. Money may or may not be involved.

barter The trading of products

Buyers' interest in price stems from their expectations about the usefulness of a product or the satisfaction they may derive from it. Because buyers have limited resources, they must allocate those resources to obtain the products they most desire. Buyers must decide whether the utility gained in an exchange is worth the buying power sacrificed. Almost anything of value—ideas, services, rights, and goods—can be assessed by a price. In our society, financial price is the measurement of value commonly used in exchanges.

◆ Terms Used to Describe Price

Value can be expressed in different terms for different marketing situations. For instance, students pay *tuition* for a college education. Automobile insurance companies charge a *premium* for protection from the cost of injuries or repairs stemming from an automobile accident. An officer who stops you for speeding writes a ticket that requires you to pay a *fine*, while a lawyer you hire to defend you in traffic court charges a *fee*. A taxi driver charges a *fare*. A *toll* is charged for the use of bridges or toll roads. *Rent* is paid for the use of equipment or an apartment. A *commission* is remitted to a broker for the sale of real estate. *Dues* are paid for membership in a club or group. A *deposit* is made to hold or lay away merchandise. *Tips* help pay food servers for their services. *Interest* is charged for a loan, and *taxes* are paid for government services. Although price may be expressed in a variety of ways, its purpose is to quantify and express the value of the items in a marketing exchange.

◆ The Importance of Price to Marketers

As pointed out in Chapter 12, developing a product may be a lengthy process. It takes time to plan promotion and to communicate benefits. Distribution usually requires a long-term commitment to dealers

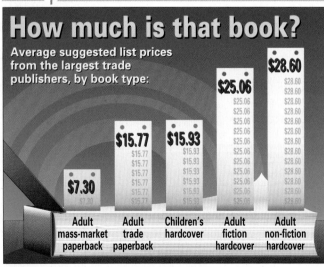

Snapshot

How much is that book?

Average suggested list prices from the largest trade publishers, by book type:

Adult mass-market paperback	Adult trade paperback	Children's hardcover	Adult fiction hardcover	Adult non-fiction hardcover
$7.30	$15.77	$15.93	$25.06	$28.60

Source: Data from Andrew Grabois, R. R. Bowker's *Books in Print.*

that will handle the product. Often price is the only thing a marketer can change quickly to respond to changes in demand or to actions of competitors. Under certain circumstances, however, the price variable may be relatively inflexible.

Price is a key element in the marketing mix because it relates directly to the generation of total revenue. The following equation is an important one for the entire organization:

$$\text{Profit} = \text{Total Revenue} - \text{Total Costs}$$
$$\text{or}$$
$$\text{Profits} = (\text{Price} \times \text{Quantity Sold}) - \text{Total Costs}$$

Prices affect an organization's profits in several ways because it is a key component of the profit equation and can be a major determinant of quantities sold. For example, price is a top priority for Hewlett-Packard in gaining market share and improving financial performance.[3] Furthermore, total costs are influenced by quantities sold.

Because price has a psychological impact on customers, marketers can use it symbolically. By pricing high, they can emphasize the quality of a product and try to increase the prestige associated with its ownership. By lowering a price, marketers can emphasize a bargain and attract customers who go out of their way to save a small amount of money. Thus, as this chapter details, price can have strong effects on a firm's sales and profitability.

Price and Nonprice Competition

Price and Nonprice Competition
Timepieces International uses price competition, whereas Rolex does not.

The competitive environment strongly influences the marketing mix decisions associated with a product. Pricing decisions are often made according to the price or nonprice competitive situation in a particular market. Price competition exists when consumers have difficulty distinguishing competitive offerings and marketers emphasize low prices. Nonprice competition involves a focus on marketing mix elements other than price.

◆ Price Competition

price competition Emphasizing price as an issue and matching or beating competitors' prices

When engaging in **price competition**, a marketer emphasizes price as an issue and matches or beats competitors' prices. To compete effectively on a price basis, a firm should be the low-cost seller of the product. If all firms producing the same product charge the same price for it, the firm with the lowest costs is the most profitable. Firms that stress low price as a key marketing mix element tend to market standardized products. A seller competing on price may change prices frequently, or at least must be willing and able to do so. For example, Best Buy, a retail consumer electronics leader, engages in price competition. To attain sales growth, Best Buy has had to reduce its prices.[4] Whenever competitors change their prices, the company usually responds quickly and aggressively. Building Customer Relationships looks at price competition in the personal computer industry.

Price competition gives marketers flexibility. They can alter prices to account for changes in their costs or respond to changes in demand for the product. If competitors try to gain market share by cutting prices, a company competing on a price

BUILDING CUSTOMER RELATIONSHIPS

Inside the PC Price War

Who is the world's leading personal computer manufacturer? IBM was the market leader during part of the 1980s and again in the early 1990s. Then Compaq took over the coveted rank of the world's number one PC maker, while up-and-coming rival Dell Computer used numerous effective marketing techniques to wrench away the top slot. After Compaq enjoyed seven years at the top, Dell pulled ahead to become the global market share leader in 2001, followed closely by Hewlett-Packard. But the rankings could change again at any time, thanks to an ongoing PC price war. In the high-stakes world of PC marketing, a market share increase of even a fraction of a percentage point translates into hundreds of thousands of units sold. For this reason, Dell, Compaq, Hewlett-Packard, and Gateway are jockeying for position, using price competition to score market share gains.

Because Dell deals directly with most customers and makes PCs to order, its costs are generally lower than those of Compaq and Gateway, which allows Dell to be very price competitive. In its bid for higher market share, Dell has been steadily cutting its prices and adding new low-price, entry-level models. The average price of a Dell PC system fell from $2,300 to $1,500, and it continues to drop. Dell maintains a separate sales force to call on business customers, who are a particular focus of Dell's reduced prices. Salespeople have fanned out across the country offering special pricing to companies that buy in volume. Some customers are switching to Dell, but others are using Dell's offers to negotiate lower pricing from competitors. Either way, customers are benefiting from the lower prices

as the intense price competition continues. "This strategy is working," says Dell's co-president. "We are not anticipating pulling back on our aggressive stance."

Compaq has been forced to respond with its own price cuts to defend its market share and remain competitive. In turn, these price cuts have lowered Compaq's sales revenues and profit margins, even as worldwide PC demand grows more slowly than in previous years. So Compaq is taking a longer-term approach by refocusing its efforts on larger computers and servers for corporate customers, a more profitable market. "There's a lot of chatter about PC price wars, but chasing prices is a very short-term strategy, and we're chasing profitable growth," explains Compaq's CEO.

Gateway, which recently lost market share as Dell strengthened its leadership position, is determined to use the PC price war to its advantage. One recent advertising campaign used the slogan "PC Price War? Cool." The campaign put the spotlight on Gateway's promise to beat the advertised price of any major competitor. But competitive pricing parity may not be enough to help Gateway catch Dell and Hewlett-Packard as the price war continues and customers become accustomed to paying ever-lower prices for ever-higher computing power.

basis can react quickly to such efforts. However, a major drawback of price competition is that competitors too have the flexibility to adjust prices. If they quickly match or beat a company's price cuts, a price war may ensue. For example, a price war has developed in the market for high-speed Internet access, with prices for cable-modem service dropping below $20 a month in some areas.[5] Telecommunications companies often compete mainly on the basis of price reductions, per-second call billing, and free calls.[6] Chronic price wars such as this one can substantially weaken organizations.

◆ Nonprice Competition

nonprice competition
Emphasizing factors other than price to distinguish a product from competing brands

Nonprice competition occurs when a seller decides not to focus on price and instead emphasizes distinctive product features, service, product quality, promotion, packaging, or other factors to distinguish its product from competing brands. Thus, nonprice competition allows a company to increase its brand's unit sales through means other than changing the brand's price. A major advantage of nonprice competition is that a firm can build customer loyalty toward its brand. If customers prefer a brand because of nonprice factors, they may not be easily lured away by competing firms and brands. In contrast, when price is the primary reason customers buy a particular brand, a competitor is often able to attract those customers through price cuts. However, some surveys show that the proportion of customers who base their purchase decisions solely on price is fairly small.[7]

Nonprice competition is effective only under certain conditions. A company must be able to distinguish its brand through unique product features, higher product quality, effective promotion, distinctive packaging, or excellent customer service. Buyers not only must be able to perceive these distinguishing characteristics but must also view them as important. The distinguishing features that set a particular brand apart from competitors should be difficult, if not impossible, for competitors to imitate. Finally, the firm must extensively promote the brand's distinguishing characteristics to establish its superiority and set it apart from competitors in the minds of buyers.

Even a marketer that is competing on a nonprice basis cannot ignore competitors' prices. It must be aware of them and sometimes be prepared to price its brand near or slightly above competing brands. Therefore, price remains a crucial marketing mix component even in environments that call for nonprice competition.

Analysis of Demand

Determining the demand for a product is the responsibility of marketing managers, who are aided in this task by marketing researchers and forecasters. Marketing research and forecasting techniques yield estimates of sales potential, or the quantity of a product that could be sold during a specific period. These estimates are helpful in establishing the relationship between a product's price and the quantity demanded.

◆ The Demand Curve

For most products, the quantity demanded goes up as the price goes down and the quantity demanded goes down as the price goes up. Intel, for example, knows that lowering prices boosts demand for its Pentium PC chips. By cutting the price of its sophisticated Pentium 4 chip from $795 to $519 in less than five months, Intel was able to keep sales growing even as the PC market suffered a slowdown.[8] Thus, an inverse relationship exists between price and quantity demanded. As long as the

$799 color laser

magicolor 2300 DL

The magicolor 2300 DL is a high-flying laser printer that's small in size and big in color. Included in its compact design is a combination of soaring speed, high-wire networking, and 2400 dpi quality—so even if you have to wing it, your prints will look brilliant! Powerful enough for workgroups, the magicolor 2300 DL is affordable enough for the home office user. Simply put...you can have it for a song—just $799. For more information call 800-523-2696.

■ 4 ppm color, 16 ppm b&w ■ 2400 dpi ■ 32 MB RAM
■ Ethernet 10/100BaseTX, USB and Parallel interfaces included
■ Windows XP/2000/NT 4/Me/98/95 compatible
■ Optional automatic duplexing ■ Up to legal size page support

OfficeMax COMPUSA Office DEPOT STAPLES

MINOLTA
QMS

The essentials of imaging

The Demand Curve
As the price of color laser printers drops, demand increases.

Space is no longer at a premium.

Introducing the Legacy
$1,368,750 (1/16th share)

Purchase now and fly at the pre-owned Hawker 800XP hourly rate ($1,990/hr)* during the first 24 months of ownership.

*Legacy Fuel Adjustment Factor and Federal Excise Tax (FET) apply.

The newest member of the Flight Options family is the 13-passenger Legacy. It offers the spaciousness of a large-cabin aircraft with the occupied hourly rate of a mid-size model. And you'll only find it here. To find out more about the terms and conditions of our purchase options, call us at 877.703.2348 or visit us at flightoptions.com.

FLIGHT OPTIONS

Fractional shares available on the following models: Legacy, Challenger 601, Citation X, Hawker 800XP, Citation 650, Citation V, Hawker 400XP, Beechjet 400A, CitationJet and King Air 8200. Flight Options, LLC is an affiliate of Raytheon Company.

Prestige Products
Private planes, such as the Legacy, are examples of luxury, or prestige products.

marketing environment and buyers' needs, ability (purchasing power), willingness, and authority to buy remain stable, this fundamental inverse relationship holds.

Figure 21.1 illustrates the effect of one variable, price, on the quantity demanded. The classic **demand curve** (D_1) is a graph of the quantity of products expected to be sold at various prices if other factors remain constant.[9] It illustrates that as price falls, quantity demanded usually rises. Demand depends on other factors in the marketing mix, including product quality, promotion, and distribution.

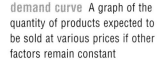 **demand curve** A graph of the quantity of products expected to be sold at various prices if other factors remain constant

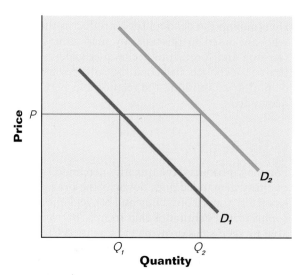

Figure 21.1 Demand Curve Illustrating the Price–Quantity Relationship and Increase in Demand

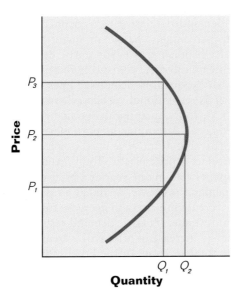

Figure 21.2 Demand Curve Illustrating the Relationship Between Price and Quantity for Prestige Products

An improvement in any of these factors may cause a shift to, say, demand curve D_2. In such a case, an increased quantity (Q_2) will be sold at the same price (P).

Many types of demand exist, and not all conform to the classic demand curve shown in Figure 21.1. Prestige products, such as selected perfumes and jewelry, tend to sell better at high prices than at low ones. These products are desirable partly because their expense makes buyers feel elite. If the price fell drastically and many people owned these products, they would lose some of their appeal.

The demand curve in Figure 21.2 shows the relationship between price and quantity demanded for prestige products. Quantity demanded is greater, not less, at higher prices. For a certain price range—from P_1 to P_2—the quantity demanded (Q_1) goes up to Q_2. After a certain point, however, raising the price backfires: if the price goes too high, the quantity demanded goes down. The figure shows that if price is raised from P_2 to P_3, quantity demanded goes back down from Q_2 to Q_1.

◆ Demand Fluctuations

Changes in buyers' needs, variations in the effectiveness of other marketing mix variables, the presence of substitutes, and dynamic environmental factors can influence demand. Restaurants and utility companies experience large fluctuations in demand daily. Toy manufacturers, fireworks suppliers, and air-conditioning and heating contractors also face demand fluctuations because of the seasonal nature of their products. The demand for online services, beef, and flat-screen TVs has changed over the last few years. Building Customer Relationships (on p. 566) examines changes in the demand and price of beef. In the case of flat-screen plasma or LCD TVs, demand accelerated as prices dropped by as much as 30 percent.[10] In some cases, demand fluctuations are predictable. It is no surprise to restaurants and utility company managers that demand fluctuates. However, changes in demand for other products may be less predictable, leading to problems for some companies. Other organizations anticipate demand fluctuations and develop new products and prices to meet consumers' changing needs.

◆ Assessing Price Elasticity of Demand

Up to this point, we have seen how marketers identify the target market's evaluation of price and its ability to purchase and how they examine demand to learn whether price is related inversely or directly to quantity. The next step is to assess price elasticity of demand. **Price elasticity of demand** provides a measure of the sensitivity of demand to changes in price. It is formally defined as the percentage change

price elasticity of demand
A measure of the sensitivity of demand to changes in price

in quantity demanded relative to a given percentage change in price (see Figure 21.3).[11] The percentage change in quantity demanded caused by a percentage change in price is much greater for elastic demand than for inelastic demand. For a product such as electricity, demand is relatively inelastic: when its price increases, say, from P_1 to P_2, quantity demanded goes down only a little, from Q_1 to Q_2. For products such as recreational vehicles, demand is relatively elastic: when price rises sharply, from P_1 to P_2, quantity demanded goes down a great deal, from Q_1 to Q_2.

If marketers can determine the price elasticity of demand, setting a price is much easier. By analyzing total revenues as prices change, marketers can determine whether a product is price elastic. Total revenue is price times quantity; thus, 10,000 rolls of wallpaper sold in one year at a price of $10 per roll equals $100,000 of total revenue. If demand is *elastic,* a change in price causes an opposite change in total revenue: an increase in price will decrease total revenue, and a decrease in price will increase total revenue. *Inelastic* demand results in a change in the same direction as total revenue: an increase in price will increase total revenue, and a decrease in price will decrease total revenue. In the hotel industry, for example, research has found that demand for hotel rooms is inelastic regardless of whether they are in budget motels or luxury hotels.[12] The following formula determines the price elasticity of demand:

BUILDING CUSTOMER RELATIONSHIPS

The Ups and Downs of Beef Prices

After the U.S. Senate issued dietary recommendations in 1977 telling Americans to eat more chicken and less red meat, per capita beef consumption in the United States began to decline. Over the next 20 years, annual demand for beef fell by as much as 31 percent, lowering the prices received by ranchers as well as at the grocery store.

However, in the late 1990s and early 2000s, the beef market changed dramatically. The price of live cattle increased to more than $1 per pound, whereas prices closer to 50 cents per pound used to be common. Market analysts credited the price increase to two factors: dietary trends and a decreased supply of cattle. The popularity of low-carb, high-protein diets such as the Atkins diet changed the way many Americans viewed beef. Once condemned as a source of fat and cholesterol, beef increasingly was seen as a healthy ingredient in a weight loss diet. Americans began demanding more beef, including more expensive cuts of beef. However, this rise in demand coincided with a decreased supply of beef resulting from a five-year drought in the American rangelands. The drought forced ranchers to reduce their herd size, and the population of cattle in the United States reached a seven-year low in 2003. This decrease in supply, coupled with the increase in demand, resulted in soaring beef prices.

U.S. beef prices fluctuated again after a cow in the state of Washington tested positive for bovine spongiform encephalopathy (BSE), or "mad cow disease," in December 2003. Although U.S. consumer demand for beef did not immediately decline, more than 50 nations fully or partially banned the import of U.S. beef. Since the export market previously accounted for approximately 10 percent of U.S. beef sales, the ban on exports resulted in a glut of beef in the domestic market. As a result, the prices ranchers received for live cattle dropped 20 percent in January 2004.

After publicity surrounding the mad cow case, grocers and restaurants began to demand more high-end, natural or organic beef, that is, from cattle raised without artificial growth hormones and locally fed with organic grain or allowed to graze on grassland. At a time when most beef prices were declining, natural beef ranchers reported an increase in demand, pushing organic beef prices up more than $1 per pound above the price of conventional cuts of beef. Natural or organic beef producers such as Coleman Natural Meats and Blue Ridge Premium Beef represent just 1 percent of overall beef production. Beef is an example of an agricultural commodity that experiences unpredictable fluctuations in demand and supply that determine market prices.

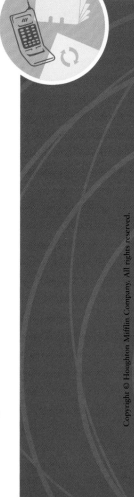

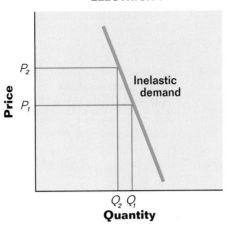

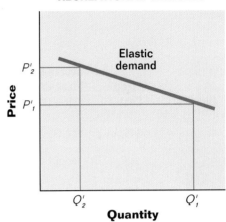

Figure 21.3 **Elasticity of Demand**

$$\text{Price Elasticity of Demand} = \frac{(\% \text{ Change in Quantity Demanded})}{(\% \text{ Change in Price})}$$

For example, if demand falls by 8 percent when a seller raises the price by 2 percent, the price elasticity of demand is −4 (the negative sign indicating the inverse relationship between price and demand). If demand falls by 2 percent when price is increased by 4 percent, elasticity is −1/2. The less elastic the demand, the more beneficial it is for the seller to raise the price. Products without readily available substitutes and for which consumers have strong needs (for example, electricity or appendectomies) usually have inelastic demand.

Marketers cannot base prices solely on elasticity considerations. They must also examine the costs associated with different sales volumes and evaluate what happens to profits.

Demand, Cost, and Profit Relationships

The analysis of demand, cost, and profit is important because customers are becoming less tolerant of price increases, forcing manufacturers to find new ways to control costs. In the past, many customers desired premium brands and were willing to pay extra for those products. Today customers pass up certain brand names if they can pay less without sacrificing quality. To stay in business, a company must set prices that not only cover its costs but also meet customers' expectations. In this section, we explore two approaches to understanding demand, cost, and profit relationships: marginal analysis and break-even analysis.

◆ Marginal Analysis

Marginal analysis examines what happens to a firm's costs and revenues when production (or sales volume) changes by one unit. Both production costs and revenues must be evaluated. To determine the costs of production, it is necessary to distinguish among several types of costs. **Fixed costs** do not vary with changes in the number of units produced or sold. For example, a wallpaper manufacturer's cost of renting a factory does not change because production increases from one to two shifts a day or because twice as much wallpaper is sold. Rent may go up, but not because the factory has doubled production or revenue. **Average fixed cost** is the fixed cost per unit produced and is calculated by dividing fixed costs by the number of units produced.

fixed costs Costs that do not vary with changes in the number of units produced or sold

average fixed cost The fixed cost per unit produced

Table 21.1   Costs and Their Relationships

1	2	3	4	5	6	
Quantity	Fixed Cost	Average Fixed Cost (2) ÷ (1)	Average Variable Cost	Average Total Cost (3) + (4)	Total Cost (5) × (1)	Marginal Cost
1	$40	$40.00	$20.00	$60.00	$ 60	
						$10
2	40	20.00	15.00	35.00	70	
						5
3	40	13.33	11.67	25.00	75	
						15
4	40	10.00	12.50	22.50	90	
						20
5	40	8.00	14.00	22.00	110	
						30
6	40	6.67	16.67	23.33	140	
						40
7	40	5.71	20.00	25.71	180	

variable costs Costs that vary directly with changes in the number of units produced or sold

average variable cost The variable cost per unit produced

total cost The sum of average fixed and average variable costs times the quantity produced

average total cost The sum of the average fixed cost and the average variable cost

marginal cost (MC) The extra cost incurred by producing one more unit of a product

Variable costs vary directly with changes in the number of units produced or sold. The wages for a second shift and the cost of twice as much wallpaper are extra costs incurred when production is doubled. Variable costs are usually constant per unit; that is, twice as many workers and twice as much material produce twice as many rolls of wallpaper. **Average variable cost**, the variable cost per unit produced, is calculated by dividing the variable costs by the number of units produced.

Total cost is the sum of average fixed costs and average variable costs times the quantity produced. The **average total cost** is the sum of the average fixed cost and the average variable cost. **Marginal cost (MC)** is the extra cost a firm incurs when it produces one more unit of a product.

Table 21.1 illustrates various costs and their relationships. Notice that average fixed cost declines as output increases. Average variable cost follows a U shape, as does average total cost. Because average total cost continues to fall after average variable cost begins to rise, its lowest point is at a higher level of output than that of average variable cost. Average total cost is lowest at 5 units at a cost of $22.00, whereas average variable cost is lowest at 3 units at a cost of $11.67. As Figure 21.4 shows, marginal cost equals average total cost at the latter's lowest level. In Table 21.1, this occurs between 5 and 6 units of production. Average total cost decreases as long as marginal cost is less than average total cost and increases when marginal cost rises above average total cost.

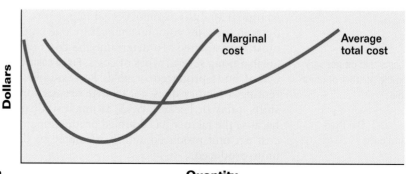

Figure 21.4 Typical Marginal Cost and Average Total Cost Relationship

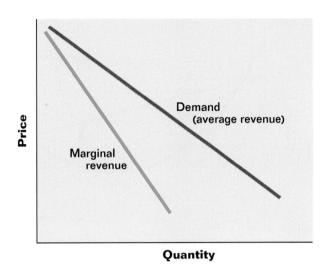

Figure 21.5 **Typical Marginal Revenue and Average Revenue Relationship**

marginal revenue (MR) The change in total revenue resulting from the sale of an additional unit of a product

Marginal revenue (MR) is the change in total revenue that occurs when a firm sells an additional unit of a product. Figure 21.5 depicts marginal revenue and a demand curve. Most firms in the United States face downward-sloping demand curves for their products; in other words, they must lower their prices to sell additional units. This situation means that each additional unit of product sold provides the firm with less revenue than the previous unit sold. MR then becomes less than average revenue, as Figure 21.5 shows. Eventually MR reaches zero, and the sale of additional units actually hurts the firm.

However, before the firm can determine whether a unit makes a profit, it must know its cost, as well as its revenue, because profit equals revenue minus cost. If MR is a unit's addition to revenue and MC is a unit's addition to cost, MR minus MC tells us whether or not the unit is profitable. Table 21.2 illustrates the relationships among price, quantity sold, total revenue, marginal revenue, marginal cost, and total cost. It indicates where maximum profits are possible at various combinations of price and cost.

Profit is maximized where MC = MR. In Table 21.2, MC = MR at 4 units. The best price is $33.75, and the profit is $45.00. Up to this point, the additional revenue generated from an extra unit sold exceeds the additional total cost. Beyond this point, the additional cost of another unit sold exceeds the additional revenue generated, and profits decrease. If the price were based on minimum average total cost—$22.00 (Table 21.1)—it would result in less profit: only $40.00 (Table 21.2) for 5 units at a price of $30.00 versus $45.00 for 4 units at a price of $33.75.

Table 21.2		Marginal Analysis: Method of Obtaining Maximum Profit-Producing Price					
1	2	3	4	5	6	7	
Price	Quantity Sold	Total Revenue (1) × (2)	Marginal Revenue	Marginal Cost	Total Cost	Profit (3) − (6)	
$57.00	1	$ 57	$57	$—	$ 60	−$ 3	
55.00	2	110	53	10	70	40	
39.00	3	117	7	5	75	42	
33.75*	**4**	**135**	**15**	**15**	**90**	**45**	
30.00	5	150	15	20	110	40	
27.00	6	162	12	30	140	22	
25.00	7	175	13	40	180	25	

*Boldface indicates the best price–profit combination.

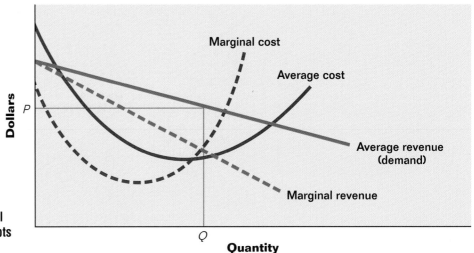

Figure 21.6 Combining the Marginal Cost and Marginal Revenue Concepts for Optimal Profit

Graphically combining Figures 21.4 and 21.5 into Figure 21.6 shows that any unit for which MR exceeds MC adds to a firm's profits, and any unit for which MC exceeds MR subtracts from profits. The firm should produce at the point where MR equals MC because this is the most profitable level of production.

This discussion of marginal analysis may give the false impression that pricing can be highly precise. If revenue (demand) and cost (supply) remained constant, prices could be set for maximum profits. In practice, however, cost and revenue change frequently. The competitive tactics of other firms or government action can quickly undermine a company's expectations of revenue. Thus, marginal analysis is only a model from which to work. It offers little help in pricing new products before costs and revenues are established. On the other hand, in setting prices of existing products, especially in competitive situations, most marketers can benefit by understanding the relationship between marginal cost and marginal revenue.

◆ Break-Even Analysis

break-even point The point at which the costs of producing a product equal the revenue made from selling the product

The point at which the costs of producing a product equal the revenue made from selling the product is the **break-even point**. If the wallpaper manufacturer has total annual costs of $100,000 and sells $100,000 worth of wallpaper in the same year, the company has broken even.

Figure 21.7 illustrates the relationships among costs, revenue, profits, and losses involved in determining the break-even point. Knowing the number of units necessary to break even is important in setting the price. If a product priced at $100 per unit has an average variable cost of $60 per unit, the contribution to fixed costs is $40. If total fixed costs are $120,000, the break-even point in units is determined as follows:

$$\text{Break-Even Point} = \frac{\text{Fixed Costs}}{\text{Per-Unit Contribution to Fixed Costs}}$$

$$= \frac{\text{Fixed Costs}}{\text{Price} - \text{Variable Costs}}$$

$$= \frac{\$120,000}{\$40}$$

$$= 3,000 \text{ Units}$$

To calculate the break-even point in terms of dollar sales volume, the seller multiplies the break-even point in units by the price per unit. In the preceding example, the break-even point in terms of dollar sales volume is 3,000 (units) times $100, or $300,000.

To use break-even analysis effectively, a marketer should determine the break-even point for each of several alternative prices. This determination allows the marketer to compare the effects on total revenue, total costs, and the break-even point

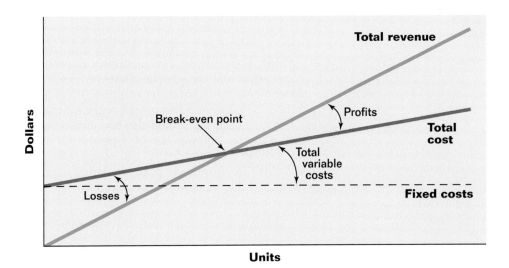

Figure 21.7 Determining the Break-Even Point

for each price under consideration. Although this comparative analysis may not tell the marketer exactly what price to charge, it will identify highly undesirable price alternatives that should definitely be avoided.

Break-even analysis is simple and straightforward. It does assume, however, that the quantity demanded is basically fixed (inelastic) and that the major task in setting prices is to recover costs. It focuses more on how to break even than on how to achieve a pricing objective, such as percentage of market share or return on investment. Nonetheless, marketing managers can use this concept to determine whether a product will achieve at least a break-even volume.

Factors Affecting Pricing Decisions

Pricing decisions can be complex because of the number of factors to consider. Frequently there is considerable uncertainty about the reactions to price among buyers, channel members, and competitors. Price is also an important consideration in marketing planning, market analysis, and sales forecasting. It is a major issue when assessing a brand's position relative to competing brands. Most factors that affect pricing decisions can be grouped into one of the eight categories shown in Figure 21.8. In this section, we explore how each of these groups of factors enters into price decision making.

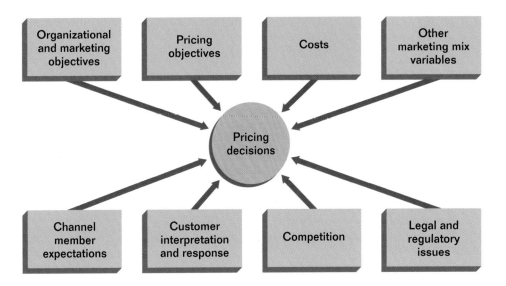

Figure 21.8 Factors That Affect Pricing Decisions

◆ Organizational and Marketing Objectives

Marketers should set prices that are consistent with the organization's goals and mission. For example, a retailer trying to position itself as value oriented may wish to set prices that are quite reasonable relative to product quality. In this case, a marketer would not want to set premium prices on products but would strive to price products in line with this overall organizational goal.

Pricing decisions should also be compatible with the firm's marketing objectives. For instance, suppose one of a producer's marketing objectives is a 12 percent increase in unit sales by the end of the following year. Assuming buyers are price sensitive, increasing the price or setting a price above the average market price would not be in line with this objective.

◆ Types of Pricing Objectives

The types of pricing objectives a marketer uses obviously have considerable bearing on the determination of prices. For example, an organization that uses pricing to increase its market share would likely set the brand's price below those of competing brands of similar quality to attract competitors' customers. A marketer sometimes uses temporary price reductions in the hope of gaining market share. If a business needs to raise cash quickly, it will likely use temporary price reductions such as sales, rebates, and special discounts. We examine pricing objectives in more detail in the next chapter.

Cost as a Pricing Consideration
Wausau discusses the cost of risk in pricing its insurance services.

◆ Costs

Clearly costs must be an issue when establishing price. A firm may temporarily sell products below cost to match competition, generate cash flow, or even increase market share, but in the long run it cannot survive by selling its products below cost. Even a firm that has a high-volume business cannot survive if each item is sold slightly below its cost. A marketer should be careful to analyze all costs so they can be included in the total cost associated with a product.

To maintain market share and revenue in an increasingly price-sensitive market, many marketers have concentrated on reducing costs. In the highly competitive computer industry, for example, IBM constantly looks for ways to lower the cost of developing, producing, and marketing computers and related products. As a cost-cutting move, the company recently relocated 4,750 managerial and engineering jobs to India, where labor costs are significantly lower.[13]

Labor-saving technologies, a focus on quality, and efficient manufacturing processes have brought productivity gains that translate into reduced costs and lower prices for customers. In an industry ravaged by labor concerns and monetary losses, Southwest Airlines has managed to stay one step ahead of its larger rivals. Southwest is the low-fare leader on more of the top 100 routes in the United States than the three largest airlines—American, Delta, and

United. One reason for the Texas-based airline's success is its ability to control costs. Southwest's per-seat mile costs are somewhat lower than those of its "big three" rivals.

Besides considering the costs associated with a particular product, marketers must take into account the costs the product shares with others in the product line. Products often share some costs, particularly the costs of research and development, production, and distribution. Most marketers view a product's cost as a minimum, or floor, below which the product cannot be priced.

◆ Other Marketing Mix Variables

All marketing mix variables are highly interrelated. Pricing decisions can influence evaluations and activities associated with product, distribution, and promotion variables. A product's price frequently affects the demand for that item. A high price, for instance, may result in low unit sales, which in turn may lead to higher production costs per unit. Conversely, lower per-unit production costs may result from a low price. For many products, buyers associate better product quality with a high price and poorer product quality with a low price. This perceived price–quality relationship influences customers' overall image of products or brands. Sony, for example, prices its television sets higher than average to help communicate that Sony televisions are high-quality electronic products. Consumers recognize the Sony brand name, its reputation for quality, and the prestige associated with buying Sony products. Individuals who associate quality with a high price are likely to purchase products with well-established and recognizable brand names.[14]

The price of a product is linked to several dimensions of its distribution. Premium-priced products are often marketed through selective or exclusive distribution; lower-priced products in the same product category may be sold through intensive distribution. For example, Cross pens are distributed through selective distribution and Bic pens through intensive distribution. Moreover, an increase in physical distribution costs, such as shipping, may have to be passed on to customers. Soaring ocean-shipping rates, for example, increased the price of imported commodities and goods in the United States when the supply of ships trailed the demand for ocean-shipping services.[15] When setting a price, the profit margins of marketing channel members, such as wholesalers and retailers, must also be considered. Channel members must be adequately compensated for the functions they perform.

Price may determine how a product is promoted. Bargain prices are often included in advertisements. Premium prices are less likely to be advertised, though they are sometimes included in advertisements for upscale items such as luxury cars or fine jewelry. Higher-priced products are more likely than lower-priced ones to require personal selling. Furthermore, the price structure can affect a salesperson's relationship with customers. A complex pricing structure takes longer to explain to customers, is more likely to confuse potential buyers, and may cause misunderstandings that result in long-term customer dissatisfaction. For example, the pricing structures of many airlines are complex and frequently confuse ticket sales agents and travelers alike.

◆ Channel Member Expectations

When making price decisions, a producer must consider what members of the distribution channel expect. A channel member certainly expects to receive a profit for the functions it performs. The amount of profit expected depends on what the intermediary could make if it were handling a competing product instead. Also, the amount of time and the resources required to carry the product influence intermediaries' expectations.

Channel members often expect producers to give discounts for large orders and prompt payment. At times, resellers expect producers to provide several support activities such as sales training, service training, repair advisory service, cooperative advertising, sales promotions, and perhaps a program for returning unsold merchandise to the producer. These support activities clearly have associated costs that a producer must consider when determining prices.

◆ Customers' Interpretation and Response

When making pricing decisions, marketers should address a vital question: How will our customers interpret our prices and respond to them? *Interpretation* in this context refers to what the price means or what it communicates to customers. Does the price mean "high quality" or "low quality," or "great deal," "fair price," or "rip-off"? Customer *response* refers to whether the price will move customers closer to purchase of the product and the degree to which the price enhances their satisfaction with the purchase experience and with the product after purchase.

Customers' interpretation of and response to a price are to some degree determined by their assessment of what they receive compared with what they give up to make the purchase. In evaluating what they receive, customers will consider product attributes, benefits, advantages, disadvantages, the probability of using the product, and possibly the status associated with the product. In assessing the cost of the product, customers likely will consider its price, the amount of time and effort required to obtain it, and perhaps the resources required to maintain it after purchase.

At times, customers interpret a higher price as higher product quality. They are especially likely to make this price–quality association when they cannot judge the quality of the product themselves. This is not always the case, however; whether price is equated with quality depends on the types of customers and products involved. Obviously marketers that rely on customers making a price–quality association and that provide moderate- or low-quality products at high prices will be unable to build long-term customer relationships.

internal reference price A price developed in the buyer's mind through experience with the product

external reference price A comparison price provided by others

When interpreting and responding to prices, how do customers determine if the price is too high, too low, or about right? In general, they compare prices with internal or external reference prices. An **internal reference price** is a price developed in the buyer's mind through experience with the product. It reflects a belief that a product should cost approximately a certain amount. As consumers, our experiences have given each of us internal reference prices for a number of products. For example, most of us have a reasonable idea of how much to pay for a six-pack of soft drinks, a loaf of bread, or a gallon of milk. For the product categories with which we have less experience, we rely more heavily on external reference prices. An **external reference price** is a comparison price provided by others, such as retailers or manufacturers. For example, a retailer in an advertisement might state, "While this product is sold for $100 elsewhere, our price is only $39.95." When attempting to establish a reference price in customers' minds by advertising a higher price against which to compare the company's real price, a marketer must make sure the higher price is realistic, because if it is not, customers will not use this price when establishing or altering their reference prices.[16] Customers' perceptions of prices are also influenced by their expectations about future price increases, by what they paid for the product recently, and by what they would like to pay for the product. Other factors affecting customers' perceptions of whether the price is right include time or financial constraints, the costs associated with searching for lower-priced products, and expectations that products will go on sale.

Value-Conscious Consumers
Allegheny Trail clothing appeals to consumers who are value conscious by offering quality at "rock bottom prices."

Buyers' perceptions of a product relative to competing products may allow the firm to set a price that differs significantly from rivals' prices. If the product is deemed superior to most of the competition, a premium price may be feasible. However, even products with superior quality can be overpriced. Strong brand loyalty sometimes provides the opportunity to charge a premium price. On the other hand, if buyers view a product less than favorably (though not extremely negatively), a lower price may generate sales.

In the context of price, buyers can be characterized according to their degree of value consciousness, price consciousness, and prestige sensitivity. Marketers that understand these characteristics are better able to set pricing objectives and policies. **Value-conscious** consumers are concerned about both price and quality of a product. **Price-conscious** individuals strive to pay low prices. **Prestige-sensitive** buyers focus on purchasing products that signify prominence and status.[17] For example, the Porsche Cayenne, one of the highest-priced sport-utility vehicles ever marketed, created record sales and profits for Porsche. Only 18 percent of Cayenne buyers had previously owned a Porsche; many of the rest were attracted to a vehicle with the prestige associated with the Porsche name.[18] On the other hand, some consumers vary in their degree of value, price, and prestige consciousness. In some segments, consumers are increasingly "trading up" to higher-status products in categories such as automobiles, home appliances, restaurants, and even pet food, yet remain price conscious regarding cleaning and grocery products. This trend has benefited marketers such as Starbucks, Sub-Zero, BMW, and Petco, which can charge premium prices for high-quality, prestige products, as well as Sam's Club and Costco, which offer basic household products at everyday low prices.[19]

value conscious Concerned about price and quality of a product

price conscious Striving to pay low prices

prestige sensitive Drawn to products that signify prominence and status

◆ Competition

A marketer needs to know competitors' prices so it can adjust its own prices accordingly. This does not mean a company will necessarily match competitors' prices; it may set its price above or below theirs. However, for some organizations (such as airlines), matching competitors' prices is an important strategy for survival.

When adjusting prices, a marketer must assess how competitors will respond. Will competitors change their prices and, if so, will they raise or lower them? In Chapter 3, we described several types of competitive market structures. The structure that characterizes the industry to which a firm belongs affects the flexibility of price setting. For example, because of reduced pricing regulation, firms in the telecommunications industry have moved from a monopolistic market structure to an oligopolistic one, which has resulted in significant price competition.

When an organization operates as a monopoly and is unregulated, it can set whatever prices the market will bear. However, the company may not price the product at the highest possible level to avoid government regulation or to penetrate a market by using a lower price. If the monopoly is regulated, it normally has less pricing flexibility; the regulatory body lets it set prices that generate a reasonable but not excessive return. A government-owned monopoly may price products below cost to make them accessible to people who otherwise could not afford them. Transit systems, for example, sometimes operate this way. However, government-owned monopolies sometimes charge higher prices to control demand. In some states with state-owned liquor stores, the price of liquor is higher than in states where liquor stores are not owned by a government body.

The automotive and aircraft industries exemplify oligopolies, in which only a few sellers operate and barriers to competitive entry are high. Companies in such industries can raise their prices, in the hope competitors will do the same. When an organization cuts its price to gain a competitive edge, other companies are likely to follow suit. Thus, very little advantage is gained through price cuts in an oligopolistic market structure.

A market structure characterized by monopolistic competition has numerous sellers with product offerings that are differentiated by physical characteristics, features, quality, and brand images. The distinguishing characteristics of its product may allow a company to set a different price than its competitors. However, firms in a monopolistic competitive market structure are likely to practice nonprice competition, discussed earlier in this chapter.

Under conditions of perfect competition, many sellers exist. Buyers view all sellers' products as the same. All firms sell their products at the going market price, and buyers will not pay more than that. This type of market structure, then, gives a marketer no flexibility in setting prices. Farming, as an industry, has some characteristics of perfect competition. Farmers sell their products at the going market price. At times, for example, corn, soybean, and wheat growers have had bumper crops and been forced to sell them at depressed market prices.

◆ Legal and Regulatory Issues

As discussed in Chapter 3, legal and regulatory issues influence pricing decisions. To curb inflation, the federal government can invoke price controls, freeze prices at certain levels, or determine the rates at which firms may increase prices. In some states and many other countries, regulatory agencies set prices on such products as insurance, dairy products, and liquor.

Many regulations and laws affect pricing decisions and activities in the United States. The Sherman Antitrust Act prohibits conspiracies to control prices, and in interpreting the act, courts have ruled that price fixing among firms in an industry is illegal. Marketers must refrain from fixing prices by developing independent pricing policies and setting prices in ways that do not even hint at collusion. Both the Federal Trade Commission Act and the Wheeler-Lea Act prohibit deceptive pricing. In establishing prices, marketers must guard against deceiving customers.

price discrimination Employing price differentials that injure competition by giving one or more buyers a competitive advantage

The Robinson-Patman Act has had a strong impact on pricing decisions. For various reasons, marketers may wish to sell the same type of product at different prices. Provisions in the Robinson-Patman Act, as well as those in the Clayton Act, limit the use of such price differentials. **Price discrimination**, the practice of employing price differentials that tend to injure competition by giving one or more buyers a competitive advantage over other buyers, is prohibited by law. However, not all price differentials are discriminatory. A marketer can use price differentials if they do not hinder competition, if they result from differences in the costs of selling or transportation to various customers, or if they arise because the firm has had to cut its price to a particular buyer to meet competitors' prices.

Pricing for Business Markets

Business markets consist of individuals and organizations that purchase products for resale, for use in their own operations, or for producing other products. Establishing prices for this category of buyers sometimes differs from setting prices for consumers. Differences in the size of purchases, geographic factors, and transportation considerations require sellers to adjust prices. In this section, we discuss several issues unique to the pricing of business products, including discounts, geographic pricing, and transfer pricing.

◆ Price Discounting

Producers commonly provide intermediaries with discounts, or reductions, from list prices. Although many types of discounts exist, they usually fall into one of five categories: trade, quantity, cash, seasonal, and allowance. Table 21.3 summarizes some reasons to use each type of discount and provides examples.

Table 21.3	Discounts Used for Business Markets	
Type	**Reasons for Use**	**Examples**
Trade (functional)	To attract and keep effective resellers by compensating them for performing certain functions, such as transportation, warehousing, selling, and providing credit	A college bookstore pays about one-third less for a new textbook than the retail price a student pays
Quantity	To encourage customers to buy large quantities when making purchases and, in the case of cumulative discounts, to encourage customer loyalty	Large department store chains purchase some women's apparel at lower prices than do individually owned specialty stores
Cash	To reduce expenses associated with accounts receivable and collection by encouraging prompt payment of accounts	Numerous companies serving business markets allow a 2% discount if an account is paid within 10 days
Seasonal	To allow a marketer to use resources more efficiently by stimulating sales during off-peak periods	Florida hotels provide companies holding national and regional sales meetings with deeply discounted accommodations during the summer months
Allowance	In the case of a trade-in allowance, to assist the buyer in making the purchase and potentially earn a profit on the resale of used equipment; in the case of a promotional allowance, to ensure that dealers participate in advertising and sales support programs	A farm equipment dealer takes a farmer's used tractor as a trade-in on a new one Nabisco pays a promotional allowance to a supermarket for setting up and maintaining a large, end-of-aisle display for a two-week period

trade (functional) discount
A reduction off the list price a producer gives to an intermediary for performing certain functions

quantity discount A deduction from list price for purchasing in large quantities

cumulative discount A quantity discount aggregated over a stated period

noncumulative discount
A one-time price reduction based on the number of units purchased, the size of the order, or the product combination purchased

Trade Discounts. A reduction off the list price given by a producer to an intermediary for performing certain functions is called a **trade**, or **functional, discount**. A trade discount is usually stated in terms of a percentage or series of percentages off the list price. Intermediaries are given trade discounts as compensation for performing various functions, such as selling, transporting, storing, final processing, and perhaps providing credit services. Although certain trade discounts are often a standard practice within an industry, discounts vary considerably among industries. It is important that a manufacturer provide a trade discount large enough to offset the intermediary's costs, plus a reasonable profit, to entice the reseller to carry the product.

Quantity Discounts. Deductions from list price that reflect the economies of purchasing in large quantities are called **quantity discounts**. Quantity discounts are used to pass on to the buyer cost savings gained through economies of scale.

Quantity discounts can be either cumulative or noncumulative. **Cumulative discounts** are quantity discounts aggregated over a stated time period. Purchases totaling $10,000 in a three-month period, for example, might entitle the buyer to a 5 percent, or $500, rebate. Such discounts are intended to reflect economies in selling and to encourage the buyer to purchase from one seller. **Noncumulative discounts** are one-time reductions in prices based on the number of units purchased, the dollar value of the order, or the product mix purchased. Like cumulative discounts, these discounts should reflect some economies in selling or trade functions.

NET SIGHTS

About.com, Inc., maintains websites about a wide variety of subjects, created by experts in their fields. **http://government.about.com/cs/ costandpricing/** *provides a huge array of information for individuals who want to learn about U.S. government accounting, costs, and pricing. Topics include cost and price forecasting, cost and price analysis, and payment methods.*

Cash Discounts. A **cash discount**, or price reduction, is given to a buyer for prompt payment or cash payment. Accounts receivable are an expense and a collection problem for many organizations. A policy to encourage prompt payment is a popular practice and sometimes a major concern in setting prices.

Discounts are based on cash payments or cash paid within a stated time. For example, "2/10 net 30" means that a 2 percent discount will be allowed if the account is paid within 10 days. If the buyer does not make payment within the 10-day period, the entire balance is due within 30 days without a discount. If the account is not paid within 30 days, interest may be charged.

cash discount A price reduction given to buyers for prompt payment or cash payment

Seasonal Discounts. A price reduction to buyers that purchase goods or services out of season is a **seasonal discount**. These discounts let the seller maintain steadier production during the year. For example, automobile rental agencies offer seasonal discounts in winter and early spring to encourage firms to use automobiles during the slow months of the automobile rental business.

seasonal discount A price reduction given to buyers for purchasing goods or services out of season

Allowances. Another type of reduction from the list price is an **allowance**, a concession in price to achieve a desired goal. Trade-in allowances, for example, are price reductions granted for turning in a used item when purchasing a new one. Allowances help make the buyer better able to make the new purchase. This type of discount is popular in the aircraft industry. Another example is a promotional allowance, a price reduction granted to dealers for participating in advertising and sales support programs intended to increase sales of a particular item.

allowance A concession in price to achieve a desired goal

◆ Geographic Pricing

geographic pricing Reductions for transportation and other costs related to the physical distance between buyer and seller

Geographic pricing involves reductions for transportation costs or other costs associated with the physical distance between buyer and seller. Prices may be quoted as F.O.B. (free-on-board) factory or destination. An **F.O.B. factory** price indicates the price of the merchandise at the factory, before it is loaded onto the carrier, and thus excludes transportation costs. The buyer must pay for shipping. An **F.O.B. destination** price means the producer absorbs the costs of shipping the merchandise to the customer. This policy may be used to attract distant customers. Although F.O.B. pricing is an easy way to price products, it is sometimes difficult to administer, especially when a firm has a wide product mix or when customers are widely dispersed. Because customers will want to know about the most economical method of shipping, the seller must be informed about shipping rates.

F.O.B. factory The price of merchandise at the factory, before shipment

F.O.B. destination A price indicating the producer is absorbing shipping costs

To avoid the problems involved in charging different prices to each customer, **uniform geographic pricing**, sometimes called *postage-stamp pricing*, may be used. The same price is charged to all customers regardless of geographic location, and the price is based on average shipping costs for all customers. Gasoline, paper products, and office equipment are often priced on a uniform basis.

uniform geographic pricing Charging all customers the same price, regardless of geographic location

Zone pricing sets uniform prices for each of several major geographic zones; as the transportation costs across zones increase, so do the prices. For example, a Florida manufacturer's prices may be higher for buyers on the Pacific Coast and in Canada than for buyers in Georgia.

zone pricing Pricing based on transportation costs within major geographic zones

base-point pricing Geographic pricing that combines factory price and freight charges from the base point nearest the buyer

freight absorption pricing Absorption of all or part of actual freight costs by the seller

Base-point pricing is a geographic pricing policy that includes the price at the factory, plus freight charges from the base point nearest the buyer. This approach to pricing has virtually been abandoned because of its questionable legal status. The policy resulted in all buyers paying freight charges from one location, such as Detroit or Pittsburgh, regardless of where the product was manufactured.

When the seller absorbs all or part of the actual freight costs, **freight absorption pricing** is being used. The seller might choose this method because it wishes to do business with a particular customer or to get more business; more business will cause the average cost to fall and counterbalance the extra freight cost. This strategy is used to improve market penetration and to retain a hold in an increasingly competitive market.

◆ Transfer Pricing

transfer pricing Prices charged in sales between an organization's units

Transfer pricing occurs when one unit in an organization sells a product to another unit. The price is determined by one of the following methods:

- *Actual full cost:* calculated by dividing all fixed and variable expenses for a period into the number of units produced

- *Standard full cost:* calculated based on what it would cost to produce the goods at full plant capacity

- *Cost plus investment:* calculated as full cost plus the cost of a portion of the selling unit's assets used for internal needs

- *Market-based cost:* calculated at the market price less a small discount to reflect the lack of sales effort and other expenses

The choice of transfer pricing method depends on the company's management strategy and the nature of the units' interaction. An organization must also ensure that transfer pricing is fair to all units involved in the transactions.

SUMMARY

Price is the value exchanged for products in marketing transactions. Price is not always money paid; barter, the trading of products, is the oldest form of exchange. Price is a key element in the marketing mix because it relates directly to generation of total revenue. The profit factor can be determined mathematically by multiplying price by quantity sold to get total revenue and then subtracting total costs. Price is the only variable in the marketing mix that can be adjusted quickly and easily to respond to changes in the external environment.

A product offering can compete on either a price or a nonprice basis. Price competition emphasizes price as the product differential. Prices fluctuate frequently, and price competition among sellers is aggressive. Nonprice competition emphasizes product differentiation through distinctive features, service, product quality, or other factors. Establishing brand loyalty by using nonprice competition works best when the product can be physically differentiated and the customer can recognize these differences.

An organization must determine the demand for its product. The classic demand curve is a graph of the quantity of products expected to be sold at various prices if other factors hold constant. It illustrates that as price falls, the quantity demanded usually increases. However, for prestige products, there is a direct positive relationship between price and quantity demanded: demand increases as price increases. Next, price elasticity of demand, the percentage change in quantity demanded relative to a given percentage change in price, must be determined. If demand is elastic, a change in price causes an opposite change in total revenue. Inelastic demand results in a parallel change in total revenue when a product's price is changed.

Analysis of demand, cost, and profit relationships can be accomplished through marginal analysis or break-even analysis. Marginal analysis examines what happens to a firm's costs and revenues when production (or sales volume) is changed by one unit. Marginal analysis combines the demand curve with the firm's costs to develop a price that yields maximum profit. Fixed costs do not vary with changes in the number of units produced or sold; average fixed cost is the fixed cost per unit produced. Variable costs vary directly with changes in the number of units produced or sold. Average variable cost is the variable cost per unit produced. Total cost is the sum of average fixed cost and average variable cost times the quantity produced. The optimal price is the point at which marginal cost (the cost associated with producing one more unit of the product) equals marginal revenue (the change in total revenue that occurs when one additional unit of the product is sold). Marginal analysis is only a model; it offers little help in pricing new products before costs and revenues are established.

Break-even analysis, determining the number of units that must be sold to break even, is important in setting price. The point at which the costs of production equal the revenue from selling the product is the break-even point. To use break-even analysis effectively, a marketer should determine the break-even point for each of several alternative prices. This makes it possible to compare the effects on total revenue, total costs, and the break-even point for each price under consideration. However, this approach assumes the quantity demanded is basically fixed and the major task is to set prices to recover costs.

Eight factors enter into price decision making: organizational and marketing objectives, pricing objectives, costs, other marketing mix variables, channel member expectations, customer interpretation and response, competition, and legal and regulatory issues. When setting prices, marketers should make decisions consistent with the organization's goals and mission. Pricing objectives heavily influence price-setting decisions. Most marketers view a product's cost as the floor below which a product cannot be priced. Because of the interrelationship among the marketing mix variables, price can affect product, promotion, and distribution decisions. The revenue channel members expect for their functions must also be considered when making price decisions.

Buyers' perceptions of price vary. Some consumer segments are sensitive to price, but others may not be. Thus, before determining price, a marketer needs to be aware of its importance to the target market. Knowledge of the prices charged for competing brands is essential to allow the firm to adjust its prices relative to competitors'. Government regulations and legislation also influence pricing decisions. Several laws aim to enhance competition in the marketplace by outlawing price fixing and deceptive pricing. Legislation also restricts price differentials that can injure competition. Moreover, the government can invoke price controls to curb inflation.

Unlike consumers, business buyers purchase products for resale, for use in their own operations, or for producing other products. When adjusting prices, business sellers consider the size of the purchase, geographic factors, and transportation requirements. Producers commonly provide discounts off list prices to intermediaries. The categories of discounts include trade, quantity, cash, seasonal, and allowance. A trade discount is a price reduction for performing such functions as storing, transporting, final processing, or providing credit services. If an intermediary purchases in large enough quantities, the producer gives a quantity discount, which can be either cumulative or noncumulative. A cash discount is a price reduction for prompt payment or payment in cash. Buyers who purchase goods or services out of season may be granted a seasonal discount. An allowance, such as a trade-in allowance, is a concession in price to achieve a desired goal.

Geographic pricing involves reductions for transportation costs or other costs associated with the physical distance between buyer and seller. With an F.O.B. factory price, the buyer pays for shipping from the factory. An F.O.B. destination price means the producer pays for shipping; this is the easiest way to price products, but it is difficult to administer. When the seller charges a fixed average cost for transportation, it is using uniform geographic pricing. Zone prices are uniform within major geographic zones; they increase by zone as transportation costs increase. With base-point pricing, prices are adjusted for shipping expenses incurred by the seller from the base point nearest the buyer. Freight absorption pricing occurs when a seller absorbs all or part of the freight costs.

 Please visit the student website at **www.prideferrell.com** for ACE Self-Test questions that will help you prepare for exams.

IMPORTANT TERMS

Price	Average variable cost	Price conscious	Allowance
Barter	Total cost	Prestige sensitive	Geographic pricing
Price competition	Average total cost	Price discrimination	F.O.B. factory
Nonprice competition	Marginal cost (MC)	Trade (functional) discount	F.O.B. destination
Demand curve	Marginal revenue (MR)	Quantity discount	Uniform geographic pricing
Price elasticity of demand	Break-even point	Cumulative discount	Zone pricing
Fixed costs	Internal reference price	Noncumulative discount	Base-point pricing
Average fixed cost	External reference price	Cash discount	Freight absorption pricing
Variable costs	Value conscious	Seasonal discount	Transfer pricing

DISCUSSION & REVIEW QUESTIONS

1. Why are pricing decisions important to an organization?
2. Compare and contrast price and nonprice competition. Describe the conditions under which each form works best.
3. Why do most demand curves demonstrate an inverse relationship between price and quantity?
4. List the characteristics of products that have inelastic demand, and give several examples of such products.
5. Explain why optimal profits should occur when marginal cost equals marginal revenue.
6. Chambers Company has just gathered estimates for conducting a break-even analysis for a new product. Variable costs are $7 a unit. The additional plant will cost $48,000. The new product will be charged $18,000 a year for its share of general overhead. Advertising expenditures will be $80,000, and $55,000 will be spent on distribution. If the product sells for $12, what is the break-even point in units? What is the break-even point in dollar sales volume?
7. In what ways do other marketing mix variables affect pricing decisions?
8. What types of expectations may channel members have about producers' prices? How might these expectations affect pricing decisions?
9. How do legal and regulatory forces influence pricing decisions?
10. Compare and contrast a trade discount and a quantity discount.
11. What is the reason for using the term *F.O.B.*?
12. What are the major methods used for transfer pricing?

APPLICATION QUESTIONS

1. Price competition is intense in the fast-food, air travel, and personal computer industries. Discuss a recent situation in which companies had to meet or beat a rival's price in a price-competitive industry. Did you benefit from this situation? Did it change your perception of the companies and/or their products?
2. Customers' interpretations and responses regarding a product and its price are an important influence on marketers' pricing decisions. Perceptions of price are affected by the degree to which a customer is value conscious, price conscious, or prestige sensitive. Discuss how value consciousness, price consciousness, and prestige sensitivity influence the buying decision process for the following products:
   a. A new house
   b. Weekly groceries for a family of five
   c. An airline ticket
   d. A soft drink from a vending machine

Internet Exercise & Resources

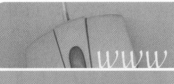

Visit **www.prideferrell.com** for resources to help you master the material in this chapter, plus materials that will help you expand your marketing knowledge, including Internet Exercise updates, ACE self-tests, hotlinks to companies featured in this chapter, and much more.

Autosite

Autosite offers car buyers a free, comprehensive website to find the invoice prices for almost all car models. The browser can also access a listing of all the latest new-car rebates and incentives. Visit this site at **www.autosite.com**.

1. Find the lowest-priced Lexus available today, and examine its features. Which Lexus dealer is closest to you?
2. If you wanted to purchase this Lexus, what are the lowest monthly payments you could make over the longest time period?
3. Is this free site more credible than a "pay" site? Why or why not?

Video Case 21.1

JetBlue's Flight Plan for Profitability

When David Neeleman sold his Utah-based airline to Southwest Airlines in 1994, he signed a contract agreeing not to compete in the air travel industry for five years. By the time the five years ended, the entrepreneur had created a new flight plan—and found $160 million in financial backing—for his full-throttle return to the skies with a customer-friendly, low-fare airline called JetBlue. Today that airline serves 22 U.S. cities and has become the number four airline flying out of New York City.

Neeleman and his management team decided to base the startup airline in New York City after they thoroughly analyzed the area's air travel patterns. "Essentially, New Yorkers were prisoners," explains John Owen, JetBlue's chief financial officer. "They had only low-quality, high-fare airlines to choose from. Their expectations were at [the] bottom." New York travelers also had to contend with crowds and delays at nearby La Guardia Airport unless they were willing to venture eight miles farther to fly from John F. Kennedy International Airport. Unlike some metropolitan airports, JFK is not a regional hub for major airlines or for low-fare carriers such as Southwest. Seizing an opportunity to trade off a slightly less convenient location for less competition and better on-time performance, Neeleman secured more than 70 takeoff and landing slots at JFK Airport, enough to accommodate JetBlue's projected growth through 2005.

Neeleman understands price is a top consideration for travelers. He therefore has sharpened his pencil to keep JetBlue's ticket prices highly competitive to attract vacationers as well as business travelers. Major carriers such as Delta typically quote dozens of fares between two locations, depending on time of day and other factors. JetBlue's everyday pricing structure is far simpler and avoids complicated requirements such as Saturday-night stayovers. Neeleman says the fares are based on demand and that JetBlue uses pricing to equalize the loads on the flights so no jet takes off empty while another is completely full. Thus, fares for Sunday-night flights tend to be higher because of higher demand, whereas Tuesday-night

flights may be priced lower due to lower demand. Still, the CEO observes that JetBlue's highest fare generally undercuts the lowest fare of its competitors.

JetBlue's promotional fares are even lower. When inaugurating service between New York and California, the airline offered a one-way fare of $99, an extraordinarily low price for a nonstop, cross-country flight. Neeleman points out that low fares stimulate traffic, which helps JetBlue weather the turbulence of tough economic times and challenges such as the fall-off in air travel that occurred after the September 11 terrorist attacks. JetBlue's flights have an average passenger load of 80 percent of full capacity, compared with an industry average load of 68.4 percent.

Neeleman and his team have made other decisions to set their startup apart from other new airline ventures. Whereas many new carriers buy used jets, JetBlue flies new, state-of-the-art Airbus A320 jets with seat-back personal video screens. Rather than squeeze in the maximum 180 seats that A320s can hold, JetBlue flies with only 162, which allows passengers more leg room. In addition, the jets are outfitted with roomier leather seats, which cost twice as much as regular seat fabric but last twice as long. More important, passengers feel pampered when they sink into the leather seats and enjoy free satellite television programming, which also differentiates JetBlue from other low-fare airlines.

Another advantage of flying new jets is higher fuel efficiency. Because of their dual engines and weight, A320s can operate on 60 percent of the amount of fuel burned by an equivalent jet built decades earlier. As a result, JetBlue has not had to raise ticket prices to compensate for rising fuel costs even as the airline expands beyond the East Coast to western destinations such as Long Beach (California) and Seattle. In addition, because JetBlue's technicians work on only one type of jet, they become highly proficient at their maintenance tasks, which saves time and money. New jets come with a five-year warranty, so JetBlue has to budget only for routine maintenance service.

From its first day of operation, JetBlue has relied on Internet bookings to minimize sales costs. Travelers who buy tickets directly through the company's website (**www.jetblue.com**) get a special discount and are also eligible for online specials, such as "Get It Together" fares designed for two people traveling together. By the airline's second year, it was selling 50 percent of its tickets via the Internet. JetBlue also set up a special web-based service to encourage travel agents to buy tickets for their customers online.

JetBlue's total costs equal about 6.5 cents per mile, well below the per-mile costs of most major competitors. In turn, its low cost structure allows the airline to keep ticket prices low while delivering a comfortable flying experience. Neeleman's decision to fly from JFK Airport also means JetBlue's on-time record is generally better than those of the big airlines, another important consideration for business travelers and vacationers alike. Not surprisingly, JetBlue flew into profitability just months after its launch, and Neeleman aims to keep the airline's revenues and profits soaring in the future.[20]

QUESTIONS FOR DISCUSSION

1. In an industry where pricing has driven many firms out of business or into bankruptcy protection, why does JetBlue compete so successfully on the basis of price?
2. How does JetBlue use pricing to deal with demand fluctuations?
3. Is a businessperson's demand for air travel likely to be relatively elastic or inelastic? Is a vacationer's demand for air travel likely to be relatively elastic or inelastic?
4. What other factors related to pricing are most important to JetBlue's management when making pricing decisions?

Case 21.2

Priceline.com Lets Online Customers Set Prices

Priceline.com, the original name-your-price website, has had a challenging few years. The site invites customers to name the price they are willing to pay for an airline ticket, a hotel room, a rental car, long-distance telephone service, a mortgage, or a new car or truck. In its first four months of operation, the company sold 40,000 airline tickets and continues to attract more than 1 million visitors a week. At peak times, it sells a ticket every 70 seconds to one of its 11 million registered customers.

However, Priceline only recently recorded its first profit since the company burst onto the Internet with much fanfare in 1998. Like other e-businesses, Priceline has employed a substantial promotional budget to build awareness and attract customers. The company has also been saddled with costs incurred by its withdrawal from ill-fated attempts to expand its product mix to include name-your-price groceries, gasoline, and insurance. On top of these challenges, Priceline is learning to deal with competition now that it is no longer the only name-your-price site on the Web.

Travel services remain Priceline's most popular offering. Unsold airline seats and hotel rooms are wasted; they cannot be stored in warehouses for later sale. Priceline.com, which provides an anonymous link between buyers and sellers, gives buyers an opportunity to pay a price they can afford and sellers the chance to reduce waste by accepting a buyer's offer. Since planes fly with more than 500,000 empty seats a day, waste and lost revenues are a major problem for airlines, and many therefore cooperate with Priceline.com.

How does Priceline.com's airline ticket service work? Using the lowest available advance purchase fares as a guideline, customers go to the Priceline site, enter their destinations and travel dates, offer a price for a ticket, and type in their credit card numbers. Travel must begin in the United States, and customers must be flexible regarding the time of day they are willing to travel. However, destinations can be worldwide, and there are no blackout dates or advance purchase requirements. After receiving an offer, Priceline searches ticket availability on participating airlines. Within an hour or less (one day for international flights), Priceline lets the customer know whether his or her offer has been accepted, charges the credit card, and processes the tickets. Customers whose offers are rejected can try again. This web-based pricing system is so original that the U.S. Patent and Trademark Office granted Priceline a patent on the method.

Shopping at Priceline.com sounds easy and economical, and most of its customers agree. Critics, however, point out some drawbacks in Priceline's airline ticket service. In addition to committing themselves to fly at hours that will not be specified until after their offers are accepted, customers must be willing to take flights that may include one or more stops or connections and possibly a long layover. Tickets are nonrefundable, cannot be changed, and earn no frequent flier miles. Some reporters who have tested Priceline's system complain the airfares are not always the lowest available and conclude that the site works best for people who must fly on short notice and can't meet advance purchase requirements for lower fares.

Customers can also use Priceline to name their price for hotel rooms in major U.S. cities. First, they enter their destination, dates, number of rooms, desired quality level of the hotel (two, three, four, or five stars), and how much they are willing to pay per night. As with the airline ticket system, they have to provide a credit card number so Priceline can lock in the reservation if it finds accommodations that meet their criteria. Priceline searches its database of participating hotels for one with a rate at or below the customer's request, books the room, buys it from the hotel, and charges the customer $5 more than the price it paid. Priceline guarantees its hotel prices and promises that if customers can find a better price for a similar room online, the company will refund the difference. This Priceline service has become so popular that it now represents more than half of all booked offers on Priceline. Customers are also reserving more rental cars, helping to boost Priceline's overall revenues and contributing to its profitability.

Although Priceline had no name-your-price competition in its early years, two other travel sites now offer variations on this pricing approach. Expedia, backed by Microsoft, offers Flight Price Matcher, a service very similar to Priceline's—so similar, in fact, that Priceline sued for patent infringement (a settlement calls for Expedia to pay royalties to Priceline).

Expedia customers don't find out which airline they are using or when their flights leave until their bids have been accepted, which takes up to 15 minutes. Hotwire.com, started by several major airlines, invites customers to bid on airline tickets, rental cars, and hotel rooms. Unlike Expedia and Priceline, Hotwire allows customers one hour to make a decision once they find out whether their price has been accepted, but they still don't learn all the details until they have agreed to the purchase.

Because travelers have become savvier about searching out special Internet deals, online travel is experiencing tremendous growth. Priceline.com hopes its name-your-price strategy will prove irresistible to a large number of these price-sensitive travelers, bringing them again and again to Priceline's site rather than to competing sites.[21]

QUESTIONS FOR DISCUSSION

1. What effect do name-your-price sites seem to be having on demand for travel services? What are the implications for price elasticity of demand?
2. Does the pricing facilitated by Priceline.com result in price or nonprice competition?
3. What are the advantages and disadvantages of Priceline.com's pricing approach for buyers? For sellers?

Setting Prices

22

OBJECTIVES

1. To describe the six major stages of the process used to establish prices

2. To explore issues related to developing pricing objectives

3. To understand the importance of identifying the target market's evaluation of price

4. To examine how marketers analyze competitors' prices

5. To describe the bases used for setting prices

6. To explain the different types of pricing strategies

Trouble in Toyland

Once upon a time, 51 percent of all toys were sold during the Christmas and Hanukkah seasons, but in 2002 only 38 percent of toys were sold in this period. Toys represent a $21 billion business in the United States, yet toy retailers, such as Toys "R" Us, are singing the holiday blues. Many accuse Wal-Mart and other discount chains of extreme price cutting on popular toys during the holidays. Toys "R" Us, once the number one toy retailer in the world, has watched its share of the toy market decline to 17 percent, while Wal-Mart, now the world's leading toy retailer, has 21 percent. Rival discount chains Target and Kmart command 9 and 4 percent of the market, respectively. Toys "R" Us is not the only toy retailer suffering. FAO Schwarz, the upscale retailer popularized in the Tom Hanks movie *Big*, has sought bankruptcy protection and is looking for a buyer for its stores.

In recent years, both Target and Wal-Mart have started their holiday advertising sooner and employed more aggressive pricing strategies than ever before. Wal-Mart, for example, sold the Hokey Pokey Elmo 30 percent below the list price and even below its wholesale cost. Target slashed the price of the Bratz disco doll set from $100 to $65 when Toys "R" Us was selling the same set for $100. A Prudential Equity Group's pricing survey of the 50 hottest toys found that Toys "R" Us prices were 5.5 percent higher than those at Wal-Mart. Moreover, private-label toys are becoming more widespread because retailers can protect their margins on these lines. At Wal-Mart, private-line toys, including a line called Kid Connection, account for 50 percent of shelf space. In contrast, roughly 20 percent of sales at Toys "R" Us are generated by private-label toys.

Although Toys "R" Us remains very competitive in terms of selection and variety of toys, discounters such as Wal-Mart and Target use toys as "loss leaders" and traffic generators, knowing they can make up the margins on a wide variety of nontoy products. When it comes to toys, consumers are extremely price sensitive, and Toys "R" Us has found the discounters' aggressive pricing strategy hard to beat. As competition in the toy market diversifies and intensifies, high-end pricing strategies and premium locations are no longer effective competitive tools. Adding to the competitive pressure is the fact that toys are now sold almost everywhere—in supermarkets and drugstores, at tourist destinations, and online, as well as in the more traditional locations.

Toys "R" Us has remodeled 75 percent of its 680 stores, freshened inventory (cutting from 14,000 items to 9,000 and focusing on profitable lines), and become more aggressive in pricing the most popular toys. Despite these efforts, sales at Toys "R" Us have continued to decline, with the largest losses occurring in video game sales. As a result, Toys "R" Us is selling its 145 Kids "R" Us clothing stores and 35 Imaginarium educational-toy stores. Some industry analysts believe to survive, Toys "R" Us will need to get even smaller, sell less profitable locations, and focus on enhancing its visibility and differential advantage against the giant discounters. As Wal-Mart continues to grow and thrive, the challenge for Toys "R" Us is to engage customers in more innovative ways. The company is already experimenting with new Geoffrey stores in Wisconsin, Texas, North Carolina, and Mississippi, providing a fun shopping experience for kids and adults alike. Perhaps by competing on entertainment value rather than price, Toys "R" Us can generate sufficient profits to prosper again.[1] ■

1 Development of pricing objectives

2 Assessment of target market's evaluation of price

3 Evaluation of competitors' prices

4 Selection of a basis for pricing

5 Selection of a pricing strategy

6 Determination of a specific price

Figure 22.1 **Stages for Establishing Prices**

W al-Mart became the world's leading toy retailer by following an everyday low price strategy, which helped the firm gain market share at the expense of more traditional toy retailers, including former market leader Toys "R" Us. Because price has such a profound impact on a firm's success, finding the right pricing strategy is crucial. Selecting a pricing strategy is one of the fundamental components of the process of setting prices.

In this chapter, we examine six stages of a process marketers can use when setting prices. Figure 22.1 illustrates these stages. Stage 1 is the development of a pricing objective that is compatible with the organization's overall and marketing objectives. Stage 2 entails assessing the target market's evaluation of price. Stage 3 involves evaluating competitors' prices, which helps determine the role of price in the marketing strategy. Stage 4 requires choosing a basis for setting prices. Stage 5 is the selection of a pricing strategy, or the guidelines for using price in the marketing mix. Stage 6, determining the final price, depends on environmental forces and marketers' understanding and use of a systematic approach to establishing prices. These stages are not rigid steps that all marketers must follow; rather, they are guidelines that provide a logical sequence for establishing prices.

Development of Pricing Objectives

pricing objectives Goals that describe what a firm wants to achieve through pricing

Pricing objectives are goals that describe what a firm wants to achieve through pricing. Developing pricing objectives is an important task because pricing objectives form the basis for decisions about other stages of pricing. Thus, pricing objectives must be stated explicitly, and the statement should include the time frame for accomplishing them.

Marketers must ensure that pricing objectives are consistent with the organization's marketing objectives and with its overall objectives because pricing objectives influence decisions in many functional areas, including finance, accounting, and production. A marketer can use both short- and long-term pricing objectives and can employ one or multiple pricing objectives. For instance, a firm may wish to increase market share by 18 percent over the next three years, achieve a 15 percent return on investment, and promote an image of quality in the marketplace.

In this section, we examine some of the pricing objectives companies might set for themselves. Table 22.1 shows the major pricing objectives and typical actions associated with them.

Table 22.1	Pricing Objectives and Typical Actions Taken to Achieve Them
Objective	**Possible Action**
Survival	Adjust price levels so the firm can increase sales volume to match organizational expenses
Profit	Identify price and cost levels that allow the firm to maximize profit
Return on investment	Identify price levels that enable the firm to yield targeted ROI
Market share	Adjust price levels so the firm can maintain or increase sales relative to competitors' sales
Cash flow	Set price levels to encourage rapid sales
Status quo	Identify price levels that help stabilize demand and sales
Product quality	Set prices to recover research and development expenditures and establish a high-quality image

◆ Survival

A fundamental pricing objective is survival. Most organizations will tolerate setbacks such as short-run losses and internal upheaval if necessary for survival. Because price is a flexible variable, it is sometimes used to keep a company afloat by increasing sales volume to levels that match expenses. For example, a women's apparel retailer may run a three-day, 60-percent-off sale to generate enough cash to pay creditors, employees, and rent.

◆ Profit

Although a business may claim its objective is to maximize profits for its owners, the objective of profit maximization is rarely operational because its achievement is difficult to measure. Because of this difficulty, profit objectives tend to be set at levels that the owners and top-level decision makers view as satisfactory. Specific profit objectives may be stated in terms of either actual dollar amounts or a percentage of sales revenues. For example, the main pricing objective for Shoebuy.com, an online shoe retailer, is to return an overall 30 percent profit. To achieve this objective, the company minimizes costs by maintaining a small work force and holding no inventory. Manufacturers ship directly to customers.[2]

◆ Return on Investment

Pricing to attain a specified rate of return on the company's investment is a profit-related pricing objective. Most pricing objectives based on return on investment (ROI) are achieved by trial and error because not all cost and revenue data needed to project the return on investment are available when setting prices. General Motors, for example, uses ROI pricing objectives.

Market Share
AT&T Wireless uses low prices to achieve market share objectives.

Introducing **the lowest international wireless calling rates. Ever.**

◆ Market Share

Many firms establish pricing objectives to maintain or increase market share, a product's sales in relation to total industry sales. Airbus Industrie, the European aircraft manufacturer that is Boeing's major competitor, uses pricing as a strategic tool for expanding market share. By offering discounts of as much as 40 percent off the list price, Airbus increased its global share of the aircraft market from 21 percent to nearly 50 percent over the past five years.[3] Many firms recognize that high relative market shares often translate into higher profits. The Profit Impact of Market Strategies (PIMS) studies, conducted over the last 30 years, have shown that both market share and product quality heavily influence profitability. Thus, marketers often use an increase in market share as a primary pricing objective.

Maintaining or increasing market share need not depend on growth in industry sales. Remember that an organization can increase its market share even if sales for the total industry are flat or decreasing. On the other hand, an organization's sales volume may increase while its market share decreases if the overall market is growing.

◆ Cash Flow

Some organizations set prices so they can recover cash as quickly as possible. Financial managers understandably seek to

Product Quality
Kohler produces high-quality plumbing products priced to compete in a high-quality category.

quickly recover capital spent to develop products. This objective may have the support of a marketing manager who anticipates a short product life cycle. Although it may be acceptable in some situations, the use of cash flow and recovery as an objective oversimplifies the contribution of price to profits. If this pricing objective results in high prices, competitors with lower prices may gain a large share of the market.

◆ Status Quo

In some cases, an organization is in a favorable position and, desiring nothing more, may set an objective of status quo. Status quo objectives can focus on several dimensions, such as maintaining a certain market share, meeting (but not beating) competitors' prices, achieving price stability, and maintaining a favorable public image. A status quo pricing objective can reduce a firm's risks by helping to stabilize demand for its products. The use of status quo pricing objectives sometimes minimizes pricing as a competitive tool, leading to a climate of nonprice competition in an industry. Professionals such as accountants and attorneys often operate in such an environment.

◆ Product Quality

A company may have the objective of leading its industry in product quality. This goal normally dictates a high price to cover the costs of achieving high product quality and, in some instances, the costs of research and development. For example, Mercedes-Benz cars are priced to reflect and emphasize high product quality. As previously mentioned, the PIMS studies have shown that both product quality and market share are good indicators of profitability. The products and brands that customers perceive to be of high quality are more likely to survive in a competitive marketplace. High quality usually enables a marketer to charge higher prices for the product. For example, by setting the price of the MACH3 razor at approximately 35 percent above the Sensor price, Gillette clearly communicates that the MACH3 is a high-quality product.

Snapshot

Would you pay top dollar?
Even in bad economic times, people with incomes over $50,000 say it is smarter to pay more for some premium-quality products.

Disagree **19%** Agree **81%**

Source: Data from *Trading Up: The New American Luxury*/The Boston Consulting Group.

Assessment of the Target Market's Evaluation of Price

Despite the general assumption that price is a major issue for buyers, the importance of price depends on the type of product, the type of target market, and the purchase situation. For example, buyers are probably more sensitive to gasoline prices than to luggage prices. With respect to the type of target market, adults may have to pay more than children for certain products. The purchase situation also affects the buyer's view of price. Most moviegoers would never pay in other situations the prices charged for soft drinks, popcorn, and candy at movie concession stands. By assessing the target market's evaluation of price, a marketer is in a better position to know how much emphasis to put on price. Information about the target market's price evaluation may also help a marketer determine how far above the competition the firm can set its prices.

Because some consumers today are seeking less expensive products and shopping more selectively, some manufacturers and retailers are focusing on the value of their products. Value combines a product's price and quality attributes, which customers use to differentiate among competing brands. Consumers are looking for good deals on products that provide better value for their money. Companies that offer both low prices and high quality, such as Target and Best Buy, have altered consumers' expectations about how much quality they must sacrifice for low prices.[4] Even retail atmospherics can influence consumers' perceptions of price: the use of soft lights and colors has been found to have a positive influence on perception of price fairness.[5] Understanding the importance of a product to customers, as well as their expectations about quality and value, helps marketers correctly assess the target market's evaluation of price.

Evaluation of Competitors' Prices

In most cases, marketers are in a better position to establish prices when they know the prices charged for competing brands. Learning competitors' prices may be a regular function of marketing research. Some grocery and department stores, for example, have full-time comparative shoppers who systematically collect data on prices. Companies may also purchase price lists, sometimes weekly, from syndicated marketing research services.

Finding out what prices competitors are charging is not always easy, especially in producer and reseller markets. Competitors' price lists are often closely guarded. Even if a marketer has access to competitors' price lists, those lists may not reflect the actual prices at which competitive products are sold because those prices may be established through negotiation.

Knowing the prices of competing brands can be very important for a marketer. Competitors' prices and the marketing mix variables they emphasize partly determine how important price will be to customers. A marketer in an industry in which price competition prevails needs competitive price information to ensure its prices are the same as, or lower than, competitors' prices.

In some instances, an organization's prices are designed to be slightly above competitors' prices to give its products an exclusive image. In contrast, another company may use price as a competitive tool and price its products below those of competitors. Category killers such as Costco, membership warehouse club and The Home Depot have acquired large market shares through highly competitive pricing.

Selection of a Basis for Pricing

The three major dimensions on which prices can be based are cost, demand, and competition. The selection of the basis to use is affected by the type of product, the market structure of the industry, the brand's market share position relative to competing brands, and customer characteristics. In this section, we discuss each basis separately. However, when setting prices, an organization generally considers two or all three of these dimensions, even if one is the primary basis on which it determines prices. For example, if an organization is using cost as a basis for setting prices, marketers in that organization are also aware of and concerned about competitors' prices. If a company is using demand as a basis for pricing, those making pricing decisions still must consider costs and competitors' prices. Fairchild Semiconductor uses software to assess all three dimensions, as well as buying behavior, manufacturing capacity, inventories, and product life cycles, in setting prices for its 44,000 products.[6]

◆ Cost-Based Pricing

cost-based pricing Adding a dollar amount or percentage to the cost of the product

With **cost-based pricing**, a dollar amount or percentage is added to the cost of the product. This approach thus involves calculations of desired profit margins. Cost-based pricing does not necessarily take into account the economic aspects of supply and demand, nor must it relate to just one pricing strategy or pricing objective. Cost-based pricing is straightforward and easy to implement. Two common forms of cost-based pricing are cost-plus and markup pricing.

cost-plus pricing Adding a specified dollar amount or percentage to the seller's cost

Cost-Plus Pricing. With **cost-plus pricing**, the seller's costs are determined (usually during a project or after a project is completed), and then a specified dollar amount or percentage of the cost is added to the seller's cost to establish the price. When production costs are difficult to predict, cost-plus pricing is appropriate. Projects involving custom-made equipment and commercial construction are often priced using this technique. The government frequently uses such cost-based pricing in granting defense contracts. One pitfall for the buyer is that the seller may increase costs to establish a larger profit base. Furthermore, some costs, such as overhead, may be difficult to determine. In periods of rapid inflation, cost-plus pricing is popular, especially when the producer must use raw materials that are fluctuating in price. In industries in which cost-plus pricing is common and sellers have similar costs, price competition may not be especially intense.

markup pricing Adding to the cost of the product a predetermined percentage of that cost

Markup Pricing. With **markup pricing**, commonly used by retailers, a product's price is derived by adding a predetermined percentage of the cost, called *markup*, to the cost of the product. Although the percentage markup in a retail store varies from one category of goods to another—35 percent of cost for hardware items and 100 percent of cost for greeting cards, for example—the same percentage is often used to determine the prices on items within a single product category, and the percentage markup may be largely standardized across an industry at the retail level. Using a rigid percentage markup for a specific product category reduces pricing to a routine task that can be performed quickly.

Markup can be stated as a percentage of the cost or as a percentage of the selling price. The following example illustrates how percentage markups are determined and points out the differences in the two methods. Assume a retailer purchases a can of tuna at 45 cents, adds 15 cents to the cost, and then prices the tuna at 60 cents. Here are the figures:

$$\text{Markup as a Percentage of Cost} = \frac{\text{Markup}}{\text{Cost}}$$

$$= \frac{15}{45}$$

$$= 33.3\% \qquad \textit{(continued)}$$

$$\text{Markup as a Percentage of Selling Price} = \frac{\text{Markup}}{\text{Selling Price}}$$

$$= \frac{15}{60}$$

$$= 25.0\%$$

Obviously, when discussing a percentage markup, it is important to know whether the markup is based on cost or selling price.

Markups normally reflect expectations about operating costs, risks, and stock turnovers. Wholesalers and manufacturers often suggest standard retail markups that are considered profitable. To the extent that retailers use similar markups for the same product category, price competition is reduced. In addition, using rigid markups is convenient and is the major reason retailers, which face numerous pricing decisions, favor this method.

◆ Demand-Based Pricing

demand-based pricing Pricing based on the level of demand for the product

Marketers sometimes base prices on the level of demand for the product. When **demand-based pricing** is used, customers pay a higher price when demand for the product is strong and a lower price when demand is weak. For example, hotels that otherwise attract numerous travelers often offer reduced rates during lower-demand periods. Some long-distance telephone companies, such as Sprint and AT&T, also use demand-based pricing by charging peak and off-peak rates. Building Customer

Demand-Based Pricing
Ski resorts use demand-based pricing.

Relationships looks at pricing in the cellphone industry. To use this pricing basis, a marketer must be able to estimate the amounts of a product consumers will demand at different prices. The marketer then chooses the price that generates the highest total revenue. Obviously the effectiveness of demand-based pricing depends on the marketer's ability to estimate demand accurately.

Compared with cost-based pricing, demand-based pricing places a firm in a better position to reach higher profit levels, assuming buyers value the product at levels sufficiently above the product's cost.

◆ Competition-Based Pricing

With **competition-based pricing**, an organization considers costs to be secondary to competitors' prices. The importance of this method increases when competing products are relatively homogeneous and the organization is serving markets in which price is a key purchase consideration. A firm that uses competition-based pricing may choose to price below competitors' prices, above competitors' prices, or at the same level. Airlines use competition-based pricing, often charging identical fares on the

Wireless Companies Ring Up Competitive Pricing Strategies

How low can it go? Intense competition among wireless carriers is dropping the price of cellphone service to ever-lower levels across the United States. According to one study, the price of wireless phone service fell more than 7 percent for two consecutive years, and continues to drop. This is because companies such as Cingular Wireless, AT&T Wireless, Sprint PCS, VoiceStream Wireless, and Verizon Wireless are all using price—often in conjunction with special promotional offers—as a major tool to build market share.

The wireless companies set different prices for different levels of phone usage, such as 200, 500, and 1,000 calling minutes during a single month. Customers may be required to sign a service contract, typically covering a minimum of one year, and face high cancellation fees if they want to leave before the end of the contract period. In addition, carriers sometimes levy an activation fee and may charge for services such as text messaging and call forwarding.

However, the monthly price usually includes valuable extras. For example, most providers throw in bonus minutes that can be used during off-peak periods (nights and weekends). Verizon Wireless has offered up to 3,000 night and weekend bonus minutes to customers who buy the

$35 monthly package with 300 anytime minutes, the $55 monthly package with 550 anytime minutes, or the $100 monthly package with 1,200 anytime minutes. One Sprint PCS plan went even further, providing 6,500 bonus minutes to customers who signed up for the $75 monthly package of 1,000 anytime minutes. Some VoiceStream Wireless plans allow unlimited weekend calls.

During special promotions, the wireless providers pile on extras to add more value and attract more customers. AT&T Wireless recently put customers in the holiday mood by offering free downloadable ring tones such as "Jingle Bell Rock." It also offered rebates to new customers who joined its Shared Advantage program, which allows five people to share the calling minutes in a monthly package. Sprint PCS has brought in new customers by offering rebates on cellphone purchases.

Teens and twenty-something customers are a particularly attractive target for the wireless industry. Eyeing this segment, Cingular Wireless invites customers to personalize their ring tones by downloading college and university fight songs for 99 cents each. Verizon is marketing prepaid cellphone cards that reduce the per-minute cost of phone usage and help customers better manage their wireless budgets. The quest for higher market share in the wireless industry is likely to spawn more price strategy variations over the coming years.

same routes. In recent years, online travel services such as Orbitz, Expedia, and Travelocity have also employed competition-based pricing.[7]

Although not all introductory marketing texts have exactly the same price, they do have similar prices. The price the bookstore paid to the publishing company for this textbook was determined on the basis of competitors' prices. Competition-based pricing can help a firm achieve the pricing objective of increasing sales or market share. Competition-based pricing may necessitate frequent price adjustments. For example, for many competitive airline routes, fares are adjusted often.

Selection of a Pricing Strategy

A pricing strategy is an approach or a course of action designed to achieve pricing and marketing objectives. Generally pricing strategies help marketers solve the practical problems of establishing prices. Table 22.2 lists the most common pricing strategies, which we discuss in this section.

Table 22.2	Common Pricing Strategies
Differential Pricing	**Psychological Pricing**
Negotiated pricing	Reference pricing
Secondary-market pricing	Bundle pricing
Periodic discounting	Multiple-unit pricing
Random discounting	Everyday low prices
	Odd-even pricing
New-Product Pricing	Customary pricing
Price skimming	Prestige pricing
Penetration pricing	
	Professional Pricing
Product-Line Pricing	
Captive pricing	**Promotional Pricing**
Premium pricing	Price leaders
Bait pricing	Special-event pricing
Price lining	Comparison discounting

◆ Differential Pricing

An important issue in pricing decisions is whether to use a single price or different prices for the same product. Using a single price has several benefits. A primary advantage is simplicity. A single price is easily understood by both employees and customers, and since many salespeople and customers dislike having to negotiate a price, it reduces the chance of an adversarial relationship developing between marketer and customer. The use of a single price does create some challenges, however. If the single price is too high, a number of potential customers may be unable to afford the product. If it is too low, the organization loses revenue from those customers who would have paid more had the price been higher.

differential pricing Charging different prices to different buyers for the same quality and quantity of product

Differential pricing means charging different prices to different buyers for the same quality and quantity of product. For differential pricing to be effective, the market must consist of multiple segments with different price sensitivities, and the method should be used in a way that avoids confusing or antagonizing customers. Customers paying the lower prices should not be able to resell the product to the individuals and organizations paying higher prices, unless that is the seller's intention. Differential pricing can occur in several ways, including negotiated pricing, secondary-market discounting, periodic discounting, and random discounting.

negotiated pricing Establishing a final price through bargaining between seller and customer

Negotiated Pricing. **Negotiated pricing** occurs when the final price is established through bargaining between seller and customer. Negotiated pricing occurs in a number of industries and at all levels of distribution. Cutler-Hammer/Eaton streamlined its contract-negotiations process for more than 90,000 products by reducing quote response times and implementing automatic acceptance of offers.[8] Even when there is a predetermined stated price or a price list, manufacturers, wholesalers, and retailers may negotiate to establish the final sales price. Consumers commonly negotiate prices for houses, cars, and used equipment.

secondary-market pricing Setting one price for the primary target market and a different price for another market

Secondary-Market Pricing. **Secondary-market pricing** means setting one price for the primary target market and a different price for another market. Often the price charged in the secondary market is lower. However, when the costs of serving a secondary market are higher than normal, secondary-market customers may have to pay a higher price. Examples of secondary markets include a geographically isolated domestic market, a market in a foreign country, and a segment willing to purchase a product during off-peak times. For example, some restaurants offer special "early-bird" prices during the early evening hours, movie theaters offer senior citizen and afternoon matinee discounts, and some textbooks and pharmaceutical products are sold for considerably less in certain foreign countries than in the United States. Secondary markets give an organization an opportunity to use excess capacity and stabilize the allocation of resources.

periodic discounting Temporary reduction of prices on a patterned or systematic basis

Periodic Discounting. **Periodic discounting** is the temporary reduction of prices on a patterned or systematic basis. Many retailers, for example, have annual holiday sales. Some women's apparel stores have two seasonal sales each year: a winter sale in the last two weeks of January and a summer sale in the first two weeks of July. Automobile dealers regularly discount prices on current models in the fall, when the next year's models are introduced. From the marketer's point of view, a major problem with periodic discounting is that because the discounts follow a pattern, customers can predict when the reductions will occur and may delay their purchases until they can take advantage of the lower prices.

random discounting Temporary reduction of prices on an unsystematic basis

Random Discounting. To alleviate the problem of customers knowing when discounting will occur, some organizations employ **random discounting**; that is, they temporarily reduce their prices on an unsystematic basis. When price reductions of a product occur randomly, current users of that brand are likely unable to predict when the reductions will occur and thus will not delay their purchases. In the automobile industry, with the increasing reliance on sales, rebates, and incentives such

THE ART OF SEDUCTION CAN'T BE TAUGHT BUT IT CAN BE BOUGHT

EXPRESS LINGERIE

SALE

Types of Discounting
Express uses random discounting to provide special value to customers.

as zero percent financing, random discounting has become nearly continuous discounting, and some analysts have expressed concern that automakers will find it difficult to "wean" consumers off the generous incentives as the economy improves.[9] Marketers also use random discounting to attract new customers. For example, Lever Brothers may temporarily reduce the price of one of its bar soaps in the hope of attracting new customers.

Irrespective of whether they use periodic discounting or random discounting, retailers often employ tensile pricing when putting products on sale. *Tensile pricing* refers to a broad statement about price reductions as opposed to detailing specific price discounts. Examples of tensile pricing would be statements such as "20 to 50% off," "up to 75% off," and "save 10% or more." Generally, using and advertising the tensile price that mentions only the maximum reduction (such as "up to 50% off") generates the highest customer response.[10]

◆ New-Product Pricing

Setting the base price for a new product is a necessary part of formulating a marketing strategy. The base price is easily adjusted (in the absence of government price controls), and its establishment is one of the most fundamental decisions in the marketing mix. The base price can be set high to recover development costs quickly or provide a reference point for developing discount prices for different market segments. When a marketer sets base prices, it also considers how quickly competitors will enter the market, whether they will mount a strong campaign on entry, and what effect their entry will have on the development of primary demand. Two strategies used in new-product pricing are price skimming and penetration pricing.

price skimming Charging the highest possible price that buyers who most desire the product will pay

Price Skimming. **Price skimming** means charging the highest possible price that buyers who most desire the product will pay. The Porsche Cayenne, for example, has a starting price of $56,000, considerably higher than those for other sport-utility vehicles.[11] This approach provides the most flexible introductory base price. Demand tends to be inelastic in the introductory stage of the product life cycle.

Price skimming can provide several benefits, especially when a product is in the introductory stage of its life cycle. A skimming policy can generate much-needed initial cash flows to help offset sizable development costs. Price skimming protects the marketer from problems that arise when the price is set too low to cover costs. When a firm introduces a product, its production capacity may be limited. A skimming price can help keep demand consistent with the firm's production capabilities. The use of a skimming price may attract competition into an industry because the high price makes that type of business appear quite lucrative. In reality, companies price new products for less than they could or should. In such cases, companies risk not only failing to maximize potential profits but also establishing a lower market value in buyers' minds.[12] New-product prices should be based on both the value to the customer and competitive products.

penetration pricing Setting prices below those of competing brands to penetrate a market and gain a significant market share quickly

Penetration Pricing. With **penetration pricing**, prices are set below those of competing brands to penetrate a market and gain a large market share quickly. In South America, for example, when Industrias Añanos introduced Kola Real to capitalize on limited supplies of Coca-Cola and Pepsi-Cola in Peru, it set an ultra-low penetration price to appeal to the low-income consumers who predominate in the region. Kola Real quickly secured one-fifth of the Peruvian market and has made significant gains in Ecuador, Venezuela, and Mexico, forcing larger soft-drink marketers to cut prices.[13] This approach is less flexible for a marketer than price skimming because it is more difficult to raise a penetration price than to lower or discount a skimming price. It is not unusual for a firm to use a penetration price after having skimmed the market with a higher price.

Penetration pricing can be especially beneficial when a marketer suspects competitors could enter the market easily. If penetration pricing allows the marketer to gain a large market share quickly, competitors may be discouraged from entering the market. In addition, because the lower per-unit penetration price results in lower per-unit profit, the market may not appear to be especially lucrative to potential new entrants.

◆ Product-Line Pricing

product-line pricing Establishing and adjusting prices of multiple products within a product line

Rather than considering products on an item-by-item basis when determining pricing strategies, some marketers employ product-line pricing. **Product-line pricing** means establishing and adjusting the prices of multiple products within a product line. When marketers use product-line pricing, their goal is to maximize profits for an entire product line rather than focusing on the profitability of an individual product. Product-line pricing can lend marketers flexibility in price setting. For example, marketers can set prices so that one product is quite profitable while another increases market share due to having a lower price than competing products.

Before setting prices for a product line, marketers evaluate the relationship among the products in the line. When products in a line are complementary, sales increases in one item raise demand for other items. For instance, desktop printers and toner cartridges are complementary products. When products in a line function as substitutes for one another, buyers of one product in the line are unlikely to purchase one of the other products in the same line. In this case, marketers must be sensitive to how a price change for one of the brands may affect the demand not only for that brand but also for the substitute brands. For example, if decision makers at Procter & Gamble were considering a price change for Tide detergent, they would be concerned about how the price change might influence sales of Cheer, Bold, and Gain.

When marketers employ product-line pricing, they have several strategies from which to choose. These include captive pricing, premium pricing, bait pricing, and price lining.

NET SIGHTS

On the U.S. government Bureau of Labor Statistics' Consumer Price Index page (**www.bls.gov/cpi/home. htm**), *visitors have access to an Inflation Calculator, news releases, and a vast amount of information on the consumer price index. Information on this site illuminates some of the complexity involved in setting prices.*

captive pricing Pricing the basic product in a product line low while pricing related items higher

Captive Pricing. With **captive pricing**, the basic product in a product line is priced low while items required to operate or enhance it are priced higher. For example, a manufacturer of cameras and film may set the price of the cameras at a level low enough to attract customers but set the film price relatively high because to use the cameras, customers must continue to purchase film.

premium pricing Pricing the highest-quality or most versatile products higher than other models in the product line

Premium Pricing. **Premium pricing** is often used when a product line contains several versions of the same product; the highest-quality products or those with the most versatility are given the highest prices. Other products in the line are priced to appeal to price-sensitive shoppers or to buyers who seek product-specific features.

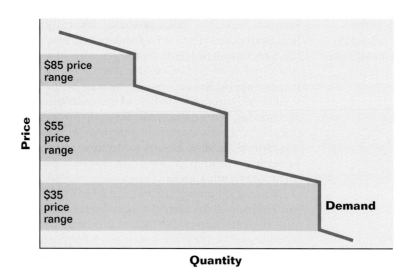

Figure 22.2 Price Lining

Marketers that use a premium strategy often realize a significant portion of their profits from premium-priced products. Examples of product categories that commonly use premium pricing are small kitchen appliances, beer, ice cream, and cable television service.

Bait Pricing. To attract customers, marketers may put a low price on one item in the product line with the intention of selling a higher-priced item in the line; this strategy is known as **bait pricing**. For example, a computer retailer might advertise its lowest-priced computer model, hoping that when customers come to the store they will purchase a higher-priced one. This strategy can facilitate sales of a line's higher-priced products. As long as a retailer has sufficient quantities of the advertised low-priced model available for sale, this strategy is considered acceptable. In contrast, *bait and switch* is an activity in which retailers have no intention of selling the bait product; they use the low price merely to entice customers into the store to sell them higher-priced products. Bait and switch is considered unethical, and in some states it is illegal as well.

bait pricing Pricing an item in a product line low with the intention of selling a higher-priced item in the line

Price Lining. When an organization sets a limited number of prices for selected groups or lines of merchandise, it is using **price lining**. A retailer may have various styles and brands of similar-quality men's shirts that sell for $15 and another line of higher-quality shirts that sell for $22. Price lining simplifies customers' decision making by holding constant one key variable in the final selection of style and brand within a line.

The basic assumption in price lining is that the demand for various groups or sets of products is inelastic. If the prices are attractive, customers will concentrate their purchases without responding to slight changes in price. Thus, a women's dress shop that carries dresses priced at $85, $55, and $35 may not attract many more sales with a drop to, say, $83, $53, and $33. The "space" between the price of $85 and $55, however, can stir changes in consumer response. With price lining, the demand curve looks like a series of steps, as shown in Figure 22.2.

price lining Setting a limited number of prices for selected groups or lines of merchandise

◆ Psychological Pricing

Learning the price of a product is not always a pleasant experience for customers. It is sometimes surprising (as at a movie concession stand) and sometimes downright horrifying; most of us have been afflicted with "sticker shock." **Psychological pricing** attempts to influence a customer's perception of price to make a product's price more attractive. In this section, we consider several forms of psychological pricing: reference pricing, bundle pricing, multiple-unit pricing, everyday low prices (EDLP), odd-even pricing, customary pricing, and prestige pricing.

psychological pricing Pricing that attempts to influence a customer's perception of price to make a product's price more attractive

reference pricing Pricing a product at a moderate level and positioning it next to a more expensive model or brand

Reference Pricing. **Reference pricing** means pricing a product at a moderate level and positioning it next to a more expensive model or brand in the hope that the customer will use the higher price as an external reference price (i.e., a comparison price). Because of the comparison, the customer is expected to view the moderate price favorably. Reference pricing is based on the "isolation effect," meaning an alternative is less attractive when viewed by itself than when compared with other alternatives. When you go to Best Buy or Circuit City to buy a DVD player, a moderately priced DVD player may appear especially attractive because it offers most of the important attributes of the more expensive alternatives on display and at a lower price. It is not unusual for an organization's moderately priced private brands to be positioned alongside more expensive, better-known manufacturer brands. On the other hand, many private store brands are raising their prices in an effort to boost these products' image.[14]

bundle pricing Packaging together two or more complementary products and selling them at a single price

Bundle Pricing. **Bundle pricing** is packaging together two or more products, usually complementary ones, to be sold at a single price. Cox Communications, for example, bundles local telephone service, high-speed Internet access, and digital cable television for one monthly fee.[15] To attract customers, the single bundled price is usually considerably less than the sum of the prices of the individual products. The opportunity to buy the bundled combination of products in a single transaction may be of value to the customer as well. Marketing research models suggest that marketers can develop heterogeneous bundles of products with optimal prices for different market segments.[16] Bundle pricing not only helps increase customer satisfaction; by bundling slow-moving products with products with higher turnover, an organization can also stimulate sales and increase revenues. It may also help build customer loyalty and reduce "churn," that is, losing dissatisfied customers to rivals.[17] Selling products as a package rather than individually may also result in cost savings. Bundle pricing is commonly used for banking, travel, and telecommunications services.

multiple-unit pricing Packaging together two or more identical products and selling them at a single price

everyday low prices (EDLP) Pricing products low on a consistent basis

Multiple-Unit Pricing. **Multiple-unit pricing** occurs when two or more identical products are packaged together and sold at a single price. This normally results in a lower per-unit price than the price regularly charged. Multiple-unit pricing is commonly used for twin-packs of potato chips, four-packs of light bulbs, and six- and twelve-packs of soft drinks. Customers benefit from the cost saving and convenience this pricing strategy affords. A company may use multiple-unit pricing to attract new customers to its brands and, in some instances, to increase consumption of them. When customers buy in larger quantities, their consumption of the product may increase. For example, multiple-unit pricing may encourage a customer to buy larger quantities of snacks, which are likely to be consumed in higher volume at the point of consumption simply because they are available. However, this is not true for all products. For instance, greater availability at the point of consumption of light bulbs, bar soap, and table salt is not likely to increase usage.

Discount stores and especially warehouse clubs, such as Sam's Club, are major users of multiple-unit pricing. For certain products in these stores, customers receive significant per-unit price reductions when they buy packages containing multiple units of the same product, such as an eight-pack of canned tuna fish.

Everyday Low Prices (EDLP). To reduce or eliminate the use of frequent short-term price reductions, some organizations use an approach referred to as **everyday low prices (EDLP)**. With EDLP, a marketer sets a low price for its products on a consistent basis rather than setting higher prices and frequently discounting them. Everyday low prices, though not deeply discounted, are set far enough below competitors'

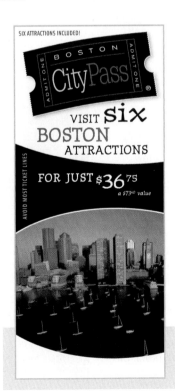

Bundle Pricing
Travel- and tour-related products are sometimes priced using bundle pricing.

prices to make customers feel confident they are receiving a fair price. EDLP is employed by retailers such as Wal-Mart and manufacturers such as Procter & Gamble. A company that uses EDLP benefits from reduced losses from frequent markdowns, greater stability in sales, and decreased promotional costs. Building Customer Relationships explores how Family Dollar Stores uses everday low prices.

A major problem with EDLP is that customers have mixed responses to it. Over the last several years, many marketers have inadvertently "trained" customers to expect and seek out deeply discounted prices. In some product categories, such as apparel, finding the deepest discount has become almost a national consumer sport. Thus, failure to provide deep discounts can be a problem for certain marketers. In some instances, customers simply don't believe everyday low prices are what marketers claim they are but are instead a marketing gimmick.

odd-even pricing Ending the price with certain numbers to influence buyers' perceptions of the price or product

Odd-Even Pricing. Through **odd-even pricing**—ending the price with certain numbers—marketers try to influence buyers' perceptions of the price or the product. Odd pricing assumes more of a product will be sold at $99.95 than at $100. Theoretically, customers will think, or at least tell friends, that the product is a bargain—not $100, but $99 and change. Also, customers will supposedly think the store could have charged $100 but instead cut the price to the last cent, to $99.95. Some

BUILDING CUSTOMER RELATIONSHIPS

Family Dollar Stores' Strategy Is Driven by Everyday Low Prices

The low-price appeal of Family Dollar Stores is evident in its name. This chain of 5,100 stores in 43 states targets families with incomes of $25,000 or less who know the value of a dollar and want to stretch it as far as possible. Rather than hold an endless series of advertised price promotions on selected merchandise, Family Dollar has an everyday low price policy that encourages customers to shop more often and buy more products. Few items sell for more than $10, and because the shelves are filled with bargain-priced household supplies, customers return every time they run out of something.

Headquartered in Matthews, North Carolina, Family Dollar first spread its stores across the South before expanding northward into Pennsylvania, Ohio, Michigan, and New York. Half of its stores are located in towns with populations of less than 15,000, towns too small even for Wal-Mart. Yet Family Dollar has thrived by opening relatively small neighborhood stores—generally less than 8,000 square feet—where customers find shorter checkout lines and less parking congestion compared to much larger stores. The company also keeps costs low by concentrating stores in a specific area to gain economies of scale from shared distribution and management supervision. As chainwide sales approach $4.8 billion, the company continues to open hundreds of stores every year, including a

growing number in urban locations abandoned by troubled retailers.

Family Dollar competes with a number of retail chains that also position themselves as low-price "dollar" stores. The largest competitor is Dollar General, which rings up $6.1 billion in annual sales at 6,700 stores. Other competitors include Dollar Tree Stores, Bill's Dollar Stores, Dollar Discount Stores of America, and 99 Cents Only Stores. Family Dollar is also feeling some competitive pressure from Wal-Mart's Neighborhood Market stores, which are a fraction of the size of a typical Wal-Mart SuperCenter and are opening in some smaller communities.

For years, Family Dollar packed its stores with high-margin apparel products and shoes. A few years ago, however, management realized the company could increase repeat business by stocking more discounted soaps, paper products, and other "hardline" products. Today hardlines make up two-thirds of the merchandise assortment, and the retailer is enjoying higher sales and higher gross profits. Even when a recession slows sales in other retail sectors, Family Dollar's everyday low pricing policy keeps sales high. "We're basically a store that meets the recurring, everyday needs of the community we're going into," explains a Family Dollar vice president. "We sell things people need on an ongoing basis. We're not recession-proof. But we are recession-resistant."

claim, too, that certain types of customers are more attracted by odd prices than by even ones. Research has found a higher-than-expected demand associated with prices ending in 9 in print advertisements.[18] Odd prices are far more common today than even prices.

Even prices are often used to give a product an exclusive or upscale image. An even price supposedly will influence a customer to view the product as being a high-quality, premium brand. A shirtmaker, for example, may print on a premium shirt package a suggested retail price of $42.00 instead of $41.95; the even price of the shirt is used to enhance its upscale image.

customary pricing Pricing on the basis of tradition

Customary Pricing. With **customary pricing**, certain goods are priced primarily on the basis of tradition. Recent economic uncertainties have made most prices fluctuate fairly widely, but the classic example of the customary, or traditional, price is the price of a candy bar. For years, a candy bar cost 5 cents. A new candy bar would have had to be something very special to sell for more than a nickel. This price was so sacred that rather than change it, manufacturers increased or decreased the size of the candy bar itself as chocolate prices fluctuated. Today, of course, the nickel candy bar has disappeared. However, most candy bars still sell at a consistent, but obviously higher, price. Thus, customary pricing remains the standard for this market.

prestige pricing Setting prices at an artificially high level to convey prestige or a quality image

Prestige Pricing. With **prestige pricing**, prices are set at an artificially high level to convey prestige or a quality image. Prestige pricing is used especially when buyers associate a higher price with higher quality. Pharmacists report that some consumers complain when a prescription does not cost enough; apparently some consumers associate a drug's price with its potency. Typical product categories in which selected products are prestige priced include perfumes, liquor, jewelry, and cars. Although traditionally appliances have not been prestige priced, upscale appliances have appeared in recent years to capitalize on the willingness of some consumer segments to "trade up" for high-quality products. These consumers do not mind paying extra for a Subzero refrigerator, a Viking commercial range, or a Whirlpool Duet washer and dryer because these products offer high quality as well as a level of prestige. The Whirlpool Duet washer and dryer, for example, are priced at $2,300 per pair—about $1,500 more than conventional washers and dryers—but offer high performance, large loads, gentle cleaning, and energy efficiency.[19] If these producers lowered their prices dramatically, the new prices would be inconsistent with the perceived high-quality images of their products.

◆ Professional Pricing

professional pricing Fees set by people with great skill or experience in a particular field

Professional pricing is used by people who have great skill or experience in a particular field. Professionals often believe their fees (prices) should not relate directly to the time and effort spent in specific cases; rather, a standard fee is charged regardless of the problems involved in performing the job. Some doctors' and lawyers' fees are prime examples, such as $55 for a checkup, $1,500 for an appendectomy, and $399 for a divorce. Other professionals set prices in other ways. Like other marketers, professionals have costs associated with facilities, labor, insurance, equipment, and supplies. Certainly costs are considered when setting professional prices.

The concept of professional pricing carries the idea that professionals have an ethical responsibility not to overcharge customers. In some situations, a seller can charge customers a high price and continue to sell many units of the product. Medicine offers several examples. If a person with diabetes requires one insulin treatment per day to survive, she or he will buy that treatment whether its price is $1 or $10. In fact, the patient surely would purchase the treatment even if the price rose. In these situations, sellers could charge exorbitant fees. Drug companies claim that despite their positions of strength in this regard, they charge ethical prices rather than what the market will bear.

Special-Event Pricing
Roche Bobois creates special events to employ special-event pricing.

◆ Promotional Pricing

As an ingredient in the marketing mix, price is often coordinated with promotion. The two variables are sometimes so closely interrelated that the pricing policy is promotion oriented. Types of promotional pricing include price leaders, special-event pricing, and comparison discounting.

Price Leaders. Sometimes a firm prices a few products below the usual markup, near cost, or below cost, which results in prices known as **price leaders**. This type of pricing is used most often in supermarkets and restaurants to attract customers by giving them especially low prices on a few items. Management hopes that sales of regularly priced products will more than offset the reduced revenues from the price leaders.

Special-Event Pricing. To increase sales volume, many organizations coordinate price with advertising or sales promotions for seasonal or special situations. **Special-event pricing** involves advertised sales or price cutting linked to a holiday, a season, or an event. If the pricing objective is survival, special sales events may be designed to generate the necessary operating capital. Special-event pricing entails

price leader A product priced below the usual markup, near cost, or below cost

special-event pricing Advertised sales or price cutting linked to a holiday, a season, or an event

comparison discounting Setting a price at a specific level and comparing it with a higher price

coordination of production, scheduling, storage, and physical distribution. Whenever a sales lag occurs, special-event pricing is an alternative that marketers should consider.

Comparison Discounting. **Comparison discounting** sets the price of a product at a specific level and simultaneously compares it with a higher price. The higher price may be the product's previous price, the price of a competing brand, the product's price at another retail outlet, or a manufacturer's suggested retail price. Customers may find comparative discounting informative, and it can have a significant impact on their purchases. However, overuse of comparison pricing may reduce customers' internal reference prices, meaning they no longer believe the higher price is the regular or normal price.[20]

Because this pricing strategy has on occasion led to deceptive pricing practices, the Federal Trade Commission has established guidelines for comparison discounting. If the higher price against which the comparison is made is the price formerly charged for the product, the seller must have made the previous price available to customers for a reasonable period of time. If the seller presents the higher price as the one charged by other retailers in the same trade area, it must be able to demonstrate that this claim is true. When the seller presents the higher price as the manufacturer's suggested retail price, the higher price must be similar to the price at which a reasonable proportion of the product was sold. Some manufacturers' suggested retail prices are so high that very few products are actually sold at those prices. In such cases, comparison discounting would be deceptive. An example of deceptive comparison discounting occurred when a major retailer put 93 percent of its power tools on sale, with discounts ranging from 10 to 40 percent. The retailer's frequent price reductions meant the tools sold at sale prices most of the year. Thus, comparisons with regular prices were deemed to be deceptive.

Determination of a Specific Price

A pricing strategy will yield a certain price. However, this price may need refinement to make it consistent with pricing practices in a particular market or industry.

Pricing strategies should help in setting a final price. If they are to do so, marketers must establish pricing objectives, have considerable knowledge about target market customers, and determine demand, price elasticity, costs, and competitive factors. Also, the way pricing is used in the marketing mix will affect the final price.

In the absence of government price controls, pricing remains a flexible and convenient way to adjust the marketing mix. The online brokerage arm of American Express, for example, sets prices on a sliding scale based on how much service support each customer uses. Customers who conduct all their securities trades without going through Amex employees pay lower prices than those who work with the firm's financial advisers to complete trades. As a result, American Express can provide the exact services each customer requires at an appropriate price.[21] In many situations, prices can be adjusted quickly—over a few days or even in minutes. Such flexibility is unique to this component of the marketing mix.

SUMMARY

The six stages in the process of setting prices are (1) developing pricing objectives, (2) assessing the target market's evaluation of price, (3) evaluating competitors' prices, (4) choosing a basis for pricing, (5) selecting a pricing strategy, and (6) determining a specific price.

Setting pricing objectives is critical because pricing objectives form a foundation on which the decisions of subsequent stages are based. Organizations may use numerous pricing objectives, including short-term and long-term ones, and different objectives for different products and market segments. Pricing objectives are overall goals that describe the role of price in a firm's long-range plans. There are several major types of pricing objectives. The most fundamental pricing objective is the organization's survival. Price usually can be easily adjusted to increase sales volume or combat competition to help the organization stay alive. Profit objectives, which are usually stated in terms of sales dollar volume or percentage change, are normally set at a satisfactory level rather than at a level designed to maximize profits. A sales growth objective focuses on increasing the profit base by raising sales volume. Pricing for return on investment (ROI) has a specified profit as its objective. A pricing objective to maintain or increase market share links market position to success. Other types of pricing objectives include cash flow, status quo, and product quality. Assessing the target market's evaluation of price tells the marketer how much emphasis to place on price and may help determine how far above the competition the firm can set its prices. Understanding how important a product is to customers relative to other products, as well as customers' expectations of quality, helps marketers correctly assess the target market's evaluation of price.

A marketer needs to be aware of the prices charged for competing brands. This allows the firm to keep its prices in line with competitors' prices when nonprice competition is used. If a company uses price as a competitive tool, it can price its brand below competing brands.

The three major dimensions on which prices can be based are cost, demand, and competition. When using cost-based pricing, the firm determines price by adding a dollar amount or percentage to the cost of the product. Two common cost-based pricing methods are cost-plus and markup pricing. Demand-based pricing is based on the level of demand for the product. To use this method, a marketer must be able to estimate the amounts of a product buyers will demand at different prices. Demand-based pricing results in a high price when demand for a product is strong and a low price when demand is weak. In the case of competition-based pricing, costs and revenues are secondary to competitors' prices.

A pricing strategy is an approach or a course of action designed to achieve pricing and marketing objectives. Pricing strategies help marketers solve the practical problems of establishing prices. The most common pricing strategies are differential pricing, new-product pricing, product-line pricing, psychological pricing, professional pricing, and promotional pricing.

When marketers employ differential pricing, they charge different buyers different prices for the same quality and quantity of products. Negotiated pricing, secondary-market discounting, periodic discounting, and random discounting are forms of differential pricing. With negotiated pricing, the final price is established through bargaining between seller and customer.

Secondary-market pricing involves setting one price for the primary target market and a different price for another market; often the price charged in the secondary market is lower. Marketers employ periodic discounting when they temporarily lower their prices on a patterned or systematic basis; the reason for the reduction may be a seasonal change, a model-year change, or a holiday. Random discounting occurs on an unsystematic basis.

Two strategies used in new-product pricing are price skimming and penetration pricing. With price skimming, the organization charges the highest price that buyers who most desire the product will pay. A penetration price is a low price designed to penetrate a market and gain a significant market share quickly.

Product-line pricing establishes and adjusts the prices of multiple products within a product line. This strategy includes captive pricing, in which the marketer prices the basic product in a product line low and prices of related items higher; premium pricing, in which prices on higher-quality or more versatile products are set higher than those on other models in the product line; bait pricing, in which the marketer tries to attract customers by pricing an item in the product line low with the intention of selling a higher-priced item in the line; and price lining, in which the organization sets a limited number of prices for selected groups or lines of merchandise. Organizations that employ price lining assume the demand for various groups of products is inelastic.

Psychological pricing attempts to influence customers' perceptions of price to make a product's price more attractive. With reference pricing, marketers price a product at a moderate level and position it next to a more expensive model or brand. Bundle pricing is packaging together two or more complementary products and selling them at a single price. With multiple-unit pricing, two or more identical products are packaged together

and sold at a single price. To reduce or eliminate use of frequent short-term price reductions, some organizations employ everyday low pricing (EDLP), setting a low price for products on a consistent basis. When employing odd-even pricing, marketers try to influence buyers' perceptions of the price or the product by ending the price with certain numbers. Customary pricing is based on traditional prices. With prestige pricing, prices are set at an artificially high level to convey prestige or a quality image.

Professional pricing is used by people who have great skill or experience in a particular field, therefore allowing them to set the price. This concept carries the idea that professionals have an ethical responsibility not to overcharge customers. As an ingredient in the marketing mix, price is often coordinated with promotion. The two variables are sometimes so closely interrelated that the pricing policy is promotion oriented. Promotional pricing includes price leaders, special-event pricing, and comparison discounting.

Prices leaders are products priced below the usual markup, near cost, or below cost. Special-event pricing involves advertised sales or price cutting linked to a holiday, season, or event. Marketers that use a comparison discounting strategy price a product at a specific level and compare it with a higher price.

Once a price is determined by using one or more pricing strategies, it will need to be refined to a final price consistent with the pricing practices in a particular market or industry.

Please visit the student website at **www.prideferrell.com** for ACE Self-Test questions that will help you prepare for exams.

IMPORTANT TERMS

Pricing objectives
Cost-based pricing
Cost-plus pricing
Markup pricing
Demand-based pricing
Competition-based pricing
Differential pricing
Negotiated pricing
Secondary-market pricing
Periodic discounting
Random discounting
Price skimming
Penetration pricing
Product-line pricing
Captive pricing
Premium pricing

Bait pricing
Price lining
Psychological pricing
Reference pricing
Bundle pricing
Multiple-unit pricing
Everyday low prices (EDLP)
Odd-even pricing
Customary pricing
Prestige pricing
Professional pricing
Price leader
Special-event pricing
Comparison discounting

DISCUSSION & REVIEW QUESTIONS

1. Identify the six stages in the process of establishing prices.
2. How does a return on investment pricing objective differ from an objective of increasing market share?
3. Why must marketing objectives and pricing objectives be considered when making pricing decisions?
4. Why should a marketer be aware of competitors' prices?
5. What are the benefits of cost-based pricing?
6. Under what conditions is cost-plus pricing most appropriate?
7. A retailer purchases a can of soup for 24 cents and sells it for 36 cents. Calculate the markup as a percentage of cost and as a percentage of selling price.
8. What is differential pricing? In what ways can it be achieved?

9. For what types of products would price skimming be most appropriate? For what types of products would penetration pricing be more effective?

10. Describe bundle pricing and give three examples using different industries.

11. What are the advantages and disadvantages of using everyday low prices?

12. Why do customers associate price with quality? When should prestige pricing be used?

13. Are price leaders a realistic approach to pricing? Explain your answer.

APPLICATION QUESTIONS

1. Price skimming and penetration pricing are strategies commonly used to set the base price of a new product. Which strategy is more appropriate for the following products? Explain.
   a. Short airline flights between cities in Florida
   b. A DVD player
   c. A backpack or book bag with a lifetime warranty
   d. Season tickets for a newly franchised NBA basketball team

2. Price lining is used to set a limited number of prices for selected lines of merchandise. Visit a few local retail stores to find examples of price lining. For what types of products and stores is this practice most common? For what types of products and stores is price lining not typical or feasible?

3. Professional pricing is used by people who have great skill in a particular field, such as doctors, lawyers, and business consultants. Find examples (advertisements, personal contacts) that reflect a professional-pricing policy. How is the price established? Are there any restrictions on the services performed at that price?

4. Organizations often use multiple pricing objectives. Locate an organization that uses several pricing objectives, and discuss how this approach influences the company's marketing mix decisions. Are some objectives oriented toward the short term and others toward the long term? How does the marketing environment influence these objectives?

Internet Exercise & Resources

T-Mobile

T-Mobile has attempted to position itself as a low-cost cellular phone service provider. A person can purchase a calling plan, a cellular phone, and phone accessories at its website. Visit the T-Mobile website at **www.t-mobile.com**.

1. Determine the various nationwide calling rates available in your city.
2. How many different calling plans are available in the your area?
3. What type of pricing strategy is T-Mobile using on its rate plans in your area?

Visit **www.prideferrell.com** for resources to help you master the material in this chapter, plus materials that will help you expand your marketing knowledge, including Internet exercise updates, ACE self-tests, hotlinks to companies featured in this chapter, and much more.

Video Case 22.1

Pricing for New Balance

William Riley founded New Balance Arch Company in Boston during the early twentieth century. Riley, an English immigrant, made arch supports and prescription footwear for people with problem feet, and was committed to helping people. His daughter and son-in-law took over the business in the 1950s and spearheaded the development of the company's first performance running shoe in 1961. Since then, New Balance has developed a reputation for quality manufacturing, superior fit, and technological innovation in athletic shoes. These are values the current owners of the company, Jim and Anne Davis, strive to maintain even in a highly competitive industry.

In the United States, New Balance operates facilities in Boston; Lawrence, Massachusetts; and three in

Maine, where the bulk of the manufacturing operations are located. The company employs about 2,000 people, about three-quarters of whom are actually involved in manufacturing. New Balance also maintains wholly owned subsidiaries in Britain, Germany, France, Australia, New Zealand, Mexico, Canada, and South Africa. It has a variety of licensees and distributorships around the globe, including Latin America, the Asia-Pacific Basin, India, and the Eastern European region, which has been merged into the European region. Like many of its competitors, New Balance has manufacturing facilities in China and Taiwan. Unlike its competitors, the company also manufactures shoes in Vietnam, but uses Vietnam solely to supply European and other marketplaces rather than the United States.

New Balance's goal is to create and market performance-oriented products that live up to their reputation and create satisfied customers. When customers buy New Balance shoes from a store, they will judge the company's products based on whether the shoes provide proper support and are appropriate for the intended activity. Indeed, at New Balance, developing a new product begins with customer needs in a particular category—for instance, running. Key decisions are made: For what type of runner will the shoe be designed? How many miles do they run? What is the runner's body makeup? A product segment, such as running shoes, will contain a spectrum of products in a range of prices, from entry level to high performance.

Although costs and prices are not the key factors in marketing athletic shoes, they are very important. At New Balance, pricing starts at the very beginning of the product development process. In the first stage of development, a separate firm is hired to prepare a marketing brief, which gives the company some information about the target customer, what special features the shoe design should include, and the target price margin to yield adequate profits.

From the beginning, the design, development, and marketing teams consider costs a part of the marketing strategy. They look at material costs, labor costs, and overhead costs, as well as any special treatments the shoe design may include, such as specially molded pieces, labels, or embroidery. This information is used to create a rough cost estimate that will be a major factor in the retail price.

Material costs are a key factor. Upscale high-performance products may contain more expensive materials and technology, and thus sell for higher prices. Lower-end products may employ less technology and use different materials that perform at a different level. This permits products at price points to serve various market segments for running shoes.

Competitors' prices are also an important part of New Balance's pricing strategy. When New Balance develops an $80 cushioning shoe, it examines $80 cushioning shoes from competitors, comparing features as well as appearance and color. New Balance often purchases competing shoes to get an idea of what is on the market and how its product stacks up to the competition. The company constantly strives to improve its products and make them stand out against the competition.

At this point, New Balance contracts with the manufacturer to make a prototype, which gives a more realistic estimate of material costs, labor costs, and the costs of any extra work needed in actually making the product. Based on these actual costs, adjustments are made to materials, manufacturing, and shoe details to meet cost standards and requirements.

Jim Sciabarrasi, Corporate Manager of Sourcing, Purchasing, and Logistics, helped develop New Balance's costing and pricing system. When Sciabarrasi joined the company, no such process was in place. One team of people would set the projected cost and another team would take charge of negotiating with the manufacturer to get that particular price. This created frustrating situations for employees. Sciabarrasi's new integrated system of product costing and development ensures that real value is created for each product.

New Balance is a brand that focuses on fit and performance for both consumers and resellers. Integrity is a core value and creates a sense of honesty and genuineness in buyer-seller relationships. The company extends its view of integrity into all marketing and advertising decisions. For example, because New Balance is "about" the value, performance, and sincerity of its products, it avoids celebrity endorsers. The company believes a customer will choose its products not because they have been endorsed by the athletic star of the week or represent a fashion statement but because they are the right shoe for that customer. However, the company has benefited from the celebrity status of some of its more famous customers, including Willie Nelson and former president Bill Clinton.[22]

QUESTIONS FOR DISCUSSION

1. What pricing objectives does New Balance seem to employ?
2. What type of pricing strategy is New Balance using?
3. What other pricing tools does New Balance employ?

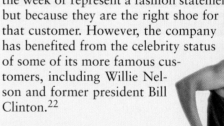

Case 22.2

General Motors Tries to Reduce Reliance on Rebates

Automakers have been using incentives to attract customers since 1912, when Henry Ford gave rebate checks to Model T buyers. The idea of incentives has remained popular throughout the years, although the offers themselves have varied, ranging from lease promotions and special financing offers to cash rebates. Incentives are a form of random discounting, temporary reductions of prices on an unsystematic basis; however, they have become almost ubiquitous in promoting sales of automobiles. Although incentives are credited with increasing sales and market share, automakers are now being criticized for abusing incentives, leading to decreased profits and poor brand image. The growing reliance on sales, rebates, and zero percent financing has made it difficult to wean consumers off incentives.

General Motors has led the auto industry in incentives since the period following the September 11, 2001, attacks, when the company launched its "Keep America Rolling" zero percent financing campaign. GM executives credit the incentive program with providing many benefits for the company, including preserving market share and keeping GM's factories running. The latter is important because GM's labor costs are relatively fixed due to its contract with the United Auto Workers union, which requires the firm to pay unemployment benefits equal to 95 percent of normal pay to any laid-off workers. Thus, even if the company cut production, its labor cost would remain the same. GM has therefore chosen to use incentives to equalize sales and production rather than cutting production to meet demand. To understand General Motors' fear of reducing incentives, it is constructive to know that every percentage point of market share translates into millions of dollars in profit, according to Morgan Stanley.

However, GM has indicated that over the next two years, it would like to reduce as much as half of the $4,300 per vehicle that it spent last year on rebates. With many new products being launched over the next few years, GM wants to enhance consumers' desire for the product rather than for a discount. For example, the company launched the Chevrolet Cobalt in the fall of 2004 with rebates no larger than $1,500, compared to the $4,000 rebate offered on the Chevrolet Cavalier that the Cobalt replaced.

The problem with incentives is that they erode profit. For example, in 2003 General Motors earned $1.1 billion on global auto sales, less than half of the $2.6 billion it netted in 2002. Rebates may also give the impression of operating in a distressed atmosphere. There is little doubt that large rebates may suggest to consumers that a product's quality and reliability are not up to par. An important element of product quality is the amount of quality a product possesses. Because this concept is relative, a company that offers deep discounts

may give consumers the impression of less quality. On the other hand, it would be desirable to use product design, styling, or other product features that would enhance and maintain a high-quality concept of the firm's product relative to competitive brands. Rebates and the cost of long-term loans can also undermine the resale value of an automaker's vehicles.

Alternatives to direct consumer incentives include discounting to dealers, who can then make decisions about how much of the discounts to pass along to consumers. Another approach is nonprice competition, using promotions that encourage consumers to visit a dealership. In 2004, for example, General Motors gave away 1,000 new cars and trucks worth $25 million to prospective buyers who visited a GM dealership. General Motors expected the giveaway to attract 40 to 50 percent more showroom traffic during months that are historically slow. Another approach is to build more niche cars that generate greater profits. Some "must-have" models include the Chevy SSR Pickup, Pontiac GTO, and Cadillac XLR. Volkswagen is also applying this approach. Volkswagen CEO Bernd Pischetsrieder says he would rather let U.S. sales fall substantially, preserving brand image and resale value, than to use incentives.

An important question for all automobile companies is how to go about reducing incentives. Because incentive-driven sales persuaded many consumers to replace their cars during the economic downturn at the beginning of the century, little pent-up demand remains for new vehicles. Worse, consumers seem to have become addicted to incentives and unwilling to make a purchase without them. Volkswagen plans to "stick to its guns" and attempt to break consumers of the incentive habit. The company's new Touareg SUV is a good example of a unique, high-quality offering that can be sold at sticker price with few deals. Time will tell whether VW can maintain this approach when it introduces the new Jettas and Passats in 2005.

While GM is working to reduce incentives, it is redesigning 90 percent of its passenger car lineup over the next three years in the hope of being able to compete on nonprice attributes. The value of marketing in this industry is illustrated by the effectiveness of price incentives to manage demand. The challenge is to find other promotional methods that can effectively communicate the benefits and value of automakers' products.[23]

QUESTIONS FOR DISCUSSION

1. What pricing objectives does General Motors seem to be using? How do these objectives help dictate the firm's use of periodic discounting and incentives?
2. What type of pricing strategy is GM using?
3. What risks does Volkswagen face in going against the industry by avoiding price incentives?

Strategic Case 8

Napster 2.0: The Cat Is Back

Napster was the brainchild of Shawn Fanning, a 17-year-old freshman at Northeastern University who left college to develop a technology to trade music over the Internet. The technology was commercialized through Napster, which allowed computer users to share high-quality digital recordings (MP3s) of music via the Internet using its proprietary MusicShare software. Napster didn't actually store the recordings on its own computers; rather, it provided an index of all the songs available on the computers of members who were logged on to the service. In other words, Napster functioned as a sort of clearinghouse where members could search by artist or song title, identify MP3s of interest, and download their choices from other members' hard drives. Napster quickly became one of the most popular sites on the Internet, claiming some 15 million users in little more than a year. Indeed, so many college students were downloading songs from Napster that many universities were forced to block the site from their systems to regain bandwidth.

From the beginning, Napster's service was as controversial as it was popular. Barely a year after its 1999 launch, Napster was sued by the Recording Industry Association of America (RIAA), which represents major recording companies such as Universal Music, BMG, Sony Music, Warner Music Group, and EMI. The RIAA claimed that Napster's service violated copyright laws by allowing users to swap music recordings for free. The RIAA also sought an injunction to stop the downloading of copyrighted songs, as well as damages for lost revenue. The RIAA argued that song swapping via Napster and similar firms had cost the music industry more than $300 million in lost sales. Metallica, a heavy-metal band, and rap star Dr. Dre filed separate lawsuits accusing Napster of copyright infringement and racketeering. Lars Ulrich, Metallica's drummer, told a Senate committee that he believed Napster users were basically stealing from the band every time they downloaded one of its songs.

The Fall of Napster   On July 26, 2000, U.S. District Judge Marilyn Patel granted the RIAA's request for an injunction and ordered Napster to stop making copyrighted recordings available for download. This order would have effectively destroyed the company by pulling the plug on its most popular feature. However, on July 28, just nine hours before Napster would have shut down, the Ninth Circuit Court of Appeals stayed that order, granting Napster a last-minute reprieve until the lawsuits could be tried in court. Despite the brief reprieve, Napster was ultimately found guilty of direct copyright infringement of RIAA members' musical recordings, and that ruling was upheld on appeal on February 12, 2001. The District Court of Appeals refuted all of Napster's defense tactics and ordered the company to stop allowing its millions of users to download and share copyrighted material without properly compensating the owners of that material.

In late September 2001, Napster agreed to pay $26 million for past distribution of unauthorized music and made a proposal that would let songwriters and musicians distribute their music on Napster for a fee. This settlement would have covered as many as 700,000 songs, but Napster still needed an agreement before it could legally distribute the music. However, after several failed attempts to reach a suitable compromise with the recording industry and with litigation expenses mounting, the company entered Chapter 11 bankruptcy proceedings in June 2002 as a last-gasp effort to reach a deal with Bertelsmann AG, Napster's strategic partner.

The final nail in the coffin for Napster came on September 3, 2002, when a Delaware bankruptcy judge blocked the sale of the company to Bertelsmann, ruling that negotiations with the German media company had not been made at arm's length and in good faith. Bertelsmann had agreed to pay creditors $8 million for Napster's assets. According to the bankruptcy petition, the company had assets of $7.9 million and debts of $101 million as of April 30, 2002. Shortly after the judge's ruling, Napster laid off nearly all of its 42-person staff and proceeded to convert its Chapter 11 reorganization into a Chapter 7 liquidation. At the time, Napster appeared to be doomed.

The Digital Music Revolution   The United States is the largest music market in the world, accounting for 40 percent of all global sales and almost 33 percent of all unit sales ($40 billion). In 2002, the average U.S. consumer spent $46.50 on music albums. However, the future of traditional music sales appears bleak. The RIAA predicted that U.S. music sales would decline by 6 percent in 2003 and total album sales by 7 percent. According to the RIAA, the number of CD shipments declined significantly, about 9 percent, from 2001 to 2002. The sale of DVDs increased, but only by a slight 4 percent.

One major reason for the decline in music sales is changing consumer preferences. Although consumers value CDs because they provide "long-term" entertainment, an RIAA survey found that many believe CDs cost too much. The RIAA's research indicates that a significant number of consumers do not fully understand the variables that play a role in the overall pricing of a CD. Consumers counter that they resent paying $13 to $18 for a CD to get only one or two popular songs. Thus, many consumers find downloading music an appealing alternative to high CD prices.

With Napster out of the picture and the RIAA bringing lawsuits against individual downloaders of music online, other online music providers were rapidly getting their houses in order. One of the first was AOL, which launched MusicNet in February 2003 with 20 music streams and 20 downloads for $3.95 per month. Apple's iTunes, which debuted in April 2003, was by far the heaviest hitter to join the foray into online music. Other services were available as well:

- Rhapsody (**www.listen.com**), a division of Real-Networks, whose RealPlayer is ubiquitous on millions of PCs. Rhapsody offers 400,000 songs for download.

- MusicMatch (**www.musicmatch.com**), a major partner with Dell, which preinstalls MusicMatch Jukebox on all new PCs. MusicMatch offers 200,000 songs for download.

- BuyMusic.com (**www.buymusic.com**), a subsidiary of Buy.com that offers 315,000 songs for download.

- walmart.com, which entered the online music business. Naturally, the discount chain would undercut the competition with 88-cents-per-song downloads.

- Amazon.com has top CDs for as low as $12.99, breakthrough artists for less, and some free downloads.

Thus, it has become clear to both sides of the music-downloading controversy that online music distribution is here to stay. It was only a matter of time until a compromise could be reached among the recording studios, the artists, and the various online music providers.

Some thorny issues remained to be resolved, however. First, because even pay-for-download services are not immune to piracy, the recording industry wanted to develop technology that would prevent downloaders from swapping files on their own even after making a legitimate purchase. To protect the artists, the industry also wanted to limit the number of times a song can be downloaded and copied. Suggestions included using the MD5 hash—a digital fingerprint—or using software that monitors sound patterns to detect illegal copies. A second issue was the development of a revenue model. Should MP3 files be available individually, as one file in a complete album, or both? Should pricing be based on a per-download basis or on an unlimited basis for a monthly subscription fee?

The Rise of Napster 2.0   In late 2002, Napster's name and assets were purchased by Roxio, a company well known for its "CD-burning" software. After much fanfare and excitement, Roxio revived Napster as Napster 2.0 on October 29, 2003. The new fee-based service offers 500,000 songs for download—giving it the largest online catalog currently available in the industry—at 99 cents per track or $9.95 per album. Users can also pay $9.95 per month for unlimited music streaming to their desktops. Perhaps most important, Napster's relaunch came with the blessing of five major record labels. Napster has also developed a number of partnerships with Microsoft, Gateway, Yahoo!, and Samsung that gave it an advantage during its relaunch. Napster's partnership with Samsung led to the creation of the Samsung YP-910GS, a 20-gigabyte digital audio player that is fully integrated with Napster 2.0. The device allows users to transfer songs from Napster directly to the unit via a USB connection. The player also boasts an integrated FM transmitter that allows users to broadcast MP3 playback through their home or car stereo systems. In addition, Napster subscribers receive the industry's leading CD creation software package, developed by parent company Roxio, as a bonus.

Although the reborn Napster currently offers the largest catalog of songs, it continues to face competition from a growing number of firms, particularly MusicNet and iTunes. MusicNet is marketed by AOL, the world's largest Internet service provider (ISP) with more than 35 million users. In addition to its massive potential user base, AOL's diverse business operations enable the company to offer music at a lower price than Napster. AOL can afford to take a volume-based approach to pricing rather than a profit-based approach. Furthermore, because MusicNet is also heavily supported by advertisers and sponsors, it can offer many different promotional packages to bolster sales.

Despite MusicNet's potential size advantages, Apple's iTunes is likely to pose the biggest threat to

Napster. iTunes currently offers more than 400,000 songs and adds thousands more weekly. It also offers a wide selection of audio books. Moreover, the popularity of Apple's iPod MP3 player confers on Apple a distinct advantage: the iPod provides customers with a perfect vehicle to get the music they desire. The iTunes software application works for both Macintosh and Windows operating systems. The service is easy to use and boasts fewer restrictions than MusicNet and other brand competitors. As a result, iTunes has developed a high customer satisfaction rating. Recently Apple partnered with PepsiCo to offer 1,000 songs free of charge to help bolster membership in iTunes.

Other competitors include the thousands of offline and online music record stores that offer CDs and other merchandise. However, given the movement in the industry toward online downloading of music, these competitors may soon become less worrisome. Moreover, there are still websites where music can be downloaded free of charge, albeit illegally. Some potential customers would rather risk getting caught than pay for the music.

As with any technology-based service, new competition is often unseen and swift. With subscribers of peer-to-peer networks, such as Kazaa, being targeted by the Recording Industry Association of America, any or all of these services may move toward a pay-for-play service to avoid being hassled by the RIAA. In addition, competition exists from major retailers such as Wal-Mart and Amazon.com and from traditional music retailers such as Tower Records, Sam Goody, Best Buy, and Circuit City. In addition, some insiders have speculated that Microsoft will launch a service of its own. Given the existing and future competition, it is imperative that Napster make its brand the market leader in a short period of time.

QUESTIONS FOR DISCUSSION

1. What factors seem to have the greatest influence on Napster 2.0's pricing decisions? Explain.
2. What appear to be Napster's primary pricing objectives?
3. Assess the level of price competition in the music industry as a whole and within the online music distribution business specifically.
4. Evaluate Napster's pricing strategy of charging 99 cents per song. Under what circumstances should the company consider changing that strategy?

Careers in Marketing

Changes in the Workplace

Between one-fourth and one-third of the civilian work force in the United States is employed in marketing-related jobs. Although the field offers a multitude of diverse career opportunities, the number of positions in each area varies. For example, millions of workers are employed in many facets of sales, but relatively few people work in public relations and marketing research.

Many nonbusiness organizations now recognize that they perform marketing activities. For that reason, the number of marketing positions in government agencies, hospitals, charitable and religious groups, educational institutions, and similar organizations is increasing. Today's nonprofit organizations are competitive and better managed, with job growth rates often matching those of private-sector firms. Another area ripe with opportunities is the World Wide Web. The federal government makes more sales to consumers online than even Amazon.com. With so many businesses setting up websites, demand will rise for people who have the skills to develop and design marketing strategies for the Web.

Many workers outplaced from large corporations are choosing an entrepreneurial path, creating still more new opportunities for first-time job seekers. Even some individuals with secure managerial positions are leaving corporations and heading to smaller companies, toward greater responsibility and autonomy. The traditional career path used to be graduation from college, then a job with a large corporation, and a climb up the ladder to management. This pattern has changed, however. Today people are more likely to experience a career path of sideways "gigs" rather than sequential steps up a corporate ladder.

Career Choices Are Major Life Choices

Many people think career planning begins with an up-to-date résumé and a job interview.[1] In reality, it begins long before you prepare your résumé. It starts with *you* and what you want to become. In some ways, you have been preparing for a career ever since you started school. Everything you have experienced during your lifetime you can use as a resource to help you define your career goals. Since you will likely spend more time at work than at any other single place during your lifetime, it makes sense to spend that time doing something you enjoy. Unfortunately, some people just work at a *job* because they need money to survive. Other people choose a *career* because of their interests and talents or a commitment to a particular profession. Whether you are looking for a job or a career, you should examine your priorities.

Personal Factors Influencing Career Choices

Before choosing a career, you need to consider what motivates you and what skills you can offer an employer. The following questions may help you define what you consider important in life:

1. *What types of activities do you enjoy?* Although most people know what they enjoy in a general way, a number of interest inventories exist. By helping you determine specific interests and activities, these inventories can help you land a job that will lead to a satisfying career. In some cases, it may be sufficient just to list the activities you enjoy, along with those you dislike. Watch for patterns that may influence your career choices.

2. *What do you do best?* All jobs and all careers require employees to be able to "do something." It is extremely important to assess what you do best. Be honest with yourself about your ability to succeed in a specific job. It may help to make a list of your strongest job-related skills. Also, try looking at your skills from an employer's perspective: What can you do that an employer would be willing to pay for?

3. *What kind of education will you need?* The amount of education you need is determined by the type of career you choose. In some careers, it is impossible to get an entry-level position without at least a college degree. Other careers may also require technical or hands-on skills. Generally, additional education increases your potential earning power.

4. *Where do you want to live?* Initially some college graduates will want to move to a different part of the country before entering the job market, whereas others may prefer to reside close to home, friends, and relatives. In reality, successful job applicants must be willing to go where the jobs are. The location of an entry-level job may be influenced by the type of marketing career selected. For example, some of the largest advertising agencies are in New York, Chicago, and Los Angeles. Likewise, large marketing research organizations are based in metropolitan areas. On the other hand, sales positions and retail management jobs are available in medium-size as well as large cities

Job Search Activities

When people begin to search for a job, they often first go online or turn to the classified ads in their local newspaper. Those ads are an important source of information about jobs in a particular area, but they are only one source. Many other sources can lead to employment and a satisfying career. Because there is a wealth of information about career planning, you should be selective in both the type and the amount of information you use to guide your job search.

In recent years the library, a traditional job-hunting tool, has been joined by the Internet. Both the library and the Internet are sources of everything from classified newspaper ads and government job listings to detailed information on individual companies and industries. You can use either resource to research an area of employment or a particular company that interests you. In addition, the Internet allows you to check electronic bulletin boards for current job information, exchange ideas with other job seekers through online discussion groups or e-mail, and get career advice from professional counselors. You can also create your own web page to inform prospective employers about your qualifications. You may even have a job interview online. Many companies use their websites to post job openings, accept applications, and interview candidates.

As you start your job search, you may find the following websites helpful. (Addresses of additional career-related websites can be accessed through the Student Career Center at **www.prideferrell.com**.)

America's Job Bank: **www.ajb.dni.us**

This massive site contains information on nearly 250,000 jobs. Listings come from 1,800 state employment offices around the country and represent every line of work, from professional and technical to blue-collar, and from entry level on up.

CareerBuild.com: **www.careerbuilder.com**

This site is one of the largest on the Internet, with more than 900,000 jobs to view. The site allows a job seeker to find jobs, post résumés, get advice and career resources, and obtain information on career fairs.

Hoover's Online: **www.hoovers.com**

Hoover's offers a variety of job search tools, including information on potential employers and links to sites that post job openings.

The Monster Board: **www.monster.com**

The Monster Board carries hundreds of job listings and offers links to related sites, such as company homepages and sites with information about job fairs.

Federal jobs: **www.fedworld.gov/jobs/jobsearch.html**

If you are interested in working for a government agency, this site lists positions all across the country. You can limit your search to specific states or do a general cross-country search for job openings.

Other web addresses for job seekers include:

www.careers-in-marketing.com

www.marketingjobs.com

www.starthere.com/jobs

www.careermag.com

www.salary.com

In addition to the library and the Internet, the following sources can be of great help when trying to find the "perfect job":

1. *Campus placement offices.* Colleges and universities have placement offices staffed by trained personnel specialists. In most cases, these offices serve as clearinghouses for career information. The staff may also be able to guide you in creating a résumé and preparing for a job interview.

2. *Professional sources and networks.* A network is a group of people—friends, relatives, and professionals—who are in a position to exchange information, including information about job openings. According to many job applicants, networking is one of the best sources of career information and job leads. Start with as many people as you can think of to establish your network. (The Internet can be very useful in this regard.) Contact these people and ask specific questions about job opportunities they are aware of. Also, ask each individual to introduce or refer you to someone else who may be able to help you in your job search.

3. *Private employment agencies.* Private employment agencies charge a fee for helping people find jobs. Typical fees can be as high as 15 to 20 percent of an employee's first-year salary. The fee may be paid by the employer or the employee. Like campus placement offices, private employment agencies provide career counseling, help create résumés, and provide preparation for job interviews. Before you use a private employment agency, be sure you understand the terms of any contract or agreement you sign. Above all, make sure you know who is responsible for paying the agency's fee.

4. *State employment agencies.* The local office of your state employment agency is a valuable source of information about job openings in your immediate area. Some job applicants are reluctant to use state agencies because most jobs available through them are for semiskilled or unskilled workers. From a practical standpoint, though, it can't hurt to consult state employment agencies. They will have information about some professional and managerial positions available in your area, and you will not be charged a fee if you obtain a job through one of these agencies.

Many graduates want a job immediately and are discouraged at the thought that an occupational search can take months. But people seeking entry-level jobs should expect their job search to take considerable time. Of course, the state of the economy and whether or not employers are hiring can shorten or extend a job search.

During a job search, you should use the same work habits that effective employees use on the job. Resist the temptation to "take the day off" from job hunting. Instead, make a master list of the activities you want to accomplish each day. If necessary, force yourself to make contacts, do job research, or schedule interviews that might lead to job opportunities. (In fact, many job applicants look at the job hunt as their actual job and "work" full time at it until they find the job they want.) Above all, realize that an occupational search requires patience and perseverance. According to many successful applicants, perseverance may be the job hunter's most valuable trait.

Planning and Preparation

The key to landing the job you want is planning and preparation—and planning begins with goals. In particular, it is important to determine your *personal* goals, decide on the role your career will play in reaching those goals, and then develop your *career* goals. Once you know where you are going, you can devise a feasible plan for getting there.

The time to begin planning is as early as possible. You must, of course, satisfy the educational requirements for the occupational area you desire. Early planning will give you the opportunity to do so. However, some of the people who will compete with you for the better jobs will also be fully prepared. Can you do more? Company recruiters say the following factors give job candidates a definite advantage:

- *Work experience.* You can get valuable work experience in cooperative work/school programs, during summer vacations, or in part-time jobs during the school year. Experience in your chosen occupational area carries the most weight, but even unrelated work experience is useful.

- *The ability to communicate well.* Verbal and written communication skills are increasingly important in all aspects of business. Yours will be tested in your letters to recruiters, in your résumé, and in interviews. You will use these same communication skills throughout your career.

- *Clear and realistic job and career goals.* Recruiters feel most comfortable with candidates who know where they are headed and why they are applying for a specific job.

Again, starting early will allow you to establish well-defined goals, sharpen your communication skills (through elective courses, if necessary), and obtain solid work experience. To develop your own personal career plan, go to the **www.pride ferrell.com** student site and access the Student Career Center. There you will find personal career plan worksheets.

The Résumé

An effective résumé is one of the keys to being considered for a good job. Because your résumé states your qualifications, experiences, education, and career goals, a potential employer can use it to assess your compatibility with the job requirements. The résumé should be accurate and current.

In preparing a résumé, it helps to think of it as an advertisement. Envision yourself as a product and the company, particularly the person or persons doing the hiring, as your customer. To interest the customer in buying the product—hiring you—your résumé must communicate information about your qualities and indicate how you can satisfy the customer's needs—that is, how you can help the company achieve its objectives. The information in the résumé should persuade the organization to take a closer look at you by calling you in for an interview.

To be effective, the résumé should be targeted at a specific position, as Figure A.1 shows. This document is only one example of an acceptable résumé. The job target section is specific and leads directly to the applicant's qualifications for the job. The qualifications section details capabilities—what the applicant can do—and also shows that the applicant has an understanding of the job's requirements. Skills and strengths that relate to the specific job should be emphasized. The achievement section ("Experiences" in Figure A.1) indicates success at accomplishing tasks or goals on the job and at school. The work experience section in Figure A.1 includes an unusual listing, which might pique the interviewer's interest: "helped operate relative's blueberry farm in Michigan for three summers." It tends to inspire rather than satisfy curiosity, thus inviting further inquiry.

Another type of résumé is the chronological résumé, which lists work experience and educational history in order by date. This type of résumé is useful for those just entering the job market because it helps highlight education and work experience.

LORRAINE MILLER
2212 WEST WILLOW
PHOENIX, AZ 12345
(416) 862-9169

EDUCATION: B.A. Arizona State University, 2004, Marketing, achieved a 3.4 on a 4.0 scale throughout college

POSITION DESIRED: Product manager with an international firm providing future career development at the executive level

QUALIFICATIONS:

- Communicates well with individuals to achieve a common goal
- Handles tasks efficiently and in a timely manner
- Understands advertising sales, management, marketing research, packaging, pricing, distribution, and warehousing
- Coordinates many activities at one time
- Receives and carries out assigned tasks or directives
- Writes complete status or research reports

EXPERIENCES:

- Assistant Editor of college paper
- Treasurer of the American Marketing Association (student chapter)
- Internship with 3-Cs Advertising, Berkeley, CA
- Student Assistantship with Dr. Steve Green, Professor of Marketing, Arizona State University
- Solo cross-Canada canoe trek, summer 2003

WORK RECORD:

2003–Present	Blythe and Co., Inc. —Junior Advertising Account Executive	
2001–2002	Student Assistant for Dr. Steve Green —Research Assistant	
2000–2001	The Men —Retail sales and consumer relations	
1998–2000	Farmer —Helped operate relative's blueberry farm in Michigan for three summers	

Figure A.1 A Résumé Targeted at a Specific Position

In some cases, education is more important than unrelated work experience because it indicates the career direction you desire despite the work experience you have acquired thus far.

Common suggestions for improving résumés include deleting useless or outdated information, improving organization, using professional printing and typing, listing duties (not accomplishments), maintaining grammatical perfection, and avoiding an overly elaborate or fancy format.[2] Keep in mind that the person who will look at your résumé may have to sift through hundreds in the course of the day in addition to handling other duties. Consequently it is important to keep your résumé short (one page is best, never more than two), concise, and neat. Moreover, you want your résumé to be distinctive so it will stand out from all the others.

In addition to having the proper format and content, a résumé should be easy to read. It is best to use only one or two kinds of type and plain, white paper. When sending a résumé to a large company, several copies may be made and distributed. Textured, gray, or colored paper may make a good impression on the first person who sees the résumé, but it will not reproduce well for the others, who will see only a poor copy. You should also proofread your résumé with care. Typos and misspellings will grab attention—the wrong kind.

Along with the résumé itself, always submit a cover letter. In the letter, you can include somewhat more information than in your résumé and convey a message that expresses your interest and enthusiasm about the organization and the job.

The Job Interview

In essence, your résumé and cover letter are an introduction. The deciding factor in the hiring process is the interview (or several interviews) with representatives of the firm. It is through the interview that the firm gets to know you and your qualifications. At the same time, the interview gives you a chance to learn about the firm.

Here again, preparation is the key to success. Research the firm before your first interview. Learn all you can about its products, its subsidiaries, the markets in which it operates, its history, the locations of its facilities, and so on. If possible, obtain and read the firm's most recent annual report. Be prepared to ask questions about the firm and the opportunities it offers. Interviewers welcome such questions. They expect you to be interested enough to spend some time thinking about your potential relationship with their organization.

Also, prepare to respond to questions the interviewer may ask. Table A.1 lists typical interview questions that job applicants often find difficult to answer. But don't expect interviewers to stick to the list given in the table or to the items appearing in your résumé. They will be interested in anything that helps them decide what kind of person and worker you are.

Make sure you are on time for your interview and are dressed and groomed in a businesslike manner. Interviewers take note of punctuality and appearance just as they do of other personal qualities. Bring a copy of your résumé, even if you already sent one to the firm. You may also want to bring a copy of your course transcript and letters of recommendation. If you plan to furnish interviewers with the names and addresses of references rather than with letters of recommendation, make sure you have your references' permission to do so.

Consider the interview itself as a two-way conversation rather than a question-and-answer session. Volunteer any information that is relevant to the interviewer's questions. If an important point is skipped in the discussion, don't hesitate to bring it up. Be yourself, but emphasize your strengths. Good eye contact and posture are also important; they should come naturally if you take an active part in the interview. At the conclusion of the interview, thank the recruiter for taking the time to see you.

In most cases, the first interview is used to *screen* applicants, that is, choose those who are best qualified. These applicants are then given a second interview and perhaps a third, usually with one or more department heads. If the job requires relocation to a different area, applicants may be invited there for these later interviews.

Table A.1	**Interview Questions Job Applicants Often Find Difficult to Answer**

1. Tell me about yourself.
2. What do you know about our organization?
3. What can you do for us? Why should we hire you?
4. What qualifications do you have that make you feel you will be successful in your field?
5. What have you learned from the jobs you've held?
6. If you could write your own ticket, what would be your ideal job?
7. What are your special skills, and where did you acquire them?
8. Have you had any special accomplishments in your lifetime that you are particularly proud of?
9. Why did you leave your most recent job?
10. How do you spend your spare time? What are your hobbies?
11. What are your strengths and weaknesses?
12. Discuss five major accomplishments.
13. What kind of boss would you like? Why?
14. If you could spend a day with someone you've known or know of, who would it be?
15. What personality characteristics seem to rub you the wrong way?
16. How do you show your anger? What type of things make you angry?
17. With what type of person do you spend the majority of your time?

Source: Adapted from The *Ultimate Job Hunter's Guidebook,* 4th ed., by Susan D. Greene and Melanie C. L. Martel. Copyright © 2004 by Houghton Mifflin Company.

After the interviewing process is complete, applicants are told when to expect a hiring decision.

After the Interview

Attention to common courtesy is important as a follow-up to your interview. You should send a brief note of thanks to the interviewer and give it as much care as you did your résumé and cover letter. A short, typewritten letter is preferred to a handwritten note or card, or an e-mail. Avoid not only typos but also overconfident statements such as "I look forward to helping you make Universal Industries successful over the next decade." Even in the thank-you letter, it is important to show team spirit and professionalism, as well as convey proper enthusiasm. Everything you say and do reflects on you as a candidate.

After the Hire

Clearly, performing well in a job has always been a crucial factor in keeping a position. In a tight economy and job market, however, a person's attitude, as well as his or her performance, counts greatly. People in their first jobs can commit costly political blunders by being insensitive to their environments. Politics in the business world includes how you react to your boss, how you react to your coworkers, and your general demeanor. Here are a few rules to live by:

1. *Don't bypass your boss.* One major blunder an employee can make is to go over the boss's head to resolve a problem. This is especially hazardous in a bureaucratic organization. You should become aware of the generally accepted chain of command and, when problems occur, follow that protocol, beginning with your immediate superior. No boss likes to look incompetent, and making him or her appear so is sure to hamper or even crush your budding career. However, there may be exceptions to this rule in

emergency situations. It is wise to discuss with your supervisor what to do in an emergency, before an emergency occurs.[3]

2. *Don't criticize your boss.* Adhering to the old adage "praise in public and criticize in private" will keep you out of the line of retaliatory fire. A more sensible and productive alternative is to present the critical commentary to your boss in a diplomatic way during a private session.

3. *Don't show disloyalty.* If dissatisfied with the position, a new employee may start a fresh job search, within or outside the organization. However, it is not advisable to begin a publicized search within the company for another position unless you have held your current job for some time. Careful attention to the political climate in the organization should help you determine how soon to start a new job campaign and how public to make it. In any case, it is not a good idea to publicize that you are looking outside the company for a new position.

4. *Don't be a naysayer.* Employees are expected to become part of the organizational team and to work together with others. Behaviors to avoid, especially if you are a new employee, include being critical of others; refusing to support others' projects; always playing devil's advocate; refusing to help others when a crisis occurs; and complaining all the time, even about such matters as the poor quality of the food in the cafeteria, the crowded parking lot, or the temperature in the office.

5. *Learn to correct mistakes appropriately.* No one likes to admit having made a mistake, but one of the most important political skills you can acquire is minimizing the impact of a blunder. It is usually advantageous to correct the damage as soon as possible to avoid further problems. Some suggestions: be the first to break the bad news to your boss; avoid being defensive; stay poised and don't panic; and have solutions ready for fixing the blunder.[4]

Types of Marketing Careers

In considering marketing as a career, the first step is to evaluate broad categories of career opportunities in the areas of marketing research, sales, industrial buying, public relations, distribution management, product management, advertising, retail management, and direct marketing. Keep in mind that the categories described here are not all-inclusive and that each encompasses hundreds of marketing jobs.

Marketing Research

Clearly, marketing research and information systems are vital aspects of marketing decision making. Marketing researchers survey customers to determine their habits, preferences, and aspirations. The information about buyers and environmental forces that research and information systems provide improves a marketer's ability to understand the dynamics of the marketplace and therefore make effective decisions.

Marketing research firms are usually employed by a client organization such as a provider of goods or services, a nonbusiness organization, a research consulting firm, or an advertising agency. The activities performed include concept testing, product testing, package testing, advertising testing, test market research, and new-product research.

Marketing researchers gather and analyze data relating to specific problems. A researcher may be involved in one or several stages of research depending on the size of the project, the organization of the research unit,

Snapshot

What jobs pay today
Median salaries for entry-level positions in the U.S.:

PAY TO:	
Customer Service Rep	$27,374
Sales Assistant	$33,638
Advertising Assistant	$33,643
Public Relations Assistant	$37,515
Assistant Merchandise Buyer	$38,571

Source: Data from http://salary.monster.com. Accessed May 13, 2004.

and the researcher's experience. Marketing research trainees in large organizations usually perform a considerable amount of clerical work, such as compiling secondary data from the firm's accounting and sales records and from periodicals, government publications, syndicated data services, the Internet, and unpublished sources. A junior analyst may edit and code questionnaires or tabulate survey results. Trainees may also participate in gathering primary data through mail and telephone surveys, personal interviews, and observation. As a marketing researcher gains experience, he or she may become involved in defining problems and developing research questions; designing research procedures; and analyzing, interpreting, and reporting findings. Exceptional personnel may assume responsibility for entire research projects.

Although most employers consider a bachelor's degree sufficient qualification for a marketing research trainee, many specialized positions require a graduate degree in business administration, statistics, or other related fields. Today trainees are more likely to have a marketing or statistics degree than a liberal arts degree. Courses in statistics, information technology, psychology, sociology, communications, economics, and technical writing are valuable preparation for a career in marketing research.

The Bureau of Labor Statistics indicates that marketing research provides abundant employment opportunities, especially for applicants with graduate training in marketing research, statistics, economics, and the social sciences. Generally, the value of information gathered by marketing information and research systems rises as competition increases, thus expanding opportunities for prospective marketing research personnel.

The major career paths in marketing research are with independent marketing research agencies/data suppliers and marketing research departments in advertising agencies and other businesses. In a company in which marketing research plays a key role, the researcher is often a member of the marketing strategy team. Surveying or interviewing customers is the heart of the marketing research firm's activities. A statistician selects the sample to be surveyed, analysts design the questionnaire and synthesize the gathered data into a final report, data processors tabulate the data, and the research director controls and coordinates all these activities so each project is completed to the client's satisfaction.

Salaries in marketing research depend on the type, size, and location of the firm, as well as the nature of the position. Overall, salaries of marketing researchers have increased slightly during the last few years. However, the specific position within the marketing research field determines the degree of fluctuation.[5] Generally, starting salaries are somewhat higher and promotions somewhat slower than in other occupations requiring similar training. The typical salary for a market analyst is $24,000 to $50,000; a marketing research director can earn $75,000 to $200,000.[6]

Sales

Millions of people earn a living through personal selling. Chapter 20 defines personal selling as paid personal communication that attempts to inform customers and persuade them to purchase products in an exchange situation. Although this definition describes the general nature of sales positions, individual selling jobs vary enormously with respect to the types of businesses and products involved, the educational background and skills required, and the specific activities sales personnel perform. Because the work is so varied, it offers numerous career opportunities for people with a wide range of qualifications, interests, and goals. The two types of career opportunities we discuss relate to business-to-business sales.

Sales Positions in Wholesaling. Wholesalers buy products intended for resale, for use in making other products, and for general business operations, and sell them directly to business markets. Wholesalers thus provide services to both retailers and producers. They can help match producers' products to retailers' needs and provide services that save producers time, money, and resources. Some activities a sales representative for a wholesaling firm is likely to perform include planning and negotiating transactions; assisting customers with sales, advertising, sales promotion, and publicity; facilitating transportation and storage; providing customers with inventory control and data processing assistance; establishing prices; and giving customers technical, managerial, and merchandising assistance.

The background needed by wholesale personnel depends on the nature of the product handled. A sales representative for a drug wholesaler, for example, needs extensive technical training and product knowledge, and may have a degree in chemistry, biology, or pharmacology. A wholesaler of standard office supplies, on the other hand, may find it more important that its sales staff be familiar with various brands, suppliers, and prices than have technical knowledge about the products. A person just entering the wholesaling field may begin as a sales trainee or hold a nonselling job that provides experience with inventory, prices, discounts, and the firm's customers. A college graduate usually enters a wholesaler's sales force directly. Competent salespeople also transfer from manufacturer and retail sales positions.

The number of sales positions in wholesaling is expected to grow about as rapidly as the average for all occupations. Earnings for wholesale personnel vary widely because commissions often make up a large proportion of their incomes.

Sales Positions in Manufacturing. A manufacturer's sales personnel sell the firm's products to wholesalers, retailers, and industrial buyers; they thus perform many of the same activities as a wholesaler's representatives. As in wholesaling, educational requirements for a sales position depend largely on the type and complexity of the products and markets. Manufacturers of nontechnical products usually hire college graduates who have a liberal arts or business degree and train them so they become knowledgeable about the firm's products, prices, and customers. Manufacturers of highly technical products generally prefer applicants who have degrees in fields associated with the particular industry and market.

Sales positions in manufacturing are expected to increase at an average rate. Manufacturers' sales personnel are well compensated and earn above-average salaries; most are paid a combination of salary and commission. Commissions vary according to the salesperson's efforts, abilities, and sales territory, as well as the type of products sold. Annual salary and/or commission for sales positions range from $63,511 to $78,348 for a sales manager and $30,000 to $52,000 for a field salesperson. A sales trainee would start at about $35,500 in business sales positions.[7]

Industrial Buying

Industrial buyers, or purchasing agents, are responsible for maintaining an adequate supply of the goods and services an organization requires for its operations. In general, industrial buyers purchase all items needed for direct use in producing other products and for use in day-to-day operations. Industrial buyers in large firms often specialize in purchasing a single, specific class of products—for example, all petroleum-based lubricants. In smaller organizations, buyers may be responsible for many different categories of purchases, including raw materials, component parts, office supplies, and operating services.

An industrial buyer's main job is to select suppliers that offer the best quality, service, and price. When the products to be purchased are standardized, buyers may base their purchasing decisions on suppliers' descriptions of their offerings in catalogs and trade journals. Buyers who purchase highly homogeneous products often meet with salespeople to examine samples and observe demonstrations. Sometimes buyers must inspect the actual product before purchasing it; in other cases, they invite suppliers to bid on large orders. Buyers who purchase equipment made to specifications often deal directly with manufacturers. After choosing a supplier and placing an order, an industrial buyer usually must trace the shipment to ensure on-time delivery. Sometimes the buyer is also responsible for receiving and inspecting an order and authorizing payment to the shipper.

Training requirements for a career in industrial buying relate to the needs of the firm and the types of products purchased. A manufacturer of heavy machinery may prefer an applicant who has a background in engineering. A service company, on the other hand, may recruit liberal arts majors. Although not generally required, a college degree is becoming increasingly important for industrial buyers who wish to advance to management positions.

Employment prospects for industrial buyers are expected to increase faster than average. Opportunities will be excellent for individuals with a master's degree in business administration or a bachelor's degree in engineering, science, or business administration. Companies that manufacture heavy equipment, computer equipment, and communications equipment will need buyers with technical backgrounds.

Public Relations

Public relations encompasses a broad set of communication activities designed to create and maintain favorable relationships between an organization and its stakeholders—customers, employees, stockholders, government officials, and society in general. Public relations specialists help clients create the image, issue, or message they wish to present and communicate it to the appropriate audience. According to the Public Relations Society of America, about 120,000 people work in public relations in the United States. Half the billings of the nation's 4,000 public relations agencies and firms come from Chicago and New York. The highest starting salaries are also found there. Communication is basic to all public relations programs. To communicate effectively, public relations practitioners must first gather data about the firm's stakeholders to assess their needs, identify problems, formulate recommendations, implement new plans, and evaluate current activities.

Public relations personnel disseminate large amounts of information to the organization's stakeholders. Written communication is the most versatile tool of public relations; thus, good writing skills are essential. Public relations practitioners must be adept at writing for a variety of media and audiences. It is not unusual for a person in public relations to prepare reports, news releases, speeches, broadcast scripts, technical manuals, employee publications, shareholder reports, and other communications aimed at both organizational personnel and external groups. In addition, a public relations practitioner needs a thorough knowledge of the production techniques used in preparing various communications. Public relations personnel also establish distribution channels for the organization's publicity. They must have a thorough understanding of the various media, their areas of specialization, the characteristics of their target audiences, and their policies regarding publicity. Anyone who hopes to succeed in public relations must develop close working relationships with numerous media personnel to enlist their interest in disseminating clients' communications.

A college education combined with writing or media-related experience is the best preparation for a career in public relations. Most beginners have a college degree in journalism, communications, or public relations, but some employers prefer a business background. Courses in journalism, business administration, marketing, creative writing, psychology, sociology, political science, economics, advertising, English, and public speaking are recommended. Some employers ask applicants to present a portfolio of published articles, scripts written for television or radio programs, slide presentations, and other work samples. Other agencies require written tests that include such tasks as writing sample press releases. Manufacturing firms, public utilities, transportation and insurance companies, and trade and professional associations are the largest employers of public relations personnel. In addition, sizable numbers of public relations personnel work for health-related organizations, government agencies, educational institutions, museums, and religious and service groups.

Although some larger companies provide extensive formal training for new personnel, most new public relations employees learn on the job. Beginners usually perform routine tasks such as maintaining files about company activities and searching secondary data sources for information to be used in publicity materials. More experienced employees write press releases, speeches, and articles, and help plan public relations campaigns.

Employment opportunities in public relations are expected to increase faster than the average for all occupations. One caveat is in order, however: competition for beginning jobs is keen. The prospects are best for applicants who have solid academic preparation and some media experience. Abilities that differentiate candidates, such as an understanding of information technology, are becoming increasingly important. Public relations account executives earn $30,000 to $45,000. Public relations agency managers earn in the $51,460 to $62,874 range.[8]

Distribution Management

A distribution manager arranges for transportation of goods within firms and through marketing channels. Transportation is an essential distribution activity that permits a firm to create time and place utility for its products. It is the distribution manager's job to analyze various transportation modes and select the combination that minimizes cost and transit time while providing acceptable levels of reliability, capability, accessibility, and security.

To accomplish this task, a distribution manager performs many activities. First, the individual must choose one or a combination of transportation modes from the five major modes available: railroads, trucks, waterways, airways, and pipelines. The distribution manager must then select the specific routes the goods will travel and the particular carriers to be used, weighing such factors as freight classifications and regulations, freight charges, time schedules, shipment sizes, and loss and damage ratios. In addition, this person may be responsible for preparing shipping documents, tracing shipments, handling loss and damage claims, keeping records of freight rates, and monitoring changes in government regulations and transportation technology.

Distribution management employs relatively few people and is expected to grow about as fast as the average for all occupations in the near future. Manufacturing firms are the largest employers of distribution managers, although some distribution managers work for wholesalers, retail stores, and consulting firms. Salaries of experienced distribution managers vary but generally are much higher than the average for all nonsupervisory personnel. Entry-level positions are diverse, ranging from inventory control and traffic scheduling to operations or distribution management. Inventory management is an area of great opportunity because of increasing global competition. While salaries in the distribution field vary depending on the position and information technology skill requirements, entry salaries start at about 40,000.[9]

Most employers of distribution managers prefer to hire graduates of technical programs or people who have completed courses in transportation, logistics, distribution management, economics, statistics, computer science, management, marketing, and commercial law. A successful distribution manager is adept at handling technical data and is able to interpret and communicate highly technical information.

Product Management

The product manager occupies a staff position and is responsible for the success or failure of a product line. Product managers coordinate most of the activities required to market a product. However, because they hold a staff position, they have relatively little actual authority over marketing personnel. Nevertheless, they take on a large amount of responsibility and typically are paid quite well relative to other marketing employees. Being a product manager can be rewarding both financially and psychologically, but it can also be frustrating because of the disparity between responsibility and authority.

A product manager should have a general knowledge of advertising, transportation modes, inventory control, selling and sales management, sales promotion, marketing research, packaging, pricing, and warehousing. The individual must be knowledgeable enough to communicate effectively with personnel in these functional areas and to make suggestions and help assess alternatives when major decisions are being made.

Product managers usually need college training in an area of business administration. A master's degree is helpful, although a person usually does not become a product manager directly out of school. Frequently several years of selling and sales management experience are prerequisites for a product management position, which is often a major step in the career path of top-level marketing executives. Product managers can earn $60,000 to $120,000, while an assistant product manager starts at about $40,000.[10]

Advertising

Advertising pervades our daily lives. Business and nonbusiness organizations use advertising in many ways and for many reasons. Advertising clearly needs individuals with diverse skills to fill a variety of jobs. Creativity, imagination, artistic talent, and expertise in expression and persuasion are important for copywriters, artists, and account executives. Sales and managerial abilities are vital to the success of advertising managers, media buyers, and production managers. Research directors must have a solid understanding of research techniques and human behavior. A related occupation is an advertising salesperson, who sells newspaper, television, radio, or magazine advertising to advertisers.

Advertising professionals disagree on the most beneficial educational background for a career in advertising. Most employers prefer college graduates. Some employers seek individuals with degrees in advertising, journalism, or business; others prefer graduates with broad liberal arts backgrounds. Still other employers rank relevant work experience above educational background.

"Advertisers look for generalists," says a staff executive of the American Association of Advertising Agencies. "Thus, there are just as many economics or general liberal arts majors as M.B.A.'s." Common entry-level positions in an advertising agency are found in the traffic department, account service (account coordinator), or the media department (media assistant). Starting salaries in these positions are often quite low, but to gain experience in the advertising industry, employees must work their way up in the system. Assistant account executives start at $25,000, while a typical account executive earns $30,000 to $50,000. Copywriters earn $30,000 to $50,000 a year.[11]

A variety of organizations employ advertising personnel. Although advertising agencies are perhaps the most visible and glamorous employers, many manufacturing firms, retail stores, banks, utility companies, and professional and trade associations maintain advertising departments. Advertising jobs are also available with television and radio stations, newspapers, and magazines. Other businesses that employ advertising personnel include printers, art studios, letter shops, and package design firms. Specific advertising jobs include advertising manager, account executive, research director, copywriter, media specialist, and production manager.

About 59 percent of advertising employees are between 25 and 44 years of age compared to 51 percent of all workers in the U.S. economy. Employment opportunities in advertising are expected to increase faster than the average for all occupations through 2008.[12]

Retail Management

Although a career in retailing may begin in sales, there is more to retailing than simply selling. Many retail personnel occupy management positions. Besides managing the sales force, they focus on selecting and ordering merchandise, promotional activities, inventory control, customer credit operations, accounting, personnel, and store security.

Organization of retail stores varies. In many large department stores, retail management personnel rarely engage in actual selling to customers; these duties are performed by retail salespeople. Other types of retail organizations may require management personnel to perform selling activities from time to time.

Large retail stores offer a variety of management positions, including assistant buyers, buyers, department managers, section managers, store managers, division managers, regional managers, and vice president of merchandising. The following list describes the general duties of four of these positions; the precise nature of their duties may vary from one retail organization to another.

A section manager coordinates inventory and promotions and interacts with buyers, salespeople, and ultimate consumers. The manager performs merchandising, labor relations, and managerial activities, and usually works more than a 40-hour workweek.

The buyer's task is more focused. This fast-paced occupation involves much travel and pressure, and the need to be open-minded with respect to new, potentially successful items.

The regional manager coordinates the activities of several stores within a given area, usually monitoring and supporting sales, promotions, and general procedures.

The vice president of merchandising has a broad scope of managerial responsibility and reports to the organization's president.

Most retail organizations hire college graduates, put them through management training programs, and then place them directly in management positions. They frequently hire candidates with backgrounds in liberal arts or business administration. Sales positions and retail management positions offer the greatest employment opportunities for marketing students.

Retail management positions can be exciting and challenging. Competent, ambitious individuals often assume a great deal of responsibility very quickly and advance rapidly. However, a retail manager's job is physically demanding and sometimes entails long working hours. In addition, managers employed by large chain stores may be required to move frequently during their early years with the company. Nonetheless, positions in retail management often offer the chance to excel and gain promotion. Growth in retailing, which is expected to accompany the growth in population, is likely to create substantial opportunities during the next ten years. While a trainee may start in the $30,000 to $47,250 range, a store manager can earn from $50,000 to $200,000 depending on the size of the store.[13]

Direct Marketing

One of the more dynamic areas in marketing is direct marketing, in which the seller uses one or more direct media (telephone, online, mail, print, or television) to solicit a response. The telephone is a major vehicle for selling many consumer products. Telemarketing is direct selling to customers using a variety of technological improvements in telecommunications. Direct-mail catalogs appeal to such market segments as working women and people who find going to retail stores difficult or inconvenient. Newspapers and magazines offer great opportunity, particularly in special market segments. *Golf Digest,* for example, is obviously a good medium for selling golfing equipment. Cable television provides many opportunities for selling directly to consumers. Home shopping channels, for instance, have been very successful. The Internet offers numerous direct marketing opportunities.

The most important asset in direct marketing is experience. Employers often look to other industries to locate experienced professionals. This preference means that if you can get an entry-level position in direct marketing, you will have an advantage in developing a career.

Jobs in direct marketing include buyers, such as department store buyers, who select goods for catalog, telephone, or direct-mail sales. Catalog managers develop marketing strategies for each new catalog that goes into the mail. Research/mail list management involves developing lists of products that will sell in direct marketing and lists of names of consumers who are likely to respond to a direct-mail effort. Order fulfillment managers direct the shipment of products once they are sold. The effectiveness of direct marketing is enhanced by periodic analysis of advertising and communications at all phases of contact with the consumer. Direct marketing involves all aspects of marketing decision making. Most positions in direct marketing involve planning and market analysis. Some direct marketing jobs involve the use of databases that include customer information, sales history, and other tracking data. A database manager might receive a salary of $53,750 to $88,750. A tele-marketing director in business-to-business sales could receive a salary of about $35,000.[14]

E-Marketing and Customer Relationship Management

Today only about 1.5 percent of all retail sales are conducted on the Internet.[15] Currently approximately one-half of all businesses order online. One characteristic of firms engaged in e-marketing is a renewed focus on relationship marketing by building customer loyalty and retaining customers—in other words, on customer relationship management (CRM). This focus on CRM is possible because of e-marketers' ability to target individual customers. This effort is enhanced over time as the customer invests more time and effort in "teaching" the firms what he or she wants.

Opportunities abound to combine information technology expertise with marketing knowledge. By providing an integrated communication system of websites, fax, telephone, and personal contacts, marketers can personalize customer relationships. Careers exist for individuals who can integrate the Internet as a touch point with customers as part of effective customer relationship management. Many Internet-only companies ("dot-coms") failed because they focused too heavily on brand awareness and did not understand the importance of an integrated marketing strategy.

The use of laptops, cellular phones, e-mail, voice mail, and other devices is necessary to maintain customer relationships and allow purchases on the Internet. A variety of jobs exist for marketers who have integrated technology into their work and job skills. Job titles include e-marketing manager, customer relationship manager, and e-services manager, as well as jobs in dot-coms.

Salaries in this rapidly growing area depend on technical expertise and experience. For example, a CRM customer service manager receives a salary in the $40,000 to $45,000 range. Database administrators earn salaries of approximately $70,500 to $90,000. With five years of experience in e-marketing, individuals responsible for online product offerings can earn from $50,000 to $85,000.

Financial Analysis in Marketing*

Our discussion in this book focuses more on fundamental concepts and decisions in marketing than on financial details. However, marketers must understand the basic components of financial analyses to be able to explain and defend their decisions. In fact, they must be familiar with certain financial analyses to reach good decisions in the first place. To control and evaluate marketing activities, they must understand the income statement and what it says about their organization's operations. They also need to be familiar with performance ratios, which compare current operating results with past results and with results in the industry at large. We examine the income statement and some performance ratios in the first part of this appendix. In the second part, we discuss price calculations as the basis for price adjustments. Marketers are likely to use all these areas of financial analysis at various times to support their decisions and make necessary adjustments in their operations.

The Income Statement

The income, or operating, statement presents the financial results of an organization's operations over a certain period. The statement summarizes revenues earned and expenses incurred by a profit center, whether a department, a brand, a product line, a division, or the entire firm. The income statement presents the firm's net profit or net loss for a month, quarter, or year.

Table B.1 is a simplified income statement for Stoneham Auto Supplies, a fictitious retail store. The owners, Rose Costa and Nick Schultz, see that net sales of $250,000 are decreased by the cost of goods sold and by other business expenses to yield a net income of $83,000. Of course, these figures are only highlights of the complete income statement, which appears in Table B.2.

The income statement can be used in several ways to improve the management of a business. First, it enables an owner or a manager to compare actual results with budgets for various parts of the statement. For example, Rose and Nick see that the total amount of merchandise sold (gross sales) is $260,000. Customers returned merchandise or received allowances (price reductions) totaling $10,000. Suppose the budgeted amount was only $9,000. By checking the tickets for sales returns and allowances, the owners can determine why these events occurred and whether the $10,000 figure could be lowered by adjusting the marketing mix.

Table B.1	Simplified Income Statement for a Retailer

Stoneham Auto Supplies
Income Statement for the Year Ended December 31, 2005

Net Sales	$250,000
Cost of Goods Sold	45,000
Gross Margin	$205,000
Expenses	122,000
Net Income	$ 83,000

* We gratefully acknowledge the assistance of Jim L. Grimm, Professor of Marketing, Illinois State University, in writing this appendix.

After subtracting returns and allowances from gross sales, Rose and Nick can determine net sales, the amount the firm has available to pay its expenses. They are pleased with this figure because it is higher than their sales target of $240,000.

A major expense for most companies that sell goods (as opposed to services) is the cost of goods sold. For Stoneham Auto Supplies, it amounts to 18 percent of net sales. Other expenses are treated in various ways by different companies. In our example, they are broken down into standard categories of selling expenses, administrative expenses, and general expenses.

The income statement shows that for Stoneham Auto Supplies, the cost of goods sold was $45,000. This figure was derived in the following way. First, the statement shows that merchandise in the amount of $51,000 was purchased during the year. In paying the invoices associated with these inventory additions, purchase (cash) discounts of $4,000 were earned, resulting in net purchases of $47,000. Special requests for selected merchandise throughout the year resulted in $2,000 in freight charges, which increased the net cost of delivered purchases to $49,000. When this amount is added to the beginning inventory of $48,000, the cost of goods available for sale during 2005 totals $97,000. However, the records indicate that the value of inventory at the end of the year was $52,000. Because this amount was not sold, the cost of goods that were sold during the year was $45,000.

Rose and Nick observe that the total value of their inventory increased by 8.3 percent during the year:

$$\frac{\$52,000 - \$48,000}{\$48,000} = \frac{\$4,000}{\$48,000} = \frac{1}{12} = 0825, \text{ or } 8.3\%$$

Further analysis is needed to determine whether this increase is desirable or undesirable. (Note that the income statement provides no details concerning the composition of the inventory held on December 31; other records supply this information.) If Nick and Rose determine that inventory on December 31 is excessive, they can implement appropriate marketing action.

Gross margin is the difference between net sales and cost of goods sold. Gross margin reflects the markup on products and is the amount available to pay all other expenses and provide a return to the owners. Stoneham Auto Supplies had a gross margin of $205,000:

Net sales	$250,000
Cost of goods sold	− 45,000
Gross margin	$205,000

Stoneham's expenses (other than cost of goods sold) during 2005 totaled $122,000. Observe that $53,000, or slightly more than 43 percent of the total, constituted direct selling expenses:

$$\frac{\$53,000 \text{ selling expenses}}{\$122,000 \text{ total expenses}} = .434, \text{ or } 43\%$$

The business employs three salespeople (one full time) and pays competitive wages. The selling expenses are similar to those in the previous year, but Nick and Rose wonder whether more advertising is necessary because the value of inventory increased by more than 8 percent during the year.

The administrative and general expenses are essential for operating the business. A comparison of these expenses with trade statistics for similar businesses indicates that the figures are in line with industry amounts.

Net income, or net profit, is the amount of gross margin remaining after deducting expenses. Stoneham Auto Supplies earned a net profit of $83,000 for the fiscal year ending December 31, 2005. Note that net income on this statement is figured before payment of state and federal income taxes.

Income statements for intermediaries and for businesses that provide services follow the same general format as that shown for Stoneham Auto Supplies in Table B.2. The income statement for a manufacturer, however, differs somewhat in that the

Table B.2	Income Statement for a Retailer

Stoneham Auto Supplies
Income Statement for the Year Ended December 31, 2005

Gross Sales			$260,000
Less: Sales returns and allowances			$ 10,000
Net Sales			**$250,000**
Cost of Goods Sold			
Inventory, January 1, 2005 (at cost)		$48,000	
Purchases	$51,000		$260,000
Less: Purchase discounts	4,000		
Net purchases	$47,000		
Plus: Freight-in	2,000		
Net cost of delivered purchases		$49,000	
Cost of goods available for sale		$97,000	
Less: Inventory, December 31, 2005			
(at cost)		52,000	
Cost of goods sold			$ 45,000
Gross Margin			**$205,000**
Expenses			
Selling expenses			
Sales salaries and commissions	$32,000		
Advertising	16,000		
Sales promotions	3,000		
Delivery	2,000		
Total selling expenses		$53,000	
Administrative expenses			
Administrative salaries	$20,000		
Office salaries	20,000		
Office supplies	2,000		
Miscellaneous	1,000		
Total administrative expenses		$43,000	
General expenses			
Rent	$14,000		
Utilities	7,000		
Bad debts	1,000		
Miscellaneous (local taxes,			
insurance, interest, depreciation)	4,000		
Total general expenses		$26,000	
Total expenses			$122,000
Net Income			**$ 83,000**

"purchases" portion is replaced by "cost of goods manufactured." Table B.3 shows the entire Cost of Goods Sold section for a manufacturer, including cost of goods manufactured. In other respects, income statements for retailers and manufacturers are similar.

Performance Ratios

Rose and Nick's assessment of how well their business did during fiscal year 2005 can be improved through use of analytical ratios. Such ratios enable a manager to

Table B.3	Cost of Goods Sold for a Manufacturer

ABC Manufacturing
Income Statement for the Year Ended December 31, 2005

Cost of Goods Sold			$ 50,000
Finished goods inventory January 1, 2005			
Cost of goods manufactured			
Work-in-process inventory, January 1, 2005		$ 20,000	
Raw materials inventory, January 1, 2005	$ 40,000		
Net cost of delivered purchases	$240,000		
Cost of goods available for use	$280,000		
Less: Raw materials inventory, December 31, 2005	$ 42,000		
Cost of goods placed in production		$238,000	
Direct labor		32,000	
Manufacturing overhead			
Indirect labor	$ 12,000		
Supervisory salaries	10,000		
Operating supplies	6,000		
Depreciation	12,000		
Utilities	$ 10,000		
Total manufacturing overhead		$ 50,000	
Total manufacturing costs		$320,000	
Total work-in-process		$340,000	
Less: Work-in-process inventory, December 31, 2005		$ 22,000	
Cost of Goods Manufactured			$318,000
			$368,000
Cost of Goods Available for Sale			
Less: Finished goods inventory, December 31, 2005			48,000
Cost of Goods Sold			$320,000

compare the results for the current year with data from previous years and industry statistics. However, comparisons of the current income statement with income statements and industry statistics from other years are not very meaningful because factors such as inflation are not accounted for when comparing dollar amounts. More useful comparisons can be made by converting these figures to a percentage of net sales, as this section shows.

The first analytical ratios we discuss, the operating ratios, are based on the net sales figure from the income statement.

Operating Ratios

Operating ratios express items on the income, or operating, statement as percentages of net sales. The first step is to convert the income statement into percentages of net sales, as illustrated in Table B.4. After making this conversion, the manager

Table B.4	Income Statement Components as Percentages of Net Sales

Stoneham Auto Supplies
Income Statement as a Percentage of Net Sales for the Year Ended
December 31, 2005

		Percentage of Net Sales
Gross Sales		103.8%
Less: Sales returns and allowances		3.8
Net Sales		100.0%
Cost of Goods Sold		
Inventory, January 1, 2005 (at cost)		19.2%
Purchases	20.4%	
Less: Purchase discounts	1.6	
Net purchases	18.8%	
Plus: Freight-in	0.8	
Net cost of delivered purchases		19.6
Cost of goods available for sale		38.8%
Less: Inventory, December 31, 2005		
(at cost)		20.8
Cost of goods sold		18.0
Gross Margin		82.0%
Expenses		
Selling expenses		
Sales salaries and commissions	12.8%	
Advertising	6.4	
Sales promotions	1.2	
Delivery	0.8	
Total selling expenses		21.2%
Administrative expenses		
Administrative salaries	8.0%	
Office salaries	8.0	
Office supplies	0.8	
Miscellaneous	0.4	
Total administrative expenses		17.2%
General expenses		
Rent	5.6%	
Utilities	2.8	
Bad debts	0.4	
Miscellaneous	1.6	
Total general expenses		10.4%
Total expenses		48.8
Net Income		**33.2%**

looks at several key operating ratios: two profitability ratios (the gross margin ratio and the net income ratio) and the operating expense ratio.

For Stoneham Auto Supplies, these ratios are determined as follows (see Tables B.2 and B.4 for supporting data):

$$\text{Gross Margin Ratio} = \frac{\text{Gross Margin}}{\text{Net Sales}} = \frac{\$205,000}{\$250,000} = 82\%$$

$$\text{Net Income Ratio} = \frac{\text{Net Income}}{\text{Net Sales}} = \frac{\$83,000}{\$250,000} = 33.2\%$$

$$\text{Operating Expenses Ratio} = \frac{\text{Total Expenses}}{\text{Net Sales}} = \frac{\$122,000}{\$250,000} = 48.8\%$$

The gross margin ratio indicates the percentage of each sales dollar available to cover operating expenses and achieve profit objectives. The net income ratio indicates the percentage of each sales dollar that is classified as earnings (profit) before payment of income taxes. The operating expense ratio calculates the percentage of each dollar needed to cover operating expenses.

If Nick and Rose believe the operating expense ratio is higher than historical data and industry standards, they can analyze each operating expense ratio in Table B.4 to determine which expenses are too high and then take corrective action.

After reviewing several key operating ratios, Nick and Rose, like many managers, will probably want to analyze all the items on the income statement. By doing so, they can determine whether the 8 percent increase in the value of their inventory was necessary.

Inventory Turnover Rate

The inventory turnover rate, or stock-turn rate, is an analytical ratio that can be used to answer the question "Is the inventory level appropriate for this business?" The inventory turnover rate indicates the number of times an inventory is sold (turns over) during one year. To be useful, this figure must be compared with historical turnover rates and industry rates.

The inventory turnover rate is computed (based on cost) as follows:

$$\text{Inventory Turnover} = \frac{\text{Cost of Goods Sold}}{\text{Average Inventory at Cost}}$$

Rose and Nick would calculate the turnover rate from Table B.2 as follows:

$$\frac{\text{Cost of Goods Sold}}{\text{Average Inventory at Cost}} = \frac{\$45,000}{\$50,000} = 0.9\%$$

Their inventory turnover is less than once per year (0.9 times). Industry averages for competitive firms are 2.8 times. This figure convinces Rose and Nick that their investment in inventory is too large and they need to reduce their inventory.

Return on Investment

Return on investment (ROI) is a ratio that indicates management's efficiency in generating sales and profits from the total amount invested in the firm. For Stoneham Auto Supplies, the ROI is 41.5 percent, which compares well with competing businesses.

We use figures from two different financial statements to arrive at ROI. The income statement, already discussed, gives us net income. The balance sheet, which states the firm's assets and liabilities at a given point in time, provides the figure for total assets (or investment) in the firm.

The basic formula for ROI is

$$ROI = \frac{\text{Net Income}}{\text{Total Investment}}$$

For Stoneham Auto Supplies, net income is \$83,000 (see Table B.2). If total investment (taken from the balance sheet for December 31, 2005) is \$200,000, then

$$ROI = \frac{\$83,000}{\$200,000} = 0.415, \text{ or } 41.5\%$$

The ROI formula can be expanded to isolate the impact of capital turnover and the operating income ratio separately. Capital turnover is a measure of net sales per dollar of investment; the ratio is figured by dividing net sales by total investment. For Stoneham Auto Supplies,

$$\text{Capital Turnover} = \frac{\text{Net Sales}}{\text{Total Investment}} = \frac{\$250,000}{\$200,000} = 1.25$$

ROI is equal to capital turnover times the net income ratio. The expanded formula for Stoneham Auto Supplies is

$$ROI = \frac{\text{Net Sales}}{\text{Total Investment}} \times \frac{\text{Net Income}}{\text{Net Sales}}$$
$$= \frac{\$250,000}{\$200,000} \times \frac{\$83,000}{\$250,000}$$
$$= (1.25)(33.2\%) = 41.5\%$$

Price Calculations

An important step in setting prices is selecting a basis for pricing, as discussed in Chapter 22. The systematic use of markups, markdowns, and various conversion formulas helps in calculating the selling price and evaluating the effects of various prices.

Markups

As discussed in the text, markup is the difference between the selling price and the cost of the item; that is, selling price equals cost plus markup. The markup must cover cost and contribute to profit; thus, markup is similar to gross margin on the income statement.

Markup can be calculated on either cost or selling price as follows:

$$\frac{\text{Markup as Percentage}}{\text{of Cost}} = \frac{\text{Amount Added to Cost}}{\text{Cost}} = \frac{\text{Dollar Markup}}{\text{Cost}}$$

$$\frac{\text{Markup as Percentage}}{\text{of Selling Price}} = \frac{\text{Amount Added to Cost}}{\text{Selling Price}} = \frac{\text{Dollar Markup}}{\text{Selling Price}}$$

Retailers tend to calculate the markup percentage on selling price.

To review the use of these markup formulas, assume an item costs \$10 and the markup is \$5:

$$\text{Selling Price} = \text{Cost} + \text{Markup}$$
$$\$15 = \$10 + \$5$$

Thus,

$$\text{Markup Percentage on Cost} = \frac{\$5}{\$10} = 50\%$$

$$\text{Markup Percentage on Selling Price} = \frac{\$5}{\$15} = 33\tfrac{1}{3}\%$$

It is necessary to know the base (cost or selling price) to use markup pricing effectively. Markup percentage on cost will always exceed markup percentage on price, given the same dollar markup, as long as selling price exceeds cost.

On occasion, we may need to convert markup on cost to markup on selling price, or vice versa. The conversion formulas are as follows:

$$\frac{\text{Markup Percentage}}{\text{on Selling Price}} = \frac{\text{Markup Percentage on Cost}}{100\% + \text{Markup Percentage on Cost}}$$

$$\frac{\text{Markup Percentage}}{\text{on Cost}} = \frac{\text{Markup Percentage on Selling Price}}{100\% - \text{Markup Percentage on Selling Price}}$$

For example, if the markup percentage on cost is $33\tfrac{1}{3}$ percent, the markup percentage on selling price is

$$\frac{33\tfrac{1}{3}\%}{100\% + 33\tfrac{1}{3}\%} = \frac{33\tfrac{1}{3}\%}{133\tfrac{1}{3}\%} = 25\%$$

If the markup percentage on selling price is 40 percent, the corresponding percentage on cost is as follows:

$$\frac{40\%}{100\% - 40\%} = \frac{40\%}{60\%} = 66\tfrac{2}{3}\%$$

Finally, we can show how to determine selling price if we know the cost of the item and the markup percentage on selling price. Assume an item costs $36 and the usual markup percentage on selling price is 40 percent. Remember that selling price equals markup plus cost. Thus, if

$$100\% = 40\% \text{ of Selling Price} + \text{Cost}$$

then,

$$60\% \text{ of Selling Price} = \text{Cost}$$

In our example, cost equals $36. Therefore,

$$0.6X = \$36$$

$$X = \frac{\$36}{0.6}$$

$$\text{Selling Price} = \$60$$

Alternatively, the markup percentage could be converted to a cost basis as follows:

$$\frac{40\%}{100\% - 40\%} = 66\tfrac{2}{3}\%$$

The selling price would then be computed as follows:

$$\begin{aligned}
\text{Selling Price} &= 66\tfrac{2}{3}\%(\text{Cost}) + \text{Cost} \\
&= 66\tfrac{2}{3}\%(\$36) + \$36 \\
&= \$24 + \$36 = \$60
\end{aligned}$$

If you keep in mind the basic formula—selling price equals cost plus markup—you will find these calculations straightforward.

Markdowns

Markdowns are price reductions a retailer makes on merchandise. Markdowns may be useful on items that are damaged, priced too high, or selected for a special sales event. The income statement does not express markdowns directly because the change in price is made before the sale takes place. Therefore, separate records of markdowns would be needed to evaluate the performance of various buyers and departments.

The markdown ratio (percentage) is calculated as follows:

$$\text{Markdown Percentage} = \frac{\text{Dollar Markdowns}}{\text{Net Sales in Dollars}}$$

In analyzing their inventory, Nick and Rose discover three special automobile jacks that have gone unsold for several months. They decide to reduce the price of each item from $25 to $20. Subsequently these items are sold. The markdown percentage for these three items is

$$\text{Markdown Percentage} = \frac{3(\$5)}{3(\$20)} = \frac{\$15}{\$60} = 25\%$$

Net sales, however, include all units of this product sold during the period, not just those marked down. If ten of these items were already sold at $25 each, in addition to the three items sold at $20, the overall markdown percentage would be

$$\text{Markdown Percentage} = \frac{3(\$5)}{10(\$25) + 3(\$20)}$$

$$= \frac{\$15}{\$250 + \$60} = \frac{\$15}{\$310} = 4.8\%$$

Sales allowances are also a reduction in price. Thus, the markdown percentage should include any sales allowances. It would be computed as follows:

$$\text{Markdown Percentage} = \frac{\text{Dollar Markdowns} + \text{Dollar Allowances}}{\text{Net Sales in Dollars}}$$

Discussion and Review Questions

1. How does a manufacturer's income statement differ from a retailer's income statement?
2. Use the following information to answer questions a through c:

TEA Company
Fiscal year ended June 30, 2005

Net sales	$500,000
Cost of goods sold	300,000
Net income	50,000
Average inventory at cost	100,000
Total assets (total investment)	200,000

a. What is the inventory turnover rate for TEA Company? From what sources will the marketing manager determine the significance of the inventory turnover rate?

b. What is the capital turnover ratio? What is the net income ratio? What is the return on investment (ROI)?
c. How many dollars of sales did each dollar of investment produce for TEA Company?

3. Product A has a markup percentage on cost of 40 percent. What is the markup percentage on selling price?
4. Product B has a markup percentage on selling price of 30 percent. What is the markup percentage on cost?
5. Product C has a cost of $60 and a usual markup percentage of 25 percent on selling price. What price should be placed on this item?
6. Apex Appliance Company sells 20 units of product Q for $100 each and 10 units for $80 each. What is the markdown percentage for product Q?

Sample Marketing Plan

This sample marketing plan for a hypothetical company illustrates how the marketing planning process described in Chapter 2 might be implemented. If you are asked to create a marketing plan, this model may be a helpful guide, along with the concepts in Chapter 2.

1 The Executive Summary, one of the most frequently read components of a marketing plan, is a synopsis of the marketing plan. Although it does not provide detailed information, it does present an overview of the plan so readers can identify key issues pertaining to their roles in the planning and implementation processes. Although this is the first section in a marketing plan, it is usually written last.

2 The Environmental Analysis presents information regarding the organization's current situation with respect to the marketing environment, the current target market(s), and the firm's current marketing objectives and performance.

3 This section of the environmental analysis considers relevant external environmental forces such as competitive, economic, political, legal and regulatory, technological, and sociocultural forces.

Star Software, Inc. Marketing Plan

1 ## I. EXECUTIVE SUMMARY

Star Software, Inc., is a small, family-owned corporation in the first year of a transition from first-generation to second-generation leadership. Star Software sells custom-made calendar programs and related items to about 400 businesses, which use the software mainly for promotion. As Star's business is highly seasonal, its 18 employees face scheduling challenges, with greatest demand during October, November, and December. In other months, the equipment and staff are sometimes idle. A major challenge facing Star Software is how to increase profits and make better use of its resources during the off-season.

An evaluation of the company's internal strengths and weaknesses and external opportunities and threats served as the foundation for this strategic analysis and marketing plan. The plan focuses on the company's growth strategy, suggesting ways it can build on existing customer relationships, and on the development of new products and/or services targeted to specific customer niches. Since Star Software markets a product used primarily as a promotional tool by its clients, it is currently considered a business-to-business marketer.

2 ## II. ENVIRONMENTAL ANALYSIS

Founded as a commercial printing company, Star Software, Inc., has evolved into a marketer of high-quality, custom-made calendar software and related business-to-business specialty items. In the mid-1960s, Bob McLemore purchased the company and, through his full-time commitment, turned it into a very successful family-run operation. In the near future, McLemore's 37-year-old son, Jonathan, will take over as Star Software's president and allow the elder McLemore to scale back his involvement.

3 ### A. The Marketing Environment

1. *Competitive forces.* The competition in the specialty advertising industry is very strong on a local and regional basis, but somewhat weak nationally. Sales figures for the industry as a whole are difficult to obtain since very little business is conducted on a national scale.

The competition within the calendar industry is strong in the paper segment and weak in the software-based segment. Currently paper calendars hold a dominant market share of approximately 65 percent; however, the software-based segment is growing rapidly. The 35 percent market share held by software-based calendars is divided among many different firms. Star Software, which holds 30 percent of the software-based calendar market, is the only company that markets

1

a software-based calendar on a national basis. As software-based calendars become more popular, additional competition is expected to enter the market.

2. *Economic forces.* Nationwide, many companies have reduced their overall promotion budgets as they face the need to cut expenses. However, most of these reductions have occurred in the budgets for mass media advertising (television, magazines, newspapers). While overall promotion budgets are shrinking, many companies are diverting a larger percentage of their budgets to sales promotion and specialty advertising. This trend is expected to continue as a weak, slow-growth economy forces most companies to focus more on the "value" they receive from their promotion dollars. Specialty advertising, such as can be done with a software-based calendar, provides this value.

3. *Political forces.* There are no expected political influences or events that could affect the operations of Star Software.

4. *Legal and regulatory forces.* In recent years, more attention has been paid to "junk mail." A large percentage of specialty advertising products are distributed by mail, and some of these products are considered "junk." Although this label is attached to the type of products Star Software makes, the problem of junk mail falls on Star's clients and not on the company itself. While legislation may be introduced to curb the tide of advertising delivered through the mail, the fact that more companies are diverting their promotion dollars to specialty advertising indicates that most do not fear the potential for increased legislation.

5. *Technological forces.* A major emerging technological trend involves personal digital assistants (PDAs). A PDA is a handheld device, similar in size to a large calculator, that can store a wide variety of information, including personal notes, addresses, and a calendar. Some PDAs, such as the Black Berry, can be loaded with a cellphone and walkie-talkie. The user can e-mail and schedule on the electronic calendar.. As this trend continues, current software-based calendar products may have to be adapted to match the new technology.

6. *Sociocultural forces.* In today's society, consumers have less time for work or leisure. The hallmarks of today's successful products are convenience and ease of use. In short, if the product does not save time and is not easy to use, consumers will simply ignore it. Software-based calendars fit this consumer need quite well. A software-based calendar also fits in with other societal trends: a move to a paperless society, the need to automate repetitive tasks, and the growing dependence on computers, for example.

 B. Target Market(s)

By focusing on commitment to service and quality, Star Software has effectively implemented a niche differentiation strategy in a somewhat diverse marketplace. Its ability to differentiate its product has contributed to superior annual returns. Its tar-

4 The analysis of current target markets assesses demographic, geographic, psychographic, and product usage characteristics of the target markets. It also assesses the current needs of each of the firm's target markets, anticipated changes in those needs, and how well the organization's current products are meeting those needs.

get market consists of manufacturers or manufacturing divisions of large corporations that move their products through dealers, distributors, or brokers. Its most profitable product is a software program for a PC-based calendar, which can be tailored to meet client needs by means of artwork, logos, and text. Clients use this calendar software as a promotional tool, providing a disk to their customers as an advertising premium. The calendar software is not produced for resale.

The calendar software began as an ancillary product to Star's commercial printing business. However, due to the proliferation of PCs and the growth in technology, the computer calendar soon became more profitable for Star than its wall and desktop paper calendars. This led to the sale of the commercial printing plant and equipment to employees. Star Software has maintained a long-term relationship with these former employees, who have added capabilities to reproduce computer disks and whose company serves as Star's primary supplier of finished goods. Star's staff focuses on further development and marketing of the software

C. Current Marketing Objectives and Performance

Star Software's sales representatives call on potential clients and, using a template demonstration disk, help them create a calendar concept. Once the sale has been finalized, Star completes the concept, including design, copywriting, and customization of the demonstration disk. Specifications are then sent to the supplier, located about 1,000 miles away, where the disks are produced. Perhaps what most differentiates Star from its competitors is its high level of service. Disks can be shipped to any location the buyer specifies. Since product development and customization of this type can require significant amounts of time and effort, particularly during the product's first year, Star deliberately pursues a strategy of steady, managed growth.

Star Software markets its products on a company-specific basis. It has an annual reorder rate of approximately 90 percent and an average customer-reorder relationship of about eight years. The first year in dealing with a new customer is the most stressful and time consuming for Star's salespeople and product developers. Subsequent years are faster and significantly more profitable.

The company is currently debt free except for the mortgage on its facility. However, about 80 percent of its accounts receivable are billed during the last three months of the calendar year. Seasonal account billings, along with the added travel of Star's sales staff during the peak season, pose a special challenge to the company. The need for cash to fund operations in the meantime requires the company to borrow significant amounts of money to cover the period until customer billing occurs.

5 Star Software's marketing objectives include increases in both revenues and profits of approximately 10 percent over the previous year. Revenues should exceed $4 million, and profits are expected to reach $1.3 million.

5 A company must set marketing objectives, measure performance against those objectives, and then take corrective action if needed.

3

III. SWOT ANALYSIS

6 Strengths are competitive advantages or core competencies that give the organization an advantage in meeting the needs of its customers.

6 **A. Strengths**

1. Star Software's product differentiation strategy is the result of a strong marketing orientation, commitment to high quality, and customization of products and support services.

2. There is little turnover among employees, who are well compensated and liked by customers. The relatively small staff size promotes camaraderie with coworkers and clients, and fosters communication and quick response to clients' needs.

3. A long-term relationship with the primary supplier has resulted in shared knowledge of the product's requirements, adherence to quality standards, and a common vision throughout the development and production process.

4. The high percentage of reorder business suggests a satisfied customer base, as well as positive word-of-mouth communication, which generates some 30 percent of new business each year.

7 Weaknesses are limitations a firm has in developing or implementing a marketing strategy.

7 **B. Weaknesses**

1. The highly centralized management hierarchy (the McLemores) and lack of managerial backup may impede creativity and growth. Too few people hold too much knowledge.

2. Despite the successful, long-term relationship with the supplier, single-sourcing could make Star Software vulnerable in the event of a natural disaster, strike, or dissolution of the current supplier. Contingency plans for suppliers should be considered.

3. The seasonal nature of the product line creates bottlenecks in productivity and cash flow, places excessive stress on personnel, and strains the facilities.

4. Both the product line and the client base lack diversification. Dependence on current reorder rates could breed complacency, invite competition, or create a false sense of customer satisfaction. The development of a product that would make the software calendar obsolete would probably put Star out of business.

5. While the small size of the staff fosters camaraderie, it also impedes growth and new-business development.

6. Star Software is reactive rather than assertive in its marketing efforts because of its heavy reliance on positive word-of-mouth communication for obtaining new business.

7. Star's current facilities are crowded. There is little room for additional employees or new equipment.

4

8 Opportunities are favorable conditions in the environment that could yield rewards for an organization if acted on properly.

8 **C. Opportunities**

1. Advertising expenditures in the United States exceed $132 billion annually. More than $25 billion of this is spent on direct-mail advertising and another $20 billion on specialty advertising. Star Software's potential for growth is significant in this market.

2. Technological advances have not only freed up time for Americans and brought greater efficiency but have also increased the amount of stress in their fast-paced lives. Personal computers have become commonplace, and personal information managers have gained popularity.

3. As U.S. companies look for ways to develop customer relationships rather than just close sales, reminders of this relationship could come in the form of acceptable premiums or gifts that are useful to the customer.

4. Computer-based calendars are easily distributed nationally and globally. The globalization of business creates an opportunity to establish new client relationships in foreign markets.

9 Threats are conditions or barriers that may prevent the organization from reaching its objectives.

9 **D. Threats**

1. Reengineering, right-sizing, and outsourcing trends in management may alter traditional channel relationships with brokers, dealers, and distributors or eliminate them altogether.

2. Calendars are basically a generic product. The technology, knowledge, and equipment required to produce such an item, even a computer-based one, are minimal. The possible entry of new competitors is a significant threat.

3. Theft of trade secrets and software piracy through unauthorized copying are difficult to control.

4. Specialty advertising through promotional items relies on gadgetry and ideas that are new and different. As a result, product life cycles may be quite short.

5. Single-sourcing can be detrimental or even fatal to a company if the buyer-supplier relationship is damaged or if the supplying company has financial difficulty.

6. Competition from traditional paper calendars and other promotional items is strong.

10 During the development of a marketing plan, marketers attempt to match internal strengths to external opportunities. In addition, they try to convert internal weaknesses into strengths and external threats into opportunities.

10 **E. Matching Strengths to Opportunities/ Converting Weaknesses and Threats**

1. The acceptance of technological advances and the desire to control time create a potential need for a computer-based calendar.

5

2. Star Software has more opportunity for business growth during its peak season than it can presently handle because of resource (human and capital) constraints.

3. Star Software must modify its management hierarchy, empowering its employees through a more decentralized marketing organization.

4. Star Software should discuss future growth strategies with its supplier and develop contingency plans to deal with unforeseen events. Possible satellite facilities in other geographic locations should be explored.

5. Star Software should consider diversifying its product line to satisfy new market niches and develop nonseasonal products.

6. Star Software should consider surveying its current customers and its customers' clients to gain a better understanding of their changing needs and desires.

 The development of marketing objectives is based on environmental analysis, SWOT analysis, the firm's overall corporate objectives, and the organization's resources. For each objective, this section should answer the question "What is the specific and measurable outcome and time frame for completing this objective?"

11 IV. MARKETING OBJECTIVES

Star Software, Inc., is in the business of helping other companies market their products and/or services. Besides formulating a marketing-oriented and customer-focused mission statement, Star Software should establish an objective to achieve cumulative growth in net profit of at least 50 percent over the next five years. At least half of this 50 percent growth should come from new, nonmanufacturing customers and from products that are nonseasonal or that are generally delivered in the off-peak period of the calendar cycle.

To accomplish its marketing objectives, Star Software should develop benchmarks to measure progress. Regular reviews of these objectives will provide feedback and possible corrective actions on a timely basis. The major marketing objective is to gain a better understanding of the needs and satisfaction of current customers. Since Star Software is benefiting from a 90 percent reorder rate, it must be satisfying its current customers. Star could use the knowledge of its successes with current clients to market to new customers. To capitalize on its success with current clients, the company should establish benchmarks to learn how it can improve the products it now offers through knowledge of clients' needs and specific opportunities for new product offerings. These benchmarks should be determined through marketing research and Star's marketing information system.

Another objective should be to analyze the billing cycle Star now uses to determine if there are ways to bill accounts receivable in a more evenly distributed manner throughout the year. Alternatively, repeat customers might be willing to place orders at off-peak cycles in return for discounts or added customer services.

Star Software should also create new products that can utilize its current equipment, technology, and knowledge base. It should conduct simple research and analyses of similar products or product lines with an eye toward developing specialty advertising products that are software based but not necessarily calendar related.

6

12 The marketing plan clearly specifies and describes the target market(s) toward which the organization will aim its marketing efforts. The difference between this section and the earlier section covering target markets is that the earlier section deals with present target markets, whereas this section looks at future target markets.

12 **V. MARKETING STRATEGIES**

A. Target Market(s)

Target market 1:   Large manufacturers or stand-alone manufacturing divisions of large corporations with extensive broker, dealer, or distributor networks

Example: An agricultural chemical producer, such as Dow Chemical, distributes its products to numerous rural "feed and seed" dealers. Customizing calendars with Chicago Board of Trade futures or USDA agricultural report dates would be beneficial to these potential clients.

Target market 2:   Nonmanufacturing, nonindustrial segments of the business-to-business market with extensive customer networks, such as banks, medical services, or financial planners

Example: Various sporting goods manufacturers distribute to specialty shop dealers. Calendars could be customized to the particular sport, such as golf (with PGA, Virginia Slims, or other tour dates), running (with various national marathon dates), or bowling (with national tour dates).

Target market 3:   Direct consumer markets for brands with successful licensing arrangements for consumer products, such as Coca-Cola

Example: Products with major brand recognition and fan club membership, such as Harley-Davidson motorcycles or the Bloomington Gold Corvette Association, could provide additional markets for customized computer calendars. Environmental or political groups represent a nonprofit market. Brands with licensing agreements for consumer products could provide a market for consumer computer calendars in addition to the specialty advertising product, which would be marketed to manufacturers/dealers.

Target market 4:   Industry associations that regularly hold or sponsor trade shows, meetings, conferences, or conventions

Example: National associations, such as the National Dairy Association or the American Marketing Association, frequently host meetings or annual conventions. Customized calendars could be developed for any of these groups.

13 Though the marketing mix section in this plan is abbreviated, this component should provide considerable details regarding each element of the marketing mix: product, price, distribution, and promotion.

13 ### B. Marketing Mix

1. *Products.* Star Software markets not only calendar software but also the service of specialty advertising to its clients. Star's intangible attributes are its ability to meet or exceed customer expectations consistently, its speed in responding to customers' demands, and its anticipation of new customer needs. Intangible attributes are difficult for competitors to copy, thereby giving Star Software a competitive advantage.

7

2. *Price.* Star Software provides a high-quality specialty advertising product customized to its clients' needs. The value of this product and service is reflected in its premium price. Star should be sensitive to the price elasticity of its product and overall consumer demand.

3. *Distribution.* Star Software uses direct marketing. Since its product is compact, lightweight, and nonperishable, it can be shipped from a central location direct to the client via United Parcel Service, FedEx, or the U.S. Postal Service. The fact that Star can ship to multiple locations for each customer is an asset in selling its products.

4. *Promotion.* Since 90 percent of Star's customers reorder each year, the bulk of promotional expenditures should focus on new product offerings through direct-mail advertising and trade journals or specialty publications. Any remaining promotional dollars could be directed to personal selling (in the form of sales performance bonuses) of current and new products.

 VI. MARKETING IMPLEMENTATION

A. Marketing Organization

Because Star's current and future products require extensive customization to match clients' needs, it is necessary to organize the marketing function by customer groups. This will allow Star to focus its marketing efforts exclusively on the needs and specifications of each target customer segment. Star's marketing efforts will be organized around the following customer groups: (1) manufacturing group; (2) non-manufacturing, business-to-business group; (3) consumer product licensing group; and (4) industry associations group. Each group will be headed by a sales manager who will report to the marketing director (these positions must be created). Each group will be responsible for marketing Star's products within that customer segment. In addition, each group will have full decision-making authority. This represents a shift from the current highly centralized management hierarchy. Frontline salespeople will be empowered to make decisions that will better satisfy Star's clients.

These changes in marketing organization will enable Star Software to be more creative and flexible in meeting customers' needs. Likewise, these changes will overcome the current lack of diversification in Star's product lines and client base. Finally, this new marketing organization will give Star a better opportunity to monitor the activities of competitors.

 ### B. Activities, Responsibility, and Timetables for Completion

All implementation activities are to begin at the start of the next fiscal year on April 1. Unless specified, all activities are the responsibility of Star Software's next president, Jonathan McLemore.

14 This section of the marketing plan details how the firm will be organized—by functions, products, regions, or types of customers—to implement its marketing strategies. It also indicates where decision-making authority will rest within the marketing unit.

15 This component of the marketing plan outlines the specific activities required to implement the marketing plan, who is responsible for performing these activities, and when these activities should be accomplished based on a specified schedule.

8

- On April 1, create four sales manager positions and the position of marketing director. The marketing director will serve as project leader of a new business analysis team, to be composed of nine employees from a variety of positions within the company.

- By April 15, assign three members of the analysis team to each of the following projects: (1) research potential new product offerings and clients, (2) analyze the current billing cycle and billing practices, and (3) design a customer survey project. The marketing director is responsible.

- By June 30, the three project groups will report the results of their analyses. The full business analysis team will review all recommendations.

- By July 31, develop a marketing information system to monitor client reorder patterns and customer satisfaction.

- By July 31, implement any changes in billing practices as recommended by the business analysis team.

- By July 31, make initial contact with new potential clients for the current product line. Each sales manager is responsible.

- By August 31, develop a plan for one new product offering, along with an analysis of its potential customers. The business analysis team is responsible.

- By August 31, finalize a customer satisfaction survey for current clients. In addition, the company will contact those customers who did not reorder for the 2005 product year to discuss their concerns. The marketing director is responsible.

- By January, implement the customer satisfaction survey with a random sample of 20 percent of current clients who reordered for the 2005 product year. The marketing director is responsible.

- By February, implement a new product offering, advertising to current customers and to a sample of potential clients. The business analysis team is responsible.

- By March, analyze and report the results of all customer satisfaction surveys and evaluate the new product offering. The marketing director is responsible.

- Reestablish the objectives of the business analysis team for the next fiscal year. The marketing director is responsible.

16 **VII. EVALUATION AND CONTROL**

A. Performance Standards and Financial Controls

A comparison of the financial expenditures with the plan goals will be included in the project report. The following performance standards and financial controls are suggested:

16 This section details how the results of the marketing plan will be measured and evaluated. The control portion of this section includes the types of actions the firm can take to reduce the differences between the planned and the actual performance.

9

- The total budget for the billing analysis, new-product research, and the customer survey will be equal to 60 percent of the annual promotional budget for the coming year.

- The breakdown of the budget within the project will be a 20 percent allocation to the billing cycle study, a 30 percent allocation to the customer survey and marketing information system development, and a 50 percent allocation to new-business development and new-product implementation.

- Each project team is responsible for reporting all financial expenditures, including personnel salaries and direct expenses, for their segment of the project. A standardized reporting form will be developed and provided by the marketing director.

- The marketing director is responsible for adherence to the project budget and will report overages to the company president on a weekly basis. The marketing director is also responsible for any redirection of budget dollars as required for each project of the business analysis team.

- Any new product offering will be evaluated on a quarterly basis to determine its profitability. Product development expenses will be distributed over a two-year period, by calendar quarters, and will be compared with gross income generated during the same period.

B. Monitoring Procedures

To analyze the effectiveness of Star Software's marketing plan, it is necessary to compare its actual performance with plan objectives. To facilitate this analysis, monitoring procedures should be developed for the various activities required to bring the marketing plan to fruition. These procedures include, but are not limited to, the following:

- A project management concept will be used to evaluate the implementation of the marketing plan by establishing time requirements, human resource needs, and financial or budgetary expenditures.

- A perpetual comparison of actual and planned activities will be conducted on a monthly basis for the first year and on a quarterly basis after the initial implementation phase. The business analysis team, including the marketing director, will report their comparison of actual and planned outcomes directly to the company president.

- Each project team is responsible for determining what changes must be made in procedures, product focus, or operations as a result of the studies conducted in its area.

10

Glossary

Accessibility The ability to obtain information available on the Internet. (6)

Accessory equipment Equipment used in production or office activities that does not become a part of the final physical product. (11)

Addressability A marketer's ability to identify customers before they make a purchase. (6)

Advertising Paid nonpersonal communication about an organization and its products transmitted to a target audience through mass media. (19)

Advertising appropriation The advertising budget for a specific time period. (19)

Advertising campaign The creation and execution of a series of advertisements to communicate with a particular target audience. (19)

Advertising platform Basic issues or selling points to be included in an advertising campaign. (19)

Advocacy advertising Advertising that promotes a company's position on a public issue. (19)

Aesthetic modifications Changes relating to the sensory appeal of a product. (12)

Agent A functional intermediary that represents buyers or sellers on a permanent basis. (16)

Aided recall test A posttest that asks respondents to identify recent ads and provides clues to jog their memories. (19)

Allowance A concession in price to achieve a desired goal. (21)

APEC An alliance that promotes open trade and economic and technical cooperation among member nations throughout the world. (5)

Approach The manner in which a salesperson contacts a potential customer. (20)

Arbitrary approach Budgeting for an advertising campaign as specified by a high-level executive in the firm. (19)

Artwork An advertisement's illustrations and layout. (19)

Asia-Pacific Economic Cooperation (APEC) An alliance that promotes open trade and economic and technical cooperation among member nations throughout the world (5)

Atmospherics The physical elements in a store's design that appeal to consumers' emotions and encourage buying. (17)

Attitude An individual's enduring evaluation of feelings about and behavioral tendencies toward an object or idea. (9)

Attitude scale A means of measuring consumer attitudes by gauging the intensity of individuals' reactions to adjectives, phrases, or sentences about an object. (9)

Automatic vending The use of machines to dispense products. (17)

Average fixed cost The fixed cost per unit produced; calculated by dividing fixed costs by number of units produced. (21)

Average total cost The sum of the average fixed cost and the average variable cost. (21)

Average variable cost The variable cost per unit produced; calculated by dividing variable costs by number of units produced. (21)

Bait pricing Pricing an item in a product line low with the intention of selling a higher-priced item in the line. (22)

Balance of trade The difference in value between a nation's exports and its imports. (5)

Barter The trading of products. (21)

Base-point pricing Geographic pricing that combines factory price and freight charges from the base point nearest the buyer. (21)

Benchmarking Comparing the quality of the firm's goods, services, or processes with that of its best-performing competitors. (2)

Benefit segmentation The division of a market according to benefits that customers want from the product. (8)

Better Business Bureau (BBB) A local, nongovernmental regulatory agency, supported by local businesses, that helps settle problems between customers and specific business firms. (3)

Brand A name, term, symbol, design, or other feature that identifies a seller's products and differentiates them from competitors' products. (13)

Brand competitors Firms that market products with similar features and benefits to the same customers at similar prices. (3)

Brand equity The marketing and financial value associated with a brand's strength in a market. (13)

Brand extension branding Using an existing brand name for an improved or new product. (13)

Brand insistence The degree of brand loyalty in which a customer strongly prefers one brand and will accept no substitute. (13)

Brand licensing An agreement whereby a company permits another organization to use its brand on other products for a licensing fee. (13)

Brand loyalty A customer's favorable attitude toward a specific brand and likelihood of consistent purchase. (13)

Brand manager The person responsible for a single brand. (12)

Brand mark The part of a brand not made up of words, such as a symbol or design. (13)

Brand name The part of a brand that can be spoken, including letters, words, and numbers. (13)

Brand preference The degree of customer loyalty in which a customer prefers one brand over competitive offerings. (13)

Brand recognition Awareness that a brand exists and is an alternative purchase. (13)

Breakdown approach Measuring company sales potential based on a general economic forecast for a specific period and the market potential derived from it. (8)

Breakeven point The point at which the costs of producing a product equal the revenue made from selling the product. (21)

Broker A functional intermediary that brings buyers and sellers together temporarily. (16)

Buildup approach Measuring company sales potential by estimating how much of a product a potential buyer in a specific geographic area will purchase in a given period, multiplying the estimate by the number of potential buyers, and adding the totals of all the geographic areas considered. (8)

Bundle pricing Packaging together two or more complementary products and selling them at a single price. (22)

Business analysis Assessing the potential of a product idea for the firm's sales, costs, and profits. (12)

Business (organizational) buying behavior The purchase behavior of producers, government units, institutions, and resellers. (10)

Business cycle A pattern of economic fluctuations that has four stages: prosperity, recession, depression, and recovery. (3)

Business market Individuals or groups that purchase a specific kind of product for resale, direct use in producing other products, or use in general daily operations; also called a *business-to-business* market. (8, 10)

Business products Products bought to use in a firm's operations, to resell, or to make other products. (11)

Business services Intangible products that many organizations use in their operations. (11)

Business-to-business buying behavior *See* Business (organizational) buying behavior.

Buy-back allowance A sum of money given to a reseller for each unit bought after an initial promotion deal is over. (20)

Buying allowance A temporary price reduction to resellers for purchasing specified quantities of a product. (20)

Buying behavior The decision processes and acts of people involved in buying and using products. (9)

Buying center The people within an organization, including users, influencers, buyers, deciders, and gatekeepers, who make business purchase decisions. (10)

Buying power Resources, such as money, goods, and services, that can be traded in an exchange. (3)

buzz marketing An attempt to create a trend or acceptance of a product through word-of-mouth communications (18)

Captioned photograph A photograph with a brief description of its contents. (19)

Captive pricing Pricing the basic product in a product line low while pricing related items higher. (22)

Cash-and-carry wholesaler A limited-service wholesaler whose customers pay cash and furnish transportation. (16)

Cash discount A price reduction given to buyers for prompt payment or cash payment. (21)

Catalog marketing A type of marketing in which an organization provides a catalog from which customers make selections and place orders by mail, telephone, or the Internet. (17)

Catalog showroom A warehouse showroom in which consumers use catalogs to place orders for products, which are then filled directly in the warehouse area and picked up by buyers in the showroom. (17)

Category killer A very large specialty store that concentrates on a major product category and competes on the basis of low prices and enormous product availability. (17)

Causal research Research in which it is assumed that a particular variable X causes a variable Y. (7)

Cause-related marketing The practice of linking products to a particular social cause on an ongoing or short-term basis. (4)

Centralized organization A structure in which top-level managers delegate little authority to lower levels. (2)

Cents-off offer A promotion that allows buyers to pay less than the regular price to encourage purchase. (20)

Channel capacity The limit on the volume of information a communication channel can handle effectively. (18)

Channel captain The dominant member of a marketing channel or supply chain. (15)

Channel of distribution *See* Marketing channel.

Channel power The ability of one channel member to influence another member's goal achievement. (15)

Client-based relationships Interactions that result in satisfied customers who use a service repeatedly over time. (14)

Client publics Direct consumers of a product of a nonbusiness organization. (14)

Closing The stage in the personal selling process when the salesperson asks the prospect to buy the product. (20)

Co-branding Using two or more brands on one product. (13)

Codes of conduct Formalized rules and standards that describe what the company expects of its employees; also called codes of ethics. (4)

Coding process Converting meaning into a series of signs or symbols; also called *encoding*. (18)

Cognitive dissonance A buyer's doubts shortly after a purchase about whether the decision was the right one. (9)

Combination compensation plan Paying salespeople a fixed salary plus a commission based on sales volume. (20)

Commercialization Refining and finalizing plans and budgets for full-scale manufacturing and marketing of a product. (12)

Commission merchant An agent that receives goods on consignment from local sellers and negotiates sales in large, central markets. (16)

Common Market of the Southern Cone (MERCOSUR) An alliance that promotes the free circulation of goods, services, and production factors, and has a common external tariff and commercial policy among member nations in South America (5)

Communication A sharing of meaning through the transmission of information. (18)

Community A sense of group membership or feeling of belonging by individual group members. (6)

Community shopping center A shopping center with one or two department stores, some specialty stores, and convenience stores. (17)

Company sales potential The maximum percentage of market potential that an individual firm within an industry can expect to obtain for a specific product. (8)

Comparative advertising Advertising that compares two or more brands on the basis of one or more product characteristics. (19)

Comparison discounting Setting a price at a specific level and comparing it with a higher price. (22)

Competition Other organizations that market products that are similar to or can be substituted for a marketer's products in the same geographic area. (3)

Competition-based pricing Pricing influenced primarily by competitors' prices. (22)

Competition-matching approach Determining an advertising budget by trying to match competitors' advertising outlays. (19)

Competitive advantage The result of a company's matching a core competency to opportunities it has discovered in the marketplace. (2)

Competitive advertising Advertising that points out a brand's special features, uses, and advantages relative to competing brands. (19)

Component parts Items that become part of the physical product and are either finished items ready for assembly or items that need little processing before assembly. (11)

Concentrated targeting strategy A market segmentation strategy in which an organization targets a single market segment using one marketing mix. (8)

Concept testing Seeking potential buyers' responses to a product idea. (12)

Consideration set A group of brands within a product category that a buyer views as alternatives for possible purchase. (9)

Consistency of quality The degree to which a product has the same level of quality over time. (12)

Consumer buying behavior Buying behavior of people who purchase products for personal or household use and not for business purposes. (9)

Consumer buying decision process A five-stage purchase decision process that includes problem recognition, information search, evaluation of alternatives, purchase, and postpurchase evaluation. (9)

Consumer contests and games Sales promotion methods in which individuals compete for prizes based on their analytical or creative skills. (20)

Consumerism Organized efforts by individuals, groups, and organizations to protect consumers' rights. (3)

Consumer jury A panel of a product's existing or potential buyers who pretest ads. (19)

Consumer market Purchasers and household members who intend to consume or benefit from the purchased products and do not buy products to make profits. (8)

Consumer products Products purchased to satisfy personal and family needs. (11)

Consumer sales promotion methods Sales promotion techniques that encourage consumers to patronize specific stores or try particular products. (20)

Consumer socialization The process through which a person acquires the knowledge and skills to function as a consumer. (9)

Consumer sweepstakes A sales promotion in which entrants submit their names for inclusion in a drawing for prizes. (20)

Contract manufacturing The practice of hiring a foreign firm to produce a designated volume of the domestic firm's product to specification; the final product carries the domestic firm's name. (5)

Control Customers' ability to regulate the information they view and the rate and sequence of their exposure to that information. (6)

Convenience products Relatively inexpensive, frequently purchased items for which buyers exert minimal purchasing effort. (11)

Cookie An identifying string of text stored on a website visitor's computer. (6)

Cooperative advertising An arrangement in which a manufacturer agrees to pay a certain amount of a retailer's media costs for advertising the manufacturer's products. (20)

Copy The verbal portion of advertisements. (19)

Core competencies Things a firm does extremely well, which sometimes give it an advantage over its competition. (2)

Corporate culture *See* Organizational culture.

Corporate strategy A strategy that determines the means for utilizing resources in the various functional areas to reach the organization's goals. (2)

Cost-based pricing Adding a dollar amount or percentage to the cost of the product. (22)

Cost comparison indicator A means of comparing the costs of advertising vehicles in a specific medium in relation to the number of people reached. (19)

Cost-plus pricing Adding a specified dollar amount or percentage to the seller's cost. (22)

Count-and-recount A sales promotion method based on payment of a specific amount for each product unit moved from a reseller's warehouse in a given period of time. (19)

Coupon A written price reduction used to encourage consumers to buy a specific product. (20)

Credence qualities Attributes that customers may be unable to evaluate even after purchasing and consuming a service. (14)

Culture The values, knowledge, beliefs, customs, objects, and concepts of a society. (9)

Cumulative discount A quantity discount aggregated over a stated period. (21)

Customary pricing Pricing on the basis of tradition. (22)

Customers The purchasers of organizations' products; the focal point of all marketing activities. (1)

Customer contact The level of interaction between provider and customer needed to deliver the service. (14)

Customer forecasting survey A survey of customers regarding the quantities of products they intend to buy during a specific period. (8)

Customer relationship management (CRM) Using information about customers to create marketing strategies that develop and sustain desirable customer relationships. (1)

Customer service audit A specialized audit in which specific consumer service activities are analyzed and service goals and standards are compared to actual performance. (22)

Customer services Human or mechanical efforts or activities that add value to a product. (12)

Cycle analysis An analysis of sales figures for a period of three to five years to ascertain whether sales fluctuate in a consistent, periodic manner. (8)

Cycle time The time needed to complete a process. (16)

Database A collection of information arranged for easy access and retrieval. (6)

Dealer brand *See* Private distributor brand.

Dealer listing An advertisement that promotes a product and identifies the names of participating retailers that sell the product. (20)

Dealer loader A gift, often part of a display, given to a retailer that purchases a specified quantity of merchandise. (20)

Decentralized organization A structure in which decision-making authority is delegated as far down the chain of command as possible. (2)

Decline stage The stage of a product's life cycle when sales fall rapidly. (11)

Decoding process Converting signs or symbols into concepts and ideas. (18)

Delphi technique A procedure in which experts create initial forecasts, submit them to the company for averaging, and then refine the forecasts. (8)

Demand-based pricing Pricing based on the level of demand for the product. (22)

Demand curve A graph of the quantity of products expected to be sold at various prices if other factors remain constant. (21)

Demonstration A sales promotion method a manufacturer uses temporarily to encourage trial use and purchase of the product or to show how a product works. (20)

Department store A large retail organization characterized by wide product mixes and organized into separate departments to facilitate marketing efforts and internal management. (17)

Depression A stage of the business cycle when unemployment is extremely high, wages are very low, total disposable income is at a minimum, and consumers lack confidence in the economy. (3)

Depth of product mix The average number of different products offered in each product line. (11)

Derived demand Demand for industrial products that stems from demand for consumer products. (10)

Descriptive research Research conducted to clarify the characteristics of certain phenomena to solve a particular problem. (7)

Differential pricing Charging different prices to different buyers for the same quality and quantity of product. (22)

Differentiated targeting strategy A strategy in which an organization targets two or more segments by developing a marketing mix for each segment. (8)

Digitalization The ability to represent a product, or at least some of its benefits, as digital bits of information. (6)

Direct-cost approach An approach to determining marketing costs in which cost analysis includes variable costs and traceable common costs but not nontraceable common costs. (22)

Direct marketing The use of the telephone, Internet and nonpersonal media to introduce products to customers who can then purchase them via mail, telephone, or the Internet. (17)

Direct ownership A situation in which a company owns subsidiaries or other facilities overseas. (5)

Direct-response marketing A type of marketing in which a retailer advertises a product and makes it available through mail or telephone orders. (17)

Direct selling Marketing products to ultimate consumers through face-to-face sales presentations at home or in the workplace. (17)

Discount store A self-service, general-merchandise store offering brand name and private-brand products at low prices. (17)

Discretionary income Disposable income available for spending and saving after an individual has purchased the basic necessities of food, clothing, and shelter. (3)

Disposable income After-tax income. (3)

Distribution The activities that make products available to customers when and where they want to purchase them. (15)

Distribution center A large, centralized warehouse that focuses on moving rather than storing goods. (16)

Diversified growth Growth that occurs when new products are developed to be sold in new markets. (2)

Drop shipper A limited-service wholesaler that takes title to products and negotiates sales but never actually takes possession of products; also known as a *desk jobber*. (16)

Dual distribution The use of two or more marketing channels to distribute the same product to the same target market. (15)

Dumping Selling products at unfairly low prices. (5)

Early adopters Careful choosers of new products. (11)

Early majority Individuals who adopt a new product just prior to the average person. (11)

Electronic commerce (e-commerce) Sharing business information, maintaining business relationships, and conducting business transactions by means of telecommunications networks. (6)

Electronic data interchange (EDI) A computerized means of integrating order processing with production, inventory, accounting, and transportation. (16)

Electronic marketing (e-marketing) The strategic process of creating, distributing, promoting, and pricing products for targeted customers in the virtual environment of the Internet. (6)

Embargo A government's suspension of trade in a particular product or with a given country. (5)

Empowerment Giving customer contact employees the authority and responsibility to make marketing decisions without seeking approval of their supervisors. (2)

Encoding *See* Coding process.

Environmental analysis The process of assessing and interpreting the information gathered through environmental scanning. (3)

Environmental scanning The process of collecting information about forces in the marketing environment. (3)

Ethical issue An identifiable problem, situation, or opportunity requiring a choice among several actions that must be evaluated as right or wrong, ethical or unethical. (4)

European Union (EU) An alliance that promotes trade among its member countries in Europe. (5)

Evaluative criteria Objective and subjective characteristics that are important to a buyer. (9)

Everyday low prices (EDLP) Pricing products low on a consistent basis. (22)

Exchange The provision or transfer of goods, services, or ideas in return for something of value. (1)

Exchange controls Government restrictions on the amount of a particular currency that can be bought or sold. (5)

Exclusive dealing A situation in which a manufacturer forbids an intermediary to carry products of competing manufacturers. (15)

Exclusive distribution Using a single outlet in a fairly large geographic area to distribute a product. (15)

Executive judgment A sales forecasting method based on the intuition of one or more executives. (8)

Experience qualities Attributes that can be assessed only during purchase and consumption of a service. (14)

Experiment A research method that attempts to maintain certain variables while measuring the effects of experimental variables. (7)

Expert forecasting survey Sales forecasts prepared by experts outside the firm, such as economists, management consultants, advertising executives, or college professors. (8)

Exploratory research Research conducted to gather more information about a problem or to make a tentative hypothesis more specific. (7)

Exporting The sale of products to foreign markets. (5)

Extended problem solving A consumer problem-solving process employed when purchasing unfamiliar, expensive, or infrequently bought products. (9)

External customers Individuals who patronize a business. (2)

External reference price A comparison price provided by others. (21)

External search An information search in which buyers seek information from sources other than memory. (9)

Family branding Branding all of a firm's products with the same name or part of the name. (13)

Family packaging Using similar packaging for all of a firm's products or packaging that has one common design element. (13)

Feature article A manuscript of up to 3,000 words prepared for a specific publication. (19)

Federal Trade Commission (FTC) An agency that regulates a variety of business practices and curbs false advertising, misleading pricing, and deceptive packaging and labeling. (3)

Feedback The receiver's response to a decoded message. (18)

Fixed costs Costs that do not vary with changes in the number of units produced or sold; costs allocated on the basis of how money was actually spent, such as rent, salaries, office supplies, and utilities. (21)

F.O.B. (free-on-board) destination A price indicating the producer is absorbing shipping costs. (21)

F.O.B. (free-on-board) factory The price of merchandise at the factory, before shipment. (21)

Focus-group interview A research method involving observation of group interaction when members are exposed to an idea or a concept. (7)

Franchising A form of licensing in which a franchiser, in exchange for a financial commitment, grants a franchisee the right to market its product in accordance with the franchiser's standards; An arrangement in which a supplier (franchiser) grants a dealer (franchisee) the right to sell products in exchange for some type of consideration. (5, 17)

Free merchandise A manufacturer's reward given to resellers that purchase a stated quantity of products. (20)

Free sample A sample of a product given out to encourage trial and purchase. (20)

Freight absorption pricing Absorption of all or part of actual freight costs by the seller. (21)

Freight forwarder An organization that consolidates shipments from several firms into efficient lot sizes. (16)

Full-cost approach An approach to determining marketing costs in which cost analysis includes variable, traceable common costs and nontraceable common costs. (22)

Full-service wholesaler A merchant wholesaler that provides the widest range of wholesaling functions. (16)

Functional discount *See* Trade discount.

Functional middlemen Intermediaries that negotiate purchases and expedite sales for a fee but do not take title to products. (15)

Functional modifications Changes affecting a product's versatility, effectiveness, convenience, or safety. (12)

GATT *See* General Agreement on Tariffs and Trade.

General Agreement on Tariffs and Trade (GATT) An agreement among nations to reduce worldwide tariffs and increase international trade. (5)

General-merchandise retailer A retail establishment that offers a variety of product lines that are stocked in depth. (17)

General-merchandise wholesaler A full-service wholesaler with a wide product mix but limited depth within product lines. (16)

General publics Indirect consumers of a product of a nonbusiness organization. (14)

Generic brand A brand indicating only the product category. (13)

Generic competitors Firms that provide very different products that solve the same problem or satisfy the same basic customer need. (3)

Geodemographic segmentation A method of market segmentation that clusters people in zip code areas and smaller neighborhood units based on lifestyle and demographic information. (8)

Geographic pricing Reductions for transportation and other costs related to the physical distance between buyer and seller. (21)

Globalization The development of marketing strategies that treat the entire world (or its major regions) as a single entity. (5)

Good A tangible physical entity. (11)

Government market A federal, state, county, or local government that buys goods and services to support its internal operations and provide products to its constituencies. (10)

Green marketing The specific development, pricing, promotion, and distribution of products that do not harm the natural environment. (4)

Gross domestic product (GDP) The market value of a nation's total output of goods and services for a given period; an overall measure of economic standing. (5)

Growth stage The product life cycle stage when sales rise rapidly and profits reach a peak, then start to decline. (11)

Heterogeneity Variation in quality. (14)

Heterogeneous market A market made up of individuals or organizations with diverse needs for products in a specific product class. (8)

Homogeneous market A market in which a large proportion of customers have similar needs for a product. (8)

Horizontal channel integration Combining organizations at the same level of operation under one management. (15)

Hypermarket A store that combines supermarket and discount store shopping in one location. (17)

Hypothesis An informed guess or assumption about a certain problem or set of circumstances. (7)

Idea A concept, philosophy, image, or issue. (11)

Idea generation Seeking product ideas to achieve organizational objectives. (12)

Illustrations Photos, drawings, graphs, charts, and tables used to spark audience interest in an advertisement. (19)

Importing The purchase of products from a foreign source. (5)

Import tariff A duty levied by a nation on goods bought outside its borders and brought in. (5)

Impulse buying An unplanned buying behavior resulting from a powerful urge to buy something immediately. (9)

Income For an individual, the amount of money received through wages, rents, investments, pensions, and subsidy payments for a given period. (3)

Individual branding A branding policy in which each product is given a different name. (13)

Industrial distributor An independent business organization that takes title to industrial products and carries inventories. (15)

Inelastic demand Demand that is not significantly altered by a price increase or decrease. (10)

Information inputs Sensations received through the sense organs. (9)

In-home (door-to-door) interview A personal interview that takes place in the respondent's home. (7)

Innovators First adopters of new products. (11)

Input-output data Information that identifies what types of industries purchase the products of a particular industry. (10)

Inseparability The quality of being produced and consumed at the same time. (14)

Installations Facilities and nonportable major equipment. (11)

Institutional advertising Advertising that promotes organizational images, ideas, and political issues. (19)

Institutional market Organizations with charitable, educational, community, or other nonbusiness goals. (10)

Intangibility Unable to be perceived by the senses or to be possessed. (14)

Integrated marketing communications Coordination of promotion and other marketing efforts for maximum informational and persuasive impact. (18)

Intended strategy The strategy the company decided on during the planning phase and wants to use. (2)

Intensive distribution Using all available outlets to distribute a product. (15)

Intensive growth Growth that occurs when current products and current markets have the potential for increasing sales. (2)

Interactivity The ability to allow customers to express their needs and wants directly to the firm in response to the firm's marketing communications. (6)

Intermodal transportation Two or more transportation modes used in combination. (16)

Internal customers A company's employees. (2)

Internal marketing A management philosophy that coordinates internal exchanges between the organization and its employees to achieve successful external exchanges between the organization and its customers. (2)

Internal reference price A price developed in the buyer's mind through experience with the product. (21)

Internal search An information search in which buyers search their memories for information about products that might solve their problem. (9)

International marketing Developing and performing marketing activities across national boundaries. (5)

Introduction stage The initial stage in a product's life cycle; its first appearance in the marketplace, when sales start at zero and profits are negative. (11)

Inventory management Developing and maintaining adequate assortments of products to meet customers' needs. (16)

Joint demand Demand involving the use of two or more items in combination to produce a product. (10)

Joint venture A partnership between a domestic firm and a foreign firm or government. (5)

Just-in-time (JIT) An inventory management approach in which supplies arrive just when needed for use in production or for resale. (16)

Kinesic communication Communicating through the movement of head, eyes, arms, hands, legs, or torso. (18)

Labeling Providing identifying, promotional, or other information on package labels. (13)

Laggards The last adopters, who distrust new products. (11)

Late majority Skeptics who adopt new products when they feel it is necessary. (11)

Layout The physical arrangement of an advertisement's illustration and copy. (19)

Learning Changes in an individual's thought processes and behavior caused by information and experience. (9)

Level of involvement An individual's intensity of interest in a product and the importance of the product for that person. (9)

Level of quality The amount of quality a product possesses. (12)

Licensing An alternative to direct investment requiring a licensee to pay commissions or royalties on sales or supplies used in manufacturing. (5)

Lifestyle An individual's pattern of living expressed through activities, interests, and opinions. (9)

Limited-line wholesaler A full-service wholesaler that carries only a few product lines but many products within those lines. (16)

Limited problem solving A consumer problem-solving process used when purchasing products occasionally or needing information about an unfamiliar brand in a familiar product category. (9)

Limited-service wholesaler A merchant wholesaler that provides some services and specializes in a few functions. (16)

Line extension Development of a product that is closely related to existing products in the line but meets different customer needs. (12)

Mail-order wholesaler A limited-service wholesaler that sells products through catalogs. (16)

Mail survey A research method in which respondents answer a questionnaire sent through the mail. (7)

Manufacturer brand A brand initiated by its producer. (13)

Manufacturers' agent An independent intermediary that represents more than one seller and offers complete product lines. (16)

Marginal cost (MC) The extra cost incurred by producing one more unit of a product. (21)

Marginal revenue (MR) The change in total revenue resulting from the sale of an additional unit of a product. (21)

Market A group of individuals and/or organizations that have needs for products in a product class and have the ability, willingness, and authority to purchase those products. (2, 7)

Market density The number of potential customers within a unit of land area, such as a square mile. (8)

Market growth/market share A strategic planning tool based on the philosophy that a product's market growth rate and market share are important considerations in determining marketing strategy. (2)

Marketing The process of creating, distributing, promoting, and pricing goods, services, and ideas to facilitate satisfying exchange relationships with customers in a dynamic environment. (1)

Marketing audit A systematic examination of the marketing group's objectives, strategies, organization, and performance. (22)

Marketing channel A group of individuals and organizations that direct the flow of products from producers to customers; also called *channel of distribution* or *distribution channel*. (15)

Marketing citizenship The adoption of a strategic focus for fulfilling the economic, legal, ethical, and philanthropic social responsibilities expected by stakeholders. (4)

Marketing concept A philosophy that an organization should try to provide products that satisfy customers' needs through a coordinated set of activities that also allows the organization to achieve its goals. (1)

Marketing control process Establishing performance standards, evaluating actual performance by comparing it with established standards, and reducing the differences between desired and actual performance. (2)

Marketing cost analysis Breaking down and classifying costs to determine which are associated with specific marketing activities. (22)

Marketing decision support system (MDSS) Customized computer software that aids marketing managers in decision making. (7)

Marketing environment The competitive, economic, political, legal and regulatory, technological, and sociocultural forces that surround the customer and affect the marketing mix. (1)

Marketing ethics Principles and standards that define acceptable marketing conduct as determined by various stakeholders. (4)

Marketing implementation The process of putting marketing strategies into action. (2)

Marketing information system (MIS) A framework for managing and structuring information gathered regularly from sources inside and outside the organization. (7)

Marketing intermediary A middleman linking producers to other middlemen or ultimate consumers through contractual arrangements or through the purchase and resale of products. (15)

Marketing management The process of planning, organizing, implementing, and controlling marketing activities to facilitate exchanges effectively and efficiently. (1)

Marketing mix Four marketing activities—product, distribution, promotion, and pricing—that a firm can control to meet the needs of customers within its target market. (1)

Marketing objective A statement of what is to be accomplished through marketing activities. (2)

Marketing orientation An organizationwide commitment to researching and responding to customer needs (1)

Marketing plan A written document that specifies the activities to be performed to implement and control the organization's marketing activities. (2)

Marketing planning The process of assessing marketing opportunities and resources, determining marketing objectives, defining marketing strategies, and establishing guidelines for implementation and control of the marketing program. (2)

Marketing research The systematic design, collection, interpretation, and reporting of information to help marketers solve specific marketing problems or take advantage of marketing opportunities. (7)

Marketing strategy A plan of action for identifying and analyzing a target market and developing a marketing mix to meet the needs of that market. (2)

Market manager The person responsible for managing the marketing activities that serve a particular group of customers. (12)

Market opportunity A combination of circumstances and timing that permits an organization to take action to reach a particular target market. (2)

Market potential The total amount of a product that customers will purchase within a specified period at a specific level of industrywide marketing activity. (8)

Market segment Individuals, groups, or organizations sharing one or more similar characteristics that cause them to have similar product needs. (8)

Market segmentation The process of dividing a total market into groups with relatively similar product needs to design a marketing mix that matches those needs. (8)

Market share The percentage of a market that actually buys a specific product from a particular company. (2)

Market test Making a product available to buyers in one or more test areas and measuring purchases and consumer responses to marketing efforts. (8)

Markup pricing Adding to the cost of a product a predetermined percentage of that cost. (22)

Maslow's hierarchy of needs The five levels of needs that humans seek to satisfy, from most to least important. (9)

Materials handling Physical handling of products. (16)

Maturity stage The stage of a product's life cycle when the sales curve peaks and starts to decline and profits continue to fall. (11)

Media plan A plan that specifies the media vehicles to be used and the schedule for running advertisements. (19)

Medium of transmission The medium that carries the coded message from the source to the receiver. (18)

Megacarrier A freight transportation firm that provides several modes of shipment. (16)

Memory The ability to access databases or data warehouses containing individual customer profiles and purchase histories and to use these data in real time to customize a marketing offer. (6)

Merchandise allowance A manufacturer's agreement to pay resellers certain amounts of money for providing special promotional efforts, such as setting up and maintaining a display. (20)

Merchant wholesaler An independently owned business that takes title to goods, assumes ownership risks, and buys and resells products to other wholesalers, business customers, or retailers. (16)

MERCOSUR An alliance that promotes the free circulation of goods, services, and production factors, and has a common external tariff and commercial policy among member nations in South America. (5)

Micromarketing An approach to market segmentation in which organizations focus precise marketing efforts on very small geographic markets. (8)

Missionary salesperson A support salesperson, usually employed by a manufacturer, who assists the producer's customers in selling to their own customers. (20)

Mission statement A long-term view, or vision, of what the organization wants to become. (2)

Modified rebuy purchase A new-task purchase that is changed on subsequent orders or when the requirements of a straight rebuy purchase are modified. (10)

Money refund A sales promotion technique offering consumers a specified amount of money when they mail in a proof of purchase, usually for multiple product purchases. (20)

Monopolistic competition A competitive structure in which a firm has many potential competitors and tries to develop a marketing strategy to differentiate its product. (3)

Monopoly A competitive structure in which an organization offers a product that has no close substitutes, making that organization the sole source of supply. (3)

Motive An internal energizing force that directs a person's behavior toward satisfying needs or achieving goals. (8)

MRO supplies Maintenance, repair, and operating items that facilitate production and operations but do not become part of the finished product. (11)

Multinational enterprise A firm that has operations or subsidiaries in many countries. (5)

Multiple sourcing An organization's decision to use several suppliers. (10)

Multiple-unit pricing Packaging together two or more identical products and selling them at a single price. (22)

NAFTA *See* North American Free Trade Agreement.

NAICS *See* North American Industry Classification System.

National Advertising Review Board (NARB) A self-regulatory unit that considers challenges to issues raised by the National Advertising Division (an arm of the Council of Better Business Bureaus) about an advertisement. (3)

Negotiated pricing Establishing a final price through bargaining between seller and customer. (22)

Neighborhood shopping center A shopping center usually consisting of several small convenience and specialty stores. (17)

New-product development process A seven-phase process for introducing products: idea generation, screening, concept testing, business analysis, product development, test marketing, and commercialization. (12)

News release A short piece of copy publicizing an event or a product. (19)

New-task purchase An initial purchase by an organization of an item to be used to perform a new job or solve a new problem. (10)

Noise Anything that reduces a communication's clarity and accuracy. (18)

Noncumulative discount A one-time price reduction based on the number of units purchased, the size of the order, or the product combination purchased. (21)

Nonprice competition Emphasizing factors other than price to distinguish a product from competing brands. (21)

Nonprobability sampling A sampling technique in which there is no way to calculate the likelihood that a specific element of the population being studied will be chosen. (7)

Nonprofit marketing Marketing activities conducted to achieve some goal other than ordinary business goals such as profit, market share, or return on investment. (14)

Nonstore retailing The selling of products outside the confines of a retail facility. (17)

Nontraceable common costs Costs that cannot be assigned to any specific function according to any logical criteria and thus are assignable only on an arbitrary basis. (22)

North American Free Trade Agreement (NAFTA) An alliance that merges Canada, Mexico, and the United States into a single market. (5)

North American Industry Classification System (NAICS) An industry classification system that will generate comparable statistics among the United States, Canada, and Mexico. (10)

Objective-and-task approach Budgeting for an advertising campaign by first determining its objectives and then calculating the cost of all the tasks needed to attain them. (19)

Odd-even pricing Ending the price with certain numbers to influence buyers' perceptions of the price or product. (22)

Off-price retailer A store that buys manufacturers' seconds, overruns, returns, and off-season merchandise for resale to consumers at deep discounts. (17)

Oligopoly A competitive structure in which a few sellers control the supply of a large proportion of a product. (3)

Online retailing Retailing that makes products available to buyers through computer connections. (17)

Online survey A research method in which respondents answer a questionnaire via e-mail or on a website. (7)

On-site computer interview A variation of the shopping mall intercept interview in which respondents complete a self-administered questionnaire displayed on a computer monitor. (7)

Opinion leader A reference group member who provides information about a specific sphere of interest to reference group participants. (9)

Opportunity cost The value of the benefit given up by choosing one alternative over another. (14)

Order getter A salesperson who sells to new customers and increases sales to current customers. (20)

Order processing The receipt and transmission of sales order information. (16)

Order taker A salesperson who primarily seeks repeat sales. (20)

Organizational (corporate) culture A set of values, beliefs, goals, norms, and rituals that members of an organization share. (4)

Outsourcing Contracting physical distribution tasks to third parties that do not have managerial authority within the marketing channel. (16)

Patronage motives Motives that influence where a person purchases products on a regular basis. (9)

Penetration pricing Setting prices below those of competing brands to penetrate a market and gain a significant market share quickly. (22)

Percent-of-sales approach Budgeting for an advertising campaign by multiplying the firm's past and expected sales by a standard percentage. (19)

Perception The process of selecting, organizing, and interpreting information inputs to produce meaning. (9)

Performance standard An expected level of performance against which actual performance can be compared. (2)

Periodic discounting Temporary reduction of prices on a patterned or systematic basis. (22)

Perishability The inability of unused service capacity to be stored for future use. (14)

Personal interview survey A research method in which participants respond to survey questions face to face. (7)

Personality A set of internal traits and distinct behavioral tendencies that result in consistent patterns of behavior. (9)

Personal selling Paid personal communication that attempts to inform customers and persuade them to buy products in an exchange situation. (20)

Physical distribution Activities used to move products from producers to consumers and other end users. (16)

Pioneer advertising Advertising that tries to stimulate demand for a product category rather than a specific brand by informing potential buyers about the product. (19)

Pioneer promotion Promotion that informs consumers about a new product. (18)

Point-of-purchase (P-O-P) materials Signs, window displays, display racks, and similar devices used to attract customers. (20)

Population All the elements, units, or individuals of interest to researchers for a specific study. (7)

Portal A multiservice website that serves as a gateway to other websites. (6)

Posttest Evaluation of advertising effectiveness after the campaign. (19)

Premium An item offered free or at a minimal cost as a bonus for purchasing a product. (20)

Premium (push) money Extra compensation to salespeople for pushing a line of goods. (20)

Premium pricing Pricing the highest-quality or most versatile products higher than other models in the product line. (22)

Press conference A meeting used to announce major news events. (19)

Prestige pricing Setting prices at an artificially high level to convey a prestige or a quality image. (22)

Prestige sensitive Drawn to products that signify prominence and status. (21)

Pretest Evaluation of advertisements performed before a campaign begins. (19)

Price The value that is exchanged for products in a marketing transaction. (21)

Price competition Emphasizing price as an issue and matching or beating competitors' prices. (21)

Price conscious Striving to pay low prices. (21)

Price discrimination Employing price differentials that injure competition by giving one or more buyers a competitive advantage and that is prohibited by law. (21)

Price elasticity of demand A measure of the sensitivity of demand to changes in price. (21)

Price leader A product priced below the usual markup, near cost, or below cost. (22)

Price lining Setting a limited number of prices for selected groups or lines of merchandise. (22)

Price skimming Charging the highest possible price that buyers who most desire the product will pay. (22)

Pricing objectives Goals that describe what a firm wants to achieve through pricing. (22)

Primary data Data observed and recorded or collected directly from respondents. (7)

Primary demand Demand for a product category rather than for a specific brand. (18)

Private brand *See* Private distributor brand.

Private distributor brand A brand initiated and owned by a reseller; also called *private brand*, *store brand*, or *dealer brand*. (13)

Private warehouse A company-operated facility for storing and shipping products. (16)

Probability sampling A sampling technique in which every element in the population being studied has a known chance of being selected for study. (7)

Process materials Materials that are used directly in the production of other products but are not readily identifiable. (11)

Producer market Individuals and business organizations that purchase products to make profits by using them to produce other products or using them in their operations. (10)

Product A good, a service, or an idea. (1)

Product adoption process The five-stage process of buyer acceptance of a product: awareness, interest, evaluation, trial, and adoption. (11)

Product advertising Advertising that promotes the uses, features, and benefits of products. (19)

Product competitors Firms that compete in the same product class but market products with different features, benefits, and prices. (3)

Product deletion Eliminating a product from the product mix when it no longer satisfies a sufficient number of customers. (12)

Product design How a product is conceived, planned, and produced. (12)

Product development Determining if producing a product is feasible and cost effective. (12)

Product differentiation Creating and designing products so that consumers perceive them as different from competing products. (12)

Product features Specific design characteristics that allow a product to perform certain tasks. (12)

Product item A specific version of a product. (11)

Product life cycle The progression of a product through four stages: introduction, growth, maturity, and decline. (11)

Product line A group of closely related product items viewed as a unit because of marketing, technical, or end-use considerations. (11)

Product-line pricing Establishing and adjusting prices of multiple products within a product line. (22)

Product manager The person within an organization responsible for a product, a product line, or several distinct products that make up a group. (12)

Product mix The total group of products that an organization makes available to customers. (11)

Product modifications Changes in one or more characteristics of a product. (12)

Product positioning Creating and maintaining a certain concept of a product in customers' minds. (12)

Professional pricing Fees set by people with great skill or experience in a particular field. (22)

Promotion Communication to build and maintain relationships by informing and persuading one or more audiences. (18)

Promotion mix A combination of promotional methods used to promote a specific product. (18)

Prospecting Developing a list of potential customers. (20)

Prosperity A stage of the business cycle characterized by low unemployment and relatively high total income, which together ensure high buying power (provided the inflation rate stays low). (3)

Proxemic communication Communicating by varying the physical distance in face-to-face interactions. (18)

Psychological influences Factors that in part determine people's general behavior, thus influencing their behavior as consumers. (9)

Psychological pricing Pricing that attempts to influence a customer's perception of price to make a product's price more attractive. (22)

Publicity A news story type of communication form about an organization and/or its products that is transmitted through a mass medium at no charge. (19)

Public relations Communication efforts used to create and maintain favorable relations between an organization and its stakeholders. (19)

Public warehouse A business that leases storage space and related physical distribution facilities to other firms. (16)

Pull policy Promoting a product directly to consumers to develop strong consumer demand that pulls products through the marketing channel. (18)

Purchasing power *See* Buying power.

Pure competition A market structure characterized by an extremely large number of sellers, none strong enough to significantly influence price or supply. (3)

Push policy Promoting a product only to the next institution down the marketing channel. (18)

Quality The overall characteristics of a product that allow it to perform as expected in satisfying customer needs. (12)

Quality modifications Changes relating to a product's dependability and durability. (12)

Quantity discount Deductions from list price for purchasing in large quantities. (21)

Quota A limit on the amount of goods an importing country will accept for certain product categories in a specific time period. (5)

Quota sampling A nonprobability sampling technique in which researchers divide the population into groups and then arbitrarily choose participants from each group. (7)

Rack jobber A full-service, specialty-line wholesaler that owns and maintains display racks in stores. (16)

Random discounting Temporary reduction of prices on an unsystematic basis. (22)

Random factor analysis An analysis attempting to attribute erratic sales variations to random, nonrecurrent events. (8)

Random sampling A type of sampling in which all units in a population have an equal chance of appearing in the sample. (6)

Raw materials Basic natural materials that become part of a physical product. (11)

Realized strategy The strategy that actually takes place. (2)

Rebate A sales promotion technique in which a consumer receives a specified amount of money for making a single product purchase. (20)

Receiver The individual, group, or organization that decodes a coded message. (18)

Recession A stage of the business cycle in which unemployment rises and total buying power declines, stifling both consumer and business spending. (3)

Reciprocity An arrangement unique to business marketing in which two organizations agree to buy from each other. (10)

Recognition test A posttest in which respondents are shown the actual ad and asked if they recognize it. (19)

Recovery A stage of the business cycle during which the economy moves from depression or recession toward prosperity. (3)

Recruiting Developing a list of qualified applicants for sales positions. (20)

Reference group Any group that positively or negatively affects a person's values, attitudes, or behavior. (9)

Reference pricing Pricing a product at a moderate level and positioning it next to a more expensive model or brand. (22)

Regional issues Versions of a magazine that differ across geographic regions. (19)

Regional shopping center A type of shopping center with the largest department stores, the widest product mix, and the deepest product lines of all shopping centers. (17)

Regression analysis A method of predicting sales based on finding a relationship between past sales and one or more independent variables, such as population or income. (8)

Reinforcement advertising Advertising that assures users they chose the right brand and tells them how to get the most satisfaction from it. (19)

Relationship marketing Establishing long-term, mutually satisfying buyer-seller relationships (1)

Reliability A condition existing when a research technique produces almost identical results in repeated trials. (7)

Reminder advertising Advertising used to remind consumers about an established brand's uses, characteristics, and benefits. (19)

Research design An overall plan for obtaining the information needed to address a research problem or issue. (7)

Reseller market Intermediaries that buy finished goods and resell them for profit. (10)

Retailer An organization that purchases products for the purpose of reselling them to ultimate consumers. (17)

Retailing Transactions in which ultimate consumers are the buyers. (17)

Retail positioning Identifying an unserved or underserved market segment and serving it through a strategy that distinguishes the retailer from others in the minds of consumers in that segment. (17)

Role Actions and activities that a person in a particular position is supposed to perform based on expectations of the individual and surrounding persons. (9)

Routinized response behavior A consumer problem-solving process used when buying frequently purchased, low-cost items that require very little search-and-decision effort. (9)

Sales analysis The use of sales figures to evaluate a firm's current performance. (22)

Sales branch A manufacturer-owned intermediary that sells products and provides support services to the manufacturer's sales force. (16)

Sales contest A sales promotion method used to motivate distributors, retailers, and sales personnel through recognition of outstanding achievements. (20)

Sales force forecasting survey A survey of a firm's sales force regarding anticipated sales in their territories for a specified period. (8)

Sales forecast The amount of a product a company expects to sell during a specific period at a specified level of marketing activities. (8)

Sales office A manufacturer-owned operation that provides services normally associated with agents. (16)

Sales promotion An activity and/or material intended to induce resellers or salespeople to sell a product or consumers to buy it. (20)

Sample A limited number of units chosen to represent the characteristics of a total population. (7)

Sampling The process of selecting representative units from a total population. (7)

Scan-back allowance A manufacturer's reward to retailers based on the number of pieces scanned. (20)

Scrambled merchandising The addition of unrelated products and product lines to an existing product mix, particularly fast-moving items that can be sold in volume. (17)

Screening Choosing the most promising ideas for further review. (12)

Search qualities Tangible attributes that can be judged before the purchase of a product. (14)

Seasonal analysis An analysis of daily, weekly, or monthly sales figures to evaluate the degree to which seasonal factors influence sales. (8)

Seasonal discount A price reduction given to buyers for purchasing goods or services out of season. (21)

Secondary data Data compiled both inside and outside the organization for some purpose other than the current investigation. (7)

Secondary-market pricing Setting one price for the primary target market and a different price for another market. (22)

Segmentation variables Characteristics of individuals, groups, or organizations used to divide a market into segments. (8)

Selective demand Demand for a specific brand. (18)

Selective distortion An individual's changing or twisting of information that is inconsistent with personal feelings or beliefs. (9)

Selective distribution Using only some available outlets to distribute a product. (15)

Selective exposure The process of selecting inputs to be exposed to the person's awareness while ignoring others. (9)

Selective retention Remembering information inputs that support personal feelings and beliefs and forgetting inputs that do not. (9)

Self-concept A perception or view of oneself. (9)

Selling agent An intermediary that markets a whole product line or a manufacturer's entire output. (16)

Service An intangible result of the application of human and mechanical efforts to people or objects; an intangible product involving a deed, a performance, or an effort that cannot be physically possessed. (11, 14)

Service heterogeneity *See* Heterogeneity.

Service inseparability *See* Inseparability.

Service intangibility *See* Intangibility.

Service perishability *See* Perishability.

Service quality Customers' perceptions of how well a service meets or exceeds their expectations. (14)

Shopping mall intercept interview A research method that involves interviewing a percentage of individuals passing by "intercept" points in a mall. (7)

Shopping products Items for which buyers are willing to expend considerable effort in planning and making purchases. (11)

Single-source data Information provided by a single marketing research firm. (7)

Situational influences Influences resulting from circumstances, time, and location that affect the consumer buying decision process. (9)

Social class An open group of individuals with similar social rank. (9)

Social influences The forces other people exert on one's buying behavior. (9)

Social responsibility An organization's obligation to maximize its positive impact and minimize its negative impact on society. (4)

Sociocultural forces The influences in a society and its culture(s) that change people's attitudes, beliefs, norms, customs, and lifestyles. (3)

Sole sourcing An organization's decision to use only one supplier. (10)

Source A person, group, or organization with a meaning it tries to share with a receiver or an audience. (18)

Spam Unsolicited commercial e-mail. (6)

Special-event pricing Advertised sales or price cutting linked to a holiday, a season, or an event. (22)

Specialty-line wholesaler A full-service wholesaler that carries only a single product line or a few items within a product line. (16)

Specialty products Items with unique characteristics that buyers are willing to expend considerable effort to obtain. (11)

Stakeholders Constituents who have a "stake," or claim, in some aspect of a company's products, operations, markets, industry, and outcomes. (4)

Standard Industrial Classification (SIC) System The federal government's system for classifying selected economic characteristics of industrial, commercial, financial, and service organizations. (10)

Statistical interpretation Analysis of what is typical or what deviates from the average. (7)

Store brand *See* Private distributor brand.

Storyboard A blueprint combining copy and visual material to show the sequence of major scenes in a commercial. (19)

Straight commission compensation plan Paying salespeople according to the amount of their sales in a given time period. (20)

Straight rebuy purchase A routine purchase of the same products by a business buyer. (10)

Straight salary compensation plan Paying salespeople a specific amount per time period. (20)

Strategic alliance A partnership formed to create competitive advantage on a worldwide basis. (5)

Strategic business unit (SBU) A division, product line, or other profit center within the parent company. (2)

Strategic channel alliance An agreement whereby the products of one organization are distributed through the marketing channels of another. (15)

Strategic philanthropy The synergistic use of organizational core competencies and resources to address key stakeholders' interests and achieve both organizational and social benefits. (4)

Strategic planning The process of establishing an organizational mission and formulating goals, corporate strategy, marketing objectives, marketing strategy, and a marketing plan. (2)

Strategic windows Temporary periods of optimal fit between the key requirements of a market and the particular capabilities of a firm competing in that market. (2)

Stratified sampling A type of probability sampling in which the population of interest is divided into groups according to a common attribute and a random sample is then chosen within each group. (7)

Styling The physical appearance of a product. (12)

Subculture A group of individuals whose characteristic values and behavior patterns are similar and differ from those of the surrounding culture. (9)

Supermarket A large, self-service store that carries a complete line of food products, along with some nonfood products. (17)

Superstore A giant retail outlet that carries food and nonfood products found in supermarkets, as well as most routinely purchased consumer products. (17)

Supply chain management Long-term partnerships among marketing channel members that reduce inefficiencies, costs, and redundancies and develop innovative approaches to satisfy customers. (15)

Support personnel Sales staff members who facilitate selling but usually are not involved solely with making sales. (20)

Sustainable competitive advantage An advantage that the competition cannot copy. (2)

SWOT analysis Assessment of an organization's strengths, weaknesses, opportunities, and threats. (2)

Tactile communication Communicating through touching. (18)

Target audience The group of people at whom advertisements are aimed. (19)

Target market A specific group of customers on whom an organization focuses its marketing efforts. (1)

Target public People interested in or concerned about an organization, a product, or a social cause. (14)

Technical salesperson A support salesperson who gives technical assistance to the firm's current customers. (20)

Technology The application of knowledge and tools to solve problems and perform tasks more efficiently. (3)

Technology assessment A procedure for anticipating the effects of new products and processes on a firm's operation, other business organizations, and society. (3)

Telemarketing The performance of marketing-related activities by telephone. (17)

Telephone depth interview An interview that combines the traditional focus group's ability to probe with the confidentiality provided by a telephone survey. (7)

Telephone survey A research method in which respondents' answers to a questionnaire are recorded by an interviewer on the phone. (7)

Television home shopping A form of selling in which products are presented to television viewers, who can buy them by calling a toll-free number and paying with a credit card. (17)

Test marketing Introducing a product on a limited basis to measure the extent to which potential customers will actually buy it. (12)

Time series analysis A forecasting method that uses historical sales data to discover patterns in the firm's sales over time and generally involves trend, cycle, seasonal, and random factor analyses. (8)

Total budget competitors Firms that compete for the limited financial resources of the same customers. (3)

Total cost The sum of average fixed and average variable costs times the quantity produced. (21)

Total quality management (TQM) A philosophy that uniform commitment to quality in all areas of the organization will promote a culture that meets customers' perceptions of quality. (2)

Traceable common costs Costs that can be allocated indirectly, using one or several criteria, to the functions they support. (22)

Trade (functional) discount A reduction off the list price a producer gives to an intermediary for performing certain functions. (21)

Trademark A legal designation of exclusive use of a brand. (13)

Trade name The full legal name of an organization. (13)

Trade salesperson A salesperson involved mainly in helping a producer's customers promote a product. (20)

Trade sales promotion methods Methods intended to persuade wholesalers and retailers to carry a producer's products and market them aggressively. (20)

Trading company A company that links buyers and sellers in different countries. (5)

Traditional specialty retailer A store that carries a narrow product mix with deep product lines. (17)

Transfer pricing Prices charged in sales between an organization's units. (21)

Transportation The movement of products from where they are made to where they are used. (16)

Trend analysis An analysis that focuses on aggregate sales data over a period of many years to determine general trends in annual sales. (8)

Truck wholesaler A limited-service wholesaler that transports products directly to customers for inspection and selection; also known as a *truck jobber* or *wagon jobber*. (16)

Tying agreement An agreement in which a supplier furnishes a product to a channel member with the stipulation that the channel member must purchase other products as well. (15)

Unaided recall test A posttest in which respondents are asked to identify ads they have recently seen but are given no recall clues. (19)

Undifferentiated targeting strategy A strategy in which an organization defines an entire market for a particular product as its target market, designs a single marketing mix, and directs it at that market. (8)

Uniform geographic pricing Charging all customers the same price, regardless of geographic location; sometimes called postage-stamp pricing. (21)

Universal product code (UPC) A series of electronically readable lines identifying a product and containing inventory and pricing information. (13)

Unsought products Products purchased to solve a sudden problem, products of which customers are unaware, and products that people do not necessarily think of buying. (11)

Validity A condition existing when a research method measures what it is supposed to measure. (7)

Value analysis An evaluation of each component of a potential purchase, including quality, design, and materials, to acquire the most cost-effective product. (10)

Value conscious Concerned about price and quality of a product. (21)

Variable costs Costs that vary directly with changes in the number of units produced or sold. (21)

Vending *See* Automatic vending.

Vendor analysis A formal, systematic evaluation of current and potential vendors. (10)

Venture team A cross-functional group that creates entirely new products that may be aimed at new markets. (12)

Vertical channel integration Combining two or more stages of the marketing channel under one management. (15)

Vertical marketing system (VMS) A marketing channel managed by a single channel member to achieve efficient, low-cost distribution aimed at satisfying target market customers. (14)

Warehouse club A large-scale, members-only establishment that combines features of cash-and-carry wholesaling with discount retailing. (17)

Warehouse showroom A retail facility in a large, low-cost building with large on-premise inventories and minimal services. (17)

Warehousing The design and operation of facilities for storing and moving goods. (16)

Wealth The accumulation of past income, natural resources, and financial resources. (3)

Wheel of retailing A hypothesis holding that new retailers usually enter the market as low-status, low-margin, low-price operators but eventually evolve into high-cost, high-price merchants. (17)

Wholesaler An individual or organization that facilitates and expedites wholesale transactions. (16)

Wholesaling Transactions in which products are bought for resale, for making other products, or for general business operations. (16)

Width of product mix The number of product lines a company offers. (11)

Willingness to spend An inclination to buy because of expected satisfaction from a product, influenced by the ability to buy and numerous psychological and social forces. (3)

World Trade Organization (WTO) An entity that promotes free trade among member nations by eliminating trade barriers and educating individuals, companies, and governments about trade rules around the world. (5)

Value A customer's subjective assessment of benefits relative to costs in determining the worth of a product. (1)

Zone pricing Pricing based on transportation costs within major geographic zones. (21)

Notes

Chapter 1

1. Sources: Better Business Bureau Marketplace Ethics Torch Award Competition Project: King's Saddlery and King Ropes, 2004; interviews with Bruce King and Mary King by Krista Ocker, Stacie Bergstrom, Kim Nissen, and Wendy Gleckler, for Linda Ferrell, University of Wyoming, Marketing Ethics class, Nov. 7, 2003.

2. "FAQs," Pepsi World, www.pepsi.com/help/faqs/faq.php?category=pepsi_brands&page=code_red (accessed Apr. 13, 2004).

3. Michael J. Weiss, "To Be About to Be," *American Demographics*, Sep. 2003, pp. 29–36.

4. "A New Way to Dial Up the Net," *Time*, Nov. 24, 2003, p. 84.

5. Grainger David, "Can McDonald's Cook Again?" *Fortune*, Apr. 14, 2003, p. 122; "McDonald's Worldwide Corporate Site," McDonald's, www.mcdonalds.com/corp.html (accessed Apr. 13, 2004).

6. Great Southern Sauce Company, www.greatsauce.com (accessed Apr. 13, 2004).

7. "Lincoln Signs Magic Johnson," *Holland Sentinel*, July 16, 2003, www.hollandsentinel.com/stories/071603/bus_071603085.shtml.

8. Shelly K. Schwartz, "Do Big Boxes Stack Up?" CNNfn, May 3, 2001, www.cnn.com.

9. "Zilliant," *Fortune*, Nov. 24, 2003, p. 210.

10. "Coke Chief Wants Anti-Obesity Effort," CNN/Money, Dec. 9, 2003, www.cnn.com; "Ruby Tuesday to Use Healthier Oil, Offer Low-Carb Items," *USA Today*, Nov. 11, 2003, www.usatoday.com/money/industries/food/2003-11-11ruby-tuesday_x.htm.

11. John Thaw, "Why Sharper Image Is Playing the Hits Again," *Business 2.0*, Nov. 2003, pp. 64–66.

12. Ajay K. Kohli and Bernard J. Jaworski, "Market Orientation: The Construct, Research Propositions, and Managerial Implications," *Journal of Marketing*, Apr. 1990, pp. 1–18; O. C. Ferrell, "Business Ethics and Customer Stakeholders," *Academy of Management Executive*, 18, May 2004, pp. 126–129.

13. Ibid.

14. Dottie Enrico, "M&M's Candies Singing the Blues," *USA Today*, Sep. 5, 1995, p. B1.

15. Alan Grant and Leonard Schlesinger, "Realize Your Customers' Full Profit Potential"; Peter C. Verhoef, "Understanding the Effect of Customer Relationship Management Efforts on Customer Retention and Customer Share Development," *Journal of Marketing*, Oct. 2003, p. 30.

16. Jagdish N. Sheth and Rajendras Sisodia, "More Than Ever Before, Marketing Is Under Fire to Account for What It Spends," *Marketing Management*, Fall 1995, pp. 13–14.

17. "2000 Worldwide Case Volume by Region," Coca-Cola 2000 Annual Report, www.cocacola.com, May 11, 2001.

18. Lynette Ryals and Adrian Payne, "Customer Relationship Management in Financial Services: Towards Information-Enabled Relationship Marketing," *Journal of Strategic Marketing*, Mar. 2001, p. 3.

19. O. C. Ferrell and Michael Hartline, *Marketing Strategy* (Mason, OH: South-Western, 2005), p. 114.

20. Vernoet, "Understanding the Effect of Customer Relationship Management Efforts on Customer Retention and Customer Share Development," pp. 17–35.

21. Werner J. Reinartz and V. Kumar, "On the Profitability of Long-Life Customers in a Noncontractual Setting: An Empirical Investigation and Implications for Marketing," *Journal of Marketing*, Oct. 2000, pp. 17–35.

22. Libby Estell, "This Call Center Accelerates Sales," *Sales & Marketing Management*, Feb. 1999, p. 72.

23. Werner J. Reinartz and V. Kumar, "The Impact of Customer Relationship Characteristics on Profitable Lifetime Duration," *Journal of Marketing*, Jan. 2003, pp. 77–99.

24. Jerry Wind and Arvind Rangaswamy, "Customization: The Next Revolution in Mass Customization," *Journal of Interactive Marketing*, Winter 2001, p. 131.

25. Ryals and Payne, "Customer Relationship Management in Financial Services," pp. 3–27.

26. Alan Brown, "How Amazon.com Sells," *eCompany*, June 2001, p. 114.

27. Natalie Mizik and Robert Jacobson, "Trading Off Between Value Creation and Value Appropriation: The Financial Implications of Shifts in Strategic Emphasis," *Journal of Marketing*, Jan. 2003, pp. 63–76.

28. Ferrell and Hartline, *Marketing Strategy*, p. 104.

29. Gordon T. Anderson, "Lights! Camera! The New $20," CNN/Money, Sep. 18, 2003, http://money.cnn.com/2003/09/16/pf/banking/marketing_new_money/.

30. "Charity Holds Its Own in Tough Times (Giving USA 2003, The Annual Report on Philanthropy for the Year 2002)," American Association of Fundraising Counsel, http://aafrc.org/press_releases/trustreleases/charityholds.html (accessed Apr. 13, 2004).

31. Michael J. Mondel, "Rethinking the Internet," *Business Week*, Mar. 21, 2001, p. 118.

32. Susan Berfield, with Diane Brady and Tom Lowry, "The CEO of Hip Hop," *Business Week*, Oct. 27, 2003, pp. 90–98.

33. Sources: Donna Hood Crecca, "Higher Calling," *Chain Leader*, Dec. 2002, p. 14; "State Fare: Finagle A Bagel, Boston," *Restaurants and Institutions*, Oct. 1, 2002, www.rimag.com/1902/sr.htm; "Finagle Sees a Return to More Normal Business Mode," *Foodservice East*, Fall 2002, pp. 1, 17; "Sloan Grads Bet Their Money on Bagels," *Providence Business News*, Oct. 25, 1999, p. 14; interview with Laura B. Trust and Alan Litchman, Feb. 25, 2003.

34. Sources: "A Brief History of CART and Champ Car Racing," Fullspeed Database, Feb. 17, 2003, www.fsdb.net/champcar/history/index.htm; "Champ Car Confirms 2004 Schedule," Racing Lines, Sep. 28, 2003, www.racinglines.com/article/archive/3/; Mark Cipolloni, "Branding CART and Their Race Cars," AutoRacing1.com, Nov. 9, 2000, www.autoracing1.com/MarkC/001109Branding.htm; Daniel Kaplan, "CART Tries Turnaround," *Sports Business Journal*, www.sportsbusinessjournal.com/article.cms?articleId=26881&s=1 (accessed July 29, 2003); Robin Miller, "New Owners Could Focus on Streets," RPM//espn.go.com/rpm/cart/2003/0810/159430.html; Robin Miller, "Pook Looking to Privatize Company," RPM//espn.go.com/rpm/cart/2003/0615/1568383.html; "Open Wheel Racing Series Pursues the Acquisition of Championship Auto Racing Teams," *Champ Car News*, Sep. 18, 2003, www.cart.com/News/Article.asp?ID=7058&print=true, Sep. 10, 2003; Chapman Rackaway, "Eccelstone to the Rescue?" Racing News Online, Oct. 23, 2002, www.racingnewsonline.com/story.do?id=55630; Bob Zeller, "CART vs. IRL: Who Won the War?" Car and Driver Online, Feb. 2004, www.caranddriver.com/article.asp?section_id=4&article_id=7719&page_number=1. Don Roy, Middle Tennessee State University, assisted in the preparation of this case.

Chapter 2

1. Sources: Fiji Water, www.fijiwater.com/site/ (accessed Apr. 8, 2004); Janet Forgrieve, "Haute Water: Celebrities Seen Sipping

Fiji Help Spike Sales, Cachet of the Mineral-Rich Drink at Local Hotels and Restaurants," *Rocky Mountain News*, July 5, 2003, pp. 1C, 5C; John Rodwan, "Bottled Water: A New Paradigm?" International Bottled Water Association, in *USA Today* regional insert, Feb. 8, 2002, www.bottledwater.org/public/pdf/USAtoday_final.pdf; "Selling Sparkling Water," *Restaurant Hospitality*, Dec. 2001, www.findarticles.com/cf_dls/m3188/12_85/80924843/p1/article.jhtml.

2. O. C. Ferrell and Michael Hartline, *Marketing Strategy* (Mason, OH: South-Western, 2005), p. 10.

3. Ibid.

4. J. Chris White, P. Rajan Varadarajan, and Peter A. Dacin, "Market Situation Interpretation and Response: The Role of Cognitive Style, Organizational Culture, and Information Use," *Journal of Marketing*, July 2003, pp. 63–79.

5. Ferrell and Hartline, *Marketing Strategy*, p. 51.

6. Lea Goldman, "Red-Hot Chili's," *Forbes*, Jan. 8, 2001, pp. 134–136.

7. Derek F. Abell, "Strategic Windows," *Journal of Marketing*, July 1978, p. 21.

8. Michael Krauss, "EBay 'Bids' on Small-Biz Firms to Sustain Growth," *Marketing News*, Dec. 8, 2003, p. 6.

9. Larry Light and David Greising, "Litigation: The Choice of a New Generation," *Business Week*, May 25, 1998, p. 42.

10. Michael McCarthy, "CD Prices Hit Sour Note with Retailers, Buyers," *USA Today*, Dec. 8, 2003, pp. 1B, 2B.

11. Ibid.

12. Douglas Bowman and Hubert Gatignon, "Determinants of Competitor Response Time to a New Product Introduction," *Journal of Marketing Research*, Feb. 1995, pp. 42–53.

13. Kathleen Kerwin, with David Welch, "'Detroit Is Missing the Boat,'" *Business Week*, Oct. 27, 2003, pp. 44–46.

14. "Our Mission," Celestial Seasonings, www.celestialseasonings.com/whoweare/corporatehistory/mission.php (accessed Apr. 8, 2004).

15. Laurence G. Weinzimmer, Edward U. Bond III, Mark B. Houston, and Paul C. Nystrom, "Relating Marketing Expertise on the Top Management Team and Strategic Market Aggressiveness to Financial Performance and Shareholder Value," *Journal of Strategic Marketing*, June 2003, pp. 133–159.

16. Stanley Holmes, "Nike's New Advice? Just Strut It," *Business Week*, Nov. 3, 2003, p. 40.

17. Jean L. Johnson, Ruby Pui-Wan Lee, Amit Saini, and Bianca Grohmann, "Market-Focused Flexibility: Conceptual Advances and an Integrative Model," *Journal of the Academy of Marketing Science* 31, no. 1 (2003), pp. 74–89.

18. Amy Barrett, "Hershey: Candy Is Dandy, But ... ," *Business Week*, Sep. 29, 2003, pp. 68–69.

19. George S. Day, "Diagnosing the Product Portfolio," *Journal of Marketing*, Apr. 1977, pp. 30–31.

20. G. Tomas, M. Hult, David W. Cravens, and Jagdish Sheth, "Competitive Advantage in the Global Marketplace: A Focus on Marketing Strategy," *Journal of Business Research*, Jan. 2001, pp. 1–3.

21. Michael J. Weiss, "To Be About to Be," *American Demographics*, Sep. 2003, pp. 28–36.

22. Nancy Einhart, "How the New T-Bird Went Off Course," *Business 2.0*, Nov. 2003, pp. 74–76.

23. Christian Homburg, John P. Workman, and Ove Jensen, "Fundamental Changes in Marketing Organization: The Movement Toward a Customer-Focused Organizational Structure," *Journal of the Academy of Marketing Science*, Fall 2000, pp. 459–478.

24. Weiss, "To Be About to Be," pp. 28–36.

25. Rajdeep Grewal and Patriya Tansuhaj, "The Chain of Effects from Brand Trust and Brand Affect to Brand Performance: The Role of Brand Loyalty," *Journal of Marketing*, Apr. 2001, pp. 67–80.

26. Steve Watkins, "Marketing Basics: The Four P's Are as Relevant Today as Ever," *Investor's Business Daily*, Feb. 4, 2002, p. A1.

27. Hemant C. Sashittat and Avan R. Jassawalla, "Marketing Implementation in Smaller Organizations: Definition, Framework, and Propositional Inventory," *Journal of the Academy of Marketing Science*, Winter 2001, pp. 50–69.

28. Ferrell and Hartline, *Marketing Strategy*, p. 257.

29. Weiss, "To Be About to Be," pp. 28–36.

30. Adapted from Nigel F. Piercy, *Market-Led Strategic Change* (Newton, MA: Butterworth-Heinemann, 1992), pp. 374–385.

31. Sybil F. Stershic, "Internal Marketing Campaign Reinforces Service Goals," *Marketing News*, July 31, 1998, p. 11.

32. Philip B. Crosby, *Quality Is Free: The Art of Making Quality Certain* (New York: McGraw-Hill, 1979), pp. 9–10.

33. Piercy, *Market-Led Strategic Change*.

34. Kenneth W. Thomas and Betty A. Velthouse, "Cognitive Elements of Empowerment: An 'Interpretive' Model of Intrinsic Task Motivation," *Academy of Management Review*, Oct. 1990, pp. 666–681.

35. Ferrell and Hartline, *Marketing Strategy*.

36. Rohit Deshpande and Frederick E. Webster, Jr., "Organizational Culture and Marketing: Defining the Research Agenda," *Journal of Marketing*, Jan. 1989, pp. 3–15.

37. Kathleen Cholewka, "CRM: Lose the Hype and Strategize," *Sales & Marketing Management*, June 2001, pp. 27–28.

38. Douglas W. Vorhies and Neil A. Morgan, "A Configuration Theory Assessment of Marketing Organization Fit with Business Strategy and Its Relationship with Marketing Performance," *Journal of Marketing*, Jan. 2003, pp. 100–115.

39. Bernard J. Jaworski, "Toward a Theory of Marketing Control: Environmental Context, Control Types, and Consequences," *Journal of Marketing*, July 1988, pp. 23–39.

40. "Saab Sales Surpass 40,000 for First Time in 16 Years," General Motors, press release, Oct. 31, 2003, www.gm.com/cgi-bin/pr_display.pl?5172.

41. "Infiniti Ranks Highest in Customer Satisfaction with Dealer Service," J. D. Powers & Associates press release, July 23, 2003, www.jdpower.com/news/releases/pressrelease.asp?ID=2003058.

42. Sources: "All About Jared," Subway, www.subway.com/subwayroot/MenuNutrition/Jared/jaredStats.aspx (accessed Apr. 8, 2004); Jessica Bujol, "Subway Restaurants Passes McDonald's in the U.S.," Subway, press release, Feb. 1, 2002, www.subway.com/subwayroot/AboutSubway/mckyd.aspx; Houghton Mifflin video, *Global Growth: The Subway Story*; "Franchise Opportunities," Subway, www.subway.com/subwayroot/Development/ (accessed Dec. 12, 2003); "Jared, the Subway Guy: Superstar," CNN, Nov. 17, 2003, www.cnn.com/2003/SHOWBIZ/TV/11/17/subway.guy.ap/; "Man Loses 245 Pounds Eating Nothing But SUBWAY® Sandwiches," Subway, Dec. 2000, www.subway.com/society/public_rel/pcr_press/011101pr.htm; "Subway® Restaurants Announces Opening of First Location in Croatia," Subway, June 2001, www.subway.com/society/public_rel/pcr_press/062501.htm; "Subway® Restaurants Announces Opening of First Location in France," Subway, June 2001, www.subway.com/society/public_rel/pcr_press/070301.htm; "Subway® Restaurants Announces Opening of First Location in Oman," Subway, Feb. 2001, www.subway.com/society/public_rel/pcr_press/020701bpr.htm; "Subway Student and Educator Resource Guide," Subway, Nov. 25, 2003, www.subway.com/StudentGuide/.

43. Sources: Marty Bernstein, "Auto Ads Create a Buzz at Cannes Festival," *Automotive News*, July 21, 2003, p. 18; Julie Cantwell, "Saturn's VUE: Attract Owners, Current and Past,"

Automotive News, Jan. 22, 2001, p. 20; Julie Cantwell, "Saturn Works to Shed Small-Car Label," *Automotive News*, Oct. 28, 2002, p. 1; Brian Corbett, "Saturn's Mission: Lassoing Those Young 'Uns," *Ward's Dealer Business*, Jan. 1, 2003; General Motors, www.gm.com (accessed Apr. 8, 2004); Earle Eldridge, "Is Beaten-Up Saturn GM's Falling Star?" *USA Today*, Dec. 5, 2003, pp. 1B, 1B; Jean Halliday, "Saturn Revamps Strategy: New Advertising Tack Moves Beyond Customer Service, Focuses on Safety, Style," *Advertising Age*, Oct. 28, 2002, p. 4; Matt Nauman, "Saturn's VUE Worthy of Consideration," Knight/Ridder Tribune News Service, May 10, 2002; Saturn, www.saturn.com (accessed Apr. 8, 2004); "Relay Is Next Step in Saturn's Drive to Grow," General Motors, press release, Dec. 4, 2003, www.gm.com/cgi-bin/pr_display.pl?5192; David Welch, "Can Saturn Get Off the Ground Again?" *Business Week*, Oct. 14, 2002, pp. 79–80; G. Chamber Williams III, "ION Recharges Saturn's Entry-Level Lineup," *Seattle Post-Intelligencer*, Jan. 17, 2003, p. F1. Don Roy, Middle Tennessee State University, assisted in the preparation of this case.

Chapter 3

1. Sources: Gail Edmondson, "This SUV Can Tow an Entire Carmaker, *Business Week*, Jan. 19, 2004, pp. 40–41; Russ Devault, "Porsche Cayenne S Peps Up SUV Field," *Atlanta Journal-Constitution*, Sep. 4, 2003; Chris Reiter, "Porsche to Offer Cheaper Version of Hot SUV," *Wall Street Journal*, Aug. 28, 2003, p. D2; Alex Taylor III, "Porsche's Risky Recipe," *Fortune*, Feb. 17, 2003, pp. 90+; Edmund Chew, "Complexity of Cayenne Surprised Project Leader," *Automotive News*, Mar. 24, 2003, p. 22; "Porsche's Strategy Shifts to Cost Cutting," *Automotive News Europe*, Aug. 25, 2003, p. 7; Neal Boudette, "Will Americans Buy More European Luxury Cars?" *Wall Street Journal*, Jan. 29, 2003, pp. D4+.
2. O. C. Ferrell and Michael Hartline, *Marketing Strategy* (Mason, OH: South-Western, 2005), p. 58.
3. Ibid.
4. Rodolfo Vazquez, Maria Leticia Santos, and Luis Ignacio Álvarez, "Market Orientation, Innovation and Competitive Strategies in Industrial Firms," *Journal of Strategic Marketing*, Mar. 2001, pp. 69–90.
5. Eberhard Stickel, "Uncertainty Reduction in a Competitive Environment," *Journal of Business Research* 51, no. 3 (2001), pp. 169–177.
6. *EContent*, November 2003, p. 23.
7. Paula Lyon Andruss, "Staying in the Game: Turning an Economic Dip into Opportunity," *Marketing News*, May 7, 2001, pp. 1, 9.
8. www.census.gov/press-release/www/2003/cb03-153.html.
9. Patrick Barta and Anne Marie Chaker, "Consumers Voice Rising Dissatisfaction with Companies," *Wall Street Journal*, May 21, 2001, p. A2.
10. Hall Dickler Kent Goldstein & Wood LLC, "Controversy over Food Advertising to Children," *AdLaw*, Oct. 20, 2003.
11. www.usdoj.gov/atr/public/press_releases/2003/201284.htm.
12. "Survey: Kids Disclose Private Details Online," CNN, May 17, 2000, www.cnn.com.
13. Jeff Bater, "FTC Says Companies Falsely Claim Cellphone Patches Provide Protection," *Wall Street Journal*, Feb. 21, 2002, http://online.wsj.com.
14. David A. Balto, "Emerging Antitrust Issues in Electronic Commerce," *Journal of Public Policy and Marketing*, Fall 2000, pp. 277-286.
15. "FTC Slams Pop-Up Spammer," *eWeek*, Nov. 6, 2003.
16. www.bankrate.com/goocalf/news/DrDon/20030221a1.asp?prodtype=cc.
17. Shelly Branch, "Questions from Rival Firms Spark Watchdog to Probe Smirnoff Ice Ads," *Wall Street Journal*, Feb. 22, 2002, http://online.wsj.com.
18. Kate MacArthur, "Government to Mediate Vodka Ad Dispute; Grey Goose, Belvedere Fight Could Drag On," *Advertising Age*, Sep. 8, 2003, p. 92.
19. Michael Zawacki, "Homework. (By the Numbers)," *Inside Business*, Aug. 2003, p. 8.
20. Debbie McAlister, Linda Ferrell, and O. C. Ferrell, *Business and Society*, (Boston: Houghton Mifflin Company, 2005), p. 85.
21. Olga Kharif, "Telemarketers' Next Target: Cell Phones; Tracking Down Wireless Numbers Will Soon Be Easier and That Means the Sales Pitches Will Find You, Wherever You Are," *Business Week Online*, Oct. 10, 2003.
22. Ibid.
23. McAlister, Ferrell, and Ferrell, *Business and Society*.
24. Vladimir Zwass, "Electronic Commerce: Structures and Issues," *International Journal of Electronic Commerce*, Fall 2000, pp. 3–23.
25. "Covisint Parts Exchange Officially Opens for Business," Bloomberg Newswire, Dec. 11, 2000, via AOL.
26. "Peace Corp. Seeks to Launch First PEO Business-to-Business Online Marketplace." Business Wire July 31, 2003, p. 2086.
27. Nicholas Negroponte, "Will Everything Be Digital?," *Time*, June 19, 2000.
28. Bureau of the Census, *Statistical Abstract of the United States*, p. 15.
29. Ibid., pp. 51, 55.
30. Ibid., p. 14.
31. Ibid., p. 9.
32. Ibid., p. 12.
33. Laura Clark Geist, "Big 3 Boost Effort to Win Minority Buyers; Growing Ethnic Groups Can Help Raise Market Share," *Automotive News*, Oct. 13, 2003.
34. "Good Translations: Targeting a Multicultural Audience Takes More Than a Dictionary: It Takes Tact, Understanding, and Relevance," *PR Week*, Aug. 18, 2003.
35. Geist, "Big 3 Boost Effort to Win Minority Buyers."
36. Sources: "Technology Briefing Internet: AOL Introduces Low-Priced Access Service," *New York Times*, Jan. 9, 2004, p. C3; Julia Angwin, "AOL to Launch Discount Dial-Up Service Called Netscape," *Wall Street Journal*, Oct. 14, 2003, p. B1; Dan Gillmore, "AOL Ends Ties with Mozilla but Helps Keep It Alive," *San Jose Mercury News*, July 30, 2003, www.mercurynews.com; "Netscape and Powered, Inc. Collaborate to Launch New Online Education Service," Business Wire, Aug. 5, 2003, www.businesswire.com; Cade Metz, "Whither Netscape?" *PC Magazine*, June 11, 2003, www.pcmagazine.com; "Direct Testimony of Jim Barksdale," MSNBC, www.msnbc.com/news/206739.asp, Sep. 4, 2001; "Netscape," *Business Now*, www.batv.com, Sep. 5, 2001; Stephen H. Wildstrom, "A Nimbler Netscape Navigator," Business Week Online, Aug. 24, 2001, www.businessweek.com.
37. Sources: "Frito-Lay Introduces New Lineup of Low-Carb Chips," *Long Island Business News*, Jan. 16, 2004; Judith Weinraub, "Getting the Fat Out," *Washington Post*, Nov. 12, 2003, p. F1; Andrea K. Walker, "Potato-Chip Maker Now Targets 'Bad Fat,'" *FSView and Florida Flambeau*, Oct. 2, 2003; Suzanne Vranica, "PepsiCo Sets Health-Snack Effort," *Wall Street Journal*, Sep. 23, 2003, p. B6; Theresa Howard, "Frito-Lay's New Stax to Take a Stand," *USA Today*, Aug. 15, 2003, p. 12B; "Snacking Now Made Easier with Frito-Lay's New Smart Snack Ribbon Label," PR Newswire, Aug. 5, 2003, www.prnewswire.com; Sonia Reyes, "Strategy: R-R-R-Ruffles Hopes Its Past Gives Future a Blast," *Brandweek*, June 23, 2003.

Chapter 4

1. Sources: "I Am Gorgeous, Aren't I?" Better Business Bureau, press release, Dec. 10, 2002 via www.bbb.org/alerts/model-talent.asp; Barbara Nordin, "The Fearless Consumer—Losing Face: 'Model Search' Hits the Doubletree," *(Charlottesville) Hook,* Feb. 27, 2003, www.readthehook.com/stories/2003%5C02%5C26%5CtheFearlessConsumerLosingF.html.
2. "Growth in Piracy Reverses Trend," *The Star Tribune,* May 28, 2001, p. D7.
3. John Hechinger and Theo Francis, "Putnam Holders Vote with Money: Exodus of $14 Billion Stirs Fears over Funds' Health at Scandal-Tainted Firm," *Wall Street Journal,* Nov. 11, 2003, http://online.wsj.com; "Putnam Chief Ousted in Fund Probe," *Wall Street Journal,* Nov. 3, 2003, http://online.wsj.com.
4. "About Avon," Avon, www.avoncompany.com/about/, (accessed Apr. 8, 2004); "The Avon Breast Cancer Crusade," Avon, www.avoncompany.com/women/avoncrusade/ (accessed Apr. 8, 2004).
5. Isabelle Maignan and O. C. Ferrell, "Antecedents and Benefits of Corporate Citizenship: An Investigation of French Businesses," *Journal of Business Research* 51, no. 1 (2001), pp. 37–51.
6. Debbie McAlister, Linda Ferrell, and O. C. Ferrell, *Business and Society: A Strategic Approach to Social Responsibility* (Boston: Houghton Mifflin, 2005), pp. 38–40.
7. B&Q, www.diy.com/, (accessed Apr. 8, 2004).
8. Archie Carroll, "The Pyramid of Corporate Social Responsibility: Toward the Moral Management of Organizational Stakeholders," *Business Horizons,* July/Aug. 1991, p. 42.
9. Thea Singer, "Can Business Still Save the World?" *Inc.,* Apr. 2001, pp. 58–71.
10. "Smucker Sued over '100 Percent' Fruit Label," CNN.com, Oct. 20, 2003, www.cnn.com/2003/LAW/10/20/food.smuckers.reut/index.html.
11. "Charity Holds Its Own in Tough Times (Giving USA 2003: The Annual Report on Philanthropy for the Year 2002)," American Association of Fundraising Council, press release, http://aafrc.org/press_releases/trustreleases/charityholds.html (accessed Apr. 8, 2004).
12. Mark Calvey, "Profile: Safeway's Grants Reflect Its People," *San Francisco Business Times,* July 14, 2003, http://sanfrancisco.bizjournals.com/sanfrancisco/stories/2003/07/14/focus9.html.
13. Thorne, Ferrell, and Ferrell, *Business and Society,* p. 335.
14. Ibid.
15. Alan K. Reichert, Marion S. Webb, and Edward G. Thomas, "Corporate Support for Ethical and Environmental Policies: A Financial Management Perspective," *Journal of Business Ethics* 25 (2000), pp. 53–64.
16. Kathleen Kerwin, with David Welch, "'Detroit Is Missing the Boat,'" *Business Week,* Oct. 27, 2003, pp. 44–46.
17. Thorne, Ferrell, and Ferrell, *Business and Society.*
18. "Certification," Home Depot, www.homedepot.com/HDUS/EN/_US/corporate/corp_respon/green_products.shtml (accessed Apr. 8, 2004).
19. "Yes, We Have No Bananas: Rainforest Alliance Certifies Chiquita Bananas," *AgJournal,* Dec. 16, 2003, www.agjournal.com/story.cfm?story_id=1047.
20. Paul Hawken and William McDonough, "Seven Steps to Doing Good Business," *Inc.,* Nov. 1993, pp. 79–90.
21. Roger Bougie, Rik Pieters, and Marcel Zeelenberg, "Angry Customers Don't Come Back, They Get Back: The Experience and Behavioral Implications of Anger and Dissatisfaction in Services," *Journal of the Academy of Marketing Science* 31, no. 4 (2003), pp. 377–393.
22. "Take Charge of Education," Target, http://target.com/target_group/community_giving/take_charge_of_education.jhtml (accessed Apr. 8, 2004).
23. "The Vibe," New Belgium Brewing Company, www.newbelgium.com/n_vibe.shtml (accessed Apr. 8, 2004).
24. Thorne, Ferrell, and Ferrell, *Business and Society.*
25. Thomas L. Carson, "Self-Interest and Business Ethics: Some Lessons of the Recent Corporate Scandals," *Journal of Business Ethics,* April 2003, pp. 389–394.
26. "2002 Cone Corporate Citizenship Study," Cone, Inc., press release, Oct. 22, 2002, www.coneinc.com/Pages/pr_13.html.
27. "Firestone: A Reputation Blowout," O. C. Ferrell, John Fraedrich, and Linda Ferrell, *Business Ethics: Ethical Decision Making and Cases* (Boston: Houghton Mifflin, 2005), pp. 313–320.
28. "Hasbro: Do Not Pass Go, Ghettopoly," *USA Today,* Oct. 23, 2003, www.usatoday.com.
29. David E. Sprott, Kenneth C. Mannign, and Anthony D. Miyazaki, "Grocery Price Setting and Quantity Surcharges," *Journal of Marketing,* July 2003, pp. 34–46.
30. Gisele Durham, "Study Finds Lying, Cheating in Teens," AOL News, Oct. 16, 2000.
31. Peggy H. Cunningham and O. C. Ferrell, "The Influence of Role Stress on Unethical Behavior by Personnel Involved in the Marketing Research Process" (working paper, Queens University, Ontario, 2004), p. 35.
32. Joseph W. Weiss, *Business Ethics: A Managerial, Stakeholder Approach* (Belmont, CA: Wadsworth, 1994), p. 13.
33. Ethics Resource Center, *The Ethics Resource Center's 2000 National Business Ethics Survey: How Employees Perceive Ethics at Work* (Washington, DC: Ethics Resource Center, 2000), p. 85.
34. O. C. Ferrell, Larry G. Gresham, and John Fraedrich, "A Synthesis of Ethical Decision Models for Marketing," *Journal of Macromarketing,* Fall 1989, pp. 58–59.
35. Barry J. Babin, James S. Boles, and Donald P. Robin, "Representing the Perceived Ethical Work Climate Among Marketing Employees," *Journal of the Academy of Marketing Science* 28, no. 3 (2000), pp. 345–358.
36. Ethics Resource Center, *2000 National Business Ethics Survey,* p. 38.
37. Ferrell, Gresham, and Fraedrich, "A Synthesis of Ethical Decision Models for Marketing."
38. Lawrence B. Chonko and Shelby D. Hunt, "Ethics and Marketing Management: A Retrospective and Prospective Commentary," *Journal of Business Research* 50, no. 3 (2000), pp. 235–244.
39. Linda K. Trevino and Stuart Youngblood, "Bad Apples in Bad Barrels: A Causal Analysis of Ethical Decision Making Behavior," *Journal of Applied Psychology* 75, no. 4 (1990), pp. 378–385.
40. Margaret M. Clark, "Corporate Ethics Programs Make a Difference, but Not the Only Difference," *HR News,* May 23, 2003, www.shrm.org/hrnews_published/archives/CMS_004611.asp.
41. Gene R. Laczniak and Patrick E. Murphy, *Ethical Marketing Decisions: The Higher Road* (Boston: Allyn & Bacon, 1993), p. 14.
42. "Social Responsibility Statement," American Apparel & Footwear Association, http://apparelandfootwear.org/4col.cfm?pageID=228 (accessed Apr. 8, 2004); "About WRAP," Worldwide Responsible Apparel Production, www.wrapapparel.org/index.cfm?page=principles (accessed Apr. 8, 2004).
43. Brian Hindo, "Teaching MCI Right from Wrong," *Business Week,* Nov. 3, 2003, p. 12.
44. Del Jones, "Law Rings up Growth in Worker Hotline Industry," *USA Today,* May 26, 2003, www.usatoday.com.
45. Edward Petry, "Six Myths about the Corporate Ethics Office," *Ethikos,* Mar./Apr. 1998, p. 4.

46. Sir Adrian Cadbury, "Ethical Managers Make Their Own Rules," *Harvard Business Review*, Sep./Oct. 1987, p. 33.

47. Andrea K. Walker, "Low-Carb Craze Puts Bread Industry on Defensive," *Austin American-Statesman*, Dec. 17, 2003, www.statesman.com/.

48. Don Tapscott and David Ticoll, "The Naked Corporation," *Wall Street Journal*, Oct. 14, 2003, http://online.wsj.com/.

49. Ferrell, Fraedrich, and Ferrell, *Business Ethics*, pp. 27–30.

50. Isabelle Maignan, "Antecedents and Benefits of Corporate Citizenship: A Comparison of U.S. and French Businesses" (Ph.D. dissertation, University of Memphis, 1997).

51. Kurschner, "5 Ways Ethical Busine\$\$ Creates Fatter Profit\$," *Business Ethics*, March/April 1996, p. 24.

52. Margaret A. Stroup, Ralph L. Newbert, and Jerry W. Anderson, Jr., "Doing Good, Doing Better: Two Views of Social Responsibility," *Business Horizons*, Mar./Apr. 1987, p. 23.

53. Sources: Peter Asmus, "Goodbye Coal, Hello Wind," *Business Ethics*, July/Aug. 1999, pp. 10–11; Robert Baun, "What's in a Name? Ask the Makers of Fat Tire," *The (Fort Collins) Coloradoan*, Oct. 8, 2000, pp. E1, E3; Rachel Brand, "Colorado Breweries Bring Home 12 Medals in Festival," *Rocky Mountain (Denver) News*, www.insidedenver.com/news/1008beer6.shtml (accessed Nov. 6, 2000); Stevi Deter, "Fat Tire Amber Ale," The Net Net, www.thenetnet.com/reviews/fat.html (accessed Apr. 8, 2004); DirtWorld.com, www.dirtworld.com/races/Colorado_race 745.htm (accessed Nov. 6, 2000); Robert F. Dwyer and John F. Tanner, Jr., *Business Marketing* (Burr Ridge, IL: Irwin/McGraw-Hill, 1999), p. 104; "Fat Tire Amber Ale," *Achwiegut (The Guide to Austrian Beer)*, www.austrianbeer.com/beer/ b000688.shtml, Mar. 5, 2001; "Four Businesses Honored with Prestigious International Award for Outstanding Marketplace Ethics," Better Business Bureau, press release, Sep. 23, 2002, www.bbb.org/alerts/2002torchwinners.asp; Julie Gordon, "Lebesch Balances Interests in Business, Community," *Coloradoan*, Feb. 26, 2003; Del I. Hawkins, Roger J. Best, and Kenneth A. Coney, *Consumer Behavior: Building Marketing Strategy*, 8th ed. (Burr Ridge, IL: Irwin/McGraw-Hill, 2001); David Kemp, Tour Connoisseur, New Belgium Brewing Company, personal interview by Nikole Haiar, Nov. 21, 2000; New Belgium Brewing Company, Ft. Collins, CO, www.newbelgium.com (accessed Apr. 8, 2004); New Belgium Brewing Company Tour by Nikole Haiar, Nov. 20, 2000; "New Belgium Brewing Wins Ethics Award," *Denver Business Journal*, Jan. 2, 2003, http://denver.bizjournals. com/denver/stories/2002/12/30/daily21.html; Dan Rabin, "New Belgium Pours It on for Bike Riders," *Celebrator Beer News*, Aug./Sep. 1998, www.celebrator.com/9808/rabin.html. This case was prepared by Nikole Haiar for classroom discussion rather than to illustrate either effective or ineffective handling of an administrative, ethical, or legal decision by management.

54. Sources: Christopher M. Byron, *Martha Inc.: The Incredible Story of Martha Stewart Living Omnimedia* (New York: John Wiley & Sons, Inc., 2002); Diane Brady, "Martha Inc. Inside the Growing Empire of America's Lifestyle Queen," *Business Week*, Jan. 17, 2000; Julie Creswell, "Will Martha Walk?" *Fortune*, Nov. 25, 2002, pp. 121–124; Mike Duff, "Martha Scandal Raises Questions, What's in Store for Kmart?" *DSN Retailing Today*, July 8, 2002, pp. 1, 45; Anne D'Innocenzio, "Charges Imperil Stewart Company," *(Fort Collins) Coloradoan*, June 5, 2003, pp. D1, D7; Shelley Emling, "Martha Stewart Indicted on Fraud," *Austin American-Statesman*, June 5, 2003, www. statesman.com; Shelley Emling, "Stewart Defends Her Name with Ad," *Austin American-Statesman*, June 6, 2003, www. statesman.com; "Feds Tighten Noose on Martha," CNN/Money, Feb. 6, 2003, http://money.cnn.com/2003/02/06/news/companies/ martha/index.htm; Charles Gasparino and Kara Scannell, "Probe of Martha Stewart's Sale of Stock Enters Its Final Phase," *Wall Street Journal*, Jan. 24, 2003, p. C7; "ImClone Probe Costly for Martha Stewart," MSNBC, Jan. 27, 2003, http://stacks.msnbc. com/news/864675.asp; Charles M. Madigan, "Woman Behaving Badly," *Across the Board*, July/Aug. 2002, p. 75; Jerry Markon, "Martha Stewart Could Be Charged as 'Tippee,'" *Wall Street Journal*, Oct. 3, 2002, pp. C1, C9; "Martha Stewart Enters Not Guilty Plea to Charges," *Wall Street Journal*, June 4, 2003, http://online.wsj.com; "Martha's Mouthpiece: We'll Deliver," CBS News, Aug. 20, 2002, www.cbsnews.com/stories/2002/ 08/20/national/main519320.shtml; "Martha Stewart Living Slides into Red, Expects More Losses," *Wall Street Journal*, Mar. 4, 2003, http://online.wsj.com; Erin McClam, "Martha Stewart Indicted in Stock Scandal," *Coloradoan*, June 5, 2003, p. A1; Amy Merrick, "Can Martha Deliver Merry?" *Wall Street Journal*, Oct. 8, 2002, pp. B1, B3; Keith Naughton, "Martha's Tabloid Dish," *Newsweek*, June 24, 2002, p. 36; Keith Naughton and Mark Hosenball, "Setting the Table," *Newsweek*, Sep. 23, 2002, p. 7; "New Witness in Martha Probe," CBSNews, Aug. 9, 2002, www.cbsnews.com/stories/2002/08/12/national/ main518448.shtml; Marc Peyser, "The Insiders," *Newsweek*, July 1, 2002, pp. 38–53; Thomas A. Stewart, "Martha Stewart's Recipe for Disaster," *Business2.com*, July 3, 2002; Jeffrey Toobin, "Lunch at Martha's," *New Yorker*, Feb. 3, 2003, pp. 38–44; Thor Valdmanis, "Martha Stewart Leaves NYSE Post," *USA Today*, Oct. 4, 2002, p. 3B.

Chapter 5

1. Sources: "The Company," Starbucks, www.starbucks.com/ aboutus/overview.asp (accessed Dec. 8, 2003); Cora Daniels, "Mr. Coffee," *Fortune*, Apr. 14, 2003, pp. 139, 140; Keith Johnson, "Starbucks Enters Market in Spain as Part of Broad Global Expansion," *Wall Street Journal*, Apr. 11, 2002, http://online. wsj.com; Ariff Kachra and Mary Crossan, "Starbucks," in Michael A. Hitt, R. Duane Ireland, and Robert E. Hoskisson, eds., *Strategic Management Competitiveness and Globalization*, 4th ed. (Mason, OH: South-Western, 2001), pp. 569–585; "Starbucks Steaming Toward Long-Term Profitability and Growth Internationally," Business Wire, June 20, 2003, www.findarticles. com/cf_0/mEIN/2003_June_20/103773499/print.jhtml; "Starbucks Timeline and History," Starbucks, www.starbucks.com/ aboutus/timeline.asp (accessed Apr. 8, 2004).

2. U. S. Census Bureau World Population Clock, www.census. gov/cgi-bin/ipc./popclockw (accessed Apr. 8, 2004); "Stronger Than Expected Growth Spurs Modest Trade Recovery," World Trade Organization press release, April 5, 2004, www.wto.org/ english/news_e/pres04_e/pr373_e/htm.

3. Anthony Bianco and Wendy Zellner, "Is Wal-Mart Too Powerful?" *Business Week*, Oct. 6, 2003, pp. 100–110; Cora Daniels, "Mr. Coffee," *Fortune*, Apr. 14, 2003, pp. 139–140.

4. Robert D. Hof, "Reprogramming Amazon," *Business Week*, Dec. 22, 2003, pp. 82–86.

5. Brian Bremner and Chester Dawson, "Can Anything Stop Toyota?" *Business Week*, Nov. 17, 2003, pp. 114–122.

6. "Product Pitfalls Proliferate in Global Cultural Maze," *Wall Street Journal*, May 14, 2001, p. B11.

7. Ibid.

8. Ibid.

9. Greg Botelho, "2003 Global Influentials: Selling to the World," CNN, Dec. 9, 2003, www.cnn.com.

10. Jeffrey G. Blodgett, Long-Chuan Lu, Gregory M. Rose, and Scott J. Vitell, "Ethical Sensitivity to Stakeholder Interests: A Cross-Cultural Comparison," *Journal of the Academy of Marketing Science* 29, no. 2 (2001), pp. 190–202.

11. Thomas G. Brashear, Elzbieta Lepkowska-White, and Cristian Chelariu, "An Empirical Test of Antecedents and Consequences of Salesperson Job Satisfaction among Polish Retail

Salespeople," *Journal of Business Research,* Dec. 2003, pp. 971–978.

12. Zeynep Gürhan-Canli and Durairaj Maheswaran, "Cultural Variations in Country of Origin Effects," *Journal of Marketing Research,* Aug. 2000, pp. 309–317.

13. Joseph Albright and Marcia Kunstel, "Schlotzsky's First China Opening Less Than Red-Hot," *Austin American-Statesman,* www.austin360.com, May 27, 1998.

14. Isabelle Maignan and O. C. Ferrell, "Nature of Corporate Responsibilities: Perspectives from American, French, and German Consumers," *Journal of Business Research,* Jan. 2003, pp. 55–67.

15. Dave Izraeli and Mark S. Schwartz, "What We Can Learn from the Federal Sentencing Guidelines for Organizational Ethics," *Journal of Business Ethics,* July 1998, pp. 9–10.

16. "U.S. Balance of Trade in Goods and Services," Kiplinger's, http://special.kiplinger.com/kbftables/usecon/trade/trade_balance_annual.htm (accessed Apr. 8, 2004).

17. Bureau of the Census, *Statistical Abstract of the United States, 2002* (Washington, DC: Government Printing Office, 2003), p. 834.

18. Ibid., pp. 824–826, 834.

19. Charles R. Taylor, George R. Franke, and Michael L. Maynard, "Attitudes Toward Direct Marketing and Its Regulation: A Comparison of the United States and Japan," *Journal of Public Policy & Marketing,* Fall 2000, pp. 228–237.

20. "European Consumers Getting Comfortable with Online Channel," CyberAtlas, July 6, 2001, http://cyberatlas.internet.com/big_picture/geographics/article/0,,5911_794321,00.html.

21. "Population Explosion!" CyberAtlas, Sep. 22, 2003, http://cyberatlas.internet.com/big_picture/geographics/article/0,1323,5911_151151,00.html.

22. Elisa Batista, "Telcos Duke It Out over Iraq," Wired News, June 27, 2003, www.wired.com/news/politics/0,1283,59410,00.html; Ben Charny, "Study: Cell Phone Use to Double," clnet, Aug. 2003, http://news.com.com/2100-1039_3-5060745.html.

23. Louisa Kasdon Sidell, "The Economics of Inclusion," *Continental,* Apr. 2001, pp. 64–67.

24. Geri Smith and Cristina Lindblad, "Mexico: Was NAFTA Worth It?" *Business Week,* Dec. 22, 2003, pp. 66–72.

25. Bureau of the Census, *Statistical Abstract of the United States, 2002,* pp. 824–826, 834; "NAFTA: A Decade of Strengthening a Dynamic Relationship," U.S. Department of Commerce, pamphlet, 2003, available at www.ustr.gov.

26. Bureau of the Census, *Statistical Abstract of the United States, 2002,* pp. 824, 834.

27. "Canada-U.S. Trade Statistics," Canada Customs and Revenue Agency, Sep. 2002, www.ccra-adrc.gc.ca/newsroom/factsheets/2002/sep/stats-e.html.

28. William C. Symonds, "Meanwhile, to the North, NAFTA Is a Smash," *Business Week,* Feb. 27, 1995, p. 66.

29. Bureau of the Census, *Statistical Abstract of the United States, 2002,* pp. 825, 834; "NAFTA: A Decade of Strengthening a Dynamic Relationship."

30. Smith and Lindblad, "Mexico: Was NAFTA Worth It?"; Cheryl Farr Leas, "The Big Boom," *Continental,* Apr. 2001, pp. 85–94.

31. "Antecedents of the FTAA Process," FTAA, www.ftaa-alca.org/View_e.asp (accessed Apr. 8, 2004); "FTAA Fact Sheet," Market Access and Compliance, U.S. Department of Commerce, www.mac.doc.gov/ftaa2005/ftaa_fact_sheet.html (accessed Apr. 8, 2004).

32. "U.S.-Brazil Split May Doom America's Free-Trade Zone," *Wall Street Journal,* Nov. 7, 2003, http://online.wsj.com.

33. "Archer Daniels to File NAFTA Claim Against Mexico," *Inbound Logistics,* Oct. 2003, p. 30.

34. Smith and Lindblad, "Mexico."

35. "The European Union at a Glance," Europa (European Union online), http://europa.eu.int/abc/index_en.htm# (accessed Apr. 8, 2004).

36. Stanley Reed, with Ariane Sains, David Fairlamb, and Carol Matlack, "The Euro: How Damaging a Hit?" *Business Week,* Sep. 29, 2003, p. 63; "The Single Currency," CNN, www.cnn.com/SPECIALS/2000/eurounion/story/currency/, July 3, 2001.

37. "Common Market of the South (MERCOSUR): Agri-Food Regional Profile Statistical Overview," Agriculture and Agrifood Canada, Oct. 2002, http://atn-riae.agr.ca/latin/e3431.htm.

38. "About APEC," Asia-Pacific Economic Cooperation, www.apecsec.org.sg/apec/about_apec.html (accessed Apr. 8, 2004).

39. Smith and Lindblad, "Mexico."

40. Clay Chandler, "How to Play the China Boom," *Fortune,* Dec. 22, 2003, pp. 141, 142.

41. Dexter Roberts and Frederik Balfour, "Is This Boom in Danger?" *Business Week,* Nov. 3, 2003, pp. 48–50.

42. "What Is the WTO?" World Trade Organization, www.wto.org/english/thewto_e/whatis_e/whatis_e.htm (accessed Apr. 8, 2004).

43. "WTO: U.S. Steel Duties Are Illegal," *USA Today,* Nov. 10, 2003, http://usatoday.com.

44. "Bush Ends Steel Tariffs," CNN/Money, Dec. 4, 2003, http://cnnmoney.com.

45. Pradeep Tyagi, "Export Behavior of Small Business Firms in Developing Economies: Evidence from the Indian Market," *Marketing Management Journal,* Fall/Winter 2000, pp. 12–20.

46. Berrin Dosoglu-Guner, "How Do Exporters and Non-Exporters View Their 'Country of Origin' Image Abroad?" *Marketing Management Journal,* Fall/Winter 2000, pp. 21–27.

47. Farok J. Contractor and Sumit K. Kundu, "Franchising Versus Company-Run Operations: Model Choice in the Global Hotel Sector," *Journal of International Marketing,* Nov. 1997, pp. 28–53.

48. Margreet F. Boersma, Peter J. Buckley, and Pervez N. Ghauri, "Trust in International Joint Venture Relationships," *Journal of Business Research,* Dec. 2003, pp. 1031–1042.

49. "What We're About," NUMMI, www.nummi.com/co_info.html (accessed Nov. 3, 2003).

50. William Q. Judge and Joel A. Ryman, "The Shared Leadership Challenge in Strategic Alliances: Lessons from the U.S. Healthcare Industry," *Academy of Management Executive,* May 2001, pp. 71–79.

51. Ibid.

52. Leslie Gornstein, "Retailers Cater to Growing U.S. Hispanic Population," *Pensacola News Journal,* June 17, 2001, p. 4B.

53. Botelho, "Selling to the World."

54. Theodore Levitt, "The Globalization of Markets," *Harvard Business Review,* May/June 1983, p. 92.

55. Deborah Owens, Timothy Wilkinson, and Bruce Keillor, "A Comparison of Product Attributes in a Cross-Cultural/Cross-National Context," *Marketing Management Journal,* Fall/Winter 2000, pp. 1–11.

56. Anil K. Gupta and Vijay Govindarajan, "Converting Global Presence into Global Competitive Advantage," *Academy of Management Executive,* May 2001, pp. 45–58.

57. Sources: "About BMW Group," BMW, www.bmw.usa.com/about/group.htm (accessed Apr. 8, 2004); "About BMW North America–Manufacturing," BMW, www.bmwusa.com/About/manufacturing.htm?dNav_loc=_root.manufacturing (accessed Apr. 8, 2004); Neal E. Boudette, "BMW's CEO Just Says 'No' to Protect Brand," *Wall Street Journal,* Nov. 26, 2003, http://online.wsj.com/; "Excerpt from 'Trading Up,'" *USA Today,* Dec. 14, 2003, www.usatoday.com/money/books/reviews/2003-12-14-trading-up-excerpt_x.thm; "Fre-

quently Asked Questions–Corporate Goals and Strategy," www.bmwgroup.com/e/nav/?/e/0_0_www_bmwgroup_com/home page/index.jsp?1_0 (accessed Apr. 8, 2004); "The Psychology of Luxury," *USA Today*, Dec. 15, 2003, www.usatoday.com/money/ books/reviews/2003-12-15-trade-book_x.htm; Joseph B. White, "DaimlerChrysler Will Launch Smart Mini Car Brand in U.S.," *Wall Street Journal*, Dec. 9, 2003, http://online.wsj.com/.
58. Sources: Rekha Balu, "Hop Faster, Energizer Bunny: Ray-ovac Batteries Roll On," *Wall Street Journal*, June 15, 1999, p. B4; "Battle of the Blades Draws Corporate Blood," Datamoni-tor, Oct. 8, 2003, www.datamonitor.com/~eb69fbdf57f24f129c 0c4f3f3ac1ccbd~/consumer/news/product.asp?pid=4D673D8B-F3F4-4A53-9BE9-BB5D806FCD14; "For Mighty Gillette, These Are the Faces of War," *New York Times*, Oct. 12, 2003, sec. 3, p. 1; The Gillette Company, www.gillette.com (accessed Apr. 8, 2004); Gillette 1999 and 2002 Annual Reports; "Gillette's Edge," *Business Week*, Jan. 19, 1998, pp. 70–77; "Gillette Sues Schick over Razor Launch," *Promo*, Aug. 14, 2003, www.promomagazine.com/ar/marketing_gillette_sues_schick/; "Wal-Mart Selling Its Own Brand of Alkaline Batteries," *Wall Street Journal*, Dec. 10, 1999, pp. C4–5. Don Roy, Middle Tennessee State University, and Michael D. Hartline, Florida State University, assisted in the development of these case materials.

Chapter 6

1. Sources: "Google History," Google, www.google.com/ corporate/history.html (accessed Apr. 15, 2004); Liane Gouthro, "Going Ga-Ga for Google," CNN, Apr. 24, 2000, www.cnn.com; Jefferson Graham, "The Search Engine That Could," *USA Today*, Aug. 26, 2003, pp. 1D, 2D; Kara Swisher, "Lifting Google's Dot-Com Shell Reveals Serious Internet Player," *Wall Street Journal*, Jan. 21, 2002, http://online.wsj.com; Betsy Cummings, "Beating the Odds," *Sales and Marketing Management*, March 2002, vol. 154, issue 3, pp. 24–28.
2. Vladimir Zwass, "Electronic Commerce: Structures and Issues," *International Journal of Electronic Commerce*, Fall 1996, pp. 3–23.
3. Stan Crock, "Lockheed Martin," *Business Week*, Nov. 24, 2003, p. 85.
4. Michael J. Mandel and Robert D. Hof, "Rethinking the Internet," *Business Week*, Mar. 26, 2001, pp. 116–122.
5. Catherine Yang, "Homeland Security Dept.," *Business Week*, Nov. 24, 2003, p. 85.
6. Fang Wu, Vijay Mahajan, and Sridhar Balasubramanian, "An Analysis of E-Business Adoption and Its Impact on Business Performance," *Journal of the Academy of Marketing Science*, Fall 2003, pp. 425–447.
7. Michael Totty, "The Researcher," *Wall Street Journal*, July 16, 2001, p. R20.
8. "Shop Around the Clock," *American Demographics*, Sep. 2003, p. 18.
9. David W. Stewart and Qin Zhao, "Internet Marketing, Business Models, and Public Policy," *Journal of Public Policy & Marketing*, Fall 2000, pp. 287–296.
10. Totty, "The Researcher."
11. Ronald L. Hess, Shankar Ganesan, and Noreen M. Klein, "Service Failure and Recovery: The Impact of Relationship Factors on Customer Satisfaction," *Journal of the Academy of Marketing Science*, Spring 2003, pp. 127–145.
12. "Turning to Tech," *Business Week*, Dec. 22, 2003, p. 83.
13. Jon Mark Giese, "Place Without Space, Identity Without Body: The Role of Cooperative Narrative in Community and Identity Formation in a Text-Based Electronic Community" (unpublished dissertation, Pennsylvania State University, 1996).
14. "Krispy Kreme's Secret Ingredient," *Business 2.0*, Sep. 2003, p. 36.

15. Robyn Greenspan, "Europe, U.S. on Different Sides of Gender Divide," CyberAtlas, Oct. 21, 2003, http://cyberatlas. internet.com/big_picture/demographics/article/0,,5901_3095681, 00.html.
16. "U.S. Internet Population Continues to Grow," CyberAtlas, Feb. 6, 2002, http://cyberatlas.internet.com/big_picture/ geographics/article/0,,5911_969541,00.html.
17. "More Work, Less Play for American Internet Users," CyberAtlas, Mar. 4, 2002, http://cyberatlas.internet.com/big_ picture/demographics/article/0,,5901_984721,00.html.
18. Robyn Greenspan, "Your Speed May Vary," CyberAtlas, Apr. 25, 2003, http://cyberatlas.internet.com/markets/broadband/ article/0,,10099_2196961,00.html.
19. "B2B E-Commerce Headed for Trillions," CyberAtlas, Mar. 6, 2002, http://cyberatlas.internet.com/markets/b2b/article/ 0,,10091_986661,00.html.
20. Laura Rush, "U.S. E-Commerce to See Significant Growth by 2008," CyberAtlas, Aug. 7, 2003, http://cyberatlas.internet. com/markets/retailing/article/0,,6061_2246041,00.html.
21. Ibid.
22. Heather Green, "FreshDirect" *Business Week*, Nov. 24, 2003, p. 104.
23. "Southwest Airlines Fact Sheet," Southwest Airlines, www.iflyswa.com/about_swa/press/factsheet.html (accessed Apr. 15, 2004).
24. Stephanie Anderson Forest, "Kinko's," *Business Week*, Nov. 24, 2003, p. 101.
25. Michael Arndt, "Yellow," *Business Week*, Nov. 24, 2003, pp. 100, 101.
26. Andrew Park, "Imperial Sugar," *Business Week*, Nov. 24, 2003, p. 98.
27. "Industry Projections," Jupiter Media Metrix, www.jmm.com/xp/jmm/press/industryProjections.xml#ususers (Accessed Mar. 4, 2002).
28. "AMZN Q3 2003 Financial Results," Amazon.com, press release, Oct. 21, 2003, http://phx.corporate-ir.net/phoenix. zhtml?c=97664&p=IROL-NewsText&t=Regular&id=461065&.
29. "Small Businesses Use Net for Customer Service, Communications," CyberAtlas, Nov. 12, 2001, http://cyberatlas.internet. com/markets/smallbiz/article/0,,10098_921821,00.html.
30. "Valpak.com Success, Growth Based on Offering Local Coupons, Commitment to Value and Strong Backing," Business Wire, Sep. 24, 2001, via www.findarticles.com.
31. Asim Ansari and Carl F. Mela, "E-Customization," *Journal of Marketing Research*, May 2003, pp. 131–145.
32. C. B. Bhattacharya and Sankar Sen, "Consumer–Company Identification: A Framework for Understanding Consumers' Relationships with Companies," *Journal of Marketing*, Apr. 2003, pp. 76–88.
33. Peter C. Verhoef, "Understanding the Effect of Customer Relationship Management Efforts on Customer Retention and Customer Share Development," *Journal of Marketing*, Oct. 2003, pp. 30–45.
34. O. C. Ferrell, Michael D. Hartline, 3d. Ed, *Marketing Strategy* (Mason, OH: South Western, 2005), p. 72.
35. Werner J. Reinartz and V. Kumar, "The Impact of Relationship Characteristics on Profitable Lifetime Duration," *Journal of Marketing*, Jan. 2003, pp. 77–99.
36. J. Bonasia, "Eyeing Growth in Customer Relationship Management Software," *Investors Business Daily*, Jan. 8, 2002, p. 7.
37. "Better Relationships, Better Business," *Business Week*, Special Advertising Section, Apr. 29, 2002.
38. Edward Prewitt, "How to Build Customer Loyalty in an Internet World," *CIO*, Jan. 1, 2002, www.cio.com/archive/ 010102/loyalty_content.html.

39. Robyn Greenspan, "Moderate, Steady CRM Growth Through 2006," CyberAtlas, July 3, 2003, http://cyberatlas. internet.com/big_picture/applications/article/0,,1301_2230361, 00.html.
40. Michael Krauss, "At Many Firms, Technology Obscures CRM," *Marketing News,* Mar. 18, 2002, p. 5.
41. Emin Babakus, Ugur Yavas, Osman M. Karatepe, and Turgay Avci, "The Effect of Management Commitment to Service Quality on Employees' Affective and Performance Outcomes," *Journal of the Academy of Marketing Science,* Summer 2003, pp. 272–286.
42. Prewitt, "How to Build Customer Loyalty in an Internet World."
43. Ibid.
44. Ibid.
45. Dennis B. Arnett, Steve D. German, and Shelby D. Hunt, "The Identity Salience Model of Relationship Marketing Success: The Case of Nonprofit Marketing," *Journal of Marketing,* Apr. 2003, pp. 89–105.
46. David Pottruck and Terry Peace, "Listening to Customers in the Electronic Age," *Fortune,* May 2000, www.business2.com/articles/mag/0,1640,7700,00.html.
47. Stephenie Steitzer, "Commercial Websites Cut Back on Collections of Personal Data," *Wall Street Journal,* Mar. 28, 2002, http://online.wsj.com.
48. Peter Loftus, "Yahoo Modifies Its Privacy Policy to Allow More Sharing of User Data," *Wall Street Journal,* Mar. 28, 2002, http://online.wsj.com.
49. Steitzer, "Commercial Websites Cut Back on Collections of Personal Data."
50. "BBBOnLine Privacy Seal," BBBOnLine, www.BBBOnLine. org/privacy/index.asp (accessed Apr. 15, 2004).
51. "European Union Directive on Privacy," E-Center for Business Ethics, www.e-businessethics.com/privacy.eud.htm (accessed Apr. 15, 2004).
52. Tim McCollum, "Some Online Marketers Are Downsizing E-Mail Campaigns," *Investor's Business Daily,* Jan. 23, 2002, p. A5.
53. "Unsolicited Commercial E-mail Advertisements (Anti-Spam Legislation) 2003 Legislative Activity," National Conference of State Legislatures, Dec. 22, 2003, www.ncsl.org/programs/lis/legislation/spam03.htm.
54. Stephen H. Wildstrom, "Can Microsoft Stamp Out Piracy?" Business Week Online, Oct. 2, 2000, www.businessweek.com.
55. William T. Neese and Charles R. McManis, "Summary Brief: Law, Ethics and the Internet: How Recent Federal Trademark Law Prohibits a Remedy Against Cyber-squatters," *Proceedings from the Society of Marketing Advances,* Nov. 4–7, 1998.
56. Sources: Computers4SURE.com, www.computers4sure.com (accessed Apr. 15, 2004); "Computers4SURE.com Awarded Three Prominent Industry Website Awards," PRNewswire, Oct. 25, 1999, via www.findarticles.com; "Engage Enabling Technologies: Ad Management Solutions with AdBureau and AdManager," Engage, Inc., case study, www.engage.com/au/solutions/cs_solutions_shop4sure.cfm (accessed Sep. 19, 2001); David Jastrow, "Attacking the B2B Market," *Computer Reseller News,* Apr. 14, 2000, http://crn.channelsupersearch.com/news/crn/15761.asp; "Office Depot and GoToMyPC Forge Relationship to Provide Remote-Access Service; Office Depot to Offer Award-Winning GoToMyPC for Remote Workers," Business Wire, June 11, 2003, via www.findarticles.com; "Office Depot Announces Acquisition of Computers4Sure.com and Solutions4Sure.com," 4SURE.com, press release, July 9, 2001, www.computers4sure. com/static/releaseOfficeDepot.asp; "Shopping4SURE.com," BATV, video, www.batv.com (accessed Sep. 20, 2001; Dec. 30, 2003); "Shopping4SURE.com, the Award Winning On-line Retailer, Chooses ICC's B2B Fulfillment Solution," Internet Commerce Corporation, press release, Dec. 15, 1999, www.icc.net/aboutICC/ICCnews/pressReleases/1215299.html; Solutions4SURE.com, www.solutions4sure.com (accessed Apr. 15, 2004, Dec. 30, 2003).
57. Sources: Karen Bannan, "Sole Survivor," *Sales & Marketing Management,* July 2001, pp. 36–41; "Company Overview," eBay, http://pages.ebay.com/community/aboutebay/overview/index.html (accessed Apr. 15, 2004); Robert Goff, "Ebay's Cop," *Forbes,* June 25, 2001, p. 42; "Fiorina Tops Fortune List of Most Powerful Women," *Mercury News,* Oct. 1, 2003, www.mercurynews. com/mld/mercurynews/business/6904474.htm; Robert D. Hof, "The eBay Economy," Business Week Online, Aug. 25, 2003, www.businessweek.com/magazine/content/03_34/b3846650.htm; Robert D. Hof, "Online Extra: Q&A with eBay's Meg Whitman," Business Week Online, May 14, 2001, www.business week.com; Julia King, "Websites Crack Down on Fraud," *ComputerWorld,* Sep. 13, 1999, p. 1113; Chuck Lenatti, "Auction Mania," *Upside,* July 11, 1999, pp. 84–92; Ellen Messmer, "Ebay Acts to Curtail Internet Fraud," *Network World,* July 24, 2000, pp. 31, 34; Jon Swartz, "'E' in eBay Might Stand for Expansion," *USA Today,* Mar. 28, 2001, www.usatoday.com; Lizette Wilson, "Businesses Build Profits Helping Others Use Ebay," *San Francisco Business Times,* May 26, 2003, http://sanfrancisco.bizjournals.com/sanfrancisco/stories/2003/05/26/story8.html; Eric Young, "Ebay Says Fixed-Price Bazaar Will Open Next Quarter," *The Standard,* May 25, 2001, www.thestandard.com.

Chapter 7

1. Sources: "VNU, Inc.," *Marketing News,* June 9, 2003, pp. H6–H8; "Insights into Today's Global Consumers," VNU, www.vnu.com/vnu/page.jsp?id=104 (accessed Apr. 15, 2004); "A Leading Information and Media Company," VNU, www.vnu. com/vnu/page.jsp?id=84 (accessed Apr. 15, 2004).
2. Jack Honomichl, "Revenues Up, but Little Real Growth," *Marketing News,* June 9, 2003, p. H3.
3. Earle Eldridge, "Move Over, Boys: Today's Hot Rodders Often Women," *USA Today,* Nov. 10, 2003, www.ustoday.com.
4. "Pizza Hut® Studies Effects of 'Pizza Deprivation' on College and High School Students," PRNewswire, via America Online, May 30, 2001.
5. Jacquelyn S. Thomas, "A Methodology for Linking Customer Acquisition to Customer Retention," *Journal of Marketing Research,* May 2001, pp. 262–268.
6. "We Know Who Our Customers Are," Lowe's 2000 Annual Report, p. 9.
7. Aaron Bernstein, with Christopher Palmeri and Roger O. Crockett, "An Inner-City Renaissance," *Business Week,* Oct. 27, 2003, pp. 64–68.
8. Brian T. Ratchford, Myung-Soo Lee, and Debabrata Talukdar, "The Impact of the Internet on Information Search for Automobiles," *Journal of Marketing Research,* May 2003, pp. 193–209.
9. Vikas Mittal and Wagner A. Kamakura, "Satisfaction, Repurchase Intent, and Repurchase Behavior: Investigating the Moderating Effects of Customer Characteristics," *Journal of Marketing Research,* Feb. 2001, pp. 131–142.
10. "Internal Secondary Market Research," Small Business Owner's Toolkit, www.lycos.com/business/cch/guidebook.html?lpv51&docNumber5P03_3020, June 23, 2001.
11. Amy Merrick, "New Population Data Will Help Marketers Pitch Their Products," *Wall Street Journal,* Feb. 14, 2001, http://interactive.wsj.com/.
12. "Information Resources, Inc.," *Marketing News,* June 9, 2003, pp. H3, H11.
13. John Harwood and Shirley Leung, "Hang-Ups: Why Some Pollsters Got It So Wrong This Election Day," *Wall Street Journal,* Nov. 8, 2003, pp. A1, A6.

14. Ibid.
15. Ibid.
16. Leonardo Felson, "Netting Limitations: Online Researchers' New Tactics for Tough Audiences," *Marketing News*, Feb. 26, 2001, www.ama.org/pubs/.
17. Alissa Quart, "Ol' College Pry," *Business 2.0*, Apr. 3, 2001.
18. "Focus Groups in Nebraska Help Market Tourism," *Marketing News*, Jan. 6, 2003, p. 5.
19. Daniel Gross, "Lies, Damn Lies, and Focus Groups," *Slate*, Oct. 10, 2003, http://slate.msn.com/id/2089677/.
20. Peter DePaulo, "Sample Size for Qualitative Research," *Quirk's Marketing Research Review*, Dec. 2000, www.quirks.com.
21. Barbara Allan, "The Benefits of Telephone Depth Sessions," *Quirk's Marketing Research Review*, Dec. 2000, www.quirks.com.
22. Jagdip Singh, Roy D. Howell, and Gary K. Rhoads, "Adaptive Designs for Likert-Type Data: An Approach for Implementing Marketing Surveys," *Journal of Marketing Research*, Aug. 1990, pp. 304–321.
23. Bas Donkers, Philip Hans Franses, and Peter C. Verhoef, "Selective Sampling for Binary Choice Models," *Journal of Marketing Research*, Nov. 2003, pp. 492–497.
24. Alison Stein Wellner, "Research on a Shoestring," *American Demographics*, Apr. 2001, www.americandemographics.com.
25. Thomas T. Semon, "Determine Survey's Purpose for Best Results," *Marketing News*, Jan. 6, 2003, p. 7.
26. "Marketing Campaigns Impact on Consumer Habits," *The Guardian*, Nov. 15, 2000, www.society.guardian.co.uk/.
27. Eunkyu Lee, Michael Y. Hu, and Rex S. Toh, "Are Consumer Survey Results Distorted? Systematic Impact of Behavioral Frequency and Duration on Survey Response Errors," *Journal of Marketing Research*, Feb. 2000, pp. 125–133.
28. Judy Strauss and Donna J. Hill, "Consumer Complaints by E-mail: An Exploratory Investigation of Corporate Responses and Customer Reactions," *Journal of Interactive Marketing*, Winter 2001, pp. 63–73.
29. Laurence N. Goal, "High Technology Data Collection for Measurement and Testing," *Marketing Research*, Mar. 1992, pp. 29–38.
30. Philip Hans Franses, "How Nobel-Worthy Economics Relates to Databases," *Marketing News*, Mar. 12, 2001, p. 14.
31. Kathleen Cholewka, "Tiered CRM: Serving Pip-Squeaks to VIPs," *Sales & Marketing Management*, Apr. 2001, pp. 25–26.
32. Merrick, "New Population Data Will Help Marketers Pitch Their Products."
33. Spencer E. Ante, "IBM," *Business Week*, Nov. 24, 2003, p. 84.
34. Joseph Rydholm, "A Global Perspective: Syndicated Survey Monitors Airline Performance Around the World," *Quirk's Marketing Research Review*, Nov. 2000, www.quirks.com/.
35. "Top 50 U.S. Research Organizations," *Marketing News*, June 9, 2003, p. H4.
36. Lambeth Hochwald, "Are You Smart Enough to Sell Globally?" *Sales & Marketing Management*, July 1998, pp. 52–56.
37. Ibid.
38. Sources: "Information Resources Inc.," *Marketing News*, June 9, 2003, pp. H10, H11; "Key Facts," *Wall Street Journal*, http://interactive.wsj.com (accessed Jan. 2, 2004); "On-Line Purchases of Consumer Packaged Goods on the Rise" (study by Information Resources, Inc.), *DSN Retailing Today*, June 4, 2001, www.findarticles.com/cf_0/m0FNP/11_40/75452753/p1/article.jhtml?term5%22Information1Resources%22; "Overview," Information Resources, Inc., www.infores.com/public/us/aboutiri/default.htm (accessed Apr. 15, 2004).
39. Sources: Patrick Goldstein, "Untangling the Web of Teen Trends," *Los Angeles Times*, Nov. 21, 2000, www.look-look.com/looklook/html/Test_Drive_Press_LA_Times2.html; Sarah Moore, "On Your Markets," *Working Woman*, Feb. 2001, p. 26; "Quest for Cool," *Time*, Sep. 2003, www.look-look.com/looklook/html/Test_Drive_Press_Time.html; Michael Quintanilla and Marian Lu, "The Very Latest in Hanging Out at the Mall," *Los Angeles Times*, July 28, 2000, www.look-look.com/looklook/html/Test_Drive_Press_LA_Times.html; "Who We Are," look-look.com, www.look-look.com (accessed Apr. 15, 2004).

Chapter 8

1. Sources: Julia Boorstin, "Disney's 'Tween Machine," *Fortune*, Sep. 29, 2003, pp. 111–114; "'Disney's Karaoke Series' Starts On a High Note," Business Wire, Sep. 23, 2003, www.businesswire.com.
2. Jeff Green, "The Toy-Train Company That Thinks It Can," *Business Week*, Dec. 4, 2000, pp. 64–69.
3. Service Corporation International, www.hoovers.com, Oct. 29, 2003.
4. Martin Croft, "The Age Old Question," *Marketing Week*, Apr. 17, 2003, p. 37.
5. Kids and Commercialism, Center for New American Dream, Dec. 4, 2003, newdream.org/campaign/kids/facts.html.
6. Bureau of the Census, *Statistical Abstract of the United States 2002*, p. 13.
7. J. D. Mosley-Matchett, "Marketers: There's a Feminine Side to the Web," *Marketing News*, Feb. 16, 1998, p. 6.
8. Marvin Maties, "The New Product Game: Why Targeting Women Is Key," *Prepared Foods*, June 2003, p. 35.
9. Ibid.
10. Joseph T. Plummer, "The Concept and Application of Life Style Segmentation," *Journal of Marketing*, Jan. 1974, p. 33.
11. "Shacking Up," *American Demographics*, Jan. 2002, p. 45.
12. Rebecca Piirto Heath, "You Can Buy a Thrill: Chasing the Ultimate Rush," *American Demographics*, June 1997, pp. 47–51.
13. Beverage World, "Beverage Market Index 2003," June 15, 2003, VNU Business Media.
14. Philip Kotler, *Marketing Management: Analysis, Planning, Implementation, and Control*, 11th ed. (Englewood Cliffs, NJ: Prentice-Hall, 2003), p. 144.
15. Charles W. Chase, Jr., "Selecting the Appropriate Forecasting Method," *Journal of Business Forecasting*, Fall 1997, pp. 2, 23, 28–29.
16. "Controlled Market Test (CMT)," ACNielsen Market Decisions, www.marketdec.com/newprodtst/default.htm (accessed Feb. 11, 2002).
17. Sources: Lynn Cowan and Cheryl Winokur Munk, "Small Broker-Dealers Look for Partners," *Wall Street Journal*, Oct. 23, 2002, p. B3C; Eve Epstein, "Dot-Com Brokerage Exploits a Market Niche," *InfoWorld*, Jan. 8, 2001, pp. 34+; "Broker Cuts Fees, Adds New Payment Plan," *Financial Net News*, Dec. 18, 2000, p. 2; "BuyandHold.com First to Introduce the Virtual Direct Stock Purchase Plan," PR Newswire, Apr. 25, 2000, www.prnewswire.com; John P. Mello, Jr., "Going Direct," *CFO*, Oct. 2000, p. 22; BuyandHold.com website, www.buyandhold.com.
18. Sources: "IKEA's Growth Limited by Style Issues, Says CEO," *Nordic Business Report*, January 21, 2004, www.nordicbusinessreport.com; "Verticalnet's Supply Chain Software Upgrade, Packaging Wins Customers," *InternetWeek*, Sep. 3, 2003, www.internetworld.com; "IKEA Sets New Heights with Cat," *Printing World*, Aug. 21, 2003, p. 3; "Stylish, Swedish, 60-ish: IKEA's a Global Phenomenon," *Western Mail*, May 20, 2003, p. 1; "Facts and Figures," IKEA, www.ikea-usa.com.

Chapter 9

1. Sources: Matt DeMazza, "Teen Magnets," *Footwear News*, Nov. 17, 2003, p. 15; Lev Grossman, "The Quest for Cool," *Time*, Sep. 8, 2003, pp. 48–54; Irma Zandl, "B-T-S: Anything

Hot?" *Marketing Insight from the Zandl Group,* Aug. 2003; Barbara White-Sax, "Teens Become Price Savvy in Search for What's Cool," *Drug Store News,* Mar. 23, 2003, pp. 17+.

2. "First Source for Car Shoppers in Online Households," *USA Today* Snapshot, Nov. 16, 2001, www.usatoday.com/snapshot.

3. Russell W. Belk, "Situational Variables and Consumer Behavior," *Journal of Consumer Research,* Dec. 1975, pp. 157–164.

4. Greg Hernandez, "Websites Meet Demand for Tickets to Popular Movies," *E-Commerce Times,* Jan. 28, 2002, www.ecommercetimes.com/perl/story/16027.html.

5. Joan Oleck, "Dieting: More Fun with a Buddy?" *Business Week,* Apr. 23, 2001, p. 16.

6. Kim Ann Zimmermann, "Safeway Enters Online Grocery Turnstile," *E-Commerce Times,* Jan. 16, 2002, www.ecommercetimes.com/perl/story/?id=15809.

7. Margaret Sheridan, "Made to Measure: Patient Satisfaction Surveys Provide Hospitals with Paths to Improvement," *Restaurants & Institutions,* Nov. 1, 2003, p. 69.

8. Laura Q. Hughes and Alice Z. Cuneo, "Lowe's Retools Image in Push Toward Women," *Advertising Age,* Feb. 26, 2001, www.adage.com/news_and_features/features/20010226/article7.html.

9. Casey Keller, "So Far, It's Easy Being Green," *New York Times,* Oct. 22, 2000, sec. 3, p. 2.

10. Julie Cook, "Making the Grade: Markets Set Their Sites on Luring Savvy, On-the-Go Teens to Dairy Products," *Dairy Field,* April 2002, p. 50.

11. 2002 American Community Survey Profile. www.census.gov. (accessed May 20, 2004).

12. Jeffrey M. Humphreys, *Georgia Business and Economic Conditions,* 63, no. 2. Second Quarter 2003, p. 4.

13. Ibid.

14. Stuart Elliott, "Campaigns for Black Consumers." *New York Times,* June 13, 2003.

15. Ibid.

16. Ibid.

17. Press release from: Daimler Chrysler Corporation. www.csrwire.com. (accessed May 20, 2004).

18. "Hawaiian Punch Announces 2003 Black History Contest" www.blackvoices.com. (accessed May 20, 2004).

19. 2002 American Community Survey Profile. www.census.gov. (accessed May 20, 2004).

20. Ethnic Analysis. www.databankusa.com. (accessed May 20, 2004).

21. Ibid.

22. "Minority Buying Power to Triple" *Dallas Morning News,* Aug. 15, 2003.

23. Stuart Elliott, "Campaigns for Black Consumers" *New York Times,* June 13, 2003.

24. Noel C. Paul, "Advertisers Slip into Spanish" *The Christian Science Monitor,* June 2, 2003.

25. Ibid.

26. 2002 American Community Survey Profile. www.census.gov. (accessed May 20, 2004).

27. "Kmart Marketing: Urban/Ethnic Strategy Remains Pillar of Competitive Advantage," *Dsn Retailing Today,* Mar. 5, 2001, pp. 44–46.

28. Greta Guest, "Analysts Commend New Kmart Ads; Campaign to Capitalize on Store's Strengths," *Detroit Free Press,* Oct. 17, 2003.

29. Christina Hoag, "Asian-Americans Are Fastest Growing Group" *Miami Herald,* Apr. 7, 2003.

30. Ibid.

31. Phuong Ly, "Immigrants Find a Taste of Home; Foreign Food Shops Expand to U.S. to Serve Old Customers—and New," *Washington Post,* Jan. 22, 2002, p. B1.

32. Sources: Maria Weiskott, "A Bear of a Challenge," *Playthings,* Oct./Nov. 2003, p. 4; Bruce Spence, "Build-A-Bear Hits Retail Sweet Spot," *The America's Intelligence Wire,* Aug. 11, 2003; Sharon Nelton, "Building an Empire One Smile at a Time," *Success,* Sep. 2000, pp. 34+; Brad Patten, "Teddy Bear Bonanza Run by Sweetheart of a System," *Washington Business Journal,* Feb. 4, 2000, p. 53; Marilyn Vise, "Corporate Culture: Build-A-Bear Workshop," *St. Louis Business Journal,* May 7, 2001, http://stlouis.bcentral.com/stlouis/stories/2001/05/07/focus11.html.

33. Sources: Gregory Jordan, "Online, Used Car Lots That Cover the Nation," *New York Times,* Oct. 22, 2003, pp. G13+; "AutoTrader.com Continues Summer Marketing Blitz with Television Buy," PR Newswire, June 30, 2003, www.prnewswire.com; Chaz Osburn, "AutoTrader Adds Online Auction Listings," *Automotive News,* Jan. 13, 2003, p. 28; Steve Jarvis, "Pedal to the Cyber-Metal," *Marketing News,* Jan. 21, 2002, pp. 6–7; "How to Translate a TV Ad into an Online Promotion," MarketingSherpa.com, Nov. 1, 2001, www.emarketingtoher.com; "AutoTrader.com Gears Up for One-of-a-Kind Interactive Online Gaming Experience," AutoTrader.com news release, Aug. 2, 2001, www.autotrader.com/about/press_releases.

Chapter 10

1. Sources: "Building the Brighton Business," *Brighton View,* 2003, pp. 1-22; Brighton website, www.brighton.com; interview with a Bryan, Texas, Brighton retailer, Dec. 18, 2003.

2. Bureau of the Census, *Statistical Abstract of the United States* (Washington, DC: Government Printing Office, 2002), p. 635.

3. Ibid.

4. Ibid., p. 326.

5. Ibid., p. 261.

6. Kimberly Hill, "Biometric ID Firm Opts for Salesforce.com," CRMDaily.com, Jan. 28, 2002, www.crmdaily.com/perl/story/&id=16031.

7. "A Talk with SBA's Subcontractor of the Year," www.smallbusinessdepot.com/success/subcontractor.html, May 26, 2000.

8. Michael A. Verespej, "Sitting Pretty," *Industry Week,* Mar. 5, 2001, www.industryweek.com.

9. Moin Uddin, "Loyalty Programs: The Ultimate Gift," *DSN Retailing Today,* Mar. 5, 2001, p. 12.

10. Frederick E. Webster, Jr., and Yoram Wind, "A General Model for Understanding Organizational Buyer Behavior," *Marketing Management,* Winter/Spring 1996, pp. 52–57.

11. Doug Bartholomew, "CEO of the Year–The King of Customers," *Industry Week,* Feb. 1, 2002, www.industryweek.com/CurrentArticles/Asp?ArticleId=1180.

12. Suzanne Sabrosk, "NAICS Codes: A New Classification System for a New Economy," *Technology Information,* Nov. 2000, p. 18.

13. Sources: Charles Davis, "Are You Being Served?" *Cards International,* Mar. 7, 2003, p. 26; Toddi Gutner, "A Dot-Com's Survival Story," *Business Week,* May 13, 2002, p. 122; Maria Bruno, "Winning Customers: Concierge Services," *Bank Technology News,* July 2001, www.electronicbanker.com/btn/articles/btnjul01-6.shtml#top; "VIPdesk Expands Web-Based Personal Assistant Service to Wireless Devices," VIPdesk news release, June 25, 2001, www.vipdesk.com; Terry Brock, "The Internet Is Not About Dot-Coms," *Business Journal of Milwaukee,* Feb. 16, 2001, p. 14; VIPdesk video; "Online Concierge Service Secures Funding," *Business Wire,* Jan. 20, 2000, www.businesswire.com.

14. Sources: "WebMD Responds to Physicians' Complaints," *Information Week,* Jan. 28, 2004; Adam L. Freeman, "WebMD Wants to Process Claims, Too," *Wall Street Journal,* Nov. 19, 2003, p. 1; "WebMD to Pay $280 Million for Medifax-EDI," *New York Times,* Oct. 23, 2003, p. C4; Milt Freudenheim, "WebMD Is Somewhat Stronger After Therapy," *New York Times,* Feb. 4, 2002, p. C5; www.webmd.com.

Chapter 11

1. Sources: Jeffrey Kluger, "Inside the Food Labs," *Time*, Oct. 6, 2003, pp. 56-60; "McDonald's Tries to Speed Things Up," *Houston Chronicle*, Oct. 22, 2003, p. 1; "McDonald's Salads, McGriddles Boost Profit," *Agence France Presse*, Oct. 22, 2003; Rhasheema A. Sweeting, "Columbus, Ohio, Helped Pilot-Test McDonald's New McGriddle Sandwich," *Columbus Dispatch*, July 10, 2003, www.columbusdispatch.com.
2. James Champy, "New Products or New Processes?" *Sales & Marketing Management*, May 2001, pp. 30–32.
3. Earle Eldridge, "Bentley Gets Buyers' Hearts Racing," *USA Today*, May 21, 2001, p. 3B.
4. Emily Nelson, "Too Many Choices," *Wall Street Journal*, Apr. 20, 2001, pp. B1, B4.
5. William P. Putsis, Jr., and Barry L. Bayus, "An Empirical Analysis of Firms' Product Line Decisions," *Journal of Marketing Research*, Feb. 2001, pp. 110–118.
6. Stephanie Clifford, "The Grill of Their Dreams," *Business 2.0*, Feb. 2002, p. 96.
7. Nelson, "Too Many Choices."
8. James Bander, "Kodak Shifts Focus from Film, Betting Future on Digital Lines," *Wall Street Journal Online*, Sep. 25, 2003, http://online.wsj.com/article/0,,SB106444156883098700,00.html.
9. Brian A. Lukas and O. C. Ferrell, "The Effect of Market Orientation on Product Innovation," *Journal of the Academy of Marketing Science*, Feb. 2000, pp. 239–247.
10. Lee G. Cooper. "Structure Marketing Planning for Radically New Products," *Journal of Marketing*, Jan. 2000, pp. 1-16.
11. Paul Davidson, "AOL Prepares to Grab Net Users from Europe's Phone Titans," *USA Today*, May 21, 2001, p. 3B.
12. O. C. Ferrell and Michael Hartline, *Marketing Strategy* (Mason, OH: South-Western, 2005), pp. 172–173.
13. Matthew Swibel, "Spin Cycle," *Forbes*, Apr. 2, 2001, p. 118.
14. Nelson, "Too Many Choices."
15. Ferrell and Hartline, *Marketing Strategy*, p. 174.
16. Adapted from Everett M. Rogers, *Diffusion of Innovations* (New York: Macmillan, 1962), pp. 81–86.
17. Ibid., pp. 247–250.
18. Susan Casey, "Object-Oriented: Everything I Ever Needed to Know About Business I Learned in the Frozen Food Aisle," *eCompany*, Oct. 2000, www.ecompany.com.
19. Ibid.
20. Louis Lavelle, "What Campbell's New Chief Needs to Know," *Business Week*, June 25, 2001, p. 60.
21. Sources: "Technology Briefing Hardware: PlayStation 2 Sales Surpass 70 Million," *New York Times*, Jan. 15, 2004, p. C21; "Sony Corp.: Scaled-Back PSX Machine to Debut in Japan Saturday," *Wall Street Journal*, Dec. 9, 2003, p. 1; "Changing the Game," *The Economist*, Dec. 6, 2003, p. 16; "Sony Corp.: PlayStation 2 Is Set to Be Sold in China Starting This Month," *Wall Street Journal*, Dec. 1, 2003, p. 1; Mark Sweney, "PlayStation 2," *Campaign*, July 25, 2003, p. 15; Byron Acohido, "Microsoft Bets on Xbox Success, but Some Skeptical," *USA Today*, Apr. 24, 2001, p. 6B; Brian Bremner, "Microsoft vs. Sony: Mortal Combat," *Business Week Online*, Apr. 3, 2001, www.businessweek.com; Misha Davenport, "Sony Still in Command at Game Show," *Chicago Sun-Times*, May 19, 2003, p. 53; "Sony Ships 60th Million PlayStation 2," *Online Reporter*, Sep. 13, 2003.
22. Sources: Heather Green, "Consumer Electronics: Free-Falling Prices and Rocketing Sales," *Business Week*, Jan. 12, 2004, pp. 99-101; Cathy Booth Thomas, "Dell Wants Your Home," *Time*, Oct. 6, 2003, pp. 48-50; Bolaji Ojo, "Equipped with Hard Drive," *EBN*, Oct. 27, 2003, p. 2; Cynthia L. Webb, "Battle of the Consumer Electronics Giants," Washingtonpost.com, Sep. 26, 2003, www.washingtonpost.com.

Chapter 12

1. Sources: Jonathan Pont, "See Ginger Run: Segway Rebounds from Last Year's Recall," *Potentials*, Jan. 2004, p. 7; "Florida Ever-Glides to Offer Tours on Segway HTs," *Electric Vehicle Online Today*, Nov. 4, 2003; Lance Ulanoff, "Segway's Devoted Inventor," *PC Magazine*, Oct. 15, 2003; "Segway Introduces New 'p Series' Model of HT," *Electric Vehicle Online Today*, Oct. 24, 2003; "Power Issue Forces Recall of All Segway Scooters," *Wall Street Journal Online*, Sep. 29, 2003, online.wsj.com/article/0,,SB106459421766454200,00.html.
2. Chung K. Kim, Anne M. Lavack, and Margo Smith, "Consumer Evaluation of Vertical Brand Extensions and Core Brands," *Journal of Business Research*, Mar. 2001, pp. 211–222.
3. Lisa Robinson, "Caller ID Add-Ons Screen Out Unidentified Callers," Reuters Newswire, via AOL, July 11, 2001.
4. Joann Muller, "Daimler and Chrysler Have a Baby," *Business Week*, Jan. 14, 2002, p. 36.
5. Robert M. McMath, "Kellogg's Cereal Mates: 'It's Not for Breakfast Anymore,'" *Failure Magazine*, Dec. 2003.
6. Lee G. Cooper, "Strategic Marketing Planning for Radically New Products," *Journal of Marketing*, Jan. 2000, pp. 1–16.
7. Lisa C. Troy, David M. Szymanski, and P. Rajan Varadarajan, "Generating New Product Ideas: An Initial Investigation of the Role of Market Information and Organizational Characteristics," *Journal of the Academy of Marketing Science*, Jan. 2001, pp. 89–101.
8. Mark Roberti, "Space-Age Electric Parka? Sir, Yes, Sir!" *Business 2.0*, Mar. 2002, pp. 28–29.
9. John Grossman, "The Idea Guru," *Inc.*, May 2001, pp. 32–41.
10. Aric Rindfleisch and Christine Moorman, "The Acquisition and Utilization of Information in New Product Alliances: A Strength-of-Ties Perspective," *Journal of Marketing*, Apr. 2001, pp. 1–18.
11. Douglas Robson, "Nike: Just Do...Something," *Business Week*, via AOL, July 2, 2001.
12. Hillary Chura, "A-B Readies Test of Energy Drink to Rival Red Bull," *Advertising Age*, www.adage.com, July 18, 2001.
13. Barry L. Bayus, Sanjay Jain, and Ambar G. Rao, "Truth or Consequences: An Analysis of Vaporware and New Product Announcements," *Journal of Marketing Research*, Feb. 2001, pp. 3–13.
14. "P&G Ends Test of Impress Plastic Wrap," *Advertising Age*, www.adage.com, July 18, 2001.
15. "P&G to Launch Hair Care for Men," *Advertising Age*, www.adage.com, July 18, 2001.
16. Adapted from Michael Levy and Barton A. Weitz, *Retailing Management* (Burr Ridge, IL: Irwin/McGraw-Hill, 2001), p. 585.
17. Doug Young, "U.S. Hotels Make Headway into Online Booking," Reuters Newswire, via AOL, June 22, 2001.
18. Patrick Barta and Anne Marie Chaker, "Consumers Voice Rising Dissatisfaction with Companies," *Wall Street Journal*, May 21, 2001, p. A2.
19. Mike Drummond, "Customer Service Woes," *Business 2.0*, June 4, 2001, www.business2.com/marketing/2001/06/service_woes.html.
20. Jack Neff, "White Clouds Could Bring Rain on P&G," *Advertising Age*, July 2, 2001, p. 4.
21. Julie Cantwell, "GM Redefines Role of Brand Managers," *Automotive News*, Jan. 14, 2002, p. 3.
22. Rajesh Sethi, "New Product Quality and Product Development Teams," *Journal of Marketing*, Apr. 2000, pp. 1–14.
23. Sources: "The WWD List," *WWD*, December 8, 2003, p. 34S; Patricia Van Arnum, "The Two Faces of the Global Cosmetics/Personal Care Market," *Chemical Market Reporter*, Dec. 1, 2003, pp. FR3+; "An Ancient Italian Recipe for Success," *European Cosmetic Markets*, Nov. 2002, p. 397; "Olive Oil–

Cosmetics and Soaps," The Olive Oil Source, www.oliveoil source.com/cosmetics.htm, Sep. 7, 2001; Jean Patteson, "Olive Oil, Essences Are Being Poured into Beauty Products," *The Morning Call,* Aug. 3, 2001, www.mcall.com/html/news/ am_mag/d_pg001oliveoil.htm; Pamela Sauer, "A Makeover for Personal Care and Cosmetics," *Chemical Market Reporter,* May 14, 2001, www.findarticles.com.

24. Sources: John S. McClenahen, "New World Leader: 3M Co.'s James McNerney, CEO of the Year," *Industry Week,* Jan. 2004, pp. 36+; Jennifer Bjorhus, "3M Unveils Drastic Shakeup of Research and Development Division," *Saint Paul Pioneer Press,* Sep. 27, 2003, www.twincities.com/mld/pioneerpress; Robert Westervelt, "3M Reorganizes R&D Effort," *Chemical Week,* Oct. 5, 2003, p. 11; Tim Studt, "3M—Where Innovation Rules," *R&D,* Apr. 2003, pp. 20+; Rita Shor, "Managed Innovation: 3M's Latest Model for New Products," *Manufacturing and Technology News* (n.d.), www.manufacturingnews.com/news/editorials/shor.html.

Chapter 13

1. Sources: "Voted & Quoted," *Advertising Age,* Sep. 1, 2003, p. 12; Maria Guzzo, "Mascots with a Mission," *Pittsburgh Business Times,* Sep. 9, 2002; Rebecca Beer, "Agencies Aren't Worried by Kellogg's Deal with Cartoon Network," *Campaign,* Aug. 9, 2002, p. 18; Theresa Howard, "Ad Icons Star in Other Brands' Commercials," *USA Today,* May 20, 2002, p. 3B; Mark McMaster, "Lessons from the Marlboro Man," *Sales & Marketing Management,* Feb. 2002, pp. 44-45.
2. Peter D. Bennett, ed., *Dictionary of Marketing Terms* (Chicago: American Marketing Association, 1995), p. 27.
3. U.S. Patent and Trademark Office, Management Discussion and Analysis, Trademark Performance, 2002.
4. David J. Lipke, "Pledge of Allegiance," *American Demographics,* Nov. 2000, pp. 40–42.
5. David A. Aaker, *Managing Brand Equity: Capitalizing on the Value of a Brand Name* (New York: Free Press, 1991), pp. 16–17.
6. Paul Davidson and Theresa Howard, "FTC Could Try to Block Pepsi-Quaker Merger," *USA Today,* May 10, 2001, p. 1B.
7. Kelly Pate, "Private Brands Help Grocers Compete, Offer Higher Profit Margins," *The Denver Post,* July 30, 2003.
8. Private Label Manufacturers Association, *PLMA's 2003 Private Label Yearbook,* p. 8.
9. "British Retailing: Chemistry Upset," *The Economist,* Feb. 24, 2001, p. 68.
10. Marcel Corstjens and Rajiv Lal, "Building Store Loyalty Through Store Brands," *Journal of Marketing Research,* Aug. 2000, pp. 281–291.
11. Mike Beirne, "Philip Morris to Put New Name, Altria, Aloft," *Brandweek,* Dec. 16, 2002, p. 4.
12. Dorothy Cohen, "Trademark Strategy," *Journal of Marketing,* Jan. 1986, p. 63.
13. Chiranjev Kohli and Rajheesh Suri, "Brand Names That Work: A Study of the Effectiveness of Different Brand Names," *Marketing Management Journal,* Fall/Winter 2000, pp. 112–120.
14. U.S. Trademark Association, "Trademark Stylesheet," no. 1A.
15. Suzanne Bidlake, "Unilever's Leaner Lineup to Get $1.6 Bil Spending Boost," *Advertising Age,* Feb. 2000; "Unilever Unveils 'Big Hit' Innovations, Brand Cull Progress," *Advertising Age,* Feb. 9, 2001, www.adage.com.
16. Vicki R. Lane, "The Impact of Ad Repetition and Ad Content on Consumer Perceptions of Incongruent Extensions," *Journal of Marketing,* Apr. 2000, pp. 80–91.
17. David Breitkopf, "Airline Co-Brand Cards Reach for New Heights," *American Banker,* Dec. 12, 2000, p. 1.

18. Alessandra Galloni, "Armani, Mercedes to Form Marketing, Design Venture," *Wall Street Journal Online,* Sep. 30, 2003, http://online.wsj.com/article/0,,SB106487258836292400,00.html.
19. Christopher Palmeri, "Mattel: Up the Hill Minus Jill," *Business Week,* Apr. 9, 2001, pp. 53–54.
20. Thomas J. Madden, Kelly Hewett, and Martin S. Roth, "Managing Images in Different Cultures: A Cross-National Study of Color Meanings and Preferences," *Journal of International Marketing,* Winter 2000, p. 90.
21. Stephanie Thompson, "Nestlé Gives Mate Update in New Package, Ad Effort," *Advertising Age,* Sep. 18, 2000, p. 8.
22. "FDA Proposed New Rules for GM Foods," *Chemical Market Reporter,* Jan. 29, 2001, p. 7.
23. Federal Trade Commission, www.ftc.gov, (Accessed May 16, 2001).
24. Sources: Jim Scott, "Grape News—Cork Being Phased Out at Premium Wineries," *North County Times (California),* June 6, 2002, www.nctimes.net; Harry Cline, "Premium Wine in Screw-Top," *Western Farm Press,* July 15, 2000, pp. 91; "PlumpJack Winery Owners Gordon Getty, Bill Getty, and Gavin Newsom Announce First Screw Cap Closures for Luxury Wine," *Business Wire,* June 5, 2000, www.businesswire.com.
25. Sources: Abraham Lustgarten, "The 100 Best Companies to Work For: Harley-Davidson," *Fortune,* Jan. 12, 2004, p. 76; Mark Yost, "Harley-Davidson Centenary Bash Brings Out Armchair 'Rebels,'" *Wall Street Journal,* Sep. 3, 2003, p. D4; Monica Davey, "Harley at 100," *New York Times,* Sep. 1, 2003, p. A1; "Harley-Davidson Reports Record Second Quarter," Harley-Davidson news release, July 16, 2003, www.harley-davidson. com; Joseph Weber, "Harley Investors May Get a Wobbly Ride," *Business Week,* Feb. 11, 2002, p. 65; Jonathan Fahey, "Love into Money," *Forbes,* Jan. 7, 2002, pp. 60–65.

Chapter 14

1. Sources: Karyn Strauss, "Move Over, Disney," *Hotels,* Jan. 2004, p. 13; "He Lives in a Pineapple Under the Sea," *Hotel & Motel Management,* Nov. 3, 2003, p. 126; Joe Flint, "Testing Limits of Licensing," *Wall Street Journal,* Oct. 9, 2003, p. B1; Diane Brady and Gerry Khermouch, "How to Tickle a Child," *Business Week,* July 7, 2003, pp. 48–50.
2. Leonard L. Berry and A. Parasuraman, *Marketing Services: Competing through Quality* (New York: Free Press, 1991), p. 5.
3. Michael Levy and Barton A. Weitz, *Retailing Management* (Burr Ridge, IL: Irwin/McGraw-Hill, 2001), p. 585.
4. The information in this section is based on K. Douglas Hoffman and John E. G. Bateson, *Essentials of Services Marketing* (Mason, OH: South-Western, 2001); Valarie A. Zeithaml, A. Parasuraman, and Leonard L. Berry, *Delivering Quality Service: Balancing Customer Perceptions and Expectations* (New York: Free Press, 1990).
5. Stephen Phillips, "Money Changer to the Masses," *Business 2.0,* Mar. 2002, p. 25.
6. J. Paul Peter and James H. Donnelly, *A Preface to Marketing Management* (Burr Ridge, IL: Irwin/McGraw-Hill, 2003), p. 212.
7. Michael D. Hartline and O. C. Ferrell, "Service Quality Implementation: The Effects of Organizational Socialization and Managerial Actions of Customer Contact Employee Behavior," *Marketing Science Institute Report,* no. 93–122 (Cambridge, MA: Marketing Science Institute, 1993).
8. Starbucks Corporation Fact Sheet, *Hoover's Online,* Nov. 14, 2003.
9. Richard B. Chase and Sriram Dasu, "Want to Perfect Your Company's Service? Use Behavioral Science," *Harvard Business Review,* June 2001, pp. 78–84.
10. Martha McKay, "AT&T to Invest $2.6 Billion in Boosting Customer Care," CRM Daily.com, Jan. 17 2002, www.crmdaily. com/perl/story/?id=15856.

11. www.smarttan.com/beta/page.php?pid=4.

12. "Kinko's Recognized in Business Week Web Smart 50," PRNewswire, Dec. 18, 2003.

13. Zeithaml, Parasuraman, and Berry, *Delivering Quality Service*.

14. Valarie A. Zeithaml, "How Consumer Evaluation Processes Differ between Goods and Services," in *Marketing of Services*, ed. James H. Donnelly and William R. George (Chicago: American Marketing Association, 1981), pp. 186–190.

15. A. Parasuraman, Leonard L. Berry, and Valarie A. Zeithaml, "An Empirical Examination of Relationships in an Extended Service Quality Model," *Marketing Science Institute Working Paper Series*, no. 90–112 (Cambridge, MA: Marketing Science Institute, 1990), p. 29.

16. Valarie A. Zeithaml, Leonard L. Berry, and A. Parasuraman, "Communication and Control Processes in the Delivery of Service Quality," *Journal of Marketing*, Apr. 1988, pp. 35–48.

17. Valarie A. Zeithaml, Leonard L. Berry, and A. Parasuraman, "The Nature and Determinants of Customer Expectations of Service," *Journal of the Academy of Marketing Science*, Winter 1993, pp. 1–12.

18. Linda Himelstein, "'Room Service, Send Up a Techie,'" *Business Week*, Apr. 9, 2001, p. 10.

19. James Zoltak, " 'When Pigs Fly' Teaches GenXers the Meaning of Customer Service," *Amusement Business*, Sep. 1, 2003.

20. Philip Kotler, *Marketing for Nonprofit Organizations*, 2nd ed. (Englewood Cliffs, NJ: Prentice-Hall, 1982), p. 37.

21. Ibid.

22. "Non-Profits Discover the Benefits of Using Software Through the Internet," *Fund Raising Management*, Apr. 2001, page 36.

23. Sources: Thomas Caywood, "Red Ink at Beleaguered Aquarium," *Boston Herald*, Aug. 15, 2003, p. 23; Jeffrey Krasner, "New England Aquarium Plunges into Financial Turmoil," *Boston Globe*, Dec. 13, 2002, www.boston.com/globe; "Press Kit," www.neaq.org; "Aquarium to Release Two Rescued Seals Saturday," New England Aquarium news release, (n.d.), www.neaq.org; "New England Aquarium," EMC website, www.emc.com; Jeffrey Krasner, "New England Aquarium Plunges into Financial Turmoil," *Boston Globe*, Dec. 13, 2002, www.bostonglobe.com.

24. Sources: "AARP to Train Older Workers for Home Depot," United Press International, Feb. 6, 2004, www.comtexnews.com; Gay Jervey, "At AARP, Pushing for Change," *New York Times*, Dec. 14, 2003, sec. 3, p. 2; David Noonan and Mary Carmichael, "A New Age for AARP," *Newsweek*, Dec. 1, 2003, pp. 42-44; Jane Elsinger Rooney, "Brand New Day," *Association Management*, Feb. 2003, pp. 46+; Gerry Romano, "Feeling Groovy? Join AARP," *Association Management*, Feb. 2001, pp. 321; David J. Lipke, "Fountain of Youth," *American Demographics*, Sep. 2000, pp. 37–40.

Chapter 15

1. Sources: Kelley L. Carter, "Hard Rock Café Falls Hard for Detroit," *Detroit Free Press*, Nov. 7, 2003, www.freep.com; "Avicon Leads Hard Rock Café's Successful Transition to Outsourced Logistics, Fulfillment, and Distribution," *Business Wire*, Dec. 1, 2003, www.businesswire.com; Hard Rock Café Selects Kuehne & Nagel Subsidiary," *Business Wire*, Nov. 24, 2003, www.businesswire.com; Sarah Hale Meitner, "United Airlines to Serve Food from Hard Rock Café," *Orlando Sentinel*, Oct. 1, 2003, www.orlandosentinel.com; Ben Worthen, "Hard Rock Goes IT," *CIO*, May 1, 2001, www.itworld.com; "History of Hard Rock Café," (n.d.), www.hardrock.com.

2. "When Complexity Pays Off," CFO, *The Magazine for Financial Executives, Winter 2003* p. 14.

3. Chester Dawson, "Machete Time," *Business Week*, Apr. 9, 2001, pp. 42–44.

4. Michael Dempsey, "In Search of the Missing Link," *The Financial Times*, Nov. 26, 2003, p. 2.

5. Lester E. Goodman and Paul A. Dion, "The Determinants of Commitment in the Distributor-Manufacturer Relationship," *Industrial Marketing Management*, Apr. 2001, pp. 287–300.

6. "Estée Lauder Sees Dept. Stores as Smaller Portion of Its Business," *Forbes*, Feb. 28, 2001, www.forbes.com/newswire/2001/02/28/rtrl94332.html.

7. Leo Aspinwall, "The Marketing Characteristics of Goods," in *Four Marketing Theories* (Boulder: University of Colorado Press, 1961), pp. 27–32.

8. Jennifer Weil and Brid Costello, "Hermes Planning to Launch a Wonder," *WWD*, Dec. 12, 2003, p. 10.

9. Wroe Alderson, *Dynamic Marketing Behavior* (Homewood, IL: Irwin, 1965), p. 239.

10. Jonathan D. Hibbard, Nirmalya Kumar, and Louis W. Stern, "Examining the Impact of Destructive Acts in Marketing Channel Relationships," *Journal of Marketing Research*, Feb. 2001, pp. 45–61.

11. Anne T. Coughlan, Erin Anderson, Louis W. Stern, and Adel I. El-Ansary, *Marketing Channels* (Upper Saddle River, NJ: Prentice-Hall, 2001), pp. 368–369.

12. Sources: "Excelligence Learning Releases Third Quarter 2003 Results," Business Wire, Nov. 5, 2003, www.businesswire.com; Nichole Cipriani, "Testing Your Child—Online," *Parenting*, May 2001, p. 21; Susan Holly, "Get Smarter," *PC Magazine*, Oct. 17, 2000, pp. 19+; www.smarterkids.com; www.excelligence.com.

13. Sources: Victoria Fraza, "Grainger Branches Out," *Industrial Distribution*, Nov. 2003, p. 18; "Top Distributor Talks Business," *Industrial Distribution*, June 1, 2003, pp. 46+; "Grainger Sets Growth Course by Expanding Market Presence," *PR Newswire*, Oct. 9, 2003, www.prnewswire.com; "Grainger Retreats, Closes Material Logic," *Industrial Distribution*, June 2001, p. 19; James P. Miller, "Firm to Close Its Troubled Chicago-Area 'E-Procurement' Business," *Chicago Tribune*, Apr. 24, 2001, http://www.chicago.tribune.com; Alan Earls, "Valuing Exchanges," *Industrial Distribution*, Sep. 2000, p. E15; "W. W. Grainger," *Hoover's Online*, http:///www.hoovers.com, Aug. 8, 2001; "W. W. Grainger," *Hoover's Handbook of American Business 2001* (Austin, TX: Hoover's Business Press, 2001), pp. 1550–1551; "Grainger Retreats, Closes Material Logic," *Industrial Distribution*, June 2001, p. 19.

Chapter 16

1. Sources: Ann Bednarz, "Footwear Maker Treads Wirelessly," *Network World*, Nov. 17, 2003, p. 23; "Psion Teklogix's Wireless Inventory Management System Implemented at Skechers," *Canadian Corporate News*, Sep. 16, 2003; Rishawn Biddle, "Skechers' Executives Dispute Wrongdoing in Distribution Deals," *Los Angeles Business Journal*, Apr. 21, 2003, pp. 3+.

2. Bureau of the Census, *Statistical Abstract of the United States* (Washington, DC: Government Printing Office, 2000), p. 543.

3. Genuine Parts Company Fact Sheet, Hoover's Online, Nov. 17, 2003.

4. Universal Corporation Fact Sheet, *Hoover's Online*, Nov. 17, 2003.

5. "Our History in a Nutshell...," Red River Foods, www. redriverfoods.com (accessed Jan. 24, 2002).

6. Mark Del Franco, Shawn Ferriolo, and Lisa Santo, "Benchmark 2001 Operations," *Catalog Age*, Mar. 15, 2001, pp. 50–54.

7. "How Federated Stays a Leader," *Inbound Logistics*, Aug. 2000, p. 36.

8. Dominic Gates, "Boeing 7E7 Site Winner Will Get Second-Plant Bonus," *Seattle Times*, Nov. 19, 2003.

9. Margaret L. Williams and Mark N. Frolick, "The Evolution of EDI for Competitive Advantage: The FedEx Case," *Information Systems Management*, Spring 2001, pp. 47–53.

10. "Manufacturing Your Way into the Warehouse Business," *Inbound Logistics*, Jan. 2002, pp. 106-108.

11. Anne T. Coughlan, Erin Anderson, Louis W. Stern, and Adel I. El-Ansary, *Marketing Channels* (Upper Saddle River, NJ: Prentice-Hall, 2001), p. 510.

12. "How Federated Stays a Leader," p. 36.

13. Daniel Machalaba, "Trucker Rewards Customers for Good Behavior," *Wall Street Journal Online*, Sep. 9, 2003, http://online.wsj.com/article/0,,SB106306661322925630000,00.html.

14. "Low Inventory, High Expectations," *Inbound Logistics*, June 2000, pp. 36–42.

15. Anne Stuart, "Express Delivery," *Inc. Tech 2001*, Mar. 15, 2001, pp. 54–56.

16. Sources: Martha McNeil Hamilton, "Delivering Life—Fast," *Washington Post*, Aug. 11, 2003, p. E1; "Quick International Courier Launches QuickOnline, Knowledge Management Tool Delivers Extremely Urgent and First-Flight-Out Transportation Solutions Through Internet," Quick International Courier news release, Apr. 18, 2001, www.quickintl.com; Margaret Allen, "Quick's Delivery Service Moving at Rapid Pace," *Dallas Business Journal*, Jan. 28, 2000, p. 24; Ken Cottrill, "Electronic Runway," *Traffic World*, Sep. 4, 2000, p. 28.

17. Sources: "Ready for RFID?" *Information Week*, Jan. 5, 2004; Anthony Bianco and Wendy Zellner, "Is Wal-Mart Too Powerful?" *Business Week*, Oct. 6, 2003, pp. 100-110; Jack Neff, "Wal-Marketing: How to Benefit in Bentonville," *Advertising Age*, Oct. 6, 2003, pp. 1+; "World-Class Merchandising Model Leverages Global Synergies," *DSN Retailing Today*, June 2001, p. 15; "Trucking Company to Expand to Accommodate Wal-Mart," *Capital District Business Review*, May 7, 2001, p. 8; Liz Parks, "Wal-Mart Gets Onboard Early with Collaborative Planning," *Drug Store News*, Feb. 19, 2001, p. 14; Jean Kinsey, "A Faster, Leaner Supply Chain: New Uses of Information Technology," *American Journal of Agricultural Economics*, Nov. 15, 2000, pp. 1123+; Alorie Gilbert, "Retail's Super Supply Chains—Wal-Mart Inks Deal to Roll Out Private Trading Hub; Kmart Readies an Overhaul of Its Planning Systems," *Information Week*, Oct. 16, 2000, p. 22; "Wal-Mart Fuels Expansion at M.S. Carriers," *Memphis Business Journal*, July 28, 2000, p. 3.

Chapter 17

1. Sources: Ricardo Sandoval, "Doughnut Chain Krispy Kreme Opens First Latin American Store Near Mexico City," *Dallas Morning News*, Jan. 27, 2004, www.dallasnews.com; Charles Haddad, "Web Smart 50: Krispy Kreme," *Business Week*, Nov. 24, 2003, p. 88; Andy Serwer, "The Hole Story," *Fortune*, July 7, 2003, pp. 52-62.

2. Bureau of the Census, *Statistical Abstract of the United States* (Washington, DC: Government Printing Office, 2002), p. 636.

3. Roger O. Crockett, "Chat Me Up...Please," *Business Week*, Mar. 19, 2001, p. EB10.

4. Sam's Club Fact Sheet and Costco Wholesale Corporation Fact Sheet, *Hoover's Online*, Nov. 17, 2003.

5. Maria Halkias, "Neiman Marcus Stores Display Catalog Items; Showrooms' Future Is Unknown," *Dallas Morning News*, May 12, 2003.

6. Jeffrey Arlan, "Retailers Jockeyed for $180 Billion in 2000 Sales: Who Are the Winners?" *DSN Retailing Today*, Feb. 5, 2001, pp. A6–A8.

7. Tanya Fogg Young, "Retail Demand over Holiday Season Likely to Be Stronger in 2003," *The State*, Nov. 24, 2003.

8. Patrick Seitz, "After a Failure, Reinvent Yourself," *Investor's Business Daily*, Dec. 8, 2003, p. A08.

9. Pete Barlas, "Rising Security Fears Will Result in Less Shopping Online: Survey," *Investor's Business Daily*, Nov. 21, 2003.

10. Scott Frey, "Complying with Do-Not-Call," *National Underwriter Life & Health—Financial Services Edition*, Dec. 8, 2003, p. 17.

11. www.donotcall.gov/FAQ, Jan. 18, 2004.

12. Jill Hecht Maxwell, "Sit! Stay! Make Money! Good Company," *Inc. Tech 2001*, Mar. 15, 2001, pp. 42–44.

13. Todd Wasserman, "Kodak Rages in Favor of the Machines," *Brandweek*, Feb. 26, 2001, p. 6.

14. "ABCs of Franchising," International Franchise Association, www.franchise.org., Nov. 19, 2003.

15. Nora Ganim Barnes, "As the Mall Falls: Is Mall Entertainment Too Little, Too Late?" *Marketing Advances in the New Millennium*, Proceedings of the Society for Marketing Advances, 2000, pp. 51–54.

16. Maureen Tkacik, "'Alternative' Teens Are Hip to Hot Topic's Mall Stores," *Wall Street Journal*, Feb. 12, 2002, http://interactive.wsj.com.

17. Rebecca Flass, "Albertson's Goes to Market," *Brandweek*, June 30, 2003, p. 13.

18. "McDonald's Corp. Plans to Test Market a String of Coffee Bars Called McCafes," *The Food Institute Report*, Sep. 15, 2003, p. 6.

19. Richard F. Yalch and Eric R. Spangenberg, "The Effects of Music in a Retail Setting on Real and Perceived Shopping Times," *Journal of Business Research*, Aug. 2000, pp. 139–147.

20. Stephen Brown, "The Wheel of Retailing: Past and Future," *Journal of Retailing*, Summer 1990, pp. 143–149.

21. Sources: "REI Climbs to New Heights Online," *Chain Store Age*, Oct. 2003, pp. 72+; Mike Gorrell, "New REI Store Opens in Salt Lake City Area," *Salt Lake Tribune*, Mar. 28, 2003, www.sltrib.com; "Retailer Eastern Mountain Sports Opens Hamburg, N.Y. Store," *Buffalo News*, Dec. 1, 2003, www.buffalonews.com.

22. Sources: Doug Desjardins, "Costco Home to Expand in '04," *DSN Retailing Today*, Dec. 15, 2003, p. 8; John Helyar, "The Only Company Wal-Mart Fears," *Fortune*, Nov. 24, 2003, pp. 158+; Doug Desjardins, "Costco Comps Up 7%, Despite 4Q Lag," *DSN Retailing Today*, Oct. 27, 2003, p. 8.

Chapter 18

1. Sources: Edward Popper, "Talking Turkey about Pop Culture," *Business Week*, Nov. 25, 2003, www.businessweek online.com; "The Jones Soda Story," Jones Soda, www.jones-soda.com/stockstuff/story.html (accessed May 6, 2004); "Jones Soda Swamped with Requests for Turkey & Gravy Soda," Jones Soda, Press Release, Nov. 20, 2003, www.jonessoda.com/stockstuff/pdf_documents/2003/tandg.pdf (accessed Dec. 22, 2003).

2. Prasad A. Naik and Kalyon Raman, "Understanding the Impact of Synergy in Multimedia Communications," *Journal of Marketing Research*, Nov. 2003, pp. 375–388.

3. Ibid.

4. "Californian Targets Youth with Text Messaging," Yahoo! News, Nov. 20, 2003, http://news.yahoo.com.

5. Rebecca Gardyn, "Swap Meet: Customers Are Willing to Exchange Personal Information for Personalized Products," *American Demographics*, July 2001, pp. 51–55.

6. Ibid.

7. Chad Terhune, "Wood Folks Hope for 'Got Milk' Success," *Wall Street Journal,* Feb. 9, 2001, p. B7.

8. "Yoplait Is Committed to Fighting Breast Cancer!" Yoplait, www.yoplait.com/breastcancer_commitment.aspx (accessed May 6, 2004).

9. Theresa Howard, "Marketing Parties' Pizazz Pulls Plenty," *USA Today,* Nov. 19, 2003, http://usatoday.com.

10. In case you do not read Chinese, the message, prepared by Chih Kang Wang, says, "In the factory we make cosmetics, and in the store we sell hope."

11. Terence A. Shimp, *Advertising Promotion,* 5th Ed. (Ft. Worth, TX: Dryden Press, 2000) p. 117.

12. Judy A. Wagner, Noreen M. Klein, and Janet E. Keith, "Selling Strategies: The Effects of Suggesting a Decision Structure to Novice and Expert Buyers," *Journal of the Academy of Marketing Science* 29, no. 3 (2001), pp. 289–306.

13. Michael J. Weiss, "To Be About to Be," *American Demographics,* Sep. 2003, pp. 28–36.

14. John S. McClenahen, "How Can You Possibly Say That?" *Industry Week,* July 17, 1995, pp. 17–19.

15. Ivonne M. Torres, Betsy D. Gelb, and Jaime L. Noriega, "Warning and Informing the Domestic International Market," *Journal of Public Policy & Marketing,* Fall 2003, pp. 216–222.

16. Mathew Boyle, "Atkins World," *Fortune,* Jan. 12, 2004, pp. 94–96.

17. Bruce Horovitz, "Color Them Beautiful—and Visible," *USA Today,* May 2, 2001, pp. B1, B2.

18. David M. Szymanski, "Modality and Offering Effects in Sales Presentations for a Good Versus a Service," *Journal of the Academy of Marketing Science* 29, no. 2 (2001), pp. 179–189.

19. Sally Beatty, "Advance Sales of Children's Ads Slacken," *Wall Street Journal,* May 11, 2001, p. B8.

20. Lorin Cipolla, "Nivea for Men Targets 2 Million Consumers," *Promo Magazine,* Nov. 13, 2003, http://promomagazine.com/ar/marketing_nivea_men_targets/index.htm.

21. "Inside Chrysler's Celine Dion Advertising Disaster," AdAge.com, Nov. 24, 2003, www.adage.com/news.cms?newsID=39262.

22. Michael McCarthy, "$250M Ad Campaign Aims to Hit Homer," *USA Today,* Apr. 3, 2001, p. 3B.

23. Reshma Kapadia, "AOL Internet Service Members Surpass 30 Million," Reuters Newswire, via AOL, June 25, 2001.

24. Jack Neff, "Gillette, Schick Fight with Free Razors," *Advertising Age,* Dec. 1, 2003, p. 8.

25. Libby Estell, "This Call Center Accelerates Sales," *Sales & Marketing Management,* Feb. 1999, p. 72.

26. Karen Lundegaard, "Car Crash Ads May Lose Impact," *The Detroit News,* Apr. 15, 2001, p. C1.

27. "Ad Space," *Business Week,* Jan. 12, 2004, p. 14.

28. "Rates and Editions," *Time,* Jan. 5, 2004, www.time-planner.com/planner/rates/index.html.

29. Vicki R. Lane, "The Impact of Ad Repetition and Ad Content on Consumer Perceptions of Incongruent Extensions," *Journal of Marketing,* Apr. 2000, pp. 80–91.

30. "Got Milk," National Fluid Milk Processor Promotion Board, www.whymilk.com (accessed May 6, 2004).

31. Scott B. MacKenzie, Philip M. Podsakoff, and Gregory A. Rich, "Transformational and Transactional Leadership and Salesperson Performance," *Journal of the Academy of Marketing Science* 29, no. 2 (2001), pp. 115–134.

32. Arun Sharma and Michael Levy, "Salespeople's Affect Toward Customers: Why Should It Be Important for Retailers?" *Journal of Business Research* 56 (2003), pp. 523–528.

33. Ken Grant, David W. Cravens, George S. Low, and William C. Moncrief, "The Role of Satisfaction with Territory Design on the Motivation, Attitudes, and Work Outcomes of Salespeople," *Journal of the Academy of Marketing Science* 29, no. 2 (2001), pp. 165–178.

34. Debbie Thorne McAlister and Robert C. Erffmeyer, "A Content Analysis of Outcomes and Responsibilities for Consumer Complaints to Third-Party Organizations," *Journal of Business Research* 56 (2003), pp. 341–351.

35. Michael Krauss, "Television Advertising in a Time of TiVo," *Marketing News,* Jan. 6, 2003, p. 4.

36. David Kiley, "Lawsuits Give Ford Publicity Problem, *USA Today,* Jan. 22, 2003, www.usatoday.com.

37. "Sears Links Appliances to Olympics," *Advertising Age,* www.adage.com, July 19, 2001.

38. John J. Burnett, *Promotion Management* (Boston: Houghton Mifflin, 1993), p. 7.

39. Betsy Spethmann, "McDonald's Plays Monopoly Again—With Best Buy," *Promo Magazine,* Oct. 15, 2003, http://promomagazine.com/ar/marketing_mcdonalds_plays_monopoly/index.htm.

40. Jack Neff, "Clorox Gives in on Glad, Hikes Trade Promotion," *Advertising Age,* www.adage.com, July 19, 2001.

41. Harald J. Van Heerde, Sachin Gupta, and Dick R. Wittink, "Is 75% of the Sales Promotion Bump Due to Brand Switching? No, Only 33% Is," *Journal of Marketing Research,* Nov. 2003, pp. 481–491.

42. Linda Tischler, "Buzz Without Bucks," *Fast Company,* Aug. 2003, pp. 78–83.

43. Alice Z. Cuneo, "Apple Transcends as Lifestyle Brand," *Advertising Age,* Dec. 15, 2003, pp. S-2, S-6.

44. Gerry Khermouch and Jeff Green, "Buzz Marketing," *Business Week,* July 30, 2001, pp. 50–51.

45. Weiss, "To Be About to Be."

46. Suzanne Vranica and Sarah Ellison, "Guess Who Won P&G's First Super Bowl Slot," *Wall Street Journal,* Dec. 5, 2003, http://online.wsj.com.

47. Rockney G. Walters and Maqbul Jamil, "Exploring the Relationships Between Shopping Trip Type, Purchases of Products on Promotion, and Shopping Basket Profit," *Journal of Business Research* 56 (2003), pp. 17–29.

48. Greg Winter, "Pepsi Looks to a New Drink to Jolt Soda Sales," *New York Times,* May 1, 2001, www.partners.nytimes.com.

49. Michael McCarthy, "Recent Crop of Sneaky Ads Backfire," *USA Today,* July 17, 2001, p. 3B.

50. Deborah L. Vence, "Marketing to Minors Still Under Careful Watch," *Marketing News,* Mar. 31, 2003, p. 5.

51. Abraham H. Maslow, *Motivation and Personality* (New York: Harper and Row, 1954).

52. Sources: "About Us," "History," "Charities," and "News and Events," Jordan's Furniture, www.jordans.com (accessed May 6, 2004); "Berkshire Hathaway Unit to Acquire Jordan's Furniture," *Boston Business Journal,* Oct. 11, 1999, www.bizjournals.com/boston/stories/1999/10/11/daily1.html; "Jordan's Furniture," *Hoover's Online,* www.hoovers.com/free/co/factsheet.xhtml?COID=99028 (accessed May 6, 2004); Massachusetts General Hospital Hotline, www.mgh.harvard.edu (accessed May 6, 2004); Barry Tatelman and Elliot Tatelman, "Why Are These People Smiling?" Blue Cross Blue Shield of Massachusetts, www.bluecrossma-values.com/barryelliot.php3 (accessed May 6, 2004); "Winners! BBB National Torch Awards: Jordan's Furniture," Better Business Bureau, www.bbb.org/BizEthics/winners/jordans.asp (accessed May 6, 2004).

53. Sources: Brian Grow and Gerry Khermouch, "The Low-Carb Food Fight Ahead," *Business Week,* Dec. 22, 2003, www.businessweek.com; Kate MacArthur, "Miller Lite Ads Turn Tables on Coors," *Advertising Age,* www.adage.com (accessed Dec. 22, 2003); Al Ries, "The Secret Behind America's Top Pasta Marketer," *Advertising Age,* 2003, www.adage.com (accessed Dec, 22, 2003); Andrea K. Walker, "Low-Carb Product Craze Puts Bread Industry on Defensive," *Austin American-Statesman,* Dec. 17, 2003, www.statesman.com.

Chapter 19

1. Sources: Apple, www.apple.com (accessed May 6, 2004); Alice Z. Cuneo, "Marketer of the Year: Apple," *Advertising Age*, Dec. 15, 2003, www.adage.com; Scott Donaton, "A Marketing Tale of the Great and the Desperate," *Advertising Age*, Dec. 15, 2003, www.adage.com.

2. "100 Leading National Advertisers," *Advertising Age*, www.adage.com/page.cms?pageId=991 (accessed Dec. 2, 2003).

3. Arundhati Parmar, "New Ads and Marketing Up Tourism to Mexico," *Marketing News*, Apr. 14, 2003, pp. 6, 8.

4. Cornelia Pechmann, Guangzhi Zhao, Marvin E. Goldberg, and Elen Thomas Reibling, "What to Convey in Antismoking Advertisements for Adolescents: The Use of Protection Motivation Theory to Identify Effective Message Themes," *Journal of Marketing*, Apr. 2003, pp. 1–18.

5. Desiree J. Hanford, "Miller Lite's Ads, Price Gives Brand Some Momentum," Dow Jones Newswires, Oct. 22, 2003, http://online.wsj.com.

6. Laurel Wentz, "Nissan Boosts Hispanic Efforts," *Advertising Age*, Dec. 1, 2003, p. 26.

7. Kate Fitzgerald, "Curves International: Diane Heavin," *Advertising Age*, Nov. 17, 2003, p. S-6.

8. Chad Terhune, "Pepsi Unveils Ad Campaign Emphasizing Food and Cola," *Wall Street Journal*, Nov. 19, 2003, http://online.wsj.com.

9. Charles Newbery, "Coke Goes Native with New Soft Drink," *Advertising Age*, Dec. 1, 2003, p. 34.

10. Chuck Bartels, "Newspaper Ads No Longer Best Fit for Dillard's," *Marketing News*, Sep. 15, 2003, p. 5.

11. "Notion of Ad Overspending Lessens with Integrated Communications," *Marketing News*, Nov. 24, 2003, pp. 28, 30.

12. William F. Arens, *Contemporary Advertising* (Burr Ridge, IL: Irwin/McGraw-Hill, 1999), p. 378.

13. Gerry Khermouch, "The Top 5 Rules of the Ad Game," *Business Week*, Jan. 20, 2003, p. 73.

14. Jean Halliday, "Z Series: Steven Wilhite," *Advertising Age*, Nov. 17, 2003, p. S-2.

15. Peter J. Danaher and Guy W. Mullarkey, "Factors Affecting Online Advertising Recall: A Study of Students," *Journal of Advertising Research* 43 (2003), pp. 252–267.

16. Tobi Elkin, "64% Respond to Wireless Ads in Market Test," *Advertising Age*, Mar. 8, 2001, www.adage.com/news_and_features/features/20010308/article3.html.

17. George E. Belch and Michael A. Belch, *Advertising and Promotion* (Burr Ridge, IL: Irwin/McGraw-Hill, 2001), pp. 576–577.

18. Thea Singer, "Can Business Still Save the World?" *Inc.*, Apr. 30, 2001, pp. 58–71.

19. "UPS Holds Official Status at Daytona International Speedway," *Business Wire*, Feb. 15, 2001, p. 2260.

20. "McDonald's Introduces New McKIDS Multi-Category, Worldwide Licensing Program," McDonald's, press release, Nov. 13, 2003, www.mcdonalds.com/corporate/press/corporate/2003/11132003/index.html.

21. Belch and Belch, *Advertising and Promotion*, p. 598.

22. Suman Basuroy, Subimal Chatterjee, and S. Abraham Ravid, "How Critical Are Critical Reviews? The Box Office Effects of Film Critics, Star Power, and Budgets," *Journal of Marketing*, Oct. 2003, pp. 103–117.

23. Sources: Robert S. Boynton, "Powder Burn," *Outside*, Jan. 1999, http://outside.away.com/magazine/0199/9901vail.html; "Destination Vail," Vail Resorts, www.vailresorts.com/ourresorts.cfm?mode=vail (accessed May 6, 2004); "Earth Liberation Front Sets Off Incendiary at Vail Colorado," FactNet, www.factnet.org/cults/earth_liberation_front/vail_fire.html (accessed Jan. 7, 2004); Robert Kreitner, *Management*, 9th ed. (Boston: Houghton Mifflin, 2004), p. 572; Sarah Love, "Investigation into Vail Fires

Continues," *Mountain Zone News*, Nov. 4, 1998, http://classic.mountainzone.com/news/vail10-21.html.

24. Sources: "Fast Facts About Microsoft," Microsoft, www.microsoft.com/presspass/inside_ms.asp (accessed May 6, 2004); David Bank and John Simons, "Microsoft Is on Defensive over Media Strategy," *Wall Street Journal*, Apr. 13, 1998, p. B8; Dan Carney, "Outreach, Microsoft Style," *Business Week*, July 23, 2001, p. 47; Amy Cortese, "Emperor of High Tech, Sultan of Spin," *Business Week*, May 18, 1998, p. 37; Mike France and Susan B. Garland, "Microsoft: The View at Halftime," *Business Week*, Jan. 25, 1999, pp. 78–82; Susan B. Garland, "A Tough Sell, but Not Impossible," *Business Week*, Jan. 18, 1999, p. 44; Thomas W. Haines, "Lesson Plan: Microsoft Hits the Hallways, Because Today's Fifth-Grader Is Tomorrow's Software Buyer," *Seattle Times*, Apr. 12, 1998, p. F1; Steve Hamm, "'I'm Humble, I'm Respectful,'" *Business Week*, Feb. 9, 1998, pp. 40–42; Geoffrey James, "Image Making at Mighty Microsoft," *Upside*, June 1998, pp. 81–86; Bradley Johnson, "Microsoft Eyes Ads in Antitrust Struggle with Justice Dept.," *Advertising Age*, Apr. 13, 1998, p. 39; Joseph Menn and Jube Shiver, "The Microsoft Decision," *Los Angeles Times*, Nov. 2, 2002, sec. 1, p. 1; Greg Miller and Leslie Helm, "Microsoft Plans Stealth Media Blitz," *Los Angeles Times*, Apr. 10, 1998, p. A1; William O'Neal, "Behold the Xbox!" *Computer Gaming World*, Mar. 1, 2001, p. 118; Rick Tetzeli and David Kirkpatrick, "America Loves Microsoft," *Fortune*, Feb. 1998, p. 801.

Chapter 20

1. Sources: David Grainger, "Can McDonald's Cook Again?" *Fortune*, Apr. 14, 2003, pp. 120–129; Kate MacArthur, "Burger Giants Dig Up Dinos for Summer Movie Tie-Ins," *Advertising Age*, Apr. 17, 2000, p. 3; Kate MacArthur, "New Tastes Offers Sampling of McD's Marketing Strategy," *Crain's Chicago Business*, Feb. 5, 2001, p. 32; "S&P: Fast-Food Chains' Ratings at Risk amid Health Concerns," Fox News, Sep. 8, 2003, www.foxnews.com/story/0,2933,96743,00.html; "Segmenting the Message," *Adweek Eastern Edition*, Apr. 17, 2000, p. 20; Amy Zuber, "McD-Disney Marketing Alliances Grow with Burger Invasion Concept's Debut," *Nation's Restaurant News*, Jan. 22, 2001, p. 4.

2. Jennifer Gilbert, "Small but Mighty," *Sales & Marketing Management*, Jan. 2004, p. 32.

3. "What a Sales Call Costs," *Sales & Marketing Management*, Sep. 2000, p. 80.

4. Dan Brekke, "What You Don't Know Can Hurt You," *Smart Business*, Mar. 2001, pp. 64–74.

5. Eli Jones, Paul Busch, and Peter Dacin, "Firm Market Orientation and Salesperson Customer Orientation: Interpersonal and Intrapersonal Influence on Customer Service and Retention in Business-to-Business Buyer–Seller Relationships," *Journal of Business Research* 56 (2003), pp. 323–340.

6. Julie T. Johnson, Hiram C. Barksdale, Jr., and James S. Boles, "Factors Associated with Customer Willingness to Refer Leads to Salespeople," *Journal of Business Research* 56 (2003), pp. 257–263.

7. Sarah Lorge, "The Best Way to Prospect," *Sales & Marketing Management*, Jan. 1998, p. 80.

8. Andy Cohen, "Success with Referrals," *Sales & Marketing Management*, Sep. 2003, p. 12.

9. J. Bonasia, "Keep Sales Up by Finding New Customers, Focusing on Strengths," *Investor's Business Daily*, Mar. 25, 2002, p. A4.

10. "Lose the Sales Act," *Sales & Marketing Management*, Jan. 2004, p. 22.

11. Stephen S. Porter, Joshua L. Wiener, and Gary L. Frankwick, "The Moderating Effect of Selling Situation on the Adaptive Selling Strategy—Selling Effectiveness Relationship," *Journal of Business Research* 56 (2003), pp. 275–281.

12. Julia Chang, "Born to Sell?" *Sales & Marketing Management,* July 2003, pp. 34+.

13. Greg W. Marshall, Daniel J. Goebel, and William C. Moncrief, "Hiring for Success at the Buyer–Seller Interface," *Journal of Business Research* 56 (2003), pp. 247–255.

14. Mark McMaster, "Express Train," *Sales & Marketing Management,* May 2002, pp. 46–52.

15. Christine Galea, "3rd Annual Compensation Survey," *Sales & Marketing Management,* May 2003, pp. 32–36.

16. Susan Mudambi, "Salesforce Compensation and the Web: Managing Change in the Information Age," *American Marketing Association,* Winter 2002, p. 489.

17. Kirk Shinkle, "All of Your People Are Salesmen: Do They Know? Are They Ready?" *Investor's Business Daily,* Feb. 6, 2002, p. A1.

18. Ibid.

19. Eilene Zimmerman, "Motivation on Any Budget," *Sales & Marketing Management,* Jan. 2004, pp. 37, 38.

20. Nora Wood, "What Motivates Best?" *Sales & Marketing Management,* Sep. 1998, pp. 71–78.

21. David Drickhamer, "Best Practices—Manufacturer Goes for the Gold," *Industry Week,* Feb. 1, 2002, www.industryweek.com/CurrentArticles/Asp/articles.asp?ArticleId51182.

22. Mudambi, "Salesforce Compensation and the Web."

23. Joseph A. Bellizzi and Ronald W. Hasty, "Supervising Unethical Sales Force Behavior: How Strong Is the Tendency to Treat Top Sales Performers Leniently?" *Journal of Business Ethics,* Apr. 2003, pp. 337–351.

24. George E. Belch and Michael A. Belch, *Advertising and Promotion* (Burr Ridge, IL: Irwin/McGraw-Hill, 2001), pp. 526–532.

25. "September Is National Coupon Month," Promotion Marketing Association, press release, Sep. 2, 2003, www.couponmonth.com/pages/news.htm.

26. Judith A. Garretson and Scot Burton, "Highly Coupon and Sale Prone Consumers: Benefits Beyond Price Savings," *Journal of Advertising Research* 43 (2003), pp. 162–172.

27. Arthur L. Porter, "Direct Mail's Lessons for Electronic Couponers," *Marketing Management Journal,* Spring/Summer 2000, pp. 107–115.

28. Ibid.

29. Patricia Odell, "Counterfeit Coupons Flood the Internet," *Promo,* Aug. 27, 2003, http://promomagazine.com/ar/marketing_counterfeit_coupons_flood/index.htm.

30. Janet Singleton, "Mail-in Rebates Aren't Worth the Trouble for Most Customers," *Denver Post,* May 6, 2001, p. D08.

31. Richard F. Beltramini and Patricia S. Chapman, "Do Customers Believe in Automobile Industry Rebate Incentives?" *Journal of Advertising Research* 43 (2003), pp. 16–24.

32. "Hotels Plan Deals to Lure Cost-Conscious Travelers," *Promo,* Apr. 11, 2001, www.marketingclick.com.

33. Jean Halliday, "GM's 'Sleep on It' Test Drives: Christopher 'C. J.' Fraleigh," *Advertising Age,* Nov. 17, 2003, p. S-8.

34. Kate MacArthur, "Sierra Mist: Cie Nicholson," *Advertising Age,* Nov. 17, 2003, p. S-2.

35. Karen J. Bannan, "Freebies in Cyberspace: Online Companies Let Consumers Pick the Samples They Want Mailed to Them," *Wall Street Journal,* Nov. 27, 2000, p. 10.

36. T. L. Stanley, " 'Bend It Like Beckham': Nancy Utley," *Advertising Age,* Nov. 17, 2003, p. S-8.

37. Lorin Cipolla, "American and United Airlines Launch Separate Sweeps," *Promo,* Nov. 11, 2003, http://promomagazine.com/ar/marketing_american_united_airlines/index.htm.

38. Sources: Based on a personal interview with Deborah Bernard of Wheelworks, Aug. 22, 2001; "Motivating the Sales Force at Wheelworks" video; Wheelworks.com (accessed Jan. 12, 2004).

39. Sources: "About IBM," IBM, www.ibm.com/ibm/us/ (accessed May 6, 2004); Jim Botkin, Bill Kegg, and Susan Valdiserri, "IBM Sales Experiences the Co-Active Magic!" The Coaches Training Institute, www.thecoaches.com/newsletter/2003/09/jbm-sales.html (accessed May 6, 2004); "IBM Leans on Business Partner Channel to Push Server Sales," Midrange Server, Aug. 14, 2002, www.Midrangeserver.com/mid/mid081402-story04.html; Erin Strout, "IBM Blue Skies Ahead," *Sales & Marketing Management,* Mar. 2003, pp. 26, 29.

Chapter 21

1. Sources: Tyler Hamilton, "What's Music Worth?" *Toronto Star,* Jan. 13, 2004, www.thestar.com; Kevin C. Johnson, "On a Not So Sour Note ... CD Sales in 2003 Dropped," *St. Louis Post-Dispatch,* Jan. 9, 2004, www.stltoday.com; Ethan Smith, "Universal Slashes Its CD Prices in Bid to Revive Music Industry," *Wall Street Journal,* Sep. 4, 2003, www.wallstreetjournal.com.

2. Rajneesh Suri and Kent B. Monroe, "The Effects of Time Constraints on Consumers' Judgments of Prices and Products," *Journal of Consumer Research,* June 2003, pp, 92+.

3. "Hewlett-Packard," case study, Professional Pricing Society, www.pricingsociety.com/casestudiesdetails3.asp (accessed May 6, 2004).

4. "Broadcast of New Vision Gets Mixed Reception from the Street," *DSN Retailing Today,* Jan. 2001, p. 16.

5. Jon Swartz, "Price War Looms for High-Speed Net Access," *USA Today,* Nov. 14, 2003, p. 1B.

6. Akshay R. Rao, Mark E. Bergen, and Scott Davis, "How to Fight a Price War," *Harvard Business Review,* Mar./Apr. 2000, pp. 107–116.

7. David Aaker and Erich Joachimsthaler, "An Alternative to Price Competition," *American Demographics,* Sep. 2000, p. 11.

8. Cliff Edwards, "Intel Inside the War Room," *Business Week,* Apr. 30, 2001, p. 40.

9. Peter D. Bennett, *Dictionary of Marketing Terms* (Chicago: American Marketing Association, 1995), p. 79.

10. "Want a Cheaper Flat-Panel TV?" CNNMoney, Dec. 4, 2003, http://money.cnn.cm/.

11. Bennett, *Dictionary of Marketing Terms,* p. 215.

12. "Study: Hotel Demand Is Price Inelastic—So What Now?" *Hotels,* July 1, 2003, p. 14.

13. Carleen Hawn, "The Global Razor's Edge," *Fast Company,* Feb. 2004, pp. 27, 28.

14. Donald Lichtenstein, Nancy M. Ridgway, and Richard G. Netemeyer, "Price Perceptions and Consumer Shopping Behavior: A Field Study," *Journal of Marketing Research,* May 1993, pp. 234–245.

15. Robert Guy Matthews, "A Surge in Ocean-Shipping Rates Could Increase Consumer Prices," *Wall Street Journal,* Nov. 4, 2003, http://online.wsj.com.

16. Bruce L. Alford and Brian T. Engelland, "Advertised Reference Price Effects on Consumer Price Estimates, Value Perception, and Search Intention," *Journal of Business Research,* May 2000, pp. 93–100.

17. Lichtenstein, Ridgway, and Netemeyer, "Price Perceptions and Consumer Shopping Behavior."

18. Gail Edmondson, "This SUV Can Tow an Entire Carmaker," *Business Week,* Jan. 19, 2004, pp. 40, 41.

19. Linda Tischler, "The Price Is Right," *Fast Company,* Nov. 2003, pp. 83+.

20. Sources: "Blue Skies: Is JetBlue the Next Great Airline—or Just a Little Too Good to Be True?" *Time,* July 30, 2001, pp. 241; J. K. Dineen, "JetBlue Offering $99 Nonstop Coast-to-Coast Flights," *New York Daily News,* Aug. 15, 2001, www.nydailynews.com; "Fact Sheet," JetBlue, www.jetblue.com/learnmore/factsheet.html (accessed Jan. 16, 2003); Dan Reed, "JetBlue Gains on Its Competition," *USA Today,* Aug. 13, 2003, p. 3B;

Darren Shannon, "Three of a Kind," *Travel Agent*, July 23, 2001, pp. 601.

21. Sources: Beth Cox, "Priceline Finds Some Room in the Hotel Market," *Internet News*, Feb. 24, 2003, www.internetnews.com; Greg Dalton, "Priceline Is Finally on the Ascent," *Industry Standard*, July 31, 2001, www.thestandard.com/article/0,1902,28394,00.html; Maryann Keller, "Inside Priceline's Sausage Factory," *Fortune*, Sep. 3, 2001, p. 42; Priceline.com, www.priceline.com (accessed May 6, 2004); "Priceline.com Incorporated," CNN/Money, http://money.cnn.com (accessed Jan. 13, 2004); Clare Saliba, "Priceline, Expedia End Patent Flap," *E-Commerce Times*, Jan. 10, 2001, http://ecommercetimes.com/perl/story/?id56605; Jay Walker, "What Price Brand Loyalty?" *Marketing Week*, June 29, 2000, p. 53.

Chapter 22

1. Sources: Dina Elboghdady, "Big Toy Retailers Pushing Own Knockoffs of Hot Sellers," *Washington Post*, Nov. 27, 2003, www.contracostatimes.com; Daren Fonda, "Will Wal-Mart Steal Christmas?" *Time*, Dec. 8, 2003, pp. 54-56; "More Work Needed at Toys "R" Us," *Business Week*, Nov. 24, 2003, www.businessweek.com; "So Many Toys, So Little Joys," *Business Week*, Nov. 24, 2003, www.businessweek.com; "Toys "R" Us, Inc.," *Hoover's Online*, www.hoovers.com/toys-"r"-us/—ID__11495—/free-co-factsheet.xhtml (accessed May 11, 2004); Amy Tsao, "Wal-Mart: Cruising for a Bruising?" *Business Week*, Nov. 14, 2003, www.businessweek.com.

2. Christopher Caggiano, "E-tailing by the Numbers," *Inc. Tech 2001*, Mar. 15, 2001, pp. 46–49.

3. Stanley Holmes, "Rumble over Tokyo," *Business Week*, Apr. 2, 2001, pp. 80–81.

4. "When Your Competitor Delivers More for Less," McKinsey Quarterly, www.mckinseyquarterly.com (accessed Jan. 6, 2004).

5. Barry J. Babin, David M. Hardesty, and Tracy A. Suter, "Color and Shopping Intentions: The Intervening Effect of Price Fairness and Perceived Affect," *Journal of Business Research*, July 2003, pp. 541–551.

6. "Fairchild Dynamic Pricing Team," Professional Pricing Society, case study, www.pricingsociety.com/casestudiesdetails.asp (accessed May 11, 2004).

7. Melanie Trottman, "Scoring Travel Discounts Gets Easier," *Wall Street Journal*, Nov. 4, 2003, http://online.wsj.com.

8. "Cutler-Hammer/Eaton Corporation," case study, Professional Pricing Society, www.pricingsociety.com/casestudiesdetails1.asp (accessed May 11, 2004).

9. "Can Detroit Break the Rebate Habit?" *Business Week*, Jan. 12, 2004, p. 110; Joann Muller, "Outpsyching the Car Buyer," *Forbes*, Feb. 17, 2003, p. 52.

10. Marla Royne Stafford and Thomas F. Stafford, "The Effectiveness of Tensile Pricing Tactics in the Advertising of Services," *Journal of Advertising*, Summer 2000, pp. 45–56.

11. Gail Edmondson, "This SUV Can Tow an Entire Carmaker," *Business Week*, Jan. 19, 2004, pp. 40, 41.

12. Michael Marn, Eric V. Roegner, and Craig C. Zawada, "Pricing New Products," *Inc.*, July 2003, http://pf.inc.com/articles/2003/07/pricing.html.

13. David Luhnow and Chad Terhune, "Latin Pop: A Low-Budget Cola Shakes Up Markets South of the Border," *Wall Street Journal*, Oct. 27, 2003, pp. A1, A18.

14. Daniel A. Sheinin and Janet Wagner, "Pricing Store Brands across Categories and Retailers," *Journal of Product & Brand Management* 12, no. 4 (2003), pp. 201–220.

15. Keith Damsell, "Telecom Bundling Seen Luring Customers," *The Globe and Mail*, Sep. 29, 2003, p. B8, via www.globe technology.com.

16. Jaihak Chung and Vithala R. Rao, "A General Choice Model for Bundles with Multiple-Category Products: Application to Market Segmentation and Optimal Pricing for Bundles," *Journal of Marketing Research*, May 2003, pp. 115–130.

17. Damsell, "Telecom Bundling Seen Luring Customers."

18. Keith S. Coulter, "The Influence of Print Advertisement Organization on Odd-Ending Price Image Effects," *Journal of Product & Brand Management* 11, no. 4 (2002), pp. 319+.

19. Linda Tischler, "The Price Is Right," *Fast Company*, Nov. 2003, pp. 83+.

20. Bruce L. Alford and Brian T. Engelland, "Advertised Reference Price Effects on Consumer Price Estimates, Value Perception, and Search Intention," *Journal of Business Research*, May 2000, pp. 93–100.

21. Nigel Cox, "Amex Charges Ahead," *Smart Business*, Apr. 2001, pp. 123–128.

22. Sources: Interviews with Jim Sciabarrasi, Christine Epplett, and Paul Heffernan of New Balance, video, Houghton Mifflin Company, 2003; "New Balance Athletic Shoe, Inc.," *Hoover's Online*, www.hoovers.com/new-balance-athletic-shoe,-inc./—ID__42602—/free-co-factsheet.xhtml (accessed May 11, 2004); "Our History," New Balance, www.newbalance.com/aboutus/misc/history.html (accessed May 11, 2004).

23. Sources: David Guilford, "Apologize for Incentives? GM Loves 'Em," *Automotive News*, Aug. 18, 2003, p. 1, via Lexis-Nexis Academic Database; Chris Isidore, "GM Execs: No Let-Up on Incentives," CNN/Money, Jan. 5, 2004, via Lexis-Nexis Academic Database; Kathleen Kerwin and David Welch, "Can Detroit Break the Rebate Habit?" *Business Week*, Jan. 12, 2004, pp. 110-111; David Kiley, "GM Tries to Cut Cord on Costly Rebates," *USA Today*, Jan. 23, 2004, pp. 1B–2B; David Kiley, "The Incentive Trap: Owing More Than Trade-in's Worth," *USA Today*, Jan. 23, 2004, p. 2B; Alisa Priddle and David E. Zoia, "Are Incentives a Carrot or Noose?" *Ward's Dealer Business*, Aug. 1, 2003, p. 8, via Lexis-Nexis Academic Database.

Appendix A

1. This section and the three that follow are adapted from William M. Pride, Robert J. Hughes, and Jack R. Kapoor, *Business* (Boston: Houghton Mifflin, 2002), pp. A1–A9.

2. Sal Divita, "Résumé Writing Requires Proper Strategy," *Marketing News*, July 3, 1995, p. 6.

3. Andrew J. DuBrin, "Deadly Political Sins," *Wall Street Journal's Managing Your Career*, Fall 1993, pp. 11–13.

4. Ibid.

5. Cyndee Miller, "Marketing Research Salaries Up a Bit, but Layoffs Take Toll," *Marketing News*, June 19, 1995, p. 1.

6. Market research—salaries: www.careers-in-marketing.com/mrsal.htm, Aug. 8, 2004.

7. www.payscale.com, May 5, 2004.

8. Ibid.

9. Ibid.

10. Product management—salaries: www.careers-in-marketing.com/pmsal.htm, Aug. 8, 2004.

11. Advertising and public relations—salaries: www.careers-in-marketing.com/adsal.htm, Aug. 8, 2004.

12. Advertising and public relations—salaries: www.careers-in-marketing.com/adsal.htm, Aug. 8, 2004.

13. www.payscale.com, May 5, 2004.

14. Ibid.

15. www.pcworld.com, May 6, 2004.

Sources

Chapter 1

Page 8: "Chrysler: Drive & Love," DaimlerChrysler, **www.chrysler.com/celine/celine.html** (accessed Dec. 11, 2003); David Kiley, "Chrysler Bets Big on Dion's Auto Endorsement Deal," June 8, 2003, *USA Today,* **http://advertising.about.com/library/weekly/aa072903a.htm**; "Kobe Bryant's Endorsement Deals," About Advertising, **http://advertising.about.com/library/weekly/aa072903a.htm** (accessed Dec. 10, 2003); Jason Stein, "Inside Chrysler's Celine Dion Advertising Disaster: Selling the Celebrity Instead of the Product," *Advertising Age,* Nov. 24, 2003, **www.adage.com/news.cms?newsId=39262**; *page 19:* Mission Foods, **www.missionfoods.com** (accessed Dec. 9, 2003); Jenalia Moreno, "Ruling Could Favor Tortilla Giant," *Houston Chronicle,* Nov. 27, 2003, pp. 1C-2C; R. R. Ramirez and P. de la Cruz, *The Hispanic Population in the United States: March 2002,* Current Population Reports, P20-545, U.S. Census Bureau, Washington, DC, 2002; Fernando Ruiz, "Companies Sue Leading Rival for Flattening Sales," *Los Angeles Times,* Oct, 30, 2003, **www.redding.com/news/business/past/20031030bus060.shtml**; "Tortilla Pioneer Sets His Sights on Britain," PM Communications, **www.pmcomm.com/mexico2/food.htm** (accessed Dec. 9, 2003).

Chapter 2

Page 32: Susan Decker, "Disposable Camera Firm Ordered to Pay," *CanWest Global Communications,* Mar. 4, 2003; "Explore the World of Fujifilm-Recycling," Fuji, **www.fujifilm.com/JSP/fuji/epartners/reclycling.jsp?nav=3** (accessed Dec. 8, 2003); "Fuji Wins Disposable-Cameras Suit," *Wall Street Journal,* Mar. 3, 2003, **http://online.wsj.com**; "Judge: Firm Must Pay for Taking Fuji's One-Use Camera Technology," *Miami Herald,* Mar. 3, 2003; "Kodak: HSE Annual Report, 2000—Single-Use Cameras," Kodak, **http://kodak.com/US/en/corp/environment/00CoprEnviroRpt/HSEsingle-use.shtml** (accessed Dec. 8, 2003); "Nonmetallics," *Recycling Today,* Mar. 15, 2001, **www.recyclingtoday.com/articles/article.asp?ID=442&CatID=&SubCatID=/**; "Picture This: Disposable Camera Could Spoil Memories," NBC5.com, Nov. 25, 2002, **www.nbc5.com/print/1806438/detail.html?use=print**; *page 46:* Ricardo Braca, "Red Bull vs. Lion in Bar-Mixer Duel," *Denver Post,* Sep. 22, 2003, **www.denverpost.com/Stories/0,1413,36%257E24769%257E1645216,00.html**; "Cool Colorado Stuff," *ColoradoBiz,* Mar. 2002, p. 47; Kenneth Hein, "A Bull's Market," *Brandweek,* May 28, 2001, via **www.findarticles.com**; "The History—The Story," Red Bull, **www.redbull.com/product/history/** (accessed Dec. 8, 2003); "Red Bull's Energy-Drink Claims May Be Hype—But Not Its Sales," Business Week Online, June 30, 2000, **www.businessweek.com**.

Strategic Case 1

"Baseball Weekly Hits Record Circulation," *PR Newswire,* Apr. 13, 1998, p. 413; "Circulation Slide for Newspapers," *Editor & Publisher,* May 10, 1997, p. 3; "Company Profile," Gannett Inc., **www.gannett.com/map/gan007.htm** (accessed Dec. 12, 2003); R. Cook, "Gannett Hits Heights in Print but Falls Short of TV Stardom," *Campaign,* Jan. 17, 1997, p. 24; R. Curtis, "Introducing Your New *USA Today,*" *USA Today,* Apr. 3, 2000, p. 27A; "Deadline," *Fortune,* July 8, 2002; pp. 78–86; J. Duscha, "Satisfying Advertiser Position Demands Now Easier," *NewsInc,* Sep. 13, 1999; Gannett Company, Inc., 1997 annual report; Gannett Company, Inc., 1999 annual report; Gannett Company, Inc., 2000 annual report; Gannett Company, Inc., 1996 Form 10-K (on file with the Securities and Exchange Commission); "Gannett's Game Plan," Gannett, **www.gannett.com/map/gameplan.htm** (accessed Dec. 12, 2003); "Giving Samples Made Easy Through *USA Today* from Shampoo to CDs," *NewsInc,* June 22, 1998; K. Jurgensen, "Quick Response; Paper Chase: *USA Today* Editor Sees Shifts in How Information Is Gener-

ated and Delivered to Readers," *Advertising Age,* Feb. 14, 2000, p. S6; K. Jurgensen, *USA Today*'s New Look Designed for Readers," *USA Today,* Apr. 3, 2000, p. 1A; A. M. Kerwin, "Daily Paper's Circulation Woes Persist into '97," *Advertising Age,* May 12, 1997, p. 26; P. Long, "After Long Career, *USA Today* Founder Al Neuharth Is Ready for More," *Knight-Ridder/Tribune Business News,* Apr. 28, 1999; J. McCartney, "*USA Today* Grows Up," *American Journalism Review,* Sep. 1997, p. 19; B. Miller, "*USA Today,* Gannett to Launch *USA Today Live,*" *Television & Cable,* Feb. 8, 2000; T. Noah, "At Least It's Free, Right?" *U.S. News & World Report,* Dec. 2, 1996, p. 60; N. Paul, "McWebsite: USA Today Online," *Searcher,* May 1999, p. 58; M. L. Stein, "Don't Sweat the Internet Says *USA Today*'s Curley," *Editor & Publisher,* Aug. 22, 1998, p. 40; M. Stone, *USA Today Online* Listens to Its Logs," *Editor & Publisher,* Aug. 7, 1999, p. 66; J. Strupp, "Accuracy Is the Aim," *Editor & Publisher,* May 1, 2000, p. 9; J. Strupp, "*USA Today* Ads Go Page One," *Editor and Publisher,* May 8, 1999, p. 40; "Where Are Newspapers Headed?" *Editor and Publisher,* June 28, 1997; R. Tedesco, "Internet Profit Sites Elusive," *Broadcasting & Cable,* Nov. 17, 1997, p. 74; "*USA Today:* A Case Study," prepared by M. Condry, R. Dailey, F. Gasquet, M. Holladay, A. Johnson, S. Menzer, and J. Miller, University of Memphis, 1997; "*USA Today* Launches New Life Section Friday Format," *PR Newswire,* Mar. 16, 1998, p. 316; "*USA Today* Launches Online Classifieds Area and 17 New Marketplace Partnerships," *Business Wire,* Apr. 15, 1997; "*USA Today* Launches Pay-Per-View Archives Service," *Business Wire,* Jan. 5, 1998; "*USA Today Online* Launches Real Time Survey System," *Business Wire,* Feb. 18, 1998; *USA Today* press kit, 1997, Gannett Company, Inc.; "*USA Today* Sells Page One Advertising Space," *PR Newswire,* May 5, 1999, p. 3517; I. Wada, "*USA Today* Marketplace Signs Up Six for On-Line Services," *Travel Weekly,* Apr. 28, 1997, p. 44. Geoffrey Lantos, Stonehill College, prepared this case for classroom discussion rather than to illustrate either effective or ineffective handling of an administrative situation. Cheryl Anne Molchan, Stonehill College, and James G. Maxham, Louisiana State University, provided research assistance on earlier versions.

Chapter 3

Page 72: "Hollywood Preaches Anti-Piracy to Schools," CNN.com, Oct. 24, 2003, **www.cnn.com**; Dan Rather and Bill Whitaker, "Whether Parents Should Be Teaching Their Children About Copyright Infringement When They're Downloading Music Off the Internet," *CBS Evening News,* Sep. 10, 2003; "12-Year-Old Settles Music Swap Lawsuit," CNN.com, Sep. 9, 2003, **www.cnn.com**; "NPD Group: Apple's iTunes Music Store Successfully Translates Brand Awareness into Usage," *Business Wire,* July 31, 2003, **www.businesswire.com**; *page 78:* Benjamin Fulford, "Gadgets We Love: 3G Phone," *Forbes,* Nov. 10, 2003, p. 170; David Pringle, Jesse Drucker, and Evan Ramstad, "Cellphone Makers Pay a Heavy Toll for Missing Fads," *Wall Street Journal,* Oct. 30, 2003, pp. 1+; John Blau, "New In-Flight Cell Phone Technology on the Horizon," *Computerworld,* July 15, 2003.

Chapter 4

Page 92: Anthony Bianco and Wendy Zellner, "Is Wal-Mart Too Powerful?" *Business Week,* Oct. 6, 2003, pp. 102–110; Cora Daniels, "Women vs. Wal-Mart," *Fortune,* July 21, 2003, pp. 79–82; Charles Fishman, "The Wal-Mart You Don't Know: Why Low Prices Have a High Cost," *Fast Company,* Dec. 2003, pp. 70–80; Daren Fonda, "Will Wal-Mart Steal Christmas?" *Time,* Dec. 8, 2003, pp. 54–56; *page 99:* Andrew Backover, "Write-Down by Qwest Grows to $40.8 Billion," *USA Today,* Oct. 29, 2002, p. B1; Andrew Backover and Greg Farrell, "Qwest Execs Charged with Fraud," *USA Today,* Feb.

26, 2003, p. B1; "Ex-Qwest Execs Indicted," CNN/Money, Feb. 25, 2003, **http://money.cnn.com/2003/02/25/technology/qwest/index. htm**; "Feds Indict Four ex-Qwest Executives," MSNBC, Feb. 25, 2003, **www.msnbc.com/news/876997.asp**; Kris Hudson, "Qwest Assessed $20 Million Fine," *Denver Post*, Oct. 25, 2002; "Qwest's Anschutz to Face Second Questioning—WSJ," Reuters, Oct. 8, 2002.

Chapter 5

Page 122: "Food Promotion Debate: The Facts," Food Standards Agency, **www.foodstandards.gov.uk/healthiereating/promotion/ promofacts/** (accessed Nov. 20, 2003); Ellen Hale, "Junk Food Super-Sizing Europeans," *USA Today*, Nov. 18, 2003, pp. 13A, 14A; "Obesity Not Just a U.S. Problem," CBS News, Feb. 28, 2003, **www. cbsnews.com/stories/2003/03/03/health/main542482.shtml**; *page 136:* Richard C. Morais, "Listen Up, Sucker," *Forbes*, Jan. 8, 2001, p. 212; Daniel Woolls, "Spanish Firm's Lollipops Have International Flavor," *Mobile Register*, May 6, 2001, p. 3F; Doris Walczyk, "Realizing Global Brand Leadership," The Business of Branding, newsletter, **www.iirusa.com/businessofbranding/index.cfm/Link=31** (accessed Dec. 17, 2003): Ian Wylie, "These Lollies Are About to Go Pop," *Fast Company*, Dec. 2002, pp. 52, 54.

Strategic Case 2

Deborah Adamson, "Trouble in Toyland," CBS MarketWatch, Mar. 8, 2000, **http://cbs.marketwatch.com/**; American Girl, **www. americangirl.com** (accessed May 27, 2003); Bandai, **www.bandai. com** (accessed May 27, 2003); "Barbie Is Banned from Russia, Without Love," *The Observer*, Nov. 24, 2002, **www.observer.co.uk/**; Lisa Bannon, "Mattel Sees Untapped Market for Blocks: Little Girls," *Wall Street Journal*, June 6, 2002, p. B-1; Lisa Bannon, "New Playbook: Taking Cues from GE, Mattel's CEO Wants Toy Maker to Grow Up," *Wall Street Journal*, Nov. 14, 2001, p. A-1; Barbie, **www.barbie.com** (accessed May 27, 2003); Sherri Day, "As It Remakes Itself, Mattel Does Same for Barbie," *New York Times*, Nov. 9, 2002, p. C-1; Hot Wheels, **www.hotwheels.com/** (accessed May 27, 2003); Debbie Howell, "Top Brands 2002: A Longing for Labels' Returns," *DSN Retailing Today*, Oct. 28, 2002, pp. 24–27; Interbrand, "The 100 Best Brands," Business Week Online, Aug. 5, 2002, **www.businessweek.com**; "Iran Enforces Barbie Ban," *Associated Press*, May 23, 2002; Kate MacArthur, "Plastic Surgery: Barbie Gets Real Makeover," *Advertising Age*, Nov. 4, 2002, pp. 4, 53; Mattel, **www.mattel.com** (accessed May 26, 2003); "Mattel Combines Girls, Boys Divisions, Cuts Management," Associated Press, Feb. 28, 2003; "Mattel, Inc. Launches Global Code of Conduct Intended to Improve Workplace, Workers' Standard of Living," Canada NewsWire, Nov. 21, 1997 (for more information on Mattel's code, contact the company at (310) 252-3524); "Mattel Lands WB Master Toy Licenses," *Home Textiles Today*, Sep. 2002, p. 14; "Mattel Swings to Better Than Expected Profit," Reuters News & Financial Intelligence, Apr. 13, 2003, **http://www.reuters.com/**; My Scene Barbie, **www.myscene.com** (accessed May 27, 2003); Christopher Palmeri, "Mattel's New Toy Story," *Business Week*, Nov. 18, 2002, pp. 72–74; J. Alex Tarquino, "Barbie & Co. Reviving Mattel," *New York Times*, March 9, 2003, Section 3, p. 7. This case was prepared by Debbie Thorne McAlister and Laura Leigh Saenz, Texas State University–San Marcos, for classroom discussion rather than to illustrate either effective or ineffective handling of an administration situation. The authors acknowledge the work of Kevin Sample on previous versions of this case.

Chapter 6

Page 154: "How You Benefit," Harris Poll Online, **http://vr. harrispollonline.com/benefit.asp** (accessed Dec. 8, 2003); "Welcome to Harris Online Poll," Harris Interactive, **www.harrisinteractive. com/** (accessed Dec. 8, 2003); **http://h.harrispollonline.com/scripts/ scywebMT.dll/Job_w12937c-214203-128230** (accessed Apr. 7,

2002); **http://h.harrispollonline.com/scripts/scywebMT.dll/ Job_w12937c-214203-128230** (accessed Apr. 7, 2002); *page 164:* "European Union Directive on Privacy," *Banking and Financial Services Policy Report*, Dec. 2002, pp. 1–5; David Scheer, "Europe's New High-Tech Role: Playing Privacy Cop to the World," *Wall Street Journal*, Oct. 10, 2003, **http://online.wsj.com**; Deborah L. Venice, "New California Privacy Law Appears Redundant to DMers," *Marketing News*, Oct. 27, 2003, p. 9.

Chapter 7

Page 185: "About Our Company," Procter & Gamble, **www.pg.com/about_pg/sectionmain.jhtml** (accessed Dec. 31, 2003); Emily Nelson, "P&G Checks Out Real Life," *Wall Street Journal*, May 17, 2000, pp. B1, B4; "National Poll Finds Home-Cooked Meal Retains Its Appeal But Appetite for Dish Washing Wanes," Cascade Complete, **www.cascadecomplete.com/cascadeCorner/surveyRes. html**, June 4, 2001; *page 191:* "Former Employee Accuses Coke of Deceptive Marketing, Contaminated Products," *Atlanta Business Chronicle*, May 20, 2003, **www.bizjournals.com/atlanta/stories/ 2003/05/19/daily12.htm**; "Lancer Expanding Coca-Cola Investigation," *Atlanta Business Chronicle*, Aug. 26, 2003, **www.bizjournals. com/atlanta/stories/2003/08/25/daily10.htm**; Jim Lovel, "Lawsuits: Coke Breaking Law to Boost Sales," *Atlanta Business Chronicle*, June 2, 2003, **www.bizjournals.com/atlanta/stories/2003/06/02/story7. html**; Chad Terhune, "How Coke Beefed Up Results of a Marketing Test," *Wall Street Journal*, Aug. 20, 2003, p. A1; "U.S. Attorney's Office Investigating Coca-Cola," *Atlanta Business Chronicle*, July 11, 2003, **www.bizjournals.com/atlanta/stories/2003/07/07/daily41.htm**; "Whitley Settles with Coke for $540,000," *Atlanta Business Chronicle*, Oct. 8, 2003, **www.bizjournals.com/atlanta/stories/2003/10/06/ daily23.htm**.

Strategic Case 3

"About FedEx Automated Solutions," FedEx, **www.fedex.com/us/ about/technology/automation.html?link=4** (accessed Dec. 30, 2003); "About FedEx Wireless Solutions," FedEx, **www.fedex.com/us/ about/technology/wireless.html?link=4** (accessed Dec. 30, 2003); "DHL/Airborne Deal Could Shake Up U.S. Express Market," *Logistics Management*, Apr. 1, 2003, **www.manufacturing.net/lm/ index.asp?layout=article&articleid=CA290554**; FedEx Corporation, 2003 Annual Report; FedEx Corporation, **www.fedex.com** (accessed Dec. 30, 2003); "FedEx Corporation," CNN/Money, **http://money. cnn.com/MGI/snap/A1878.htm** (accessed Dec. 30, 2003); "FedEx to Buy Kinko's for $2.4B," CNN/Money, Dec. 30, 2003, **http://money. cnn.com/2003/12/30/news/companies/kinko_fedex/index.htm**; "FedEx to Create Shanghai Hub Office," *AirWise News*, Oct. 24, 2003, **http://news.airwise.com/stories/2003/10/1066964235.html**; "FedEx Ground Opens 'Super Hub,'" *Transportation & Distribution*, Nov. 2000, pp. 12–13; Linda Grant, "Why FedEx is Flying High," *Fortune*, Nov. 10, 1997, p. 155; Nicole Harris, "Flying into a Rage?" *Business Week*, Apr. 27, 1998, p. 119; Michele Kayal, "FedEx Launches Sunday Service Amid Skepticism," *Journal of Commerce*, Mar. 11, 1998, p. 1A; Kristin S. Krause, "Handling the Holiday Crush," *Traffic World*, Dec. 4, 2000, p. 33; Betsy McKay and Rick Brooks, "FedEx Will Buy Kinko's for $2.4 Billion in Cash," *Wall Street Journal*, Dec. 30, 2003, **http://online.wsj.com/article_ print/,,SB107278969871498900,00.html**; Theo Mullen, "Delivery Wars Go High-Tech—FedEx Ground Sends Message with $80M Investment to Improve Package Tracking," *Internetweek*, Oct. 23, 2000, p. 18; Jayne O'Donnell, "FedEx–Postal Service Alliance Delivers Goods," *USA Today Online*, Jan. 11, 2001, **www.usatoday.com/ money/**; "Post Office, FedEx to Work Together," *USA Today Online*, Jan. 10, 2001, **www.usatoday.com/money/**; Monica Roman, "FedEx Hitches Up a New Trucker," *Business Week*, Nov. 27, 2000, p. 66; Marc L. Songini, "FedEx Expects CRM System to Deliver," *Computerworld*, Nov. 6, 2000, p. 10; Richard Tomkins, "The Bear and the

Alligator Enter into a Race to Deliver," *Financial Times,* Mar. 13, 1998, p. 30; "UPS Wants Fed Probe into DHL–Airborne Deal," *San Francisco Business Times,* Mar. 27, 2003, **www.bizjournals.com/ sanfrancisco/stories/2003/03/24/daily40.html**; Michael Weingarten and Bart Stuck, "No Substitutions?" *Telephony,* Feb. 2, 1998, p. 26. This case was prepared with the assistance of Michael D. Hartline, Florida State University.

Chapter 8

Page 214: Michelle Conlin, "Unmarried America," *Business Week,* Oct. 20, 2003, pp. 106–116; Mary Wiltenburg and Amanda Paulson, "All in the (Mixed-Race) Family," *Christian Science Monitor,* Aug. 28, 2003, p. 3; D'Vera Cohn, "Live-Ins Almost as Likely as Marrieds to Be Parents," *Washington Post,* Mar. 13, 2003, p. A1; *page 217:* Robert Strauss, "Appealing to Youth, Selling to the Not-So-Young," *New York Times,* Oct. 22, 2003, p. G37; Ann D. Middleman, "The New Mature Market: How Mature Is It?" *MarketingNewz,* May 1, 2003, **www.ientry.com**; Arundhati Parmar, "Knowledge of Mature Market Pays Reward," *Marketing News,* April 28, 2003, pp. 5–6.

Chapter 9

Page 239: Todd Wasserman, "Sharpening the Focus," *Brandweek,* Nov. 3, 2003, pp. 28+; Bruce Horovitz, "Shop, You're on Candid Camera," *Money,* Nov. 6, 2002, p. 1B; *page 252:* Eliot Tiegel, "Multicultural Focus for McDonald's," *Television Week,* Sep. 8, 2003, p. 20; Tammy Mastroberte, "Shell Unveils Multicultural Marketing Campaign," *Convenience Store News,* Aug. 25, 2003, p. 10; Laurel Wentz, "Pepsi Puts Interests Before Ethnicity," *Advertising Age,* July 7, 2003, p. S4; "Advertisers Use Their Census," *Crain's New York Business,* June 9, 2003, p. 22.

Chapter 10

Page 267: Arnold S. Relman, "Your Doctor's Drug Problem," *New York Times,* Nov. 18, 2003, p. A25; "New OIG Pharmaceutical Compliance Guidance Raises Questions About Financial Relationships," *Mondaq Business Briefing,* July 10, 2003, **www.mondaq. com**; Tim Bonfield, "Drug Firms' Gifts to Docs Draw Scrutiny," *Cincinnati Enquirer,* Oct. 3, 2002, **www.enquirer.com**; Julie Appleby, "Feds Warn Drugmakers: Gifts to Doctors May Be Illegal," *USA Today,* Oct. 2, 2002, **www.usatoday.com**; Helen Jung, "Some Doctors Are Getting Awful Tired of Visits from Drug-Industry Sales Reps," *Associated Press,* June 14, 2002, LexisNexis; Melinda Ligos, "Gimme! Gimme!" *Sales and Marketing Management,* March 2002, pp. 33–40; *page 269:* Anne Kadet, "Sold on eBay," *SmartMoney,* Jan. 2004, pp. 92–98; "Buy or Sell in Bulk on eBay," *HardwareCentral,* Sep. 8, 2003; Jane Salodof MacNeil, "Beyond eBay," *Inc.,* Mar. 2002, p. 124; Peralte C. Paul, "Atlanta-Based Online Auction Equipment Maker Sees Surge in Big-Name Customers," *Atlanta Journal–Constitution,* Jan. 2, 2002, **www.ajc.com**; Janet Patton, "First Open Online Cattle Auction Rated a Success in Kentucky," *Lexington Herald-Leader,* Aug. 29, 2001, **www.kentuckyconnect.com**.

Strategic Case 4

Scott Van Voorhis, "Reebok Pitching Licensing Deal to MLB," *Boston Herald,* Jan. 15, 2004, p. 40; Wayne Niemi, "Chasing China: With Several Major Athletic Players Betting Big on China, the Sneaker Wars Are Heating Up," *Footwear News,* Dec. 15, 2003, p. 12; Jennifer Carofano, "The Turnaround Gunning for the No. 1 Spot in Athletic Footwear, Reebok Cranked Up the Heat in 2003," *Footwear News,* Dec. 8, 2003, p. 22; Elizabeth Olson, "Being Chased by the Big Boys," *New York Times,* Nov. 27, 2003, p. C4; Joseph Pereira and Stephanie Kang, "Phat News: Rappers Choose Reebok Shoes," *Wall Street Journal,* Nov. 14, 2003, p. B1; Polly Devaney, "Reebok Shoots from the Hip-Hop in Sneaker Wars," *Marketing Week,* July 31, 2003, p. 21; David Lipke, "Reebok Targets Men with New NYC Store," *Daily News Record,* Oct. 27, 2003,

p. 14; Morag Cuddeford Jones, "Reebok Has Spring in Its Step," *Brand Strategy,* Oct. 2003, p. 9; Rosemary Feitelberg, "Eve to Rap Up Reebok Classic," *Women's Wear Daily,* Mar. 20, 2003, p. 8; **www.hoovers.com**.

Chapter 11

Page 296: "Nokia Announces Two New Games for N-Gage Game Deck," *Nordic Business Report,* Feb. 9, 2004, **www. nordicbusinessreport.com**; Gerry Khermouch, "Cell Phones: America Zooms in on Camera Phones," *Business Week,* Dec. 22, 2003, pp. 44–45; Andy Reinhardt, "Nokia's Big Leap," *Business Week,* Oct. 13, 2003, pp. 50–52; Ali Quassim, "Nokia Phone Game Hits Big," *Advertising Age,* Feb. 24, 2003, p. 15; *page 301:* "Has Kodak Missed the Moment?" *The Economist,* Jan. 3, 2004, pp. 46–47; "Analysis: Kodak Moves into New Arena with SDP," *Print Week,* Dec. 4, 2003, p. 20; James Bandler, "Kodak Shifts Focus from Film, Betting Future on Digital Lines," *Wall Street Journal,* Sep. 25, 2003, pp. A1+.

Chapter 12

Page 323: Based on information from "Staples to Pay $850,000 Penalty," ConsumerAffairs.com, May 22, 2003, **www. consumeraffairs.org**; Russell Mokhiber, "Household's Predatory Plea," *Multinational Monitor,* Oct./Nov. 2002, pp. 6+; Erin Strout, "To Tell the Truth," *Sales & Marketing Management,* July 2002, pp. 40–47; Philip Reed, "Low Down, Low Payments!" *Edmunds. com,* April 25, 2002, **www.edmunds.com**; *page 327:* Joann Muller, "Global Motors," *Forbes,* Jan. 12, 2004, pp. 62–68; "Chevrolet's Cavalier Continues to Deliver Strong Sales, GM Reports," *Vindicator* (Youngstown, OH), Dec. 3, 2003, **www.vindy.com**; Dave Guilford, "As Olds Folds, GM Fights to Keep Owners," *Automotive News,* Aug. 11, 2003, p. 6; David Welch, "Headed for That Showroom in the Sky," *Business Week,* July 21, 2003, p. 52; Brian E. Albrecht, "Oldsmobile Era Long and Glorious," *Plain Dealer* (Cleveland), June 1, 2003, p. F1.

Chapter 13

Page 343: Sarah Ellison, "Kraft's Stale Strategy," *Wall Street Journal,* Dec. 18, 2003, p. B1; Matthew Boyle, "Brand Killers," *Fortune,* Aug. 11, 2003, pp. 88–100; *page 351:* Arundhati Parmar, "Marketers Ask: Hues on First?" *Marketing News,* Feb. 15, 2004, pp. 8–10; Jim Butschli, "Inks Bring Benefits to Label Printer," *Packaging World,* July 3, 2003, p. 17; Pamela Paul, "Color by Numbers," *American Demographics,* Feb. 2002, pp. 30–35; Carol Angrisani, "The Silent Salesman," *Supermarket News,* Feb. 11, 2002, p. 15.

Chapter 14

Page 369: Kortney Stringer, "Hard Lesson Learned: Premium, No-Frills Rental Cars Don't Mix," *Wall Street Journal,* November 3, 2003, **www.online.wsj.com/article/0.SB106782013621302600.00.html**; Jorge Sidron, "Vanguard's Plan for Brands: Divide and Conquer," *Travel Weekly,* Nov. 3, 2003, p. 27; *page 381:* John Bissell, "Opening the Doors to 'Cause Branding,'" *Brandweek,* Oct. 27, 2003, p. 30; Jeff Bailey, "Nonprofits Can Provide Brand Name That Sells," *Wall Street Journal,* Sep. 23, 2003, p. B11; Bonnie Jennings Steele, "Brand Names for Volunteerism?" *Charity Channel,* Apr. 2, 2003, **www. charitychannel.com**.

Strategic Case 5

Brad Stone, "Greetings, Earthlings: Satellite Radio for Cars Is Taking Off and Adding New Features—Now Broadcasters Are Starting to Fight Back," *Newsweek,* Jan. 26, 2003, p. 55; "In Brief, Radio: XM Radio Ends '03 with 1.36 Million Users," *Los Angeles Times,* Jan. 8, 2004, p. C3; Stephen Holden, "High-Tech Quirkiness Restores Radio's Magic," *New York Times,* Dec. 26, 2003, pp. E1+; Dan Thanh Dang, "Satellite Radio Industry Continues to Grow, Enter

Mainstream," *Baltimore Sun,* Nov. 16, 2003, **www.sunspot.net**; David Welch, "Satellite Radio: Two for the Road," *Business Week,* Nov. 24, 2003, p. 144+; David Pogue, "Satellite Radio Extends Its Orbit," *New York Times,* Dec. 18, 2003, p. G1.

Chapter 15

Page 396: "Barnes & Noble Implements i2 Solutions to Increase Distribution Center Efficiencies Nationwide," *Canadian Corporate News,* May 8, 2001, **www.comtextnews.com**; "Barnes & Noble Selects Retek to Support Supply Chain Planning and Optimization," Barnes & Noble news release, Jan. 10, 2001, **www.prnewswire.com**; Herb Greenberg, "Dead Mall Walking," *Fortune,* May 1, 2000, p. 304; Tom Andel, "Logistics@Barnesandnoble.com,"*Material Handling Management,* Jan. 2000, p. 39; "Mezzanines Help Support Store and Web Demand," *Material Handling Management,* Jan. 2000, 14SCF; *page 405:* "Office Depot's E-Diva," *Business Week,* Aug. 6, 2001, pp. EB221; David Stires, "Office Depot Finds an E-Business That Works," *Fortune,* Feb. 19, 2001, p. 232.

Chapter 16

Page 429: Jordan K. Speer, "Collaboration Station," *Apparel,* Dec. 2003, pp. 44+; Gabriel Kahn, "Made to Measure: Invisible Supplier Has Penney's Shirts All Buttoned Up," *Wall Street Journal,* Sep. 11, 2003, p. 1+; *page 437:* Doris Hajewski, "OshKosh B'Gosh to Close Two Factories," *Milwaukee Journal Sentinel,* Dec. 13, 2003, p. 3D; Rachel Gecker, "An Overall Inbound Success," *Inbound Logistics,* Nov. 2003, pp. 56–58.

Chapter 17

Page 455: Based on information from "Repeat Performers," *Business Week,* Jan. 12, 2004, p. 68; Crayton Harrison, "Dell Copies Automakers' Financing Deals," *Dallas Morning News,* Jan. 2, 2004, **www.dallasnews.com**; Sam Diaz, "Dell Succeeds by Breaking Silicon Valley Rules," *San Jose Mercury News,* Dec. 17, 2003, www. mercurynews.com; J. Bonasia, "Supply Chain Issues Take on New Urgency," *Investor's Business Daily,* Feb. 27, 2002, p. A10; Joan Magretta, "The Power of Virtual Integration: An Interview with Dell Computer's Michael Dell," *Harvard Business Review,* Mar.–Apr. 1998, pp. 74–84; "I'm Going Full Blast," *Business Week,* Sep. 24, 2001, **www.businessweek.com**; *page 458:* Boonsong Kositchitethana, "Conoco Boosts Presence While Rivals Close Service Stations. 160 Service Stations Planned by 2003," *Bangkok Post,* Mar. 30, 2001, **www.siamfuture.com/thainews/thnewstxt.asp?tid=579**; Sutthinee Sattarugawong, "Ban Rai Coffee House," Masters in Marketing Program, Competitive Strategies course, Thammasat University, Bangkok, Thailand, Winter 2002; Nareeat Wiriyapong, "Convenience Store: Conoco Set to Invest Bt3bn," *The Nation,* June 5, 2000, **www.siamfuture.com/thainews/thnewstxt.asp?tid=169**.

Strategic Case 6

Sources: "Home Depot to Focus on Modernization, New Ventures in '04," *DSN Retailing Today,* Jan. 26, 2004, pp. 7+; Tiffany Montgomery, "Home Depot to Open Its Largest Store in the Nation in Anaheim Hills, Calif.," *Orange County Register,* Jan. 23, 2004, **www.ocregister.com**; Tony Wilbert, "Home Depot Refocuses Expo Unit," *Atlanta Journal-Constitution,* Jan. 18, 2004, **www.ajc.com**; "Home Depot Buys a Supplier to Homebuilders," *New York Times,* Jan. 7, 2004, p. C3; "Home Depot Debuts Catalog," *Chain Store Age,* Dec. 2003, p. 110; Kathleen Hickey, "Seasoning the Warehouse," *Journal of Commerce,* Nov. 24, 2003, pp. 31+.

Chapter 18

Page 476: "Editorial: 'Got Cereal?' Plan Is OK with Limits," *Advertising Age,* Feb. 18, 2002, p. 13; William A. Roberts, Jr., "A Vulnerable Position," *Prepared Foods,* Feb. 2002, pp. 13+; Stephanie Thompson, "Kellogg's Kickstart," *Advertising Age,* Jan. 7, 2002,

p. 2; Stephanie Thompson, "Rivals Back $50 Mil Cereal Campaign," *Advertising Age,* Feb. 11, 2002, pp. 1, 46; *page 493:* "About KFC: KFC Sets the Record Straight," KFC, press release, Oct. 28, 2003, **www.kfc.com/about/pr/102803.htm**; K. MacArthur, "KFC Pulls Controversial Health-Claim Chicken Ads," *Advertising Age,* Nov. 18, 2003, **www.adage.com/news.cms?newsId=39220**; A. D. Mathios and P. Ippolito, "Health Claims in Food Advertising and Labeling: Disseminating Food Information to Consumers," in Elizabeth Frazao, ed., *America's Eating Habits: Changes and Consequences,* Agriculture Information Bulletin No. 750, 1999, USDA Economic Research Service, Food and Rural Economics Division, pp. 189-212, available at **www.ers.usda.gov/publications/aib750/aib750k.pdf**; A. W. Matthews and B. Steinberg, "FTC Examines Health Claims in KFC's Ads," *Wall Street Journal,* Nov. 19, 2003, pp. B1, B2; Ira Teinowitz, "CARU's Role in KFC Advertising Debacle Revealed: Children's Marketing Watchdog Releases Fried Chicken Case File," *Advertising Age,* Dec. 05, 2003, **www.adage.com/news.cms?newsId=39339**.

Chapter 19

Page 509: "Latest News Release: P&G Committed to Sustain 4–6% Top Line and Double-Digit Bottom-Line Growth," Procter & Gamble, press release, **www.pgnews.com** (accessed Dec. 22, 2003); Jeff Neff, "P&G Announces 20 Brand Tie-In with Survivor," *Advertising Age,* Dec. 18, 2003, **www.adage.com**; "Shopping Guide," Bravo, **www.bravotv.com** (accessed Dec. 22, 2003); *page 518:* Tom Daykin, "Communities Force Big Box Retailers to Rethink Designs," *Milwaukee Journal Sentinel,* June 14, 2001, **www.jsonline.com/bym/biz2biz/ jun01/daykcoll5061401a.asp**; "Friends of Saybrook, Inc.: Welcome to the Effort to Help Protect Our Small Town," Nov. 2, 2001, **www.connix.com/~fndssayb/**; Anne Hatchitt, "Wal-Mart Withdraws Plans for SW Austin Store," *Austin Business Journal,* Oct. 2, 2003, **www.bizjournals.com/austin/stories/2003/09/29/daily25.html?page= 1**;Constance L. Hays, "Wal-Mart Ads Don't Discount Criticism," *Austin American-Statesman,* Aug. 14, 2003, **www.statesman.com**; "One Reason Why Wal-Mart Can Sell for Less," **http://209.157. 64.200/focus/f-news/1044225/posts** (accessed Jan. 5, 2004); Amy Smith, "Wal-Mart Is Everywhere," *Austin Chronicle,* Sep. 5, 2003, **www.austinchronicle.com/issues/dispatch/2003-09-05/pols_naked3. html**.

Chapter 20

Page 532: Julia Chang, "Codes of Conduct," *Sales & Marketing Management,* Nov. 2003, p. 22; Betsy Cummings, "Do Customers Hate Salespeople? Only If They Commit One of These Six Deadly Sins of Selling," *Sales & Marketing Management,* June 2001, pp. 44–51; Melinda Ligos, "Gimme! Gimme!" *Sales & Marketing Management,* Mar. 2002, pp. 32–40; "60% of B2B Firms Not Following Up with Prospective Customers," *Direct Marketing,* Nov. 2001, p. 10; Christopher Stewart, "Desperate Measures," *Sales & Marketing Management,* Sep. 2003, pp. 32–36; Anthony J. Urbaniak, "After the Sale—What Really Happens to Customer Service," *American Salesman,* Feb. 2001, pp. 14–17; *page 539:* Betsy Cummings, "Welcome to the Real Whirled," *Sales & Marketing Management,* Feb. 2001, pp. 87–88; Rekha Balu, "Whirlpool Gets Real with Customers," *Fast Company,* Dec. 1999, pp. 74, 76; "Fact Sheet," Whirlpool, **www.whirlpoolcorp.com** (accessed Jan. 9, 2004); Amy Milshtein, "Livin' It," Steelcase, 2003, **www.steelcase.com/en/pdf/ knowledgepapers/LivinIt.pdf**; "Whirlpool Corporation," Hoover's Online, **www.hoovers.com** (accessed Jan. 9, 2004).

Strategic Case 7

"About Us," Cabelas, **www.cabelas.com** (accessed Oct. 8, 2003); "Academy Sports & Outdoor, Ltd.," Hoover's Online, **www. hoovers.com** (accessed Oct. 8, 2003); Rick Alm, "Tourist Attraction May Be Looking at KCK as Site," *Kansas City Star,* June 27, 2000, p. D21; Andrew Backover, "Bass Pro Opener in Grapevine Reels in

Thousands," *Fort Worth Star-Telegram*, Mar. 26, 1999, p. 1; Andrew Backover, "Tackling the Competition—Smaller Stores Plan to Keep an Eye on Bass Pro Shops," *Fort Worth Star-Telegram*, Mar. 25, 1999, p. 1; "Bass Pro's Kansas City Project in Jeopardy," *Columbia Daily Tribune*, Oct. 9, 2002, p. 14A; Bass Pro Shop *2000 Master Catalog*; Robert Baun, "Sporting Goods Giant Takes First Colo. Store to Loveland," (Fort Collins) *Coloradoan*, Sep. 4, 2000, pp. A1, A2; Cabela's *Master Catalog Spring 2000 Edition I* and *Master Catalog Fall 2003 Late-Season Edition*; Bob Carr, "Communities Rush to Finance Bass Pro and Cabela's Stores," *Sporting Goods Business*, May 2003, p. 10; O. K. Carter, "Bass Pro Shop Opening in Grapevine," *Fort Worth Star-Telegram*, Mar. 19, 1999, p. 2; Ray Carter, "Oklahoma Supreme Court Upholds OKC in Bass Pro Shops Challenge," *Journal Record Legislative Report*, June 25, 2003, News Section; "Corporate Office," Gander Mountain, **www.gandermountain.com** (accessed Oct. 8, 2003); Mark Couch, "Bass Pro Shops Not Hooked on Bannister Area," *Kansas City Star*, July 25, 2000, p. D23; Mark P. Couch, "TIF Panel Tries to Land Bass Pro," *Kansas City Star*, May 11, 2000, p. C1; Gordon Dickson, "Store Angles for Easy Opener Traffic Control," *Fort Worth Star-Telegram*, Mar. 24, 1999, p. 1; Bob Edwards, "Communities Across the Country Offer Tax Incentives to Lure Bass Pro Shop to Town," National Public Radio, Sep. 1, 2003, transcript; D'Arcy Egan, "A Hot Lure: Megastores," (Cleveland) *Plain Dealer*, Sep. 7, 2000, p. 6D; Tim Eisele, "Famous Outdoors Store Right Next Door," *Capital Times*, July 17, 2002, p. 6D; "Factory Stores," L. L. Bean, **www.llbean.com** (accessed Oct. 8, 2003); "Future Store—Toronto Bass Pro Shops Outdoor World," "Future Store—Myrtle Beach, SC Bass Pro Shops Outdoor World Retail Store," "Future Store—Oklahoma City, OK Bass Pro Shops Outdoor World Retail Store," "Future Store—Hampton, VA Bass Pro Shops Outdoor World Retail Store," and "Future Store—Las Vegas, NV Bass Pro Shops Outdoor World Retail Store," all from Outdoor World, **www.outdoorworld.com/site/future_stores.cfm** (accessed Oct. 2, 2003); "Gander Mountain Company," Hoover's Online, **www.hoovers.com** (accessed Oct. 8, 2003); "General Retail Store Information," Cabelas, **www.cabelas.com** (accessed Oct. 8, 2003); Jamaal Glenn, "Bass Pro Unveils Design," *Columbia Missourian*, Aug. 31, 2002, p. 6A; Kevin Helliker, "Hunter Gatherer: Rare Retailer Scores by Targeting Men Who Hate to Shop," *Wall Street Journal*, Dec. 17, 2002, p. A1; "History," Gander Mountain, **www.gandermountain.com** (accessed Oct. 8, 2003); "In the Beginning" and "The Growth of Tracker Marine," Bass Pro Shops, **www.basspro.com** (accessed Oct. 2000); Joanne Kimberlin, "Hampton Reels in a Bass Pro Shop," *The Virginian-Pilot*, Feb. 5, 2002, p. D1; "L. L. Bean Today," L. L. Bean, **www.llbean.com** (accessed Oct. 2000 and Oct. 2003); Matt Maile, "OKC, VA Town Face Similar Bass Pro Shops Issues," *The Journal Record*, Apr. 24, 2002, News Section; Paul Miller, "Bass Pro Focuses on Its Channels," *Catalog Age*, Mar. 1, 2002, p. 5; Dave Moore, "Bass Pro Inks Deal for Shop on Vandiver," *Columbia Daily Tribune*, July 26, 2003, p. 1A; Linda A. Moore, "Bass Pro Shops Will Open Sport Warehouse," *The Commercial Appeal*, Feb. 13, 2002, p. C1; Bob Niedt, "Aurelius Hooks Bass Pro Shops," *The Post-Standard*, Nov. 13, 2002, p. A1; Bob Niedt, "What Bass Has in Store for Auburn," *The Post-Standard*, Aug. 12, 2003, p. A1; "Our History," Cabelas, **www.cabelas.com** (accessed Oct. 2000 and Oct. 2003); "Outdoor World Springfield, MO," Bass Pro pamphlet; Jon Pepper, "Michigan Version of Bass Pro Shop to Boost Tourism," *Detroit News*, Apr. 5, 1998, p. C1; "Program Planning Guidelines," OW Incentives, **www.owincentives.com** (accessed Oct. 3, 2002); "Recreational Equipment, Inc.," Hoover's Online, **www.hoovers.com** (accessed Oct. 8, 2003); "REI Store Directory," REI, **www.rei.com/stores/storeloc.html** (accessed Oct. 8, 2003); "REI to Open Store in Hillsboro, Oregon," REI, news release, **www.rei.com/aboutrei/newsroom.html** (accessed Oct. 8, 2003); Tim Renken, "Outdoors Stores Bring Big Business, Tourists Galore," *St. Louis Post-Dispatch*, Aug. 17, 2002, p. 23; "Retail Stores," L. L. Bean, **www.llbean.com** (accessed Oct. 8, 2003); Kelly Ryan, "Grapevine's Bass Pro Shops to Open Soon," *Dallas Morning News*, Feb. 28, 1999, p. 11A; "Springfield's Famous Bass Pro Shops Is Expanding into Texas," *St. Louis Post-Dispatch*, Feb. 21, 1998, p. 6; "Store Locator," Gander Mountain, **www.gandermountain.com** (accessed Oct. 8, 2003); "Store Map & Directory Outdoor World Grapevine, Texas," Bass Pro Shop pamphlet; Karen Talaski, "Outdoors Store Opens," *Detroit News*, May 19, 2000, p. 1; "Tanger Acquires Bass Pro Tract," *Wall Street Journal*, Nov. 16, 1999, p. A6; David Tobin, "Fingerlakes Mall Snags Tax Break for Bass Pro," *The Post-Standard*, Mar. 19, 2003; David Tobin, "How Local Ties Helped CNY Lure Bass Pro Shops," *The Post-Standard*, Sep. 4, 2003, p. A1; Mike Troy, "Gander Mtn. Fires at—and Hits—Retailtainment Bull's-Eye," *DSN Retailing Today*, Apr. 7, 2003, pp. 5, 50; Todd Vinyard, "Bassin' Businessman—Career Built on Enthusiasm," *The Commercial Appeal*, May 19, 2002, p. D12; visits by the case author to Outdoor World stores in Grapevine, Texas, and Springfield, Missouri, and to the L. L. Bean Store in Freeport, Maine, May and June, 2000; visits by the case author to the Outdoor World store in Springfield, Missouri, Mar. 2003, to the Sportsman's Warehouse in St. Charles, Missouri, Sep. 2003, to the Cabela's in Dundee, Michigan, Feb. 2002, and to the Cabela's in Owatonna, Minnesota, Aug. 2002; "Welcome to Outdoor World Dallas-Ft. Worth Texas," Bass Pro Shop pamphlet; Susanne Williams, "Bass Pro Shop Also a Contentious Issue in OKC," *Virginia Business Observer*, May 6, 2002, News Section. This case was researched and written by Dr. Neil Herndon, Department of Marketing at the University of Missouri–Columbia, for classroom discussion rather than to illustrate either effective or ineffective handling of an administrative situation.

Chapter 21

Page 562: Tim McDonald, "Dell Beats Out Compaq for First Time," *E-Commerce Times*, Apr. 20, 2001, **www.ecommercetimes.com/perl/story/9120.html**; Tim McDonald, "Gateway Takes Offensive in PC Price War," *E-Commerce Times*, May 31, 2001, **www.ecommercetimes.com/perl/story/10140.html**; Ken Popovich, "PC Price Wars Begin to Shake Loyalties—Dell, Compaq Battle for Users by Slashing Prices," *eWeek*, Apr. 30, 2001, p. 1; Rebecca Sausner, "Dell Pegs New PC Price Point Below $600," *E-Commerce Times*, June 4, 2001, **www.ecommercetimes.com/perl/story/10240.html**; Amy Schatz, "Dell Takes Top Spot in 2003 Sales," *Austin American-Statesman*, Jan. 15, 2004, **www.statesman.com**; "John G. Spooner, "Study: PC Prices Rocking to the Bottom," Clnet, Apr. 4, 2003, **http://zdnet.com/2100-1103-995560.html**; Martin Veitch, "Compaq Builds Corporate Line to Challenge IBM in Enterprise," *IT Week*, Feb. 19, 2001, p. 22; Leah Beth Ward, "Dell Vows to Persist with Price Strategy: Firm Says Cuts Led to Market Share Gains," *Dallas Morning News*, May 18, 2001, p. 1D; *page 566:* "Cattlemen Credit Atkins Diet for High Demand in Beef," (Fort Collins) *Coloradoan*, Nov. 17, 2003, p. E4; Blaine Harden, "Low-Carb Diet Fad, Thinner Herds Fatten Wallets of Ranchers," *Wall Street Journal*, Dec. 23, 2003, **http://online.wsj.com/**; Scott Kilman and Tamsin Carlisle, "U.S. Meatpackers Lay Off Workers amid Export Ban," *Wall Street Journal*, Jan. 12, 2004, **http://online.wsj.com/**; Sue Kirchhoff, "Natural Beef Industry Might See Boost from Mad Cow Fears," *USA Today*, Jan. 12, 2004, pp. 1B, 2B.

Chapter 22

Page 593: Michele Kessler, "Big Companies Get on Board with Net Calls," *USA Today*, Nov. 28, 3004; Dan Meyer, "Carriers Try to Pick Up Marginal Users with Cheap Calling Plans," *RCR Wireless News*, Mar. 11, 2002, pp. 3+; Margo McCall, "Giving the Gift of Wireless," *Wireless Week*, Dec. 17, 2001, pp. 1+; Becca Mader, "Being Young and Wireless: Companies Target Teens and College Crowd with 'Hip' Features," *Baltimore Business Journal*, Nov. 16, 2001, p. 11;

page 600: Ken Clark, "Where the Dollar Is King," *Chain Store Age Executive,* Feb. 2001, p. 35; "Dollar General Corporation," Hoover's Online, **www.hoovers.com/dollar-general/--ID__13220—/free-co-factsheet.xhtml** (accessed Jan. 19, 2004); "Family Dollar Stores, Inc.," Hoover's Online, **www.hoovers.com/family-dollar-stores, -inc./--ID__10546--/free-co-factsheet.xhtml** (accessed Jan. 19, 2004); "Family Dollar to Join S&P 500," *Business Journal of Charlotte,* July 31, 2001, **http://charlotte.bcentral.com/charlotte/stories/2001/ 07/30/daily23.html**; Adelia Cellini Linecker, "Family Dollar Uses 'Hardline' Stance to Get a Leg Up in Discount Battles," *Investor's Daily Business,* May 23, 2001, p. 1; Tim Schooley, "Discounter Finds Plenty to Like Here," *Pittsburgh Business Times,* May 18, 2001, p. 3.

Strategic Case 8

"GartnerG2 Says 'Big 5' Record Labels Must Standardize Digital Music Delivery to Profit from the Market Opportunity," The Gartner Group, press release, Aug. 29, 2001, **http://gartner.com/5_about/ press_releases/2001/pr20010829c.html**; Stephen Hinkle, "RIAA, Surrender Now!" Dmusic.com, **http://news.dmusic.com/print/5026**

(accessed Nov. 20, 2003); Bob Keefe, "Music File-Sharers Hit by New Round of Lawsuits," *Austin American-Statesman,* Jan. 22, 2004, **www.statesman.com**; "Napster, But in Name Only," Wired News, July 28, 2003, **www.wired.com/news/digiwood/ 0,1412,59798,00.html**; "Napster Fact Sheet," Napster, **www. napster.com/facts.html** (accessed Jan. 21, 2004); "Napster Quote Sheet," Napster, **www.napster.com/quotes.html** (accessed Jan. 21, 2004); Michael Pastore, "The Online Music Debate Rambles On," Cyberatlas, July 24, 2000, **http://cyberatlas.internet.com/markets/ retailing/article/0,,6061_420571,00.html**; Plunkett Research, **www.plunkettresearch.com/technology/infotech_trends.htm** (accessed Nov. 20, 2003); "U.S. Electronic Media and Entertainment," the-infoshop.com, **www.the-infoshop.com/study/fi13558_electronic_ media.html** (accessed Nov. 20, 2003); Andrew Wallmeyer, "Wal-Mart to Offer Songs at 88 Cents a Download," *Wall Street Journal,* Dec. 18, 2003, **http://online.wsj.com**. Michael D. Hartline and O. C. Ferrell prepared this case for classroom discussion rather than to illustrate effective or ineffective handling of an administrative, legal, or ethical situation.

Credits

CHAPTER 1

p.3: Photodisc Green/Getty Images. p.5: Courtesy of Morgan Stanley. p.7: Reprinted with permission of Cultivator Advertising and Design. p.7: Reprinted with permission of Cultivator Advertising and Design. p.11: © 2004 BMW of North America, LLC, used with permission. The BMW name and logo are registered trademarks. Photo by Mervyn Franklyn/M Represents Inc. p.15: Reprinted with permission of Federated Merchandising Group. p.19: Brand X Pictures/Getty Images. p.20: Reprinted with permission of LG Electronics U.S.A., Inc. All rights reserved. Photo by Andrew Zuckerman. p.21: Reprinted with permission of The Nature Conservancy. p.24: Photodisc Green/Getty Images. p.25: Brand X Pictures/Getty Images.

CHAPTER 2

p.28: © John and Lisa Merrill/CORBIS. p.31: Courtesy of the Gillette Company. p.32: © Alan Towse; Ecoscene/CORBIS. p.34: Courtesy of Wendy's International, Inc. p.35: General Motors Corp. Used with permission, GM Media Archives. p.38: Copyright, State Farm Mutual Automobile Insurance Company, 2004. Used by permission. p.39: Reprinted with permission of Publicis. Courtesy of Hewlett-Packard. p.43 (top): Reprinted with permission of Microsoft Corporation. p.43 (bottom): Reprinted with permission of Microsoft Corporation. p.46: David Young-Wolff/PhotoEdit, Inc. p.50: Photodisc Collection/Getty Images.

STRATEGIC CASE 1

p.55: Photodisc Collection/Getty Images.

CHAPTER 3

p.59: Photo by Porsche AG via Getty Images. p.61 (left): Courtesy of American Honda Motor Co., Inc. p.61 (right): Reprinted with permission of Toyota Motors North America, Inc. p.63 (left): © The Procter & Gamble Company. Used by permission. p.63 (right): Courtesy of the Gillette Company. p.65 (left): Courtesy of Wendy's International, Inc. p.65 (right): Reprinted with permission of Oakwood Worldwide. p.72: Photo Courtesy of Apple Computer Corp. via Getty Images. p.75 (left): Courtesy of General Electric. p.75 (right): Rob & Ann Simpson/VIREO. Reprinted with permission of Home Depot & The National Wildlife Federation. p.76: Reprinted with permission of Dell, Inc. p.78: Photodisc Green/Getty Images. p.81 (left): Reprinted with permission of Unilever Bestfoods. p.81 (right): Reprinted with permission of Bayer Corporation. p.86: The Image Bank/Getty Images.

CHAPTER 4

p.88: Rubberball Productions/Getty Images. p.89: Reprinted with permission by AVEDA Corporation. Photo by David Meredith and Greg Kadel. Model: Raica. p.99: Photodisc Green/Getty Images. p.94: Courtesy of Newman's Own. p.95 (left): Reprinted with permission of Hitachi America, LTD. p.95 (right): Courtesy of the European Commission. p.96: Courtesy of ENERGYCONSERVATIONPOSTERS.com, 800-875-1725. Made in USA. p.98: Reprinted with permission of Verizon Communications, Inc. p.106: Reprinted with permission of Business Ethics, 2845 Harriett Avenue Suite 207, Minneapolis MN 55408. www.business-ethics.com. p.110: Copyright The Procter & Gamble Company. Used by permission. p.113: Photodisc Green/Getty Images.

CHAPTER 5

p.118: Photodisc Green/Getty Images. p.120 (top): General Motors Corp. Used with permission, GM Media Archives. p.120 (bottom): General Motors Corp. Used with permission, GM Media Archives. p.122: Brand X/Getty Images. p.124: Reprinted with permission of

Ernst & Young. p.125: Courtesy of Pitney Bowes, Inc. p.127: Reprinted with permission of Yellow Transportation. p.134: Courtesy of J.P. Morgan Chase & Co. Used with permission. p.139: David Young-Wolff/PhotoEdit, Inc. p.140: Michael Newman/PhotoEdit, Inc.

STRATEGIC CASE 2

p.143: Photodisc Blue/Getty Images.

CHAPTER 6

p.147: Photodisc Green/Getty Images. p.149: Reprinted with permission from the J.M. Smucker Company. p.153: Photo by Roy Zipstein ©. Ad courtesy pf Expedia.com. p.154: Courtesy of Napster, LLC. p.156: Courtesy of Ebay. p.157: Reprinted with permission of Freightgate, Inc. p.160: SAS and all other SAS Institute Inc. product or service names are registered trademarks or trademarks of SAS Institute Inc. in the USA and other countries. ® indicates USA registration. Other brand and product names are trademarks of their respective companies. Copyright © 2003 SAS Institute Inc. Cary, NC, USA. All rights reserved. p. 163: Reprinted with permission of SurfControl. Created by Bandujo, Donkers and Brothers. Photo by Tim Bradley/Tim Bradley.com. p.164: Comstock Images/Getty Images. p.170: Photodisc Green/Getty Images.

CHAPTER 7

p.172: Photodisc Red/Getty Images. p.173: Reprinted with permission of Decision Analyst, Inc. p.179: Reprinted with permission of Apian Software, Inc. p.181: Reprinted with permission of Harris Interactive, Inc. p.182: Reprinted with permission of Delve. p.185: Photodisc Green/Getty Images. p.186: Reprinted with permission of Teradata, a division of NCR. p.188: Courtesy of HarrisInteractive.com. Photo by Time & Life Pictures/Getty Images. p.193: Reprinted with permission of Global Market Insite (GMI). p.196: Brand X Pictures/Getty Images. p.197: Digital Vision/Getty Images.

STRATEGIC CASE 3

p.199: George Hall/CORBIS.

CHAPTER 8

p.203: Photodisc Green/Getty Images. p.205 (left): ™/® DOVE is a registered trademark of Mars, Incorporated and its affiliates. It is used with permission. Mars, Incorporated is not associated with William M. Pride, O. C. Ferrell, or Houghton Mifflin Company. p.205 (right): Reprinted with permission of Ricoh Corporation, Courtesy of Gigante Vaz Partners. p.208 (left): Reprinted with permission of A. T. Cross. p.208 (right): Reprinted with permission of New York Marriott Marquis Hotels. p.210 (left): Reprinted with permission of The Eveready Battery Company, Inc. and Wilkinson Sword GmBH. All rights reserved. p.210 (right): Reprinted with permission of The Eveready Battery Company, Inc. and Wilkinson Sword GmBH. All rights reserved. p.212 (top): Reprinted with permission of Hacienda Mexican Restaurants. p.212 (bottom): Copyright State Farm Mutual Automobile Insurance Company, 2003. Used by Permission. p.216: Company: Teva; Agency: Frank Creative Workgroup; Execution: "The Kayak Never Showed Up"; Product Featured: Haze; Creative Director: David Karstad; Photographer: Dawn Kish; Product Photographer: Mark Aimerito; Ad ran in Sept. 03 *National Geographic Adventure*. p.217: Rubberball Productions/Getty Images. p.223: Courtesy of MapInfo Corporation. One Global View, Troy, NY 12180. p.230: Photodisc Green/Getty Images.

CHAPTER 9

p.232: Photodisc Green/Getty Images. p.234 (left): Reprinted with permission of Bell-Carter Foods, Inc. p.234 (right): Courtesy of FORD Global Technologies, Inc. p.236: Reprinted with permission with Culligan International Company. p.237: Reprinted with permission of Publicis/Courtesy of Ray Brown Productions/Photo by Michael Haber. p.241: M. C. Escher's "Sky and Water I" © 2004 The M. C. Escher Company–Baarn–Holland. All rights reserved. p.244: Reprinted with permission of McKee Wallwork Henderson. p.246: Courtesy of American Honda Motor Co., Inc. Copyright by Stephen Wilkes Photography. p.247: Reprinted with permission of KPMG LLP, the US member firm of KPMG International. p.251: Copyright of Procter and Gamble Company. Used by permission. p.252: Rob Elliott/AFP/Getty Images. p.257: Brand X Pictures/Getty Images. p.258: AP/Wide World Photos.

CHAPTER 10

p.260: Courtesy of Morgan Fitzgerald's, Bryan, TX. p.262: Reprinted with permission of TRI-K Industries, Inc. p.263: Reprinted with permission of Richard Sisson. Courtesy of American Valve, Inc. p.265: Reproduced courtesy of ERB Industries, Inc. p.266: Trademarks and copyrights use herein are properties of the United States Postal Service and are used under license to Houghton Mifflin Company. All rights reserved. p.267: Brand X Pictures/Getty Images. p.268: Courtesy of Pitney Bowes, Inc. p.270 (left): BROTHER® is a trademark of Brother Industries, Ltd. and P-touch® and Multifunction Center® are trademarks of BROTHER International Corporation. © BROTHER INTERNATIONAL CORPORATION 2003–2004. p.270 (right): Reprinted with permission of Everest Partners, L. P. Creative by Gregg Floyd, GAF Advertising/Design. p.271: Courtesy of the National Peanut Board. p.274: Reprinted with permission of Websense, Inc. p.275: Reprinted with permission of Altria Group, Inc. p.281: Comstock Images/Getty Images. p.282: Thinkstock/Getty Images.

STRATEGIC CASE 4

p.283: David Young-Wolff/PhotoEdit Inc.

CHAPTER 11

p. 287: Rubberball Productions/Getty Images. p.288 (top): Reprinted with permission of Washington Wild Things. Michael Giunta, Copywriter. David Hughes, Art Director. p.288 (bottom): Reprinted with permission of The Central Philadelphia Transportation Management Association. p.290 (left): READYMOP ™ is a registered trademark of The Clorox Company. Used with permission. p.290 (right): Reprinted with permission of La-Z-boy S. p.292 (left): Reprinted with permission of Olympia Group, Inc. p.292 (right): Reprinted with permission of Presperse Inc. p.293: Reprinted with permission of Penguin Brands. p.295: Reprinted with permission of Energizer. p.296: Jack Hollingsworth/CORBIS. p.298: Reprinted with permission of The Quaker Oats Company. p.302: Reprinted with permission of This Old House Ventures. p.307: Brand X Pictures/Getty Images.

CHAPTER 12

p.310: Michael Macor/San Francisco Chronicle/CORBIS SABA. p.312 (left): Advertisement provided courtesy of Frito-Lay, Inc. p.312 (right): Reprinted with permission of Starbucks. p. 313: Courtesy of FORD Global Technologies LLC. p.314: Reprinted with permission of Logitech. p.321: Reproduced with permission by New Balance Athletic Shoes, Inc. and EURO RSCG Worldwide/Photography by Leon Steele. p.322: Reprinted with permission of Glastron Boats. p.323: Richard Hamilton Smith/CORBIS. p.324: Courtesy of Audi of America, Inc. p.325 (left): Reprinted with permission of Red Bull of North America. p.325 (right): Reprinted with permission of Stonyfield Farm. p.331: C Squared Studios/Getty Images. p.333: Ryan McVay/Royalty Free/Getty Images.

CHAPTER 13

p.336: AP/Wide World Photos. p.337: Reprinted with permission of The Quaker Oats Company. p.339: Reprinted with permission of the Andrew Jergens Company. p.340 (left): © 2004 Kellogg NA Co. ™, ® Kellogg NA CO. p.340 (right): KELLOGG'S® TONY'S CINNA-

MON KRUNCHERS™ is a registered trademark of the Kellogg Company. All Rights Reserved. Used with permission. p.342: Tony Freeman/PhotoEdit, Inc. p.343: Photodisc Collection/Getty Images. p.345: © 2004 Kimberly-Clark Worldwide, Inc. Reprinted with Permission. p.347: Reprinted with permission of Inter-American Foods. p.348: Reprinted with permission of Marriott International. p. 350: Courtesy of Stull Technologies. p.352: Courtesy of ConAgra Foods, Inc. p.353: Copyright the Procter & Gamble Company. Used by permission. p.358: Photodisc Green/Getty Images. p.360: Thinkstock/Getty Images.

CHAPTER 14

p.362: Royalty Free/Corbis Images. p.365: Reprinted with permission of Mount Sinai Medical Center Courtesy of DeVito/Vendi. p.367 (top): Courtesy of Jeffery Wirth and the Wirth Companies.com. p.367 (bottom): Trademarks and copyrights used herein are properties of the United States Postal Service and are used under license to Houghton Mifflin Company. All Rights Reserved. p.369: Lawrence Manning/Corbis Images. p.371: © 2003 Hertz Systems, Inc. Hertz is a registered service mark and trademark of Hertz System, Inc. Photo by Stephen Marks/Getty Images. p.373: Courtesy of Hotels.com. p.376: Reprinted with permission of Smith Barney a subsidiary of Citigroup Global Markets, Inc. Photo by Corbis Images. p.378: Ad courtesy of Starwood Hotels & Resorts Worldwide, Inc., a Maryland Corporation. p.379 (left): Reprinted with permission of THE HOLE IN THE WALL GANG FUND, INC. p.379 (right): Reprinted with permission of Earth Share. p.380: Reprinted with permission of the Pan-Mass Challenge. p.385: Photodisc Collection/Getty Images. p.387: Rubberball Productions/Getty Images.

STRATEGIC CASE 5

p.388: Thinkstock/Getty Images.

CHAPTER 15

p.391: C Squared Studios/Getty Images. p.393: Reprinted with permission of Motion Industries, Inc. p.395 (left): Reprinted with permission of Transentric. p.395 (right): Courtesy of NxTrend Technology, Inc. p.396: James A. Sugar/CORBIS. p.399: Reprinted with permission of BALDOR ELECTRIC COMPANY. p.401 (left): PHILADELPHIA is a registered trademark used with permission of Kraft Foods. p.401 (right): Reprinted with permission of Tropicana Products, Inc. p.402 (left): Courtesy of Procter & Gamble. Used by permission. p.402 (right): Reprinted with permission of Leanna Bard, Marketing Consultant. Courtesy of Green Design Furniture. p.404: Reprinted with permission of Benjamin Moore Paints. p.412: Photodisc Green/Getty Images. p.413: Photodisc Green/Getty Images.

CHAPTER 16

p.416: Photodisc Green/Getty Images. p.418: Reprinted with permission of Merit Abrasive Products, Inc. p.426: Courtesy of BAX Global. Used by permission. p.427: Courtesy of Siemens Logistics and Assembly Systems. p.428: Reprinted with permission of GERS retail systems. p.429: Photodisc Blue/Getty Images. p.430: Reprinted with Permission of PEAK Technologies, Inc. p.433: Courtesy of Roadway Express, Inc. p.435: Courtesy of FedEx Corporation. Used by Permission. p.436: Courtesy of Aperum. p.437: Brand X Pictures/Getty Images. p.441: Thinkstock/Getty Images.

CHAPTER 17

p.444: Marianna Day Masseu/ZUMA/CORBIS. p.446: Leon C. Diehl/PhotoEdit, Inc. p.448: AP/Wide World. p.450: Reprinted with permission by Crate and Barrel. Photo courtesy of Dave Jordano Photography. p.451: Michael Newman/PhotoEdit, Inc. p. 452: Copyright 2004 Land's End, Inc. Used with permission. p.454: Courtesy of Orbitz. p.457: Courtesy of Merry Maids LP. p.458: Photodisc Blue/Getty Images. p.461: © Judy Griesedieck/CORBIS. p.463: Reprinted with permission of Triversity Inc. p.467:

C Squared Studios/Getty Images. p.468: Najlah Feanny–Hicks/ CORBIS SABA.

STRATEGIC CASE 6

p.470: PictureArts/CORBIS.

CHAPTER 18

p.473: Brand X Pictures/Getty Images. p.474: Reprinted with permission of Catalina Marketing Corporation. p.475: Reprinted with permission of the American Dairy Association. p.476: Royalty-Free/ CORBIS. p.478: Reprinted with permission of Ditto.com. p.481: Reprinted with permission of the Almond Board of CALIFORNIA. p.482: Reprinted with permission of Eastland Park Hotel. p.485: Reprinted with permission of Hitachi, Ltd. p.487: Courtesy of Expedia Corporate Travel. p.490: Reproduced with permission of XEROX. p.494: Reprinted with permission of the Media Campaign Resource Center (MCRC) of The Centers for Disease Control. p.496: Photodisc Green/Getty Images. p.498: C Squared Images/Getty Images.

CHAPTER 19

p.500: Bill Aron/PhotoEdit, Inc. p.501: Bill Aronson/PhotoEdit, Inc. p.502: Courtesy of the Campbell Soup Company. p.504: Reprinted with permission of Unilever and KLONDIKE (R). Courtesy of CARBSMART, Inc. p.505: Reprinted with permission of BROWN COW. p.507: Created by RDA International, Inc. Reproduced with permission of Car and Driver Magazine, Hachette Filipacchi Media U.S. p.510: © The Procter & Gamble Company. Used by permission. p.514: Reproduced with permission of XEROX. p.517: Reprinted with permission of World Wildlife Fund. Photo by Jerry Ellis/ Minden Pictures. p.518: AP/Wide World Photos. p.519: Reprinted with permission of Boston Children's Museum. p.526: © CORBIS.

CHAPTER 20

p.528:Bo Zaunders/CORBIS. p.531: Reprinted with permission of infoUSA, Inc. p.532: Photodisc Green/Getty Images. p.533: Reprinted with permission of Sanyo Presentations Technology.

p.534: Reprinted with permission of WebEx Communications, Inc. p.535: Reprinted with permission of Liveperson. p.538: Reprinted with permission of Careerbuilder.com. p.540: Courtesy of Caesars Tahoe. p.542: Reprinted with permission of Omaha Steaks. p.546: Reprinted with permission of Consumer Promotions Department of Binney and Smith, Design Creative of Think 360°. p.547: Courtesy of Continental Airlines. p.548: Courtesy of Starwood Hotels and Resorts. All rights reserved. p.553: Thinkstock/Getty Images.

STRATEGIC CASE 7

p.555: Photodisc Green/Getty Images.

CHAPTER 21

p.559: Tom Grill/CORBIS. p.561 (left): Reprinted with permission of Timepieces International. p.561 (right): Reprinted with permission of Rolex Watch U.S.A., Inc. p. 562: Bill Aron/PhotoEdit, Inc. p.564 (left): Images provided by kind courtesy of KONICA MINOLTA PRINTING SOLUTIONS U.S.A., INC., and Digital Vision. p.564 (right): Courtesy of Flight Options, LLC. p.566: Photodisc Green/Getty Images. p.572: Reprinted with permission of Wausau Insurance Companies. p.574: Courtesy of Allegheny Trail Corp. p.575: Reprinted with permission of Gorilla Mobile. p.578: Reproduced with permission of XEROX. p.582: AP/Wide World Photos.

CHAPTER 22

p.586: AP/Wide World Photos. p.588: Courtesy of AT&T Wireless. p.589: Photography courtesy of Kohler Co. p.592: Reprinted with permission of Ski Butternut. Matt Sawyer, Managing Director; Nancy Emerson, Designer. p.593: Tom Grill/CORBIS. p.594: Reprinted with permission of Quantum Corp. p.596: David Young-Wolff/PhotoEdit, Inc. p.599: Courtesy of CITYPASS, INC. p.600: Comstock Images/Getty Images. p.602: Reprinted with permission of Roche-Bobois. p.606: Rubberball Productions/Getty Images.

STRATEGIC CASE 8

p.608: AP/Wide World Photos.

Name Index

Aaker, David A., N12, N17
Abell, Derek F., N2
Acohido, Byron, N11
Albright, Joseph, N6
Alderson, Wroe, N13
Alford, Bruce L., N17, N18
Allan, Barbara, N9
Allen, Margaret, N14
Álvarez, Luis Ignacio, N3
Anderson, Erin, N13, N14
Anderson, Gordon T., N1
Anderson, Jerry W., Jr., N5
Andreessen, Marc, 84
Andretti, Michael, 26
Andruss, Paula Lyon, N3
Angwin, Julia, N3
Ansari, Asim, N7
Anschultz, Phillip, 99
Ante, Spencer E., N9
Arens, William F., N16
Arlan, Jeffrey, N14
Arndt, Michael, N7
Arnett, Dennis B., N8
Asmus, Peter, N5
Aspinwall, Leo, N13
Atkins, Richard, 497
Avci, Turgay, N8

Babakus, Emin, N8
Babin, Barry J., N4, N18
Bacanovic, Peter, 115
Balasubramanian, Sridhar, N7
Balfour, Frederik, N6
Ballmer, Steve, 405
Balto, David A., N3
Bander, James, N11
Bank, David, N16
Bannan, Karen J., N8, N17
Barksdale, Hiram C., Jr., N16
Barlas, Pete, N14
Barnes, Nora Ganim, N14
Barrett, Amy, N2
Barta, Patrick, N3, N11
Bartels, Chuck, N16
Bartholomew, Doug, N10
Basuroy, Suman, N16
Bater, Jeff, N3
Bateson, John E.G., 368, N12
Batista, Elisa, N6
Baum, Jeff, 397
Baun, Robert, N5
Bayus, Barry L., N11
Beales, Howard, 73
Beatty, Sally, N15
Beazley, Patty, 377
Bednarz, Ann, N13
Beer, Rebecca, N12
Begemann, Kurt, 552
Beirne, Mike, N12
Belch, George E., N16, N17
Belch, Michael A., N16, N17
Belk, Russell W., N10

Bellizzi, Joseph A., N17
Beltramini, Richard F., N17
Bennett, Peter D., N12, N17
Berfield, Susan, N1
Bergen, Mark E., N17
Bernard, Deborah, N17
Bernstein, Aaron, N8
Bernstein, Marty, N2
Berry, Leonard L., 368, N12, N13
Best, Roger J., N5
Bhattacharya, C.B., N7
Biagi, Luca, 122
Bianco, Anthony, N5, N14
Biddle, Rishawn, N13
Bidlake, Suzanne, N12
Biel, Jessica, 248
Bjorhus, Jennifer, N12
Blodgett, Jeffrey G., N5
Boersma, Margreet F., N6
Boles, James S., N4, N16
Bonasia, J., N7, N16
Bond, Edward U., III, N2
Boorstin, Julia, N9
Botelho, Greg, N5
Botkin, Jim, N17
Boudette, Neal E., N3, N6
Bougie, Roger, N4
Bowman, Douglas, N2
Boyle, Mathew, N15
Boynton, Robert S., N16
Brady, Diane, N1, N5, N12
Branch, Shelly, N3
Brand, Rachel, N5
Brashear, Thomas G., N5
Breitkopf, David, N12
Brekke, Dan, N16
Bremner, Brian, N5, N11
Brin, Sergey, 147
Brock, Terry, N10
Brown, Alan, N1
Brown, Stephen, N14
Bruno, Maria, N10
Bryant, Kobe, 8
Buckley, Peter J., N6
Buffet, Warren, 496
Buffett, Jimmy, 444
Bujol, Jessica, N2
Burnett, John J., N15
Burton, Scot, N17
Busch, Paul, N16
Byron, Christopher M., N5

Cadbury, Sir Adrian, N5
Caggiano, Christopher, N18
Cali, Consuelo, 332
Calvey, Mark, N4
Cantwell, Julie, N2, N3, N11
Carmichael, Mary, N13
Carney, Dan, N16
Carroll, Archie, N4
Carson, Thomas L., N4
Carter, Kelley L., N13

Casey, Susan, N11
Caywood, Thomas, N13
Chaker, Anne Marie, N3, N11
Champy, James, N11
Chandler, Clay, N6
Chang, David, 100
Chang, Julia, N17
Chapman, Patricia S., N17
Charny, Ben, N6
Chase, Charles W., Jr., N9
Chase, Richard B., 370, N12
Chatterjee, Subimal, N16
Chelariu, Cristian, N5
Chew, Edmund, N3
Cholewka, Kathleen, N2, N9
Chonko, Lawrence B., N4
Chung, Jaihak, N18
Chura, Hillary, N11
Cipolla, Lorin, N15, N17
Cipolloni, Mark, N1
Cipriani, Nichole, N13
Clark, Dick, 444
Clark, Jim, 84
Clark, Margaret M., N4
Clark, Maxine, 256, 257
Clifford, Stephanie, N11
Cline, Harry, N12
Clinton, Bill, 606
Cohen, Andy, N16
Cohen, Dorothy, N12
Coleman, Richard P., 249, 250
Combs, Sean "P Diddy," 283
Coney, Kenneth A., N5
Conover, John, 358
Conroy, Erin, 232
Contractor, Farok J., N6
Cook, Julie, N10
Cooper, Lee G., N11
Corbett, Brian, N3
Corstjens, Marcel, N12
Cortese, Amy, N16
Costello, Brid, N13
Cottrill, Ken, N14
Coughlan, Anne T., N13, N14
Coulter, Keith S., N18
Cowan, Lynn, N9
Cox, Beth, N18
Cox, Nigel, N18
Cravens, David W., N2, N15
Crecca, Donna Hood, N1
Creswell, Julie, N5
Crock, Stan, N7
Crockett, Roger O., N8, N14
Croft, Martin, N9
Crosby, Philip B., N2
Crossan, Mary, N5
Cuneo, Alice Z., N10, N15, N16
Cunningham, Peggy H., N4

Dacin, Peter A., N2, N16
Dalton, Greg, N18
Damsell, Keith, N18

Organization Index

AAMCO, 458
AARP The Magazine, 387
ABC, 252
Abercrombie & Fitch, 462
About.com, Inc., 577
Accenture, 371
Acklands Ltd., 413
ACNielsen Company, 172, 178, 190
  (table), 225, 319, 458, 486
Acorn, 215
Acura, 47
Adidas, 129, 135
Advertising Age, 190 (table), 500
AIDS Action Committee, 497
Airbus A320, 582
Airbus Industrie, 588
AirCell, 78
Air China, 134
AirTran, 64
Ajax dishwashing liquid, 344
Alamo Rent-a-Car, 369
Albertson's, 196, 448, 452, 518
Alcohol and Tobacco Tax and Trade
  Bureau, 75
Alitalia, 134
Allegheny Trail, 574 (illus.)
Allstate, 372
Almond Board of California, 481 (illus.)
Altria Group, 275 (illus.), 344, 506 (table)
Amana refrigerators, 82, 160
Amazon.com, 14, 38, 39, 119, 150, 151
  (illus.), 160, 445, 559, 610
American Airlines, 548, 572
American Apparel & Footwear Associa-
  tion, 104
American Association of Retired Persons
  (AARP), 386–387
American Cancer Society, 497
American Demographics, 190 (table)
American Express, 6, 93, 281, 341 (table),
  347, 370
American Life, 370
American Marketing Association, 104–105
  (table), 166–167 (table)
American Museum of Natural History, 379
American Red Cross, 497
American Valve, 263 (illus.)
America Online (AOL), 85, 152, 165, 370,
  481, 506 (table), 609
America's Electric Utility Companies, 82
America's Job Bank, A–2
Amoco, 7
AmSouth Bank, 14
Amway, 455
ANC Rental Car, 369
Anheuser-Busch, 46, 318, 352 (table), 503
A&P, 448
Aperum, 436 (illus.)
Apian, 179 (illus.)
Applebee's, 81
Apple Computer, 11, 36, 72, 185, 488,
  500, 501, 610

Arbitron, 190 (table), 486
Archer Daniels Midland, 72, 127
Arizona School Facilities Board, 99
Giorgio Armani, 348
Arm & Hammer, 8, 347, 352
Arthritis Foundation, 497
Aston Martin, 59
Atkins Nutritionals, 497–498
AT&T, 90 (table), 348, 348 (illus.), 371,
  497, 592
AT&T Wireless, 588 (illus.), 593
AuctionDrop, 170
Auctionworks, 269
Audi, 38, 324 (illus.), 387
Autobytel, 152, 156, 160
AutoNation, 170
Auto Shack, 345
Autosite, 581
AutoTrader.com, 257–258
AutoZone, 345
Aveda, 90 (illus.), 400
Averitt Express, 437
Avia, 219
Avon Products, 89, 90, 90 (table), 455,
  479
A&W's Great Root Beer, 121

Bakersfield Californian, 475
Baldor, 399 (illus.)
Ban deodorant, 339 (illus.)
Ban Rai Coffee House bar, 458
Barbie dolls, 142–144, 504
Barnes & Noble, 445, 454
Baseball Weekly, 55
Baskin-Robbins, 133 (table), 457 (table)
Bass Pro Shops, 555–556
BAX Global, 426 (illus.)
Bayer, 18, 81 (illus.)
BBBOnLine (Council of Better Business
  Bureaus), 163, 163 (illus.)
BehaviorBank, 218
Behavior Scan (IRI), 196, 515
Beiersdorf, 480
Bell South, 253
Benjamin Moore Paints, 404 (illus.)
Ben & Jerry's, 11, 517
Bennigan's restaurants, 30
Bentley, 403
Bergen Brunswig Corporation, 420
Berkshire Hathaway Inc., 496
Bertelsmann AG, 608
Best Buy, 92, 419, 487, 559, 562, 590,
  599, 610
Best Products, 450
BET cable channel, 528
Better Business Bureau (BBB), 74, 88, 163
  (illus.)
Bic pens, 573
Billpoint, 170
Bill's Dollar Stores, 600
Bioland, 292 (illus.)
Bissell, 184

Bizjournals.com, 224
Bizrate.com, 169
BJ's Warehouse Club, 449
Black Entertainment Television, 252
Bloomberg Report, 190 (table)
Bloomingdale's, 426, 461
Blue Cross Blue Shield of Massachusetts,
  497
Bluefly, 152
Blue Lobster Bowl, 385
Blue Ridge Premium Beef, 566
BMG, 608
BMW, 11 (illus.), 38, 59, 138–140, 341
  (table), 388, 483, 509, 575
The Body Shop, 446, 521
Boeing Company, 271, 427
The Bon Marché, 426
Borden, 36
Boston Children's Museum, 519 (illus.)
Boston Consulting Group (BCG), 36
Boston Market, 81
Bounty paper towels, 36
BP, 18, 135 (table)
BP-Amoco, 434
B&Q, 90
Bradlees, 447
Braun, 141
Bravo, 509
Bridgestone/Firestone, 98
Brighton, 260
Brooks Brothers, 429
Brother, 270 (illus.)
Brown Cow, 505 (illus.)
Budweiser, 113, 341 (table), 478, 498,
  501 (illus.)
Buick, 6, 327
Build-A-Bear, 256–257
Burdine's, 426
Bureau of Consumer Protection (Federal
  Trade Commission), 73
Bureau of Labor Statistics, 597
Burger King, 5, 80, 133 (table), 191, 458,
  484, 493, 528
Burlington Coat Factory, 451
Business Ethics magazine, 106 (illus.), 114
Business for Social Responsibility (BSR),
  112
Business Software Alliance, 455
Business Week, 190 (table)
BuyandHold.com, 228–229

Cable News Network, 55
C.A.C.I., Inc., 215
Cadillac, 119, 344
Cadillac Catera, 327
Cadillac Eldorado, 327
Cali Cosmetics, 331–332
California Department of Health Services,
  494
California Milk Processor Board, 476
California Prune Growers, 245
Calvin Klein, 429

Subject Index